Our Social World

Seventh Edition

To our beloved coauthor, Keith A. Roberts. His love for teaching through deep learning lives on in this book and in the lives of the many, many teachers and students he touched.

Our Social World

Introduction to Sociology

Seventh Edition

Jeanne H. Ballantine

Wright State University

Keith A. Roberts

Emeritus, Hanover College

Kathleen Odell Korgen

William Paterson University

Los Angeles | London | New Delhi
Singapore | Washington DC | Melbourne

FOR INFORMATION:

SAGE Publications, Inc.
2455 Teller Road
Thousand Oaks, California 91320
E-mail: order@sagepub.com

SAGE Publications Ltd.
1 Oliver's Yard
55 City Road
London EC1Y 1SP
United Kingdom

SAGE Publications India Pvt. Ltd.
B 1/I 1 Mohan Cooperative Industrial Area
Mathura Road, New Delhi 110 044
India

SAGE Publications Asia-Pacific Pte. Ltd.
18 Cross Street #10-10/11/12
China Square Central
Singapore 048423

Acquisitions Editor: Jeff Lasser
Editorial Assistant: Tiara Beatty
Content Development Editor: Liza Neustaetter
Production Editor: Laureen Gleason
Copy Editor: Mark Bast
Typesetter: C&M Digitals (P) Ltd.
Proofreaders: Jeff Bryant, Sue Irwin, Theresa Kay
Indexer: Robie Grant
Cover Designer: Scott Van Atta

Printed in Canada

Library of Congress Cataloging-in-Publication Data

Names: Ballantine, Jeanne H., author. | Roberts, Keith A., author. | Korgen, Kathleen Odell, 1967- author.

Title: Our social world : introduction to sociology / Jeanne H. Ballantine, Wright State University, Keith A. Roberts, Hanover College, Kathleen Odell Korgen, William Paterson University.

Description: Seventh Edition. | Thousand Oaks : SAGE Publications, [2019] | Revised edition of the authors' Our social world, [2018] | Includes bibliographical references and index.

Identifiers: LCCN 2018039606 | ISBN 9781544333533 (pbk. : alk. paper)

Subjects: LCSH: Sociology. | Sociology—Cross-cultural studies.

Classification: LCC HM586 .B35 2019 | DDC 301—dc23
LC record available at https://lccn.loc.gov/2018039606

This book is printed on acid-free paper.

19 20 21 22 23 10 9 8 7 6 5 4 3 2 1

BRIEF CONTENTS

© Alexander Spatari/Moment/Getty Images

DETAILED CONTENTS

© Lisa Maree Williams/Stringer/Getty Images

© iStock.com/Christian Mueller

© iStock.com/Imgorthand

© REUTERS/Gonzalo Fuente

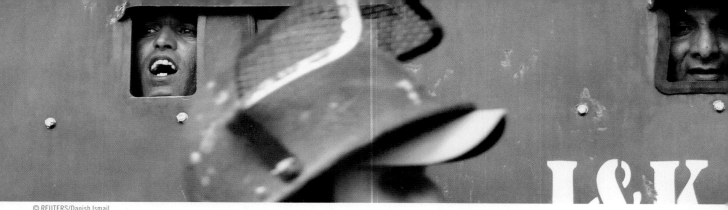
© REUTERS/Danish Ismail

PART IV: INSTITUTIONS   287

Chapter 10: Family: *Partner Taking, People Making, and Contract Breaking*   292

© Getty/Scott Olson/Staff

© AFP/Getty Images

© Bettmann/Getty Images

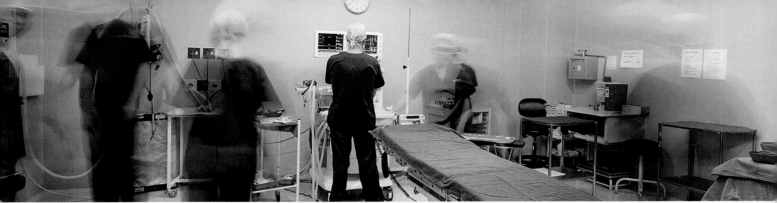

Chapter 14: Health Care: *An Anatomy of Health and Illness*   420

© Dirk Meister/Moment/Getty Images

© Getty/YASUYOSHI CHIBA/Staff

© REUTERS/Jonathan Ernst

PREFACE

To Our Students

This book will change how you view the social world—and your place in it. You will gain a sociological perspective on the world that will change what you notice and how you make sense of your social world. Some of you will become sociology majors. All of you will find the subject matter of this course relevant to your personal and professional lives. You will learn how society works—and how you can influence it, develop interpersonal skills, and gain new information about social life in small groups and global social systems. As the broadest of the social sciences, sociology has a never-ending array of fascinating subjects to study.

Sociology and this book ask you to think outside the box. Why? The best way to become a more interesting person, to grow beyond the old familiar thoughts and behaviors, and to make life exciting is to explore new ways to view your social world. The world in which we live is intensely personal and individual, with much of our social interaction occurring in intimate groups of friends and family. Our most intense emotions and most meaningful links to others are at this small-group "micro" level of social life. *As you use this book, apply what you read to your life and those in your social world.* This will make the book relevant to you and help you apply what you learn to your own life.

However, these intimate micro-level links in our lives are influenced by larger social structures and global trends. The social world you face in the job market of the 21st century is influenced by changes and forces that are easy to miss. Like the wind, which can do damage even if the air is unseen, social structures are themselves so taken for granted that it is easy to miss seeing them. However, their effects can be readily identified. Sociology's perspectives will help you to better understand your family, friends, work life, leisure time, and your place in a diverse and changing world.

Becoming Literate in Sociology

Each day you have routines, many of them involving other people and groups to which you belong or have a connection. Think about your roommate, classes, sports team, Greek organization, college you attend, and country in which you live. All these groups—and many more—make up your social world. Just as you learn the ideas, principles, theories, and frameworks in your other science and social science courses, so, too, sociology has key ideas, theories, frameworks, and models that fit together to give a picture of the social world and literacy in the field of sociology. Your text and course will introduce you to key elements that make up your individual social world. Each chapter provides a slice of the total sociological pie, and each different ingredient adds to the whole. When you finish this course you will have achieved basic literacy in sociology. You will see how you as an individual fit into your social world.

The following table shows an outline of the sociological competencies you will begin to learn in this course that will aid you in getting a job and navigating life. Advanced courses in sociology go into more depth in these competencies.

Essential Competency	Significance (Students Will . . .)
Apply sociological theories to understand social phenomena	Be able to identify how sociological concepts and theories relate to everyday life
Critically evaluate explanations of human behavior and social phenomena	Possess a critical lens for understanding human behavior and societies
Apply scientific principles to understand scientific methods and data	Articulate the importance of evidence and scientific methods for explanations and social phenomena
Rigorously analyze social scientific data	Be able to identify the characteristics of high-quality data and methods in sociological research
Use sociological knowledge to inform policy debates and promote public understanding	Use their sociological knowledge and skills to engage with and impact the world around them

The Social World Model

A well-constructed course needs to be organized around a central question, one that leads to other questions and intrigues the participants. For you to understand sociology as an integrated whole rather than a set of separate chapters in a book, we have organized this book around the *social world model*. The social world model demonstrates the relationships among individuals (micro level); organizations, institutions, and subcultures (meso level); and national societies and global structures (macro level). At the beginning of each chapter, a visual diagram of the model illustrates this idea as it relates to the topic of that chapter. This opening includes examples of issues related to the topic that have implications for the social world, influencing and being affected by other parts of society. No aspect of society exists in a vacuum. Note that this model does not assume that everyone always gets along or that relationships are always harmonious or supportive. Sometimes different parts of society compete for resources and conflict with one another over policies.

This micro- to macro-level analysis is a central concept in the discipline of sociology. It will help you to develop a *sociological imagination*, an ability to see the complex links among various levels of the social system, from the micro level of close relationships to the macro level of globalization. Within a few months, you may not remember all the specific concepts or terms that have been introduced, but if the way you see the world has been transformed during this course, a key element of deep learning has been accomplished. Learning to see things from alternative perspectives is a precondition for critical thinking. This book attempts to help you recognize connections between your personal experiences and problems and larger social forces of society. Thus, you will be learning to take a new perspective on the social world in which you live.

A key element of that social world is diversity. We live in societies in which people differ in a host of ways: ethnicity, socioeconomic status, religious background, political persuasion, gender, sexual orientation, and so forth. The most productive and creative organizations and societies are those that are highly diverse. This is the case because people with different backgrounds solve problems in different ways. When people with such divergences come together, the outcome of their problem-solving can create new solutions to vexing problems. Thus, diversity is a blessing in many ways to a community or society. However, diversity often creates challenges as well. Misunderstanding and "us" versus "them" thinking can divide people. These issues are explored throughout this book. We now live in a global village, and in this book, you will learn something about how people on the other side of the village live and view the world.

We hope you enjoy the book and get as enthralled with sociology as we are. It genuinely is a fascinating field of study.

Jeanne H. Ballantine

Jeanne H. Ballantine
Wright State University

Keith A. Roberts

Keith A. Roberts
Emeritus, Hanover College

Kathleen Odell Korgen

Kathleen Odell Korgen
William Paterson University

Your authors—teaching "outside the box"

INSTRUCTORS

How to Make This Book Work for You

How to reach students at their ability and interest levels and provide sociological principles they can grasp and use underlies the content and features of this book. Based on current pedagogical theory and recommendations for the beginning sociology course, the following discussion provides a curriculum map for the chapters and an introduction to the use of the *sociological literacy framework*.

Special features woven throughout each chapter support the themes of the book. These will help students comprehend and apply the material and make it more understandable and interesting. These features are also designed to facilitate deep learning, to help students move beyond rote memorization, and to increase their ability to analyze and evaluate information.

For students to understand both the comparative global theme and sociology as an integrated whole rather than as a set of separate chapters in a book, we have organized this book around the *social world model* that demonstrates the relationships among individuals (micro level); organizations, institutions, and subcultures (meso level); and societies and global structures (macro levels of analysis) (see following discussion). At the beginning of each chapter, a visual diagram of the model illustrates this idea as it relates to the topic of the chapter, including how issues related to the topic have implications at various levels of analysis in the social world.

Sociological Literacy Framework

In the past few years, sociologists in the teaching movement have developed a framework for teaching key topics and competencies in introductory sociology courses (Ferguson and Carbonaro, 2015). The individual ideas are not new, but together they lay out a comprehensive framework for teaching our discipline, and they provide a guide for what students should understand and be able to do when they complete the introductory course. Broad enough to include the topics we typically teach in the introductory course, the framework places loose parameters around the field and organizes content into a comprehensive and comprehendible format. *Our Social World* uses the key ideas and concepts in the framework for a systematic presentation aimed at undergraduate students and an up-to-date presentation of sociology's core content.

The framework represents what "students of sociology should understand" after completing an introductory sociology course, as determined by several working groups of teacher-scholars and sociologist task forces.* "To Our Students" includes a box outlining the six essential competencies.

"Think About It"

So that students can become curious, active readers, we have posed questions at the outset of each chapter that we hope are relevant to everyday life but are also tied to the micro-meso-macro levels of analysis that serve as the theme of the book. The purpose is to transform students from passive readers who run their eyes across the words into curious, active readers who read to answer a question and to be reflective. Active or deep reading is key to comprehension and retention of reading material (Roberts and Roberts 2008). Instructors can also use this feature to encourage students to think critically about the implications of what they have read. Instructors might want to ask students to write a paragraph about one of these questions before coming to class each day. These questions might also provide the basis for in-class discussions.

Students should be encouraged to start each chapter by reading and thinking about these questions, looking at the topics outlined in "What Will You Learn in This Chapter?," and asking some questions of their own. This will mean that they are more likely to stay focused, remember the material long-term, and be able to apply it to their own lives.

---

* For further information, see Ferguson and Carbonara, 2016.

A Global Perspective and the Social World Model

This book incorporates a global perspective throughout so that students can see not only how others live different but rewarding lives, but also the connections between others' lives and their own. Students will need to think and relate to the world globally in future roles as workers, travelers, and global citizens. Our analysis illustrates the interconnections of the world's societies and their political and economic systems and demonstrates that what happens in one part of the world affects others.

This global approach attempts to instill interest, understanding, and respect for different groups of people and their lifestyles. Race, class, and gender are integral parts of understanding the diverse social world, and these features of social life have global implications. The comparative global theme is carried throughout the book in the main text, in examples, and in boxes and selection of photos. As students read this book, they should continually think about how the experiences in their private world are influenced by and may influence events at other levels: the community, organizations and institutions, the nation, and the world.

Opening Vignettes

Chapters typically open with an illustration relevant to the chapter content that will grab the attention of students. For instance, in Chapter 2, "Examining the Social World," the case of Hector, a Brazilian teenager living in poverty in a favela, is used to illustrate research methods and theory throughout the chapter. In Chapter 4, "Socialization," Craig Kielburger, who at the age of 12 founded a major nonprofit organization fighting child labor practices around the world, begins the discussion. Chapter 7 opens with the royal wedding of Prince Harry and Meghan Markle. Chapter 15 begins with the experiences of Sally Ride, the first American woman in outer space. These vignettes are meant to interest students in the upcoming subject matter by helping them relate to a personalized story. In several cases, the vignettes serve as illustrations throughout the chapters.

Public Sociology and Sociologists in Action

Public sociology has become a major initiative within sociology, and students are often interested in what can be done with sociology outside of the academy. With that in mind, in each chapter we feature professional or student "Sociologists in Action" who describe how they use sociology to make a positive impact on society.

"Thinking Sociologically" Questions

Following major topics, students will find thought-provoking questions that ask them to think critically and apply the material they just read to some aspect of their lives or the social world. This feature encourages students to apply the ideas and concepts in the text to their lives, to develop critical thinking skills, and to use the material for better recall. These questions can be the basis for in-class discussions and can be assigned as questions to start interesting conversations with friends and families to learn how the topics relate to their own lives.

"Engaging Sociology"

Perhaps the most innovative feature in this book is called "Engaging Sociology"—and the double entendre is intentional. We want students to think of sociology as engaging, informative, and fun. These features—such as applying a population pyramid to the business world, taking a survey to understand why differences in social and cultural capital can make first-generation students feel alienated on a college campus, and reading a map and learning to analyze the patterns—help students understand how interesting and useful sociology can be.

Special Features

Featured inserts provide even more in-depth illustrations of the usefulness of the sociological perspective to understand world situations or events with direct relevance to a student's life. The "Sociology in Our Social World" features focus on a sociological issue or story, often with policy implications. "Sociology Around the World" takes readers to another part of the globe to explore how things are different (or how they are the same) from what they might experience in their own lives.

Key Concepts, Examples, and Writing Style

Key terms that are defined and illustrated within the running narrative and that appear in the glossary appear in **bold** with an italicized definition following. Other terms that are defined but are of less significance are italicized. The text is rich in examples that bring sociological concepts to life for students. Each chapter has been student tested for readability. Both students and reviewers describe the writing style as reader-friendly, often fascinating, and accessible—but not watered down.

Social Policy and Becoming an Involved Citizen

Most chapters include discussion of social policy issues and the relevance of sociological findings to current social debates. Furthermore, because students sometimes feel helpless and do not know what to do about social issues that concern them at macro and meso levels, we have concluded every chapter with a few ideas about how they might become involved as active citizens, even as undergraduate students. Some suggestions in the "Contributing to Our Social World: What Can We Do?" section may be assigned as extra credit, service learning, or term projects.

Summary Sections and Discussion Questions

Each chapter ends with review material: a "What Have We Learned?" feature that includes a "Key Points" bulleted summary of the chapter's core material. The summary is followed with probing discussion questions that ask students to go beyond memorization and apply the material in the chapter to their own lives. Research indicates that unless four discrete sections of the brain are stimulated, the learning will not be long term and deep but surface and short term (Zull 2002). These questions are carefully crafted to activate all four critical sections of the brain.

A Little (Teaching) Help From Our Friends

Whether the instructor is new to teaching or an experienced professor, there are some valuable ideas in this text that can help invigorate and energize the classroom. As we noted earlier, substantial literature on teaching methodology tells us that student involvement is key to the learning process. In addition to the engaging questions and exercises in the text, there are teaching suggestions in the supplements and teaching aids for active learning in large or small classes.

Instructor Teaching Site

A password-protected instructor teaching site, available at edge.sagepub.com/ballantine7e, provides integrated sources for all instructor materials, including the following key components for each chapter:

- The *test bank*, available in Word and ExamView, contains multiple-choice, true/false, short-answer, and essay questions for each chapter. The test bank provides you with a diverse range of prewritten options as well as the opportunity to edit any question and/or insert your own personalized questions to assess students' progress and understanding effectively.

- Editable, chapter-specific Microsoft *PowerPoint slides* offer you complete flexibility in easily creating a multimedia presentation for your course and highlight essential content, features, and artwork from the book.

- *Lecture notes* summarize key concepts on a chapter-by-chapter basis to help with preparation for lectures and class discussions.

- *Chapter-specific discussion questions* can help you launch classroom interaction by prompting students to engage with the material and by reinforcing important content.

- Lively and stimulating *ideas for class activities* can be used in class to reinforce active learning. The activities apply to individual or group projects.

- And much more!

Interactive E-Book

Our Social World is also available as an interactive e-book, which can be packaged with the text for just $5 or purchased separately. This interactive e-book includes premium video resources.

SAGE Coursepacks

SAGE coursepacks make it easy to import our quality instructor and student resource content into your school's learning management system (LMS) with minimal effort. Intuitive and simple to use, SAGE coursepacks give you the control to focus on what really matters: customizing course content to meet your students' needs. The SAGE coursepacks, created specifically for this book, are customized and curated for use in Blackboard, Canvas, Desire2Learn (D2L), and Moodle.

In addition to the content available on the SAGE edge site, the coursepacks include the following:

- *Pedagogically robust assessment tools* that foster review, practice, and critical thinking and offer a better, more complete way to measure student engagement, including the following:

- *Diagnostic chapter pretests and posttests* that identify opportunities for student improvement, track student progress, and ensure mastery of key learning objectives

- *Assignable premium video and SAGE Stats data activities* that bring concepts to life, increasing student engagement and appealing to different learning styles; the activities feed to your gradebook

- *Integrated links to the e-book version* that make it easy to access the mobile-friendly version of the text, which can be read anywhere, anytime

Student Study Site

An open-access student study site, available at edge.sagepub.com/ballantine7e, provides a variety of additional resources to build students' understanding of the book content and extend their learning beyond the classroom. Students will have access to the following features for each chapter:

- *E–flash cards and web quizzes.* These mobile-friendly resources reinforce understanding of key terms and concepts outlined in the chapters.

- *SAGE journal articles.* Exclusive full-text journal articles have been carefully selected for each chapter. Each article supports and expands on the concepts presented in the chapter.

- *Video, audio, and web links.* These carefully selected web-based resources feature relevant articles, interviews, lectures, personal stories, inquiries, and other content for use in independent or classroom-based explorations of key topics.

- *MCAT guide.* This guide summarizes the content in each chapter, highlighting the relevant topics tested on the MCAT (Medical College Admission Test). Each chapter entry also contains links to resources that allow students to understand and explore specific topic areas in more detail.

- And much more!

What Is New in the Seventh Edition?

In this major revision we have updated all data, added many new studies, and added new emphases in sociology, such as environmental sociology. The following list provides a summary of key changes:

- Thoroughly revised Chapter 15, bringing Urban Sociology and Population under the umbrella of Environmental Sociology and adding a new section on climate change.

- Included new Sociologists in Action features, such as Richard M. Carpiano's "Connecting Personal Health to Community Life" (Chapter 14).

- Revised the Engaging Sociology features, with opportunities for data analysis by students.

- Updated the Contributing to Our Social World: What Can We Do? features to provide new recommendations for how students can get involved.

- Added new and updated figures and maps.

- Added many new topics, including the influence of robots and artificial intelligence on workers, race relations in the Trump era, issues related to transgender identity and gender fluidity, sexual harassment in the workplace, declining marriage rates, the impact of tracking for students at all academic achievement levels, smoking as an example of health and inequality in the United States, gun violence and the student movement to control access to guns, and Facebook's handling of Russian interference in the 2016 election.

The core elements of the book—with the unifying theme and the social world model at the beginning of every chapter—have not changed.

Finally, although we had been told that the writing was extraordinarily readable, we have tried to simplify sentence structure in places. In short, we have tried to respond to what we heard from all of you—both students and instructors (and yes, we *do* hear from students)—to keep this book engaging and accessible.

A PERSONAL NOTE TO THE INSTRUCTOR

What is truly distinctive about this book? This text tries to break the mold of the typical textbook synthesis, a cross between an encyclopedia and a dictionary. *Our Social World* is a unique course text that is *a coherent essay on the sociological imagination—understood globally.* We attempt to radically change the feel of the introductory book by emphasizing coherence, integrating themes, and current knowledge about learning and teaching (such as the sociological literacy framework), but we also present much traditional content. Instructors will not have to throw out the well-honed syllabus and begin from scratch, but they can refocus each unit, so it stresses understanding of micro-level personal troubles within the macro-level public issues framework. Indeed, in this book, we make clear that the public issues must be understood as global.

Here is a text that engages students. *They* say so! From class testing, we know that the writing style, structure of chapters and sections, Thinking Sociologically features, wealth of examples, and other instructional aids help students stay focused, think about the material, and apply it to their lives. It neither bores them nor insults their intelligence. It focuses on deep learning rather than memorization. It develops sociological skills of analysis rather than emphasizing memorization of vocabulary. Key concepts and terms are introduced but only in the service of a larger focus on the sociological imagination. The text is both personal and global. It speaks to sociology as a science as well as addresses public or applied aspects of sociology. It has a theme that provides integration of topics as it introduces the discipline. This text is an analytical essay, not a disconnected encyclopedia.

As one of our reviewers noted,

Unlike most textbooks I have read, the breadth and depth of coverage in this one is very impressive. It challenges the student with college-level reading. Too many textbooks seem to write on a high school level and give only passing treatment to most of the topics, writing in nugget-sized blocks. More than a single definition and a few sentences of support, the text forces the student deep into the topics covered and challenges them to see interconnections.

Normally, the global perspective angle within textbooks, which seemed to grow in popularity in the past two decades, was implemented by using brief and exotic examples to show differences between societies—a purely comparative approach rather than a globalization treatment. They gave, and still give to a large extent, a token nod to diversity. This textbook, however, forces students to take a broader look at similarities and differences in social institutions around the world and structures and processes operating in all cultures and societies.

So, our focus in this book is on deep learning, especially expansion of students' ability to role-take or "perspective-take." Deep learning goes beyond the content of concepts and terms and cultivates the habits of thinking that allow one to think critically. Being able to see things from the perspective of others is essential to doing sociology, but it is also indispensable to seeing weaknesses in theories or recognizing blind spots in a point of view. Using the sociological imagination is one dimension of role-taking because it requires a step back from the typical micro-level understanding of life's events and fosters a new comprehension of how meso- and macro-level forces—even global ones—can shape the individual's life. Enhancement of perspective-taking ability is at the core of this book because it is a *prerequisite* for deep learning in sociology, and it is the core competency needed to *do* sociology. One cannot do sociology unless one can see things from various positions on the social landscape.

This may sound daunting for some student audiences, but we have found that instructors at every kind of institution have had great success with the book because of the writing style and instructional tools used throughout. We have made some strategic decisions based on these principles of learning and teaching. We have focused much of the book on higher-order thinking skills rather than memorization and regurgitation. We want students to learn to think sociologically: to apply, analyze, synthesize, evaluate, and comprehend the interconnections of the world through a globally informed sociological imagination. However, we think it is also essential to do this with an understanding of how students learn.

Many introductory-level books offer several theories and then provide critiques of the theories. The idea is to teach critical thinking. We have purposefully refrained from extensive critique of theory (although some does occur) for several reasons. First, providing critique to beginning-level students does not really teach critical thinking. It trains them to memorize someone else's critique. Furthermore, it simply confuses many of them, leaving students with the feeling that sociology is just contradictory ideas, and the discipline really does not have anything firm to offer. Teaching critical thinking needs to be done in stages, and it needs to take into account the building steps that occur before effective critique is possible. That is why we focus on the concept of deep learning. We are working toward building the foundations necessary for sophisticated critical thought at upper levels in the curriculum.

Therefore, in this beginning-level text, we have attempted to focus on a central higher order or deep learning skill—synthesis. Undergraduate students need to grasp this before they can fully engage in evaluation. Deep learning involves understanding of complexity, and some aspects of complexity need to be taught at advanced levels. Although students at the introductory level are often capable of synthesis, complex evaluation requires some foundational skills. Thus, we offer contrasting theories in this text, and, rather than telling what is wrong with each one, we encourage students through Thinking Sociologically features to analyze the use of each and to focus on honing synthesis and comparison skills.

Finally, research tells us that learning becomes embedded in memory and becomes long-lasting only if it is related to something that learners already know. If they memorize terms but have no unifying framework to which they can attach those ideas, the memory will not last until the end of the course, let alone until the next higher-level course. In this text, each chapter is tied to the social world model that is core to sociological thinking. At the end of a course using this book, we believe that students will be able to explain coherently what sociology is and construct an effective essay about what they have learned from the course as a whole. Learning to develop and defend a thesis, with supporting logic and evidence, is another component of deep learning. In short, this text provides instructors with the tools to teach sociology in a way that will have a long-term impact on students.

Organization and Coverage

Reminiscent of some packaged international tours, in which the travelers figure that "it is Day 7, so this must be Paris," many introductory courses seem to operate on the principle that it is Week 5, so this must be deviance week. Students do not sense any integration, and at the end of the course, they have trouble remembering specific topics. This book is different. A major goal of the book is to show the integration between topics in sociology and between parts of the social world. The idea is for students to grasp the concept of the interrelated world. A change in one part of the social world affects all others, sometimes in ways that are mutually supportive and sometimes in ways that create intense conflict.

Although the topics are familiar, the textbook is organized around levels of analysis, explained through the social world model. This perspective leads naturally to an integrated discussion in which all topics fit clearly into an overall view, a comparative approach, and discussions of diversity and inequality. It hangs together!

As seen in the table of contents, the book includes 16 chapters plus additional online materials, written to fit into a semester or quarter system. It allows instructors to use the chapters in order, or to alter the order, because each chapter is tied into others through the social world model. We strongly recommend that Chapter 1 be used early in the course because it introduces the integrating model and explains the theme. Also, if any chapters on institutions are used, the section opener Institutions may be useful to include as well. Otherwise, the book has been designed for flexible use.

Instructors may also want to supplement the core book with other materials, such as those suggested on the Instructor Teaching Site. While covering all the key topics in introductory sociology, the cost and size of a mid-sized book allows for this flexibility. Indeed, for a colorful introductory-level text, the cost of this book is remarkably low—roughly half the cost of most other popular introductory texts.

A Unique Program Supporting Teaching of Sociology

There is one more way in which *Our Social World* has been unique among introductory sociology textbooks.

In 2007, the original authors (Ballantine and Roberts) teamed with SAGE to start a new program to benefit the entire discipline. Using royalties from *Our Social World*, we helped establish the SAGE Teaching Innovations & Professional Development Award (now the SAGE Publishing Keith Roberts Teaching Innovations Award), designed to prepare a new generation of scholars within the teaching movement in sociology. People in their early career stages (graduate students, assistant professors, newer PhDs) can be reimbursed $600 each for expenses entailed while attending the day-long American Sociological Association (ASA) Section on Teaching and Learning's preconference workshop. The workshop is on the day before ASA meetings. In 2007, 13 young scholars—graduate students or untenured faculty members—received this award and benefited from an extraordinary workshop on learning and teaching. Since then, more than two dozen other SAGE authors have supported this program from textbook royalties, and hundreds of young scholars have been beneficiaries. We are pleased to have had a hand in initiating and continuing to support this program.

We hope you find this book engaging. If you have questions or comments, please contact us.

Jeanne H. Ballantine

Jeanne H. Ballantine
Wright State University
jeanne.ballantine@gmail.com

Kathleen Odell Korgen

Kathleen Odell Korgen
William Paterson University
korgenk@wpunj.edu

ACKNOWLEDGMENTS

Knowledge is improved through careful, systematic, and constructive criticism. The same is true of all writing. This book is of much greater quality because we had such outstanding critics and reviewers. We, therefore, wish to honor and recognize the outstanding scholars who served in this capacity. These scholars are listed on this page and the next.

People also served in a variety of other capacities, including as authors of our Sociologists in Action pieces and some of our Sociology in Our Social World boxes. David Yamane drafted early versions of the discussion of denominationalism and church polity in the religion chapter. Sandra Enos revised and updated the Contributing to Our Social World: What Can We Do? feature.

All three of us are experienced authors, and we have worked with some excellent people at other publishing houses. However, the team at SAGE Publications was truly exceptional in support, thoroughness, and commitment to this project. Our planning meetings were fun, intelligent, and provocative. Jeff Lasser provided wonderful support as the SAGE sociology publisher. Folks who have meant so much to the quality production of this book include Liza Neustaetter, content development manager, Laureen Gleason, production editor, Mark Bast, copy editor, Tiara Beatty, editorial assistant, Sheri Gilbert, permissions editor, and Kara Kindstrom, senior marketing manager. We have become friends and colleagues with the staff at SAGE Publications. They are all greatly appreciated.

Thanks to the following reviewers:

Sabrina Alimahomed, *University of California, Riverside*

George Ansalone, *Florida Gulf Coast University*

Richard Ball, *Ferris State University*

Fred Beck, *Illinois State University*

Jessica Bishop-Royse, *DePaul University*

Charles Bittner, *Texas Woman's University*

Stacye Blount, *Fayetteville State College*

Christopher Bradley, *Troy University, Division of Social Sciences*

David L. Briscoe, *University of Arkansas at Little Rock*

W. Trevor Brooks, *Austin Peay State University*

James A. Crone, *Hanover College*

April Cubbage, *Saddleback College*

David R. Dickens, *University of Nevada, Las Vegas*

Jamie M. Dolan, *Carroll College (MT)*

Amy Donley, *University of Central Florida*

Kevin Doran, *Indiana University, Bloomington*

Obi N. I. Ebbe, *University of Tennessee at Chattanooga*

Maureen Ellis-Davis, *Bergen Community College*

Sandra Enos, *Bryant University*

Lance Erickson, *Brigham Young University*

Jo Ry-Anne Feller, *Palm Beach State College*

Stephanie Funk, *Hanover College*

Loyd R. Ganey Jr., *Western International University*

Skylar C. Gremillion, *Louisiana State University*

Mary Grigsby, *University of Missouri–Columbia*

Chris Hausmann, *University of Notre Dame*

Todd A. Hechtman, *Eastern Washington University*

Robert B. Jenkot, *Costal Carolina University*

Kristina Jensen, *Boise State University*

Keith Kerr, *Blinn College*

Lisa L. Kuecker, *Western New Mexico University*

Leslie C. Lamb, *State University of New York, Empire State College Center for Distance Learning*

Naomi Latini, *Troy University*

Elaine Leeder, *Sonoma State University*

Jason J. Leiker, *Utah State University*

Stephen Lilley, *Sacred Heart University*

David A. Lopez, *California State University, Northridge*

Crystal V. Lupo, *Auburn University*

Akbar Madhi, *Ohio Wesleyan University*

Gerardo Marti, *Davidson College*

Laura McCloud, *Ohio State University*

Meeta Mehrotra, *Roanoke College*

Melinda S. Miceli, *University of Hartford*

Leah A. Moore, *University of Central Florida*

Nirmal Niroula, *Coastal Carolina University*

Boniface Noyongoyo, *University of Central Florida*

Katy Pinto, *California State University at Dominguez Hills*

R. Marlene Powell, *University of North Carolina at Pembroke*

Suzanne Prescott, *Central New Mexico Community College*

Antonia Randolph, *University of Delaware*

Olga Rowe, *Oregon State University*

Paulina Ruf, *Lenoir-Rhyne University*

Sarah Samblanet, *Kent State University*

Martha L. Shockey-Eckles, *Saint Louis University*

Toni Sims, *University of Louisiana–Lafayette*

Terry L. Smith, *Harding University*

Frank S. Stanford, *Blinn College*

Tracy Steele, *Wright State University*

Rachel Stehle, *Cuyahoga Community College*

Amy Stone, *Trinity University*

John Stone, *Boston University*

Hephzibah V. Strmic-Pawl, *Coastal Carolina University*

Stephen Sweet, *Ithaca College*

Debra K. Taylor, *Johnson County Community College*

Ruth Thompson-Miller, *Texas A & M University*

Tim Ulrich, *Seattle Pacific University*

Natasha Vannoy, *Logan University*

Thomas L. Van Valey, *Western Michigan University*

Connie Veldink, *Everett Community College*

Dennis Veleber, *Montana State University Northern*

Kristie Vise, *Northern Kentucky University*

Chaim I. Waxman, *Rutgers University*

Lisa Munson Weinberg, *Florida State University*

Debra Welkley, *California State University at Sacramento*

Matthew West, *Bevill State Community College*

Debra Wetcher-Hendricks, *Moravian College*

Deborah J. White, *Collin County Community College*

Jake B. Wilson, *University of California, Riverside*

Laurie Winder, *Western Washington University*

Robert Wonser, *College of the Canyons*

Luis Zanartu, *Sacramento City College*

John Zipp, *University of Akron*

PART I

UNDERSTANDING OUR SOCIAL WORLD

The Scientific Study of Society

Can an individual make a difference in the world or in a community? How does your family influence your chances of gaining a college degree and a high-paying job? If you were born into a poor family, what are your chances of becoming wealthy? How does your level of education impact your likelihood of marrying—and staying married? Why are Generation Zers less likely to have sex than Generation Xers? How can sociology help you understand and be an effective member of society?

Those are some of the questions you will be able to answer as you develop a deeper understanding of our social world. Sociology is valuable because it gives us new perspectives on our personal and professional lives and because sociological insights and skills can help all of us make the world a better place. Sociology can change your life—and help you change the world.

By the time you finish reading the first two chapters, you should have an initial understanding of what sociology is, what you can gain from studying sociology, the roots of the sociological perspective, and how sociologists carry out research. We invite you to view our social world through a sociological lens and learn how you can use sociology to make a difference in your life, your community, and the world.

CHAPTER 1

© Alexander Spatari/Moment/Getty Images

SOCIOLOGY

A Unique Way to View the World

▲ Sociology involves a transformation in the way one sees the world—learning to recognize the complex connections among our intimate personal lives, large organizations, and national and global systems.

MICRO

ME (MY FAMILY AND CLOSE FRIENDS)

LOCAL ORGANIZATIONS AND COMMUNITY
My school, place of worship, hangouts

MESO

NATIONAL ORGANIZATIONS, INSTITUTIONS, AND ETHNIC SUBCULTURES
My political party, ethnic affiliation

MACRO

SOCIETY
Type of national government and economic system

GLOBAL COMMUNITY
United Nations, World Bank, Doctors Without Borders, multinational corporations

WHAT WILL YOU LEARN IN THIS CHAPTER?

This chapter will help you to do the following:

1.1 Explain the sociological perspective

1.2 Describe why sociology can be useful for us

1.3 Show how the social world model works, with examples

This model illustrates a core idea carried throughout the book—how your own life is shaped by your family, community, society, and world, and how you influence them in return. Understanding this model can help you to better understand your social world and to make a positive impact on it.

THINK ABOUT IT

Micro: Small groups and local communities	How can sociology help me understand my own life and my social world?
Meso: National institutions, complex organizations, and ethnic groups	How do sociologists help us understand and even improve our lives in work organizations and health care organizations?
Macro: National and global systems	How might national and global events affect my life?

The womb is apparently the setting for some great body work. It may win the prize for the strangest place to get a back massage, but, according to a scientific article, by the 4th month of gestation, twin fetuses begin reaching for their "womb-mates," and by 18 weeks, they spend more time touching their siblings than themselves or the walls of the uterus (Weaver 2010). Fetuses that have single-womb occupancy tend to touch the walls of the uterus a good deal to make contact with the mother. Nearly 30% of the movement of twins is directed toward their companions. Movements such as stroking the back or the head are more sustained and more precise than movements toward themselves—touching their own mouths or other facial features. As one team of scholars put it, we are "wired to be social" (Castiello et al. 2010). In short, humans are innately social creatures.

The social world is not merely something that exists outside us. As the story of the twins illustrates, the social world is also something we carry inside. We are part of

it, we reflect on it, and we are influenced by it, even when we are alone. The patterns of the social world engulf us in ways both subtle and obvious, with profound implications for how we create order and meaning in our lives. We need others—and that is where sociology enters.

Sometimes it takes a dramatic and shocking event for us to realize just how deeply embedded we are in our social relationships in the social world that we take for granted. "It couldn't happen in the United States," read typical world newspaper accounts. "This is something you see in the Middle East, Central Africa, and other war-torn areas. . . . It's hard to imagine this happening in the economic center of the United States." Yet on September 11, 2001, shortly after 9 a.m., a commercial airliner crashed into New York City's World Trade Center, followed a short while later by another pummeling into the paired tower. This mighty symbol of financial wealth collapsed. After the dust settled and the rescue crews finished their gruesome work, nearly 3,000 people were dead and many others injured. The world as we knew it changed forever that day. This event taught U.S. citizens how integrally connected they are with the international community.

Such terrorist acts horrify people because they are unpredictable and unexpected in a normally predictable world. They violate the rules that support our connections to one another. They also bring attention to the discontent and disconnectedness that lie under the surface in many societies—discontent that can come to the surface and express itself in hateful violence. Such discontent and hostility are likely to continue until the root causes are addressed.

Terrorist acts represent a rejection of the modern civil society we know. The terrorists themselves see their acts as justifiable, as a way they can strike out against injustices and threats to their way of life. Few outside the terrorists' inner circle understand their thinking and behavior. The events of 9/11 forced U.S. citizens to realize that, although they may see a great diversity among themselves, people in other parts of the world view

▲ Within hours of their birth in October 2010, Jackson and Audrey became highly fussy if the nurses tried to put them in separate bassinets. Shortly after birth they were both put in a warmer, and Jackson cried until he found Audrey, proceeding to intertwine his arms and legs with hers. Twins, like all humans, are hard-wired to be social and in relationships with others.

© Keith Roberts

U.S. citizens as all the same; they are despised by some for what they represent—consumerism, individualism, freedom of religion, and tolerance of other perspectives. The United States is a world power, yet its values challenge and threaten the views of many people around the world. For many U.S. citizens, a sense of loyalty to the nation was deeply stirred by the events of 9/11. Patriotism abounded. The nation's people became more connected to one another as a reaction to an act against the United States.

A similar sense of patriotism and connectedness arose in the United States immediately after the radical Islamic bombings and shootings at the Boston Marathon in 2013, Chattanooga in 2015, San Bernardino in 2015, and Orlando in 2016. First responders were held up as heroes and symbols of U.S. pride and perseverance in the face of terrorist attacks. However, most mass killings in the United States have not involved Islamic terrorists (Bump 2016). As Émile Durkheim, one of the founders of sociology, first pointed out, acts that break normal rules of behavior, as terrorism does, can unite the rule-following members of society (Durkheim [1895] 1982).

Most of the time, we live with social patterns that we take for granted as routine, ordinary, and expected. These social patterns help us to understand what is happening and to know what to expect. Unlike our innate drives, social expectations come from those around us and guide (or constrain) our behaviors and thoughts. Without shared expectations among humans about proper patterns of behavior, life would be chaotic. Our social interactions require some basic rules, and these rules create routine and normalcy in everyday interaction. It is strange if someone breaks the expected patterns. For the people in and around the World Trade Center on September 11, 2001, the Boston Marathon finish line on April 15, 2013, Sandy Hook Elementary School in Newtown, Connecticut, on December 14, 2012, and Stoneman Douglas High School in Parkland, Florida, on February 14, 2018, the social rules governing everyday life were brutally violated.

This chapter examines the social ties that make up our social world, as well as sociology's focus on those connections. You will learn what sociology is, what sociologists do, how sociology can be used to improve your life and society, and how the social world model helps us understand society and our social world work.

What Is Sociology?

Sociology is *the scientific study of social life, social change, and social causes and consequences of human behavior.* Sociologists examine how society both shapes and is

▲ The terrorist bombing of the 2013 Boston Marathon inspired residents in the Boston area and marathon runners to stand strong in the face of terrorism. The 2014 Boston Marathon attracted even more participants and spectators.

shaped by individuals, small groups of people, organizations, national societies, and global social networks. For you this means learning how what you do affects other people—and how they affect your life.

Unlike the discipline of psychology, which focuses on the attributes, motivations, and behaviors of individuals, sociology focuses on group patterns. Whereas a psychologist might try to explain behavior by examining the personality traits of individuals, a sociologist would examine the positions or tasks of different people within the group and how these positions influence what individuals think and do. Sociologists seek to analyze and explain why people interact with others and belong to groups, how groups like the family or you and your friends work together, why some groups have more power than other groups, how decisions in groups are made, and how groups deal with conflict and change. Sociologists also examine the causes of social problems, such as delinquency, child abuse, crime, poverty, and war, and ways they can be addressed.

Two-person interactions—*dyads*—are the smallest units studied by sociologists. Examples of dyads include roommates discussing their classes, a professor and student going over an assignment, a husband and wife negotiating their budget, and two children playing. Next in size are small groups consisting of three or more interacting people who know each other—a family, a neighborhood or peer group, a classroom, a work group, or a street gang. Then come increasingly larger groups—organizations such as sports or scouting clubs, neighborhood associations, and local religious congregations. Among the largest groups contained within nations are ethnic groups and national organizations or institutions, such as Google or

▲ Here children experience ordered interaction in the competitive environment of a soccer game. What values, skills, attitudes, and assumptions about life and social interaction do you think these kids are learning?

Facebook, the Republican and Democratic national political parties, and national religious organizations like the Southern Baptists. Nations themselves are still larger and can sometimes involve hundreds of millions of people. In the past several decades, social scientists have increasingly focused on **globalization**, *the process by which the entire world is becoming a single interdependent entity*. Of particular interest to sociologists is how these various groups are organized, how they function, how they influence one another, and why they can come into conflict.

THINKING SOCIOLOGICALLY

Identify several dyads, small groups, and large organizations to which you belong. Did you choose to belong, or were you born into membership in these groups? How does each group influence who you are and the decisions you make? How do you influence each of the groups?

Ideas Underlying Sociology

The idea that one action can cause or result in something else is a core idea in all science. Sociologists also share several ideas that they take for granted about the social world. These ideas about humans and social life are supported by considerable evidence, and they are no longer matters of debate or controversy. They are considered to be true. Understanding these core assumptions helps us see how sociologists approach the study of people in groups.

People are social by nature. This means that humans seek contact with other humans, interact with one another,

and influence and are influenced by the behaviors of others. Furthermore, humans need groups to survive. Although a few individuals may become socially isolated as adults, they could not have reached adulthood without sustained interactions with others. The central point here is that we become who we are because other people and groups constantly influence us.

People live much of their lives belonging to social groups. It is in social groups that we interact with family, friends, and fellow workers; learn to share goals and to cooperate with others in our groups; develop identities that are influenced by our group affiliations; obtain power over others—or are relatively powerless; and have conflicts with others over resources we all want. Our individual beliefs and behaviors, our experiences, our observations, and the problems we face are derived from connections to our social groups.

Interaction between the individual and the group is a two-way process in which each influences the other. In our family or on a sports team, we can influence the shape and direction of our group, just as the group provides the rules and decides the expected behaviors for individuals.

Recurrent social patterns, ordered behavior, shared expectations, and common understandings among people characterize groups. Consider the earlier examples of the chaos created by 9/11 and other bombings and mass shootings. These events were so troubling because they were unexpected, even though such events are becoming more common. Normally, a degree of continuity and recurrent behavior is present in human interactions, whether in small groups, large organizations, or society.

The processes of conflict and change are natural and inevitable features of groups and societies. No group can remain unchanged and hope to perpetuate itself. To survive, groups must adapt to changes in the social and physical environment, yet rapid change often comes at a price. It can lead to conflict within a society—between traditional and new ideas and between groups that have vested interests in particular ways of doing things. Rapid change can give rise to protest activities; changing in a controversial direction or failing to change fast enough can spark conflict, including revolution. Governments in several Latin American countries have been challenged or overthrown, springing from citizens' discontent with corrupt or authoritarian rule. The problem is finding acceptable replacement governments to take over what has been overthrown.

The previous ideas underlying sociology will be relevant in each of the topics we discuss. As you read this book, keep in mind these basic ideas that form the foundation of sociological analysis: People are social; they live and carry out activities largely in groups; interaction influences both individual and group behavior; people share common behavior patterns and expectations; and processes such as change and conflict are always present. Thus, in several important ways, sociological understandings provide new lenses for looking at our social world.

THINKING SOCIOLOGICALLY

Try this throughout the book: Apply the core ideas underlying sociology, just discussed, to understand the groups to which you belong—a class, team, religious organization, work group, or other. You can better understand these groups by applying these ideas to examples you can relate to rather than memorizing abstract ideas.

Sociological Findings and Commonsense Beliefs

Through research, sociologists have shown that many commonly held beliefs are not actually true, and some "commonsense" ideas have been discredited by sociological research. Here are three examples.

Belief: Most of the differences in the behaviors of women and men are based on "human nature"; men and women are just different from each other. Research shows that biological factors certainly play a part in the behaviors of men and women, but the culture (beliefs, values, rules, and way of life) that people learn as they grow up determines who does what and how biological tendencies are played out. A unique example illustrates this: In the nomadic Wodaabe tribe in Africa, women do most of the heavy work, whereas men adorn themselves with makeup, sip tea, and gossip (Cultural Survival 2010; Drury 2015; Zaidi 2017). Each year, the group holds a festival where men adorn makeup and fancy hairstyles, and show their white teeth and the whites of their eyes to attract a marriage partner. Such dramatic variations in the behavior of men and women around the world are so great that it is impossible to attribute behavior to biology or human nature alone; learned behavior patterns enter in.

Belief: Racial groupings are based on biological differences among people. Actually, racial categorizations are socially constructed (created by members of society), and beliefs vary among societies and over time within societies. A person can be seen as one race in Brazil and another in the United States. Even within the United States, racial categories have changed many times. All one has to do is look at old U.S. Census records to see how racial categories change over time—even within the same nation (Chappell 2017)! We discuss construction of the concept of race in Chapter 8.

© Getty Images/Oliver Strewe

▲ In the early 20th century, immigrants to the United States of Irish and Italian ancestry were not considered "White" in Virginia and several other states. In some cases where parochial schools were not an option, Irish and Italian children were forced to go to racially segregated public schools with Black students.

Belief: Most marriages in the United States do not last. There is not a simple answer to this belief! Marriage and divorce rates differ by age, education level, income, location, and other variables. Those who marry at age 18 or before, have less education, and have lower levels of income than the average person have the highest divorce rates (Kennedy and Ruggles 2014). Those who are middle class or higher tend to have more stable marriages, and most of their marriages do not end in divorce. Overall, noted researcher Paul Amato predicts that the lifetime risk of divorce is from 42% to 45%; "throw in permanent separations that don't end in divorce, then the overall likelihood of marital disruption is pushing 50 percent" (DePaulo 2017; Pew Research Center 2018a; Stanton 2018). Thus, research shows that divorce rates average below 45% depending on demographic variables.

As these examples illustrate, the discipline of sociology provides a method to assess the accuracy of our commonsense assumptions about the social world. To improve the lives of individuals in our communities and in societies around the world, decision makers must have accurate information. Sociological research can be the basis for more rational and just social policies—policies that better meet the needs of all groups in the social world. The *sociological imagination*, discussed next, helps us gain an understanding of social problems.

The Sociological Imagination

Events in our social world affect our individual lives. If we are unemployed or lack funds for a college education, we may say this is a personal problem. Yet broader social issues are often at the root of our situation. The sociological imagination holds that we can best understand our personal experiences and problems by examining their broader social context—by looking at the big picture.

Many individual problems (*private troubles*) are rooted in social or *public issues* (what is happening in the social world outside one's personal control). Distinguished sociologist C. Wright Mills called the ability to understand this *complex interactive relationship between individual experiences and public issues* the **sociological imagination**. For Mills, many personal experiences can and should be interpreted in the context of large-scale forces in the wider society (Mills 1959).

Consider, for example, someone you know who has been laid off from a job. This personal trauma is a common situation during a recession. Unemployed persons often experience feelings of inadequacy or lack of self-worth because of the job loss. Their unemployment, though, may be due to larger forces such as a machine taking over their job, unsound banking practices, corporate downsizing, or a corporation taking operations to another country where labor costs are cheaper and there are fewer environmental regulations on companies. People may blame themselves or each other for personal troubles such as unemployment or marital problems, believing that they did not try hard enough. Often, they do not see the connection between their private lives and larger economic and social forces beyond their control. They fail to recognize the public issues that create private troubles.

If you are having trouble paying for college, that may feel like a very personal trouble. High tuition rates, though, relate to a dramatic decline in governmental support for public higher education and financial aid for students. The rising cost of a college education is a serious public issue that our society needs to address. Individuals, alone, cannot reduce the high price of college.

As you learn about sociology, you will begin to notice how social forces shape individual lives and group behavior. This knowledge helps us understand aspects of everyday life we take for granted. In this book you will learn to view the social world and your place in it from a sociological perspective as you develop your *sociological imagination*. Connecting events from the global and national levels to the personal and intimate level of our own lives is the core organizing theme of this book.

THINKING SOCIOLOGICALLY

How has divorce, poverty, or war caused personal troubles for someone you know? Give examples of why it is inadequate to explain these personal troubles by examining only the personal characteristics of those affected.

Questions Sociologists Ask—and Don't Ask

Think about this—everything a sociologist asks must be answerable through research. Perhaps you have had late-night discussions with your friends about the meaning of life, the existence of God, the ethical implications of genetically modified food, or the morality of abortion. These are philosophical issues that sociologists, like other scientists, cannot answer through scientific research. What sociologists *do* ask are questions about people in social groups and organizations—questions that can be studied scientifically. Sociologists may research how people feel about the previous issues (the percentage of people who want genetically modified food to be labeled, for example), but sociologists do not determine the right or wrong answers to such value-driven opinions. They are more interested in how people's beliefs influence their behavior. They focus on issues that can be studied objectively and scientifically—looking for causes or consequences.

Sociologists might ask, *Who gets an abortion, why do they do so, and how does the society, as a whole, view abortion?* These are matters of fact that a social scientist can explore. However, sociologists avoid making ethical judgments about whether abortion is always acceptable, sometimes acceptable, or always wrong. In their private lives, sociologists and other scientists may have opinions on controversial philosophical issues, but these should not enter into their scientific work.

Likewise, sociologists might ask, *What are the circumstances around individuals becoming drunk and acting drunk?* This question is often tied more to the particular social environment than to the availability of alcohol. Note that a person might become intoxicated at a fraternity party but not at a family member's wedding reception where alcohol

▲ Binge drinking, losing consciousness, vomiting, or engaging in sexual acts while drunk may be sources of storytelling at a college party but can be offensive at a wedding reception.

is served. The expectations for behavior vary in each social setting. The researcher does not make judgments about whether use of alcohol is good or bad, or right or wrong, and avoids—as much as possible—opinions regarding responsibility or irresponsibility. The sociologist does, however, observe variations in the use of alcohol in different social situations and the resulting behaviors. The focus of sociology is on facts, what causes behaviors, and the results.

THINKING SOCIOLOGICALLY

Consider the information you have just read. What are some questions sociologists might ask about drinking and drunkenness? What are some questions sociologists would not ask about these topics, at least while in their role as researchers?

The Social Sciences: A Comparison

Not so long ago, our views of people and social relationships were based on stereotypes, intuition, superstitions, supernatural explanations, and traditions passed on from one generation to the next. Natural scientists (e.g., chemists, astronomers, biologists, and oceanographers) first used the scientific method, a model later adopted by social scientists. Social scientists, including sociologists, anthropologists, psychologists, economists, cultural geographers, historians, and political scientists, apply the scientific method to study social relationships, to correct misleading and harmful misconceptions about human behavior, and to guide policy decisions. Consider the following examples of specific studies various social scientists have conducted.

Consider an *anthropologist* who studies garbage. He examines what people discard to understand what kind of lives they lead (Bond 2010). *Anthropology* is the study of humanity in its broadest context. It is closely related to sociology, and the two areas have common historical roots and sometimes overlapping methodologies and subject matter. However, anthropologists have different specialties in four major subfields within anthropology: physical anthropology (which is related to biology), archaeology, linguistics, and cultural anthropology (sometimes called *ethnology*). This last field has the most in common with sociology. Cultural anthropologists study the culture, or way of life, of a society.

A *psychologist* may wire research subjects to a machine that measures their physiological reaction to a violent film clip and then ask them questions about what they were feeling. *Psychology* is the study of individual behavior and mental processes (e.g., sensation, perception, memory, and thought processes). It differs from sociology in that it focuses on individuals rather than on groups, institutions, and societies. Although there are different branches of psychology, most psychologists are concerned with individual motivations, personality attributes, attitudes, perceptions, abnormal behavior, mental disorders, and the stages of normal human development.

A *political scientist* studies opinion poll results to predict who will win the next election, how various groups of people are likely to vote, or how elected officials will vote on proposed legislation. *Political science* is concerned with government systems and power—how they work, how they are organized, the forms of government, relations among governments, who holds power and how they obtain it, how power is used, and who is politically active (Domhoff 2018). Political science overlaps with

▲ Anthropologists can learn about a society by studying what it throws away. Consider this picture of children rummaging through a garbage dump in India just to survive. What do you think they would learn about you from your garbage?

sociology, particularly in the study of political theory and the nature and uses of power.

Many economists study the banking system and market trends to try to predict trends and understand the global economy. *Economists* analyze economic conditions and explore how people organize, produce, and distribute material goods. They are interested in supply and demand, inflation and taxes, prices and manufacturing output, labor organization, employment levels, and comparisons between postindustrial, industrial, and nonindustrial nations.

What these social sciences—sociology, anthropology, psychology, political science, and economics—have in common is that they study aspects of human behavior and social life. Social sciences share many common topics, methods, concepts, research findings, and theories, but each has a different focus or perspective on the social world. Each of these social science studies relates to topics also studied by sociologists, but sociologists focus on human interaction, groups, and social structure, providing the broadest overview of the social world.

THINKING SOCIOLOGICALLY

Consider the issue of unemployment in the United States. What is one question in each discipline that an anthropologist, psychologist, political scientist, economist, and sociologist might ask about the social issue of unemployment?

Why Does Sociology Matter?

Sociology helps us to understand our relationships with other people; it can inform social policy decisions; and we can use skills developed through sociology in a wide range of career fields.

Why Study Sociology?

The sociological perspective helps us to be more effective as we carry out our roles as life partners, workers, friends, family members, and citizens. For example, an employee who has studied sociology may better understand how to work with groups and how the structure of the workplace affects individual behavior, how to approach problem-solving, and how to collect and analyze data. Likewise, a schoolteacher trained in sociology may have a better understanding of classroom management, student motivation, the causes of poor student learning that have roots outside the school, and why students drop out. Consider the example in the following Sociology in Our Social World feature, which explores who drops out, why, the consequences of dropping out, and other variables that shape the professional life of teachers and academic success of students.

A sociological perspective allows us to look beneath the surface of society and notice social patterns that others tend to overlook. When you view our social world with a sociological perspective, you

1. become more self-aware by understanding your social surroundings, which can lead to opportunities to improve your life;

2. have a more complete understanding of social situations by looking beyond individual explanations to include group analyses of behavior;

3. understand and evaluate problems more clearly, viewing the world systematically and objectively rather than only in emotional or personal terms;

4. gain an understanding of the many diverse cultural perspectives and how cultural differences are related to behavioral patterns;

5. assess the impact of social policies;

6. understand the complexities of social life and how to study them scientifically;

7. gain useful skills in interpersonal relations, critical thinking, data collection and analysis, problem-solving, and decision-making; and

8. learn how to change your local environment and the larger society.

HIGH SCHOOL DROPOUTS:
CAUSES, CONSEQUENCES, AND CURES

"Cesar entered Hacienda Middle School in the Los Angeles School District in the sixth grade. He lived with his mother and three younger siblings in a garage that was divided into sleeping quarters and a makeshift kitchen with no running water. His mother, who spoke only Spanish, supported the family by working long hours at a minimum-wage job" (Rumberger 2011:1). Because Cesar missed lots of school and did not complete assignments, he failed the first quarter. However, a dropout prevention program helped him begin to pass courses. By eighth grade peer pressure and gangs became part of his life. He was involved in a fight in school and was "transferred"—but stopped going to school. Cesar became a dropout (Rumberger 2011).

Sociologists studying education look for causes and results of students dropping out versus staying in school. Dropouts are defined as "16- through 24-year-olds who are not enrolled in school and have not earned a high school credential (either a diploma or an equivalency credential such as a GED certificate)" (National Center for Education Statistics 2017a). The percentage of high school dropouts has decreased from 12% in 1990 to approximately 6% in 2017. The decline for White students was from 9% to 5%, for Blacks from 13% to 7%, and for Hispanics from 32% to 12%. This narrowed the gap between White and Hispanic students by 23% (McFarland, Stark, and Cui 2018; U.S. Department of Education 2015). The U.S. dropout rate is currently at an all-time low due to improvements in graduation rates to 84.1% overall and lower dropout rates for students of color, low-income students, English language learners, and students with disabilities (America's Promise Alliance 2018).

Yet sociologists, educators, parents, and policymakers, among others, are concerned about dropout rates because of economic factors—dropouts have difficulty finding jobs, pay fewer taxes, and often receive public assistance. If they do find a job, they earn about $8,000 a year less than high school graduates and $26,500 a year less than college graduates (Alliance for Excellent Education 2018). Unemployment rates for dropouts are 7.7% compared to 2.5% for college graduates (Bureau of Labor Statistics 2017c). Dropouts have poorer health, use more health services, and die younger. They also are more likely to engage in criminal behavior and spend time in prison. They are less likely to vote or be engaged in civic activities. Dropouts cost the nation an estimated $1.8 billion every year in lost tax revenue alone ("High School Dropouts Cost $1.8 Billion Every Year" 2013).

Why do students drop out? A few reasons stand out:

- High rates of absenteeism
- Low levels of school engagement
- Low parental education
- Work or family responsibilities
- Problematic/deviant behavior
- Moving to a new school in ninth grade
- Attending school with lower achievement scores (Child Trends 2013b)

Sociologists and others propose many solutions for the dropout problem. Dropout counselors can identify students at risk and work with them, finding programs and curricula suited to their needs. Schools designed for at-risk students attempt to address issues in the students' lives such as living situations, poverty, poor health, lack of nutrition, gang membership, and other barriers to success (Diggs 2014). By understanding the causes of students dropping out we can address the problem (National Dropout Prevention Center/Network 2015).

This book introduces you to most major topics in sociology, as outlined in *the sociological literacy framework*: the sociological eye (or the sociological imagination); social structure (from micro to macro levels); socialization (the relationship between ourselves and society); stratification (social inequality); and social change and social reproduction (major change processes and how social structures reproduce themselves) (ASA 2017).

What Do Sociologists Do?

Graduates with a bachelor's degree in sociology who seek employment immediately after college are most likely to find their first jobs in social services, administrative assistantships, sales and marketing, or management-related positions. The kinds of employment college graduates with a sociology major get are listed

**Occupational Categories for
Sociology Graduates' First Jobs**

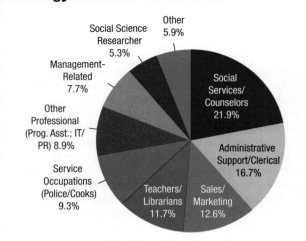

Source: Based on "21st Century Careers With an Undergraduate Degree in Sociology," American Sociological Association, 2009.

in Figure 1.1. With graduate degrees—a master's or a doctoral degree—sociologists usually become college teachers, researchers, clinicians, or consultants (Bureau of Labor Statistics 2018a). Some work for governments, whereas others work for businesses or public service nonprofit organizations.

Many sociologists work outside of academia, using their knowledge and research skills to address the needs of businesses, nonprofit organizations, and government. For example, they may work in human resources departments and as consultants for businesses. In government jobs, they provide data such as population projections for education and health care planning. In social service agencies, they help provide services to those in need, and in health agencies, they may be concerned with outreach to immigrant communities. Both sociologists who work in universities and those who work for business or government can use sociological tools to improve society. You will find examples of some jobs sociologists are doing in the Sociologists in Action boxes throughout the book. In addition, at the end of some chapters you will find a discussion of policy related to that chapter topic.

THINKING SOCIOLOGICALLY

From what you have read so far, how might sociological tools (e.g., social interaction skills and knowledge of how groups work) be useful to you in your anticipated major and career or current job?

What Do Employers Want?

Ask employers what they want in a new hire, and the focus is likely to be on writing, speaking, and analytical skills—especially when the new employee will be faced with complex problems. Other desired skills include the ability to cope with change; work effectively in diverse teams; gather and interpret quantitative information; and other "soft skills" such as leadership, communication, and collaboration (Beaton 2017). Indeed, having a combination of social skills and math and computer skills is the best predictor of landing a job that is unlikely to be replaced by technological automation and tends to do better than most other areas in pay (Deming 2015). The left column in Table 1.1 indicates what employers want from college graduates; the right column indicates the skills and competencies that are part of most sociological training. Compare the two, noting the high levels of overlap.

We now have a general idea of what sociology is, what sociologists do, and what jobs students with sociology degrees tend to seek. It should be apparent that sociology is a broad field of interest; sociologists study all aspects of human social behavior. The next section of this chapter shows how the parts of the social world that sociologists study relate to each other, and it outlines the model you will follow as you continue to learn about sociology.

THINKING SOCIOLOGICALLY

Imagine that you are a mayor, legislator, police chief, or government official. You must make many decisions each day. What method of decision-making will you use: your own intuition or assumptions, information gathered by social science research, or some other method? What are some advantages or disadvantages to each decision-making method?

The Social World Model

Think about the different groups you depend on and interact with daily. You wake up to greet members of your family or your roommate. You go to a larger group—a class—that exists within an even larger organization—the college or university. Understanding sociology and the approach of this book requires a grasp of **levels of analysis**—that is, *social groups from the smallest to the largest.* It may be relatively easy to picture small groups such as a family, a group of friends, a sports team, or a sorority or fraternity. It is more difficult to visualize large groups, such as corporations—Target, Nike,

What Employers Want and What Sociology Majors Can Deliver

Employers Who Want Colleges to "Place More Emphasis" on Essential Learning Outcomes		Traits and Knowledge That Are Developed in Most Sociological Training
Knowledge of Human Culture	**(% Seeking)**	**Skills and Competencies**
1. Global issues	72	• Knowledge of global issues • Sensitivity to diversity and differences in cultural values and traditions
2. The role of the United States in the world	60	• Sociological perspective on the United States and the world
3. Cultural values and traditions—U.S. and global	53	• Understanding diversity • Working with others (ability to work toward a common goal)
Intellectual and Practical Skills	**(% Seeking)**	
4. Teamwork skills in diverse groups	76	• Effective leadership skills (ability to take charge and make decisions) • Interpersonal skills (working with diverse coworkers)
5. Critical thinking and analytic reasoning	73	• Analysis and research skills • Organizing thoughts and information • Planning effectively (ability to design, plan, organize, and implement projects and to be self-motivated)
6. Written and oral communication	73	• Communication skills (listening, verbal and written communication) • Working with peers • Effective interaction in group situations
7. Information literacy	70	• Knowledge of how to find information one needs—online or in a library
8. Creativity and innovation	70	• Flexibility, adaptability, and multitasking (ability to set priorities, manage multiple tasks, adapt to changing situations, and handle pressure) • Creative ways to deal with problems
9. Complex problem-solving	64	• Ability to conceptualize and solve problems • Ability to be creative (working toward meeting the organization's goals)
10. Quantitative reasoning	60	• Computer and technical literacy (basic understanding of computer hardware and software programs) • Statistical analysis
Personal and Social Responsibility	**(% Seeking)**	
11. Intercultural competence (teamwork in diverse groups)	76	• Personal values (honesty, flexibility, work ethic, dependability, loyalty, positive attitude, professionalism, self-confidence, willingness to learn) • Working with others; ability to work toward a common goal
12. Intercultural knowledge (global issues)	72	• Knowledge of global issues

Source: American Sociological Association 2009; Hansen and Hansen 2003; WorldWideLearn 2007. See also Association of American Colleges and Universities and Hart Research Associates 2013.

Apple, General Motors Company, Starbucks, Google, or Facebook—or organizations such as local or state governments. The largest groups include nations or international organizations, such as the sprawling networks of the United Nations or the World Trade Organization. Groups of various sizes shape our lives. Sociological analysis involves an understanding of these groups that exist at various levels of analysis and the connections among them.

The **social world model** helps us picture *the levels of analysis in our social surroundings as an interconnected series of small groups, organizations, institutions, and societies.* Sometimes these groups are connected by mutual support and cooperation, but other times there are conflicts and power struggles over access to resources. What we are asking you to do here and throughout this book is to develop a sociological imagination—the basic lens used by sociologists. Picture the social world as connected levels of increasingly larger circles. To understand the units or parts of the social world model, look at the model shown here (and at the beginning of each chapter).

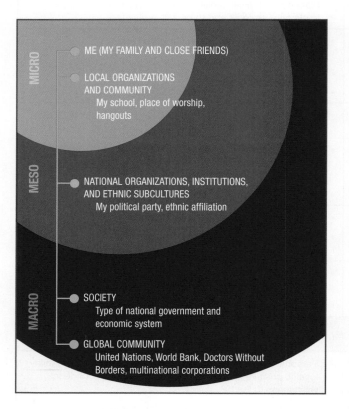

MICRO

ME (MY FAMILY AND CLOSE FRIENDS)

LOCAL ORGANIZATIONS
AND COMMUNITY
My school, place of worship,
hangouts

MESO

NATIONAL ORGANIZATIONS, INSTITUTIONS,
AND ETHNIC SUBCULTURES
My political party, ethnic affiliation

MACRO

SOCIETY
Type of national government and
economic system

GLOBAL COMMUNITY
United Nations, World Bank, Doctors Without
Borders, multinational corporations

We use this social world model throughout the book to illustrate how each topic fits into the big picture: our social world. The social world includes both *social structures* and *social processes.*

Social Structures

Picture the human body, held together by bones and muscles. The organs or *units* that make up that body include the brain, heart, lungs, and kidneys. In a similar manner, **social units** are *interconnected parts of the social world ranging from small groups to societies.* These social units include dyads (two people); small groups like the members of a family; community organizations including schools and religious groups; large-scale organizations such as political parties or state and national governments; and global societies, such as the United Nations.

All of these social units connect to make up the **social structure**—*the stable patterns of interactions, statuses (positions), roles (responsibilities), and organizations that provide stability for the society and bring order to individuals' lives.* Think about these parallels between the structure that holds together the human body and the structure that holds together societies and their units.

Sometimes, however, the units within the social structure are in conflict. For example, a religion that teaches that some forms of birth control are wrong may conflict with the health care system regarding how to provide care to women. This issue has been in the U.S. news because many religious organizations and religious business owners have fought against the requirements of the 2010 Affordable Care Act in the United States that employers provide birth control to those who wish to receive it.

Social institutions are *organized, patterned, and enduring sets of social structures that provide guidelines for behavior and help each society meet its basic survival needs.* Think about the fact that all societies have some form of family, education, religion, politics, health care, and economics; in more complex societies there are also essential structures that provide science, media, advanced health care, and a military. These are the institutions that provide the rules, roles, and relationships to meet human needs and guide human behavior. They are the units through which organized social activities take place, and they provide the setting for activities essential to human and societal survival. For example, we cannot survive without an economic institution to provide guidelines and a structure for meeting our basic needs of food, shelter, and clothing. Likewise, society would not function without political institutions to govern and protect its members. Most social units fall under one of the main institutions just mentioned.

Like the human body, society and social groups have a structure. Our body's skeleton governs how our limbs are attached to the torso and how they move. Like the system of organs that make up our bodies—heart, lungs, kidneys,

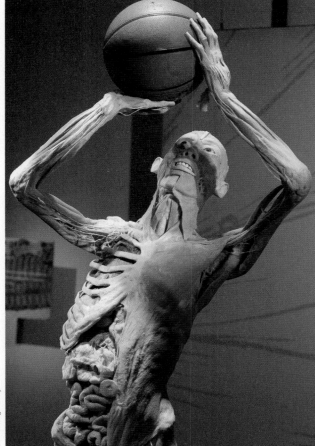

© AFP/Stringer/Getty

▲ All social institutions are interrelated, just as the parts of the body are interdependent: If the skeletal system of the body breaks down, the muscular system and nervous system are not far behind.

and bladder—all social institutions are interrelated. Just as an illness in one organ affects other organs, a dysfunction in one institution affects the other institutions. A heart attack affects the flow of blood to all other parts of the body. Likewise, if many people are unable to afford medical treatment, the society is less healthy, and there are consequences for families, schools, workplaces, and society as a whole.

The **national society**, one of the largest social units in our model, includes *a population of people, usually living within a specified geographic area, connected by common ideas and subject to a particular political authority.* It also features a social structure with groups and institutions. In addition to having relatively permanent geographic and political boundaries, a national society has one or more languages and a unique way of life. In most cases, national societies involve countries or large regions where the inhabitants share a common identity as members. In certain other instances, such as the contemporary United

Kingdom, a single national society may include several groups of people who consider themselves distinct nationalities (e.g., Welsh, English, Scottish, and Irish) and those individuals from former colonies. Such multicultural societies may or may not have peaceful relations.

THINKING SOCIOLOGICALLY

Can you think of any human activities that do not fall into one of the institutions just mentioned? How might change in one national institution, such as health care, affect change in other national institutions, such as the family and the economy?

Social Processes

If social structure is similar to the human body's skeletal structure, social processes are similar to what keeps the

© Getty Images/Peter Turnley/Contributor

▲ This refugee mother and child from Mozambique represent the smallest social unit, a dyad. In this case, they are trying to survive with help from larger groups such as the United Nations.

body alive—a beating heart, the lungs processing oxygen, and the stomach processing nutrients. **Social processes** *take place through actions of people in institutions and other social units.* The process of *socialization* teaches individuals how to behave in their society. It takes place through actions in families, educational systems, religious organizations, and other social units. Socialization is essential for the continuation of any society because through this process members of society learn the thoughts and actions needed to survive in their society. Another process, *conflict,* occurs between individuals or groups over money, jobs, and other needed or desired resources. The process of *change* also occurs continuously in every social unit; change in one unit affects other units of the social world, often in a chain reaction. For instance, change in the quality of health care can affect the workforce; a workforce in poor health can affect the economy; instability in the economy can affect families, for breadwinners lose jobs; and family economic woes can affect religious communities because devastated families cannot afford to give money to churches, mosques, or temples.

Sociologists try to identify, understand, and explain the processes that take place within social units. Picture these processes as overlying and penetrating our whole social world, from small groups to large societies. Social units would be lifeless without the action brought about by social processes, just as body parts would be lifeless without the processes of electrical impulses shooting from the brain to each organ or the oxygen transmitted by blood coursing through our arteries to sustain each organ.

Our Social World and Its Environment

Surrounding each social unit, whether a small family group or a large corporation, is an **environment**—*the setting in which the social unit works, including everything that influences the social unit, such as its physical and organizational surroundings and technological innovations.* Just as each individual has a unique environment with family, friends, and other social groups, each social unit has an environment to which it must adjust. For example, your local church, mosque, synagogue, or temple may seem autonomous and independent, but it depends on its environment, including its national organization, for guidelines and support; the local police force to protect the building from vandalism; and the local economy to provide jobs to members so that the members, in turn, can support the organization. If the religious education program is going to train children to understand the scriptures, local schools are needed to teach the children to read. A religious group may also be affected by

other religious bodies, competing with one another for potential members from the community. These religious groups may work cooperatively—organizing a summer program for children or jointly sponsoring a holy day celebration—or they may define one another as evil, each trying to malign or stigmatize the other. Moreover, one local religious group may be composed primarily of professional and businesspeople and another group mostly of laboring people. The religious groups may experience conflict in part because each serves a different socioeconomic constituency in the environment. The point is that to understand a social unit *or* the human body, we must consider the *structure* and *processes* within the unit as well as the interaction with the surrounding environment.

Perfect relationships or complete harmony among the social units is unusual. Social units, be they small groups or large organizations, are often motivated by self-interest and the need for self-preservation, with the result that they compete with other units for resources (e.g., time, money, skills, and the energy of members). Therefore, social units within a society are often in conflict. Whether groups are in conflict or they cooperate does not change their interrelatedness; units are interdependent and can be studied using the scientific method.

THINKING SOCIOLOGICALLY

Think of an example of a social unit to which you belong. Describe the environment of the social unit. How does the environment influence that social unit?

Studying the Social World: Levels of Analysis

Picture for a moment your sociology class as a social unit in your social world. Students (individuals) make up the class, the class (small group) is offered by the sociology department, the sociology department (a large group, including faculty and students) is part of the college or university, and the university (an organization) is located in a community. The university follows the practices approved by the social institution (education) of which it is a part, and education is an institution located within a nation. Practices the university follows are determined by a larger accrediting agency that provides guidelines and oversight for educational institutions. The national society, represented by the national government, is shaped by global events such as technological and economic competition among nations, natural disasters, global climate change, wars, and terrorist attacks. Such events influence national policies and goals, including policies for the educational system. Thus, global issues and conflicts may shape the content of the curriculum taught in the local classroom, from what is studied to the textbooks used.

As discussed, each of these social units is referred to as a *level of analysis* (two students in a discussion group, to a society or global system; see Table 1.2). These levels are illustrated in the social world model at the beginning of each chapter, and their relation to that chapter's content is shown through examples in the model.

Micro-Level Analysis. A focus on *individual or small-group interaction in specific situations* is called **micro-level analysis**. The micro level is important because one-to-one and small-group interaction form the basic foundation of all social groups and organizations to which we belong, from families to corporations to societies. We are members of many groups at the micro level.

To understand micro-level analysis, consider the problem of spousal abuse. Why does a person remain in an abusive relationship, knowing that each year thousands of people are killed by their partners and millions more are severely and repeatedly battered? To answer this question, several possible micro-level explanations can be considered. One view is that the abusive partner has convinced the abused person that she or he is powerless in the relationship or "deserves" the abuse. Therefore, the abused person gives up in despair of ever being able to alter the situation. The abuse is viewed as part of the interaction—of action and reaction—and some partners come to see abuse as what composes normal interaction.

Another explanation for remaining in the abusive relationship is that battering is a familiar part of the person's everyday life. However unpleasant and unnatural this may seem to outsiders, it may be seen by the abused as a "normal" and acceptable part of intimate relationships, especially if she or he grew up in an abusive family.

Another possibility is that an abused woman may fear that her children would be harmed or that she would be harshly judged by her family or religious group if she "abandoned" her mate. She may have few resources to make leaving the abusive situation possible. To study each of these possible explanations involves analysis at the micro level because each issue posed here focuses on interpersonal interaction factors rather than on large society-wide trends or forces. Moving to the next level, meso-level analysis leads to different explanations for abuse.

Meso-Level Analysis. **Meso-level analysis** involves looking at *intermediate-sized units smaller than the nation but larger than the local community or even the region*. This level includes national institutions (such as the economy of a country, the national educational system, or the political system within a country), nationwide organizations (such as a political party, a soccer league, or a national women's rights organization), and ethnic groups that have an identity as a group (such as Jews, Mexican Americans, or Native Americans in the United States). Organizations, institutions, and ethnic communities are smaller than the nation or global social units, but they are still beyond the everyday personal experience and control of individuals. They are intermediate in the sense of being too large to know everyone in the group, but they are not as

▼ TABLE 1.2

Levels of Analysis and Education

	Level	Parts of Education
Micro-level analysis	Interpersonal	Sociology class; professor and student interacting; study group cramming for an exam
	Local organizations	University; sociology department
Meso-level analysis	Organizations and institutions	State boards of education; National Education Association
	Ethnic groups within a nation	Islamic madrassas or Jewish yeshiva school systems
Macro-level analysis	Nations	Policy and laws governing education
	Global community	World literacy programs

large as nation-states. For example, state governments in the United States, provinces in Canada, prefectures in Japan, or cantons in Switzerland are at the meso level and usually more accessible and easier to change than the national bureaucracies of these countries.

In discussing micro-level analysis, we used the example of domestic violence. Recognizing that personal troubles can often be related to public issues, many social scientists look for broader explanations of spousal abuse, such as social conditions at the meso level of society (Straus 2017; Straus, Gelles, and Steinmetz 2006). When a pattern of behavior in society occurs with increasing frequency, it cannot be understood solely from the viewpoint of individual cases or micro-level causes. For instance, sociological findings show that fluctuations in spousal or child abuse at the micro level are related to levels of unemployment in meso-level organizations and macro-level government economic policies. Frustration resulting in abuse erupts within families when poor economic conditions make it nearly impossible for people to find a stable and reliable means of supporting themselves and their families. The message here is that meso-level economic issues in the society need to be addressed in order to decrease domestic violence.

Macro-Level Analysis. Studying the largest social units in the social world, called **macro-level analysis**, involves looking at *entire nations, global forces (such as international organizations), and international social trends*. Macro-level analysis is essential to our understanding of how larger societal forces and global events shape our everyday lives. A natural disaster, such as recent droughts and floods in North America and West Africa, and massive hurricanes in Central America and the Caribbean, may change the foods we can serve at our family dinner table because much of what we consume comes from other parts of the world. (Figure 1.2 shows some of the deadliest natural disasters in 2017.) Likewise, a political conflict on the other side of the planet can lead to war, which means that a member of your family may be called up on active

▼ FIGURE 1.2

Loss Events Worldwide in 2017: Geographic Overview

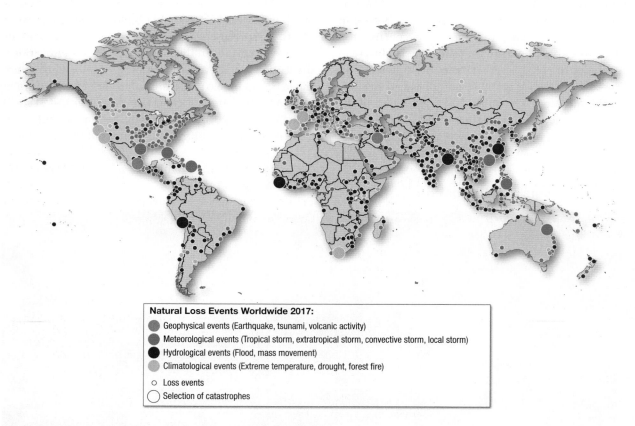

Natural Loss Events Worldwide 2017:

● Geophysical events (Earthquake, tsunami, volcanic activity)
● Meteorological events (Tropical storm, extratropical storm, convective storm, local storm)
● Hydrological events (Flood, mass movement)
● Climatological events (Extreme temperature, drought, forest fire)

○ Loss events
◯ Selection of catastrophes

Source: Münchener Ruckversicherungs-Gesellschaft, NatCatService 2018.

duty and sent into harm's way more than 7,000 miles from your home. Each member of the family may experience individual stress, have trouble concentrating, and feel ill with worry. The entire globe has become an interdependent social unit. If we are to prosper and thrive in the world today, we need to understand connections that go beyond our local communities. We are, indeed, members of the global community.

Patterns such as domestic violence can be examined at each level of analysis. Violence against women (especially rape) occurs at different rates in different societies, with some having a *culture of rape* (Kristof and WuDunn 2009). Recent gang rapes of a Danish tourist and young teenagers and the death of an 8-year-old girl from a gang rape became headline news and shone a spotlight on the culture and lack of law enforcement in some isolated parts of India that encourage violence against women (Gowen 2018; McCoy 2014). The most consistent predictor of violence against women is a macho conception of masculine roles and personality. Societies or subgroups within society that teach males that the finest expression of their masculinity is physical strength and domination tend to have more battered women (Mayeda 2013).

India is far from the only nation with some parts of the culture that generate violence against women. The United Nations estimates that 35% of women worldwide experience physical or sexual violence in their lives; in some nations that figure is 70% (UN Women 2017). South Africa has one of the highest levels of rape in the world, with one in four men having raped a woman and 46% of those more than once (U.S. Department of State 2015). The men tend to show no remorse because the behavior is "accepted" by their segments of society; it is "macho" (Lindow 2009). Recent studies profile rape behavior; on college campuses, these rapes are associated with heavy drinking, perceived pressure to have sex, "rape myths" such as no means yes, a peer group that uses hostile language to describe women, and rape porn. Men scoring high on tests of empathy are less likely to rape (Murphy 2017).

Understanding individual human behavior often requires investigation of the larger societal beliefs and values that support that behavior. Worldwide patterns may tell us something about a social problem and offer new lenses for understanding that problem.

Distinctions between the levels of analysis are not always sharply delineated. The micro level shades into the meso level, and the lines between the meso level and the macro level are blurry on the continuum. Still, it is clear that in some micro-level social units, you know everyone, or at least every member of the social unit is only two degrees of separation away. In other words, every person in the social unit knows someone whom you also know. Try the next Engaging Sociology box to test your understanding of levels of analysis and the sociological imagination.

We all participate in meso-level social units that are smaller than the nation but that can be huge. For example, thousands or even millions of individuals join organizations such as the NRA, MoveOn.org, or the environmental group 350.org. Those involved participate in marches and dialogues online and contribute money to these organizations. People living thousands of miles from one another united financially and in spirit to support candidates in the 2016 U.S. presidential election and 2018 midterm elections. We share connections with the members of these organizations, and our lives are interconnected, even if we never meet face to face.

The macro level is even more removed from the individual, but its impact can change our lives. For example, decisions by lawmakers in Washington, D.C., can seem distant, but decisions by Congress and the president may determine whether your own family has health care coverage (and of what quality) and whether the United States will lead or stymie global efforts to address climate change. These government leaders will also determine whether interest rates on federal student loans for U.S. students go up.

The social world model presented in each chapter illustrates the interplay of micro-, meso-, and macro-level forces related to that chapter's sociological content. Figure 1.3 shows how this micro-to-macro model should be seen as a continuum.

The Social World Model and This Book

The social world engulfs each of us from the moment of our birth until we die. Throughout our lives, each of us is part of a set of social relationships that provides

▼ FIGURE 1.3

The Micro-to-Macro Continuum

Micro social units   Meso social units   Macro social units

ENGAGING SOCIOLOGY

MICRO-MESO-MACRO

The distinctions between levels of analysis are gray rather than precise. Levels of analysis should be viewed as a *continuum*—from micro to macro social units. Clear criteria help identify groups at each level. One criterion is size (number of people) of the group. A second is the geographic range of influence:

- intimate or very close personal relationships (micro);

- social units in the local community (micro);

- social units that cover a large geographic region (like a state or commonwealth) and even nationwide groups that—despite size—are still a small portion of the entire nation (meso);

- the nation itself (macro); and

- units with global influence (macro).

A third criterion is degree of separation. If you know someone personally, that is one degree of separation. If you do not know the mayor of your town, but you know someone who knows the mayor, that is two degrees of separation. If you have a friend or a relative who knows someone who is a friend or relative of the governor in your state or province, that is three degrees of separation. Some research indicates that every person on the planet is within seven degrees of separation from every other human being. Let us see what these mean for various levels of analysis in our social world.

Micro-level groups are small, local-community social units such as families and school classrooms within which everyone knows everyone else or knows someone who also knows another member. So the degree of separation is usually not more than two degrees.

Meso-level groups are social units of intermediate size, such as state governments (with limited geographic range), ethnic groups, and religious denominations (with large geographic range but population sizes that make them a minority of the entire nation). Typically, the group is large enough that members have never heard the names of many other members. Many members may have little access to the leaders, yet the group is not so large as to make the leaders seem distant or unapproachable. Almost anyone within the social unit is only three or four degrees of separation apart. Everyone in the unit knows someone who is an acquaintance of yours.

Macro-level groups are large social units, usually bureaucratic, that operate at a national or a global level, such as national governments or international organizations. Most members are unlikely to know or have communicated with the leaders personally or know someone who knows the leaders. The "business" of these groups is of international importance and implication. A macro-level system is one in which most of the members are at least five degrees of separation from one another—that is, they know someone who knows someone who knows someone who knows someone who knows the person in question.

★ ★ ★ ★ ★ ★

Engaging Sociology

─────────────────────────

1. Micro social units

─────────────────────────

2. Meso social units

─────────────────────────

3. Macro social units

Look at the following list of social units. Identify which level each group is most likely to belong to: (1) micro, (2) meso, or (3) macro. Why did you answer as you did? The previous definitions should help you make your decisions. Again, some are "on the line" because this is a continuum from micro to macro, and some units could legitimately be placed in more than one group. Which ones are especially on the line?

_____ Your nuclear family

_____ The United Nations

_____ A local chapter of the Lions Club or the Rotary Club

_____ Your high school baseball team

_____ India

_____ NATO (North Atlantic Treaty Organization)

_____ The First Baptist Church in Muncie, Indiana

_____ The World Bank

_____ A family reunion

_____ Amazon.com, Inc. (international)

_____ The Department of Education for the Commonwealth of Kentucky	_____ The Roman Catholic Church (with its headquarters at the Vatican in Rome)
_____ The show choir in your local high school	_____ Australia
_____ African Canadians	_____ The Chi Omega national sorority
_____ The Dineh (Navajo) people	_____ Boy Scout Troop #187 in Minneapolis, Minnesota
_____ Canada	
_____ The Republican Party in the United States	_____ Al-Qaeda (an international alliance of terrorist organizations)
_____ The World Court	
_____ A fraternity at your college	_____ The provincial government for the Canadian province of Ontario
_____ The International Monetary Fund (IMF)	
_____ The Ministry of Education for Spain	_____ The United States of America

guidelines for how we interact with others and how we see ourselves. This does not mean that human behavior is strictly determined by our links to the social world. Humans are more than mere puppets whose behavior is programmed by social structure. It does mean, however, that the individual and the larger social world influence each other. We are influenced by, and we have influence on, our social environment. The social world is a human creation, and we can and do change that which we create. It influences our behaviors, and we influence our social world. In this sense, social units are constantly emerging and changing in the course of human action and interaction.

The difficulty for most of us is that we are so caught up in our daily concerns that we fail to see and understand the social forces at work in our personal lives. What we need are conceptual and methodological tools to help us gain a more complete and accurate perspective on the social world. The ideas, theories, methods, and levels of analysis employed by sociologists are the very tools that will help give us that perspective. To use an analogy, each different lens of a camera gives the photographer a unique view of the world. Wide-angle lenses, close-up lenses, telephoto lenses, and special filters each serve a purpose in creating a distinctive picture or frame of the world. No one lens provides the complete picture. Yet the combination of images produced by various lenses allows us to examine in detail aspects of the world we might ordinarily overlook. That is what the sociological perspective gives us: a unique set of lenses to see the social world around us with deeper understanding. In seeing the social world from a sociological perspective, we are better able to understand who we are as social beings.

Throughout this book, we use the social world model as the framework for understanding the social units, processes, and surrounding environment. We look at each social unit and process. We take the unit out, examine it, and then return it to its place in the interconnected social world model so that you can comprehend the whole social world and its parts, like putting a puzzle together. Look for the model at the beginning of every chapter. We also explain the micro-, meso-, and macro-level dimensions of issues throughout the text. Test your understanding of these concepts by identifying the levels of analysis in the following Engaging Sociology.

Our next chapter asks the following: When we say we know something about society, how is it that we know? What is considered evidence in sociology, and what lens (theory) do we use to interpret the data? We now turn to how we gather data to help us develop hypotheses, test theories, and understand the social world.

MICRO-MESO-MACRO: AN APPLICATION EXERCISE

Imagine there has been a major economic downturn (recession) in your local community. Identify three possible events at each level (micro, meso, and macro) that might contribute to the economic troubles in your town.

The micro (local community) level:

1. _____

2. _____

3. _____

The meso (intermediate—state, organizational, or ethnic subculture) level:

1. _____

2. _____

3. _____

The macro (national/global) level:

1. _____

2. _____

3. _____

WHAT HAVE WE LEARNED?

How can sociology help you see new aspects of your life and change society? Throughout this book you will find ideas and examples that will help answer these questions. You will learn how to view the social world through a sociological lens and use the *sociological imagination*. Understanding how the social world works from the micro through the meso to the macro level helps us interact more effectively in it. Using the sociological imagination enables us to see how individual troubles can be rooted in social issues and are best addressed with an understanding of the meso and macro level. This knowledge enables us to be better family members, workers, citizens, and members of the global community.

We live in a complex social world with many layers of interaction. If we really want to understand our own lives, we need to comprehend the levels of analysis that affect our lives and the connections between those levels. To do so wisely, we need both objective lenses for viewing this complex social world and accurate, valid information (facts) about the society. As the science of society, sociology can provide both tested empirical data and a broad, analytical perspective, as you will learn in the next chapter. Here is a summary of points from Chapter 1.

KEY POINTS

- Humans are, at our very core, social animals—more akin to pack or herd animals than to individualistic cats.

- Sociology is based on scientific findings, making it more predictable and reliable than opinions or commonsense beliefs in a particular culture.

- A core idea in sociology is the sociological imagination. It requires that we see how our individual lives and personal troubles are shaped by historical and structural events that go beyond our everyday lives. It also prods us to see how we can influence our society.

- Sociology is a social science and, therefore, uses the tools of the sciences to establish credible evidence to understand our social world. As a science, sociology is scientific and objective rather than value laden.

- Sociology has practical applications, including those that are essential for the job market.

- Sociology focuses on social units or groups, on social structures such as institutions, on social processes that give a social unit its dynamic character, and on their social environments.

- The social world model is the organizing theme of this book. Using the sociological imagination, we can understand our social world best by clarifying the interconnections among micro, meso, and macro levels of the social world. Each chapter of this book focuses on one major topic in sociology using society at these three levels of analysis.

DISCUSSION QUESTIONS

1. Think of a problem that impacts you personally (e.g., the high cost of tuition, unemployment, or divorce) and explain how you would make sense of it differently if you viewed it as (a) only a personal problem or (b) influenced by a public issue. How do possible solutions to the problem differ depending on how you view it?

2. How can sociology help you become a more informed citizen and better able to understand how government policies impact society?

3. What are three ways the sociological perspective can help you succeed in college and the workforce?

4. Think of some of the ways the social institutions of government and education are connected. Why is it in the interest of the government to support higher education? How has government support (or lack of support) impacted your college experience?

5. Imagine you would like to look at reasons behind the high college dropout rate in the United States. How might your explanations differ based on whether your analysis was on the micro, meso, or macro level? Why? Which level or levels would you focus on for your study? Why?

KEY TERMS

environment   16

globalization   6

levels of analysis   12

macro-level analysis   18

meso-level analysis   17

micro-level analysis   17

national society   15

social institutions   14

social processes   16

social structure   14

social units   14

social world model   14

sociological imagination   8

sociology   5

CONTRIBUTING TO OUR SOCIAL WORLD: WHAT CAN WE DO?

At the end of this and all subsequent chapters, you will find suggestions for work, service learning, internships, and volunteering that encourage you to apply the ideas discussed in the chapter. Suggestions for Chapter 1 focus on student organizations for sociology majors and nonmajors.

at your school, consider forming one with the help of a faculty member. Sociologists also have an undergraduate honors society, Alpha Kappa Delta (AKD). Visit the AKD website at alphakappadelta.org to learn more about the society and what it takes to qualify for membership or to form a chapter.

At the Local (Micro) Level

- *Student organizations and clubs* enable you to meet other students interested in sociology, carry out group activities, get to know faculty members, and attend presentations by guest speakers. These clubs are usually not limited to sociology majors. If no such organization exists for sociology students

At the Organizational or Institutional (Meso) Level

- *State, regional, and specialty (education, criminology, social problems, and so forth) sociological associations* are especially student-friendly and feature publications and sessions at their annual meetings specifically for undergraduates. The

American Sociological Association lists regional and specialty organizations and their website addresses, with direct links to their home pages at www.asanet.org/news-events/calendar.

At the National or Global (Macro) Level

- *The American Sociological Association (ASA)* is the leading professional organization of sociologists in the United States. Visit the ASA website at www.asanet.org and take a look around. You will find many programs and initiatives of special interest to students. If you are interested in becoming a sociologist, be sure to look at the links under the heading "News on the Profession." ASA also sponsor an Honors Program at the annual meeting that introduces students to the profession and gives them a heads-up on being successful in sociology. For more information go to www.asanet.org/teaching-learning/undergraduate-student-resources/honors-program.

- *The International Sociological Association (ISA)* serves sociologists from around the world. Every 4 years, the ISA sponsors a large meeting. Specialty groups within ISA hold smaller conferences throughout the world during the other years. Check out www.isa-sociology.org.

$SAGE edge™

Get the tools you need to sharpen your study skills. SAGE edge offers a robust online environment featuring an impressive array of free tools and resources.

Access practice quizzes, eFlashcards, video, and multimedia at **edge.sagepub.com/ballantine7e**

EXAMINING THE SOCIAL WORLD

How Do We Know What We Know?

▲ Science is about knowing—through careful systematic investigation. Of course there are other ways of seeking knowledge, such as finding a good library on a beach!

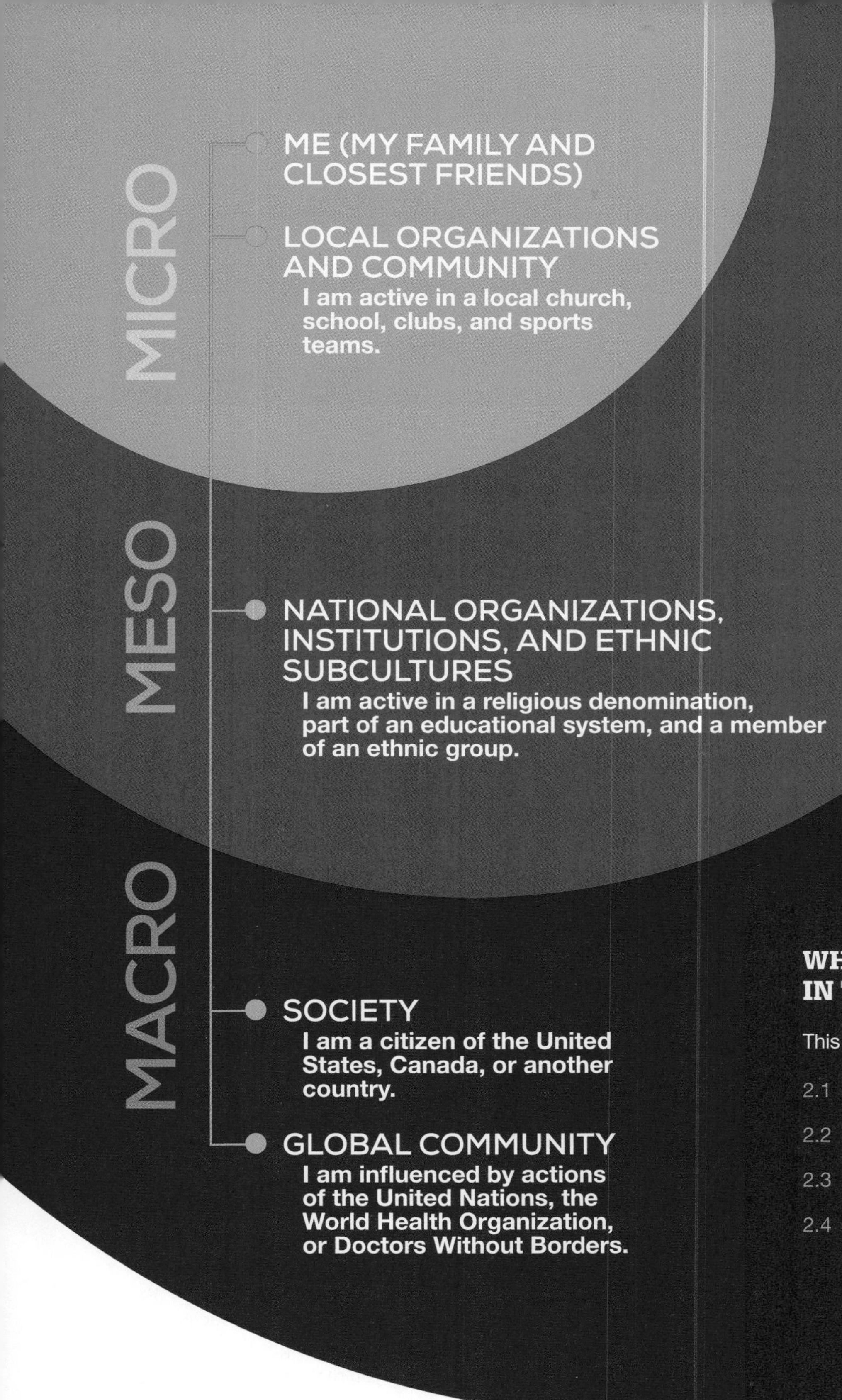

MICRO

ME (MY FAMILY AND CLOSEST FRIENDS)

LOCAL ORGANIZATIONS AND COMMUNITY
I am active in a local church, school, clubs, and sports teams.

MESO

NATIONAL ORGANIZATIONS, INSTITUTIONS, AND ETHNIC SUBCULTURES
I am active in a religious denomination, part of an educational system, and a member of an ethnic group.

MACRO

SOCIETY
I am a citizen of the United States, Canada, or another country.

GLOBAL COMMUNITY
I am influenced by actions of the United Nations, the World Health Organization, or Doctors Without Borders.

WHAT WILL YOU LEARN IN THIS CHAPTER?

This chapter will help you to do the following:

2.1 Outline the development of sociology

2.2 Describe key theoretical perspectives

2.3 Explain the scientific approach

2.4 Outline the basic steps of the scientific research process

THINK ABOUT IT

Micro: Small groups and local communities	When you are trying to convince neighbors or people in your community to accept your opinion, why are facts and evidence important?
Meso: National institutions, complex organizations, and ethnic groups	How do sociologists gather accurate data about families, educational institutions, or ethnic groups?
Macro: National and global systems	How can theories about national and global interactions help us understand our own lives at the micro level?

Let us travel to the Southern Hemisphere to meet a teenage boy, Hector. He is a 16-year-old, living in a favela (slum) on the outskirts of São Paulo, Brazil. He is a polite, bright boy, but his chances of getting an education and a steady job in his world are limited. Like millions of other children around the world, he comes from a poor rural family that migrated to an urban area in search of a better life. However, his family ended up in a crowded slum with only a shared spigot for water and one string of electric lights along the dirt road going up the hill on which they live. The sanitary conditions in his community are appalling—open sewers and no garbage collection—and make the people susceptible to various diseases. His family is relatively fortunate, for they have cement walls and wood flooring but no bathroom, running water, or electricity. Many adjacent dwellings are little more than cardboard walls with corrugated metal roofs and dirt floors.

Hector wanted to stay in school but was forced to drop out to help support his family. Since leaving school, he has picked up odd jobs—deliveries, trash pickup, janitorial work, and gardening—to help pay for the family's dwelling and to buy food to support his parents and six siblings. Even when he was in school, Hector's experience was discouraging. He was not a bad student, and some teachers encouraged him to continue, but other students from the city teased the favela kids and made them feel unwelcome. Most of his friends dropped out before he did. Hector often missed school because of other obligations: looking for part-time work, helping a sick relative, or taking care of a younger sibling. The immediate need to put food on the table outweighed the long-term value of staying in school. What is the bottom line for Hector and millions like him? Because of his limited education and work skills, obligations to his family, and limited opportunities, he most likely will continue to live in poverty along with millions of others in this situation.

Sociologists are interested in factors that influence the social world of children like Hector: family, friends, school, community, and the place of one's nation in the global political and economic structural systems. Sociologists use social theories and scientific methods to examine and understand poverty and many other social issues. In this chapter, you will learn about some of the different data collection methods sociologists use to collect information and the theories they use to make sense of their data.

Sociological research helps us to understand how and why society operates and how we might change it. It can also help you make sense of why people in your family, neighborhood, college campus, and workplace act the way they do. You will, no doubt, find yourself in a situation where conducting a research study will help your organization or community.

© Getty/Christopher Pillitz/Contributor

▲ Slum dwellers of São Paulo, Brazil. Hector lives in a neighborhood with shelters made of available materials such as boxes, with no electricity or running water and poor sanitation.

This chapter introduces you to the basic tools used to plan studies and gather dependable information on topics of interest. It will also help you understand how sociology approaches research questions. To this end, we begin this chapter by discussing the development of sociology as a discipline and the core principles of sociology's major theoretical perspectives. We then explore sociology as a science—core ideas that underlie any science: how to collect data, ethical issues involving research, and practical applications and uses of sociological knowledge. We start with the beginnings and emergence of sociology as a field of study.

Development of Sociology

Throughout recorded history, humans have been curious about how and why society operates as it does. Long before the development of science, religion and philosophy influenced the way individuals thought about the world. Both approaches to understanding society had a strong moral tone. For example, Plato's *Republic*, written around 400 BCE, outlines plans for an ideal state—complete with government, family, economic systems, class structure, and education—designed to achieve social justice. These philosophers' opinions were derived from abstract reflection about how the social world should work, but they were not tested scientifically.

The first person on record to suggest a systematic approach to explain the social world was North African Islamic scholar Ibn Khaldun (1332–1406). Khaldun was particularly interested in understanding the feelings of solidarity that held tribal groups together during his day, a time of great conflict and wars (Alagha 2017; Alatas 2006). With this beginning came the rise of modern sociology.

Rise of Modern Sociology

Several conditions from the 1600s to the 1800s gave rise to sociology. First, European nations were imperial powers extending their influence and control by establishing colonies in other cultures. This exposure to other cultures encouraged at least some Europeans to learn more about the people in and around their new colonies. Second, they sought to understand the rapid changes in their own societies brought about by the Industrial Revolution (which began around the middle of the 1700s) and the French Revolution (1789–1799). Finally, advances in the natural sciences demonstrated the value of the scientific method, and some wished to apply this scientific method to social sciences and to understanding the social world.

© Getty/DEA/G. DAGLI ORTI

© SOPA Images/LightRocket/Getty Images

▲ The Bastille, a state prison in Paris, France, and a symbol of oppression, was seized by the common people during the French Revolution, a social upheaval that forced social analysts to think differently about society and social stability. Today, rallying points for social movements and revolutions such as we see in Venezuela illustrate that uprisings of the common people are still changing societies.

In the early and mid-1800s, no one had clear, systematic explanations for why the old social structure, which had lasted since the early Middle Ages, was collapsing or why cities were exploding with migrants from rural areas. French society was in turmoil, members of the nobility were being executed, and new rules of justice were taking hold. Churches were made subordinate to the state, equal rights under the law were established for citizens, and democratic rule emerged. These dramatic changes marked the end of the traditional monarchy and the beginning of a new social order.

In this setting the scientific study of society emerged. Two social thinkers, Henri Saint-Simon (1760–1825) and Auguste Comte (1798–1857), decried the lack of systematic data collection or objective analysis in social thought. These Frenchmen argued that a science of society could help people understand and perhaps control the rapid changes and unsettling revolutions taking place.

Comte officially coined the term *sociology* in 1838. His basic premise was that common ways of understanding the world at that time, through religious or philosophical speculation about society, did not provide an adequate understanding of how to solve society's problems. Just as the scientists compiled basic facts about the *physical* world, so, too, was there a need to gather scientific knowledge about the *social* world. Only then could leaders systematically apply this scientific knowledge to improve social conditions.

Comte asked two basic questions: What holds society together and gives rise to a stable order rather than anarchy? Further, why and how do societies change? Comte conceptualized society as divided into two parts: (1) *social statics*, aspects of society that give rise to order, stability, and harmony, and (2) *social dynamics*, forces that promote change and evolution (even revolution) in society. Comte was concerned with what contemporary sociologists and the social world model in this book refer to as *structure* (social statics) and *process* (social dynamics). By understanding these aspects of the social world, Comte felt that leaders could strengthen society and respond appropriately to change. His optimistic belief was that sociology would be the "queen of sciences," guiding leaders to construct a better social order (Comte [1855] 2003).

Sociology continued developing as scholars tried to understand further changes brought about by the Industrial Revolution. Massive social and economic transformations in the 18th and 19th centuries brought about restructuring and sometimes the demise of political monarchies, aristocracies, and feudal lords. Scenes of urban squalor were common in Great Britain and other industrializing European nations. Machines replaced both agricultural workers and cottage (home) industries because they produced an abundance of goods faster, better, and cheaper. Peasants were pushed off the land by new technologies and migrated to urban areas to find work; at the same time, a powerful new social class of capitalists was emerging. Industrialization brought the need for a new skilled class of laborers, putting new demands on an education system that had served only the elite. Families now depended on work and wages in the industrial sector to stay alive.

These changes stimulated other social scientists to study society and its problems. The writings of Émile Durkheim, Karl Marx, Harriet Martineau, Max Weber, W. E. B. Du Bois, and many other early sociologists set the stage for the development of sociological theories. Du Bois, an African American who had to deal with racism within and without academia, was the first scholar in North America to have a truly scientific program for the study of society, beginning prior to 1900 (A. Morris 2015). Accompanying the development of sociological theory was the use of the scientific method—the systematic gathering and recording of reliable and accurate data to test ideas. In the next section, we turn to sociology's major theoretical perspectives.

Sociology's Major Theoretical Perspectives

A **theoretical perspective** is *a basic view of society that guides sociologists' research and analysis. Theoretical perspectives are the broadest theories in sociology, providing overall approaches to understanding the social world and social problems.* Sociologists draw on major theoretical perspectives at each level of analysis to guide their research and to help them understand social interactions and social organizations. **Theories** *are statements or explanations regarding how and why two or more facts are related to each other and the connections between these facts.* A good theory also allows social scientists to make *predictions* about the social world.

Recall the description of the social world model presented in Chapter 1. It stresses the levels of analysis—smaller units existing within larger social systems. Some theories are especially useful when trying to understand small micro-level interactions, whereas others tend to be used to make sense of large macro-level structures. Either type of theory—those most useful at the micro or macro level—can be used at the meso level, depending on the research question being asked.

To illustrate four of the major theoretical perspectives on the social world, we delve into our examination of Hector's circumstances, introduced at the beginning of this chapter.

Micro- to Meso-Level Theories

If we wanted to study Hector's interactions with his friends and their influence on him or his school performance, we would turn to micro- and meso-level theories to guide our research. Two theories most often used at the micro and meso levels of analysis are *symbolic interaction theory* and *rational choice theory*.

Symbolic Interaction Theory.

Symbolic interaction theory (also called social constructionism or interpretative theory) *sees humans as active agents who create shared meanings of symbols and events, and then interact on the basis of those meanings.*

Let's break that down: Through our interactions, we learn to share common ideas, understand what to expect from others, and gain the capability to influence society. As we interact, we make use of **symbols**, *actions or objects that represent something else and therefore have meaning beyond their own existence*—such as flags, wedding rings, words, and nonverbal gestures. Such symbolic communication (e.g., language) helps people construct a meaningful world. Humans continually create and re-create society through their construction and interpretation of the social world. More than any other theory in the social sciences, symbolic interaction theory stresses the active role of individuals in creating their social environment, called *human agency.*

George Herbert Mead (1863–1931), one of the founders of the symbolic interaction perspective, explored how humans define or make sense of situations (G. H. Mead [1934] 1962). He placed special emphasis on human interpretations of gestures and symbols (including language) and the meanings we attach to our actions. He also examined how we learn our social *roles* in society, including expected behaviors, rights, obligations, responsibilities, and privileges assigned to a social status (such as mother, child, teacher, and friend) and how we learn to carry out these roles. Indeed, as we will see in Chapter 4, Mead insisted that our notion of who we are—our *self*—emerges from social experience and interaction with others. Language is critical to this process, for it allows us to step outside of our own experience and reflect on how others see us. Indeed, human language is a unique and powerful human trait, as is illustrated in the next Sociology in Our Social World.

These ideas of how we construct our individual social worlds and have some control over them represent one approach of symbolic interactionism (known as the Chicago School). Another symbolic interaction approach (the Iowa School) makes a clear link between a person's individual identity and her or his position within organizations. This connects the micro and the meso level of the social system (Kuhn 1964). If we hold several positions—honors student, club president, daughter, sister, student, athlete, thespian, middle-class person—those positions form our *self*. We will interpret new situations in light of our social positions, some of which are important and anchor how we see the social world. Once a core *self* is established, it guides and shapes the way we interact with people in many situations—even in new social settings (Kuhn 1964). Thus, if you are president of an organization and have the responsibility for overseeing the organization, part of your self-esteem, your view of responsible citizenship, and your attitude toward life will be shaped by that position. Thus, the Iowa School of symbolic interaction places less emphasis on individual choice but more on recognizing the link among the micro, meso, and macro levels of society (Carrothers and Benson 2003; Stryker 1980).

To summarize, the modern symbolic interaction theory emphasizes the following:

- People continually create and re-create society through interacting with one another.

- People interact by communicating with one another through the use of shared symbols.

- We learn who we are (our sense of self) and our place in society through interacting with others.

Critique of Symbolic Interaction Theory. Each theory has its critics, those who disagree with some aspect of the theory. That is how scientists critique their ideas and develop new theories. Although symbolic interaction theory is widely used by sociologists today, it is often criticized for neglecting the macro-level structures of society that affect human behavior. By focusing on interpersonal interactions, large-scale social forces such as an economic depression or a political revolution that shape human destinies are given less consideration. With the focus on the ability of each individual to create his or her meaning in social situations (called *agency*), symbolic interaction has often been less attuned to important macro-level issues of social class position, social power, historical circumstances, or international conflict between societies (Carter and Fuller 2015; Meltzer, Petras, and

SOCIOLOGY IN OUR SOCIAL WORLD

HUMAN LANGUAGE AND THE MARVEL OF A COLLEGE CLASSROOM

A college classroom is a magical place, and this is true mostly because of human language. Human language is distinctive. All other species communicate with a fairly limited number of sounds they can make. Other animals, except perhaps for dolphins, whales, and chimpanzees, communicate only about something that is happening in the present time and location like a threat (Phillips 2013).

Each human language identifies about 50 sounds that come to be designated as meaningful language. In English, this includes such sounds as *sss*, *mmm*, *nnn*, *ttt*, *kkk*, *bbb*, and *ooo*. We take this designated collection of sounds and combine them in various ways to make words: *cat*, *dog*, *college*, *student*. This ability to combine sounds into words and words into sentences allows you to say something to your instructor that she or he has never heard any other human say before. The sounds are familiar, as are the words themselves, but you may combine them in a novel way that causes a new idea to occur to your listener. This is actually the root of much humor. For example, you can say a sentence or tell a story that has such a surprising ending that it causes the listener to laugh.

Your animal companions at home clearly have memory. They can recognize you when you get home. Your dog may well remember the other pups in his litter. However, they cannot remember together. They cannot gather to recall and share stories about good-old dad the way you

can recall the quirky traits of your professors with friends. Your dogs and cats cannot plan for the future—planning a litter reunion for next summer, for example.

The fact that our communication is a *distinctive feature system* allows something unique: temporal and spatial sharing. We can remember together our experiences of the past, and we can pass ideas from one person to another. We can discuss the ideas of people who have died and have perhaps been gone for more than a century. A mare cannot transmit to her colt the racing ideas of Man o' War, the great racehorse of the 1920s, let alone the experiences of horses involved in the Trojan War, or even the triple-crown 1970s derby winner, Secretariat. However, whether in a classroom or a pub, humans can discuss the ideas of Plato, or Muhammad, or Karl Marx. Further, because of words humans can take other perspectives—to vicariously visit the other side of the planet or to go back in history to experience a time when an entirely different set of ideas about life was common.

When we come into a classroom, something mysterious, something amazing, happens. Language allows us to see things from a new point of view. What a remarkable gift that we can share ideas and see things through the eyes of someone different from ourselves, and it is largely because of the human *distinctive feature system* of communication. What an interesting species to study! What a marvel that we can do so in a classroom.

Reynolds 1975). For example, if we focused only on how Hector interacts with his family and friends in trying to determine why he dropped out of school, we would overlook macro forces (e.g., how the lack of government supports for poor families impacted his decision to drop out of school). Another critique is that it is difficult to study abstract ideas like the development of the self, key to symbolic interaction theory.

Despite these limitations, theorists from the symbolic interaction perspective have made significant contributions to understanding the development of social identities and interactions that underlie groups, organizations, and societies. Many of these studies are discussed throughout the book.

Rational Choice (Exchange) Theory. According to **rational choice theory**, *humans are fundamentally*

concerned with self-interests, making rational decisions based on weighing costs and rewards of the projected outcome of an action. Someone from this perspective would say Hector would picture the situation as if it were a mental balance sheet: For example, on the plus side, staying in school may lead to opportunities not available to the uneducated. On the minus side, school is a negative experience, and the family needs help to feed its members now, so going to school is a "waste of time." Which side will win depends on Hector's balance sheet and on family and friends' influence over the rewards versus costs.

Rational choice theory, also called *exchange theory*, has its roots in several disciplines—economics, behavioral psychology, anthropology, and philosophy (Cook, O'Brien, and Kollock 1990). Social behavior is seen as an exchange activity—a transaction in which resources are given and received (Blau 1964; Homans 1974). Every interaction involves an exchange of something valued: money, time, material goods, attention, sex, allegiance, and so on. People stay in relationships because they get something from the exchange, and they leave relationships that have more costs than benefits for them. They constantly evaluate whether there is reciprocity or balance in a relationship, so that they are receiving as much as they give. Simply stated, people are more likely to act if they see some reward or success coming from their behavior. The implication is that self-interest for the individual is the guiding element in human interaction.

In summary, rational choice theory involves the following key ideas:

▲ According to rational choice theory, people avoid cost or pain and seek benefits. Thus, people in authority try to control others—like this woman—by imposing cost for behaviors that are unwanted. The cost for this woman for speeding is an expensive ticket, and the city council and police hope it will lead to more desired behaviors in her future.

© iStock/Pamela Moore

- Human beings are mostly self-centered, and self-interest drives their behavior.

- Humans calculate costs and benefits (rewards) in making decisions.

- Humans are rational in that they weigh choices to maximize their own benefits and minimize costs.

- Every interaction involves exchanges entailing rewards and penalties or expenditures.

- A key element in exchanges is reciprocity—a balance in the exchange of benefits.

- People keep a mental ledger in their heads about whether they owe someone else or that person owes them.

Critique of Rational Choice Theory. Rational choice theorists see human conduct as self-centered, with rational behavior implying that people seek to maximize rewards and minimize costs. They give little attention to micro-level internal mental processes, such as self-reflection. Charitable, unselfish, or altruistic behavior is not easily explained by this view. Why would a soldier sacrifice his or her life to save a comrade? Why would a starving person in a Nazi concentration camp share a crust of bread with another? Proponents of rational choice counter the criticism by arguing that if a person feels good about helping another that, in itself, is a reward that compensates for the cost.

THINKING SOCIOLOGICALLY

How can symbolic interaction and rational choice perspectives help explain everyday behavior? For example, how might a theorist from each perspective explain why people tend to hold the door for a person walking behind them? How would each of the previous micro theories answer this question a bit differently?

Meso- and Macro-Level Theories

Meso- and macro-level theories consider large units in the social world: organizations (e.g., General Motors or the Episcopal Church), institutions (such as family, education, religion, health care, politics, or economies), societies (e.g., Canada or Mexico), or global systems (e.g., the World Trade Organization or World Bank). For example, Hector's government at the national and international levels affects his life in a variety of ways. As Brazil industrializes, the nature of jobs and the modes of communication change. Local village cultures adjust as the entire nation gains more uniformity of values, beliefs, and norms. Similarly, resources such as access to clean water may be allotted at the local level, but local communities need national and sometimes international support to access resources, as illustrated by tribal elders from Tanzania in the photo on the next page. We can begin to understand how the process of modernization influences Hector, this village in Tanzania, and other people around

▲ The Tanzanian village elders in this photo continue to have authority to make local (micro-level) decisions about the traditional irrigation canals being improved in their village, but their expanded water supply is possible in part because of international financial support (meso- and macro-level decisions).

the globe by looking at two major macro-level perspectives: the structural-functional and conflict theories.

Structural-Functional Theory. **Structural-functional theory**, also called functional theory, *assumes that all parts of the social structure (groups, organizations, and institutions), the culture (values and beliefs), and social processes (e.g., legislators working to create a law, an instructor teaching a child, or laws passed to bring about positive social change) work together to make the whole society run smoothly and harmoniously.* To understand the social world from this perspective, we must look at how the parts of society (structure) fit together and how each part contributes to the maintenance of society. For instance, two functions (purposes) of the family include having children and teaching them to be members of society. These and other functions help perpetuate society, for without reproducing and teaching new members to fit in, societies would collapse.

Émile Durkheim (1858–1917) is considered the founder of the functionalist perspective. He theorized that society is made up of necessary parts that fit together into a working whole. Durkheim believed that individuals conform to the rules of societies because of a *collective conscience*—the shared beliefs in the values of a group (Durkheim 1947). People grow up sharing the same values, beliefs, and rules of behavior as those around them. Gradually, individuals internalize these shared beliefs and rules. A person's behavior is, in a sense, governed from within because it feels right and proper to behave in

accordance with what is expected. As such, the functionalist perspective of Durkheim and subsequent theorists places emphasis on social consensus, which gives rise to stable and predictable patterns of order in society. Because people need groups for survival, they adhere to the group's rules so that they do not stand apart from it. This means that most societies run in an orderly manner, with most individuals fitting into their positions in society.

Functions, *consequences of an action or behavior*, can be manifest or latent. **Manifest functions** are *the planned outcomes of interactions, social organizations, or institutions.* Some of the planned consequences of the microwave oven, for instance, have been to allow people to prepare meals quickly and easily, facilitating life in overworked and stressed modern families. **Latent functions** are *unplanned or unintended consequences of actions or of social structures* (Merton 1938, [1942] 1973). Some of the unplanned consequences of microwave ovens were the creation of a host of new jobs and stimulation of the economy as people wrote new cookbooks and as businesses were formed to produce microwavable cookware and prepared foods ready for the microwave.

Latent functions can be functional (helpful) or dysfunctional (bad for the organization or society). Functional actions contribute to the stability or equilibrium of society whereas **dysfunctions** are *those actions that undermine the stability or equilibrium of society* (Merton 1938). For example, by allowing people to prepare meals without using a stove or conventional oven, the microwave oven has contributed to some young people having no idea how to cook, thus making them highly dependent on expensive technology and processed foods, and in some cases adding to problems of obesity.

From a functionalist theory perspective, it is important to examine the possible functional and dysfunctional aspects of life in society in order to maintain harmony and balance.

In summary, the structural-functional perspective

- examines the macro-level organizations and patterns in society;

- looks at what holds societies together and enhances social continuity;

- considers the consequences or *functions* of each major part in society;

- focuses on the way the structure (groups, organizations, and institutions), the culture, and social processes work together to make society function smoothly; and

- notes manifest functions (which are planned), latent functions (which are unplanned or secondary), and dysfunctions (which undermine stability).

Critique of the Structural-Functional Perspective. Some ideas put forth by functional theorists are so abstract that they are difficult to test with data. Moreover, functionalism does not explain social changes in society, such as conflict and revolution. It assumes a stable world. As we try to understand the many societal upheavals in the world, from suicide bombings in major cities to economic ups and downs in stock markets and trade relations, it is clear that dramatic social change is possible. The functionalist assumption is that if a system is running smoothly, it must be working well because it is free from conflict. It assumes that conflict is harmful, even though we know that stability may come about because of ruthless dictators suppressing the population. In short, stability is not always good, and conflict signifies tensions in societies.

THINKING SOCIOLOGICALLY

Describe a manifest and a latent function of the system of higher education in the United States today. Is the latent function dysfunctional? Why or why not?

Conflict Theory. In many ways, conflict theory turns the structural-functional theory on its head. **Conflict theory** contends that *conflict is inevitable in any group or society*. It claims that inequality and injustice are the source of the conflicts that permeate society. Resources and power are distributed unequally in society, so some members have more money, goods, and prestige than others. The rich protect their positions by using the power they have accumulated to keep others in their places. From the perspective of poor people such as Hector, it seems the rich get all the breaks. Most of us want more of the resources in society (e.g., money, good jobs, education, nice homes, and cars), causing the possibility of conflict between the *haves* (those who control resources) and the *have-nots* (those who lack resources). These conflicts sometimes bring about a change in society.

▲ Although the microwave oven and fast-food restaurants have had many benefits for a society in a hurry, one dysfunction is the deterioration of health, especially due to obesity.

Modern conflict theory has its origins in the works of Karl Marx (1818–1883), a German social philosopher who lived in England during the height of 19th-century industrial expansion. Capitalism had emerged as the dominant economic system in Europe. *Capitalism* is an economic system in which individuals and corporations, rather than the state, own and control the means of production (e.g., factories). As they compete for profits, some win while others lose.

Marx recognized the plight of workers toiling in factories in the new industrial states of Europe and viewed the ruling elites and the wealthy industrial owners as exploiters of the working class. Marx wrote about the new working class crowded in urban slums, working long hours under appalling conditions, without earning enough money for decent housing and food. Few of the protections enjoyed by many (but not all) workers today—such as retirement benefits, health coverage, sick leave, the 40-hour workweek, and restrictions against child labor—existed in Marx's time.

Marx maintained that two classes, the capitalists (also referred to as the *bourgeoisie* or "haves"), who owned the **means of production** (*property, machinery, and other means of creating saleable goods or services*), and the laborers working for the "haves" (also referred to as the *proletariat* or "have-nots") would continue to live in conflict until the workers shared more equally in the profits of their labor. The more workers came to understand their plight, the more aware they would become of the injustice of their situation. Eventually, Marx believed, workers would rise up and overthrow capitalism, forming a new, classless society. Collective ownership—shared ownership of the means of production—would be the new economic order (Marx and Engels [1848] 1969).

The idea of the bourgeoisie (the capitalist exploiters who own the factories) and the proletariat (the exploited workers who sell their labor) has carried over to analysis of modern-day conflicts among groups in society. For example, from a conflict perspective, Hector in Brazil and millions like him in other countries are part of the reserve labor force—a cheap labor pool that can be called on when labor is needed and disregarded when demand is low, thus meeting the changing labor needs of industry and capitalism. This pattern results in permanent economic insecurity and poverty for Hector and those like him.

Many branches of the conflict perspective have grown from the original ideas of Marx. Here, we mention four contributions to conflict theory, those of American sociologists Harriet Martineau ([1837] 1962), W. E. B. Du Bois ([1899] 1967), Ralf Dahrendorf (1959), and Lewis Coser (1956). As you can see, social conflict has been a major focus of their sociological investigations.

Harriet Martineau (1802–1876), generally considered the first female sociologist, wrote several books that contribute to our understanding of modern sociological research methods and provided a critique of the failure of the United States to live up to its democratic principles, especially as they related to women. She argued that social laws influence social behavior and that societies can be measured on their social progress (including how much freedom they give to individuals and how well they treat the most oppressed members of society). Her work represents the foundation of current feminist and conflict theories (Martineau 1838).

Another early American conflict theorist was W. E. B. Du Bois (1868–1963), the first African American to receive a doctorate from Harvard University. After being denied full-time positions at White universities, Du Bois founded a sociology program in 1898 at Atlanta University, a Black college. There, he established a significant research center and trained a generation of Black social scientists. In 1899, he published *The Philadelphia Negro* (one of the first truly scientific studies in North America), and in 1903, he completed a classic sociological work, *The Souls of Black Folk*. His work was truly groundbreaking (Morris 2015).

Du Bois, like other early sociological theorists, believed that although research should be scientifically rigorous and fair-minded, the ultimate goal of sociological work was social improvement—not just human insight. Throughout his life, Du Bois documented and lambasted the status of Black Americans, noting that African Americans were an integral part of U.S. society but not fully accepted into it.

Du Bois helped establish the National Association for the Advancement of Colored People (NAACP). He stressed the need for minority groups to become advocates for their rights—to object loudly when those in power act to disadvantage minorities—and to make society more just

▲ Harriet Martineau (left) published a critique of the United States' failure to live up to its democratic principles 11 years before Karl Marx's most famous work, but she was not taken seriously as a scholar for more than a century because she was female—the first feminist theorist. Karl Marx (center) is known as the founder of conflict theory. W. E. B. Du Bois (right) continued the development of conflict theory and was among the first to apply that theory to U.S. society, especially to issues of race.

(Du Bois [1899] 1967). He was—and continues to be—an inspiration for many sociologists who believe that their findings should be used to create a more humane social world (Mills 1956).

A half century later, in 1959, Ralf Dahrendorf (1929–2009) argued that society is always in the process of change and affected by forces that bring about change. Dahrendorf refined Marx's ideas in several ways. He pointed out that capitalism had survived, despite Marx's prediction of a labor revolt, because of improved conditions for workers (e.g., unions, the establishment of labor laws, and workplace regulations). Dahrendorf also maintained that, instead of divisions based on ownership, conflict had become based on authority.

Dahrendorf noted that those with lower-status positions, such as Hector, could form interest groups and engage in conflict with those in higher positions of authority. *Interest groups*, such as the members of Hector's favela, share a common situation or common interests. In Hector and his neighbors' case, these interests include a desire for sanitation, running water, electricity, jobs, and a higher standard of living. From within such interest groups, *conflict groups* arise to fight for changes. There is always potential for conflict when those without power realize their common position and form interest groups. How much change or violence is brought about depends on how organized those groups become.

Dahrendorf's major contribution is the recognition that conflict over resources results in conflict not just between the proletariat and the bourgeoisie but among a multitude of interest groups, including old people versus young people, rich versus poor, one region of the country versus another, Christians versus non-Christians, and so forth. This acknowledges multiple rifts in the society based on interest groups.

Whereas Marx emphasized the divisive nature of conflict, other theorists have offered a modified theory of conflict in society. American theorist Lewis Coser took a different approach to conflict from that of Marx, arguing that it can strengthen societies and the organizations within them. According to Coser, problems in a society or group lead to complaints or conflicts—a warning message to the group that all is not well. Resolution of the conflicts shows that the group is adaptable in meeting the needs of its members, thereby creating greater loyalty to the group. Thus, conflict provides the message of what is not working to meet people's needs, and the system adapts to the needs for change because of the conflict (Coser 1956; Simmel 1955).

In summary, conflict theorists advance the following key ideas:

- Conflict and the potential for conflict underlie all social relations.

- Groups of people look out for their self-interest and try to obtain resources and make sure they are distributed primarily to members of their own group.

- Social change is desirable, particularly changes that bring about a greater degree of social equality.

- The existing social order reflects powerful people imposing their values and beliefs on the weak.

Critique of Conflict Theory. First, many conflict theorists focus on macro-level analysis and lose sight of the individuals involved in conflict situations, such as Hector and his family. Second, empirical research to test conflict theory is limited. The conflict perspective often paints a picture with rather broad brushstrokes. Research to test the picture involves interpretations of broad spans of history and is more difficult to claim as scientific. Third, conflict theorists tend to focus on social stress, power dynamics, and disharmony. Conflict theory is not very effective in explaining social cohesion and cooperation. Fourth, many critics of conflict theory argue that altruism and cooperation are common motivations in human behaviors but not recognized by conflict theory.

THINKING SOCIOLOGICALLY

Imagine you are a legislator. You have to decide whether to cut funding for a senior citizens' program or slash a scholarship program for college students. You want to be reelected, and you know that approximately 90% of senior citizens are registered to vote and most actually do vote. You also know that less than half of college-age people are likely to vote. These constituencies are about the same size. What would you do, and how would you justify your decision? How does this example illustrate conflict theory?

Multilevel Analysis. Many of the more contemporary theorists try to bridge the gap between micro and macro levels of analysis, offering insights relevant at each level. We examine two of these next.

Max Weber's Contributions. Max Weber (1864–1920), a German-born social scientist, has had a lasting effect on sociology and other social sciences. Weber (pronounced VAY-ber) cannot be pigeonholed easily into one of the theoretical categories or one level of analysis, for his contributions include both micro- and macro-level analyses. His emphasis on *Verstehen* (meaning deep empathetic understanding in humans) gives him a place in micro-level theory, and his discussions of power and bureaucracies give him a place in meso- and macro-level theory (Weber 1946).

Verstehen stems from the interpretations or meanings individuals at the micro level give to their social experiences. Weber argued that to understand people's behaviors, you must step into their shoes and see the world as they do. Following in Weber's footsteps, sociologists try to understand both human behavior and the meanings that people attach to their experiences. In this work, Weber is a micro theorist who set the stage for symbolic interaction theorists.

However, the goal-oriented, efficient new organizational form called bureaucracy was the focus of much of Weber's writing at the meso level. This organizational form was based on **rationality** (*the attempt to reach maximum efficiency with rules that are rationally designed to accomplish goals*) rather than relying on long-standing tradition for how things should be done. As we describe in Chapter 5, Weber's ideas about society at the meso level have laid the groundwork for a theoretical understanding of modern organizations.

Weber also attempted to understand macro-level processes. For instance, in his famous book *The Protestant Ethic and the Spirit of Capitalism* (Weber [1904–1905] 1958), he asked how capitalists (those who have money and control production) understood the world around them. His work was influenced by Marx's writings, but whereas Marx focused on economic conditions as the key factor shaping history and power relations, Weber argued that Marx's focus was too narrow. Weber felt that politics, economics, religion, psychology, and people's ideas are interdependent—affecting each other. In short, Weber thought that society was more complex than Karl Marx's theory, which focused only on two groups—the haves and the have-nots—in conflict over economic resources.

Feminist Theory. Feminist theory also uses multi-level analysis and has foundations in the conflict perspective. **Feminist theory** *critiques the hierarchical power structures that disadvantage women and other minorities* (Cancian 1992; P. Collins 2008). Proponents note that men form an interest group intent on preserving their privileges. Feminists also argue that sociology has been dominated by a male perspective that does not give a complete view of the social world.

Some branches of feminist theory come from interaction perspectives, emphasizing the way gender socialization, cues, and symbols shape the nature of many human interactions. Thus, feminist theory moves from macro-level analyses (e.g., looking at national and global situations that give privileges to men) to micro-level analysis (e.g., looking at inequality between husbands and wives in marriage). In particular, feminist theory points to the importance of gender as a variable influencing social patterns (Burn 2011; Kramer and Beutel 2014; Lorber 2009; Messerschmidt et al. 2018).

People face inequality due to multiple factors, and it is the interplay of these factors that interests Patricia Hill Collins. An important contemporary scholar, Collins examines the discrimination and oppression people face because of their race, class, gender, sexuality, or nationality, all of which are interconnected. Collins (2008; Collins and Bilge 2016) uses the term *intersectionality*, meaning individuals have multiple identities (e.g., race, class, and gender) that intersect and impact their lives and opportunities.

▲ Patricia Hill Collins, an innovative feminist scholar, has challenged sociologists to look at the ways experiences of race, social class, gender, and sexuality intersect and reinforce one another.

© Photo courtesy of Patricia Hill Collins

THINKING SOCIOLOGICALLY

To what extent are human beings free agents who can create their own social world and come up with their own ideas about how to live their lives? To what extent are our lives determined or influenced by the social systems around us and by our positions in the economic and political system? Is this different for different people, and why?

Using Different Theoretical Perspectives

Each of the theoretical perspectives described in this chapter begins from a set of assumptions about humans. Each makes a contribution to our understanding, but each has limitations or blind spots, such as not taking into account other levels of analysis (Ritzer 2011). Figure 2.1 provides a summary of cooperative versus competitive perspectives to illustrate how the theories differ.

The strength of a theory depends on its ability to explain and predict behavior accurately. Each theoretical perspective focuses on a different aspect of society and level of analysis and gives us a different lens through which to view our social world. Depending on the questions we ask, different theories will be appropriate; the social world model helps us picture the whole system and determine which theory or theories best suits our needs in analyzing a specific social process or structure.

Middle-Range Theories. Often, sociologists use *middle-range theories*, those theories that explain specific aspects of social life—such as deviant behavior, racial prejudice, and civic engagement—to make sense of the data they gather (Merton 1968). These theories tend to fall under the umbrella of one of the four major theoretical perspectives described earlier. For example, Erving Goffman, coming from a symbolic interactionist perspective, focused on the impact of *stigmas* (social characteristics that distinguish a person or group of people from other members of society) in social interactions. His analysis of the impact of stigmas and the midrange theory of social stigma he developed out of it provides one piece of the overall puzzle of explaining social interaction in society.

THINKING SOCIOLOGICALLY

Consider the issue of homelessness in cities around the world. How could each of the theories discussed in this chapter be used to help us understand the problem of homelessness?

Theory and Research Methods. Scientists, including sociologists, often use theories to predict changes in society and under what conditions they are likely to occur. Theory tells the researcher what to look for and what concepts or variables need to be measured. However, explanations about the relationships between social variables need to be tested. This is where *research methods*—the procedures one uses to gather data—are relevant. Data must be carefully gathered and then used to assess the accuracy of theory. If a theory is not supported by the data, it must be reformulated or discarded. Theory and research are used together and are mutually dependent.

To study Hector's life in Brazil, researchers might focus on the micro-level interactions between Hector and his family members, peers, teachers, and employers as factors that contribute to his situation. For example, one theory could be that Hector's family has socialized him to believe that certain activities (for example, working) are more realistic or immediately rewarding than others (such as attending school). A meso-level focus might examine the influence of the organizations and institutions—such as the business world, the schools, and the religious communities in Brazil—to see how they shape the forces that affect Hector's life. Alternatively, the focus might be on macro-level analysis—the class structure (rich to poor) of the society and the global forces, such as

▼ FIGURE 2.1
Cooperative Versus Competitive Perspectives

	Macro analysis	Micro analysis
Humans viewed as cooperative (people interact with others on the basis of shared meanings and common symbols)	*Structural-Functional Theory*	*Symbolic Interactionism Theory*
Humans viewed as competitive (behavior governed by self-interest)	*Conflict Theory* (group interests)	*Rational Choice Theory* (individual interests)

trade relations between Brazil and other countries, that influence opportunities for Brazilians who live in poverty.

Whatever the level of analysis, as social *scientists*, sociologists use scientific methods of gathering evidence to disprove or to support theories about society.

Ideas Underlying Science

Throughout most of human history, people came to "know" the world by the traditions passed down from one generation to the next. Things were so because authoritative people in the culture said they were so. Often, there was reliance on magical, philosophical, or religious explanations of the forces in nature, and these explanations became part of tradition. For example, just 260 years ago, the conventional wisdom was that lightning storms were a sign of an angry god, not electricity caused by meteorological forces. As ways of knowing about the world shifted, tradition, religion, and magic as the primary means to understand the world were challenged. With advances in the natural sciences, observations of cause-and-effect processes became more systematic and controlled.

The scientific approach is based on several core ideas: First, there are real physical and social worlds that can be studied scientifically. Second, there is a certain order to the world, with identifiable patterns that result from a series of causes and effects. The world is not merely a collection of unrelated random events; rather, events occur in a systematic sequence and in patterns—that is, they are *causally* related. Third, the way to gain knowledge of the world is to subject it to empirical testing. **Empirical knowledge** is founded on *information gained from evidence (facts), rather than intuition.* **Evidence** refers to *facts and observations that can be objectively observed and carefully measured using the five senses (sometimes enhanced by scientific instruments).*

Consider the alternative to evidence. As early as middle school grades, children in some schools are asked to distinguish factual news stories from "fake news" stories, news that has little to no basis in facts that can be verified. Students are asked to look for half-truths, misinformation, and unsubstantiated claims by looking for the validity, accuracy, and reliability of information and sources. These are not always present in stories from Facebook, Twitter, and other social and news media sites (Barron 2017). For knowledge to be scientific, it must come from phenomena that can be observed and measured. Phenomena that cannot be subject to measurement are not within the realm of scientific inquiry. For example, what religion is "best" or the existence of God, the devil, heaven, hell, and the soul cannot be observed

and measured and therefore cannot be examined scientifically. Religion, however, can be studied scientifically by looking at the role it plays in society and our lives, its impact on our values and behavior (the sociology of religion), the historical development of specific religious traditions (the history of religion), or the emotional comfort and stability it brings to people (the psychology of religion). Finally, science is rooted in **objectivity**; that is, *one must take steps to ensure that one's personal opinions or values do not bias or contaminate data collection and analysis.* Scientists are obliged not to distort their research findings so as to promote a particular point of view. Scientific research is judged first on whether it relies on careful efforts to be objective. Social scientists, like all scientists, must explain what the data reveal, not what they wish it would reveal! Researchers must be open to finding results that support *or* disprove their **hypothesis** (*an educated guess or prediction*) about the research being conducted.

Failure to meet these standards—empirical knowledge, objectivity, and scientific evidence—means that a study is not scientific. Someone's ideas can seem plausible and logical but may still not be supported by the facts. This is why evidence is so important. Sociology is concerned with using accurate evidence, and it is important to know what is or is not considered accurate. Perhaps you have seen an episode of *Law and Order*, *Criminal Minds*, *NCIS*, or *Elementary* on television. These series depict the importance of careful collection of data and commitment to objective analysis. Sociologists deal with different issues, but the same sort of concern for accuracy in gathering data guides their work. When sociologists establish theories as to why society works as it does, they must test those theories using scientific methods.

How Sociologists Study the Social World

Suppose you have a research question you want to answer, such as "Why do boys like Hector drop out of school?" For your research to be scientific, you must follow the basic steps of the scientific research process.

A. PLANNING A RESEARCH STUDY

- *Step 1.* Define a topic or problem that can be studied scientifically.

- *Step 2.* Review existing relevant research studies and theory to refine the topic and define **variables**, *concepts (ideas) that can vary in frequency of occurrence from one time, place, or* *person to another* (such as age, ethnicity, religion, and level of education).

- *Step 3*. Formulate hypotheses or research questions and determine how to define and measure the variables.

B. DESIGNING THE RESEARCH PLAN AND METHOD FOR COLLECTING THE DATA

- *Step 4*. Design the research plan that specifies how the data will be gathered.
- *Step 5*. Select a **sample**, *a group of systematically chosen people who represent a much larger group to study.*
- *Step 6*. Collect the data using appropriate research methods.

C. MAKING SENSE OF THE DATA

- *Step 7*. Analyze the data and relate it to previous findings on the topic, concluding exactly what the study says about the research question(s) from Step 3.
- *Step 8*. Draw conclusions and present the report, including suggestions for future research and policy recommendations (if appropriate). The study is then ready for peer review—critique by other social scientists. Publicize findings and recommendations supported by the peer review.

Planning a Research Study

To study Hector's situation, the researcher uses Step 1 to define a topic or problem, including the variables to be studied. Step 2 requires the researcher to review past studies on related topics to see what has been done and how variables were defined in other studies. This review provides the basis for Step 3.

In Step 3, to formulate hypotheses, the researcher must link concepts, such as poverty or dropping out of school, to specific measurements. For example, the researcher could hypothesize that poverty is a major cause of favela teenagers dropping out of school because they need to earn money for their families. Who is a dropout might be determined by school records indicating whether that child has attended school during the past 6 months. Poverty could be defined as having a low annual income—say less than half of the average income for that size of family in the country—or by assessing ownership of property such as cattle, automobiles, and indoor plumbing. It is important

for researchers to be clear, precise, and consistent in how they define and measure their variables.

In order to conduct research to test a theory, researchers formulate a hypothesis, a statement they can test to determine if it is true. This is called *deductive research*. It starts with a theory that you then test. *Inductive research*, on the other hand, starts with observations that then lead to hypothesis development and, potentially, theory formation. Researchers make an observation and then begin to collect more data to determine if what they witnessed initially was a social pattern. Once they start to notice social patterns, they can begin to analyze those patterns using appropriate existing theories, or they can create a new theory if existing ones do not provide needed explanations.

THINKING SOCIOLOGICALLY

Think of a research question based on a theoretical perspective. For example, you might ask how Hector's peers affect his decisions, using a micro-level theory. Then write a hypothesis and identify your variables in the hypothesis.

Whether you use inductive or deductive research, you must always carefully define your variables and determine how they interact with and relate to one another. The relationship between variables is central to understanding *causality*. Causal reasoning and other statistical terms are discussed in the next Sociology in Our Social World.

Designing the Research Plan and Method for Collecting the Data

Researchers must always make clear how they collect their data. Every research study should be replicable—capable of being repeated—by other researchers. So, enough information must be given to ensure that another researcher could repeat the study and compare results.

The appropriate data collection method depends on the level(s) of analysis of the research question (micro, meso, or macro) the researcher is asking. For example, if you want to answer a macro-level research question, such as the effect of poverty on students dropping out of school in Brazil, you should focus on large-scale social and economic data sources such as the Brazilian census. To learn about micro-level issues, such as the influence of peers on an individual's decision to drop out of school, you will need to examine small-group interactions at the micro level. Figure 2.2 illustrates the different levels of analysis.

BEING CLEAR ABOUT CAUSALITY

Sociology as a science tries to be very careful about language—more precise than we usually are in our everyday conversations. What do we really mean when we say that something *causes* something else? At the heart of the research process is the effort to find causal relationships (i.e., one variable causes another one to change). The following key terms are important in understanding how two variables (concepts that vary in frequency and can be measured) are related.

CORRELATION

X ⬌ Y

- **Correlation** refers to *a relationship between variables (such as poverty and low levels of education), with change in one variable associated with change in another*. The hypothesis earlier predicts that poverty and teenagers dropping out of school are related and vary together. That is, when the poverty level is high, dropping out of school is also high. If we claim a correlation, however, that is only the first step. We have not yet established that change in one variable *causes* a change in the other.

CAUSE AND EFFECT VARIABLES

X ⟶ Y

- **Cause-and-effect relationships** occur when there is *a relationship between variables so that one variable stimulates a change in another*. Once we have determined that there is probably a relationship, or correlation (the fact that the two variables, such as poverty and dropping out of school, both occur in the same situation), we need to take the next step: analyzing which comes first and seeing if one variable causes change in another. The **independent variable** is *the variable in a cause-and-effect relationship that comes first in a time sequence and causes a change in another variable*—the **dependent variable**. If we hypothesize that poverty causes Hector and others to drop out of school, *poverty* is the independent variable in this hypothesis and *dropping out of school* is the dependent variable, dependent on the level of poverty. In determining cause and effect, the independent variable must always precede the dependent variable in the time

sequence if we want to try to determine whether the independent variable causes a change in the dependent variable.

SPURIOUS RELATIONSHIPS

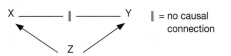

- **Spurious relationships** occur when there is *no causal relationship between the independent and dependent variables, but they vary together, often due to a third variable affecting both of them*. For example, if the quantity of ice cream consumed is highest during those weeks of the year when most drownings occur, these two events are correlated. However, eating ice cream did not *cause* the increase in deaths. Indeed, hot weather may have caused more people both to purchase ice cream and to go swimming, with the larger number of swimmers resulting in more drowning incidents. The connection between ice cream and drownings is a *spurious relationship*.

CONTROLS

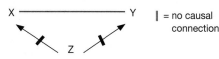

- **Controls** are *steps used by researchers to eliminate all variables except those related to the hypothesis—especially those variables that might be spurious*. Using controls helps ensure that the relationship is not spurious. Using the ice cream example, we might have studied beaches where lots of ice cream was sold and beaches where none was available in order to compare water death incidents. If there was no difference in death rates, the drownings could not have been caused by the ice cream.

- Correlation alone can never prove causality. We need studies conducted over time, with control groups, to establish causal relationships. For example, cigarette use correlates with lung cancer. The causal relationship was only proved, however, by comparing lung cancer rates among similar groups of people whose only difference was whether they smoked.

The Social World Model and Levels of Analysis

Micro Level		
Individual	Hector	
Small group	Hector's family and close friends	
Local community	The favela; Hector's local school, church, neighborhood organizations	
Meso Level		
Organizations	Brazilian corporations, Catholic Church, and local school system in Brazil	
Institutions	Family; education; political, economic, and health systems in the region or nation of Brazil	
Ethnic subcultures	Native peoples, African-Brazilians	
Macro Level		
National society	Social policies, trends, and programs in Brazil	
Global community of nations	Status of Brazil in global economy; trade relations with other countries; programs of international organizations or corporations	

Designing the Research Plan. Step 4 is vitally important because the researcher evaluates the various methods used to collect data for research studies and selects one or more that are appropriate for the research question. These include questionnaires, interviews, observational studies, secondary data analysis, content analysis, and experiments. Some methods produce *quantitative* (numerical) data whereas others supply *qualitative* (nonnumerical) data such as individuals' responses to interviews. Questionnaires and secondary data analysis tend to be quantitative and used when conducting macro- and meso-level studies. Interviews, observational studies, and content analysis usually produce qualitative data or a blend of quantitative and qualitative data and are primarily used for micro-level research. Some studies include both quantitative and qualitative data.

Interviews are *research conducted by talking directly with people and asking questions in person or by telephone.* Structured interviews consist of an interviewee asking respondents a set list of questions with a choice of set answers. Unstructured and semistructured interviews, which allow respondents to answer questions in a more open-ended manner, allow for follow-up and additional questions as they evolve in response to what the researcher learns as the research progresses.

Questionnaires contain *questions and other types of items designed to solicit information appropriate to analysis of research questions* (Babbie 2014). They are convenient for collecting large amounts of data because they can be distributed by mail or sent by e-mail to many respondents at once.

▲ Census questionnaires are taken in the United States and many other countries every 10 years. Sometimes it is difficult to gather accurate data on the entire population, as in the case of homeless people or those in remote areas. Census worker Danielle Forino gathered data in Maine, where she had to use an all-terrain vehicle and sometimes snowshoes in remote sections of the North Maine Woods.

© AP Photo/Robert F. Bukaty

Observational studies (also called field research) involve *systematic, planned observation and recording of interactions and other human behavior in natural settings (where the activity normally takes place, rather than in a laboratory).*

They can take different forms: (1) observations in which the researcher actually participates in the activities of the group being studied or (2) observations in which the researcher is not involved in group activities but observes or records the activity. It is important for observers to avoid influencing or altering group functioning and interaction by their presence.

THINKING SOCIOLOGICALLY

If you were trying to compare how effectively two professors teach a research methods course offered in your department, what variables might you use, and what variables might you need to control? How would you set up your study? What methods would you use?

Secondary analysis *uses existing data, information that has already been collected in other studies—including data banks, such as the national census.* Often, large data-collecting organizations, such as the United Nations or a country's census bureau, the national education department, or a private research organization, will make data available for use by researchers. Consider the question of the dropout rate in Brazil. Researchers can learn a great deal about the behavior of school dropouts as a group from analysis of information gathered by ministries or departments of education. Likewise, if we want to compare modern dropout rates with those of an earlier time, we may find data from previous decades to be invaluable. Secondary analysis can be an excellent way to do meso- or macro-level studies that reveal large-scale patterns in the social world.

Content analysis entails *the systematic categorizing and recording of information from written or recorded sources—printed materials, videos, radio broadcasts, or artworks.* With content analysis (a common method in historical research and the study of organizations), sociologists can gather the data they need from printed materials—books, magazines, newspapers, laws, letters, comments on websites, e-mails, videos, archived radio broadcasts, or even artwork. They develop a coding system to classify the source content. A researcher trying to understand shifts in Brazilian attitudes toward youth poverty in favelas could do a content analysis of popular magazines to see how many pages or stories were devoted to child poverty in the Brazilian media in each decade

from the 1960s to the present. Content analysis has the advantage of being relatively inexpensive and easy to do. It is also *unobtrusive*, meaning that the researcher does not influence the participants being investigated by having direct contact with them. Furthermore, examining materials in historical sequence can be effective in recognizing patterns over time.

An example of historical research using existing materials to examine social patterns is illustrated in the next Sociology in Our Social World. In this case the researcher, Virginia Kemp Fish, studied records and writings of early women sociologists in Chicago to discover their contributions to sociology and to the betterment of society.

In **experiments**, *all variables except the one being studied are controlled so researchers can study the effects on the variable under study.* An experiment usually requires an **experimental group**, in which *subjects in the group are exposed to the variable being studied; this process is to test the effects of that variable on human behavior,* and a **control group**, in which *the subjects are not exposed to the variable the researcher wants to test.* The control group provides a baseline with which the experimental group can be compared, as shown in the example of Hector.

Experiments conducted in a lab can often provide the most accurate test of cause and effect. They make it possible to control most variables (eliminating irrelevant spurious variables) and determine the sequence in which variables affect each other. By separating the sample into experimental and control groups, the researcher can see if the study's independent variable makes a difference in the behavior of people who are exposed to that variable compared with those who are not. Psychologists use lab experiments, but few sociologists use this method because many sociological questions cannot be studied in controlled settings. For example, Hector's environment in the favela cannot be studied in a laboratory setting.

Control and experimental research projects outside of a lab setting are more common among sociologists. For example, researchers may want to determine whether a new teaching method using technology might help children from Hector's favela. Researchers can do so by comparing a control group, exposed to the usual teaching method, and an experimental group, provided with the new method or experimental technology. We must ensure that the control and experimental groups of children are at the same academic level and that the teachers are equally motivated and prepared when teaching both classes. With this carefully designed research project, we can conclude that the new approach increases learning if the children in the experimental group score

THE HULL HOUSE CIRCLE: HISTORICAL CONTENT ANALYSIS IN SOCIOLOGY

▲ Jane Addams: social researcher, critic, and reformer.

Hull House was a settlement house in Chicago, one of several such residences established in urban immigrant neighborhoods. Settlement houses created a sense of community for residents and offered a multitude of services to help residents and neighbors negotiate poverty. In addition to offering services, Hull House was the location for a group of women social researchers, reformers, and activists. Well-known social activist Jane Addams (1860–1935), who received a Nobel Peace Prize, was one of them. These women had obtained college degrees in some of the few fields then open to women (political science, law, economics), and they used their education and skills to help others and to do research on social conditions, contributing to the development of the science of sociology. Until recently, women sociologists, such as the members of the Hull House Circle, have not

received much attention for their contributions to the science of sociology. Yet some of the earliest social survey research was conducted by the women connected with Hull House, sometimes employing the Hull House residents to collect data. For example, these women led the first systematic attempt to describe an immigrant community in an American city, a study found in *Hull House Maps and Papers* (Residents of Hull House [ca.1895] 1970).

Historical research can be an important source of data for sociological analysis, for historical circumstances help us understand why things evolved to the present state of affairs. Virginia Kemp Fish, who originated the designation Hull House Circle, researched historical literature to learn more about the lives and contributions of these women and their place in the sociological literature. She examined records, letters, biographies, and other historical sources to piece together their stories (Fish 1986). By studying their writings and activist work, Fish showed how they supported each other's work and scholarship and provided emotional encouragement and intellectual stimulation. Fish also considered women's professional styles as compared with the styles of men. Whereas men often received their training and support from a mentor (an older, established, and respected man in the field), the women of Hull House operated within a network of egalitarian relationships and interactions.

According to Fish's research, the data and documents collected by their leader, Jane Addams, and other Hull House women provide baseline information that has been used as a starting point or comparison for later studies—for social researchers in the fields of immigration, ethnic relations, poverty, health care, housing, unemployment, work and occupations, delinquency and crime, war, and social movements.

significantly higher on the final exam than those in the control group.

Triangulation refers to *the use of two or more methods of data collection to enhance the amount and type of data for analysis and the accuracy of the findings.* To study Hector's situation, a research study could use macro-level quantitative data on poverty and on educational statistics in Brazil and micro-level interviews with Hector and his peers to determine their goals and attitudes toward education. If all

findings point to the same conclusion, the researcher can feel much more confident about the study results.

Selecting a Sample. It would be impossible to interview or send a questionnaire to every school dropout in Brazil to determine why the teenage dropout rate is so high. It is possible to study a portion of that population, however. In Step 5, the research design process includes determining how to make sure the study includes people who

© Getty Images/Benjamin Lowy/Getty Images News

▲ Social scientists are not the only professionals who use triangulation. Journalists also consult a variety of sources, including social scientists, to put together news broadcasts.

are typical, that is, representative, of the total group (or population) you want to learn about. This involves careful selection of a *sample*, a group systematically chosen to represent a much larger group.

Researchers use many types of samples. A common one, the representative sample, attempts to accurately reflect the group being studied so that the sample results can be generalized or applied to the larger group or population. In the case of studying why so many boys from Hector's favela drop out of school, a representative sample for a study could be drawn from all 13- to 16-year-olds in his region or city in Brazil.

The most common form of representative sample is the *random sample*. All people in the population being studied have an equal *chance* of being selected for the study. By observing or talking with this smaller group selected from the total population under study, the researcher can get an accurate picture of the total population and have confidence that the findings apply to the larger group. Developing an effective sampling technique is often a complex process. In the case of Brazil, people constantly move in and out of the favela. Those who have just arrived may not have the same characteristics as those who have been living there a long time, but it is important to have a sample that represents the whole group being studied. Samples also must be large enough to accurately represent a population and to use statistical programs to analyze the data. If you take a methods course, you will delve further into these details of sampling and data analysis discussed next.

Collecting the Data. We have now made a research plan and selected our methods to use and our sample. In Step 6 we actually collect the data following our research plan. Once we have data, we have to determine what to do with the data to answer our research question.

Making Sense of the Data

Once you have collected your data from your sample, you have to analyze it.

Analyzing the Data. In Step 7, the researcher uses statistical and other techniques to analyze what the data say in order to answer the research question. Imagine that you have 100 interviews from residents of Hector's favela, plus a notebook full of field observation notes from "hanging out" with the youth there. What do you do with the data? Social researchers use multiple techniques to analyze data, but whatever techniques they use, they look for patterns in the data and then use theories and findings from past research on the topic to make sense of those patterns.

Presenting the Findings. One of the last steps in the research process, Step 8, is to draw conclusions and present the final report. The report includes a discussion of the results, draws conclusions as to whether the hypotheses were supported or answers were found for the research question, interprets the results, and (if appropriate) makes recommendations on how to use the findings. This report is usually reviewed by other social scientists, and feedback on the study is provided to the researcher. After this step, the report (if it holds up to peer review) may be publicly disseminated. As part of the presentation and discussion of results, reports often contain tables or figures presenting summaries of data to help the reader easily understand the patterns found in the data. The next Engaging Sociology (pages 48–49) provides useful tips on reading research tables found in journal articles, newspapers, and magazines.

Ethical Issues in Social Research

What happens if a scientist conducts research that has negative impacts on the participants? It is due to this concern that most universities and other research organizations, especially those receiving public money, have *human subjects review boards.* The boards review the proposed research plans and methods to be sure they will *not* hurt the subjects. Of special concern are research projects in medical sciences, but social scientists must also have their research reviewed.

Sociologists and other scientists are bound by the ethical codes of conduct governing research. The American Sociological Association (ASA) code of ethics outlines standards that researchers are expected to observe when doing research, teaching, and publishing. They include

- explaining the uses and consequences of the research and gaining informed consent from respondents;

- taking steps to ensure the privacy of respondents;

- being objective, reporting findings and sources fully;

- making no promises to respondents that cannot be honored;

- accepting no support that requires violation of these principles;

- completing contracted work; and

- delineating responsibilities in works with multiple authors.

Examples of unethical research include studying people without their knowledge or consent, including only data that support the results you would like to see, and violating the confidentiality of your subjects by revealing their identities. The bottom line is that researchers must do everything they can to protect their subjects from harm.

THINKING SOCIOLOGICALLY

Distinguish the differences in each of these approaches to gathering data in sociology and identify a potential ethical problem in each approach:

experiments

observational studies

interviews

questionnaires

content analysis

secondary analysis

Putting Sociology to Work: Public Sociology

Most early sociologists—including Lester Ward, the first president of the American Sociological Association—promoted sociology as a means for improving society (Calhoun 2007). As the discipline of sociology grew from its early days and became an acknowledged social science, some sociologists advocated for "pure" research disconnected from social policy issues and the public sphere. Throughout the history of the discipline, sociologists have debated their proper role in society.

However, like physicists, chemists, and geologists, many sociologists believe that, in addition to pure research, there are both important practical applications of the discipline and many policy issues that need to be informed by good social science. Today, there is a movement to recall the roots of sociology and make sociology more *public,* that is, of use to society. **Public sociologists** *use sociological tools to understand and inform citizens about how society works and to improve society.* Some help create and advocate for social policies that their research indicates will have a positive impact on society. Public sociologists—whether professors or those in a variety of professions outside academia—share a common goal: to better understand how society operates *and* to make practical use of their sociological findings to better society (Pickard and Poole 2007).

Some public sociologists work outside of academia and use sociological knowledge and research skills to address organizational needs or problems in government, education, health care settings, social service agencies, and businesses. They work for clients or organizations that often determine the research questions they will address. Depending on their positions, they may be known as sociological practitioners, applied sociologists, clinical sociologists, policy analysts, program planners, or evaluation researchers, among other titles. They focus on pragmatic ways to improve organizations or society, sometimes recommending major changes and sometimes proposing modest policy proposals.

Some sociology professors build a public sociology emphasis into their courses, hoping not only to work with students to improve the social environment in which they live but also to foster important skills for students entering the job market. The next Sociologists in Action feature (page 50) describes one such effort.

HOW TO READ A RESEARCH TABLE

A statistical table is a researcher's labor-saving device. Quantitative data presented in tabular form are clearer and more concise than the same information presented in several written paragraphs. A good table has clear signposts to help the reader avoid confusion. For instance, Table 2.1 shows many of the main features of a table, and the list that follows explains how to read each feature.

HEADNOTE (or subtitle): Many tables will have a headnote or subtitle under the title, giving information relevant to understanding the table or units in the table.

For this table, the reader is informed that it includes all persons over the age of 25 and the units are reported in thousands.

TITLE: The title provides information on the major topic and variables in the table.

"Educational Attainment by Selected Characteristics: 2017"

HEADINGS AND STUBS: Tables generally have one or two levels of headings under the title and headnotes. These instruct the reader about what is in the columns below.

In this table, the headings indicate the level of education achieved so that the reader can identify the percentage with a specified level of education.

The table also has a stub: the far-left column under "Characteristic." This lists the items that are being compared according to the categories found in the headings. In this case, the stub indicates age, sex, and race/ethnicity.

▼ TABLE 2.1

Educational Attainment by Selected Characteristics: 2017, for Persons 25 Years Old and Over, Reported in Thousands

MARGINAL TABS: In examining the numbers in the table, try working from the outside in. The marginals, the figures at the margins of the table, often provide summary information.

In this table, the first column of numbers is headed "Population (1,000)," indicating (by thousands) the total number of people in each category who were part of the database. The columns to the right indicate—by percentages—the level of educational attainment for each category.

Characteristic	Percentage of Population—Highest Level						
	Population (1,000)	Not a High School Graduate	High School Graduate	Some College but No Degree	Associate's Degree[1]	Bachelor's Degree	Advanced Degree
Total persons	216,921	10.4	29	16.3	10.4	21.3	12.9
Age							
25–34 yrs old	44,250	7.8	26.1	18.4	10.4	25.7	11.6
35–54 yrs old	82,072	10.1	27	15.3	11.2	22.5	14.3
55 yrs and older	90,599	12.2	32	16.3	9.6	18.1	12.2

CELLS: To make more detailed comparisons, examine specific cells in the body of the table. These are the boxes that hold the numbers or percentages.

In this table, the cells contain data on educational achievement by age, sex, and race/ethnicity (for Asians, Whites, Blacks, and Hispanics).

▼ TABLE 2.1

Educational Attainment by Selected Characteristics: 2017, for Persons 25 Years Old and Over, Reported in Thousands (Continued)

UNITS: Units refer to how the data are reported. They could be in percentages, in number per 100 or 1,000, or in other units.

In this table, the data are reported first in raw number in thousands and then in percentages.

FACTS FROM THE TABLE: After reviewing all this information, the reader is ready to make some interpretations about what the data mean.

In this table, the reader might note that young adults are more likely to have a college education than older citizens, though those in the middle age bracket are more likely to have graduate degrees. In addition, people with Asian backgrounds have the highest levels of education. What other interesting patterns do you see?

		Percentage of Population—Highest Level					
Characteristic	Population (1,000)	Not a High School Graduate	High School Graduate	Some College but No Degree	Associate's Degree[1]	Bachelor's Degree	Advanced Degree
Sex							
Male	104,325	10.9	30	16.2	9.3	21	12.7
Female	112,597	10	28	16.6	11.4	21.6	13.1
Race/Ethnicity							
Asian	13,183	9	20	9.4	6.3	30.5	24.3
White[2]	171,046	10	30	16.1	10.5	21.8	12.7
Black[2]	26,455	12.6	33	20.1	10.3	15.1	8.8
Hispanic	32,660	29.5	31	14.5	8.1	12.2	5.1

Source: U.S. Census Bureau (2017).

[1] Includes vocational degrees.

[2] For persons who selected this race group only.

Features of the table adapted from Broom and Selznick (1963).

SOURCE: The source note, found under the table, points out the origin of the data. It is usually identified by the label "Source."

Under this table, the source note says "U.S. Census Bureau (2017)."

FOOTNOTES: Some tables have footnotes, usually indicating something unusual about the data or where to find more complete data.

In this table, two footnotes are provided so that the reader does not make mistakes in interpretation.

USING SOCIOLOGY TO IMPROVE CAMPUS LIFE AND GAIN MARKETABLE SKILLS

I did not become a sociologist to live in an ivory tower. Rather, I envisioned busting down the castle gate and doing work that would have a positive impact. As a result of my orientation to sociology, I created a Public Sociologies course in which students learn skills relevant to their careers and lives—gathering and analyzing data to understand and address social issues on our campus and in the wider community. One issue my students have worked on is interpersonal violence on campus. Students can play an important role in preventing such violence through a variety of strategies. For example, they might personally intervene if they see a couple arguing, call a resource who can diffuse the situation (such as a resident assistant or campus safety officer), or simply state their discomfort when a friend talks about women in a sexist way.

A number of bystander intervention training programs now attempt to teach these skills. Our campus chose to use the Green Dot program, a violence prevention program that focuses on peers and culture. My students and I agreed that we would help our Women's Center to evaluate the effectiveness of the Green Dot program. To do this, my students had to learn and then use research and evaluation skills.

My students designed the initial survey instrument and tested the survey with a diverse sample of their fellow students so that they could refine the measures. The following spring, my class fielded the baseline wave of the survey. They came up with a sampling strategy (using randomly selected course sections) and went through the approval process with our Institutional Review Board (IRB) to make sure that we protected our human subjects. The students distributed the surveys and entered all of the data into a computer program. Finally, we did statistical analysis of the data and prepared a report for our Women's Center and the Public Prevention and Education Committee of the New Jersey Governor's Advisory Council Against Sexual Assault.

Students in the sociology major worked on this project for over 3 years, eventually gathering three waves of data from over 1,000 students about their experiences with interpersonal violence, as well as their intentions to intervene to prevent violence. An important finding was that 1 in 5 of our female students and 1 in 10 of our male students had experienced interpersonal violence. Even more striking, two thirds of our students knew someone who had experienced interpersonal violence. We were also able to provide evidence that students who had received Green Dot training were more likely to intervene as active bystanders than students who had not. Being able to show the prevalence of the issue and the effectiveness of our prevention strategy were important for securing institutional resources to expand the program.

Through this experience, Public Sociologies students were able to engage in an important evaluation project that helped them develop real-world research skills. A number of my students have gone on to work in jobs that require them to consume and produce research, and to bridge theory and practice (e.g., social workers, police officers, and market researchers, to name a few). You can too!

* * * * * * *

Kristin Kenneavy is an associate professor of sociology at Ramapo College of New Jersey where she works closely with the Center for Student Involvement to promote community-based learning and scholarship, and continues to research interpersonal violence prevention.

So far, we have focused on what sociology is and how sociologists know what they know and do the research they do. The rest of the book examines our social world as informed by methods and theory discussed in this chapter. The next chapter explores how you can understand your culture and society at the various levels of analysis in our social world.

WHAT HAVE WE LEARNED?

Theories serve as lenses to help us create research questions and to make sense of the data we gather using various research strategies. The data themselves can be used to test the theories, so there is an ongoing reciprocal relationship between theory (the lens for making sense of the data) and research (the evidence used to test the theories). The most important ideas in this chapter concern what sociology considers data or evidence and how sociology is a science. These ideas form the framework for the content of sociology.

The core features of *scientific* research are (a) a commitment to using the scientific method to collect, analyze, and understand data through systematic processes of testing using the five senses (sometimes enhanced by scientific instruments); (b) allowing ourselves to be convinced by the evidence rather than by our preconceived ideas; (c) absolute integrity and objectivity in how we conduct and report on our research; and (d) continual openness to having our findings reexamined and new interpretations proposed. We must always consider the possibility that we have overlooked alternative explanations of the data and alternative ways to view the problem.

Science—including social science—does not consist of just facts to be memorized. Science is a process made possible by a social exchange of ideas, a clash of opinions, and a continual search for truth. Knowledge in the sciences is created by vigorous debate. We hope you will engage in the creation of knowledge by entering into these debates.

KEY POINTS

- Attempts to understand society have existed for at least two and a half millennia, but gathering of scientific evidence to test hypotheses and validate claims is a modern idea.

- Theories are especially important to science because they raise questions for research, and they explain the relationships among facts. Sociology has four primary, overriding theoretical perspectives or paradigms: symbolic interaction theory, rational choice theory, structural-functional theory, and conflict theory. Other perspectives, such as feminist theory, serve as correctives to the main paradigms. Most of these theories are more applicable at either the micro to meso level or at the meso to macro level.

- Sociology is a science used to study society, and therefore it is essential to understand what is—and what is not—considered data or evidence. For a scientist, this means that ideas must be tested empirically, that is, scientifically.

- As social scientists, sociologists use eight systematic steps to gather data and test theories about the social world.

- The *independent variable* is the variable in a cause-and-effect relationship that comes first in a time sequence and causes a change in another variable—the *dependent variable*.

- Major methods for gathering data in sociology include questionnaires, interviews, observational studies, secondary data analysis, content analysis, and experiments.

- Quantitative data come in the form of numbers (e.g., derived from questionnaires or some secondary sources such as the census), and qualitative data come in nonnumerical forms (e.g., derived from semistructured and unstructured interviews or observational studies).

- Use of multiple methods—triangulation—increases confidence in the findings.

- Scientific confidence in results requires representative samples, usually drawn randomly.

- Responsible research requires sensitivity to the ethics of research—ensuring that gathering scientific data does no one harm.

- Public sociologists use sociological tools to understand and inform citizens about how society operates and to improve society.

DISCUSSION QUESTIONS

1. If you were to examine the relationship between the government and the economy in the United States today, which of the four major theoretical perspectives outlined in the chapter would be most helpful? Why?

2. Imagine you would like to conduct a sociological study of the students with whom you attended the fourth grade to determine what key factors influenced their academic achievements. Which of the four major

theoretical perspectives would you employ in your study? Why?

3. Why do research questions have to be asked in a precise way? Give an example of a precise research question. How do precise questions make it possible for you to test and measure your topic?

4. Sociologists must be continually open to having their findings reexamined and new interpretations proposed. Describe a time when you changed your mind due to new information. Was it difficult for you to change your mind? Why or why not?

5. Why is the ability to be open to new ideas and interpretations and to be objective so vital to the scientific perspective? Do you think you could carry out this aspect of the scientific process successfully—no matter how you feel about a topic? Why or why not?

6. If you were to conduct a study to measure student satisfaction with a particular academic department on campus, what research method(s) would you use? Why? How would the method(s) you select vary according to (a) the size of the department and (b) the type of information you sought?

KEY TERMS

cause-and-effect relationships   42

conflict theory   35

content analysis   44

control group   44

controls   42

correlation   42

dependent variable   42

dysfunctions   34

empirical knowledge   40

evidence   40

experimental group   44

experiments   44

feminist theory   38

functions   34

hypothesis   40

independent variable   42

interviews   43

latent functions   34

manifest functions   34

means of production   34

objectivity   40

observational studies   44

public sociologists   47

questionnaires   43

rational choice theory   32

rationality   38

sample   41

secondary analysis   44

spurious relationships   42

structural-functional theory   34

symbolic interaction theory   31

symbols   31

theoretical perspective   30

theories   30

triangulation   45

variables   40

CONTRIBUTING TO OUR SOCIAL WORLD: WHAT CAN WE DO?

At the Local (Micro) Level

- *Local volunteer coordinating organizations* give creative outlets to students allowing them to demonstrate their awareness and learning of the world around them through different tasks, volunteering, civil engagement, and literary skills. Volunteer Match (www.volunteermatch.org) links volunteers to virtual opportunities both in nearby communities and across the globe. Virtual volunteering is an excellent way to extend humanitarian reach across the globe as well as locally. If your college or university has a service-learning office, it will offer connections to many service opportunities, sometimes linked to specific fields of study. Many colleges and universities also offer Academic Service Learning (ASL) credit in which course assignments include such community work under the supervision of the instructor.

At the Organizational or Institutional (Meso) Level

- *State agencies* often have ongoing projects to gather data for more accurate information about the state and the needs of its citizens. Go to www.nationalservice.gov/about/contact-us/state-service-commissions to find volunteer opportunities through your state government.

At the National or Global (Macro) Level

- *The U.S. Bureau of the Census* is best known for its decennial (every 10 years) enumeration of the population, but its work continues each year as it prepares special reports, population estimates, and regular publications (including *Current Population Reports*). Visit the bureau's website at www.census.gov and explore the valuable and extensive quantitative data and other information available. Visit your local Census Bureau office or go to www.census.gov/about/census-careers/opportunities/programs/student.html to find volunteer and other opportunities for students at the Census Bureau.

$SAGE edge™

Get the tools you need to sharpen your study skills. SAGE edge offers a robust online environment featuring an impressive array of free tools and resources.

Access practice quizzes, eFlashcards, video, and multimedia at **edge.sagepub.com/ballantine7e**

PART II

SOCIAL STRUCTURE, PROCESSES, AND CONTROL

Picture a house. First, there is the foundation, then the wood frame, and then the walls and roof. This provides the framework or *structure*. Within that structure, activities called *processes* take place—electricity to turn on lights and appliances, water to wash in and drink, and people to carry out these processes. If something goes wrong in the house, we take steps to control the damage and repair it.

Now compare that picture of a house with a society. The *social structure* of a society, its groups and organizations, is the framework of society. The *social processes* are the dynamic activities of society that take place within those structures. This section begins with a discussion of the structure of society, followed by the processes of culture and socialization through which individuals are taught cultural rules—how to live effectively within their society's structure. Although socialization of individuals takes place primarily at the micro level, we explore its implications at the meso and macro levels as well.

If we break the social structure into parts, such as the wood frame, walls, and roof of a house, it is the groups and organizations (including large organizations, or bureaucracies) that are parts of the social structure. To work smoothly, these organizations depend on people's loyalty so that the participants do what society and its groups need to survive. However, these components do not always work well together. Things break down. Leaders in societies try to control disruptions and deviant individuals in order to maintain their control of social structures, whatever their goals may be.

As we explore the next few chapters, we continue to examine social life at the micro, meso, and macro levels, for as individuals we are profoundly shaped by social processes and structures at larger and more abstract levels, all the way to the global level.

© iStock.com/Christian Mueller

SOCIETY AND CULTURE

Hardware and Software of Our Social World

▲ Depending on what resources are available where we live and what is considered usable and edible, we put something out to eat. It might be a juicy hamburger, dog meat, or bugs. What we consider food is influenced by the organization of food production, distribution, technology, and the culture—ideas about what is edible. In the opening photo, an international market is bustling with activity as people shop for the kinds of foods considered nutritious and tasty in their culture.

MICRO

ME (AND MY FAMILY)

LOCAL ORGANIZATIONS
AND COMMUNITY
Local soccer teams and scout
troops have a microculture.

MESO

NATIONAL ORGANIZATIONS,
INSTITUTIONS, AND ETHNIC
SUBCULTURES
Ethnic groups have a subculture.

MACRO

SOCIETY
A nation has a national culture.

GLOBAL COMMUNITY
Multinational organizations like
the World Health Organization
have a global culture.

WHAT WILL YOU LEARN IN THIS CHAPTER?

This chapter will help you to do the following:

3.1 Describe the structure (the "hardware") of our social world

3.2 Illustrate how culture affects individuals, groups, and societies

3.3 Provide examples of microcultures, subcultures, countercultures, and global cultures

3.4 Compare key ideas in the symbolic interactionist, functionalist, and conflict perspectives on culture

3.5 Explain why culture (the "software") from one society does not always "fit" with the structure ("hardware") of another society

THINK ABOUT IT

Micro: Small groups and local communities	How do microcultures (such as your fraternity, study group, or athletic team) influence you?
Meso: National institutions, complex organizations, and ethnic groups	How do subcultures (such as your ethnic group) and countercultures (such as youth gangs) shape the character of your nation and influence your own life?
Macro: National and global systems	How do your nation's social structures and culture influence who you are; what opportunities are available to you; and how you dress, eat, work, and live your life?

What is considered edible, even delectable, to people in one society may be repulsive to those in another. Taste and how people eat differ greatly, depending on the culture in which one lives and what is available in that culture.

Mrs. Ukita, the mom in the Ukita family, rises early to prepare a breakfast of miso soup and a raw egg on rice. The father and two daughters eat quickly and rush out to catch their early morning trains to work and school in Kodaira City, Japan. The mother cares for the house; does the shopping; and prepares a typical evening meal of fish or meat, vegetables, and rice for the family.

The Ahmed family lives in a large apartment building in Cairo, Egypt. The 12 members of the extended family include the women who shop for and cook the food: vegetables, including peppers, greens, potatoes, squash, and tomatoes; garlic, onions, and spices; and rice, along with pita bread and often fish or meat. The adult men work in shops in one of the many bazaars, while the school-age children attend school and then help with the chores.

At the Aznaq and Za'atan refugee camps in Jordan, Syrian refugees face food insecurity. Some refugee families who are registered with the United Nations High Commissioner for Refugees receive cash vouchers to buy limited amounts of food available. Other families receive weekly rations with bare essentials for existence. Sometimes shipments of food are not possible due to hostilities, and people go hungry.

The Walker family from Norfolk, Virginia, grabs dinner at a fast-food restaurant on their way to basketball practice and an evening meeting. Because of their busy schedules and individual activities, they cannot always find time to cook and eat together—a behavior that would be unthinkable in most societies around the world.

Although most diets include some form of grain and starch, locally available fruits and vegetables, and perhaps meat or fish, broad variations in food consumption exist even within one society. Yet all of these differences have something in common: Each represents a society with a unique culture that includes growing or buying food, preparing and eating it, storing food, and cleaning up after eating. Food preparation is only one aspect of our *way of life*, common for all humans and necessary for survival. Ask yourself why you sleep on a bed, brush your teeth, or listen to music with friends. Our way of life is called *culture*.

Culture refers to *the way of life shared by a group of people—the knowledge, beliefs, values, rules or laws, language, customs, symbols, and material products (such as food, houses, and transportation) within a society that help meet human needs.* Culture provides guidelines for living. We are seldom conscious of learning our culture, but learning culture puts our social world in an understandable framework, providing a tool kit we can use to help construct the meaning of our world and behaviors in it (Bruner 1996; Nagel 1994). We compare culture with software because it is the human ideas and input that make the society work. Otherwise, society would just be structures, like the hard drive of a computer or framework of a house, with no processes to bring it alive.

A **society** is *an organized and interdependent group of individuals who live together in a specific geographic area, who interact more with each other than they do with outsiders, who cooperate for the attainment of common goals, and who share a common culture over time.* In most cases, societies are the same as the countries that make up the world. Each society includes key parts called institutions—family, education, religion, politics, economies, and health care or medicine—that help humans meet basic needs. This structure that makes up society is what we refer to here as the hardware, like the hard drive mentioned earlier. Culture, the software, is learned, transmitted, shared, and reshaped from generation to generation. All activities in the society, whether educating young members, preparing and eating dinner, selecting leaders for the group, finding a mate, or negotiating with other societies, are guided by cultural rules and expectations. In each society, culture provides the social rules for how individuals carry out necessary tasks.

Society—organized groups of people—and *culture*—their way of life—are interdependent. The two are not the same thing, but they cannot exist without each other, just as computer hardware and software are each useless without the other.

This chapter explores the ideas of society and culture and their relation to each other, what society is and how it is organized, how it influences and is influenced by culture, what culture is, how and why culture develops, the components of culture, cultural theories, and policy issues. After reading this chapter, you will have a better idea of how you learn the ways of your society and culture.

Society: The Hardware

The structures that make up society include the micro-level positions we hold (parent, student, and employee); the groups to which we belong (family, work group, and clubs); and the larger groups, organizations, or institutions in which we participate (educational, political, and economic organizations). This "hardware" (structure) of our social world provides the framework for "software" (culture) to function.

Societies, usually countries but sometimes distinct sovereign groups within countries (such as Native Americans), differ because they exist in different locations with unique resources—mountains, coastal areas, jungles, and deserts. Although human societies have become more complex over time, especially in recent history, people have been hunters and gatherers for 99% of human existence. Only a few groups remain hunters and gatherers today. As Table 3.1 illustrates, if all human history were to be compressed into the lifetime of an 80-year-old person, humans would have started cultivating crops and herding animals for their food supply only a few months ago. Note the incredible rate of change that has occurred just in the past 2 centuries.

THINKING SOCIOLOGICALLY

What major changes took place in your grandparents' lifetimes that affect the way you and your family live today?

Societies are organized in particular patterns shaped by factors that include the way people procure food, the

▲ Traditional, rural Mayan women in Guatemala make tortillas or *boxboles*. Food preparation, as well as consumption, is a communal experience among these people with customs to be followed.

availability of resources, contact with other societies, and cultural beliefs. For example, people can change from herding to farming only if they have the knowledge, skills, and desire to do so and only in environments that will support agriculture. As societies develop, changes take place in the social structures and relationships between people. For example, in industrialized societies, relationships between people typically become more formal because people must interact with strangers and not just their relatives. It is important to note that not all societies go through all stages. Some are jolted into the future by political events or changes in the global system, and some resist pressures to become modernized and continue to live in simpler social systems.

Evolution of Societies

The Saharan desert life for the Tuareg tribe is pretty much as it has been for centuries. In simple traditional

One Million Years of Human History Compressed Into One 80-Year Lifetime

Approximate Time ·	Age	Event in Human History	
2.5 million years ago	Birth	*Homo habilis* is born—the first ancestor to make/use tools and have culture; evidence of sharing food, congregating, and probably sharing housing	
2 million years ago	2 years old	*Homo erectus* shows early evidence of family structures; findings of longer life spans and three generations alive simultaneously	
15,000 years ago	79 years old	Six months ago: North America settled by early humans, hunters and gatherers	
11,000 years ago	79 years old	Five months ago: In the Middle East, the first agricultural communities, indicating food cultivation	
10,000 years ago	79 years old	Twenty weeks ago: The last ice age is over; humans spread more widely over the planet	
5,000 years ago	79 years old	Ten weeks ago: Humans began to cast and use metals and built the pyramids	
2,000 years ago	79 years old	Seven weeks ago: Beginning of the Common Era (under the Holy Roman Empire)	
220 years ago	79 years old	Two and a half weeks ago: The United States began a new experiment with democracy	
100 years ago	79 years old	Yesterday morning: The airplane was invented	
30–50 years ago	80th birthday	Yesterday afternoon: Humans first set foot on the moon; after dinner, we broke the DNA (genetic) code and invented the first cell phone	

http://starchild.gsfc.nasa.gov/ Images/ StarChild/space_level2/ aldrin_big.gif

societies, individuals are assigned to comparatively few social positions or statuses. Today, however, few societies are isolated from global impact. Even the Tuareg are called on to escort adventurous tourists through the desert for a currency new to them and unneeded until recently. In such traditional societies, men teach their sons everything they need to know, for all men do much the same jobs, depending on where they live: hunting, fishing, or farming and protecting the community from danger. Likewise, girls learn their jobs—such as child-care, fetching water, food preparation, farming, weaving, and perhaps house building—from their mothers. In contrast, in more complex societies, such as industrial or "modern" societies, thousands of interdependent job statuses are based on complex divisions of labor with designated tasks.

Émile Durkheim ([1893] 1947), an early French sociologist, pictured a continuum between simple and complex societies. He described simple premodern societies as held together by **mechanical solidarity**—*social cohesion and integration based on the similarity of individuals in the group, including shared beliefs, values, and emotional ties between members of the group.* Furthermore, the division of labor is based largely on male/female distinctions and age groupings; everyone fulfills his or her expected social positions. This provides the glue that holds the society together. The entire society may involve only a few hundred people, with no meso-level institutions, organizations, or subcultures. Prior to the emergence of nation-states, there was no macro level either—only tribal groupings.

According to Durkheim, as societies transformed, they became more complex through increasingly multi-faceted divisions of labor and changes in the ways people carried out necessary tasks for survival ([1893] 1947). **Organic solidarity** refers to *social cohesion (glue) based on division of labor, with each member playing a highly specialized role in the society and each person being dependent on others due to interdependent, interrelated tasks.* The society has cohesion regardless of whether people have common values and shared outlooks. Prior to the factory system, for example, individual cobblers made shoes to order. With the Industrial Revolution, factories took over the process, with many individuals carrying out interdependent tasks. The division of labor is critical because it leads to new forms of social cohesion based on interdependence, and much less on familial and emotional ties. Gradual changes from mechanical (traditional) to organic (modern) society also involve harnessing new forms of energy and finding more efficient ways to use them (Nolan and Lenski 2014). For example, the use of steam engines and coal for fuel triggered the Industrial Revolution, leading to the development of industrial societies.

As societies changed toward organic solidarity, they added large organizations and institutions. The meso level—institutions and large bureaucratic organizations—became more influential for individuals and families. Still, as recently as 200 years ago, even large societies had little global interdependence, and life for the typical citizen was influenced mostly by events at the micro and meso levels. As communication and transportation around the world developed and expanded, the global level grew.

As you read about each of the following types of societies, from the simplest to the most complex, notice the presence of these variables: (a) division of labor, (b) interdependence of people's positions, (c) increasingly advanced technologies, and (d) new forms and uses of energy. Although none of these variables alone is *sufficient* to trigger evolution to a new type of society, they may all be *necessary* for a transition to occur.

According to Durkheim, then, in traditional societies with mechanical solidarity, interpersonal interaction and community life at the micro level were the most important aspects of social life. Meso- and macro-level societies developed as a result of changes toward more organic solidarity. As societies become more complex, meso- and macro-level institutions evolve and become more important, and have increasingly profound impacts on the lives of individuals.

Hunter-Gatherer Societies. In the Kalahari Desert of southwestern Africa live hunter-gatherers known as the !Kung. (The ! is pronounced with a click of the tongue.) The !Kung live a nomadic life, moving from one place to another as food supplies become available or are used up. As a result, they carry few personal possessions and live in temporary huts, settling around water holes for a few months at a time. Settlements are small, rarely more than 20 to 50 people, for food supplies are not plentiful enough to support large, permanent populations (Lee 1984). !Kung women gather edible plants and nuts, while !Kung men hunt. Beyond division of labor by gender and age, however, there are few differences in roles or status.

In **hunter-gatherer societies**, *people rely on the vegetation and animals occurring naturally in their habitat to sustain life.* Generally, life is organized around kinship ties and reciprocity—that is, mutual assistance—for the well-being of the whole community. When a large animal is killed, people gather from a wide area to share in the bounty, and great care is taken to ensure that the meat is distributed fairly. Resources are shared among the people, but sharing is regulated by a complex system of mutual obligations. A visitor who eats food at another's hearth is expected to repay that hospitality in the future.

▲ Hunting and gathering societies, like these Botswana Bushmen, do still exist, but they are increasingly affected by modern societies and technologies. These hunters make notes of their most recent excursion on a GPS app on their smartphone.

The !Kung are a typical hunter-gatherer society. People make their clothing, shelter, and tools from available materials or obtain goods through trade with other nearby groups. People migrate seasonally to new food sources. Population size remains small because the number of births and deaths in the society are balanced.

From the beginning of human experience until recently, hunting and gathering (or foraging) were the sole means of sustaining life. These early humans developed cultures and skills necessary for survival. Although few hunting and gathering societies exist in today's crowded and modernizing world, we can learn some interesting aspects about the relationship between culture and human skills from those that do exist. For example, studies of the hunting-gathering group the Semaq Beri of the Malay Peninsula indicate that they have developed superior smell and recognition of scents, in part because identifying odors is key to their culture and survival (Klein 2018).

Other types of societies emerged only recently. Today, only a handful of societies still rely on hunting and gathering (Nolan and Lenski 2014). The hunter-gatherer lifestyle is becoming extinct largely because no society is isolated in today's world.

Herding and Horticultural Societies.

A seminomadic herding society, the Masai of Kenya and Tanzania move camp to find grazing land for their animals and set up semipermanent shelters for the few months they will remain in one area. Settlements consist of huts constructed in a circle with a perimeter fence surrounding the compound. At the more permanent settlements, the Masai grow short-term crops to supplement their diet.

Herding societies *have food-producing strategies based on domestication of animals whose care is the central focus of their activities.* Domesticating animals has replaced hunting them. In addition to providing food and other products, cattle, sheep, goats, pigs, horses, and camels represent forms of wealth that result in more social prestige for members of the group with large herds.

Horticultural societies are *those in which the food-producing strategy is based on domestication of plants, using digging sticks and wooden hoes to cultivate small gardens.* They may also keep domesticated animals, but they focus on simple agriculture or gardening. They cultivate tree crops, such as date palms or bananas, and plant garden plots, such as yams, beans, taro, squash, or corn. This is more efficient than gathering wild vegetables and fruits. Both herding and horticultural societies differ from hunter-gatherer societies in that they settle in one place, occasionally moving to another when water becomes scarce or land is depleted; make their living by cultivating food; and have some control over their food production (Ward and Edelstein 2014).

The ability to control food sources was a major turning point in human history. Societies became more settled and stored surpluses of food, which led to increases in population size. A community could contain as many as 3,000 individuals. More people, surplus food, and greater accumulation of possessions encouraged the development of private property and created new status differences between individuals and families. Forms of social inequality started to become pronounced.

The technological breakthrough that moved many societies from the horticultural to the agricultural stage was the plow, introduced more than 6,000 years ago. It marked the beginning of the agricultural revolution in Europe, the Middle East, and other parts of the world, and it brought about massive changes in social structures in many societies. The end of the horticultural stage also saw advances in irrigation systems, the fertilization of land, crop rotation, more permanent settlements, land ownership, human modification of the natural environment, higher population density (cities), and power hierarchies.

Agricultural Societies.

Pedro and Lydia Ramirez, their four young children, and Lydia's parents live as an extended family in a small farming village in Nicaragua. The family plows the land with the help of strong animals such as horses and oxen, uses fertilizers, and waters the garden when needed. The Ramirezes' way of life is typical in an agricultural society. **Agricultural societies** *rely primarily on raising crops for food but make use of technological advances such as the plow, irrigation, animals, and fertilization to continuously cultivate the same land.* The continuous cultivation of the same land results in permanent settlements and greater food surpluses. Agricultural societies use energy more efficiently than foraging societies. For example, the plow circulates nutrients better than a digging stick, and when an animal pulls the plow, the farmer uses strength beyond that of a person. As increasingly sophisticated agricultural technology resulted in surplus food, the size of population centers increased to as much as a million or more.

As surpluses accumulated, land in some societies became concentrated in the hands of a few individuals. Wealthy landowners built armies and expanded their empires. During these periods, fighting for land took precedence over technological advances. War was prevalent, and societies were divided increasingly into rich and poor classes. Those who held the land and wealth could control the labor sources and acquire serfs or slaves. Thus, the feudal system was born. Serfs (the peasant class) were forced to work the land for their survival. Food surpluses also allowed some individuals to leave the land and to trade goods or services in exchange for food. For the first time, social inequality became extensive enough to divide society into social classes. At this point, religion, political power, a standing army, and other meso-level institutions and organizations came to be independent of the family. The meso level became well established.

As technology advanced, goods were manufactured in cities. Peasants moved from farming communities, where the land could not support the large population, to rapidly growing urban areas, where the demand for labor was great. It was not until the mid-1700s in England that the next major transformation of society began to take place, resulting largely from technological advances and additional harnessing of energy. (See Figure 3.1 for a timeline of this transformation.)

Industrial Societies. The Industrial Revolution involved the harnessing of steam power and the manufacture of gasoline engines, permitting machines to replace human and animal power. A tractor can plow far more land in a week than a horse, and an electric pump can irrigate more acres than an ox-driven pump. As a result of such new technologies, raw mineral products such as ores, raw plant products such as rubber, and raw

▲ Plows, essential for agricultural societies to develop, were pushed by people and then pulled by animals and later machines. Harnessing energy ever more effectively is a prerequisite to a society becoming more complex.

animal products such as hides could be transformed into mass-produced consumer goods. The Industrial Revolution brought about enormous changes in occupations, the division of labor, production of goods, and social structures.

Industrial societies *rely primarily on mechanized production resulting in greater division of labor based on expertise.* Economic resources were distributed more widely among individuals in industrial societies, but inequities between owners and laborers persisted. Wage earning gradually replaced slavery and serfdom, and highly skilled workers earned higher wages, leading to the rise of a middle class. Farm workers moved from rural areas to cities to find work in factories that produced consumer goods. Cities grew, and many became populated by millions of people.

Family and kinship patterns at the micro level also changed. Agricultural societies need large, land-based extended family units to do the work of farming (recall

Timeline of the Industrial Revolution, 1712–1903

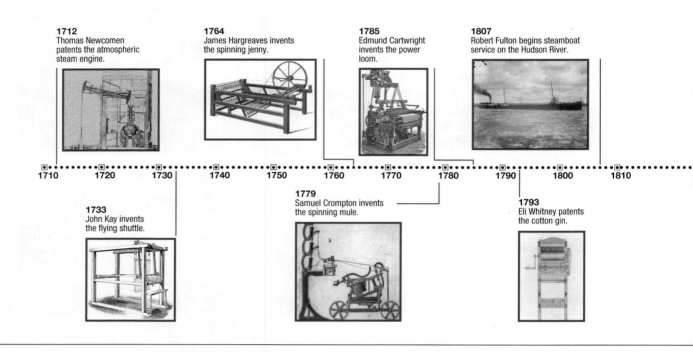

1712
Thomas Newcomen patents the atmospheric steam engine.

1764
James Hargreaves invents the spinning jenny.

1785
Edmund Cartwright invents the power loom.

1807
Robert Fulton begins steamboat service on the Hudson River.

1710   1720   1730   1740   1750   1760   1770   1780   1790   1800   1810

1733
John Kay invents the flying shuttle.

1779
Samuel Crompton invents the spinning mule.

1793
Eli Whitney patents the cotton gin.

how the Ramirez parents, grandparents, and children in Nicaragua all help out at harvest time), but industrial societies need individuals with specific skills, the ability to move to where the jobs are, and smaller families to support. Family roles change. Children are an asset in agricultural societies and begin work at an early age. However, from a purely economic perspective, children become a liability in an industrial society because they contribute less to the finances of the family.

Meso- and macro-level dimensions of social life expand in industrializing societies and become more influential in the lives of individuals. National institutions and multinational organizations develop. Today, for example, global organizations such as the World Bank, the World Court, the United Nations, and the World Health Organization address social problems and sometimes even make decisions that change national boundaries or national policies. Corporations such as Nike and Gap are multinational organizations (located in many countries). Some voluntary associations—such as Doctors without Borders, which serves medical needs, and Amnesty International, which lobbies for human rights—do their work across the globe.

Perhaps the most notable characteristic of the industrial age is the rapid rate of change compared with other stages of societal development. The beginning of industrialization in Europe was gradual, based on years of population movement, urbanization, technological development, and other factors of modernization. Today, however, societal change occurs so rapidly that societies at all levels of development are being drawn together into a new age—the postindustrial era. As you will see, this rapid change and globalization have caused disruption in many societies, and reactions to the change vary widely.

Postindustrial or Information Societies. **Postindustrial societies** are *those that have moved from human labor and manufacturing to automated production and service jobs, largely processing information.* Postindustrial societies require workers with high levels of technical and professional education. Those without technical education are less likely to find rewarding employment in the technological revolution. This results in new class lines being drawn, based in part on skills and education in new technologies, and can influence political participation and voting preferences, attitudes toward technology, and other factors of modern life.

The shift to an information-based society has also enhanced cross-border workplaces. As your authors finished chapters for this book, they were sent to India for

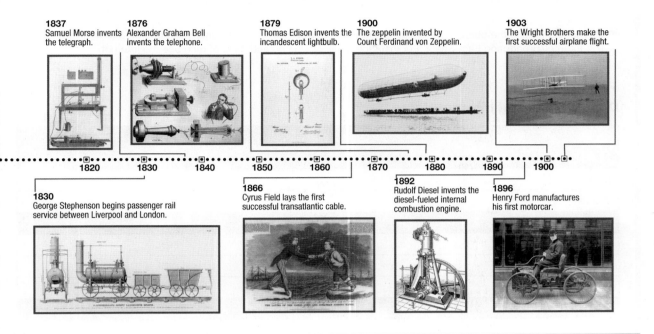

1837
Samuel Morse invents the telegraph.

1876
Alexander Graham Bell invents the telephone.

1879
Thomas Edison invents the incandescent lightbulb.

1900
The zeppelin invented by Count Ferdinand von Zeppelin.

1903
The Wright Brothers make the first successful airplane flight.

1820   1830   1840   1850   1860   1870   1880   1890   1900

1830
George Stephenson begins passenger rail service between Liverpool and London.

1866
Cyrus Field lays the first successful transatlantic cable.

1892
Rudolf Diesel invents the diesel-fueled internal combustion engine.

1896
Henry Ford manufactures his first motorcar.

typesetting in the evening; due to the time change with India being 9 hours and 30 minutes ahead of the U.S. East Coast, chapters were returned to the United States by the next morning. Technology, the efficiency of overnight delivery, and the lower cost of production have led many publishing companies to turn to businesses halfway around the world for much of the book production process. As India and other developing countries increase their trained, skilled labor force, they are being called on by national and multinational companies to carry out global manufacturing processes. India has some of the world's best technical training institutes and modern **technology**—*the practical application of tools, skills, and knowledge to meet human needs and extend human abilities.* Although many people in India live in poverty, a relatively new middle class is rapidly emerging in major business centers around the country.

After World War II, starting in the 1950s, the transition from industrial to postindustrial society began in the United States, Western Europe, and Japan. This shift was characterized by movement from human labor to automated production and from a predominance of

▲ This Buddhist monk uses modern technology, including a laptop that can connect him with colleagues on the other side of the globe.

manufacturing jobs to a growth in service jobs, such as computer operators, bankers, scientists, teachers, public relations workers, stockbrokers, and salespeople. More than two thirds of all jobs in the United States now reside in organizations that produce and transmit information, thus the reference to an *information age*. Daniel Bell

DEMOGRAPHICS OF INTERNET USERS

The following is the percentage of each group of U.S. adults who use the Internet, according to the Pew Internet/Broadband Fact Sheet. For instance, 88% of women and 89% of men use the Internet.

▼ TABLE 3.2

Demographics of Internet Users

	Percentage Who Use the Internet
All Adults	89%
Men	89%
Women	88%
Race/Ethnicity	
White	89%
Black	87%
Hispanic	88%
Age	
18–29	98%
30–49	97%
50–64	87%
65+	66%
Household Income	
Less than $30,000/year	81%
$30,000–$49,999	93%
$50,000–$74,999	97%
$75,000+	98%
Educational Attainment	
Less than high school graduate	65%
High school graduate	84%
Some college	93%
College graduate	97%

Source: The Pew Research Center's Internet/Broadband Fact Sheet 2018.

Note: Surveys conducted 2000–2018. Data for each year based on a pooled analysis of all surveys conducted during that year. Data for Hispanics includes only surveys that included Spanish-language interviews.

Engaging Sociology

Interview 10 people you know to find out about their Internet use, keeping records on the gender, age, race or ethnicity, educational attainment, and income bracket of each. Then compare your figures with those in Table 3.2. Are they similar? If not, what possible geographic, social class, or other factors might cause your figures to be different from those in this national survey?

describes this transformation of work, information, and communication as *the third technological revolution* after industrialization based on steam (the first technological revolution) and the invention of electricity (the second technological revolution) (Bell 1973). According to Bell, the third technological revolution was the development of the computer, which has led to this postindustrial era or information age. To examine this transformation, see Table 3.2 in the Engaging Sociology feature on the opposite page.

Postindustrial societies rely on new sources of power such as atomic, wind, thermal, and solar energy and new uses of computer automation. Former sources of power such as coal, oil, and gas are in less demand as renewable energy sources grow in affordability and accessibility. Computer-controlled robots have taken over many jobs once carried out by humans. The control of information and the ability to develop technologies or provide services have become key sources of money and power.

Values of 21st-century postindustrial societies favor scientific and creative approaches to problem-solving, research, and development, along with attitudes that support the globalization of world economies. Satellites, cell phones, fiber optics, and especially the Internet continue to transform postindustrial societies of the information age, linking people from societies around the world. Globalization is a force that cannot be stopped.

In a study of postmodern communities, sociologist Richard Florida links creativity to the local cultural climate and to economic prosperity. His research has important practical applications and is useful to policymakers in local communities. As his research in the next Sociologists in Action makes clear, the organization of society and the means of providing the necessities of life have a profound impact on values, beliefs, lifestyle, and other aspects of culture.

THINKING SOCIOLOGICALLY

Why do some communities attract creative people? What are some characteristics of these communities? What might be advantages—or disadvantages—to living in a creative community? Would you like to live in such a community? Why or why not? How do you think growing up in such a community would impact your choice of a career and friends?

What will the future bring? Futurologists predict new trends based on current activities and predictions of new advances and technologies on the horizon. Among the many ideas for the future, technological advances dominate the field. Predictions include the increasing use of cell phones connecting the poorest corners of the globe with the rest of the world. One billion mobile phone users are predicted for China by 2020, with 80% of the population having cell phones. With discovery and efficient use of energy being central to sociocultural evolution, alternative energy sources from wind to solar power will become essential to meet demand. Plug-in hybrids, natural gas, and electric batteries may replace gasoline motors. One million hydrogen-fueled cars are predicted for the United States by the year 2035, and far more for Europe and Japan. Gas may be on the way out. Rechargeable batteries that run for 40 hours without interruption will run most home appliances by 2030. Other energy advances include LEDs (light-emitting diodes); energy on demand from mix-and-match sources; "smart" home devices; "smart" city infrastructures to meet needs for energy, transit, and roads; breathalyzer cars; extinguishers that put out forest fires with sound; edge-of-space balloon rides; and so much more (Kleinman 2014; Science Focus 2016). Brain computer interfaces will give paralyzed people the ability to control their environments (National Institutes of Health 2012). These are just a few of the many predictions of what will affect societies and alter human interactions.

In much of this book we focus on complex, multilevel societies, for this is the type of social environment in which most of us reading this book now live. Much of this book also focuses on social interaction and social structures, including interpersonal networking, the growth of bureaucratic structures, social inequality within the structure, and the core institutions necessary to meet the needs of individuals and society. In short, *hardware*—society—is the focus of many subsequent chapters. The remainder of this chapter focuses primarily on the social *software*—culture.

Culture: The Software

Culture, the way of life shared by a group of people, includes the ideas and "things" passed on from one generation to the next in a society, including knowledge, beliefs, values, rules and laws, language, customs, symbols, and material products. It varies greatly as we travel across the globe. Each social unit of interdependent people, whether at the micro, meso, or macro level, develops a unique way of life with guidelines for the actions and interaction of individuals and groups within society.

As you can see, the sociological definition of culture refers to far more than "high or elite culture" shared by a

THE CREATIVITY CLASS AND SUCCESSFUL COMMUNITIES

Like the transformations of societies from the hunter-gatherer to the horticultural stage or from the agricultural to the industrial stage, our own current transformation seems to have created a good deal of "cultural wobble" within society. How does one identify the elements or the defining features of a new age while the transformation is still in progress? This was one of the questions that intrigued sociologist Richard Florida, who studied U.S. communities.

Professor Florida visited especially prosperous communities that seemed to be on the cutting edge of change in U.S. society. In these communities, he did individual interviews and focus-group interviews. *Focus-group interviews* are semistructured group interviews with seven or eight people where ideas can be generated from the group by asking open-ended questions. He also used existing (secondary) data collected by various U.S. government agencies, especially the U.S. Bureau of Labor Statistics and the Census Bureau. The collected data helped Professor Florida identify the factors that attracted creative people to certain areas.

Currently, more than one third of the jobs in the United States—and almost all the extremely well-paid professional positions—require creative thinking. These include not just the creative arts but scientific research; computer and mathematical occupations; education and library science positions; and many media, legal, and managerial careers. People in this "creative class" have an enormous amount of autonomy in their work; they are given problems to solve and the freedom to figure out how to do so. Florida found that modern businesses flourish when they hire highly creative people.

Florida's research led him to collaborate with Gary Gates, a scholar who was doing research on communities hospitable to gays and lesbians. Gates and Florida were amazed to find that their lists were nearly identical. Florida found that creative people thrive on diversity—ethnic, gender, religious, and otherwise—for when creative people are around others who think differently, it tends to spawn new avenues of thinking and problem-solving. Tolerance of difference and even the enjoyment of individual idiosyncrasies are hallmarks of thriving communities.

Florida is now very much in demand as a consultant to mayors and urban-planning teams, and his books have become required reading for city council members. Some elected officials have decided that fostering an environment that attracts creative people leads to prosperity because business will follow. Key elements of creative communities include local music and art festivals, organic food grocery stores, legislation that encourages interesting mom-and-pop stores (and keeps out large "box stores" that crush such small and unique endeavors), quaint and locally owned bookstores and distinctive coffee shops, provisions for bike and walking paths throughout the town, and ordinances that establish an environment of tolerance for people who are "different."

★ ★ ★ ★ ★ ★

Richard Florida heads the Martin Prosperity Institute at the Rotman School of Management at the University of Toronto, and the Creative Communities Leadership Program. He earned his bachelor's degree from Rutgers University and his doctorate in urban planning from Columbia University (Florida 2017).

---

select few—such as fine art, classical music, opera, literature, ballet, and theater—and also far more than "popular culture"—such as reality TV, professional wrestling, YouTube, and other mass entertainment. *Popular culture* is mass produced and consumed and becomes part of everyday traditions through its practices, beliefs, and material objects. It influences public opinion and values. Music, a form of pop culture, has many forms; for example, rap music often focuses on urban culture's politics, economics, and inequality and provides an outlet for frustrations through musical commentary. Much of pop culture has been shaped by technology, as we see in texting and social media. The rapid change in this aspect of popular culture is illustrated in the next Engaging Sociology.

Characteristics of Culture

Culture has certain characteristics in common that define and illustrate the purposes it serves for our societies. What are these common elements?

All people share a culture with others in their society. Culture provides the rules, routines, patterns, and expectations for carrying out daily rituals and interactions. Within a society, the process of learning how to act is

POP CULTURE TECHNOLOGY TIMELINE

© Getty/Bernhard Lang

1996: Google makes its debut.

2002: Amazon Web Services debuts, followed in 2006 by Amazon Elastic Compute Cloud.

2004: Mark Zuckerberg debuts Facebook while still a college student.

2005: YouTube is created by Chad Hurley, Steve Chen, and Jawed Karim.

2009: "Killer apps" from Microsoft and Google debut.

2013: Wristbands to collect biological data and living, breathing running shoes debut.

2014: Video glasses with head-mounted display screen debut, and smartwatches connect to the Internet and smartphones.

2015: Three-dimensional computer cursors and robotic exoskeletons are controlled by human thoughts.

2018: Genetically modified future challenges humans to think about the relationship between technology and society (Illing 2018).

How surprising to think that digital telephones, high-speed lines for computers, digitized print media, and the World Wide Web were all invented within about the past half century, many within the last 20 years. Vinyl records, dial telephones, VHS tapes, and more recently CDs and DVDs have been surpassed by smartphones and streamed and downloaded movies and music. Slim laptops, tablets, and handheld computers have replaced bulky desktop computers. The following timeline shows the advances of the Internet and World Wide Web in recent years; the point of this timeline is to illustrate the rapid advance of technology and the place it holds in our lives. Technology is now a primary conveyor of culture, especially pop culture.

An Internet and World Wide Web Timeline

1946: The first general-purpose computer is created, developed for military purposes.

1951: The first civilian computer is created.

1971: The first personal computer (PC) is launched.

1978: Cellular phone service begins.

1982: Invention of high-speed communications network leads to the Internet.

1984: Apple's Macintosh introduces the first PC with graphics.

1991: The Internet opens to commercial use; the World Wide Web is launched.

The continuing rapid advances in technology have paralleled the development of shared pop culture in the United States and around the world, culture that is accessible to everyone. Music groups from other continents have gained audiences in the United States, with some becoming instant success stories through YouTube.

Engaging Sociology

1. Identify four innovations that you feel are particularly significant. What are some ways in which they have impacted your life?

2. Identify three positive and three negative ways these rapid advances in technology might impact less developed parts of the world.

3. How can the spread of pop culture across the globe (a) bring different societies closer together and (b) cause tensions within and between societies?

called socialization (discussed in Chapter 4). From birth, we learn the patterns of behavior approved in our society.

Culture evolves over time and is adaptive. What is normal, proper, and good behavior in hunter-gatherer societies, where cooperation and communal loyalty are critical to the hunt, differs from appropriate behavior in the information age, where individualism and competition are encouraged and enhance one's position and well-being.

The creation of culture is ongoing and cumulative. Individuals and societies continually build on existing culture to adapt to new challenges and opportunities. Your culture shapes the behaviors, values, and institutions that seem natural to you. Culture is so much a part of life that you may not even notice behaviors that outsiders find unusual or even abhorrent. You may not think about it when handing food to someone with your left hand, but in some other cultures, such an act may be defined as disgusting and rude.

The transmission of culture is the feature that most separates humans from other animals. Some societies of higher primates have shared cultures but do not systematically enculturate (teach a way of life to) the next generation. Primate cultures focus on behaviors relating to obtaining food, use of territory, protection, and social status. Human cultures have significantly more content and are mediated by language. Humans are the only mammals with cultures that enable them to adapt to and even modify their environments so that they can survive on the equator, in the Arctic, or even beyond the planet.

THINKING SOCIOLOGICALLY

Imagine playing a game of cards with four people in which each player thinks a different suit is trump (a rule whereby any card from the trump suit wins over any card from a different suit). In this game, one person believes hearts is trump, another assumes spades is trump, and so forth. What would happen? Try it with some friends. How would the result be similar to a society with no common culture?

Ethnocentrism and Cultural Relativity

"What's morally acceptable? It depends on where in the world you live" (Poushter 2014). In a study of 40 countries around the world about what is morally acceptable—and not—researchers at the Pew Research Center found that 78% of respondents around the world say

extramarital affairs are morally unacceptable (84% in the United States), compared with 46% responding that premarital sex was unacceptable (30% in the United States). Other morality issues included gambling (62% unacceptable), homosexuality (59%), abortion (56%), alcohol use (42%), divorce (24%), and contraception use (14%). The point is that what is morally acceptable varies across societies, causing judgments of others based on one's own standards. *The tendency to view one's own group and its cultural expectations as right, proper, and superior to others* is called **ethnocentrism**—*ethno* for ethnic group and *centrism* for centered on. However, even within a diverse society, what is considered morally acceptable can vary between subgroups and change over time. In the United States, for example, 56% of respondents in 2017 felt it is not necessary to believe in God to have good values, compared to 49% in 2011 (Smith 2017a). As you can see, social values, beliefs, and behaviors can vary dramatically within one society and from one society to the next. These differences can be threatening and even offensive to people who judge others according to their own perspectives, experiences, and values.

If you were brought up in a society that forbids premarital or extramarital sex, for instance, you might judge many from the United States to be immoral. In a few Muslim societies, people who have premarital sex may be severely punished or even executed, because such behavior is seen as an offense against the faith and the family and as a weakening of social bonds. It threatens the lineage and inheritance systems of family groups. In turn, some Americans would find such strict rules of abstinence to be strange and even wrong.

As scientists, sociologists must rely on scientific research to understand behavior. The scientific method calls for *objectivity*—the practice of considering observed behaviors independently of one's own beliefs and values. The study of social behavior, such as that cited earlier by the Pew Research Center, requires both sensitivity to a wide variety of human social patterns and a perspective that reduces bias. This is more difficult than it sounds because sociologists themselves are products of society and culture. All of us are raised in a particular culture that we view as normal or natural. Yet not every culture views the same things as "normal."

Societies instill some degree of *ethnocentrism* in their members because ethnocentric beliefs hold groups together and help members feel that they belong to the group. Ethnocentrism promotes loyalty, unity, high morale, and conformity to the rules of society. Fighting for one's country, for instance, requires some degree of belief in the rightness of one's own society and its causes.

Ethnocentric attitudes also help protect societies from rapid, disintegrating change. If most people in a society did not believe in the rules and values of their own culture, the result could be widespread dissent, deviance, or crime.

Unfortunately, ethnocentrism can lead to misunderstandings between people of different cultures. The same ethnocentric attitudes that strengthen ties between some people may encourage hostility, racism, war, and genocide against others—even others within the society—who are different. Virtually all societies tend to "demonize" their adversary—in movies, the news, and political speeches—especially when a conflict is most intense. Dehumanizing another group with labels makes it easier to torture or kill its members or to perform acts of discrimination and brutality against them. We see this in the current conflict in Syria in which both sides in the conflict feel hatred for each other. However, as we become a part of a global social world, it becomes increasingly important to understand and accept those who are "different." Despite current hostile images, bigotry and attitudes of superiority do not enhance cross-national cooperation and trade in the long run—which is what the increasing movement toward a global

village and globalization entails. The map in Figure 3.2 challenges our ethnocentric view of the world.

THINKING SOCIOLOGICALLY

What strikes you about the map? What is your reaction? How would you see this map through ethnocentric eyes and through the eyes of a cultural relativist?

U.S. foreign relations illustrate how ethnocentrism can produce hostility. Many U.S. citizens are surprised to learn that the United States—a great democracy; world power; and disseminator of food, medicine, and technological assistance to developing nations—is despised in many countries. Anti-U.S. sentiments in South America, the Middle East, Asia, and Europe have brought this reality to life through television broadcasts of demonstrations against the U.S. government. Across the globe, 38% of people in 30 nations now say U.S. power and influence pose a major threat to their countries, up from 13% in

▼ FIGURE 3.2

"Southside Up" Global Map

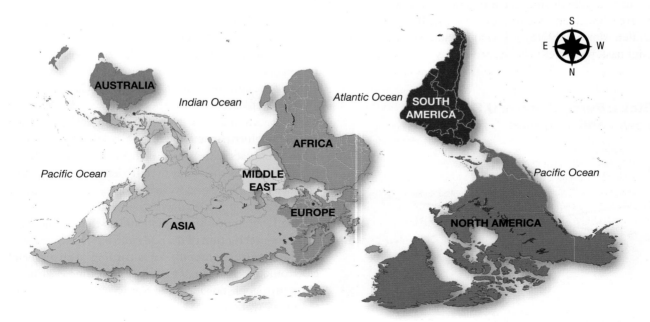

Source: Map by Anna Versluis.

Note: This map illustrates geographic ethnocentrism. U.S. citizens tend to assume it is natural that north should always be "on top." The fact that this map of the world is upside down, where south is "up," seems incorrect or disturbing to some people. Most people think of their countries or regions as occupying a central and larger part of the world.

2013. This is now comparable to worries over Chinese and Russian power in the world (Manevich and Chwe 2017). The countries with the most negative opinion of the United States, according to polls, include Jordan (83%), Russia (81% unfavorable, up from 33% in 2010), Palestinian territories (70%), Pakistan (62%), Lebanon (60%), Turkey (58%) and China (49%) (Wike, Stokes, and Poushter 2015). In the most recent polls of public attitudes toward the United States, 72% of Turks and 61% of Mexicans report negative feelings toward the country (Manevich and Chwe 2017; see Figure 3.3). One cause for the unfavorable feelings in these countries is the political dominance of the United States and the perceived threat it poses to other people's way of life. In many places of the world, people believe the U.S. government and its citizens think only about their own welfare as their country exploits weaker nations. U.S. tourists are sometimes seen as loudmouthed ignoramuses whose ethnocentric attitudes prevent them from seeing value in other cultures or from learning other languages.

Note that even referring to citizens of the United States as "Americans"—as though people from Canada, Mexico, Central America, and South America do not really count as Americans—is seen as ethnocentric by many people from these other countries. *America* and the *United States of America* are not the same thing, but many people in the United States, including some presidents, fail to make the distinction, much to the dismay of other North, South, and Central Americans. If you visit the United Mexican States (Mexico's official name), people might ask you where you are from. Say "America," and

they, too, will say they are from America. Say "North America," and Mexicans will say "From Canada or the United States of America?"

Not all ethnocentrism is hostile; some of it is just a reaction to the strange ways of other cultures. An example is making judgments about what is proper food to eat and what is just not edible. Although people everywhere must eat, we can see widespread cultural differences in what people eat, as noted in the first part of this chapter. Some New Guinea tribes savor grasshoppers; Europeans and Russians relish raw fish eggs (caviar); Inuit children may find seal eyeballs a treat; some Indonesians eat dog; and some Nigerians prize termites. Whether it is from another time period or another society, variations in food can be shocking to those who do not eat the delicacies.

In contrast to ethnocentrism, **cultural relativism** *requires setting aside cultural and personal beliefs and prejudices to understand another group or society through the eyes of its members and using its own community standards.* Instead of judging cultural practices and social behavior as good or bad according to one's own cultural practices, the goal is to be impartial in learning the purposes and consequences of practices and behaviors of the group under study. Cultural relativism does not require that social scientists accept or agree with all of the beliefs and behaviors of the societies or groups they study. Yet it allows them to try to understand those practices in the social and cultural contexts in which they occur.

Being tolerant and understanding is not always easy. Some behaviors or ideas in other cultures can be difficult for even the most objective observer to understand. The notion of being "on time," for example, which is so much a part of the cultures of the United States, Canada, Japan, and parts of Europe, is a rather bizarre concept in some societies. Among most Native American people, such as the Dineh (Apache and Navajo), "clock time" is used when in contact with White institutions such as schools but of little use in their daily lives. To let a piece of machinery such as a cell phone govern the way one constructs and lives life is accommodated when necessary, but the Dineh orientation to time is that one should do things according to the natural rhythm of the body and other "timepieces" in nature (e.g., the moon), not according to an artificial electronic mechanism. This concept of time is difficult for many people outside some Native American cultures to grasp (Wells 2008). Misunderstandings occur when North Americans think that "Native Americans are always late" and jump to the erroneous conclusion that "Indians" are undependable. Native Americans, on the other hand, think Whites are neurotic about letting some

▼ FIGURE 3.3
Global Perceptions of U.S. Power and Influence

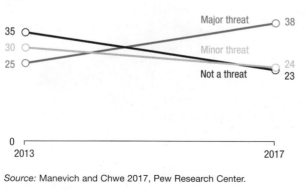

U.S. power and influence is a __ to our country

Source: Manevich and Chwe 2017, Pew Research Center.

Note: Percentages are global medians across 30 countries.

SOCIOLOGY IN OUR SOCIAL WORLD

CLOCK TIME AND BODY TIME

In the *Dance of Life*, Edward T. Hall explores the difference between "clock time" and "body time." In the history of humankind, clock time is a relatively recent phenomenon. Obviously, contemporary clocks are much more precise than just looking at where the sun is or even examining a sundial to tell time. Clocks have become both more precise and ever-present in our modern Western culture. Moreover, before the Western world began to have its influence in more remote areas of the Global South, some cultures did not have a time unit of less than half a day. Being "late" is less likely to happen if a single unit of time covers several hours. In the modern world, in our sporting events, and in our space exploration program, hundredths and even thousandths of seconds matter. Some of the ice skating speed racing events at the Olympics were won or lost by .001 of a second.

Clock time is externalized and objectified, as opposed to body time, which is internalized and subjective. Moreover, we in the Western or "modern" world are so obsessed with clock time that we wear clocks on our bodies or keep clock time ever present via smartphones. Many wristwatches and virtually all smartphones now have stopwatches on them. Clock time is so normalized in our culture that some people evaluate worship services or sermons based on their length; God forbid that a sermon message should exceed 20 minutes!

Body time has to do with our intuitive sense of time as it is experienced, including internal rhythms such as breathing and heartbeat. On one of my first trips to the U.S. Southwest, I visited Taos Pueblo and discovered that a corn dance was to occur later that day. I asked a stupid question: "When will the dance begin?" Answer? "When the Taos elders feel that the community is moving in a common rhythm." The start time had nothing to do with a clock. Notions of "using time," "saving time," or "time as money" are bizarre where body time is the dominant cultural motif.

Why do concepts of time matter? First, Western culture seems to be out of touch with body time. Yet the externalization of time (measurement by instruments) may put us out of touch with internal rhythms. We often eat when the clock says it's time for lunch, not when our bodies tell us they need food. Second, when clock time begins to supersede body time and natural rhythms, our heart rate and respiration rhythms can speed up, and we stress out. Third, using different research methods, Edward Hall found an interesting social consequence related to rhythm that pointed to the same conclusion: When a spirit of harmony and solidarity exists in a group, the people tend to move to a common rhythm. Perhaps this is why so many groups—college Greek societies, faith communities, and civic groups like the Kiwanis—all have times when they sing together. Singing gets the group moving in a common rhythm, and this, in turn, creates feelings of social integration and solidarity.

Source: Hall, Edward T. 1984. *The Dance of Life: The Other Dimension of Time.* New York: Penguin Random House.

By Keith A. Roberts. Your coauthor studied and traveled among Native American groups, often with groups of students, and was fascinated by their cultures.

---

instrument control them (Basso 1996; Farrer 2011; Hall 1981, 1983). The Sociology in Our Social World above looks at some of the social consequences of using "clock time" instead of "body time."

THINKING SOCIOLOGICALLY

Small, tightly knit societies with no meso or macro level often stress cooperation, conformity, and personal sacrifice for the sake of the community. Complex societies with established meso- and macro-level linkages tend to be more individualistic, stressing personal uniqueness, individual creativity, and critical thinking. Why do you think this is the case?

Components of Culture: Things and Thoughts

Things (material objects) and thoughts (nonmaterial ideas) make up our culture. Together they provide the guidelines for our lives.

Material Culture: The Artifacts of Life. **Material culture** *includes all the human-made objects we can see or touch, all the artifacts of a group of people*—grindstones for grinding cassava root, microwave ovens for cooking, bricks of mud or clay for building shelters, hides or woven cloth for making clothing, books or computers for conveying information, tools for reshaping environments, vessels for carrying and sharing food, and weapons for dominating and subduing others.

Some material culture is from the local community; it is of micro-level origin. The kinds of materials with which homes are constructed and the materials used for clothing often reflect the geography and resources of the local area. Houses are an especially good example of material culture, because they result from local ideas of what a "home" looks like and shape the interactions and attitudes of people in the society. Likewise, types of jewelry, pottery, musical instruments, or clothing reflect tastes that emerge at the micro and meso levels of family, community, and subculture. At a more macro level, national and international corporations interested in making profits work hard to establish trends in fashion and style that may cross continents and oceans.

Material culture helps drive the globalization process. Workers in Asia and Central American countries now make many of our clothes. Our shoes may come from the Philippines. The last banana you ate probably grew in Costa Rica, Guatemala, Honduras, or Panama. That romantic diamond engagement ring—a symbol that represents the most intimate tie—may well be imported from a South African mine using low-paid or even slave labor. Our cars consist of parts produced on nearly every continent.

THINKING SOCIOLOGICALLY

Think of examples of material culture that you use daily: stove, automobile, cell phone, computer, refrigerator, clock, money, and so forth. How do these material objects influence your way of life and the way you interact with others? How would your behavior be different if one of these material objects, say iPhones or money, did not exist?

▲ Homes are good examples of material culture. Their construction is influenced not only by local materials but also by ideas of what a home should be. Homes shape the context in which family members interact, so they can influence the nonmaterial culture—including beliefs, values, and symbols. Houses, like clothes, act as symbols that communicate levels of prestige.

▲ Coaches and players use hand signals to cue each other into an upcoming play or to convey what defense or offense to set up—an example of nonverbal communication.

Nonmaterial Culture: Beliefs, Values, Rules, and Language. Saluting the flag, saying a blessing before meals, flashing someone an obscene gesture, and a football coach signaling what defensive formation to run for the next play are all acts with symbolic meaning. In the case of the salute and the prayer, the acts undergird a belief about the nation or about a higher spiritual presence. In each case something is communicated, yet each of these acts refers to something more abstract than any material object.

Nonmaterial culture refers to *the thoughts, language, feelings, beliefs, values, and attitudes that make up much of our culture.* It is the invisible and intangible parts of culture that involve society's rules of behavior, ideas, and beliefs that shape how people interact with others and with their environment. Although we cannot touch the nonmaterial components of our culture, they pervade our life and influence how we think, feel, and behave. Nonmaterial culture is complex, comprising four main elements: values, beliefs, norms or rules, and language.

Values are *shared judgments about what is desirable or undesirable, right or wrong, and good or bad.* They express the basic ideals of any group of people. In industrial and postindustrial societies, for instance, a good education is highly valued. That you are in college shows you have certain values toward learning and education. Gunnar Myrdal, a Swedish sociologist and observer of U.S. culture, referred to the U.S. value system as the American creed, so much a part of the way of life that it acquires the power of religious doctrine (Myrdal 1964). We tend to take our core values for granted, including freedom, equality, individualism, democracy, free enterprise, efficiency, progress, achievement, and material comfort (Williams 1970).

SOCIAL JUSTICE IN A GUATEMALAN VILLAGE

▲ Rigoberta Menchú Tum

In her 57 years, Rigoberta Menchú Tum experienced the closeness of family and cooperation in village life. These values are important in Chimel, the Guatemalan hamlet where she lived. She also experienced great pain and suffering with the loss of her family and community. A Quiche Indian, Menchú became famous throughout the world in 1992, when she received the Nobel Peace Prize for her work to improve conditions for Indian peoples.

Guatemalans of Spanish origin hold the most power in Guatemala and have used Indians almost as slaves. Some of the natives were cut off from food, water, and other necessities, but people in Menchú's hamlet helped support each other and taught children survival techniques. Most people had no schooling. Menchú's work life in the sugarcane fields began at age 5. At 14, she traveled to the city to work as a domestic servant. While there, she learned Spanish, which helped her be more effective in defending the rights of the indigenous population in Guatemala. Her political coming of age occurred at age 16, when she witnessed her brother's assassination by a group trying to expel her people from their native lands.

Menchú's father started a group to fight the repression of the indigenous and poor, and at 20, Menchú joined the movement, Comité de Unidad Campesina (CUC, meaning "Peasant Unity Committee"), which the government claimed was communist inspired. Her father was murdered during a military assault, and her mother was tortured and killed. Menchú moved to Mexico with many other exiles to continue their nonviolent fight for rights and democracy.

The values of the native population represented by Menchú focus on respect for and a profound spiritual relationship with the environment, equality of all people, freedom from economic oppression, the dignity of her culture, and the benefits of cooperation over competition. The landowners tended to stress freedom of people to pursue their individual self-interests (even if inequality resulted), the value of competition, and the right to own property and to do whatever one desired to exploit that property for economic gain. Individual property rights were thought to be more important than preservation of indigenous cultures. Economic growth and profits were held in higher regard than religious connectedness to the earth.

The values of the native population and those of the landowners are in conflict. Only time will tell if the work of Indian activists such as Rigoberta Menchú Tum and her family will make a difference in the lives of this indigenous population.

At the meso and macro level, conflicts may arise between groups in society because of differing value systems. For example, there are major differences between the values of various Native American groups and the dominant culture—whether that dominant culture is in North, Central, or South America (Lake 1990; Sharp 1991). Consider the story in the Sociology Around the World above about Rigoberta Menchú Tum and the experiences of Native American populations living in Guatemala.

The experiences of Rigoberta Menchú Tum provide some examples of clashes between dominant and less powerful groups within a single nation. What are some examples of cultural conflict among groups in your society? Which (if any) reflect the types of cultural clashes experienced by Rigoberta? How do these conflicts impact the stability of the overall society? Why?

The conflict in values between First Nations and the national cultures of Canada, the United States, and many Latin American countries has had serious consequences. For example, cooperation is a cultural value that has been passed on through generations of Native Americans. Their survival has always depended on group cooperation in the hunt, in war, and in daily life. The value of cooperation can place native children at a disadvantage in North American schools that emphasize competition. Native American and Canadian First Nations children experience more success in classrooms that stress cooperation and sociability over competition and individuality (Lake 1990; Mehan 1992).

Beliefs are *ideas we hold about life, about the way society works, and about where we fit into the world.* They are expressed as specific statements that we hold to be true. Many Hindus, for example, believe that fulfilling behavioral expectations of one's own social caste will lead to rewards in one's next birth, or incarnation. In the next life, good people will be born into a higher social status. In contrast, some Christians believe that one's fate in the afterlife depends on whether one believes in certain ideas—for instance, that Jesus Christ is one's personal savior. Beliefs come from traditions established over time, sacred scriptures, experiences people have had, and lessons given by parents and teachers or other individuals in authority. Beliefs, based on values, influence the choices we make. For example, one value might be that the environment is worth preserving. A belief based on that value would be that humans should make efforts to curb climate change.

Values and beliefs, as elements of nonmaterial culture, are expressed in two forms: an ideal culture and a real culture. **Ideal culture** consists of *practices, beliefs, and values regarded as most desirable in society, and are consciously taught to children.* Not everyone, however, follows the approved cultural patterns, even though people may say they do. Sometimes our values contradict one another. **Real culture** refers to *the way things in society are actually done.* For example, family time and money are both highly valued in U.S. society. However, in order to make money, we often have to sacrifice time with our families.

Norms are *rules of behavior shared by members of a society and rooted in the value system.* Examples include our rather routine behaviors, from saying "Hi" to people we meet to obeying traffic signs. Norms range from religious warnings such as "Thou shalt not kill" to the expectation in many societies that young people will complete their high school education. Sometimes the origins of particular norms are clear. Few people wonder, for instance, why there is a norm to stop and look both ways at a stop sign. Other norms, such as the rule in many societies that women should wear skirts but men should not, have been passed on through the generations and have become unconsciously accepted patterns and a part of tradition. Sometimes we may not know how norms originated or even be aware of norms until they are violated.

Norms generally fall into two categories—folkways and mores—based largely on their importance and people's response to the breach of those norms. *Folkways* are customs and usually desirable behaviors, but they are not strictly enforced. Examples of folkways include responding appropriately and politely when introduced to someone, speaking quietly in a library, not scratching your genitals in public, using proper table manners, and covering your mouth when you cough. Violation of these norms causes people to think you are weird or even uncouth but not necessarily immoral or criminal.

Mores are norms that most members observe because they have great moral significance in a society. Conforming to mores is a matter of right and wrong, and violations of many mores are treated very seriously. The person who deviates from mores is considered immoral or criminal. Being faithful in a marriage has been among the stronger mores in U.S. society, though this has been gradually changing with high-profile cases in the news. Table 3.3 provides examples of violations of folkways and mores.

Taboos are the strongest form of mores. They concern actions considered unthinkable or unspeakable in the culture. For example, most societies have taboos that forbid incest (sexual relations with a close relative) and prohibit defacing or eating a human corpse. Taboos are most common and numerous in societies without centralized governments to establish formal laws and to maintain jails.

Taboos and other moral codes are of the utmost importance to a group because they provide guidelines for what is right and wrong. Yet behaviors that are taboo in one situation may be acceptable at another time and place. The incest taboo is an example found in most cultures, yet the application of the incest taboo varies greatly across cultures. Ivory Coast and China have no laws forbidding incest except in special cases, and many countries qualify what blood relatives can marry

▼ TABLE 3.3

Violations of Norms

Folkways: Conventional Polite Behaviors *Violations viewed as "weird"*
Swearing in a house of worship
Wearing blue jeans to the prom
Using poor table manners
Picking one's nose in public

Mores: Morally Significant Behaviors *Violations viewed as "immoral"*
Lying or being unfaithful to a spouse
Buying cigarettes or liquor for young teens
Having sex with a professor as a way to increase one's grade
Parking in handicap spaces when one is in good physical condition

under what circumstances (Quora 2016). In medieval Europe, if a man and a woman were within seven degrees of relatedness and wanted to marry, the marriage could be denied by the priest as incestuous. (Your first cousin is a third degree of relatedness from you.) Of course, in Europe, exceptions were made for the royal families, where cousins often married. By contrast, the Balinese sometimes permit twins to marry because it is believed they have already been intimately bonded together in the womb (Henley 2008; Leslie and Korman 1989). In some African and Native American societies, one cannot marry a sibling but might be expected to marry a first cousin. As Table 3.4 illustrates, the definition of what is and what is not incest varies even from state to state in the United States (Greenspan 2018).

Laws are *norms formally encoded by those holding political power in society,* such as laws against stealing property or killing another person. The violator of a law is likely to be perceived not just as a weird or an immoral person but also as a criminal who deserves formal punishment. Many mores are passed into law, and some folkways are also made into laws with formal punishments imposed for their violation. Behaviors may be folkways in one situation and mores or laws in another, with gradually more serious consequences. For example, nudity or various stages of near nudity may be only mildly questionable in some social settings (the beach or certain fraternity parties) but would be offensive in others (a four-star restaurant or a house of worship) and against the law in some situations, incurring a penalty or sanction.

Sanctions *reinforce norms through rewards and penalties.* Sanctions vary with the importance of the norm and can range from a parent frowning at a child who fails to use proper table manners to a prison term or death sentence. **Formal sanctions** are *rewards or punishments conferred by recognized officials.* Fines for parking illegally, failing grades for plagiarism, and expulsion for bringing drugs or weapons to school are formal negative sanctions your school might impose. Positive sanctions include honors and awards.

Informal sanctions are *unofficial rewards or punishments such as smiles, frowns, gossip, or ignoring someone.* A private word of praise by your professor after class about how well you did on your exam would be an informal positive sanction; gossip or ostracism by other students because of the clothes you wear would be an informal negative sanction. Most often, adherence to norms is ingrained so deeply that our reward is simply "fitting in."

Language is *the foundation of every culture. It conveys verbal, written, and nonverbal messages among members of society.* The mini-drama between infant and adult is played out every day around the world as millions of infants

▼ TABLE 3.4

Incest Taboos in the United States: States That Allow First-Cousin Marriage

Alabama	Connecticut	Hawaii	New Mexico	South Carolina
Alaska	District of Columbia	Maryland	New York	Tennessee
California	Florida	Massachusetts	North Carolina	Vermont
Colorado	Georgia	New Jersey	Rhode Island	Virginia
States that allow first-cousin marriage only under certain conditions such as marriage after a certain age or inability to bear children: Arizona, Illinois, Indiana, Maine, Utah, and Wisconsin.				

Source: Wikipedia 2018.

learn the language of the adults who care for them. In the process, they acquire an important part of culture, which is learned. Although many animals can communicate with a limited repertoire of sounds, the ability to speak a language is unique to humans (Phillips 2013). Transport a baby from France to the Arapesh tribe in New Guinea and another baby from New Guinea to France, and each will learn to speak the language and adhere to the culture in which it is brought up. Language conveys verbal, written, and nonverbal messages among members of society. Simply put, without language there would be little, if any, culture. Through the use of language, members of a culture can pass on essential knowledge to children and can share ideas with other members of their society. Work can be organized, and the society can build on its experiences and plan its future. Through language, members express their ideas, values, beliefs, and knowledge, a key ingredient in the ability of humans to sustain social life.

Language takes three primary forms: spoken, written, and nonverbal. There are over 7,100 languages spoken in the world. About 3,700 language groups are small, with fewer than 10,000 native speakers. The most common first languages are shown in Figure 3.4. English is the top Internet language around the world with 1.05 billion users. Chinese is next with 804 million users, Spanish with 516 million, and Arabic with 436 million users (Internet World Stats 2017).

Written language enables humans to store ideas for future generations, accelerating the accumulation of ideas on which to build. It also makes possible communication over distances. Members of a society learn to read these shared symbols.

Nonverbal language consists of gestures, facial expressions, and body postures. Communications scholars say this mode carries 93% of the message—55% in the facial expressions and 38% in the voice (vocal elements and intonation). That leaves 7% of the message coming from the actual words said (Debenham 2014; Fields 2015; Mehrabian 1972). Every culture uses nonverbal language to communicate, and just like verbal language, those cues may differ widely among cultures.

The power to communicate nonverbally is illustrated in American Sign Language, designed for the hearing challenged and the mute. Complex ideas can be transmitted without vocalizing a word. Indeed, one can argue that the deaf have a distinctive culture of their own rooted in large part in the unique sign language that serves them (discussed in Sociology in Our Social World on page 82). In addition, technology has aided communication among the hearing impaired through text messaging.

THINKING SOCIOLOGICALLY

Think about a time when you were trying to understand what someone was saying and you could not hear the words (at a concert, a bar, or a loud party). Did you rely on the other person's nonverbal communication to interpret what he or she was trying to convey? Explain.

Our language also plays a critical role in our perceptions of our world and organization of our thoughts, according to many linguists. The *linguistic relativity theory* posits that the people who speak a specific language make interpretations of their reality based on the language—they notice certain things and may fail to notice certain other things. Language is influenced by history and sociopolitical factors, and the structure of the language affects how people conceptualize their world (Sapir 1929, 1949; Whorf 1956). Think about this: "A person's 'picture of the universe' or 'view of the world' differs as a function of the particular language or languages that person knows" (Kodish 2003:384). Most current linguistic scholars agree that, although language does not totally determine thinking, it does influence thinking (Casasanto 2008; Levinson 2000; Wolff and Holmes 2011). For example, recent research confirms that in some Native Alaskan cultures where life depends on the elements, there are more than 50 words for *snow*, each giving members of the group a description that could mean life or death—wet snow, dry

▼ FIGURE 3.4

The World's Most Spoken Languages (in Millions)

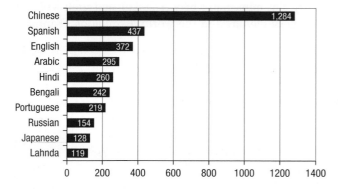

Language	Millions
Chinese	1,284
Spanish	437
English	372
Arabic	295
Hindi	260
Bengali	242
Portuguese	219
Russian	154
Japanese	128
Lahnda	119

Source: From "The World's Most Spoken Languages," Niall McCarthy, February 12, 2018, Statista. https://www.statista.com/chart/12868/the-worlds-most-spoken-languages.

Note: Each language also includes associated member languages and varieties.

snow, heavy snow, melting snow, and so forth (Krupnik et al. 2010; Robson 2013). The Inuit also have 17 words for various types of ice, for they must be able to distinguish types of solidified water (Ice 2015). Children in different cultures will learn about the world within the framework provided by their language.

In the English language people tend to associate colors with certain qualities in a way that may add to the problem of racist attitudes (Levinson 2000). The definition of the word *black* includes "dismal," "boding ill," "hostile," "harmful," "inexcusable," "without goodness," "evil," "wicked," "disgrace," and "without moral light." The word *white*, on the other hand, is defined as "honest," "dependable," "morally pure," "innocent," and "without malice" (Merriam-Webster 2014; *Webster's Unabridged English Dictionary* 1989). If the linguistic relativity thesis is correct, it is more than a coincidence that bad things are associated with the *black sheep* of the family, the *blacklist*, or *Black Tuesday* (when the U.S. stock market dropped dramatically and crashed in 1929).

This association of blackness with negative images and meanings is not true of all languages. The societies that have negative images for *black* and positive images for *white* are the same societies that associate negative qualities with people of darker skin. Blackness associated with something evil is not true of many African languages (Jordan 2012). The use of *white* as a synonym for good or innocent—as in reference to a *white noise machine* or a *white lie*—may contribute to a cultural climate that devalues people of color. In essence, the language may influence our perception of color in a manner that contributes to racism. Interestingly, there is empirical evidence supporting this claim of color symbolism. Athletic teams that wear black uniforms have more penalties called on them than teams with lighter-colored uniforms (De los Santos 2017; Frank and Gilovich 1988).

When grouped together, material and nonmaterial components form cultural patterns. People's lives are organized around these patterns. For example, family life includes patterns of courtship, marriage, child-rearing, and care of the elderly.

We have seen that material artifacts and nonmaterial beliefs, values, norms, and language compose the basic components of culture. Next, we explore the theoretical explanations for culture.

Society, Culture, and Our Social World

Whether people eat termite eggs, fish eggs, or chicken eggs, societies always have a culture, and culture is

▲ White and black colors have symbolic meaning—with phrases like "blackballed from the club" or "black sheep of the family" indicating negative judgment associated with blackness. Research shows that teams wearing black are called for more fouls than teams wearing white.

always linked to a society. Culture provides guidelines for behaviors and actions at each level of society, from the global system to the individual family. The social world model at the beginning of the chapter, with its concentric circles, represents the micro to macro levels of society. Smaller social units such as a school operate within a larger community that is also part of a region and the country. The culture determines what takes place in each of these units. There is a social unit—or structural "hardware"—and a culture—or "software"—at each level.

Microcultures: Micro-Level Analysis

Micro-level analysis focuses on social interactions in small groups. Groups of people, if those people meet with regularity and have some common interests or purpose, will develop insider language, jokes, symbols, and ways of interacting that may differ from other groups in which those same people participate. The social unit at this level of analysis only affects a portion of one's daily life (a bowling league, a book group, or a poker club) or shapes a limited time period of one's life (such as a Greek organization, Boy Scout troop, or a soccer team for 8-year-old girls). The social unit at the meso or macro level affects larger groups or societies and has more long-term impacts. So a **microculture** is *a culture that develops at*

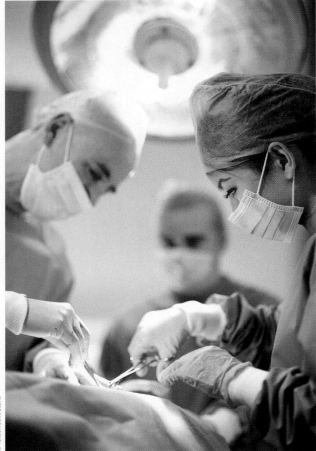

Hospitals provide one example of a microculture. Hospital employees share terminology, rules of interaction, and values regarding objectifying human body parts so that the patient is not sexualized.

the micro level in groups or organizations and affects only a segment of one's life or influences a limited period of one's life. Other classic examples from sociology include a street gang, a college sorority, and a business office.

Hospitals are communities of people who share a *microculture*. People in different-colored uniforms scurry around carrying out their designated tasks, part of the division of labor in the organization; each uniform has symbolic significance indicating positions at the hospital. Hospital workers interact among themselves to attain goals of patient care. They have a common in-group vocabulary, a shared set of values, a hierarchy of positions with roles and behaviors for each position, and a guiding system of regulations for the organization—all of which shape interactions during the hours when each member works in the hospital. Yet the hospital microculture may have little relevance to the rest of the employees' everyday

lives. Microcultures may survive over time, with individuals coming in and leaving as workers and patients, but in a complex society, no one lives his or her entire life within a microculture. The values, rules, and specialized language used by the hospital staff continue as one shift ends and other medical personnel enter and sustain that microculture. Outside that microculture, a different set of norms takes over.

Every organization, club, and association is a social group and therefore must have a culture (a microculture) with its own set of rules and expectations. Schools develop their own unique cultures and traditions; as students graduate and move out of that microculture, others move into it and perpetuate the microculture. However, some microcultures exist for a limited period of time or for a special purpose. A summer camp microculture may develop but exists only for that summer. The following summer, a different culture may evolve because of new counselors and campers. A girls' softball team may develop its own cheers, jokes, insider slang, and values regarding competition or what it means to be a good sport, but next year, the girls may be realigned into different teams, and the transitory culture of the previous year will change. In contrast to microcultures, *subcultures* continue across a person's life span.

Subcultures and Countercultures: Meso-Level Analysis

A **subculture** *is smaller than the nation but, unlike a microculture, is large enough to support people throughout the life span* (Dowd 2017; Gordon 1970). Many ethnic groups within the larger society have their own subcultures with their own sets of conventions and expectations. Picture a person, perhaps yourself, who is African Canadian, Chinese Canadian, or Hispanic Canadian, living within an ethnic community that provides food, worship, and many other resources. Despite unique cultural traits, that person is still a Canadian, living within the national laws, norms, and way of life. It is just that the person's life has guidelines from the subculture in addition to the dominant culture of the society.

Because the social unit, such as the ethnic groups mentioned earlier, plays a more long-term and pervasive role in the life span of group members than a summer camp or a sorority (microcultures), we analyze subcultures at the meso level. (Table 3.5 illustrates the connection between the social units at each level and the type of culture at that level.)

Note that many of the categories into which we group people are not subcultures. For example, redheads,

▼ TABLE 3.5

Level of Social Units and of Culture

Social Unit (People who interact and feel they belong)	Culture (The way of life of that social unit)
Dyads, small groups, local community	Microculture
Ethnic community or social class community	Subculture
National society	Culture of a nation
Global system	Global culture

left-handed people, tall people, individuals who read *People* magazine, people who are single, visitors to Chicago, and Netflix watchers do not make up subcultures because they do not interact as social units or share a common way of life. A motorcycle gang, a college fraternity, and a summer camp are also not subcultures because they affect only a segment of one's life (Gordon 1970; Yablonski 1959).

In the United States, subcultures include ethnic groups, such as Mexican American and Korean American; restricted religious groups, such as the Orthodox Jews in New York City; and social class groups, including the elite upper class on the East and West Coasts of the United States. The superwealthy have networks, exclusive clubs, and the Social Register, which lists the names and phone numbers of the elite, so they can maintain contact with one another. They have a culture of opulence that differs from middle-class culture, and this culture is part of their experience throughout their lives.

Many societies have subcultures based on ethnicity or religion or other historical characteristics, but broad-based subcultures with extensive social networks can emerge in other ways as well. Perhaps the most fascinating is the deaf subculture in the United States, explained in the next Sociology in Our Social World.

A give-and-take exists between subcultures and the dominant culture, with each contributing to and influencing the other. Sometimes the differences between the two lead to tension and conflict. When conflict between a subculture and the larger culture becomes serious and important norms of the dominant society are violated, a different type of culture may emerge as an outcome of the conflict.

A **counterculture** is *a group with expectations and values that contrast sharply with the dominant values of a particular society* (Yinger 1960). An example of a counterculture is the Old Order Amish of Pennsylvania and Ohio. The Amish drive horse-drawn buggies and seldom use

▲ Subcultures, such as the Orthodox Jewish faith community, impact their members throughout life—from infancy to death. Here, an Orthodox Jewish boy prepares to pray according to Jewish law by wrapping the leather strap of his tefillin around his arm and a tallit (prayer shawl) around his shoulders.

electricity or modern machines. They reject many mainstream notions of success and replace them with their own work values and goals. The Old Order Amish prefer to educate their children in their own communities, insisting that their children not go beyond an eighth-grade education in the public school curriculum. They also do not use automobiles or conventional tractors. The Amish are pacifists and will not serve as soldiers in the national military.

Some countercultures such as the Amish continue over time and can sustain members throughout their life cycle. Like subcultures, they may operate at the meso level, but unlike subcultures they reject mainstream culture. Moreover, some countercultural groups, such as punk rock groups or violent and deviant teenage gangs, are short-lived or are relevant to people only at a certain age. These countercultural groups operate at the micro level but create more conflict with the dominant culture than microcultures.

DEAF SUBCULTURE IN THE UNITED STATES

by Thomas P. Horejes

The deaf subculture possesses its own language, norms, and social networks that are unique to the deaf. American Sign Language (ASL) has its own conversational rules and social norms such as mandatory eye gaze and appropriate facial expressions. Like other subcultures, the deaf subculture celebrates its own arts and entertainment, including deaf poetry, deaf music, deaf theater, and deaf cinema. The arts of the deaf subculture are often expressed visually through perspectives, experiences, and/or metaphors only understood by those who are fluent in ASL and a part of the deaf subculture. There are social gatherings and events by associations within the deaf subculture that host annual conferences and tournaments ranging from the Deaf World Softball Championships to the Rainbow Alliance of the Deaf (an LGBTQIA organization). As with other subcultures, there is a deaf history and heritage passed on from generation to generation.

Many of the 5% to 10% of deaf children born to deaf parents are immediately enculturated into their own deaf subculture. In contrast, a large majority (90%–95%) of deaf children (including myself, born to hearing parents) start with an identity from the larger world (hearing society). As we progress throughout life, however, our identities become negotiated as we become more aware of a subculture—a deaf subculture that each of us has embraced differently. Some reject the deaf subculture in favor of total immersion into hearing society whereas others navigate in the deaf subculture but in different ways. In addition to those born deaf, many individuals become deaf later in life due to age, illness, or even prolonged exposure to loud sounds.

Regardless of how one becomes deaf, some individuals rely on technology (hearing aids or cochlear implants), communicate with hearing individuals via spoken or written English or through an ASL interpreter, and express willingness to join a workplace dominated by members of the hearing society. Other deaf individuals become fully immersed into the deaf subculture or what they call the deaf "world." They may attempt to depart from the hearing culture by rejecting values and beliefs possessed by the hearing society such as assistive-listening devices and speech therapy, and by not placing their deaf child in hearing schools. These people typically attend only deaf plays, read about deaf history, take on jobs where communication is through sign language, and forbid any voiced language in favor of equal "access" in all aspects of their daily activities. One common denominator in shaping deaf identity and deaf subculture is language: the incorporation of sign language in the deaf individual's life.

★ ★ ★ ★ ★ ★

Thomas P. Horejes received his PhD at Arizona State University in justice studies and teaches sociology at Gallaudet University, the world's only university with programs and services specifically designed to accommodate students who are deaf or hard of hearing. He is the author of *Social Constructions of Deafness: Examining Deaf Languacultures in Education* (Washington, DC: Gallaudet University Press, 2012).

Yet other types of countercultures seek to withdraw from society, to operate outside its economic and legal systems, or even to bring about the downfall of the larger society. Examples include survivalist groups such as racist militia and skinheads, who reject the principles of democratic pluralism. In the United States, the number of anti-government "patriot" groups has increased dramatically over the past decade (Anderson 2017). They believe "that the federal government is conspiring to take U.S. citizens' guns and destroy their liberties as it paves the way for a global 'one-world government'" (Potok 2013a:1). Countercultures are not necessarily bad for society. According to conflict theory, which was introduced in Chapter 2, the existence of counterculture groups is clear evidence that there are contradictions or tensions within a society that need to be addressed. Countercultures often challenge the unfair treatment of groups in society that do not hold power. They sometimes develop into social organizations or protest groups. Extremist religious and political groups, whether Christian, Islamic, Hindu, or any other, may best be understood as countercultures against Western or global influences that they perceive as threatening to their way of life. Figure 3.5 illustrates the types of cultures in the social world and the relationship between countercultures and their national culture. Countercultures, as depicted, view themselves and are viewed by others as "fringe" groups—partial outsiders within a nation.

**Cultures at Various Levels
in the Social World**

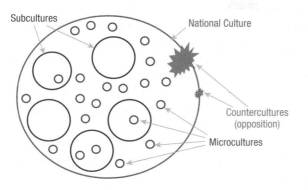

THINKING
SOCIOLOGICALLY

Describe a counterculture group whose goals are at odds with those of the dominant culture. Do you see any evidence to show that the group is influencing behavioral expectations and values in the larger society? What effect, if any, do countercultures have on your life?

National and Global Culture:
Macro-Level Analysis

Canada is a national society, geographically bounded by the mainland United States to the south, the Pacific Ocean and Alaska to the west, the Atlantic Ocean to the east, and the Arctic to the north. The government in Ottawa passes laws that regulate activities in all provinces (which are similar to states or prefectures), and each province passes its own laws on regional matters. These geographic boundaries and political structures make up the national society of Canada.

National Society and Culture. The *national society* (introduced in Chapter 1) is a population of people, usually living within a specified geographic area, who are connected by common ideas, cooperate for the attainment of common goals, and are subject to a particular political authority. Within the nation, there may be smaller groups, such as ethnic, regional, or tribal subcultures, made up of people who identify closely with others in the group Most nations have a **national culture** of *common values and beliefs that tie citizens of a nation together.* The national culture affects the everyday lives of most citizens. Within some countries of Africa and

the Middle East, on the other hand, local subcultures including ethnic or religious loyalties are much stronger than any sense of national culture, in part because the nation-state boundaries were originally *imposed* by foreign colonial powers. Subcultural differences divide many nations. Consider the loyalties of Shiites, Sunnis, and Kurds in Iraq to their subcultures, where the national culture struggles for influence over its citizens through laws and military force.

In colonial America, people thought of themselves as Virginians or Rhode Islanders rather than as U.S. citizens. Even during the "War Between the States" of the 1860s, the battalions were organized by states and often carried their state banners into battle. The fact that some Southern states still call it the War Between the States rather than the Civil War communicates the struggle over whether to recognize the nation or states as the primary social unit of loyalty and identity. People in the United States today are increasingly likely to think of themselves as U.S. citizens (rather than as Iowans or Floridians), yet the national culture determines only a few of the specific guidelines for everyday life. The sense of *nation* has grown stronger in most industrialized societies over the past century, and the primary identity is likely to be "United States" or "Canadian" citizen.

Global Society and Culture. Several centuries ago there was no "global culture," but with expanding travel and trade, economic interdependence of different countries, international political linkages, global environmental concerns, and most recently technology allowing for communication throughout the world, people now interact across continents in seconds. *Globalization* refers to the process by which the entire world is becoming a single sociocultural entity—more uniform, more integrated, and more interdependent. The globalization process brings increased connectedness, uniformity, and interdependency across the planet (Eitzen and Zinn 2012; Martell 2016). It also brings conflicts at the national and regional levels as cultures clash.

Western political and economic structures dominate in the development of this global society, largely as a result of the domination of Western (European and U.S.) worldviews and Western control over resources. For example, the very idea of governing a geographic region with a bureaucratic structure known as a nation-state is a fairly new notion. Formerly, many small bands and tribal groupings dominated areas of the globe. However, with globalization, nation-states now exist in every region of the world.

Global culture includes *behavioral standards, symbols, values, and material objects that have become common across the globe* (International Beliefs and Values Institute 2012). We need to understand global culture to engage in human rights issues, global education, conflict resolution, sustainability, and religious and cultural understanding. For example, beliefs that monogamy is normal; that marriage should be based on romantic love; that people have a right to life, liberty, and the pursuit of happiness; that people should be free to choose their leaders; that women should have rights such as voting; that wildlife and fragile environments should be protected; and that everyone should have a cell phone and television set are spreading across the globe (Newman 2017).

During the 20th century, the idea of the primacy of individual rights, civil liberties, and human rights spread around the world, creating conflicts within nations that traditionally lacked democratic institutions and processes. Backlashes against these and other Western ideas also can be seen in the acts of groups that have embraced terrorism (Eitzen and Zinn 2012; Timsit 2017). This has resulted in Western societies fighting terrorism when terrorist groups see themselves as trying to preserve their culture (Morey and Yaqin 2011; Peek 2011).

Still, these trends are aspects of the emerging global culture. Even 100 years ago, notions of global cooperation and competition would have seemed bizarre (Lechner and Boli 2012). However, in nations around the world, people who travel by plane know they must stand in line, negotiate airport security, squeeze their bodies into confined spaces, and stay seated in the airplane until they are told they can get up (Lechner and Boli 2012). Regardless of nationality, we know how to behave in any airport in the world.

▲ Many simple norms or beliefs about how to behave in public—like waiting in line for a train—have become accepted in cultures throughout the world.

As the world community becomes more interdependent and addresses issues that can only be dealt with at the global level (such as global warming, massive human rights violations as in the Syrian or Yemen revolution or Sudanese war, international terrorism, global food shortages, and global financial crises), the idea of a common "software" of beliefs, social rules, and common interests takes on importance. Common ideas for making decisions allow for shared solutions to conflicts. Global culture at the macro level affects our individual lives, and its influence will only increase.

However, global culture is not the only pattern that is new. Today, we see a counterculture at the global level. Stateless terrorist networks such as al-Shabaab, al-Qaeda, ISIS, Boko Haram, and the Taliban reject the values of international organizations and agreements such as the World Court, the Geneva Convention, and other international systems designed to resolve disputes. Terrorists do not recognize the sovereignty of nations and do not acknowledge some global values of respect for life or for civil discourse. This counterculture at the global level is a more serious threat than those at the micro and meso levels, in part because it does not fit into the global system of nations and its norms. (See the discussion of terrorism in Chapter 13.)

THINKING SOCIOLOGICALLY

Make a list of social groups of which you are a part. Place these groups into categories of microculture, subculture, national culture, and global culture. Consider which of them affects only a portion of your day or week (such as your place of work) or only a limited time in your entire life span. Consider which groups are smaller than the nation but will likely influence you over much of your life. To what cross-national (global) groups do you belong? Do you belong to fewer groups at the national culture and global culture levels than at the micro level? If so, why do you suppose that is the case?

Theories of Culture

Cultural Theory at the Micro Level

To understand our interactions with family and friends, we turn to the micro level of analysis. Although external forces at the national and global (macro) levels shape us in many ways, that is not the whole story as we see when we examine the symbolic interaction approach to culture.

Symbolic Interaction Theory. How amazing it is that babies learn to share the ideas and meanings of complex cultures with others in those cultures. Symbolic interaction theory considers how we learn to share the meanings of symbols, whether material or nonmaterial. Cultures contain many symbols, such as rings, flags, and words that stand for or represent some thing or some idea. A ring means love and commitment. A flag represents national identity and is intended to evoke patriotism and love for one's country. A term such as *middle class* conjures up images and expectations of what that term means, a meaning shared with others in that group. Together in our groups and societies, we define what is real, normal, and good.

Symbolic interaction theory maintains that our humanness comes from the impact we have on each other through these shared understandings of symbols that humans have created. When people create symbols, such as a new greeting (e.g., a fist bump instead of a handshake) or a symbolic shield for a fraternity or sorority, they come to have an existence and importance for the group.

Symbolic interaction theory pictures humans as consciously and deliberately creating their personal and collective histories. The theory emphasizes the part that verbal and nonverbal language and gestures play in the shared symbols of individuals and the smooth operation of society. More than any other theory in the social sciences, symbolic interaction stresses the active decision-making role of individuals—the ability of individuals to do more than conform to the larger forces of the society.

Many of our definitions of what is "normal" are shaped by what others around us define as "normal" or "good." The **social construction of reality** is *the process by which individuals and groups shape their reality through social interaction.* Our construction of what we see as reality, influenced by our social relations, has a profound effect on our daily lives, our life chances, and what we believe is possible in our lives. One illustration of this is the notion of what is beautiful or ugly. In the late 18th and early 19th centuries, in Europe and the United States, beaches were considered eyesores because there was nothing there but crushed stone and dangerous water. A beach was not viewed as a place to relax in a beautiful environment. Likewise, when early travelers to the West encountered the Rocky Mountains, with soaring granite rising to snow-capped peaks, the idea was that these were incredibly ugly wounds in the earth's surface. The summits were anything but appealing. We now see both as beautiful, but the social construction of scenery has not always been so (Lofgren 1999, 2010). So even what we experience as relaxing and peaceful in nature is shaped by how our society constructs those experiences.

▲ In the late 1700s and early 1800s, this mountain view would have been considered an eyesore—too ugly to enjoy and an obstacle to progress. The social construction of reality—the definition of what is beautiful in our culture—has changed dramatically over the past 2 centuries.

This notion that individuals shape culture and that culture influences individuals is at the core of symbolic interaction theory. Other social theories tend to focus on the meso and macro levels.

THINKING SOCIOLOGICALLY

Think about how you communicate with one or more of your close friends. What are some of the symbols you use to communicate with one another? How do these forms of communication indicate that you are close friends and help you feel connected to them?

Cultural Theories at the Meso and Macro Levels

How can we explain such diverse world practices as eating termites and worshipping cows? Why have some societies allowed men to have four wives, whereas others—such as the Shakers—have prohibited any sex between men and women? Why do some groups worship their ancestors, others have many gods, and yet others believe in a single divine being? How can societies adapt to extremes of climate and geographical terrain—hot, cold, dry, wet, mountainous, and flat? Humankind has evolved practices so diverse that it would be hard to find a practice that has not been adopted in some society at some time in history.

To explain these cultural differences, we refer to two already familiar perspectives that have made important contributions to understanding culture at the meso and macro levels: structural-functional and conflict theories.

Structural-Functional Theory. Structural-functional theorists (also called functionalists) ask why members of an ethnic subculture or a society engage in certain practices. To answer, they look at how those practices contribute to the survival or social solidarity of the group or society as a whole. Consider the reverence for cattle in India. The *sacred cow* is protected, treated with respect, and not slaughtered for food. The reasons relate to India's ancient development into an agricultural society that required sacrifices. Cattle were needed to pull plows and to provide a source of milk and dried dung for fuel. Cows gained religious significance because of their importance for the survival of early agricultural communities. They must, therefore, be protected from hungry people for the long-term survival of the group. Protecting cows was functional; that is, the practice served a purpose for society (Harris 1989).

Functionalists view societies as composed of interdependent parts, each fulfilling certain necessary functions or purposes for the total society (Radcliffe-Brown 1935). Shared norms, values, and beliefs, for instance, serve the function of holding a social group together. At a global macro level, functionalists see the world moving in the direction of having a common culture, potentially reducing we-versus-they thinking and promoting unity across boundaries. Synthesis of cultures and even the loss of some cultures are viewed as a natural result of globalization. But read on!

Although most cultural practices serve positive functions for the maintenance and stability of society, some practices, such as slavery and those using child labor, may be functional for those in power but dysfunctional for minority groups or individual members of society. The fact that some societies are weak or have died out suggests that their way of life may not have been functional in the long run. Consider the case of Haiti, a country weakened, in part, because all the forests have been cut down to provide firewood. The resulting erosion made much of the land unusable for growing crops and led to a scarcity of food (Diamond 2012; FAO 2016). Add to the existing poverty and hunger the devastation brought about by two earthquakes in 2010 that damaged or destroyed most buildings, followed by a hurricane and a cholera epidemic. The country and its people must rely on external support and donations from other countries to survive as it tries to rebuild.

The functionalist perspective has been criticized because it fails to consider how much dysfunction a

society has, how much conflict a society can tolerate, and how much unity is necessary for a society to survive. Some critics argue that functional theory overemphasizes the need for consensus and integration among different parts of society, thus ignoring conflicts that may point to problems such as inequality in societies (Dahrendorf 1959).

Conflict Theory. With rapid change from processes of globalization, many global citizens face uncertain futures. These rapid changes result in excitement for those who see prosperity and success in the global trends, to those who see threats to their familiar ways of life. How do different theoretical perspectives try to make sense of the changes? Whereas functionalists assume consensus exists because all people in society have learned the same cultural values, rules, and expectations, conflict theorists do not view culture as having this uniting effect. Conflict theorists describe societies as composed of meso-level groups—class, ethnic, religious, and political groups—vying for power. Each group protects its own self-interests and struggles to make its own cultural ways dominant in the society. Instead of consensus, the dominant groups may impose their cultural beliefs on minorities and other subcultural groups, thus laying the groundwork for conflict. Conflict theorists identify tension between meso and macro levels, whereas functionalists tend to focus on harmony and smooth integration between those levels.

Conflict theorists argue that the people with privilege and power in society manipulate institutions such as religion and education. In this way, average people learn the values, beliefs, and norms of the privileged group and accept the dominant group's beliefs, self-interests, power,

▲ Conflict theorists believe that society is composed of groups, each acting to meet its own self-interests. In 2018, Greek taxi drivers rallied against Uber, which charges cheaper rates because it employs mostly part-time workers and does not pay benefits. According to public transportation associations, car-booking services undermine the livelihoods of taxi drivers.

and advantage. The status of the privileged will likely be secure. In many school districts, for instance, schools that serve lower-class children teach obedience to authority, punctuality, and respect for superiors—behaviors that make for good laborers and compliant workers. The children of the affluent, meanwhile, are more likely to attend schools stressing divergent thinking, creativity, and leadership, attributes that prepare them to occupy the most professional, prestigious, and highly rewarded positions in society. Conflict theorists point to this control of the education process by those with privilege as part of the overall pattern by which the society benefits the rich.

Conflict theory can also help us understand global dynamics. Many poor nations feel that the global system protects the self-interests of the richest nations and that those rich nations impose their own culture, including their ideas about economics, politics, and religion, on the poorer nations of the Global South. Some scholars believe there is great richness in local customs that is lost when homogenized by cultural domination of the powerful nations (Eitzen and Zinn 2012; Ritzer and Dean 2014).

Conflict theory is useful for analyzing the relationships between societies (at a macro level) and between subcultures (at a meso level) within complex societies. It also helps illuminate tensions in a society when local (micro-level) cultural values clash with national (macro-level) trends. Conflict theory is not as successful, however, in explaining simple, well-integrated societies in which change is slow to come about and cooperation is an organizing principle.

Actually, conflict may contribute to a smoother-running society in the long run. German sociologist Georg Simmel (1858–1918) and American sociologist Lewis Coser (1913–2003) blended insights from functional and conflict perspectives, insisting that conflict sometimes serves a positive purpose. One example is that it can alert societal leaders to problem areas that need attention; conflict can also serve to bond people together in opposition to others. Both scholars agree that some degree of conflict is essential for any group to be viable—which is a pretty strong statement about how important conflict is (Coser, 1956; Simmel 1904, 1955).

Middle-Range Theories

The perspectives just discussed are comprehensive and cover a wide scope. They are paradigms that explain much behavior and many social patterns, but they are hard to test. *Middle-range theories* of culture bridge the gap between empirical data and abstract or broad general paradigms. R. K. Merton (1968) coined the term and argued that middle-range theories could be used to break down abstract theories into smaller parts to test, thus providing data that could be generalized to a large group.

For example, Pettigrew, Tropp, Wagner, and Christ (2011) examined more than 500 studies that tested the intergroup contact hypothesis, a middle-range theory that maintains that intergroup contact, under appropriate conditions, can reduce prejudice. Through looking at the results of the 500-plus studies, Pettigrew showed that the positive effects of such intergroup contact are universal—across racial, ethnic, national, age, and gender groups.

Fit Between Hardware and Software

Computer software cannot work with incompatible machines. Some documents cannot be easily transferred to a different piece of hardware, although sometimes a transfer can be accomplished with significant modification in the formatting of the document. The same is true with the hardware of society and the software of culture. For instance, consider the size of families: The value (software) of having a large extended family, typical in agricultural societies, does not work well in the structure (hardware) of industrial and postindustrial societies that are mostly urban and crowded. Children in urban settings are generally a liability compared with those who work on the farm in agricultural societies. In short, there are limits to what can be transferred from one type of society to another, and the change or "formatting" may mean the new beliefs transferred to a different social setting are barely recognizable.

Attempts to transport U.S.-style "software" (culture)—individualism, capitalism, freedom of religion, and democracy—to other parts of the world illustrate that these ideas are not always successful in other settings. The hardware of societies may be able to handle more than one type of software or set of beliefs, but there are limits to the adaptability. Thus, we should not be surprised when ideas from one society are transformed into something different when they are imported to another society. If we are to understand the world in which we live and if we want to improve it, we must first fully understand other societies and cultures.

THINKING SOCIOLOGICALLY

Team sports are a core component of most societies. How does participating in team sports help prepare people to successfully navigate life in the United States? In other societies? For example, what lessons learned through playing on an organized team might be relevant to life in the competitive business world or in a cooperative, noncompetitive society?

Because there is such variation among societies and cultures in what they see as *normal*, how do we learn our particular society's expectations? The answer is addressed in the next chapter. Each society relies on the process of socialization to teach the culture to its members, especially new members, such as babies and immigrants. Humans go through a lifelong process of socialization to learn social and cultural expectations. The next chapter discusses the ways in which we learn our culture and become members of society.

WHAT HAVE WE LEARNED?

Individuals and small groups cannot live without the support of a larger society, the hardware of the social world. Without the software—culture—there could be no society, for there would be no norms to guide our interactions with others in society. Humans are inherently social and learn their culture from others. Furthermore, as society has evolved into more complex and multilevel social systems, humans have learned to live in and negotiate conflicts among multiple cultures, including those at micro (microcultures), meso (subcultures), and macro (societal and global cultures) levels. Life in an information age society demands adaptability to different sociocultural contexts and tolerance of different cultures and subcultures. This is a challenge to a species that has always had tendencies toward ethnocentrism.

KEY POINTS

- *Society* refers to an organized and interdependent group of individuals who live together in a specific geographic area, interact with each other more than with outsiders, cooperate to attain goals, and share a common culture over time. Each society has a culture, the way of life shared by a group of people, including ideas and "things" that are passed on from one generation to the next; the culture has both material and nonmaterial components.

- Societies evolve from very simple to more complex, from the simple hunter-gatherer society to the information societies of the postindustrial world.

- The study of culture requires that we try to avoid ethnocentrism (judging other cultures by the standards of our own culture). Instead, we should use the view of cultural relativism, so that we can understand culture from the standpoint of those inside it.

- Just as social units exist at various levels of our social world, from small groups to global systems, cultures exist within different levels of the social system—microcultures, subcultures, national cultures, and global cultures. Some social units at the micro or meso level stand in opposition to the dominant national culture, and they are called countercultures.

- Various theories offer different lenses for understanding culture. Whereas symbolic interaction illuminates the way humans bring meaning to events (thus generating culture), functionalist and conflict theories examine cultural harmony and conflict between cultures, respectively.

- The metaphor of hardware (society's structure) and software (culture) describes the interdependent relationship of society and culture, and as with computers, there must be some compatibility between the structure of a society and the culture. If there is none, either the cultural elements that are transported into another society will be rejected or the culture will be "reformatted" to fit the society.

DISCUSSION QUESTIONS

1. Think about the different types of societies described in this chapter. In which type of society (hunter-gatherer, herding, horticultural, agricultural, industrial, or postindustrial) would you prefer to live? Why? In which would you most likely be (a) economically successful and (b) content? Why?

2. This chapter points out that today material culture "drives the globalization process." Read the labels on your clothing and look around at what your classmates are wearing and carrying and come up with some examples that support that point.

3. Think of a subculture to which you belong. What are the norms, values, and material artifacts that distinguish members of your subculture from those who do not belong to it?

4. Every classroom has norms of behavior. Some are mores, and some are folkways. Describe two of each in a typical classroom at your school. How are both enforced? How do you help enforce these norms?

5. Are you part of a counterculture? Why or why not? In what ways might a counterculture benefit a society?

KEY TERMS

agricultural societies 63

beliefs 76

counterculture 81

cultural relativism 72

culture 58

ethnocentrism 70

formal sanctions 77

global culture 84

herding societies 62

horticultural societies 62

hunter-gatherer societies 61

ideal culture 76

industrial societies 63

informal sanctions 77

language 77

laws 77

material culture 73

mechanical solidarity 61

microculture 79

national culture 83

nonmaterial culture 74

norms 76

organic solidarity 61

postindustrial societies 64

real culture 76

sanctions 77

social construction of reality 85

society 58

subculture 80

technology 65

values 74

CONTRIBUTING TO OUR SOCIAL WORLD: WHAT CAN WE DO?

At the Local (Micro) Level

- *Immigrant and refugee aid groups* are ethnically oriented organizations that assist recent immigrants in dealing with adjustment to life in a new country at the local level. Contact one of these local groups and explore the possibility of volunteering or serving as an intern. You should be able to determine if one is in your area by Googling the name of your town or city, the name of the ethnic group, and "immigrant aid group" or "refugee aid group."

At the Organizational or Institutional (Meso) Level

- *Ethnic group* organizations and clubs focus on the interests of specific ethnic groups: Arabic Americans, Chinese Americans, Italian Canadians, Polish Canadians, and so on. You may have one or more groups on your own campus. Contact one of these groups (of your own background or of a background that differs from your own). Arrange to attend one of the group's meetings and learn about the subculture and activities in which its members are involved. To find an ethnic association on campus, call your campus activities office. To find one in your local area, try Googling the name of the ethnic group, "club," and the name of your town or city.

At the National or Global (Macro) Level

- *The United Nations Permanent Forum on Indigenous Issues* assists indigenous (native) people around the world who face threats to their cultures, languages, and basic rights as the process of globalization accelerates. We have experienced this in North America in relation to Native American and Inuit populations, but it is occurring throughout the world. Visit the forum's website at www.un.org/development/desa/indigenouspeoples and contact the forum about the possibility of volunteering.

- *Cultural Survival* is an example of a leading nongovernmental organization (NGO) engaged in action-oriented programs. The organization partners with indigenous people to "defend their lands, languages, and cultures." Look at their website (www.culturalsurvival.org) for internship and volunteer opportunities.

$SAGE edge™

Get the tools you need to sharpen your study skills. SAGE edge offers a robust online environment featuring an impressive array of free tools and resources.

Access practice quizzes, eFlashcards, video, and multimedia at **edge.sagepub.com/ballantine7e**

© iStock.com/Imgorthand

SOCIALIZATION

Becoming Human and Humane

▲ Our close family and friends (micro level) and the organizations and institutions we belong to (meso level) teach us how to be human and humane in our society. We learn skills, as well as values such as loyalty and compassion, by watching others.

MICRO

ME (MY FAMILY AND CLOSEST FRIENDS)

LOCAL ORGANIZATIONS AND COMMUNITY
Families and friends serve as agents of socialization.

MESO

NATIONAL ORGANIZATIONS, INSTITUTIONS, AND ETHNIC SUBCULTURES
Citizens are socialized for national loyalty and patriotism.

MACRO

SOCIETY
Political parties and religious denominations transmit values.

GLOBAL COMMUNITY
People are socialized for tolerance and respect across borders.

WHAT WILL YOU LEARN IN THIS CHAPTER?

This chapter will help you to do the following:

4.1 Summarize the nature versus nurture debate and the sociological perspective on it

4.2 Predict the impact of isolation and neglect on children

4.3 Defend the position that groups at each level in our social world have a stake in how we are socialized

4.4 Describe how we develop a "self" through interacting with others

4.5 Explain how micro- and meso-level agents of socialization influence individuals

4.6 Discuss how macro-level agents of socialization can impact children today

4.7 Identify policy questions that rely on an understanding of socialization

Micro: Small groups and local communities	What does it mean to have a "self"? How have your family, local religious congregation, and schools shaped who you are?
Meso: National institutions, complex organizations, and ethnic groups	How do various subcultures or organizations of which you are a member (your ethnic group, political party, or religious affiliation) influence who you are and your position in the social world?
Macro: National and global systems	What would you be like if you were raised in a different country? How might globalization or other macro-level events—such as a terrorist attack on your country—impact you and your sense of self?

Canadian preteen Craig Kielburger happened to see an article about a 12-year-old boy in Pakistan, Iqbal Masih, a child who had escaped slavery and was murdered for speaking out against child labor. Iqbal was Craig's age, so the story stunned him. Curious about what child labor was, he learned that there are 250 million child laborers ages 5 to 17 around the world, about 1 in 4 in the poorest, least developed countries (UNICEF 2018). He was appalled. Although only 12, he mobilized his classmates and they started a nonprofit called Free the Children. It became an international organization that has won a number of awards for its contributions to better the lives of oppressed children (Free the Children 2015). Craig, now in this 30s, and his brother Marc cofounded another organization called Me to We that sells socially conscious products and services that helps to fund Free the Children.

© Finbar O'Reilly/Reuters

▲ Unlike Craig Kielburger, who was socialized to create a gentler and more humane world, some children grow up in a world of hostility and violence. Children as young as 5 in the Democratic Republic of the Congo have been kidnapped or sold to be child soldiers in rebel armies. They are socialized through abuse by their captors and forced to obey and kill "enemies" in order to survive themselves. They do not look at the world as a friendly place.

Many people are concerned primarily about their own self-interests, yet even as a child Craig seemed to care about people he had never met. He was motivated to act on that concern, but why? Sociologists would point largely to his upbringing—his *socialization*. Coming from a religious background that stressed compassion and justice, and being raised in a family that stressed awareness of people different from themselves, his mother, Theresa Kielburger, ensured that her children had direct experiences in the world around them. She commented to a journalist, "Kids become so desensitized by television and the media. It's important to sensitize them, and you have to do it when they are young" (Langlois 2015). She used small gestures—like stopping to have a conversation with a homeless person rather than just ignoring the person or giving away pocket change—as a way to communicate values of caring and humaneness. She often asked her boys to imagine what it feels like to be the kid in class whom everyone teases, thereby enhancing an ability to see things from the perspective of others. Craig also reported that a central family motto was "The only failure in life is not trying," so he developed a sense of *agency*—of his ability to make choices and to act, even while he was still a child (Kielburger 2009:13). Eventually, both brothers became major human rights activists in Canada, and Craig received an International Human Rights Award and has twice been nominated for the Nobel Peace Prize (World of Children 2012). This type of altruism clearly seems to be developed by an environment that fosters understanding, tolerance, and caring for the plight of others, yet many children are not exposed to this type of upbringing.

In this chapter we examine the process of socialization, how it involves development of our *selves*, and the many directions that process can take, depending on one's experiences in life.

Socialization is *the lifelong process of learning to become a member of the social world, beginning at birth and* *continuing until death.* It is a major part of what the family, education, religion, and other institutions do to prepare individuals to be members of their social world. In some cases, a negative socialization experience from peers or adults results in a damaged self-concept.

From the day they are born, infants are interactive, ready to be socialized into membership in the human social world. As they cry, coo, or smile, they gradually learn that their behaviors elicit responses from other humans. This **interaction** is *the exchange of verbal and nonverbal messages.* These form the basic building blocks of socialization through which a child learns his or her culture and becomes a member of society. This process of interaction shapes the infant into a human being with a social self—the perception we have of who we are.

Three main elements provide the framework for socialization: human biological potential, culture, and individual experiences. Babies enter this world unsocialized, totally dependent on others to meet their needs and completely lacking in social awareness and an understanding of the rules of their society. Despite this complete vulnerability, they have the potential to learn the language, norms, values, and skills needed in their society. Socialization is necessary not only for the survival of the individual but also for the survival of society and its groups. The process continues in various forms throughout our lives as we enter and exit social positions—from school and work to retirement to death.

In this chapter, we explore the nature and importance of socialization and how individuals become socialized. We also look at development of the self, who or what socializes us, macro-level issues in the socialization process, and a policy example illustrating socialization. First, we briefly examine an ongoing debate: Which is more influential in determining who we are—our genes (nature) or our socialization into the social world (nurture)?

Nature *Versus* Nurture—or *Both* Working Together?

What is it that makes us who we are? Is it our biological makeup or the family and community in which we grow up? One side of the contemporary debate regarding nature versus nurture seeks to explain the development of the self and human social behaviors—violence, crime, academic performance, mate selection, economic success, gender roles, and other behaviors—by examining biological or genetic factors that are the basis for social behavior (Harris 2009). Sociologists call this *sociobiology,* the systematic study of the biological basis of all forms of social behavior, including sexual and parental

▲ Socialization starts at the beginning of life as babies interact intensively with their parents, observing and learning what kinds of sounds or actions elicit response from adults.

behavior, in all kinds of organisms including humans (Wilson 1978). Researchers in these fields claim that our human genetic makeup wires us for social behaviors (Pinker 2002; E. Wilson 1978, 2000, 2012).

The idea is that we perpetuate our own biological family and the human species through our social behaviors. Human groups develop power structures, are territorial, and protect their kin. Examples of behaviors that sociobiologists see as rooted in the genetic makeup of the species include a mother ignoring her own safety to help a child, soldiers dying in battle for their comrades and countries, communities feeling hostility toward outsiders or foreigners, and people defending property lines against intrusion by neighbors. Sociobiologists say that these behaviors continue because they result in an increased chance of survival of the family, one's group, and the species as a whole (Dennis 2017; Pinker 2002; E. Wilson 1980, 2000, 2012).

Most sociologists believe that sociobiology has flaws. Sociobiology is a *reductionist* theory; that is, it often reduces complex social behaviors to single inherited traits such as an altruism gene, an aggression gene, or any other behavioral gene. However, evidence for such inherited traits is weak, at best. Sociologists point to the fact that there are great variations in the way members of different societies and groups behave. People born in one culture and raised in another adopt social behaviors common to the culture in which they grow up, not based on inherited traits (S. Gould 1997). If a specific social behavior is genetic, then it should be present regardless of the culture in which humans are raised. What sets humans apart from other animals is not so much our biological heritage but our ability to learn the ways of our culture through socialization.

THE INTRIGUING CASE OF GENES VERSUS THE ENVIRONMENT

Can we pass on major life events, especially traumatic ones, through our genes to the next generation? Recent research suggests an expanding field of research may provide insights into this genes (nature) versus environment (nurture) question. Until recently, most related research focused on animals, but recent studies on humans raise questions that challenge existing beliefs. Referred to as "epigenetic inheritance," new studies go against the idea that genetic inheritance comes only from the DNA code of the parent to offspring. The findings suggest that the effects of traumatic parental experiences can be passed on from generation to generation (Thomson 2015).

Researchers in England studied Jews who were traumatized in World War II in concentration camps, by torture or by having to live in hiding from Nazis. They also studied their children, controlling for any traumas the children may have had or the parents may have discussed. They compared this data with Jewish families living outside of Europe during the Holocaust (to see their methodology, go to the article cited nearby). The results show effects of trauma from environmental factors such as torture and confinement in the genes of children of the people who had experienced trauma (Yehuda et al. 2015).

Studies like the one just described show the interconnections between human environment and biology. Most importantly, for sociologists, they show that the impact of environment on people can be passed down to future generations. This makes the need to understand and learn how to positively shape our environment all the more relevant (Sample 2015).

Most sociologists recognize that individuals are influenced by biology, which limits the range of human responses and creates certain needs and drives, but they believe that nurture is far more important in shaping the individual. Some sociologists propose theories that consider both nature and nurture. Alice Rossi, former president of the American Sociological Association, has argued that we need to build both biological and social theories—or biosocial theories—into explanations of social processes such as parenting (Rossi 1984). One group of sociologists has developed a theory called evolutionary sociology, which takes seriously the way our genetic makeup—including a remarkable capacity for language—shapes our range of behaviors. However, biological research also shows that living organisms are often modified by their environments and the behaviors of others around them—with even biological or genetic structure becoming modified due to social interaction and experiences (De Waal 2016; Dobbs 2013; Machalek and Martin 2010).

Biology influences human behavior, but human action and interaction can also modify biological traits. For example, our cultural values shape what we eat today and whether we share food with the less privileged in our society. Further, as the Sociology Around the World above describes, recent research on Holocaust survivors has shown that trauma experiences can be so severe that they are passed on genetically to the next generation (Sample 2015; Thomson 2015; Yehuda et al. 2015). The bottom line is that even our biological traits may be shaped by social factors. Socialization is key in the process of becoming human and becoming humane.

Importance of Socialization

If you have lived on a farm, watched animals in the wild, or seen television nature shows, you probably have noticed that many animal young become independent shortly after birth. Horses are on their feet in a matter of hours, and by the time turtles hatch from eggs, their parents are long gone. Many species in the animal kingdom do not require contact with adults to survive because their behaviors are inborn and instinctual. Generally speaking, the more intelligent the species, the longer the period of gestation and of nutritional and social dependence on the mother and family. Humans clearly take the longest time to socialize their young and to teach them how to survive. Even among primates, human infants have the longest gestation and dependency period, generally 6 to 8 years. Chimpanzees, very similar to humans in their DNA, take only 12 to 28 months (see Table 4.1). This extended dependency period for humans—what some have referred to as the *long childhood*—allows each human being time to learn

▼ TABLE 4.1

Dependence on Adults Among the Primates

Primate Form	Pregnancy Period	Period of Absolute Nutritional Dependency on Mother or Mother Surrogate	Nursing Period	Social Independence
Human	266 days	1 year or more	1–2 years	6–8 years
Ape: chimpanzee	235 days	3–6 months	2–3 months	12–28 months
Monkey: rhesus	166 days	1–3 weeks	2–4 weeks	2–4 months
Lemur	111–145 days	1–3 days	2–14 days	2–3 weeks

Note: Lemurs and monkeys, among the less complex members of the primate order, depend on adults for food for a much shorter time than do apes and humans. The period of dependence affords human infants time to absorb the extensive knowledge important to the survival of the species.

the complexities of culture. This suggests that biology and social processes work together.

Normal human development involves learning to sit, crawl, stand, walk, think, talk, and participate in social interactions. Ideally, the long period of dependence allows children the opportunity to learn necessary skills, knowledge, and social roles through affectionate and tolerant interaction with people who care about them. Yet what happens if children are deprived of adequate care or even human contact? The following section illustrates the importance of socialization by showing the effects of deprivation and isolation on normal socialization.

Isolated and Abused Children

What would children be like if they grew up without human contact or only negative interactions? Among the most striking examples are the few cases we know of severely abused and neglected children whose parents kept them isolated in cellars or attics for years without providing even minimal attention and nurturing. When these isolated children were discovered, typically they suffered from profound developmental disorders that endured throughout their lives (Curtiss 1977; K. Davis 1947). Most experienced great difficulty in adjusting to their social world's complex rules of interaction, which people normally start to learn from infancy onward. Recent medical studies also show how social

isolation and deprivation in early life harm brain development and can result in mental health problems (C. Y. Johnson 2012).

In case studies comparing two girls, Anna and Isabelle, who experienced extreme isolation in early childhood, Kingsley Davis (1947) found that even minimal human contact made some difference in their socialization. Both "illegitimate" girls were kept locked up by relatives who wanted to keep their existence a secret. Both were discovered at about age 6 and moved to institutions where they received intensive training. Yet the cases were different in one significant respect: Prior to her discovery by those outside her immediate family, Anna experienced virtually no human contact, was fed only milk, and

▲ This family shares a playful moment together as they interact with one another. Even in such carefree moments, parents act as socializing agents for their children.

when found was barely alive. She saw other individuals only when they left food for her. Anna could not sit, walk, or talk and learned little in the special country school in which she was placed. When she died from jaundice at age 10, she had learned the language and skills of a 2- or 3-year-old.

When found, Isabelle was physically ill from an inadequate diet and lack of sunshine. She made only croaking sounds and gestures. During her first 6 years she lived in a darkened room with her deaf-mute mother, who provided some human contact. Isabelle, unlike Anna, did progress. She learned to talk and played with her peers. After 2 years, she reached an intellectual level approaching normal for her age but remained about 2 years behind her classmates in skill and competency levels. By age 14, she was attending regular school, participating in social activities, and was near normal for her age (K. Davis 1940, 1947; Foley and Harris 2014).

Contemporary cases of children neglected or abused in their family settings, forced into slavery or prostitution, or fighting wars reinforce the importance of early social interaction. Although not totally isolated, these children experience problems and disruptions in the socialization process. They have to deal with socially toxic abusive, violent, and dead-end environments with harmful developmental consequences for these children (War Child 2014). Consider the case of the Chibok schoolgirls from northern Nigeria's Borno State. On April 14, 2014, 276 students were kidnapped by Boko Haram, an extremist Islamic terrorist organization, with more girls kidnapped from Dapchi, Nigeria, in February 2018. Although a few escaped, most of the girls were forced into sexual relationships and made to marry Boko Haram fighters. Some girls were forced to fight alongside their captors or to become suicide bombers. The socialization process for these girls became very negative, something they will live with for life (*The Guardian* 2018).

Other young children have been forced into armies as soldiers or to work on plantations as slaves. A recent video, *Invisible Children*, went viral on YouTube, showing the plight of children kidnapped by Joseph Kony's Lord's Resistance Army into a world of drugs, sex, and violence (Terra Networks 2013). Most will have a difficult time integrating back into society after their traumatic experiences, even if they have a chance to do so. Some organizations are trying to help the released children readjust to their societies.

These cases illustrate the devastating effects of isolation, neglect, and abuse early in life on the socialization process. To develop into social beings, humans need more from their environments than food and shelter. They need positive contact; a sense of belonging; affection; safety; and someone to teach them language, knowledge, and skills. Through this socialization experience into the world, every person develops a *self*. Before we examine the development of the self in depth, however, we consider the complexity of socialization in the multilevel (micro, meso, and macro) social world.

Socialization and the Social World

Ram, a first grader from India, had been in school in Iowa for only a couple of weeks. The teacher was giving the first test. Ram did not know much about what a test meant, but he rather liked school, and the red-haired girl next to him, Elyse, had become a friend. He was catching on to reading a bit faster than she, but she was better at the number exercises. They often helped each other learn while the teacher was busy with a small group in the front of the class. The teacher gave each child the test, and Ram saw that it had to do with numbers. He began to do what the teacher had instructed the children to do with the worksheet, but after a while, he became confused. He leaned over to look at the page Elyse was working on. She hid her sheet from him, an unexpected response. The teacher looked up and asked what was going on. Elyse said that Ram was "cheating." Ram was not quite sure what that meant, but it did not sound good. The teacher's scolding of Ram left him baffled, confused, and entirely humiliated.

This incident was Ram's first lesson in the individualism and competitiveness that govern Western-style schools. His teacher was socializing him into a new set of values. In his culture of origin, competitiveness is discouraged, and individualism is equated with selfishness and rejection of community. Often, athletic events end in a tie so that no one will feel rejected. Indeed, a well-socialized person would rather lose in a competition than cause others to feel badly because they lost. Like Ram, each of us learns the values and beliefs of our culture. In Ram's case, he moved from one cultural group to another and had to adjust to more than one culture within his social world. Many migrants and immigrants around the world go through similar experiences. Some immigrants face humiliation and bullying as they learn the social norms of their new culture.

At the micro level, most parents teach children proper behaviors to be successful in life, and peers influence children to "fit in" and have fun. In fact, the process of socialization in groups allows the self to develop as individuals learn to interact with others in their culture. *Interaction theory*, focusing on the micro level, forms the basis of this chapter. At the meso level, religious denominations and political groups teach their versions of the truth, and educational systems teach the knowledge and skills considered by leaders as necessary for functioning in society. At the nationwide macro level, television ads encourage viewers to be more masculine or feminine, buy products that will make them better and happier people, and join the military or other institutions. From interactions with our significant others to dealing with government bureaucracy, most activities are part of the socialization experience that teaches us how to function in our society.

Keep in mind that socialization is a lifelong process. Even your grandparents are learning how to live at their stage of life. The process of socialization takes place at each level of analysis—micro, meso, and macro—linking the parts of society. Groups at each level have a stake in how we are socialized because they all need trained and loyal group members to survive. Organizations need citizens who have been socialized to devote the time, energy, and resources that these groups rely on to survive and meet their goals. For example, volunteer and charitable organizations cannot thrive unless people are willing to volunteer their energy, time, skills, and money. Lack of adequate socialization means social organizations will not receive the support they need to thrive—or even, possibly, survive.

Most perspectives on socialization focus on the micro level because much of socialization takes place in an individual's family, with peers, and in small groups. However, meso- and macro-level theories add to our understanding of how socialization prepares individuals for their roles in the larger social world. *Structural-functionalist perspectives* of socialization tend to see organizations at different levels supporting each other. For example, families often organize holidays around patriotic themes, such as a national independence day, or around religious celebrations. These activities can strengthen family members' commitment to the nation and buttress the moral values emphasized in churches, temples, and mosques. All of these values, in turn, help prepare individuals to support national political and economic systems.

At the meso level, the purposes and values of organizations or institutions sometimes directly contrast with one another or conflict with other parts of the social system. From the *conflict perspective*, the linkages between various parts of the social world are based on competition with or even direct opposition to another part. Socialization into a nation's military forces, for example, stresses patriotism and ethnocentrism, sometimes generating conflict and hostility toward other groups and countries. Demands from various organizations for people's time, money, and energy may leave little to give to our religious communities or even our families. Each organization and unit competes to gain our loyalty in order to claim some of our resources.

Conflict can occur in the global community as well. For example, religious groups often socialize their members to identify with humanity as a whole ("the family of God"). However, in some cases, nations do not want their citizens socialized to identify with those beyond their borders. Leaders of nations may seek to persuade Christians to kill other Christians, Jews, or Muslims, whom they define as "the enemy." If religion teaches that all people are "brothers and sisters" and if religious people object to killing, the nation may have trouble mobilizing its people to arms when the leaders call for war. Quaker, Mennonite, and Amish religious groups, among others, promote peace and refuse to engage in warfare.

THINKING SOCIOLOGICALLY

What would happen if all religious groups taught that all people are "brothers and sisters" and that we should not take the life of a fellow human?

Conflict theorists believe that those who have power and privilege use socialization to manipulate individuals so that they will support the power structure and the self-interests of the elite. For example, parents decide how they would like to raise their children and what values they want to instill in them, but as their children enter school, parents must share the socialization process with school personnel who teach curricula established and approved by those in power in society. One reason why some parents choose to homeschool their children is to control external influences on the socialization process.

Whether we stress harmony in the socialization process or conflict rooted in power differences, the development of a sense of self through the process of socialization is an ongoing, lifelong process. Let us now focus on the micro level: How does the *self* develop? How did *you* develop your sense of self?

THINKING SOCIOLOGICALLY

Although the socialization process occurs primarily at the micro level, it is influenced by events at each level in the social system. Give examples of family, community, subcultural, national, or global events that influenced how you were socialized or how you might socialize your child.

Development of the Self: Micro-Level Analysis

Have you seen a young child, 3 years or under, using a tablet, smartphone, or other interactive device? Some research shows that the impact of mobile devices on preschool children can be detrimental to their social-emotional, sensorimotor, problem-solving, math and science, and reading skills. Preschool children who use such devices do not develop as much empathy as children who spend more time in social interaction during unstructured play with peers. Using mobile devices can also affect their ability for self-regulation of behavior and early literacy skills (Walters 2015).

On the other hand, educational television and mobile device programs can get parents reading to young children and help children who are closer to school age gain technological skills (Pearson 2018). Still, researchers suggest more direct human-to-human interaction, and designated "family time" is beneficial for young children's socialization. Children under 30 months learn primarily from human interaction. We are talking here about the development of the *self*.

A baby is born with the potential to develop a *self*, the main product of the socialization process. Fundamentally, **self** refers to *the perceptions we have of who we are*. This process starts at birth. Throughout the socialization process, our self develops largely from the way others respond to us—praising us, disciplining us, ignoring us, and so on. The development of the self allows individuals to interact with other people and to learn to function at each level of the social world.

Humans are not born with a sense of self. It develops gradually, beginning in infancy and continuing throughout adulthood as we interact with others. Individual biology, culture, and social experiences all play a part in shaping the self. The hereditary blueprint each person brings into the world provides broad biological outlines, including particular physical attributes, temperament, and a maturational schedule. Each person is also born into a family that lives within a particular culture, illustrating that nature is shaped by nurture. This hereditary blueprint, in interaction with family and culture, helps create each unique person, different from any other person yet sharing the types of interactions by which the self is formed.

Most sociologists, although not all, believe that we humans are distinct from other animals in our ability to develop a self and to be aware of ourselves as individuals or objects (Irvine 2004). Consider how we refer to ourselves in the first person—*I* am hungry, *I* feel foolish, *I* am having fun, and *I* am good at basketball. We have a conception of who we are, how we relate to others, and how we differ from and are separate from others in our abilities and limitations. We have an awareness of the characteristics, values, feelings, and attitudes that give us our unique sense of self (W. James [1890] 1934; G. Mead [1934] 1962).

THINKING SOCIOLOGICALLY

Who are some of the people who have been most significant in shaping your *self* at different stages in your life? How have their actions and responses helped shape your self-concept as musically talented, athletic, intelligent, kind, assertive, clumsy, or any of the other hundreds of traits that might make up your *self*?

© iStock.com/quintanilla

▲ This child is learning something about technology and no doubt receiving other messages through play. Besides how to work an electronic device, what other messages might this child be learning?

The Looking-Glass Self and Role-Taking

Ty: "Hi! What's up?" (Ty has had his eye on this girl in his class, so he approaches her before class.)

Valerie: "Nothin' much."

Ty: "So what do you think of our sociology class?"

Valerie: "It's OK." (She turns around, spots a friend, and walks away.) "Hey Julie, did you get your soc assignment done?"

Ty is left to reflect on how to interpret Valerie's response. Take this common interaction and apply it to interactions you have had. First you approach someone and open a conversation (or someone approaches you); second, the person takes you up on the conversation—or not; third, you evaluate the individual's response and modify your behavior based on your interpretation. These steps make up the process called the *looking-glass self*, and they are repeated many times each day. We now explore these seemingly simple interactions that are key to developing our self through the socialization process.

The looking-glass-self idea is part of *symbolic interaction theory* and offers important insights into how individuals develop the self. Two of the major scholars in this approach were Charles H. Cooley ([1909] 1983) and George Herbert Mead ([1934] 1962). Cooley believed that the self is a social product, shaped by interactions with others from the time of birth. He likened interaction processes to looking in a mirror, whereby each person reflects an image of the other.

> Each to each a looking-glass
>
> Reflects the other that doth pass (Cooley [1909] 1983:184; Emerson, 1904).

For Cooley ([1909] 1983), the **looking-glass self** is *a reflective process that develops the self based on our interpretations and on our internalization of the reactions of others* ([1909] 1983). In this process, Cooley believed there are three principal elements, shown in Figure 4.1: (1) We imagine how we appear to others, (2) others judge our appearance and respond to us, and (3) we react to that feedback. We experience feelings such as pride or shame based on what we imagine this judgment of others means, and respond based on our interpretation. Moreover, throughout this process, we actively try to manipulate other people's view of us to serve our needs and interests. This is one of the many ways we learn to be boys or girls—the image we see reflected back to us lets us know whether we have behaved in socially acceptable ways according to gender expectations in our social setting. The issue of gender socialization in particular is discussed in Chapter 9. Of course, this does not mean our interpretation of the other person's response is correct, but our interpretation does determine how we respond.

THINKING SOCIOLOGICALLY

Think about a recent conversation you had with someone you don't know well. What might be several interpretations of that interaction?

Our self is influenced by the many "others" with whom we interact, and our interpretations of their reactions feed into our self-concept. Recall that the isolated children failed to develop this sense of self precisely because they lacked interaction with others, and the kidnapped girls had negative socialization experiences during captivity.

Taking the looking-glass-self idea a step further, Mead explained *that individuals take others into account by imagining themselves in the position of that other*, a process called **role-taking**. When children play mommy and daddy, doctor and patient, or firefighter, they are imagining themselves in another's shoes. Role-taking allows humans to view themselves from the standpoint of others. This requires mentally stepping out of our own experience to imagine how others experience and view the social world. Through role-taking, we begin to see who we are from the standpoint of others. In short, role-taking allows humans to view themselves as objects, as though they were looking at themselves through the eyes of another person. For some individuals, role-taking helps develop empathy for others—the bullied student, the homeless person on the street, the person with a disability. For Mead, role-taking is a prerequisite for the development of our sense of self.

▼ FIGURE 4.1

The Looking-Glass-Self Process of Self-Development

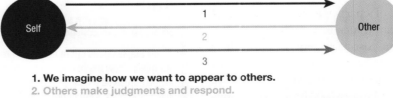

1. **We imagine how we want to appear to others.**
2. Others make judgments and respond.
3. **We experience feelings and react based on our interpretations.**

BLACK MEN AND PUBLIC SPACE

By Brent Staples

My first victim was a woman—White, well dressed, probably in her early 20s. I came upon her late one evening on a deserted street in Hyde Park, a relatively affluent neighborhood in an otherwise mean, impoverished section of Chicago. As I swung onto the avenue behind her . . . she cast back a worried glance. To her, the youngish black man—broad, 6 feet 2 inches with a beard and billowing hair, both hands shoved into the pockets of a bulky military jacket—seemed menacingly close. After a few more glimpses, she picked up her pace and was running in earnest. Within seconds, she disappeared into a cross street.

That was more than a decade ago. I was 22 years old, a graduate student newly arrived at the University of Chicago. It was in the echo of that terrified woman's footfalls that I first began to know the unwieldy inheritance I'd come into. . . . It was clear that she thought herself the quarry of a mugger, a rapist, or worse. Suffering a bout of insomnia, however, I was stalking sleep, not defenseless wayfarers. . . . I was surprised, embarrassed, and dismayed all at once. Her flight . . . made it clear that I was indistinguishable from the muggers who occasionally seeped into the area from the surrounding ghetto. . . . And I soon gathered that being perceived as dangerous is a hazard in itself. I only needed to make an errant move after being pulled over by a policeman. Where fear and weapons meet—and they often do in urban America—there is always the possibility of death.

In that first year, my first away from my hometown, I was to become thoroughly familiar with the language of fear.

At dark, shadowy intersections, I could cross in front of a car stopped at a traffic light and elicit the *thunk, thunk, thunk, thunk* of the driver—Black, White, male, or female—hammering down the door locks. On less traveled streets after dark, I grew accustomed to but never comfortable with people crossing to the other side of the street rather than pass me.

After dark, on the warrenlike streets of Brooklyn where I live, I often see women who fear the worst from me. They seem to have set their faces on neutral, and with their purse straps strung across their chests bandolier-style, they forge ahead as though bracing themselves against being tackled. I understand, of course, that . . . women are particularly vulnerable to street violence, and young Black males are drastically overrepresented among the perpetrators of that violence. Yet these truths are no solace against the kind of alienation that comes of being ever the suspect.

Over the years, I learned to smother the rage I felt at so often being taken for a criminal. Not to do so would surely have led to madness. I now take precautions to make myself less threatening. I move about with care, particularly late in the evening. . . . And on late-evening constitutionals, I employ what has proved to be excellent tension-reducing measures: I whistle melodies from Beethoven and Vivaldi and the more popular classical composers. Even steely New Yorkers hunching toward nighttime destinations seem to relax, and occasionally they even join in the tune. Virtually everybody seems to sense that a mugger wouldn't be warbling bright, sunny selections from Vivaldi's *Four Seasons*. It is my equivalent of the cowbell that hikers wear when they know they are in bear country.

Source: Staples (2001). Reprinted with permission from Brent Staples.

The Sociology in Our Social World above describes a situation experienced by Brent Staples, an African American journalist. It illustrates the relationship between our development of self through the looking-glass self and role-taking, and stereotypes. Many *stereotypes*—rigid images of members of a particular group—surround young African American males in the United States. Think about the human cost of stereotypes and their effect on the socialization process as you read the essay. If one's sense of self is profoundly influenced by how we see others respond (the looking-glass self) and one's ability to role-take by imagining oneself in another's shoes, how might the identity of a young African American boy be affected by news reports and public images of Black males?

THINKING SOCIOLOGICALLY

Brent Staples goes out of his way to reassure others that he is harmless. How might one's sense of self be influenced by being perceived as dangerous and untrustworthy? How might such stereotypes affect one's physical and mental well-being?

Mead ([1934] 1962) also argued that role-taking is possible because humans have a unique ability to use and respond to symbols. *Symbols*, first described in Chapter 2, are actions or objects that represent something else and therefore have meaning beyond their own existence. Language and gestures are examples, for they carry specific meaning for members of a culture. Symbols such as language allow us to give names to objects in the environment and to infuse those objects with meanings. Once the person learns to symbolically recognize objects in the environment, the self can be seen as one of those objects. This starts with possessing a name that allows us to see our self as separate from other objects. If we said the name LeBron James, most people would immediately think of the same person: an extraordinary athlete, now with the Los Angeles Lakers, who largely turned around the fortunes of the Miami Heat professional basketball team to win back-to-back NBA championships and brought Cleveland, in 2016, their first-ever NBA championship.

In the process of symbolic interaction, we take the actions of others and ourselves into account. We may blame, encourage, praise, punish, or reward ourselves. An example would be a basketball player missing the basket because the shot was poorly executed and thinking, *What did I do to miss that shot? I'm better than that!* Reflexive behavior, being able to look at oneself and one's behaviors as though from the outside looking in, includes the simple act of taking mental notes or mentally talking to one's self.

Parts of the Self

The self is composed of two distinct but closely related parts according to the symbolic interaction perspective—dynamic parts in interplay with one another (Mead [1934] 1962). The most basic element of the self is what symbolic interactionist George Herbert Mead refers to as the ***I***, *the spontaneous, unpredictable, impulsive, and largely unorganized aspect of the self.* The *I* initiates behavior without considering the possible social consequences. We can see this at work in the "I want it now" behavior of a baby or a toddler. Cookie Monster, on the children's television program *Sesame Street*, illustrates the *I* in every child, gobbling cookies at every chance and insisting on more *now*.

The *I* continues as part of the self throughout life but is controlled or tempered by the social expectations that surround individuals. In developmental stages from early childhood on, humans become increasingly influenced by interactions with others who instill society's rules. Children develop the ability to see their *self* as others see them (role-taking), allowing them to critique the behavior initiated by the *I*. Mead called this reflective capacity of the

self the *Me*. The **Me** is *the part of the self that has learned the rules of society through interaction and role-taking, and it controls the I and its desires.* Just as the *I* initiates the act, the *Me* gives direction to the act. In a sense, the *Me* channels the impulsive *I* in an acceptable manner according to societal rules and restraints yet meets the needs of the *I* as best it can. When we stop ourselves just before saying something and think to ourselves, *I'd better not say that*, it is our *Me* monitoring and controlling the *I*. Notice that the *Me* requires the ability to take the role of the other, to anticipate the other's reaction.

THINKING SOCIOLOGICALLY

For college students there are many temptations that tantalize and lure the *I*. What are some of these temptations, and how does the *Me* control them (or not)?

Stages in the Development of the Self

The process of developing a social self occurs gradually and in stages from birth to death. Mead identified three critical stages—(1) the imitation stage, (2) the play stage, and (3) the game stage—each of which requires the uniquely human ability to engage in role-taking (Mead [1934] 1962).

In the **imitation stage**, *children under 3 years old prepare for role-taking by observing others and imitating their behaviors, sounds, and gestures.* The **play stage** involves *a child, usually from 3 to 5, being able to see things (role-take) from the perspective of one person at a time: simple role-taking or play-acting.* Listen to children who are 3 to 5 years old play together. You will notice that they spend most of their time telling each other what to do. One of them will say something like, "You be the mommy, and José can be the daddy, and Zoe, you be the dog. Now you say, 'Good morning, Dear,' and I'll say, 'How did you sleep?' and Zoe, you scratch at the door like you want to go out." They will talk about their little skit for 15 minutes and then enact it, with the actual enactment taking perhaps 1 minute. Small children mimic or imitate role-taking based on what they have seen as they learn and practice future roles (Handel, Cahill, and Elkin 2007).

Society and its rules are initially represented by **significant others**—*parents, guardians, relatives, siblings, or important individuals whose primary and sustained interactions are especially influential* for the individual. That is why much of the play stage involves role-taking based on these significant people in the child's life. The child does not yet understand the complex relations and multiple role players in the social world outside the immediate family. Children may have a sense of how their mommy or daddy sees them, but children are not yet able to comprehend how they are seen by the larger social world. Lack of role-taking ability is apparent when children say inappropriate things, such as, "Why are you so fat?"

The third stage in the process of developing a social self, the **game stage**, is *when a child develops the ability to take the roles of multiple others concurrently and to conform to societal expectations.* The child goes beyond the significant other, such as a parent, to value the opinion of all peers or the expectations of the community.

Have you ever watched a team of young children play T-ball (a pre–Little League baseball game in which the children hit the ball from an upright rubber device that holds the ball) or observed a soccer league made up of 6-year-olds? If so, you have seen Mead's point illustrated vividly. In soccer (or football), 5- or 6-year-old children will not play their positions despite constant urging and cajoling by coaches. They all run after the ball, with little sense of their interdependent positions. Likewise, a child in a game of T-ball may pick up a ball that has been hit, turn to the coach, and say, "Now what do I do with it?" Most still do not quite grasp throwing it to first base, and the first-base player may actually have left the base to run for the ball. It can be hilarious for everyone except the coach when a hit that goes 7 feet turns into a home run because everyone is scrambling for the ball.

Prior to the game stage, the vision of the whole process is not possible. When children enter the game stage at about age 7 or 8, they are developmentally able to play the

roles of various positions and enjoy a complex game. Each child learns what is expected and the interdependence of roles because she or he is able, at this stage, to respond to the expectations of several people simultaneously (Hewitt and Shulman 2011; Meltzer 1978). This allows the individual to coordinate his or her activity with others.

In moving from the play stage to the game stage, children's worlds expand from family and day care to neighborhood playmates, school, and other organizations. *This process gradually builds up a composite of societal expectations that the child learns from family, peers, and other organizations,* what Mead refers to as the **generalized other**. The child learns to internalize the expectations of society—the generalized other—over and above the expectations of any *significant others.* Behavior comes to be governed by abstract rules ("no running outside of the baseline" or "no touching the soccer ball with your hands unless you are the goalie") rather than guidance from and emotional ties to a significant other. Children become capable of moving into new social situations such as school, organized sports, and (eventually) the workplace to function with others in both routine and novel interactions.

The common human experience of feeling embarrassed illustrates how the *generalized other* becomes internalized into one's conception of self. Making an inappropriate remark at a party or having another call undue attention to one's appearance can cause embarrassment. Feeling embarrassed may occur when one violates a social norm and then thinks about how others view that behavior. According to this role-taking view, we see ourselves as objects from the standpoint of others, and we judge ourselves accordingly. Very young children, however, do not feel embarrassment when they do things such as soil their pants or make inappropriate comments because they have not incorporated the *generalized other.* They have not yet learned the perspective of others.

The capacity to feel embarrassed is not only an indicator of having internalized the generalized other but also a uniquely human outcome of our role-taking ability (Hewitt and Schulman 2011; Koschate-Reis 2009). Some children face challenges to their self from teasing and bullying that result in fear, shame, embarrassment, and guilt. These feelings affect the bullied child's sense of self and can influence the self into adulthood.

As children grow, they identify with new in-groups, such as a neighborhood, a college sorority, or the military. We learn new ideas and expand our understanding. Some individuals ultimately come to think of themselves as part of the global human community. Thus, for many individuals, the social world expands through

© iStock.com/wind-moon

▲ Very young children who play soccer do not understand the role requirements of games. They all—including the goalie—want to chase after the ball. Learning to play positions and understand the roles in a complex situation is a critical step in the future socialization of the young child.

socialization. However, some individuals never develop this expanded worldview, remaining narrowly confined and drawing lines between themselves and others who are different. Such narrow boundaries often result in prejudice against others.

THINKING SOCIOLOGICALLY

Who are you? Write down 15 to 20 roles or attributes that describe who you are. How many of these items are characteristics associated with the *Me*—nouns such as *son, mother, student,* and *employee*? Which of the items are traits or attributes—adjectives such as *shy, sensitive, lonely, selfish,* and *daring*? How do you think each of these was learned or incorporated into your conception of your *self*?

Socialization Throughout the Life Cycle

In all societies, individuals move from one stage to the next in the socialization process. Socialization is a life-long process with many small and large passages. Infants begin the socialization process at birth. In childhood, one rite of passage is a child's first day at school—entrance into the meso-level institution of education. This turning point marks a child's entry into the larger world. The standards of performance are now defined by the child's teachers, peers, friends, and others outside the home.

Adolescence is an important stage in Western industrial and postindustrial societies, but this stage is far from universal. Indeed, it is largely an invention of complex industrial societies over the past 2 centuries, characterized by extensive periods of formal education and dependency on parents (Papalia, Martorell, and Feldman 2014). Adolescence is, in a sense, a structurally produced mass identity crisis because Western societies lack clear rites of passage for adolescents. Teens come to view themselves as a separate and distinct group with their own culture, slang vocabulary, clothing styles, and opinions about appropriate sexual behavior and forms of recreation. Some social scientists today argue that adolescence is continuing into the mid-20s as young people struggle to enter adulthood, remaining economically and socially semidependent (Roberts 2018; Stetka 2017).

Much of our adult years are spent in work and home life, including marriage and parenting roles for many. It is not surprising, then, that graduation from one's final alma mater (whether it be high school, college, or graduate school) and acceptance of one's first full-time job serve as rites of passage into adulthood in modern societies.

Most social scientists emphasize the importance of *rites of passage*—celebrations or public recognitions when individuals shift from one status to another—naming ceremonies, school graduations, marriages, and retirements. The importance of this shift resides in how others come to perceive the individual differently, the different expectations that others hold for the person, and changes in how the person sees himself or herself.

THINKING SOCIOLOGICALLY

Find someone who has grown up in a different culture and ask her or him about rites of passage from adolescence to adulthood where she or he was raised. How are the patterns similar to or different from your own?

Even the retired and elderly members of society are constantly undergoing socialization and resocialization in the process of developing their sense of self. The type of society influences the socialization experience of the elderly and how they carry out their roles, as well as their status in society. Consider the changes that have taken place in the lifetimes of those born before 1945, as described by one elder:

> We were born before television, before polio shots, frozen foods, Xerox, plastic contact lenses, Frisbees, and the Pill. . . . We never heard of artificial hearts, word processors, yogurt, and guys wearing earrings. For us time sharing means togetherness—not computers and condominiums. (Grandpa Junior 2006)

The elderly are vitally important to the ongoing group in more settled agricultural societies. They are the founts of wisdom and carry group knowledge, experiences, and traditions valued in societies where little change takes place. In industrial and postindustrial countries that continually undergo rapid changes, the wisdom of the elderly is not as relevant. Yet the number of elderly people is growing rapidly as medical science keeps people alive longer, diets improve, retirees have more resources, and diseases are brought under control. Average life expectancy in all of Europe's 28 countries was 81 years in 2016, with a gender gap favoring women by 5.4 years (Eurostat 2018). The average life expectancy in the United States

▲ Some retirees, rather than taking up hobbies, decide on a part-time job, like this man who enjoys people and is now a greeter at Walmart. Others take on a postretirement job because they need the income.

for those born in 2017 was 76 years for men and 81 years for women.

In modern systems, social participation by the elderly often drops after retirement. Retirement is a rite of passage to a new status, like that of marriage or parenthood, for which there is little preparation. As a result, retired people sometimes feel a sense of uselessness when they abruptly lose their occupational status. Retirees in Western societies generally have many years of life yet to live. The most socially satisfied retirees tend to develop hobbies, attend classes, enjoy sports, volunteer their time, travel, or have new jobs they can pursue after they retire. The point is that even your grandparents are going through a period of socialization, as are parents entering the empty nest stage.

Dying is the final stage of life (Kübler-Ross 1997). Death holds different meanings in different cultures: passing into another life, a time of judgment, a waiting for rebirth, or a void and nothingness. In some religious groups, people work hard or do good deeds because they believe that they will be rewarded in an afterlife or with rebirth to a better status in the next life on earth. Thus, beliefs about the meaning of death can affect how people live their lives and how they cope with dying and death. Each stage of the life cycle involves socialization into new roles in the social world. Many social scientists have studied these developmental stages and contributed insights into what happens at each stage (Clausen 1986; Gilleard and Higgs 2015; Handel et al. 2007; Papalia, Feldman, and Martorell 2015; Piaget 1989; Putt 2014). For example, some sociologists focus their research on the study of old age (gerontology) and death and dying.

Death ends the lifelong process of socialization, a process of learning social rules and roles and adjusting to them (see the photos of death rituals on the next page). When an individual has passed on, society continues. New members are born, are socialized into the social world, pass through roles once held by others, and eventually give up those roles to younger members. Cultures provide guidelines for each new generation to follow. The social world perpetuates itself and outlives the individuals who populate it.

THINKING SOCIOLOGICALLY

How were you socialized to view death and dying? What have you learned in your family about how to cope with death? Is death a taboo topic? If so, why?

Process of Resocialization

If you have experienced life in the military, a boarding school, a convent, a mental facility, or a prison, or had a major transition in your life such as divorce or the death of a spouse or child, you have experienced resocialization. **Resocialization** is *the process of shedding one or more social positions and taking on others, which involves learning new norms, behaviors, and values suitable to the newly acquired status* (Goffman 1961). Sometimes resocialization takes place in a *total institution*—a place that cuts people off from the rest of society and totally controls their lives during the process of resocialization. These include prisons, mental hospitals, monasteries, concentration camps, boarding schools, and military barracks. Bureaucratic regimentation and the manipulation of residents for the convenience of the staff is part of the routine (Goffman 1961).

We often associate resocialization with major developmental stages in adult life—leaving home to go to college or take a job, having a baby, divorce, retirement, and widowhood. Changes in status present opportunities to move in new and often exciting directions, such as going to college. Resocialization can also mean adjusting to living alone, raising children alone, loneliness, and possible financial problems.

Sometimes, resocialization occurs when individuals are forced to correct or reform behaviors defined as undesirable or deviant. Prison rehabilitation programs provide one example. However, research suggests that the difficulty in resocializing prisoners is rooted in the nature of the prison environment itself. Prisons are often coercive and violent environments, which may not provide the social supports necessary for bringing about positive change in a person's attitudes and behaviors.

Although resocialization is the goal of self-help groups such as Alcoholics Anonymous, Gamblers

▲ Death rituals differ depending on the culture and religion of the group. In India (top left), this body is being cremated on the banks of the holy Ganges River to release the soul from earthly existence. The closest relative lights the funeral pyre. The top right photo shows the Muslim tradition of washing and wrapping the dead before burial in Najaf, Iraq. At the bottom left, a U.S. Honor Guard carries a casket with the remains of U.S. Air Force personnel at Arlington National Cemetery. A celestial burial master (bottom right) feeds the body of a dead Tibetan to the vultures in northwest China's Qinghai province. In Tibetan regions, the practice is known as *jhator*, which literally means "giving alms to the birds"; people there believe in rebirth and see no need to preserve the body.

Anonymous, Parents Anonymous, drug rehabilitation groups, and weight loss groups, relapse is common among participants. Some public sociologists work on trying to understand why there are such high rates of reversion to previous patterns of behavior. Former prison inmates are at especially high risk of repeating a crime, so public sociologists want to know what might make the resocialization "stick." This is explored further in the discussion of policy. Clearly not all socialization or all resocialization is positive or functional. Sometimes resocialization alienates people from others and can contribute to violence or even terrorism. The next Sociology Around the World feature examines resocialization of young people into the terrorist group ISIS (or ISIL).

Multiple individuals, groups, and institutions are involved in the socialization process. These socialization forces are referred to as agents of socialization.

Agents of Socialization: The Micro-Meso Connection

Agents of socialization are *the transmitters of culture— the people, organizations, and institutions that help us define our identity and teach us how to thrive in our social world.* Agents are the mechanism by which the self learns the values, beliefs, and behaviors of the culture. Agents of socialization help new members find their place, just as they prepare older members for new responsibilities in society. At the micro level, one's family, one's peer group, and local groups and organizations help people know how they should behave and what they should believe. At the meso level, formal sources of learning (e.g., education and religion) and informal sources of learning (e.g., the media and books) are all agents that contribute to socialization. They transmit information to children and to adults throughout their lives.

ISIS RECRUITMENT

Why do a small proportion of young people become radicalized and join terrorist organizations like ISIS (Islamic State in Iraq and Syria, also referred to as ISIL and Daesh) or other terrorist groups? To combat terrorist groups, we need to try to understand what attracts young people to such destructive, sometimes barbaric activities so that we can counter the negative impacts of *resocialization*.

Potential jihadi, strongly influenced by social media (often Facebook), often feel they have nothing to lose by becoming jihadists. In countries like England, Belgium, and France, a small percentage of youth from Muslim backgrounds feel alienated in societies in which their religion is looked upon as "different." They become disaffected with their poor or middle-class lives and seek both meaning and adventure. For some, the idea of becoming a martyr makes death palatable, even desirable (Weaver 2015).

One half of ISIS fighters are born outside of the Middle East, and over 4,000 come from the West (Europe and other Global North countries). Most are males in their early 20s, of South Asian and Middle Eastern origins and with some university education. Recruiters begin the process of resocialization by appealing to youth looking for new meaning in life and drawing distinctions between the values of the Western world and a "new Islamic world order."

Reports on recruitment of child soldiers from many countries shows children as "victims of brutal violence, exploited for supporting roles, subjected to indoctrination and conscription, and often used as child soldiers, spies, or suicide bombers" (UNODC 2018). Understanding the recruitment tactics begins the process of tackling the root causes of the problem.

Carefully planned recruitment strategies involve the resocialization of disaffected young people into jihadists (Gunaratna 2018). Steps include (a) establishing first contact (often through social media), (b) drawing out the personal stories and frustrations of potential recruits, (c) laying out the possibility of a new path with new values and ways of doing things, (d) encouraging potential recruits to form a new identification with ISIS and against the West's non-Muslim way of life, and (e) promising a home and connections in a new caliphate (Islamic state) that will eventually spread throughout the world. Through this resocialization process, ISIS recruiters make new recruits feel that they have a purpose and power in a world from which they feel alienated (Torok 2015). These approaches can be especially appealing to those who see no opportunities in their lives or futures; many Palestinian youths fall into this category, among others who lack hope.

In ISIS recruiting efforts, potential jihadis learn about ISIS's expansionist philosophy and absolute rule by fear; for infidels (nonbelievers), the message is "convert or die" (Torok 2015). Some recruits are vulnerable to indoctrination through exposure to graphic imagery (such as beheadings) in the name of ISIS's "pure Islam" and claims by recruiters that they are living under "righteous Islamic rule" (Torok 2015). YouTube propaganda videos that "normalize" jihad and martyrdom give disaffected young people an alternative to their present lives. Recruits begin to anticipate excitement and acceptance and the promise of a good life on earth and martyrdom in heaven should they die. Leaving family and their former lives for a cause becomes a goal.

Efforts to prevent young people from being resocialized into a small, radicalized group of jihadis, alien to most peaceful and peace-loving Muslims, requires intervening in this resocialization process. Unfortunately, some efforts have resulted in Muslim organizations facing suspicion and civil rights abuses by law enforcement agencies and fellow citizens and can cause feelings of alienation and fuel the jihadi cause (Kundnani 2012).

THINKING SOCIOLOGICALLY

As you read this section, make a list of socializing agents at the micro, meso, and macro levels. Indicate two or three central messages each agent of socialization tries to instill in people. Do these messages conflict, and if so, why?

In early childhood, the family acts as the primary agent of socialization, passing on messages about respect for property and authority and the value of love and loyalty (Handel et al. 2007). **Peer groups**—*people who are roughly equal in some status within the society, such as the same age or the same occupation*—are also important, especially during the teenage years. Some writers even argue that the peer group is the most important *agent* in the socialization process of children and teens (Aseltine 1995; Harris 2009). Each agent has its own functions and is important at different stages of the life cycle, but meso-level institutions play a more active role as one matures. For example, schools and religious bodies become more involved in socialization as children reach 6 years old and older, compared with when they were preschool age (Rosenqvist 2017).

Formal agents of socialization are *official or legal agents (e.g., families, schools, teachers, and religious organizations) whose purpose it is to socialize the individual into the values, beliefs, and behaviors of the culture.* For example, a primary goal of families is to teach children to speak and to learn proper behavior. In addition, schoolteachers educate by giving formal instruction, and religious organizations provide moral instruction. (These formal agents of socialization are discussed in Chapters 10–12.)

Informal agents of socialization are *unofficial influential agents that shape values, beliefs, and behaviors in which socialization is not the express purpose.* Examples include peers, the media, books, advertising, and the Internet. They bring us continuous messages even though their primary purpose is not socialization but entertainment or selling products. Children watch countless advertisements on television, many with messages about what is good and fun to eat and how to be more attractive, more appealing, smarter, and a better person through the consumption of products. This bombardment is a particularly influential part of socialization for children and teenagers.

Lessons from one agent of socialization generally complement those from other agents. Parents work at home to support what school and religion teach. However, at times, agents provide conflicting lessons. For example, family and faith communities often give teens messages that conflict with those of peer groups regarding sexual activity and drug use. This is an example of mixed messages given by formal and informal agents.

THINKING SOCIOLOGICALLY

What confusion might be created for children when the formal and informal agents of socialization provide different messages about values or acceptable behaviors? Is this contradiction something that parents should be concerned about? Why or why not?

© iStock.com/oscarhdez

▲ As children become teenagers, peers become increasingly important socializing agents, shaping their norms, values, and attitudes.

Micro-Level Socialization

Perhaps the most important micro-level formal agent of socialization is our own family—parents, siblings, and other family members. One way in which families teach children what is right and wrong is through rewards and punishments, called *sanctions*. Children who lie to their parents may receive a verbal reprimand or a slap on the hand, be sent to their rooms, have a "time out," or receive a spanking, depending on differences in child-rearing practices among families. These are examples of negative sanctions. Conversely, children may be rewarded for good behavior with a positive sanction, such as a smile, praise, a cookie, or a special event. The number and types of sanctions dispensed in the family shape the socialization process, including development of the self and the perceptions we have of who we are and even whether we are good and clever or bad and stupid. Note that family influence varies from one culture to another.

In Japan, the mother is a key agent in the process of turning a newborn into a member of the group, passing on the strong group standards and expectations of family, neighbors, community, and society through the use of language and emotion. The child learns the importance of depending on the group and therefore fears being cast out. The need to belong creates pressure to conform to expectations, and the use of threats and the fear of shame help socialize children into Japanese ways (Brinkerhoff et al. 2014; Hendry 1987). The social class of the mother and gender of the child affects the socialization experience provided by the mother; for example, many women

© Getty Images/Tibor Bognar/Corbis Documentary

▲ A Japanese mother helps her son at Heian Shinto Shrine during Shichi-go-san Matsuri, also called the Seven-Five-Three Festival, a celebration with prayers of long life for children aged 3 to 7.

In contrast to the values of conformity and fitting into the group espoused in many Asian countries, in the United States most parents teach their children to value friendliness, cooperation, orientation toward achievement, social competence, responsibility, and independence. However, subcultural values and socialization practices may differ within the diverse groups in the U.S. population. Conceptions of what makes a "good person" or a "good citizen" and varied goals of socialization bring about differences in the process of socialization around the world.

Meso-Level Socialization

Meso-level agents also work to socialize people into specific cultural values and roles they must learn to fulfill. Education and religion are two obvious influences—both being institutions with primary responsibility for socialization. We discuss those in more detail in Chapters 11 and 12; here we illustrate meso-level socialization influences with a focus on social class and the media.

Social Class. Our education level, our occupation, the house we live in, what we choose to do in our leisure time, the foods we eat, and our religious and political beliefs are just a few aspects of our lives affected by socialization. Applying what we know from sociological research, the evidence strongly suggests that socialization varies by *social class* (as seen in the example about Japanese children earlier) (Yamamoto 2015). **Social class** refers to *the wealth, power, and prestige rankings that individuals hold in society* (Paxton and Pearce 2009). Meso-level patterns of distribution of resources, based, in part, on the economic opportunities created by state and national policies, affect who we become.

Upper-middle-class and middle-class parents in the United States usually have above-average education and managerial or professional jobs. They tend to pass on to their children the skills and values necessary to succeed in the subculture of their social class. Subcultures, you will recall, operate at the meso level of the social system. Subcultural values such as autonomy, creativity, self-direction (the ability to make decisions and take initiative), responsibility, curiosity, and consideration of others are especially important for middle-class success and are part of middle-class subculture (Kohn 1989). If the child misbehaves, for example, middle-class parents typically analyze the child's reasons for misbehaving, and punishment is related to these reasons. Sanctions often involve instilling guilt and denying privileges.

Working-class parents tend to pass on to children their cultural values of respect for authority and conformity to

see their daughters as caregivers of the family in the future, thus influencing the daughters' type of education and educational attainment (Yamamoto 2015).

Nonconformity is a source of shame in Japan. The resulting ridicule is a powerful means of social control. In some cases, the outcast is physically punished by peers. Thus, to bring shame on oneself or the family is behavior to be avoided. In the most extreme cases, young people have committed suicide because they did not conform to group expectations or succeed in school or a job and felt profoundly ashamed as a result.

THINKING SOCIOLOGICALLY

How did agents of socialization influence who you are today, and how did your experience differ from that of the Japanese children just described?

rules, lessons that will be useful if the children also have blue-collar jobs (Kohn 1989). Immediate punishment with no questions asked if a rule is violated functions to prepare children for positions in which obedience to rules is important to success. Children are expected to be neat, clean, well-mannered, honest, and obedient students and workers (MacLeod 2008). Socialization experiences for boys and girls are also often different, following traditional gender-role expectations of the working-class subculture.

Members of each class, as you can see, socialize their children to be successful in their social class and to meet expectations for adults of that class. Schools, like families, participate in this process and socialize children to adapt to the settings in which they grow up and are likely to live. Children's social class position on entering school, in turn, affects the socialization experiences they have in school (Ballantine, Hammack, and Stuber 2017). The result is the *reproduction of class*, as young people are socialized into the social class of their parents.

Social class, however, is only one of many influencing agents of socialization. As we saw in *Black Men and Public Space* (p. 100), race and ethnicity are important factors in socialization, as is gender. We discuss gender socialization in more detail in Chapter 9, but note here that race, class, and gender act as structural constraints on many members of the population, as they receive different messages about who they are and how they should behave. Therefore, it is important to recognize the interplay of these variables in people's lives.

© Getty/Jeff Randall

▲ This parent passes on a love for the piano to his young son. Because of the social class of this father, his son is likely to receive many messages about creativity, curiosity, and self-direction.

Electronic Media

Take a moment to consider the impact of rapidly growing screen time on the socialization process. Television, computers, and other electronic devices are important *informal agents* of socialization at the meso level. They can be categorized as intermediate-sized social units—larger than a local community but smaller than a nation. However, their impact reaches from the micro to macro levels, from individuals and families to nation-states and global agencies. Electronic media shape global policies at the macro level and affect family interactions at the micro level.

Internet users now number over 4 billion, over half of the world's population; the fastest growth of users is in Africa (Kemp 2018), and the largest number of users are in China, followed by India not far behind. In all of North America, 70% of the population had at least one social networking account in 2017, including 81% in the United States (Statista 2018b). The rapid change in electronic usage around the world is affecting the socialization process, world interconnectedness, and how people

communicate from the micro to macro levels. Figure 4.2 shows the use of social media in the United States in 2018 (Smith and Anderson 2018).

Young adults and millennials spend more time on their mobile phones and catch up on TV shows through that medium. By the time an average child in the United States reaches age 18, he or she will have spent more time watching television than doing any other single activity besides sleeping. Although TV is still the most watched media, other electronic forms are catching up and in some cases surpassing TV (Dunn 2017).

THINKING SOCIOLOGICALLY

What impact do you think the introduction of electronics and social media has on families in the Global South developing countries, especially in rural areas?

Social Media Use in the United States

% of U.S. adults who say they use the following social media sites online or on their cellphone

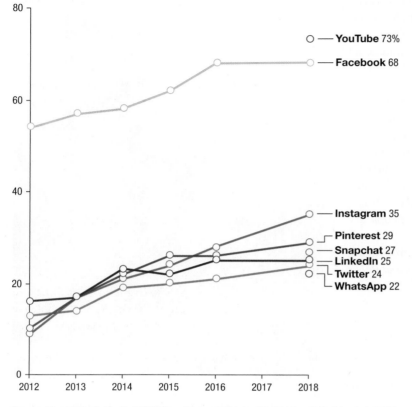

- YouTube 73%
- Facebook 68
- Instagram 35
- Pinterest 29
- Snapchat 27
- LinkedIn 25
- Twitter 24
- WhatsApp 22

Source: "Social Media Use in 2018." Pew Research Center, Washington, D.C. (March 1, 2018), http://www.pewinternet.org/2018/03/01/social-media-use-in-2018.

Note: Pre-2018 telephone poll data are not available for YouTube, Snapchat, or WhatsApp.

▲ These children illustrate how electronic devices influence the socialization process. Notice that they are not even all sharing the same device, and this influences the way they relate to each other.

On average, children 9 years and under in the United States are on their screens more than 2 hours a day; pediatricians agree that this affects their socialization experience, often negatively, depending on the amount and type of screen time. Children are spending much more time on mobile devices than they are reading, being read to, or playing outside. In addition, children from lower-income families (under $30,000 a year) spend more time with screen media than children from homes making more than $75,000 a year, a screen difference of 1 hour and 39 minutes daily (Howard 2017). Couch potato behavior cuts down on active play and brain development.

Mass media moguls influence what electronic media reaches children. These meso-level social institutions can influence the socialization of children within the most intimate of environments—the micro-level family. However, what influence they have depends on parental decisions about access to media. Parents oversee children's media experiences, what they are allowed to watch and for how long (Ofcom 2017). Parents who play an active role in helping children understand the content of television and computer games can have a powerful effect on mitigating media's negative impacts and enhancing the positive aspects of media. The media usage habits of parents can also influence how their children respond to media (National Consumers League 2013).

Online Social Networking

Today, almost all teens in the United States are online. Whereas just 25% of teens see friends in person every day outside of school, 55% text their friends daily (Lenhart 2015). Over half of teens (61% of boys and 52% of girls) have met a friend online through social networking sites (e.g., Instagram or Snapchat) or online gaming sites. Girls who meet a friend online tend to do so through networking sites whereas boys are about equally likely to make a friend through an online game site (Lenhart 2015). One out of five teens has met a friend in person that they got to know online.

Although social networking sites can help people meet new friends, feel connected, and gain support from others, they can also lead to some negative consequences. For teens, in particular, social media sites can be full of friendship, drama, and bullying. As Figure 4.3 shows, 45% of teens say they are online almost constantly—an almost 100% increase in just 3 to 4 years. (Anderson and Jiang 2018; Lenhart 2015). Interaction via electronics is a major part of the socialization process.

Frequency of Internet Use by U.S. Teens

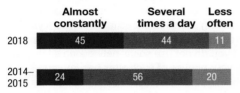

% of U.S. teens who say they use the internet, either on a computer or a cellphone . . .

	Almost constantly	Several times a day	Less often
2018	45	44	11
2014–2015	24	56	20

Source: Anderson and Jiang (2018), Pew Research Center.

Note: The "less often" category includes teens who say they use the Internet "about once a day," "several times a week," and "less often."

The next Engaging Sociology looks at social network usage across various demographic groups. Examine this issue in more depth by answering the questions following Table 4.2.

The Tsarnaev brothers—Tamerlan and Dzhokhar—were apparently well-adjusted teens while in high school, but they were deeply influenced by Internet exchanges and by political websites. Eventually, they teamed together to plot the Boston Marathon bombings on April 15, 2013. Three people were killed, and roughly 280 people were injured, many losing limbs. The actions of these young men were spawned when they adopted ideologies deeply antagonistic to the United States through Internet socialization. In a country that values free speech, controlling such antisocial influences is a real dilemma for law enforcement (Crary and Lavoie 2013).

Perhaps the most important aspect of television and computers is something we do not fully understand but that has frightening potential. For the first time in human history, we have powerful agents of socialization in the home from a child's birth onward. Time spent watching television or playing computer games means less time spent engaging in interaction with family members, caregivers, and peers. Intimate family bonds formed of affection and meaningful interaction are being altered by the dominant presence of electronic media in the home. In addition, those who control the flood of mass media messages received by children may have different interests and concerns than parents.

Without a doubt, a significant part of the informal socialization process occurs with the assistance of electronic equipment that shares the home with parents and siblings and that commands a significant portion of a child's time and attention. We also know that macro forces, such as globalization, have influenced school curricula and media content. We move next to a discussion of some of the national and global processes that influence socialization.

Socialization and Macro-Level Issues

Sense of Self in a New Global Context

Immigration patterns and ethnic conflicts around the world have resulted in a fairly new phenomenon: transnationalism. *Transnationalism* refers to multiple ties and interactions linking people and institutions across the borders of nation-states (UNESCO 2017). Many people crossing borders as immigrants, fleeing war and violence or seeking better economic opportunities, have multinational social relations that link together their original societies with their new locations. This means that an individual or a family has national loyalty to more than one country. Often, transnationalism occurs after the migration of war refugees, whose roots lie in their country of origin and whose close family members may continue to live far away. Recent transnational migrations due to wars include Somalis moving to Kenya's Dadaab refugee camp, Rohingya fleeing Myanmar for refugee camps in Bangladesh, and Syrians who have fled to European and other Middle Eastern countries (Refugees Deeply 2018).

Consider the socialization process of transnational children raised in war-torn countries. In the Palestinian territories, especially Gaza, and in Israeli settlements along the border, children grow up with fear and hatred that result in major influences on their socialization. Some war refugees spend childhoods in refugee camps and may never return to their native countries. For people experiencing transnationalism, there are conflicting messages about culturally appropriate behaviors and the obligations of loyalty to family and nation. Events of a national or global nature directly impact how an individual is socialized—with some of the socializing influences being from outside one's country of residence.

However, one need not migrate to another country to experience global pressures and added socialization

ENGAGING SOCIOLOGY

USES AND CONSEQUENCES OF SOCIAL NETWORKING

▼ TABLE 4.2

Who Uses Social Networking Sites

Percentage of U.S. adults within each group who use at least one social media site

All Internet Users	69%
Men	65%
Women	73%
18–29	88%
30–49	78%
50–64	64%
65+	37%
High school grad or less	60%
Some college	72%
College +	79%
Less than $30,000/year	63%
$30,000–$49,999	74%
$50,000–$74,999	74%
$75,000+	77%

Source: Pew Research Center (2018a, 2018b, 2018c).

Engaging Sociology

1. Among the demographic variables of sex, age, education, and income, which one has a significant impact on who uses social networking sites?

2. How does the impact of historical time period on the socialization process help explain the differences in social media usage described in the table?

3. How has your own use (or nonuse) of social networking sites influenced (a) with whom you interact and (b) how you communicate with people? (Or if you do not use social networking sites, discuss how your nonuse of such sites has impacted your relationships with those who are users.)

4. Overall, do you think the increase in the use of social networking sites has had more of a positive or negative impact on (a) your life (micro level), (b) your social class and educational institution (meso level), and (c) your society (macro level)? Why?

influences. The Internet and smartphones have increasingly created connectedness to other parts of the world and an awareness of global interdependencies. Some commentators have even suggested that the Internet is a threat to the nation-state because it allows individuals to be socialized through friendships, loyalties, and norms that are not in the interests of the state (Drori 2006). Ideas of social justice or progress may be shaped not just by the government that rules the country but by international human rights organizations and ideas obtained from the Internet that cross borders. In recent uprisings in some Middle Eastern and North African countries, social networking kept movement participants in touch with others in the uprisings and with outside media and supporters. Socialization agents now include electronic communication beyond local and

national boundaries, and provide information, contacts, and friendships across borders and boundaries. Figure 4.4 on Internet use around the world illustrates not only variability of access but also how widespread this access has become. One interesting question is how access or lack of access will influence the strength of "us" versus "them" feelings between citizens of different countries, insofar as sense of self is connected to belonging to a group—to a sense of *we*.

At a time when people lived in isolated rural communities and did not interact with those unlike themselves, there was little price to pay for being bigoted or chauvinistic toward those who were different. However, we now live in a global village where we or our businesses will likely interact with all kinds of people in a competitive

Internet Users per 100 People

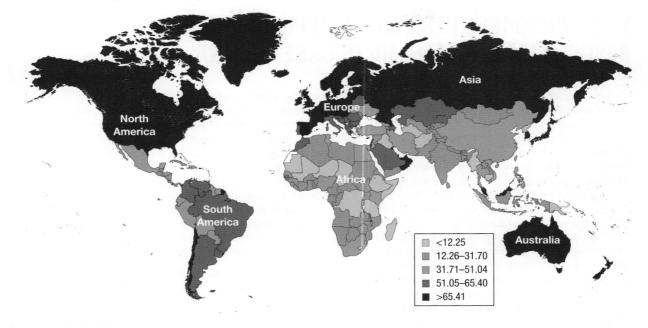

<12.25
12.26–31.70
31.71–51.04
51.05–65.40
>65.41

Source: World Bank 2016.

environment. If we hold people in low regard because they are unlike us or because we think they are destined for hell, there may be a high cost for this animosity. Therefore, training in cultural sensitivity toward those "others" has become an economic and a political issue in many communities.

The reality is that children today live in a globalized world. An increasing number of children around the world learn multiple languages to enhance their ability to communicate with others. Some college campuses require experiences abroad as part of the standard curriculum because faculty members and administrators feel that a global perspective is essential in our world today and part of a college education. Global sensitivity and tolerance of those once considered "the other" has become a core component of curricula today.

Sometimes, global events can cause a different turn—away from tolerance and toward defensive isolation. When 19 young men from Saudi Arabia and other Middle Eastern countries crashed planes into the World Trade Center in New York City and into the Pentagon in Washington, DC, the United States was shocked and became mobilized to defend itself and its borders. The messages within schools and from the government suddenly took a more patriotic turn. So this event and other terrorist acts, clearly tragedies rooted in global political

conflicts, did intensify the boundaries between people and loyalty to the nation-state. Global forces are themselves complex and do not always result in more tolerance.

Indeed, the only thing we can predict with considerable certainty is that in this age of sharing a small planet, the socialization of our citizens will be influenced by events at the macro level, whether national or global.

THINKING SOCIOLOGICALLY

How can events at the macro level (national or global) influence our individual socialization experience at the micro level? Consider world events such as wars and trade conflicts, education, religion, and other world events that affect most global citizens.

Policy and Practice

Should preschoolers living in poverty be socialized in the "enriched" environments of day care settings? Should adolescents work while going to school? Should we place emphasis in high school and college on in-group loyalty and patriotism or on developing a sense of global citizenship? Should new parents be required to take

SOCIOLOGISTS IN ACTION
David S. Kirk

EVIDENCE-BASED RESEARCH AND PUBLIC POLICY: RESOCIALIZATION AFTER HURRICANE KATRINA

I have spent much of my professional career using the tools of sociology to examine the myriad consequences of criminal justice policies in the United States. Part of my focus has been on the influence of communities on the *resocialization* of ex-prisoners. Research reveals that on leaving prison ex-prisoners tend to be geographically concentrated in a relatively small number of neighborhoods within metropolitan areas; they often return to the very same neighborhoods and find themselves surrounded by the friends and neighbors (socializing agents) that helped lead them to criminal behavior in the first place. Thus, it is not surprising that large proportions of ex-prisoners end up back in prison within just 3 years. The hope for ex-prisoners is that they will become *resocialized*, shedding their criminal identity as they learn the norms, behaviors, and values of law-abiding citizens.

These well-known facts about crime and justice in the United States serve as the backdrop of my research on prisoner reentry, the process of leaving prison and returning to the community. The tragedy of Hurricane Katrina, which devastated the Gulf Coasts of Louisiana and Mississippi in August 2005, afforded me a unique opportunity to examine what would happen if ex-prisoners did not return home to their old neighborhoods upon exiting prison. Katrina provided a natural experiment for investigating the importance of residential change because it forced some people to move who otherwise would not have. Residential change may serve as a catalyst for sustained behavioral change by providing an opportunity for individuals to separate from the former contexts and associates that facilitated their prior criminal behavior. A fresh location enhances resocialization efforts.

As I had hypothesized, prisoners exiting incarceration following Hurricane Katrina were much less likely to reside in the New Orleans neighborhoods where they resided prior to incarceration. Among those who did return to the same parish (a parish is the equivalent of a county) where they resided prior to incarceration, 26% were reincarcerated within 1 year of release from prison. By comparison, only 11% of offenders who moved to a new parish faced reincarceration 1 year after leaving prison. Based on these results, I concluded that separating individuals from their former residential environment reduces their likelihood of recidivism. Moving allows an individual to separate from the peers and routine activities that contributed to his or her criminal behavior in the past.

One critical component of disseminating information about scientific discoveries is to communicate the implications of the research. For instance, in most states, prisoners released on parole are legally required to return to their county of last residence, contributing to a return to old neighborhoods. So, parole policies, although designed to enhance public safety, may in fact undermine it. One implication of my research that I have discussed with key policymakers is that removing the institutional barriers to residential change may enhance public safety by lessening repetition of crime. Additionally, providing incentives for individuals to move to new neighborhoods, such as public housing vouchers, may benefit public safety. In my experience, redesigning public policies is part of a methodical process that involves good science, communication of results, and further testing in a real-world environment to determine effectiveness.

★ ★ ★ ★ ★ ★

David S. Kirk, PhD, is Professorial Fellow in Sociology at Nuffield College, University of Oxford, England. This excerpt is adapted from *Sociologists in Action: Sociology, Social Change, and Social Justice* (Sage 2014).

child-rearing classes? How should job training programs be structured? How can communities use the talents and knowledge of retirees? Can the death process be made easier for the dying person and the family? These are all policy questions—issues of how to establish governing principles that will enhance our common life.

One vexing problem for communities and societies is how to resocialize people during or after their experiences in prisons so they are prepared to be contributing and functioning members of society. In the Sociologists in Action feature above, David Kirk shows how he used lessons from the aftermath of Hurricane

Katrina to solve an ex-prisoner puzzle and make policy recommendations.

These policy questions rely on an understanding of socialization—how socialization influences our beliefs and our positions on issues facing society. For example, making decisions about how to provide positive early childhood education experiences at a time when young children first learn the ways of their culture depends on understanding the socialization they receive at home and at school. The quality of childcare we provide for young children will affect not only how well-trained our future workforce is but also whether the children turn out to be productive citizens or a drain on society. Likewise, resocializing those who have run afoul of the law can turn them into law-abiding citizens. These are all questions public sociologists work on and can help to answer.

> Now that we have some understanding of the process of socialization, we look at the next level in the process of interaction and how individuals become members of small groups, networks, and large complex organizations.

WHAT HAVE WE LEARNED?

Human socialization is pervasive, penetrating, and lifelong. We cannot understand what it means to be human without comprehending the impact of a specific culture on us; the influence of our close associates; and the complex interplay of pressures at the micro, meso, and macro levels. Indeed, without social interaction, there would not even be a self. We humans are, in our most essential natures, social beings. This chapter opens our eyes to the ways in which we become the individuals we are. We move next to a discussion of how we use our socialization in interactions with groups and organizations as members of society.

KEY POINTS

- Human beings come with their own biological makeup, but most of what makes us uniquely human we learn from our culture and society—through socialization. Humans who live in isolation from others do not receive the socialization necessary to be part of culture and are sometimes barely human.

- The self consists of the interaction of the *I*—the basic impulsive human with drives, needs, and feelings—and the *Me*. We develop a reflective self through role-taking and seeing how others might view us.

- The self is profoundly shaped by others, but it also has agency—that is, it can be an initiator of action and a maker of meaning.

- The self develops through stages, from mimicking others (the play stage) to more intellectually sophisticated abilities such as role-taking and seeing how various roles complement each other (the game stage).

- The self is modified as it moves through life stages, and some of those stages require major resocialization—shedding old roles and taking on new ones as one enters new statuses in life.

- A number of agents of socialization are at work in each of our lives, communicating messages relevant at the micro, meso, or macro level of social life. At the meso level, for example, we may receive different messages about what it means to be a "good" person depending on our ethnic, religious, or social-class subculture.

- Some of these messages may be in conflict with each other, as when global messages about tolerance for those who are different conflict with a nation's desire to have absolute loyalty and a sense of being superior to other nations.

1. Cooley's idea of the looking-glass self helps us understand how we think other people view us, and this in turn influences our view of ourselves. How has your sense of your ability to succeed in college been influenced by the feedback you have processed from those around you (particularly teachers, peers, and family members)?

2. Socialization occurs throughout the life cycle. Into what role have you been socialized most recently? Who were the primary agents in this socialization process? Did you find the process relatively easy or difficult? Why?

3. Sociological studies have shown that middle-class and working-class parents tend to socialize their children differently. Explain the differences and describe how they relate to how you were socialized by your family of origin.

4. How has your socialization been influenced by television, video games, and other electronics? Do you think the extent to which these informal agents of socialization influence children these days has a positive or a negative impact on our society? Why?

5. If you were asked to create government policies to promote positive socialization experiences that would strengthen our society, what might you propose? Why?

KEY TERMS

agents of socialization   105

formal agents of socialization   107

game stage   102

generalized other   102

I   101

imitation stage   101

informal agents of socialization   107

interaction   93

looking-glass self   99

Me   101

peer groups   106

play stage   101

resocialization   104

role-taking   99

self   98

significant others   101

social class   108

socialization   92

CONTRIBUTING TO OUR SOCIAL WORLD: WHAT CAN WE DO?

At the Local (Micro) Level

In every community, numerous opportunities exist for volunteer work helping children from economically and otherwise disadvantaged backgrounds to succeed in school. *Opportunities to help disadvantaged children succeed in school include tutoring or mentoring in the local schools.*

- *Head Start centers for poor preschool children* often have opportunities to do something concrete to help children. An education faculty member at your college can give you contact information or go to the association's website at www.nhsa.org.

- *Help in a local Boys and Girls Club* that provides socialization experiences for children through their teens. You can find a club near you by going to www.bgca.org/whoweare/Pages/FindaClub.aspx.

- *Take service learning course* credits. Locate the service learning office at your college or university to learn about service learning programs on your campus that help disadvantaged children.

At the National or Global (Macro) Level

Literacy is a vital component of socialization yet remains an unmet need in many parts of the world, especially in the less-developed countries of Africa and Asia.

- *World Education* provides training and technical assistance in nonformal education in economically disadvantaged communities worldwide. Go to the organization's website at www.worlded.org to learn about its wide variety of projects and volunteer or work opportunities.

- *CARE International* (www.care-international.org) and *Save the Children* (www.savethechildren.org) provide funding for families to send children to school and to receive specialized training.

- *WE Charity* (wecharity.org) is a Canadian-based organization that empowers young people to help other young people. Through its "award winning development model" they have been "changing lives in more than eight countries around the world." Go to the organization's website to learn how you can work with others to help create more educational opportunities for children. This organization provides multiple ways to track the impact of your donation.

- *UNESCO (the United Nations Educational, Scientific, and Cultural Organization)* promotes literacy around the world in many ways. Learn more about its efforts at en.unesco.org/themes/éducation. Opportunities exist for fund-raising, internships, and eventually jobs with these organizations.

$SAGE edge™

Get the tools you need to sharpen your study skills. SAGE edge offers a robust online environment featuring an impressive array of free tools and resources.

Access practice quizzes, eFlashcards, video, and multimedia at **edge.sagepub.com/ballantine7e**

CHAPTER 5

© Press Association via AP Images

INTERACTION, GROUPS, AND ORGANIZATIONS

Connections That Work

▲ Human interactions result in connections—networks—that make life more fulfilling and our economic efforts more productive. These connections link everything from micro groups to large bureaucratic organizations.

MICRO

ME (MY FAMILY AND CLOSEST FRIENDS)

LOCAL ORGANIZATIONS AND COMMUNITY
Networks form in local organizations like civic and alumni groups.

MESO

NATIONAL ORGANIZATIONS, INSTITUTIONS, AND ETHNIC SUBCULTURES
Ethnic organizations, political parties, and religious denominations are important to many people.

MACRO

SOCIETY
Citizens of a nation develop connections and a common identity.

GLOBAL COMMUNITY
The United Nations, international courts, and transnational corporations influence our lives.

WHAT WILL YOU LEARN IN THIS CHAPTER?

This chapter will help you to do the following:

5.1 Demonstrate the impact social networks can have on the lives of individuals

5.2 Provide examples of how verbal and nonverbal interaction guide our behavior

5.3 Describe the needs primary and secondary groups meet for individuals and society

5.4 Show how the characteristics of bureaucracy apply to formal organizations

5.5 Explain why networking with people from different cultures has become increasingly important

THINK ABOUT IT

Micro: Small groups and local communities	How does interaction with family and friends affect who you are, what you do, and what you believe?
Meso: National institutions, complex organizations, and ethnic groups	Is bureaucratic red tape necessary and inevitable?
Macro: National and global systems	What are some ways national trends, such as the decline in the percentage of U.S. citizens who smoke, influence your quality of life? What are some ways networks across the globe affect your daily life, your education, and your chosen profession?

Imagine that you cannot use your cell phone (or anyone else's). How would your behavior (and your mood) change? As of 2018, 95% of all U.S. adults own a cell phone, and 77% own smartphones. These figures are almost identical for men and women, but 100% of those aged 18 to 29 own a cell phone, and 94% own a smartphone. The number drops to 85% cell phone ownership among those over 65 years, and 46% for smartphones. Ownership is slightly lower for less educated persons and those with lower incomes. Not surprisingly, younger users are more dependent than older users (Pew Research Center 2018a). Over three fourths of U.S. citizens are on their phone daily, with 26% online constantly (Perrin and Jiang 2018). Most U.S. owners, including 92% of young adults aged 18 to 29, use their smartphones to avoid boredom. Almost half (47%) of young adults and one out of three (32%) of those aged 30 to 49 use their smartphones to avoid people around them (Smith 2015). How would you cope without being connected? Our constant access to media and communication technology has changed how we act and with whom we interact. Smartphones enable us to both connect and disconnect from others.

©iStockphoto.com/FatCamera

▲ No longer are paper and pencil the sole tools of learning. From as early as kindergarten on, students use electronic devices and the Internet at school.

THINKING SOCIOLOGICALLY

Explain how smartphones and other technologies have changed the way you communicate with others, compared to when your parents or grandparents were your age.

In the mid-1980s Jeanne, one of the authors of this book, took a leave of absence to conduct some research in Japan. A benefit of that leave was that she escaped the distraction of ringing phones and could concentrate. Fax was almost unknown, and e-mail hardly existed for the civilian population. In 2016, when she taught on Semester at Sea, she had instant contact with her office, publisher, and family over the international Internet superhighway, even in the middle of the ocean. She could insert earphones into her laptop computer and have a Skype conversation by voice or pick up a mobile phone and call her family or coauthor. What a change in the span of a couple of decades! Technology is developing rapidly and, as mentioned in Chapter 4, connects peoples and countries of the world through global networks.

This chapter lays the groundwork for understanding how we fit into the structure of our social world—exploring the link between the individual and the social structure. The process starts when we are born and continues with group activities as we join playgroups, preschool, and kindergarten classes. It broadens as we become members of larger organizations and bureaucracies within universities, workplaces, national political parties, and national and international religious organizations. First, we consider how networks and connections link individuals and groups to different levels of analysis. Then, we focus on micro-level interactions, meso-level groups, and meso- and macro-level organizations and bureaucracies. Finally, we consider macro-level national and global networks.

Networks and Connections in Our Social World

Try imagining yourself at the center of a web, such as a spider's web. Attach the threads that spread from the center first to family members and close friends, on out in the web to peers, then to friends of friends. Some thread connections are close and direct. Others are more distant but connect more and more people in an ever-expanding web.

Have you ever used the Six Degrees of Kevin Bacon search tool? Perhaps you have heard that just about any actor can be connected to Kevin Bacon in six or fewer steps. It is also true that the typical person in the United States is now fewer than six steps (or degrees) removed from any other person in the country. Stanley Milgram and his associates studied social networks by selecting several target people in different cities (Korte and Milgram 1970; MacMillan 2018; Milgram 1967). Then, they identified *starting persons* in cities more than 1,000 miles away. Each starting person was given a folder with instructions and the target person's name, address, and occupation, as well as a few other facts. The starting person was instructed to mail the folder to someone he or she knew on a first-name basis who lived closer to or might have more direct networks with the target person than the starting person had. The number of links in the chain to complete delivery ranged from two to 10, with most having five to seven intermediaries. This is the source of the reference to "six degrees of separation" and the original inspiration for the Kevin Bacon game.

More recently, research by scientists at Facebook and the University of Milan showed that the average number of acquaintances separating any two people in the world was 4.74. Within the United States the separation was only 4.37 people (Markoff and Sengupta 2011). Now among the 2.2 billion people active on Facebook, the average connection is 3.57 intermediaries or "degrees of separation" (Bhagat et al. 2016). Clearly, networks are powerful linkages and create a truly small world.

Our **social networks**, then, refer to *individuals linked together by one or more social relationships, connecting us to the larger society.* Our social networks provide us with *social capital*, access to people who can help us get jobs or favors. Networks begin with micro-level contacts and exchanges between individuals in private interactions and expand to small groups and then to large (even global) organizations

▲ Supporters of Myanmar leader Aung San Suu Kyi take a selfie as they look at the official results of the elections on a giant screen. Within seconds, their friends anywhere in the world could see them at the election rally through the photo on their Facebook pages.

(Granovetter 2007; Tolbert and Hall 2008). The stronger people's networks, the more influential they can be in another person's life (see Figure 5.1).

The blue circle represents an individual—perhaps you—and the yellow dots represent your friends and acquaintances. The lines represent personal relationships between individuals. Your network, then, looks a bit like a spider's web.

Networks at the Micro, Meso, and Macro Levels

Networks span the micro, meso, and macro levels of analysis. For example, at the *micro level,* you develop

▼ FIGURE 5.1

Networks: A Web of Connections

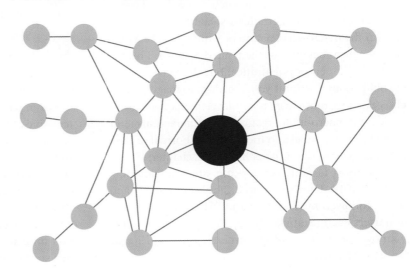

close friends in college—bonds that may continue for the rest of your life. You introduce your friends from the student government to your roommate's friends from the soccer team, and the network expands and your social capital increases. These acquaintances may have useful information about which professors to take, what campus organizations to join, and how to get a job in your field. You most likely carry out all of these interactions both in person and online.

When you graduate from your university, you will be part of the university's alumni association, and this may become important to you for social contacts, business connections, or help with settling in a new location. When people refer to the "old boy network," they are talking about contacts made through general associations with people such as alumni. Men have used networks successfully in the past, and networks of working women—new girl networks—are expanding rapidly as exemplified by the #MeToo movement's mobilization of thousands of people for marches and rallies. One of the reasons for the persistent inequality in our society is that members of certain groups may not have access to these privilege-enhancing networks.

THINKING SOCIOLOGICALLY

Map your social network web (as far as you can). What advantages do you get from your network? How might this network help you to advance your interests or chosen career?

Networks also link groups at different levels of analysis. In fact, you are linked through networks to (a) micro-level college, athletic, and faith communities; (b) meso-level formal, complex organizations such as a political party or national fraternity and ethnic or social class subcultures; and (c) the macro-level nation of which you are a citizen and global entities such as the United Nations. These networks may open opportunities, but they also may create obligations that limit your freedom to make your own choices. As we move from micro-level interactions to larger meso- and macro-level organizations, interactions tend to become less personal and more formal. Formal organizations are explored in the latter half of this chapter.

The most famous networking site is Facebook. As of April 2018, Facebook had 2.2 billion monthly active users, followed by YouTube and WhatsApp at 1.5 million users each (Statista 2018a). As a way of examining your own networks, try the exercise in the next Engaging Sociology feature.

We can network through Facebook, LinkedIn, Twitter, Instagram, and other sites, and we can keep in touch constantly through text messaging. However, this means that people spend more time interacting with a piece of technology and may feel less comfortable interacting face-to-face with someone. Likewise, online courses are, in one sense, less intimate. The instructor and the student may never meet face-to-face. Yet, through the Internet, more people can take college-level courses than ever before. We are only beginning to understand the implications of this technology on human interaction, learning, and interpersonal skills.

The Process of Interaction: Connections at the Micro Level

Each morning as you rouse yourself, you consider what the day might bring. You evaluate what is in store for you, what roles you will play during the day, and with whom you are likely to interact.

Should you wear the ragged but comfy jeans and T-shirt? Perhaps that will not work today because there is that class trip to the courthouse. Something a bit less casual is in order. Then, you are meeting with your English professor to discuss the last essay you wrote. What approach should you take? You could act insulted that she failed to think of you as a future J. K. Rowling, Suzanne Collins, or John Green. Maybe a meek, mild "Please tell me what I did wrong; I tried so hard" approach would work. She seems a nice, sympathetic sort. After class, there is a group of students who chat in the hall. It would be nice to meet them. What strategy should you use? Tell a joke? Make small talk? Talk to the students individually so you can get to know each before engaging the whole group? Each of these responses is a strategy for interaction, and each might elicit different reactions.

Elements of Social Interaction

"Let's have a drink!" Such a simple comment might have many different meanings. We could imagine two thirsty children playing together, men going to a bar after work, a couple of friends getting together to celebrate an event, fraternity brothers at a party, or a couple on a date. In all of these cases, **social interaction** consists of *two or more individuals purposefully relating to each other*.

Having a drink, like all *interaction*, involves action on the part of two or more individuals; is directed toward a goal that people hope to achieve (e.g., meeting someone, planning an event, relaxing over a beer); and takes place in a social context that includes cultural norms and rules

NETWORKING VIA FACEBOOK

If you are on Facebook, go to your Facebook account and note the number of friends you have listed. Then, look at them carefully to see if you can answer the following questions:

1. What is the age range of the friends on your list?

2. What is the gender composition of your list?

3. How many members of each of the following racial, ethnic, or global links are on your list?

    ___ African Americans

    ___ Whites

    ___ Hispanics

    ___ Asians

    ___ Other racial or ethnic group (or some combination)

    ___ International contacts

4. What is the socioeconomic status of your friends?

    ___ Blue collar (families in which the primary wage earner works for an hourly wage)

    ___ Middle class (families in which the primary wage earner earns a salary of less than $100,000 per year)

    ___ Professional (families in which the primary wage earner earns a salary of $100,000 to $500,000 per year)

    ___ Highly affluent corporate executive (families in which the primary wage earner earns a salary of $500,000 to $10 million per year)

    ___ Upper class (families in which much of the wealth is inherited and annual income is in the multimillions)

★ ★ ★ ★ ★ ★

Engaging Sociology

1. Now look at the data you have collected. What have you learned about your own networks?

2. How much socioeconomic, age, race, ethnic, and global diversity do the data reveal about your networks?

---

governing the situation, setting, and other factors shaping the way people perceive the circumstances. The action, goal, and social context help us interpret the meaning of statements such as "Let's have a drink."

The norms governing the particular social context tell us how to behave. Recall from Chapter 3 that *norms* are rules that guide human interactions. People assume that others will share their interpretation of a situation. These shared assumptions about proper behavior provide the cues for your own behavior and become a part of your social self. You look for cues to proper behavior and rehearse in your mind your actions and reactions. In the "Let's have a drink" scenario, the dress, mannerisms, speech, and actions you consider appropriate depend on expectations from your socialization and past experience in similar situations. You will, no doubt, have learned to dress and act differently depending on whether you are having the drink with an old friend, a boss, or a potential romantic partner. In turn, you will expect that the person with whom you are drinking will be making the same sort of decisions on what to wear and how to behave when you get together.

Although most people assume that talking, or *verbal communication*, is the primary means of communication between individuals, words themselves are actually only a part of the message. In most face-to-face communication, they make up less than half of the communication, with body language and tone of voice accounting for the rest (Fields 2015; Mehrabian 1971). Words account for 7% of the overall message, tone of voice 38%, and body language 55% (Debenham 2018). We communicate primarily through **nonverbal communication**—*interactions without words using facial expressions, the head, eye contact, body posture, gestures, touch, walk, status symbols, and personal space* (Cherry 2012; Givens 2012). We learn these important elements of communication through socialization as we grow up.

People who travel to a country other than their own often use gestures as they try to be understood. Like spoken language, however, nonverbal gestures vary from culture to culture. Communicating with others in one's own language can be difficult enough. Add to this the complication of individuals with different languages, cultural expectations, and personalities using different nonverbal

▲ In North America, friends interact at a close distance, 1.5 to 4 feet—as in the photo on the top. A more formal setting calls for a distance of 4 to 12 feet, which can feel cold and intimidating, as in the photo on the bottom.

messages, and misunderstandings are likely. Although one may master another written and verbal language, nonverbal messages are the hardest part of another language to master because they are specific to a culture and learned through socialization from an early age.

Consider the following example: You are about to wrap up a major business deal. You are pleased with the results of your negotiations, so you give your hosts the thumb-and-finger A-OK sign. In Brazil, you have just grossly insulted your hosts—it is the equivalent of giving them "the finger." In Japan, you have asked for a small bribe. In the south of France, you have indicated the deal is worthless. Intercultural communication takes more than knowing the language of a different culture.

Another example of nonverbal communication involves personal space. Most people have experienced social situations, such as parties, where someone gets too close. One person backs away, the other moves in again, and the first backs away again—into a corner or a table with nowhere else to go. Perhaps the person approaching

was aggressive or rude, but it is also possible that the person held different cultural norms or expectations in relation to personal space.

The amount of personal space an individual needs to be comfortable or proper varies with the cultural setting, gender, status, and social context of the interaction. Individuals from Arab countries are often comfortable at very close range. However, people from Scandinavia generally need a great deal of personal space. Consider the following four categories of social distance and social space based on a study of middle-class people in the United States, though there may be some variation within the middle class depending on ethnicity. Each category applies to particular types of activity (Hall and Hall 1992).

1. *Intimate distance:* from zero distance (touching, embracing, kissing) to 18 inches. Children may play together in such proximity, and adults and children may maintain this distance, but between adults, this intimate contact is reserved for private and affectionate relationships.

2. *Personal distance:* from 18 inches to 4 feet. This is the public distance for most friends and for informal interactions with acquaintances.

3. *Social distance:* from 4 feet to 12 feet. This is the distance for impersonal business relations, such as a job interview or class discussions between students and a professor. This distance implies a more formal interaction or a significant difference in the status of the two people.

4. *Public distance:* 12 feet and beyond. This is the distance most public figures use for addressing others, especially in formal settings and in situations in which the speaker has a high status.

Personal space also communicates one's position in relation to others. The higher the position, the greater the control of space. In social situations, individuals with higher positions spread out, prop their feet up, put their arms out, and use more sweeping gestures.

THINKING SOCIOLOGICALLY

Describe a time when you experienced miscommunication. Who was involved? What happened? How can what you are reading in this chapter help you to explain why the miscommunication occurred?

Theoretical Perspectives on the Interaction Process

Sociologists study interactions, including verbal and nonverbal communication, to better understand why people behave the way they do. Symbolic interactionists and rational choice theorists examine how and why people communicate with one another. As you will see, their different perspectives lead them to focus on different aspects of interactions and come up with distinctive conclusions as to why they occur.

Symbolic Interaction Theory. With whom do you interact? What determines whether the interaction will continue or stop? How do you know how to behave and what to say around

When a U.S. presidential candidate or any possible head of state speaks, it is not only the Secret Service that keeps people at a formal distance. It is a sense of awed respect for the office: 12 feet or more is the standard distance kept between high-status public figures and other people.

© AP Photo/Julie Jacobson

each other? What other processes are taking place as you "talk" to each other? Why do you act differently with different people?

Symbolic interactionism is based on the idea that humans create society through interacting with one another. We act toward people and objects on the basis of the meanings those people or things have for us. The meanings are derived by individuals as they interact with others. Together, through our interactions with one another, we agree that objects, gestures, and phrases like "Let's have a drink" symbolize certain things. Likewise, the word *hello* can signify the beginning of a conversation, and *goodbye* signifies the end of one because we agree on the meanings of those words and agree to act accordingly. Symbols are the key to understanding human life, and we go about the task of fitting our actions together through our shared perceptions and meanings of those symbols. Through our mental manipulation of symbols and interpretation of meaning, we *define situations* and determine how we should act in a given situation or how we should make sense of it. More than any other theory in the social sciences, symbolic interactionism stresses the agency—the active decision-making role—of humans within their societies (Charon 2010; Hewitt and Shulman 2011).

Have you ever laughed at a joke you did not hear or understand because those around you laughed? In ambiguous situations, humans look to others to see how they have made sense of the situation or interaction taking place—do people around us look frightened,

annoyed, bored, or amused? When in doubt, we tend to follow the cues of those around us. Once one person defines the situation and acts, especially if that person is highly regarded or self-confident, others will often accept that response as "normal." This is how social interaction is involved in the *social construction of reality*—the process by which individuals and groups shape reality through social interaction. This notion of reality then takes on a life of its own, often constraining and even coercing people to conform (Berger and Luckmann 1966; Hewitt and Shulman 2011; J. O'Brien 2011; Ritzer 2013). For example, our career goals tend to be influenced by those with whom we interact. If you had been a woman in the United States in the 1910s, you would be unlikely to think you could pursue a career in the "male" field of engineering.

However, socially constructed constraints can be challenged by individuals and groups, and lead to different realities that begin to influence people's perceptions of what is true and what is possible. For example, until recently, it seemed impossible for gay and transgender people in the military to gain acceptance. If you were gay, the choice seemed to be to choose a different path or keep your sexual orientation hidden. This changed in 2011, with the repeal of the ban on openly gay service personnel in the military.

A different approach to interaction analysis—called *dramaturgy*—analyzes life as a play or drama on a stage, with scripts and props and scenes to be played. The play we put on creates an impression for our

▲ Depicted here are Japanese yen. Your local store or restaurant will not accept yen in exchange for a piece of furniture or the meal you just consumed, any more than it would accept Monopoly money. We exchange goods and services based on some pieces of paper because we have a general agreement that this is "good currency"—a social construction of reality.

audience. In everyday life, individuals learn new lines to add to their scripts through the socialization process, including influence from family, friends, films, and television. They perform these scripts for social audiences to maintain certain images, much like the actors in a play.

Consider the following familiar example: Every day in high schools around the world, teenagers go on stage—in the classroom or the hallway with friends and peers and with adult authorities who may later be giving grades or writing letters of reference. The props these students use include their style of clothing, a backpack, a smartphone, and a smile or a "cool" look. The set is the classroom, the cafeteria, and perhaps the athletic field. The script is shaped by the actors: Teachers and coaches may establish an authoritarian relationship with students; classmates engage in competition for grades; peers seek social status among companions. The actors include hundreds of teens struggling with issues of identity, adapting to changing bodies, and attempting to be accepted and avoid humiliation and bullying. Each individual works to assert and maintain an image through behavior, clothing, language, and friends.

Each part or character an individual plays and each audience requires a different script. For example, interacting with peers at a bar differs from meeting a professor in her office. As we perform according to society's script for the situation, we take into consideration how our actions will influence others. By carefully managing the image we project—a process called *impression management*—we try to create an impression that

works to our advantage. Most of the time, we engage in *frontstage* behavior. This is the largely scripted behavior we use with strangers or casual acquaintances. A poor or unacceptable performance, such as wearing out-of-style clothes or spilling our lunch, is embarrassing both for us and for our audience. We learn to develop strategies to cover up weaknesses or failures, such as laughing at a joke even though we do not understand it.

Sometimes we avoid situations that will require us to play a role with which we are unfamiliar or uncomfortable. Have you ever avoided interacting with a certain group of people because you were unsure of how to act when around them or decided against trying out for a team or a theater production or running for office because you were afraid you might not make it or it was not an "in" thing to do? We learn to avoid those performance activities that are likely to result in humiliation or failure or that contradict the image we have worked to create.

At home or with close friends with whom we are more intimate, we engage in *backstage* behavior, letting our feelings show and behaving in ways that might be unacceptable for other audiences (Goffman 1967, [1959] 2001). We feel that with them we can relax and be our "true" selves, without possible negative repercussions. So, as you can see, dramaturgical analysis, and its frontstage and backstage concepts, can help us to better understand our interactions and how our behavior changes with the setting.

THINKING SOCIOLOGICALLY

Describe some ways in which your life feels like a dramatic production. Identify frontstage and backstage behaviors you carry out daily.

Rational Choice Theory. Rational choice or exchange theorists look at a different aspect of interaction: the rewards and costs of interaction for the individual and why individuals continue in relationships. Rational choice theorists argue that the choices we make are guided by reason (*rational choices*). If the benefits of the interaction are high and if the costs are low, the interaction will be valued and sustained. Every interaction involves calculations of self-interest, expectations of reciprocity (a mutual exchange of favors), and decisions to act in ways that have current or eventual payoff for the individual (Smelser 1992).

Reciprocity is a key concept for rational choice theorists. The idea is that if a relationship is imbalanced over a period of time, it will become unsatisfying. As theorists from this perspective see human interaction, each person tends to keep a mental ledger of who "owes" whom. If I have done you a favor, you owe me one. If you have helped me in some way, I have an obligation to you. If I then fail to comply or even do something that hurts you, you will likely view it as a breach in the relationship and have negative feelings toward me. Moreover, if one person has more power in the relationship, there is an imbalance in what each brings to the relationship.

Consider decision-making in families—what to purchase or where to vacation, for example. The person with the least interest or stake in the relationship is the person who brings more resources (financial, physical, social, and personal) to the relationship. That person could easily leave the relationship. The person who offers less to the relationship or who has fewer assets is more dependent on the relationship. This person is likely to give in when there is a disagreement about spending or decisions about vacations. Thus, the person with "less interest" in the relationship and more resources gets her or his way. Scholars refer to this relationship as the *principle of least interest*.

Sometimes a person may engage in a behavior where there is little likelihood of reciprocity from the other person—as in cases where the behavior is altruistic or self-giving. Rational choice theorists would argue that there is still a benefit to the person. It might be enhanced feelings of self-worth for helping someone in need, positive recognition from others or for work well done, hope for a reward in the afterlife, or just the expectation of indirect reciprocity. This latter notion is akin to the idea of *paying it forward* or being rewarded in the future or indirectly. Group-based social identity, which stems from interdependent relationships, often leads people to help others in the group, even though the person they help might not directly help them in return. However, if they are in a similar situation, they could hope for and expect someone in the group to come to their assistance (Gouldner 1960; J. Turner 2003; Whitham 2017).

Social Status: Individuals' Link to Groups

As you will recall, a **status** is *a social position in society*. We interact with others and they react to us based, in part, on the statuses we hold. We interact differently when in the daughter status with our parents, in a student status with our professor, or in friend status with our peers. Each individual holds many statuses, and this combination of statuses held by any individual is called a *status set*—for instance, daughter, sister, worker, teammate, and student.

Statuses affect the type of interactions individuals have. In some interactions (as with classmates), people are equals. In other situations, individuals have interchanges with people who hold superior or inferior statuses. If you are promoted to supervisor, your interaction with former peers and subordinates will change. Consider the possible interactions shown in Figure 5.2, in which the first relationship is between equals and the others are between those with unequal statuses.

With a friend, these status relationships are constantly being negotiated and bargained: "I'll do what you want tonight, but tomorrow I choose." By contrast, when individuals are in dominant or subordinate positions, power or deference affects their interactions. As pointed out in rational choice theory, the more powerful person, such as one who has more wealth or privilege, can interrupt in a conversation with his or her partner and show less deference in the interaction (Wood 2008).

People have no control over certain statuses they hold. These **ascribed statuses** are *often assigned at birth and do not change during an individual's lifetime*. Age cohort, sex, and ethnicity are examples. For example, whereas a few people undergo sex transformations, for most people sex is an ascribed characteristic. Ascribed statuses are assigned to a person without regard for personal desires, talents, or choices. In some societies, the caste or social position into which one is born (e.g., "untouchables" or Dalits in India) is an ascribed status because it is usually impossible to change within one's lifetime.

Achieved status, on the other hand, *is chosen or earned by the decisions one makes, the interest or effort one puts into an activity, and sometimes by personal ability*. Attaining a higher education, for example, improves an individual's occupational opportunities and thus his

▼ FIGURE 5.2

Types of Status Relationships Experienced by You

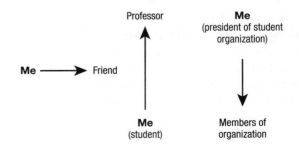

or her achieved status. Being a guitarist in a band is an achieved status and so is being a criminal, for both are earned positions based on the person's own decisions and actions.

At a particular time in life or under certain circumstances, one of an individual's statuses may become most important and take precedence over others; this is called a **master status**. Whether it is an occupation, parental status, or something else, it dominates and shapes much of an individual's life, activities, self-concept, and position in the community for a period of time. For a person who is very ill, for instance, that illness may occupy a master status, needing constant attention from doctors; influencing social relationships; and determining what that person can do in family, work, or community activities (Roberts 2018).

THINKING SOCIOLOGICALLY

What are your statuses? Which ones are ascribed, and which are achieved statuses? Do you have a master status? How do these statuses affect the way you interact with others in your network of relationships?

Relationship Between Status and Role

Every status (position) in your network includes certain behaviors and obligations as you carry out **roles**, *the expected behaviors, rights, obligations, responsibilities, and privileges assigned to a social status*. Roles are the dynamic, action part of statuses in a society. They define how each individual in an interaction is expected to act (Linton 1937). The role of a person holding the status of college student includes behaviors and obligations such as attending classes, studying, taking tests, writing papers, and interacting with professors and other students. We enter most statuses with some knowledge of how to carry out the roles dictated by our culture. Through the process of socialization, we learn roles by observing others; watching television and films; reading; and being taught by family members, teachers, and others how to carry out the status.

Both statuses (positions) and roles (behavioral expectations of people holding the status or position) form links with other people in the social world because they must be carried out in relationships with others. For example, a father has certain obligations (or roles) toward his children and their mother. The position of father exists not on its own but in relationship to significant others who have reciprocal ties.

Your status of student requires certain behaviors and expectations, depending on whether you are interacting with a dean, a professor, an adviser, a classmate, or a prospective employer. This is because the role expectations of the status of student vary as one interacts with specific people in other statuses. In Figure 5.3, the student is the subject, and the others are those with whom the student interacts in the status of student.

Within a group, individuals may hold both formal and informal statuses. One illustration is the formal status of high school students such as class year and the informal roles in cliques that are not part of the formal school structure. These cliques or "adolescent societies" show levels of networks, clusters, segregation, and hierarchy within and between them. A student may be known, for example, as one of the popular crowd, a jock, a nerd, a loner, a clown, a prep, or an outcast based on either a rank-ordered caste system in school or cliques that develop based on other characteristics of members (McFarland et al. 2014). Individual schools have their own clique structure; consider cliques in the film *Mean Girls*—JV and Varsity Jocks, Asian Nerds, and Desperate Wannabes to name several ("Mean Girls Cliques" 2014). Each of these roles takes place in a status relationship with others: teacher-student, peer-peer, coach-athlete, for example. Social networks may be based on ascribed characteristics, such as age and sex, or on achieved status, such as education, occupation, or common interests. These links, in turn, form the basis for social interactions and group structures (R. Hall 2002). However, at times, individuals cannot carry out their roles as others expect them to, creating role strain or conflict.

▼ FIGURE 5.3

Types of Interactions Students Have With Reciprocal Status Holders

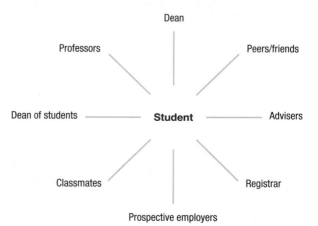

Role Strain and Role Conflict. Most people have faced times in their lives when they simply could not carry out all the obligations of a status, such as student—write two papers, study adequately for two exams, complete the portfolio for the studio art class, finish the reading assignments for five classes, and memorize lines for the oral interpretation class—all in the same week. Every status carries role expectations, the way the status is supposed to be carried out according to generally accepted societal or group norms. Yet in these cases, individuals face **role strain**, the *tension among roles within a status*. Role strain causes the individual to be pulled in many directions by various obligations of the single status, as in the example regarding the status of student.

To resolve role strain, individuals can cope in several possible ways, such as passing the problem off lightly (and thus not doing well in classes); considering the dilemma humorous; becoming highly focused and pulling a couple of all-nighters to get everything done; or becoming stressed, tense, fretful, and immobilized because of the strain. Most often, individuals set priorities based on their values and make decisions accordingly: "I'll work hard in the class for my major and let another one slide."

Role conflict refers to *conflict between the roles of two or more social statuses*. It differs from role strain in that it is conflict *between* the roles of two or more statuses, rather than tension among roles within one of the statuses. For example, college athletes face role conflicts from competing demands on their time (Adler and Adler 1991, 2004). They must complete their studies on time, attend practices and be prepared for games, perhaps attend meetings of a Greek house to which they belong, and get home for a little brother's birthday. Stress-coping strategies have to be developed for such situations, depending on personal characteristics and social support systems (Wendling, Kellison, and Sagas 2018). Similarly, a student may be going to school, holding down a part-time job to help make ends meet, and raising a family. If the student's child gets sick, the status of parent comes into conflict with that of student and worker. In the case of role conflict, the person may choose—or be informed by others—which status is the master status. Figure 5.4 illustrates the difference between role strain and role conflict.

THINKING SOCIOLOGICALLY

Using Figure 5.4 as a model, write down the statuses you hold in your social world and the roles you perform in these statuses. Then, list three examples of role conflicts and three examples of role strains that you experience.

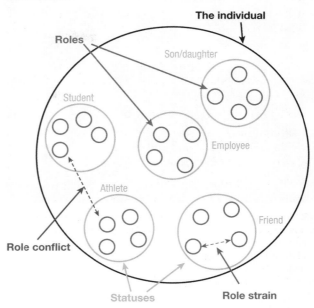

Each individual has many statuses: a status set. Each status has many roles: a role set. A conflict between two roles of the same status is a role strain. A conflict between the roles of two different statuses is a role conflict.

Most statuses and accompanying roles come and go. For example, you will not always be a student. You may or may not be married at different points in your life. You will retire from your job. As people grow older, they disengage from some statuses and engage in new and different statuses and roles.

Our statuses connect us to and make us integral parts of meso- and macro-level organizations. Our place within the social world, then, is guaranteed, even obligatory, because of statuses we hold—within small groups (family and peers), in larger groups and organizations (school and work organizations), in institutions (political parties or religious denominations), and ultimately as citizens of the society and the world (citizens and workers in global corporations). Each of these statuses connects us to a group setting.

Groups in Our Social World: The Micro-Meso Connection

Groups refer to *units involving two or more people who interact with each other because of shared common interests, goals, experiences, and needs* (Drafke 2008). As we have seen, humans are social beings. We become members of society and gain a sense of self through social interaction. Groups meet our social needs for belonging and

© Getty Images/Handout

▲ Suicide bombers are willing to commit altruistic suicide—to die voluntarily for the good of the group—to further their cause. They are deeply integrated into their own social network, and the cause of the group is seen as more important than the individual's life. Reem Slaleh Raiyshi, a mother of two children from Gaza, blew herself up at the Erez Crossing between Israel and the Gaza Strip. Many in her community viewed this as altruistic suicide—for the group.

acceptance, support us throughout our lives, and place restrictions on us. We also need groups for protection, to obtain food, to manufacture goods, and to get jobs done. Groups can be small, intimate environments—micro-level interactions with family or friends—or they can become large, meso-level organizations. In any case, it is through our group memberships that the micro and meso levels are connected.

Not all collections of individuals are groups. For instance, your family is a group, but people shopping at a mall or waiting for a bus are not a group because they do not regularly interact or acknowledge shared common interests.

Groups form through a series of succeeding steps. Consider people forming a soccer team in a new league: The first step is initial interaction. If the interactions with the other members are rewarding and meet individuals' needs, the individuals will attempt to maintain the benefits the group provides and form a team (T. Mills 1984). In the second step, a collective goal emerges. For example, team members may work together to plan practice and game schedules, buy uniforms, and advertise the games. In the third and final step, the group attempts to expand its collective goals by building on the former steps and by pursuing new goals. For example, the team may reach out to new players, to coaches, and to supporters for funding.

As noted, groups impact both society and individuals. Neither would function properly without groups.

The importance of groups becomes especially clear when we consider two social problems: anomie and suicide.

Group Solidarity, Anomie, and Suicide

Who commits suicide? Did you know that the answer to this is closely related to an individual's group affiliations? Early sociologist Émile Durkheim took a unique approach to making sense of suicide trends. In his book *Suicide*, Durkheim ([1897] 1964) discussed the social factors contributing to suicide. Using existing statistical data to determine suicide rates in European populations, Durkheim looked at variables such as sex, age, religion, nationality, and the season in which the suicide was committed. His findings demonstrate that individual problems cannot be understood without also understanding the group context in which they occur.

Durkheim found that Protestants committed suicide more often than Catholics, urban folks more often than people living in small communities, people in highly developed and complex societies more frequently than those in simple societies, and people who lived alone more than those situated in families. The key variable linking these findings was the degree to which an individual was integrated into a group—that is, the degree of social bond with others. Those who belonged to more tightly knit groups were least likely to commit suicide, whereas those whose lives were less tied to those of others were most likely to kill themselves. Durkheim described this type of suicide, when the individual feels little social bond to the group or society and lacks familial ties, as *egoistic suicide*.

A second type, *anomic suicide*, occurs when a society or one of its parts is in disorder, turmoil, or rapid change and lacks clear norms and guidelines for social behavior. With the rapid changes and continued breakdown of institutional structures in many modern and modernizing societies, religious and political groups may vie for power and offer contrasting definitions of reality. Social controls (police and military forces) may be strained, and leaders struggle to cope with the turmoil and lack of consensus. The result of the collapse of norms is **anomie**, *the state of normlessness that occurs when the rules for behavior in society break down under extreme stress from rapid social change or conflict* (Merton 1938). This anomie tends to lead to higher rates of suicide.

Durkheim's third type of suicide, *altruistic suicide*, differs from the others in that it involves such a strong bond and group obligation that the individual is willing to die for the group. Self-survival becomes less important than group survival (Durkheim [1897] 1964). Examples of altruistic suicide include the young suicide bombers in Iraq, Afghanistan, and Pakistan carrying out suicide missions against their country's police forces and sometimes against NATO or American military forces, which they have defined as invading forces. U.S. military Medal of Honor recipients who sacrificed their own lives to save those of the men in their units are another example. These suicides usually include social groups that have clear norms and high consensus about values arising from their religious or political beliefs.

Durkheim's work revealed that suicide rates are strongly influenced by social and psychological factors that can operate at the meso or macro level. His findings and those of others show that groups impact our lives and even our desire to continue living (Hall 2002; Nolan, Triplett, and McDonough 2010). No individual is an island. The importance of groups and social influence from various levels in the system is an underlying theme of this text. To more fully understand the influence of groups over us, though, we must become familiar with the different types of groups in which we interact.

Types of Groups

Each of us belongs to several types of groups. Some groups provide intimacy and close relationships, whereas others meet different needs. Some are required affiliations, and others are voluntary. Some provide personal satisfaction, and others are obligatory or necessary for survival.

Primary groups are at the most micro level and *characterized by cooperation among close, intimate, long-term relationships.* Your family members and best friends, school classmates, and close work associates are all of primary importance in your everyday life. Primary groups provide a sense of belonging and shared identity. Group members care about you, and you care about the other group members, creating a sense of loyalty. Approval and disapproval from the primary group influence the activities you choose to pursue. Belonging to the group is the main reason for membership. The group is of intrinsic value—enjoyed for its own sake—rather than for some utilitarian value such as making money.

For individuals, primary groups provide an anchor point in society. You were raised in a primary group: your family. You hold many statuses and play a variety of roles in primary relationships: those of child, sibling, partner, parent, relative, close friend, and so on. You

meet with other members face-to-face or keep in touch on a regular basis and know a great deal about their lives. What makes them happy or angry? What are sensitive issues? In primary groups you share values, say what you think, let down your hair, dress as you like, and share your concerns and emotions and successes and failures (Goffman 1967, [1959] 2001). Charles H. Cooley, who first discussed the term *primary group*, saw these relationships as the source of close human feelings and emotions—love, cooperation, and concern (Cooley [1909] 1983).

Secondary groups are *those with formal, impersonal, and businesslike relationships, and they are often temporary and based on a specific limited purpose or goal.* Secondary groups are usually large and task-oriented because they have a specific purpose to achieve and focus on accomplishing a goal. In the modern world, people cannot always live under the protective wing of primary-group relationships. As children grow, they move from the security and acceptance of primary groups—the home and neighborhood peer group—to a secondary group—the large school classroom, where each child is one of many students vying for the teacher's (and others') approval and competing for rewards. Similarly, the work world requires formal relations and procedures: applications, interviews, and contracts. Employment is based on specific skills, training, and job knowledge—competence to carry out the role expectations in the position.

Because each individual in a secondary group carries out a specialized task, communication between members is often specialized as well. Contacts with doctors, store clerks, and even professors are generally formal and impersonal parts of organizational life. Sometimes associations with secondary groups are long lasting; sometimes they are of short duration, as in the courses you are taking this term. Secondary groups operate at the meso and macro levels of our social world, but they affect individuals at the micro level.

As societies modernize, they evolve from small towns and close, primary relationships to predominantly urban areas with more formal, secondary relationships. In the postindustrial world, with family members scattered across countries and around the world, secondary relationships have come to play ever greater roles in people's lives. Large work organizations may provide day care, health clinics, financial planning, courses to upgrade skills, and sports leagues.

Small micro-level and large macro-level groups often occur together. Behind most successful secondary groups are primary groups. Consider the small work group within

Primary and Secondary Group Characteristics

	Primary Group	Secondary Group
Quality of relationships	Personal orientation	Goal orientation
Duration of relationships	Usually long-term	Variable, often short-term
Breadth of activities	Broad, usually involving many activities	Narrow, usually involving a few largely goal-directed activities
Subjective perception of relationships	As an end in itself (friendship, belonging)	As a means to an end (to accomplish a task, earn money)
Typical examples	Families, close friendships	Coworkers, political organizations

a large organization that eats together or goes out for a beer on Friday afternoons. These relationships help individuals feel a part of the larger organization, just as residents of large urban areas have small groups of neighborhood friends. Table 5.1 summarizes some of the dimensions of primary and secondary groups.

Problems in primary groups can affect performance in secondary groups. Consider the problems of a student who has an argument with a partner or roommate, or experiences a failure of his or her family support system due to divorce or other problems. Group support can diminish during times of family stress and affect group relationships in other parts of one's life (Drafke 2008). Because self-concepts and social skills begin to develop in early childhood and need primary group support, a young child who is a victim of trauma or separation, left out, teased, or bullied can develop low self-esteem and be less effective in social situations (Oswalt 2018).

▲ Many colleges find that having a sports program facilitates loyalty and sense of belonging to the in-group. Even where such an in-group does not originally exist, an athletic team can create an in-group.

THINKING SOCIOLOGICALLY

In the past, raising children was considered a family task, done by the primary family group. Today, many children are in childcare settings, often run by secondary groups. What differences do you see between the experiences a child receives in a family and in childcare? What might be the advantages and disadvantages of each? Can a secondary group provide care comparable with that provided by a family? Can the secondary group provide better care than families? What variables (such as family situation) might affect the child? How and why?

Reference groups are *composed of members who act as role models and establish standards against which members measure their conduct.* Individuals look to reference groups to set guidelines for behavior and decision-making. Successful businesses can serve as reference groups for other businesses. The term is often used to refer to models in one's chosen career field. Ethnic groups can also be reference groups. Ethnic groups can provide adolescent members with strong reference group standards by which to judge themselves. The stronger the ethnic pride and identification, the more some teens may separate themselves from contact with members of other ethnic groups (Schaefer and Kunz 2007). This can be functional or dysfunctional for the teens, as with in-groups and out-groups.

An **in-group** is *one to which an individual feels a sense of loyalty and belonging.* It also may serve as a reference group. (Any group may fit into more than one category.) An **out-group** is *one to which an individual does not belong, but more than that, it is a group that competes with or acts in opposition to an in-group.*

Membership in an in-group may be based on sex, race, ethnicity, social class, religion, political affiliation, the school one attends, an interest group such as the fraternity or sorority one joins, or the area where one lives. People tend to judge others according to their own in-group identity. Members of the in-group—for example, supporters of a high school team—often feel hostility toward or reject out-group members—boosters of the rival team. The perceived outside threat or hostility is often exaggerated, but it does help create the in-group members' feelings of solidarity. Another example might be the "preps" in a high school who control many resources because they control the school's student council and many of the leadership positions in the school. They are an in-group, but the punks or burnouts (the out-group) reject the preps and seek alternatives to the activities planned by the preps. Unfortunately, these feelings of hostility can result in prejudice and ethnocentrism, overlooking the individual differences of in-group and out-group members.

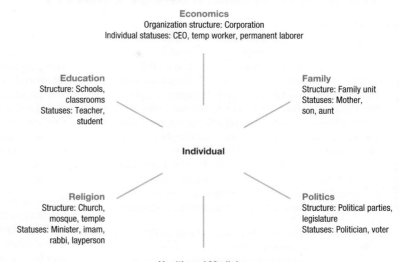

▼ FIGURE 5.5

Our Social World: Institutions, Organizations, and Individual Status

THINKING SOCIOLOGICALLY

What are some examples of your own group affiliations? Draw a diagram of your primary groups, secondary groups, peer groups, reference groups, and in-groups and out-groups.

Organizations and Bureaucracies: The Meso-Macro Connection

Our days are filled with activities that involve us with complex organizations: from the doctor's appointment to college classes; from the political rally for the issue we support to worship in a church, temple, or mosque; and from paying state sales tax for our toothpaste to buying a sandwich at a fast-food franchise. Figure 5.5 shows the institutions of society, each made up of thousands of organizations (e.g., medical organizations, educational organizations, religious groups, economic corporations, political movements, and the government itself) and each following the cultural norms of the society. We have statuses and roles in each group, and these link us to networks and the larger social world. We now look at how the modern forms of these organizations developed.

How Modern Organizations Evolved

Recall from Chapter 3 the discussion of types of societies, from hunter-gatherer to postindustrial. Each type of society entails different organizational structures (Blau 1956; P. Nolan and Lenski 2014). The development of modern organizations and bureaucracies began with the Industrial Revolution in the 1700s and 1800s. Increasingly complex organizations required and helped create what Max Weber called the **rationalization** of social life—*the attempt to maximize efficiency by creating rules and procedures focused solely on accomplishing goals* (Weber 1947). No longer were decisions made by tradition, custom, or the whim of a despot. Instead, trained leaders planned policies to achieve organizational efficiency. Tasks became more specialized, and some manual jobs were taken over by machines. People were expected to behave in purposeful, coordinated ways to advance organizational efficiency.

Formal organizations (also called *modern "rational" organizations*), *composed of complex secondary groups deliberately formed to pursue and achieve certain goals*, were created to standardize production and increase productivity, precision, and speed. They are called formal organizations because of the written charters, constitutions, bylaws, and procedures that govern them. Google, General Electric (GE), the Red Cross, the National Basketball Association (NBA), the Republican Party, and your university are all examples of formal organizations.

Bureaucracies are *specific types of very large formal organizations that have the purpose of maximizing efficiency. They are characterized by set relations among participants, clearly laid-out procedures and rules, and the pursuit of stated*

THE MCDONALDIZATION OF SOCIETY

The process of rationalization described by Max Weber—the attempt to reach maximum bureaucratic efficiency—comes in a new modern version, expanded and streamlined, exemplified by the fast-food restaurant businesses that began to spread in the 1950s and chain "box" stores now found around the world. Efficient, rational, predictable sameness is sweeping the world—from diet centers such as Weight Watchers to NutriSystem to 7-Eleven and from Walmart to Gap clothing stores with their look-alike layouts. Most major world cities feature McDonald's or Kentucky Fried Chicken in the traditional main plazas of train stations, serving familiar fare to flustered foreigners and curious native consumers.

The McDonaldization of society, as George Ritzer calls it, refers to several trends: First, *efficiency* is maximized by the sameness—same store plans, same mass-produced items, and same procedures. Second is *predictability*, the knowledge that each hamburger or piece of chicken will appear and taste the same, leaving nothing to chance. Third, everything is *calculated* so that the organization can ensure that everything fits a standard— every burger is cooked the same number of seconds on each side. Fourth, there is *increased control* over employees and customers so there are fewer variables to consider—including substitution of technology for human labor as a way to ensure predictability and efficiency.

What is the result of this efficient, predictable, planned, automated new world? According to Ritzer, the world is becoming more dehumanized, and efficiency is replacing individual creativity and human interactions. The mom-and-pop grocery, bed and breakfasts, and local craft or clothing shops are rapidly becoming a thing of the past. This process of the McDonaldization of society, meaning principles of efficiency and rationalization exemplified by fast-food chains, is coming to dominate more and more sectors of our social world (Ritzer 2015). Although there are aspects of this predictability that we all like, it also entails a loss of the uniqueness and local flavor that individual entrepreneurs bring to a community.

Some large corporations have started a movement toward *Starbuckization* to impress consumers tired of McDonaldization. For examples, Starbucks, with its own music mixes, comfortable seats, and Wi-Fi, makes customers feel like they are purchasing a cultural product along with their coffee. This culture, however, is as controlled as any other McDonaldized endeavor, making Starbucks a McClone at its core.

McDonaldization is so widespread and influential that many modern universities are now McDonaldized. A large lecture hall is an efficient way of teaching sociology or biology to many students at once. Similarly, massive online classes, PowerPoint presentations, multiple-choice exams, and a limited choice of textbooks for professors increase the predictability of content in course offerings. Finally, grade point averages and credit hours completed are calculated— and efficient—ways to judge student accomplishments.

goals. Bureaucratization evolved as the most efficient way of producing products economically for mass markets (Ritzer 2015).

An example of a bureaucratic organization can be found in the fast-food empires and chain "box" stores spreading all around the world. The Sociology Around the World feature above describes the trend toward the "McDonaldization" of society—sociologist George Ritzer's pop culture term for rationalization in organizations.

THINKING SOCIOLOGICALLY

To what extent do you think your college is McDonaldized? Is this a problem? If so, what can you and your fellow students do to address the problem of the McDonaldization of higher education? If no, should McDonaldization of higher education be expanded? Explain.

Formal Organizations and Modern Life

Think about the many organizations that regularly affect your life: the legal system that passes laws, your college, your workplace, and voluntary organizations to which you belong. Human interactions take place in formal organizations, and formal organizations require human interaction to meet their organizational needs. Some organizations, such as the local chapter of the Rotary Club or troop of the Girl Scouts, function at the micro level. Everyone is in a face-to-face relationship with every other member of the organization. However, those local groups are part of a nationwide meso-level organization. At the macro level, the federal government in the United States is a complex formal organization that influences the lives of every citizen and organization in the nation. Meanwhile, multinational corporations and entities like the United Nations are global in their reach.

▲ The Mall of America near Minneapolis is the largest mall in North America, with 4.3 miles of storefront footage, 520-plus stores on five stories, 4.2 million total square feet, and 25 amusement park rides. Yet many of the stores look like clones of one another, and this cathedral to consumerism can feel like an experience in the McDonaldization of society.

Some organizations provide us with work necessary for survival. Others are forced on us—prisons, psychiatric hospitals, military draft systems, and even education up until a certain age. Still others are organizations we believe in and voluntarily join—scouts, environmental groups, sports leagues, and religious organizations. Residents of the United States tend to join voluntary organizations at higher rates than people in many other countries, with 68 million volunteering in 2017 (Charities Aid Foundation 2012; Statista 2017).

Characteristics of Bureaucracy

If you have been to a Caribbean, African, Asian, or Middle Eastern market, you know that the bartering system is used to settle on a mutually agreeable price for goods. This system requires personal encounters and involves intense interaction between the seller and the buyer, but it also takes more time and is less efficient

than the buying process to which shoppers from North America are accustomed. Bartering can be frustrating to the uninitiated visitor used to the relative efficiency and predictability of bureaucracy: going to a store, selecting a product, and paying a set price. As societies become more complex, they tend to adopt bureaucratic forms of organization.

At the beginning of the 20th century, Max Weber (1864–1920) looked for the reasons behind the transition from traditional society to bureaucratic, capitalist society. He wanted to understand why bureaucracy came to dominate the forms of organization in some countries more rapidly than in others. Weber found that bureaucracies arose first in more democratic nations with capitalist, industrial economic systems. As these countries established systems of government and economics whereby positions were granted based on merit, rather than tradition, their economies could grow much faster. This growth, in turn, required more efficient and rational means of organization—bureaucratization (Weber 1947).

Weber's concept of the *ideal-type bureaucracy* refers to the dominant and essential characteristics of organizations designed for reliability and efficiency (Weber 1947). The term simply describes an organization with a particular set of traits, not necessarily a good or perfect organization. Any particular bureaucracy is unlikely to have all of the characteristics of the ideal type, but the degree of bureaucratization is measured by how closely an organization resembles the core characteristics of the ideal type. The following shows Weber's ideal-type bureaucracy with examples related to schools today:

1. *Division of labor based on technical competence.* Administrators lead but do not teach, and instructors teach only in areas of their certification; staff are assigned positions for which their credentials make them most qualified, and recruitment and promotion are governed by formal policies.

2. *Administrative hierarchy.* There are a specified chain of command and designated channels of communication, from school board to superintendent to principal to teacher.

3. *Formal rules and regulations.* Written procedures and rules—perhaps published in an administrative manual—spell out system-wide requirements, including discipline practices, testing procedures,

curricula, sick days for teachers, penalties for student tardiness, field trip policies, and other matters.

4. *Impersonal relationships.* Formal relationships tend to prevail between teachers and students and between teachers and administrative staff (superintendents, principals, and counselors); written records and formal communication provide a paper trail for all decisions.

5. *Emphasis on rationality and efficiency to reach goals.* Established processes are used, based on the best interests of the school. Efficiency is defined in terms of the lowest overall cost to the organization in reaching a goal, not in terms of personal consequences.

Although the list of characteristics makes bureaucracies sound formal and rigid, informal structures allow organizational members to deviate from rules both to meet the goals of the organization more efficiently and to humanize an otherwise uncaring and sterile workplace. The *informal structure* includes the unwritten norms and the interpersonal networks people use within an organization to carry out roles. Likewise, although bylaws, constitutions, or contracts spell out the way things are supposed to be done, people often develop unwritten shortcuts to accomplish goals. For example, the U.S. Postal Service has rules specifying that letter carriers are not supposed to walk across people's lawns, yet if they did not find shortcuts, it would take much longer for mail to be delivered.

Informal norms are not always compatible with those of the formal organization. For example, what if the norm in your work group at your organization or in your class is to do the least amount of work possible? Have you ever been pressured *not* to work hard by your coworkers or fellow students? Consider the following example from a famous classical study. In the Western Electric plant near Chicago, the researchers found that new workers were quickly socialized to do "a fair day's work" and those who did more or less than the established norm— what the work group thought was fair—were considered "rate busters" or "chiselers" and experienced pressure from the group to conform. These informal norms help give workers a degree of power but make the formal goals of the organization harder to achieve (Roethlisberger and Dickson 1939). They also indicate a lack of clear communication or enforcement of the rules of the bureaucratic system.

THINKING SOCIOLOGICALLY

How closely does each of Weber's characteristics of ideal-type bureaucracy describe your college or work setting? Is your college highly bureaucratized, with many rules and regulations? Are decisions based on efficiency and cost-effectiveness, educational quality, or both? To what extent is your work setting characterized by hierarchy and formal rules governing your work time? To what extent is it shaped by informal relationships?

Issues in Bureaucracies

Despite the fact that some informal norms and red tape can hamper bureaucratic efficiency, bureaucracies are likely here to stay. They are the most efficient form of modern organization yet devised. Nonetheless, several individual and organizational problems created by bureaucratic structures are important to understand. These deficiencies arise from our roles in organizations or our interactions with organizations. Consider several examples of problems that can arise in bureaucracies: decreased levels of professionalism in bureaucracies, alienation, oligarchy, and goal displacement.

Bureaucracy, some argue, can be the number one enemy of *professionalism*, referring to those who usually work independently or autonomously. Bureaucracy reduces the individual professional's autonomy. First, bureaucrats assume that authority rests in the person who holds an organizational status or title in the hierarchy rather than the person with the most expertise. Second, bureaucrats tend to reward people with external rewards, such as bonuses, rather than internal motivations, such as greater freedom in how they do their work. Third, bureaucrats focus on the needs of the organization as primary rather than on the needs of the client or professional. For example, a scientist hired by a tobacco company faced a dilemma when his research findings did not support the company position that nicotine is not addictive. They wanted him to falsify his research, a violation of professional ethics. The potential clash between professionals and bureaucracy raises key concerns as universities, hospitals, and other large organizations are governed increasingly by bureaucratic principles (K. Roberts and Donahue 2000).

Alienation, feeling uninvolved, uncommitted, unappreciated, and unconnected to the group or society, occurs when workers are assigned routine, boring tasks or dead-end jobs with no possibility of advancement. Marx believed that alienation is a structural feature of capitalism, with serious consequences: Workers lose their sense of purpose and become dehumanized and objectified in their work, creating a product that they often do not see completed and for which they do not get the profits (Marx [1844] 1964). Workers who see possibilities for advancement put more energy into the organization, but those stuck in their positions are less involved and put more energy into activities outside the workplace (Kanter 1977).

THINKING SOCIOLOGICALLY

Why might giving workers increased autonomy, more participation in decision-making, and stockholder shares in the company enhance commitment and productivity in your place of work? What might be some risks or downsides to such worker input and freedom?

Oligarchy, the concentration of power in the hands of a small group, is a common occurrence in bureaucratic organizations. In the early 1900s, Robert Michels, a French sociologist, wrote about the *iron law of oligarchy*, the idea that power becomes concentrated in the hands of a small group of leaders in political, business, voluntary, or other organizations. Initially, organizational needs, more than the motivation for power, cause these few stable leaders to emerge. As organizations grow, however, a division of labor emerges so that only a few leaders have access to information, resources, and the overall picture. This, in turn, causes leaders who enjoy their elite positions of power to become entrenched (Michels [1911] 1967).

Goal displacement occurs when the original motives or goals of the organization are displaced by new, secondary goals. Organizations are formed to meet specific goals. For example, religious organizations are established to worship a deity and serve humanity on behalf of that deity, schools are founded to educate children, and social work agencies are organized to serve needy citizens. Yet over time, the original goals may not be met or become less important as other motivations and interests emerge. These organizations can sometimes become focused on the benefits they can bring to patrons or employees, rather than on fulfilling the goals for which they were established (Merton 1938; Whyte 1956). For example, in 2015, many high-ranking members of the Federation Internationale de Football Association (FIFA), international soccer's governing body, were charged with using the organization to enrich themselves through bribery, racketeering, fraud, and money laundering (Florio 2018; M. Miller, 2015; Sweeney 2016).

© Reuters/Desmond Boylan

© Reuters/Sara Farid

▲ Women in many countries tend to have low-paid, dead-end jobs that result in alienation. Most, however, need the work to support themselves and their families, such as the women in these photos.

THINKING SOCIOLOGICALLY

In what areas of your college or workplace do you see goal displacement? In other words, where do you see decisions being driven by goals other than the original purpose of the group or organization?

Diversity and Equity in Organizations. In a global and diverse society, it makes sense to have a diverse workforce. The interaction of people who see things differently because of religious beliefs, ethnic backgrounds, countries of origin, and gender experiences increases productivity and creativity in many organizations. Having a wide range of perspectives can lead to better problem-solving (Florida 2004). Successful business owners, government offices, and the military feel they need to have a diverse group of employees to thrive (CNN Wire 2017). That is also one reason why colleges promote diversity on campus. The U.S. Supreme Court has held several hearings on affirmative action admissions programs in higher education, programs meant to promote diversity on campuses and prepare a diverse workforce by actively seeking qualified underrepresented minority students for admission. However, groups affected by diversifying colleges have filed legal challenges, arguing that special consideration amounts to discrimination against their more-qualified applicants, as measured by grades and test scores. The Supreme Court has upheld race-conscious admissions, but by a very slim margin. The president and his administration could weigh in on the issue as well. In other words, the issue is still contentious and unsettled (Thomason 2017).

Big business also has weighed in on affirmative action in college admissions. In 2012, fifty large corporations, including Walmart, Pfizer, Halliburton, and American Express, joined together to write a brief in support of affirmative action programs in higher education. More recently, Apple, Microsoft, Procter and Gamble, and other Fortune 500 companies repeated the plea (Parloff 2015). Although these corporations gave most of their political donations to Republicans, they supported the Obama administration's arguments in favor of affirmative action, because they know a diverse workforce is good for business (M. Wilson 2012).

Despite efforts to diversify the workplace, women and other minorities in bureaucracies are underrepresented in upper-management positions. For example, "the proportion of managers at U.S. commercial banks who were Hispanic rose from 4.7% in 2003 to [just] 5.7% in 2014, white women's representation dropped from 39% to 35%, and black men's from 2.5% to 2.3%" (Dobbin and Kalev 2016).

National and Global Networks: The Macro Level

Understanding people unlike us, networking with people from different cultures, and being open to new ideas have become core competencies in our globalizing social world. Increasingly, colleges require study-abroad programs, and corporations seek multilingual employees with cultural competence in diverse settings. One young college graduate with a sociology degree found that she could use her sociology skills in leading groups of college-age students in international travel experiences. She explains this use of sociology in the next Sociologists in Action.

With modern communication and transportation systems and the ability to transfer ideas and money with a touch of the keyboard, global networks are superseding national boundaries. Some businesses are global and can easily move their physical headquarters from one nation to another (Ritzer 2015). This has helped many companies avoid paying millions of dollars in taxes. Apple, a multinational company, managed to reduce its taxes by billions of dollars through "routing profits through Irish subsidiaries and the Netherlands and then to the Caribbean" (Duhigg and Kocieniewski 2013). This practice is now common in that many corporations can move freely from nation to nation, in search of the largest profit possible.

Profit, efficiency, and calculability are highly prized in multinational corporations. However, as these Western notions of public life are exported to other countries, a severe backlash has occurred in some nations. In many Middle Eastern Islamic countries, for example, these values clash with Muslim loyalties and priorities. The result has been high levels of anger at the United States and Western Europe. Many scholars believe that Middle Eastern anger at the United States is based not just on opposition to freedom and democracy but also on what some Middle Easterners see as the crass greed and impersonal organizational structures being imported into their micro-, meso-, and macro-level worlds. They feel that their very culture is threatened (Ritzer 2015).

Radical fundamentalist movements—groups fueled by religious beliefs and socioeconomic stressors and that view the world in absolutes—are mostly antimodernization movements turned militant (Antoun 2008). They have emerged in Christian, Jewish, Islamic, Sikh, and other groups, largely as a response to perceived threats to their ways of life (Singer 2018). Some aspects of global terrorism and international conflict are a response to the way the Western world organizes its social life and exports it to other parts of the world. These conflicts, in turn, have resulted in the mobilization of the armed forces in the United States and other countries. A consequence is that members of your own family might be serving abroad even as you read these pages.

THINKING SOCIOLOGICALLY

How has global interaction been transformed during your lifetime through Internet technology? Give an example of how you can learn about what is happening in, say, Syria right now by using the Internet. Does this make you feel more connected to people there? Why or why not?

USING SOCIOLOGY IN INTERNATIONAL TRAVEL AND INTERCULTURAL EDUCATION

After graduating from college with a bachelor's degree in sociology, I left the country to backpack through Mexico and Central America. Eventually, I found a job leading groups of teenagers on alternative-education trips abroad. What struck me on meeting my first group was that I had very few students who initially understood the sociological perspective that I took for granted and that was so helpful in dealing with others. At times, my students would make fun of the way things were done in other countries, calling them "weird" or "stupid." They would mock the local traditions, until we discussed comparable traditions in U.S. culture. These students were not mean or unintelligent. In fact, they loved the places we were seeing and the people we were meeting. They just thought everything was new, strange, and often weird. They had been socialized to understand their own society's ways as "right" and "normal." They were fully absorbed in the U.S. society, and they had never questioned it before.

It was rewarding to apply concepts from my textbooks in the real world. My co-leaders and I learned to have fun while encouraging our students to become more socially conscious and analytical about their travel experience. They had to learn to understand "odd" gestures, like pointing with the lips or side-to-side nodding. We would use these experiences to discuss nonverbal communication and gestures that we take for granted in U.S. culture.

We would encourage our novice travelers to interact with the people around them, which helped them understand the struggles facing immigrants and non–English speakers in the United States. We would force them to have conversations while standing toe-to-toe with each other, and they would finish with backaches from leaning away from one another. We would not allow them to explain their behavior with "because it's creepy to stand so close together," even though this was the consensus. "Why do you feel uncomfortable?" we would ask. "Why is this weird?" The answer has to do with social constructions of what is "normal" in any society.

Of course, while traveling internationally, one is surrounded by various other sociological issues, such as different racial or ethnic conflicts, gender roles, or class hierarchies, and learning about these issues was a part of our program as well. Without realizing it, many group conversations and meetings began to remind me of some of my favorite undergraduate sociology classes. "Study sociology!" I would say. Traveling abroad on my own and leading programs overseas were extremely fascinating experiences, and it was incredibly rewarding to be able to use my sociology degree every day on my job.

★ ★ ★ ★ ★ ★ ★

Elise Roberts graduated from Macalester College with a major in sociology. After leading these tours, she earned a master's degree in international social work from Colombia University and is now the executive director of Witness for Peace.

Our networks play a major role in setting norms and controlling our behaviors, usually resulting in our conformity to the social expectations of those in our network. This, of course, contributes to the stability of the entire social system because deviation can threaten the existence of "normal" patterns, as we see in the next chapter.

Each of us has a network of people and groups that surround us. The scope of our networks has broadened with the increased complexity of societies and includes the global social world. Indeed, it is sometimes hard to recognize how far our networks reach. Although some of our social experiences are informal (unstructured), we are also profoundly affected by another phenomenon of the past 3 centuries—highly structured bureaucracies. As a result of both, our experiences and personal lives are far more extensively linked to meso- and macro-level events and to people and places on the other side of the globe than were those of our parents. If we hope to understand our lives, we must understand this broad context. Although it may have been possible to live without global connections and bureaucratic systems several centuries ago, these networks are intricately woven into our lifestyles and our economic systems today. The question is whether we will control these networks or they will control us.

KEY POINTS

- People in the modern world are connected through one acquaintance to another in a chain of links, referred to as networks, that can now span the globe.

- We interpret interpersonal interactions at the micro level through unspoken assumptions based on the social context, nonverbal communication, and the physical space between people.

- Many of our behaviors are shaped by the statuses (social positions) we hold and the roles (expectations associated with a status) we play. However, our multiple-status occupancy can create role conflicts (between the roles of two statuses) and role strains (among the role expectations of a single status).

- When the norms of behavior are unclear, we may experience anomie (normlessness), and when anomie spreads in a society, suicide rates rise.

- Various types of groups affect our behavior—from primary and secondary groups to peer groups and reference groups.

- At the meso and macro levels, formal organizations in the contemporary modern world are bureaucratized. Bureaucratic organizations are ruled by rational calculation of the organization's goals rather than by tradition or emotional ties, tend to expand, are governed by impersonal formal rules, and stress efficiency and rational decision-making.

- Bureaucracies often create particular issues that may make them inefficient or destructive, such as alienation, oligarchies, and goal displacement.

- In a global and diverse society, it makes sense to have a diverse workforce. Discrimination against minorities in promotion and hiring is irrational and dysfunctional for organizations.

- Some scholars think that this impersonal mode of organizing social life—so common in the West for several centuries now—is a critical factor in anti-American and anti-Western resistance movements.

DISCUSSION QUESTIONS

1. Think about your social network. How useful might it be in helping you get a job (or a better job) once you graduate from college? Why?

2. Have you ever experienced role strain because of your status as a student? Explain why or why not. If so, how did/do you cope with it?

3. Most college students, particularly those with family, work, and/or sports team obligations, deal with role conflict. Describe a time when you dealt with a conflict between the roles you carry out. What did you do about it? How might colleges and universities diminish role conflict among students?

4. To what primary and secondary groups do you belong? How does your involvement (or lack thereof) in primary groups on your campus impact your feelings of attachment to your school?

5. Would you rather live in a bureaucratic society or in a society without bureaucratic forms of organizations? Why?

6. How does the informal structure at your college or university impact how the school functions? Does it do more to help or hurt students? Why?

achieved status   127

anomie   130

ascribed status   127

bureaucracies   133

formal organizations   133

groups   129

in-group   132

master status   128

out-group   132

primary groups   131

rationalization   133

reference groups   132

role conflict   129

role strain   129

roles   128

secondary groups   131

social interaction   122

social networks   121

status   127

CONTRIBUTING TO OUR SOCIAL WORLD: WHAT CAN WE DO?

At the Local (Micro) Level

- *Tutoring and mentoring* programs help students struggling with their studies. Contact your school's student affairs or tutoring office and arrange to observe and/or volunteer in a program. Helping students build *social capital*, which includes knowing people who can help them to obtain the help they need, can increase their chances of success.

- *Workers' centers* for employed people not represented by unions have developed in many metropolitan areas, often with the aid of local clergy. Workers' centers help these workers to organize and develop the social capital to obtain better wages, benefits, and workplace dignity. For a list of workers' centers, go to www.iwj.org/worker-center-network/ locations.

At the Organizational or Institutional (Meso) Level

- Social capital theory can also be applied to meso-level *community organizations* that work to build power and implement social change, such as *IAF* (*the Industrial Areas Foundation*) (www.industrialareasfoundation.org), *Gamaliel* (www.gamaliel.org), and the *Freelancers Union* (www.freelancersunion.org). Find a group affiliated with one of these organizations near you.

- *Unions* also develop social capital for their members. Although far fewer U.S. citizens are unionized today than in past decades, membership in a union can improve the economic prospects of workers. For some workers, this can make the difference between living in poverty and obtaining a living wage. With 2 million members, the *Service Employees International Union* (*SEIU*) is the fastest growing union in North America. Internships with unions like SEIU are a great way to learn about organizing and social capital. You can find information about internships on the SEIU website (www.seiu.org).

- *The Anti-Defamation League* (www.adl.org), *the American-Arab Anti-Discrimination Committee* (www.adc.org), and *the National Association for the Advancement of Colored People* (www.naacp.org) are examples of organizations that defend the rights of minority groups. These organizations often use volunteers or interns and can provide you with the opportunity to learn about the extent to which social contacts and networks play a role in managing social conflict.

At the National or Global (Macro) Level

- Well-run *microfinance organizations* can help poor people, particularly women, gain social capital and economic independence. Three well-known and respected groups are *CRS* (*Catholic Relief Services*) (www.crs.org), *FINCA* (www.finca.org), and *Kiva* (www.kiva.org). Check out their websites to learn how you can support their efforts.

⑤SAGE edge™

Get the tools you need to sharpen your study skills. SAGE edge offers a robust online environment featuring an impressive array of free tools and resources.

Access practice quizzes, eFlashcards, video, and multimedia at **edge.sagepub.com/ballantine7e**

CHAPTER 6

© REUTERS/Gonzalo Fuente

DEVIANCE AND SOCIAL CONTROL

Sickos, Weirdos, Freaks, and Folks Like Us

▲ We often think of deviants as bad people who do not care about rules or other members of society; we contrast them to people like us. Sometimes, though, people need to commit deviant acts to change unjust social structures and to topple tyrants. Further, enforcement of conformity is often experienced as authoritarian.

MICRO

ME (MY FAMILY AND CLOSE FRIENDS)

LOCAL ORGANIZATIONS AND COMMUNITY
People violate local ordinances and commit thefts.

MESO

NATIONAL ORGANIZATIONS, INSTITUTIONS, AND ETHNIC SUBCULTURES
People violate state laws, and they commit crimes using corporations.

MACRO

SOCIETY
People commit federal crimes; the national government itself may commit crimes such as torture.

GLOBAL COMMUNITY
Crimes may result in global environmental destruction or violations of human rights across national boundaries.

WHAT WILL YOU LEARN IN THIS CHAPTER?

This chapter will help you to do the following:

6.1 Describe who is deviant and why

6.2 Compare key ideas in the differential association, labeling, rational choice, structural-functional, and conflict perspectives of deviance

6.3 Provide possible explanations for why the crime rate has fallen in recent years

6.4 Describe types of organized crime and crime by organizations prevalent today

6.5 Give examples of crimes committed at the national and global level today

6.6 Explain which theoretical perspective would be most useful in explaining the function of prisons in U.S. society today

THINK ABOUT IT

Micro: Small groups and local communities	Are you deviant? Who says so? Why do some people in your community become deviant whereas others do not?
Meso: National institutions, complex organizations, and ethnic groups	What are the consequences of organized crime or occupational crime for large bureaucratic organizations?
Macro: National and global systems	What are the costs—and the benefits—of deviance for a nation? How can a global perspective on crime enhance our understanding of international and national criminal activities?

Wafa did not stand out from the girls around her as she grew up, but she was destined to make world headlines—as the first female suicide bomber in the Palestinian-Israeli conflict. She was the age of most university students reading this book, but she never had an opportunity to attend college. Her task was to smuggle explosives across the Israeli border for the intended bomber, her brother. Instead, on January 27, 2002, she chose to blow up herself and an Israeli soldier. She was declared a martyr, a *sahida*, by the al-Aqsa Martyrs Brigade, and the organization took credit for the attack. The group's political leadership gave approval of her act, opening the way for other women to follow. Since Wafa's death, over 67 other Palestinian women have been suicide bombers, and more than 100 have been captured by Israelis in failed bombing attempts (Cashman 2017; Turner 2015). Why did this happen? Women are not supposed to blow themselves up but instead to stay home and give birth. What motivated Wafa to commit suicide and take another life in the process? Was she driven by ideology to participate in the Palestinian-Israeli struggle? Did social and structural factors affect her decision? Most important, was she deviant in carrying out this act, and according to whom?

Wafa Idris grew up in Palestine. She was married at a young age but did not produce children. As a result, her husband divorced her and remarried. She had no future, for who would want a barren, divorced woman in a society that values women for their purity and their childbearing ability? She was a burden to her family. Her way out of an impossible and desperate situation was to commit suicide, bringing honor and wealth to her family and redeeming herself in the process. Other women who followed Wafa have similar stories: Most shared an inability to control their own lives in the patriarchal (male-controlled) society (Gonzalez-Perez 2011; Handwerk 2004; Sawicki 2016; Victor 2003).

Our question is this: Are such women deviant criminal terrorists, hapless victims of terrorist groups, mentally ill "crazies," invisible victims in a patriarchal society, or martyrs who should be honored for their acts? Who says so? Each of these views is held by someone interested in this situation. From this opening example, we can begin to see several complications that arise when defining deviance and deviants. In this chapter, we consider who is deviant, under what circumstances, and in whose eyes.

First, we discuss **deviance**—*the violation of social norms*—and the social control mechanisms that keep most people from becoming deviant. Occasionally, most of us violate a norm, and depending on its importance and on the severity of the violation, we may be seen as deviant. Wearing strange clothes may be seen as amusing and nonconformist once in a while, but you will be labeled deviant if you do so regularly. If enough people start wearing similar clothes, however, this once deviant act will no longer be deviant. Getting a tattoo or wearing torn, skin-tight jeans to school are good examples of once-deviant acts now considered normal behavior in many communities. We also examine **crime** in this chapter, *deviant actions for which there are formal penalties imposed by the government, such as fines, jail, or prison sentences.*

You may be surprised to learn that we are all deviant at some times and in some places, and almost all of us have committed crimes. The self-test in the next Engaging Sociology illustrates this point.

What Is Deviance?

Whereas some acts, such as murder, assault, robbery, and rape, are considered deviant in almost every time and place, some deviant acts may be overlooked or even viewed as understandable under certain circumstances,

WHO IS DEVIANT?

Please jot down your answers to the following self-test questions. There is no need to share your responses with others.

Have you ever engaged in any of the following acts?

1. Stolen anything, even if its value was under $10
2. Used an illegal drug
3. Misused a prescription drug
4. Used tobacco prior to age 18
5. Drank alcohol prior to age 21
6. Engaged in a fistfight
7. Carried a concealed knife or gun
8. Used a car without the owner's permission
9. Driven a car after drinking alcohol
10. Downloaded a movie without paying for it
11. Offered sex for money
12. Damaged property worth more than $10
13. Skipped school
14. Arrived home after your curfew
15. Accepted or transported property that you had reason to believe might be stolen
16. Taken a towel from a hotel room after renting the room for a night

All of these are delinquent acts (violations of legal standards), and most young people are guilty of at least one infraction. However, few teenagers are given the label of *delinquent*. If you answered yes to any of the preceding questions, you committed a crime in many states. Your penalty or sanction for the infraction could range from a stiff fine to several years in prison—*if* you got caught!

Engaging Sociology

1. Do you think of yourself as being deviant? Why or why not?
2. Are deviants only those who get caught? For instance, if someone steals your backpack but avoids being caught, is he or she a deviant?
3. Who is considered deviant—and by whom?

---

such as when a family steals water and diapers from a destroyed supermarket after a natural disaster.

Some acts of deviance are considered serious offenses in one society but tolerated in another. Examples include prostitution, premarital or extramarital sex, gambling, corruption, and bribery. Even within a single society, different groups may define deviance and conformity differently. The state government may officially define alcohol consumption by 19-year-olds as deviant, but on a Saturday night at a fraternity party, the 19-year-old "brother" who does *not* drink may be viewed as deviant by his peers. What do these cases tell us about deviance?

Deviance is socially constructed and dependent on the time and social context. Members of groups in societies define (construct) what is deviant. As we noted earlier, these socially constructed definitions of deviance can change over *time* and depend on the social situation or *context* in which the behavior occurs.

If we take the same behavior and place it in a different social context, perceptions of whether the behavior is deviant may well change. For example, in Greece,

Spain, and other Mediterranean countries, the clothing norms on beaches are very different from those in most of North America. Topless sunbathing by women is not at all uncommon, even on beaches designated as family beaches. The norms vary, however, even within a few feet of the beach. Women will sunbathe topless, lying only

▲ Dressing as a medieval knight would typically be considered deviant behavior, but when the setting is Renaissance Fair it is socially acceptable and even expected.

10 feet from the boardwalk where concessionaires sell beverages, snacks, and tourist items. If these women become thirsty, they cover up, walk the 10 feet to purchase a cola, and return to their beach blankets, where they again remove their tops. To walk onto the boardwalk topless would be considered highly deviant.

THINKING SOCIOLOGICALLY

Have you ever dressed or styled your hair in a deviant way? Why? Did you have any role models to guide you on how to do so? If so, does this mean you really were *not* being deviant? Why or why not? Who determines whether your clothes or hairstyle are deviant?

An individual's status or group may be defined as deviant. Some individuals have a higher likelihood of being labeled deviant because of the group into which they were born, such as a particular ethnic group, or because of a distinguishing mark or characteristic, such as a facial anomaly. Others may escape being considered deviant because of their dominant status in society. The higher one's status, the less likely that one will be suspected of violating norms and the less likely that any violations will be characterized as criminal. Who would suspect that a respectable, white-collar husband and father is embezzling funds from his company?

The looting following Hurricane Katrina was addressed differently depending on whether it was done by White or Black Americans (Huddy and Feldman 2006; Thompson 2009). The media showed photos of

© istock/muldoon

▲ Deviance is socially constructed. Is this man deviant by virtue of his appearance? Why or why not? For a photo essay and further thinking about deviance as social construction, visit edge.sagepub.com/ballantine7e.

Black "looters" who "stole food," but the same media described Whites who "broke into grocery stores" in search of food as "resourceful." Likewise, gays and lesbians are often said to be deviant and accused of flaunting their sexuality. Heterosexuals are rarely accused of "flaunting" their sexuality, regardless of how overtly flirtatious or underdressed they may be. So, one's group membership or ascribed traits may make a difference in whether one is defined as deviant.

Deviance can be functional for society. As structural-functionalists point out, deviance serves vital functions by setting examples of unacceptable behavior, providing guidelines for behavior necessary to maintain social order, and bonding people through their common rejection of the deviant behavior. Deviance is also functional because it provides jobs for those who deal with deviants—police, judges, social workers, and so forth (Gans 2007). Furthermore, deviance can signal problems in society that need to be addressed and can therefore stimulate positive change.

Sometimes deviant individuals break the model of conventional thinking, thereby opening society to new and creative paths of thinking. Scientists, inventors, activists, and artists have often been rejected in their time but have been honored later for accomplishments that positively affected society. Famous artist Vincent van Gogh, for example, lived in poverty and suffered from schizophrenia. During his life, his artistic gifts were overlooked, but he became recognized as a renowned painter after his death. His paintings now sell for millions of dollars. Likewise, Nelson Mandela, Martin Luther King Jr., and Mahatma Gandhi were once considered deviant and dangerous, but today they are regarded as social justice heroes.

THINKING SOCIOLOGICALLY

Think of examples in your life that illustrate the *relative nature of deviance*. For instance, which of your behaviors are deviant in one setting but not in another, or were deviant when you were younger but not deviant now?

Crime: Deviance That Violates the Law

Governments create laws and impose formal sanctions—punishments—for some acts of deviance, and the social disapproval associated with being convicted of these violations results in the perpetrator being identified as "criminal." *When members of society are in general agreement about the seriousness of certain crimes*, these acts are referred to as **consensus crimes** (Brym and Lie 2007; Goodman and Brenner 2002; Hagan and Rymond-Richmond 2009). *Predatory crimes* (crimes—usually violent—against humans, such as premeditated murder, forcible rape, and kidnapping for ransom) are consensus crimes in most nations and are described later in this chapter.

Just as what is considered deviant varies over time and place, so does what is regarded as criminal behavior. For example, at the end of the 1920s, 42 of the 48 U.S. states had laws forbidding interracial marriage (see Figure 6.1). Legislatures in half of these states removed those restrictions by the 1960s, but 16 states still had antimiscegenation laws on the books until 1967 when the U.S. Supreme Court ruling in *Loving v. Virginia* made these laws unconstitutional. Today, this legal ban on interracial marriage has been eliminated completely, illustrating that most laws change to reflect the times and sentiments of the majority of people. The *Obergefell v. Hodges* U.S. Supreme Court

▲ Until recently, this same-sex couple would have been considered deviant in the United States. Today, the United States and Canada both recognize same-sex marriages.

ruling in 2015 that legalized same-sex marriages throughout the nation provides a more recent example of how laws and attitudes can change dramatically over time (Liptak 2015).

▼ FIGURE 6.1

Historical Restrictions on Interracial Marriage in the United States

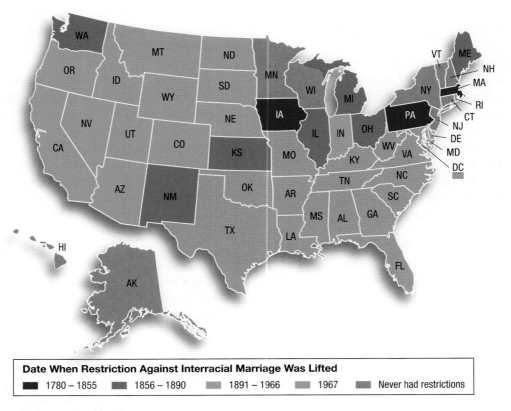

Date When Restriction Against Interracial Marriage Was Lifted

■ 1780 – 1855   ■ 1856 – 1890   ■ 1891 – 1966   ■ 1967   ■ Never had restrictions

Source: Wallenstein (2002). Map by Anna Versluis.

We now look at theoretical perspectives that help explain deviance, how some deviant acts become crimes, and what policies might control or reduce crime.

What Causes Deviant Behavior? Theoretical Perspectives

Helena is a delinquent. Her father deserted the family when Helena was 10, and before that, he had abused Helena and her mother. Her mother has all she can cope with; she is just trying to survive financially and keep her three children in line. Helena gets little attention and little support or encouragement in her school activities. Her grades have fallen steadily. As a young teen, she sought attention from boys, and in the process, she became pregnant. Now, the only kids who have anything to do with her are others who have been in trouble; her friends are other young people who have also been labeled delinquent. Helena's schoolmates, teachers, and mother see her as a delinquent troublemaker, and it would be hard for Helena to change their views and her status.

How did this happen? Helena's situation is, of course, only one unique case. Sociologists cannot generalize from Helena to other cases, but they do know from their studies that there are thousands of teens with similar problems. Next we consider some theories of deviance that help us recognize and explain patterns among delinquent teens like Helena.

Throughout history, people have proposed explanations for why some members of society "turn bad"—from biological explanations of imbalances in hormones and claims of innate personality defects to social conditions within individual families or in the larger social structure. Biological and psychological approaches focus on personality disorders or abnormalities in the body or psyche of individuals, but they generally do not consider the social context in which deviance occurs.

Sociologists place emphasis on understanding the interactions, social structure, and social processes that lead to deviant behavior, rather than on individual characteristics. They consider the socialization process and interpersonal relationships, group and social class differences, cultural and subcultural norms, and power structures that influence individuals to conform to or deviate from societal expectations. Theoretical explanations about why people are deviant influence social policy decisions and strategies to curb deviant behavior and deal with deviants.

Some theories explain particular types of crime better than others (say, theft as opposed to sexual assault), just as some illuminate micro-, meso-, or macro-level processes better than others. Taken together these theories help us understand a wide range of deviant and criminal behaviors.

Micro-Level Explanations of Deviance

No one is born deviant. Why do some people learn to become deviant and others learn to follow the norms of society? Symbolic interaction and rational choice theories focus primarily on micro-level answers to this question.

Symbolic Interaction Approaches to Deviance: Differential Association. Symbolic interactionists focus on how our interactions with others influence whether we commit deviant acts. One interactionist approach, differential association theory, describes how people learn to commit delinquent acts through their social relationships with peers and family members.

Differential association theory *focuses on the process of learning deviant behavior from those with whom we interact (e.g., family, peers, fellow employees)* (Hagan 2016; Sutherland, Cressey, and Luckenbil 1992). Helena, for example, is surrounded by people who make dropping out of school and other delinquent acts seem normal. If her close friends and siblings were also sexually active as teens, her teen pregnancy might not be remarkable and might even be a source of some prestige with her group of peers.

According to differential association theory, the possibility of becoming deviant depends on four factors related to associating with a deviant group: the *duration* of time spent with the group, the *intensity* of interaction, the *frequency* of interaction, and the *priority* of the group in one's friendship network (Sutherland et al. 1992). If people have regular and frequent exposure to deviance among their longtime, close friends, they are likely to learn to behave in deviant ways.

Some theorists contend that life in poverty often involves immersion in a distinctive subculture in which poor people learn delinquent behavior patterns through socialization. The values, beliefs, norms, and practices that have evolved in poor communities over time can often encourage violation of laws. Just as upper-class youth learn norms that help them to succeed in middle- and upper-class areas of society, lower-class youth may learn other behaviors that help them to survive in their poor neighborhoods. These very same behaviors that help them survive, though, have been defined as delinquent and criminal by

▲ According to differential association theory, people who abuse drugs, like this young woman, tend to learn this behavior through close associations with other illicit drug users. They come to see the drugged state as enjoyable and learn the techniques for using the drugs.

those with privilege (Bettie 2003; Chambliss 1973; Vance 2016).

Following this perspective, J. D. Vance's *Hillbilly Elegy* describes how people in the poor, predominantly White rust belt towns in which he grew up are socialized into a "learned helplessness." They learn to think that other people (especially those in the government) are to blame for their woes and that hard work will not help them escape their poverty. The result is that they focus on immediate gratification (like drinking and opioid abuse) rather than on earning an education and attaining and keeping a job (Vance 2016). Vance's book explains how he escaped this fate, thanks to the influence of his grandparents and to a stint in the Marines during which he became resocialized.

Elijah Anderson's book, *Code of the Street* (2000), on the other hand, describes two types of groups that coexist in poor, inner-city Black neighborhoods: "decent people" and "street people." "Street-oriented people" learn a code of the street that involves hanging out on the street with peers; seeking immediate gratification through sex, violence, and drugs; and adopting a certain look with their clothes and jewelry—an image expected by the group. Peers become more important than society's social control agents. "Decent families" accept mainstream values and often find support systems in church communities or other organizations. To survive in such neighborhoods and avoid violent sanctions from street-oriented peers, however, those from decent families may dress and carry themselves in a way that conforms with the street-oriented image. The result is that other members of society, including the police, view both the street-oriented and those from decent families as deviant (Anderson 2000).

As mentioned, we know that members of all social classes commit crimes, and no socioeconomic class has a monopoly on violence, corruption, or dishonesty. However, *labeling theory* explains why some individuals and groups are more likely to be caught and punished for deviance.

Symbolic Interaction Approaches to Deviance: Labeling. **Labeling theory** *explains how people can be labeled deviant after committing a deviant act, which can then lead them to carry out further acts that reflect that label.* Labels (such as "juvenile delinquent") are symbols that have meanings affecting an individual's self-concept and the way others see the individual.

Labeling theorists define two stages in the process of becoming a deviant. **Primary deviance** is *a violation of a norm that may be an isolated act or an initial act of rule breaking*, such as a young teenager shoplifting something on a dare by friends. Most people commit acts of primary deviance. However, many of us avoid being labeled "deviant" when we commit one of these primary acts. Remember how you marked the deviant behavior test that you took at the beginning of this chapter? If you have engaged in deviant acts, you were probably not labeled deviant for the offense. If you had been so labeled, you might not be in college or taking this class.

If an individual continues to violate a norm and begins to take on a deviant identity as a result of being labeled as deviant, this is referred to as **secondary deviance**. Secondary deviance becomes publicly recognized, and the individual is identified as deviant, beginning a deviant career. If a teenager like Helena is caught and prosecuted for shoplifting, her act becomes known. She may spend time in a juvenile detention center, and parents of other teens may not want their children associating with

▲ Shoplifting, when done by young people without a criminal record, often provides an example of primary deviance.

her. Employers and store managers may refuse to hire her. Soon, there are few opportunities open to her because others expect her to be delinquent. The teen may continue performing the deviant acts and associating with delinquent acquaintances, in part because few other options are available. Society's reaction, then, is what defines a deviant person and may limit options for that person to change the label (Lemert 1951, 1972).

The process of labeling individuals and behaviors takes place at each level of analysis, from individual to society. If community or societal norms and laws define a behavior as deviant, individuals are likely to believe it is deviant. Sanctions against juvenile delinquents can have the effect of reinforcing the deviant behavior by (a) increasing alienation from the social world, (b) forcing increased interaction with deviant peers, and (c) motivating juvenile delinquents to positively value and identify with the deviant status (Conyers and Calhoun 2015; Kaplan and Johnson 1991).

A **self-fulfilling prophecy** occurs when *a belief or a prediction becomes a reality, in part because of the prediction.* A false perception of a person, perhaps based on a stereotype, can become true if it provokes behavior that fulfills that false perception or stereotype. For example, James is 8 years old and already sees himself as a "bad" kid who will end up in prison, just like his father, whom he has never met. His mother tells him he was born bad because he resembles his father, and his teachers and peers tell him he is bad because he struggles in school. In keeping with the idea of a self-fulfilling prophecy, James accepts the label and acts accordingly, refusing to do his homework and stealing other kids' lunch money. Unless someone—such as an insightful teacher—steps in to give him another image of himself, James is likely to end up in prison—not because he was born "bad" but because he was treated by others as if he were bad and learned that image of himself (Merton 1948).

THINKING SOCIOLOGICALLY

What labels do you carry? How do you know you carry these labels? How do they affect your self-concept and behavior?

A major explanation of why certain individuals and groups are labeled deviant has to do with their status and power in society—a concern of conflict theory. Those on the fringes, away from power—the poor, minorities, members of new religious movements, or others who

in some way do not fit into the dominant system—are more likely to be labeled as deviants. On the other hand, because the powerful have the influence to define what is acceptable, they tend to avoid the deviant label. Their behavior, even when it has a negative impact on society, is less likely to be labeled as deviant or criminal.

A study by William J. Chambliss illustrates the process of labeling in communities and groups. Perhaps during your high school years you witnessed situations similar to that described in his study (Chambliss 1973). Chambliss looked at the behavior of two small peer groups of boys and at the reactions of community members to their behavior. The Saints, boys from "good" families, were some of the most delinquent boys at Hannibal High School. Although the Saints were constantly occupied with truancy, drinking, wild driving, petty theft, and vandalism, none was officially arrested for any misdeed during the 2-year study. The Roughnecks, who were from less affluent families, were constantly in trouble with the police and community residents, even though their rate of delinquency was about equal to that of the Saints.

What was the cause of the disparity in the labeling of these two groups? Community members, the police, and teachers alike labeled the boys based on their perceptions of the boys' family backgrounds and social class. The Saints came from stable, White, upper-middle-class families; were active in school affairs; and were precollege students whom everyone expected would become professionals. In fact, the Saints almost all did become professionals, living up to their images in the community. On the other hand, the general community feeling was that the Roughnecks would amount to nothing. They carried around a negative label that was hard to change. Two Roughnecks ended up in prison, two became coaches, and little is known of the others. For a number of these boys, the prophecy became self-fulfilling (Chambliss 1973).

Labels are powerful and can **stigmatize** an individual—*branding the person with a negative mark that discredits a person's claim to a "normal" identity.* This process can be extended to a number of issues, including obesity, as the next Sociology in Our Social World illustrates.

THINKING SOCIOLOGICALLY

On your campus, what physical characteristics can affect people's self-perception or cause them to be labeled as different or even deviant by others?

STIGMATIZING FATNESS

By Leslie Elrod

▲ Obesity in America.

The United States is now the fattest country in the world. "American society has become 'obesogenic,' characterized by environments that promote increased food intake, unhealthy food, and physical inactivity." One in five Hispanic and Black and almost one in seven White children and adolescents are obese (Centers for Disease Control and Prevention [CDC] 2009, 2017c). Approximately one in four adults is obese (Hales, Carroll, Fryar, and Ogden 2017).

The obsession with thinness and body image in U.S. culture can make being overweight particularly painful for many. When a physical attribute is assigned social significance, violators of this norm are likely to endure negative labeling because of perceived physical imperfections. According to Cooley's theory (1902,

[1909] 1983) of *the looking-glass self*, we generally define ourselves based on how we think others perceive us. Obese people in the United States tend to suffer lower self-esteem and have negative self-images, thus creating heightened levels of psychological distress. The obese, labeled as self-indulgent, gluttonous, lazy, sloppy, and selfish, experience social condemnation. Some research shows that even doctors tend not to be as nice to their overweight patients as they are to their thin ones, to whom they give more warmth, increased empathy, and better care (Kolata 2016; Parker-Pope 2013).

Socialized by the media to believe that their physical appearance should be a valuable commodity, obese women tend to experience greater stigmatization than obese men. Such messages come from images in ads, magazines, television programming, and movies as well as merchandizing directed toward females of all ages. These messages portray unrealistic images of women. In fact, as real women grew heavier, models and "beautiful" women were portrayed as increasingly thinner. "In 1965, the average female fashion model weighed about 8% less than the average American women," By the 1990s, that figure had jumped to 23% less (Kilbourne 1999). Failing to meet this standard of beauty not only jeopardizes a woman's happiness but also challenges her femininity.

Although eating disorders have long been associated with upper-class White girls and women, research has found consistent rates of anorexia and bulimia across racial and ethnic groups and greater rates of binge eating among Hispanics, Asians, and Blacks compared to non-Hispanic Whites. Moreover these issues impact boys and men as well as girls and women (Marques et al. 2011). This is a clear indication that more attention must be paid to the dangers of unrealistic body images in the media and the stigmatization of fatness.

★ ★ ★ ★ ★ ★ ★

Leslie Elrod is associate professor of sociology at University of Cincinnati, Blue Ash College. Two of her specialties are sociology of the body and deviance.

Rational Choice Approaches to Deviance. Rational choice theory, as noted in previous chapters, suggests that when individuals make decisions, they calculate the costs and benefits to themselves. They consider the balance between pleasure and pain. Turning to crime is therefore a conscious, rational, and calculated decision made after weighing the costs and benefits of alternatives. Rational choice theorists believe that punishment—imposing high "costs" for criminal behavior, such as fines, imprisonment, or even the death penalty—is the best way to dissuade criminals from choosing the path of crime. When the cost outweighs the potential benefit and opportunities are restricted, it deters people from thinking that crime is a "rational" choice (Earls and Reiss 1994; G. Walters 2015; Winslow and Zhang 2008).

▲ Rational choice theorists would note that this little girl is weighing the costs and benefits of taking cookies, and the benefits are looking pretty sweet!

Positive sanctions reward those behaviors approved by society. This is why schools have honor ceremonies, companies reward their top salespeople, and communities recognize civic leadership with "Citizen of the Year" awards. All these actions enhance the rewards for conventional behavior. Negative sanctions (or punishments) increase the cost to those who deviate from the norm. They range from fines for traffic violations to prison sentences for serious crimes, and even death in many states, for acts considered most dangerous to society.

Applying rational choice theory to crime prevention has led to measures that focus on making it harder and less rewarding to commit crimes. For example, improved lighting, especially at night (making it harder to commit a crime unnoticed), marking goods that may be stolen (for easy tracking and recovery), and creating positive alternatives to crime (such as summer jobs for teens) make crime both harder and less appealing (Clarke 1997; Freilich and Newman 2017).

THINKING SOCIOLOGICALLY

Think of a time when you committed a deviant act or avoided doing so despite a tempting opportunity. What factors influenced whether you conformed to societal norms or committed a deviant act?

Meso- and Macro-Level Explanations of Deviance

Whereas micro-level interactions can lead a person to become and to be labeled as deviant, meso- and macro-level analysis can help us gain a greater understanding of the societal factors leading to deviance. As we have noted, meso-level analysis focuses on ethnic subcultures, organizations, and institutions. Macro-level analysis focuses on national and global social systems.

Structural-functional theories of deviance include (1) *social control theory*, which focuses on the processes a society or group uses to ensure conformity to its norms and expectations; (2) *anomie*, the breakdown of societal norms guiding behavior, which leads to social disorganization; and (3) *strain theory*, which shows that the difference between definitions of success (goals) in a society and the means available to achieve those goals can lead to deviant behavior.

Structural-Functional Approaches to Deviance: Social Control. One of sociology's central concepts is social control—why people obey norms (Hagan 2016). If human beings were truly free to do whatever they wanted, they would likely commit more deviant acts. Yet to live near others and with others requires individuals to control their behaviors based on social norms and sanctions—in short, social control. **Social control theory** examines *the processes a society or group uses to ensure conformity to its norms and expectations.*

The roots of social control theory can be traced back to Émile Durkheim's (1858–1917) work on suicide (Meier 2017). Recall that Durkheim noted that people who have more social attachments are less likely to commit suicide than those who have fewer social connections. Those who are less bonded to society are more likely to commit deviant acts, such as suicide. Travis Hirschi built on Durkheim's work on suicide to develop social control theory.

Control theory contends that people are bonded to others by four powerful factors:

1. *Attachment* to other people who respect the values and rules of the society. Individuals do not want to be rejected by those with whom they are close or by whom they admire.

2. *Commitment* to conventional activities (such as school and jobs) that they do not want to jeopardize.

3. *Involvement* in activities that keep them so busy with conventional roles and expectations that they do not have time for mischief.

4. *Belief* in the social rules of their culture, which they accept because of their childhood socialization and indoctrination into those conventional beliefs.

These factors decrease the likelihood that a person will commit deviant acts (Hirschi [1969] 2002).

In addition to these factors, social control theorists point out that two primary forces shape our tendency to conform. The first is internal controls, those voices within us that tell us when a behavior is acceptable or unacceptable, right or wrong. The second is external controls—society's formal or informal controls against deviant behavior. Informal external controls include smiles, frowns, hugs, and ridicule from family members, friends, and close acquaintances (Gottfredson and Hirschi 1990). Formal external controls come from the legal system through the police, judges, juries, and social workers. Societies can influence both forces through societal institutions (e.g., family, education, government) that teach us the norms of society (which we internalize) and punish those who violate the norms.

Structural-Functional Approaches to Deviance: Anomie.

Sociologists use the term *anomie*, or the state of normlessness that occurs when rules for behavior in society break down under extreme stress from rapid social change or conflict (Merton 1968). Durkheim first described this normlessness as a condition of weak, conflicting, or absent norms and the changes in values that arise when societies are disorganized. As discussed in Chapter 5, this situation is typical in rapidly urbanizing, industrializing societies, at times of sudden prosperity or depression, during rapid technological change, during a war, or when a government is overthrown (or, on television, during a zombie apocalypse).

Imagine you grew up in a small village where your family and all those around you have been farmers for as far back as anyone can remember. You were raised to become one yourself and thought you would raise your children to become farmers, as well. Over the past few years, though, due to climate change, the rains have not come and the fields no longer support crops. You have no choice but to leave everyone and everything you have ever known to try to find work in the nearest city. This may thrust you into a situation where norms of interaction—including mutual support and friendliness—are very different and you might feel like you are in a different country.

Millions of people are now living out similar stories. Villagers in industrializing countries in Africa, Asia, and Latin America find themselves pushed off marginally productive rural lands and pulled into rapidly expanding cities to seek better lives and means for survival. They hope to find good jobs in these urban areas, but when they arrive, they often face disappointment. Poor, unskilled, and homeless, they move into crowded apartments or shantytowns of temporary shacks and try to adjust to the new style of life, which often includes unemployment. Old village norms that have provided the guidelines for proper behavior crumble, sometimes without clear expectations emerging to take their places. The lack of clear norms in the rapidly changing urban environment leads to high levels of social disorganization and deviant behavior.

This general idea of anomie led a group of Chicago sociologists to study the social conditions of that city that correlate with deviance. The Chicago School, as the research team is known, linked life in transitional slum areas to the high incidence of crime. Certain neighborhoods or zones in the Chicago area—generally inner-city transitional zones with recent settlers—have always had high delinquency rates, regardless of the group that occupied the area. Low economic status, ethnic heterogeneity, residential mobility, family disruption, and competing value systems (because of the constant transitions) led to community disorganization. Although new immigrant groups have replaced the older groups over time, the delinquency rate has remained high because each

▲ The autocratic Yemeni president, Abdrabbuh Mansour Hadi, claimed that protests against him were leading to anomie and general social chaos. In this image, Yemeni army soldiers try to stop antigovernment protesters. Hadi resigned in January 2015 under siege by a rebel group called the Houth. Social order or stability has been an issue since then.

Merton's Strain Theory

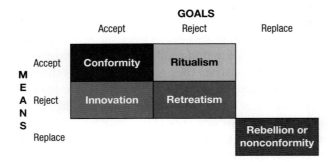

generation of newcomers experiences anomie (Shaw and McKay 1929).

Structural-Functional Approaches to Deviance: Strain.

What happens when you know what your goal is but you cannot find a socially acceptable path to reach it? How do you proceed? **Strain theory** contends that *the opportunity or limitations embedded in the structures of society may contradict and undermine the goals and aspirations society encourages for its members, creating strains that lead to deviance.*

Strain theory suggests that the gap between an individual's or a society's *goals* and the legitimate ways of attaining those goals—*the means*—can lead to strain in the society (Merton 1968). Individuals may agree with the society's *goals* for success (say, financial affluence) but may not be able to achieve them using socially acceptable means. The strain created can lead to deviance. Merton uses U.S. society as an example because it places a heavy emphasis on success as measured by wealth and social standing. He outlines five ways by which individuals adapt to the strain. Figure 6.2 shows these five types and their relationship to goals and means.

To further illustrate strain theory, we trace the choices of a lower-class student who realizes the value of an education and knows it is necessary to get ahead but has problems finding time to study because she has to work many hours a week to help support her family.

1. *Conformity* means embracing the society's definition of success and adhering to the established and approved means of achieving success. If the student takes this path, she will work hard despite the obstacles, pulling all-nighters and trying to do well in school to achieve success and a good job placement. She will use legitimate, approved means—education and hard work—to reach goals that the society views as worthy.

2. *Innovation* refers to the use of illicit means to reach approved goals. In this scenario, our student uses illegitimate means to achieve her education goals. She may cheat on exams or get papers from Internet sources. Success in school is all that matters. How she attains that success does not matter.

3. *Ritualism* involves strict adherence to the culturally prescribed rules, even though individuals give up on the goals they hoped to achieve. If our student goes down this route, she will no longer think she can get good grades and succeed in college but, as a matter of pride and self-image, she will continue to try hard and to attend school. She will conform to expectations, but with no sense of purpose. She will just do what she is told.

4. *Retreatism* refers to giving up on both the goals and the means. In this case, the student either bides her time, not doing well, or drops out, giving up on job goals. She abandons or retreats from the goals of a professional position in society and the means to get there. She may even turn to a different lifestyle—for example, becoming a user of drugs and alcohol—as part of the retreat.

5. *Rebellion* entails rejecting socially approved ideas of success and the means of attaining that success. It replaces those with alternative definitions of success and alternative strategies for attaining new goals. In this option, rebelling against the dominant cultural goals and means, our student leaves her family, abandons thoughts of college and a profession, and joins a radical political or religious group or becomes a terrorist, seeking to destabilize the government and establish a new type of society.

Deviant behavior results from retreatism, rebellion, and innovation. According to Merton, the reasons why individuals resort to these behaviors lie in the social conditions that prevent access to success, not in their individual biological or psychological makeup (Merton 1968).

The structural-functional approaches to deviance focus on what occurs if deviance disrupts the ongoing social order. They explore what causes deviance, how to prevent disruptions, how to keep change slow and nondisruptive, and how deviance can be useful to the ongoing society. However, anomie and strain theories fail to account for class conflicts and inequities, which conflict theorists argue cause deviance.

Conflict Theory Approaches to Deviance. As you will recall from previous chapters, conflict theorists assume that conflict among groups is inevitable. Conflict theory focuses on a meso- and macro-level analysis of deviance, looking at deviance as the result of social inequality or of the struggle among groups for power.

Wealthy and powerful elites want to maintain their control and high positions (Domhoff 2014b). They have the power to pass laws and define what is deviant, sometimes by effectively eliminating the opposition groups. The greater the cultural difference between the dominant group and other groups in society, the greater the possibility of conflict. This is because if minority groups establish countercultures, they act in opposition to the norms of the dominant groups and may destabilize society.

Some conflict theorists blame capitalist systems for the unjust administration of law and unequal distribution of resources, arguing that the ruling class uses the legal system to further the capitalist enterprise (Quinney 2002). The dominant or ruling class defines deviance, applies laws to protect its interests, represses efforts to make laws more just, and, in effect, may force those in subordinate classes to carry out actions that the dominant class has defined as deviant. These deviant actions become necessary for survival when the affluent restrict legitimate avenues to resources. In most cases, the dominant class consists of one racial or ethnic group that distinguishes itself from the racial or ethnic groups found in the subordinate classes. So, conflict and definitions of deviance often have racial and ethnic implications as well as social class dimensions. When people believe that those in power treat them unfairly, they have less loyalty to the society and to its rules.

To reduce deviance and crime, conflict theorists believe that we must change the structure of society. For instance, legal systems in many countries claim to support equal and fair treatment for all, but when one looks at the law in action, another picture emerges, as seen in the next Engaging Sociology. Recall the example of the Saints and Roughnecks; the students from powerful families and higher social classes received favored treatment. Unequal treatment of groups that differ from the dominant group—the poor, working class and racial or ethnic minorities in particular—is rooted in the legal, political, and occupational structures of societies.

A Multilevel Analysis of Deviance: Feminist Theories. As we have indicated in previous chapters, feminist theories sometimes take a macro approach akin to conflict theory and sometimes are more micro in approach. In either case, feminist theorists consistently argue that traditional theories do not give an adequate picture or understanding of women's situations. These theorists look for explanations of violence against women and the secondary status of most women in gender relations and social structures. Although there are several branches of feminist theory, most see the macro-level causes of abuses suffered by women as rooted in the capitalist patriarchal system.

One result of women's secondary status brought to light by the #MeToo movement is that they are often victims of sexual crimes, and those who commit such crimes against women do not face severe, or in some cases *any*, punishment. Criminal acts against women, including honor killings, sex trafficking, and rape, take place around the world (U.S. Department of State 2017). Globally, 35% of women have experienced physical or sexual violence by an intimate partner or sexual violence by someone else at some point during their lives (UNWomen 2017). Often, women are blamed for "letting it happen" (Boy and Kulczycki 2008; Mahendru 2017). The next Sociology Around the World feature illustrates this pattern.

THINKING SOCIOLOGICALLY

How might a feminist theorist explain why some women face punishment for being raped? Do you agree with this perspective? Why? What is the counterargument to your position?

▲ Protesters demonstrate during Stanford University graduation in protest against a judge's decision to sentence a former Stanford University swimmer to just 6 months in prison for rape.

MARIJUANA USE VERSUS MARIJUANA ARRESTS

Today, we can see evidence of disparity in treatment of Black and White Americans who use marijuana in states where it is illegal. See Figures 6.3a and 6.3b.

Engaging Sociology

1. What are the respective percentages of White and Black Americans who use marijuana?

2. What are the respective percentages of White and Black Americans arrested for marijuana use?

3. Of the theories described in this chapter, which offers the most convincing explanation for the discrepancy in the answers to Questions 1 and 2? Why?

▼ FIGURE 6.3A

Marijuana Use by Race, 2001–2014

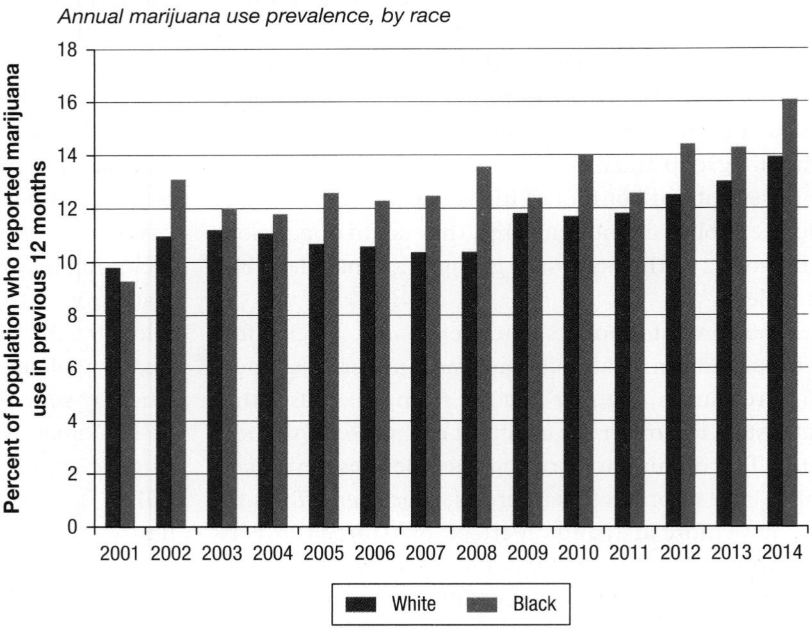

Annual marijuana use prevalence, by race

Source: Matthew, Dayna, and Richard Reeves. 2017. "Trump Won White Voters, but Serious Inequities Remain for Black Americans." January 13. Reprinted with permission from Brookings Institution Press.

▼ FIGURE 6.3B

Arrest Rates for Marijuana Possession by Race, 2001–2014

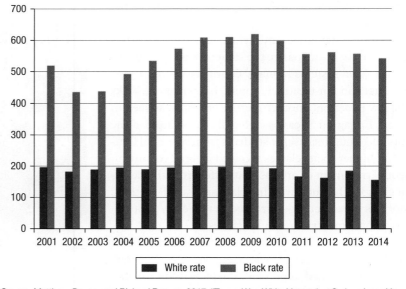

Arrest rate per 100,000 for marijuana possession, by race

Source: Matthew, Dayna, and Richard Reeves. 2017. "Trump Won White Voters, but Serious Inequities Remain for Black Americans." January 13. Reprinted with permission from Brookings Institution Press.

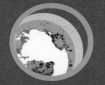

BLAMING THE VICTIM: EXTREME CASES

Every woman fears being raped—being forced into having sex against her will. In most countries, rape is considered a crime punishable by imprisonment—yet only a small percentage of estimated rapes are reported. In a few countries or regions, the legal system is based on strict interpretations of religious books by those who practice rigid and absolutist interpretations of the faith, in an attempt to guard against loss of a woman's virtue, shame, and illegitimate children. These laws also maintain patriarchal control. Recent rape laws proposed in Afghanistan would have permitted marital rape, and some people threw stones at women who rallied against the proposed law. Cases in other countries show the contentious nature of this issue.

Although the following examples are rare, they show the extremes to which communities can go to protect the "virtue" of women and the family. A young Pakistani woman, Mukhtar Mai, was ordered to be raped as punishment for the acts of her brother. He was found with a woman from another, more powerful tribe. In 2004, officials from small towns and villages in Pakistan

ordered about 400 rapes as punishment for both sexual and nonsexual offenses. These rapes are not sanctioned by higher levels of the Pakistani government, and sometimes the rapists are arrested by state or national officials. Often, however, they escape punishment. Six of the 14 men who raped Mai have been charged with rape, and Mai has asked that the men not be acquitted (O'Shea 2005). However, on April 21, 2011, five of the six alleged rapists were freed by the courts, and Mai says she fears for her life (Shackle 2012; Taseer 2011).

In Afghanistan, a 24-year-old woman sits in prison, sentenced—without a trial—for adultery. She refused to have sex with her brother-in-law when her family was away. The result? She was accused of, and imprisoned for, attempted adultery. With her in the prison is Sumaira, who was raped and impregnated by her uncle when she was 16. Her crime? Adultery (Mahendru 2017).

Although these are extreme cases, these true stories powerfully illustrate the low status of women in some areas of the world.

According to feminist theory, the work of women in the private sphere—including housework, childbearing, and childcare—is undervalued, as are the women who carry out these roles. In some societies, women are the property of their husbands, with men's strength and physical force the ultimate means of control over women. In Afghanistan, for example, women are not even referred to by their own names in public. Afghan women are generally referred to as "Aunt" by those they encounter outside their homes. Some phrases often used by husbands to refer to their wives when in public include "Mother of children," "My household," or "My weak one" (Mashal 2017).

Some branches of feminist theory argue that men exploit and usurp women's labor power, sexuality, and even their very identity. This patriarchal system is reproduced through new generations socialized to view inequality between the sexes as "normal" and "natural." Only deviants veer from the cultural expectations of this "normal" behavior.

No one theory of deviance can fully explain the social construction of deviance and why people commit deviant acts. Depending on the level of analysis (micro, meso, or macro) of the questions sociologists

wish to study, some theories are more helpful than others. Each, though, provides a needed angle to view and understand deviant behavior. In the following sections, we explore in more detail the micro-meso-macro connections as they apply to one manifestation of deviance—crime.

THINKING SOCIOLOGICALLY

Meso- and macro-level social forces can be even more powerful than micro-level forces in explaining deviance. What might be the factors at the meso and macro levels that contribute to deviance such as prostitution or shoplifting? Pick a recent example of deviance now in the news. Which sociological theories help explain this deviant behavior?

Crime and Individuals: Micro-Level Analysis

No doubt you have heard news reports about crime rates. These rates come from yearly reports on the occurrences of individual criminal acts. They indicate whether the

rate of crime is increasing or decreasing and help determine the effectiveness of attempts to curb crime. To have
accurate information on crime rates, however, we must
measure and categorize types of crimes correctly. We
now look at various means of collecting and categorizing
crime data.

How Much Crime Is There?

How do sociologists and law enforcement officials know
how much crime occurs? Not all crime is reported to the
police, and when crime is reported, the methods of collecting data may differ. Each country has its own methods of keeping crime records. For instance, the official
record of crime in the United States is found in the U.S.
Federal Bureau of Investigation's (FBI) *Uniform Crime
Reports* (UCR). The FBI relies on information submitted voluntarily by law enforcement agencies and divides
crimes into two categories: Type I and Type II offenses.
Type I offenses, also known as *FBI index crimes*, are murder, forcible rape, robbery, aggravated assault, burglary,
larceny-theft, motor vehicle theft, and arson. Type II
offenses include fraud, simple assault, vandalism, driving under the influence of alcohol or drugs, and running
away from home. In fact, there are hundreds of Type II
crimes. Figure 6.4, the Crime Clock, summarizes UCR
records on Type I offenses. To examine trends in crime,
social scientists calculate a rate of crime, usually per
100,000 people.

Although the UCR data provide a picture of how
much crime gets *reported* to the police and leads to arrest,
the FBI does not provide complete information on how
much crime there is in the United States. The UCR does
not show most corporate, or white-collar, crimes, and

many street crimes are not reported for a host of reasons.
Further, sometimes a crime reported to the police does
not lead to an arrest; or an arrest is made, but the case is
never prosecuted; or a prosecutor initiates prosecution,
but the case never comes to trial. A majority of cases end in
plea bargains—a suspect agrees to plead guilty to a lesser
charge, perhaps because the suspect expresses feelings of
guilt, because the person does not have the resources to
fight the charges with a good attorney, or because the suspect is willing to exchange information for a lighter sentence. The state prefers plea bargains because going to trial
is expensive for the state. The reduction in the number of
cases at each level of the criminal justice system contributes
to the difficulty of determining accurate crime rates.

Self-reporting surveys—asking individuals what criminal acts they have committed—provide another way to
measure crime rates. Criminal participation surveys typically focus on adolescents and their involvement in delinquency. *Victimization surveys* ask people how much crime
they have experienced. The Bureau of Justice Statistics
carries out the National Crime Victimization Survey each
year. The NCVS indicates that the tendency to report
crime to the police varies by the type of crime, with violent victimizations having the highest reporting rate.

THINKING SOCIOLOGICALLY

Imagine that you work for the Bureau of Justice Statistics.
Congress asks you to predict how many FBI agents will be
needed to deal with different types of crime. How would
you go about determining this, and what data sources might
you use?

▼ FIGURE 6.4

2016 Crime Clock

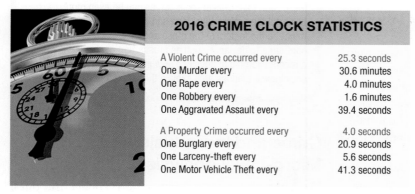

2016 CRIME CLOCK STATISTICS

A Violent Crime occurred every	25.3 seconds
One Murder every	30.6 minutes
One Rape every	4.0 minutes
One Robbery every	1.6 minutes
One Aggravated Assault every	39.4 seconds
A Property Crime occurred every	4.0 seconds
One Burglary every	20.9 seconds
One Larceny-theft every	5.6 seconds
One Motor Vehicle Theft every	41.3 seconds

Source: U.S. Department of Justice (2017).

Although discrepancies in crime
reports are often difficult to reconcile,
each measurement instrument provides
a different portion of the total crime picture. By using several data-gathering
techniques (triangulation), a more accurate picture of crime begins to emerge. All
data-gathering techniques indicate that
the rate of violent and nonviolent crime
in the United States has dropped since
the mid-1990s, so we can be confident
that the crime rate has really fallen. As
Figure 6.5 indicates, in 1993, there were
747.1 violent crimes per 100,000 residents, but in 2016, that number was 386.3
(Gramlich 2018).

▼ FIGURE 6.5

Trends in Violent Crime and Property Crime, 1993–2016

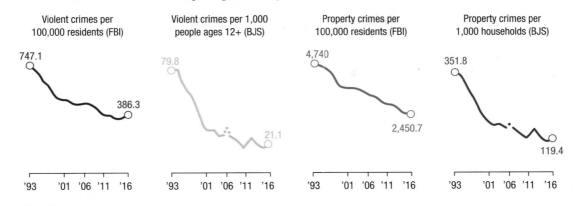

Source: Gramlich (2018).

Note: FBI figures include reported crimes only. Bureau of Justice Statistics (BJS) figures include unreported and reported crimes. The 2006 and 2016 BJS estimates are not comparable to those in other years due to methodological changes.

Researchers have yet to come to a consensus as to why crime has declined. Some ideas now under review include these:

- Changing demographics: a decline in the number of young people (those most likely to commit crimes)

- Rising rates of incarceration (though those rates have declined over the past few years)

- New policing strategies, including computer-assisted planning and closer focus on gun use by youth

- Greater access to abortion after the 1973 *Roe v. Wade* Supreme Court decision, which led to fewer unwanted children (relatively more likely to commit crimes due to their negative treatment)

- The phasing out of lead in gasoline in the 1970s (lead can cause brain damage related to violent behavior) (Cohn et al. 2013; Wilson 2015)

- Informal sources of social control from residents and organizations in communities, including local nonprofits focused on violence reduction and community building (Sharkey 2017)

Though crime is down, it is still the common subject of news headlines. Crime reporting is relatively inexpensive because reporters can rely on information about index crimes that officials regularly make public. So, the crimes that grab the attention of average citizens of countries around the world tend to be violent crimes committed by individuals or small groups. The following are some types of micro-level crimes.

Types of Crime

Predatory Crimes. Citizens of the United States tend to be most afraid of violent predatory crimes (consensus crimes—usually violent—against humans, such as premeditated murder, forcible rape, and kidnapping for ransom). Many citizens feel they cannot trust others. Some keep guns to protect themselves from this perceived danger. Some neighborhoods *are* dangerous; however, as noted earlier, the total violent crime victimization rate has declined over the past several decades. Next, we discuss other crimes committed by individuals—but stay tuned because most criminologists believe there are more serious crimes, to be discussed under meso- and macro-level deviance.

Crimes Without Victims. *Acts committed by or between individual consenting adults* are known as **victimless** or **public order crimes**. These can include prostitution, gambling, drug use, and public drunkenness. Although these crimes do not result in victimization, they are deemed harmful to society (and thus, criminal) because they violate the dominant values and norms. Although illegal, they may be tolerated (the police may look the other way) as long as they do not become highly visible. For example, it would be rare for police in the United States to crack down on a low-stakes monthly poker game friends play behind closed doors.

Americans' Support for Legalizing Marijuana Continues to Rise

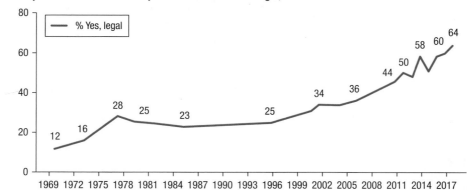

Do you think the use of marijuana should be made legal, or not?

Source: "Record-High Support for Legalizing Marijuana Use in U.S.," by Justin McCarthy, October 25, 2017.

▼ FIGURE 6.7

Where Some Use of Marijuana Is Legal

Marijuana Legalization Status
- ■ Medical marijuana broadly legalized
- ■ Marijuana legalized for recreational use
- ■ No broad laws legalizing marijuana

Source: Governing. 2017. "State Marijuana Laws in 2017 Map." Retrieved July 31, 2017 (http://www.governing.com/gov-data/state-marijuana-laws-map-medical-recreational.html).

Victimless crimes involving drugs result in a variety of policies, from execution in Iran and hanging in Malaysia to legalization in Holland. As noted earlier, U.S. drug policies have led to huge numbers of people being imprisoned. The vast majority (84% in 2015) were for possession of small amounts of drugs, and numbers of drug arrests have increased since President Trump took office (Drug Policy Alliance 2017).

Support for the legalization of marijuana has increased dramatically over the past 3 decades, however, as seen in Figure 6.6. In turn, proposals to legalize drugs in the United States have gained traction. As Figure 6.7 shows, 26 states and Washington, DC, have legalized some marijuana use (Governing 2017).

Fears among some that marijuana legalization would lead to increased drug use among teens have not materialized. Colorado legalized the recreational use of marijuana in 2012. A 2015 survey showed that 21% of Colorado teens had used marijuana in the past 30 days. This was a slight *decline* from the 25% who reported using marijuana in 2009, before pot was legal. Four out of five Colorado teens said they don't ever use it (Colorado Department of Public Health & Environment 2016; Ingraham 2016).

▲ This photo shows how what we consider deviant can change over time. The people who paid for the billboard support legalization of marijuana, maintaining that it is less dangerous than beer or football.

THINKING SOCIOLOGICALLY

Can a person be victimized by drugs even if he or she willingly uses them? Many prostitutes consent to sex acts only because poverty or drug addiction leaves them with few other options and because, like many women without resources, they are vulnerable to domination by men. Are illegal drug use and prostitution really "victimless crimes," or should drug users and prostitutes be considered victims?

Hate Crimes. A **hate crime** is a "*criminal offense against a person or property motivated in whole or in part by an offender's bias against a race, religion, disability, ethnic origin or sexual orientation*" (FBI 2017). The FBI reported 6,121 hate crimes in 2016, up from 5,462 in 2014, with the breakdown by bias indicated in Figure 6.8. Hate crimes are underreported, with many victims not believing the police can help them (FBI 2017; Langton, Planty, and Sandholtz 2013; Potok 2013a).

Those who commit hate crimes feel rage against the victim as a representative of a group they despise. Often, they believe this group threatens their lifestyle and economic security. In the case of some White

▼ FIGURE 6.8

Breakdown of the 6,121 Single-Bias Hate Crime Incidents Reported in 2016

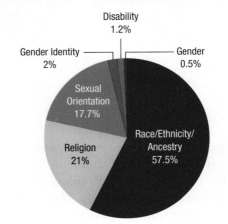

Source: FBI (2017).

supremacy movement members, philosophical, political, and even religious principles guide their beliefs (Blee 2008).

As minority groups gain notoriety *or* acceptance in society, they can face more hate crimes. For example, hate crime incidents against Muslim Americans increased after September 11, 2001, and the Boston Marathon bombings in 2013, carried out by Muslim extremists. The number of White supremacist groups increased dramatically after Barack Obama, the first

Crime and Organizations: Meso-Level Analysis

Crime control efforts are part of the social structure of modern societies. First, as societies modernize, there is an almost universal tendency for crime rates to increase dramatically due to the anomie that new migrants and the poor experience in urban areas where old norms are no longer relevant (Merton 1938). Second, as societies become modernized and urban, they become more reliant on meso-level formal or bureaucratic mechanisms of control rather than small community pressures and conformity. They develop a criminal justice system.

Crimes Involving Organizations and Institutions

Jeanne, one of the authors of this book, recently got a call from a fraud office at an online retailer saying that her credit card had been compromised. Someone had ordered online items from Atlanta-based Bloomingdale's, Coach, and DSW (Designer Shoe Warehouse) using her credit card—and it was not Jeanne! Credit card fraud and identity theft are two types of organized crime prevalent today.

Some crimes are committed by highly organized, hierarchically structured syndicates formed for the purpose of achieving their economic objectives through criminal behavior. On the other hand, legitimate corporations also commit crimes. Their crimes are often serious, but the public image of such organizations is not criminal, so they are not always suspected or caught. We look first at organized criminal organizations and then at crimes committed by people within their legitimate occupations and organizations.

Organized Crime. **Organized crime** refers to *ongoing criminal enterprises by an organized group whose ultimate purpose is economic gain through illegitimate means* (Siegel 2011). Our image of this type of crime is sometimes glamorized in classic films such as *No Country for Old Men*, *The Godfather*, *Goodfellas*, *Gangs of New York*, and more recently *The Bling Ring*, *American Hustle*, and *Prisoners* (Lyttelton 2017). On television, *The Sopranos* is the ultimate media "mob" depiction. Despite the alluring view of these idealized stories, organized crime is a serious problem in many countries. It is essentially a counterculture with a hierarchical structure, from the boss down to the underlings. The organization relies on power, control, fear, violence, and corruption. This type of deviance is a particular problem when

▲ These photos reveal how various subcultures can have sharply different views on what they consider deviant. They also help illustrate why hate crimes tend to increase as minority groups gain more power in society and their definitions of reality come to be normalized.

U.S. president of color, was elected, and antigay hate crimes have become more common since the success of the same-sex marriage movement (Park and Mykhyalyshyn 2016; Peek 2011). More recently, hate crimes have risen since the election of Donald Trump, and White nationalist groups, emboldened by the hate rhetoric so prevalent during the presidential campaign, have conducted "unprecedented" recruitment campaigns on college campuses after the presidential election (CBS News 2017).

One form of hate crime that has gotten little attention is hostile attacks on people with one or more disabilities. Jack Levin tells of his entry into this area of research in the next Sociologists in Action.

These examples represent only a few of the many types of micro-level crimes, characterized by individual or small-group actions. We now turn to crime in organizations and institutions at the meso level. Organizations usually commit the crimes most harmful to society.

THREE TIMES THE VIOLENCE

A few years ago, I was asked to serve as a speaker in England on the topic of what the British call "disablist violence"—hate crimes committed against people with emotional, intellectual, and physical disabilities. For decades, I had studied hate crimes based on race, religion, gender, and sexual orientation, but it never occurred to me that people with disabilities might be victimized by widespread and sometimes extraordinary levels of violence. According to anonymous victim accounts from the Bureau of Justice Statistics, each year, the 54 million Americans with disabilities experience serious violence at a rate nearly 3 times that of the general population. Their rate for sexual assault is almost 4 times that of Americans who are considered to be able-bodied.

After returning from England, I decided not to just drop my newly acquired information about the plight of people with disabilities. As someone who regards himself as a public sociologist, I was eager to communicate my findings as widely as possible. First, I wrote an article titled "The Invisible Hate Crime" for an issue of *Pacific Standard* magazine (www.psmag.com/politics-and-law/the-invisible-hate-crime-27984). Then, I authored an article about the topic for *Disability, Hate Crime, and Violence*, edited by Roulstone and Mason-Bish.

Finally, I teamed up with producer Bill Lancaster (a colleague at Northeastern University who, years earlier, had asked me to appear on several episodes of Geraldo Rivera's then-popular talk show). We decided to produce a documentary that would help give some visibility to what seems to be an unacknowledged hate crime.

After a couple of years gathering interviews and incidents, we put together a 15-minute film designed to stimulate debate and conversation among students and practitioners—especially those in or going into careers in criminal justice and social work.

Our film, *Three Times the Violence* (http://original.livestream.com/webshare/video?clipId=pla_af5ee04c-ee39-4617-bbdd-48059fc22684), was meant to increase public and professional awareness of the special vulnerability people with disabilities have to extraordinary violence. We were intent on helping to remove disablist violence from the shadows and bring it into the spotlight. After all, the first step in combating these shameful incidents is an acknowledgment that they exist.

We don't have to change the law on hate crimes against people with disabilities—that has already happened at the federal level—but we must change the thinking of ordinary people who consider only race, religion, or sexual orientation as grounds for bigotry. Many people with disabilities are harmed more by the way others treat them than by their intellectual, psychiatric, or physical disadvantage. This unfortunate fact has been widely ignored by otherwise decent Americans, who, when they think of hate crimes, tend to focus only on people wearing sheets, armbands, steel-toe boots, or Nazi tattoos.

★ ★ ★ ★ ★ ★

A prolific author, public speaker, and commentator, Jack Levin, PhD, is professor emeritus at Northeastern University and codirector of the Brudnick Center on Violence and Conflict.

---

societies experience rapid change and anomie and where social controls break down.

Marginalized ethnic groups that face discrimination may become involved in a quest to get ahead through organized crime. Earlier in U.S. history, Italians were especially prominent in organized crime, but today many ethnic and racial groups are involved. Organized crime around the world has gained strong footholds in countries in transition (Felbab 2017). For example, in Russia, the move from a socialist to a market economy has provided many opportunities for criminal activity. The *Mafiya* is estimated to include over 90,000 people, and some estimate that its members control 70% to 80% of all private

business in Russia and 40% of Russia's wealth. It is heavily involved in human trafficking and the heroin drug trade, originating in Afghanistan. The Mafiya also now seems connected to the security services in the Russian government and is used by the state for its own purposes (Galeotti 2017; Matthews 2014; Schmalleger 2012).

Organized crime usually takes one of three forms: (1) the sale of illegal goods and services, including gambling, loan sharking, trafficking in drugs and people, selling stolen goods, and prostitution; (2) infiltrating legitimate businesses and unions through threat and intimidation and using bankruptcy and fraud to exploit and devastate a legitimate company; and (3) racketeering—the extortion of funds in exchange for protection (i.e., not being hurt). Activities such as a casino or trash collection service often appear to be legitimate endeavors on the surface but may be cover operations for highly organized illegal crime rings. Transnational organized crime takes place across national boundaries, using sophisticated electronic communications and transportation technologies. The major crime clans in the world include the Yakuza, a collection of Japan-based gangs; the Russian Mafiya, composed of hundreds of criminal groups; the Italian Mafia; and Mexican drug cartels (Adelstein 2015; Matthews 2014). The Russian Mafiya and its close relations with the Russian government has become better known in the United States recently, with news stories about President Trump's alleged business relations with Russian mobsters and Russian interference in elections in the United States (Neuhauser 2018; Petropoulos and Engel 2017; Sanger 2018).

Occupational Crime. Bernard (Bernie) Madoff, a well-respected investor and former chair of the NASDAQ stock exchange, developed a Ponzi scheme that was probably the largest investment fraud Wall Street has ever seen. The scheme defrauded and wrecked thousands of investors, public pension funds, charitable foundations, and universities of billions of dollars, with more than $65 billion missing from investor accounts when the scam became public in 2008. Named after Charles Ponzi, the first to be caught (in 1919), Ponzi schemes involve promises of large returns on investments, paying old investors with money from new investors. Money is simply shifted among investors to make it appear as though the investments earn money ("The Madoff Case" 2009). Meanwhile, those running the scam pocket enormous sums of the money invested.

Ponzi schemes are one example of **white-collar** or **occupational crime**, *a violation of the law committed by an individual or a group in the course of a legitimate, respected occupation or financial activity* (Hagan 2016). Occupational crime is committed for personal or group gain, can be committed by individuals from virtually any social class, and can occur at any organizational level.

These crimes receive less attention than violent crimes because they are less visible, do not always cause obvious physical injury to identifiable people, and are frequently committed by people in positions of substantial authority and prestige. Reports of violent crimes that appear on the television news each night attract more attention. Yet occupational crime is far costlier in money, health, and lives. Victims of financial scams who have lost their life savings or workers who have lost their good health because of unsafe and illegal work conditions are well aware of this.

Sociologists divide occupational crimes into four major categories: (1) against the company, (2) against employees, (3) against customers, and (4) against the general public or other organizations (Hagan 2016).

Crimes against the company include pilfering (using company resources such as the photocopy machine for personal business) and employee theft (taking company supplies for your own use, stealing from the cash register, and embezzlement). Those who commit occupational crimes say they do so for several reasons. First, they feel little or no loyalty to the organization, especially if it is large and impersonal. It is like stealing from nobody, they say. Second, workers feel exploited and resentful toward the company. Stealing is getting back at the company. Third, the theft is seen as a "fringe benefit" or "informal compensation" that they deserve. Such workers may spend time on a side business while at work or take paper and ink cartridges for their printer at home. Fourth, workers may steal because of the challenge. It makes the job more interesting if they can get away with it. It is important to note that these people do not see themselves as criminals, especially compared with "street" criminals (Altheide et al. 1978).

The other three types of corporate crime benefit the company at the expense of employees or members of the larger society. *Crimes against employees* refer to corporate neglect of worker safety. In 1970 the U.S. government established the Occupational Safety and Health Administration (OSHA) to help enforce regulations to protect workers, but there are still many problems. When comparing deaths by homicide and those due to injuries or illnesses from work-related causes, people in the United States are *7* times more likely to be killed by job-related hazards than murdered outside of work (Reiman and Leighton 2017).

Neglect of worker safety is a particularly serious problem in many developing or peripheral countries trying to attract multinational corporations with low taxes, cheap labor, and few regulations. The decisions of many corporations and factory owners illustrate *rational choice theory*. Too often they decide the benefits (profit) that come from exploiting labor outweigh the costs (harm to workers). The collapse of a shoddily constructed factory building in Bangladesh that killed 1,127 workers in 2013 is a powerful example of what can result from this type of thinking.

As *strain theorists* point out, almost all corporations want to make the greatest short-term profit possible,

▲ Employees in the Rana Plaza building in Bangladesh made clothing for many multinational apparel companies who failed, along with the building owner, to ensure that they had a safe place to work. This is an example of corporate crime against employees.

and one (deviant) method to do that is to cut costs at the expense of worker safety. Government regulatory agencies responsible for reducing environmental hazards and workplace dangers do not have sufficient staff to police companies for adherence to laws. Internationally, there is little oversight. Multinational corporations generally look for the cheapest labor costs and fewest environmental regulations; governments of poor countries try to attract foreign corporations to keep the poor populace employed regardless of the environmental or workplace health and safety consequences.

Wage theft, underpaying or not paying workers, is another widespread corporate crime that harms millions of workers. Many employers do not pay workers their due wages by requiring them to work "off the clock," not paying them minimum wage, stealing their tips, not paying them overtime, refusing to give them their last check, or simply not paying them at all. Seventeen percent, almost one in six, low-wage workers are victims of wage theft. A 2017 study in the 10 U.S. states with the largest populations revealed that 2.4 million low-income workers

lose nearly a quarter of the wages they earn to wage theft (about $3,300 dollars per year). This is no doubt much less than the true amount of money lost to wage theft, given the fact that relatively few people report it for fear of retribution (Cooper and Kroeger 2017; Meixell and Eisenbrey 2014).

Consumers, as well as workers, can be victims of corporate crime. *Crimes against customers* involve acts victimizing patrons, such as selling dangerous foods or unsafe products, consumer fraud, deceptive advertising, and price-fixing (i.e., setting prices in collusion with another producer). The purpose of advertising is to convince customers to buy the product—appealing to their vanity, sexual interests, or desire to keep up with their neighbors. Sometimes these techniques cross the line between honesty and deception, and customers purchase defective and even dangerous products—all with the full knowledge of company officials.

Crimes against the public include acts by companies that negatively affect large groups of people. One example is hospitals or medical offices that overbill the federal government's health insurance programs Medicare and Medicaid, or insurance companies pressuring hospitals to discharge patients too early to save on costs. Surreptitiously dumping pollutants into landfills, streams, or the air is another crime against the public. Proper disposal of contaminants can be costly and time-consuming for a company, but shortcuts can cause long-term effects for the public. Pollutants from industrial wastes have caused high rates of birth defects and other physical harm (Kihal-Talantkite, Zmirou-Navier, Padilla, and Deguen 2017; National Geographic 2017). For examples of white-collar environmental crimes, see the U.S. Department of Justice's Press Room page (www. justice.gov/enrd/press-room).

These examples help illustrate that white-collar crime hurts more people than all violent street criminals put together (Coleman 2006; Reiman and Leighton 2017).

THINKING SOCIOLOGICALLY

Why are meso-level crimes (occupational or white-collar crimes) more dangerous and costlier to the public than micro-level crimes? Why do they get so much less attention?

National and Global Crime: Macro-Level Analysis

As we have seen, national boundaries continue to blur as people migrate around the globe and many corporations move headquarters across national lines in search of lower costs and higher profits. As we have discussed, crime syndicates, too, are multinational, as they move money, goods, and people surreptitiously across borders. Likewise, terrorist organizations have no boundaries. We now turn to the macro-level crimes of terrorism, election interference, corruption, and cybercrime.

Terrorism is *the calculated use of unlawful violence or threat of unlawful violence to inculcate fear; it is intended to coerce or intimidate governments or societies in the pursuit of goals that are generally political, religious, or ideological* (U.S. Department of Defense 2014). Terrorist groups can be anarchist, state sponsored, right wing or left wing, nationalist, or religious (Rice 2013; Schmalleger 2006). Table 6.1 shows the major types of terrorist groups.

Governments can commit *state-organized crime.* Often overlooked by the public and by social scientists, this form of crime includes acts defined by law as criminal but committed by state or government officials. For

▼ TABLE 6.1

Types of Terrorist Groups

Anarchist	Some contemporary antiglobalization groups
State sponsored	Hezbollah (Iran), Abu Nidal Organization (Syria)
Right wing	Neo-Nazis, skinheads, White supremacists
Left wing	Revolutionary Armed Forces of Colombia (FARC); Revolutionary People's Liberation Party-Front (Turkey)
Nationalist	Irish Republican Army, Basque Fatherland and Liberty
Religious	Al-Qaeda, Hamas, ISIS (Iraq and Syria), Aum Shinrikyo (Japan)

example, a government might be complicit in smuggling, assassination, or torture, which is then justified in terms of "national defense." Government offices may also violate laws that restrict or limit government activities such as eavesdropping.

In some countries, political prisoners, such as the Guantánamo Bay detainees held in Cuba by the United States, are imprisoned for long periods without charges, without access to lawyers, and without trials, and some have been tortured, violating both national and international laws (Center for Constitutional Rights 2017). The U.S. Supreme Court has ruled (2006 and 2008) that the U.S. administration violated the rights of those held at Guantanamo (Global Security 2009). The Obama administration planned to abide by the Supreme Court rulings and tried to shut down the facility but failed in its attempt to move all the prisoners from Guantánamo Bay. As we write, 41 detainees remain at "Gitmo," and the Trump administration plans on refilling it with prisoners (Kheel 2017). Although countries may violate their own laws, it is difficult to prosecute when the guilty party is the government.

Russia's use of fake news to influence elections in the United States, Canada, and Europe and increase racial and ethnic tensions provides another example of state-organized crime. For example, in recent elections, Russian agents used social media platforms like Facebook, Instagram, and Twitter to spread negative stories about political candidates (such as Hillary Clinton, German prime minister Angela Merkel, and French president Emmanuel Macron) and immigrants. These stories were designed to sway voters away from political figures and policies that might threaten people in power in Russia and encourage social upheaval in Europe, Canada, and the United States. These tactics are not new, and many nations have used them, but today they have much greater reach and influence, thanks to unsuspecting—and often easily manipulated—social media users (Dorell 2017; Huggler and Oliphant 2017). Russia even managed to infiltrate some states' voting systems during the 2016 election (though there is no evidence that it tampered with votes). In 2018, the chief of the U.S. Department of Homeland Security, Kirstjen Nielsen, declared "It is clear that our cyber adversaries can now threaten the very fabric of our republic itself" (Reuters 2018).

Bribery and corruption, other forms of state-run (or supported) crimes, are the way of life in many countries. According to the most recent analysis by Transparency International, New Zealand and Denmark have the least and Syria, South Sudan, and Somalia have the most corruption (Transparency International 2018). The institutions perceived to be most affected by corruption globally include political parties, the police, the judiciary, legislatures, and business. Figure 6.9 indicates levels of corruption in various countries around the world.

THINKING SOCIOLOGICALLY

Sometimes government officials and even heads of state are the perpetrators of crimes. When, if ever, is it justified for a government official to violate the law of the nation?

Since the presidential election of 2016, more people in the United States believe their government officials are corrupt. A poll by Transparency International reveals that

- 44% of Americans believe that corruption is pervasive in the White House, up from 36%, and

- almost 7 out of 10 people believe the government is failing to fight corruption, up from half in 2016.

(Transparency International 2017b:para. 6).

The forms of global corruption are too extensive to catalog here, so we will settle for an illustration of one of the newest manifestations of global crime against people and property: cybercrime. Internet deviance or cyberspace crime is growing at an incredible rate. This new world of crime ranges from online identity theft and gambling to

▼ FIGURE 6.9

Corruption Percentage Index, 2017

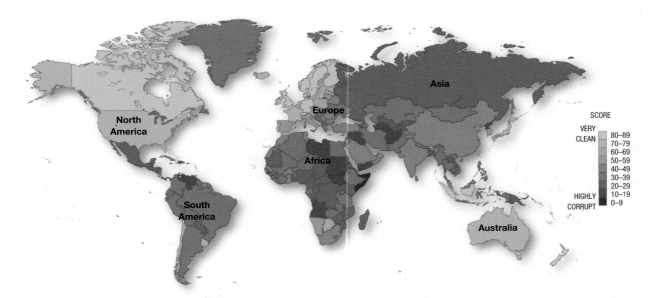

Source: Reprinted from CPI 2017. Copyright CPI 2017 Transparency International: the global coalition against corruption. Used with permission.

Note: Data for Africa are WHO estimates.

cybersex and pornography, to hate sites and stalking, to hacking into government and military files, to terrorist recruiting sites.

Corporations are finding it necessary to spend increasing amounts of money on protecting themselves from cyberattacks but still often find themselves vulnerable. Recent attacks include the following:

- Russian hackers intruding into U.S. election websites in 21 states during the 2016 presidential election (Reuters 2018)

- Hackers stealing data, including social security numbers and driver's license numbers, from approximately 143 million customers of Equifax, one of the biggest consumer credit agencies in the United States (Bernard et al. 2017)

- Cyberattackers hitting HBO, threatening to release yet unaired episodes of *Game of Thrones* (Victor 2017)

- Shadow brokers infiltrating the NSA and gathering NSA tools then used in the global WannaCry ransomware attack that crippled the National Health Service facilities and hospitals in the United Kingdom and the Petya/Not Petya attack that greatly harmed the Ukrainian government facilities in 2017 (Newman 2017)

In 2017, Congress passed and President Trump signed legislation to authorize a National Computer Forensics Institute within the U.S. Secret Service. The institute trains state and local officials on how to look for and find digital evidence of cybercrime (Chalfant 2017). No government has yet found an effective means to halt cyberattacks. We turn now to another macro-level issue: a comparison of crime across nations.

Cross-National Comparison of Crimes

The vending machine was on the corner near the Ballantines' house in Japan. The usual cola, candy, and sundries were displayed, along with cigarettes, beer, whiskey, sake, and pornographic magazines. Out of curiosity, Jeanne and her family watched to see who purchased what from the machines, and not once did they see teenagers sneaking the beer, cigarettes, or porn. It turns out that the Ballantines were not the only ones watching! The neighbors also kept an eye on who did what. Because of the stigma attached to deviant behavior in Japan, teens tend to avoid violating norms, and vigilant neighbors help

keep the overall amount of deviance low. The many eyes in the neighborhood remind people that deviant behavior is unacceptable and provide informal social control over those who might be tempted to commit crimes.

Japan and the United States are both modern, urban, industrial countries, but their crime rates and the way they deal with deviant behavior and crimes differ. The overall crime rate in the United States is 4 times that of Japan and the U.S. murder rate is almost 5 *times* higher. Japan has 1.02 murders for every 100,000 people, whereas the United States has 5.0 per 100,000 residents (NationMaster 2017).

How can these extreme differences in crime rates be explained? Researchers look at cultural differences: Japan's low violent crime rate is due in part to Japan's culturally homogeneous society and loyalty to a historic tradition of cooperation that provides a sense of moral order, a network of group relations, strong commitment to social norms, and respect for law and order. The example of vending machines in Japan illustrates this idea. In addition, guns are outlawed and much harder to come by in Japan.

Japan does not attain its lower crime rate through heavy investment in its criminal justice system. In fact, the Japanese government actually spends far less of its gross national product on the police, courts, and prisons than does the United States. For many crimes in Japan, the offender may simply be asked to write a letter of apology. This is frequently a sufficient sanction to deter the person from further violation of the law. The humiliation of writing an apology and the fear of shame and embarrassing one's family are strong enough to curb deviant behavior (Lazare 2004; Smith 2014). Figure 6.10 provides a picture of the homicide rates per 100,000 individuals in the population in various parts of the world.

Although comparing cross-national data on crime is difficult because of variations in the definitions of crime and the measurements used, comparisons do give us some insight into what types of crimes are committed, under what circumstances, and how often. Two sources of international data are Interpol (the International Criminal Police Organization) and the United Nations. Although these organizations collect and present data, they have limited ways of checking the accuracy of the data they receive from countries.

Global Crimes

Increasingly, crimes are global in nature. Some scholars use the *world systems theory* to understand global crime, arguing that the cause of global crime lies in the

Intentional Homicide Rates (per 100,000 People), 2015

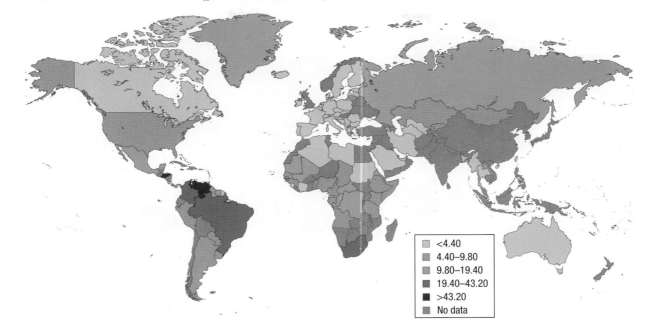

▢	<4.40
▨	4.40–9.80
▨	9.80–19.40
▨	19.40–43.20
■	>43.20
▨	No data

Source: The World Bank (2018a).

global economy, the inequalities between countries, and the competition between countries for resources and wealth. As a result of the capitalist mode of production, an unequal relationship has arisen between core nations (the developed, wealthy nations in the Global North) and peripheral nations (the Global South). Core nations often take unfair advantage of peripheral nations. Peripheral nations, in turn, must find ways to survive in this global system, and they sometimes turn to illegal methods—such as violating global environmental standards—to achieve their goals (Chase-Dunn and Anderson 2006; United Nations Environmental Programme 2017). Semiperipheral nations, though not wealthy, have many natural resources. Benefiting from extensive trade, they are less vulnerable than the poorest nations. Figure 6.11 helps you see where some of these core, peripheral, and semiperipheral nations are located.

As you look at this map, note that the developed or affluent countries are almost all located in the Northern Hemisphere. Although some poor countries are north of the equator, the pattern is obvious. To avoid some misleading implications of the words *developed* and *developing*, many scholars now prefer the term *Global South* to refer to less affluent nations. If you hear this term, this map should help you see why it refers to developing or poor countries.

Controlling Crime: Social Policy Considerations

What is the best way to control crime? Although all modern societies have criminal justice systems, their crime prevention strategies vary. We now look at the mechanisms used by societies to curb deviant behavior and punish deviants.

Dealing With Crime: The Criminal Justice Process

Structural-functionalists see the justice system as a crucial means of ensuring order and social control in society. Conflict theorists, on the other hand, argue that the criminal justice system works in the interest of those in power, at the expense of other members of society. It is in the interests of those in power to maintain the image that crime is primarily the work of outsiders and the poor. This deflects citizen discontent and hostility from the powerful and helps them retain their positions of power (Reiman and Leighton 2017). Conflict theorists point out that there will always be crime in society because the powerful will make sure that some things and some people are labeled deviant.

Depending on whether one uses a structural-functional or conflict theoretical perspective, criminal justice policy generally focuses either on how to deter deviant

Core, Semiperipheral, and Peripheral Countries of the World

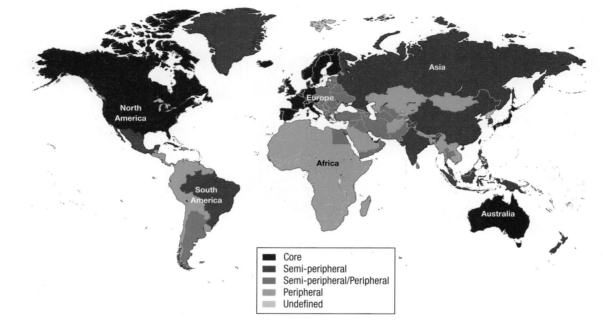

Core
Semi-peripheral
Semi-peripheral/Peripheral
Peripheral
Undefined

Source: Map by Anna Versluis.

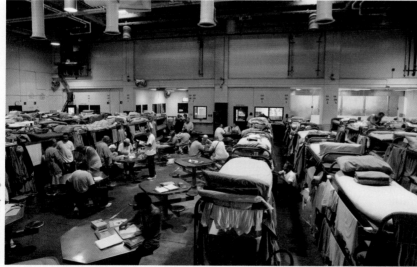

▲ The United States has 5% of the world's population but 22% of all prisoners. Conditions in prisons, like this Mule Creek State Prison in California, are not conducive to rehabilitation, and the incarcerated are disproportionately minorities.

Prisons. Prisons are a form of *total institution* that completely controls the prisoners and regulates all their activities. Inmates' lives are drastically changed through the processes of *degradation*, which marks the individual as deviant, and *mortification*, which breaks down the individual's original self as the inmate experiences resocialization (Goffman 1961; Irwin 1985; Irwin and Owen 2007). The inmate cannot have any personal property. Guards allow prisoners only limited communication and often verbally abuse inmates. Uniforms and standard buzz cuts (for men) are required, and inmates have strictly controlled schedules.

Conflict theorists believe that social class and demographic makeup of prisons reveal that prisons are mostly about controlling or "managing" poor people and people of color, not about public safety. The (preincarceration) income of men in prison is about half that of nonincarcerated men (Rabuy and Kopf 2015). As Figure 6.12 shows, Black and Hispanic people are still much more likely to be imprisoned than White people in the United States.

acts or on the injustices of the criminal justice system. In the United States today, prisons provide one of the primary means of controlling individual criminal behavior. Think about which theoretical perspective, structural-functionalism or conflict theory, you would use to better understand the function of prisons in U.S. society as you read the following section.

The recent decrease in incarceration rates in the United States stems from more people being released from prison due to overcrowding and fewer lockups for minor offenses. The Trump administration, however, has promised to reinvigorate the "War on Drugs" and "zero tolerance policies" (which prevent judges from adjusting punishments to fit particular circumstances), which keep the prison population in the United States high compared with that in any other Global North country (Horwitz 2017), as indicated in Figure 6.13. See Figure 6.14 for an illustration of how these policies enacted in the 1980s and 1990s led to a rapid rise in the prison population, despite a decrease in the crime rate.

THINKING SOCIOLOGICALLY

Why do you think the United States has 5% of the world's population but 22% of the world's prisoners? Has this impacted your life? How and why? How do you think your age, gender, social class, and race influenced your answer?

▼ FIGURE 6.12

Federal and State Imprisonment by Race

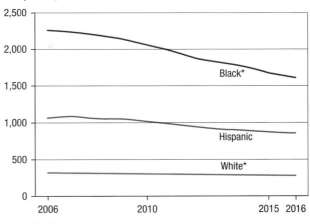

Rate per 100,00 residents

Source: Carson (2018).

Note: Jurisdiction refers to the legal authority of state or federal correctional officials over a prisoner, regardless of where the prisoner is held. Counts are based on prisoners with sentences of more than 1 year. Imprisonment rate is per 100,000 U.S. residents age 18 or older.

*Excludes persons of Hispanic origin.

▼ FIGURE 6.13

Global Incarceration Rates (per 100,000 People)

U.S. incarcerates a larger share of its population than any other country

Incarceration rate per 100,000 people of any age

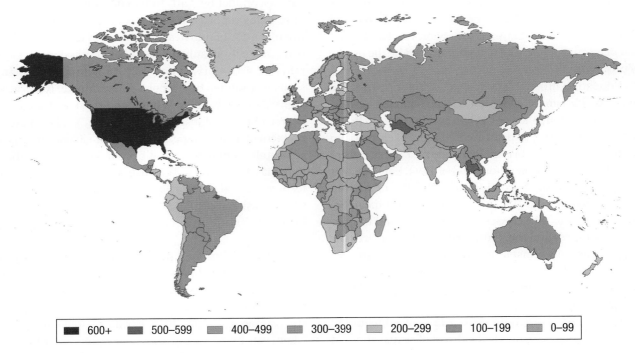

■ 600+ ■ 500–599 ■ 400–499 ■ 300–399 ■ 200–299 ■ 100–199 ■ 0–99

Source: Gramlich (2018b), Pew Research Center.

▼ FIGURE 6.14

U.S. State and Federal Prison Population, 1925–2016

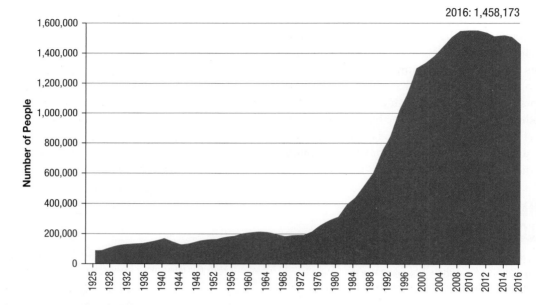

2016: 1,458,173

Source: The Sentencing Project (2018).

Purpose of Prisons. What purpose do you believe prisons serve? From the structural-functional perspective, prisons serve several purposes for society: (1) fulfilling the desire for revenge or retribution; (2) removing dangerous people from society; (3) deterring would-be deviants; and (4) rehabilitating deviants through counseling, education, and work training programs inside prisons (Johnson 2002). However, in prison, inmates are exposed to more criminal and antisocial behavior, so rehabilitation and deterrence goals are often undermined by the nature of prisons.

Educating inmates is a deterrence policy proven to work. Recidivism rates for inmates who take classes while in prison are much lower (43%) than for those who do not. Moreover, such inmates are 17% more likely to attain a job once they leave prison. Pell grants for inmates were abolished in the Prison Reform Act of 1994, but President Obama created the Second Chance Pell Pilot Program in 2015 that, as of 2018, has allowed 12,000 incarcerated students to take classes via 67 colleges and universities. Congress and the Trump administration are now considering fully reinstating the Pell grant programs for inmates. Until they do so, however, relatively few inmates will have access to an education while in prison (Davis et al. 2013; Green 2018).

Even more disturbing than a lack of educational opportunities for inmates is the threat of sexual abuse in prison. According to a recent Bureau of Justice Statistics analysis, mandated by the Prison Rape Elimination Act of 2003, sexual abuse against inmates is a serious problem, even in facilities for juveniles. Among juveniles incarcerated, 5.9% of inmates in male-designated facilities and 1.5% in female-designated facilities reported sexual misconduct by staff. In female-only facilities, 5.3% of inmates reported a youth-on-youth sexual assault, whereas 1.5% of inmates in male-only facilities reported being sexually assaulted by another youth. Among adult inmates, 4% in prison and 3.2% in jail reported being sexually assaulted by staff or a fellow inmate. Rates were highest among women, Whites, and those with a college degree (Bureau of Justice Statistics 2017). This ongoing problem of assault, rape, and threat of violence in prison so brutalizes inmates that it becomes difficult for them to reenter society as well-adjusted citizens ready to conform to societal norms (Fathi 2009; Hensley, Koscheski, and Tewksbury 2005; Liptak 2008; U.S. Department of Justice 2017).

Prisons and Profit. There is money to be made from locking people up. Prisons in the United States were traditionally run by local, state, or federal governments. Today, however, for-profit companies house 8% of state and federal prisoners (Geiger 2017). Private prisons can save on labor costs by providing lower wages and fewer benefits than correctional officers in state and federal prisons receive and offering fewer services for prisoners.

Profits are also found through hiring out inmate labor. Both the federal and state government and private prison companies use prison labor to save money. State and federal governments use prisoners to clean and cook in prisons and to make goods, such as uniforms and license plates. Today, however, prison labor is also a billion-dollar industry in which prisoners earn less than a dollar an hour for their labor when working for companies like Victoria's Secret, Boeing, and Starbucks. Both prisons that hire out prisoners and the companies that employ them save money through this practice. The employers are legally obliged to pay just the minimum wage, and the prisons get to garnish most of these low wages for "legal financial obligations" covering the cost of keeping inmates imprisoned (Bozelko 2017; "Prison Labour" 2017; Scherrer and Shah 2017). As of 2017, about 15% of inmates were hired out to companies for their labor.

In 2016, the U.S. Justice Department under President Obama announced that it would stop using private prisons. Deputy Attorney General Sally Yates announced that the decision was based on research showing private prisons are less safe and provide fewer correctional services than those run by the government (Amnesty International 2016; Williams 2018; Zapotosky and Harlan 2016). Some states have stopped using them for these reasons, but more than two dozen states use them to save money, and President Trump, who supports the use of private prisons, has reversed the Obama decision (Gidda 2017).

The big money these days in imprisoning people is in detention facilities housing undocumented immigrants. They started to grow under President Obama, and now President Trump's immigration policies have helped make this a booming business. Detention facilities for undocumented immigrants are now growing at a much faster rate than regular prisons. In the week following President's Trump election, stock prices for the two largest for-profit detention companies, GEO and CoreCivic, grew by 20% and 40%, respectively (Burnett 2017). As of 2017, 50%–60% of all detained immigrants were in private, for-profit facilities (Dickerson 2017; Hoover 2017). Seeking to increase profits, some private detention facilities have been accused of forcing immigrants to work as custodians for little or no pay, so they would not have to hire paid custodians. It is legal to force convicted criminals to work for less than minimum wage, but it is against the law to coerce undocumented immigrants to do so (Dickerson 2017; Hoover 2017).

The Death Penalty. Crimes of murder, assault, robbery, and rape usually receive severe penalties because citizens consider them the most dangerous. The most controversial (and irreversible) method of control is for the state to put the deviant to death. The most common argument for using the death penalty, more formally known as capital punishment, is to deter people from crime. The idea is that not only will the person who has committed the crime be punished, but also others will be deterred from committing such a crime because they know that the death penalty is a possibility for them too.

However, the death penalty does not deter murder (Alarcon and Mitchell 2011; Radelet and Lacock 2009). In addition, it costs far more to use the death penalty than prison as a punishment. Because of the costs of a capital trial, various appeal processes (many of which are mandated by law to avoid mistakes), and special death row incarceration requirements, the cost is much greater than for life imprisonment. For example, a study in Oklahoma revealed that cases pursuing the death penalty were 3.2 times costlier than those seeking life in prison (Collins et al. 2016).

Moreover, more murders occur in states with the death penalty than in those without it. The average murder rate in death penalty states was 5.5 per 100,000 persons, whereas the average murder rate of states without the death penalty was 4.3. Thirty-one states still allow the death penalty, but movements are now underway in several states to abolish it for financial and religious reasons (Death Penalty Information Center 2017).

Few Global North countries use the death penalty, and in 2007 the United Nations passed a resolution calling on all nations to abolish it as "cruel and unusual punishment" (Amnesty International 2012; UN News Center 2010). As Figure 6.15 indicates, however, 57 nations still use the death penalty.

THINKING SOCIOLOGICALLY

How can you explain the higher murder rates in U.S. states that have the death penalty? Why do you think the United States still allows the death penalty when most nations do not?

Race and class status relate to who receives the death penalty. In most U.S. states with capital punishment, a disproportionate number of minority and lower-class individuals are put to death. Of those executed since 1976, 56% have been White and 34% Black. Yet the

Global Status of the Death Penalty, 2018

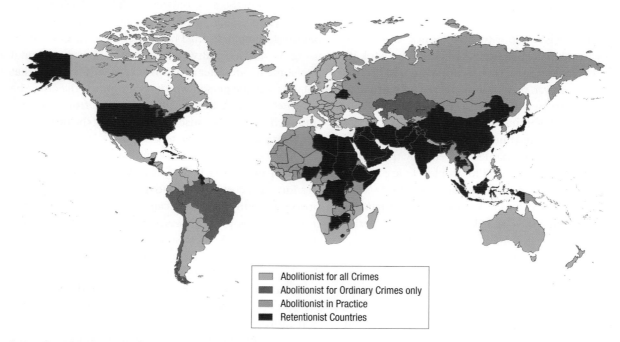

Abolitionist for all Crimes
Abolitionist for Ordinary Crimes only
Abolitionist in Practice
Retentionist Countries

Source: Death Penalty Information Center (2018).

percentage of Blacks in the total population is less than 13%. Although just 50% of all murder victims are White, 75% of all murder cases that end in the death penalty have a White victim (Death Penalty Information Center 2017). When Maryland became the 18th state to abolish the death penalty in 2013, the governor of the state said, "Maryland has effectively eliminated a policy that is proven not to work. Evidence shows that the death penalty is not a deterrent, it cannot be administered without racial bias, and it costs three times as much as life in prison without parole" (Sutton 2013).

These problems with the death penalty have led to a search for alternative means to deter crime and spurred policy analysts to rethink assumptions about what factors are effective in controlling human behavior.

Alternative Forms of Social Control

The disturbing reality is that, despite the high rates of incarceration in the United States, **recidivism rates—** *the likelihood that someone who is arrested, convicted, and imprisoned will later be a repeat offender—*are also very high. More than half of all men who do time in prison will be confined again for a crime. This means that as

a specific deterrent or for rehabilitation, imprisonment does not work very well (Siegel and Bartollas 2016). What options does government have?

Based on the understanding that most criminal behavior is learned through socialization, that criminals can be resocialized, and that tax dollars can be saved, several sociological theories of crime suggest early community intervention to reduce crime rates. Some of these ideas include high-quality schools, preventing young people from entering the criminal justice system in the first place, and methods of treatment other than brutalizing incarceration for those who do find themselves in trouble with the law. Each of these approaches increases the social capital of criminals and those at risk of becoming criminals. You will recall from Chapter 5 that *social capital* refers to social networks within and among groups that give us access to important resources, such as jobs. Increasing an individual's social capital by increasing educational attainment, job skills, and the ability to take advantage of available resources can reduce the chances of that person going to prison in the first place and of recidivism.

Research also shows the impact of employment on recidivism. Often ex-offenders cannot obtain a job because of their criminal record, thus increasing their likelihood of ending up back in prison (Minor, Persico, and Weiss 2017). To help ex-offenders overcome discrimination by employers in the hiring process, a Ban the Box campaign has urged government and other employers to not include a box on applications that requires job candidates to report whether they have a criminal record. This gives ex-offenders the opportunity to be considered, at least in the first stages of the hiring process, on their qualifications, rather than automatically dismissed because of their criminal record. As of 2017, 29 states and the federal government have adopted the policy, and 9 states no longer allow the conviction question on private employer applications (Avery and Hernandez 2017).

Seeing how other countries control crime can also help nations lower their incarceration rates. There is a wide range of options available for dealing with deviance other than harsh (and expensive) punishments. For example, what can the United States learn from how other nations deal with drugs? How might the legalization of marijuana in some U.S. states affect incarceration rates?

Sociologists use comparative studies and evaluation research of current policies to help determine the best strategies for crime and recidivism deterrence. For example, evidence shows that prison education, substance abuse, and job training programs can be used to reduce criminal justice expenses by allowing some prisoners to "earn" reduced sentences. These programs also lead to lower recidivism rates. Once prisoners are released, recidivism rates can also be reduced through individualized plans based on their needs and likelihood of reoffending and cognitive programs that help ex-offenders recognize the impact of their attitudes on their actions (Council of State Governments Justice Center 2015; Lawrence 2009).

THINKING SOCIOLOGICALLY

How has what you read in this chapter affected your ideas about deviance, crime, and the criminal justice system?

One of the dominant characteristics of modern society is social inequality, and, as we have seen, inequality is often an issue in criminal activity. Indeed, many of our social problems are rooted in issues of inequality. Extreme inequality may even be a threat to the deeper values and dreams of a society, especially one that stresses individualism and achievement. In the following three chapters, we look at three types of inequality: socioeconomic, ethnic or racial, and gender-based inequity.

WHAT HAVE WE LEARNED?

Deviance is socially constructed and varies across time and societies. What is considered deviant now may not be considered deviant in another place or time. All societies must fashion responses to deviant behaviors that can threaten their stability and safety. The criminal justice system tends to be a conservative force in society because of its focus on ensuring social conformity.

To make our society run more smoothly, we must understand why deviance and crime happen. Good policy must be based on accurate information and careful analysis of the information. We must also understand that deviance and conformity operate at various levels in the social world: micro, meso, and macro. In addition, it is important to understand that there may be positive aspects of deviance for any society, from uniting society against deviants to providing creative new ways to solve problems.

KEY POINTS

- Deviance—the violation of social norms, including those that are formal laws—has both positive and negative consequences for individuals and for society.

- We can use many sociological theories to explain deviance—rational choice, symbolic interaction's anomie, and labeling theories at the micro level; structural-functional theory's social control, differential association, and strain theory; and conflict and feminist theory at the meso and macro level.

- Many of the formal organizations concerned with crime (such as local law enforcement and the media) focus on crimes involving individuals—predatory crimes, crimes without victims, and hate crimes—but the focus on these crimes may blind us to occupational crimes that are more harmful and costlier to society.

- At the meso level, organized and occupational crimes cost billions of dollars and pose a great risk to thousands of lives. Occupational crime may be against the company, employees, customers, or the public.

- At the macro level, national governments sometimes commit state-organized crimes, sometimes in violation of their own laws or in violation of international law. These crimes may be directed against their own citizens (usually minorities) or people in other countries. Russia's attempts in recent years to influence elections and sow discontent in other nations through hacking polling sites and using social media sites provides examples of state-organized crimes.

- Controlling crime has generated many policy debates, from the use of prisons to the death penalty to alternative approaches to the control of deviance.

DISCUSSION QUESTIONS

1. List five acts that were once considered deviant but are now considered acceptable or even courageous. Have you ever committed a deviant act because you believed it was the moral thing to do? If yes, please explain why. If not, in what sort of situation might you consider carrying out a deviant act?

2. Have you ever been labeled deviant? Why or why not? How does your social class, level of education, gender, race or ethnicity, and nation of origin impact the chances you will be considered deviant in your country?

3. Which of the following theories of deviance described in the chapter—rational choice, differential association, labeling theory, social control, anomie and social disorganization, strain theory, and conflict theory—best explain the recent increase in cheating among college students? Why?

4. Why is occupational crime not given as much attention as violent crime? What are some examples of occupational crimes that hurt millions of Americans every day? Have you ever been the victim of one of these crimes? What would you suggest policymakers do to curb these crimes?

5. How do conflict theorists explain the makeup of prisoners in the U.S. prison system? Do you agree with their explanation? Why or why not?

6. How can social capital help keep people out of prison and help former prisoners avoid returning to prison? How will your social capital help you conform (or not?) to the norms of society?

KEY TERMS

At the Local (Micro) Level

- *LGBTQIA groups* support lesbian, gay, bisexual, transgender, queer/questioning, intersex, and asexual/aromantic students. The Consortium of Higher Education LGBT Resource Professionals, a national organization of college and university groups, maintains a website at www.lgbtcampus.org. Regardless of your own identity or orientation, consider contacting your campus LGBTQIA group, attending meetings, and participating in its support and public education activities.

- *Boys and Girls Clubs* provide local programs and services to promote healthy development by instilling a sense of competence, usefulness, belonging, and influence in young people. Organizations for youth like Boys and Girls Clubs need interns and volunteers to provide role models for youth. Consider volunteering to help children with homework or activities. You can find a club near you by going to www.bgca.org/whoweare/Pages/FindaClub.aspx.

At the Organizational or Institutional (Meso) Level

- The extensive and rapidly growing *criminal justice system* in the United States focuses on crime prevention, law enforcement, corrections, and rehabilitation. Identify the aspect of the system that interests you most and, using faculty and community contacts, select an appropriate organization for volunteer work, an internship, or a job.

- *Criminal courts* play a central role in the administration of criminal justice, and trials are often open to the public. Attending a trial and/or contacting a judge or magistrate could provide a good introduction to the court system and some of the people who work within it.

- *Crime prevention programs* are designed to reduce crime. You can find information about such programs at the National Crime Prevention Council at www.ncpc.org/programs. To obtain a better understanding of what types of crime prevention programs are most effective, go to the Center for the Study and Prevention of Violence's (CSPV) Blueprints website at www.colorado.edu/cspv/blueprints.

At the National or Global (Macro) Level

- *The Polaris Project* works to reduce global trafficking in women and children (www.polarisproject.org). Volunteers participate in letter-writing campaigns, support antitrafficking legislation, and conduct research on the problem. Many social enterprises give their profits back to help stop human trafficking, including https://www.whotheyare.com/single-post/2017/09/21/5-Social-Enterprises-that-Help-Survivors-of-Human-Trafficking-Create-a-New-Start. Consider supporting these organizations.

- *The Equal Justice Initiative* (EJI) works with individuals, communities, and policymakers to curb discriminatory treatment in the criminal justice system due to poverty or racial bias. You can find information about EJI internships for recent college graduates and law students at www.eji.org/fellowships-internships.

$SAGE edge™

Get the tools you need to sharpen your study skills. SAGE edge offers a robust online environment featuring an impressive array of free tools and resources.

Access practice quizzes, eFlashcards, video, and multimedia at **edge.sagepub.com/ballantine7e**

PART III

INEQUALITY

Why are you rich, whereas others in your sociology class or community are poor—or vice versa? Why do some people rise to the top of society with wealth, power, and prestige at their fingertips, and others languish near the bottom? Does ethnicity, race, or gender affect your position in society? What are your chances of moving out of your current social position? These are the underlying questions in the following three chapters. They focus on stratification, how individuals and groups are layered or ranked in society according to how many valued resources they possess or to which they have access (e.g., wealth, power, and prestige). *Inequality* is a social condition in which privileges, opportunities, and substantial rewards are given to people in some positions in society but denied to others. At the bottom of the human hierarchy are those starving and diseased world citizens who have no hope beyond mere survival for either themselves or their families. This contrasts with corporate executives and some world leaders who have billions of dollars at their disposal. The implications of social stratification extend from the individual all the way to global social networks.

Sometimes the basis for social stratification and inequality is one's socioeconomic status, but other characteristics such as race, ethnicity, gender, sexual orientation, nationality, religion, or age can also help determine where you fall in the social stratification system. These differences often result in strong feelings like "us" versus "them" thinking.

In this section, we focus on issues of social inequality related to social class, race, ethnicity, and gender. Chapter 7 focuses on local and global socioeconomic stratification resulting in inequality; subsequent chapters examine ethnic, racial, and gender stratification.

© Reuters/Romeo Ranoco

STRATIFICATION

Rich and Famous—or Rags and Famine?

▲ Will you live under the bridge or above it—rags or riches? Whereas hard work can often make a difference, your success also depends on your society's system of stratification and amount of inequality.

MICRO

ME (AND MY RAGS OR RICHES)

LOCAL ORGANIZATIONS AND COMMUNITY
How I am regarded by my peers.

MESO

NATIONAL ORGANIZATIONS, INSTITUTIONS, AND ETHNIC SUBCULTURES
Institutions support the privileged; ethnic subcultures are often disadvantaged.

MACRO

SOCIETY
The privileged control resources, health care, economic markets, and tax rates.

GLOBAL COMMUNITY
Rich countries have more access to resources than poor ones.

WHAT WILL YOU LEARN IN THIS CHAPTER?

This chapter will help you to do the following:

7.1 Describe what social stratification means for individuals and groups

7.2 Compare key theoretical perspectives on stratification

7.3 Explain how achieved and ascribed characteristics impact individuals' life chances

7.4 Explain what affects your chances for social mobility

7.5 Compare pluralist and power elite perspectives on stratification

7.6 Discuss inequality and poverty from a sociological perspective

THINK ABOUT IT

Micro: Small groups and local communities	Why are some people in your community wealthier than others?
Meso: National institutions, complex organizations, and ethnic groups	How do institutions—such as the family, education, religion, health, politics, and the economy—help keep people in the class they were born into?
Macro: National and global systems	Why are some nations affluent and others impoverished? How does the fact that we live in a global society affect you and your social position?

Pomp and circumstance surrounded the May 19, 2018, royal wedding of Prince Harry and Meghan Markle. All eyes in Britain and many eyes around the world were glued to their TVs and computer monitors. Thousands waited for hours to see the happy couple in person, as they lined the royal route to the palace. The bill for the entire wedding (security included) is estimated at around $43 million (Elkins 2018).

A member of a royal family, such as Prince Harry of Britain, grows up in a privileged world, with wealth, prestige, and access to power. A regal lifestyle includes formal receptions, horse races, polo games, royal hunts, state visits, and other social and state functions. The family has several elegant residences at its disposal. However, like most royalty, Harry—and now Meghan—also live within the confines of their elite status, with its strict expectations and limitations. They cannot show up for a beer at the local pub or associate freely with commoners.

Members of the royal family cannot even protect their loved ones from the abuse of bigoted commentary, as Harry discovered shortly after his and Markle's

relationship became public. Once their relationship became known, Markle, who has a White father and Black mother, faced an onslaught of both racism and sexism in the media. Through a statement by his communications director, Prince Henry declared that "Markle has been subject to a wave of abuse and harassment. Some of this has been very public—the smear on the front page of a national newspaper; the racial undertones of comment pieces; and the outright sexism and racism of social media trolls and web article comments" (Scobie 2016). Although there is no official royalty in the United States, wealthy entrepreneurs, stock brokers and bankers, and entertainment and sports figures hold positions that allow for a life of comfort similar to that of royalty, without the restrictions and intense media coverage.

On the other hand, rags and famine pervade the planet. Hidden from the public eye in Britain and the United States are people with no known names and no swank addresses; some have no addresses at all. Around the globe, wars, natural disasters, famines, economic crises, slavery, and human trafficking point to the presence

▲ Prince Harry, Duke of Sussex, and Meghan, Duchess of Sussex (born Rachel Meghan Markle), on their wedding day on May 19, 2018. Prince Harry is currently sixth in the line of succession to the British crown.

▲ The United States does not have royalty with inherited thrones and titles. However, it does have enormous gaps in wealth, with some people living in splendor and luxury beyond the imagination of the average citizen.

of inequality. **Inequality** is *a social condition in which privileges, opportunities, and substantial rewards are given to people in some positions in society but denied to others.*

Inequality leaves many people particularly vulnerable when natural and human-made disasters strike. Residents in poorer nations and poorer areas within nations face the brunt of climate change. For example, as deserts continue to grow across northern China, thousands of nomadic herders have become "ecological migrants," forced off their native lands into uncertain economic and social futures. Thanks to climate change–induced desertification, their land is no longer habitable (Haner et al. 2016).

As noted in Chapter 6, climate change and economic hard times have pushed many low-income people from their rural homes to cities in hopes of finding jobs. However, with few jobs for unskilled and semiskilled workers in today's postindustrial service economies, many of the poor are left homeless. They live in abandoned buildings or sleep in unlocked autos, on park benches, under bridges, on beaches, or anywhere they can stretch out and hope not to be attacked or harassed. In the United States, cities such as Houston, Los Angeles, Washington, DC, and New York try to cope with the homeless by setting up sanitary facilities and temporary shelters, especially in bad weather. Cities also rely on religious and civic organizations to run soup kitchens and shelters.

Extreme poverty has fallen (almost in half) over the past couple of decades, but the figures are still staggering. Nearly 1 billion people still live on less than $1.90 a day (World Bank 2017). Children raised in families with the lowest incomes grow up in poverty, with lack of electricity, clean water, education, sanitation, health care, and adequate food. They die of preventable diseases.

In some areas of the world, such as India and sub-Saharan Africa, the situation is particularly desperate, and many families are starving. At daybreak, a cart traverses the city of Kolkata, India, picking up bodies of diseased and starved homeless people who have died on the streets during the night. Mother Teresa, who won the Nobel Peace Prize for her work with those in dire poverty, established a home in India where these people could die with dignity. She also founded an orphanage for children who would otherwise wander the streets begging or lie on the sidewalk dying. The micro- and meso-level efforts of Mother Teresa and her fellow Missionaries of Charity are noble but only a small bandage on a massive macro-level social problem.

Despite the awful conditions experienced by those living on the street, homeless people are not the lowest group on the social hierarchy. It may surprise you

▲ New York, like most cities, has a large homeless population. This person seeks shelter and some sleep in a New York subway station.

to know that **slavery**—*when an individual or a family is bound in servitude as the property of a person or household, bought and sold, and forced to work*—is alive and flourishing around the world. It exists in every nation—even in the United States and other Global North nations (Free the Slaves 2018). In 2016, Great Britain noted 2,255 slavery offenses in Wales and England (Yeginsu 2017). Throughout the world, an estimated 40.3 million people live as slaves (Walk Free Foundation 2018). Women and girls make up a slight majority of slaves. Slaves find themselves auctioned off or lured into slavery each year by gangs, pimps, and cross-border syndicates to work in forced labor or prostitution, as child soldiers or brides in forced marriages, or on plantations or in factories. Children make up more than one out of every four slaves (Free the Slaves 2018).

The countries with the highest percentage of their population enslaved are North Korea, Uzbekistan, Cambodia, India, and Qatar; those with the least are Luxembourg, Ireland, Norway, Denmark, Switzerland, Austria, Sweden and Belgium, the United States and Canada, and Australia and New Zealand. The latter are relatively politically stable, economically prosperous nations with lower levels of conflict and more efforts to combat slavery. The next Sociology Around the World looks at how slavery has become part of chocolate and coffee production in some areas of the world.

In the slavery of the 19th century, slaves were expensive, and there was some economic incentive to care about their health and survival so that they could be productive workers. In the new slavery, humans are cheap and replaceable. There is little concern about working them to death, especially if they are located in remote cacao, coffee, tea, or sugar cane plantations. By current dollars, a slave in the southern United States in the mid-1800s

CHOCOLATE AND COFFEE: A MORAL DILEMMA?

Yum! Chocolate and coffee are addictive, and most of us depend on one or both. The average U.S. citizen eats over 11 pounds of chocolate (that's the equivalent of 120 bars) a year, and 83% drink coffee (Perez 2013). The ugly side of chocolate treats is that children, often used as slave labor, pick most of the cocoa beans in West Africa (Ivory Coast and Ghana) where 70% of all chocolate is produced. "Boys and girls, usually between the ages of 12 and 16 but some as young as 7, are smuggled from neighboring countries such as Mali and Burkina Faso, and sold to cocoa bean plantation owners . . . forced to engage in grueling manual labor, carrying extremely heavy bags, working with machetes and pesticides" (Food Empowerment Project 2015; Nall 2012: para. 3, O'Keefe 2016). Others are sent out by their families to work on plantations, so that they can earn money instead of going to school.

Large chocolate companies (e.g., Hershey, Mars, Cadbury, and Nestle) have made some steps to reduce their reliance on slave labor and to train and support farmers who treat their workers with dignity and refuse to use child and slave labor. Many farmers find this difficult to do, however, because they make so little from selling their chocolate. For example, "the average farmer in Ghana in the 2013–14 growing season made just 84¢ per day, and farmers in Ivory Coast a mere 50¢. That puts them well below the World Bank's new $1.90 per day standard for extreme poverty" (O'Keefe 2016). Until the average farmer makes more money, it will be difficult to eradicate slave labor on cocoa bean farms.

As in the chocolate-producing countries of West Africa, slavery remains widespread in Brazil, the world's largest exporter of coffee. One third of all coffee comes from Brazil, where "coffee pickers often face debt bondage, non-existent work contracts, exposure to deadly pesticides, lack of protective equipment, and accommodation without doors, mattresses or drinking water" (Danwatch 2016; *The Guardian* 2016: para. 4).

How can we get our coffee and chocolate fixes and help solve the problem? Free the Slaves, Mercy Project, Slavery Footprint, Ark of Hope for Children, and other organizations work to prevent child slavery. *Fair trade certified* products are free from abuse and exploitive labor practices; fair wages are paid, health and safety are observed, and sustainable methods are used. Supporting organizations that fight for children's rights can go a long way toward making our chocolate and coffee guilt-free. The two logos provided here are common indicators of fair trade products.

would have cost the equivalent of $40,000 today, but contemporary slaves can be procured from poor countries for an average of $90 (Bales 2012; The CNN Freedom Project 2017).

Ongoing efforts by public sociologists, among others, seek to do away with modern-day slavery. A sociologist at the forefront of the current movement to eradicate slavery is featured in the next Sociologists in Action.

STOPPING SLAVERY IN THE 21ST CENTURY

Becoming an abolitionist sociologist crept up on me. The first tiny prodding was a leaflet I picked up at an outdoor event in London. The front of the leaflet read "There Are Millions of Slaves in the World Today." I was a university professor, and I confess to an unpleasant mixture of pride and hubris in my reaction to the bold title of the leaflet. Having been involved in human rights for many years, I thought, *How could this be true if I don't know about it already?*

I came to understand why this issue was invisible. Slavery was hidden under a thick blanket of ignorance, concealed by the common assumption that it was extinct. With slavery illegal in every country, criminal slaveholders kept their activities hidden.

As I built up a picture of slavery, every new set of facts generated new questions. I began to realize that a large-scale research project was needed, and I went in search of modern slavery, traveling to India, Pakistan, Thailand, Mauritania, and Brazil—often going undercover as I studied slave-based businesses in each country. The result was the book *Disposable People: New Slavery in the Global Economy* (Bales 1999, 2004, 2012).

In 2000, I, with three others, helped found Free the Slaves, the American sister organization of Anti-Slavery International, the world's oldest (1787) and original human rights group. Free the Slaves works with local partners to liberate slaves around the world and change the systems that allow slavery to exist. In addition to addressing the crime of enslavement, this work often involves confronting gender inequality, racism, ethnic and religious discrimination, and the negative outcomes of global economic growth. We have learned that freedom and empowerment are viral and that freed slaves will stop at nothing to stay free and help others to liberty.

Not every part of liberation and reintegration requires sociological training, but it would be very hard to be successful without it. Without carefully constructed longitudinal surveys of villages in slavery we could never have demonstrated the *freedom dividend*, the powerful and positive economic change that comes to whole communities when slavery is abolished. Without training in the empathetic understanding of a social researcher we could never have developed the *slavery lens*, a way of seeing this hidden crime, that the U.S. government now requires of all of its foreign aid program workers. Without learning about the complex interplay of culture, society, economics, politics, and social vulnerability, we would never be able to build the unique methodologies of liberation tailored to specific and culturally rooted forms of slavery. There is nothing like the ugly reality of a crime like slavery to push young sociologists to do their best work—using solid social science to change the world.

★ ★ ★ ★ ★ ★

Kevin Bales is a sociologist and professor of contemporary slavery at the Wilberforce Institute for the Study of Slavery and Emancipation (WISE) at the University of Hull, England, and cofounder of Free the Slaves in Washington, DC. This excerpt is taken from Korgen, White, and White's (2013) *Sociologists in Action: Race, Class, Gender, and Intersections*.

THINKING SOCIOLOGICALLY

Why do you think slavery exists today? List micro, meso, and macro forces at work that support modern slavery. What steps should be taken to combat each and eradicate slavery?

As we can see from the previous examples, our social world is stratified in ways that result in high levels of inequality. The rest of this chapter discusses (a) why stratification is important, (b) systems of stratification, (c) the consequences of social rankings for individuals, (d) whether one can change social class positions (social

▲ Child laborers make up at least a third of the workforce at an aluminum factory in Dhaka, Bangladesh, in 2016.

mobility), (e) characteristics of major stratification systems, (f) poverty and social policies to address it, and (g) the global digital divide.

Importance of Social Stratification

Consider your own social ranking in society. You were born into a family that holds a position in society: upper, middle, or lower class. The position of your family influences the neighborhood in which you live and where you

© iStockPhoto.com/Freezing Rain

© REUTERS/Gary Hershorn

▲ Even the sports one plays—such as polo or stickball—are greatly influenced by social class and convey different kinds of social and cultural capital. Polo clearly requires a good deal of economic capital in order to play, whereas stickball requires only a ball and a straight stick.

shop, go to school, play sports, engage in the arts or other activities, and attend religious services. Most likely, you and your family carry out the tasks of daily living in your community with people who share your social class status.

Your position in the stratification system affects the opportunities available to you and the choices you make in life. Note the social world model at the beginning of the chapter. It provides a visual image of the social world and socioeconomic stratification. The stratification process affects everything from individuals' social rankings at the micro level of analysis to positions of countries in the global system at the macro level.

Social stratification refers to *how individuals and groups are layered and ranked in society according to their access to and possession of valued resources.* The society's culture (rules, values, beliefs, and artifacts) determines and legitimizes the society's system of sorting its members.

Each society also determines what it considers to be valued resources. For example, in an agricultural society, members are ranked according to how much land or how many animals they own. In an industrial society, ownership of the *means of production* (machinery that can produce goods) and occupational skills determine class status. In postindustrial information societies, education, access to technology, and control of information dissemination are key determinants in the ranking process.

What members of each society value and the criteria they use to rank other members depends on events in the society's history, its geographic location, its level of development in the world, its political philosophy, and the decisions of those in power. The more powerful individuals tend to get the best positions, the most desirable mates, and the greatest opportunities. They may have power because of birth order, personality characteristics, age, physical attractiveness, education, intelligence, wealth, race, family background, occupation, religion, or ethnic group—whatever the basis for power is in that particular society. Those with relatively high amounts of power have advantages that perpetuate their power, and they try to hold on to those advantages through laws, customs, power, ideologies, and sometimes force. Note that each level of analysis—micro, meso, and macro—adds to our understanding of the stratification process.

Micro-Level Prestige and Influence

Remember how some of your peers on the playground were given more respect than others? Their high regard may have come from belonging to a prestigious family, having a dynamic or domineering personality, being good at games, or owning symbols that distinguished them—"cool" clothing or shoes, a desirable bicycle, or expensive toys. This is stratification at work.

Property, power, and prestige are accorded to those who have **cultural capital** (*knowledge, skills, language mastery, style of dress, and values that provide a person with access to a particular status in society*) and **social capital** (*connections or networks with people who have influence*). Individual qualities, such as leadership skills, an engaging personality, self-confidence, quick-wittedness, and physical attractiveness, or ascribed characteristics, such as sex or race, influence cultural and social capital. Interactions with meso-level organizations help shape the influence of these individual traits.

Meso-Level Access to Resources

Many of the resources we use come from institutions at the meso level: family, education, religion, economic and political institutions, and health care. We first learn our social status and the roles associated with it through our interactions with family members. The socialization we undergo in our families influences how we see ourselves, how others perceive us, and our access to resources such as education and jobs. For example, we learn grammar and manners from our families; that in turn affects how our teachers and peers view and judge us. Educational organizations treat children differently according to their social status, revealed through such symbols as language

(e.g., if we speak standard English) and manners (e.g., not interrupting, saying please and thank you when appropriate, and addressing adults by their proper titles). Our education can result in differential access to prestigious jobs and affect our social status in society—and therefore our position in the social stratification hierarchy.

Macro-Level Factors Influencing Stratification

The global economic position of a nation affects the opportunities available to individuals in that nation, illustrating that macro-level factors also influence placement in the stratification system (see Figure 7.1). Haiti provides a powerful illustration of this fact. Located on the island of Hispaniola in the Caribbean, Haiti is the poorest country in the Western Hemisphere and one of the poorest countries in the world, with little technology, few resources, ineffective government, a weak educational system, and an occupational structure based largely on subsistence farming. Even its forest resources are essentially gone due to desperately poor people cutting down the last trees for firewood and shelters, leaving the land to erode (Diamond 2005; World Bank 2017).

The 2010 earthquake and floods added to Haitians' economic woes and misery. Residents were driven from what meager shelters they had and then faced a cholera epidemic

▼ FIGURE 7.1

Gross National Income per Capita in 2016

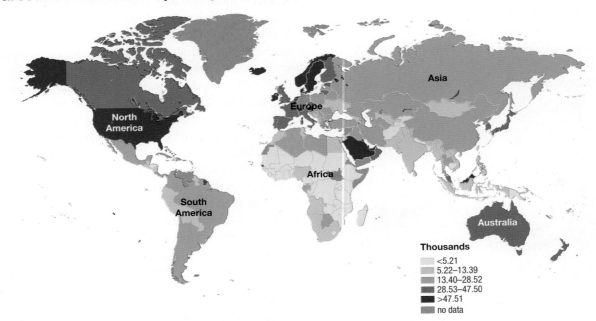

Thousands
<5.21
5.22–13.39
13.40–28.52
28.53–47.50
>47.51
no data

Source: World Bank 2018b.

from contaminated water. Haitians now have few opportunities to get ahead and be successful. This is but one example of macro-level factors (failing economy; eroded land; lack of infrastructure, such as schools and health facilities; and lack of opportunity to participate in the global economy) affecting the opportunities available to people in the country. A major influx of international money has allowed for some public projects, but progress is slow as political tensions and instability increase ("Haiti" 2015).

Almost all societies stratify members, and societies themselves are stratified in the world system, so that each individual or nation experiences the world in unique ways related to its position. Stratification is one of the most powerful forces that we experience, but we are seldom conscious of how it works or how pervasive it is in our lives. This is the driving question sociologists ask when developing theories of stratification: How does it work?

THINKING SOCIOLOGICALLY

Place yourself in the center of the social world model. Working outward from micro-level interactions toward the meso-level institutions and the macro-level global stratification system, indicate what has influenced where you fall in the stratification system.

Theoretical Explanations of Stratification

As we traverse the world, we see continuous examples of rich and poor—those who have more resources than they need and those who do not have enough to survive. Why

is the distribution of resources so uneven? Is the unequal distribution inevitable, healthy, or harmful for society?

Sociologists have developed theories to explain social stratification, based on the lens through which they view society. These explanations range from individual micro-level to national and global macro-level theories (e.g., symbolic interaction, rational choice, structural-functional, and conflict theories).

Micro-Level Theory

Our now familiar theories that relate to the micro level help us again, this time to understand differences among individuals in the stratification hierarchy.

Symbolic Interaction Theory. Have you ever been to a party where almost everyone came from a social class that had either much more or much less money than you? Even if you have not, you can probably imagine what it would be like. Awkward! Each social group has norms that members learn through the socialization process. These norms are recognized within that group and can make clueless outsiders feel uncomfortable.

People learn what is expected in their groups—family, peer group, social class—through interaction with others. For instance, children are rewarded or punished for behaviors appropriate or inappropriate to their social position. The socialization process transmits and perpetuates our positions in the social stratification system. Learning our position means learning values, speech patterns, consumption habits, appropriate group memberships (including political, economic, and religious affiliations), and even our self-concept. This knowledge provides us with the cultural capital necessary to interact effectively with people who share our social position.

Cultural knowledge is learned by children at home; they then bring that with them to school. Some home environments teach children to obey rules and authority, and to develop hands-on skills, such as repairing houses and cars. Other families teach children by expanding vocabularies; developing good grammar; experiencing concerts, art, and theater; visiting historical sites; providing reading materials; and modeling engagement with reading. The higher-class parents tend to stress thinking and questioning skills as opposed to primarily obeying authority figures. The result of this learning at home is that all children attain cultural capital that helps them interact with others at their social class level. The class difference in the types of cultural capital, though, means that children from the middle and upper classes or higher castes are more likely to get the best education, setting

© iStockphoto.com/tomazi

▲ Look at all those forks and knives. Some people know what to do with each of them! Knowing which fork or knife to use for each course of a meal is a sign of cultural capital that can influence your chances of acceptance into elite society or success on a job interview.

them up to be future leaders with better life chances. Schools place children into courses and academic groups, influenced in part by the labels children receive due to their cultural capital. In this way, children's home experiences and education help reproduce the social class systems and perpetuate the family's social class position in society (Ballantine, Hammack, and Stuber 2017).

Like language, other symbols can also represent social positions. Clothing, for example, sets up some people as special and privileged. In the 1960s, wearing blue jeans was a radical act by college students to reject status differences—showing solidarity with and support for the working class. Today, many young people wear expensive designer jeans that low-income people cannot afford. Drinking wine that most people do not have the means to buy, driving a Jaguar rather than a less expensive car, and living in a home that has six or eight bedrooms and is 5,000-plus square feet are expressions of *conspicuous consumption*—displaying goods in a way that others will notice and that will presumably earn the owner respect (Veblen 1902). Thus, purchased products become symbols intended to define the person as someone of high status in the stratification hierarchy.

Privacy can also symbolize affluence. For example, in most of the Global North, one symbol of middle-class "decency" is the right to bathe and do one's grooming in private. Indeed, many young people in the United States have their own bedrooms and expect no interruptions when sprucing up for the day. Homeless people in the United States do not have this luxury, and in India, bathing on the streets is not uncommon. Privacy requires money.

A core idea in symbolic interaction theory is that reality is constructed, that as we figure out what our circumstances mean, we construct the reality in which we live. This idea is explored further in the next Sociology in Our Social World.

Rational Choice Theory.

As you know, rational choice theorists focus on individuals and the way they make decisions regarding their own self-interest. From this view, people make decisions based on their perception of costs and benefits. Some people evaluate potential benefits with a view to the long-term. They are willing to endure short-term expense or "pain" if the long-term gains are substantial. To take this view, one needs a sense of *delayed gratification*—being able to delay rewards or benefits until later. People who are willing or in a position to do this—living austerely now to experience prosperity later—may be more likely to have upward mobility and to experience greater affluence later. You are probably practicing delayed gratification as you read these words, focusing on

▲ In India, many people must bathe in public in whatever water supply they can find. Even many people with homes do not have their own water supply. Privacy for one's grooming is a symbol of privilege for the affluent.

paying for and succeeding in college now, while planning to use a college degree to gain a professional, well-paying job in the future. Thus, rational choice theorists would look at how personal choices influence one's place in the social system. The idea is that one's socioeconomic position is shaped largely by individual decisions. What, though, influences those individual decisions?

In high school, many college prep students make "rational" decisions to become involved in athletic programs, student council, the Spanish Club, leadership roles in the National Honor Society, or community service because they want to list those involvements on college applications. They commit effort now—sometimes in activities they care little about—in hopes of having a payoff in admission or scholarships to the college of their choice. Those same students become discouraged with classmates who will not help with student council activities or with building the junior class float. However, for young people whose parents did not go to college and whose past experiences do not lead them to believe that they, themselves, could ever attain a college degree, spending time decorating a float makes no sense. It is not seen as a rational choice. Thus, past experiences and social position can influence the way one evaluates costs and benefits.

These micro-level theories help us to understand how our daily interactions and decisions can impact our social positions (and vice versa) within society's stratification hierarchy. We now look at theories that examine the larger social structures, processes, and forces that affect stratification and inequality: structural-functional theory and various forms of conflict theory.

UNDERSTANDING URBAN HOMELESS PEOPLE

Homeless people may find themselves sleeping under bridges or in parks, vacant lots, cars, or unused subway tunnels. On any given night, there are an estimated 549,928 homeless people in the United States (National Alliance to End Homelessness 2017). In *Down on Their Luck: A Study of Homeless Street People*, a classic sociological text on homelessness, David Snow and Leon Anderson identified key variables that distinguished different types of homelessness and uncovered a wide range of causes, circumstances, and coping methods among the homeless. They studied the micro culture of street people, how they lend each other support and help each other make sense of their circumstances. Their work points to many forces at work on the homeless, from global economic trends to the way their families relate to them.

One question Snow and Anderson addressed is how homeless people affirm a positive sense of self in this humiliating situation. After all, to be a person of worth in American society is to (a) own some property, (b) have someone who cares about you enough to take you in if you are really desperate, and (c) occupy a significant status in society by earning some money and having a career or position deserving of respect. The homeless not only lack all these, but their master status—"homeless person"—is one that elicits disrespect. "Dignity and worth are not primarily individual characteristics, but instead flow from the roles we play," write the authors (Snow and Anderson 1993:9). To be

homeless, then, is far more than to be without a residence or shelter. It is to be without a place to restore one's dignity. So how do the homeless cope?

Snow and Anderson uncovered a number of coping strategies during their interviews with homeless urban people. Sometimes, the homeless people explained away their circumstances as temporary "bad luck" or part of a normal cycle in which they just happened to be on the down end for a short period of time. Others distanced themselves from the role of homelessness, pointing out that they were "different" from other homeless people, "did not really belong," and did not really deserve to be seen as homeless at all. Some people coped by fictive storytelling, pointing to pronounced achievements in the past (often fictionalized or embellished) or creating stories of phenomenal things they would accomplish when they get on their feet. By affirming another identity in the past or the future, their self-esteem was salvaged. However, perhaps the most surprising strategy to preserve self-worth was to embrace the role of being homeless with pride—to boast about how one was the best at being a survivor, the best at being a friend to the homeless, or the best at rejecting shallow values of materialism in our commercial society. They had defined reality in a way that affirmed their strengths and allowed them to see themselves in a positive light. They had changed the social construction of reality, at least among themselves (Snow and Anderson 1993).

Meso- and Macro-Level Theories

Structural-Functional Theory. Structural-functionalists view stratification within societies as an inevitable, and generally necessary, part of the social world. The stratification system provides individuals a place or position in the social world and motivates them to carry out their roles. Societies survive by having an organized system into which each individual is born and raised and contributes to the maintenance of the society.

The basic elements of the structural-functional theory of stratification were explained by Kingsley Davis and Wilbert Moore (1945), and their work still provides the main ideas of the theory today. Focusing on stratification by considering the rewards given to people in various occupations, they argue the following:

1. *Value of positions.* Some positions are more important to society than others. For example, society needs people to fill occupations that require specialized training and long hours, such as physicians and CEOs. Societies must motivate talented individuals to prepare for and occupy the most important and difficult positions.

2. *Preparation requires talent, time, and money.* To motivate talented individuals to make the sacrifices necessary to prepare for difficult positions such as a physician or CEO, differential rewards of income, prestige, power, or other valued goods must be offered. Thus, a doctor and a CEO receive high income, prestige, and power as incentives.

3. *Unequal distribution of rewards.* The differences in rewards, such as pay for most-valued positions, in turn, lead to the unequal distribution of resources—or inequality—for occupations in society. The result is that stratification is inevitable.

Look at the example of poverty. Some sociologists argue that poverty serves certain *functions* for society, thus making it difficult to eliminate (Gans 1971, 1995). Some people may actually benefit from having poor people kept poor. Consider the following points:

1. *Poverty provides us with a convenient scapegoat—* someone to blame for individual and societal problems. We can put the blame for poverty on the poor individuals themselves. That way we can ignore the meso- and macro-level causes of poverty—like economic and political systems—and maintain the present way those institutions operate for the benefit of those now in positions of power.

2. *Having poor people creates many jobs for those who are not poor,* especially in the "helping" professions such as social workers and law enforcement jobs such as police, judges, and prison workers.

3. *The poor provide an easily available group of surplus laborers* to do undesirable jobs when needed.

4. *The poor reinforce and legitimize our own lives and institutions.* Their existence allows the rest of us to feel superior to someone, enhancing our self-esteem.

5. *Their violation of mainstream values* helps reaffirm the values among the affluent (Gans 1971, 1995).

In the mid-20th century, structural-functional theory was the dominant theory used to explain stratification. However, it has been criticized for its inability to explain why some people in society who do not provide vital services for society (e.g., professional basketball players, rappers, and hedge fund managers) receive great rewards. It also does not explain why CEOs now make so much more money compared with the typical nonsupervisory worker than they once did. For example, in 1965, CEOs made, on average, 18 times the average worker's salary. In 2015, the average pay of CEOs at the S&P 500 Index companies was 335 times the pay of the average nonsupervisory worker in their field (AFL-CIO 2016). Functionalist explanations of stratification have also been critiqued for an inability to fully explain the conflict societies experience. This is the primary focus of conflict theory.

Conflict Theory. Conflict theorists see stratification as the outcome of struggles for dominance and scarce resources, with some individuals in society taking advantage of others. Individuals and groups act in their own self-interest by trying to exploit others, leading inevitably to a struggle between those who have advantages and want to keep them and those who want a larger share of the pie.

Conflict theorist Karl Marx (1818–1883) described four possible ways to distribute wealth, according to (1) what each person needs, (2) what each person wants, (3) what each person earns, or (4) what each person can take. It was this fourth way, Marx believed, that was dominant in competitive capitalist societies (Cuzzort and King 2002; Marx and Engels 1955).

Marx viewed the stratification structure as composed of two major economically based social classes: the *haves* and the *have-nots.* The haves consist of the owners (capitalist bourgeoisie), whereas the have-nots are the working class (proletariat). The struggle over resources between the haves and have-nots is a cause of conflict. The haves control what Marx called the *means of production—* property, machinery, and cash owned by capitalists—the valued resources in society (Marx [1844] 1964). The haves dominate because the lower-class have-nots cannot accumulate enough money and power to change their positions. The haves use their dominance of the economic institution in society to influence the other social institutions. In the process they shape the norms and values of the society to make the distribution of resources seem "fair" and justified. Laws, religious beliefs, and educational systems spread ideas that support the domination of the haves. This keeps the have-nots from understanding their own self-interests and is why working-class people often support politicians whose policies really favor the wealthiest 1%. The haves' control of political structures, policies, and police and military forces ensures their continued dominance in society.

The unorganized lower-class have-nots cannot overcome their exploitation until they develop a *class consciousness*—a shared awareness that they, as a class, have interests that differ from those of the haves. They need to understand that what is good for the haves is bad for the have-nots. Marx contended that, with the help of enlightened intellectuals (like him), the working class would develop a class consciousness, rise up, and overthrow the haves, culminating in a classless society in which wealth would be more equally shared (Marx and Engels 1955).

Unlike the structural-functionalists, then, conflict theorists maintain that money and other rewards are not necessarily given to those in the most important positions in society. Can we argue that a rock star or baseball player

© Al Powers/Invision/AP

© Melissa Phillip/Houston Chronicle via AP

▲ Who do you think makes more money, Leonardo DiCaprio (here at the Oscars) or these emergency personnel? What does this imply about the structural-functionalist argument that societies motivate (through higher salaries) individuals to prepare for and occupy the most critically important and challenging positions?

Some theorists criticize Marx for his focus on only the economic system, pointing out that noneconomic factors enter into the stratification struggle as well. Max Weber (1864–1920), another influential theorist, agreed with Marx that class conflict is inevitable, that economics is one of the key factors in stratification systems, and that those in power try to perpetuate their positions. However, he added two other influential factors that he argued also work to determine stratification: power and prestige. Sometimes these are identified as the "three Ps"—property, power, and prestige. Depending on the type of economic and political era, one P tends to be more important than the others (prestige in feudal times, property in the industrial era, and power in the postindustrial period), but usually, having one P gives a person access to the other two, as well.

Recent theorists suggest that by using the three Ps, we can identify five classes—capitalists, managers, small-business owners or the petty bourgeoisie, workers, and the underclass—rather than just the haves and have-nots. *Capitalists* own the means of production, and they purchase and control the labor of others. *Managers* sell their labor to capitalists and manage the labor of others for them. The *petty bourgeoisie*, such as small-business owners, own some means of production but control little of the labor of others; they have modest prestige, power, and property (Sernau 2010). *Workers* sell their labor to capitalists and are low in all three Ps. Finally, the *underclass* has virtually no property, power, or prestige.

Even though median income has risen over the past couple of years, the distribution of wealth and income in the United States is more uneven today than at any time since before the Great Depression hit in 1929. **Income** is *money received from work or investments* whereas **wealth** is *the worth of a person based on his or her financial holdings (stocks, bank accounts, and investment income) and property (homes, cars) minus debt*. Today, the richest 20 people in the United States are wealthier than the entire bottom 50% of the U.S. population (152 million people) (Collins and Hoxie 2015). In the world, the richest 1% own more than the other 99% of the combined world's population (Byanyima 2015).

Workers have also become more anxious about declining wages and job insecurity. Since the 1990s, companies have begun to outsource more and more jobs. Fewer people now work for one company in a stable position, with benefits and some sense of job security, and more work in temporary positions as consultants (without benefits and job security). Some economists refer to this as the *Uberization* of the job market, referring to the fast-growing ride sharing company Uber that directly employs only

is more necessary for the survival of society than a teacher or police officer? Yet it takes most teachers (even those with a master's degree) an entire career to earn as much as many celebrities earn in a matter of months.

As you can see, not all of Marx's predictions have come true. Whereas many nations have labor laws that require owners to pay workers a minimum wage and provide safe working conditions and that prohibit discrimination on the basis of race, gender, or religion, inequality still exists throughout the world. Even societies that claim to be classless, such as China, have privileged classes and peasants. In recent years, the Chinese government has allowed more private ownership of shops, businesses, and other entrepreneurial efforts, motivating many Chinese citizens to work long hours at their private businesses to "get ahead." The only classless societies are a few small hunter-gatherer groups that have no extra resources that would allow some members to accumulate wealth.

▲ Uber, the online transportation company, employs more than 2 million drivers worldwide. Only a small percentage of them are full-time employees with secure work hours and benefits.

© Bloomberg/Getty Images

12,000 of the 750,000 people who work (at least indirectly) for the company in the United States (Bhuiyan 2017; O'Brien 2017). Hiring people as consultants allows employers greater flexibility. They can hire and fire as needed and do not have to worry much about employees organizing to demand higher compensation or better benefits. This is great for employers but not so great for most workers, who must wonder for how long they can count on getting a paycheck, how many hours of work they might get each week, and how much their next "gig" might pay.

THINKING SOCIOLOGICALLY

> How would conflict theorists explain the fact that, as Senator Bernie Sanders often points out, the average pay of CEOs at the S&P 500 Index companies is 335 times the pay of the average nonsupervisory workers in their field? Or that the richest 1% in the world own more than the combined wealth of the other 99%? Does their argument make sense? Why or why not?

Evolutionary Theory of Stratification: A Synthesis

Evolutionary theory, developed by Gerhard Lenski, borrows assumptions from both structural-functional and conflict theories to determine how scarce resources are distributed and how that distribution results in stratification (Lenski 1966; Nolan and Lenski 2014). The basic ideas are that (a) to survive, people must cooperate; (b) despite this, conflicts of interest occur over important decisions that benefit one individual or group over another; (c) valued items such as money and status are always in demand and in short supply; (d) there is likely to be a struggle over these scarce goods; and (e) customs or traditions in a society often prevail over rational criteria in determining distribution of scarce resources. After the minimum survival needs of both individuals and the society are met, power determines who gets the surplus: prestige, luxury living, the best health care, and so forth. Lenski believes that privileges (including wealth) flow from having power, and prestige usually results from having access to both power and privilege (Hurst 2006).

Lenski tested his theory by studying societies at different levels of technological development, ranging from simple to complex. He found that the degree of inequality increases with technology until it reaches the advanced industrial stage. For instance, in subsistence-level hunter-gatherer societies, little surplus is available, and everyone's needs are met to the extent possible. As surplus accumulates in agrarian societies, those who acquire surpluses also control power, and they use this to benefit their friends and relations. However, they must share at least some of the wealth or fear being overthrown.

When societies finally reach the advanced industrial stage, there should be less inequality. Industrialization brings surplus wealth, a division of labor, advanced technology, and interdependence among members of a society. No longer can one individual control all of the important knowledge, skills, or capital resources. The surplus can be spread to more people without diminishing that received by those who have the most. Therefore, this should eliminate the extreme gaps between haves and have-nots because resources would normally be more evenly distributed. Also, at this point in history, societies tend to have constitutions and recognize the rights of citizens, making it harder to exploit them.

Evolutionary theory takes into consideration an idea shared by the structural-functionalists and rational choice theorists—that talented individuals need to be motivated to make sacrifices. This produces motivated, competent, and well-educated people in the most important social statuses. The theory also recognizes exploitation leading to inequality, a factor that conflict theorists find in systems of stratification.

Whereas some inequality may be useful in highly complex societies, as functionalists have argued, evolutionary theorists note that extraordinary amounts of inequality may undermine motivation and productivity. The most talented people will not even try to attain the most demanding and important jobs if upward mobility seems impossible. Therefore, high levels of inequality do not make sense for a healthy industrial or postindustrial society (Nolan and Lenski 2014).

Each of the theories already discussed—symbolic interaction, rational choice, structural-functional, conflict, and evolutionary theory—provides a different explanation for understanding stratification in modern societies. These theories provide the basis for micro- to macro-level discussions of stratification. Our next topic looks at some factors that influence an individual's position in a stratification system and the ability to change that position.

THINKING SOCIOLOGICALLY

Why is the income gap between the rich and the poor currently increasing in the United States? Which theory seems most helpful in explaining this pattern? What are some possible ramifications of this widening income gap?

Individuals' Social Status: The Micro Level

You are among the world's elite. Less than 7% of the world's population has a college degree (Erickson and Vonk 2012). Being able to afford the time and money for college is a luxury beyond the financial or personal resources of almost 93% of people in the world. However, the global number of college students is expanding rapidly as countries such as China provide more higher-education opportunities to support their growing economies. Because the demand for a college education far exceeds the opportunity in China, many Chinese college students study abroad, adding to their opportunities and enhancing China's knowledge of the world. Chinese students make up the largest number of international students studying in the United States (Witherell 2016).

In the United States, access to higher education is greater than in many other countries because there are more levels of entry—including technical colleges, community colleges, state universities, and private 4-year colleges. However, with limited government help, most students must have enough financial resources to cover tuition and the cost of living.

The prestige of the college that students choose can also make a difference in their future opportunities. Students born into wealth can afford private preparatory schools and tutors to help them raise their SAT and ACT test scores, which increases their chances of gaining acceptance to prestigious colleges. Such colleges offer social networking and other opportunities not available to those attending the typical state university or nonelite

college (Jaschik 2013; Persell 2005). In turn, these social networks can help them land lucrative professional positions.

Prestigious colleges do not benefit all students equally, however. For a variety of reasons, ascribed characteristics, such as gender, can affect your chances for success in life—no matter what school you attend. Gender socialization and embedded gender stratification systems may make it difficult for women to rise in the occupational hierarchy. Many Japanese women, for example, earn college degrees but leave employment after getting married and having children, because of both gender socialization and gender discrimination in the workforce (*The Japan Times* 2016). We examine gender stratification in more depth in Chapter 9, but note that it intersects with socioeconomic status and must be viewed as part of a larger pattern resulting in inequality in the social world.

Individual Life Chances

Life chances refer to one's opportunities, depending on both achieved and ascribed statuses in society. That you are in college, probably have health insurance and access to health care, and are likely to live into your late 70s or 80s are factors directly related to your life chances. Let us consider several examples of how placement in organizations at the meso level affects individual experiences and has global ramifications.

Education. Although education is valued by most individuals, the cost of books, clothing, shoes, transportation, childcare, and time taken from income-producing work may be insurmountable barriers to school attendance for many people. One's level of education affects many aspects of life, including economic, political, religious, and family attitudes and behavior. Generally speaking, the higher the education level, the more active individuals are in political life; the more mainstream or conventional their religious affiliation; and the more likely they are to marry, remain married, and have good health.

Health, Social Conditions, and Life Expectancy. If you have a sore throat for an extended period of time, you will probably go see a doctor. Yet many people in the world will never see a doctor. Access to health care requires doctors and medical facilities, money for transportation and treatment, access to childcare, and released time from other tasks. Often, the poor do not have these luxuries. In contrast, the affluent eat better food; are less exposed to polluted water and unhygienic conditions;

and are able to pay for health insurance, medical care, and drugs when they do have ailing health. As a result, they tend to live much longer than poorer people.

Examining causes of death among different classes illustrates the drastic differences in access to health care among people at different places in the stratification hierarchy. For example, in the poor Global South, shorter life expectancies and deaths, especially among children, are due to controllable infectious diseases such as cholera, malaria, AIDS, typhoid, tuberculosis, and other respiratory ailments. In contrast, in affluent countries, heart disease, stroke, and lung cancer are the most common causes of death, and most deaths are of people above the age of 65. With improvements in immunizations, mosquito nets to prevent malaria, better sanitation and water quality, access to medicines, better nutrition, and female literacy, life expectancy rises. Yet the chance to live a long and healthy life is a privilege available primarily to those living in wealthy countries. Indeed, despite medical advances, the gap in life spans between the wealthy and those with low incomes has been widening since 1970 (Tavernise 2016).

By studying Table 7.1 in the next Engaging Sociology feature, you can compare life expectancy with two other measures of life quality for the poorest and richest countries: the gross domestic product (GDP) per capita income—the average purchasing power each person has per year—and the infant mortality rates (death rates for babies). Note that life expectancy in poor countries is as low as 51 years in Chad and Guinea-Bissau, Africa (many of the people in these countries are subsistence farmers), as high as 89 years in the wealthy country of Monaco, and 85 in Japan and Singapore. In the United States, life expectancy is 80 (World Factbook 2017d). Average annual GDP is as low as $700 in Central African Republic and as high as $139,100 in Liechtenstein and $124,900 in Qatar. The average U.S. GDP is $59,500 a year (World Factbook 2017b). Infant mortality is as high as 110.6 deaths per 1,000 births in Afghanistan (more than 1 in 10) and as low as 2 in Iceland and 1.8 in Monaco. In the United States, the estimated 2015 rate is 5.8 deaths per 1,000 births (World Factbook 2017c).

THINKING SOCIOLOGICALLY

How do some specific factors at the micro, meso, and macro levels affect your life expectancy and that of your family members?

One does not have to look beyond the borders of the United States to see the relationship between health and wealth. The United States has much larger gaps between rich and poor people than most other wealthy nations, and that has led to a corresponding gap in health and life expectancy among social classes, much wider than that in other highly developed nations. As the video *In Sickness and In Wealth: Health in America* (2008) reveals, there is "a health-wealth gradient" in the United States, in "which every descending rung of the socioeconomic ladder corresponds to worse health." Today, in some areas of the United States life expectancy varies between the rich and the poor by 20 years (Dwyer-Lindgren et al. 2017).

Life chances are determined, in part, by the per capita income of individuals. If people are poor, they have little disposable income. This means a life of poverty and less access to education, health, and other social conditions that determine life chances and lifestyle.

Individual Lifestyles

Your individual **lifestyle** includes *your attitudes, values, beliefs, behavior patterns, and other aspects of your place in the world, as shaped by socialization.* As individuals grow up, the behaviors and attitudes consistent with their culture and their family's status in society become internalized through the process of socialization. Lifestyle is not simply a matter of having money. Acquiring money—say, by winning a lottery—cannot buy a completely new lifestyle (Bourdieu and Passeron 1977). This is because values and behaviors are ingrained in our self-concept from childhood. A person may gain material possessions, but that does not mean she has the lifestyle of the upper-class rich and famous. Remember the awkward party when you were around people of a different social class? Even if you suddenly made the same amount of money as they do, you would not know the norms associated with that social class. Some examples of factors related to your individual lifestyle that tend to differ among social classes include attitudes toward achievement, family life and child-rearing patterns, religious membership, and political involvement.

Attitudes Toward Achievement. Attitudes toward achievement differ by social status and are generally closely correlated with life chances. As noted previously, motivation to get ahead and beliefs about what we can achieve are in part products of our upbringing and the opportunities we see as available to us. These attitudes differ greatly depending on the opportunity structure around us, including what our families and friends see

LIFE EXPECTANCY, PER CAPITA INCOME, AND INFANT MORTALITY

Analyzing the meaning of data can provide an understanding of the health and well-being of citizens around the world. A country's basic statistics, including life expectancy, per capita gross national product, and infant mortality, tell researchers a great deal about its economic health and vitality.

1. What questions do the data in Table 7.1 raise regarding differences in mortality and life expectancy rates around the world?

2. Considering what you know from this and previous chapters and from Table 7.1, what do you think are some differences in the lives of citizens in the richest and poorest countries?

▼ TABLE 7.1

Life Expectancy, Infant Mortality, and per Capita Income, Selected Poor and Rich Countries

Poor Countries	Life Expectancy (in Years) (2017 est.)	Infant Mortality (Deaths per 1,000 Births)	Per Capita GDP ($)	Rich Countries	Life Expectancy (in Years)	Infant Mortality (Deaths per 1,000 Births)	Per Capita GDP ($)
Chad	50.6	85.4	2,400	Iceland	83.1	2.1	52,100
Guinea-Bissau	51	85.7	1,800	Japan	85.3	2.0	42,700
Afghanistan	51.7	110.6	1,900	Singapore	85.2	2.4	90,500
Zambia	52.7	61.1	4,000	Switzerland	82.6	3.6	61,400
Central African Republic	52.8	86.3	700	Australia	82.3	4.3	49,900
Nigeria	53.8	69.8	5,900	Sweden	82.1	2.6	51,300
Uganda	55.9	56.1	2,400	Canada*	81.9	4.5	48,100
Burkina Faso	55.9	72.2	1,900	France	81.9	3.2	43,600
Mali	60.3	69.5	2,200	United States**	80	5.8	59,500

Source: World Factbook 2017c and 2017d for infant mortality and life expectancy; World Factbook 2017b for per capita GDP.

Note: Infant mortality is per 1,000 live births.

*Canada is 21st in life expectancy.

**United States is 43rd in life expectancy.

Most figures are 2017 estimates.

as possible and desirable. For example, the primary concern of poor families in poor nations may be to put food on the family's table. They may view education as a luxury not appropriate for people of their social class. In Global North countries, opportunity is available for most children to attend school at least through high school and often beyond. However, some students do not learn to value achievement in school due to lack of support from their primary socializing agents: family, peers, and teachers (Ballantine, Hammack, and Stuber 2017).

Family Life and Child-Rearing Patterns. Attitudes toward achievement are not the only things that differ among socioeconomic groups. Child-rearing patterns also vary and serve to reinforce one's attitude toward achievement and social position in society. When you were growing up, were your afterschool hours, weekends, and summers filled with adult-organized activities (e.g., formal lessons, youth sports, camps), or were you pretty much free to play on your own, watch TV, or hang out with friends or extended family? A family's social class location shapes the daily rhythms of family life (Duncan and Murnane 2011; Lareau 2003).

Differences in parenting behavior can lead to the "transmission of differential advantages to children" (Lareau 2003:5). Through their socialization by their parents, middle-class children are better able to navigate the educational and, later, professional occupational worlds than working-class children. This, in turn, influences the social class destinies of each group (Duncan and Murnane 2011; Lashbrook 2009).

Religious Membership. Religious affiliation also correlates with the social status variables of education, occupation, and income. For instance, in the United States, upper-class citizens are found disproportionately in Episcopalian, Unitarian, and Jewish religious groups, whereas lower-class citizens tend to be attracted to Nazarene, Southern Baptist, Jehovah's Witness, and other holiness and fundamentalist sects. Although there are exceptions, such as Catholicism, most religious groups attract members predominantly from one social class, as Chapter 12 illustrates (Roberts and Yamane 2016).

Political Involvement. Political party identification and general ideological beliefs affect voting, and they are, in turn, affected by social factors such as race, religion, region of the country, social class, gender, marital status, and age (Interuniversity Consortium for Political and Social Research 2011). Throughout the world, the lower the social class, the more likely people are to vote for parties that support greater distribution of wealth, and the higher the social status, the more likely people are to be conservative on economic issues—consistent with protecting their wealth (Domhoff 2014; Kerbo 2008). However, those with lower levels of education and income tend to vote conservatively on many social issues relating to minorities and civil liberties (e.g., rights for lesbians, gays, bisexual, and transgender people; access to birth control and abortions; and voter registration laws) (Gilbert 2011; Kerbo 2008).

Money also influences who can run successful campaigns. For example, during the 2016 congressional elections, the average candidate running for a position in the House of Representatives or the Senate spent, respectively, $462,980 and $1,467,360. During the presidential campaign of 2016, Hillary Clinton and Donald Trump (along with their allies) raised, respectively, $1.4 billion and $957.6 million. This contributes to the fact that those with more money, who can help support such campaigns, also have more influence in elections (Center for Responsive Politics 2017; King 2012).

Status Inconsistency. Some people experience high status on one trait, especially a trait achieved through education and hard work, but may experience low standing in another area. For example, a professor may have high prestige but low income. Max Weber called this unevenness in one's social standing *status inconsistency*. In societies with high levels of racism and sexism, racial minorities and women in high-status positions experience *status inconsistency*. If their lowest ascribed status is treated as most important, they are likely to experience discontent with the current system and become more liberal politically (Weber 1946).

Life experiences such as hunger, the unnecessary early death of family members, or the pain of seeing one's child denied opportunities are all experienced at the micro level, but their causes are usually rooted in events and actions at other levels of the social world. This brings us to our next question: Can an individual move up or down in a stratification system?

THINKING SOCIOLOGICALLY

Describe your own lifestyle and life chances. How do these relate to your socialization experience and your family's position in the stratification system? What difference do they make in your life today and for what you think you will accomplish in the future? What can you do to improve your life chances?

Social Mobility: The Micro-Meso Connection

The LeBron Jameses and Andrew Lucks of the world make millions of dollars—at least for the duration of their playing careers. For professionals in the world of sport, each hoop, goal, or touchdown throw is worth thousands of dollars. These riches give hope to those in rags that if they "play hard," they too may be on the field or court making millions. The problem is that the chances of

▲ This young street basketball player has dreams of glory on the courts. Despite many grand hoop dreams, few experience dramatic social mobility through sports.

making it big are so small that such hopes are some of the cruelest hoaxes perpetrated on poor young African Americans and others in the lower or working class today. It is a false promise to think of sports as the road to wealth when chances of success are extremely limited (Dufur and Feinberg 2007; Edwards 2000; Hattery and Smith 2012). Moreover, if young people put all of their hopes and energies into developing their muscles and physical skills, they may lose the possibility of moving up in the social class system, which requires obtaining an education to develop their minds and technical skills.

Those few minority athletes who do "make it big" and become models for young people tend to experience *stacking*, holding certain limited positions in a sport. Moreover, those young players who make it into the major leagues may have done so by going in right after high school or leaving college after a single year. This thwarts their post–athletic career opportunities. When retired from playing, few Black athletes rise in the administrative hierarchy in the sports of football and baseball. (Basketball has a better record of hiring Black coaches and managers.) For example, in Division I football, nearly half of players are Black men, but only 11% of, or 14, head coaches are Black; this stems in part from the

pipeline that leads to coaching positions. Quarterbacks often become coaches, but less than one tenth of college quarterbacks are Black (Johnson 2017).

Social mobility refers to *the extent of individual movement up or down in the class system, changing one's social position in society—especially relative to one's parents* (Gilbert 2011). What is the likelihood that your status will be different from that of your parents over your lifetime? Will you start a successful business? Marry into wealth? Win the lottery? Experience downward mobility due to loss of a job, illness, or inability to complete your education? What factors at different levels of analysis might influence your chances of mobility? These are some of the questions addressed in this section and the next.

Four issues dominate the analysis of mobility: (1) types of social mobility, (2) methods of measuring social mobility, (3) factors that affect social mobility, and (4) whether there is a "land of opportunity" for those wishing to improve their lot in life.

Types of Social Mobility

Mobility can be up, down, or sideways. *Intergenerational mobility* refers to change in social class status compared with one's parents, usually resulting from education and occupational attainment. If you are the first to go to college in your family and you become an engineer, this represents intergenerational upward mobility. The amount of intergenerational mobility—that is, the number of children who move up or down in the social structure compared with where their parents are—measures the degree to which a society has an *open class system*. The more movement there is between classes, the more open the class system.

You can change positions at the same level in the stratification system. For example, you could move from your job as a postal worker and become a firefighter. This type of mobility is called *horizontal mobility*. You have changed your position, but your income, power, and social prestige remain essentially the same.

Intragenerational mobility (not to be confused with *intergenerational mobility*) refers to a change in position within a single individual's life. For instance, if you begin your career as a teacher's aide and end it as a school superintendent, that is upward intragenerational mobility. However, mobility is not always up. *Vertical mobility* refers to movement up *or* down in the hierarchy and sometimes involves changing social classes. You may start your career as a waitress, go to college part-time, get a degree in computer science, and get a more prestigious and higher-paying job, resulting in upward mobility. Alternatively, you could lose a job and take one at a lower status and pay. In recent years, people at all levels of the occupational structure have experienced downward intragenerational mobility after being laid off from one job and having difficulty finding another at the same level and pay grade.

How Much Mobility Is There? Measures of Social Mobility

One traditional method of measuring mobility is to compare fathers with sons and, in more recent research, with daughters. Determining the mobility of women is more difficult because they often have lower-level positions and their mothers may not have worked full-time, but one conclusion is that both women's and men's occupational attainment is powerfully influenced by class origins. As Figure 7.2 indicates, the level of social mobility in the United States is lower than in most other Global North nations (Corak 2016). This figure shows correlations, and a lower number in this case means the more likely it is that sons will end up in the same (or higher) social class as their fathers.

Men, in particular, have experienced stagnant or even declining wages over the past several decades. As Figure 7.3 on the next page reveals, in 1973, the inflation-adjusted median income for men was $54,030, whereas in 2016 it was $51,640. So, men, on average, made $2,400 less in 2016 than they did in 1973. This decline in wages helped spur the resentment that prompted White working-class men to overwhelmingly support Donald Trump in the 2016 presidential election (Hochschild 2016).

Factors Affecting an Individual's Mobility

Why are some people successful at moving up the ladder, whereas others lag behind? Mobility is driven by many factors, from your family's background to global economic variables. One's chances to move up depend on micro-level factors (e.g., cultural capital, socialization, personal characteristics, and education) and meso- and macro-level factors (e.g., the occupational structure and economic status of regions and countries; population changes in the number of births, deaths, or people migrating; the numbers of people vying for similar positions; discrimination based on gender, race, or ethnicity; and the global economic situation).

Studying mobility can be a complicated process because these key variables are interrelated. Macro-level forces (such as the occupational structure and economic status in a country) are related to meso-level factors (such as access to education and type of economy) and micro-level factors (such as socialization, family background, and education level) (Blau and Duncan 1967).

Researchers from Harvard and Berkeley conducted the largest study on inequality in the United States to

▼ FIGURE 7.2

Intergenerational Earnings: The Lower the Number, the Higher the Social Mobility

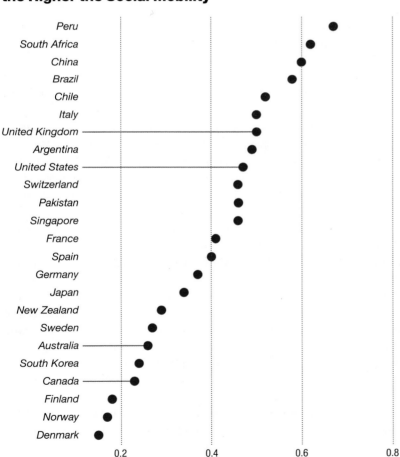

Source: Corak, Miles. 2016. "Economic Mobility." In "State of the Union: The Poverty and Inequality Report," ed. Stanford Center on Poverty and Inequality, special issue, *Pathways Magazine*. Reprinted with permission from The Stanford Center on Poverty and Inequality and author Miles Corak.

Note: The horizontal distance displays the intergenerational earnings elasticity between fathers and sons.

Ratio and Median Earnings of Full-Time, Year-Round Male Workers 15 Years and Older: 1960 to 2016

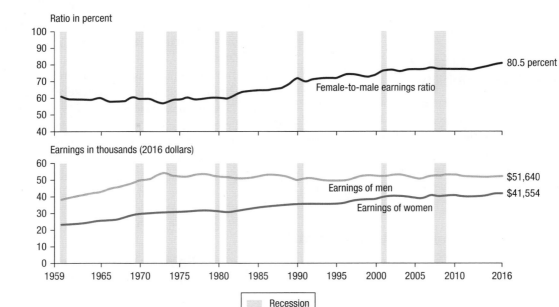

Source: Semega, Fontenot, and Kollar 2017.

date (Chetty et al. 2014). Their research revealed large regional variations in mobility (as seen in Figure 7.4). For example, they found that "the probability of a child born into the poorest fifth of the population in San Jose, California making it to the top fifth is 12.9%, not much lower than in Denmark. In Charlotte, North Carolina, [however,] it is 4.4%, far lower than anywhere else in the rich world" ("Mobility Measured" 2014).

The researchers noted five factors that help explain the levels of mobility in different areas of the United States: "residential segregation (whether by income or race); the quality of schooling; family structure (e.g., how many children live with only one parent); 'social capital' (such as taking part in community groups); and inequality (particularly income gaps among those outside the top 1%)." They point out that "social mobility is higher in integrated places with good schools, strong families, lots of community spirit and smaller income gaps within the broad middle class" ("Mobility, Measured" 2014). We now look in more detail at a few of the variables that can make a difference in your chances for mobility.

Family Background, Socialization, Marriage, and Education. Whether you marry and whom you marry can move you up or down the social class ladder. As men's

wages have fallen over the past few decades and more women have joined the workforce, household incomes (rather than just male incomes) play more of a role in people's social class positions. As people increasingly tend to marry those of similar income levels, marriage makes even more of an impact on family income. Two high-income earners make much more than two low-income earners (and *much* more than one low-income or even middle-income worker) (Carbone and Cahn 2014; Pew Charitable Trusts 2012).

As we have noted throughout this chapter, our family background has a major influence on our chances for upward mobility on the social class ladder. For example, recent research discusses the continuing social class *word gap* between children from different classes. By the time they are 4 years old, children from high-income families know about 4 million more words than those from low-income backgrounds (Kamenetz 2018). These numbers represent a gap in the range of words they hear at home and illustrate the difference family background and socialization can make in education and future opportunities (Brookings 2017; Hart and Risley 2003). A University of Chicago study recommends a *3-Ts* approach—tune in, talk more, and take turns—to increase vocabulary. Because language usage at home

Location and Social Mobility for a Child in the Bottom Fifth of Income in the United States

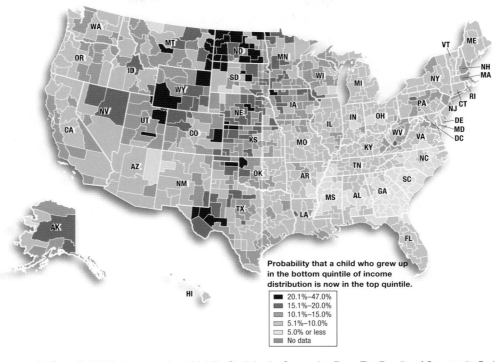

Probability that a child who grew up in the bottom quintile of income distribution is now in the top quintile.

- 20.1%–47.0%
- 15.1%–20.0%
- 10.1%–15.0%
- 5.1%–10.0%
- 5.0% or less
- No data

Source: Chetty, R., Hendren, N., Saez, E. (2014). Intergenerational Mobility Statistics by Commuting Zone. The Equality of Opportunity Project. http://www.equality-of-opportunity.org/index.php/data.

Note: Commuting zones are geographic areas that help define local economies and labor markets—where people live and work, independent of political boundaries.

impacts school success, that in turn plays a role in a child's chances of getting into college and climbing the stratification ladder.

THINKING SOCIOLOGICALLY

How might your vocabulary affect your success in school? How might an expanded vocabulary affect your opportunities in life (for example, impressing a potential employer)? What can you do to increase your vocabulary?

A college degree potentially helps those at the bottom of the stratification system move up and helps those in the middle and upper classes to remain in those higher positions. This positive impact on social class position relates to the fact that, as Figure 7.5 on the next page reveals, employment rates and earnings tend to go up dramatically with a college degree. For example, in 2016, the unemployment rate for adults over 25 years old was 5.2%

for those with a high school degree but just 2.7% for those with a degree from a 4-year college. The median weekly earnings were $1,156 for those with a four-year degree but just $692 for those with only a high school diploma (Bureau of Labor Statistics 2017a).

However, as Figure 7.6 on the next page indicates, there is a huge difference in access to higher education. In 2014, among all bachelor's degrees awarded by age 24, 54% went to children from families in the top quartile of income earning, as opposed to 10% from the bottom quartile (Cahalan et al. 2016). Further, this is not just a matter of more capable students succeeding in college. As Figure 7.7 on page 203 demonstrates, a high-income student with just mediocre math scores has the same chances of earning a BA as a low-income student with the highest test scores. If U.S. society were truly a **meritocracy**, *positions would be allocated in a social group or organization according to individuals' abilities and credentials.* One would expect cognitive ability to be the most important variable.

Even when a young person from a low-income background is admitted to a college or university, she or he may

Earnings and Employment Rates by Educational Attainment

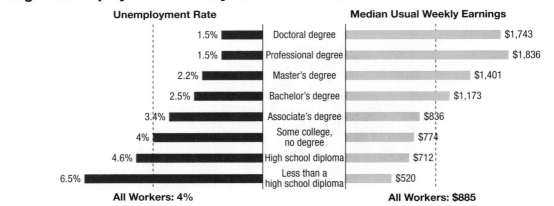

Unemployment Rate		Median Usual Weekly Earnings
1.5%	Doctoral degree	$1,743
1.5%	Professional degree	$1,836
2.2%	Master's degree	$1,401
2.5%	Bachelor's degree	$1,173
3.4%	Associate's degree	$836
4%	Some college, no degree	$774
4.6%	High school diploma	$712
6.5%	Less than a high school diploma	$520

All Workers: 4%   **All Workers: $885**

Source: Bureau of Labor Statistics 2017.

▼ FIGURE 7.6

Differences in Bachelor's Degree (by age 24) by Family Income

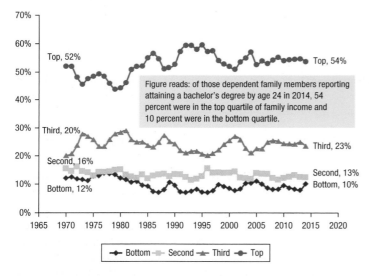

Figure reads: of those dependent family members reporting attaining a bachelor's degree by age 24 in 2014, 54 percent were in the top quartile of family income and 10 percent were in the bottom quartile.

Top, 52% / Top, 54%
Third, 20% / Third, 23%
Second, 16% / Second, 13%
Bottom, 12% / Bottom, 10%

◆ Bottom — Second ▲ Third ● Top

Source: Cahalan, Margaret, Perna, Laura, Yamashita, Mika, Ruiz, Roman, Franklin, Khadish. 2016 Indicators of Higher Education Equity in the United States, 2016 Historical Trend Report, Washington, DC: Pell Institute for the Study of Opportunity in High Education, Council for Opportunity in Education (COE) and Alliance for Higher Education and Democracy of the University of Pennsylvania (PennAHEAD).

be at a disadvantage in the classroom and feel alienated from past social ties. The culture of 4-year colleges, particularly elite ones, is typically the culture of the well-educated upper-middle class and may be different and uncomfortable for those from other class backgrounds (Foster 2015). The alienation many first-generation poor and working-class students experience at 4-year colleges is explored in more detail in the next Engaging Sociology.

Economic Vitality and Population Trends. The economic health of a nation and population trends can also influence an individual's chances for social mobility. As noted earlier, the economic vitality of a country affects the chances for individual mobility, because there will be fewer positions at the top if the economy is stagnant. Macro-level factors such as a country's economy and its place in the global system shape the employment chances of individuals.

The *fertility rates*, or number of children born at a given time, influence the number of people looking for jobs and their chance of moving up in society. For example, the U.S. nationwide baby boom following World War II resulted in a flood of job applicants and downward intergenerational mobility for the many who could not find work comparable to their social class at birth. In contrast, the smaller group following the Baby Boomer generation had fewer competitors for entry-level jobs. Baby Boomers hold many of the executive and leadership positions today, so promotion has been hard for the next cohort. As Boomers retire, opportunities will open up, and mobility should increase.

Gender, Race, Ethnicity, and Earnings. Gender, race, and ethnicity also impact rates of social mobility. For example, Blacks tend to remain poor or fall from the middle class more often than people in other racial groups (Rodrigue and Reeves 2015). Likewise, whereas women have made some gains, they also still make less money than men. Table 7.2 shows median weekly earnings of full-time workers by race or ethnicity and gender. Moreover, despite being, on average, more educated than

▼ FIGURE 7.7

Advantage of Wealth in College Success

B.A. completion rate in three socioeconomic groups, ranked in four groups of math test scores

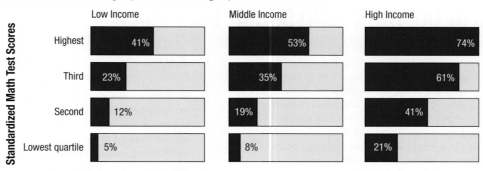

A low-income college student with top math scores has the same chance of graduating with a bachelor's degree (41%) as a rich student with mediocre scores.

Source: Dynarski 2015a, 2015b; National Center for Educational Statistics 2015.

▼ TABLE 7.2

Median Weekly Earnings by Race or Ethnicity and Gender

	Men	Women	Women's Earnings as a Percentage of Men's Earnings	Women's Earnings as a Percentage of White Men's Earnings
All	$941	$770	82%	NA
White	$971	$795	82%	82%
Black	$710	$657	93%	68%
Asian	$1,207	$903	75%	62%
Hispanic/Latino	$690	$603	87%	83%

Note: Hispanic workers may be of any race. Based on median weekly earnings of full-time wage and salary workers aged 16 and over.

Source: U.S. Bureau of Labor Statistics 2018.

men (34% of women compared to 26% of men earn a BA by the time they are 29) women are still woefully underrepresented in upper-level management positions. Only 6% of, or 29, CEOs of S&P 500 companies are women (Bureau of Labor Statistics 2016; Catalyst 2017).

Interdependent Global Market. All members of an economy are vulnerable to international events and swings in the global marketplace. If the Chinese or U.S. stock market hiccups, it sends ripples through world markets. If high-tech industries in Japan or Europe falter, North American companies in Silicon Valley, California, may go out of business, costing many professionals their lucrative positions. In ways such as these, the interdependent global economies affect national and local economies, and that, in turn, affects individual families. As the information in this chapter indicates, mobility for the individual, a micro-level event, is linked to a variety of events at other levels of the social world. Whether individuals move from "rags to riches" is not determined solely by their personal ambition and work ethic.

THINKING SOCIOLOGICALLY

Think of family members or friends who have recently lost or acquired jobs. Using your sociological imagination, how can you connect those individual experiences to the national and global economy? How do you think the national and global economies will impact your experience in the marketplace after you earn your college degree?

Is There a "Land of Opportunity"? Cross-Cultural Mobility

Television shows bombard us with images of rich bachelors and the desirability of marrying a millionaire to improve our status in life. By playing a game of trivia or being challenged on an island on a TV show, we too might "strike it rich." Another possibility is that we might win the lottery by buying a ticket at our local convenience store. In reality, these quick fixes and easy get-rich-fast

ENGAGING SOCIOLOGY

FIRST-GENERATION COLLEGE STUDENTS: ISSUES OF CULTURAL AND SOCIAL CAPITAL

Socioeconomic classes develop subcultures that can be quite different from one another, and when one changes subcultures, it can be confusing and alienating. College campuses provide an example because they are dominated by middle-class cultures. First-generation college students often find themselves in a world as alien as visiting another country. Students whose parents went to college are more likely to have cultural and social capital that helps them understand their professors, who are generally part of the middle-class culture. Answer the following survey questions. How might your own cultural and social capital cause you to feel at home or alienated, privileged or disprivileged, in a college environment?

A. Which of the following experiences were part of your childhood?

- ☐ Had a library of books (at least 50 adult books) in your childhood home
- ☐ Had parents who read a newspaper daily
- ☐ Had parents who subscribed to news magazines (e.g., *Time*, *The Economist*)
- ☐ Listened to music as a family, including classical or instrumental music such as harp or flute
- ☐ Traveled to at least 20 other states or to at least 5 other countries
- ☐ Took regular trips to the library
- ☐ Took regular trips to museums
- ☐ Attended plays (theater productions) and concerts
- ☐ Played a musical instrument
- ☐ Took dance lessons
- ☐ Listened to National Public Radio (NPR)
- ☐ Watched PBS (Public Broadcasting Service) on television

B. Which of the following *relationships* were part of your childhood?

- ☐ My parents knew at least two influential people in my community on a first-name basis—such as the mayor, members of the city council, the superintendent of schools, the governor, and the district's representative to Congress.
- ☐ The regional leader of my religious group—church, temple, or mosque—knew and respected my family.
- ☐ My parents knew, on a first-name basis, at least three CEOs of corporations.
- ☐ When I entered new situations in high school, it was likely that my parents were known by the coaches, music directors, summer camp directors, or others "running the show."
- ☐ When I came to college, one or more professors and administrators at the college knew my parents, a sibling, or another family member.
- ☐ I have often interacted directly and effectively (in a nonadversarial way) with authority figures.

Engaging Sociology

1. If you experienced many of the items under *A* at home, you had fairly high cultural capital. If you marked most of the items under *B*, you had a lot of social capital. If you did not, you may find the culture of a 4-year college campus to be alien and even confusing. How well does your background match up with the cultural capital of a college?

2. Which of the following aspects of a college campus do you think might make a first-generation student feel most alienated at your college: *economic* capital (money), *social* capital (networks with those who have resources), or *cultural* capital (knowledge of important aspects of the culture)? Why?

Source: Survey constructed in part using ideas from Morris and Grimes, 1997.

plans are seldom realized, and the chances of us profiting are slim indeed.

The question for this section concerns your realistic chances for mobility and whether you have a better chance to improve your status by moving to some other country.

The answer is not simple. Countless immigrants have sought better opportunities in new locations. Their economic future depended on the historical period, economic conditions, attitudes toward immigrants, their job skills, and their ability to blend into the new society.

During economic growth periods, many immigrants have found great opportunities for mobility in the United States and Europe. However, opportunities for upward mobility have changed significantly with globalization. Multinational corporations look for the cheapest sources of labor in the Global South, with low taxes, few labor unions and workplace safety regulations, and many workers needing jobs. This has drained away low-skilled manufacturing jobs from Global North countries, making it even more essential to have advanced educational credentials (such as a bachelor's or master's degree).

Most jobs in the United States today focus on providing services. These service-sector jobs tend to require either a great deal of education (e.g., computer engineers or doctors) or minimal training (e.g., nurse's aides, fast-food workers, or security guards). The low-skill jobs do not pay well, and labor unions, with declining memberships and political clout, have increasingly limited influence on the wages and working conditions of workers. The result is a shrinking middle class in the United States, as shown in Figure 7.8.

This inequality trend exists throughout the world. Although the new factories for multinational industries springing up in Global South countries such as Malaysia, Mexico, and the Philippines provide opportunities for mobility to those of modest origins, much of the upward mobility in the world is taking place among those who come from small, highly educated families with individualistic achievement-oriented values. They tend to be positioned to take advantage of the changing occupational structure and high-tech jobs. Their education and social and cultural capital allow them to work effectively in multiple nations. As the gap between rich and poor individuals widens, education becomes more important (Gratton 2012; Ireland 2016; Rothman 2005).

THINKING SOCIOLOGICALLY

What social factors in your society limit or enhance the likelihood of upward social mobility for you and other members of your generation? Explain.

Major Stratification Systems: Macro-Level Analysis

Mansa works on a plantation in Mozambique. He tries in vain to pay off his debt. Like his parents, he and his wife and children, however hard they work, will always be in debt because they cannot pay the amount due for their hut or food from the owner's store. Basically, they are slaves—they do not have control over their own labor. They were born into this status, and there they will stay.

Imagine being born into a society in which you have no choices or options in life because of your family background, age, sex, or ethnic group. You can neither select an occupation that interests you nor move to another location. You see wealthy aristocrats parading their advantages and realize that this will never be possible for you. You can never own land or receive the education of your choice.

This situation is reality for millions of people in the world—they are born this way and will spend their lives this way. In **ascribed stratification systems**, *characteristics beyond the control of individuals—such as family background, age, sex, and race—determine their position in society.* In contrast, **achieved stratification systems** *allow individuals to earn positions through their ability, efforts, and choices.* In an open class system, it is possible to achieve a higher ranking by working hard, obtaining education, and choosing an occupation that pays well.

Ascribed Status: Caste and Estate Systems

Caste systems are *the most rigid ascribed stratification systems. Individuals are born into a status, which they retain*

▼ FIGURE 7.8

The Shrinking Middle Class in the United States

% of adults in each income tier

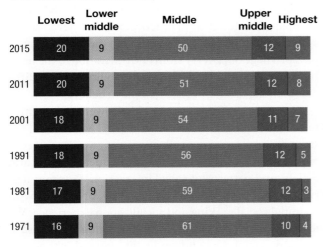

	Lowest	Lower middle	Middle	Upper middle	Highest
2015	20	9	50	12	9
2011	20	9	51	12	8
2001	18	9	54	11	7
1991	18	9	56	12	5
1981	17	9	59	12	3
1971	16	9	61	10	4

Source: Pew Research Center 2015i.

Note: Adults are assigned to income tiers based on their size-adjusted household income in the calendar year prior to the survey year. Figures may not add up to 100% due to rounding.

throughout life. That status is deeply embedded in religious, political, and economic norms and institutions. Individuals born into caste systems have predetermined occupational positions, marriage partners, residences, social associations, and prestige levels. A person's caste is easily recognized through clothing, speech patterns, family name and identity, skin color, or other distinguishing characteristics. From their earliest years, individuals learn their place in society through the process of socialization. To behave counter to caste prescriptions would be to go against religion and social custom and to risk not fitting into society. That can be a death sentence in some societies.

In caste-based societies, the institution of religion works together with the family, education, economy, and political institutions to shape both expectations and aspirations and to keep people in their prescribed places. For example, Hindu ideas dictate that violating the caste prescriptions can put one's next *reincarnation* (or rebirth in the Hindu tradition) in jeopardy. Stability in Hindu societies is maintained in part by the belief that people can be reborn into a higher status in the next life if they fulfill expectations in their ascribed position in this life.

The clearest example of a caste system is found in India, a predominantly Hindu society. The Hindu religion holds that individuals are born into one of four *varnas*, broad caste positions, or into a fifth group below the caste system, the *outcaste* group. The first and highest varna, called *Brahmans*, originally was made up of priests and scholars but now includes many leaders in society. The second varna, *Kshatriyas* or *Rajputs*, includes the original prince and warrior varna and now embraces much of the army and civil service. The *Vaishyas*, or merchants, are the third varna. The fourth varna, the *Sudras*, includes peasants, farmers, artisans, and laborers. The final layer, below the caste system, encompasses profoundly oppressed people—"a people put aside"—referred to as untouchables, outcastes, *Chandalas* (a Hindu term), and *Dalits* (the name preferred by many "untouchables" themselves). Although the Indian Constitution of 1950 granted full social status to these citizens, and a law passed in 1955 made discrimination against them punishable, deeply rooted traditions can be difficult to change. Caste distinctions are still prevalent, especially in rural areas.

Estate systems are characterized by *the concentration of economic and political power in the hands of a small minority of political-military elite, with the peasantry tied to the land* (Rothman 2005). They existed in ancient Egypt, the Incan and Mayan civilizations, Europe, China, and Japan. In estate systems an individual's rank and legal rights are clearly spelled out, and arranged marriages and religion bolster the system. In Europe, during the Middle Ages, knights defended the realms and the religion of the nobles. Behind every knight in shining armor were peasants, sweating in the fields and paying for the knights' food, armor, and campaigns. For farming the land owned by the nobility, peasants received protection against invading armies and enough of the produce to survive. Their lives were often miserable. If the yield of crops was poor, they ate little. In a good year, they might save enough to buy a small parcel of land. A very few were able to become independent in this fashion. Today, similar systems exist in some Central and South American, Asian, and African countries on large banana, coffee, cacao, and sugar plantations.

THINKING SOCIOLOGICALLY

What might be some advantages, for both the society and the individuals living in it, of a society where status was ascribed rather than achieved? Do you think you would enjoy living in such a society? Why or why not?

Achieved Status: Social Class in the United States

In contrast to ascribed status systems, *achieved stratification systems* maintain that everyone is born with common legal status and equality before the law. In principle, all individuals can own property and choose their own occupations. However, in practice, most achieved status systems, like the class system found in the United States, pass privilege or poverty from one generation to the next. Individual upward or downward mobility is more difficult than the ideology invites people to believe.

Social class refers to the wealth, power, and prestige rankings that individuals hold in society. Members of the same social class have similar incomes, wealth and economic positions, lifestyles, levels of education, cultural beliefs, and patterns of social interaction. Our families, rich or poor and educated or unskilled, provide us with an initial social ranking and socialization experience. We tend to feel a kinship and sense of belonging with those in the same social class and tend to live, attend school, and work with people from our social class. We think alike, share interests, and probably look up to the same people as a reference group.

Our social class position is based on the three main factors in the stratification system: (1) property, (2) prestige, and (3) power. This is the trio—the three *P*s—that, according to Max Weber, determines where individuals rank in relation to each other (Weber 1946, 1947). By *property* (wealth), Weber refers to owning or controlling the means of production. *Power*, the ability to control others, includes not only the means of production but also the position one holds. *Prestige* involves the esteem and recognition one receives, based on wealth, position, or accomplishments. Chances of being granted high prestige improve if one's patterns of behavior, occupation, and lifestyle match those valued in the society (e.g., in U.S. society today that would include physicians, military officers, judges, CEOs, and college professors).

Although these three dimensions of stratification are often found together, this is not always so. Recall the idea of *status inconsistency*: an individual can have a great deal of prestige yet not command much wealth (Weber 1946). Consider winners of the prestigious Nobel Peace Prize such as Wangari Maathai, a Kenyan environmentalist who won the prize for starting a movement to plant trees and for her political activism, or Betty Williams and Mairead Corrigan of Northern Ireland, founders of the Community of Peace People who won for their efforts to find a peaceful end to their country's conflicts. None of them was rich, but each made contributions to the world that gained them universal prestige. Likewise, some people gain enormous wealth through crime or gambling, but this wealth may not be accompanied by respect or prestige.

Some theorists see power as the key element in systems of stratification. Conflict theorists maintain that those who hold power control the economic capital and the means of production in society. Consistent with Marx, many recent conflict theorists argue that a **power elite** composed of *top leaders in corporations, politics, and the military* rules society (Domhoff 2014).

These interlocking groups of elites grow up together, attending the same private schools and belonging to the same private clubs. There is an unspoken agreement to protect each other's positions and ensure that their power is not threatened. Those not in this interlocking elite group do not hold real power and have little chance of breaking into the inner circles (Domhoff 2014; Dye 2002, 2014; Mills 1956).

Pluralist power theorists, on the other hand, argue that *power is not held exclusively by an elite group but is shared among many power centers, each of which has its own self-interests to protect* (Ritzer and Goodman 2004; Zdan 2017). Well-financed special interest groups (e.g., the insurance industry, dairy and cattle farmers, or truckers' trade unions) and professional associations (e.g., the American Medical Association or American Bar Association) have considerable power through collective action. From the pluralist perspective, officials who hold political power are vulnerable to pressure from influential interest groups, and each interest group competes for power with others. Creating and maintaining this power through networks and pressure on legislators is the job of lobbyists. For example, in the intense U.S. debate over health care legislation, interest groups from the medical community, insurance lobbies, and citizens' groups wield their power to influence the outcome, but because these major interests conflict and no one group has the most power, no one group has attained all it wants. Some groups want to nationalize health care and others want to completely privatize it; the current health care legislation does neither. The core idea of pluralist theorists, then, is that many centers of power create at least some checks and balances on those in elite positions.

Social Classes in the United States

Imagine that you are a politician. The public is clamoring for more help for the middle class. Flash back to the most recent U.S. presidential campaign. All the candidates were talking about the middle class. Did you ever hear the politicians define what they meant? You probably did not, because the broader and more inclusive the definition, the more useful it is to politicians trying to appeal to a range of voters.

When given a choice among lower, middle, and upper class, almost all Americans will say they are middle class. When given a choice that includes working and upper-middle class, however, 51% say they are middle or upper-middle class, and another 48% define themselves as working class (Newport 2015a).

Most social scientists measure social class by looking at the income, education, and profession of respondents. Sometimes, social scientists break down members of the middle class into two groups: the white-collar middle class and the working class. Most white-collar workers have a college education, have professions with salaries (rather than jobs where they are paid by the hour), work in an office setting, and earn within a specified range around the median income. Members of the working class work for hourly wages, do manual labor, and do not usually have a college degree.

How does today's popular culture on TV and in films, magazines, and music reflect interests of different social classes? How are rich and poor people depicted? Who appears responsible for their wealth or poverty—the individuals, the society, or some other combination? Do any of these depictions question the U.S. class system?

Poverty and Social Policy

Nothing describes poverty more vividly than hunger. Stories about hunger and famine in Global South countries fill the newspapers. Chronic hunger has declined by 216 million people since 1990 (Food and Agriculture Organization, International Fund for Agricultural Development, World Food Program 2015). Yet, around the world, nearly 794 million people, or roughly 1 in every 9 people on earth, still go to bed hungry every night. Figure 7.9 shows where hunger is most severe.

One hardly expects to see hunger in rich countries, yet in the United States 1 in 8 people are hungry some of the time (Feeding America 2017). States most severely affected by food insecurity (lack of consistent access to food) include Alabama, Arkansas, Kentucky, Louisiana, Mississippi, and Ohio (Coleman-Jensen et al. 2016). Households led by single women are especially likely to be food insecure, with 30% lacking sufficient food. Race also influences the likelihood of food insecurity. One out of four Black (25%) and a little more than one out of five Hispanic (22%) households are food insecure (Coleman-Jensen et al. 2016).

Most people living in poverty have no property-based income and no permanent or stable work, only casual or intermittent earnings in the labor market. They often depend on help from government agencies or private organizations to survive. In short, they have personal troubles in large part because they have been unable to establish linkages and networks in the meso- and macro-level organizations of our social world. Most of the gap is due to structural issues, with the wealth gap becoming

▼ FIGURE 7.9

2017 Global Hunger Index by Severity

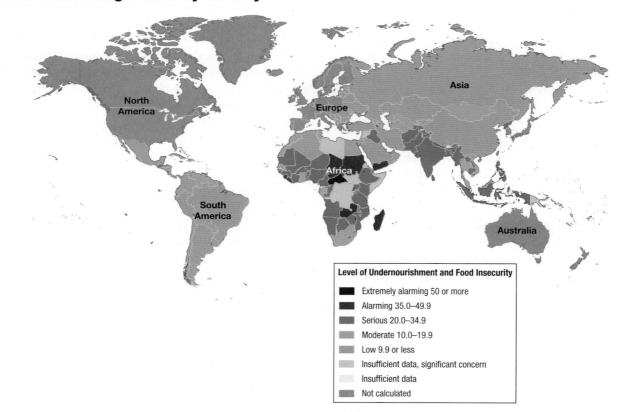

Level of Undernourishment and Food Insecurity

■ Extremely alarming 50 or more
■ Alarming 35.0–49.9
■ Serious 20.0–34.9
■ Moderate 10.0–19.9
■ Low 9.9 or less
■ Insufficient data, significant concern
■ Insufficient data
■ Not calculated

Source: Global Hunger Index 2018. Used with permission from the International Food Policy Research Institute.

so extreme that the top 1% of the world's population owns more wealth than the rest of the population, and just *eight* men own more wealth than the poorest half of the world's population (Oxfam 2017).

Here are the world's nine richest people for 2018:

1. Jeff Bezos: American founder, chairman, and chief executive of Amazon.com (net worth: $112 billion)

2. Bill Gates: American cofounder of Microsoft (net worth: $90 billion)

3. Warren Buffett: American CEO and largest shareholder in Berkshire Hathaway (net worth: $84 billion)

4. Bernard Arnault: French chairman and CEO of LVMH Moet Hennessy Louis Vuitton (net worth: $72 billion)

5. Mark Zuckerberg: American chairman, CEO, and cofounder of Facebook (net worth: $71 billion)

6. Amancio Ortega: Spanish founder of Inditex, which owns the Zara fashion chain (net worth: $70 billion)

7. Carlos Slim Helu: Mexican owner of Grupo Carso (net worth: $67 billion)

8. (tie) Charles Koch: CEO, Koch Industries (net worth: $60 billion)

9. (tie) David Koch: Executive vice president, Koch Industries (net worth: $60 billion)

Source: "Richest People" 2018.

THINKING SOCIOLOGICALLY

How does your family's ability to provide food for its members at the micro level largely depend on its connectedness to the meso and macro levels of society?

Sociologists recognize two basic types of poverty: (1) absolute poverty and (2) relative poverty. **Absolute poverty**, *not having resources to meet basic needs,* means no prestige, very little access to power, no accumulated wealth, and insufficient means to survive. Some die of easily cured diseases because the bodies of those in absolute poverty are weakened by chronic and persistent hunger and almost total lack of medical attention.

Relative poverty occurs when *one's income falls below the poverty line, resulting in an inadequate standard of living relative to others in the individual's country.* In the United States, relative poverty means shortened life expectancy, higher infant mortality, and poorer health. Whereas few people starve on the street and suffer from the easily cured diseases more common among the poor in Global South nations, food insecurity and the stress and hardships of relative poverty lead to more health problems and earlier deaths for the poor in the United States and other Global North nations with high levels of inequality.

The *feminization of poverty* refers to the trend in which single females with children make up a growing proportion of those in poverty. In 2016, among those ages 18 to 64, 9.7% of males and 13.4% of females in the United States lived in poverty. Table 7.3 shows how much income it would take to remove one from the poverty line. Also in 2016, more than 1 in 10 adults (10.7%) and almost 1 in

▼ TABLE 7.3

Poverty Thresholds for 2017 by Size of Family

Size of Family Unit	Weighted Average Threshold
One person	$12,752
Two people	$16,414
Three people	$19,173
Four people	$25,283
Five people	$30,490
Six people	$35,069

Source: U.S. Census Bureau 2018.

in poverty find themselves without a home. Families now make up over one third (35%) of the homeless population (National Alliance to End Homelessness 2017).

The Obama administration made a concerted effort to combat homelessness and used social scientific research to do so. Studies have shown that "mainstream housing, health, education, and human service programs must be fully engaged and coordinated to prevent and end homelessness" (Sullivan, 2013). Research also reveals that providing a wide range of services for the homeless, including providing housing first, while addressing mental health and additional issues actually saves taxpayers money in the long run "by interrupting a costly cycle of emergency room visits, detoxes, and even jail terms" (Sullivan 2013). Despite rising levels of inequality, the number of homeless has declined by 14% since 2010 (U.S. Department of Housing and Urban Development 2016).

How can we effectively address inequality? First, we must become aware of the problem. As this chapter has described, almost every society has some system of stratification. We do not all have the same chances of "making it." Most of us, though, do not fully realize the extent of the inequality in the society we call home. For example, in one study, a nationally representative sample of U.S. citizens was shown three charts that displayed different distributions of wealth ranging from somewhat equal to very unequal. When asked which of the three charts illustrated how wealth was distributed in the United States, most respondents chose the chart that actually described wealth distribution in Sweden, the nation with the *lowest level* of economic inequality in the world. The chart most often picked by respondents as an "ideal" distribution of wealth illustrated an even *more equitable* distribution of wealth than that found in Sweden (Norton and Ariely 2011). Figure 7.10 shows the actual U.S. wealth distribution plotted against the estimated and ideal distributions across all respondents. Responses varied a bit by age, income, and political party, but there was overall agreement that America would be better off with a smaller wealth gap (Weissmann 2014).

THINKING SOCIOLOGICALLY

What distribution of wealth and income would you favor for your nation, and why?

▲ A homeless girl (top) walks in the rain in Dhaka, Bangladesh. The child's family has little power to improve its situation or her life chances. Compare her circumstances with those of the boy and girl in their parents' arms on a yacht.

5 children (18%) were in poverty (Semega, Fontenot, and Kollar 2017). If you were raised by a single mother, you have a greater chance of experiencing poverty. Among single-parent households, more than 1 out of 4 (26.6%) led by a female compared to 13.1% led by a male were in poverty (Semega, Fontenot, and Kollar 2017). Some of those

After reading this chapter, you understand that the United States has higher levels of inequality and poverty

▼ FIGURE 7.10

Wealth Inequality in the United States: Actual, Estimated, and Perceived Ideal Percentage of Wealth Owned

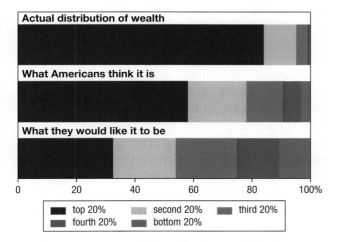

Source: Perspectives on Psychological Science 2011 6:9, Michael I. Norton and Dan Ariely, "Building a Better America One Wealth Quintile at a Time"; Weissmann, Jordan, 2014, "Americans Have No Idea How Bad Inequality Really Is," *Slate*, September.

Note: The actual U.S. wealth distribution plotted against the estimated and ideal distributions across all respondents. Because of their small percentage share of total wealth, both the "4th 20%" value (0.2%) and the "Bottom 20%" value (0.1%) are not visible in the "Actual" distribution.

The bar labeled "What Americans Think It Is" represents the *actual* distribution of wealth in Sweden.

and less class mobility than most other wealthy nations. Once we understand the extent of inequality and poverty, we can start to develop ways to address these issues. We can also critique poverty reduction programs now under way in different nations and help to create more effective ones, if needed.

Solutions to Poverty: Policy Considerations

Government programs exist in the United States and many other countries to help individuals through difficult times, especially during economic downturns. The stated goal of most public and private poverty reduction and welfare programs is to change factors that perpetuate poverty, but this requires money, jobs, and remodeling our social institutions. Sociologists and other social scientists work to understand social problems. They also devise programs to mitigate them and evaluate programs in existence to help ensure that only effective programs continue to receive funds. Some policymakers suggest attacking the problem of poverty institution by institution, offering incentives

for family stability, for students to finish high school, and for job training.

Welfare, Workfare, and Other Aid Programs. Most Global North countries provide assistance to citizens who need help when they are unemployed, sick, or elderly. The United States established the Great Society programs of the 1960s and 1970s as part of the "War on Poverty" of that era. Some of these programs still exist, including the Special Supplemental Nutrition Program for Women, Infants, and Children (WIC), which provides nutritional help, and Head Start, which provides early childhood education. Both programs have received high grades for effectiveness. Yet child poverty rates are still high compared with those of other Global North countries, with the United States ranked 30th. Whereas only 3% of Denmark's children live in poverty, over 20% of children in the United States do so (OECD 2016a).

In addition to micro-level incentives such as childcare and work training, success in helping people out of poverty depends on meso- and macro-level economic conditions. Jobs are now threatened by both globalization (companies can move to locations where labor is cheapest) and automation. Both blue- and white-collar workers face competition from computers and robots due to the second trend. Jobs that require routine tasks, from assembly line work to reading x-rays and CAT scans, can be done more efficiently by machines than humans. One study indicates that by 2030, half of all jobs in the United States will no longer exist due to such changes (Frey and Osborne 2013).

Our social institutions, as well as individuals, must adjust for our society to survive in an era of automation and artificial intelligence. For example, our education system must focus more on training children and adults to adjust to new technologies and continually learn new skills. Meanwhile, our government must invest in technological developments that can allow our nation to compete effectively with others (*The Economist* 2016). Employees must have access to retraining programs so they can adjust to these changes without fear of losing their job (and health insurance) as employment opportunities change. In Sweden, where the government supplies health insurance and free education and companies provide extensive retraining programs, 80% of people have positive views toward robots and artificial intelligence. Meanwhile, in the United States, 73% of the population are "worried" about robots and computers replacing human workers (European Commission 2017; Pew Research Center 2017b).

Recalling what you have learned about poverty, how would you develop a plan to attack the problem of poverty within your community or nation, taking into account micro, meso, and macro levels of analysis? Consider job training, changing family values, providing childcare for working parents, raising the minimum wage—or other tactics. First describe the root causes of poverty and then suggest solutions.

Bridging the National and Global Digital Divide: Macro-Level Stratification

Global economic and political institutions increasingly produce and transmit information through digital technology. Few tools are more important than computers, smartphones, and the Internet. In nearly every salaried and professional position, computer knowledge and ability to navigate the Internet are critical employment skills. The *digital divide* refers to the gap between those with knowledge and access to information technology and those without it. The lines of the divide are drawn by the position of the country in the world, socioeconomic status of citizens, and urban versus rural residence (World Economic Forum 2015).

As Internet technology expands, it brings the world to remote villages, opening new horizons and options and changing lifestyles. Some poor countries are transitioning into the electronic age and making policies that facilitate rapid modernization. They are passing over developmental stages that rich Global North countries went through. As an illustration, consider the impact of the smartphone in Kenya. Today, almost every household in Kenya has a smartphone. These phones have transformed individuals' ability to move and earn money and have lifted many Kenyans out of poverty. Safaricom, the biggest mobile network in Kenya, started a money transfer service in 2007. Along with the technology, it established a network of 150,000 agents who can distribute cash across Kenya. The result? Almost all Kenyans now have access to loans and the ability to transfer money across the nation. This has allowed many individuals, particularly women, to start their own businesses and to support their families. Approximately 185,000 women moved from subsistence farming to owning their own businesses and 194,000 households were raised out of poverty (Rosenberg 2017; Suri and Jack 2017). The growing use of smartphones has helped shrink the digital divide more than anything else.

© Elise Roberts

© Arthur Dries/Stone/Getty Images

▲ In Laos, where many people live in grass houses such as this one (left), families do not have access to electronic devices or the Internet. Their homes and their life chances stand in stark contrast to those of the children seen here working on computers—seen as necessary equipment.

We leave this discussion of stratification systems, including class systems, with a partial answer to the question posed at the beginning of this chapter: Why are some people rich and others poor? In the next two chapters, we expand the discussion to include other variables in stratification systems—race or ethnicity and gender. By the end of these chapters, the answer to the opening question—why some have riches and some have only rags—should be even clearer. Socioeconomic status is important as a measure in any society, but it is not the sole basis for stratification. In the next chapter, we look at the role of race and ethnicity in social inequality.

WHAT HAVE WE LEARNED?

The issue of social stratification calls into question the widely held belief in the fairness of our economic system. By studying this issue, we better understand why some individuals experience prestige (respect) and control power and wealth at the micro, meso, and macro levels of the social system, whereas others have little access to those resources. Few social forces affect your personal life at the micro level as much as stratification. That includes the decisions you make about what you wish to do with your life or whom you might marry. Indeed, stratification played a role in why you are reading this book.

KEY POINTS

- *Stratification*—the layering or ranking of people within society—is one of the most important factors shaping the life chances of individuals. This ranking is influenced by micro, meso, and macro forces and resources.

- Depending on the theoretical perspective, stratification can be viewed as either functional or harmful for society and its members.

- The United States has less social mobility and higher levels of inequality and poverty than most other Global North nations.

- For individuals, where they stand in the system of stratification is highly personal, but it is influenced by the way the social system works at the meso and macro levels—due to access to education; the problems created by gender, racial, and ethnic discrimination; and the vitality of regions and the global economy.

- People without much social capital have fewer connections to the meso and macro levels and are less likely to attain power, wealth, and prestige.

- Some macro systems stress ascribed status (assigned to one, often at birth, without consideration of one's individual choices, talents, or intelligence). Other systems purport to be open and based on achieved status (depending on one's contributions to the society and one's personal abilities and decisions).

- Poverty is a difficult social problem, one that can be costly to a society as a whole. Various efforts at the micro, meso, and macro levels have had mixed results, partly because it is in the interests of those with privilege to have an underclass to do the unpleasant jobs.

- Technology is both a contributor to and a possible remedy for inequality, in that the digital divide creates problems for the poor, but electronic innovations can connect individuals to financial structures and opportunities.

DISCUSSION QUESTIONS

1. Were you surprised to learn that among rich nations, life expectancy in the United States is among the lowest? Explain. What sociological theory best explains this fact? Support your answer.

2. How has the social class of your parents and your upbringing influenced your success in school and your professional aspirations?

3. What is the social class of most of the people with whom you hang out? Why do you think you tend to associate with people from this social class?

4. Describe factors at the (a) micro, (b) meso, and (c) macro levels that impact your ability to move up the social class ladder.

5. How do the forces that have led to the shrinking of the middle class impact your chance of becoming (or remaining) a member of the (a) middle, (b) upper-middle, or (c) upper class after you graduate from college?

6. How can bridging the global digital divide lead to decreased inequality across the world? How does your ready access (or lack of access) to a computer and the Internet impact *your* life chances?

KEY TERMS

CONTRIBUTING TO OUR SOCIAL WORLD: WHAT CAN WE DO?

At the Local (Micro) Level

- *Volunteer to serve a meal* at an area soup kitchen. Your campus activities office should be able to help you find one in your area and even connect you with a group on campus that regularly volunteers at one.

- *Organize a Walk for Water Challenge,* where students simulate the challenge faced by women and children who walk great distances to gain access to clean water each day. Design this event to raise awareness of this issue and perhaps use this as an occasion to raise some funds for your favorite clean water charity. You can learn how to organize your walk at www .watermission.org.

- *Tip service people in cash.* Housekeepers in hotels and motels, maids, meal servers at restaurants, and food delivery employees may depend on tips to survive. To make it more likely that they receive the tips intended for them, be sure to tip in cash, rather than using a credit card.

At the Organizational or Institutional (Meso) Level

- *Habitat for Humanity* pairs volunteers with current and prospective homeowners in repairing or constructing housing for little or no cost. Habitat projects are under way or planned for many communities in the United States and around the world. See the organization's website at www.habitat.org for more details and to see if you can volunteer for a project in your area.

- Founded in the early 1990s, *AmeriCorps* includes a variety of programs from intensive residential programs to part-time volunteer opportunities in communities across the United States. For more information, go to the organization's website at www.americorps.gov.

At the National or Global (Macro) Level

- *The Peace Corps* involves a serious, long-term (2-year) commitment, but most who have done it agree that it is well worth the time and energy. The Peace Corps is an independent agency of the U.S. government, founded in 1961. Volunteers work in foreign countries throughout the world, helping local people improve their economic conditions, health, and education. The Peace Corps website (www.peacecorps .gov) provides information on the history of the organization, volunteer opportunities, and reports of former and present volunteers.

- *Grameen Bank* (www.grameenfoundation.org), a micro-credit organization, was started in Bangladesh by Professor Muhammad Yunus, winner of the 2006 Nobel Peace Prize. It makes small-business loans to people who live in impoverished regions of the world and who have no collateral for a loan. Consider doing a local fund-raiser with friends for the Grameen Bank or other micro-credit organizations, such as FINCA (www.finca.org), Kiva (www.kiva.org), and Care International (www.care-international.org).

- WE is a youth-focused organization whose international programs help free people across the globe from the cycle of poverty by providing clean water, schools, health care, and sanitation. You can learn more about this organization and how you can join its efforts at www.we.org.

$SAGE edge™

Get the tools you need to sharpen your study skills. SAGE edge offers a robust online environment featuring an impressive array of free tools and resources.

Access practice quizzes, eFlashcards, video, and multimedia at **edge.sagepub.com/ballantine7e**

CHAPTER 8

© REUTERS/Danish Ismail

RACE AND ETHNIC GROUP STRATIFICATION

Beyond "Us" and "Them"

▲ As human beings, we are all part of "us," but there is a tendency to define those who look or behave differently as "them." Those labeled as "them" are often separated from "us," even dehumanized and mistreated by "us."

MICRO

● **ME (AND MY RACE AND ETHNICITY)**

● **LOCAL ORGANIZATIONS AND COMMUNITY**
Locally, members of ethnic groups may experience exclusion and prejudice.

MESO

● **NATIONAL ORGANIZATIONS, INSTITUTIONS, AND ETHNIC SUBCULTURES**
Policies in large organizations may discriminate—intentionally or unintentionally.

MACRO

● **SOCIETY**
National laws or court rulings often set policies that relate to discrimination.

● **GLOBAL COMMUNITY**
Racial and ethnic hostilities around the world may result in wars, genocide, and "ethnic cleansing."

WHAT WILL YOU LEARN IN THIS CHAPTER?

This chapter will help you to do the following:

8.1 Distinguish between racial and ethnic groups

8.2 Describe the difference between prejudice and discrimination

8.3 Provide examples of dominant and minority group contact in the world today

8.4 Outline effects of prejudice, racism, and discrimination on minority and dominant groups

8.5 Describe efforts to reduce racial and ethnic inequality at the micro, meso, and macro levels of analysis

THINK ABOUT IT

DeBrun was a well-liked African American college student, actively involved in extracurricular activities at his selective liberal arts college. Like many college students, he enjoyed both alcohol consumption on weekends and the outrageous things that happened when people were inebriated. However, DeBrun's anger, normally kept in check, tended to surface when he was drunk. One weekend, some racial slurs were thrown around at a party, and when one of the perpetrators pushed DeBrun too far—including a sucker punch—DeBrun exploded in a fury of violence. No one died, but there were some serious injuries—the worst inflicted by the muscular DeBrun—and at one point a knife was pulled. DeBrun was expelled from college, and felony charges were leveled against him. Because there had been a weapon—one that did not belong to DeBrun but at one point ended up in his hand—the college president would not consider readmission. The local White prosecutor, who saw a powerfully built young Black man with tattoos and dreadlocks, assumed that this campus leader was a "thug" and insisted on the most severe felony charges and penalties.

DeBrun, who had no previous encounters with law enforcement, ended up with a felony record and 2 years in prison. Because of both state and federal laws, the felony charges meant that he no longer qualified for federal financial aid. Because his family had very few resources, his hopes for a college degree were crushed. As a convicted felon, he would not be able to vote in many states for the rest of his life, his future employment prospects were greatly diminished, and his family's hopes that he would be their first college graduate were crushed. The president of the college was not a bigot, but the professors who knew DeBrun well were convinced that neither his expulsion, nor his arrest, nor his conviction as a serious felon would have occurred had he been White.

DeBrun's experience represents a way that African American males can experience a different United States of America than White males. The cause is not necessarily personal bigotry by people in power. Differential treatment and harmful actions against minorities can sometimes occur at individual and small-group levels, but they are particularly problematic at the meso or institutional level. They lead to different racial groups having very different life experiences, and life chances, within the same nation.

In a recent study, sociologists interviewed Black and White schoolchildren whose ages ranged from 11 to 14 and asked them, "What would happen if an alien entered your room at night and turned you into a Black [or White] child?" The majority (65%) of the White children and an overwhelming majority (93%) of the Black children thought their lives would be different if their race changed (Risman and Banerjee 2013).

What do you think? Would your life change if your race changed? Imagine that you were given the opportunity to choose your own racial and ethnic background. What would you do? Why? How do you think your life would be different if you chose a different racial and ethnic background? In this chapter, we explore racial and ethnic stratification. In doing so, we look at related issues, such as the social construction of race, prejudice, racism, and discrimination. Some are micro-level issues, whereas others are best addressed at the meso and macro levels.

What Characterizes Racial and Ethnic Groups?

In this section, we consider the characteristics of racial and ethnic groups and their positions within the stratification system. **Minority groups** are *groups of people with distinct physical or cultural characteristics who are singled out* *from others in their society for differential and unequal treatment.* Racial and ethnic minority groups, like all minority groups, are subject to discrimination.

Minority Groups

Several factors characterize minority groups and their relations with dominant groups in society (Dworkin and Dworkin 1999). Minority groups

1. can be distinguished from the group that holds power by physical appearance, dress, language, or religion;

2. are excluded from or denied full participation at the meso level of society in economic, political, educational, religious, health, and recreational institutions;

3. have less access to power and resources within the nation and are evaluated less favorably, based on their characteristics as minority group members;

4. are stereotyped, ridiculed, condemned, or otherwise defamed, allowing dominant group members to justify and not feel guilty about unequal and poor treatment; and

5. develop collective identities to insulate themselves from the unaccepting world; this in turn perpetuates their group identity by creating ethnic or racial enclaves, intragroup marriages, and segregated group institutions such as religious congregations.

THINKING SOCIOLOGICALLY

Based on the preceding list of minority group characteristics, explain how membership in dominant or minority groups influences people's interactions at the micro (family and friends), the meso (institutional), and the macro levels of society.

Minority and majority status can change over time and among societies. For example, throughout England's history, wars and assassinations changed the ruling group from Catholic to Protestant and back several times. Today, in Iraq, Shiite Muslims are dominant, but they

▲ In the Republic of South Africa, Blacks are almost three quarters of the population, but they are still considered a minority group because they face racial discrimination and have far less access to economic power and privilege than White South Africans, who compose 8% of the population.

© Gideon Mendel/Corbis via Getty Images

were a minority group and Sunni Muslims were the dominant group when Saddam Hussein ruled Iraq.

As in the case of Iraq under Saddam Hussein, dominant groups are not always the numerical majority. In the case of South Africa, possession of advanced European weapons placed the native African Bantu population under the rule of a relatively small number of White British and Dutch descendants in what became a complex system of planned discrimination called *apartheid*. From 1948 to 1994, each major racial group in South Africa—White, "Indian" (meaning Asian), Colored (meaning mixed race), and Black—had its own living area, and members carried identification cards showing the "race" to which they belonged. Racial classification and privilege were defined by the laws of the dominant group.

Concept of Race

Race is *a socially created concept that identifies a group as "different," usually on the basis of ancestry or certain physical characteristics.* This allows members of the groups to be singled out for dissimilar treatment. Most attempts at racial classifications have been based on appearance, such as skin color and shade, stature, facial features, hair color and texture, head form, nose shape, eye color and shape, and height. As you will see, though, racial categories are social constructions that vary over time and place.

Social Construction of Race. From our earliest origins in Ethiopia and around the Olduvai Gorge in East Africa, about 200,000 years ago, *Homo sapiens* slowly spread around the globe, south through Africa, north to Europe, and across Asia. Original migration patterns of early humans over thousands of years are shown in Figure 8.1. As the map shows, most theorists believe that humans crossed Asia and the Bering Straits to North America around 20,000 BCE and continued to populate North and South America (Diamond 1999, 2005). However, continuing archaeological research indicates that indigenous human populations may have reached South America well before the map indicates (Bower 2016; Mann 2005). The point is that mixing of peoples over the centuries has left few if any genetically isolated people, only gradations in appearance as one moves around the world. Thus, the way societies choose to define race has come about largely through what is culturally convenient for the dominant group. The next Sociology in Our Social World provides insight into the origins of racial categories that have had a major impact on history and form the basis for many conflicts today.

In 1978, the United Nations, concerned about racial conflicts and discrimination based on scientifically inaccurate beliefs, issued a Declaration on Race and Race Prejudice prepared by a group of eminent scientists from around the world. This declaration and similar statements by other scientific groups pointed out the harmful effects of racist arguments, doctrines, and policies. The conclusion of their document upheld that (a) all people are born free and equal both in dignity and in rights, (b) racial prejudice impedes personal development, (c) conflicts (based on race) cost nations money and resources, and (d) racism foments international conflict. Racist doctrines lack any scientific basis, in that all people belong to the same species and have descended from the same origin. In summary, problems arising from race relations are social, not biological, in origin. Differential treatments of groups based on "race" falsely claim a scientific basis for classifying humans.

THINKING SOCIOLOGICALLY

How would you describe the other people in your sociology class? Do you use racial terms for everyone? Why or why not? How does your own racial background influence how much you notice the racial characteristics of others? Why?

▼ FIGURE 8.1

The Spread of Humans Around the World

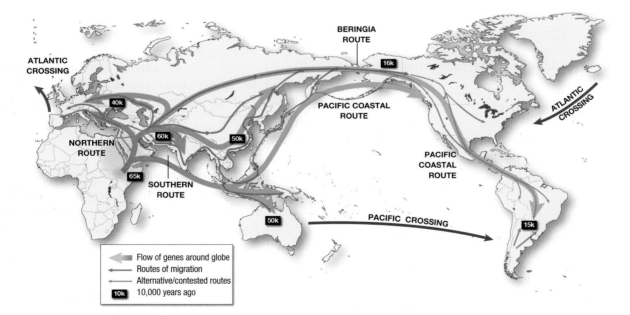

Source: Phys.org 2009.

This map shows the historical spread of humans around the globe and the approximate time periods of the movements.

HISTORICAL ATTEMPTS TO DEFINE RACE

Throughout history, political and religious leaders, philosophers, and scientists have struggled with the meaning and significance of race. Carl von Linné (Linnaeus) created the first systematic (and hierarchical) classification of all living species based on the study of fossils. In 1758, he published *Systema Naturae*, indicating four "different" types of humans: Americanus (Native Americans), Asiaticus, Africanus, and Europeanus (Cashmore and Troyna 1990). Johann Blumenbach was the first to use the word *race* in his 1775 classification system of humans: Caucasian, Mongolian, Ethiopian, American, and Malay. Others proposed lists of as many as 30 "races."

By the 19th century, race began to take on a biological meaning, with theories emerging about inherent inequalities among races to justify slavery and colonialism. For example, U.S. senator John Calhoun declared in 1840 that Africans were incapable of self-care and would become mentally ill under the "burden of freedom." Therefore "it is a mercy to him to give him the guardianship and protection" of slavery (Deutsch 1944; Feagin 2012:71). During this same time period, Joseph Arthur—also known as Comte de Gobineau (1816–1882)—argued that each race has specific characteristics, and he attributed the demise of great societies to the mixing of the White race with other races he deemed inferior. His book *Essay on Inequality of the Human Races* (1853–1855) earned him the title "father of modern racism."

Charles Darwin's *On the Origin of Species* also influenced thinking in this area ([1859] 1909). Among Darwin's many ideas was that human races *might* represent the stages or branches of a tree of evolution. This idea implied that those groups of humans who were biologically best suited to the environment would survive. From Darwin's ideas emerged the concepts of *survival of the fittest* and *ever-improving races*.

These two late-19th-century concepts were taken out of context and became the foundation for a number of theories of superior races. For instance, in 1899, the Brit-turned-German Houston Stewart Chamberlain published an anti-Semitic work in which he argued that northern and western European populations were superior ([1899] 1911). He argued for racial purity, a theme the Nazis later adopted (Cashmore and Troyna 1990).

In the United States, lawyer and eugenicist Madison Grant published *The Passing of the Great Race* in 1916, claiming the superiority of the "Nordic race." Grant proposed a eugenics or breeding program to "save" this "endangered" racial strain. The argument was later discredited after Nazis took this effort to the extreme during the Holocaust, and later scientific discoveries led to the knowledge that there are more genetic variations among than between races (American Anthropological Association [1998] 2016).

Mein Kampf was Adolf Hitler's contribution to the concept of a superior race (1939). In it, he conceptualized just two races: Aryans and Others. He focused attention on several groups, particularly Jews, whom he blamed for the economic and social problems of Germany. In the name of German purity, millions of Jews, Poles, Roma, gay men, and others deemed "less human" were exterminated. The extent to which Hitler succeeded exemplifies what can happen when one group feels superior to others, blames other groups for its shortcomings, and has the power to act against those minorities.

Looking through history, one can see many more examples of how racial categorizations have been misused across time and societies. For example, in the United States, Irish and Italians were once seen as distinct races viewed as inferior to the White race. These examples help reveal that racial categories are social, rather than biological, constructions.

Symbolic Interactionist Analysis of the Social Construction of Race. Why are sociologists concerned about a concept that has little scientific accuracy and is ill defined? The answer is its *social significance*. The social reality is that people's group membership can influence how they are treated by others and how they view themselves. Remember the *looking-glass self* concept—we see ourselves based on how we think others perceive us. Our self-concept can be greatly affected by whether we see ourselves as members of a dominant or minority racial group.

Strangely, we might be seen as part of a dominant group in one society and a minority group in another. For example, imagine it is 1970 and you have White parents, three White grandparents, and one Black grandparent. Imagine, too, that no one would guess by your appearance that you had an ancestor who was not White. In South Africa, you would be treated as "Colored" (in between Black and White); in many U.S. states, you would be defined as Black; and in Brazil, you would be perceived as White (Kottak 2014).

In 1977, the U.S. Office of Management and Budget issued a directive to ensure consistent ethnic and racial categories for both statistical and administrative goals. Federal programs directed toward specific racial and ethnic groups and the U.S. Census use these categories. Many very different groups have been combined under the five racial and ethnic categories: (1) American Indian or Alaska Native, (2) Asian or Pacific Islander, (3) Black, (4) Hispanic, and (5) White. (Hispanic/Latino Americans are an ethnic group and can be of any race.) For example, in North America, those racially classified as Native American or Alaska Native use 600 independent tribal nation names to identify themselves, including the Ojibwa (Chippewa), the Dineh (Navajo), the Lakota (Sioux), Unangax (Aleut), and many others. Most consider themselves very different from other "Native American" groups. Some even fought against one another in past wars. Likewise, in the U.S. Census, people of Korean, Filipino, Chinese, Japanese, and Malaysian descent are all identified as *Asian Americans*, but they come from very different cultures (including some that were once mortal enemies). In addition, people from (or who have ancestors from) Bolivia, Mexico, Cuba, and many other nations are grouped together in an ethnic category called *Hispanics* or *Latinos*, even though they may not think of themselves as being alike.

When government aid is tied to such categories, people must identify as such to receive funds. When federal funds for social services were made available to Asian Americans or American Indians, these diverse people began to think of themselves as part of a larger grouping for political purposes (Esperitu 1992). The federal government essentially created a racial group by naming and providing funding to that group. If people wanted services (health care, legal rights, and so forth), they had to become a part of a particular group—such as "Asian Americans."

Before civil rights laws were passed in the United States in the 1960s, a number of states had laws that spelled out distinct treatments for different racial groups. These were commonly referred to as Jim Crow laws.

States in the South passed laws defining who was Black and subject to discriminatory laws. In many cases, it was difficult to determine to which category an individual belonged. For instance, Blacks in Georgia were defined as people with any ascertainable trace of "Negro" blood in their veins. In Missouri, one eighth or more "Negro" blood was the standard, whereas in Louisiana, 1/32 Negro blood defined someone as Black. In Texas the father's race determined the race of the child. Even the U.S. Census Bureau finds categories that indicate race or ethnicity to be confusing and complex. Over the history of the United States, the classifications have changed many times.

THINKING SOCIOLOGICALLY

Visit the Pew Research Center's "What Census Calls Us: A Historical Timeline" (www.pewsocialtrends.org/interactives/multiracial-timeline) to learn how U.S. Census racial and ethnic categories have changed over time. List at least two changes among the many throughout the history of the United States and then describe some social forces behind those changes. How does this timeline provide evidence that racial categories are social constructions?

Continuing Significance of Race. The civil rights legislation of the 1960s that prohibited racial discrimination in voting, housing, and employment has helped diminish discrimination. Unfortunately, though, racial discrimination still exists, and the combination of the impact of past and present discrimination has led to disparities in wealth and income among Black, Hispanic, and White Americans. As Tables 8.1 and 8.2 make clear, income levels for Blacks, Hispanics, and Whites, even when controlling for education level, are still quite disparate. A clear racial economic hierarchy exists with White Americans on the top and other racial groups below.

Education levels minimize, but do not eradicate, the gap in unemployment rates by race or ethnicity. Figure 8.2 displays the differences.

▼ TABLE 8.1

Race or Ethnicity and Family Income

	White	Black	Hispanic
Median family annual income	$65,041	$39,490	$47,675

Source: Semega, Fontenot, and Kollar 2017; U.S. Census Bureau.

Earnings by Educational Level and Race or Ethnicity for Adults 25 and Older

Education	White Income	Black Income	Hispanic Income
High school degree/GED	$32,399	$27,490	$30,198
Associate degree	$40,484	$35,747	$35,454
Bachelor's degree	$54,004	$48,878	$46,298
Master's degree	$65,499	$56,880	$60,866

Source: U.S. Census Bureau 2017c.

▼ FIGURE 8.2

Unemployment Rates by Race or Ethnicity

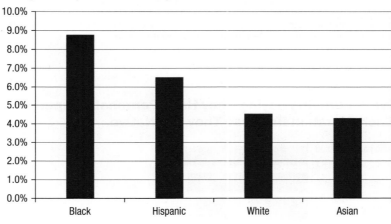

Average Monthly Rate from January 2000 to December 2016

Source: Andolfatto 2017.

Differences in *wealth* (one's income, property, and total assets) by race are even more stark. As Figure 8.3 indicates, in the United States, Whites have 13 times the wealth of Blacks and 10 times the wealth of Hispanics. In 2013, the median White family had $142,000 in wealth, compared with $11,000 for the median Black family (Kochhar and Fry 2014).

This racial economic hierarchy is due to current as well as past discrimination. For example, in one well-known study, Black, White, and Hispanic applicants (of similar age, similar physical appearance, and the same level of educational attainment and qualifications) responded to help wanted ads for jobs in the low-wage sector in New York City. The results showed that Whites received a callback about the position or job offer 31% of

the time compared with 25.2% for Hispanics and 15.2% for Blacks. Other studies reveal that among equally qualified job candidates, those with lighter skin tones are more likely to be selected than those with darker skin (Harrison 2010; Harrison and Thomas 2009). A study published in 2017 shows that officials in local government offices, including libraries, sheriff offices, county clerks, and school districts' offices, are 4% less likely to respond to e-mails from those with Black-sounding names than those with White-sounding names (Giuletti, Tonin, and Vlassopoulos 2017). When they do respond to those they assume are Black, they are 8% less likely to respond politely.

Being Black also exposes one to a string of humiliating, frustrating, and sometimes dangerous situations.

Wealth Gaps Based on Race Have Grown Since the Great Recession

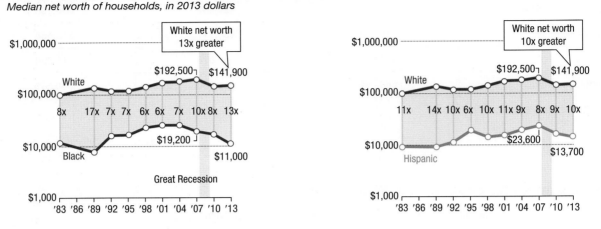

Racial, Ethnic Wealth Gaps Have Grown Since Great Recession
Median net worth of households, in 2013 dollars

Source: Kochhar and Fry, "Wealth inequality has widened along racial, ethnic lines since end of Great Recession," Pew Research Center, Washington, DC (December 2014), www.pewresearch.org/fact-tank/2014/12/12/racial-wealth-gaps-great-recession.

▼ FIGURE 8.4

Percentage of Native Americans Saying They Have Personally Experienced Discrimination in Each Situation Because They Are Native

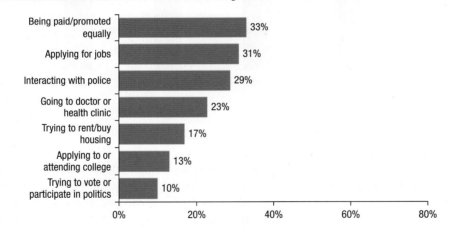

Source: Brewer, Graham. November 18, 2017. "As Native Americans Face Job Discrimination, A Tribe Works to Employ Its Own." NPR. Retrieved November 19, 2017. Alyson Hunt/NPR.

For example, the chances of being pulled over by the police are 5 times higher for Blacks than Whites in cities as diverse as Torrington, Connecticut, and Chicago, Illinois. Moreover, despite the fact that, when pulled over, Whites are more likely to have drugs or illegal materials in their cars than Blacks, Blacks have their cars searched for drugs or contraband far more often

(LaFraniere and Lehren 2015; Police Accountability Task Force 2016).

American Indians also face discrimination today. Figure 8.4 shows how many have experienced discrimination in areas ranging from trying to vote to receiving equal pay and promotion opportunities in the workplace (Brewer 2017). Discrimination and poor health care

© Getty Images/Hill Street Studios/Blend Images

▲ One constant frustration for Blacks is being pulled over for DWB—driving while Black. Blacks are many times more likely to be stopped, humiliated, and even endangered than are Whites.

services have contributed to shorter life spans for Native Americans. Today, the life expectancy of American Indians and Alaskan Natives is 4.4 years less than the average life expectancy of all other races combined (73.7 years compared to 78.1 years) (Indian Health Service 2016).

THINKING SOCIOLOGICALLY

Were you aware of the race-based disparities in income and wealth? Why do you think income and wealth among races differ, even when controlling for education?

Black and American Indian children have lower rates of upward mobility and higher rates of downward mobility than other children. Not even being born into a wealthy family can shield these children from race-based economic inequality. For example, whereas

White children born into wealth are 5 times as likely to stay rich as fall into poverty, Black children born into wealthy families have almost as great a chance of falling into poverty as they do remaining wealthy (Chetty et al. 2018).

This economic gap, however, is almost all due to inequality among Black and White males. In 99% of neighborhoods in the United States, Black men earn less than White men raised by families with comparable incomes. On average, however, Black women tend to make slightly *higher* incomes than White women raised in families with similar incomes (Chetty et al. 2018).

Fortunately, new research indicates environmental factors that can increase the life chances of Black men. We now know that Black men raised in areas with low poverty, high rates of present fathers, and low levels of racial bias among Whites tend to stay out of prison and have higher incomes. Efforts to reduce racial inequality across generations need to be aimed at creating more such neighborhoods (Chetty et al. 2018).

Ethnic Groups

Ethnic groups *are based on cultural factors: language, religion, dress, foods, customs, beliefs, values, norms, a shared group identity or feeling, and sometimes loyalty to a homeland, monarch, or religious leader.* Members are grouped together because they share a common cultural heritage, often connected with a national or geographical identity. There can be many ethnic groups under one racial category (e.g., Black Americans include African immigrants, West Indian immigrants, and African Americans). Visits to ethnic enclaves in large cities in the United States give a picture of ethnicity. Indian, Chinese, and Dominican neighborhoods may have non-English street signs and newspapers, ethnic restaurants, culture-specific houses of worship, and clothing styles that reflect the ethnic subculture.

Census 2010 data show the ethnic ancestry of millions of Americans and their distribution across the United States. Those with German ancestry make up the largest group at almost 50 million, followed by African Americans at 41 million, Irish at 36 million, Mexicans at 32 million, and English at 30 million. Twenty million claim "American" as their ancestry. American Indians and Alaska Natives, the original Americans, make up about 5 million people (O'Connor, Lubin, and Spector 2013).

Figure 8.5 shows where each ethnic group, by county, has the largest concentration, though this does not necessarily mean the group makes up more than 50% of the population of that county.

Ancestry With Largest Population in Each County, 2010

Legend:
- African American
- American Indian
- American or Unknown
- British
- French
- German
- Irish
- Italian
- Mexican or Spanish
- Scandinavian
- Other

Source: Lombard 2014.

Multiracial Populations: Immigration, Intermarriage, and Personal Identification

"Push" factors drive people from some countries, and "pull" factors draw them to other countries. The most common push-pull factors today are job opportunities, the desire for peace and security, individual liberties, and availability of medical and educational opportunities. The target countries of migrants are most often in North America, Australia, or Western Europe, and the highest emigration rates are from Africa, Eastern Europe, Central Asia, and South and Central America.

Immigration into the United States from every continent has led to a diverse population, with 13% of the current U.S. population born elsewhere (López and Radford 2017). As Figure 8.6 reveals, among the Black population, the foreign-born have tripled in number since 1980. Today, almost one out of ten (8.7%) are foreign-born. About half are from the Caribbean (Anderson 2015).

With new immigration, increasing rates of intermarriage, and many more individuals claiming multiracial identification, color lines are changing (DaCosta 2007; Korgen 2016; Lee and Bean 2004, 2007). Seven percent

of adults come from more than one racial background (based on their own, their parents', or their grandparents' racial heritage) and 10% of children living with two parents have parents of different races. Figure 8.7 illustrates the heritage of the current multiracial population in the United States.

Some Americans, including growing numbers of those with mixed racial heritage, prefer not to identify themselves racially (Hochschild, Weaver, and Burch 2012; Khanna, 2016; Rockquemore and Brunsma 2008). Some scholars, such as Eduardo Bonilla-Silva, say, however, that although the racial hierarchy is shifting, it persists. Bonilla-Silva argues that the United States is moving from a Black-White racial hierarchy to a three-tiered racial hierarchy with the top positions held by *Whites*: "'traditional' whites; new 'white' immigrants; and, in the near future, assimilated Latinos, some multiracials (light-skinned ones), and individual members of other groups (some Asian Americans, etc.)" (Bonilla-Silva and Embrick 2005:33). Next will come a middle group consisting of "*honorary Whites* (most light-skinned Latino Americans, Japanese Americans, Korean Americans, Asian Indian [Americans], Chinese Americans, the bulk of multiracials . . . and most

▼ FIGURE 8.6

Immigrants as Part of the Black U.S. Population

Immigrants Are a Growing Share Among Black Americans . . .

% of U.S. Black population that is foreign born

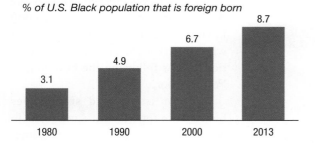

1980	1990	2000	2013
3.1	4.9	6.7	8.7

. . . As the Black Immigrant Population Has More Than Quadrupled Since 1980

Total foreign-born Black population in the U.S., in thousands

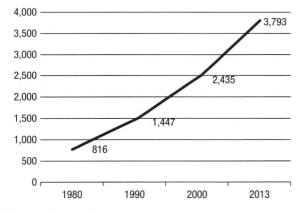

816, 1,447, 2,435, 3,793

Source: Anderson 2015.

Middle Eastern Americans)" (Bonilla-Silva and Embrick 2005:33). The bottom group, the "*collective Black*," will contain Black Americans, dark-skinned Latino Americans, Vietnamese Americans, Cambodian Americans, Laotian Americans, and maybe Filipino Americans. The lines are moving, but the racial hierarchy remains (Bonilla-Silva, 2009; Bonilla-Silva and Embrick 2005).

THINKING SOCIOLOGICALLY

Identify one dominant and one minority group in your community or on campus. Where does each group fit into the stratification system in the United States? How are the life chances of individuals in these groups influenced by factors beyond their control?

Prejudice: Micro-Level Analysis

Have you ever found yourself in a situation in which you were viewed as different, strange, or undesirable? Perhaps you have felt the sting of rejection, based not on judgment of you as a person but solely because of the ethnic or racial group into which you were born. Then again, you may have been insulated from this type of rejection if you grew up in a homogeneous community or in a privileged group. Where and when we are born can determine how we are treated, our life chances, and many of our experiences and attitudes.

Prejudice influences dominant–minority group relations. **Prejudice** refers to *preconceived attitudes about a group, usually negative and not based on facts.* Prejudiced individuals lump together people with certain characteristics without considering individual differences. In this section we also look at *stereotyping*, when prejudiced individuals use distorted, oversimplified, or exaggerated ideas to categorize a group of people and attribute personal qualities to them. Whereas prejudice and stereotypes can be stimulated by events such as conflicts at the institutional level and war at the societal level, attitudes are held by individuals and can be best understood as a micro-level phenomenon.

Prejudice refers to attitudes rather than actions. **Discrimination**, on the other hand, is *differential treatment and harmful actions against minorities.* These actions at the micro level might include refusal to sell someone a house because of the religion, race, or ethnicity of the buyer or not hiring someone because of her or his minority status (Feagin and Feagin 2012). Discrimination in the legal system, such as laws that deny opportunities or resources to members of a particular group, operates largely at the meso or macro level, discussed later in this chapter.

Nature of Prejudice

Prejudice is an understandable response of humans to their social environment. To survive, every social group or unit—a sorority, sports team, civic club, or nation—needs to mobilize the loyalty of its members. Each organization needs to convince people to voluntarily commit energy, skills, time, and resources so the organization can meet its needs. As people commit themselves to a group, they invest a portion of themselves and feel loyalty to the group. This loyalty leads to a preference for the group and attempts to distinguish it from others. It is important to recognize prejudice, though, and how it can foster discriminatory actions.

Percentage of Multiracial U.S. Adults

Percentage of all U.S. adults who have at least two races in their background (based on races of self, parents, or grandparents)

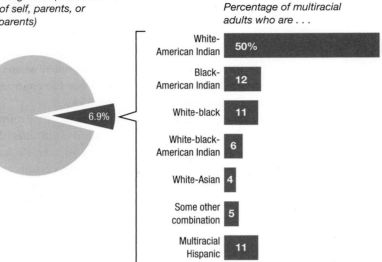

Percentage of multiracial adults who are . . .

White-American Indian	50%
Black-American Indian	12
White-black	11
White-black-American Indian	6
White-Asian	4
Some other combination	5
Multiracial Hispanic	11

6.9%

Source: Pew Research Center 2015g.

Note: Multiracial adults are two or more races (based on backgrounds of self, parents, or grandparents). Multiracial subgroups and "some other combination" are non-Hispanic and mutually exclusive. The multiracial Hispanic subgroup includes Hispanics who are also any two or more races. Multiracial subgroups may not add up to 100% because of rounding.

▲ After Japan bombed Pearl Harbor on December 7, 1941, more than 110,000 Japanese Americans, including those pictured here, were forcibly removed from many western states and sent to relocation camps.

In wartime, the enemy may be depicted in films or other media as villains. During World War II, American films often showed negative stereotypes of Japanese and German people. These negative images helped lead to the decision to intern more than 110,000 Japanese Americans, the majority of whom were U.S. citizens, in detention camps following the bombing of Pearl Harbor.

Similar issues and stereotypes have arisen for Muslim Americans in recent years. For example, hate crimes against Muslims spiked after the attacks on New York's World Trade Center on September 11, 2001; the Boston Marathon bombings on April 15, 2013; and during and after the 2016 presidential election in the United States (Potok 2015; Southern Poverty Law Center 2017b). The number of anti-Muslim hate groups tripled (34 to 101) from 2015 to 2016. In 2017, half of the people in the United States believed that at least some U.S. Muslims are anti-American. Candidate and President Donald Trump's anti-Muslim rhetoric helped make this a partisan issue. As Figure 8.8 reveals, more Republicans than Democrats have a negative view toward Muslims. This political divide holds true in Europe, as well. In Europe, those with right-wing political ideologies have more negative feelings toward Muslims than do those with left-wing political perspectives (Lipka 2017a).

Explaining Racial Discrimination at the Micro Level

Why do individuals commit acts of racial discrimination? Why would people be so angry at racial minorities that they would act to harm them? The following is one theory that has attempted to explain acts of racial discrimination.

Views About Anti-Americanism Among U.S. Muslims

How many Muslims in the U.S., if any, are anti-American?

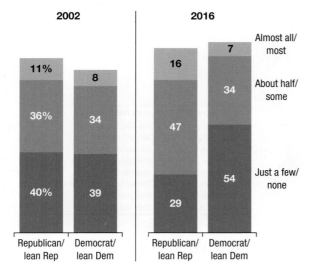

2002

11% — Republican/lean Rep (Almost all/most)
8 — Democrat/lean Dem (Almost all/most)
36% — Republican/lean Rep (About half/some)
34 — Democrat/lean Dem (About half/some)
40% — Republican/lean Rep (Just a few/none)
39 — Democrat/lean Dem (Just a few/none)

2016

16 — Republican/lean Rep (Almost all/most)
7 — Democrat/lean Dem (Almost all/most)
47 — Republican/lean Rep (About half/some)
34 — Democrat/lean Dem (About half/some)
29 — Republican/lean Rep (Just a few/none)
54 — Democrat/lean Dem (Just a few/none)

Almost all/most
About half/some
Just a few/none

Republican/lean Rep   Democrat/lean Dem

Source: "Muslims and Islam: Key findings in the U.S. and around the world." Pew Research Center, Washington, D.C. (August 9, 2017), http://www.pewresearch.org/fact-tank/2017/08/09/muslims-and-islam-key-findings-in-the-u-s-and-around-the-world.

Frustration-Aggression Theory. On June 17, 2015, Dylann Roof "entered the church, asked for the pastor, and sat next to him during Bible study before opening fire. 'I have to do it,' he said, according to [reports]. 'You rape our women and you're taking over our country. You have to go'" (Robles, Horowitz, and Dewan 2015). After being charged with murder, he admitted to killing nine people in a historic African American church in South Carolina (Croft and Smith 2017). According to frustration-aggression theory, many of those who carry out acts of racial discrimination feel angry and frustrated because they cannot attain what they desire. Frustration-aggression theory focuses largely on poorly adjusted people who express their frustration through aggressive attacks on others. From all accounts, Dylann Roof, a 21-year-old high school dropout with a history of heavy drug use and scrapes with the law, was a poorly adjusted young man with racist beliefs (Horowitz et al. 2015; Robles et al. 2015).

When people cannot take out their aggression on its source and turn it on innocent victims, they are *scapegoating*. The word *scapegoat* comes from the Bible (see Leviticus 16:5–22). Once a year, a goat (which was obviously innocent) was laden with parchments on which people had written their sins. The goat was then sent out to the desert to die. This was part of a ritual of purification, and the creature took the blame for the sins committed by the people. Scapegoating occurs when a minority group is blamed for the failures of others. It is often difficult to look at oneself to seek reasons for failure but easy to transfer the blame for one's failure to others. Individuals who feel they are failures in their jobs or other aspects of their lives may turn the blame toward minority groups. From within such a prejudiced mind-set, violence toward the out-group may seem acceptable. Hate groups evolve when people with such mind-sets unite.

As Figure 8.9 reveals, there are active hate groups in every state, but some states have more than others. Figure 8.10 shows how the number of hate groups has increased dramatically over the past two decades. As society changes, hate groups grow and fall in numbers. For example, from 2016 to 2017, the number of neo-Nazi hate groups increased 22% and the number of Ku Klux Klan groups fell by 49% (Southern Poverty Law Center 2018).

▲ The shooting of Blacks in the United States has shaken the country and spawned the Black Lives Matter movement. Pallbearers release doves over the casket of one of the nine people killed in the shooting at Emanuel AME Church in Charleston, South Carolina, in 2015. They were engaged in a Bible study when attacked.

Active Hate Groups in 2017

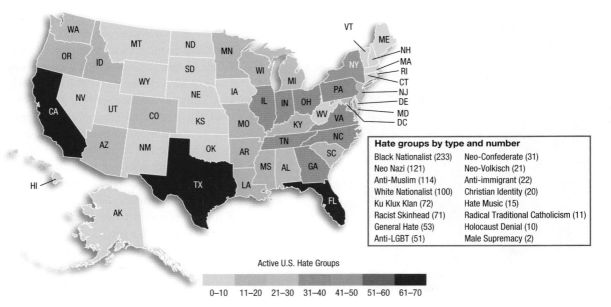

Hate groups by type and number	
Black Nationalist (233)	Neo-Confederate (31)
Neo Nazi (121)	Neo-Volkisch (21)
Anti-Muslim (114)	Anti-immigrant (22)
White Nationalist (100)	Christian Identity (20)
Ku Klux Klan (72)	Hate Music (15)
Racist Skinhead (71)	Radical Traditional Catholicism (11)
General Hate (53)	Holocaust Denial (10)
Anti-LGBT (51)	Male Supremacy (2)

Active U.S. Hate Groups

0–10 11–20 21–30 31–40 41–50 51–60 61–70

Source: Southern Poverty Law Center 2018.

Color-Blind Ideology and Racism Evasiveness

A bigot is someone who blindly insists that certain people are so different that they are inferior—even, perhaps, less than human. Hate groups in the United States, Europe, and many other countries justify themselves on the basis of bigoted thinking. They loudly proclaim that those outside their racial or ethnic group deserve to face discrimination.

Many other people are not bigoted but simply oblivious to racial inequality and the hidden privileges that Whites experience in U.S. society. They do not want to hear about the realities of racial inequality. In fact, they maintain that race no longer matters. A racial ideology that grew out of opposition to affirmative action programs in the 1980s, the *color-blind ideology*, is now the dominant racial ideology in the United States (Bonilla-Silva 2009; Brunsma 2006; Korgen and Brunsma 2012). Promoters of the color-blind ideology maintain that we should all act as though we are "color-blind" when it comes to race and avoid the topic in personal interactions. However, for many people of color, their blackness or brownness is so integral to their identity that to say one is color-blind is to fail to see the whole person. They feel they are being made invisible and forced to be part of the mainstream culture—to be assimilated (Dalton 2012; Dyer 2012; Feagin 2012).

Those who have a color-blind perspective on race do not notice the "invisible privileges" of Whites in U.S. society (Rothenberg 2015). Consider the following privileges that most people who are part of the dominant group take for granted (McIntosh 2002:97–101):

- I can avoid spending time with people who mistrust people of my color.

- I can protect my children most of the time from people who might not like them.

- I can criticize our government and talk about how I fear its policies and behavior without being seen as a cultural "outsider" or unpatriotic.

- I can easily buy posters, postcards, picture books, greeting cards, dolls, toys, and children's magazines featuring people of my race.

- I can arrange my activities so that I will never have to experience feelings of rejection owing to my race.

THINKING SOCIOLOGICALLY

What is your reaction to this list? How does your own racial or ethnic background influence your reaction?

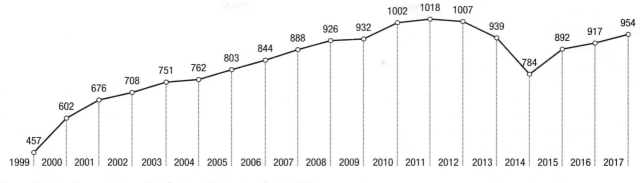

▼ FIGURE 8.10

Hate Groups, 1999–2017

Source: Reprinted by permission of the Southern Poverty Law Center 2018.

The color-blind ideology leads people to practice "racism evasiveness." For indeed, "what people are ultimately avoiding when they say they do not see color, when they overlook differences in power, or avoid 'race words' is racism" (Beeman 2015:131). Therefore, the color-blind perspective on race allows discrimination hidden within the society's institutions to remain in place. Advocates of the color-blind racial ideology reject blatant bigotry as crude and ignorant but fail to recognize that their own actions may perpetuate inequalities at the institutional or meso level.

Today, the color-blind ideology has been challenged as never before by the spread of racist events and ideology on social media. It's difficult to think that racism is not a problem when you can see videos of unarmed Black people being shot on your phone. These horrific events, kept in public view through smartphones and the efforts of organized groups like Black Lives Matter, have made more people recognize racial inequality and the fact that racial prejudice and discrimination still exist in the United States at both the individual and the institutional levels. As former president Jimmy Carter describes it, "Recent reports showing high unemployment and incarceration rates among black people, 'combined with the white police attacks on innocent Blacks' has 'reawakened' the country to the fact that racism was not resolved in the 1960s and 70s" (Goodstein 2016:para. 8).

Discrimination: Meso-Level Analysis

Dear Teacher, I would like to introduce you to my son, Wind-Wolf. He is probably what you would consider a typical Indian kid. He was born and raised on the reservation. He has black hair, dark brown eyes, and an olive complexion, and, like so many Indian children his age, he is shy

and quiet in the classroom. He is 5 years old, in kindergarten, and I can't understand why you have already labeled him a "slow learner." He has already been through quite an education compared with his peers in Western society. He was bonded to his mother and to the Mother Earth in a traditional native childbirth ceremony. He has been continuously cared for by his mother, father, sisters, cousins, aunts, uncles, grandparents, and extended tribal family since this ceremony. . . .

Wind-Wolf was strapped (in his baby basket like a turtle shell) snugly with a deliberate restriction on his arms and legs. Although Western society may argue this hinders motor-skill development and abstract reasoning, we believe it forces the child to first develop his intuitive faculties, rational intellect, symbolic thinking, and five senses. Wind-Wolf was with his mother constantly, closely bonded physically, as she carried him on her back or held him while breast-feeding. She carried him everywhere she went, and every night he slept with both parents. Because of this, Wind-Wolf's educational setting was not only a "secure" environment, but it was also very colorful, complicated, sensitive, and diverse.

As he grew older, Wind-Wolf began to crawl out of the baby basket, develop his motor skills, and explore the world around him. When frightened or sleepy, he could always return to the basket, as a turtle withdraws into its shell. Such an inward journey allows one to reflect in privacy on what he has learned and to carry the new knowledge deeply into the unconscious and the soul. Shapes, sizes, colors, texture, sound, smell, feeling, taste, and the learning process are therefore functionally integrated—the physical and spiritual, matter and energy, and conscious and unconscious, individual and social.

It takes a long time to absorb and reflect on these kinds of experiences, so maybe that is why you think my Indian child is a slow learner. His aunts and grandmothers taught him to count and to know his numbers while they sorted materials for making abstract designs in native baskets. He was taught to learn mathematics by counting the sticks we use in our traditional native hand game. So he may be slow in grasping the methods and tools you use in your classroom, ones quite familiar to his white peers, but I hope you will be patient with him. It takes time to adjust to a new cultural system and learn new things. He is not culturally "disadvantaged," but he is culturally different. (Lake 1990:48–53)

This letter expresses the frustration of a father who sees his son being labeled and discriminated against by the school system without being given a chance. *Discrimination*, introduced earlier in this chapter, refers to differential treatment and harmful actions taken against members of a minority group. It can occur at individual and small-group levels but is particularly problematic at the organizational and institutional levels—the meso level of analysis.

THINKING SOCIOLOGICALLY

> How might schools unintentionally misunderstand Wind-Wolf and other minority children in ways that have negative consequences for children's success?

Institutional racial discrimination is *any meso-level institutional arrangement that favors one racial group over another; this favoritism may result in intentional or unintentional consequences for minority groups.* This form of discrimination results from the normal or routine part of the way an organization operates that systemically disadvantages members of one group. Jim Crow laws, passed in the late 1800s in the United States that enforced racial segregation, and laws that barred Jews in Germany from living, working, or investing in certain places are examples of intentional discrimination embedded in organizations.

Institutional discrimination can occur because of racial stereotypes that funnel racial groups into different institutions or areas within an institution. This discrimination can occur without laws but simply based on practice driven by people's perceptions of differences among racial groups. We can see this in sports. Sociologists view sports as a social institution that is both an institution itself, with its own patterned sets of behavior, and a group of organizations influenced by social forces such as race, gender, and social class. These social forces influence the demographics of neighborhood pickup games, organized teams, leagues, coaches, and team owners. The next Sociology in Our

Social World looks at the influence of racial stereotypes in the National Football League (NFL).

Often, institutional racial discrimination is done unintentionally. For example, in some states, local funding of schools leads to schools with racial minorities receiving fewer funds than most predominantly White schools. This type of funding policy can be supported by nonracists who simply want local control over schools. Whether intended or not, though, such a policy benefits a particular race at the expense of others. As you can see, racial discrimination does not have to be the result of a nasty or mean-spirited person bullying others; it often operates independently of prejudice (Bonilla-Silva 2003; Rothenberg 2015).

Side-effect discrimination and past-in-present discrimination are two other types of unintentional institutional discrimination (Feagin and Feagin 1986; Rydgren 2004). **Side-effect discrimination** refers to *practices in one institutional area that have a negative impact because they are linked to practices in another institutional area; because institutions are interdependent, discrimination in one results in unintentional discrimination in others.* Figure 8.11 illustrates this idea. Each institution uses information from the other institutions to make decisions. So, discrimination in one can lead to discrimination in others.

▼ FIGURE 8.11

Side-Effect Discrimination

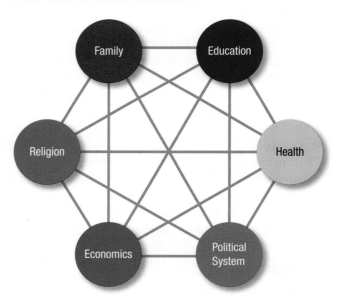

Note: Each circle represents a different institution—family, education, religion, health, political-legal system, and economics. These meso-level systems are interdependent, using information or resources from the others. If discrimination occurs in one institution, the second institution may unintentionally borrow information or practices that result in discrimination. In this way, discrimination occurs at the meso level without awareness by individuals at the micro level.

SOCIOLOGY IN OUR SOCIAL WORLD

RACIAL STEREOTYPES LEAD TO RACIAL INEQUITY IN THE NFL

Sasha Aronson

Sports is often used as an example of how racial tensions can be transcended on the field of play. However, like all social institutions, sports also reflects the racism imbedded within American society. The National Football League (NFL), the pinnacle of football, America's most popular sport, provides an example of the persistence of racial inequity in sports—and the United States (Nooran 2018; "Pro Football" 2016). Racial stereotypes—revealed in coaches' decisions on where to place players, sportswriters' published reflections, and recruiters' analyses—lead to a funneling of players into positions based on race and to an NFL with mostly Black players and White head coaches.

Studies of newspaper articles in the 1970s demonstrated that among players in "central positions" (players in the middle of the action, such as quarterbacks or centers), Whites were far more likely than Blacks to be described in terms of the mental abilities needed for those positions. In contrast, Black players tended to be portrayed as "natural" athletes but not equipped with the intelligence to lead a team. Black players' achievements were associated with innate, physical ability whereas White players earned success through hard work (Marjoribanks and Farquharson 2011). A 2004 study found that these racial stereotypes were common in descriptions of players in *all* positions—not just those in central positions (Woodward 2004).

A 2017 *Washington Post* analysis of media portrayals of White and Black quarterback prospects from 2008 to 2016 found that a White quarterback was *still* more likely to be described in "terms of intangible internal qualities for which he himself is responsible," whereas a Black quarterback had a higher chance of being described "in terms of physical characteristics, to be judged erratic and unpredictable, and to have his successes and failures ascribed to outside forces" (Monroe, Boylan, and McMahon 2017).

The perception of Black athletes as physical athletes and Whites as "smart" athletes has led to the relative paucity of Black head NFL coaches. As of 2017, there were only 8 non-White head coaches on NFL teams. This means that 70% of players in the NFL are Black, and 75% of the league's head coaches are White (Gaines 2017).

The Rooney Rule, enacted in 2002, mandates that every NFL team hiring a coach must interview a non-White person before making a final decision. This rule has had limited impact, however, because 94% of head coaches hired over the past 20 years were promoted from a coordinator position or a college head coaching position—and the overwhelming majority of those coaches are White (and many are former quarterbacks).

So, although all players may compete on the football field as equals, racial stereotypes still tend to influence the positions in which they play, how they are perceived, and who coaches them. Sports is not immune to the stereotypes in the larger society—and we need to recognize this fact to successfully combat racial inequity on and off the playing field.

Sasha Aronson is a student at Tulane University.

Side-effect discrimination occurs when discrimination in the criminal justice system leads to discrimination in the employment sector. For example, in an interview conducted by one of the authors, a probation officer in a moderate-sized city in Ohio said that he had never seen an African American in his county get a not-guilty verdict and that he was not sure it was possible. He had known of cases in which minorities had pled guilty to a lesser charge even though they were innocent because they did not think they could receive a fair verdict in that city. When people apply for jobs, however, they are usually required to report the conviction on the application form. Employers discriminate against applicants with a criminal record, whether or not the applicant was guilty of the crime. Side-effect discrimination is *unintentional discrimination*; the criminal justice system has reached an unjust verdict, and the potential employer is swayed unfairly.

A second example of side-effect discrimination shows how Internet access can play a role in institutionalized discrimination and privilege. For example, in the early 2000s in Alaska, 15.2% of the population was Native, but Natives held only 5% of state jobs, and 27.3% of Native men and 16% of Native women were unemployed (AAANativeArts 2011; U.S. Census Bureau 2011). The State of Alaska used the Internet as its primary means of advertising and accepting applications for state jobs (State of Alaska 2006). In the early 2000s, however, Internet access was unavailable in the 164 predominantly

© Design Pics Inc/Alamy Stock Photo

▲ In this rural Alaskan village, finding jobs through the Internet is not an option.

Native villages in Alaska—a state so large and spread out that it is 2.2 times the size of Texas and has only 1.2 people per square mile (Denali Commission 2001; Hudson 2011). State officials may not have been intentionally trying to prevent Aleuts, Inupiats, Athabaskans, or other Alaska Natives from gaining access to state jobs, but the effect was institutionalized discrimination. Although efforts have been made in recent years to expand Internet access, as of 2016, 67% of rural Alaskans still do not have access to broadband Internet (Federal Communications Commission 2016).

THINKING SOCIOLOGICALLY

Imagine you run a business that is hiring people. You routinely do a criminal background check on applicants and discard the applications of those with a criminal record. You have just read this chapter and realize that some of that information may be a source of unintended side-effect discrimination for a minority group member. What will you do now? Why?

Past-in-present discrimination refers to *practices from the past that may no longer be allowed but that continue to have consequences for people in the present* (Feagin and Feagin 1986; Verbeek and Penninx 2009). Examples of this abound if you dig deep enough. For example, in Mississippi, during the 1950s, state expenditures to educate a White child averaged $147 per pupil, whereas the average was $34 per Black pupil in segregated schools (Luhman and Gilman 1980). Such blatant segregation and inequality in use of tax dollars is no longer legal, and this may seem like ancient history. Yet some African Americans who were in school in the 1950s and 1960s are

receiving low Social Security checks because their earning power was diminished due to their poor schooling. One result is that they cannot help pay for their grandchildren to go to college. This is not ancient history to them; it affects their opportunities and those of their children and grandchildren today.

As you can see, then, the great disparity in wealth between White and Black Americans described earlier relates to the legal discrimination many generations of Black Americans experienced in the past. Another reason for the great racial disparity in wealth lies in racially discriminatory housing practices common before the Fair Housing Act of 1968 and that continue in subtler forms today (e.g., steering Black people toward low-income minority neighborhoods, not showing them as many housing options as White home seekers, offering them subprime loans even when they qualify for better, conventional loans). These practices allowed more Whites than Blacks to buy homes and to pass down the wealth invested in their homes to their children. They also made it (and continue to make it) more likely for Whites than Blacks to invest in homes that will appreciate in value, as those in stable, middle-class neighborhoods tend to do (Desmond 2017; Leonhardt 2015).

Even today, Blacks with middle-class incomes are more likely than middle-class Whites and Asian Americans to live in low-income neighborhoods, and those homes do not grow in value over time, so net worth does not grow (Reardon, Fox, and Townsend 2015). In order to gain a good, affordable (not a subprime) loan for a house, you need to have accumulated enough wealth for a down payment.

Children who live in low-income neighborhoods tend to have relatively few life chances. Those raised in low-income neighborhoods with poor schools, high crime rates, and fewer two-parent families have less chance of moving up in social class in their lifetimes than other children (Chetty and Hendren 2015). Therefore, it is past-in-present *and* contemporary discrimination that lead to relatively high percentages of middle-income Black families raising their children in low-income neighborhoods, factors that perpetuate racial inequality (Leonhardt 2015).

There are steps government can take to address such discrimination, including integrating school systems. We can see the positive effects of such efforts. New Jersey has one of the most economically, racially, and ethnically segregated school systems in the nation, but some districts have kept up integration efforts to the benefit of their students. For example, in 1971, the affluent and largely

RELATING AND USING KEY CONCEPTS

Table 8.3 indicates the levels at which discrimination can operate and how such acts can be intended or unintended.

Engaging Sociology

1. Define and give an example of the term(s) or concept(s) in each of the boxes.

2. Identify ways that each of these elements of intergroup conflict might foster the others.

3. Describe how you might take steps to counter each of the various types of discrimination.

▼ TABLE 8.3

Understanding Key Concepts

	Micro Level	Meso and Macro Level
Conscious and Intended	*Prejudice and individual acts of direct discrimination*	*Direct institutional discrimination*
Unconscious and Unintended	*Color-blind perspective*	*Indirect institutional discrimination* *Side-effect discrimination* *Past-in-present discrimination*

White, suburban Morris township and the racially, economically diverse, and urban town of Morristown were court-ordered to combine their school districts to promote racial integration. As Morristown has changed demographically since then, with more students of immigrant, Hispanic backgrounds than African American now, the school district has continually adjusted and worked to create schools that welcome and work for students of all backgrounds.

Today, none of the schools in the Morris school district are predominantly one race or ethnicity. This has not pleased all families, some of whom claim that the districts spend inordinate money helping students from Spanish-speaking families learn English. However, the district works hard to prevent White flight by creating attractive programming and investing in computer programs and laptops that allow students to work at their own pace. Moreover, studies have shown that diverse schools can benefit *all* students. White students in diverse schools tend to score just as highly on tests, work harder, and become more comfortable working in diverse settings than those in predominantly White schools (National Center for Education Statistics 2015; Spencer 2016).

With a sociological eye, it is easy to see how events from the past continue to echo into today, creating

▲ This sign was posted directly opposite the Sojourner Truth homes, a U.S. federal housing project constructed in Detroit, Michigan, after World War II. A riot was caused by White neighbors' attempts to prevent Black tenants from moving in. Note the use of flags as a symbol indicating that only Whites are real Americans—African Americans do not belong.

barriers for some citizens and clear paths for others. The Engaging Sociology feature above explores how discrimination can occur at different levels and in intentional or unintentional ways.

▲ One of the most horrific results of discriminatory racial or ethnic policies was the Holocaust, the murder of 11 million people, including 6 million Jews, by the Nazi government in Germany under Adolf Hitler. This photo is difficult to view, but this is the consequence of bigotry that leads to genocide.

THINKING SOCIOLOGICALLY

How do the different types of discrimination, as discussed previously, help us understand world conflicts, such as the intense hostility between Palestinians and Jews in the Middle East?

Dominant and Minority Group Contact: Macro-Level Analysis

Meso level analysis is essential to understanding the primary issues of racism in contemporary Global North

countries, but ultimately the tone for interracial relationships is set at the macro level. The first question is how those in power decide to structure relationships between racial and ethnic groups.

Dominant Group Policies to Manage Racial and Ethnic Relations

Dominant–minority relations depend on the time, place, and circumstances. However, dominant groups tend to structure or manage the dominant and minority relationships with one of five policies, indicated in Figure 8.12.

Genocide is *the systematic effort of one group, usually the dominant group, to destroy a minority group by killing them.* Examples of race- and ethnicity-based genocide exist throughout history. In the 13th century, Mongols under Temüjin Genghis Khan destroyed entire nations in their path. Germany's Adolf Hitler sent Jews and other non-Aryan groups into concentration camps to be gassed in the 1930s and 1940s. In Rwanda, in the mid-1990s, members of the Hutu tribe committed mass murders of people from the Tutsi tribe. As recently as 2015, the terrorist group ISIS tried to wipe out the Yazidis, a religious minority group, in Iraq. Genocide has existed at many points in history, and it still exists today. These examples illustrate the lethal consequences of racism, one group at the meso level systematically killing off another, often a minority, to gain control and power.

Subjugation refers to *the subordination of one group to another that holds power and authority.* Haiti and the Dominican Republic are two countries sharing the island

▼ FIGURE 8.12

Types of Dominant–Minority Group Relations

Most Hostile to "Others"				Most Accepting of "Others"
Genocide	Subjugation	Population Transfer	Assimilation	Pluralism
Extermination of minorities	Oppression, slavery	Removal to new location	Cultural blending of groups	Groups share in legitimacy and power

of Hispaniola in the Caribbean. Because many Haitians are poor, they are lured by promises of jobs in the sugarcane fields of the Dominican Republic. However, many are forced to work long hours for little pay and not allowed to leave until they have paid for housing and food, which may be impossible to do on their low wages.

Slavery is one form of subjugation that has existed throughout history. When the Roman Empire defeated other lands, the captives became slaves. This included ancient Greeks, who also kept slaves at various times in their history. African tribes enslaved members of neighboring tribes, sometimes selling them to slave traders, and slavery has existed in Middle Eastern countries such as Saudi Arabia. As we saw in Chapter 7, slavery is flourishing in many parts of the world today and even exists in the United States.

Segregation, a specific form of subjugation, separates minorities from the dominant group and deprives them of access to the dominant institutions. Jim Crow laws, instituted in the southern United States after the end of Reconstruction after the Civil War, legislated separation between racial groups—separate facilities, schools, and neighborhoods (Bonilla-Silva 2017; Feagin and Feagin 2010). **Population transfer** refers to *the removal, often forced, of a minority group from a region or country.* Generally, the dominant group wants land or resources. For example, Native Americans in the United States were removed to reservations. The Cherokee people were forced to walk from Georgia and North Carolina to new lands west of the Mississippi—a "Trail of Tears" along which 40% of the people perished, so that Whites in these states could have access to Cherokee land. As noted earlier, during World War II, Japanese Americans were forcibly moved to "relocation centers" and had their land and property confiscated. In 1972, Idi Amin, dictator of Uganda, gave Asian Ugandans 36 hours to pack their bags and leave—even though it had been the homeland for many of them from birth—because they had great economic resources that he argued should belong to native Ugandans.

Assimilation refers to *the social and cultural merging of minority and dominant groups.* It is often a voluntary process during which members of a minority group choose to adopt the values, norms, and institutions of the dominant group. Assimilation is more likely to occur when the minority group is similar in culture and appearance to the dominant group. For instance, in the United States, the closer a group is to being White and English speaking, the faster its members will be assimilated into the dominant group, adopting the culture and blending in further through intermarriage. Whereas some assimilation happens naturally when different groups interact in housing, schooling, employment, political circles, family groups, friendships, and social relationships, assimilation policies in certain times and places have forced ethnic minorities to change their cultural attributes (e.g., language, religions, style of eating) to avoid ridicule or even death (Marger 2012).

Forced assimilation occurs when members of a minority group are compelled to suppress their cultural identity. For example, in the late 1800s and early 1900s, Native American children in the United States and Canada were forced to leave their families and go to White-run boarding schools. There, they had to cut their hair, attend Christian religious services, dress as Whites did, and speak only in English.

Pluralism occurs when *each ethnic or racial group in a country maintains its own culture and separate set of institutions but has recognized equality in the society.* For example, Switzerland has four dominant cultural language groups: French, German, Italian, and Romansh (or Rumantsch). The government and schools use and teach all of these official languages. Each group respects the rights of the

▲ This picture of Chinatown in San Francisco helps illustrate that the United States is a pluralistic society.

PLURALISM: A LONG-STANDING HISTORY IN THE UNITED STATES

▲ This Jewish synagogue, the oldest in the United States, proudly displays a letter from George Washington enshrining pluralism in the new nation's policies.

It is no surprise that the oldest Jewish synagogue in the United States is in Rhode Island, for separation of church and state and tolerance of other religious traditions was a founding principle of the colony of Rhode Island. After George Washington was elected president of the new nation, he received a letter from that early Jewish congregation in Newport, Rhode Island, asking about his policies of pluralism or multiculturalism (though those words had not been coined yet). In response in 1790, Touro Synagogue received a handwritten letter signed by President Washington (and now proudly on display at the synagogue) embracing an open and "liberal" policy toward all American citizens, regardless of origin or religious affiliation. In this letter, George Washington affirmed a policy of pluralism from the very beginning of the country's existence as a nation. Passages from that letter follow.

★ ★ ★ ★ ★ ★

The Citizens of the United States of America have a right to applaud themselves for having given to mankind examples of an enlarged and liberal policy: a policy worthy of imitation. . . . It is now no more that toleration is spoken of, as if it was by the indulgence of one class of people, that another enjoyed the exercise of their inherent natural rights. For happily the Government of the United States, which gives to bigotry no sanction, to persecution no assistance, requires only that they who live under its protection should demean themselves as good citizens.

. . . May the children of the Stock of Abraham, who dwell in this land, continue to merit and enjoy the good will of the other Inhabitants; while everyone shall sit in safety under his own vine and fig tree, and there shall be none to make him afraid. May the father of all mercies scatter light and not darkness in our paths, and make us all in our several vocations useful here, and in his own due time and way everlastingly happy.

—G. Washington

other groups to maintain a distinctive language and way of life. In Malaysia, three groups share power: Malays, Chinese, and Indians. Although the balance is not completely stable because Chinese and Indians have higher levels of education and hold more political and economic power than the native Malays, most Malaysians want to maintain a pluralistic society. Although tensions do exist in both nations, both Switzerland and Malaysia represent examples of pluralist societies. Legal protection of smaller or less powerful groups is often necessary to have pluralism. In the United States, religious pluralism (at least among religions practiced by White Americans), as a policy, was embraced by the nation's first president, George Washington, as explained in the Sociology in Our Social World feature above.

THINKING SOCIOLOGICALLY

Think of examples from current news stories of positive and harmful intercultural contact. Where do your examples fit on the continuum from genocide to pluralism? What is your reaction to each? How do your experiences of intercultural context influence your reaction to these examples?

Minority Reactions to Prejudice, Discrimination, and Racism

How have minority groups dealt with their status? Five reactions are common: assimilation, acceptance, avoidance, aggression, and change-oriented actions directed at the social structure. The first four are micro-level responses; they do not address the meso- and macro-level issues.

Micro-Level Coping Strategies. *Passing* is a means of avoiding the prejudice and discrimination associated with minority group membership. Some minority group members, if their appearance allows them to do so, attempt to *pass* as members of the dominant group. This strategy usually involves abandoning their own culture and turning their back on family roots and community ties, a costly strategy in terms of self-esteem and sense of identity. People who select this coping strategy must deny their minority background and live with the fear that it will be exposed. They often live in constant anxiety, feeling as though they must hide something about themselves. Passing—which is a form of assimilation—also cuts people off from their family members, ancestors, and communities. This often severs them from a part of their identity, so the personal cost of assimilation can be high.

Acceptance is another reaction to minority status. Some members of minority groups have learned to live with their minority status and do not challenge the system. They may or may not hold deep-seated hostility, but they ultimately conclude that change in the society is not likely and acceptance may be the rational means to survive within the existing system.

There are many possible explanations for this seeming indifference. For example, religious beliefs allow poor Hindus in India to believe that if they accept their lot in life, they will be reincarnated in a higher life form. If they rebel, they can expect to be reincarnated into a lower life form. Their religion is a form of social control. In other cases, members of minority groups believe that they are, in fact, inferior and, therefore, should be treated that way. Socialized in a society that treats them as second-class citizens, they begin to accept this image of themselves. Others may simply fear the negative consequences of refusing to accept their minority status.

Avoidance entails coping with minority group status through shunning all contact with the dominant group. This can involve an active and organized attempt to leave the culture or live separately as some political exiles have done. For example, in the United States, Marcus Garvey organized a Back-to-Africa movement in the 1920s, encouraging Blacks to give up on any hope of justice in American society and to return to Africa. Today, the Nation of Islam advocates for the separation of Black peoples whose ancestors were slaves from White people and for Black children to be taught only by Black

▲ The Penumbra Theatre in St. Paul, Minnesota, uses the performing arts to promote social change. It fosters laughter at socially absurd norms and ideas, often a form of biting commentary. As the theater company tells the story of African Americans in the United States, the performers carry out their mission to use theater to "teach, criticize, comment, and model."

teachers (Nation of Islam ND; Southern Poverty Law Center 2017c).

Aggression resulting from anger and resentment over minority status and from subjugation may lead to retaliation or violence. Direct confrontation can be costly to those lacking political or economic power. So, aggression often takes one of two forms: indirect aggression or displaced aggression. Indirect aggression includes biting assertiveness in the arts—literature, art, racial and ethnic humor, and music—and in job-related actions such as inefficiency and slowdowns by workers. The arts can represent indirect aggression or efforts toward social change, as shown in the photo nearby. Displaced aggression, on the other hand, involves hostilities directed toward individuals or groups other than the dominant group, such as happens when youth gangs attack other ethnic or racial gangs in nearby neighborhoods. They substitute aggression against the dominant group by acting out against other minority groups.

The four responses discussed thus far address the angst and humiliation that individual minorities feel. Each strategy allows an individual to try to cope, but none addresses the structural causes of discrimination. The final strategy is *change-oriented action*.

Meso- and Macro-Level Efforts to Bring Change: Resistance. Passing, acceptance, and avoidance are forms of adaptation to the existing structures. Aggression, if not used strategically, can also work to support the status quo by creating opposition to changes that would help the minority group. Yet rather than accepting the current system and adapting to it, minority groups may choose strategic resistance. Resistance to the White framing of what life is like in the United States can take place through offering positive definitions of one's racial or ethnic group and preserving pride in one's culture (Feagin 2012). This was at work in the "Black is beautiful" theme that emerged early in the civil rights movement. That movement led to more books and films that relate the stories of courage, stamina, and contribution by minority groups. These media images and those of the more recent Black Lives Matter campaign provide a challenge and an alternative to those developed through the White perceptions of minority groups and U.S. history.

Efforts to change cultural attitudes toward minority groups have been complemented by work within the legal system to challenge unjust laws. The National Association for the Advancement of Colored People (NAACP) sought to bring about legal changes through lawsuits that created new legal precedents supporting racial equality. Often, these lawsuits addressed side-effect discrimination—a meso-level problem. Many other associations for minorities—including the Anti-Defamation League (founded by Jews) and La Raza Unida (a Mexican American organization)—also seek to address problems both within organizations and institutions (meso level) and in the nation as a whole (macro level).

One of the most important efforts to bring change in the United States has been nonviolent resistance. The model for nonviolent resistance by minority groups comes from Mahatma Gandhi who, from 1915 to 1947, led the struggle for India's independence from Britain. Although Britain clearly had superior weapons and armies, Indian boycotts, sit-ins, and other forms of resistance eventually led to British withdrawal as the ruling colonial power. This strategy has been used by workers and students to bring about change in many parts of the world.

In the United States, Martin Luther King Jr. followed in the nonviolent resistance tradition of Gandhi, who sought to change India's laws so that minorities could have equal opportunities within the society. King's strategy involved nonviolent popular protests, economic boycotts, and other challenges to racially discriminatory norms of society. His nonviolent disruptive efforts brought attention to the plight of Black people in the United States and created the political pressure needed to pass the civil rights legislation of the 1960s.

Martin Luther King Jr. (who majored in sociology in college) and many other public sociologists (e.g., W. E. B. Du Bois) have used their training to address issues of discrimination through empowerment and change. Their efforts to strategically counter the power of the dominant group have helped create a more equitable society for all residents of the United States.

Some NFL football players kneel during the national anthem in an organized effort to draw attention to racial discrimination in the criminal justice system. College football players at the University of Missouri carried out a nonviolent action against racism in November 2015. Angered by the university president's lack of support for students of color who had reported racist incidents, 30 Black players organized themselves, gained the support of their head coach, and said they would not play in the upcoming game unless the president of the university resigned. The forfeiture of the game would have cost the university more than a million dollars. Facing intense pressure, the university president did resign, and the University of Missouri began actions to address the concerns of minority students (Pearson and Sutton 2015; Svrluga 2015). Such action provides a great example of how organized nonviolent resistance can impact society—though social change rarely happens so fast.

▲ Mahatma Gandhi, leader of the Indian civil disobedience movement, led nonviolent protests against unjust laws, such as a march to collect salt, an illegal act.

Theoretical Explanations of Dominant–Minority Group Relations

Given that dominant–minority group relations take place on the micro, meso, and macro levels, we must use a wide variety of theoretical perspectives to fully understand these types of group interactions. For example, psychological and social-psychological theories are most relevant when examining prejudice in individuals and small groups. To understand discrimination embedded in institutions, studying meso-level organizations is helpful, and to understand the pervasive nature of prejudice and stereotypes over time in various societies, cultural explanations are useful. Finally, we must turn to macro-level theories to understand national and global group relations.

Structural-Functional Theory. Some functionalists point out that prejudice, discrimination, and institutional racism are dysfunctional for society, resulting in the loss of human resources, costs to societies due to poverty and crime, hostilities between groups, and disrespect for those in power. For example, Durkheim divided social inequalities into *internal* (based on people's natural abilities) and *external* (those forced on people). He argued that the existence of *external inequality* in an industrial society indicates that its institutions are not functioning properly. Because an industrial society needs all of its members doing what they do best for it to function most effectively, external inequality—like racial discrimination—that prevents some people from fulfilling their innate talents damages all of society (Durkheim [1893] 1947). Prejudice, discrimination, and institutional racism, then, are dysfunctional for society, resulting in the loss of human resources, costs to societies due to poverty and crime, hostilities between groups, and disrespect for those in power (Schaefer 2012).

However, other functionalists note that maintaining a cheap pool of laborers (e.g., members of a minority group) who are in and out of work serves several purposes for society. Not only does this minority group function to provide a ready labor force for dirty work or menial unskilled jobs, but these laborers also serve other functions for society. Having minority groups makes possible occupations that service the poor, such as social work, public health, criminology, and the justice and legal systems. The oppressed buy goods others do not want— day-old bread, old fruits and vegetables, and secondhand clothes (Gans 1971, 1994). In short, having a supply of people in desperate need at the bottom of the social structure, according to some analysts, has some useful functional aspects, and this makes change more difficult.

Conflict Theory. Conflict theorists argue that creating a less powerful group protects the dominant group's advantages. Because privileges and resources are usually limited, those who have them want to keep them. According to conflict theory, one strategy used by privileged people is to perpetrate prejudice and discrimination against minority group members. For example, in the 1840s, as the United States set out to build a transcontinental railroad, large numbers of laborers emigrated from China to do the hard manual work. When the railroad was completed and competition for jobs became stiff, the once-welcomed Chinese became targets of bitter prejudice, discrimination, and sometimes violence. Members of this minority group banded together in towns or cities for protection, founding the Chinatowns we know today (Kitano, Aqbayani, and de Anda 2005). Non-Chinese Asian groups suffered discrimination as well, because the bigoted generalizations were applied to all Asians (Winders 2004).

Karl Marx argued that exploitation of the lower classes is built into capitalism because it benefits the ruling class. Unemployment creates a ready pool of laborers to fill the marginal jobs, with the pool often made up of identifiable minority groups. This pool allows people to remain in their higher-level positions and prevents others from moving up in the stratification system and threatening their jobs.

Three critical factors contribute to animosity between groups, according to one conflict theorist: First, if two groups of people can each be identified by their appearance, clothing, or language, then us-versus-them thinking and ethnocentrism may develop. However, this by itself does not mean there will be long-term hostility between the groups. Second, if the two groups compete for scarce resources that both want, hostilities are likely to arise. The resources might be the best land or cattle, the highest-paying jobs, access to the best schools for one's children, energy resources such as oil, or positions of prestige and power. If the third element is added to the mix—one group having much more power than the other—then intense dislike between the two groups and misrepresentation of each group by the other is fairly certain to occur (Noel 1968).

The group with more power uses that power to ensure that its members (and their offspring) get the most valued resources. However, because they do not want to see themselves as unfair and brutish people, they develop stereotypes and derogatory characterizations of "those other people" so that it seems reasonable and justified not to give "them" access to the valued resources. Discrimination (often at the macro level) comes first, and bigoted ideology comes later to justify the discrimination (Noel 1968). Thus, macro- and meso-level conflicts can lead to micro-level attitudes.

Split labor market theory, a branch of conflict theory, characterizes the labor market as having two main types of jobs. The primary market involves clean jobs, largely in supervisory roles, and provides high salaries and good advancement possibilities, whereas the secondary market involves undesirable, hard, and dirty work, compensated with low hourly wages and few benefits or career opportunities. In the United States and other White-dominated nations, competition for low-wage jobs pits racial minorities against each other and low-income Whites. By encouraging division and fostering antagonism between worker groups, employers reduce threats to their dominance and get cheaper labor in the process. Workers do not organize against employers who use this dual system because they are distracted by the antagonisms that build up among themselves—hence, the *split labor market* (Bonacich 1972, 1976; Martinez 2008). This theory maintains that competition, prejudice, and ethnic animosity serve the interests of the powerful owners of capital because that atmosphere keeps the laboring classes from uniting.

Conflict theory has taught us a great deal about racial and ethnic stratification. However, conflict theorists often focus on people with power intentionally oppressing others to protect their own self-interests. They often depict the dominant group as made up of nasty, power-hungry people. As we have seen in the meso-level discussion of side-effect and past-in-present discrimination, racial discrimination is often subtle and unconscious and can continue even without conscious ill will among those in the dominant group.

THINKING SOCIOLOGICALLY

Do you think the split labor market perspective is useful when examining the racial and ethnic hierarchy in the United States? Why or why not? Can you see any evidence on your campus or in your local community to support the split labor theorists' view of racial and ethnic stratification?

Policies Governing Minority and Dominant Group Relations

The dominant ethnic group in northern Sudan is composed of Arabs—led by President Omar al-Bashir and his armies. In South Sudan, a newly formed country, the citizens are dark-skinned Africans who have a very different culture. Until a tenuous peace was brokered by the United Nations, the southern Sudanese people were tortured and killed and their villages burned by the more powerful northern Sudanese. Two issues at stake are (1) cultural and ethnic differences and (2) oil reserves. Conflict over oil, primarily located near the border between the two countries, plus a civil war in South Sudan, has made the peace plan tenuous. Whereas the hope was that the new border would separate warring factions, skirmishes continue to threaten the peace. In this case, macro-level policies from the United Nations and world powers intervened to stop the atrocities, but this has not eliminated the meso-level causes of conflict: cultural differences and resources such as land and oil. Remember that conflict over resources is usually the cause of animosity between groups.

War, famine, and economic dislocation force families to seek new locations where they can survive and perhaps improve their circumstances. Refugees may end up in a new country, perhaps on a new continent. The degree of acceptance children and their families find in their newly adopted countries varies depending on the government's policies, the group's background, economic conditions in the host country, and whether the refugee group poses a threat to residents (Rumbaut and Portes 2001). Some formerly refugee-friendly countries are closing their doors to immigration because of the strain on their economy and fear of terrorism. In this section, we consider the policies that emerge when dominant and minority groups interact.

Policies to Reduce Prejudice, Racism, and Discrimination

In the preceding pages, we considered some of the costs to individuals, groups, societies, and the global community inflicted by discriminatory behavior and policies. Discrimination's influence is widespread, from slavery and subjugation to unequal opportunities in education, work and political arenas, and every other part of the social world. If one accepts the premise that discrimination is destructive to both individuals and societies, then ways must be found to address the root problems effectively.

From our social world perspective, we know that no problem can be solved by working at only one level of analysis. A successful strategy must bring about change at every level of the social world: individual attitudes, organizational discrimination, cultural stereotypes, societal stratification systems, and national and international structures. However, most current strategies focus on only one level of analysis. Table 8.4 shows some of the programs enacted to combat prejudice, racism, and discrimination at the individual, group, societal, and global levels.

THINKING SOCIOLOGICALLY

Do you think walls such as the one pictured nearby create more positive or negative repercussions? Why and for whom?

▼ TABLE 8.4

Problems and Solutions

Types of Problems at Each Level	Types of Solutions or Programs at Each Level
Individual level: stereotypes and prejudice	Therapy, tolerance-education programs
Group level: negative group interaction	Positive contact, awareness by majority of their many privileges
Societal level: institutionalized discrimination	Education, media, legal system revisions
Global level: deprivation of human rights	Human rights movements, international political pressures

Individual or Small-Group Solutions. Programs to address prejudice and stereotypes through human relations workshops and group encounters can achieve goals at the micro level. Two groups with strong multicultural education programs are the Anti-Defamation League and the Southern Poverty Law Center's Teaching Tolerance program. Both groups provide schools and community organizations with literature, videos, and other materials aimed at combating intolerance and discrimination toward others. Schools can also create interracial friendship opportunities with racially integrated classrooms where students of different racial and ethnic backgrounds interact regularly (The Century Foundation 2016; Cheng and Xie 2013; Ellison and Powers 1994).

Group Contact. Some social scientists advocate organized group contact between dominant and minority group members to improve relations and break down stereotypes and fears. Although not all contact reduces prejudice, many studies have shown the benefits of structured contact. Some essential conditions for success are equal status of the participants, noncompetitive and nonthreatening contact, and projects or goals on which to cooperate (McBride 2015).

In a classic study of group contact, social psychologists Muzafer Sherif and Carolyn Sherif and their colleagues ran summer camps for 11- and 12-year-old boys and studied how they interacted with one another under different circumstances. On arrival, the boys were divided into two groups that competed periodically. The fiercer the competition, the more hostile the two cabins of boys became toward each other. The experimenters tried several methods to resolve the conflicts and tensions:

1. *Appealing to higher values (be nice to your neighbors):* This proved of limited value.

2. *Talking with the natural leaders of the groups (compromises between group leaders):* The group leaders agreed, but their followers did not go along.

3. *Bringing the groups together in a pleasant situation (a mutually rewarding situation):* This did not reduce competition; if anything, it increased it.

4. *Introducing a superordinate goal that could be achieved only if everyone cooperated:* This technique worked. The boys were presented with a dilemma: The water system had broken, or a fire needed to be put out, and all were needed to solve the problem. The groups not only worked together, but

▲ This photo shows a section of the border wall built to keep undocumented immigrants from crossing the U.S.–Mexican border and entering the United States. Some believe that walls of this sort foster us-versus-them thinking.

their established stereotypes eventually began to fade away. Such a situation in a community might arise from efforts to get a candidate elected, a bill passed, or a neighborhood improved. At the global macro level, representatives from hostile countries could sit together to solve issues that threatened all nations (Sherif and Sherif 1953).

College students can be actively engaged in this level of change by confronting and challenging bigotry and stereotypes, as is illustrated in the next Sociologists in Action.

Positive group contact experiences can be effective in improving relations in groups at a micro level by breaking down stereotypes, but to solidify the positive gains, we must also address institutionalized inequalities.

Institutional and Societal Strategies to Improve Group Relations.
Sociologists contend that institutional and societal approaches to reduce discrimination get closer to the core of the problems and affect larger numbers of people than do micro-level strategies. Changes at the macro level that can impact racial and ethnic stratification include legislation and government programs, like the U.S. Commission on Civil Rights and the Equal Employment Opportunity Commission, that enforce laws mandating racial and ethnic equality. Laws

requiring equal treatment of minorities, such as the Civil Rights Act of 1964, prohibit discrimination on the basis of race, religion, sex, or nation of origin. These laws have resulted in increased tolerance and opened doors once closed to minorities. In 1965, the Voting Rights Act outlawed discrimination in voting laws, allowing millions of Black citizens in southern states to vote for the first time. Today, the racial and ethnic makeup of the current members of Congress is more diverse than ever, with the number of Hispanics and Asians increasing over 100% since 2001. Still, although Whites make up 62% of the population, they comprise more than their share of members of Congress. In 2017, 81% of the members of Congress were White (Bialik and Krogstad 2017).

In the United States, presidents may also take executive action to end discrimination. For example, in 1948, Harry Truman moved to successfully end military segregation, and subsequent presidents have urged the passage of civil rights legislation and equal employment opportunity legislation. Affirmative action laws, first implemented during Lyndon Johnson's administration, have been used to fight pervasive institutional racism. The following discussion addresses the goals and forms of policies under the umbrella of affirmative action.

Affirmative Action.
As a societal policy for change, affirmative action actually involves three different policies:

CHALLENGING BIGOTRY TOWARD THE ROMA

In the spring of 2013, a group of students from St. John's University in Queens, New York, were involved in a study-abroad program in Rome, Italy, and performed weekly service work in a Roma (Gypsy) population to better understand an ethnic group that experienced discrimination. In the process we, as college students, learned we could raise awareness of the discrimination against the Roma and its impact. We worked one-on-one with Roma children living in Monachina, a settlement camp of Roma that is not officially recognized, but is tolerated, by the Italian government. Through our work at the camp, interviewing Italians knowledgeable about the Roma, and interacting closely with one of the families at Monachina, my peers and I were able to better understand the Roma lifestyle and the discrimination they face in Rome.

To deepen our understanding of the Roma population in Rome, we interviewed two Italian women involved in a *doposcuola* (afterschool) program at Monachina. These women had been visiting Monachina for several years and understood the culture at the camp and the views of Italians toward the Roma. We also read and researched all we could about the Roma to supplement the information given to us by the women involved in the doposcuola program. The Roma who reside in Rome, and other European cities, have come from dozens of different countries. Most have fled political unrest in their home countries. The Roma at the Monachina camp, for example, migrated to Rome in the early 1990s when the country of Yugoslavia dissolved and ethnic wars broke out across the area.

Italians were not pleased by the arrival of the Roma. Generally, Italians stereotype them as an inferior ethnic group that is lazy, dirty, uncooperative, and unwilling to assimilate into Italian culture. This has led to a self-fulfilling prophecy. The discrimination the Roma face prevents them from obtaining reputable jobs, owning property, receiving a good education, and generally integrating into Italian society.

Our response to this discrimination against the Roma, which we saw evidenced in the Monachina community, was to raise awareness. We invited students from several U.S. universities to visit Monachina with us and meet the Roma. Through this experience, they gained a deeper understanding of the Roma and how they are an oppressed minority group in Italian society. They were able to see that the stereotype of all Roma being lazy pickpockets was far from the truth. We also took time to discuss with them how this discrimination negatively impacts Italian society, as well as all other European countries that host these Roma populations and see them through the eyes of negative stereotypes. Being seen only as a societal nuisance hurts both the life chances of the Roma and their ability to fully contribute to the societies in which they live.

After experiencing the plight of the Roma population firsthand, my peers and I were able to use our sociological imagination to relate what we saw to the social issue of racial and ethnic discrimination. Sociology has taught me that a well-functioning society has institutions that support and respect the rights and dignity of all its members. Seeing the discrimination against the Roma at the Monachina camp in Rome has brought this truth home to me in a very real way and made me more committed than ever to teach others that racial and ethnic discrimination hurts everyone in a society—not just those who are its direct victims.

★ ★ ★ ★ ★ ★

Anna Misleh graduated from St. John's University in Queens, New York, with a major in sociology. She now works for the Center of Concern, a Catholic social justice organization in Washington, DC.

Strict affirmative action, its simplest and original form, involves taking affirmative or positive steps to make sure that unintentional discrimination does not occur. It mandates, for example, that an employer who receives federal monies advertise a position widely and not just through internal or friendship networks. If the job requires an employee with a college education, then by federal law, employers must recruit through minority and women's colleges as well as state and private colleges in the region. If employers are hiring in the suburbs, they are obliged to contact unemployment agencies in poor and minority communities as well as those in their affluent neighborhoods.

After taking these required extra steps, employers are expected to hire the most qualified candidate who applies, regardless of race, ethnicity, sex, religion, or other external characteristics. The focus is on providing opportunities for the best-qualified people. For many people, this is the meaning of affirmative action, and it is inconceivable that this could be characterized as reverse discrimination, for members of the dominant group will be hired if they are, in fact, the most qualified. These policies do not overcome the problem that qualified people who have been marginalized may be competent but do not have the traditional paper credentials that document their qualifications (Gallagher 2004).

A *quota system*, the second policy, is a requirement that employers *must* hire a certain percentage of minorities. For the most part, quotas are now unconstitutional. They apply only in cases where a court has found a company to have a substantial and sustained history of discrimination against minorities.

Preference policies are the third form, the one that has created the most controversy among opponents of affirmative action. Preference policies are based on the concept of equity, the belief that sometimes people must be treated differently in order to be treated fairly. This policy was enacted to level the playing field, which was not rewarding highly competent people because of institutional racism. To overcome these inequalities and achieve certain objectives (e.g., a diverse workforce to serve a diverse population), employers and educational institutions take account of race or sex by making special efforts to hire and retain workers or accept students from groups that have been underrepresented. In many cases, these individuals bring qualifications others do not possess. Consider the following examples.

A goal of the medical community is to provide access to medical care for underserved populations. There is an extreme shortage of physicians on the Navajo reservation. Thus, a Navajo applicant for medical school might be accepted, even if her scores are slightly lower than those of another candidate's, because she speaks Navajo and understands the culture. One could argue that she is more qualified to be a physician on the reservation than someone who knows nothing about Navajo society but has a slightly higher grade point average or test score. Some argue that tests should not be the only measure to determine the merit of applicants.

Likewise, an African American police officer may have more credibility in an African American neighborhood and may be able to defuse a delicate conflict more effectively than a White officer who scored slightly higher on a paper-and-pencil placement test. Thus, being a member of a particular racial or ethnic group can actually make one more qualified for a position.

Many colleges and universities admit students because they need an outstanding point guard on the basketball team, an extraordinary soprano for the college choir, or a student from a distant state for geographic diversity. These students are shown preference by being admitted with lower test scores than some other applicants because they are *differently qualified*. Many colleges also give preference to children of former graduates—called legacies. To achieve gender balance, at some schools male students are given preference, even if more qualified females apply. Giving underrepresented racial minority students preference follows this same reasoning.

A landmark case filed in a Detroit district court in 1997 alleged that the University of Michigan gave unlawful preference to minorities in undergraduate admissions and in law school admissions. In this controversial case, the court ruled that these undergraduate admissions were discriminatory because numbers rather than individualized judgments were used to make the admission determination (University of Michigan Documents Center 2003). Consider the next Engaging Sociology feature and decide whether you think the policy was fair and whether only race and ethnicity should have been deleted from the automatic preferences allowed.

In 2013 and again in 2016, the Supreme Court ruled that affirmative action was permissible to achieve the goal of a diverse student body. The Court has also warned that not all such programs will pass constitutional muster, that universities must verify that they are unable to achieve sufficient diversity without using racial considerations (Liptak 2013, 2016).

The Supreme Court has refused, however, to counter state bans on affirmative action. In April 2014, the Supreme Court upheld a ban on affirmative action in public higher education in Michigan that was approved by 58% of Michigan voters, arguing that a lower court did not have the authority to overturn the referendum. Thus, publicly funded colleges in Michigan cannot grant preferential treatment on the basis of race, sex, color, ethnicity, or national origin (Mears 2014). So now all such policies are illegal in Michigan, as well as at public universities in Arizona, California, Florida, Nebraska, New Hampshire, Oklahoma, and Washington (The Council of State Governments 2016). The Trump administration has also taken aim at various universities' affirmative action policies and is challenging them in court (Savage 2017).

The question remains: Should preferences be given to accomplish diversity? Some people feel that programs involving any sort of preference for underrepresented minorities are unfair and should not be allowed. Others believe that such programs do much more good than harm. They have encouraged employers, educational institutions, and government to look carefully at hiring policies and minority candidates, and many more

PREFERENCE POLICIES AT THE UNIVERSITY OF MICHIGAN

To enhance diversity on the campus—a practice that many argue makes a university a better learning environment and enhances the academic reputation of the school—many colleges have preference policies in admissions. However, the University of Michigan was sued by applicants who felt they were not admitted because others replaced them on the roster due to their racial or ethnic background.

The University of Michigan is a huge university where a numbering system is needed to handle the volume (tens of thousands) of applicants; the admissions staff cannot make a decision based on personal knowledge of each candidate. Thus, they give points for each quality they deem desirable in the student body. A maximum of 150 points is possible, and a score of 100 would pretty much ensure admission. The university feels that any combination of points accumulated according to the following formula will result in a highly qualified and diverse student body.

For academics, up to 110 points are possible:

- 80 points for grades (a particular grade point average in high school results in a set number of points; e.g., a 4.0 results in 80 points, and a 2.8 results in 56 points)

- 12 points for standardized test scores (ACT or SAT)

- 10 points for the academic rigor of high school (so all students who go to tougher high schools earn points)

- 8 points for the difficulty of the curriculum (e.g., points for honors curriculum versus keyboarding courses)

For especially desired qualities, including diversity, up to 40 points are possible for any combination of the following (but no more than 40 in this "desired qualities" category):

- Geographical distribution (10 for Michigan resident, an additional 6 for underrepresented Michigan county)

- Legacy—a direct relative has attended Michigan (4 points for a parent, 1 point for a grandparent or sibling)

- Quality of submitted essay (3 points)

- Personal achievement—a special accomplishment that was noteworthy (up to 5 points)

- Leadership and service (5 points each)

- Miscellaneous (only one of these can be used):
  - __ Socioeconomic disadvantage (20 points)
  - __ Underrepresented racial or ethnic minority (Black, Hispanic, or Native American) (20 points; disallowed by the court ruling)
  - __ Men in nursing (5 points)
  - __ Scholarship athlete (20 points)
  - __ Provost's discretion (20 points; usually the son or daughter of a large financial donor or of a politician)

In addition to race or ethnicity, athleticism, socioeconomic disadvantage, having a relative who is an alum, and being the child of someone who is noteworthy to the university are also considered. Some schools also give points for being a military veteran. The legal challenge to this admissions system was based only on the points given for race or ethnic background, not on the other reasons for which some students are given preference.

★ ★ ★ ★ ★ ★ ★

Engaging Sociology

1. Does this process seem reasonable as a way to get a diverse and highly talented incoming class of students? Why or why not?

2. Does it significantly advantage or disadvantage some students? Explain.

3. Should there be preferences for predominantly White students—such as "legacy" students, whose family members attended the university? Why or why not?

4. How would you design a fair system of admissions, and what other factors would you consider?

competent minority group members are working in the public sector as a result of these policies. What is the most equitable thing to do?

Global Movements for Human Rights

The rights granted to citizens of any nation used to be considered the business of each sovereign nation, but after the Nazi Holocaust, German officers were tried at the Nuremberg Trials, and the United Nations passed the Universal Declaration of Human Rights. Since that

▲ Some human rights movements focus on international justice issues in countries around the world. Amnesty International is one such movement, with chapters throughout the United States and world. This Moroccan protester wears a blindfold that reads in Arabic "Stop torture." This is part of a 2014 Amnesty International demonstration on United Nations International Day in Support of Victims of Torture.

time, many international organizations have been established, often under the auspices of the United Nations, to deal with health issues, world poverty and debt, trade, security, and many other issues affecting world citizens—the World Health Organization, the World Bank, the World Trade Organization, and numerous regional trade and security organizations.

The United Nations and privately funded advocacy groups speak up for international human rights as a principle that transcends national boundaries. The most widely recognized private group is Amnesty International, a watchdog group that lobbies on behalf of human rights and supports political prisoners. When Amnesty International was awarded the Nobel Peace Prize in 1997, the group's visibility dramatically increased. Some activist sociologists have formed groups such as Sociologists Without Borders, or SSF (*Sociólogos Sin Fronteras*; www.sociologistswithoutborders.org), a transnational organization committed to the idea that "all people have equal rights to political and legal protections, to socioeconomic security, to self-determination, and to their personality."

Everyone can make a positive difference in the world, and one place to start is in our own communities (see Contributing to Our Social World). We can counter prejudice, discrimination, and socially embedded racism in our own groups by teaching children to see beyond "us" and "them" and by speaking out for fairness and against stereotypes and discrimination.

Socioeconomic inequality and racial and ethnic stratification create many problems for a society. However, a full understanding of inequality also requires insights into discrimination based on gender. We turn to issues of gender inequality in Chapter 9.

WHAT HAVE WE LEARNED?

If there is competition over resources in a society, groups tend to form. Groups with the most power become dominant, and those with less power become minority groups. Those with the most power stratify their society in ways that ensure their group has more access to power, money, and status. Racial and ethnic prejudice and discrimination at the micro, meso, and macro levels work to uphold dominant–minority group relations.

- Race is a social construction.

- Racial and ethnic stratification are common throughout the world. Racial and ethnic minority groups have less power and less access to resources than dominant groups.

- Prejudice operates at the micro level of society whereas discrimination can occur at the micro, meso, and macro levels.

- The racial ideology of color-blindness does not acknowledge the reality of racial discrimination and leads to racism evasiveness.

- At the meso level, institutionalized discrimination operates through two processes: side effect and past-in-present. These forms of discrimination are unintended and unconscious—operating separately from any prejudice of individuals in the society.

- The policies of the dominant group may include genocide, subjugation, population transfer, assimilation, or pluralism.

- The costs to society from racial discrimination are high, including loss of human talent and resources.

- The coping devices used by minorities include five main strategies: assimilation, acceptance, avoidance, aggression, and organizing for societal change. Only the last of these addresses the meso- and macro-level causes.

- Policies to address problems of prejudice and discrimination range from individual and small-group efforts at the micro level to institutional, societal, and even global social movements.

- Affirmative action includes three distinct sets of policies that have different outcomes.

DISCUSSION QUESTIONS

1. Have you ever experienced being stereotyped because of your race or ethnicity? Why or why not? How can racial stereotypes harm societies, as well as groups and individuals?

2. What is the difference between the color-blind perspective on race and blatant bigotry? How does the color-blind ideology lead to racism evasiveness? Why is it often so difficult to recognize and address racial discrimination in the United States today?

3. Give two examples, respectively, of both side-effect discrimination and past-in-present discrimination. How have they impacted you and your life chances? Why?

4. We know that efforts to reduce prejudice, racism, and discrimination must take place at all levels (micro, meso, and macro). Most organizations, though, must choose one level on which to focus their particular efforts. If you were going to start an organization to decrease racial or ethnic prejudice, would you focus on the micro, meso, or macro level? Why? Explain what your organization would do.

5. Do you agree with preferences for college applicants at the University of Michigan who are scholarship athletes or the sons or daughters of a large donor or politician, but not for racial or ethnic minorities? Why, or why not? Was the Supreme Court correct in ruling that a referendum passed by voters in Michigan should trump concerns about diversity? Why?

KEY TERMS

assimilation 237

discrimination 227

ethnic groups 225

genocide 236

institutional racial discrimination 232

minority groups 218

past-in-present discrimination 234

pluralism 237

population transfer 237

prejudice 227

race 219

side-effect discrimination 232

subjugation 236

At the Local (Micro) Level

- *African American, Arab American, and Native American student associations* are examples of student organizations dedicated to fighting bigotry and promoting understanding and the rights of racial and ethnic minorities. Identify one of these groups on your campus and arrange to attend a meeting. If appropriate, volunteer to help with its work.

- Consider purchasing only fair trade certified coffee and chocolate, and encouraging your school to sell fair trade products. *Equal Exchange*, a fair trade pioneer, has some resources for promoting fair trade in your community (http://blog.equalexchange.coop/fundraising-catalog-success).

At the Organizational or Institutional (Meso) Level

- *The Leadership Conference on Civil and Human Rights* is a national coalition dedicated to combating racism and its effects. It maintains a website that includes a directory of its membership of more than 200 organizations (www.civilrights.org). On its website you can find a "take action" link that will help you to explore ways in which you can participate in its efforts.

- *Teaching Tolerance* (www.splcenter.org/teaching-tolerance), a program of the Southern Poverty Law Center, has curriculum materials for teaching about diversity and a program for enhancing cross-ethnic cooperation and dialogue in schools. Check into internship opportunities in local primary and secondary schools and explore ways in which the Teaching Tolerance approach can be incorporated into the curricula in your school district with local teachers and administrators.

- *Blacks Lives Matter* is committed to struggling together and to imagining and creating a world free of anti-Blackness, where every Black person has the social, economic, and political power to thrive. You can learn more about the organization and how to join or be an ally at www.blacklivesmatter.com.

At the National or Global (Macro) Level

- The *Anti-Defamation League* (www.adl.org) acts to "stop the defamation of the Jewish people and to secure justice and fair treatment to all." Members of this organization develop and implement educational programs on interfaith/intergroup understanding, scrutinize and call attention to hate groups, monitor hate speech on the Internet, and mobilize communities to stand up to bigotry throughout the United States and abroad. Job listings, summer internships, and opportunities in Israel and other locations are listed on the ADL website.

- *Partnership with Native Americans* "is committed to championing hope for a brighter future for Native Americans living on remote, isolated and impoverished reservations." To do so, it partners with tribal and other groups on the ground in the tribal regions of the Plains and Midwest. You can find out how to support the work of this group and its partners by going to www.nativepartnership.org.

- *Cultural Survival* and the *UN Permanent Forum on Indigenous Issues* (www.culturalsurvival.org and www.un.org/development/desa/indigenouspeoples) focus on preserving indigenous culture and advancing the rights of indigenous people worldwide.

- *Amnesty International* campaigns against abuses of human rights. It relies heavily on volunteers organized into chapters, many of them campus-based. You can join the organization and learn how to participate in its action through its website at www.amnesty.org. Consider joining or starting one on your campus.

$SAGE edge™

Get the tools you need to sharpen your study skills. SAGE edge offers a robust online environment featuring an impressive array of free tools and resources.

Access practice quizzes, eFlashcards, video, and multimedia at **edge.sagepub.com/ballantine7e**

© iStockPhoto.com/Jason Doiy

GENDER STRATIFICATION

She/He—Who Goes First?

▲ Social inequality is pervasive in gender relations, and although in some societies women are treated with deference, they are rarely given first access to positions of significant power or financial reward. The men often "go first."

MICRO

ME (AND MY GENDER)

LOCAL ORGANIZATIONS
AND COMMUNITY
Peers, neighbors, teachers,
and religious congregations
socialize us into gender
expectations.

MESO

NATIONAL ORGANIZATIONS,
INSTITUTIONS, AND ETHNIC
SUBCULTURES
Organizations and institutions limit access to
many positions based on gender.

MACRO

SOCIETY
National policies provide
sex-based privileges.

GLOBAL COMMUNITY
Gender status is determined by
laws and power structures; the
United Nations champions equal
rights for women.

WHAT WILL YOU LEARN IN THIS CHAPTER?

This chapter will help you to do the following:

9.1 Give examples of meso- and macro-level gender stratification

9.2 Describe the difference between sex and gender

9.3 Identify agents of gender socialization

THINK ABOUT IT

Micro: Small groups and local communities	How does being female or male affect your thoughts, behaviors, and opportunities? Why do some people face violence in their homes and communities because of their gender or sexual orientation?
Meso: National institutions, complex organizations, and ethnic groups	What can be done in our organizations and institutions to make men and women more equal in pay and promotions?
Macro: National and global systems	Why do women have second-class status in many societies?

When Emma Watson won an MTV Movie Award in 2017, she did not win for the category of best actress in a movie. There were no separate male actor and female actress categories. Instead, MTV opted for a single, genderless category. MTV based the decision to have one genderless category on the belief that the traditional, binary gender categories of man and woman do not fit everyone. They, like more and more people and organizations in the United States, are acknowledging that socially constructed identities such as gender have worked to promote inequality that benefits some at the expense of others. As we discuss later in the chapter, gender categories can limit the freedom and choices of all people, including boys and men.

In this chapter, we distinguish and define the closely related and often confused categories of gender, sex, and sexuality. Gender has traditionally been tied to a person's sex identity as male or female, based on their physical attributes. For those like Gavin Grimm, who are born with the physical attributes of one sex but identify with the gender traditionally assigned to another sex, life can be difficult when their communities do not allow them to live as they identify. MTV might recognize the reality of gender fluidity, but many people in positions of power do not.

Gavin, a high school student in Gloucester County, Virginia, is not allowed to use the boys' bathroom in his school. His principal had allowed him to do so, but the school board overruled that decision. Gavin sued, and the appeals court ruled in his favor, citing the Title IX federal law that bans sex discrimination. The court's ruling noted an "Education Department letter that said 'a school generally must treat transgender students consistent with their gender identity.'" Shortly after President Trump took office, however, his administration withdrew the Education Department letter and directed schools to allow students only to use the bathrooms associated with their physical attributes at birth or risk losing federal funding (Williams 2017). As we write these words, Gavin

and many other transgender students across the nation are prohibited from using the bathroom labeled for the gender with which they identify.

When we combine gender issues with race, ethnicity, and class, we get a better understanding of the stratification system and why people hold the positions they do in society. At the micro level, we consider gender socialization or how girls and boys learn to be gendered individuals. At the meso and macro levels we consider gender stratification, or placement of individuals in the society's stratification system. A discussion of costs and consequences of gender stratification plus policy implications ends this chapter.

Sex, Gender, and the Stratification System

You name it, and some society has probably done it! Gender relations are no exception. Variations around the world show that most roles and identities are not biological but rather socially constructed. In Chapter 7, we discussed factors that stratify individuals into social groups (castes and classes), and in Chapter 8, we discussed the roles that race and ethnicity play in stratification. Add the concepts of sex and gender, and we have a more complex and complete picture of how class, race, ethnicity, and gender together influence the experiences that make us who we are and our positions in society. Consider the following examples from societies that illustrate some interesting human social constructions based on sex and gender. We will then move to more familiar societies.

The Wodaabe, a subgroup of the Fulani ethnic group, are herders and traders in the Sahel region of Africa (especially Niger and Nigeria). The men would be defined as effeminate by most Western standards. Fulani men are like birds, showing their colorful feathers to attract females. They take great care in doing their hair, applying makeup, and dressing to attract women. They also gossip with each other while sipping their tea.

▲ Wodaabe men in Niger, Africa, appear to reverse gender notions. They go to great pains with makeup, hair, and jewelry to ensure that they are highly attractive, a pattern thought by many people in other parts of the world to be associated with females.

▲ Muslim girls and women in some parts of the world cover their faces when in public. The display of skin, even in a classroom, would be immoral to many Muslims. However, in other Muslim countries such coverings would be unusual.

Meanwhile, the women are cooking meals, caring for the children, cleaning, tending to the animals, planting small gardens, and preparing for the next move of this nomadic group (Beckwith 1993; Human Planet 2012; Saharan Vibe 2007). These patterns have developed over time and carry on as traditions. The point is that groups have developed cultural norms over time, often independently of other groups, that cause gender behaviors to differ widely.

Under ISIS in some Middle Eastern countries and Taliban rule in Afghanistan, women cannot be seen in public without a total body covering that meets strict requirements (Human Rights Watch 2016a). Those not obeying can be stoned to death. Women cannot hold public positions or work outside their homes. In Afghanistan, when the Taliban rule an area, women who are ill cannot be examined by a physician because all doctors are male. Instead, they have to describe their symptoms to a doctor through a screen (Makhmalbaf 2003; Trust in Education 2013).

In every society, certain tasks must be carried out by individuals and organizations for members to survive. Responsibilities include raising children, providing people with the basic necessities (such as food, clothing, and shelter), having leaders, defending the society, and solving conflicts. One's sex and age are often used to determine who holds what positions and who carries out what tasks. Each society develops its own way to meet its expectations and its own interpretations of right and wrong gender role behaviors. This results in gender role variations from one society to the next. If the genders are identified as fundamentally different, distinguishing symbols

such as dress, head coverings, hairstyles, and, of course, roles become important for each gender's identity.

THINKING SOCIOLOGICALLY

Why do you think societies in different corners of the globe develop such radically different ways of organizing their gender roles?

Sex and Sexuality

At birth, when doctors say, "It's a . . .!" they are referring to the distinguishing primary characteristics that determine sex—that is, the penis or vagina. **Sex** is *a biological term referring to genetic, anatomical, and hormonal differences between males and females*. Sometimes, however, people are born with ambiguous genitalia. Approximately 1 in 1,500 babies are born with genitalia not fitting the typical definitions of male or female (the *intersexed*) (Fausto-Sterling 2000). In Global North countries, these babies often undergo surgeries to clarify their gender, with hormonal treatments and possible further surgery at adolescence (Chase 2000). However, governments in some Global North countries are discouraging surgeries in favor of more acceptance of intersexed individuals. A law in Germany, for example, allows the category of *indeterminate gender* on birth certificates, recognizing *intersex* as a third indeterminate gender option with surgery seen as unnecessary. Australian laws also acknowledge the intersex status (Agius 2013).

In the United States, in 2016, 55-year-old Sara Kelly Keenan, born with male genes (X and Y chromosomes), female genitalia, and mixed internal reproductive organs, successfully petitioned the New York City Department of Health and Mental Hygiene (DOHMH) for a new birth certificate listing her as "intersex." Hers was the first such birth certificate issued in the United States (O'Hara 2016). In 2017, California became the first state to allow residents to attain a new birth certificate in a nonbinary gender designation. Oregon and Washington, D.C., now provide gender-neutral options on driver's licenses (Caron 2017).

Transgender describes *someone who is challenging, questioning, or changing gender from that assigned at birth to a chosen gender—male to female, female to male, transitioning between genders, or genderqueer (challenging gender norms)* (Kinsey Institute for Research in Sex, Gender, and Reproduction 2012; Lorber and Moore 2011:6). Gavin Grimm, the high school student discussed earlier, transitioned from a girl to a boy. He started his second year of high school with a new name and a school record that indicated he was a boy. All went well until parents of some of his classmates began to complain about his use of the boys' bathroom. As Figure 9.1 indicates, a recent study using data from state-level population surveys estimates that 1 in 137 (0.7%) of 13- to 17-year-olds identify as transgender today.

The reason many people have a hard time with gender fluidity and that societies go to great lengths to assign a sex to an infant is that sex constitutes a major organizing principle in societies. Despite emphasis on "achieved status" in modern societies, society's expectations guiding roles and statuses are largely ascribed—determined by a person's sex.

▼ FIGURE 9.1

Percentage of Individuals Who Identify as Transgender by Age

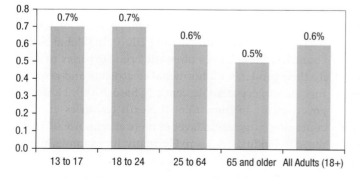

Source: Herman, Jody L., Andrew R. Flores, Taylor N. T. Brown, Bianca D. M. Wilson, and Kerith J. Conron 2017. *Age of Individuals Who Identify as Transgender in the United States.* The Williams Institute, UCLA School of Law.

Our attraction to others is expressed by our sexuality and our sexual identity. Most people identify as heterosexual (attracted to other sex), homosexual (same sex), bisexual (both sexes), or "varied" (such as transgendered). In most societies, our sexual identities follow the prevailing belief that a "normal" girl or boy will be sexually attracted to and eventually have sex with someone of the other sex (Lorber and Moore 2011). However, as we have seen, sex is not always a straightforward distinction and is as social as it is biological.

Sexuality refers to *culturally shaped meanings both of sexual acts and of how we experience our own bodies—especially in relation to the bodies of others.* Strange as it may seem, sexuality is socially constructed. A sex act is a social enterprise, with cultural norms defining what is normal and acceptable in each society, how we should feel, and hidden assumptions about what the act means (Steele 2005). Even what we find attractive is culturally defined. For a period in China, men found tiny feet a sexual turn-on—hence, some women bound their feet to be attractive to men. In some cultures, legs are the attraction, and in others, men are fascinated by breasts. Likewise, the ideal male body as depicted in popular magazines in contemporary Western cultures is "over 6 feet tall, 180 to 200 pounds, muscular, agile, with straight white teeth, a washboard stomach, six-pack abs, long legs, a full head of hair, a large penis (discreetly shown by a bulge), broad shoulders and chest, strong muscular back, clean shaven, healthy, and slightly tanned if White, or a lightish brown if Black or Hispanic" (Lorber and Moore 2011:89–90). We grow up learning what is appealing.

As individuals mature, they are expected to adopt the behaviors appropriate to their anatomical features as defined by their society. In addition to the physical sex differences between males and females, a few other physical conditions are commonly believed to be sex linked, such as a prevalence of color blindness, baldness, learning disabilities, autism, and hemophilia in males. Yet some traits that members of society commonly link to sex are actually learned through socialization. There is little evidence, for instance, that emotions, personality traits, or ability to fulfill most social statuses is determined by inborn physical sex differences. However, the social messages urging people to conform to expectations for their sex category are strong. What is defined as normal behavior for a male, a female, or an intersexed person in one society could get one killed in another.

Gender

Gender refers to *a society's notions of masculinity and femininity—socially constructed meanings associated with being male or female—and how individuals construct their identity in terms of gender within these constraints.* Gender identity, then, is how individuals form their identity using the categories of sex and gender and negotiate the constraints they entail. The examples at the beginning of this section illustrate some differences in how cultures are structured around gender.

Statuses are positions within the structures of society, and roles are expected behaviors within those statuses (Rothenberg 2015). **Gender roles**, then, are those *commonly assigned tasks or expected behaviors linked to an individual's sex-determined statuses* (Lips 2013). Members of each society learn the structural guidelines and positions expected of males and females (West and Zimmerman 1987). Our positions, which affect access to power and resources, are embedded in institutions at the meso level, with culture defining what is right and wrong. There is not some global absolute truth governing gender or gender roles. Although both vary across cultures, gender is a learned cultural idea, and gender roles are part of the structural system of roles and statuses in a society.

In summary, although the terms *sex, sexuality,* and *gender* are often used interchangeably, they do have distinct meanings. Individuals who negotiate the meanings attached to gender and sexuality are *doing gender,* a process discussed later in this chapter (Schoepflin 2011; West and Zimmerman 1987).

Sex, Gender, and Sexuality: The Micro Level

"It's a boy!" brings varying cultural responses. In many Western countries, that exclamation results in blue blankets, toys associated with boys (e.g., footballs, soccer balls, and trucks), roughhousing, and gender socialization messages. In some Asian societies, boys are sources for great rejoicing, whereas girls may be seen as a burden. Abortion rates in some countries are much higher when ultrasound tests show that the fetus is female (United Nations Population Fund 2017). In China and India, *female infanticide* (killing of newborn girl babies) is sometimes practiced in rural areas, in part because the cost to poor families of raising a girl and paying the dowry to get the daughter married all diminish the value of girls. In China, the male preference system has been exacerbated by the government's edict that most couples may have only one child,

although this law has recently been relaxed (T. Phillips 2015). As a result of government policy and female infanticide and abortion, a sex imbalance developed and is now causing other problems such as a shortage of brides.

At the micro level, we can trace stages in an individual's life as a female or male: early childhood socialization, school and community activities and experiences, adult statuses and roles of females and males, and so on through the life cycle. At each stage are messages that reinforce appropriate gender behavior. Cultural traditions learned from birth guide individuals into "proper" gender roles. These gender expectations are inculcated into children by parents, siblings, grandparents, neighbors, peers, and even day care providers. If we fail to respond to the expectations of these significant people in our lives, we may experience negative sanctions: teasing, isolation and exclusion, harsh words, and stigma. Therefore, children usually learn to conform, at least in their public behavior.

The lifelong process of gender socialization continues once we reach *school age* and become more involved in activities separate from our parents. Other people in the community—teachers, religious leaders, coaches, and peers—influence us. We are grouped by sex in many of these social settings: boys versus girls, us versus them. Even if our parents are not highly traditional in their gender expectations, we still experience many expectations to conform from peers, school, and other sources. Transgender people and nonbinary people, those who do not identify with any gender, are challenging these norms, but socializing institutions, like families and schools, still

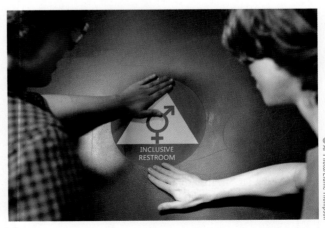

▲ Two students place a new sticker on the door at the ceremonial opening of a gender-neutral bathroom at Nathan Hale High School in Seattle. Since 2012 Seattle has mandated that transgender students be able to use the bathrooms and locker rooms of their choice; one high school has had a transgender bathroom for 20 years. The issue has been highly controversial in other parts of the country.

steer most people into the gender roles assigned to their sex at birth.

With adulthood, the differential treatment and stratification of the sexes take new forms. Men traditionally have more networks and statuses, as well as greater access to resources outside the home. This has resulted in many women around the world having less power because they depend more on husbands or fathers for resources. The subtitle of this chapter asks, "Who goes first?" When it comes to the question of who walks through a door first, the answer is that in many Western societies, *she* does—or at least, formal etiquette would suggest this is proper. The strong man steps back and defers to the weaker female, graciously holding the door for her, and women are served first at restaurants. This seems little compensation for the fact that doors are often closed to women at the meso and macro levels of society.

Language can be powerful in shaping the behavior and perceptions of people, as discussed in Chapter 3. Have you ever been in a classroom or meeting when a woman makes a point that is barely acknowledged, but when a man later says pretty much the same thing, he is applauded for his fine idea? The dilemma for women is whether to speak up and be considered aggressive, bossy, or hostile or to say less and appear weak (Sandberg and Grant 2015). In addition, women tend to adopt speech patterns to avoid appearing aggressive, often ending sentences with tag questions, that is, ending a declarative statement with a short tag that turns it into a question: "That was a good idea, don't you think?" This pattern may cause male business colleagues to think women are insecure or uncertain about themselves, preventing a woman from getting the job or the promotion. The women themselves may view it as an invitation to collaboration and dialogue. On the flip side, when women stop using these "softening" devices, they may be perceived as strident, harsh, or "bitchy" (Sandberg 2013; Wood and Reich 2006). Women also tend to use more words related to psychological and social processes, whereas men prefer more discussion of objects and impersonal topics (Coates 2013; Newman et al. 2008).

Some negative words tend to be used to describe women, rather than men. Have you ever heard a man described as a "man slut" or a "man whore"? Note the need for the "man" to distinguish them from the typical (woman) slut or whore. The word *spinster* is supposed to be the female synonym for *bachelor*, yet it has very different connotations. Even the more newly coined *bachelorette* is not usually used to describe a highly appealing, perhaps lifelong role. What might be the implications of these differences?

THINKING SOCIOLOGICALLY

Until recently, words like *mankind* and phrases like "all men are created equal" were commonly used to refer to all humans. How do such changes in language relate to changes in society? What are some other ways that our language usage has changed as traditional gender roles have been challenged in recent decades?

Sex, Gender, and Sexuality: The Meso Level

By whatever age is defined as being an *adult* in a society, members are expected to assume leadership roles and responsibilities in the institutions of family, education, religion, government, economics, health care, and the military. Our roles in these institutions often differ depending on our sex, which determines our placements and many of our experiences in the social world (Brettell and Sargent 2012). This makes it difficult—but not impossible—for women to attain the most powerful and financially rewarding positions in a society.

Many countries do not consider the military the proper place for women, although some have alternative service options. In the United States, combat roles for women were not fully open until 2016 (K. Kamarck 2016). Israel is one of the few countries to have female conscription, though women are restricted from some jobs.

In most societies, sex and age stipulate when and how we experience *rites of passage*—rituals and ceremonies in institutions that mark a change of status in the family and community—the meso levels of society. These rites include any ceremonies or recognitions that admit one to adult duties and privileges (Brettell and Sargent 2012). Rites of passage are institutionalized in various ways: religious rituals such as the Jewish male bar mitzvah or the female bat mitzvah ceremonies; education celebrations such as graduation ceremonies, which often involve caps and gowns of gender-specific colors or place females on one side of the room and males on the other; and different ages at which men and women are permitted to marry. Other institutions also segregate members by sex. For example, in very traditional Greek Orthodox Christian churches and Orthodox Jewish synagogues, men sit on one side of the sanctuary and women on the other. In mosques, women are often put in separate and removed spaces for prayer.

Sex, Gender, and Sexuality: The Macro Level

People around the world go to school, drive cars, and work, but in some parts of the world, school, driving, and work are forbidden for women. Fifteen-year-old Malala Yousafzai, a girl from northwest Pakistan, was shot and severely wounded by a Taliban gunman for both going to school and speaking out for other girls to have educational opportunities (Mehsud 2012). The Taliban, a regional organization that extends beyond the local boundaries, is opposed to girls going to school due to their beliefs about proper gender roles. Malala gained worldwide fame and, since her recovery, has spoken out about the right for education for all children. She was the youngest person ever to win the Nobel Peace Prize for her work, given to her in 2014. She now works through the Malala Fund to advocate for a minimum of 12 years of education for girls throughout the world, particularly in the Global South (Malala Fund 2017).

When we turn to the national and global level, we witness inequality between the sexes separate from any form of personal prejudice or animosity toward women. Patterns of social action embedded in the entire social system may influence women and men, providing unrecognized privileges or disadvantages. This is called *institutionalized privilege* or *disprivilege*.

Men still, overwhelmingly, dominate governments. Women make up just 23.4% of national legislators across the world (Inter-Parliamentary Union 2018a; Londoño 2017). In the November 2018 U.S. midterm elections, women won more than 100 seats in Congress, an all-time record (Gaudiano 2018). Women comprise 19% of all national representatives in the U.S. Congress, below the world average (Center for American Women and Politics 2017).

The nation with the highest percentage of women (61.3%) in the national parliament or congress is Rwanda (sub-Saharan Africa)—one of only two countries (Bolivia being the other) to reach or surpass 50%. Canada is 59th among nations, and the United States, between Indonesia and Kyrgyzstan, ranks 100th—well below many Global North countries like Sweden (#5),

▲ In 2017, 20 women served as the head of their nations, including Jacinda Ardern, the youngest prime minister (New Zealand) in the world and the second modern head of state to give birth while in office.

Norway (#10), Spain (#13), and France (#14) (Inter-Parliamentary Union 2018b). Nations like Rwanda, with political systems that stress proportional representation and gender quotas for government positions, have more women in political offices (Londoño 2017; Yoon 2011a, 2011b). Without such systems and quotas, democratization of governmental systems is sometimes linked to a *decrease* in representation by women, a sad reality for those committed to establishing democracy around the world (Fallon, Swiss, and Viterma 2012). Globally, women's access to power and prestige is highly variable, with some African and northern European countries leading when it comes to gender equity in government (see Table 9.1). As you study Table 9.1, note that researchers find the needs and interests of women are not fully represented unless a critical mass of female representatives is reached, and that critical mass is usually about 35% (Yoon 2011b).

Cross-cultural analyses confirm that gender roles, having evolved over centuries, can be transformed by sweeping government reforms, economic upheaval, or wars. In many societies, though, gender roles are passed down from one generation to the next. The fact that women in China generally work outside the home, whereas women in some Muslim societies hardly venture

Nations With the Highest Percentage of Women in National Parliaments (Governments) 2018

Rank	Country	% Women Lower or Single House	Upper House or Senate
1	Rwanda	61.3%	38.5%
2	Bolivia	53.1%	47.2%
3	Cuba	48.9%	--
4	Nicaragua	45.7%	--
5	Sweden	43.6%	--
6	Mexico	42.6%	36.7%
7	South Africa	42.1%	35.2%
8	Finland	42%	--
9	Senegal	41.8%	--
10	Norway	41.4%	--

Source: Inter-Parliamentary Union 2018b, www.ipu.org. Reprinted with permission of the Inter-Parliamentary Union (IPU).

from their homes is due to differences in cultural norms about proper gender roles dictated by traditions, religious beliefs, and governments and learned through the socialization process.

Consider the example of Japan where one of the lowest birth rates in the world has led to a sharp population decline and an aging population as fewer children are born to replace older generations. Women, even highly educated ones, have traditionally left their jobs when a child was born because of norms favoring the stay-at-home mom and the difficulty of juggling work and family. However, with Japan's shrinking population resulting in fewer workers to support the aging population, the prime minister (head of the government) is advocating more state-funded childcare and other supports so that more women can stay in the labor force and have children. It may take some time to overcome traditions, but government intervention in the economy may help Japan deal with its economic problems (Soble 2015).

Gender Socialization: Micro- and Meso-Level Analyses

"Sugar and spice and everything nice—that's what little girls are made of. Snips and snails and puppy dog tails—that's what little boys are made of." As this verse implies, different views of little girls and little boys start at birth, based on gender and stereotypes about what is biologically natural. Behavioral expectations stem from cultural beliefs about the nature of men and women, and these expectations can guide socialization from the earliest ages and in intimate primary group settings.

Gender role socialization is the process by which people learn the cultural norms, attitudes, and behaviors deemed appropriate for a particular gender. Socialization reinforces the "proper" gender behaviors and punishes the improper behaviors. This process, in turn, reinforces gender stereotypes. In many societies, traits of gentleness, passivity, and dependence are associated with femininity, whereas boldness, aggression, strength, and independence are identified with masculinity. For instance, in most Western societies, aggression in women is considered unfeminine, if not inappropriate or disturbing (Sandberg and Grant 2015). Likewise, the gentle, unassertive male is often looked on with scorn or pity, stigmatized as a "wimp."

Gender stereotypes in the United States are less rigid than in the past, but they are still a big part of popular culture and influence the perspectives and behaviors of children and adults. In one recent study, researchers told 5- and 6-year-olds a story about a very, very smart person. When asked to guess the gender of the person in the story, the 5-year-olds guessed a person of their own gender. By the time they turned 6, however, both boys and girls were guessing that the really, really smart person in the story was a man. And girls, starting at the age of 6, became less interested in activities the researchers said were for very, very smart people. Through the gender socialization process, both the boys and the girls had internalized the notion that really, really smart people tend to be men (Bian, Leslie, and Simpian 2017).

Stages in Gender Socialization

Bounce that rough-and-tumble baby boy and cuddle that precious, delicate little girl. Thus begins gender socialization, starting at birth and taking place through a series of life stages, discussed in Chapter 4 on socialization. Examples from infancy and childhood show how socialization into gender roles takes place.

Infancy. Learning how to carry out gender roles begins at birth. Parents in the United States describe their newborn daughters as soft, delicate, fine featured, little, pretty, cute, awkward, and resembling their mothers. They depict their sons as strong, firm, alert, and well-coordinated—and treat them as such (Lindsey 2015). Although gender stereotypes have declined in recent years, they continue to affect the way we handle and treat male and female infants.

Clothing, room decor, and toys also reflect notions of gender. An interesting fact is that only a century ago pink was considered the "manly" color, and self-respecting men were steered away from the very soft feminine color—blue ("Finery for Infants" 1893). A trade publication, *Earnshaw's Infants' Department,* published an article in June 1918 advising parents that "the generally accepted rule is pink for the boys, and blue for the girls. The reason is that pink, being a more decided and stronger color, is more suitable for the boy, while blue, which is more delicate and dainty, is prettier for the girl." In 1927, *Time* magazine printed a chart showing sex-appropriate colors for children: pink is for boys—blue for girls (Maglaty 2011). Moreover, prior to the 20th century, both boys and girls in the United States were dressed mostly in frilly dresses until they were about 6 (Maglaty 2011).

Childhood. Once they are out of infancy, research shows that boys receive more encouragement than girls to be independent and exploratory. More pressure is put on boys to behave in "gender-appropriate" ways, with an emphasis on achievement, autonomy, and aggression (Kramer and Beutel 2014). One recent study indicates that fathers tend to use more language related to achievement ("win," "proud") with sons but more language associated with feelings such as sadness with daughters. This supports past research that shows that boys are more likely to be pushed into competitive modes of thought and less likely to be encouraged to express sadness and other emotions than girls (Mascaro et al. 2017). Boys are socialized into this "boy code" that provides rigid guidelines for their behavior as described in the next Sociology in Our Social World.

THINKING SOCIOLOGICALLY

What evidence do you see of the "boy code" when you observe your friends and relatives? What is the impact of the boy code? Is there a similar code for girls?

Girls are trained to express aggression in subtler yet still harmful ways: through gossip, rumors, name-calling, backbiting, and excluding other girls from social activities (Beran 2012). The stereotype of the catty, self-involved, and obsessed-with-social-status version of women can be seen on a wide range of media today,

▲ Children, like the girl in this picture, begin to conform to gender expectations once they are old enough to understand that their sex is permanent.

particularly reality television. These pervasive images of women in the media help perpetuate the stereotype of girls and women as socially aggressive (Behm-Morawitz, Lewallen, and Miller 2016).

Names for children also reflect stereotypes about gender. Boys are more often given strong, hard names ending in consonants. The top 10 names given to boys in 2018 were Liam, Noah, Elijah, Logan, Mason, James, Aiden, Ethan, Lucas, and Jacob ("Top 100" 2018a). Girls are more likely to be given soft, pretty names with vowel endings, such as most of the 2018 top 10: Emma, Olivia, Ava, Isabella, Sophia, Mia, Amelia, Charlotte, Abigail, and Emily ("Top 100" 2018b).

Alternatively, girls may be given feminized versions of boys' names—Roberta, Jessica, Josephine, Nicole, Michelle, Donna, Charlotte, Georgia, or Antonia. Sometimes traditional boys' names are given to girls without first feminizing them. Names such as Lynn, Stacey, Tracey, Faye, Dana, Jody, Lindsay, Robin, Carmen, Kelly, Kim, Beverly, Ashley, Dana, Carol, Shannon, and Leslie used to be names exclusively for men, but within a decade or two after they were given to girls, parents stopped using them for boys (Kean 2007). So a common name for males may, for a time, be given to either sex, but then ultimately given primarily to girls. The pattern rarely goes in the other direction. Once feminized, the names seem to have become tainted and unacceptable for boys.

As children are rewarded for performing proper gender roles, these roles are reinforced, setting the stage for gender-related interactions, behaviors, and choices in later life. We now turn to meso-level agents of gender socialization.

THE BOY CODE

The old boy network in American society favors adult men over women. This system actually starts with the "boy code," rules about boys' proper behavior. Young boys learn the code from parents, siblings, peers, teachers, and society in general. They are praised for adhering to the code and punished for violating its dictates. William Pollack (1999) writes that boys learn several stereotyped behavior models exemplifying the boy code:

1. "The sturdy oak": Men should be stoic, stable, and independent; a man never shows weakness.

2. "Give 'em hell": From athletic coaches and movie heroes, the consistent theme is extreme daring, bravado, and attraction to violence.

3. "The 'big wheel'": Men and boys should achieve status, dominance, and power; they should avoid shame, wear the mask of coolness, and act as though everything is under control.

4. "No sissy stuff": Boys are discouraged from expressing feelings or urges perceived as feminine—dependence, warmth, empathy.

The boy code is ingrained in society; by 5 or 6 years of age, boys are less likely than girls to express hurt or distress. They have learned to be ashamed of showing feelings and of being weak. This gender straitjacket, according to Pollack, causes boys to conceal feelings to fit in and be accepted and loved. As a result, some boys, especially in adolescence, become silent, covering any vulnerability and masking their true feelings. This affects boys' relationships, performance in school, and ability to connect with others. It also causes young males to put on what Jackson Katz calls the "tough guise," when young men and boys emphasize aggression and violence to display masculinity (Katz 2006, 2016). Moreover, if fathers emphasize competition and toughness, their sons are much more likely to become bullies and are likely to

have few deep friendships, especially in the later teen years (Kindlon and Thompson 2000; Way 2011).

Although boys are innately as capable of expressing emotion as girls, they learn to suppress emotions—except for anger, which is seen as a legitimate masculine emotion (Kindlon and Thompson 2000). This inability to share feelings, these scholars found, has serious repercussions for inner well-being and for healthy relationships (*Mindful Relations* 2015). Yet many boys are a part of a resistance movement against the boy code (Way 2011). They have intimate relationships with male friends—sharing emotions, vulnerabilities, and secrets—especially during childhood and early adolescence. Sadly, research shows that although most boys deeply value intimate same-sex friendships, those ties, under pressure from the boy code, can weaken considerably by late adolescence, and many boys struggle privately with the loss. However, some men form more supportive and less competitive relationships with other men, and there are likely to be continued changes in and broadened definitions of "appropriate" behavior for men (Kimmel and Messner 2013; Way 2011).

Pollack suggests that we can help boys resist norms that are destructive to them by

1. giving some undivided attention each day just listening to boys;

2. encouraging a range of emotions;

3. avoiding language that taunts, teases, or shames;

4. looking behind the veneer of "coolness" for signs of problems;

5. expressing love and empathy;

6. dispelling the "sturdy oak" image; and

7. advocating a broad, inclusive model of masculinity (Pollack 1999).

Meso-Level Agents of Gender Socialization

Clues to "proper" gender roles surround children in materials produced by corporations (e.g., books, toys, and games), in technology and mass media images, in educational settings, and in religious organizations and beliefs. In Chapter 4, you learned about agents of socialization. Those agents play a major role in teaching children proper gender roles. The following examples demonstrate how organizations and institutions in societies teach and reinforce gender assumptions and roles.

Corporations. Corporations create many materials that help socialize children into conduct socially approved for their gender. Publishers, for example, produce books that present images of expected gender behavior. The language and pictures in preschool picture books, elementary school children's books, stories for teenagers, and school textbooks are steeped in gender role messages, reflecting society's expectations and stereotypes. In a study of children's books published in the United States during the 20th century, researchers found males more frequently represented than females throughout the entire time period (McCabe et al. 2011). Studies on more recent books have found some change in this pattern—even an overcorrection in some cases—but many children's books still show stereotyped images of females, especially those with animal or other types of nonhuman characters (D. A. Anderson and Hamilton 2005; Diekman and Murmen 2004; Houlis 2011). Recent lists of books that defy gender stereotypes have been created for parents who wish to present gender-neutral images to their children, but most parents are not aware of these options (Krueger 2015).

Producers of toys and games also contribute to traditional messages about gender. Wall posters and store-bought toys fill rooms in homes of children in the Western world, and it is usually quite clear which are boys' rooms and which are girls' rooms. Each toy or game prepares children for future gender roles. Choices ranging from college major to occupational choice appear to be affected by these early choices and childhood learning experiences (Deerwester 2013).

Boys' rooms are filled with sports equipment, army toys, building and technical toys, and cars and trucks. Girls' rooms have fewer toys, and most are related to dolls and domestic roles. Boys have more experience manipulating blocks, Tinkertoys, LEGO bricks, and Erector Sets—toys paralleling masculinized activities outside the home in the public domain, from constructing and building trades to military roles and sports. Girls prepare for domestic roles with toys related to domestic activities and play with Barbie dolls that stress physical appearance, consumerism, and glamour. Toy stores are generally divided into distinct boys' and girls' sections, shaping parents' and children's choices, and girls' and boys' future skills and interests (Abadi 2013). One recent study connected higher scores on spatial development for boys to their greater use of spatial toys (building blocks, LEGO, K'nex, puzzles) (Jiroute and Newcombe 2015). The bottom line is that gender portrayals are unequal, and the females presented in books, video games, television shows, and toys tend to be in stereotypical roles—showing women in supportive roles, as socially catty, in need of rescue, or as sexually alluring.

Mass Media. Mass media comes in many forms—magazines, ads, movies, music videos, and Internet sites—and is a major agent of socialization into gender roles. We can see its influence all around us, even during a typical

▲ Mattel's Barbie dolls and other girls' toys have been criticized for their extremely traditional and highly sexualized images of young women. The second photo is of a boys' toy department; note the difference in images as well as the color shades. What is communicated?

weekend evening for many boys. It is Friday night, and a group of adolescent males gather to play games in one house. In a house down the street a boy sits alone in front of a screen but is engaged in play with several other boys who are playing in different locations. All the boys are playing their favorite game, World of Warcraft (WoW).

In the United States, almost all teens (95%) own or have access to a smartphone, and most use social media regularly. As Figure 9.2 indicates, a strong majority of teens use Instagram and Snapchat. More than 1 out of 3 teens say they use Snapchat more than any other online platform (including YouTube) (Anderson and Jiang 2018).

Seventy-one percent of all teens play video games, with 83% of teen boys and 59% of teen girls involved (Pew Research Center 2015b). For teen boys, video games become key elements in friendships, helping them establish and maintain friendships either in the same room or over the Internet (Lenhart 2015). Teen girls love to play many different games too, often role-playing games such as Dragon Age, Assassin's Creed Syndicate, Star Wars, and games that feature match-3 or social family/farming genres (Campbell 2017). Whereas video games are social for boys, more girls play them alone without a mic to chat (Marcotte 2015). Media makes the connection to others for many teens, especially boys.

Adolescents identify with characters in video games and often view them as role models (Mou and Peng 2009). However, girls are generally peripheral to the action. Notice the next time you are around people playing video games that the fighting characters are typically male and often in armor. When fighting women do appear, they are usually clad in skin-revealing bikini-style attire—odd clothing in which to do battle!

When, in recent years, women in the gaming world began to speak out about their stereotypical portrayal, these women were viciously attacked. Some even received death threats from anonymous trolls online. Over the past decade, more women have become involved in both playing and creating games, but the pushback against their entrance into this world, and women's desires to see themselves portrayed more equitably in it, have resulted in a fierce backlash from some antiwomen gamers (Parker 2017).

A similar, though not as blatant, backlash occurs in the workplace, when women ask for raises and promotions. In U.S. corporations today, women are about 10% more likely than men to ask for a raise, reassignment, or promotion, but when they do so they are also 30% more likely than men who ask to receive feedback that they are "bossy," "intimidating," or "aggressive." They are also less likely to be granted their request than men (McKinsey & Company 2018).

THINKING SOCIOLOGICALLY

Why are video and role-playing games primarily a "boy social thing"? How do you see girls using social media? What effect might girls' and boys' different technology activities have on their futures?

Some recent action films include adventurous and competent girls and women, helping to counter images of sexy and helpless females. *The Hunger Games* heroine, Katniss Everdeen, has become a brave idol for teenage girls; Mattel has even made a Barbie version of the heroine. *Star Wars* features strong women, and *Wonder Woman* had both a woman director and star. These new examples of women in strong leadership roles may help change images, although highly competent females are still seen less frequently than men in the media. In addition, in 2016, just 7% of the top-grossing 250 films in the United States were directed by women—a decline of 2% from 2015 (Lauzen 2017).

Young men and women, desiring to fit in, can be influenced in harmful ways by messages from the media. For instance, the epidemic of steroid use or hormones among boys to stimulate muscle growth results from a desire to be successful in sports and have an appealing body image. Professional athletes set an example, and the dark side of steroids, especially for teen boys, is often overlooked: acne, mood swings, depression, elevated suicide attempts, aggressive behavior, high blood pressure, heightened sex characteristics, and liver damage (Global Sports Development 2013). Adolescent girls are more prone to dieting, bingeing, and purging (Stephen et al. 2014). Dieting among girls, driven in part by ads, is a health concern in the United States and some other countries. Studies show that 40% to 60% of children ages 6 to 12 are worried about their weight. Eighty percent of 10-year-olds have dieted. Over

▼ FIGURE 9.2

Online Platforms Among Teens

YouTube, Instagram, and Snapchat are the most popular online platforms among teens

% of U.S. teens who . . .

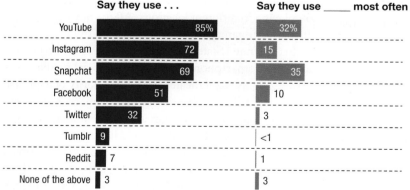

	Say they use . . .	Say they use _____ most often
YouTube	85%	32%
Instagram	72	15
Snapchat	69	35
Facebook	51	10
Twitter	32	3
Tumblr	9	<1
Reddit	7	1
None of the above	3	3

Source: "Teens, Social Media & Technology 2018." Pew Research Center, Washington, D.C. (May 31, 2018), http://www.pewinternet.org/2018/05/31/teens-social-media-technology-2018.

Note: The survey was conducted from March 7 to April 10, 2018. Figures in the first column add to more than 100% because multiple responses were allowed. The question about the most-used site was asked only of respondents who use multiple sites; results have been recalculated to include those who use only one site. Respondents who did not give an answer are not shown.

half (53%) of 13-year-old girls and more than three out of four (78%) 17-year-old girls have issues with their bodies (Hepworth 2010; C. Roberts 2012).

Television is another part of the media that works as a powerful socializing agent. The average person in the United States watches 5 hours and 4 minutes of television every day (Nielsen 2016). Seventy percent of children ages 8 to 18 have TVs in their bedrooms, many of these hooked up to cable or satellite (Uzoma 2015). Children ages 2 to 11 watch, on average, over 100 hours of TV each month; add to that time with other devices, and the time increases by another 50% (Nielsen 2014). Television often presents a simple, stereotyped view of life, from advertisements to situation comedies to soap operas. Women in television shows and ads, especially those working outside the home, are often depicted as having problems in carrying out their role responsibilities.

Educational Systems. Girls and boys often have very different experiences in school. As noted in the following examples, education systems socialize children through classroom, lunchroom, and playground activities; students' popularity and recognition; sports and Title IX programs; and teachers' attitudes and expectations. In academics, girls achieve at a higher level than boys overall. However, in college and graduate studies that lead to high-paying jobs such as high-level physics and math courses, girls lag. Recent concerns over the number of scientists and engineers needed and the lack of women pursuing these careers points to the subtle and blatant biases against women, especially women of color.

Many social scientists agree that socialization and stereotypes are major contributors to the gender gap in science and math. In a study of Israeli and European elementary classrooms, girls were judged less able in math than boys by their teachers, though anonymous tests showed girls performed as well as or better than boys (Lavy and Sand 2015). In societies where math is considered gender-neutral, girls score on par with their male classmates. For example, in Shanghai-China, Singapore, Hong Kong–China, and Chinese Taipei, girls scored as well as their boy peers on the international PISA test taken by 15-year-olds around the world (Organisation for Economic Co-operation and Development [OECD] 2015a).

Despite higher average scores for boys in math, 14% of boys compared to 9% of girls failed to meet basic standards in math, reading, and science on the most recent PISA test (OECD 2015a). One key reason boys' educational attainment has fallen behind girls in general (with the exception of math and science) relates to how boys and girls spend their time. Boys, on average, spend 1 hour

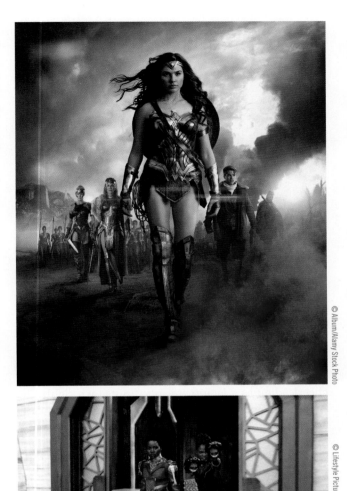

▲ *Wonder Woman* (2017) and *Black Panther* (2018) are both films that feature women in strong leadership roles.

a week less on homework, more time playing video games, and less time reading for fun than girls.

Gender Inequality, Sports, and Leadership Development in Schools. Although boys may be falling behind girls academically, they are still more likely than girls to be socialized at school to become leaders. Participation in athletics, especially team sports, can foster skills in teamwork, strategic thinking, and anticipating counteractions by a competitor, useful skills in business and government. It can also bring children attention and help them become comfortable in the limelight. In middle school and high school sports, even when there are both boys' and girls' basketball teams, more spectators come to the boys' contests than to the girls' games. Thus, few people know the female athletes

© Getty/Win McNamee/Staff

▲ Sara Seager, professor of planetary science and physics at the Massachusetts Institute of Technology, speaks at a press conference on potentially habitable worlds elsewhere in the universe. She is a researcher in the forefront of what really is "rocket science."

Explain why you think there is a gap between men and women playing sports at high school and college levels: limited opportunity, lack of interest among girls, or other factors such as profits from sports? What, if anything, should be done about the gap?

by name. In fact, female cheerleaders have a much more visible position. Girls are more likely to be noticed when standing on the sidelines cheering for the boys' teams than when playing on a girls' team. One effort to level the playing field in sports is the redefinition of cheerleading as a legitimate sport in its own right. The American Medical Association now argues that the risks and rigors of cheerleading require trained coaches and more safety measures, thus qualifying it as a varsity sport (Tanner 2014). The bottom line is that there are far more visible positions for boys than for girls in middle and high school, allowing them to be recognized and become leaders.

Title IX of the U.S. Education Amendments of 1972 was a major legislative attempt to level the educational and sports playing field. Passed in order to bar gender discrimination in schools receiving federal funds, this legislation mandates equal opportunity for participation in school-sponsored programs (Lindsey 2015). The law has reduced or eliminated blatant discrimination in areas ranging from admissions and health care to counseling and housing, sex-segregated programs, financial aid, dress codes, and other areas of concern. However, the biggest impact of Title IX legislation has been in athletics.

Women's athletic programs and scholarship opportunities have grown since 1972 but still lag behind those for men. By 2015, the number of women competing in college sports had climbed from 30,000 to almost 3.27 million; about 2 in 5 high school girls participate in varsity sports (Wong 2015). However, NCAA colleges still spend only 44% of their athletic dollars on women's sports (Dusenbery and Lee 2012). Advocates for Title IX argue that there is still work to be done to level the playing field (Title IX 2015).

Religious Organizations. Religious organizations serve as agents of gender socialization by defining, reinforcing, and perpetuating gender roles and cultural beliefs. Religious teachings provide explanations of proper male and female roles. Although the specific teachings vary, the three major monotheistic religions that affirm only one God—Christianity, Islam, and Judaism—are traditionally patriarchal, stressing separate female and male spheres (Kramer and Beutel 2014).

Some interpretations of the Adam and Eve creation story in the Hebrew Bible (the Old Testament in the Christian Bible) state that man was created first and that men are, therefore, superior. Because Eve, created from the rib of man, was the enticer to the first sin, she has kept women forever in an inferior, second-class position. For these and other reasons, in some branches of these religions, women are restricted in their roles within the family and religious organizations. They cannot be priests in Catholic churches and cannot vote on business matters in some religious organizations. However, recent work by feminist scholars challenges the notion of patriarchy in Judaic and Christian history, pointing out that women may have played a much broader role in religious development than currently recognized (Hunter College Women's Studies Collective 2005). Even *Yahweh*—the name for God in the Hebrew Bible—had both male and female connotations, and when God was referred to as a source of wisdom in the "wisdom literature" (Psalms, Proverbs, and so forth), feminine pronouns and references were used (Borg 2001). Increasingly, denominations are granting women greater roles in the religious hierarchies, ministries, and priesthood.

Women in Judaism lived for 4,000 years in a patriarchal system where men read, taught, and legislated while women followed (Lindsey 2015). Today, three of the five main branches of Judaism allow women equal participation, illustrating that religious practices do change over time. However, Hasidic and Orthodox Jews have a division of labor between men and women following old laws, with designated gender roles for the home and religious life.

Some Christian teachings have treated women as second-class citizens, even in the eyes of God. For this reason, some Christian denominations have excluded women from a variety of leadership roles and told them they must be subservient to their husbands. Other Christians point to the admonition by Saint Paul that, theologically speaking, the distinction between men and women is not relevant and that women and men are not spiritually different.

Traditional Hindu religion painted women as seductresses, strongly erotic, and a threat to male spirituality and asceticism. To protect men from this threat, women were kept totally covered in thick garments and veils and seen only by men in their immediate families. Today, Hinduism comes in many forms, most of which honor the woman's domestic sphere of life—as mothers, wives, and homemakers—while also accepting women in public roles (Lindsey 2015).

Traditional Islamic beliefs also portrayed female sexuality as dangerous to men, although many women in Islamic societies today are full participants in the public and private sphere. The Quran (also spelled Qur'an or Koran), the Muslim sacred scripture, has a few passages that seem to favor men, but most of the text actually supports women's rights (Aslan 2011). Still, aspects of the traditional Sharia law, strict Islamic law, have carried over in several countries and among some groups. It has been used to punish women accused of violating rules about gender behavior (Mydans 2002; Proudman 2012).

Women in strict literalist Muslim societies such as Algeria, Iran, Syria, and Saudi Arabia are separated from men (except for fathers, brothers, and husbands) in work and worship. They generally remain covered. *Purdah*, which means curtain, refers to practices of seclusion and separate worlds for women and men in Islamic cultures. Screens in households and veils in public enforce female modesty and prevent men from seeing women where this is dictated (Ward and Edelstein 2016). In the days of Muhammad, only his wives wore such veils for privacy, and there were no commandments in the Quran instructing women to be covered, so these patterns are more cultural and national than Islamic religious requirements. In any case, today some women argue that the veil they wear is for modesty, for cosmetic purposes, or to protect them from the stares of men.

Meso-level religious systems influence how different societies interpret proper gender roles and how sometimes these belief systems change with new interpretations of scriptures. (Further discussion of the complex relationship between religion and gender appears in Chapter 12.) From family and education to media and religion, meso-level agents of socialization teach and reinforce "appropriate" gender roles in each society.

Gender Stratification: Meso- and Macro-Level Processes

The phrase **glass ceiling** refers to *processes that limit the progress of women and other minorities.* Men, on the other hand, often ride the "glass escalator," especially in traditionally female occupations. Even if they do not seek to climb in the organizational hierarchy, occupational social forces push them up the job ladder to the higher echelons (Williams 2013). The next Engaging Sociology provides an exercise to think about how our ideas may subtly maintain the glass ceiling and glass escalator by defining "leadership" the same way we define masculinity.

Women and Men at Work: Gendered Organizations

"How can I do it all—marriage, children, education, career, social life?" Many college students ask this question. They already anticipate a delicate balancing act. Work has been central to the definition of masculinity in U.S. society, and for 6 decades women ages 25 to 54 saw increased participation in the U.S. labor force (Kramer and Beutel 2014). Participation climbed to a high of 74% in 1999; today it has fallen to 69%, in part because of lack of support for working parents of young children and also because young women plan "career pauses" for family (Miller 2015b). In many other Global North countries, the percentage of women in the labor force is growing, with family supportive policies making this possible (C. Miller and Alderman 2014).

Among countries of the Global North, Sweden has the highest percentage of working women, with 72% working (compared with 76% of men) (OECD 2015). Yet even in Sweden, with its parental leave and other family-friendly policies, women and men feel pressures of work and family responsibilities (Gunnarsdottir et al. 2015). Dual-career marriages raise questions about child-rearing, power relations, and other factors in juggling work and family.

ENGAGING SOCIOLOGY

MASCULINITY AND FEMININITY IN OUR SOCIAL WORLD

1. Mark each characteristic with an *M* or an *F* depending on whether you think it is generally defined by society as a masculine or feminine characteristic.

    _____ achiever

    _____ aggressive

    _____ analytical

    _____ caring

    _____ confident

    _____ dynamic

    _____ deferential (defers to others; yields with courtesy)

    _____ devious

    _____ intuitive

    _____ loving

    _____ manipulative

    _____ nurturing

    _____ organized

    _____ passive

    _____ careful

    _____ powerful

    _____ sensitive

    _____ strong

    _____ relationship oriented (makes decisions based on how others will *feel*)

    _____ rule oriented (makes decisions based on *abstract procedural rules rather than people's feelings*)

2. Next, mark an *X* just to the right of 10 characteristics you think are essential qualities for a leadership position in a complex organization (e.g., business or government). You might want to ask 20 of your acquaintances to do this and then add up the scores for *masculinity*, *femininity*, and *leadership trait*.

3. Do you (and your acquaintances) tend to view leadership as having the same traits as those marked "masculine" or "feminine"? What are the implications of your findings for the "glass ceiling" or "glass escalator"?

4. How might correlations between the traits of leadership and gender notions help to explain the data on income in Table 9.2?

▼ TABLE 9.2

U.S. Income by Educational Level and Sex—Full-Time Workers

Education	Men	Women
9th–12th grade (no diploma)	$39,640	$26,009
High school graduate (or GED)	$48,027	$34,682
Associate degree	$59,481	$45,999
Bachelor's degree	$88,428	$61,747
Master's degree	$108,337	$76,788
Doctorate	$142,758	$102,843
Professional degree	$187,857	$116,912

Source: U.S. Census Bureau 2016b.

Around the world, workplaces have gendered relationships: ratios of female to male workers, gender reflected in subordinate-supervisor positions, and distribution of positions among men and women. This, in turn, affects our experiences in the workplace. Consider the example of mothers breastfeeding their babies. Must they quit their jobs or alter their family schedules or switch to feeding their babies formula instead of breast milk if the workplace does not provide a space for breastfeeding? Some workplaces accommodate family needs, but many do not.

Using data from the OECD, the *Economist* constructed a "glass-ceiling index" using five indicators: the number of men and women, respectively, with college educations; female labor force participation; the gender wage gap; the proportion of women in senior positions in corporations and professions; and net childcare costs compared with incomes. Cross-national comparisons indicate that Finland, Norway, Sweden, Poland, France, Hungary, and Denmark have the best conditions for working women. Nations that scored least women-friendly in employment were Turkey, Japan, and South Korea where few women obtain top jobs. Among the 26 nations that were studied, Canada ranked 10th and the United States ranked 20th for women's employment conditions (*The Economist* 2018). The results of the ranking appear in Figure 9.3.

▼ FIGURE 9.3

Glass Ceiling Index, 2018

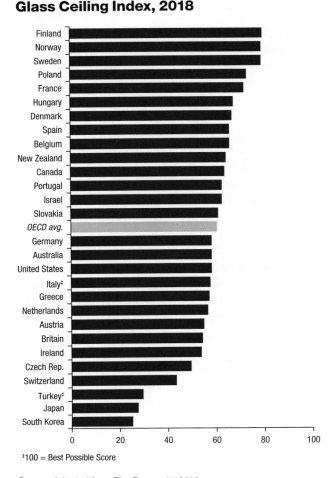

‡100 = Best Possible Score

Source: Adapted from *The Economist* 2018.

Sexual Harassment in the Workplace. As the millions of women (and some men) who have publicly shared their own experiences with sexual harassment in the workplace have made clear, the workplace is often not a safe place. According to the U.S. Equal Employment Opportunity Commission (EEOC) (2016:8), "when [women] employees were asked, in surveys using probability samples, whether they have experienced one or more specific sexually-based behaviors, such as unwanted sexual attention or sexual coercion," 40% responded affirmatively. In a poll asking men if they engaged in sexual harassment at work (from telling sexual jokes that some people might find offensive to offering or implying rewards for sex or punishing a worker from withholding sex), one in three men admitted to such behavior (Patel, Griggs, and Miller 2017). An ABC News/*Washington Post* poll (2011) revealed that 10% of men have also faced sexual harassment at work. Unfortunately, studies show that 90% of those who have experienced sexual harassment in the workplace never file a formal complaint because they fear retribution. This fear is based on fact, for a 2003 study reveals that 75% of women who do speak up about sexual harassment at work face punishment for doing so (U.S. EEOC 2016). Fortunately, the many women who have come forward to expose public figures such as Harvey Weinstein, Larry Nassar, and Louis C.K., spurred on by social media campaigns (e.g., #MeToo) throughout the world, have encouraged more women (and men) to do so and to demand change.

Although standard sexual harassment training in the workplace tends to be ineffective, other strategies to curb such behavior do work. Research has shown that "bystander" sexual harassment trainings, which focus on how community members can actively work to stop and prevent harassment, are the most effective (Moynihan et al. 2015; Potter and Moynihan 2011). Unlike traditional trainings, which teach people what they should not do, bystander trainings teach people tactics to disrupt sexual harassment in nonconfrontational ways that support the victim. Promoting more women, and thereby institutionalizing gender equity in workplaces, is the most effective strategy of all (Dobbin and Kalev 2017; Lucas 2003).

THINKING SOCIOLOGICALLY

If corporate structures were reversed so that women organized the workplace, how might the workplace environment change? How might these changes impact women, men, and their families?

Institutionalized Gender Discrimination

Gender stratification at the meso level—like race and ethnic stratification—can occur independently of any overt prejudice or ill will by others. It becomes part of the social system, and we are not even conscious of it. *Discrimination* is often built into organizations and cultural expectations and includes both intentional and unintentional actions or structures that have consequences harmful to minorities. It is embedded in institutions.

You will recall from the previous chapter that *side-effect discrimination* involves practices in one institutional area that have a negative impact because they are linked to practices in another institutional area. Institutions are interdependent, so discrimination in one can result in unintentional discrimination in others. For example, when roles of women in family life are determined by rigid gender expectations, women find it more difficult to devote themselves to gaining job promotions. In addition, as long as little girls learn through socialization to use their voices and hold their bodies and gesture in ways that communicate deference, employers assume a lack of the self-confidence necessary for major leadership roles. If women are paid less than men, despite the same levels of education (see Table 9.2 on page 268), they are less likely to have access to the best health care or be able to afford a down payment for a house, unless they are married. This makes women dependent on men in a way that most men are not dependent on women.

A factor affecting differences in incomes is the type of academic degrees men and women receive (e.g., engineering rather than education). However, even when these differences are factored in, men still make considerably more, on average, than women with identical levels of experience and training.

▲ This little girl looks cute but not very powerful or confident. When women tilt their heads—either forward or to one side—they also look like they lack confidence, and this hurts their chances of promotion in the corporate world.

Past-in-present discrimination, discussed in Chapter 8, refers to practices from the past that may no longer be allowed but that continue to affect people today. For example, in a Midwest appliance industry investigated by one of the authors, there is a sequence of jobs one must hold to be promoted up the line to floor supervisor. This requirement ensures that the floor supervisor understands the many aspects of production at the plant. One of the jobs involves working in a room with heavy equipment that cuts through and bends metal sheets. The machine is extremely powerful and could easily cut off a leg or hand if the operator is not careful. Because of the danger, the engineers designed the equipment so it would not operate unless three levers were activated at the same time. One lever was triggered by stepping on a pedal on the floor. The other two required reaching out with one's hands so that one's body was extended. When one was spread-eagled to activate all three levers, there was no way one could possibly have a part of one's body near the blades.

It was brilliant engineering, but there was one unanticipated problem: The hand-activated levers were 5 feet, 10 inches off the ground and 5 feet apart. Few women had the height and arm span to run this machine, and therefore, no women had yet made it through the sequence of positions to the higher-paying position of floor supervisor. The equipment cost millions of dollars, so it was not likely to be replaced. Neither the engineers who designed the machine nor the upper-level managers who established the sequence of jobs to become floor supervisor had deliberately tried to exclude women. Indeed, they were perplexed when they looked at their employee figures and saw so few women moving up through the ranks. The cause of women's disadvantage was not mean-spirited men but features of the system that had unintended consequences resulting in past-in-present discrimination. A machine built in the past to service workers at that time is still in use and now disqualifies women for an important job. The barriers women face, then, are not just matters of socialization or other micro-level social processes. The nature of sexism is often subtle yet pervasive in society, operating at the meso and macro levels as institutional discrimination.

Another example of how prejudices and discrimination in the past can still affect us in the present can be seen in children's books, discussed earlier. Although recent books show expansion in the roles of males and females, the tens of thousands of older, classic books in public and school libraries mean that a parent or child picking a book off of the shelf is still likely to select a book that has old stereotypical views of boys and girls.

Men often get defensive and angry when people talk about sexism in society because they feel they are being attacked or asked to correct past injustices. However, the empirical reality is that the playing field is not level for men and women. Most men do not do anything to intentionally harm women, and they may not feel prejudiced toward women, but sexism operates so that men are given privileges they never asked for and may not even recognize. As Figure 9.4 reveals, men are more likely to be hired and promoted at every level in the corporate pipeline, with women of color at even more of a disadvantage than White women in the hiring and promotion processes.

Sexism and strict gender roles for men and women hurt boys and men, not just girls and women. The fact that women do not make as much as men hurts their male partners and offspring, as well as the women themselves. Moreover, men, as well as women, are confined to gender roles that restrict their behavior and their work and family lives.

Gender Stratification: Micro- to Macro-Level Theories

Recent research by some biologists and psychologists has considered whether there are innate differences in the makeup of women and men that affect behavior. For instance, males produce more testosterone, a hormone found to be correlated with aggression. Research shows that in many situations, males tend to be more aggressive and concerned with dominance. Other traits, such as nurturance, empathy, and altruism, show no clear gender difference (Fausto-Sterling 1992; Sapolsky 2014).

▼ FIGURE 9.4

Race and Gender Representation in the U.S. Corporate Pipeline in 2017

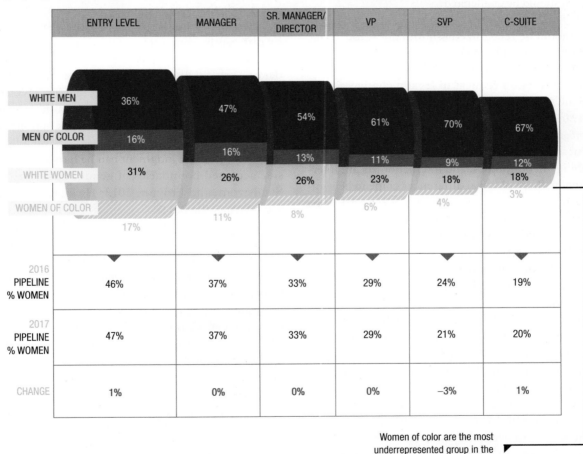

	ENTRY LEVEL	MANAGER	SR. MANAGER/ DIRECTOR	VP	SVP	C-SUITE
WHITE MEN	36%	47%	54%	61%	70%	67%
MEN OF COLOR	16%	16%	13%	11%	9%	12%
WHITE WOMEN	31%	26%	26%	23%	18%	18%
WOMEN OF COLOR	17%	11%	8%	6%	4%	3%
2016 PIPELINE % WOMEN	46%	37%	33%	29%	24%	19%
2017 PIPELINE % WOMEN	47%	37%	33%	29%	21%	20%
CHANGE	1%	0%	0%	0%	−3%	1%

Women of color are the most underrepresented group in the corporate pipeline—behind White men, men of color, and White women.

Source: Exhibit from "Women in the Workplace 2017," October 2017, McKinsey Global Institute, www.mckinsey.com. Copyright © 2018 McKinsey & Company. All rights reserved. Reprinted by permission.

Note: VP = vice president, SVP = senior vice president, C-suite = top senior executives.

Although biological and psychological factors make up part of the difference between females and males, our focus here is on the major contribution that *social factors* make in the social statuses of males and females in human society. This section explores social theories that explain gender differences.

Symbolic Interaction Theory: Micro-Level Analysis

Traditional notions of gender are hard to change. Confusion over "proper" masculine and feminine roles creates anxiety and even anomie in a society. People want behavioral guidelines. Thus, many believe it is best to adhere to traditional notions of gender that are reinforced by religious or political dogmas, making those ideas appear sacred, absolute, and beyond human interference. Others believe the male prerogatives and privileges of the past were established by men to protect their rights and should be challenged.

Today, as noted earlier, some people believe that gender should be recognized as fluid, not static. Some people refuse any kind of gender identity. In 2017, in a groundbreaking decision, a judge in Oregon granted Patrick Abbatiello's request to legally change gender from male to *agender* and use the single name "Patch" (Flood 2017).

Symbolic interactionists look at how gender is socially constructed. Sex is the biological reality of different "plumbing" in our bodies, and interactionists are interested in how those physical differences come to be symbols, resulting in different social rights and rewards. The meaning assigned to one's sex is connected to notions of masculinity and femininity. The symbolic interaction perspective has been forceful in insisting that notions of proper gender behavior are not intrinsically related to a person's sex. Rather, gender is a socially created or constructed idea.

More than any other theory, symbolic interaction stresses the idea of *human agency*—the notion that humans not only are influenced by the society in which they live but also actively help create it (Charon 2010; Hewitt and Shulman 2011). In a classic study of elementary children in classrooms and on playgrounds, Barrie Thorne (1993) found that although teachers influenced the children, the children themselves were active participants in creating the student culture that guided their play. As children played with one another, Thorne noticed the ways in which they created words, nicknames, distinctions between one another, and new forms of interaction. This is a very important

point: Humans do not just passively adopt cultural notions about gender; they *do gender*. They create it as they behave and interact with others in ways that define "normal" male or female conduct (West and Zimmerman 1987). *Doing gender* is an everyday, recurring, and routine occurrence. It is a constant ongoing process that defines each situation and takes place in organizations and between individuals. Understanding the process of *doing gender* helps us understand why we think and act as we do.

When children are in ambiguous situations, they may spontaneously define their sex as the most relevant trait about themselves or others. When children act as if gender matters, they are helping make it a reality for those around them. As the next child adopts the "definition of reality" from the first, acting as if sex is more important than hair color or eye color, it makes gender the most prominent characteristic in the mind of the next child. Yet each child could choose to ignore gender and decide that something else is more important. This is part of *human agency*—the freedom to define reality differently from others. The same principle applies to adults. When a person "chooses" to recognize gender as a critical distinction between two individuals or two groups, that person is "doing gender." We *do gender* all the time, every day. In fact, we cannot avoid it! It is present in our interactions, and we are conscious that we will be judged by others on how well we follow our gender roles. That judgment can be harsh if we go outside accepted boundaries of gender behavior (Cahil, Sandstrom, and Froyum 2013; Hewitt and Shulman 2011; Schoepflin 2011).

Through interaction, people do gender, and although this process begins at a micro level, it has implications all the way to the global level. The next section explores meso- and macro-level forces that shape gender and stratification based on sex. One example of doing gender is illustrated in eating—as discussed in the next Sociology in Our Social World. This shows how gender socialization affects our attitudes toward everyday events that we take for granted.

THINKING SOCIOLOGICALLY

How do you "do gender"? How did you learn these patterns of behavior? How do you think people would react if you did not follow the expected behavior patterns assigned to your gender in your social setting? How comfortable would you feel when violating those gender norms? Why?

GENDER AND FOOD

By Jacqueline Bergdahl

Behavior is generally considered *gendered* when it has symbolic meaning that differs for men versus women. Food is gendered—embedded with symbolic meanings. Women are more likely than men to be the primary food preparer in households, even though there are more male professional chefs than female ones. Women are more likely to bake than men, and men are more likely to grill than women. Food practices are shaped by gender, even though we prefer to think that what and how we eat are due to personal preferences, rather than larger social forces.

Some food items are considered to have a gender. Meat, potatoes, and coffee are foods that many people consider to be masculine, whereas yogurt and fruit are feminine, and chicken and oranges are gender neutral (Rappoport, 2003). When researchers asked subjects to sort the pictures of food items into men's foods and women's foods, salad, couscous, and stir-fry were generally considered women's foods whereas pizza, hot dogs, macaroni and cheese, pot roast, and bacon cheeseburgers were considered men's foods (McPhail et al. 2012). Some argue that part of these differences could be biological, for men generally require more calories to maintain their greater muscle mass than women, but generally these expectations about who eats what have more to do with cultural gender constructions than the physicality of bodies (McPhail et al. 2012).

Women were more adventurous than men when it came to food choices, whereas ease of preparation and consumption were the primary considerations for men.

Men were also found to be less concerned about their health, more reluctant to eat vegetables, and more likely to prefer spicy foods. Most participants in the study considered meat, and particularly red meat, to be men's food.

Some foods were less gendered. Fish was generally considered women's food because it is healthy and light, but some respondents considered fish men's food because men like to catch and eat their own fish. Sushi was seen by some as women's food because of its appearance but as men's food by others because it contained raw fish. Despite gendered ideas about food, all of the subjects involved in the study denied that their eating was gendered. All identified their food preferences as a matter of individual choice, not the result of social patterns or forces (McPhail et al. 2012).

Why is it important to understand that food is gendered—that it has symbolic as well as nutritional substance? It allows us to see that our behavior is under the influence of larger structural forces. We may recognize the influence generally (in this case by being willing to sort food photographs into piles according to gender), but we prefer to view our own behavior as simply a matter of choice. Until we acknowledge the effects of gender in all spheres, it will be difficult to eradicate gender inequality. Thinking about how food is gendered is a way of seeing the effects of gender in our lives and would make interesting dinner conversation.

★ ★ ★ ★ ★ ★ ★

Jacqueline Bergdahl is a professor of sociology at Wright State University. She studies food, gender, and obesity, among other topics.

Structural-Functional and Conflict Theories: Meso- and Macro-Level Analyses

Meso and macro-level theories provide the big picture related to gender issues. When the government passes laws that affect women (or men), like abortion or birth control laws, they affect individual women at the micro level. Likewise, laws related to child custody, payment of child support, and other laws related to marriage and divorce are made by state and national governmental offices and enforced by courts. In the following sections we visit our familiar theories as they relate to gender issues.

Structural-Functional Theory. From the structural-functional perspective, each sex has a role to play in the interdependent groups and institutions of society. Some early theorists argued that men and women carry out different roles and are, of necessity, unequal because of the needs of societies and practices that have developed since early human history. Social relationships and practices that have proven successful in the survival of a group are likely to continue and to be reinforced by society's norms, laws, and religious beliefs. Thus, relationships between women and men believed to support survival are maintained. In traditional hunter-gatherer, horticultural, and pastoral societies, for instance, the division of labor and social roles are based on sex and age. The females often take on the primary tasks of childcare and, while doing so, take on the gardening, food preparation, and other duties near the home. Men do tasks that require movements farther from home, such as hunting, fishing, and herding.

As societies industrialize, roles and relationships change due to structural changes in society. Émile Durkheim described a gradual move from traditional societies held together by *mechanical solidarity* (the glue based on shared beliefs, values, and traditions) to modern societies united through *organic solidarity* (social coherence based on division of labor, with each member playing a highly specialized role) (Durkheim [1893] 1947). According to early functionalists, gender-based division of labor exists in modern societies because it is efficient and useful to have different but complementary male and female roles. They believed this helps members of society to accomplish essential tasks and maintains societal stability (Lindsey 2015).

In the structural-functionalist view of the traditional Global North family in the 20th century, the father worked, the mother stayed at home, and they had two or more children. The female played the expressive role through childbearing, nursing, and caring for family members in the home. The male carried out the instrumental role by working outside the home to support the family (Dilon 2009; Parsons and Bales 1953). Although this pattern was relevant for White middle-class and wealthier families during the Industrial Revolution and for some decades before and after World War II, when men returned to take jobs women had held during the war, it characterizes relatively few families in the United States now. Today, more children are being raised by single moms than by married couples, and the turnover in partners has created complex families not seen before (Aulette 2010; Coontz 2016). Fewer people are marrying, and those who do marry tend to do so later in life than in previous decades.

Conflict Theory. Conflict theorists view gender relations through the lens of power. Men are the *haves*—controlling the majority of power positions and most wealth—and women are the *have-nots*. According to conflict theorists, males control the means of production and protect their privileged status by keeping women in subordinate roles.

A classical conflict explanation of gender stratification is found in the writings of Karl Marx's colleague, Friedrich Engels ([1884] 1942). In traditional societies, where size and strength were essential for survival, men were often dominant, but women's roles were respected as important and necessary to the survival of the group.

Men hunted, engaged in warfare, and protected women. Over time, male physical control was transformed into control by ideology, by the dominant belief system itself. Capitalism and inheritance traditions strengthened male dominance by making more wealth available to men and their sons. Women became dependent on men, and their roles were transformed into "taking care of the home" (Engels [1884] 1942).

Ideologies based on traditional beliefs and values have continued to be used to justify the social structure of male domination and subjugation of women. It is in the interest of the dominant group, in this case men, to maintain a position of privilege. Conflict theorists believe it unlikely that those in power by virtue of sex, race, class, or political or religious ideology will voluntarily give up their positions as long as they are benefiting from them. By keeping women in traditional gender roles, men maintain control over institutions and resources (Collins 1971).

Other Theoretical Perspectives

Some theories cross over the micro and macro levels of analysis so regularly that they need separate treatment. These approaches add much to our understanding of gender.

Feminist Theory. Most feminist theorists agree with Marx and Engels that gender stratification is based on power struggles, not biology. They argue, however, that Marx and Engels failed to consider fully a key variable in women's oppression: patriarchy. Patriarchy involves a few men dominating and holding authority over all others, including women, children, and less powerful men (Arrighi 2000; Lindsey 2015). According to feminist theorists, no matter what the economic or political system, women will continue to be oppressed by men until patriarchy is eliminated. They argue for bringing about a new and equal ordering of gender relationships to eliminate the patriarchy and sexism of current gender stratification systems (Kramer and Beutel 2014).

Feminist theorists try to understand the causes of women's lower status and seek ways to change the systems to provide more opportunities, to improve the standard of living, and to give women control over their bodies and reproduction. Feminist theorists also feel that little change will occur until group consciousness is raised so that women understand the system that limits their options and do not blame themselves for their situations. Today, social media outlets help spread feminist messages and mobilize women and men to support gender equality (UN Women 2018). The Women's Marches in 2016 and 2017, in which millions of women (and men) participated across the world, were sparked by a Facebook post and then organized almost entirely online (Bianco 2017).

As societies become technologically advanced and need an educated workforce, women of all social classes and ethnic groups around the world are likely to gain more equal roles. Women are entering institutions of higher education in record numbers, and evidence indicates they are needed in the world economic system and the changing labor force of most countries. The economies of countries in which women are not integrated into the economic system generally lag behind other countries. Feminist theorists examine these global and national patterns, but they also note the role of patriarchy in micro-level interpersonal situations—such as domestic violence.

Violence against women perpetuates gender stratification, as is evident in the intimate environment of many homes. Because men have more power in the larger society, they often have more resources within the household as well (an example of side-effect discrimination). Women often depend on the man of the house for his resources, meaning they must yield on many decisions. Power differences in the meso- and macro-level social systems also contribute to power differentials and vulnerability of women in micro-level settings. In addition, women have fewer options when considering whether to leave an abusive relationship. Although there are risks of staying in an abusive relationship, many factors enter into a woman's decision to stay or leave; rational choice theory has been used by some researchers to evaluate the gains and losses from staying versus leaving (Copp et al. 2013; Estrellado and Loh 2013). The following Sociology Around the World discusses one form of violence perpetuated predominantly against women: rape.

In summary, feminist analysis finds gender patterns embedded in the social institutions of family, education, religion, politics, economics, and health care. If the societal system is patriarchal, ruled by men, the interdependent institutions are likely to reflect and support this system. Feminist theory helps us understand how patriarchy at the meso and macro level can influence patriarchy at the micro level and vice versa.

THINKING SOCIOLOGICALLY

Imagine you were asked to reduce domestic violence in your society. How would you address it differently if you looked at it as a social issue, rather than just as a problem for the individuals directly affected by it?

▲ Men—like these Jordanians—are much more likely than women to play cards, games, or sports together, developing networks that enhance their power and their ability to "close deals." When women are not part of the same networks, they are denied the same insider privileges.

Interaction of Class, Race, and Gender. Some feminist theorists look at the ways in which discrimination related to class, race, and gender intersects in society (Anderson and Collins 2016). In the process, some groups face multiple forms of oppression that reinforce one another.

Zouina is Algerian in her background and ethnicity, but she was born in France to her immigrant parents. She lived with them in a poor immigrant suburb of Paris until she was forced to return to Algeria for an arranged marriage to a man who already had one wife. That marriage ended, and she returned to her "home" in France. Since she returned to France, Zouina has been employed wherever she can find work. The high unemployment rate and social and ethnic discrimination, especially against foreign women, makes life difficult.

The situation is complex. Muslim women from Tunisia, Morocco, and Algeria living in crowded slum communities outside Paris face discrimination in the workplace and their communities (Lazaridis 2011; Šeta 2016). Expected to be both good Muslim women and good family coproviders—which necessitates working in French society—they face ridicule, or even violence, when they wear their hijabs (coverings) in public. As religious symbols, hijabs are not allowed in schools, and in 2017, the European Court of Justice ruled that employers can legally fire employees for refusing to remove their headscarves at work (*The Local* 2017). However, they encounter derision in their community if they do not wear them. They are caught between two cultures and may be the scapegoats for frustrated young men who cannot find work due to high unemployment rates and discrimination.

RAPE AND ITS VICTIMS

For many women around the world, rape is the most feared act of violence and the ultimate humiliation. Rape is a sexual act but closely tied to aggressive male behavior. Often it is a power play to intimidate, hurt, and dominate women. As a weapon of war, rape humiliates the enemies who cannot protect their women (Audette 2014; Larsen 2013). Some societies are largely free from rape whereas others are prone toward rape. Why the difference?

When a society is relatively tolerant of interpersonal violence, holds beliefs in male dominance, and strongly incorporates ways to separate women and men, rape is more common ("Male Dominance Causes Rape" 2008; Pazzanese 2013; Sanday and Goodenough 1990). Rape is also more common when gender roles and identities are changing and norms about roles and interaction between women and men are unclear.

An alarming problem is rape on college campuses in the United States. What does this say about the United States, where some studies indicate 1 in 5 college women are victims of rape (Kahn 2018)?. These figures are most likely low given that only an estimated 32% of rapes and attempted rapes are reported (Bureau of Justice Statistics 2016).

Men who hold more traditional gender roles view rape very differently than both women and less traditional men. The former tend to attribute more responsibility to the female victim of a rape, believe sex rather than power is the motivation for rape, and look less favorably on women who have been raped. Moreover, many males who are sexually aggressive toward women do not define their behavior as rape. This points to the stereotypes and misunderstandings that can occur because of gendered beliefs and attitudes. Rape causes deep and lasting problems for women victims as well as for men accused of rape because of "misreading" women's signals. Some college men define gang rape as a form of male bonding. To them, it is no big deal. The woman is just the object and instrument. Her identity is immaterial (Barry and Choksi 2013).

Many citizens and politicians see rape as an individualized, personal act, whereas social scientists tend to see it as a structural problem that stems from negative stereotypes of women, subservient positions of women in society, and patriarchal systems of power. Many social scientists believe that rape will not be substantially reduced unless our macho definitions of masculinity are changed (Jewkes et al. 2015; McEvoy and Brookings 2008). The recent public allegations of rape against many prominent men, including Harvey Weinstein and Russell Simmons, have put a spotlight on this problem.

Women of color in the United States also face multiple barriers on their "unlevel playing field." In the more than 15 million households headed by women, their wages are necessary for families to survive. Yet they are faced with a gender-based wage gap across industries, occupations, and education levels. "Women in the United States who work full time, year round are paid $10,876 less annually than men who work full time, year round" (National Partnership for Women and Families 2015:1). Table 9.3 shows the median weekly earnings of workers in the United States by race and sex and helps illustrate how racism and sexism can reinforce one another and lead to the "double marginalization" of women of color.

These examples illustrate that race, class, and gender have crosscutting lines that may affect one's status in society. Women of color can face the triple status determinants of being poor (class) women (gender) and of color (race or ethnicity). Lesbians and women identifying as bisexual, transgender, or queer face yet another form of oppression that intersects with the other three.

▼ TABLE 9.3

Median Weekly Earnings of Workers by Race and Sex and Women's Percentage of Men's Earnings, 2017

Race or Ethnicity	Male	Female	Women's Percentage of Men's Earnings
Asian American	$1,207	$903	75%
White	971	795	82
Black or African American	710	657	93
Hispanic or Latino	690	603	87

Source: Bureau of Labor Statistics 2017e.

SOCIOLOGY AROUND THE WORLD

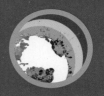

DOWRY AND DEATH: SOME DANGERS OF MARRIAGE

Dowry is a long-standing tradition in India, Bangladesh, Pakistan, Sri Lanka, and other mostly patriarchal countries. It involves the resources—the money, goods, or estate—that a woman brings to her husband or his family to support a marriage (*Black's Law Dictionary* 2015). When a son is married, the son's family receives a dowry. Though once a practice of the wealthy, it is now most common in poorer families where sons are often more "valuable" than daughters because they will receive a dowry, and a dowry can amount to the equivalent of a year's salary. The idea of dowry is one of reciprocity; that is, the wife's family is also contributing something to the well-being of the younger generation. The bride receives her inheritance at the time of the wedding rather than at the time of death of her parents.

Although dowry payments were officially prohibited in India by the Dowry Prohibition Act in 1961, this traditional practice is still widespread (Prasad and Srivastava 2016). Misunderstandings surrounding dowry agreements and payments can even result in a practice called bride burnings, in which brides are murdered by being pushed into cooking fires. These marriages are typically arranged between families and generally do not involve consent or love. It is a business deal. When the business deal fails or results in disagreement, the bride may be found soaked in kerosene or other flammable liquid and burned to death, usually in the kitchen. Authorities often rule these bride burnings as suicides. The husband can then seek another bride and another dowry. In 2016, 20 women were killed every day in dowry-related incidents. And these are only the reported cases—the actual death toll is much higher. Even when the crimes are reported, few of the perpetrators are found guilty and face punishment (Prasad and Srivastava 2016).

Women's groups in South Asia have formed to protest against both dowries and the problems they bring, especially to poor young women who have no power or options. Some women's shelters and burn wards in hospitals have been established. The Dowry Project, established in 1995, does research on bride burning. However, traditions are strong and poverty great; bride burnings are likely to continue until the penalties make it unprofitable and the guilty are punished.

THINKING SOCIOLOGICALLY

How have race, class, and gender intersected in your life and impacted your life chances? Do you think your experience is common among other members of your local community? Why or why not?

Sexual orientation, age, nationality, and other factors also have the effect of either diminishing or increasing minority status of specific women, and feminist theorists and activists are paying increasing attention to these intersections (Collins and Bilge 2016; Rothenberg 2014). Chapter 8 discussed the fact that race and class lines may be either crosscutting or parallel. In the case of gender, there are always crosscutting lines with race and social class. However, gender always affects one's prestige and privilege within that class or ethnic group (see Sociology Around the World at the top of this page). Thus, to get a full picture, these three variables—race, class, and gender—need to be considered simultaneously.

Gender, Sexuality, and Minority Status

We have already learned that sex, gender, and sexuality are complex concepts. **Heterosexism** is *an assumption that every person is heterosexual, legitimizing heterosexuality as the only normal lifestyle and marginalizing persons who do not identify as heterosexual* (Gender Equity Resource Center 2013). Heterosexism operates at all levels of society: micro, meso, and macro (Swank, Fahs, and Frost 2013).

Homophobia—*intense fear and hatred of homosexuality and homosexuals, whether male or female*—is highly correlated with and perhaps a cause of people holding traditional notions of gender and gender roles (S. Shaw and Lee 2005). This concept, which operates on the micro level, was coined by a psychologist who noted that intense hatred of LGBTQIA people is due to a personality disorder or illness (Weinberg 1972). LGBTQIA stands for

▲ A transsexual (Hijra) dances at a gathering in Bangladesh, where a group met in the capital to demand government action to provide legal protection from persecution. Hijras are treated as social outcasts but assigned a special status. They typically earn a living by singing, dancing, and other performances.

lesbian, gay, bisexual, transgender, queer or questioning, intersex, and asexual. Various other acronyms are used, such as LGBT or GLBTQ, but we will be consistent and inclusive by using LGBTQIA.

LGBTQIA people have existed in every society throughout time, but their treatment has varied considerably. They have been accepted and even required for certain positions at some times and places and rejected or outlawed in others. In some societies, gay and transgender individuals have been placed in a separate sexual category with special roles. For example, the Hijras in India and some other areas in South Asia are usually physiological males who have feminine gender identity. Many live in Hijra communities and have designated roles in Indian festivals and celebrations.

Some societies ignore the existence of LGBTQIA members of the community. Some consider them to have psychological illnesses or forms of depraved immorality. Some societies even consider these forms of sexuality a crime (as in the majority of African nations today and in most states in the United States during much of the 20th century). In at least eight countries in Africa and the Middle East—Afghanistan, Iran, Iraq, Mauritania, Pakistan, Saudi Arabia, Sudan, and Yemen—many of them following Sharia law, to be found guilty of homosexuality can result in the death penalty (International Lesbian, Gay, Bisexual, Trans and Intersex Association 2017). The reality is that deviation from a society's gender norms, such as attraction to a member of the same sex, may cause one to experience minority status (see Figure 9.5).

▼ FIGURE 9.5

Sexual Orientation Laws Around the World

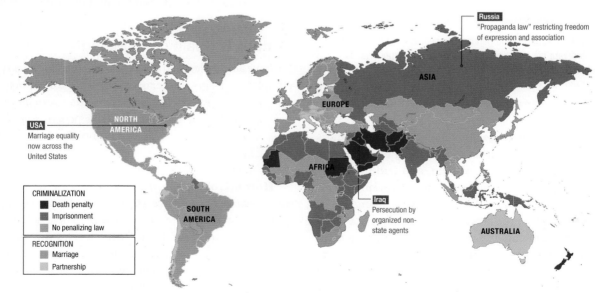

Source: International Lesbian, Gay, Bisexual, Trans and Intersex Association 2017.

Some members of the LGBTQIA community deviate from traditional notions of masculinity and femininity and therefore from significant norms of many societies. This may result in hostile reactions and stigma from the dominant group. Indeed, homosexual epithets are often used to reinforce gender conformity, particularly among men, and to intimidate anyone who would dare to be different from the norm. Because in many societies women economically depend on men, their status in society is typically based on their relationship with men. Therefore, lesbians—women attracted to other women—are in some instances perceived as a threat to men's power (Burn 2011; Ward and Edelstein 2016).

The mass media have begun to include LGBTQIA characters in films such as *Moonlight* (2016) *Behind the Candelabra* (2013), *Dallas Buyers Club* (2013), *In Bloom* (2013), *Beginners* (2011), *A Single Man* (2009), *Milk* (2008), *Shelter* (2007), and *Brokeback Mountain* (2005). In 2016 alone, 71 films featured gay themes (IMDb 2017). It is now commonplace to see positive images of gay (and, increasingly, transgender) characters on television shows (e.g., *Pretty Little Liars*, *Glee*, *Modern Family*, *Grey's Anatomy*, *Transparent*, and *Orange Is the New Black*). In addition, there are many well-known lesbian and gay news commentators and talk show hosts, including Anderson Cooper and Ellen DeGeneres, reflecting an increased level of acceptance of LGBTQIA people in many nations.

These media portrayals both reflected and helped drive attitudinal changes toward same-sex marriage. In 2001, 35% of U.S. citizens supported same-sex marriage and 57% opposed it; in 2016, 55% supported and 37% opposed (Pew Research Center 2018d). Figure 9.6 illustrates the percentage of U.S. adults who favor and oppose same-sex marriage in different years.

In June 2015, the United States Supreme Court ruled that all states must honor same-sex marriages. However, LGBTQIA people do not have many of the other rights that heterosexuals enjoy. One of the most important rights is the freedom to work. Despite indications of greater openness in attitudes, only 19 states and Washington, D.C., prohibit employers from firing workers based on their sexual or gender identity. Three more protect workers from being fired for their sexual (but not their gender) identity (Bellis 2016). Moreover, since the 2016 presidential election, when voices of intolerance gained traction, polls that measure comfort with LGBTQIA issues and discrimination faced by those who identify as LGBTQIA have shown, for the first time, a decline in comfort among non-LGBTQIA people and an

▼ FIGURE 9.6

Percentage of U.S. Adults Who Favor/Oppose Same-Sex Marriage

Public support for same-sex marriage reaches new milestone

% who _____ allowing gays and lesbians to marry legally

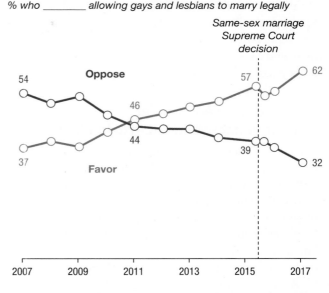

Source: "Support for Same-Sex Marriage Grows, Even Among Groups That Had Been Skeptical." Pew Research Center, Washington, D.C. (June 26, 2017), http://www.people-press.org/2017/06/26/support-for-same-sex-marriage-grows-even-among-groups-that-had-been-skeptical.

Note: The survey was conducted from June 8–18, 2017. The data for 2007–2015 are based on yearly averages. "Don't know" responses are not shown.

increase in discrimination against those who identify as LGBTQIA (GLAAD 2018).

So, although attitudes toward LGBTQIA rights have expanded in the past couple of decades, those who identify as LGBTQIA still face discrimination at the micro, meso, and macro levels of society. Note how each of these levels influences the others and how meso-level institutions such as government and religion control personal relationships. In sexuality and love, as in everything else, the micro, meso, and macro levels are connected in complex ways.

THINKING SOCIOLOGICALLY

What are the attitudes of your family members to rights for those who identify as LGBTQIA? What are some societal changes that have influenced their attitudes? Do older and younger members of your family share the same perspective on LGBTQIA issues? Why, or why not?

Costs and Consequences of Gender Stratification

The consequences of gender stratification affect every level of society. They impact life chances for individuals and how institutions, nations, and the global society function. As illustrated in the following examples, sex- and gender-based stratification limit individual development and cause problems in education, health, work, and other parts of the social world.

Psychological and Social Consequences: Micro-Level Implications

For both women and men, rigid gender stereotypes can be constraining. Individuals who hold highly sex-typed attitudes feel compelled to behave in stereotypical ways—ways consistent with the pictures they have in their heads of proper gender behavior (Kramer and Beutel 2014). However, rigid stereotypes and resulting sexism can limit our activities, behaviors, and perspectives. This hurts both men and women in their personal and work lives.

According to a recent study by the Centers for Disease Control and the University of Georgia, high masculinity in males sets up rigid standards for male behavior and has been correlated with anxiety, guilt, neuroses, and poor health outcomes, whereas less rigid masculine expectations are associated with emotional stability, sensitivity, warmth, and enthusiasm (Adams 2016). By confining people to certain ways of behaving, gender roles hurt both individuals and society by stifling creativity and allowing only certain people to carry out specific functions in society.

Results of Gender Role Expectations. Women in many societies are expected to be beautiful, youthful, and sexually interesting and interested, while at the same time preparing the food, caring for the children, keeping a clean and orderly home, bringing in money to help support the family, and being competent and successful in their careers. Multiple, sometimes contradictory, expectations for women can cause stress and even serious psychological problems. The resulting strain contributes to depression and certain health problems such as headaches, nervousness, and insomnia; thus, up to 40% more women than men develop mental health conditions. Women are more likely to report problems such as depression and anxiety. Men describe themselves as depressed or anxious less often but are more likely to turn to substance abuse or anger than women (Anxiety and Depression Association of America 2016; National Institute of Drug Abuse 2016).

Gender expectations also affect women's and men's self-concepts and body images. As noted earlier, beautiful images jump out at us from billboards, magazine covers, and TV and movie screens. Both women and men are affected negatively by these images. In a recent poll, only 25% of women and men felt very or extremely satisfied with their appearances and weight (Frederick et al. 2016). In the United States, close to 30 million people suffer from eating disorders, with 85% to 90% of those being female. Women are more likely to have eating disorders and often receive help, but men are less likely to seek help when they do have a problem, resulting in serious health problems including death (ANAD 2015; James 2013).

THINKING SOCIOLOGICALLY

How much time, energy, and money do you spend on your physical appearance? Why? From what socializing agents did you learn how to judge your physical appearance? Overall, how have those socializing agents impacted how you view yourself?

Men tend to die earlier than women, in part due to environmental, psychological, and social factors. Causes of death or illness in Global North countries such as heart disease, stroke, cirrhosis, cancers, accidents, and suicide are linked in part to the role expectations that males should appear tough, objective, ambitious, unsentimental, and unemotional—traits that require men to assume great responsibility and suppress their feelings (Tull 2012). So, gender expectations can have a substantial cost for men as well as women.

Societal Costs: Meso- and Macro-Level Implications

Gender stratification creates costs for societies around the world in a number of ways. *Poor educational achievement* of female children leads to the loss of human talents and resources, a serious cost for societies. *Social divisiveness*—us-versus-them thinking based on sex—can create alienation, if not hostility, and this can result in physical or emotional aggression, discrimination, and violence against women.

Human capital—the resources of the human population—is central to social prosperity in societal systems. Yet resistance to expanding women's public sphere and professional roles is often strong. For example, 62.5% of

Japanese women participate in the labor force, compared with 80.6% of men. If women's participation matched that of men's, the country's working population would grow by 7 million people, raising output. However, many women are reluctant to take on additional responsibilities because of the expectations at work, with family, and the lack of childcare. As an aging population, Japan is losing workers and the economy is showing the strain. Working conditions in Japan and Korea are not always favorable for women. Those countries have among the highest gender wage gaps in the world at 26.6% and 36.6%, respectively, and the largest wage gaps among Global North countries (OECD 2015b). *The Global Gender Gap Report* ranked Japan 114 out of 144 countries in terms of gender disparities at work (World Economic Forum 2017). Although Japanese women score higher in science than men and are almost half of university graduates, few can break through the glass ceiling they face in the job market. Among the 36 nations with the largest economies, Japan has the fewest women in senior corporate positions (*Wall Street Journal* 2016).

Changing Gender Stratification and Social Policy

Women in factories around the globe face dangerous conditions and low pay. Sweatshops exist because poor women in rapidly urbanizing Global South nations have few other options for work and because people in rich countries want to buy the cheap products that perpetuate the multinational corporate system. For example, over 1 million Mexicans work in maquiladoras (foreign-owned manufacturing and assembly plants) in Mexican border towns for very low wages.

These maquiladoras are owned by U.S., European, and Japanese conglomerates and hire primarily unskilled young women at very low wages. In 2017, the average seamstress in a maquiladora made $147.00 a week (including benefits), for a shift from 6:00 a.m. to 3:45 p.m., 5 days a week (Jan 2017). Maquiladora workers produce electronic equipment, clothing, plastics, furniture, appliances, and auto parts, most of which are shipped to the United States (Jan 2017). The maquiladoras are but one example of multinational corporations based in the Global North using workers in the Global South to make their products for very little money and in harsh working conditions.

One result of companies offering low wages and poor working conditions is the exploitation of (mostly female) factory workers in Global South nations. Another is the loss of jobs and lower pay for workers in the United States. So the "race to the bottom" by multinationals (seeking the lowest price for labor) is affecting earnings of men and women in the United States. We live in an interconnected world.

What can be done about the abusive treatment of women workers around the world? This is a tough issue: Governments have passed legislation to protect workers, but governments also want the jobs and tax dollars that multinational corporations bring and therefore do little to enforce regulations. International labor standards are also difficult to enforce because multinational corporations are so large and located in many parts of the world. Trade unions have had little success attracting workers to join because companies squash their recruiting efforts immediately.

One way activist groups protest for fair wages and conditions for workers is to adopt practices that have worked for other groups facing discrimination in the past. Consider the following strategies used by groups to combat unfair labor practices: holding nonviolent protests, including sit-down strikes and walkouts; encouraging

© UNESCO/Dominique Rogers

▲ Women in Thailand produce shoes for extremely low pay. These jobs are better than no employment at all, but before pressures from Global North societies changed their cultures, most people were able to feed their families on farms in small villages.

EMPOWERING MARGINALIZED GROUPS

My projects, many in India, include studying gender inequality, social movements, and how those who are disadvantaged organize to claim basic needs and rights, including ending violence against women and reducing HIV risks.

My initial research examined organized action by Dalit (the lowest caste, sometimes referred to as the "untouchables") groups in India as they challenged caste-based prejudice and the power of the dominant upper castes. I focused on strategies for empowerment of rural women and on their experiences during the establishment of national-level Dalit organizing. I also looked at the underrepresentation of Dalits in the Indian women's movement and the rise of a Dalit women's movement. The efforts to reach across and mobilize along class and caste lines going on in India have broad implications for movement organizing in many countries.

In Karnataka, a state in southern India, my research focused on a specific government initiative for rural Dalit women, the *Mahila Samakhya* program. I detailed the consciousness-raising effects of the gains in social power for these poor, mostly illiterate, women. For instance, as they recognized the importance of being able to read and write, the women's collectives demanded interventions such as adult literacy night programs. Recognizing the intersections between social and economic power for women's empowerment, this research has evolved into an action and research project promoting the economic power of these women by training them to start small businesses.

Power as a theme continues in my project on intimate partner violence and HIV prevention. I examine two major aspects of HIV prevention efforts: (1) how the structure and leadership of community organizations (COs) impact their risk reduction efforts and (2) the mechanisms used by high-risk groups to cope with intimate partner violence and to reduce risk of HIV. High-risk groups in India are women in sex work, transgender people, and men having sex with men.

My research shows that COs serve as spaces for sharing experiences and information that can be vital for the well-being of those most at risk from HIV, such as women in sex work and transgender people. They share advice grounded in experience about how to cope with physical violence and verbal and mental abuse from partners and husbands. My findings on COs help policymakers and nonprofits learn from members of marginalized groups about how they cope with intimate partner violence and integrate that information into policymaking to reduce the risk of HIV.

Sociology provides me with theoretical and methodological tools to gather and analyze data on the lives of poor women, women in sex work, and transgender people. It also drives me to consider how my own background influences my research. By using these sociological tools, I show how marginal people can gain power and push policymakers to make effective policies.

★ ★ ★ ★ ★ ★ ★

Mangala Subramaniam is Professor of Sociology & Butler Chair and Director of the Susan Bulkeley Butler Center for Leadership Excellence in the Office of the Provost, Purdue University.

---

companies to help the communities in which their factories are located; using the Internet to carry the message to others; carrying out boycotts against companies that mistreat employees; employing the arts, storytellers, and teachers to mobilize resistance; and building on traditions of student, community, and religious activism (Maquila Solidarity Network 2017). Most of these strategies require organized movements, but such efforts may antagonize the companies so much that they move to other countries. It is a delicate balance. To be successful, the fair labor effort must be as globalized as the corporations whose practices they wish to impact. Other organized efforts to empower marginalized people, including women, take place across the world. The Sociologists in Action at the top of this page provides an example of how sociologists can assist in this work.

THINKING SOCIOLOGICALLY

Take a look at the clothing in your closet and drawers. Figure out where it was made by looking at the nations listed on the tags. Chances are, if it is sold by a global corporation and produced in a Global South nation, it was made by workers in a sweatshop. Would you be willing to pay more for clothing to help ensure that those who make it secure a higher wage? Why or why not?

At women's conferences around the world, policymakers debate how to create solutions to women's problems. Most United Nations member countries have at least fledgling women's movements fighting for the improved status of women and their families. These movements attempt to change laws and other social practices that negatively impact women. One example is the Better Factories movement in Cambodia (Kampuchea), sponsored by the International Labour Organization, that works to address worker problems, especially those of garment workers (International Labour Organization 2017). Such efforts are but one example of how organized people can impact society and work together to address gender discrimination. In addition, some sociologists have dedicated their professional careers to using sociological skills to help women gain more power and access to resources.

And why should we care? The status and treatment of women affects not only the individuals but their families, husbands and partners, children, and community. Supporting women is supporting communities.

Inequality based on class, race, ethnicity, and gender takes place at all levels of analysis and is often entrenched at the meso level within the institutions found in every society—family, education, religion, government, economics, and health care. Complex societies incorporate other institutions as well, including science and technology, sports, and the military. We turn next to a discussion of institutions in our social world.

WHAT HAVE WE LEARNED?

At the beginning of this chapter, we asked how being born female or male affects our lives. Because sex is a primary variable on which societies are structured and stratified, our sex affects our public- and private-sphere activities, our health, our ability to practice religion or participate in political life, our opportunities for education, and just about everything we do.

KEY POINTS

- Whereas sex is biological, notions of gender identity and gender roles are socially constructed, learned, and vary across cultures and time periods. They confine people of all genders to roles that constrain their choices and opportunities in life.

- Notions of gender are first taught in micro settings—in the intimacy of the home—but reinforced at the meso and macro levels.

- Although *she* may go first in micro-level social encounters (served first in a restaurant or the first to enter a doorway), *he* goes first in meso and macro settings—with the doors open wider for men to enter leadership positions in organizations and institutions.

- Greater access to resources at the meso level makes it easier to have entrée to macro-level positions, but it also influences the respect one receives in micro settings.

- Much of the gender stratification today is unconscious and unintended—not caused by angry or bigoted men who purposefully oppress women. Gender inequality is rooted in institutionalized privilege and disprivilege.

- Various social theories shed different light on the issues of inequality in gender roles assigned to various sexes.

- For modern postindustrial societies, there is a high cost for treating women like a minority group—individually for the people who experience it and collectively for the society, which loses many potential contributions from women. Gender inequality hurts both men and women.

DISCUSSION QUESTIONS

1. Describe some of the ways socializing agents (e.g., family, peers, the media, religion, and schools) encouraged you to conform to traditional gender norms. Do you think you will encourage (or have you encouraged) your own children to conform to traditional gender norms? Why or why not?

2. Give two examples of side-effect gender discrimination that lead to economic inequality between men and women.

3. How does gender socialization influence who runs for office and for whom we vote? How are female politicians treated by the media, compared with male politicians? How has that impacted your own perception of female politicians?

4. How does gender discrimination harm society? What could be done on your campus to improve the status of women or men? How might you join these efforts?

5. How do strict gender roles and gender inequality hurt men?

6. What are your career goals? Do they follow traditional gender roles? Why or why not? How has your gender socialization impacted your career plans?

7. More women than men are now in college. How do you think this fact will impact gender roles on campus and in the larger society?

KEY TERMS

Gender 257

gender roles 257

glass ceiling 267

heterosexism 277

homophobia 277

sex 255

sexuality 256

transgender 256

CONTRIBUTING TO OUR SOCIAL WORLD: WHAT CAN WE DO?

At the Local (Micro) Level

- Schedule an interview with the director or other staff members of the human resources or affirmative action offices on your campus to learn about your school's policies regarding gender discrimination. What procedures exist for hiring? Do women and men receive the same salaries, wages, and benefits for equal work? Explore the possibility of working as a volunteer or an intern in the office, specifically in the area of gender equity.

At the Organizational or Institutional (Meso) Level

- *The National Organization for Women (NOW)* is the world's leading advocate for gender equity. It deals with issues such as reproductive rights, legislative outreach, economic justice, ending sex discrimination, and promoting diversity. The organization's website, www.now.org, lists contact information, state and regional affiliates, and NOW jobs and internships (now.org/about/job-and-internships).

- *Sociologists for Women in Society (SWS)*, an organization that "works to improve women's lives through advancing and supporting feminist sociological research, activism and scholars," provides many resources for students. SWS provides students with scholarships, opportunities to be

mentored, and an award to recognize students who improve the lives of women through activism. Visit the SWS website at www.socwomen.org.

- *The NEW Leadership National Network at the Center for American Women and Politics* is an annual 6-day residential summer program that "educates college women about the important role that politics plays in their lives and encourages them to become effective leaders in the political arena." To learn more about NEW Leadership and to find out how to apply to the program, go to www.cawp.rutgers.edu/education_training/NEW_Leadership/overview.

At the National or Global (Macro) Level

- *MADRE*, an international women's rights organization, works primarily in less-developed countries. You can find numerous opportunities for working on issues of justice, human rights, education, and health on its website at www.madre.org.

- The *#MeToo movement* has had a major impact on how the larger community views violence against women, especially in the workplace. What began as a grassroots effort has turned into a worldwide movement to end sexual violence. You can join the movement and find many resources for victims of sexual harassment and domestic violence at www.metoomvmt.org.

- *Equality Now*, an international nongovernmental organization, provides many venues for those interested in promoting equality for women and curbing gender violence and discrimination. You can find out more about this organization at www.equalitynow.org.

- *The United Nations Inter-Agency Network on Women and Gender Equality* works on global issues, including violence against women and women's working conditions. Its WomenWatch website at www.un.org/womenwatch contains news, information, and ideas for contributing to the worldwide campaign for women's rights.

PART IV

INSTITUTIONS

Picture a house, a *structure* in which you live. Within that house are the actions and activities that bring the house alive—the *processes*. Flip a switch, and the lights go on because the house is well-wired. Adjust the thermostat, and the room becomes more comfortable, as the *structural features* of furnace or air-conditioning systems operate. If the structural components of the plumbing and water heating systems work, you can take a hot shower when you turn the knob. These actions, the *processes*, taken within the structure make the house livable. If something breaks down, you need to get it fixed so that everything works smoothly.

Institutions, too, provide a structure for society, a framework that promotes stability. Processes are the action dimension within institutions—the activities that take place. They include the interactions among people; socialization in families, schools, and religious institutions; decision-making in organizations and political institutions; and other actions in each society and the world. These processes are often dynamic and can lead to significant change within the structure—like a decision about whether new homeowners should remodel their kitchen. Institutions are meso-level structures because they are larger in scope than the face-to-face social interactions of the micro level, and yet they are smaller than the nation or the global system. However, each institution includes processes at all levels of analysis, micro to macro, as we shall see from the examples in the following chapters.

Institutions such as family, education, religion, politics, economics, and health care include certain necessary actions, patterns, and expectations that differ in each society. They are interdependent and mutually supportive, just as the plumbing, heating system, and electricity in a house work together to make a home functional. However, a breakdown in one institution or conflict over limited resources between institutions affects the whole society, just as a malfunction in the electrical system may shut the furnace off and cool down the water heater.

Importance of Institutions

Institutions are not anything concrete that you can see, hear, touch, or smell. The concept of institutions is a way of describing and understanding how society works. For example, the institution of family meets certain needs found in almost all societies. Family as an institution refers to the behavior of thousands of people, which—taken as a whole—forms a social structure. Think of your own family. It has unique ways of interacting and raising children, but it is part of a community with many families. Those many families, in turn, are part of a national set of patterned behaviors we call the family. This pattern meets the basic needs of the society for producing and socializing new members and providing an emotionally supportive environment. Table IV.1 illustrates the impact of social institutions in society at each level of analysis.

Institutions do not dictate exactly how you will carry out the roles within your individual family. However, they do specify certain needs families will meet and statuses (e.g., spouse/partner, parent, child) that relate to each other in certain mutually caring ways and fill certain seminegotiable roles. An institution provides a blueprint (much like a local builder needs a blueprint to build a house). In your local version of the institution, you may make a few modifications to the plans to meet your individual micro-level needs. Still, through this society-encompassing structure and interlocking set of statuses, the basic needs for individuals at the micro level and for society at the macro level are met.

Institutions, then, *are organized, patterned, and enduring sets of social structures that provide guidelines for behavior and help each society meet its basic survival needs. Although institutions operate mostly at the meso level, they also act to integrate micro and macro levels of society.* Let us look more deeply at this definition.

1. *Organized, patterned, and enduring sets of social structures* means that institutions refer to a complex set of groups or organizations, statuses within those groups, and norms of conduct that guide people's behavior. These structures ensure socialization of children, education of the young, a sense of meaning in life, companionship, and production and distribution of needed goods (e.g., food, clothing, automobiles, cell phones, and computers) for the members of the society. If this patterned behavior were missing, these needs might not be addressed. At the local level, we may go to a neighborhood school and attend religious services at a congregation we favor. These are local organizations—*franchises*, if you will—of much more encompassing structures (education and religion) that provide guidelines for education or address issues of meaning of life for an enormous number of people. The Catholic church in your town, for example, is a local franchise of an organization transnational in scope and global in its concerns.

2. *Guidelines for behavior* help people know how to conduct themselves and obtain basic needs in their society. Individuals and local organizations carry out the institutional guidelines in each culture, but the exact ways they do so vary by locality. In local franchises of the political system, people know how to govern and how to solve problems at the local level because of larger norms and patterns provided by the political institution. Individual men and women operate a local hospital or clinic (a local franchise of the medical institution) that follows a national blueprint of how to provide health care. The specific activities of a local school, likewise, abide by the guidelines and purposes of the larger goals of "formal education" in a given nation.

3. *Meeting basic survival needs* is a core component of institutions because societies must meet needs of their members; otherwise the members die or the society collapses. Institutions, then, are the structures that support social life in a large bureaucratized society. Common to all industrialized societies are family, education, health care, economics, politics, and religion.

4. *Integrating micro and macro levels of society* is also critical because one of the collective needs of society is coherence and stability—including some integration among the various levels of society. Institutions help provide that integration for the entire social system. They do this by meeting needs at the local franchise level (e.g., food at the grocery store, education at the local school, and health care at the local clinic) while, at the same time, coordinating national and global organizations and patterns.

If all this sounds terribly abstract, that is because institutions *are* abstractions. You cannot touch institutions, yet they are as real as air, love, or happiness. In fact, in the modern world institutions are as necessary to life as is air, and they help provide love and happiness that make life worth living.

Impact of Institutions at Each Level of Analysis

	Family	Education	Economic Systems	Political Systems	Religion	Health Care
Micro (local "franchises" of institutions)	Your family; local parenting group; local Parents Without Partners; county family counseling clinic	Your teacher; local neighborhood school; local school board	Local businesses; local chamber of commerce; local labor union chapter	Neighborhood crime watch program; local city or county council	Your local religious study group or congregation	Your doctor and nurse; local clinic; local hospital
Meso (institutions, complex organizations, ethnic subcultures, state/provincial systems)	The middle-class family; the Hispanic family; the Jewish family	State/provincial department of education; American Federation of Teachers*	State/provincial offices of economic development; United Auto Workers*	State/provincial governments; national political parties; each state or province's supreme court	National denominations/movements (e.g., United Methodist Church or American Reform Judaism)	HMOs; Minnesota Nurses Association; American Medical Association
Macro (national and global social systems and trends)	Kinship and marriage structures, such as monogamy versus polygamy; global trends in family, such as choice of partners rather than arranged marriages	National education system; United Nations Girls' Education Initiative	Spread of capitalism around the world; World Bank; International Monetary Fund; World Trade Organization	National government; United Nations; World Court; G-7 (most powerful seven nations in the world)	Global faith-based movements and structures; National Council of Churches; World Council of Churches; World Islamic Council; World Jewish Congress	National health care system; World Health Organization; transnational pandemics

* These organizations are national in scope and membership, but they are considered meso level here because they are complex organizations *within* the nation.

Development of Modern Institutions

If we go all the way back to early hunting and gathering societies, there were no meso or macro levels of social experience. People lived their lives in one or two villages, and although a spouse might come from another village or one might move to a spouse's clan, there was no national or state governance, and certainly no awareness of a global social system. In those earlier times, family and community provided whatever education was needed, produced and distributed goods, paid homage to a god or gods, and solved conflicts and disputes through a system of familial (often patriarchal) power distribution. One social unit, the family, served multiple functions, from education to religion to health care and an economic base.

As societies have become more complex and differentiated, multiple levels of the social system and various new institutions have emerged. Sociology textbooks in the 1950s identified only five basic institutions: family, economic systems, political systems, religion, and education (with compulsory formal education not established in every state until the 20th century). These five institutions were believed to be the core structures that met the essential needs of individuals and societies in an orderly way.

Soon thereafter, *medicine* moved from the family and small-town doctors and became another institution. Medicine has become bureaucratized in hospitals, medical labs, professional organizations, and other complex structures that provide health care. *Science* is also now something more than flying kites in thunderstorms in one's backyard, as Ben Franklin did. It is a complex system that provides training, funding, research institutes, peer review, and professional associations to support empirical research. New information is the lifeblood of an information-based or postindustrial society. Science, discussed in Chapter 16, is now an essential institution. Although it is arguable whether sports is an essential component for social viability, sports has clearly become highly structured in the past 50 years, and many sociologists consider sports an institution. The mass media and military also fall into the category of institutions in more advanced countries. When considering whether a structure constitutes an institution, ask yourself the following questions: (a) Does the structure meet the basic needs of the society for survival? (b) Has it become a complex organization providing routinized structures and guidelines for society? (c) Is it national or even global in its scope, while also having pervasive local (micro) impact?

THINKING SOCIOLOGICALLY

Using Table IV.1, try placing other modern-day institutions (e.g., mass media, science, sports, the military) in the framework. Where do organizations you belong to fit into the institutional structure?

Connections Among Institutions

The Great Recession of 2007–2009 illustrates how institutions can impact one another. Many individuals in the United States became unemployed as credit dried up and companies reduced their payrolls. Their families then also faced various stresses that come with an unemployed breadwinner. In turn, the government faced pressure because citizens expected political leaders to intervene and find ways to bring the nation out of an economic recession. At the same time, religious congregations experienced increased demands at their food banks and soup kitchens *and* declining contributions from religious congregants who lost their jobs. Funding for schools also suffered during the Great Recession, because tax revenues fell.

Connections among meso-level institutions are a common refrain in this book. As you read these chapters, notice that change in one institution affects others. Sociologists studying the legal system, mass media, medicine, science, sports, or the military as institutions raise similar questions and want to know how these institutions influence the micro, meso, and macro levels of a society. We begin with the family—an institution that is such an intimate part of our lives and is often called the most basic institution of society.

CHAPTER 10

© Getty/Chicago Tribune/Contributor

FAMILY

....

Partner Taking, People Making, and Contract Breaking

▲ Through the institution of the family, we take partners and "make people"—both biologically and socially speaking. Although families can experience conflict, violence, and contract breaking, they can also give us a sense of belonging, love, and great joy.

MICRO

ME (AND MY FAMILY)

**LOCAL ORGANIZATIONS
AND COMMUNITY**
Family is the basic unit
of action within a community.

MESO

**NATIONAL ORGANIZATIONS,
INSTITUTIONS, AND ETHNIC
SUBCULTURES**
Families socialize children into social
roles so they can function in society.

MACRO

SOCIETY
Governments develop
family policies.

GLOBAL COMMUNITY
International organizations
support families and
children.

WHAT WILL YOU LEARN IN THIS CHAPTER?

This chapter will help you to do the following:

10.1 Discuss how definitions of families are socially constructed and change over time

10.2 Give examples of how each major theory approaches family

10.3 Explain how new families start in most Global North societies

10.4 Diagram and explain how the institution of family interacts with other institutions

10.5 Discuss why different societies react differently to same-sex marriage

10.6 Describe global patterns and policies that affect families and give examples

Micro: Small groups and local communities	How do people find life partners?
Meso: National institutions, complex organizations, and ethnic groups	Why is family seen as the core or basic institution of society?
Macro: National and global systems	What, if anything, should be done by government to strengthen families? What are some common and different traits among families around the world?

A Guatemalan family in a rural village prepares for the day's chores. Maria Hernandez prepares the breakfast as Miguel cares for the animals. The children fix their lunches of tortillas, beans, rice, and banana to take to school. When they return home, they will help with the farm chores. They live together with their extended family, several generations of blood relatives living side by side.

It is morning in Sweden. Anders and Karin Karlsson are rushing to get to their offices on time. They hurry their children, a 12-year-old son and an 8-year-old daughter, out the door to school. All will return in the evening after a full day of activities and join together for the evening meal. In this dual-career family, common in many postindustrial societies, both parents are working professionals.

The gossip at the village water well this day in Niger, Africa, is about the rich local merchant, Abdul, who has just taken his fourth and last wife. She is a beautiful girl of 15 from a neighboring village. She is expected to help with household chores and bear children for his already extensive family unit. Several of the women at the well live in affluent households where the husband has more than one wife.

▲ In recent decades, the definition of family has broadened in many areas of the world to include families with parents of the same sex, like these two families.

Tom and Henry in Minneapolis, Minnesota, recently adopted Ty into their family. The married couple share custody of the 2-year-old boy. In 2016, laws prohibiting same-sex couples from adopting were struck down, and adoption by same-sex couples is now legal throughout the United States (Reilly 2016). Tom has chosen to stay home with Ty until he starts kindergarten. It's a stretch, but they are able to make ends meet on just Henry's salary.

Dora, a single mom with two children, lives next door to Tom, Henry, and Ty. She bundles the children off to school before heading to her job. After school, she has an arrangement with other neighbors to care for the children until she gets home.

What do these very different scenes have in common? Each describes a family, yet not everyone or every society agrees on what constitutes a family. Only groupings officially recognized as families by governments tend to receive hundreds of privileges and rights, such as health insurance and inheritance rights; therefore, each society defines what a family is for legal, economic, and political purposes. In this chapter, we discuss changing characteristics of families, theoretical perspectives on the family, family dynamics, the family as an institution, family issues, and policies regarding marriage and family dissolution.

Families come in many shape, size, and color combinations. We begin our exploration of this institution with a discussion of what family *is*.

What Is a Family?

Who defines what constitutes a family: individuals, the government, or religious groups? Is a family just Ma, Pa, and the kids? Let us consider several definitions. The U.S. Census Bureau defines *family* as "a group of two people or more (one of whom is the householder) related by birth, marriage, or adoption and residing together; all such people (including related subfamily members) are considered as members of one family" (U.S. Census Bureau 2015b). Thus, a family in the United States might be composed of siblings, cousins, a grandparent and grandchild, or other groupings. Some religious groups and governments define family as a mother, father, and their children, whereas others include several spouses, multiple generations, or several siblings living under the same roof.

The definition and the typical composition of family change as societies and social norms change. The traditional composition of married parents with a mother who tends to the household, a father who brings in most of the income, and biological children living in an intact family compose just under 70% of U.S. families today, with 22% of children living with a single mother and 4% living with a single father. Figure 10.1 illustrates the change in family structures from 1960 to 2017 (U.S. Census Bureau 2017d).

As noted earlier, the family is often referred to as the most basic institution of any society. First, it is the place where we learn many of the norms for functioning in the larger society. Second, most of us spend our lives in the security of a family. People are born and raised in families, and many will die in a family setting. Through good and bad, sickness and health, most families provide for our needs, both physical and psychological. Therefore, families meet our primary, most basic needs. Third,

major life events—marriages, births, graduations, promotions, anniversaries, religious ceremonies, holidays, funerals—take place within the family context and are celebrated with family members. In short, family is where we invest the most emotional energy and spend much of our leisure time.

The family is capable of satisfying a range of social needs: belonging to a group, economic support, education or training, raising children, religious socialization, resolution of conflicts, and so forth. One cannot conceive of the economic system providing emotional support for each individual or the political system providing socialization and personalized care for each child. Only family can carry out these functions and those of other institutions (Benokraitis 2015).

In families, we *make people*—not just biologically but socially, through the socialization process. In the family, we take an organism that has the potential to be fully human, and we mold this tiny bit of humanity into a caring, compassionate, productive person—at least that is the ideal plan.

In Global North societies, most individuals are born and raised in the **family of orientation**, *the family into which we are born or adopted*. This family consists of

▼ FIGURE 10.1

Living Arrangements of Children Under 18 in the United States: 1960–2017

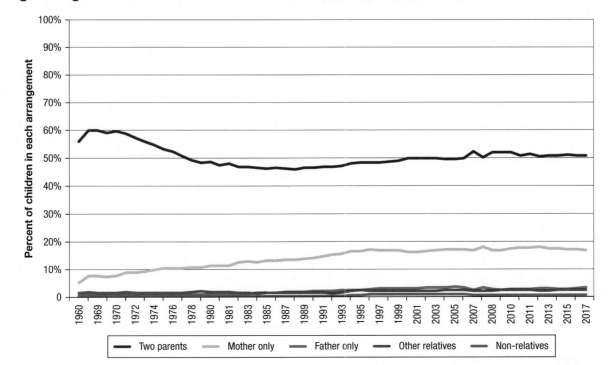

Source: U.S. Census Bureau, Decennial Census, 1960, and Current Population Survey, Annual Social and Economic Supplements, 1968 to 2017.

▲ Living in the mountains of Nepal, the Chepang family lives a simple life, but the children learn many survival skills, and their most basic needs, physical and psychological, are met.

parent(s) and possibly sibling(s). Individuals receive early socialization and learn the language, norms, core values, attitudes, and behaviors of the community and society within families. A **family of procreation** is *the family we create ourselves.* We find a life mate and/or have children. The transmission of values, beliefs, and attitudes from our family of orientation to our family of procreation generally preserves and stabilizes the family system. Because family involves emotional investment, we have strong feelings about what form it should take.

Whether we consider families at micro, meso, or macro levels, sociological theories can help us understand the role of families in our social world.

Theoretical Perspectives on Family

Things on the family front are not always a fairy tale. Consider the case of Felice, a young mother locked into a marriage that provides her with little satisfaction. For the first year of marriage, Felice tried to please her husband, Tad, but gradually he seemed to drift further away. He began to spend evenings out. Sometimes, he came home drunk and yelled at or hit her. Felice became pregnant shortly after their marriage and had to quit her job. This increased the financial pressure on Tad, and they fell behind in paying the bills.

Then came the baby. They were both ecstatic at first, but Tad soon reverted to his old patterns. Felice felt trapped. She was afraid and embarrassed to go to her parents. They had warned her against marrying so young without finishing school, but she was in love and had gone against their wishes. She and Tad had moved away from their hometown, so she was out of touch with her old support network and had few friends in her new neighborhood. Her religious beliefs told her she should

try to stick it out, suggesting that the trouble was partly her fault for not being a "good enough wife." Lacking a job or skills to get a job that paid more than minimum wage, she could not live on her own with a baby. She thought of marriage counseling, but Tad refused to consider this and did not seem interested in trying to work out the problems. He had his reasons for behaving the way he did, including feeling overburdened with the pressure of caring for two dependents. The web of this relationship seems difficult to untangle, but sociological theories provide us with some tools to analyze such family dynamics.

Micro-Level Theories of Family and the Meso-Level Connection

To understand our own families it is useful to think about how our familiar micro-level theories—symbolic interaction and rational choice—help give us new understanding and perspectives.

Symbolic Interaction Theory. Symbolic interaction theory can help us understand Felice's situation by explaining how individuals learn their particular behavior patterns and ways of thinking. We create relationship roles through socialization and interaction with others. Felice, for example, developed certain expectations and patterns of behavior by modeling her experiences on her family of orientation (the family into which she was born), observing others, and developing expectations based on her initial interactions with Tad. Tad developed a different set of expectations for his role of husband, modeled after his father's behavior. His father had visited bars after work, had affairs with other women, and expected "his woman" to be at home and to accept this without question.

Two related concepts in symbolic interaction theory (introduced in Chapters 2 and 3) are the *social construction of reality* and the *definition of a situation.* What significant others around us accept as ordinary or acceptable shapes our definition of normal family relations. Children who grow up in homes where adults argue or hit one another or shout at one another with sarcastic put-downs may come to think of this behavior as typical or a normal part of family life. They simply have known no other type of interaction. Thus, without seeing other options than what they have learned, they may create a similar pattern of family interaction in their own families of procreation (the families they create). Concepts such as *family*, *partner*, or *parenting* may mean something very different to the person sitting beside you in class or to a potential mate.

One of the great challenges of newlyweds is meshing their ideas about division of labor, family holidays, discipline of children, spousal relations, and economic necessities, along with their assumptions about being in a committed relationship. A new couple socially constructs a new relationship, blending the models of life partnership from their own childhood homes or creating an entirely new model as they jointly define their relationship. Furthermore, the meaning of one's identity and one's obligations to others change dramatically when one becomes a parent. The mother and father have to work out what this means for each of them, for their interactions with each other and for their interactions with the child. This brings us back to a central premise of symbolic interaction: Humans are active agents who create their social structure through interaction. We not only learn family patterns, we *do family* just as we *do gender* in the sense that we create roles and relationships and pass them on to others as "normal."

Institutional arrangements at the meso level shape our individual identities and family patterns. For example, religious bodies, legal systems, and other government entities define the roles of "wife" and "husband." Each U.S. state actually spells out in its legal codes the duties of husbands and wives. Those who do not fulfill these duties may be in "neglect of duty." These family roles are embedded at the macro level in ways that many people do not realize.

Rational Choice Theory. Rational choice theory can also shed light on Felice's situation, helping us understand why people seek close relationships and why they stay in abusive relationships. As discussed in Chapter 2, rational choice theory asserts that individuals evaluate the costs and rewards of engaging in interaction. We look for satisfaction of our needs—emotional, sexual, and economic—through interaction. Patterns in the family are reinforced to the extent that exchanges benefit members. When the costs outweigh the rewards, the relationship is unlikely to continue. Women in abusive relationships weigh the costs of suffering abuse against the rewards of having social

legitimacy, income, social and religious acceptance, a home, and companionship. Many factors enter into the complex balance of the exchange. Indeed, costs and benefits of various choices are often established by meso-level organizations and institutions: insurance programs, health care options, and legal regulations that make partnering decisions easy or difficult.

This cost-benefit consideration also includes whether there is *reciprocity*—"if you scratch my back, I'll scratch yours." Rational choice theorists maintain that humans will not extend assistance to others unless they think there will be a payback and some balance in the relationship. If people feel like they give more than they receive, the relationship turns sour. This pattern is no less true of family relationships than any other human interactions. Humans are ultimately seen in this perspective as focused on self-interest.

According to rational choice theorists, an exchange calculation shapes even the mate selection process. People estimate their own assets—physical, intellectual, social, and economic—and try to find the "best deal" they can make, someone with at least the level of resources they possess, even if those assets are in different areas. If Shannon marries Dana, who has more assets, this gives Dana more power and forces Shannon to put up with things that equal partners would not tolerate. As noted in Chapter 5, this is called *the principle of least interest*—the person with least interest has more power because the person with most interest (most invested in the relationship) is likely to give in when there is conflict rather than jeopardize the relationship. Cost/benefit, according to this view, affects the forming of the relationship and the power and influence in the relationship.

Meso- and Macro-Level Theories of the Family

Structural-Functional Theory. Why do all societies have families? One answer is that families fulfill certain essential purposes, or functions, that enhance survival of individuals and societies. Traditionally, there have been at least six ways the family has contributed to the stability of the society, according to structural-functional theory.

Sexual Regulation. Physically speaking, any adult human could engage in sex with any other human. However, in practice, no society allows total sexual freedom. Every society attempts to regulate the sexual behavior of its members in accordance with its own particular values. This is most often accomplished through marriage. Regulation ensures that this strong biological drive is satisfied in an orderly way that does not create ongoing disruption, conflict, or jealousy. Certain people are "taken" and "off limits" (Ward and Edelstein 2016).

Reproduction and Replacement. Societies need children to replace members who die, leave, or are incapacitated. Reproduction is controlled to keep family lineage and inheritance clear. Parent and caretaker roles are clearly defined and reinforced in many societies by ceremonies: baby showers, birth announcements, christenings, and naming ceremonies that welcome the child as a member of the family. In some places, such as New Guinea, procreation is so important that a young girl who has had children before marriage is more desirable because she has established her fertility. This practice is possible in matriarchal societies where the child is absorbed into the female side of the family.

Socialization. The family is the main training ground for children. In our families, we begin to learn values and norms, proper behavior, roles, and language. In most societies, schools, religious organizations, and other institutions carry out later socialization, but the family remains the most important initial socializing agent to prepare us for roles in society. Parents do most of the socializing in the family, but siblings, grandparents, and other relatives are important socializing agents as well.

Emotional Support and Protection. Families are the main source of love and belonging in many societies, giving us a sense of identity, security, protection, and safety from harm. The family is one place where people may experience unqualified acceptance and feelings of being cherished. Stories of runaway youth and incidents of family violence and neglect are reminders that this function is not always successfully provided in families. Still, the family is usually the environment most capable of meeting this need.

Status Assignment. Our family of orientation is the most important determinant of our social status, life chances, and lifestyles. It strongly affects our educational opportunities, access to health care, religious and political affiliations, and values. In fact, in societies with caste systems, the ascribed position at birth is generally the position at death. Although, in class societies, individuals may achieve new social statuses, our birth positions and the early years of socialization have a strong impact throughout life on who and what we are.

Economic Support. Historically, the family was a unit of production—running a farm, a bakery, or a cobbler shop. Although this function is still predominant in many societies, the economic function carried out in individual families has pretty much disappeared in most Global North families. However, the family remains an economic unit of consumption. Who paid for your clothing, food, and other needs as you were growing up? Who helps many of you pay your college tuition and expenses? Taxing agencies, advertising and commercial enterprises, workplaces, and other social organizations also treat the family as the primary economic unit.

Functional theorists ask about the consequences of what takes place in the family for other parts of the society. They note that the micro-level processes of the family meet structural needs of society at the meso and macro levels (e.g., in the United States, the need for motivated workers who thrive on competition). Each part of the system, according to functionalists, works with other parts to create a functioning society.

Changing Family Functions. As societies change, so do family systems. The sociohistorical perspective of family tells us that changes in intimate relationships—sexuality, marriage, and family patterns—have occurred over the centuries. Major transitions from agricultural to industrial to postindustrial societal systems change all

© Kate Ballantine

▲ Families vary a great deal from one culture to another; this polygynous family from Tibet illustrates one variation, a man with several wives. If the members of a family work well together, they provide support, a sense of identity, and feelings of belonging and caring.

the institutions within those societies. The institution of family in agricultural societies is often large and self-sufficient, with families producing their own food and providing their own shelter; this is not the case in contemporary urban societies. Industrialization and urbanization typical in 18th- and 19th-century Europe and the United States created a distinct change in roles (for those who were not enslaved). The wife and child depended on the husband who "brought home the bread." The family members became consumers rather than independent and self-supporting coworkers on a farm.

In addition to evolving roles, other changes in society have brought shifts to the family. Improved technology, for example, brought medical advances, new knowledge and skills to be passed on in schools, recreation outside the family unit organized according to age groups, and improved transportation. Socialization is increasingly done in schools, and in some cases teachers have become substitute parents. They do a great deal of the preparation of the child for the larger world. However, family remains a critical institution in society. Most families still function to provide stable structures to carry out early childhood socialization and to sustain love, trust, affection, acceptance, and an escape from the impersonal world.

THINKING SOCIOLOGICALLY

How does your family interact with educational and economic institutions? For example, how did the family in which you were raised influence your success in school and your chances of attaining a good job?

Conflict Theory. Conflict theorists study both individual family situations and broad societal family patterns. They argue that conflict in families is natural and inevitable. It results from the struggle for power and control in the family unit and in the society at large. As long as there is an unequal allocation of resources, conflict will arise. Family conflicts take many forms. For instance, conflicts occur over allocation of resources, a struggle that may be rooted in conflict between men and women in the society: Who makes decisions, who gets money for clothes or a car, who does the dishes? On the macro level, family systems are a source of inequality in the general society, sustaining class inequalities by passing on wealth, income, and education opportunities for their own members or perpetuating disadvantages such as poverty and lack of cultural capital.

▲ Various societies use different symbols to indicate marriage. The mangalsutra made of brass is an Indian symbol of Hindu marriage, consisting of a gold ornament strung from a thread or a gold chain. It is comparable to a Western wedding ring, worn by a woman until her husband's death. In the bottom photo, the aprons worn by these Tibetans indicate that they are married.

Yet some conflict theorists argue that conflict within the family can be positive because it forces constant negotiation among individual family members and may bring about change that can strengthen the unit as a whole (Coser 1964; Simmel 1922; Sprey 1969). Believing that

▲ In Kimukunda village in southern Uganda, orphaned siblings ages 4 to 8 return from working as daily laborers on a nearby farm. Their parents died of AIDS, and their 60-year-old grandmother now takes care of them. Together they struggle to fulfill the functions of a family.

conflict is both natural and inevitable, these theorists focus on root causes of conflict and how to deal with the discord. For conflict theorists, there is no assumption of a harmonious family. The social world is characterized more by tension and power plays than by social accord.

An Alternative Theory for Analysis of the Family

Feminist theory, which can be either a micro- or macro-level theory, is one approach to analysis of family and the place of family within the society that offers a different lens for understanding interaction within family structures.

Feminist Theory. Because women often occupy very different places in society than men, feminist theorists argue the need for a feminist perspective to understand family dynamics. Feminist scholars (some of whom are men)

begin by placing women at the center of their research, not to suggest their superiority but to spotlight them as subjects of inquiry and as active agents in the working of society. In doing so they uncover and examine biases rooted in patriarchal assumptions (Donovan 2012; Eshleman and Bulcroft 2010).

A micro-level branch of feminist theory, the interpretive approach, considers women within their social contexts—the interpersonal relations and everyday reality facing women as they interact with other family members. It does not ignore economic, political, social, and historical factors, but focuses on the ways women construct their reality, their opportunities, and their place in the family and community. According to feminist theorists, this results in a more realistic view of family and women's lives than many other theories provide.

Applying this feminist approach to understand Felice's situation, for example, the theorists would consider the way she views her social context and the way she assesses her support systems. This approach is similar to Max Weber's concept of *Verstehen*—understanding people and social units from *within* the experience—and has much in common with symbolic interaction theory, because it focuses on what interaction means to the women themselves. Felice's religious background, her reference group of close women friends, and her parents and siblings can have a profound effect on how she understands marriage, her rights and responsibilities within family roles, and her view of herself as mistreated or not.

Many branches of feminist theory have roots in conflict theory and therefore tend to be more macro in focus. These theorists argue that patterns of patriarchy and dominance lead to inequalities for women. One of the earliest conflict theorists, Friedrich Engels (Karl Marx's close associate), argued that the family was the chief source of female oppression and that until basic resources were reallocated within the family, women would continue to be oppressed. However, he said that as women become aware of their collective interests and oppression, they will insist on a redistribution of power, money, and jobs (Engels [1884] 1942).

One vivid example of how women and men can be viewed as groups with competing interests is through a feminist analysis of domestic violence. In the United States, almost 1 in 4 women and 1 in 7 men experience severe physical abuse by an intimate partner in their lifetime (Smith et al. 2017). Recent United Nations data indicate that 1 in 3 women in the world has experienced physical or sexual abuse, and some men openly admit having raped or abused women with no consequences. Although women's situation has improved in many areas, especially in education, there is a long way to go

Women with their upper bodies painted pose as they take part in a protest against domestic violence against women on International Women's Day.

to eliminate brutality (Sengupta 2014; United Nations Population Fund 2014; UNWomen 2016).

Feminist theorists point out that changes in the patriarchal family structure, education and employment opportunities for women, and childcare availability can lead to greater freedom of choice, equality, and autonomy for women.

Family Dynamics: Micro-Level Processes

The Agabi family belongs to the Hausa tribe of West Africa. They share a family compound composed of huts or houses for each family unit with houses for the head of the household (the husband) and each of his wives and her young children, plus one building for greeting guests, one for cooking, one for the older children, and one for washing. The compound is surrounded by an enclosure. Each member of the family carries out certain tasks: food preparation, washing, childcare, farming, herding—whatever is needed for the well-being of the group. Wives live with their husbands' families. Should there be a divorce, the children generally belong to the husband's household because in this tribe the family lineage is patrilineal, through the father's side.

The eldest male of the Hausa tribe is the leader and makes decisions for the group. When a child is born, he presides over a ceremony to name and welcome the child into the group. When the child reaches marrying age, the eldest male then plays a major role in choosing a suitable mate. On his death, the power he has held passes to his eldest son, who, along with his brothers, inherits the family property.

However, the eldest Agabi son has moved away from the extended family to the city, where he works in a factory to support himself. He lives in a small room with several other migrants. He has met a girl from another tribe and may marry her, but he will have to do so without his family's blessing. He will probably have a small family because of money and space constraints in the city. His lifestyle and even values have already altered considerably. These micro-level changes are connected to a global trend of urbanization and industrialization altering cultures around the world and changing family life.

Families can be studied at each level of analysis: as interdependent micro-level social units with family members in the immediate household, as meso-level institutions that can be seen as economic units, and as part of the macro-level social system. Many individual family issues that seem very intimate and personal are actually affected by cultural norms and forces at other levels (such as migration, urbanization, and economic conditions). Likewise, decisions of individuals at the micro level affect meso- and macro-level social structures (such as size of families). Individual families are, in essence, local franchises of a larger social phenomenon.

THINKING SOCIOLOGICALLY

What kinds of changes in families would you anticipate as societies change from agricultural to industrial to information technology economies and as individuals move from rural to urban areas? What changes has your family undergone over several generations?

Mate Selection: How Do New Families Start?

At the most micro level, two people get together to begin a new family unit. In the middle of 2017, the world population was approximately 7.4 billion people, but your partner was or will not be randomly selected from the entire global population (U.S. Census Bureau 2017b). Even in Global North societies, where we think individuals have free choice of marriage partners, mate selection is not an entirely individual choice. Indeed, mate selection is highly limited by geographical proximity, ethnicity, age, social class, and a host of other variables. As we shall see, micro- and macro-level forces influence each other even in a process as personal as mate selection.

Norms Governing Choice of Marriage Partners: Societal Rules and Intimate Choices. A number of cultural rules—meso- and macro-level expectations—govern the choice of a mate in any society. Most are unwritten cultural norms. They vary from culture to culture, but in every society we learn the cultural norms from an early age. One of the cultural norms is **exogamy**, *norms governing the choice of a mate that require individuals to marry outside of their own immediate group.* The most universal form of exogamy is the *incest taboo,* including restrictions against father–daughter, mother–son, and brother–sister marriages. Some countries, and about half the U.S. states, also forbid first cousins to marry (see Table 3.3 on page 77). Others, such as some African groups and many Syrian villages, encourage first-cousin marriages to solidify family ties and property holdings.

Exogamy not only prevents inbreeding that might perpetuate some biological abnormalities but also alleviates sexual jealousy within groups. For example, if father and son became jealous about who was sleeping with the wife, mother, or sister, relationships would be destroyed and parental authority sabotaged. Likewise, if the father was always going to the daughter for sexual satisfaction, the mother–daughter bond would be severely threatened (Williams, Sawyer, and Wahlstrom 2017). No society can allow this to happen to its family system. Any society that failed to have an incest taboo self-destructed long ago. Some societies require village exogamy (marriage outside one's own village) because it bonds different villages together and reduces the likelihood of armed conflict between neighboring groups.

On the other hand, norms of **endogamy** *require individuals to marry inside certain human boundaries, whatever the societal members see as protecting the homogeneity of the group.* The purpose is to encourage group bonding and solidarity and to help minority groups survive in societies with different cultures. Endogamous norms may require individuals to select mates of the same race, religion, social class, ethnic background, or clan (Williams, Sawyer, and Wahlstrom 2017). Examples of strictly endogamous religious groups include the Armenian Iranians, Orthodox Jews, Old Order Amish, Jehovah's Witnesses, Iranian Yazidi, and the Parsis of India. Such practices result in less biologically diversified groups but protect the minority identity (Belding 2004).

Each group may have different definitions of where the exogamy boundary is. For Orthodox Hasidic Jews, marriage to a Reform Jew is exogamy—strictly forbidden. For the Amish, the marriage of a Hostetler Amish woman to a Beachy Amish man is beyond consideration. Marriage of a Hopi to a Navajo has also been frowned on as marriage to an "other"—even though many Anglos would think of this as an endogamous marriage of two Native Americans. In the United States, among members of married couples of all ages, 7 in 10 (69%) share the same religion. However, as Figure 10.2 shows, among recently wed couples, only 6 in 10 do so (Murphy 2015).

▼ FIGURE 10.2

Recently Married Americans More Likely to Marry Outside the Faith

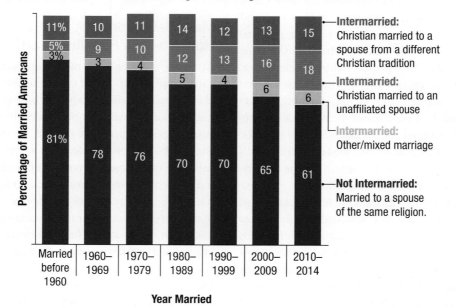

Source: "Interfaith marriage is common in U.S., particularly among the recently wed," Pew Research Center, Washington, DC (June, 2015), http://www.pewresearch.org/fact-tank/2015/06/02/interfaith-marriage.

Note: Figures may not add to 100% due to rounding.

Whether marriages are arranged or entered into freely, both endogamy and exogamy limit the number of possible mates. Most people also choose a mate with similar social characteristics—age, race, place of residence, educational background, political philosophy, moral values, and psychological traits—a practice called *homogamy*. Going outside the expected and accepted group in mate selection can make things tough for newlyweds who need family and community support.

So cultural norms of societies limit individual decisions about micro-level matters such as choice of a spouse, and they do so in ways that most individuals do not consciously recognize. Exogamy and endogamy norms and expectations generally restrict the range of potential marriage partners. Some of these norms are weakening, however, as the rapidly rising number of interracial marriages in the United States reveals. Still, the question remains: How do we settle on a life partner?

▲ Child marriage is especially common in parts of West, East, and Central Africa; the Middle East; and South Asia. In some countries, as many as 1 out of every 10 girls is married by the time she is 15 years old, some as young as 10, and nearly half are married by age 18. An Indian groom in this photo puts vermilion, the holy mark of Hindu marriage, on the forehead of his child bride.

Finding a Mate. In most societies, mate selection takes place through arranged marriages, free-choice unions, or some combination of the two. In either case, selection is shaped by cultural rules of the society.

Adah and Shray of India met for the first time for tea after a matchmaker had worked with each one's family to find a suitable mate. If they get along and do not object to the match, the wedding will be planned. Adah and Shray's experience is a typical one in India today. A recent poll indicates that 84% of married young adults (18–34) in India had arranged marriages (Harikrishnan 2017).

Meanwhile, in Afghanistan, Abdul's father has arranged a marriage for him with a girl from a nearby village. This marriage will solidify bonds between the families and the villages, reducing the chance of future conflict. Love has nothing to do with such arranged marriages, but political and economic factors matter big time! Some marriages are based on individual choice and love, and some are based on what is good for the family and community group.

Arranged marriages involve *a pattern of mate selection in which someone other than the couple—elder males, parents, or a matchmaker—selects the marital partners*. This method of mate selection is most common in traditional, often patriarchal, societies. For many girls in traditional Muslim societies, marriage is a matter of necessity, for their support comes from the family system. In poorer areas, girls are often seen as burdens, and they are raised with the expectation that they will marry into another family and take care of someone else's parents.

Arranged marriages are often used to create and strengthen economic arrangements and political alliances between family groups as illustrated in the previous examples. Beauty, youth, talent, and pleasant disposition can sometimes bring a high bride price and a good match. Should the young people like each other, it is icing on the cake. Daughters must trust that their families will make the best possible matches for them. Most often, the men hold the power in this vital decision.

Where arranged marriages are the norm, love has a special meaning. The man and woman may never have set eyes on each other before the wedding day, but respect and affection often grow over time as the husband and wife live together. People from societies with arranged marriages are assured a mate and have difficulty comprehending marriage systems based on love, romance, and courtship—factors believed to be insufficient grounds for a lifelong relationship. They wonder why anyone would want to place themselves in a marriage market, with all the uncertainty and rejection. Such whimsical and unsystematic methods would not work in many societies, where the structure of life is built around family systems.

Free-choice marriage is *a pattern of mate selection in which the partners select each other based primarily on* *romance and love.* The idea that each person has the right to choose a partner with minimal interference from others has become increasingly prevalent as societies around the world become more Westernized, women gain more rights and freedoms, and families exert less control over their children's choice of mates (Eshleman and Bulcroft 2010). The percentage of arranged marriages in Japan fell below the percentage of love marriages in the 1960s. Today, just 5% of marriages in Japan are arranged ("Miai: Meetings to Arrange Marriages" 2017).

The Internet facilitates romance and mate selection in many modern societies. Dating sites have grown exponentially since Match.com began in 1995 when only 14% of U.S. adults were Internet users. With 9 in 10 U.S. adults online today, dating sites have gained in numbers and acceptance; research shows 59% polled agree that "online dating is a good way to meet people." Twenty-seven percent of 18- to 24-year-olds, as well as many from other age groups, have used online dating, and 5% of those in committed relationships are with someone they met online (Smith and Anderson 2016).

Many of the e-dating services claim that their profiles and processes are based on social science research. The burgeoning business in e-romance introduces people with common interests, backgrounds, ages, and other variables. Several popular sites and apps include eHarmony, Match.com, Tinder, and OKCupid. If the reported average of 438 members who marry every day after being paired through eHarmony is an indication, many would-be mates are finding their partners online (eHarmony 2017). Many specialized niche dating services have sprung up based on race, religion, sexual orientation, occupation, and other interests.

THINKING SOCIOLOGICALLY

Recent studies reveal a lower divorce rate among those who met online than those who met in more traditional ways. How might a rational choice or symbolic interaction theorist explain those findings?

Starting with the assumption that eligible people are most likely to meet and be attracted to others who have similar values and backgrounds, sociologists have developed various mate selection theories, several of which view dating as a three-stage process—a series of sequential decisions (see Figure 10.3).

The notion of mate selection described previously is sometime referred to as a filter theory. It is as though you

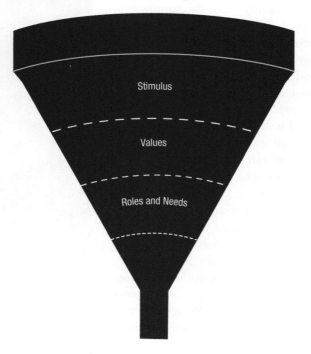

▼ FIGURE 10.3

Mate Selection "Filtering"

Stimulus

Values

Roles and Needs

were sifting for gold, and the first filter holds out the large stones, the second filter holds back pebbles, and the third filter stops sand, but the flakes of gold come through. Each stage in the mate selection process involves filtering some people out of the process. For you there may be other filter factors as well—such as religious similarities or common ethnicity.

Who Holds the Power? Authority in Marriage

Power relations, another micro-level issue shaped by cultural norms at the macro level, affect the interactions and decision-making in individual families. Two areas that have received particular sociological attention are decision-making in marriage and work roles.

Decision-Making in Marriage. Cultural traditions establish the power base in society and family: patriarchy, matriarchy, or egalitarianism. The most typical authority pattern in the world is patriarchy, or male authority. Matriarchy, female authority, is rare. Even where the lineage is traced through the mother's line, males usually dominate decision-making.

Egalitarian family patterns—in which power, authority, and decision-making are shared between the spouses and perhaps with the children—are emerging, but they are not yet a reality in most households. For example, research indicates that in many U.S. families, decisions concerning vacation plans, car purchases, and housing are reached democratically. Still, most U.S. families are not fully egalitarian. Males generally have a disproportionate say in major decisions, such as whether to move to a new city or buy a new home (Lindsey 2015). Social scientists find no evidence of inherent intellectual or personality foundations for male authority, as opposed to female authority (Kramer and Beutel 2014; Ward and Edelstein 2016).

Sociologists using *resource theory* to explain why men tend to have more power than women in families look at connections between resources outside the family and power inside the family. They argue that the spouse with more resources—education, occupational prestige, and income—has more power within the family. If only one spouse brings home a paycheck, the other is usually less powerful (Jory and Yodanis 2014).

In families where the wife is a professional, however, other factors in addition to outside resources may enter into the power dynamic (Jory and Yodanis 2014; Lindsey 2015). As noted in Chapter 9, regardless of who has greater resources, men in two-earner couples tend to have more say in financial matters and less responsibility for children and household tasks.

Who Does the Housework? The *second shift*, a term coined by Arlie Hochschild, refers to the housework and childcare that employed women do after their "first-shift" jobs (Hochschild 1989). The gap in housework done by men and women has closed dramatically in recent decades but not disappeared; one study indicates that women spend 2.19 hours and men 1.41 hours per day doing household chores. On an average day, 84% of women, compared with 68% of men, spend some time doing household activities. Further, 24.3% of women compared to 15.6% of men engage in childcare every day (U.S. Bureau of Labor Statistics 2018). (These childcare percentages are both relatively low because many parents have grown children. But if childcare was divided evenly between mothers and fathers, these percentages would be similar.) The next Engaging Sociology (page 306) shows the breakdown in hours spent by men and women at various household activities.

Social science research shows a clear positive relationship between equity in households and successful marriages. Husbands who do an equal share of the household chores actually report higher levels of satisfaction with the marriage, and such couples are less likely to divorce (Dockterman 2014; Lorillard 2011). As Figure 10.4 indicates, most married people think sharing housework is a key factor in making marriages work.

▼ FIGURE 10.4

Key Factors in Successful Marriages

% of married adults who say ___ is 'very important' to a successful marriage

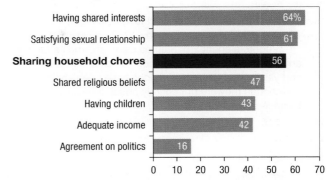

Source: Geiger 2016.

The success or failure of a marriage depends in large part on patterns that develop early in the marriage for dealing with the everyday situations, including power relationships and division of labor.

Maintaining both a job and a family can be difficult. It can be especially so for those in the *sandwich generation*, who find themselves caring for both dependent children and frail parents. Because employment obligations and family responsibilities often conflict, this is a major source of stress for people, and that tension has been the focus of sociological research. The next Sociologists in Action feature (page 307) focuses on the work of one public sociologist to reduce conflicts between company duties and other life priorities.

Family as an Institution: Meso-Level Analysis

We experience family life at a personal level, but the sum total of hundreds of thousands of families interacting in recognizable patterns results in *family as an institution* at the meso level. In this section, we look at the structure and parts of family as an institution, and the family and its relationship to other institutions. Some of the changes in the family have resulted from—or caused—changes in other institutions.

Structure and Parts of the Family Institution

The family institution varies among societies in some interesting ways. For example, depending on the society, a man may marry one woman, more than one woman, or another man. Institutions lay out the general framework

ENGAGING SOCIOLOGY

HOUSEHOLD TASKS BY GENDER

In many families, household tasks are highly gendered. As recently as the 1980s, wives and daughters spent 2 or 3 times as much time as fathers and sons in household tasks such as cleaning, laundry, and yardwork. However, the tides have been shifting, and though they are not entirely equal, they are more balanced.

★ ★ ★ ★ ★ ★ ★

Engaging Sociology

1. What is the division of labor (by gender) for household maintenance in your family?

2. How did it evolve?

3. Is it considered fair by all participants?

4. How does it compare with the data in Figure 10.5?

▼ FIGURE 10.5

Percentage of Men and Women Who Engage in Some Type of Household Tasks Each Day

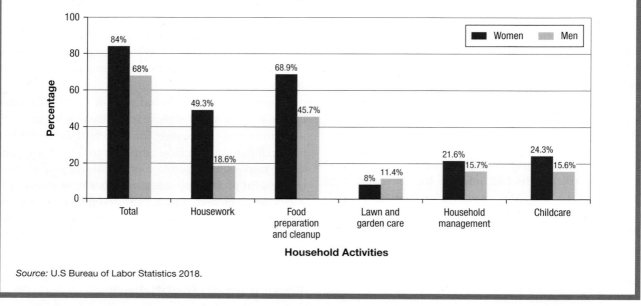

Source: U.S Bureau of Labor Statistics 2018.

for families in any society and include types of marriages, extended and nuclear families, and other structural models of families. Individual families are local expressions of a larger system of families that make up the institution of family in a society.

Types of Marriages. Monogamy and polygamy are the main forms of marriage found around the world. **Monogamy** refers to *marriage of two individuals* and is the most familiar form of marriage in industrial and postindustrial societies. **Polygamy**, *marriage of one person to more than one partner at the same time*, is most often found in agricultural societies where multiple spouses and children mean more help with the farmwork. There are

two main forms of polygamy—*polygyny* and *polyandry.* Anthropologist George Murdock found that *polygyny,* a marital system in which a husband can have more than one wife, was allowed (although not always practiced) in 709 of the 849 tribal groups and societies he cataloged in his classic *Ethnographic Atlas* (1967). Only 16% (136 societies) were exclusively monogamous (Barash 2002). Polygyny is limited due to the expense of maintaining a large family, the high cost of brides in some societies, religious and political pressures, plus a global movement toward monogamy. Also, there are seldom enough extra women to go around. Polygyny tends to increase during or immediately after wars when war casualties result in reduced numbers of men.

HELPING ORGANIZATIONS REDUCE WORK-LIFE CONFLICTS

Today, many employees are also raising kids, caring for elders and other relatives, and looking for ways to contribute to their communities. My research has looked at how organizations can change to better fit the current reality: Today's workforce is juggling multiple responsibilities on and off the job. Those organizational changes would benefit men and women at all ages and life stages.

Recently, I joined other sociologists (including Phyllis Moen), psychologists, organizational scholars, public health researchers, and economists to conduct the Work, Family, and Health Study. Our study addresses a big question: Can we make changes in workplaces that reduce employees' strain—their sense of being torn between work and the rest of their lives? We brought a change initiative, called STAR (Support. Transform. Achieve. Results.), to the information technology division of a Fortune 500 company. We then conducted a true field experiment; half of the work groups in this division participated in the STAR initiative and half were our control group who continued working under the preexisting company policies. We also surveyed the adolescent children of all employees to better understand how work policies impact family life.

STAR involved two main components: (1) training managers to express their support for employees' personal and family lives and (2) participatory workshops where teams talked about how they could effectively get their jobs done while increasing flexibility in terms of time and place of work. One goal was to make flexible work practices the new normal, rather than allowing flexibility for just a few mothers or fathers.

Our findings revealed that, compared to the control group, STAR employees experienced less work-life conflict and improved their sense of having "enough time" to be with family. STAR employees' work hours and subjective work demands (such as expectations to work hard and efficiently) did not differ from the control group, so the improvements in the work-life domain were felt without an increase or decrease in the time spent at work. Compared to those whose parents were in the control group, the adolescent children of employees in STAR also fared better in terms of time with their parent, sleep quality, and emotional well-being. Finally, STAR increased employees' job satisfaction and made them less likely to choose to leave the firm (which affects the company's costs via recruiting and training new staff). Our study demonstrates that work organizations can change to reduce work-life conflicts without harming the firm—getting the same work done and increasing employee commitment.

It has been exciting to do interdisciplinary research that looks carefully at the way work is organized and identifies positive—and feasible—solutions that can be implemented by companies. We are currently analyzing how similar initiatives could be adapted for a variety of settings, including those with hourly workers, who tend to have less freedom in the workplace than professional workers.

★ ★ ★ ★ ★ ★ ★

Erin L. Kelly is a sociologist and professor in work and organization studies at the MIT Sloan School of Management and affiliated with the Institute for Work and Employment Research. You can learn more about the STAR initiative at workfamilyhealthnetwork.org.

Polyandry, a marital system in which a wife has more than one husband, is practiced in less than 1% of the world's societies. Murdock found only four societies in the world that practice polyandrous marriage. In one such society, the Todas of Southern India, brothers can share a wife (O'Connel 1993). The Marquesan Islanders also allow wives to have more than one husband. A Tibetan practice originating in the country's system of land ownership and inheritance permits a woman to marry several men, usually brothers (O'Connel 1993). This often happens when the men are poor and must share a single plot of land to eke out a meager livelihood, so they decide to remain a single household with one wife.

Members of Global North societies often find the practice of polygamy hard to understand, just as those from polygamous societies find monogamy strange. Some societies insist on strict monogamy: Marriage to one other person is lifelong, and deviation from that standard is prohibited. Yet most Global North societies practice what could be called a variation of polygamy—*serial monogamy*. With high divorce and remarriage rates, Western societies have developed a system of marrying

▲ Members of this polyandrous family—consisting of brothers married to the same woman—pose for a photo in front of their tent in northwest China (which does not officially permit such marriages). The children—no matter who is their biological father—call the oldest brother "father" and all the other brothers "uncle."

several spouses, but one at a time. One has spouses in a series rather than simultaneously.

Extended and Nuclear Families. The mom, dad, and children monogamous model familiar in many industrialized parts of the world is not as typical as it appears to those from such societies. From a worldwide perspective, it is only one of several structural models of family.

Extended families include *two or more adult generations that share tasks and living quarters.* This may include brothers, sisters, aunts, uncles, cousins, and grandparents. In most extended family systems, the eldest male is the authority figure. This is a common pattern around the world, especially in agricultural societies. Some ethnic groups in the United States, such as Mexican Americans and some Asian Americans, live in extended monogamous families with several generations under one roof. This is financially practical and helps group members maintain their traditions and identity.

With major changes caused by industrialization, family patterns began to change: decline of the extended family system, changing authority patterns, changing status of women, changing economic functions, free choice of mate selection, decline in family size, changing attitudes toward sex and marriage, and declining functions within the family (Mondal 2015). The **nuclear family**, consisting of *two parents and their children—or any two of the three—* became more common. A worldwide movement toward more nuclear families is under way because of urbanization, fewer arranged marriages, and growing equality between men and women (Burn 2011; Goode 1970; Mondal 2015).

No matter what form it takes in a society, the family, like all of the other major institutions, is interdependent at the meso level with each of the other institutions. For example, if the health care institution is unaffordable or not functioning well, families may not get the care they need to prevent serious illness. If the economy goes into a recession and jobs are not available, families experience stress, abuse rates increase, and marriages are more likely to become unstable.

THINKING SOCIOLOGICALLY

Under what social and economic circumstances would an extended family be helpful? Under what circumstances would it be a burden? Would you rather live in an extended or nuclear family unit? Why?

Economic Institution and the Family

The family is the primary economic unit of consumption, so what happens when economic times are rough? Tough economic times can lead to fewer marriages and more suffering families. Low-income families, especially single-parent families headed by women, are particularly hard-hit and often have to struggle for survival. In some cases, families are so financially devastated that they become homeless—an especially difficult situation for children.

▲ In many societies, the family is still the primary unit of economic production. This family of farmers selling mangoes waits for customers at the side of a road on the outskirts of Havana, Cuba.

Poverty and Families in the United States

The poverty threshold for a family of four was $25,100 in 2018, and for a single person it was $12,140 (Federal Register 2018). The 2016 poverty rate, the most recent available, was 12.7%. However, for children under 18, the poverty rate was higher: 18% in 2016 (Semega, Fontenot, and Kollar 2017). The poverty rate in the United States was 2.3% higher in 2014 than in 2007, reflecting the recession's continuing effect on some families (U.S. Census Bureau 2015b). Table 10.1 shows the poverty threshold in 2018.

The *feminization of poverty*, discussed in earlier chapters, is a global problem. It occurs where single motherhood is widespread and where there are few policies to reduce poverty, especially for this group (Williams et al. 2013). One cause of single-parent families has been divorce. However, the change in birth rates in which more children are born to single women is also a factor. Table 10.2 shows the shift in 30 years from 18.4% to 40.3% of babies born outside of marriage in the United States (Centers for Disease Control and Prevention [CDC] 2017c).

Recent research has shown a relationship between the decline in marriage and the loss of manufacturing jobs and increased inequality in the United States. As Figure 10.6 reveals, the marriage rate in the United States has fallen dramatically over the past half century. In 1960, 72% of adults over the age of 18 were married, whereas today just 50% of adults are married. Those who do marry tend to be more highly educated than those who do not (Parker and Stepler 2017). Just 26% of poor and 39% of working-class men and women in the United States ages 18 to 55 are

▲ This young woman sits at the wheel of her car with all of her possessions inside and her children in the back seat. These are not conditions that make for effective parenting.

▼ TABLE 10.1

2018 Poverty Guidelines for the 48 Contiguous States and the District of Columbia

Persons in Family/Household	Poverty Guideline
1	$12,140
2	16,460
3	20,780
4	25,100
5	29,420
6	33,740
7	38,060
8	42,380

Source: Federal Register 2018.

Note: For families/households with more than 8 persons, add $4,320 for each additional person.

▼ TABLE 10.2

Percentage of Births to U.S. Unmarried and Married Women

Year	Births to Unmarried Women (%)	Births to Married Women (%)
2015	40.3	59.7
2014	40.3	59.7
2013	40.6	59.4
2010	40.8	59.2
2005	36.9	63.1
2000	33.2	66.8
1995	32.2	67.8
1990	28.0	72.0
1985	22.0	78.0
1980	18.4	81.6

Source: CDC 2017c; ChildStats.gov 2017; DeParle and Tavernise 2012.

Percentage of Adults (18+) in the United States Who Are Married

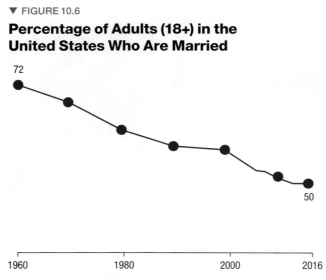

Source: Parker and Stepler 2017.

Note: Data from 2013–2016 include individuals in same-sex marriages. Adults who are separated are not classified as married.

married, whereas 56% of middle- and upper-class people in the United States are married. These figures would be even more skewed without immigrants, who tend to be both working class or poor and married (Wilcox and Wang 2017). As more men with a high school education or less find themselves without a pathway to middle-class wages, fewer find themselves marriageable.

THINKING SOCIOLOGICALLY

Why do you think fewer people are marrying these days? How has this trend influenced your views on marriage? Why? What are the potential societal repercussions of declining marriage rates?

The connection between marriageable men and falling marriage rates was first made 2 decades ago and is attributed to poor, inner-city African American males unable to find jobs due to the deindustrialization of cities (Wilson 1996). Today, these same economic patterns can be found among White men with low levels of education. Marriage has, increasingly, become an institution for the well-educated middle and upper classes (Autor, Dorn, and Hansen 2017; Parker and Stepler 2017).

Some argue that culture, rather than economics, is to blame for the declining marriage rate and for families living in poverty from one generation to the next. They maintain that a culture of poverty, a set of attitudes and values characterized by a sense of hopelessness and passivity, low aspirations, feelings of powerlessness and inferiority, and present-time orientation (concern only for the present and not planning for the future) is passed from one generation to the next (Lewis 1961). However, many sociological researchers support the argument that poverty itself causes the values and attitudes that develop as survival mechanisms in poor communities. They argue that poverty is largely a result of macro-level factors such as government policies, not the values and attitudes of the poor. Therefore, we should not *blame the victims* of poverty (MacLeod 2008). As more White people have fallen from the working class into poverty, more people are beginning to recognize how economic factors influence cultural views, including those toward marriage.

Socioeconomic Status and Parenting. Poverty is not the only way the economic system affects families. Complex societies develop significant inequalities, especially under capitalism. The inequalities are passed on to the next generation through social capital (important contacts and networks) and cultural capital (knowledge about the culture that enhances social mobility). In Chapter 7 (Stratification) we discussed the fact that what one learns from one's family, including the way one approaches life, can enhance or restrain social mobility. The way parents in different classes raise their children has important implications for their economic circumstances.

Upper- and middle-class parents engage in the *concerted cultivation* of their kids. They schedule their children in multiple activities, engage in more elaborate verbal communication with them, and intervene on their behalf with teachers and other authority figures. Working-class parents, other than providing daily essentials, tend to be more hands-off, an approach that researcher Annette Lareau labeled the "accomplishment of natural growth" (Lareau 2003:238). Their kids engage in more casual, unstructured play; have fewer opportunities to hear and use extended vocabularies; and are left to fend for themselves in dealings with adults. Their parents tell them what to do with orders, rather than reasoning with them, as many middle- and upper-class parents do with their children. Their parents also tend to use more physical punishment than middle-class parents, who use guilt, reasoning, time-outs, and other nonphysical sanctions to control children's behavior. These differences help shape children's assumptions about how authority is exercised and whether it is acceptable to challenge authority figures.

Thus, social class factors influence parenting, and parenting, in turn, influences one's prospects for social mobility and affluence within the system. The economic system and family system are linked and interrelated.

Dual-Worker Families. A different kind of economic influence can be seen in dual-career marriages. Two incomes may relieve economic strain on a household, but family life in dual-worker families may be complicated. Browse through the checkout-line magazine racks next time you are in a grocery store. Note the number of articles offering advice on how to cope with stress and overload or how to budget time, cook meals in minutes, rise to the top, and "make it" together. Stress, role conflict, and work overload are common, but most couples are aware of these strains and have chosen or feel financially compelled to combine marriage, sometimes children, and dual careers.

A debate emerged after Anne-Marie Slaughter, the director of policy planning in the U.S. State Department, left her position to spend more time with her family (Slaughter 2015). Slaughter said in explaining her departure that smart, productive career women often find they have to give up ambitions because institutional social mores make it difficult to have successful family lives and high-powered careers. This raised the question: *Can* women "have it all"—family and satisfying professional lives? The debate is not whether there are ambitious and talented women but whether the structure and norms of the workplace and society are allowing women to exercise their full potential in the current system.

In many Global North societies, government and industry support dual-career families with various family-friendly policies: readily available childcare facilities, parental leaves for childbirth and illness, and flexible work hours or telecommuting (working from one's home). These policies allow families to combine work and family lives and even have some time for leisure. The United States, however, has been slower than other Global North countries to adopt family-friendly policies. The U.S. government passed the Family and Medical Leave Act in 1993, allowing for 12 weeks of unpaid leave for the birth of a baby or care of a newborn, foster care or adoption, serious health issues in the immediate family, or serious medical conditions of the employee (U.S. Department of Labor 2013). However, few employees can afford to take unpaid time off, and less than 20% of employers offer parental leave for fathers (Sahadi 2016).

Even in places where paid leave for fathers is guaranteed under law, it can be difficult to get many fathers to take it, for fear it will hurt their careers. If taking parental leave becomes a normal practice for both mothers and fathers, however, gender equity will increase in the workplace, as well as in households (Patnaik 2015).

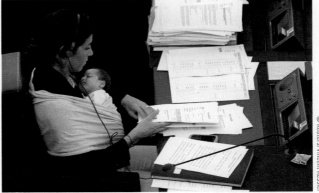

▲ Although the U.S. government's Family and Medical Leave Act allows for 12 weeks of unpaid leave for the birth and early care of a newborn or adoptee, few employees can afford the leave without pay. Because many also cannot afford the high cost of day care centers, they find themselves in a situation like this mother.

To raise the percentage of men taking parental leave, the Canadian province of Quebec, which already had leave policies and insurance programs for parents of newborns, established a 5-week paid leave *just* for new fathers. Whereas under the previous plan, most fathers transferred their leaves to their partners and did not take time off themselves, the new plan did not allow them to transfer their leaves. They could simply either use them or lose them. The result was a jump from 21% to 53% of fathers taking leaves after the birth of their children (Patnaik 2015).

There is some good news on the parental leave front in the United States today. More large U.S. companies (e.g., Netflix, Facebook, Amazon, and eBay) have created or expanded programs for employees who are new fathers, as well as those who are new mothers, to take time off with their newborn. Many leaders of large corporations, such as Starbucks and Walmart, say increased competition for workers and the major tax break for corporations passed under President Trump and the Republican-led Congress led them to increase family benefits for workers, including hourly workers (who make up 59% of the workforce) (Miller 2018).

In 2015, President Obama signed an executive order requiring federal contractors to provide up to 7 days a year of paid sick leave, and four states, California, New Jersey, New York, and Rhode Island, and some cities, including New York, Portland, and San Francisco, now have paid parental leave policies (Sahadi 2016). However, the U.S. government still does much less than other countries to ensure that parents can take time off to have a baby and keep their jobs. Figure 10.7 indicates the legal requirements of parental leave in several countries.

▼ FIGURE 10.7

Weeks of Paid Maternity Leave

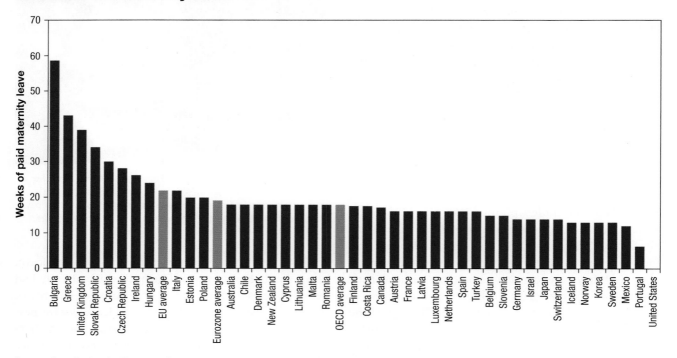

Source: Organisation for Economic Co-operation and Development (OECD) 2017, Social Policy Division - Directorate of Employment, Labour and Social Affairs. https://www.oecd.org/els/soc/PF2_1_Parental_leave_systems.pdf.

As we have seen, family is a diverse and complex social institution. It interacts with other institutions and in some ways reinforces them. As a basic institution, the family plays a role in the vitality of the entire nation. So, it should not be surprising that at the macro level, many national and global policy decisions concern how to strengthen the family institution.

THINKING SOCIOLOGICALLY

What are the challenges facing dual-worker families? What social policies might relieve some of the stress on families with two working parents?

National and Global Family Issues: Macro-Level Analysis

An effective way to explore macro-level issues pertaining to families is through policy matters that impact families. After exploring issues of national concern—same-sex families and divorce—we look at some global trends in marriage and family life.

Same-Sex Marriage

As same-sex relationships have become more widely acknowledged and accepted in the Global North, increasing numbers of gay and lesbian couples live together openly as families. Denmark was the first country to recognize same-sex unions in 1989, granting legal rights to such couples. In 2001, the Netherlands was the first country to allow same-sex marriages. The U.S. Supreme Court declared same-sex marriages legal in all 50 states on June 26, 2015. As of June 2018, 22 countries allowed same-sex couples to marry. Some countries, however, punish openly gay and lesbian individuals. As noted in Chapter 9, some nations include death as an appropriate punishment.

In the United States, support for same-sex marriage has rapidly increased, and the number of married couples is now estimated to be between 170,000 (according to the Pew Research Center) and 390,000 (according to a Gallup poll). There are an estimated 1.2 million U.S. adults living in same-sex domestic partnerships (Cohn 2015; Schwartz 2015). Most scholars acknowledge that this is probably an underreporting because of continuing stigma in reporting that one is gay, lesbian, or bisexual.

One reason many people in the lesbian, gay, and bisexual communities in the United States fought for the legalization of same-sex marriage was because same-sex partnerships were *insufficiently institutionalized*, making them somewhat less stable and creating ambiguity about their roles and rights (Cherlin 1978; Stewart 2007). Same-sex marriage advocates argue that if we actually believe that stable relationships and families make for a healthier and more stable society, then families with same-sex adults need public recognition.

Divorce: Contract Breaking

Is the family breaking down? Is it relevant in today's world? Although most cultures extol the virtues of family life, the reality is that not all partnerships work. Trust may be violated, family members may be abusive, and relationships can deteriorate. So we cannot discuss family life without also recognizing the often painful side of family life that results in contract breaking.

Some commentators view declining marriage rates and problems created by divorce as evidence that the family is losing importance. They see enormous problems created by divorce. There are costs to adults, who suffer guilt and failure; to children from divided homes; and to the society that does not have the stabilizing force of intact lifelong partnerships. Many children around the world, including in the United States, grow up in homes without both natural parents present. For example, 23% of children in the United States live in mother-only families and 4% in father-only families. In 2015, about 7 out of 10 children up to age 17 lived in two-parent families, but this varied by ethnicity: 34% of African American, 48% of American Indian, 58% of Hispanic, 75% of White, and 84% of Asian American children lived with two married parents (ChildStats.gov 2017; Kids Count 2017).

As Figure 10.8 reveals, the makeup of families in households is increasingly diverse. Less than half of children in the United States today grow up with married parents in their first marriage (Pew Research Center 2015j). Some scholars and policy analysts view this as dysfunctional instability. Other commentators argue that marriage is not so much breaking down as adapting to a different kind of social system. As recently as the late 19th century, the average length of a marriage was only 13 years—mostly because life expectancy was relatively short. "Til death do us part" was not as long a time then as it is today, when average life expectancy in Global North countries reaches into the 80s (Coontz 2016).

▼ FIGURE 10.8

Growing Diversity in Family Living Arrangements

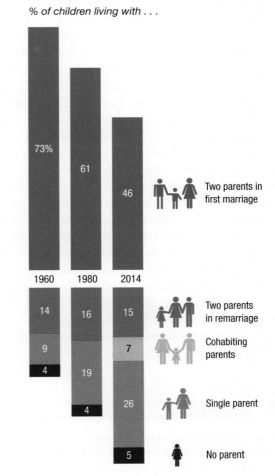

% of children living with . . .

Source: Pew Research Center 2015j.

Note: Based on children under 18. Data regarding cohabitation are not available for 1960 and 1980; for those years, children with cohabiting parents are included in "one parent." For 2014, the total share of children living with two married parents is 62% after rounding. Figures do not add up to 100% after rounding.

THINKING SOCIOLOGICALLY

Micro-level issues of divorce are often rooted in the personalities and relationships of the individuals involved. Talk with friends and family members who have divorced about micro-level factors that contributed to the dissolution of their marriages. Now, based on information from this chapter, make a list of meso-level factors (e.g., religious, economic, legal, educational) that contribute to or reduce divorce rates. What connections do you see between the micro and meso factors?

Macro-level social issues also contribute to divorce. These in turn result in micro-level individual family problems. The reason for the dramatic increases in the U.S. divorce rate after the early 1970s was a policy change: no-fault divorce laws. For centuries in the United States, in order to get a divorce one had to prove that the other party was in breach of the marriage contract. When U.S. divorce laws became more lenient in the 1970s, there was a boomlet of divorces, stimulated by the increasing number of women who entered the labor force and changed family dynamics.

All this makes divorce in the United States much easier to obtain than in earlier decades. Some critics believe this easing has led to a *divorce culture*—a society in which people assume that marriages are fragile rather than assuming that marriages are for life (a *marriage culture*) (Emery 2013).

Despite this perception, divorce rates for most groups in the United States have been dropping since the early 1980s. The divorce rate has fallen from 5.9 per 1,000 citizens in 1979 to 4 per 1,000 in 2000 and 3.1 per 1,000 in 2015 (CDC 2017a). Figure 10.9 shows that divorce rates today are as low as they were in 1970. There is also variation by region of the country. Figure 10.10 indicates where in the United States divorce rates are the highest. You may be surprised at which states have especially high or low divorce rates. Why do you think there would be so much variation by state?

THINKING SOCIOLOGICALLY

In your social group, do most people have parents who have remained married to one another? Why? What social and economic factors played a role in your answer?

Divorce and Its Social Consequences. Many find the emotional aspects of divorce most difficult. Divorce is often seen as a failure, rejection, or even punishment. Moreover, a divorce often involves splitting with more than just a spouse. It often entails separating from some family and friends, a religious community, and other social contexts in which one's identity is tied to one's marriage (Amato 2000). No wonder divorce is so wrenching. Unlike simple societies, most modern ones have no ready mechanism for absorbing people back into stable social units such as clans.

Adjustment to divorced status varies by gender: Men typically have a harder time emotionally adjusting to singlehood or divorce than women. Divorced men must often leave not only their wives but also their children, and whereas many women have support networks, fewer men have developed or sustained deep supportive relationships outside marriage. Finances, on the other hand, are a bigger problem for divorced women and their children than for men. Women are more likely to be living in poverty than men across all racial and ethnic groups in the United States. Single mothers are almost twice as likely to be in poverty as single fathers. Support from the noncustodial parent can help relieve poverty, yet only 46% of custodial parents receive all the child support payments they are due (Grall 2016).

Divorce also entails other costs for children whose lives are often turned upside down. Many children move to new houses and locations, leave one parent and friends, and must make adjustments to new schools and reduced resources. Adjustment depends on the age of the children and the manner in which the parents handle the divorce. Further, children in families with high levels

▼ FIGURE 10.9

Divorce Rates in the United States From 1950 to 2016

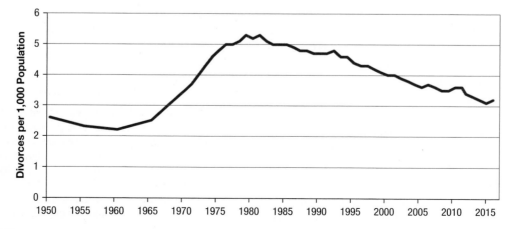

Source: CDC 2017a.

U.S. States With Highest and Lowest Divorce Rates

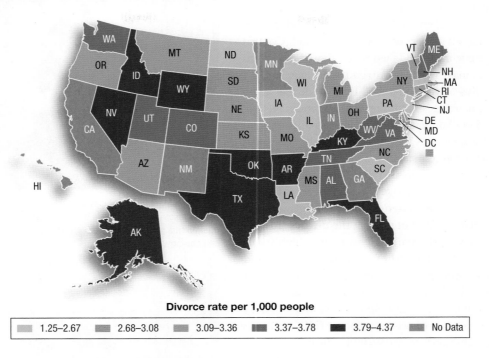

Divorce rate per 1,000 people

1.25–2.67	2.68–3.08	3.09–3.36	3.37–3.78	3.79–4.37	No Data

Source: CDC 2017b.

▲ Divorce often results in major feelings of failure, rejection, and isolation.

of marital conflict may be better off in the long-term if their parents divorce (Conley 2014; Rhoades 2008; Yu et al. 2010).

Overall, children have an easier time with divorce if they can remain in their home and in their familiar school, keep both parents in their lives, and maintain their friendship networks. Grandparents, too, can provide stability during these traumatic times.

Marriage, Divorce, and Public Sociology

Family systems around the world are changing in similar ways, pushed by industrialization and urbanization, migration to new countries or refugee status, changing kinship and occupational structures, and many other influences from outside the family. The most striking changes include greater choice of spouse, more equal status for women, equal rights in divorce, neolocal residency (when partners in a married couple live separate from either set of parents), and bilateral kinship systems (tracing lineage through both parents) (McKie and Callan 2012). However, countermovements in some parts of the world call for strengthening of marriage through modesty of women, separation of the sexes (in both public and private spheres), and rejection of some Global North trends such as high divorce rates.

National Family Patterns and Policies in the United States

As discussed, obtaining a divorce in the United States is relatively easy compared with the process in many other countries. All 50 U.S. states now have no-fault provisions based on "irreconcilable differences" or "irreconcilable breakdown of the marriage" (Benokraitis 2015). Conservative U.S. organizations, such as the Family Research Council, maintain that the family is being challenged by many forces that weaken the family structure and impede it from carrying out its purpose (Family Research Council 2014). They argue that the United States should go back to fault divorce to make it less easy to end a marriage in what they consider this "divorce culture." They argue that many couples enter marriages assuming that the marriage will probably not last. An assumption of impermanence is no way to begin a marriage, they believe, insisting that pro-family policies promote stability and are a precursor to healthy relationships. With this in mind, some policy analysts have advocated for laws to make it harder to get a divorce, forcing people to try harder to make the marriage work.

Other scholars think that making the divorce process more restrictive would leave many women in highly vulnerable positions in relationships with abusive men, and although such a strategy may create more marriages that stay together, it would not necessarily create healthy ones. Healthy marriages are what help society, not unhappy ones, say the defenders of no-fault divorce (HG.org 2014; Leon 2009; Nock, Sanchez, and Wright 2008).

THINKING SOCIOLOGICALLY

Would it strengthen marriages to remove all no-fault divorce laws and return to a fault divorce where one member of the couple must prove that the other person was in breach of contract? Why or why not? If you were making divorce policies, what would you do? What are the positive and negative aspects of your policy?

Global Family Patterns and Policies

Family life, which seems so personal and intimate, is actually linked to global patterns. For example, marriage rates are falling in most Global North nations, some rather dramatically (OECD 2016b). Increased access to contraceptives and desire to establish careers before starting families are two key reasons behind increasing numbers of young people deciding to delay or even forgo marriage. These trends have, in turn, led to a decreased birth rate in many of these countries. On the other hand, in some other nations, government policies limit families' access to birth control and knowledge about family planning. These regulations lead to more out-of-wedlock births and impact the economic circumstances of people who have no choice but to raise large families.

Because governments make policies that influence families, the interaction between policymakers and social

▲ Government policies can affect the size of nuclear families. One of the most vivid examples is the one-child policy in China. China relaxed this policy in 2013, allowing families to have two children if one parent was an only child.

▲ Global forces, such as ethnic holocausts that create refugees, can strain and destroy families. This is a scene of a refugee camp in Syria.

scientists can lead to laws based on better information and more comprehensive analysis of possible consequences. This is part of the contribution of public sociology—providing accurate information and analysis for wise public policy decisions.

Do marriage and divorce rates indicate that the family is in crisis? To answer this question, we need information on current world patterns and historical trend lines. The next Sociology Around the World provides cross-cultural data on marriage and divorce rates.

We have been talking about an international trend (divorce rates) regarding an institution (the family) and the impact it has on individual family members. Processes at the macro and meso levels affect the micro level of society, and decisions at the micro level (i.e., to dissolve a marriage) affect the community and the nation. The various levels of the social world are indeed interrelated in complex ways.

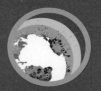

CROSS-CULTURAL DIFFERENCES IN FAMILY DISSOLUTION

Family conflict and disorganization occur when members of the family unit do not or cannot carry out roles expected of them by spouses, other family members, the community, or society. This may be due to voluntary departure (divorce, separation, desertion), involuntary problems (illness or other catastrophe), a crisis caused by external events (war or deteriorating economic conditions), or failure to communicate role expectations and needs. Many of these role failures are a direct consequence of societal changes due to globalization. Once again, the social world model helps us understand macro-level trends and patterns that affect us in micro-level contexts.

Divorce is still limited in some parts of the world, and it may be an option for only one gender. In some Arab countries, only the husband has had the right to declare "I divorce thee" in front of a witness on three separate occasions, after which the divorce is complete. The wife returns, sometimes in disgrace, to her family of orientation, whereas the husband generally keeps the children in the patriarchal family and is free to take another wife. Only recently is divorce initiated by the wife coming to be accepted in some countries, although the grounds for divorce by women may be restricted (Khazaleh 2009). Despite a seemingly easy process for men to divorce, the rate remains rather low in many Global South countries because family ties and allegiances are severely strained when divorces take place. Thus, informal pressures and cultural attitudes restrain tendencies to divorce.

Still, when family turmoil and conflict are too great to resolve or when the will to save the family disappears, the legal, civil, and religious ties of marriage may be broken. The methods for dissolving marriage ties vary, but most countries have some form of divorce. Table 10.3 compares marriage and divorce rates in selected industrial countries. Notice that although the divorce rate in countries such as the United States is high, the marriage rate is also high.

▼ TABLE 10.3

Marriage and Divorce Rates in Selected Countries, 1980–2014

Country	Marriages per 1,000 Persons in Population				Divorces per 1,000 Persons in Population			
	1980	1990	2000	Most recent data	1980	1990	2000	Most recent data
Canada	7.8	6.8	5.1	4.4 (2008)	2.5	2.8	2.3	2.1 (2008)
Denmark	5.2	6.1	7.2	5.0 (2014)	2.7	2.7	2.7	3.4 (2014)
France	7.2	5.1	5.0	3.7 (2012)	1.5	1.9	1.9	2.1 (2011)
Germany	6.3	6.5	5.1	4.8 (2014)	1.8	1.9	2.4	2.1 (2014)
Ireland	6.4	5.1	5.5	4.5 (2012)	n/a	n/a	0.7	0.6 (2012)
Italy	5.7	5.6	5.0	3.1 (2014)	0.8	0.5	0.7	0.9 (2014)
Netherlands	6.4	6.5	5.5	3.9 (2014)	1.8	1.9	2.2	2.1 (2014)
Spain	5.9	5.7	5.4	3.4 (2014)	n/a	0.6	0.9	2.2 (2014)
Sweden	4.7	4.5	4.7	5.5 (2014)	2.4	2.3	2.4	2.7 (2014)
United Kingdom	6.6	7.4	5.2	4.5 (2011)	2.6	2.7	2.6	2.0 (2012)
United States	10.2	9.8	8.3	6.9 (2014)	5.2	4.7	4.1	3.2 (2014)

Source: OECD 2016b.

The family is a powerful socializing agent and the first social experience of most human beings. As children grow up and branch out from the embrace of the family, the social environments they experience first are usually the local school and a religious organization. These provide lifelong training for participation in society. We turn to the institution of education next.

WHAT HAVE WE LEARNED?

Despite those who lament the weakening of the family, the institution of family is here to stay. Its form may alter as it responds and adapts to societal and global changes, and other institutions will continue to take on functions formerly reserved for the family. Still, the family is an institution crucial to societal survival, and whatever the future holds, the family will adapt in response to changes in other parts of the social world. It is a resilient institution that shapes the way we partner and "make people" in any society.

Our happiest and saddest experiences are integrally intertwined with family. Family provides the foundation through which individuals' needs are met. Societies depend on families as the unit through which to funnel services. It is the political, economic, health, educational, religious, and sexual base for most people and essential for societies.

KEY POINTS

- Families are diverse entities at the micro level, having a wide range of configurations, but families also collectively serve as a core structure of society—an institution—at the meso and macro levels.

- The family is sometimes called the most basic unit of society, for it is a core unit of social pairing into groups (partner taking), a primary unit of procreation and socialization (people making), and so important that when it comes unglued (contract breaking), the whole social system may be threatened.

- Various theories—rational choice, symbolic interactionism, functionalism, conflict theory, and feminist theory—illuminate different aspects of family and help us understand its conflicts, stressors, and functions.

- At the micro level, people come together in partner-taking pairs, but the rules of partner taking (exogamy/endogamy, free choice/arranged marriage, polygamy/monogamy) are meso and macro level.

- Power within a partnership—including distribution of tasks and authority—is assigned through intimate processes largely controlled by rules imposed from another level in the social system. Distributions of household chores can influence the happiness and marital stability of couples.

- At the macro level, nations and even global organizations try to establish policies that strengthen families. Issues of concern to some analysts include cohabitation patterns, same-sex households (including same-sex marriage), declining marriage and birth rates in Global North nations, and contract breaking (divorce).

DISCUSSION QUESTIONS

1. What do you believe is the ideal makeup of a family? Why? How does your description relate to the functions the family performs in society?

2. Which of the main theoretical perspectives discussed in this chapter (functionalist, conflict, rational choice, and feminist) is most useful when examining the families with which you are familiar? Why?

3. Does (or did) your family expect you to marry someone of a particular (a) race or ethnicity, (b) social class, (c) educational background, or (d) religion? Why or why not? How do you think endogamous norms impact (a) individual marriages and (b) society?

4. How were household chores distributed among family members when you were growing up? Were there any

gender patterns? Are you or do you plan on carrying out a similar distribution of chores in your own family? Why?

5. Do you think the establishment of no-fault divorce laws has been good or bad for (a) the institution of the family in the United States, (b) married couples, and (c) children? Explain your answers.

6. Have you or will you wait until you have established a career before considering marriage or having children? Why? What social and economic forces influence such decisions? What have been (or might be) the repercussions of these decisions?

KEY TERMS

arranged marriages   303

endogamy   302

exogamy   302

extended families   308

family of orientation   295

family of procreation   296

free-choice marriage   303

institutions   288

monogamy   307

nuclear family   308

polygamy   307

CONTRIBUTING TO OUR SOCIAL WORLD: WHAT CAN WE DO?

At the Local (Micro) Level

- *Support groups for married or partnered students* respond to the needs of an ever-increasing number of undergraduate students living on or near campus with spouses, partners, and children. If your campus has a support group, arrange to attend a meeting and work with members to help them meet the challenges associated with their family situation. If such a group does not exist, consider forming one.

- Is there *day care available on your campus*? Day care on campus can be invaluable for parents. If there is, look at the cost and availability of care for the children of faculty, staff, and students. If there is not a day care, look at the possibilities of creating, funding, and staffing one. How might it benefit the college or university, as well as the families it will serve?

At the Organizational or Institutional (Meso) Level

- *Support groups for multigeneration households* provide an important opportunity to support this growing population. Approximately one in five households contains more than one generation of adults.

- *House builders* have begun to change how they design some houses to meet the needs of multigeneration households. Contact your local *Habitat for Humanity chapter* (www.habitat

.org) and ask if you can help the organization create more homes suitable for such households. You can find some ideas for such homes at www.chicagotribune.com/classified/realestate/ct-re-0619-multigenerational-housing-20160616-story.html.

At the National or Global (Macro) Level

- *Influencing marriage policies* is another way for sociology students to make a difference in our social world. Select a family-related issue about which you feel strongly—pro or con—for example, requiring counseling before couples can divorce. Find out about the laws of the United States or your state regarding the issue. Next, identify your members in the U.S. House of Representatives (www.house.gov), the Senate (www.senate.gov), and/or your state legislature (www.ncsl.org/about-us/ncslservice/state-legislative-websites-directory.aspx). Contact those people via letter or e-mail, stating your views and get others to join you in a letter-writing or calling campaign.

- *Family Voices* is a national multi-issue advocacy group for children. The organization strives to improve the lives of children and their families, particularly those with special needs. You can learn about the issues on which this group is working and join its efforts by going to its website at www.familyvoices.org.

- *Hofstra University* maintains a resource site on international family law at http://people.hofstra.edu/lisa_a_spar/intlfam/intlfam.htm where you can learn more about the field.

$SAGE edge™

Get the tools you need to sharpen your study skills. SAGE edge offers a robust online environment featuring an impressive array of free tools and resources.

Access practice quizzes, eFlashcards, video, and multimedia at **edge.sagepub.com/ballantine7e**

© Getty/Scott Olson/Staff

EDUCATION

What Are We Learning?

▲ In schools, students learn much more than the three Rs. The communities in which learning occurs play a major role in what and how students learn and the place of education within societies.

MICRO

ME (AND MY TEACHERS
AND CLASSMATES)

LOCAL ORGANIZATIONS
AND COMMUNITY
**Neighborhood schools and
classrooms within those
schools affect our
everyday lives.**

MESO

NATIONAL ORGANIZATIONS,
INSTITUTIONS, AND ETHNIC
SUBCULTURES
**State or provincial funding, regulations, and
learning standards affect local schools.**

MACRO

SOCIETY
**National policies are also
developed to improve
schools.**

GLOBAL COMMUNITY
**United Nations programs try
to improve education in poor
countries.**

WHAT WILL YOU LEARN
IN THIS CHAPTER?

This chapter will help you to do the following:

11.1 Describe why an educated citizenry is
important for a nation's economy

11.2 Compare rational choice and
symbolic interaction explanations for
why students succeed—or don't—in
school

11.3 Illustrate the bureaucratization of
education

11.4 Describe how schools contribute to
the reproduction of social class

11.5 Provide examples of how society's
culture influences educational policy

THINK ABOUT IT

Micro: Small groups and local communities	What did you learn—both formally and informally—in your local school?
Meso: National institutions, complex organizations, and ethnic groups	How do families help or hurt children's school achievement?
Macro: National and global systems	How is education changing in your nation? Why is education a major concern around the world?

Tomás is considered a failure. At 9 years of age, he cannot read, write, or get along with his peers, and—out of frustration—he sometimes misbehaves. His parents have told Tomás over and over that he will not amount to anything if he does not shape up. His teachers have noticed that he is slow to learn and has few friends. So two strikes against him are the judgments of his parents and his teachers. The third strike is Tomás's own acceptance of the label *failure*. He has little evidence to contradict their judgment. Tomás is an at-risk child, identified as having characteristics inclining him toward failure in school and society. He will likely drop out of school and may even get in trouble with the law unless caring people intervene, encouraging him to realize his potential.

Tomás goes to school in Toronto (Ontario), Canada, but he could live in any country. Although successful children develop a positive self-concept that helps them deal with disappointments and failures, children like Tomás internalize failures. Successful children negotiate the rules and regulations of school, and school provides them with necessary skills for future occupations. Tomás carries a label of *failure* with him that impedes his chances for academic success and a good job. What factors could change the educational outcomes for students such as Tomás?

At least Tomás is (for now) in the education system. *Schooling*—learning skills such as reading and math via systematic instruction, by a trained professional—is a luxury some children will never know. On the other hand, in most urban areas around the world and in all areas of affluent countries, formal education has become a necessity. Education of the masses in a school setting is a modern concept that developed when literacy and math skills became essential for many jobs (even if just to read instructions for operating machinery). Literacy is also necessary for the smooth functioning of societies with democratic forms of government. Citizens must be able to read information about elected officials and proposed policies to participate effectively in a democracy.

In this chapter, we explore the state of the world's education, micro-level interactions in educational organizations, what happens in schools after the school bell rings, education at the macro level, whether education is the road to opportunity, and educational social policy issues.

State of the World's Education: An Overview

Every society educates its children. Most societies create national education systems for this task. **Formal education**—*schooling that takes place in a prescribed setting with the goal of teaching a set curriculum*—has expanded dramatically in the past several decades as higher percentages of students in many countries attend school and learn to read and write.

Global macro-level organizations concerned with education contribute to efforts to educate the world population. For example, UNESCO (the United Nations Educational, Scientific, and Cultural Organization) provides teacher training, curricular guidance, and textbook sources. It also gathers and disseminates international statistics on educational achievement. A nation's level of development, cultural values, and political ideology influences the development of *curriculum*, the courses taught in schools and the overall goals of their educational systems. What is considered essential knowledge to be taught in schools is based largely on a country's level of development, its cultural values and political ideology, and guidelines from international standards.

A literate population is necessary for economic development and expansion, a thriving political system, and the well-being of the citizenry. In the world today, 750 million adults (two thirds of whom are women) cannot read or write (UNESCO 2017b). Although literacy rates, overall, have improved dramatically over the past 50 years, as Figure 11.1 shows, in some poor Global South countries in Southeast Asia and sub-Saharan Africa, many 15- to 24-year-olds are illiterate (lacking basic reading skills) (UNESCO Institute for Statistics 2017).

▼ FIGURE 11.1

Youth Literacy Rate, Population 15–24 Years

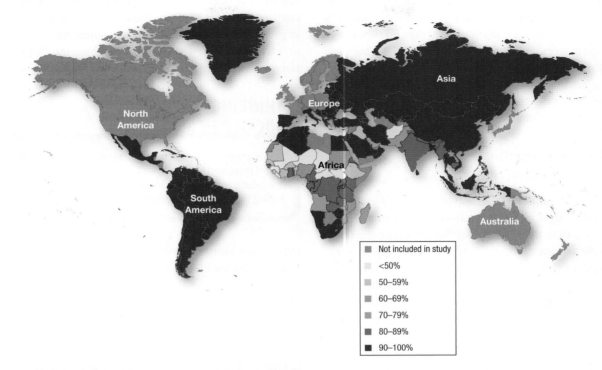

■	Not included in study
░	<50%
▓	50–59%
▒	60–69%
▒	70–79%
■	80–89%
■	90–100%

Source: Reprinted with permission from UNESCO Institute for Statistics 2017.

They will have difficulty attaining employment in the global economy.

Among Global North nations, students from some nations are better prepared for the global economy than others. The Organisation for Economic Co-operation and Development (OECD) tests people ages 16 to 24 in 72 nations on both basic knowledge questions and questions that require them to apply knowledge. Among OECD nations, Japan, Estonia, Finland, and Canada have the highest scores (OECD PISA 2015). These high scores translate into youth prepared to step into the global economy. Higher scores can also lead to economic growth. For example, if the United States improved its math and science scores, so that it ranked 19th rather than 24th among the 33 OECD nations, the better educated workforce would expand the economy and lead to $900 billion more in government revenue (Lynch 2015).

Education issues make an impact at all levels of our social world—from individuals, to local communities, to nations, and even at the global level. The next section looks at various issues in education from different theoretical perspectives and explains how the institution of education functions in society.

▲ Overcrowding in classrooms is not uncommon in Global South countries, such as Sierra Leone, where these schoolboys work to gain the skills they will need to "make it" in our global economy.

The Ins and Outs of Local Schools: Micro-Level Interactions in Educational Organizations

The process of education takes place at the micro level in the classrooms and corridors and on the playgrounds of

CHAPTER 11 • EDUCATION: WHAT ARE WE LEARNING? ■ **323**

local schools, with instructors and students who enact the everyday drama of teaching and learning. At the micro level, much sociological analysis has focused on interpersonal exchanges within the classroom and the school as a social setting within a community. At this level, sociologists look at roles and statuses in educational settings and the informal norms and interaction patterns that evolve in those settings. We begin by reviewing two micro-level theories and how they make sense of some common in-school interactions.

Micro-Level Theories: Individuals Within Schools

Symbolic Interaction Perspective and the Classroom. As discussed previously, symbolic interaction theory focuses on how people interact based on the meaning they have assigned to various traits, behaviors, or symbols (such as clothing). Children actively create distinctions among individuals and groups, becoming agents in determining the social reality in which they live. Popularity, a major issue for many children, especially in middle and high school years, is mostly a function of being well known. Students may increase their popularity by being attractive, representing the school in an athletic contest, or holding a leadership position. The difficulty is that there are few such positions, leading to a competition in which some students have less chance of winning than others.

Classrooms are small societies of peers that tend to reflect the interaction patterns and socioeconomic hierarchies of the larger world (Durkheim 1956). In the United States, children from families that cannot afford to purchase trendy clothing or other status symbols or send their children to sports training or camps have less chance of being popular. Those who have access to material and symbolic resources that give them high visibility have an advantage in the competition for popularity. They often gain special privileges in the school (e.g., if elected to a student office or captain of a sports team) and are more likely to develop leadership skills and to feel good about themselves—forms of social and cultural capital (Vijayakumar 2012).

The micro interactions of the school help form our sense of self. The extensive time we spend in school from 6 to 18 years of age has an enormous impact on how we see ourselves. How we think our peers view us can begin to mold our sense of competence, intelligence, and likability.

The larger school organization creates a structure that influences how individuals make sense of their reality and interact with others. Some symbolic interaction theorists, including those representing the Iowa School, emphasize the link between the self and meso-level positions or statuses (Stryker 2000). Official school positions—such as president of the student council, senior class president, or varsity athletic team member—become important elements of one's *self*.

THINKING SOCIOLOGICALLY

Describe how (a) your teachers and (b) your classmates in high school influenced how you view yourself. Why did they have this influence on you? Has your view of yourself changed since leaving high school? Why or why not?

Rational Choice Theory and Education Settings. Rational choice theory, as you will recall, focuses on the cost-benefit analysis that individuals undertake in virtually everything they do. What are the costs—in terms of money, relationships, self-esteem, or other factors—and what are the benefits?

How might weighing costs and benefits influence decisions about education? Students who consider dropping out of school go through some analysis of costs to themselves—for example, a student may decide to tough out a rough high school experience to preserve the chance of going to college and attaining a professional position someday. Similarly, teachers make rational choices about staying in or leaving the teaching profession. As Figure 11.2 shows, the median salary for teachers is considerably lower than that of similarly educated workers. For example, in 2016, teachers made about 80% of what nonteachers with a similar level of education made. So, most teachers do not enter or stay in the field for the money.

However, attrition rates vary considerably by school district. According to the National School Board Association, "Teacher turnover in high-poverty, high-minority urban schools can top 20% annually. Among new teachers, as many as half walk away from the profession in their first five years" (National School Board Association 2017:1). Some teachers leave because they are retiring, but about two thirds leave for other reasons, mostly dissatisfaction with teaching (Carver-Thomas and Darling-Hammond 2017). Causes of this loss range from lack of leadership and support to lower levels of resources, lack of professional development, and stresses created by a wide range of needs of students and families (National School Board Association 2017).

Median Income of Teachers Versus Nonteachers

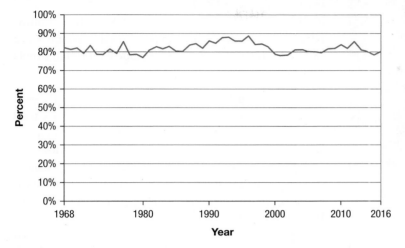

Source: "What should we pay teachers?" Dick Startz, September 20, 2017. Reprinted with permission from Brookings Institution Press.

Note: The chart shows the ratio of median income for teachers to non-teachers with a bachelor's degree or more, between ages 22 and 26, who report being in the labor force, and who report at least $1 of earnings.

THINKING SOCIOLOGICALLY

Think of the teachers you had before college. What seem to be the costs and benefits of the various roles teachers fulfill? Do you think that most teachers base their actions on this kind of rational choice calculation?

Schools are important organizations in local communities, sources of pride and unifying symbols of identity. Local communities rally around their schools. Moreover, in many communities, the school system is a large employer with real importance to the economic vitality of the area. At the micro level, much of the sociological analysis has focused on the school as a social setting within a community. At the meso level, sociologists look at schools as organizations with roles and statuses, informal norms, and interaction patterns that evolve in educational settings.

Statuses and Roles in the Education System

Students, teachers, staff, and administrators hold statuses, or positions, in educational systems. These statuses are part of the larger school organization at the meso level, and individuals hold them only during their time in the organization. The roles associated with each status in educational organizations bring both obligations and challenges. When those in each status agree on expected behaviors (role expectations), schools function smoothly. When they do not agree, conflicts can arise.

Students and the Peer Culture of Schools. In a private Rwandan secondary school, students crowd onto benches. They are quiet, respectful, and hardworking. They know that they are in a privileged position, and many students are lined up to take their places on the bench should they not carry out their roles, work hard, and succeed. Although they have no written texts, students write down the lectures in their notebooks and memorize the material. In some countries such as Rwanda, going to high school is a privilege. In others such as the United States, it is a necessary part of life that many students resist.

Schools exist to serve students and to expand their skills and knowledge. Still, many dynamics within a school may undermine that primary objective. The role expectations of anyone in the status of student can be complicated by variables such as ethnicity, gender, sexual orientation, and socioeconomic standing. Thus, the experience of being a student can be quite different for different students. Consider the life of a child who can afford the latest clothes, iPhone, and test preparation tutoring and can join clubs and sports activities instead of having to work versus a student who has to work every day after school to help pay for rent and other basic necessities. Their lives outside of school impact their lives inside the school in many ways.

Harassment is another factor that affects some children's student status. In the past school year, nearly half of all students in Grades 7 through 12 dealt with sexual harassment, and 87% of those report it had a negative impact on them (AAUW 2017; CRDC 2017; Churches 2017). Abuse was verbal, physical, and electronic, with over 30% experiencing harassment through electronic media such as Twitter and Facebook—cyberbullying (Alvarez 2013). Girls reported more harassment than boys (52% compared to 35%). Yet 79% of public schools reported no incidents of sexual harassment, meaning no students came forward to report cases or that staff do not recognize these complaints as sexual harassment. Researchers looking at middle school students found similar results in a 2016 study, noting that girls and White students are most likely to experience sexual harassment (Espelage et al. 2016). These persistent findings occur

▲ LGBTQIA-friendly student organizations, as well as inclusive curriculum, can help change school cultures and make them safer environments for LGBTQIA students.

despite a 1999 Supreme Court ruling that obligated all schools that receive federal funding to stop such harassment (Oyez 2015).

Although the climate for LGBTQIA students has improved over the past several years, such students are still more likely than other students to face harassment. Two thirds (66%) of LGBTQIA students experience harassment at school (Lahaie 2016). The good news, according to research by GLSEN, an LGBTQIA advocacy organization, is that LGBTQIA students at schools that use "an LGBTQIA-inclusive curriculum were more likely to report that their classmates were somewhat or very accepting of LGBTQIA students (76 percent vs. 42 percent)" (Lahaie 2016:para. 7). So, school administrators and teachers can make the school experience more positive and safer for their students through simple revisions in curricula.

Gender, Race, Ethnicity, and Academic Success. Research for several decades has shown that boys tend to be favored and given more privileges by teachers, and score higher in some academic areas than girls. However, in recent years, girls—who tend to study more and be more compliant in school than boys—have achieved greater academic success. In the United States, girls seem more capable of fulfilling the roles expected in schools than do boys. One indicator of girls' success in education in the United States is the *feminization* of higher education. Since 1980, more women in the United States have gone to and graduated from college than men. As Figure 11.3 shows, over the past decade, among young adults, women have started to earn college degrees in much higher numbers than men.

College graduation rates also vary markedly by race and ethnicity, as seen in Figure 11.4. Those of Asian and White (non-Hispanic descent) continue to be much more likely to have college degrees than other members of the U.S. population.

▼ FIGURE 11.3

Percentage of Population 25 Years and Older With Bachelor's Degree or Higher by Sex: 1945–2017

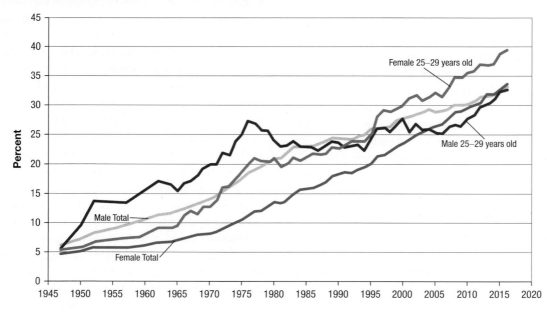

Source: U.S. Census Bureau 2017f.

Percentage of Population 25 Years and Older With a Bachelor's Degree or Higher by Race and Hispanic Origin: 1988–2015

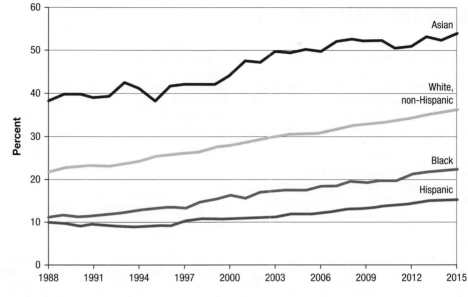

Source: U.S. Census Bureau 2017f.

Clearly, the experience of being a student is not the same for all, with gender, ethnicity, race, sexual orientation, and socioeconomic factors shaping the experience and affecting learning. Research such as that presented in the next Sociology in Our Social World discusses concerns raised about gender differences, especially in U.S. schools.

Teachers: The Front Line. Teachers in the classroom occupy the front line in implementing the goals of the school, community, and society. Teachers serve as gatekeepers, controlling the flow of students, activities, resources, and privileges. One scholar estimated that teachers have more than a thousand interactions a day in their roles as classroom managers (Jackson 1968).

As primary socializers and role models for students, teachers are expected to support and encourage students and, at the same time, judge their performance—giving grades and recommendations. This creates role strain, which can interfere with the task of teaching and contribute to teacher burnout. U.S. teachers are held accountable for students' progress, as measured on standardized tests. Although teachers play a role in how students do on these tests, other factors, such as the influence of students' families and peers, also influence test scores. This can cause stress for teachers and an overemphasis on teaching material that will

help students earn high scores on standardized tests (Dworkin and Tobe 2012).

In some nations of the world, like Japan and Finland, teachers are treated with great respect and honor. They receive salaries and respect commensurate with those in industry and professions such as law and medicine (Ballantine, Hammack, and Stuber 2017). In Europe, many high schools are organized like universities. Teachers think of themselves as akin to professors. Raising the respect for teaching requires better recruiting and training, and upgrading the status and pay of teachers (Ingersoll and Collins 2017). For example, we may learn something from Finland, which tops other OECD nations in test scores. Finland has very competitive teaching programs, and all teachers, even in primary schools, must have a master's degree. Teachers have higher-than-average salaries, freedom to create their own curriculum, and high status in their society ("How Finnish Schools Shine" 2012).

THINKING SOCIOLOGICALLY

Who should create curricula for public schools? Who should enforce high teacher standards—the federal, state, or local government, or teacher unions? Explain your answers and describe how to carry out what you envision.

WHERE THE BOYS ARE—
AND WHERE THE MEN ARE NOT

"The Fragile Girl," "The War Against Boys," "Failing at Fairness," "How America's Schools Cheat Girls," "Women Are Leaving Men in the Dust," "School-to-Prison Pipeline"—these are just a few article titles that illustrate the debate about whether girls or boys have the bigger advantage in schools. For many years, concern focused on factors that inhibited girls' educational attainment in school; boys were outperforming girls on standardized tests and level of education attained. Starting in the late 1980s, however, as girls' achievement levels increased, some researchers began to highlight how boys have fallen behind girls in school.

Among recent SAT test takers, 44% of boys and 56% of girls were in the top 10% of their high school class. The average GPA of girls was 3.45 compared to 3.30 for boys (College Board 2016:5). Boys are more likely than girls to drop out before graduation (Child Trends 2018).

Boys lacking a high school diploma face an uncertain future. With the manufacturing sector, unskilled jobs, and pay levels dropping, inflation-adjusted yearly earnings for men without a high school diploma fell 20% from 1990 to 2013 (Irwin 2015; Kearney, Hershbein, and Jacome 2015). Many boys and young men ages 16 to 24 are disconnected—neither in school nor employed.

A disproportionate number of youth who have not completed high school end up incarcerated, creating a "school-to-prison pipeline." Of state prison inmates, 68% have no high school degree. In many states, spending on corrections and prisons has grown much faster than funds spent on education (Prison Policy Initiative 2015).

In 2015, college enrollment reached almost 10 million for women, but only 7.5 million for men, and projections show the gap widening (NCES 2015). So we *do* know where many men are *not*: in high school and higher education. This is cause for concern for individual boys, men and their families, and for society, due to lost talent, income, and increased prison costs.

Administrators: Managers of the School System. Key administrators—superintendents, assistant superintendents, principals and assistant principals, and head teachers—hold the top positions in the educational hierarchy of local schools. They are responsible for a long list of tasks: issuing budget reports; engaging in staff negotiations; hiring, firing, and training staff members; meeting with parents; carrying out routine approval of projects; managing public relations; preparing reports for boards of directors, local education councils, legislative bodies, and national agencies; keeping up with new regulations; and many other tasks.

Principals, school leaders, make an immense impact on schools. They have the most power to impact the culture of the school and the learning environment for students. Schools that have positive, talented principals who work collaboratively with teachers tend to perform far better than others. In fact, researchers have found that recruiting, supporting, and retaining effective principles is an essential part of efforts to improve schools (Brooks 2018; The Wallace Foundation 2013).

The Informal System:
What Really Happens Inside a School?

It is the first day of high school, and the teacher asks a question. Should you respond or let someone else answer? If you respond, the teacher might be impressed, but the other students might think you are showing off or trying to become the teacher's pet. What if you answer incorrectly and sound foolish? Does that scenario sound familiar to you?

The informal system of schooling includes the unspoken, unwritten, and implicit norms of behavior that we learn in school. These norms may be created or enforced by teachers or by the student peer culture. The informal system does not appear in written goal statements or course syllabi but nevertheless influences our experience in school in important ways. Dimensions of the informal system include the hidden curriculum, the educational climate, the value climate, power dynamics, and coping strategies in the classroom.

The **hidden curriculum** refers to *the implicit messages learned in school through the other three Rs of school:*

rules, routines, and regulations (Ballantine, Hammack, and Stuber 2017; Snyder 1971). It includes everything not explicitly taught, such as unstated social and academic norms. Students must learn and respond to these rules to be socially accepted and succeed in the education system (Snyder 1971).

In many societies, children attend preschool and kindergarten, which provide the basis for schooling in the society. During these early school years, teachers teach children to follow rules, to cooperate with each other, and to accept the teacher as the boss who gives orders and controls how time is spent (Gracey 1967). Sometimes students learn that being tardy has a bigger impact on grades than whether one has learned the material.

According to functional theorists, it is through the hidden curriculum that students learn the expectations, behaviors, and values necessary to succeed in school and society. For conflict theorists, the hidden curriculum is a social and economic agenda that maintains class differences. Many working-class schools stress order and discipline, teaching students to obey rules and accept their lot as responsible, punctual workers (Willis 1979). More is expected of elites, and in higher-income schools, students have greater responsibility and opportunities for problem-solving that result in higher achievement (Anyon 1980; Brookover and Erickson 1975).

THINKING SOCIOLOGICALLY

What are some examples of the hidden curriculum you learned in your K–12 education? How has this training impacted how you act now in college?

Educational Climate of Schools. Schools can be comfortable and stimulating or stifling and unfriendly places. Some have an atmosphere of excitement about learning, with artwork and posters on the walls and enthusiastic noises coming from classrooms. In other schools, students tend to speak as little as possible, for fear of some form of punishment (either from their peers or teachers). These are aspects of **school climate**, *a general social environment that characterizes aspects of a school's social climate* (Brookover, Erickson, and McEvoy 1996).

School architecture, classroom layouts, teacher expectations, and student groupings by age and ability all affect the educational and cultural climate of the school. School ceremonies and rituals also contribute to the climate—logos, symbols, athletic events, pep rallies,

▲ Four-year-old preschoolers recite the Pledge of Allegiance. Developing patriotism is part of the implicit and informal curriculum of schools—and sometimes part of the formal curriculum.

and award ceremonies. Teachers' use of discipline and encouragement, the organization of tasks and opportunities for student interaction, and the grouping and seating arrangements also influence classroom climates. These aspects of the school experience can create an atmosphere that celebrates or stifles student achievement (Ballantine, Hammack, and Stuber 2017).

Teachers' responses to class, ethnicity or race, and gender differences also create climates that have subtle but profound impacts on students' experiences and learning. For example, studies indicate that teachers give boys more attention, in part to keep them controlled and attentive. They call on them and encourage them to speak up more often than girls. Teachers can usually count on girls to behave without such attention (Raina 2012; Sadker and Sadker 2005; Spade 2004). Another study found that teachers unconsciously tend to groom White girls for academic attainment yet encourage Black girls to emphasize social relationships over academic work. Teachers tend to train White boys for high attainment and high-status social roles, while focusing on carefully monitoring and controlling Black boys in the classroom. This disparate treatment leads to inequality in the way teachers and administrators discipline students. For example, Black students are 3 times as likely as White students to be suspended. American Indians, just 1% of students, make up 2% of those suspended each year. Students of color also tend to receive harsher punishments than White students for similar infractions (NPR 2014; U.S. Department of Education for Civil Rights 2012; U.S. Government Accountability Office 2018).

This inequality in school punishments can have long-lasting impacts. Using a nationally representative sample of students with similar delinquency and socioeconomic backgrounds, researchers examined the educational and criminal justice records of students suspended for the first time and nonsuspended students 12 years after the first group of students were suspended. The suspended students were less likely to have graduated high school or college and were more likely to have spent time in prison or on probation than the nonsuspended students (despite their otherwise similar backgrounds) (Rosenbaum 2018).

Teachers' perceptions of students help shape the school climate and influence achievement in other ways. Table 11.1 illustrates teacher expectations. Note that all are social variables that impact learning in the classroom.

Value Climate of Schools. The *value climate* of a school impacts students' motivations and aspirations. Schools that appreciate diversity and practice integration within classrooms can help more students succeed. High

expectations of students by teachers can also make a difference and lead to higher college enrollments. Students expected to do very well generally rise to meet these expectations (Downey and Pribesh 2004; Morris 2005; "The Power of High Expectations" 2011). Whether throughout the school or in a particular classroom, the atmosphere that pervades the learning environment has an impact on students' educational achievement and, ultimately, their life chances.

The climate in a high school can also work to perpetuate inequality, as it prepares students for certain types of higher educational experiences. For example, Lisa Nunn (2014) looked at the cultural ideas of success exemplified at three types of schools: "Alternative High," "Comprehensive High," and "Elite Charter." Alternative High teachers focus on helping their predominantly low-income, racial minority students achieve "success through effort." They downplay the influence of

▼ TABLE 11.1

Teacher Expectations

Teachers are influenced by the same stereotypes as others, and those perceptions can lead to lower expectations for some children. The following factors can create lower expectations for certain groups of students.	
Sex	Boys and girls are sometimes the recipients of low academic expectations because of beliefs about boys' maturation and assumptions about girls' mathematics skills.
Socioeconomic status	Low expectations are typically held for children from families with low income and education levels, low-status jobs, and an undesirable neighborhood residence.
Race and ethnic identifiers	Teachers are less likely to expect African American, Hispanic, and Native American students to succeed. They are also less likely to expect them to attend college. In contrast, school personnel often have high expectations for Asian American students.
School location	Rural and inner-city schools often have lower expectations than suburban schools. This sometimes evolves into a negative "can't do anything" climate.
Appearance and neatness	Lower expectations are associated with clothes and grooming that are out of style, made of cheaper material, not branded, or purchased at thrift or discount stores. Poor handwriting and other sloppiness in presentation can also create assumptions about the intellectual abilities of students.
Oral language patterns	Nonstandard English grammar and vocabulary can lead to lower expectations for students.
The halo effect	There is a tendency to measure a student's current achievement based on past performance evaluations of the child. Therefore, blind grading—evaluation of student work without knowledge of who wrote the material until after it is graded—is important.
Seating position	Lower expectations are typically transmitted to students who sit on the sides and in the back of a classroom.
Student behavior	Teachers tend to have lower academic expectations of students with nonacademic behaviors deemed inappropriate by middle-class standards.
Tracking or grouping	Students in lower academic tracks are presumed to have been placed there for a good reason (i.e., they have limited capacities and cannot be expected to learn at a high level), yet, in some cases, placements may have been arbitrary or incorrect.

Source: Adapted from *Creating Effective Schools: An In-Service Program for Enhancing School Learning Climate and Achievement* by Wilbur B. Brookover, Fritz J. Erickson, and Alan W. McEvoy. Copyright © 1997, 1982, Wilbur B. Brookover, Fritz J. Erickson, and Alan W. McEvoy. Published by Learning Publications, Inc.

intelligence and, instead, instill in students the idea that they can achieve success through hard work. Teachers at Alternative High allow students to redo assignments again and again, if necessary, in order to complete them correctly. Comprehensive High, with a more economically and racially diverse student body, uses both "success through effort" and "success through intelligence" approaches. Students there note that they must both work hard and have enough intelligence to understand and complete academic work by themselves. At the Elite Charter school, teachers assume that their students (91% of whom have parents who attended college) are intelligent. They focus on encouraging their students to display initiative and compete with one another to show elite colleges their intellectual curiosity and prowess. Indeed, the competition creates a pressure cooker environment, for students constantly compare grades with one another. In creating these different cultural definitions of success, these schools train their students for varying levels of higher education institutions, with the Alternative High students best prepared for community colleges and the Elite Charter students ready for the most prestigious colleges and universities in the nation.

THINKING SOCIOLOGICALLY

How might teachers and school administrators unintentionally create a school culture that perpetuates inequality in society?

Power Dynamics and Coping Strategies in the Classroom. For teachers, getting students to cooperate and to follow instructions can be challenging. Some students wish to wrest control from teachers and gain some freedom from the rules of the classroom or school. Both students and teachers develop strategies to cope with pressures and difficult situations. Student coping strategies range from complete compliance to outright rebellion. Do the following five strategies sound familiar? They are adapted from Merton's (1938) strain theory of deviance (see Chapter 6) and represent strategies students use to cope with school pressures:

- *Conformity:* acceptance of goals and means—doing the schoolwork expected

- *Innovation:* finding alternative or unapproved methods to achieve conventional goals—cheating or plagiarizing to pass a course or to win an academic contest

- *Retreatism:* rejection of goals and means—rebelling against school establishment by not conforming or cooperating

- *Ritualism*: indifference toward goals—"getting by" through following rules but not learning anything

- *Rejection with replacement:* rejection of goals and means in favor of another strategy—being a discipline problem or dropping out of school to pursue other activities (Hammersley and Turner 1980; Merton 1968)

Teachers try to elicit cooperation and participation from students by creating a cost-benefits ratio that favors compliance. For example, they explain to students the need for an education in today's economy, give them positive reinforcements for their efforts (praise and good grades), and punish them for a lack of effort (with bad grades) and violating rules (with detentions and suspensions).

After the School Bell Rings: Meso-Level Analysis of Educational Organizations

Schools can be like mazes, with passages to negotiate, hallways lined with lockers, and classrooms that set the scene for the education process. Schools are mazes in a much larger sense as well. They involve complex interwoven social systems at the meso level—the state agencies above the local community that affect a school's operations. At this level, we encounter the formal organization of the school system in a more bureaucratized form.

Formal Education Systems

Formal education came into being in the Western world in 17th-century Europe. Schools were seen as a way for Catholics to indoctrinate people into religious faith and for Lutherans to teach people to read so that they could interpret the Bible for themselves. The first compulsory education was provided by a Lutheran monastery in Germany in 1619. By the 19th century, schooling was seen as necessary to teach the European lower classes better agricultural methods, skills for the rapidly growing number of factory jobs, national loyalty, and obedience to authorities (Gatto 2003). After 1900, national state school systems were common in Europe and its colonial outposts and former colonial empires. These systems shared many common organizational structures, curricula, and methods, as nations borrowed ideas from other countries. The Prussian model, with strict discipline and ties to the military, became popular in Europe in the 1800s, for example.

Thus, formal education systems came into being when other social institutions required new roles, skills, and knowledge that parents could not teach. Knowledge needed by the young became too complex to be taught informally in families through example, moral lessons, and stories. Industrializing societies required workers with reading and math skills. As economies and societies transformed, schooling that formerly served only the elite gradually became available to the masses.

The post–World War II period from 1950 to 1970 brought about a rapid rise in education, with worldwide enrollment in primary schooling jumping from 36% to 84% and secondary enrollment going from 13% to 36% (Boli 2002). As of 2015, of all eligible children in the world, 81% were enrolled in primary school and 67% in secondary school (Global Partnership for Education 2017). Figure 11.5 shows enrollment by region of the world (UNESCO 2016).

As education became mandatory, schools emerged as major formal organizations and eventually developed extensive bureaucracies. We now turn to an examination

of the bureaucratic school structure. As we do so, think about how the bureaucratization of education has impacted your own school experience.

Bureaucratic School Structure

Organizational requirements of education systems at a meso level can influence the personal student-teacher relationship at the micro level. The meso-level formal bureaucratic atmosphere that permeates many schools arose because it was cost-effective, efficient, and productive. Bureaucracy provided a way to document and process masses of students coming from different backgrounds. Recall Weber's bureaucratic model of groups and organizations, discussed in Chapter 5:

1. Schools have a division of labor among administrators, teachers, students, and support personnel. The roles associated with the statuses are part of the school structure. Individuals hold these roles for a limited time and are replaced by others coming into the system.

2. The administrative hierarchy incorporates a chain of command and channels of communication.

3. Specific rules and procedures in a school cover everything from course content to discipline in the classroom and use of the schoolyard.

4. Personal relationships are downplayed in favor of formalized relations among members of the system, such as placement on the basis of tests and grades.

5. Rationality governs the operations of the organization; people are hired and fired depending on their qualifications and how well they do their jobs (unless or until they attain tenure) (Weber 1947).

One result of bureaucracy is that some children's special needs—such as personal problems or learning difficulties—are not always met (Kozol 2006; Sizer 1984; Waters 2012). Impersonal

▼ FIGURE 11.5

Out-of-School Rate by Region and Sex, 2014

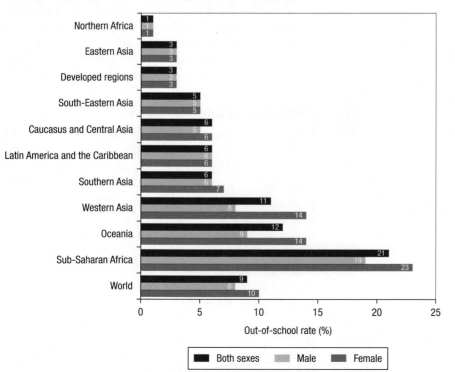

Out-of-school rate (%)

■ Both sexes ■ Male ■ Female

Source: UNESCO Institute for Statistics 2016.

rules can lock people into rigid behavior patterns, leading to apathy and alienation. In schools, these feelings cause passivity or acting out among students, which, in turn, frustrates teachers. Children like Tomás in the opening example do not fit into neat cubbyholes that bureaucratic structures invariably create. These children view school not as a privilege but as a requirement imposed by an adult world. Caught between the demands of an impersonal bureaucracy and individual goals for their students, teachers cannot always give every child the personal help she or he needs. Thus, we see how organizational requirements of education systems at a meso level can influence the personal student-teacher relationship at the micro level. This is another example of how the social world model helps us understand human behavior in organizations.

Education and the Social Institution of Family

We discuss interactions among meso-level institutions throughout this book. For example, the social institutions of family and education impact each other in many ways, some of which we have already mentioned. When children enter kindergarten or primary school, they bring their prior experience, including socialization experiences and cultural capital from a parent or parents, brothers, sisters, and other relatives. Family background, according to many sociologists, is the single most important influence on children's school achievement. Children succeed in large part because of what their parents do to support them in their education (Egalite 2016).

Most families stress the importance of education, but they do so in different ways. Middle-class parents in the Global North tend to manage their children's education, visiting schools and teachers, having educational materials in the home, and holding high expectations for their children's achievement. In these families, children learn the values of hard work, good grades, and deferred gratification for reaching goals.

Often, teachers' perceptions of their students and behavior toward them are influenced by their interactions with parents. Middle- and upper-class parents are more likely to ask about their children's progress, consult with teachers on strategies to help them learn better at home and in the classroom, and make it clear that they want teachers to focus on their children. Parents from lower-socioeconomic-status families tend to be less involved in their children's schooling, with less time to help with homework and fewer interactions with

▲ When children are hungry, they are not likely to concentrate on learning. Thus, provision of quality nutrition for low-income children has become an issue in educational programs. The U.S. federal government has stepped in to provide support and standards for nutrition in schools.

teachers. Language barriers (for new immigrants), lack of time (for single parents and those working many hours per week), and views toward teachers (as authority figures who should be left alone to do their job) are some of the reasons many lower-income parents do not play an active role in their children's schooling (Cheung and Pomerantz 2012). Children who must make educational decisions on their own have a greater likelihood of doing poorly or dropping out of school (Jaeger 2011).

Wealthier students also tend to be healthier students—another advantage in the educational institution. Healthier children do better academically (American Academy of Pediatrics 2016). Children from low-income families tend to have less access to nutritious food and safe areas to play. Providing a variety of healthy food choices at school and devising ways to make exercise fun and available for all students can impact the health gap between poor and wealthier students, as well as educational inequality. Recognizing the connection between health and educational achievement, as well as the obesity epidemic, the Obama administration, in 2012, established higher nutritional standards for school lunches, working to ensure that low-income students who rely on free or reduced-price lunches have healthy meals to eat (Nixon 2012).

THINKING SOCIOLOGICALLY

Provide some examples of links between academic success in schools and at least two other social institutions.

Educational Decision-Making at the Meso Level

Who should have the power to make decisions about what children learn? In relatively homogeneous countries such as Japan and Sweden, centralized goal setting and school decisions are possible. The process of making educational decisions typically causes little controversy. In contrast, heterogeneous societies such as Canada, Israel, and the United States include many different racial, ethnic, regional, and religious subcultures, each with its own needs and interests. In many such nations, without a strong central government that controls the educational system, teachers, administrators, school boards, parents, and interest groups all claim the right to influence the curriculum. Consider the following examples of influences from micro and macro levels on the educational institution, a meso-level organization.

Local-Level Influences. At the U.S. local community level, curricular conflicts occur routinely over the selection of reading material and sex education courses, as well as over any content thought to contain obscenity, sex, nudity, political or economic bias, profanity, slang or nonstandard English, racism or racial hatred, and antireligious or presumed anti-American sentiment. For

example, under pressure, the school system in Tucson, Arizona, suspended its Mexican American studies program in 2012 because some parents and politicians argued that it "promote[d] resentment toward a race or class of people." In 2017, a federal judge in Arizona ruled that the closure of the program violated the rights of Mexican American students and was "motivated by racial animus" (Strauss 2017). Another example comes from Family Friendly Libraries, an online grassroots interest group that started in Virginia and argues that the popular *Harry Potter* books should be banned from school libraries. Members of this group believe the series promotes the religion of witchcraft (DeMitchell and Carney 2005). Banned books in the past have included *The Wonderful Wizard of Oz, Rumpelstiltskin, Anne Frank: The Diary of a Young Girl, Madame Bovary, The Grapes of Wrath, Adventures of Huckleberry Finn*, Shakespeare's *Hamlet*, Chaucer's *The Miller's Tale*, and Aristophanes's *Lysistrata* (Ballantine and Hammack 2015). Table 11.2 shows the most frequently challenged books in 2017.

A growing number of large city school districts, concerned with teen pregnancy and sexually transmitted diseases, including AIDS, now provide teens with sex education, information about contraception, counseling, and sometimes condoms. Decisions about sex education curricula are often fraught with controversy.

▼ TABLE 11.2

The 10 Most Challenged Books for Children of 2017

	Title	Reasons Given for Banning
1	*Thirteen Reasons Why* written by Jay Asher	Discusses suicide
2	*The Absolutely True Diary of a Part-Time Indian* written by Sherman Alexie	Includes profanity and situations deemed sexually explicit
3	*Drama* written and illustrated by Raina Telgemeier	Includes LGBTQIA characters and considered "confusing"
4	*The Kite Runner* written by Khaled Hosseini	Includes sexual violence and thought to "lead to terrorism" and "promote Islam"
5	*George* written by Alex Gino	Includes a transgender child
6	*Sex Is a Funny Word* written by Cory Silverberg and illustrated by Fiona Smyth	Addresses sex education and believed to lead children to "want to have sex or ask questions about sex"
7	*To Kill a Mockingbird* written by Harper Lee	Contains violence and uses the N-word
8	*The Hate U Give* written by Angie Thomas	Contains drug use, profanity, and offensive language and considered "pervasively vulgar"
9	*And Tango Makes Three* written by Peter Parnell and Justin Richardson and illustrated by Henry Cole	Features a same-sex relationship
10	*I Am Jazz* written by Jessica Herthel and Jazz Jennings and illustrated by Shelagh McNicholas	Addresses gender identity

Source: American Library Association 2017, American Library Association Office for Intellectual Freedom.

Many oppose sex education in schools, believing it should be left to families and religious institutions. Some argue that these programs encourage premarital sex rather than abstinence and teach teens how to have sex. However, the number of sexually active teens has dropped in recent years, and most high school students are not sexually active (Centers for Disease Control and Prevention 2018b).

The birth rate among teens has also fallen—most dramatically among teens of color, as Figure 11.6 reveals. Reasons for the teen birth decline include less sex, more widespread information about pregnancy prevention, greater use of contraceptives like IUDs and the morning-after pill, and media portrayals of teen pregnancy that show the hardships associated with it (e.g., *16 and Pregnant, Teen Mom, The Secret Life of the American Teenager*) (Patten and Livingston 2016).

National-Level Influences. Whether the national government should control education is not a question in most societies. Education is centralized in almost all countries in the world other than the United States. Because the U.S. Constitution leaves education in the hands of each state, however, in the United States the involvement of the federal government has been more limited and often controversial. Even in

▲ Federal education policies put in place in recent decades attempt to close education gaps between social classes and races and provide the resources needed for all children to learn and contribute to society.

the United States, though, the federal government wields significant influence through its power to make federal funds available for special programs, such as special education and bilingual education. The government may withhold funds from schools not in compliance with federal laws and the U.S. Constitution. For example, the federal government, courts, and public opinion forced all-male military academies to become coeducational, despite the schools' resistance to such change. School changes as a result of the Civil Rights Act and the Americans with Disabilities Act are other examples of federal government influence on local schools through the enforcement of federal laws. Schools now accommodate people with various disabilities—people who in the past would have been left out of the system. With their classroom experiences and working with other teachers and children, many differently abled children can participate fully in society. However, as the following Sociology in Our Social World shows, this process is not always smooth.

▼ FIGURE 11.6

Births per 1,000 Females Ages 15–19, 2007–2014

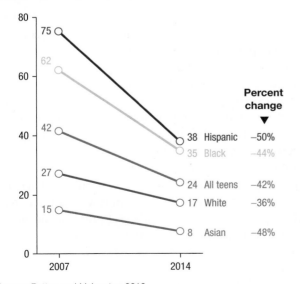

	2007	2014		Percent change ▼
	75	38	Hispanic	−50%
	62	35	Black	−44%
	42	24	All teens	−42%
	27	17	White	−36%
	15	8	Asian	−48%

Source: Patten and Livingston 2016.

Note: These data only account for live births. Hispanics are of any race. Blacks and Whites only include non-Hispanics. Asians include Pacific Islanders.

THINKING SOCIOLOGICALLY

The previous discussion shows that educational needs at the micro (individual), meso (institutional or ethnic group), and macro (national) level can differ significantly. This raises the question of who makes decisions and whether individual needs or societal needs take precedence. What do you think? Should schools focus primarily on individual or societal needs? Why?

Decisions about education tend to be deeply political from the local to national level, and not easy to make in

SOCIOLOGY IN OUR SOCIAL WORLD

DISABILITY AND INEQUALITY

By Robert M. Pellerin

Living with a visual disability for over 40 years has provided me with lived experience. I have also been doing research on experiences of others with disabilities as part of my PhD research. My results show that having a disability puts people at a disadvantage in education, employment, media images, and personal relationships. Technologies for those with disabilities have advanced, legislation has been introduced and sometimes passed, and advocacy for rights abounds, but some methods of communication, such as print media, do not work. Additionally, most of the technology from which those with visual impairment could benefit is unaffordable, and most mainstream companies do not include features that would make products disability-friendly. The bottom line is that many of us are ready, willing, and able to advance in education and be productive citizens, but we are often precluded from positions because of our disabilities and difficulty obtaining accommodation.

Disability in the United States has undergone a significant transition since the late 1800s. Most of those who have helped bring disability to the forefront have been American veterans who were wounded in war and notable figures like Helen Keller who influenced societal perceptions of disability. The most well-known legislative acts seeking to end exclusion and increase participation in areas of education and employment are the Rehabilitation Act of 1973 and the Americans with Disabilities Act (ADA) of 1990. Prior to the 1970s, people with disabilities were excluded from public education. Due to advocacy and legislation, today approximately 95% of school-aged students with disabilities attend public school (National Center for Education Statistics 2017b). Legislation regarding full inclusion has not proven as useful as planned, although exposure to students with disabilities has increased comfort levels of teachers and nondisabled students.

Despite disability rights legislation, the unemployment rate for people with a disability is more than double (10.5% to 4.6%) that of those without a disability (Bureau of Labor Statistics 2017d). I believe that until society views people as having unique abilities and strengths as opposed to disabilities, stigma will predominate and society will be deprived of talents and qualities from which all can benefit.

★ ★ ★ ★ ★ ★ ★

Robert Pellerin earned an interdisciplinary sociology and psychology PhD in family studies from Union Institute and University. His research has been on employment barriers for people with visual disabilities, and he is currently a clinician doing marriage and family therapy in California.

---

diverse societies. Everyone, though, can agree that education should provide a road to opportunity. We now turn to a macro-level analysis of how education relates to stratification.

Education, Society, and the Road to Opportunity: The Macro Level

In Dalton, Georgia, Mexican students make up over half the school-age population. In the school that researcher Hector Tobar visited there, 80% of the students were first- or second-generation Mexican Americans. The town has established programs to help Spanish-speaking students learn English (Jordon 2014). They had been unable to recruit bilingual teachers to this rural community, so the community hired teachers from Mexico for 3-year terms and sent some of its own teachers to Mexico to learn the language and become knowledgeable about the cultural and educational systems there. Since that time, some of the teachers from Mexico have decided to stay in Dalton. The teachers instruct in both English and Spanish. The state support for education covers less than half of the cost, which means that the town's carpet factories and local taxpayers (many of them low income) cover most of the expenses. The cofounder of the Georgia Project, which assisted new immigrants in their adjustment to Dalton, believes that the carpet factories made a self-interested decision when they decided to support the local schools. "The factories need the workers, and the workers come with families. . . . Without good schools for the workers' children, the county would leave itself wide open to a whole host of social problems down the road. Giving Dalton's Mexican kids a decent education was the sensible thing to do, 'pure self-interest'" (Diggs 2011:59–60).

Educational decisions made by states and national governments affect individual families and their kids, communities, states, and national economic and education systems. The next section focuses on the role of education in the stratification system. As you will see, education is deeply interwoven into the macro-level inequalities of a society.

Why Societies Have Education Systems: Macro-Level Theories

Over the past decade, India has increased its funding for public school and the literacy rate has risen dramatically, from half the population to 74% (*The Economist* 2017a). However, in some rural areas of India and other Global South countries, little more than basic literacy is considered necessary or possible, especially for girls. Basic literacy is a goal for all citizens in most countries, but it is sometimes limited to urban areas in the Global South where only basic academic skills (literacy, mathematics, and science) are seen as essential to find employment.

Village children in many Global South countries around the world go to the community school, but when the family needs help in the fields or with childcare, older children often stay at home. Even though attending several years of school is mandated by law in most countries, not all people become literate. Child marriage, migration of families, lack of competent teachers, child labor, and fears for the children's safety to and from school (especially for girls) also increase the dropout rate among poor children in the Global South (Sampath 2016).

Functionalist Perspective on Education. Functional theorists argue that formal and informal education serve certain crucial purposes in society, especially as

▲ Does it matter how one gets to school? These children who live near Inle Lake in Myanmar (Burma) take a gondola school bus—the only option for them.

© Elise Roberts

societies modernize. The functions of education as a social institution are outlined in Table 11.3. Note that some functions are planned and formalized (manifest functions), whereas others are unintended and unorganized—the informal results of the educational process (latent functions). Latent functions of schooling are often just as important to the society as manifest functions. For example, imagine what would happen to economic productivity if schools did not care for children during the day, releasing parents from childcare responsibilities so they can work.

In the functionalist view, the structure and processes within the educational institution remain stable when they help society function smoothly and achieve its goals. Government proposals for education reforms

▼ TABLE 11.3
Key Functions of Education

Manifest Functions (intended, formalized)
• Teach students the skills necessary to become educated, effective participants of society
• Socialize children to be productive members of society
• Select individuals for key positions in society
• Promote social participation, change, and innovation
• Enhance personal independence and social development

Latent Functions (unintended, informal)
• Confine and supervise underage citizens
• Weaken parental controls over youths
• Provide opportunities for peer cultures to develop
• Provide contexts for the development of friendships and mate selection

can stem from complaints from business owners about inadequately prepared workers and other indications of poor educational outcomes, such as the nation's students falling behind in international test comparisons or achievement gaps among races and ethnicities, sexes, or socioeconomic classes. We look at each of these functions of education in more detail next.

Teach Students the Skills Necessary to Become Educated, Effective Participants of Society. This function is the most obvious. Schools help students cultivate the skills needed for jobs. They also teach students to read, think clearly, and understand the history of their country in order to be active and effective members of a democratic society.

Socialize Children to Be Productive Members of Society. Societies use education to pass on essential information of a culture—especially the values, skills, and knowledge necessary for survival. Sometimes this process occurs in formal classrooms and other times in informal places. For example, in West African villages, children may have several years of formal education in a village school, but they learn what is right and wrong, values, and future roles informally by observing their elders and by "playing" at the tasks they will soon undertake for survival. The girls help pound cassava root for the evening meal, and the boys build model boats and practice negotiating the waves and casting nets.

In postindustrial Global North societies, elders and family members cannot teach all the skills necessary for survival. Formal schooling emerged as a meso-level institution to meet the needs of macro-level industrial and postindustrial societies, furnishing the specialized training required by rapidly growing and changing technology. Schools also teach students culture beyond what some families in heterogeneous societies can provide. Diverse groups must learn common rules that maintain the social order, for example. These rules come from the dominant culture of the society, and schools teach them through both their regular and hidden curriculum (Brint, Contreras, and Matthews 2001).

Select Individuals for Positions in Society. Students take standardized tests, receive grades at the end of the term or year, and ask teachers to write recommendation letters. These activities are part of the selection process prevalent in competitive societies with formal education systems. Individuals accumulate credentials—grade point averages, standardized test scores, and degrees—that determine the colleges or job opportunities available to them, the fields of study or occupations they can

pursue, and ultimately their positions in society. In some societies, education systems enact this social function through tracking, **ability grouping** (*placing students into different-level groups within classes*), grade promotion and retention, high-stakes and minimum-competency testing, and pullout programs that contribute to job training, such as vocational education and service learning.

Thus, from a functionalist perspective, education outfits people for making a living in their society, contributing to the economy and maintaining the stability of society. Income levels and standards of living for individuals, families, communities, states, and nations relate positively to education levels. Consider Figure 11.7 in the next Engaging Sociology, showing how states in the United States rank in education levels.

Promote Social Participation, Change, and Innovation. History and civics classes enable students to understand and become active in their society's system of government. Schools also teach critical thinking and analytical skills, and familiarity with information systems—computers, Internet resources, electronic library searches, and so forth. These plus written and oral communication skills help students participate in and influence society.

Enhance Personal Independence and Social Development. In school, children are taught educational and social skills and ethical conduct that will enable them to function in society. For example, in addition to the three *R*s, they learn to get along with others, resolve disputes, stay in line, follow directions, obey the rules, take turns, be kind to others, be neat, tell the truth, listen, plan ahead, work hard, meet deadlines, and so on (Neuman 2005).

Conflict Perspectives on Stratification and Education. A small percentage of students around the world receive elite educations, but many others are fortunate to receive any education. Conflict theorists emphasize the role of education in social stratification and competition between groups. They focus on the impact education or lack thereof has on children's life chances and opportunities in society.

Consider the following example of social stratification in education: Attendance at an elite school is a means of attaining high social status. Graduates of elite private high schools in countries around the world attend the best universities and become leaders of government, business, and the military. Preparatory (prep) schools in England, Japan, the United States, and many other countries traditionally have been the training ground for the sons and

CONSEQUENCES OF EDUCATIONAL ATTAINMENT

▼ FIGURE 11.7

Ranking of Education Levels of States

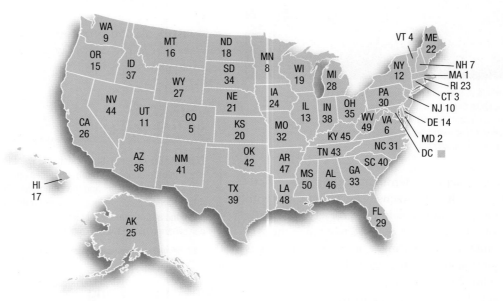

Source: Bernardo 2018. Reprinted with permission from WalletHub.

Engaging Sociology

1. How does your state rank?

2. How might the economy of a state be affected when an especially low percentage of the population has a higher education?

3. What kinds of businesses, industries, or professionals are more likely to locate in a state with a high percentage of college-educated citizens?

4. Do you think some businesses might be attracted to states where relatively few people have a college education? Why or why not?

5. How might educational levels in a state influence its political, health, and science institutions?

6. Look at the states that have especially high or especially low levels of education. What might be some causes for these varying levels?

7. Come up with at least two questions this map raises.

---

daughters of the elite. In the United States, 10% of K–12 students attend private schools (National Center for Education Statistics 2017c). Selective private schools tend to be very expensive, giving affluent members of society the most access to them (Domhoff 2014; Wade 2012). Such schools perpetuate elevated prestige and "repro- duce social class." Many leaders of former colonized countries have had the opportunity to study abroad, perpetuating Global North influence in Global South countries. Those not born into positions of advantage

have limited chances to participate in elite education and leadership positions.

According to conflict theory, when elites of society protect their educational advantages, the result is **repro- duction of class**—*the socioeconomic positions of one gen- eration passing on to the next.* This process takes place in part through the socialization of young people into adult work roles and compliance with the modern economic and political institutions and their needs. Schools teach students from lower socioeconomic positions to obey

▲ Schoolgirls in Kenya wait for classes to begin. Children like this, whose parents can afford to send them to school, will have more life chances than those who cannot attain an education. Conflict theorists point out that inequality is deeply embedded in the institution of education.

authority and accept the dominant ideology that justifies social inequality. If citizens believe that those with the best educations and jobs in their society personally earned them, they are not motivated to change the system. By promoting the legitimacy of the system, schools serve the interests of the privileged (Bowles and Gintis 2002; R. Collins 2014).

At a macro level, conflict theorists see institutions, including education, as tools of powerful affluent groups, used to ensure that their self-interests are met. This can be seen when looking at who completes college. Students from high-income families have 5 times the chance of completing college as those from low-income families (60% to 14%) (Bjorklund-Young 2016). Educational opportunities are manipulated in ways that keep the sons and daughters of the "haves" in positions of privilege, whereas lower-class children are prepared for less prestigious and less rewarding positions in society.

Conflict theorists point out that if schools do not provide equal educational opportunities for all children in a society, then students cannot compete equally in the job market. Today, disparities in the public school system in the United States are common. For example, Black and Hispanic students have less access to high-level classes and highly qualified teachers. In fact, "Black students are more than four times as likely as white students to attend schools where one-fifth of their teachers do not meet all the requirements for state teaching certifications. (Hispanic students are twice as likely to be in that situation.)" (Rich 2014).

Critics of increasing efforts to promote school choice and charter schools (publicly funded independent schools) fear that public schools might be left with

the least capable students and teachers, further stratifying an already troubled system. Students often gain entrance into charter schools through a lottery for which some, but not all, parents register. This can result in a "creaming process" that leaves traditional public schools with students whose parents are less involved in their education.

Having explored some lenses through which sociologists analyze education systems, we now focus on the classrooms and corridors of local schools, and key players where the everyday drama of teaching and learning plays out.

THINKING SOCIOLOGICALLY

Consider the community in which you went to high school. Do you think the education there enhances upward social mobility and serves all students and the community, or serves the affluent, reproducing social class and training people to fulfill positions at the same level as their parents, or is it some combination of the two? Explain.

Can Schools Bring About Equality in Societies?

Equal opportunity exists when all people have an equal chance of achieving high socioeconomic status in society regardless of their class, ethnicity, race, or gender (Riordan 2004). James Coleman describes the meaning and goals of equal educational opportunity:

- To provide a common curriculum for all children regardless of background

- To allow children from diverse backgrounds to attend the same school

- To provide equality within a given locality (Coleman 1968, 1975, 1990)

Equal educational opportunity means that *children are provided with equal facilities, financing, and access to school programs.* Schools in poor neighborhoods or rural villages around the world, however, often lack the basics—safe buildings, school supplies and books, and funds to operate. Students who live in these areas fall disproportionately to the bottom of the educational hierarchy. Many children face what seem to be insurmountable barriers to educational success, such as poverty, lack of health care, homelessness, hunger, and pressure to drop out to help the family (Kozol 2012; Noguera 2011). These conditions at home and in neighborhoods affect children's achievement in school and on standardized test scores (Boger and Orfield 2009; J. S. Coleman 1990).

Who Gets Ahead and Why? The Role of Education in Stratification

Any school or educational institution is supposed to be a *meritocracy*, a social group or organization in which people are allocated to positions according to their abilities and credentials, as in level of education attained. This, of course, is consistent with the principles of a meritocratic social system where the most qualified person is promoted and decisions are impersonal and based on "credentials" (Charles, Roscigno, and Torres 2007). Still, in societies around the world, we see evidence that middle-class and elite children receive more and better education than equally qualified poor children. Children do not attend school on an equal footing, and in many cases, meritocracy does not exist at all.

Three practices that tend to lead to inequality in schools—testing, tracking, and funding—illustrate how schools perpetuate and reproduce social class and social stratification systems. They also give clues as to what might be done to mitigate inequality in education.

Assessing Student Achievement: Testing. Testing is one means of placing students in schools according to their achievement and merit and of determining academic progress. Yet many scholars, including sociologists of education, argue that standardized test questions, the vocabulary employed, and testing situations disadvantage lower-class, minority, and immigrant students. These disadvantages often result in lower scores among these groups, relegating these students to lower tracks in the education system (Gardner 1987, 1999; Kruse 2016, M. Smith 2008).

Moreover, higher-income parents have the means to seek educational opportunities outside of school that give their children a further edge over other students on standardized tests. Families with more economic resources can provide more chances to learn through travel, going to museums, and mixing with members of the elite. They can also provide a **shadow education**, *learning opportunities outside of school, such as tutoring, test prep, and summer programs* that help prepare students for tests such as the SAT and ACT. Shadow education gives those students an advantage in the college selection process that relies, in part, on standardized test scores. The good news for those without the means to pay for test prep programs is that Khan Academy, working with the College Board, now offers free services online. Students from the graduating class of 2017 who took advantage of it increased their scores by 55 points more from the PSAT to the SAT than those who did not (Danilova 2017). This can help even the playing field, a little, between high school students of different socioeconomic classes. Table 11.4 in the next Engaging Sociology shows differences in ACT and SAT scores depending on sex, race, and ethnic group. Answer the questions posed as you engage with the following sociological data.

Student Tracking. Judgments by school administrators, counselors, and teachers can affect children for a lifetime. Decisions to separate students based on their abilities, for example, influence the peers, teachers, and curricula student experience. Tracking and streaming are two common forms of separating students by ability in schools. *Tracking* separates students into different-level classes within a school. *Streaming*, practiced in Europe and Asia but not in the United States, separates students into different secondary schools. These practices have the goal of allowing educators to more effectively address the needs of students of different abilities.

Many sociologists of education have argued against tracking in U.S. schools, pointing out that it contributes to the stratification process that perpetuates inequality. Research finds that levels at which students are tracked correlate with factors such as the child's background and ethnic group, language skills, appearance, and other socioeconomic variables. Students from lower social classes and minority groups tend to be clustered in the lower tracks and complete fewer years of school (Loveless 2013). In other words, track placement is not always a measure of a student's ability. It can be arbitrary, based on teachers' first impressions or questionable test results.

On the other hand, tracking provides many benefits for teachers and some students. In tracked classes, teachers do not have to slow down to help some students catch up, while trying to make sure that their more advanced students are not bored. Students tend to make more progress when working in groups with similar academic aptitudes. For example, in comparing Massachusetts middle schools that track students with those that have "detracked" students, researchers found that schools that track in math courses have more advanced math

TEST SCORE VARIATIONS BY GENDER AND RACE OR ETHNICITY

Evaluate your testing experiences and compare them with those of other groups.

▼ TABLE 11.4

ACT and SAT Scores by Gender and Race or Ethnicity, 2016

ACT Score	Average	SAT Score	Average
Composite, total scores	20.9	SAT Writing, all students	495
Male	20.9	Male	493
Female	20.9	Female	494
White	22.2	White	511
Black/African American	17	Black/African American	415
American Indian/Alaska Native	17.7	American Indian/Alaska Native	447
Hispanic	18.7	Hispanic	436
Asian American	24	Asian American	534
SAT Score	**Average**	**SAT Score**	**Average**
SAT Critical Reading, all students	494	SAT Math, all students	508
Male	495	Male	524
Female	493	Female	494
White	528	White	533
Black/African American	430	Black/African American	415
Hispanic	448	Hispanic	436
Asian American	529	Asian American	534
American Indian/Alaska Native	468	American Indian/Alaska Native	471

Source: ACT 2016; College Board 2016.

★ ★ ★ ★ ★ ★ ★

Engaging Sociology

1. Do you think your scores were an accurate measure of your ability or achievement? Why or why not?

2. Do you think your race or ethnicity, social class, or gender affected your scores? Why or why not?

3. Have your scores affected your life chances? Are there ways in which you have been privileged or disprivileged in the testing process?

4. What might be some causes of the variation in test scores between groups or categories of students?

students than those that do not. High-achieving students learn more when they are around other high achievers (Loveless 2009).

Less talked about are the negative impacts of tracking and streaming for stronger students. Research shows that some forms of ability grouping can cause some academically strong students to have lower academic self-concepts than similar students who attend school with mostly low-achieving students. "Specifically, when students are tracked either between schools or constantly within schools (across all subjects and not just course-by-course), high-track students have lower self-concepts and low-track students have higher self-concepts than their individual achievement predicts" (Salchegger 2016:406). These reflect the "little fish in a big pond" and "big fish in a little pond" syndromes. A capable student continually surrounded by even more capable students will have a lower sense of his or her academic efficacy than an equally capable student who experiences school with less capable students. The result is that many highly capable students pursue careers beneath their ability, (falsely) thinking they could do no better (Salchegger 2016).

Sociologists now know enough about the possible negative repercussions of tracking in the United States to emphasize that, if a school district does place students into different ability groups or tracks, it should find ways to eliminate possible race, class, and gender bias, and students should be tracked in each subject independently, not in a single track for all subjects. Students should have opportunities to move among tracks, as their progress indicates they should.

THINKING SOCIOLOGICALLY

Were you tracked in any subjects? What effect, if any, did this have on you? What effect did tracking have on friends of yours? How might tracking shape friendship networks?

School Funding. The amount of money available to fund schools affects the types of programs they

© Getty/RJ Sangosti/Contributor

▲ Funding is a serious issue in many school districts, and rather than raise taxes, some school systems, such as this one in Colorado, have decided to sell advertising on the sides of school buses. Having a particular product "endorsed" by the school and exposed daily to children raises concerns for some citizens.

can offer, an important issue for nations that must compete in the global social and economic system. Money for education, in some societies, comes from central governments and, in others, from a combination of federal, state, and local government and private sources, such as tuition, religious denominations, and philanthropies. In Uganda, for example, the government runs the schools, but most of the funding comes from tuition paid by each student or by the student's family.

In the United States, public school spending comes from local property taxes, as well as state and federal funds. On average, state governments provide 46% of education funding for elementary and secondary school budgets from income taxes, corporate taxes, sales taxes, and fees. Local governments provide about 45%, mostly from property taxes. About 9% of education funding comes from the federal government (Musu-Gillette and Cornman 2016).

The Elementary and Secondary Education Act, first passed by Congress in 1965, requires equitable state and local funding for high-poverty and low-income schools. States must send more money to low income districts that have less money coming in from the local community than do high-income districts. As Figure 11.8 reveals, however, despite that ruling, most states have not provided enough money to make up for different levels of local funding. Some areas have more money for their schools than others.

Per-Student Elementary and Secondary School Expenditures

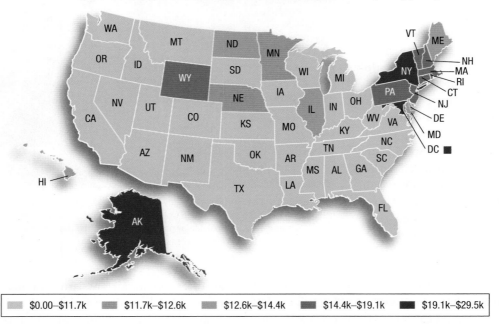

Per Pupil Elementary and Secondary School Total Expenditures (State) (2015)

$0.00–$11.7k $11.7k–$12.6k $12.6k–$14.4k $14.4k–$19.1k $19.1k–$29.5k

Source: Data sources: Education Week, U.S. Census Bureau. Map by Alyson Hurt and Katie Park/NPR. From "Why America's Schools Have a Money Problem," NPR, April 18, 2016. Reprinted with permission.

Education and Public Policy

Although the past century brought some improvement in equality of education, much remains to be done to level the playing field. Various policies have been put into place throughout the years in attempts to improve educational systems. We now turn to educational policy issues in the United States and throughout the globe.

Educational Policies in the United States

Although the U.S. high school graduation rate (83%) is higher than ever (NCES 2017d), most students do not graduate from high school ready for college or a career. In 2017, only 27% of high school students who took the ACT met the college readiness benchmark in all four subjects (English, reading, math, and science) (ACT 2017). It is also important to remember that one out of three high school students does not even take the test. If all students did so, it is likely that even a smaller percentage would be deemed college-ready (Jaschik 2016a).

Under the Obama administration, education policy focused on creating common standards that students in all states would have to reach. As noted earlier, most states (42) have adjusted their curriculum to follow the Common Core standards (Common Core Standards Initiative 2017). Under the Trump administration, policies have shifted toward efforts to increase school choice, promoting charter schools that use public school funds and vouchers that allow individuals to use the tax money they would have paid to fund public schools to pay for their children to attend private schools. The idea is that private schools, competing for students and funding, will do a better job than public schools.

The Harlem Children's Zone's Promise Academy provides one example of a charter school. Unlike most others, however, it is part of an effort to address the needs of the larger community around it. Its founder, Geoffrey Canada, grew up in the South Bronx, was raised by a single mom, and then had a lucky break. He moved to the suburbs to live with his grandparents and went on to earn a college degree in sociology and psychology from Bowdoin College and a master's degree from the Harvard Graduate School of Education. Having been given the opportunity to earn an elite education, Canada used his knowledge and connections to found the Harlem Children's Zone (HCZ) in New York.

Covering a 97-block neighborhood area, HCZ serves over 12,300 youth and 12,400 adults, providing social, medical, and educational services for free (Hollander

2014). For those in the zone who do not win the school's admissions lottery into HCZ's Promise Academy, HCZ still provides services, including parenting classes, preschool language classes, school preparation classes, and SAT tutoring. HCZ supports the idea that strong communities produce strong schools and well-educated children.

The Promise Academy has long days and a short summer vacation, a dress code, and strict discipline. The school also provides students with meals and after-school and Saturday tutoring and enrichment programs. The student–teacher ratio is 6 to 1. For students who work hard and achieve, there are rewards. Some get free trips to Disneyland for good grades, and others get paid for good high school grades. Students who attended HCZ's Promise Academy performed impressively better than those from the same background who attended a typical public school in New York City (Croft and Whitehurst 2010).

The Zone is not cheap to run at $16,000 per student (not including afterschool programs, administrative and building costs, student rewards, and so on) compared to the $14,452 spent on each public school student in New York City, but, as Canada points out, the costs of a child ending up in the criminal justice system are much greater (CNNMoney 2017).

Sociologists can assist efforts to improve schools in many ways, including evaluations of charter schools like HCZ's Promise Academy. Mark Berends, featured in the next Sociologists in Action, has used his research to inform the school choice debate.

Global Policy Issues in Education

Approaches to learning tend to reflect a society's social and economic values. Countries with capitalist economic systems are more likely to have an education system that stresses individualism and competition, pitting students against one another for the best grades and opportunities. Socialist economic systems often encourage cooperation and collaboration among students, with the collective needs of society viewed as more important than those of individuals (Rankin and Aytaç 2006).

Political and economic trends outside a country can also have an impact on the education system within the country. For example, as China has become a more powerful economic nation and trading partner with the United States, many U.S. schools have added Mandarin classes to their curriculum. Also, since 9/11, many colleges and universities have developed courses covering issues of terrorism.

▲ The French government does not permit public displays of religion and forbids Islamic girls and women from wearing the traditional head covering (hijab) to school. Government officials believe hijabs contribute to the "us" versus "them" polarization between Muslims and non-Muslims.

Gender equity in education has improved but remains a concern in some areas. Two thirds of countries have reached gender equity in primary school enrollment, but "130 million girls between the age of 6 and 17 are out of school and 15 million girls of primary-school age—half of them in sub-Saharan Africa—will never enter a classroom" (The World Bank 2017c).

The benefits of gender equity in education are many—and improve the lives of all members of society. Educated girls and women

- reduce the likelihood of children becoming brides;

- have fewer and healthier children;

- contribute to their families' economic well-being;

- increase the economic prosperity of their society; and

- pass these benefits on to the next generation (World Bank 2017b).

Unfortunately, the shooting of Nobel Prize winner Malala Yousafzai at age 15 by the Taliban in Pakistan for her support of girls' education and the kidnapping of hundreds of schoolgirls by the terrorist organization Boko Haram (which means "no Western education") in Nigeria are vivid reminders of the continuing hostility toward education for girls in some areas of the world.

Sometimes, however, unequal access to education can be fixed relatively easily. For example, the availability of clean drinking water is a major issue in the Global South. Because women must spend as many as 6 hours

SOCIOLOGISTS IN ACTION
Mark Berends

USING RESEARCH TO INFORM THE SCHOOL CHOICE DEBATE

From the time I was in graduate school, I've engaged in education research that informs controversial, contentious issues. In my early years, I looked at ability grouping and tracking. During my days at the RAND Corporation, I studied the school reforms of New American Schools, the largest privately funded educational reform initiative at that time. At Vanderbilt University and now at the University of Notre Dame, I conduct research on school choice.

Undertaking such projects is not for the faint of heart. Proponents and opponents alike have scrutinized my work for arguments that support their positions and then criticized it where support could not be found. Nonetheless, I believe research on controversial educational policies and reforms is an important space for sociologists to inhabit. Sociologists have a great deal to offer about which reforms and policies work, the circumstances in which they work, and for whom they work. Sociologists have the opportunity to employ the most rigorous methods available, both qualitative and quantitative, guarding against issues of potential selection bias. What's more, sociologists have a long tradition of debunking certain myths about educational policies and reforms, which in this day and age is badly needed.

In my most recent research on school choice, I am examining Indiana's charter schools and its voucher initiative, the Indiana Choice Scholarship Program (ICSP). The program, which is the largest in the United States, provides school vouchers (or scholarships) to families so they can send their children to the schools of their choice, whether public or private, religious or nonreligious. The ICSP—and school choice writ large—is controversial because many think that any market-based reform is dominated by business rather than educational interests and funnels public money to private schools or to school reform businesses. For researchers, the challenge is to move beyond the "horse race" comparisons of charter versus public or public versus private to consider the conditions under which each type of school works. That is, how each type either ameliorates or exacerbates inequalities among different student groups (e.g., class, race/ethnicity, gender, and language). In the meantime, policymakers remain entrenched in the fights that go on before school district boards, in state houses, and the federal government.

My approach is to remain as objective and impartial as possible to better provide the evidence to both critics and advocates of school choice. I tend not to campaign either for or against school choice or for one type of school over another. Indeed, individual experiences vary significantly within and between different types of schools. By systematically comparing schools, we can better understand the conditions under which school choice is effective or not—and for whom. For me, such an approach has led to many opportunities to inform various stakeholders and move us toward providing effective educational opportunities for all students, no matter what type of school they attend.

* * * * * *

Mark Berends is a professor of sociology and education at Notre Dame, where he directs the Center for Research on Educational Opportunity.

You can learn more about Dr. Berends's research on school vouchers in Indiana in the National Public Radio story "School Vouchers Get 2 New Report Cards" at www.npr.org/sections/ed/2017/06/26/533192616/school-vouchers-get-a-new-report-card.

a day carrying water home, their daughters often stay home from school to care for their younger siblings. Others stay home from school because their school has no running water or bathrooms. One in ten girls in sub-Saharan Africa does not attend school when having their menstrual cycle (Water Aid 2017). Indeed, research by WaterAid estimates that in the Global South, 263 million school days are lost each year due to water-related issues and diseases. When wells are built and usable water becomes more accessible, girls' school attendance immediately increases (WaterAid 2013).

In both the Global South and Global North, girls who cannot afford pads and tampons miss out on school during the days they menstruate. Some states in the United States have addressed this by ordering schools to stock tampons and pads in school bathrooms. As of 2018, California, Illinois, and New York had passed such legislation (Hinckley 2018).

How can the cost associated with pads and tampons impact one girl's education, and gender equity on the local, national, and global levels?

Educational Challenges in the Global North

A major concern in Global North countries in the information age is this: What will become of those students who do not complete enough education to attain the skills needed today and in the near future? In these countries, high school used to prepare most young people for a job. By the 1990s in the Global North, high school had become preparation for college, which was itself necessary to find a decent job in the globalizing world. What of those who may not want to attend or are not capable of succeeding in college? In European nations, such as Germany, students who do not attend college can gain work training through apprenticeships that prepare them for jobs that require certain skill sets (e.g., baker, mechanic, computer technician). This idea meets the need of the companies training students in skilled labor through apprenticeships and the need for younger workers to get a decent-paying job (Schwartz 2013).

As governments develop educational policies, we again see the interconnections of our social world. Curricula and modes of delivery of education respond to global events, international markets, and technological advances. They are also shaped by micro-level effectiveness or ineffectiveness of teachers in individual classrooms. The macro-level concerns and micro-level processes come together in education, with the ultimate objective of preparing individuals in each classroom to meet the needs of the community, state, nation, and world.

▲ These women are carrying water. Their daughters are often needed to either fetch the water or stay home with young children while the mothers tote the filled water jugs, making school attendance for girls difficult.

▲ Education, especially in the Global North, is becoming increasingly high tech. Nao, a robot manufactured by French company SoftBank Robotics, allows a sick child in the hospital to vicariously be present in the classroom. This robot is controlled by 7-year-old Jonas, who is suffering from leukemia and has regular chemotherapy preventing him from attending school.

After the family, education is one of the first institutions that a child encounters, and like the family, it is primarily concerned with the process of socialization of the populace. Another institution deeply concerned with socialization and the inculcation of values into young people is religion. Both religion and education tend to address issues of "what" and "why," but whereas education tends to focus on answers that have to do with knowledge—causality and the relationship between facts—religion tends to address questions of ultimate meaning in life. We turn in the next chapter to a sociological perspective on religion.

WHAT HAVE WE LEARNED?

Education systems are typically viewed as a means to reduce inequality, source of upward mobility, way to improve the economy, and path for reducing prejudice in society. However, institutions such as education also have a vested interest in stability. Schools foster patriotism and loyalty toward the political system, families support schools and education, and education is expected to support the economic vitality of the nation. Institutions and organizations are driven by interest in their own survival, and risk-taking behaviors on behalf of change are not necessarily those that foster survival. Taking risks may threaten those who have power, privilege, and influence. It should not be surprising, therefore, that education does more to enhance stability, carrying out what powerful policymakers feel is important, than to create change. Still, those who seek to improve society see tremendous potential in education as an agent of change, if its influence can be harnessed.

KEY POINTS

- Education is one of the primary institutions of society, focusing on the socialization of children and adults into their cultures so that they become contributing members.

- At the micro level, various statuses and roles interact within a school, and classrooms develop their own cultures that may or may not enhance learning.

- What we learn in schools goes far beyond the formal curriculum. We also learn a *hidden curriculum* that helps socialize us into our roles in schools and society.

- At the micro level, social theory is attentive to interaction in classrooms and local schools, using concepts of symbolic interaction or cost-benefit analysis to understand the climate of learning.

- At the meso level, education can be seen as a bureaucratic organization, with the pluses and minuses that come with bureaucratization.

- At the macro level, national governments often try to see that their national needs are met by shaping educational policy, and their actions often create tension with administrators and teachers at the meso and micro levels who do the actual work of running schools and teaching.

- Macro-level theories focus on how education supports the social system (functionalism) or on how education serves the interests of the "haves" and reproduces social inequality (conflict theory).

- Educating is also a global concern, with curriculum influenced by global, as well as national, events.

DISCUSSION QUESTIONS

1. Why is a good system of education important for a democracy? How can gaining a sociological perspective help people become more effective participants in a democratic society?

2. Who were the most popular kids in your high school? What made them popular? How did the reasons for their popularity vary based on their gender?

3. How do functionalist and conflict theorists describe the *hidden curriculum* in schools? What description best matches your own school experience? Why?

4. Do you think there should be tracking in schools? Why, or why not? How has tracking (or an absence of tracking) in your schools impacted your education and sense of yourself as a student? How does tracking in schools impact society?

5. This chapter describes several ways social class influences educational success. How has the social class of the family in which you were raised influenced your educational achievement? How did it influence your selection of a college to attend?

6. How do schools reproduce and perpetuate social stratification? If you had the power and desire to use the school system to reduce inequality, what policies would you implement? What do you think the chances are of your policies actually being put into place? Why?

KEY TERMS

ability grouping   338

equal educational opportunity   340

formal education   322

hidden curriculum   328

reproduction of class   339

school climate   329

shadow education   341

At the Local (Micro) Level

- Some colleges and universities have established programs called *FIGs* (*first-year interest groups*) to assist first-year students as they adjust to college and help them form a community with other students. Learn more about FIGs at schools such as the University of Wisconsin (figs.wisc.edu), the University of Washington (fyp.washington.edu), and the University of Missouri (reslife.missouri.edu/fig). If your school does not have a FIG program, try to initiate one.

- Every college and university provides opportunities for students to *tutor and mentor other students*. Ask the chair of your department or an office that coordinates mentoring how you can help!

At the Organizational or Institutional (Meso) Level

- Most primary schools welcome *reading and math tutors*, volunteers and service learning students, who can read to young students and tutor them in reading and math. Contact a faculty member on your campus who specializes in early childhood education and investigate the opportunities for such volunteer work.

- *Volunteers of America* (www.voa.org) chapters organize to provide low-income and homeless children with school supplies and backpacks every year through "Operation Backpack." You can learn more about the program and how to locate your local VOA chapter at the VOA website or by Googling "VOA" and "Operation Backpack" and the name of your state.

At the National or Global Level

- *Teach for America* (www.teachforamerica.org), a national organization modeled along the lines of AmeriCorps and Peace Corps, places recent college graduates in short-term (approximately 2-year) assignments teaching in economically disadvantaged neighborhood schools. "Teach for America is the national corps of outstanding recent college graduates and professionals of all academic majors and career interests who commit 2 years to teach in urban and rural public schools and become leaders in the effort to expand educational opportunity. . . . [Its] mission is to build the movement to eliminate educational inequity by enlisting our nation's most promising future leaders in the effort."

- *Teaching abroad* provides an opportunity to make a difference in the lives of children. Consider teaching English abroad through one of many organizations that sponsor teachers. Visit www.globaltesol.com, www.teachabroad.com, www.jetprogramme.org, and related websites. Also explore Teach for All (teachforall.org), a spin-off of Teach for America that has 45 partners across the globe with a mission "to expand educational opportunity around the world by increasing and accelerating the impact of social enterprises that are cultivating the leadership necessary for change."

CHAPTER 12

© AFP/Getty Images

RELIGION

The Social Meaning of Sacred Meaning

▲ Religion takes many forms and is expressed in many ways, but it is always about a sense of meaning and purpose in life. That meaning and actions associated with it affect many aspects of daily life.

MICRO

○ ME (AND MY FAITH COMMUNITY)

○ LOCAL ORGANIZATIONS AND COMMUNITY
People find meaning and support in a local church, temple, or mosque.

MESO

● NATIONAL ORGANIZATIONS, INSTITUTIONS, AND ETHNIC SUBCULTURES
Religious groups and denominations influence family life, government, education, and the economy.

MACRO

● SOCIETY
Religious groups foster national social movements and influence the national culture.

● GLOBAL COMMUNITY
Transnational religious organizations cross national borders, and religious outreach programs span the globe.

WHAT WILL YOU LEARN IN THIS CHAPTER?

This chapter will help you to do the following:

12.1 Explain the components and functions of religion

12.2 Discuss the process of becoming religious

12.3 Describe how the United States became a "denominational society"

12.4 Compare the functionalist and conflict perspectives on religion

12.5 Predict the future role of religion in the modern world

12.6 Understand how social trends regarding same-sex relationships affect core affirmations and policies of faith communities

THINK ABOUT IT

Micro: Small groups and local communities	How do various local religious congregations interact with the local community in your town?
Meso: National institutions, complex organizations, and ethnic groups	How does the institutionalization of a religion help it survive? Why do ethnic groups often practice specific religions or branches of religions?
Macro: National and global systems	How do religions foster solidarity and conflict within your country? How do religions help solve world problems (e.g., war, poverty, hunger, disease, bigotry) or help create them?

Abu Salmaan, a Muslim father and shopkeeper in Syria, prays frequently in keeping with the commands of the Quran, the holy book of his faith. Like his neighbors, when he hears the call to prayer, he goes to the village square, faces Mecca, and prostrates himself, with his head to the ground, to honor God and pray for peace. Doing this 5 times a day is a constant reminder of his ultimate loyalty to God, whom he calls Allah. As part of the larger Abrahamic religious tradition (which includes Judaism, Christianity, and Islam), he believes in one God and accepts the Hebrew Bible and the authority of Jeremiah, Isaiah, Amos, and Jesus as prophets. He believes that God also revealed truth through another voice—that of Muhammad. He is devoted, worshipping as commanded by the Quran, cherishing his family as directed by his scriptures, giving generously to charities, and making business decisions based on the moral standards of a God-loving Muslim.

Jennifer Quillin is a member of a congregational church (United Church of Christ) in Minneapolis. She attends worship services almost every week, and she works with her church to address justice issues—environmental, racial, and even global. Roughly a third of the congregation is gay or lesbian, and her state's approval of same-sex marriage was supported by a vigorous legislative campaign by her church. Jennifer is deeply involved in an interfaith social action association that she and her congregation see as a direct expression of Christian faith. The minister often mentions that the role of ministers is not to be "chaplains to the empire, but prophets for the resistance." Jennifer opposes prayer in schools because she thinks this would make some children feel ostracized. She values diversity and acceptance of other traditions.

Tuneq, knowledgeable Netsilik Inuit (Eskimo) hunter that he is, apologizes to the soul of the seal he has just killed. He shares the meat and blubber with his fellow hunters, and he makes sure that every part of the seal is used or consumed—skin, bones, eyes, tendons, brain, and muscles. His Inuit religion provides rules that help enforce an essential ecological ethic among these arctic hunters to preserve the delicate natural balance. His faith has taught Tuneq that if he fails to honor the seal by using every morsel or if he violates a rule of hunting etiquette, an invisible vapor will come from his body and sink through the ice, snow, and water. This vapor will collect in the hair of Nuliajuk, goddess of the sea. In revenge, she will call the sea mammals to her so the people living on the ice above will starve.

Before going to bed, Nandi Nwankwo from Nigeria sets out a bowl of milk and some food for the ancestors who, he believes, are present outside the family's dwelling at night. Respected ancestors protect family members, but they are also a powerful and even frightening force in guiding social behavior. Children learn that they must behave, or the ancestors will punish them.

These are but a few examples from the world's many and varied religious systems. What they have in common is that each system provides directions for appropriate and expected behaviors and serves as a form of social control for individuals within that society. Religious sanctions that encourage conformity are strong. Indeed, they are made *sacred*, a realm of existence different from mundane everyday life. Religion pervades the lives of people of faith so completely it becomes the fabric of their daily existence (McGuire 2008). It cannot be separated from the rest of the social world. Members of societies believe so strongly in their religions that conquests and wars throughout history have been based on spreading or defending the faith.

Sociologists are interested in these relationships—in the way social relationships and structures affect religion and in the consequences of religion for individuals and for society. In this chapter, we explore religion as a complex social phenomenon that interrelates with other processes and institutions of society. We investigate what religion does for individuals; how individuals become religious;

how religion and modern societies interact; and what religious policies have to say about teen sexuality, gay rights, and other social issues.

What Does Religion Do for Us?

What do people have to gain from religious practices, beliefs, and organizations? Religion helps explain the meaning of life, death, suffering, injustice, and events beyond our control. As sociologist Émile Durkheim pointed out, humans generally view such questions as belonging to a realm of existence different from the mundane or profane world of our everyday experience (Durkheim [1915] 2002). He called this separate dimension the *sacred realm*. This sacred realm elicits feelings of awe, reverence, and even fear. It is viewed as being above normal inquiry and doubt. Religious guidelines, beliefs, and values dictate "rights and wrongs," provide answers to the big questions of life, and instill moral codes and ideas about the world in members of each society or subculture. For these reasons, religions can have enormous control over people's attitudes and behavior (Ammerman 2009, 2013; Durkheim [1915] 2002).

Religion is more than a set of beliefs about the supernatural. It often *sacralizes* (makes sacred and unquestionable) the culture in which we live, the class or caste position to which we belong, the attitudes we hold toward other people, and the morals to which we adhere. Religion impacts our lifestyle, gender role, and social status. Around the world, billions of people believe they have found the truth—the ultimate answers—in their religions. Many are willing to die for their faith.

Note the various wars between Hindus and Muslims in India and Pakistan, between Catholics and Protestants in Northern Ireland, or between the two Muslim sects of Sunni and Shi'ite in several Muslim countries. Although the root causes of these wars are political and economic, religious differences help polarize "us" versus "them" sentiments. Religion can convince the members of each group that God is on their side.

THINKING SOCIOLOGICALLY

Consider your own religious tradition. Which of the purposes or functions of religion mentioned does your religious faith address? If you are not part of a faith community or do not hold religious beliefs of a particular group, are there other beliefs or groups that fulfill these functions for you?

Components of Religion

Religion normally involves at least three components: (1) a faith or worldview that provides a sense of meaning and purpose in life (the *meaning system*); (2) a set of interpersonal relationships and friendship networks (the *belonging system*); and (3) a stable pattern of roles, statuses, and organizational practices (the *structural system*) (Roberts and Yamane 2016).

The meaning system operates mostly at the micro level; the belonging system is also critical at the micro level but part of various meso-level organizations as well; and the structural system tends to have its major impact at the meso and macro levels. These components of religion may reinforce one another and work in harmony toward common goals, or there may be conflict among them.

Meaning System. The *meaning system* of a religion includes the ideas and symbols it uses to provide a sense of purpose in life and to help explain why suffering, injustice, and evil exist. It provides a big picture to account for events that would otherwise seem chaotic and irrational. For example, although the loss of a family member through death may be painful, many people find comfort and hope in their religion's teachings on the meaning of life and death.

Meaning systems of religion reflect the needs of the societies in which the religion is practiced. Because each culture has different problems to solve, the precise needs reflected in each society's meaning system vary. In agricultural societies, the problems revolve around growing crops and securing the elements necessary for crops—water, sunlight, and good soil. Among the Zuni of New Mexico and the Hopi of Arizona, for example, water for crops is a critical concern. These Native American people typically grow corn in a climate that averages roughly 10 inches of rain per year, so it is not surprising that the central focus of their religious dances and of their supernatural beings—kachinas—is to bring rain. In other societies, the death rate is so high that high fertility has been necessary to perpetuate the group. Thus, fertility goddesses take on great significance. In some other societies, strong armies and brave soldiers have been essential to preserve the group from invading forces; hence, gods or rituals of war have been popular.

Belonging System. *Belonging systems* are profoundly important in most religious groups. A belonging system refers to the interpersonal networks and emotional ties that develop among adherents of a faith. Many people remain members of religious groups not so much

▲ Buddhist monks pray at Bayon Temple in Angkor Thom, Cambodia. Their religious system gives them a sense of meaning and purpose in life but also provides social ties.

individualized that *sacralization* of common values can no longer occur. Therefore, religious groups almost always eventually develop a system of control and screening of new revelations. Religious leaders in designated statuses have the authority to interpret theology and define the essentials of the faith.

Religious groups also need methods of designating leaders, raising funds to support their organizations, and ensuring continuation of the group. To teach the next generation the meaning system, members need to develop a formal structure to determine the content and form of their educational materials, and then they must produce and distribute them. If the religion is to survive past the death of a charismatic leader, it must undergo institutionalization. In other words, it must establish a *structural system* of established statuses, norms, ways to access resources, and routine procedures for addressing problems.

Because religion is one institution in the larger society, it is interdependent and interrelated with the political, economic, family, education, health, media, and other social institutions. Changes in any one of these areas can bring change to religion, and changes in religion can bring changes to other institutions of society. Consider the furor in parts of the United States over the decision of some school districts to teach "intelligent design," the idea that living things were created under the design of an intelligent being (i.e., God), as part of the science curriculum in public schools. The conflict reverberates in congregations, schools, legislative chambers, courts, and scientific communities.

Although some people dislike the idea of organized religion, one insight of sociology is that a group cannot survive in the modern world unless it undergoes *routinization of charisma.* That is, religious organizations must develop established roles, statuses, groups, and routine procedures for replacing leaders after death and obtaining resources to survive more than a generation (Weber 1947).

At the local level, a formal religious structure develops, with committees doing specific tasks, such as overseeing worship, maintaining the building, recruiting religious teachers for children, and raising funds. These committees report to an administrative board that works closely with the clergy (the ordained ministers) and has much of the final responsibility for the life and continued existence of the people who regularly gather for religious services, referred to as the *congregation*. The roles, statuses, and committees make up the structural system. The structure is every bit as important as the meaning system if the group is to thrive.

because they accept the meaning system of the group but because that is where they find their belonging system—their friendship and kinship network. A prayer group may be the one area in their lives in which people can be truly open about their personal pain and feel safe to expose their vulnerabilities. This builds bonds and belonging. For many religious people, their religious group is a type of extended family that tends to become more important as their own families age. The religious groups that have grown the fastest in recent years are those that have devised ways to strengthen the sense of belonging and to foster friendship networks within the group.

Structural System. A religion involves a group of people who share a common meaning system. However, if each person interprets the group's beliefs in his or her own way and if each attaches his or her own meanings to the symbols, the meaning system becomes so

Like any other formal organization in society, meso-level religious structures consist of individuals and committees doing specialized tasks. Contemporary branches of Christianity in the United States, for example, may have national commissions on global outreach, evangelism, worship, world peace, social justice, and so forth. In addition, bishops, presbyters, or other leaders provide guidelines for pastors who lead their own congregations. Most religious organizations are, among other things, bureaucracies. The formal organization may be caught up in some of the dysfunctions that can plague any organization: goal displacement, the iron law of oligarchy, alienation, and other problems discussed in Chapter 5.

The three components of religion—meaning, belonging, and structure—are interconnected and interdependent. One member of a faith community may be committed to the meaning system, another to the belonging system through strong friendship networks, and a third to the structural system, making large financial donations to a congregation even though he or she rarely attends services. In most cases, however, commitment to one of these systems will reinforce commitment to the others. They usually go together (see Figure 12.1).

THINKING SOCIOLOGICALLY

Think about the meaning, belonging, and structural systems of a religion with which you are familiar. How do these elements influence—and how are they influenced by—the larger social world, from individual to national and global systems?

▼ FIGURE 12.1

Three Components of Religion

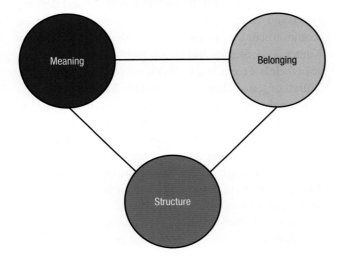

Becoming Part of a Faith Community: Micro-Level Analysis

We are not born religious, although we may be born into a religious group. We learn our religious outlook and behaviors through socialization, just as we learn our language, customs, norms, and values. Our family usually determines the religious environment in which we grow up, whether it is all-encompassing or closer to a one-day-a-week commitment. We start imitating religious practices, such as praying before bed or saying grace before dinner, before we understand these practices intellectually. Then, as we encounter the unexplainable events of life, religion is there to provide meaning. Gradually, religion becomes an ingrained part of many people's lives.

It is unlikely that we will adopt a faith not practiced in our society. For instance, if we were born in most parts of India, we would be raised in and around the Hindu, Muslim, and Sikh faiths. In most Arab countries, we would become Muslim; in South American countries, we would likely become Catholic or evangelical Christian; and in many Southeast Asian countries, Buddhist. Although our religious affiliation may seem normal and typical to us, no religion has a majority of the people in the world as its adherents, and we may in fact be part of a rather small minority religious group when we think in terms of the global population. Figure 12.2 shows this explicitly.

Learning the meaning system of a religious group is both a formal and an informal process. In some cultures, religious faith pervades everyday life. For the Amish, farming without machines or the use of electricity is part of their Christian teachings, which affect their total lifestyle. Formal teaching in most religions takes place primarily in the temple, church, or mosque. This formal teaching may take the form of bar or bat mitzvah classes, Sunday school, or parochial school. Informal religious teaching occurs when we observe others "practicing what they preach."

Again, the meaning (believing) and belonging systems are linked in important ways. Most people do not belong to a religious group because they accept its belief system, at least initially. Rather, they come to believe because they want to belong and are socialized to feel they are an integral part of the group (Greeley 1972; Roberts and Yamane 2016). Research on people who switch religious affiliations or join new religious movements (NRMs) indicates that loyalty to a friendship network usually comes first, followed by commitment to the meaning and structural systems. In many cases,

Religious Adherence Around the Globe

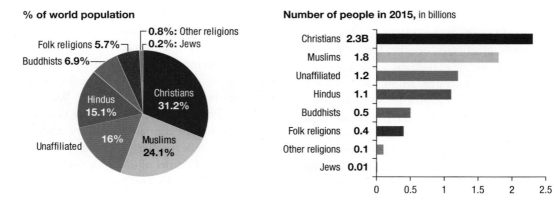

Christians are the largest religious group in 2015

% of world population

- **0.8%:** Other religions
- **0.2%:** Jews
- Folk religions **5.7%**
- Buddhists **6.9%**
- Christians **31.2%**
- Hindus **15.1%**
- Unaffiliated **16%**
- Muslims **24.1%**

Number of people in 2015, in billions

Christians	**2.3B**
Muslims	**1.8**
Unaffiliated	**1.2**
Hindus	**1.1**
Buddhists	**0.5**
Folk religions	**0.4**
Other religions	**0.1**
Jews	**0.01**

0   0.5   1   1.5   2   2.5

Source: Hackett and McClendon 2017.

▲ The bat mitzvah, shown here, is an initiation ceremony into the faith for Jewish girls.

accepting a new meaning system is the final rather than initial stage of change (Roberts and Yamane 2016).

There is more fluidity in religious membership now than at any other time in history. Historically, most people remained part of the same religious group for a lifetime. Current studies, however, show that 34% of U.S. citizens have either left the religious group in which they were raised for another religion or no longer have any religious affiliation (Pew Research Center 2015f). Increased interreligious marriage plays a role in changing religions, in that 39% of current marriages involve spouses with different religious affiliations. Most often, the change is to a different branch of the same umbrella religion (e.g., from one form of Christianity to another) (Pew Forum on Religion and Public Life 2015).

Because changing religious groups occurs most often through change of friendship networks or marriage, religious groups frequently try to control the boundaries and protect their members from outside influences. The Amish in the United States have done this by living in their own communities and attempting to limit schooling of their children by outside authorities. To help perpetuate religious beliefs and practices, most religious groups encourage endogamy, marrying within the group. For example, Orthodox Jews have food taboos and food preparation requirements that limit the likelihood they will share a meal with "outsiders." To have a wedding in the Catholic Church, Catholics who want to marry a non-Catholic must receive permission from their local bishop to marry "despite the disparity of cult" between them.

Religious groups also try to socialize members to make sacrifices of time, energy, and financial resources on behalf of their faith. If one has sacrificed and devoted one's resources and energy for a cause, one is likely to feel a commitment to the organization—the structural system (Kanter 2005; Sherkat and Ellison 1999). Single young people in their late teens and early 20s who are members of the Church of Jesus Christ of Latter-Day Saints (Mormons) are strongly encouraged to devote 2 years of their lives to missionary work. They must save money in advance to support themselves. This sacrifice of other opportunities and investment of time, energy, and resources in the church creates an intense commitment to the organization. Few of them later feel that they have wasted those years or that the investment was unwise (Barlow and Givens 2015). So, commitment to the structural system is connected to strong commitment to the meaning and belonging systems.

▲ Mormons (Latter-Day Saints) are expected to spend 2 years as missionaries as young adults, a process that increases their commitment to the faith.

▲ A Romanian Roma woman uses different tubs to wash upper- and lower-body clothing and men's and women's apparel separately so that they will not become spiritually defiled.

The survival of a religious group depends in part on how committed its members are and whether they share freely of their financial and time resources. Most religious groups try, therefore, to socialize their members into commitment to the meaning, belonging, and structural systems of their religion.

THINKING SOCIOLOGICALLY

How did you or individuals you know become committed to a faith tradition? Did you (or they) think about the process as it occurred, or were you (or they) born into it? If you left a religious organization, why did you leave?

Symbols and the Creation of Meaning: A Symbolic Interactionist Perspective

Dina is appalled as she walks passed the Laundromat. The *gaje* (the term Roma use to refer to non-Roma) just do not seem to understand cleanliness. These middle-class North American neighbors of hers are concerned about whether their clothes are *melalo*—dirty. In contrast, they pay no attention to whether they are *marime*—defiled or polluted in a spiritual sense. She watches in disgust as a woman not only places the clothing of men, women, and children in a single washing machine but also includes clothing from the upper and lower halves of the body together. No respectable Roma (sometimes called Gypsies by outsiders) would allow such mixing, and if it did occur, the clothing could be used only as rags. The laws of spiritual purity make clear that the lower half of the body is defiled. Anything that

comes in contact with the body below the waist or that touches the floor becomes marime and can never again be considered *wuzho*—truly "clean." Food that touches the floor becomes filthy and inedible.

Ideally, a Roma woman would have separate washtubs for men's upper-body clothing, men's lower-body clothing, women's upper-body clothing, women's lower-body clothing, and children's clothing. Roma know too well that the spirit of Mamioro brings illness to homes that are marime. The lack of spiritual cleanliness of non-Roma causes Roma to minimize their contact with these gaje, to avoid sitting on a chair used by a gaje, and generally to recoil at the thought of assimilation into the larger culture (Sutherland 1986, 2001; Sway 1988).

How we make sense of the world takes place through meaning systems, as illustrated in the previous example. Roma interpret objects and actions in ways that differ from members of the larger society, and the different meanings result in different behaviors and sometimes distancing from "outsiders."

Symbolic interaction theory focuses on how we make sense of and construct our worlds. When we see religious symbols, we react to them based on our experiences with and understanding of the religion they symbolize. Think about how you feel attracted to, or perhaps put off by, someone who wears a cross or another religious symbol, such as a yarmulke, worn by Orthodox Jewish men to cover the crown of the head, or a head scarf worn by Muslim women. Symbols affect micro-level interaction—the way we feel about people and whether we are inclined to form a relationship.

It is the meaning system that most interests symbolic interactionists—the worldview or conceptual framework by which people make sense of life and cope with

▲ Navajo medicine man Albert Laughter performs a healing ceremony to care for veterans. He has been contracted with the Department of Veterans Affairs to treat Native American veterans suffering from problems like post-traumatic stress with traditional Navajo rituals and healing methods.

suffering and injustice. Religious meaning systems are made up of three elements: myths, rituals, and symbols.

Myths are *stories that transmit values and embody ideas about life and the world.* When sociologists of religion use the word *myth*, they are not implying that the story is untrue. A myth may relate historical incidents that actually occurred, fictional events, or abstract ideas, such as reincarnation. Regardless of the literal truth or fiction of these stories, myths transmit values and a particular outlook on life. If a story, such as the exodus from Egypt of ancient Hebrew people, elicits some sense of sacredness, communicates certain attitudes and values, and helps make sense of life, then it is a myth. The Netsilik Eskimo myth of the sea goddess Nuliajuk (explained in the third story that opened this chapter) reinforces and makes sacred the value of conservation in an environment of scarce resources. It provides messages for appropriate behavior in that group. Thus, whether a myth is factual is irrelevant. Myths are always "true" in some deeper metaphorical sense. Indeed, stories that do not carry truth or deep meaning are simply not myths.

Rituals are *ceremonies or repetitive practices, often used to invoke a sense of awe of the divine and to make certain ideas sacred.* Ceremonies may include music, dancing, kneeling, praying, chanting, storytelling, and other symbolic acts. A number of religions, such as Islam, emphasize devotion to orthopraxy (conformity of behavior) more than orthodoxy (conformity to beliefs or doctrine) (Preston 1988; Tipton 1990). Praying 5 times a day while facing Mecca, mandated for the Islamic faithful, is an example of orthopraxy.

Often, rituals involve acting out myths. In almost all Christian churches, the cleansing of the soul is enacted by immersing people in water or pouring water on the head during baptism. Likewise, Christians frequently reenact the Last Supper of Jesus (Communion or Eucharist) as they accept their role as modern disciples. Among the Navajo, rituals enacted by a medicine man may last as long as 5 days. An appropriate myth is told, and sand paintings, music, and dramatics lend power and unique reality to the myths.

The group environment of the ritual is important. Ethereal music, communal chants, and group actions such as kneeling or taking off one's shoes when entering the shrine or mosque create an aura of separation from the everyday world and a mood of awe so that the beliefs seem eternal and beyond question. They become sacralized. Rituals also make ample use of symbols.

As you will recall from earlier chapters, a *symbol* is an object or action that represents something else and therefore has meaning beyond its own existence (e.g., flags and wedding rings). Because religion deals with the transcendent—a realm that cannot be experienced or proven with the five senses—sacred symbols are a central part of religion. They have a powerful emotional impact on the faithful and reinforce the sacredness of myths.

Sacred symbols store an enormous amount of information and can deliver that information with powerful immediacy. Seeing a cross, for example, can flood a Christian's consciousness with a whole series of images, events, and powerful emotions concerning Jesus and his disciples. Tasting the bitter herbs during a Jewish Seder service is meant to elicit memories of the story of slavery in Egypt, recall the escape under the leadership of Moses, and send a moral message to the celebrant to work for freedom and justice in the world today. The mezuzah, a plaque consecrating a house, fixed to the doorpost of a Jewish home, is a symbol reminding the occupants of their commitment to obey God's commandments and reaffirming God's commitment to them as a people. Because symbols are often heavily laden with emotion and can

358 ■ *PART IV • INSTITUTIONS*

elicit strong feelings, they are used extensively in rituals to represent myths.

Myths, rituals, and symbols are usually interrelated and interdependent (see Figure 12.3). Together, they form the meaning system—a set of ideas about life or the cosmos that seem uniquely realistic and compelling. They reinforce rules of appropriate behavior and even political and economic systems by making them sacred. They can also control social relationships among different groups. The Roma revulsion at the filthy marime practices of middle-class Americans, like the Kosher rules for food preparation among the Jews, creates boundaries between "us" and "them" that nearly eliminate prospects of marriage or even of close friendships outside the religious community. Some scholars think that these rituals and symbolic meanings are the key reason why Roma and Jews have survived for millennia as distinct groups without being assimilated or absorbed into dominant cultures. The symbols and meanings have created barriers that prevent the obliteration of their cultures (Roberts and Yamane 2016).

When symbolic interactionists study religion, they tend to focus on how symbols influence people's perception of reality. Symbolic interactionists stress that humans create, shape, and interpret the meaning of events. Clearly, no other institution focuses as explicitly on shaping and interpreting the meaning of life and its events as religion.

▼ FIGURE 12.3

The Meaning System of Religion Is Composed of Three Interrelated Elements

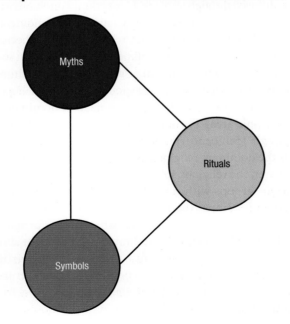

THINKING SOCIOLOGICALLY

In a religious tradition with which you are familiar, how do symbols and sacred stories reinforce a particular view of the world or set of values and social norms?

Seeking Eternal Benefits: A Rational Choice Perspective

Rational choice theorists maintain that people decide whether they should join or leave a religious group by asking about the benefits and the costs. Do the benefits outweigh the costs? The benefits, of course, are nonmaterial when it comes to religious choices—feeling that life has meaning, belonging to a community, gaining a sense of communion with God, confidence in an afterlife, and so forth (Iannaccone 2010; Warner 1993).

The rational choice approach views churchgoers as consumers out to meet their needs or obtain a "product." It depicts churches as entrepreneurial establishments, or "franchises," in a competitive market, with "entrepreneurs" (clergy) as leaders. Competition for members leads churches, for example, to "market" their religion to consumers. Converts, and religious people generally, are regarded as active and rational agents pursuing self-interests. To grow, churches must meet "consumer demand" (Finke and Stark 2005; Jelen 2002). Religious groups produce religious "commodities" (rituals, meaning systems, a sense of belonging, symbols, and so forth) to meet the "demands" of consumers (Christiano, Swatos, and Kivisto 2008).

Rational choice theorists believe that aggressive religious entrepreneurs who seek to produce religious products appealing to a target audience will reap the benefits of a large congregation. As competitive enterprises, churches, temples, and mosques must make investments of effort, time, and resources to attract and keep potential buyers. There are many religious entrepreneurs seeking to increase the number of people in their congregations. The challenge for the various groups is to beat the competition by meeting the demand of the current marketplace (Finke and Scheitle 2013; Finke and Stark 2005). For instance, because the U.S. Constitution separates church from state, organized religions have had to offer their product on an open market, in competition with other religions. This has prompted most religions in the United States to put much energy into recruiting more followers.

Not everyone agrees that religion is a competitive enterprise. This strictly utilitarian economic analysis of religion seems counter to the way most religious people understand their own behavior. As one religious scholar put it,

> It is one thing to describe a person's decision to join a church *as if* the person were trying to maximize his or her benefits; it is something different to claim that the person's *actual* thought in joining measured his or her potential gains against potential losses. (McGuire 2002:298–299)

Whereas costs and benefits may exist, people may not consciously measure them when determining whether to join a religious organization.

THINKING SOCIOLOGICALLY

Does the rational choice explanation for religious behavior seem correct to you? Why? Is religious behavior similar to self-interested economic behavior? Why or why not?

Religion and Modern Life: Meso-Level Analysis

Cassandra is a chaplain at a hospital in Minneapolis. She works closely with doctors and other professionals in health care who value her work. Many of the physicians at her hospital are convinced that when people have emotional support, feel a sense of love and connection, and have hope for the future, their health is more likely to improve. Cassandra prays for the people she counsels, but she also is convinced that God often works through

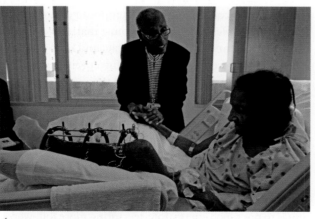

▲ Chaplains, members of the religious institution, often work closely with professionals in another institution—health care. Here we see a hospital chaplain at work.

science and modern medicine. The clergy and medical professionals collaborate as a team to help people either recover from ill health or face death with dignity.

We begin this meso-level discussion by exploring various types of religious organizations and then examining how religion as an institution interacts with other institutions. As you will see, different religions structure themselves in various ways. All, though, interact with the other social institutions in society.

Types of Religious Organizations

The unique history of religious organizations in the United States led Andrew Greeley to describe the country as a "denominational society" (Greeley 1972). In doing so, though, he stressed the heterogeneity among religious denominations in the American colonies and then the United States, which as a nation is religiously diverse in two senses: multiple religious groups living side by side with no single faith tradition being dominant, and church and state given their own autonomous realms by the U.S. Constitution (Stark and Finke 2000).

Denominations and Denominationalism. In the United States and most other Western countries, local congregations tend to be part of larger centralized organizations. These *centralized coordinating bodies or associations that link local congregations with a similar history and theology* are called **denominations**.

In the long history of human society, denominationalism is a unique and rather recent way of organizing religion (Ammerman 2006). For most of human history, religion was diffused through all of life. Under these conditions, religion and the rest of life have been seamless and undifferentiated (Bellah 1970). Over time, religion gradually became distinct from other social institutions in most Western societies, particularly in political or governmental structures. The result is that specifically religious organizations arose.

Initially, a single religious organization dominated a geographic area. Throughout the Middle Ages (the 5th through 15th centuries) the Roman Catholic Church was the dominant religious group in Europe. Eventually, however, the religious sphere itself came to be diverse, as various groups within the Catholic Church developed distinct missions (the Dominicans, the Jesuits, and so forth). It became more distinct when the Reformation (1517–1648) launched Protestantism and brought about the emergence of different, oppositional Christian groups with varied beliefs and organizational structures. Most of them were splinter groups that broke away from Catholicism, such as the Lutherans (Gorski 2000).

Each religious group attempted to become the official government-approved church in its territory. Conflict rather than peaceful coexistence came to characterize Europe, and many people were forced to flee the lands in which they were raised because of their faith.

Some of those driven out of Europe for religious reasons were followers of the Calvinist Puritan movement seeking to reform the Church of England, a church that split from the Catholic Church in 1534 largely because King Henry VIII wanted to legitimize a divorce. The Puritans ended up playing a major role in the founding of the New England colonies and, in so doing, created religious establishments of their own. Four of the colonies (Rhode Island, Delaware, New Jersey, and Pennsylvania) were religiously diverse and had no state-sponsored church. As a result, no single religious group established dominance or control in North America. This development led to necessary peaceful coexistence: religious pluralism and official separation of church and state.

Freedom of religion and prohibition of a state-endorsed church are key conditions for denominationalism. When scholars refer to the United States as a "denominational society," they mean a society characterized by religious congregations united into denominations that are presumed equal under the law and that generally treat other religious bodies with mutual respect. Because of this organizational pattern of religious pluralism, there are hundreds of denominations in the United States (Mead, Hill, and Atwood 2005). Indeed, the *Handbook of Denominations in the United States* lists 34 Baptist denominations alone (Olson, Atwood, Mead, & Hill 2018). Denominationalism has become a global phenomenon. The *World Christian Encyclopedia* reports 33,830 denominations within Christianity worldwide, and the World Christian Database has extensive data on 9,000 of those denominations (World Christian Database 2015).

Although diversity within Protestantism was a key force for denominationalism, it has become fully incorporated by all major religious groups in the United States. Some scholars have even identified Jewish "denominationalism" in reference to the four branches of Judaism—Orthodox, Conservative, Reform, and Reconstructionist (Jewish Outreach Institute 2015). The Nation of Islam and American Society of Muslims are distinctively American Islamic denominations (though the former is often viewed negatively by traditional Muslims). Some denominations of Islam are more global (Sunni and Shi'ite are the largest). Buddhism and Hinduism also have different branches or schools. Like Islam, they were brought to America in large numbers only recently, so it remains to be seen whether there will be an evolution of those branches into recognizable denominations in the United States.

Denominational Structures and the Micro-Meso Connection. The organizational structures of U.S. denominations vary. Most, however, are congregational, episcopal, or presbyterian (Ammerman 2006). Note that these are *not* the same as churches by those names, but rather the organizational structure (or "polity") of a number of churches.

In a *congregational* polity or structure, the authority of the local congregation is supreme. For example, the thousands of Baptist and United Church of Christ congregations in the United States hire and fire their own ministers, control their own finances, own their own property, decide whether to ordain women, and make other decisions about the congregation themselves (Ammerman 1990, 2009).

The *episcopal*—also called "hierarchical"—pattern of governance places ultimate authority over local churches in the centralized hands of bishops (the word *episcopal* means "governed by bishops"). Each of the Roman Catholic Church's nearly 20,000 U.S. congregations (or "parishes") is geographically defined. They are clustered into "dioceses" under the authority of local bishops and, ultimately, the bishop of Rome—the pope. In an episcopal structure, a bishop, in consultation with his or her executive staff, decides who will be the priest or minister of each local church. A committee of the local congregation may be consulted, but the bishop has the final say. Christian churches that have some form of episcopal organization include Anglican, Episcopalian, Eastern Orthodox, Methodist, African Methodist Episcopal (AME), AME Zion, and some Lutherans. So, the local United Methodist church building in your community is actually owned by the larger denomination and is only maintained by the local congregation, and a bishop decides who will be the minister for the community.

Presbyterian polity, quite simply, is a middle ground between episcopal (with a bishop having tremendous power) and congregational (where the congregation has total authority). In presbyterian polity, authority is shared so that neither a single local congregation nor the hierarchy can trump the other. The Presbyterian Church is the best example of this compromise position. Presbyterian structure usually involves a local board—called a session—in a congregation that can make decisions. Organizations composed of groups of congregations at regional and national levels, in order of regional to national, are typically called presbyteries, synods, and then the national assembly. Almost all Reformed churches use this approach: Dutch Reformed, Swiss Reformed, and the Presbyterian Church, which is an offshoot of the Scottish Reformed tradition. Table 12.1 provides some examples of which churches tend to follow which polity.

Polity or Organizational Structures of Selected Churches

Congregational Polity	Episcopal Polity	Presbyterian Polity
United Church of Christ (Congregational)	Roman Catholic	Reformed Churches
National Baptist	Episcopal	Dutch Reformed
Southern Baptist	Anglican	Swiss Reformed
Christian Church (Disciples of Christ)	United Methodist	French Reformed
Churches of Christ	African Methodist Episcopal	Church of Scotland
Unitarian Universalists	Evangelical Lutheran	Presbyterian Church USA

▲ One cannot tell by looking at these buildings, but the organizational structure and who owns them is quite different. The Methodist church on the left is episcopal in structure, the Presbyterian church in the center has a presbyterian organization, and the Congregational church on the right has a congregational structure.

Although denominational structure or polity strongly affects the structure of a local congregation and how it works, the social environment can also cause a certain amount of adaptation. The tendency to assimilate to the organizational patterns in the social environment impacts religious groups as much as it does individuals, as shown in the next Sociology in Our Social World.

New Religious Movements (NRMs) or Cults

New religious movements, or NRMs, arise to meet specific needs not met through traditional religious organizations. If an NRM survives for several generations, becomes established, and gains some legitimacy, it becomes a completely new religious tradition rather than a new denomination of an existing faith. So, an **NRM** is *the beginning phase of an entirely new religion. Cult* was once the common term for this kind of movement, but the media and the public have so completely misused the word that its meaning has become unclear and often

negative. The term *cult*, as sociologists have historically used it, is simply descriptive, not judging the group as good, bad, or kooky. Most sociologists of religion now prefer to use the term *NRM* (Christiano et al. 2008; Monahan, Mirola, and Emerson 2016).

NRMs are either imported into a country as immigrants enter from other lands or founded on a new revelation (or insight, often directly from God) by a charismatic leader. They are usually out of the mainstream religious system, at least in their early days. Christianity, Buddhism, and Islam all began as NRMs or cults. The estimated number of NRMs in North America at the turn of the century was 1,500 to 2,000 (Melton and Blaumann 2010; Nichols, Mather, and Schmidt 2006). There are an estimated 10,000 more NRMs in Africa, with especially rapid growth in Nigeria, and perhaps tens of thousands more worldwide (Ibrahim 2013; Religious Worlds 2007).

An NRM usually originates with a charismatic leader, someone who claims to have received a new insight, usually straight from God. For example, Reverend Sun

SOCIOLOGY IN OUR SOCIAL WORLD

ISLAM, MOSQUES, AND ORGANIZATIONAL STRUCTURE

Most mosques in the United States are relatively new, with almost all founded after 1970. Since 2000, the number of mosques has increased 74%. At the turn of the century, there were 1,209 mosques in the United States. As of 2018, there were approximately 2,600 (Grossman 2012; Sinclair Broadcast Group 2018).

According to Islamic scholar Ihsan Bagby, "Most of the world's mosques are simply a place to pray. . . . A Muslim cannot be a member of a particular mosque" because mosques belong to God, not to the people (Bagby 2003:115). In some countries, mosques are government supported. The role of the imam—the leader of a mosque—is simply to lead prayers 5 times a day and to run the services on the Sabbath, including delivery of a sermon. Unlike many Christian and Jewish leaders in the United States, an imam does not run an organization and does not need formal training at a seminary. In the United States, mosques, like other religious organizations, cannot depend on government funding and need to adapt to the congregational model: recruiting members who will support it. Many mosques feature multiple meeting spaces and have become community centers rather than simply a place to pray. Religious education, traditionally managed largely by extended families, also now takes place in many U.S.

mosques. Religious holidays are celebrated at the mosque rather than with families, and life cycle celebrations (births and marriages) are events for the congregation. This is a major change in the role of the mosque and the imam for many Muslims.

Mosques in the United States tend to be attended primarily by immigrants or African Americans. African American mosques represent only 27% of the total number of mosques, and these are in some important ways different in organizational structure from those attended by immigrants. Most importantly, 93% of African American mosques are led by an imam, compared with only 38% of immigrant-attended mosques.

Just 33% of all mosques in the United States have a paid, full-time imam, and only 13% of imams have a master's degree in theology, which is the standard expected for most mainstream Christian and Jewish clergy. So, despite having exceptionally high levels of well-educated members in professional and managerial positions, Islamic mosques are less bureaucratized, with less emphasis on professional credentials, membership roles, or denominational connections. Mosques have already made some adjustments to U.S. society, however, and will likely assimilate further to the religious organizational patterns of the larger society.

Myung Moon founded an NRM called the Unification Church, whose members are often referred to as *Moonies*. While claiming to be a part of Christianity, the Unification Church has its own additional scripture to complement the Bible, and Reverend Moon has a standing in the Unification Church equal to Jesus—an idea offensive to most Christian groups.

Some NRMs have ended in tragedy: In 1997, 39 members of the Heaven's Gate NRM committed group suicide. They believed supernatural beings were coming to take them away in a flying saucer and that they had to kill themselves so that their souls could board the spaceship (Wessinger 2000).

Most new religious groups, however, are not dangerous to members. Furthermore, most religious groups now accepted and established were stigmatized as strange or evil at some time. Early Christians, for example, were characterized by Romans as dangerous cannibals. In the 19th century and early decades of the 20th century

in the United States, Roman Catholics were depicted in the media as dangerous, immoral, and anti-American (Bromley and Shupe 1981). When we encounter media reports about NRMs, we should remember that not all cults are like the tragic, sensational ones.

NRMs tend to be hard to study because the members feel they might be persecuted for their faith and beliefs. Witchcraft (or Wicca) is one example of a religion forced to remain secretive; the next Sociology in Our Social World explores the strategies of one sociologist to examine this religious community.

THINKING SOCIOLOGICALLY

What factors might lead to the birth of an NRM? Imagine the leaders of an NRM have asked you for advice on how they might succeed. What advice would you give them?

SOCIOLOGY IN OUR SOCIAL WORLD

WITCHCRAFT IN THE UNITED STATES

▲ Wiccans participate in a lunar ritual in Illinois.

In *A Community of Witches: Contemporary Neo-Paganism and Witchcraft in the United States*, Helen Berger applies sociological analysis to conduct a fascinating study of contemporary Wicca (Berger 1999). She carried out participant observation in a newly formed coven in New England. A coven is a small congregation of witches, usually with no more than 10 or 12 members. It took considerable effort to establish trust with the members, but this method of gathering data allowed her to experience firsthand the close-knit support group and the actual behaviors and interactions within the group. A national organization provided her with a wealth of printed material produced by Neo-Pagans and allowed her entry to several national Neo-Pagan festivals, where she observed the rituals. She also did in-depth, open-ended interviews with 40 members from a number of covens. By using a variety of methods, Berger was able to gain in-depth information and get an idea of whether her qualitative data accurately described most covens.

Wicca was established in the first half of the 20th century from various pieces of occult lore. Every member is clergy, all priests and priestesses; worship is of two deities, a god and a goddess, and the rites and rituals are learned at initiation. It comes from a feminist perspective, believing in a goddess and emphasizing gender equality, though some branches of Wicca include men. It also celebrates the spiritual unity of humans with nature and has a strong ecology ethic. The religion encourages self-awareness, self-transformation, and an intuitive approach to decision-making (rather than using logic). As a nature-based religion, it also celebrates the senses and embraces sexuality, fertility, and being at one with the universe.

Religion and Other Social Institutions

The dominant religion in any society generally supports the dominant political system and ideology of the society. It also closely relates to the economic and education systems and legitimates the family system through sacred rites of passage for marriage, birth, and death. Religion interacts with the health system, as well. Some religions establish rules related to health care. Also, those who regularly attend religious services are healthier (and happier) than those who do not (Li et al. 2016).

Religion not only supports other institutions but may also experience support or pressure from these other institutions. For example, due to AIDS and rapid population growth, especially in poor Catholic nations, a number of international organizations, political movements, governments, religious groups, and educational institutions have encouraged the Catholic Church to ease its strict ban on artificial birth control. Pope Francis has indicated some openness to accepting the use of condoms to prevent the spread of AIDS, saying the Church should focus on more important issues (like hunger and inadequate housing) rather than stopping people from using condoms (Associated Press 2015; Nadeau 2017). If the Catholic Church does not change and adapt with the times, it must expend considerable effort to defend its position to keep from losing credibility in the eyes of members and nonmembers alike. We now consider the relationship between religion and three other social institutions: family, politics, and economics.

Religion and Family. Our parents provide our first contact with religion. They may say prayers, attend worship services, and talk about proper behavior as defined by their religious group. Many religions recognize Mother's Day, Father's Day, and Grandparents' Day, thereby honoring and connecting parenting and family ties to the religion. Many of the sacred ceremonies in religion are family affairs: births, christenings or naming of new members, marriages, and funerals. Jews, Muslims, and Latter-Day Saints (Mormons) are especially known for their many ceremonies and gatherings designed specifically for family units, and their moral codes place a high value on family loyalty and responsibility.

Various faiths spread distinct messages on how marriage partners should relate to one another and raise a family. For example, some fundamentalist Christian groups (those that believe in a literal interpretation of the Bible) produce parenting manuals and manifestos to guide families that promote their perspective on family life. Some of these have created controversy because of their emphasis on hierarchical and authority-centered parenting models (Carlson and Mero 2005; Grille 2005; Swan 2017). The conservative Christian organization Focus on the Family has a syndicated newspaper column, radio programs, books, DVDs, and a monthly magazine that it uses to spread its perspective on family life.

Sometimes tensions can arise between family and religion over social control. Among the Amish, for example, if the bishop orders a member of the church "shunned," the family must comply and refuse to speak to or associate with that person. If the family does not comply, it will be ostracized by the other members of the community (Frater 2012; Hostetler 1993).

Religion and Politics: Theocracies and Civil Religion. Religious groups and political systems may interrelate in various ways, ranging from hostile conflict to religious groups fully embracing and legitimizing political structures and leaders. In a pure **theocracy**, or rule by God, *religious leaders, like those in Iran, rule society in accordance with God's presumed wishes.* In other nations, political, rather than religious, leaders govern, but an official state religion receives support from tax money. Sweden, Britain, and Italy are examples of societies with state religions. In China, citizens have some limited freedom to practice certain religions, but the Chinese government gives itself the right to select religious leaders (like the Dalai Lama and Catholic bishops serving in China). Some

countries, such as the former Soviet Union, have outlawed religion altogether so that nothing competed with loyalty to the nation. The continuum in Figure 12.4 shows the possible relationships between church and state.

Although religion often reinforces the power of the state, it may also be a source of conflict and tension on issues regarding morality, justice, and legitimate authority. Even in the United States, which professes separation between church and state matters, religious groups seek to influence policies such as prayer in school, selection of textbooks and reading matter, and abortion laws. In some countries, religious groups strongly oppose the government and seek to undermine the authority and power of political leaders. In Nazi Germany, for example, some church leaders formulated the Barmen Declaration in opposition to Hitler. Many Christian groups in South Africa opposed apartheid. In some parts of Latin America, church leaders work for human rights and more equitable distribution of land and resources. Indeed, depending on the organizational structure, religion can provide a source of authority that offers a real challenge to the power of the state when that government has become oppressive, as shown in the next Sociology Around the World.

In simple homogeneous societies, religion serves as a kind of glue, making sacred the existing social system by offering it supernatural legitimacy. In complex and heterogeneous societies, on the other hand, no single religion can provide the core values of the culture. In such circumstances, an alternative form of religion called civil religion frequently evolves. **Civil religion** is *the set of beliefs, rites, and symbols that sacralize the values of the society and place the nation in the context of transcendent meaning, often giving it divine significance* (Yamane 2007). The beliefs, symbols, and rituals (e.g., the Pledge

▼ FIGURE 12.4

Links Between Religion and the State

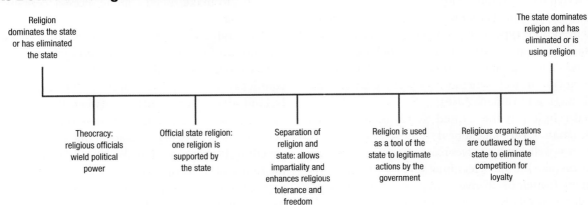

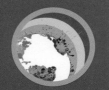
TRANSNATIONAL RELIGION: THE CATHOLIC CHURCH AND POLITICAL SYSTEMS

The Roman Catholic Church was one of the first truly transnational organizations, external to any one nation and including representation from many countries. It must be sympathetic to the circumstances of people in many nations, for its membership and its organizational reach span the globe. It cannot align itself with the economic and political interests of one nation or set of nations without risking the alienation of tens of millions of members in another part of the world (Roberts and Yamane 2016).

Sometimes, however, multinational religious organizations such as the Catholic Church can have a real impact on the social and economic policies within a nation, protecting the welfare of the people against a tyrannical state. In Poland during the 1970s and 1980s, the citizenry often felt colonized by a foreign power—the Soviet Union. The communist government in Poland was extremely unpopular, but the people had no real way to make the government more responsive to their needs. In 1983, only 3% of Poles surveyed felt that the government-dominant political hierarchy represented the interests of the Polish people. In contrast, 60% identified the Catholic Church and the pope as protecting Polish interests (Tamney 1992).

The Catholic Church became a major power broker in negotiations between unions and the government in Poland (Tamney 1992). Catholic bishops sometimes took on a role akin to union leaders and, in so doing, became major players in the political future of the country.

Because Polish bishops were ultimately responsible to the pope and had a source of support external to the nation, they experienced a good deal of independence from the Communist Party in power. Clergy supported by a church financed with tax dollars would not have had the same freedom to challenge the government. The global nature of the Catholic Church influenced the role bishops could play in the Polish situation.

In many single-nation religious denominations, the primary function of churches is to support the political power of the state or affirm an ethnic or national identity (Turner 1991b). Poland is an especially intriguing case in that a single religion tended to be identified with national pride and culture, but that religion was global in nature. That combination provided an exceptionally strong platform for challenging governmental policies not in the interests of the citizens (Tamney 1992).

A religion that crosses national boundaries can also foster suspicion among members of society who do not belong to it. For example, until a few decades ago, many people in the United States suspected the national loyalty of Roman Catholics, derisively calling them "papists." Likewise, Jews have often been accused of maintaining dangerous, subversive ties because of their international networks with others who share their faith. Muslims in the United States face these same suspicions today. When a religion transcends national boundaries, it carries both benefits and risks for individuals and the state. This is true of any religious tradition.

---

of Allegiance, the national anthem, saluting the flag) serve to create a sense of sacredness about the nation and for what that nation stands. Although civil religion lacks the structural system of organized religion, it is often supported by various types of patriotic groups. These small voluntary associations develop intense belonging systems, and civil religion tends to strengthen the sense of belonging citizens feel as members of that society (Bellah 1992; Roberts and Yamane 2016).

Civil religion in the United States is not explicitly Christian, for it must appeal to those who are non-Christian as well, but it involves reference to God in many areas of civilian life and a legitimation of the U.S. political system. It attempts to give the nation and the government supernatural blessing and authority (Bellah 1970).

It also calls the nation to a higher standard of justice and may be used by change agents, such as Dr. Martin Luther King Jr., to make social change more acceptable and compelling.

Although civil religion is supposed to unite a country and reinforce the values shared by its citizens, in some nations, civil religion can itself be a point of intense conflict (McGuire 2002; Yamane 2007). In Northern Ireland, part of the conflict between Protestants and Catholics is over civil religion. Protestants and Catholics not only come from different economic strata and different ethnic backgrounds but also have different visions for the future of the country and different ideas about what gives the country its special place in history. These disparate outlooks and backgrounds make a unified civil religion very difficult to achieve. Recently, in the United States, protests at NFL games during the national anthem, traditionally a unifying symbol of civil religion, have laid bare racial divisions in the nation. Many football players have taken a knee during the anthem to draw attention to racial injustice faced by people of color in the United States and to advocate for social change. In turn, their protests have enraged defenders of the traditional symbol of the anthem who believe it blasphemous to refuse to stand during the national anthem.

THINKING SOCIOLOGICALLY

How does civil religion manifest itself in your country? Give specific examples.

Religion and the Economy: The Protestant Ethic and Capitalism. Why do most of us study hard, work hard, and strive to get ahead? Why are you sacrificing time and money now—taking this and other college courses—when you might spend that money on an impressive new car? Our answers probably have something to do with our moral attitudes about work, about people who lack ambition, and about the proper way to live. Max Weber provided an answer to this question with his research on the relationship between the Protestant work ethic and capitalism. He gathered information by studying many documents, including the diaries of Calvinists (a branch of Protestantism), sermons and religious teachings, and other historical papers (Weber [1904–1905] 1958).

Weber noted that the areas of Europe where the Calvinists had the strongest followings were the same areas where capitalism had grown the fastest. Weber argued that four elements in the Calvinist Protestant faith created the moral and value system necessary for the growth of capitalism: predestination, a calling, self-denial, and individualism.

1. *Predestination* meant that one's destiny—whether one would eventually go to heaven or hell—was predetermined. Nothing anyone did would change what was to happen. Because God was presumed to be perfect, he was not influenced by human deeds or prayer. Those people who were chosen by God were referred to as the *elect* and were assumed to be a small group. Therefore, people looked for signs of their status—salvation or damnation. High social

▲ Civil religion blends reverence for the nation with more traditional symbols of faith. Shown here is a chapel at Punchbowl, the Pacific cemetery for U.S. military personnel, located in Hawaii. Note the relative prominence of the flags beside the altar.

status was sometimes viewed as a sign of being among the elect. This view motivated people to succeed in *this* life, so that they would appear to be headed toward salvation in the next.

2. The *calling* referred to the concept of doing God's work. Each person was put on earth to serve God, and each had a task to do in God's service. One could be called by God to any occupation, so the key was to work very hard and with the right attitude. Because work was a way to serve God, laziness or lack of ambition came to be viewed as a sin. These ideas helped create a society in which people's self-worth and their evaluation of others were tied to a work ethic. The Calvinists, therefore, worked hard.

3. *Self-denial* involved living a simple life. If one had a good deal of money, one did not spend it on a lavish home, expensive clothing, or various forms of entertainment. Such consumption would be offensive to God. Therefore, people worked hard and began to accumulate resources, saving or investing in a business. This self-denial was tied to an idea that we now call *delayed gratification*, postponing the satisfaction of one's present wants and desires in exchange for a future reward. The reward they sought was in the afterlife. Because Calvinists believed in predestination, they did not expect to *earn* salvation through this way of life, but they believed that they could demonstrate to themselves and others that they were among the elect.

4. *Individualism* meant that each individual faced his or her destiny alone before God. Previous Christian theology had emphasized group salvation, the idea that an entire community would be saved or damned together. The stark individualism of Calvinistic theology stressed that each individual was on his or her own before God. Likewise, in the emerging capitalist economic system, individuals were on their own. The person who thrived was an individualist who planned wisely and charted his or her own course. Religious individualism and economic individualism reinforced one another (Weber [1904–1905] 1958).

The Protestant ethic that resulted from these elements stressed hard work, simple living, and rational decision-making by individualists. Businesspeople and laborers spent long hours working at their calling and reinvested profits into new equipment or expansion of the company. The rise of individualism allowed people to focus on their own efforts to accumulate and reinvest wealth—and not feel guilty for doing so. The growth of the Calvinist Protestant church led to major changes in cultural values, which, in turn, helped transform the economy into a capitalistic system (Weber [1904–1905] 1958).

Gradually, the capitalistic system, stimulated by the Protestant ethic, spread to other countries and to other religious groups. Many of the attitudes about work and delayed gratification no longer have a supernatural focus, but they are part of the larger cultural value system nonetheless. They influence our feelings about people who are not industrious and our ideas about why some people are poor.

Weber recognized that other factors also had to be present for capitalism to develop, but he believed that the set of moral values and attitudes Calvinism instilled in the people was critical. Whereas Marx argued that religion encouraged workers to stay in their places and allowed the capitalists to exploit the system and maintain their elite positions, Weber focused on the change brought about in the economic system as a result of religious beliefs and values.

Religion is a major part of the economy. In the United States, 32% of all funds donated in 2015 went to religious organizations, more than to any other type of organization (Cramer & Associates 2016). In most countries, religions (a) employ clergy and other people who serve the church, (b) own land and property, and (c) generate millions through collections and fund-raising. Some of this money goes to salaries and the upkeep of buildings, some to charitable and advocacy activities, and some to investments. Religious ventures continue to expand into many areas, from shopping centers to homes and apartment buildings for the elderly.

In the United States, televangelism and megachurches (congregations with upwards of 10,000 members) are multimillion-dollar industries with sophisticated marketing strategies. The televangelism industry, for example, involves the sale of books, CDs, and DVDs and donations of hundreds of millions of dollars by listeners. These megachurches become corporations and use information from the corporate world (e.g., how to structure their organization and market their product) to increase their chances of success. Indeed, many televangelists and megachurches preach a version of the "gospel of prosperity"—that God wants people to be prosperous and even wealthy. They argue that worshipping God in their style and giving to their church will contribute to wealth. This embracing of the search for wealth fits with the interests of capitalists and capitalism.

There are other ways in which religion and economic institutions are linked. When large religious organizations take a moral stand on poverty, for example, they may influence government investment into the economy. Moreover, troubled economic times tend to lead to the creation of certain kinds of religious movements. For example, millenarian religious movements, which anticipate the end of the world, almost always gain adherents when economic prospects are bleak (Roberts and Yamane 2016).

Religion interacts with and impacts the other major social institutions in society, but the interaction between religion and society is a two-way street. Whereas religions can influence other social institutions, religions also find themselves influenced by the society in which they exist.

▲ Megachurches, such as this one in Guatemala, sometimes draw 20,000 to 30,000 worshippers on a weekend and offer high-entertainment worship and a range of other services. These churches are run—and marketed—like a business.

THINKING SOCIOLOGICALLY

In postindustrial societies, the media influence religion and individuals' views toward religion. How have these messages influenced your views toward religion? Why?

Religion in Society: Macro-Level Analysis

As an integral part of society, religion meets the needs of individuals and of the social structure. In this section, we explore functionalist and conflict theories as we consider some functions of religion in society, the role of religion in supporting stratification systems, and various conflicts within societies and in the global system.

Contribution of Religion to Society: A Functionalist Perspective

Regardless of their personal belief or disbelief in the supernatural, sociologists of religion acknowledge that religion has important social consequences. Functionalists contend that religion has some positive consequences—helping people answer questions about the meaning of life and providing part of the glue that helps hold a society together. Let us look at some of the social functions of religion, keeping in mind that the way religion affects society varies depending on the structure of the society and the time period.

Social Cohesion. Religion helps individuals feel a sense of belonging and unity with others, a common sense of purpose with those who share the same beliefs. It serves to hold social units together and gives the members a sense of camaraderie. You will recall that Durkheim's widely cited study of suicide stresses the importance of belonging to a group, such as a congregation (Durkheim ([1897]1964). Research shows that communities with religious homogeneity and a high rate of congregational membership have lower rates of suicide (Ellison, Burr, and McCall 1997; Lotfi, Ayar, and Shams 2012). In societies with competing religions, or religions inconsistent with other values of society, however, religions may reduce cohesion and even be a source of conflict and hatred (Bainbridge and Stark 1981; Durward and Marsden 2011). As mentioned earlier, societies with competing religions often develop a civil religion—a theology of the nation—that serves to bless the nation and to enhance conformity and loyalty.

Legitimating Social Values and Norms. Functionalists note that religion often sacralizes social norms—grounds them in a supernatural reality or a divine command that makes them larger than life. Whether those norms have to do with care for the vulnerable, the demand to work for peace and justice, the immorality of extramarital sex, the sacredness of a monogamous heterosexual marriage, or proper roles for men and women, the foundations of morality from scripture create feelings of absoluteness. This lends stability to society: Agreement on social control of deviant behavior is easier, and society needs to rely less on coercion and force to get citizens to follow social norms. Of course, the absoluteness of the norms also makes it more difficult to change them as the society evolves. This inflexibility is precisely what pleases religious conservatives and distresses theological liberals, with the latter often seeking new ways to interpret the norms.

Social Change. Depending on the time and place, religion can work for or against social change. Some religions fight to maintain the status quo or return to norms from an earlier era. This is true of many fundamentalist religions—whether they are branches of Christian, Jewish, Hindu, or Islamic faiths—that seek to simplify life in the increasingly complex industrial world. Other religious traditions support or encourage change. For example, Japan made tremendous strides in industrialization in a short time following World War II, in part because the Shinto, Confucian, and Buddhist religions provided no obstacles and, in fact, supported the changes needed to move their economy forward. In the United States, African American religious leaders led the civil rights movement in the 1950s and 1960s, using the established networks and communication channels created by African American religious organizations (Diana and McAdam 2003; Lincoln and Mamiya 1990; McAdam 1999).

Some public sociologists have focused on progressive faith movements, offering analytical feedback on strengths and weaknesses of social change movements and helping activists see what strategies might be most effective for promoting change (Delehanty 2015; Yukich 2013). One example is Grace Yukich, a sociologist who has worked on immigration issues and on interfaith alliances for change. The next Sociologists in Action feature describes why she became interested in studying religious issues from a sociological perspective and how she helps bring together sociologists and social activists working for peace and understanding.

THINKING SOCIOLOGICALLY

Which religious groups in your community have a stabilizing influence, and which ones have a disruptive influence? Which faith communities make the existing system seem sacred and beyond question? Which push for more social equality and less ethnocentrism toward others? Are there mosques, temples, or churches in your local area that oppose the government's policies, or do they all foster unquestioning loyalty?

Link Between Religion and Stratification: A Conflict Perspective

At times, religions reinforce socially defined differences between people, giving sacred legitimacy to racial prejudice, gender bias, and inequality. Conflict theory considers the ways in which religion relates to stratification and the status of minority groups. Our religious ideas and values and the way we worship are shaped not only by the society into which we are born but also by our family's position in the stratification system. Religion serves different primary purposes for individuals, depending on their positions in society. People of various social statuses differ in the type and degree of their involvement in religious groups.

Class Base of Religion. Conflict theorist Karl Marx stated clearly his view of the relationship between religion and class—religion perpetuates the prevailing power structure (Marx [1844] 1963). For the proletariat or working class, religion is a sedative, he asserted, a narcotic that dulls people's sensitivity to and understanding of their desperate situation. He labeled religion the "opiate of the people." Faith provides workers an escape from reality—from the tedium and suffering in everyday life.

At the same time, Marx noted, it can help those in power discourage workers from rebelling, by promising life in the hereafter if they work hard and contentedly. Some religions justify the positions of those who are better off by saying they have earned it.

Because the needs and interests of socioeconomic groups differ, most societies have class-based religions. With some exceptions (e.g., Catholics and Muslims) in the United States, religious affiliation tends to correlate with social class measures such as education, occupation, and income (Pyle 2006; Smith and Faris 2005). Table 12.2 indicates the specific links between denominational affiliation

▼ TABLE 12.2

Socioeconomic Profiles of American Religious Groups

Religious Group	Education Level: % With at Least a College Degree	Annual Household Income: % Over $100,000
Hindu	77	36
Unitarian	67	43
Jewish	59	44
Episcopal Church in USA	56	35
Buddhist	48	13
Presbyterian Church (USA)	47	32
United Church of Christ	46	29
Orthodox Christian	39	29
United Methodist	37	26
Muslim	34	20
Latter-Day Saint (Mormon)	33	20
Lutheran Church–Missouri Synod	32	22
Evangelical Lutheran in America	26	26
Catholic	26	19
Nones (no affiliation)	21	29
Southern Baptist	19	16
Assemblies of God	15	10
African Methodist Episcopal	n/a	10
Black Baptist	14	7
American Baptist	13	9
Jehovah's Witness	9	4

Source: Masci 2016; Pew Research Center Religious Landscape Study 2018.

n/a = not available

SOCIOLOGISTS IN ACTION
Grace Yukich

FROM RELIGIOUS VIOLENCE TO PEACE AND UNDERSTANDING

On September 11, 2001, my college roommate and I watched the World Trade Center towers fall. Sitting in front of our television, I felt angry, confused, and scared. As a White, middle-class American college student, I had little direct experience with religious violence or with religions that were not Christian. *Why did this happen?* I wondered. *The terrorists are Muslim—is something wrong with Islam?* I was not alone in jumping to this conclusion. Many Americans began blaming *all* Muslims for the terrorist attacks. Muslim Americans often faced discrimination and fear from their neighbors.

Looking back, I am so glad I was taking a sociology class at the time. It enabled me to move from my knee-jerk reaction to a new understanding of the attacks. Sociology asks us to question our assumptions about other groups of people, to "take the role of the other" by putting ourselves in their shoes. Through sociological research, I found out that all religions have a history of violence, including Christianity, the majority religion in the United States. I also discovered that most of the world's Muslims did not believe in using violence against people they disagreed with; instead, they worked with people from other religions to create peace. I became a sociologist so I could keep studying how people from different backgrounds, including different religions, work together to create a fairer, more peaceful world. From this research, a picture emerged of Christians, Jews, Muslims, Buddhists, and Hindus overcoming their differences to achieve shared goals. My book, *One Family Under God: Immigration Politics and Progressive Religion in America* (2013), shows how people from different faiths are working together for immigration reform.

In 2011, I, along with three others, founded *Mobilizing Ideas*, a blog that brings everyday activists working for social change together with the social movement scholars who study them. Focusing on issues from the LGBTQIA rights movement to the use of Twitter for antiracist activism (#BlackLivesMatter), the blog seeks to create conversation and to amplify the voices of people whose stories are not often heard in the mainstream media. Like my focus on religious difference, the blog's goal of highlighting unheard voices goes to the heart of sociology's focus on taking the role of the other. When we hear a perspective that differs from our own, it can feel frustrating or even threatening. Sociology asks us to move beyond that initial fear. Instead of stereotyping other people, we should take the responsibility of learning more about how economics, politics, race, and religion have shaped their perspectives—and our own. By adopting a sociological approach, we can recognize our commonalities with others and understand and even appreciate our differences. Building this understanding may be the only way to a less violent, more peaceful, and more just world.

★ ★ ★ ★ ★ ★

Grace Yukich is a sociologist and assistant professor of sociology at Quinnipiac University in Hamden, Connecticut. She is the cofounder and editor in chief of *Mobilizing Ideas*, which you can read online at http://mobilizingideas.wordpress.com.

and socioeconomic measures in the United States today. Some religious traditions tend to attract lower- and working-class worshippers because they focus on the problems and life situations faced by people in the lower social classes. People with higher social status attend worship more regularly and know more about the historical and social context of scriptures than do people with less education and income, but people with lower socioeconomic status are more likely to pray and read scripture daily (Masci 2016; Pew Research Center Religious Landscape Study 2018).

Max Weber referred to this *pattern of people belonging to religious groups that espouse values and characteristics compatible with their social status and self-interests* as **elective affinity** (Weber 1946). For example, people in laboring jobs usually find obeying the rules of the workplace and adhering to the instructions of the employer or supervisor essential for success on the job (Bowles and Gintis 1976; MacLeod 2008). Likewise, the faith communities of the poor and the working class tend to stress obedience, submission to "superiors," and the absoluteness of religious standards. The values of the workplace are reenacted and legitimated in churches to help socialize children to adapt to noncreative laboring jobs.

Many people in affluent congregations are paid to be problem solvers and break the mold of conventional thinking. They will not do well professionally if they merely obey rules. Instead, they must help create rules while trying to solve organizational or management problems (Bowles and Gintis 1976). It is not surprising, then, that the denominations of the affluent (Unitarian Universalist, Jewish, Episcopalian, Presbyterian, and United Church of Christ) are more likely to value tolerance of other perspectives, religions, or values and to view factors that limit individual opportunity (e.g., institutional racism and sexism) as evil. They tend to embrace tolerance of differences and condemn rigidity, absolutism, and conventionalism. Their religious communities are likely to encourage each member to work out his or her own theology, within limits, and value divergent thinking and a streak of independence (Roberts and Yamane 2016; Roof 1999).

Whatever the belief, one's religion and one's social status are correlated to everything from life expectancy, the likelihood of divorce, and mental health to attitudes regarding sexual behavior, abortion, and fetal stem cell research.

THINKING SOCIOLOGICALLY

How do the social class and religious affiliation of people you know relate to this discussion? How do denominations in your community whose members have higher-than-average levels of education (Unitarians, Jews, Episcopalians, Presbyterians, United Church of Christ members) differ from those with less educated members?

Racial Bias, Gender Prejudice, and Religion. Most religious groups profess to welcome all comers. Many, however, have practiced discrimination against some group at some time, often related to political and economic factors in the society. In fact, some studies show positive relationships among religion, prejudice, and discrimination. However, it is important to recognize that religion has multiple and even contradictory effects on societies. For example, most Christian denominations have formal statements that reject racial prejudice as un-Christian. The meaning system teaches tolerance. However, informal group norms in a local congregation—the belonging system—may be tolerant of ethnic jokes and may foster distrust of certain races. Among Whites in the United States, for instance, active church members have historically displayed more prejudice than inactive church members or the unchurched (Chalfant and Peck 1983; Roberts and Yamane 2016).

The structural system of religion can also play a role in supporting prejudice and discrimination. Promotions to larger churches are usually awarded to well-liked ministers, who have growing, harmonious congregations and financially sound organizations. Such ministers are sometimes reluctant to speak out forcefully on issues such as racial or gender equality, for fear of offending their parishioners. Bishops may not promote a minister or priest to a larger church if his or her current congregation is racked with dissention and donations have declined. Even though the denomination's meaning system may oppose prejudice, the structural system may reward clergy who do not defend that meaning system and who allow bigotry to remain unchecked (Campbell and Pettigrew 1959; Roberts and Yamane 2016).

Sometimes both the structural and informal systems of a religion can support discrimination. For example, although women tend to be more spiritual (as discussed in the next Engaging Sociology) and religiously active than men, they have been treated as second-class citizens in most religions. This is starting to change. In some denominations, they now hold leadership positions. Many Christian and Jewish denominations, for example, have female ministers and rabbis (Chaves 2004; Religious Tolerance 2015). Several Christian denominations allow women to become bishops. More conservative denominations and conservative members within more moderate denominations, however, oppose moves to grant women leadership positions.

The Anglican Church of England's internal division among progressives who support, and social conservatives who oppose, allowing women to be bishops has made headlines in recent years, with both groups vociferously arguing for their sides (Jourdan 2013). Similar divisions exist within the Catholic Church, but because of the organizational structure of the church, there is less open debate. Almost 6 out of 10 (59%) Catholics in the United States support the ordination of women priests (Smith and Masci 2018).

Men and women sit separately in some houses of worship today. These include some Christian, Islamic, and Jewish worship services. Religious rules regarding attire also help reinforce the differentiation of the sexes in some houses of worship.

Although most mainline Christian denominations now have official statements on the equality of women and formal policies against discrimination in ordaining or hiring women pastors, the official meaning system does not tell the whole story. Again, religious structures

WOMEN AND SPIRITUALITY

Figure 12.5 indicates that there is a spirituality gap.

▼ FIGURE 12.5

The Spirituality Gap in the United States

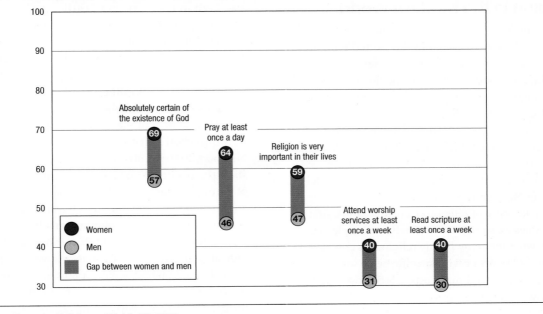

Source: Pew Forum on Religion and Public Life 2016.

★ ★ ★ ★ ★ ★ ★

Engaging Sociology

1. Are you convinced by this evidence that women are more spiritual than men? Why or why not?

2. If so, why do you think this is the case? If not, why do the data seem to suggest less involvement of men?

3. Is the message of religious communities and faith traditions (e.g., altruism, self-sacrifice, trusting others) less in tune with the everyday experiences of men than of women?

---

play a role. Local congregational search committees who screen and hire new ministers usually care deeply about the survival and health of the local church. Studies show that often members of these committees are themselves not personally opposed to women in the pulpit, but they believe that others in their church would be offended if they hired a woman and would stop coming and giving money to the church. Thus, the local belonging and structural systems of the religion may perpetuate unequal treatment of clergywomen, even if the meaning system says they are equal (Chaves 2004; Lehman 1985). The United Methodist Church granted women the right to become pastors over 60 years ago, but only 2.2% of the senior pastors in United Methodist churches with large denominations are women (Bloom 2017).

As noted, some religions may reinforce and legitimize social prejudices, whereas others may be powerful forces for change and greater equality in a society. Religion elicits strong emotions and influences people's definition of reality. Religion has promoted social strife, but it has also been the motivation for altruism and service to others, and a major contributor to social solidarity.

Religion in the Modern World

Name almost any religion, and a group representing that faith can probably be found in the United Kingdom, the United States, Canada, Kenya, and several other countries where religious diversity is the norm. In the United States, religious pluralism has been a founding principle since Roger Williams founded the state of Rhode Island in 1636 and advocated religious toleration and separation of church and state. This makes for a complex religious pattern. In this section, we look at the vitality of major religions in North America, with empirical data that track religious trends over time.

To make sense of religious trends, we must first define the variables we want to measure. For example, if we want to know whether being highly religious is correlated with other social factors or with specific behaviors, how do we measure religiosity? This question is discussed in the next Engaging Sociology.

Is Religion Dying or Reviving?

The percentage of people in the United States who are unaffiliated with a religion has increased markedly over the last decade. As of 2014, 23% of people in the United States consider themselves "atheist, agnostic or 'nothing in particular'" (Pew Forum on Religion and Public Life 2015). Younger people are those most likely to be religiously unaffiliated. Today, more than one out of three (36%) younger millennials (those born from 1990 to 1996) are unaffiliated (Pew Research Center 2015f). Many of the unaffiliated, however, consider themselves spiritual. Among those not affiliated with a religious community, roughly half say that spirituality is important to their lives—calling themselves spiritual but not religious (Alper 2015; Pew Forum on Religion and Public Life 2012a). Spirituality is a more individual experience of feeling there is something sacred in life beyond the realm of the everyday empirical world, whereas religion is a communal or social expression of that outlook.

Religion has declined in influence in Canadian life, as well. The percentage of the population unaffiliated with a religion jumped from 4% in 1970 to 24% in 2011 (Pew Research Center 2013). Despite the growth in the number of religiously unaffiliated, the indicators of religious commitment in both the United States and Canada are higher than those in most other religiously pluralistic nations. It is still safe to say that religion and spirituality have a significant influence in both U.S. and Canadian society.

Religious affiliation in the United States today is also high in comparison to earlier periods in U.S. history. In the days of colonial America, only about 17% of the population belonged to a church (Finke and Stark 1992). Today, 56% of people in the United States belong to a church, synagogue, or mosque (down from a high of 76% in 1950) (Gallup 2016). Another measure of religious strength is belief in God. Gallup poll results indicate that 86% of the U.S. population believes in God or a universal spirit or higher power (Gallup 2015b; Newport 2012e). Table 12.3 and Figure 12.6 on page 375 show the results from Gallup polls regarding indicators of the importance of religion in people's lives.

Attendance at worship in a church, temple, or mosque is also an indicator of religious involvement. Although attendance rates vary by faith community, Gallup polls indicate self-reports of attendance have been fairly steady in the United States for almost 80 years at 36% to 49% of the population, with the 36% current rate nearly matching the 37% rate in 1940 (Gallup 2016) (see Figure 12.7). Figure 12.8, however, shows significant geographical variations in rates of weekly attendance at a house of worship.

Religion in the United States has adjusted to changes in society and taken on new forms. For example, the number of Protestants in the United States has declined from two thirds of the population to less than half (48%) in the past 30 years, as the country has become more religiously diverse. This decline stems in part from decreasing numbers of White Protestant families (due to the changing ethnic composition of the country) and an increase in the number that no longer affiliate with any faith community (Pew Forum on Religion and Public Life 2012a, 2012b; Pew Research Center 2015f). The latter half of the 20th century also saw a wide range of religious groups forming and growing in North America, from the occult and astrology to New Age spirituality and Zen Buddhism. Today, approximately 38% of U.S. adults hold a creationist view of human origin, indicating the strong influence of fundamentalist Christianity in the United States. Creationists reject the theory of evolution and believe that the creation story of the Earth found in the Bible is scientifically factual (Gallup 2017).

DETERMINING WHAT IT MEANS TO BE RELIGIOUS

- Study the list of items in Table 12.3. Do factors such as belief in God, church membership, and frequency of attendance seem like good measures of one's religiosity? Why might the answer to this question indicate something other than the depth of one's religious faith?

- Attendance at Sabbath worship varies greatly, with Mormons and members of the conservative Church of Christ reporting weekly attendance at about 68%; Muslims at 56%; mainline Methodists, Presbyterians, Lutherans, and Roman Catholics at 43%–45%; and Jews at 15%. Given the fact that attendance varies so much by religious group, does this mean that members of some groups are less religious, or does it mean attendance is not a very good measure of religiosity for some groups?

- Is asking whether religion is very important in one's life, whether one believes religion answers problems in life, or how much confidence one has in religious organizations a good indicator of a person's religiosity? (See Figure 12.6 for indications of how stable "importance in life" has been over time.) What might be some misleading dimensions of using one or more of these measures to indicate religiosity?

- Some scholars have argued that how religious beliefs affect one's behavior is a good indicator of

religiosity. So in studying Islam, Judaism, or some forms of Christianity, one measure of religiosity has been how much one gives to charitable causes—both to one's faith community and to people living in poverty. Is this measure an accurate way to understand levels of religious influence in society? Why or why not?

- Imagine you have been asked to conduct a study to determine the religiosity of various demographic groups in the United States. How would you define religiosity?

▼ TABLE 12.3

Leading Religious Indicators in the United States (by Percentage)

Belief in God	86%
Member of a church or synagogue	59
Religion *very important* in life	56
Pray daily	55
High confidence in organized religion	42
Say they attended worship in past week	39

Source: Gallup 2015b.

▼ FIGURE 12.6

How Important Is Religion in Your Life (in the United States, by Percentage)?

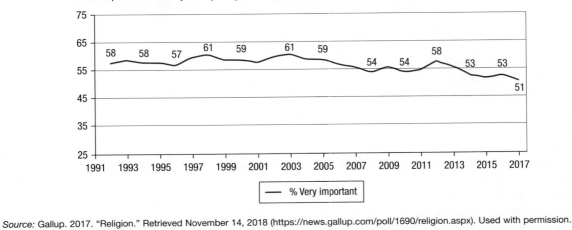

How important would you say religion is in your life?

Values along the line (left to right): 58, 58, 57, 61, 59, 61, 59, 54, 54, 58, 53, 53, 51

Legend: — % Very important

Source: Gallup. 2017. "Religion." Retrieved November 14, 2018 (https://news.gallup.com/poll/1690/religion.aspx). Used with permission.

Weekly Attendance at Church, Synagogue, or Mosque in the United States: Annual Averages

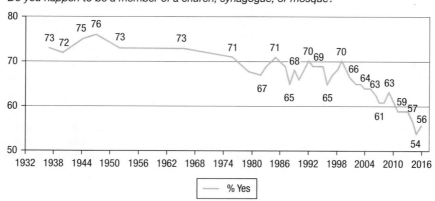

Do you happen to be a member of a church, synagogue, or mosque?

— % Yes

Source: Five Key Findings on Religion in the U.S., Frank Newport, December 23, 2016.

▼ FIGURE 12.8

Weekly Religious Service Attendance, 2014

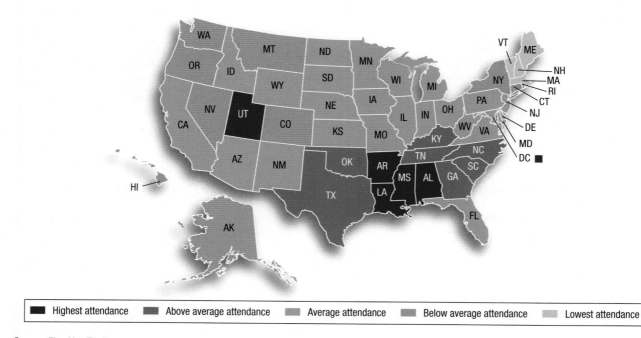

■ Highest attendance ■ Above average attendance ■ Average attendance ■ Below average attendance ■ Lowest attendance

Source: Five Key Findings on Religion in the U.S., Frank Newport, December 23, 2016.

Religious identity influences how people view the world and their political choices. The religiosity of candidates has been raised in political campaigns throughout the history of the United States. In June 2012, just as the 2012 presidential primaries ended, 18% of the population said that they would not vote for a Mormon. Despite this, the "highly religious" tended to support Romney over Obama—except for "highly religious" Hispanic Catholics who leaned toward Obama (Newport 2012 a, 2012b, 2012d).

Independent and Democratic voters reply almost identically to questions about the importance of religion in their lives. Republicans, however, are much more likely to say they are highly religious, as Table 12.4 indicates.

Political Party Identification Within Partisan Groups in the United States, 2016

	Republicans	Independents	Democrats
	%	%	%
Highly religious	51	33	33
Moderately religious	29	30	30
Not religious	20	37	37

Note: Based on 173,229 interviews conducted January 2 through December 19, 2016.

Source: Five Key Findings on Religion in the U.S., Frank Newport, December 23, 2016.

Demographic changes in the makeup of the United States and Canada have influenced the religious landscape. Although two out of every three native-born U.S. citizens are Protestant, two out of every three Christian immigrants are Catholic. This influx of Catholic immigrants has helped the Catholic Church maintain the membership of a steady percentage of U.S. citizens. Some other religious faiths are represented among those new U.S. residents as well (Lipka 2015; Pew Forum on Religion and Public Life 2012b).

Looking at religion throughout the world reveals an overall growth in the percentage of the population that is religious. A recent Pew study notes that, if trends persist, by 2060:

- The number of Muslims will nearly equal the number of Christians around the world.

- Atheists, agnostics, and other people who do not affiliate with any religion will make up a declining share of the world's total population because of their relatively low birth rate.

- The global Buddhist and Hindu populations will be slightly less than they are today, whereas the Jewish population will be about the same as it is currently.

- India will retain a Hindu majority but also will have the largest Muslim population of any country in the world, surpassing Indonesia.

- Four out of every 10 (42%) Christians in the world will live in sub-Saharan Africa (Pew Research Center 2017a).

Religion and Secularization: Micro-, Meso-, and Macro-Level Discord

Secularization refers to *the diminishing influence and role of religion in everyday life.* At the meso and macro level, religion becomes one of many institutions in the society—no longer having authority in governing, health, and other realms. Secularization at the micro level involves a movement away from supernatural and sacred interpretations of the world and toward decisions based on empirical evidence and logic. Before the advent of modern science and technology, religion helped explain our social and physical world. However, the scientific method, its emphasis on logical reasoning, and the fact that there are many different religions rather than one have challenged religious and spiritual approaches to the world. As part of micro-level secularism, we might expect to see most individuals working out their own faith systems rather than adhering to the faith affirmations of their denomination or religious leaders. If secularization were uniform, it might look like the pattern indicated in Table 12.5.

However, we have seen that most indicators of traditional religiosity—belief in God, attendance, affirmation that religion affects all of life, and confidence in religious organizations—are high. Religion is still a strong force in the lives of many individuals. However, it does not have the extensive control over other institutions of education, health, politics, or family that it once did. In most Global North countries, it is just one institution among others, rather than the dominant one. In 2016, 76% of people in the United States believed that religion is losing its influence throughout the country. As you can see in Figure 12.9, the last time poll data indicated that nearly as many people felt this way was in 1971, during an era of great social unrest (massive Vietnam War protests; publication of the Pentagon papers, which caused many people to lose faith in government; and the second wave of the women's movement (Gallup 2016).

Some scholars have argued that secularization is an inevitable and unstoppable force in the modern postindustrial world (Dobbelaere 2000; Gorski and Altinordu 2008). Others argue that secularization is far from inevitable and that it has almost reached its limit (Gardom 2011; Stark 2000). Our social world model helps us understand that, like religion, secularization is a complex phenomenon that occurs at several levels and affects each society differently (Chaves and Gorski 2001; Yamane 1997).

Secularization may be occurring at the societal level, but the evidence noted earlier suggests that this is not as

Secularization in the Social World

	Institutional Differentiation (Separation of Religion So It Does Not Dominate Other Institutions)	Decision-Making
Micro Level	Individuals emphasize being "spiritual rather than religious," formulate their own meaning system or theology, and may believe that spirituality has little to do with other aspects of their lives.	Decision-making among individuals is based on individual self-interest without concern for the teachings of the religious group or the clergy.
Meso Level	Organizations look to other social associations for accepted practices of how to operate, not to religious organizations and authorities.	Decision-making about an organization's policies is based on analyses of possible consequences, rather than on scripture, theological arguments, or proclamations of religious authorities.
Macro Level	In the larger society, government, education, and the economic institutions are independent and autonomous from religious organizations.	Decision-making about social policies uses logic, empirical data, and cost/benefit analysis rather than scripture, theological arguments, or proclamations of religious authorities.

▼ FIGURE 12.9

Perception of the Influence of Religion in the United States

At the present time, do you think religion as a whole is increasing its influence on American life or losing its influence?

Yearly averages

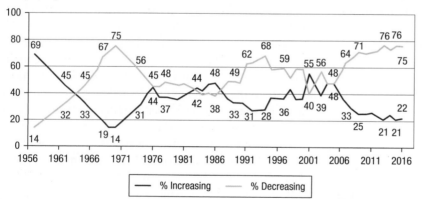

Source: Gallup 2016.

pervasive at the individual level (Chaves and Gorski 2001; Gardom 2011). When religious faith guides people's everyday lives—their conduct on the job, their political choices, their sexual behavior, or their attitudes toward race relations—then secularization at the micro level is weak and religious influence is strong. Faith still matters to many people.

Secularization is more obvious at the meso and macro levels. For example, religiously affiliated organizations (e.g., Catholic nursing homes, Presbyterian colleges, Jewish social service foundations) make most, though not all, of their decisions about how to deliver services or whom to hire or fire based on systematic policies designed for organizational efficiency, not religious dogma. Likewise, policies in the society at large are usually made with little discussion of the theological implications (health care policies are one notable exception, as we discuss in Chapter 14). In morally ambiguous cases, policymakers defend positions with human rights arguments, rather than ideas on what is sinful—again suggesting that society has become secular at the macro level (Roberts and Yamane 2016; Yamane 1997). On the other hand, debates about prayer in schools, abortion, same-sex marriage, and economic inequality; the involvement of religious leaders in political issues; and the influence of religion in presidential politics indicate a continuing impact of religion on the meso and macro levels in U.S. society. *Secularization* even at the macro level is not complete.

In short, most sociologists of religion believe that religion continues to be a particularly powerful force at the individual level whereas secularization is more pervasive at the meso and macro levels (Roberts and Yamane 2016; Sommerville 2002). At the global level, no theological authority has the power to define reality or determine policies, and secularization is well established. Perhaps this

▲ Despite the process of secularization in some parts of the world, the sense of awe before the holy remains strong for many people. This enormous Buddha at the Yungang Buddhist Caves at Wuzhou Mountain in China has been a source of veneration for generations.

▲ Although religious faith is very strong at the micro level in the United States, public policy and the operation of organizations and government are secularized—based on principles of pluralism and rational deliberation. This town council prays as it opens its monthly meeting, after the Supreme Court ruled that prayers are allowed in this setting if there is a long tradition of having prayer. Was the Court's ruling a wise decision? Visit edge.sagepub.com/Ballantine7e for an interactive photo essay about the balance between religious and secular practices.

is one reason why conservatives of nearly every religious faith are leery of global processes and global organizations, such as the United Nations. Our global political

organizations are governed by rational-legal (secular) authority, not religious doctrines.

THINKING SOCIOLOGICALLY

What might be the results if a society is secularized at the meso and macro levels but much less so at the micro level? Is this a problem? Does it create problems for decision-making and social coherence? Is separation of church and state, with government policies based on secular calculations of the interests of the nation, a good or bad idea? Why or why not?

Religion: Fostering War or Peace?

Can religion bring peace to the world? Most religious systems advocate living in harmony with other humans and with nature, yet peace has not been the reality. Although Christianity, Judaism, and Islam embrace a world of peace and justice, Christian denominations often foster nationalistic loyalty—with displays of the flag and even pledges of allegiance to the flag during worship. This endorsement of national pride can foster "us" versus "them" thinking and undermine peace.

Congregations that take peace activities seriously may decline in membership and financial stability if seen as "un-American," whereas those that foster in-group or nationalistic sentiments can attract large numbers. So the structural system may actually undermine the message of the meaning system because growth and financial vitality are major concerns for many local church leaders. Despite the rhetoric, fiscal concerns can actually trump claims to worship the Prince of Peace. The linking of nationalistic loyalty to religion can also lead to the conflation of nation and God and, in some cases, the perception that leaders are divinely chosen.

Liberal theologies suggest that God may speak to people through a variety of channels, including the revelations of other religious traditions. Whereas religious leaders may feel that their theology provides the fullest and most complete expression of God's truth, some hold that other faiths also provide paths to salvation. This pluralism has resulted in more tolerance, but it may also be an indication of secularization of theology itself.

Members of fundamentalist groups—whether they are Jewish, Muslim, or Christian—generally believe in a literal interpretation of their holy books. They usually believe that they have the only truth, which they must defend and spread. This generates ethnocentrism and sometimes hatred, causing people to fight and die to defend their belief systems and way of life. Fundamentalist religious groups attempt to preserve their distinctive identities (Marty and Appleby 1991, 2004). They seldom believe in pluralism or tolerance of other beliefs but rather believe that they have the only true religion. Consequently, they resist and defend themselves against threats to their beliefs and way of life (Ebaugh 2005; Stern 2003).

Conflict between religious groups is especially intense if there are also ethnic and economic differences between the groups. On the other hand, cross-cutting social categories reduces social hostilities, as Figure 12.10 illustrates. When you are in a group that includes adherents of different religions, ethnicities, and socioeconomic classes, it becomes much less likely that you will vilify people from those other groups. They no longer—as a category—can be seen as uniformly evil or as the enemy. This is what is meant by crosscutting divisions.

If the conflict is over ethnicity and economics, a common religious heritage can lessen the likelihood of violent confrontation. Likewise, some religious groups (including Christians, Jews, and Muslims) have joined together in peaceful enterprises such as attempts to ban nuclear weapons or to address global poverty or climate change. These common purposes provide for cooperation and collaboration, thus lessening animosity and us-versus-them thinking.

Many countries today make clear separations between religion and the state because of their histories of religious hostilities. The conflicts in Europe between Protestant and Catholic religious groups were brutal. Intense religious in-group loyalties led to a willingness to kill those following other religions or other denominations of the same faith. The horrific religious conflicts in European societies—known as the Hundred Years' War—did not reach closure until the beginning of the Enlightenment period in the mid-1600s. Acceptance of other religious traditions and separation of religion from the state were needed to restore civility (Dobbelaere 1981, 2000; Lambert 2000).

The global rise of *religious fundamentalism* appears to be a local reaction against global modernization (Dunn 2015; Fernandez 2011; Salzman 2008). Rapid global change has resulted in *anomie* as people confront

- threats to traditional cultures and religious perspectives,
- the increasing secularization of society,
- the threat to the material self-interests of religious organizations, and
- increased interdependence among nations.

All these threats have strengthened religious nativism, and they can incline a group to armed combat with adversaries (Fernandez 2011).

THINKING SOCIOLOGICALLY

What specific religious beliefs or behaviors might influence the way in which religions and countries relate to one another? How might religious organizations influence international relations? For example, how might anti-Muslim prejudice by Christians influence U.S. relations with predominantly Islamic countries? How might the growing persecutions of Christians around the world, particularly in Global South nations, impact U.S. international relations?

Religion, Technology, and the World Wide Web

Technology and the Internet affect not only nations but also religions. From television broadcasts of megachurch services to Muslim chat rooms using technology to communicate, religious messages travel in new ways.

Prior to the wide distribution of religious texts to people who were not ordained priests, the hierarchies of Christendom controlled what was disseminated as truth. The common (and typically illiterate) member of the local

▼ FIGURE 12.10

Lines of Differentiation Between "Us" and "Them"

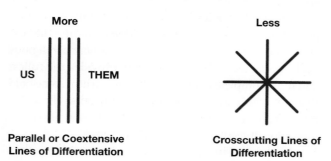

Likelihood of Hostilities

More — US | THEM — Less

Parallel or Coextensive Lines of Differentiation

Crosscutting Lines of Differentiation

Note: Imagine that each line represents a division in society between groups based on religion, ethnicity, political party, economic status, language spoken, skin color, or other factors. Parallel lines of differentiation divide people in each conflict along the same lines. *Crosscutting lines* cut the differences, so that people who were part of "them" in a previous antagonism become part of "us" in the present discord. This lessens the likelihood of deep and permanent hostilities within a social unit.

church did not have any basis for challenging the pope or other church leaders. Those leaders were the authority. However, Martin Luther, founder of the Lutheran Church, used the printed word in many powerful ways. He and other reformers claimed that the Bible alone was the ultimate source of truth and religious authority. The church leaders were to be believed only insofar as they were faithful to the scriptures. Luther himself used the printed word to spread his version of Christian truth, and he did so with a vengeance. He not only wrote more than the other dissenters; he outpublished the entire legion of Vatican defenders.

The invention of the printing press in 1450 allowed Luther to widely distribute his 95 Theses, written in 1517, containing his objections against Catholic Church practices. With his publications in the common languages of the people, rather than in Latin, Luther launched the Protestant Reformation and changed the course of religious history. It is doubtful whether this could have happened without the printing press. The printing press had similar revolutionary effects within Judaism (Brasher 2004).

Today, television and multimedia worship have enhanced the marketing of religion, including the modification of aspects of the faith to meet "consumer" demand (Ebaugh 2005; Roberts and Yamane 2016; Sargeant 2000). Tens of millions of religious websites relay information about an extraordinarily wide range of religious beliefs and practices. Even conservative Christians such as the late Jerry Falwell, who once dubbed the Internet an evil Tower of Babel, have used it to spread their message.

It is too early to tell for sure what impacts these most recent technologies might have on religions around the world, but one outcome is clear: The Internet allows instant access to information about religions that otherwise might be obscure or nonexistent for many people. For example, a relatively small number of ISIS members have been able to use social media, especially videos on Facebook, YouTube, and Twitter, very effectively to spread their absolutist religious perspective and recruit new followers (Greenemeier 2017).

Social Policy: Same-Sex Marriage, Gay or Lesbian Clergy, and Transgender People

Ordination of gay ministers and same-sex marriage in churches make for heated debate over church policy and threaten to split some denominations. More Americans favor same-sex marriage than oppose it, and in 2015 the Supreme Court declared that the Constitution guarantees U.S. citizens the right to same-sex marriage (Liptak 2015). Many religious groups, however, still view marriage as a union between a man and a woman and do not recognize same-sex marriages.

For religious people, marriage is a two-step process, in that they have both the government and their religious group recognize it. Marriage is sanctified by religious ceremony in all major religious groups, and some religious bodies have recently officially sanctioned weddings for same-sex couples. The U.S. Constitution guarantees that the government will recognize same-sex marriages, but that does not mean all religious groups will. Many of the largest denominations (e.g., Roman Catholic Church, Southern Baptist Church, United Methodist Church, Church of Jesus Christ of Latter-Day Saints [Mormons], Orthodox Judaism) define marriage as between a man and a woman and prohibit same-sex marriage.

However, a growing number of denominations have begun to allow same-sex marriages. The Unitarian Universalist Association of Congregations sanctioned them in 1996, the United Church of Christ began to perform same-sex marriages in 2005, and the Presbyterian Church (USA) accepted this position in 2015, as did Reform Judaism (1996) and Reconstructionist Judaism (1992). Attitudes among at least some people in the pews are changing: 64% of White mainline Protestants and 58% of Catholics in the United States now support same-sex marriage. Although fewer Black Protestants (39%) and White evangelical Protestants (27%) support such marriages, support has been increasing in these religious groups as well (Pew Research Center 2016b).

One of the most controversial issues in several mainline denominations is over ordination of gays and lesbians as ministers. For example, in 2003, when the Episcopal Church in the United States elected gay clergyman Gene Robinson as bishop, nearly 1,000 Episcopal congregations in the United States and Canada broke away and formed the Anglican Church in North America. Likewise, African Anglican leaders made clear their "outrage" over the Church of England's decision to allow gay clergy to become bishops, declaring their communion with the mother church "broken" (Anglican Church in North America 2013; Zaimov 2013).

Many religiously affiliated people also still oppose the recognition and acceptance of transgender people. A 2017 Pew Research poll, for example, revealed that although 62% of nonreligiously affiliated people believe "it is possible for someone to be a gender different from their sex at birth," 63% of Christians do not (Smith 2017b). Yet, just as support for same-sex marriage and gay and lesbian clergy has increased across the United States and within some religious organizations, so has support for the recognition of transgender people (Brown 2017).

In our social world, religious organizations influence society, and the larger society influences religious groups. Today, catalysts for change in religious organizations include (1) secularization in society—especially in the Global North—that emphasizes placing people in leadership roles based on competence and commitment rather than on traits beyond their control (e.g., skin color, gender, or sexual orientation) and (2) globalization and social media, which help spread religious messages across the world.

THINKING SOCIOLOGICALLY

How has religion impacted your views about same-sex marriage? What other institutions have impacted your attitudes toward same-sex marriage? Which have influenced you more? Why?

Religion deals with issues of meaning and, like education, serves as a core socialization agent in society. It provides socialization of members of society on important values, which sometimes makes cooperation more possible within a society. However, conflict cannot always be overcome by appeals to values, and sometimes the issues between individuals and groups come down to matters of power and access to resources. In the next chapter, we turn to the institutions of politics and economics and examine the influence of power and privilege in society and in our own lives.

WHAT HAVE WE LEARNED?

Religion is a powerful force in the lives of people around the world. It typically elicits passions and deep loyalties, and in so doing, it can stimulate great acts of self-sacrificing charity or horrible atrocities and intergroup bigotries. People's religious affiliations strongly relate to their nationality, ethnic and racial groups, and lifestyles. Religion is the one institution in most societies that consistently professes a desire for peace and goodwill, yet there may be inconsistencies between what people say and what they do. Religion can provide us with the hope that the world's problems may be dealt with in humanitarian ways.

Religion can provide a sense of purpose in our lives, and religious symbols come to have sacred meaning. Systems of meaning, belonging, and structure are interdependent components of religion.

Humans in the modern world tend to be spiritual. They may also live in states with massive governmental bureaucracies that hold power, and they participate in economic systems that produce and distribute the goods and services needed for survival. The next institutions we examine are politics and economics—how power relations are negotiated at each level in the social world.

KEY POINTS

- Religion makes our most important values sacred, operating through three interconnected systems: (1) a meaning system, (2) a belonging system, and (3) a structural system.

- We become committed through these three systems, by our attachment to a reference group that becomes a belonging system, by making investments in the organization (the structural system), and by holding as real the system of ideas (the meaning system).

- At the micro level, symbolic interaction theory illuminates how the meaning system works, with an interaction of myths, rituals, and symbols coming to define reality and making the values and the meaning system sacred. Rational choice

theory focuses on the costs and benefits that influence the decisions individuals make about religious commitments. It also examines how religious organizations go about seeking a "market share" in the competition for members.

- Denominationalism organizes religious life when there are multiple religious groups, without one being clearly dominant over the others, and when religious authority is separated from governmental authority. New Religious Movements (NRMs) also arise in pluralistic social contexts.

- At the macro level of analysis, functionalists maintain that religion can serve as a kind of glue to help solidify the country and can meet the basic needs of the populace. In contrast, conflict theorists focus on the ways in which religion reinforces conflicts and inequalities in society, whether socioeconomic, racial, or gender.

- In the United States and Canada, secularization is dominant at the meso and macro levels but does not seem to be as strong at the micro level. This is a source of tension in societies.

- At the global level, religion can be involved in issues of war and peace (sometimes unwittingly undermining peace), and its influence in this area has expanded through television and the Internet.

- Same-sex marriage and the ordination of gay or lesbian clergy are examples of religious policy issues causing considerable controversy among religions and their denominations.

DISCUSSION QUESTIONS

1. What are some ways that religion and government are interdependent and interrelated in the United States?

2. If you are a person of faith and affiliated with a religious community, how did you become so? If you are not, explain why. How did your family members and peers influence your views toward religion?

3. What motivates you to work hard and try to succeed professionally? Think about how Weber perceived the relationship between the development of the capitalist economic system and thoughts about sacrifice and work.

Does it relate to your answer to the first part of this question? Why or why not?

4. Do you think religion is more of a unifying or divisive force in (a) the United States and (b) the world today? Why? Do you have many friends from different religious groups? Why or why not?

5. What do you think might happen to society if religion did not exist? Why? How would an absence of religion impact you personally?

KEY TERMS

civil religion   365

denominations   360

elective affinity   371

myths   358

NRMs   362

rituals   358

secularization   377

theocracy   365

CONTRIBUTING TO OUR SOCIAL WORLD: WHAT CAN WE DO?

At the Local (Micro) Level

- *Campus religious foundations or ministries.* Most colleges and universities, including many of those not affiliated with a religion, have religious groups on campus. If you are not already a member and would like to join such an organization on your campus, contact a student representative or faculty sponsor, attend a meeting, and become involved. Most of these organizations participate in various types of outreach work, including volunteering for soup kitchens, food pantries, or thrift stores for the poor. If you attend a religiously affiliated college or university, you will find many and varied options.

At the Organizational or Institutional (Meso) Level

- *College-based religious organizations.* Many religious campus organizations such as the Newman Foundation (Roman Catholic; http://newmanfnd.org), InterVarsity (Christian; www.

intervarsity.org), Muslim Students Association (MSA; http://msanational.org), and Hillel Foundation (Jewish; www.hillel.org) are branches of larger organizations. You can find out more about them and how to start or join a chapter by going to their websites.

- *American Atheists* (www.atheists.org) provides similar services to atheists. According to the group's website, "Now in its fourth decade, American Atheists is dedicated to working for the civil rights of Atheists, promoting separation of state and church, and providing information about Atheism." Volunteers assist in this work through contributions, research, and legal support.

At the National or Global (Macro) Level

Several religious groups are committed to working for justice and peace at the national and global levels.

- *Tikkun Community* (www.tikkun.org) is an interreligious organization, started by progressive members of the Jewish community, to "mend, repair, and transform the world." It is an "international community of people of many faiths calling for social justice and political freedom."

- *American Friends Service Committee* (www.afsc.org), a Quaker organization, "includes people of various faiths who are committed to social justice, peace, and humanitarian service."

- *Catholic Relief Services* (www.crs.org) "carries out the commitment of the Catholic bishops of the United States to assist the poor and vulnerable" in over 100 countries.

- *Lutheran World Relief* (www.lwr.org) "extends the hand of Christian love to people overcoming poverty and injustice in 50 countries."

These and similar faith-based organizations sponsor many relief, peace, and justice projects around the world. You can find out more about volunteer and internship opportunities by going to their websites.

---

⑤SAGE edge™

Get the tools you need to sharpen your study skills. SAGE edge offers a robust online environment featuring an impressive array of free tools and resources.

Access practice quizzes, eFlashcards, video, and multimedia at **edge.sagepub.com/ballantine7e**

CHAPTER 13

© Bettmann/Getty Images

POLITICS AND ECONOMICS

Probing Power; Dissecting Distribution

▲ Power probes every aspect of our lives with intimidating force, even as economic distribution cuts across the social fabric. Sociology helps us probe and dissect the sources and consequences of each.

MICRO

ME (AND MY FAMILY)

LOCAL ORGANIZATIONS AND COMMUNITY
Power struggles and finances influence how well a local fraternity or a women's civic club functions.

MESO

NATIONAL ORGANIZATIONS, INSTITUTIONS, AND ETHNIC SUBCULTURES
State or provincial governments, political parties, and corporations within the state affect quality of life.

MACRO

SOCIETY
National governments and court systems set rules that resolve conflicts and establish standards for conducting business.

GLOBAL COMMUNITY
Cross-national organizations such as the United Nations and the World Court and global human rights movements like Amnesty International set standards for nations.

WHAT WILL YOU LEARN IN THIS CHAPTER?

This chapter will help you to do the following:

13.1 Describe the sociological definition of power

13.2 Discuss the importance of power and privilege in societies

13.3 Compare the key points of the pluralist and elite theories of power

13.4 Explain why some people participate in political systems and others do not

13.5 Describe the major types of governmental systems in operation today

13.6 Provide examples of the threats political systems can face from internal and external groups vying for power

Micro: Small groups and local community	How do people in your local community use power in constructive or destructive ways?
Meso: National institutions, complex organizations, ethnic groups	How does the political institution interact with the economic institution? How are different racial and ethnic groups affected by power and privilege?
Macro: National and global systems	How does economic instability threaten a national government? Why do struggles over power and privilege often evolve into war and terrorism?

Imagine that a nuclear disaster has occurred. The mortality rate is stunning. The survivors gather together for human support and collectively attempt to meet their basic survival needs. They come from varying backgrounds and have diverse skills. Before the disaster, some—the stockbroker and the business executive, for instance—earned more money and held higher social status than the others, but that is in the past. Faced with the new and unfamiliar situation, different skills are more immediately important for survival.

Where should this group begin? Think about the options. Some sort of organization seems essential, a structure that will help the group meet its needs. Food, shelter, and medical care are paramount. Those with experience in agriculture, building trades, and health care are likely to take leadership roles to provide these initial necessities. As time goes on, the need for clear norms and rules emerges. These survivors decide that all members must work—must contribute their share of effort to the collective survival. At first, these norms are unwritten, but gradually some norms and rules are declared more important than others and are recorded, with sanctions (penalties) attached for noncompliance. Survivors form committees to deal with group concerns, and a semblance of a judicial system emerges. One person is appointed to coordinate work shifts and others to oversee emerging aspects of this small society's life. This scenario could play out in many ways.

What is happening? A social structure is evolving. Not everyone in the group will agree with the structure, and some people will propose alternatives. Whose ideas will be adopted? Leadership roles may fall to the physically strongest, or perhaps the most persuasive, or those with the most skills and knowledge for survival. Those most competent at organizing may become the leaders, but that outcome is by no means assured.

In our world of power and privilege, a war, an invading power, an environmental disaster, or a revolutionary overthrow of an unstable government can change the form of a political system overnight, necessitating rapid reorganization. The daily news brings stories of governments overthrown by military leaders in coups, with new governments emerging to fill the gap, as has been happening

▲ Former secretary of state and senator Hillary Clinton and billionaire businessman and former reality TV star Donald Trump campaign during the 2016 presidential campaign. The election led to Republicans gaining control of the executive branch of the U.S. government as well as the House and Senate.

in various parts of the Middle East and Africa. The opening scenario and the political activity in our modern society share a common element: power. The concept of power is critical to understanding many aspects of our social world.

In this chapter, we focus primarily on the political and economic dimensions of society, because both political and economic systems enforce the distribution of power and resources in a society. Political systems involve the power relationships between individuals and larger social institutions. Economic systems produce and distribute goods and services. Not everyone gets an equal share, thus giving some citizens privileges that others do not have.

We consider the nature of power, politics, and economics at each level in our social world: individuals and power; political systems and the distribution of power and privilege through political and economic institutions; and national and global systems of governance, including international conflicts, war, and terrorism. We also look at how different theoretical perspectives view issues of power and privilege. Because the topic of economics has been explored in many chapters of this book, we put more emphasis on political systems and their relation to economic systems.

THINKING SOCIOLOGICALLY

Imagine that global climate change has caused massive flooding on your island nation. Only a few people have survived. How would you construct a new social system? What are the issues you would need to resolve to build a new society?

What Is Power?

Power is an age-old theme in many great scholarly discussions. Social philosophers since Socrates, Plato, and Aristotle have addressed the issue of political systems and power. Machiavelli, an early 16th-century Italian political philosopher, is perhaps best known for his observation that "the ends justify the means." His understanding of how power was exercised in the 15th, 16th, and 17th centuries significantly influenced how monarchs used the powers of the state (the means) to obtain wealth, new territories, and trade dominance (the ends) (Machiavelli [1532] 2010).

The most common definition of power used in social sciences today comes from Max Weber, who saw **power**

as *the ability of a person or group to realize its own will in group action, even against resistance of others who disagree* (Weber 1947). Building on Weber's idea of power, we can identify various power arenas. Two key arenas of power are the nation-state and the economic system. The leaders of a national government attempt to control the behavior of individuals through (a) *physical force and the threat of violence* (through a police force); (b) *symbolic control*, such as the manipulation of people (through control of the media); and (c) *rules of conduct* that channel behavior toward desired patterns (through laws). For example, the dictator and military in Syria have used torture, rape, and death to intimidate dissidents and their families and used the media to present the opposition as terrorists. The opposition has also used force and social media but does not have the same degree of power.

Control of the economy is another important source of power. Conflict theorists argue that those with power over the economy can control government officials (who depend on campaign contributions from the wealthy) and can convince the public that what is good for the wealthy is good for everyone. The members of the middle and working classes become convinced via the media that further tax breaks and advantages to the wealthy are—in the long run—in their own self-interest. In the United States, the media is largely controlled by wealthy owners of large corporations. Five companies—Time Warner, Disney, News Corporation, Bertelsmann, and Viacom (formerly CBS)—control 90% of television, radio, and newspaper outlets, and they often protect the interests of wealthy owners in the way they present news (Lutz 2012; Scheiber and Cohen 2015; Sommer 2014).

Power and Privilege in Our Social World

Power can be found at even micro levels of interaction, from individuals to family groups. In family life, relations often involve negotiation and sometimes conflict over how to run a household and spend money. Interactions between parents and children also involve power issues, as parents socialize their children. Indeed, the controversy over whether spanking is an effective discipline or an abusive imposition of pain is a question of how parents use their power to teach their children and control their behavior.

At the meso level, power operates in cities, counties, and states or provinces. Governments make decisions about which corporations receive tax breaks to locate

▲ Individual campaign workers in local communities try to influence voters at the micro level to determine who will wield power in meso and macro systems.

their plants within the region. They pass laws that regulate everything from how long one's grass can grow before a fine is imposed, to how public schools will be funded. Therefore, people have an interest in influencing governments by contributing to political campaigns and helping elect the people who support their views. Interest groups such as environmental advocacy, flat tax, and gay rights organizations also wield power and try to influence the political process at the meso level. Locally organized groups can force change that influences politics at the local, state or provincial, national, or global level.

Power processes pervade and cut across micro, meso, and macro levels. Locally organized groups can force change that influences politics at the local, state or provincial, national, or global level. Provincial or state laws shape what can and cannot be done at the local level. These laws may either limit or enhance the ability of citizens to protest or express their views, by determining where and when protests can occur. At the macro level, laws at the national and global levels influence state, provincial, and county politics and policies. Global treaties, for example, affect national autonomy. Reluctance to yield national autonomy is the main reason the United States and a few other countries have refused to ratify seemingly benign global treaties, such as the Convention on the Rights of the Child (United Nations Human Rights Office of Commissioner 2017).

Power can also be understood in terms of the allocation of economic resources in a society and what factors influence patterns of resource distribution. Both economic and political systems are important in sociologists' consideration of power distribution in any society. Let us first consider the theoretical lenses that help us understand power and politics.

Theoretical Perspectives on Power and Privilege

Do you and I have any real decision-making power? Can our voices or votes make a difference, or do leaders hold all the power? Many sociologists and political scientists have studied these questions and found several answers to who holds power and the relationship between the rulers and the ruled.

Among the common theoretical perspectives on power are our familiar ones: symbolic interaction, rational choice, structural-functional, and conflict theories. *Symbolic interaction* theorists focus on symbols and constructions of reality that help some people assume power. A core concern is the legitimacy of power, or whether those who are ruled accept the right of their leaders to have power over them. *Rational choice* theorists emphasize that people calculate their own self-interests and make choices—including political choices—based on perceived benefits and costs to themselves. Much analysis of voting behavior has to do with how people vote to advance themselves but also how they sometimes fail to understand which policies would truly be economically advantageous to them.

Focusing on the macro level, *structural-functionalists* believe that citizens legitimize political systems by supporting them through their votes or traditions. They do this because political systems serve important functions, or purposes, in society. They establish and coordinate societal goals—for example, promoting stability, providing law and order, engaging in relations with other countries, providing protection, and meeting social needs. *Conflict theorists* believe that the state protects the privileged position of a few, allowing them to consolidate power and wealth, and perpetuate inequalities that keep them in power. This power elite theory stems from conflict theory's contention that power is concentrated in the hands of an elite few and the masses have little power.

Micro- and Meso-Level Perspectives: Legitimacy of Power

Symbolic interactionists look at how loyalty to the power of the state is created—a loyalty so strong that citizens are willing to die for the state in a war. In the early years of the United States, citizens' loyalty tended to be mostly to individual states. Even as late as the Civil War, Northern battalions fought under the flag of their own states rather than that of the United States.

Most people in the United States now tend to think of themselves as U.S. citizens more than Virginians, Pennsylvanians, or Oregonians, and they are willing to defend the whole country. National symbols such as anthems and flags help create loyalty to nations. The treatment of flags illustrates the social construction of meaning around national symbols. The next Sociology in Our Social World explores this issue.

THINKING SOCIOLOGICALLY

Do you think wearing a shirt or sweater with the U.S. stars and stripes in some sort of artistic design is an act of desecration of the flag or a statement of patriotism? Why or why not? How does this illustrate that respect is "socially constructed"?

Socialization of individuals at the micro level generally instills a strong sense of the legitimacy and authority of the reigning government in a society. This includes loyalty to a flag or other symbol that represents the nation, as illustrated earlier. Individuals learn their political and economic attitudes, values, and behaviors—their political socialization—from family, schools, the media, and their nation. For example, national leaders provide much of the information for newspapers and other media and can spin that information to suit their needs and manage the perceptions of the public. Governments also play a role in what is taught in schools, which shapes attitudes of the citizenry regarding democracy, capitalism, socialism, and other political and economic systems (Glasberg and Shannon 2011; Zajda 2015).

Social Constructions of Politics: Legitimacy, Authority, and Power. Max Weber distinguished between legitimate and illegitimate power. *Power that is considered legitimate and rightful by those subject to it* is **authority** (Weber 1947). Governments are given legitimate power when citizens acknowledge that the government has the right to exercise power over them. They adhere to a judge's rulings because they recognize that court decrees are legitimate. In contrast, illegitimate

▲ This man no doubt feels he is expressing his patriotism, yet technically he is violating the U.S. Flag Code and "desecrating" the American flag. During the Vietnam War, protesters risked being attacked for dressing this way and "disrespecting" the flag and the country.

▼ FIGURE 13.1

Weber's Power Formula

Consent + force = power

Consent > force = legitimate power (authority)

Force > consent = illegitimate power (e.g., dictatorship)

power, or coercion, includes living under force of a military regime or being kidnapped or imprisoned without charge. These distinctions between legitimate and illegitimate power are important to our understanding of how leaders or political institutions establish the right to lead. To Weber, illegitimate power is sustained by brute force or coercion (see Figure 13.1). Authority, on the other hand, is granted by the people subject to the power. They believe in the legitimacy of the authority, so they willingly obey (Weber 1946).

How Do Leaders Gain Legitimate Power? Generally, leaders with legitimate power gained their positions in one of three ways.

SOCIOLOGY IN OUR SOCIAL WORLD

THE FLAG, SYMBOLISM, AND PATRIOTISM

Flags have become pervasive symbols of nations, helping to create a national identity (Billig 1995). In some countries, loyalty to the nation is taught with daily pledges to the flag at work or school. National loyalty becomes sacred, and that sacredness is embedded in the flag as a symbol of patriotism.

In the United States, the design of the flag and the respect of the public for it illustrate key ideas in symbolic interaction theory. The stars and stripes each have specific meaning related to states and the nation. Care of the U.S. flag is an interesting example of symbolism and respect for that symbol. Flag etiquette instructions make it clear that flying a flag that is faded, soiled, or dirty is considered an offense to the flag. We are told to either burn or bury a damaged flag as a way to honor and respect it.

Some citizens and legislators have proposed a constitutional amendment prohibiting burning of the U.S. flag as part of a protest against American policies. In 2006, for example, the Senate came within one vote of sending the flag-burning constitutional amendment to the individual states for ratification ("Flag-Burning" 2006). Supporters want flag burners punished and disrespect for the flag outlawed.

Those who oppose this amendment feel that only tyrannical countries limit freedom of speech, that the principle of free speech is central to democracy and must be allowed even if a sacred symbol is at stake. Indeed, opponents of the amendment think passing such a law would be a desecration of what that flag stands for. Supporters and opponents of the amendment have each attached different meanings to what is considered desecration of the national symbol. In the meantime, if you have a tattered or fading flag, burning it is the way you honor that flag—so long as you do so in private!

Other aspects of the U.S. Flag Code, which specifies what is considered official respect for or desecration of the flag, are interesting precisely because many people violate this code while they believe themselves to be displaying their patriotism (Sons of Union Veterans of the Civil War 2010).

1. The flag should *never* be used for advertising in any manner whatsoever. It should not be embroidered on cushions, handkerchiefs, or scarves or reproduced on paper napkins, carry-out bags, wrappers, or anything else that will soon be thrown away.

2. No *part* of the flag—depictions of stars and stripes that are in any form other than that approved for the flag design itself—should ever be used as a costume, a clothing item, or an athletic uniform.

3. Displaying a flag after dark should not be done unless it is illuminated, and it should not be left out when it is raining.

4. The flag should never be represented flat or horizontally (as many marching bands do). It should *always* be aloft and free.

5. The flag should under no circumstances be used as a ceiling covering (U.S. Flag Code 2008).

According to the standards established by U.S. military representatives and congressional action, any of these forms of display may be considered a desecration of the flag, yet the meaning most citizens give to these acts may be quite different. Symbolic interactionists are interested in the meaning people give to actions and how symbols themselves inform behavior.

---

1. *Traditional authority* is passed on through generations, usually within a family line, so that positions are inherited. Tribal leaders in African societies pass their titles and power to their sons. European and Japanese royal lines pass from generation to generation (though Japan still only allows males to become emperor). Usually called a monarchy, this has been a common form of leadership throughout history. Authority is seen as "normal" for a family or person because of tradition. It has always been done that way, so few dare to challenge it. When authority is granted based on tradition, authority rests with the position rather than the person. The authority is easily transferred to another heir of that status.

2. *Charismatic authority* is power based on a claim of extraordinary, even divine, personal characteristics. Charismatic leaders often emerge at times of change, when strong, new leadership is needed. For charismatic leaders, unlike traditional authority leaders, the right to lead rests with the person, not the position. Followers believe power is rooted in the personality of a dynamic

individual. This is an inherently change-oriented and unstable form of leadership because authority resides in a single person. The most common pattern is that, as stability reemerges, power will become institutionalized—rooted in stable routine patterns of the organization. Charismatic leaders are effective during transitional periods but often replaced by rational-legal leaders once affairs of state become stable.

Some examples of charismatic religious leaders include Jesus, Muhammad, Ann Lee (founder of the Shakers in the United States), and Joseph Smith (founder of the Mormon Church). Charismatic political leaders include Mao Zedong in China and Mahatma Gandhi in India. Both men led their countries to independence and had respect from citizens that bordered on awe. One charismatic leader today is Emmanuel Macron, who became the youngest ever president of France in 2017 and led his brand-new political party to a majority of seats in the French National Assembly.

3. *Rational-legal authority* is the most typical type of legitimate power in modern nation-states. Authority is given not to a particular person but to the position the person holds. Such authority is often found in political and economic bureaucracies in the modern states. For example, the president of the United States has authority due to the office he holds, just as does the CEO of a corporation. Individuals are granted authority because they have proper training or have proven their merit.

Each of these three types of authority is a legitimate exercise of power because the people being governed give their consent, at least implicitly, to the leaders (Weber 1947, [1904–1905] 1958). However, on occasion, leaders overstep their legitimate bounds and rule by force. Some of these rulers, such as Muammar Gaddafi in Libya and Hosni Mubarak of Egypt, are challenged and overthrown.

Self-Interest as a Path to Legitimacy. In contemporary democratic politics, politicians and political commentators often explicitly refer to the self-interests of voters. This reflects the *rational choice perspective* that humans tend to vote for their own benefit, regardless of whether the actions of government would be fair to all citizens.

Both U.S. Republican and Democratic Parties try to convince the public and donors that their policies will serve their self-interests. Democrats tend to argue that their government policies benefit citizens directly, with government

▲ Thailand's King Maha Vajiralongkorn participates in a religious ceremony in Bangkok in 2018. He inherited the throne after his father, King Bhumibol Adulyadej, died in 2016. This is an example of traditional authority.

▲ French president Emmanuel Macron greets an adoring crowd in July 2018. Macron became the youngest president in the history of France when he assumed office in May 2017.

programs for the middle and working classes, such as government support for preschool and higher education. Republicans, on the other hand, often stress that less government and lower taxes create a greater stimulus to the economy than anything the government can do. Again, the appeal is to self-interests. Members of both political parties promise to help those who support and vote for them, once they are put in positions of power.

Many voters do not understand the issues at play in elections and vote for people who support policies that would actually harm them. To make it even more complex, some people vote based on values—right to life, support for the needy, or protection of the environment, for example—because they think it is the right thing to do. The policy may not be in the person's self-interest—unless the person is considering the interest of his or her children and grandchildren or long-term noneconomic interests, such as a desire to build a society pleasing to God.

Macro-Level Perspectives: Who Rules?

Pluralist Model of Power. As noted in previous chapters, the pluralist model holds that power is distributed among various groups so that no one group has complete power. According to pluralists, it is primarily through interest groups that you and I influence decision-making processes. Groups such as unions or environmental organizations represent our interests and act to keep power from being concentrated in the hands of an elite few (Dahl 1961; Dye and Zeigler 1983; Zdan 2017).

Two examples of interest groups in the United States are the Tea Party and Indivisible movements. The Tea Party began as a small group of disaffected individuals opposed to government expansion but became a major influence on Republican Party politics (Skocpol and Williamson 2012). Citizens join such a movement because of a common core of concerns—for example, concern over the size of the national debt, a desire for lower taxes, and a deep distrust of the federal government and power in a centralized location (Tea Party 2016; U.S. Debt Clock 2016; U.S. Government Accountability Office 2015). The group elected a substantial number of its members to the U.S. Congress and had a strong influence over the direction of the Republican-led House of Representatives (Martin and Meckler 2012; Skocpol and Williamson 2012). The Indivisible movement, in contrast, is comprised of progressives motivated to take action after the election of Donald Trump (who was supported by the Tea Party movement) in 2016. Their goal has been to help Democrats take control of Congress from the Republicans and block much of President Trump's agenda.

Interest groups can influence laws and policies by mobilizing large numbers of voters or political donors. Examples include efforts to influence health care reform in the United States; combat global climate change; and reform government, business, and banking industry practices. AARP (formerly the American Association of Retired People); Common Cause; National Rifle Association (NRA); Bread for the World; Focus on the Family; the Family Research Council; the Service Employees International Union; American Enterprise Institute; and other consumer, environmental, religious, and political action groups have had impacts on policy decisions. According to pluralists, shared power is found in each person's ability to join groups and influence policy decisions and outcomes.

National or international nongovernmental organizations (NGOs or INGOs) can have a major impact on global issues and policymaking, as exemplified by BRAC, formerly the Bangladesh Rural Advancement Committee, Save the Children, Doctors Without Borders, and Islamic Relief International (Briner 2015; Global Journal 2013; NG Advisor 2017). NGOs exert influence on power holders because of the numbers they represent, the money they control, the issues they address, and the effectiveness of their spokespeople or lobbyists. Sometimes they form coalitions around issues of concern such as the environment, human rights, health care, or women's and children's issues. The efforts of religious, business, and labor unions for immigration reform provide an example of such a coalition. Each of these groups, with its own set of constituents, believes that immigration reform is in its best interest.

According to pluralists, multiple power centers offer the best chance to maintain democratic forms of government because no one group dominates and many citizens are involved. Although an interest group may dominate decision-making on a specific issue, no one group dictates all policy. On the other hand, some theorists maintain that only a small group of elite people really have much power.

Elite Model. The power elite model asserts that it is inevitable that a small group of elite will rule societies. As we discussed in earlier chapters, they argue that this is the nature of individuals and society and that pluralists are imagining a world that does not exist. Individuals have limited power through interest groups, but real power is held by the power elite that play central roles in both Republican and Democratic political parties in the United States (Domhoff 2008; 2014; Dye 2002; Mills 1956). They wield power through their institutional roles (e.g., as holders of high-level governmental offices, heads of political think tanks and lobbying organizations, CEOs of global corporations and financial institutions) and make decisions about war, peace, the economy, wages, taxes, justice, education, welfare, and health issues—all of which have a serious impact on citizens. These powerful elites attempt to maintain, perpetuate, and even strengthen their rule.

Robert Michels, a well-known political philosopher, believed that elite rule is inevitable. He described this pattern of domination as the *iron law of oligarchy*. In democratic and totalitarian societies alike, leaders have influence over who succeeds them and to whom they give political favors. This influence eventually leads those in elite positions to abuse their power (Michels [1911] 1967).

Social philosopher Vilfredo Pareto expanded on this idea of abuse of power, pointing out that abuse would cause a counter group to challenge the elite for power. Eventually, as the latter group gains power, its members would become corrupt as well, and the cycle—a *circulation of elites*—would continue (Pareto [1911] 1955). Corruption in many countries illustrates this pattern. Somalia, South Sudan, North Korea, and Syria were ranked as most corrupt in 2017 (Transparency International 2017a).

C. Wright Mills also argued that there is an invisible but interlocking power elite in U.S. society, consisting of leaders in military, business, and political spheres, wielding their power from behind the scenes. They make the key political, economic, and social decisions for the nation and manipulate what the public hears (Mills 1956).

According to the power elite model of G. William Domhoff, a few wealthy citizens of the United States "rule America." In a series of books titled *Who Rules America?* he describes how the members of this elite group form a cohesive economic-political and policymaking power structure that represents their interests. Through interactions from a very young age in private clubs and schools, the elite socialize with one another and prepare to become "rulers." One can see today that many of those who hold top positions on corporate boards or in policymaking think tanks attended the same private preparatory schools and Ivy League colleges—Brown, Columbia, Cornell, Dartmouth, Harvard, University of Pennsylvania, Princeton, and Yale—and created lasting connections (Domhoff 2008, 2014; Howard 2007; Persell and Cookson 1985).

Domhoff analyzed leaders of large corporations and financial institutions and showed that their common characteristics promote a network of connections, or "higher circles," and constitute a pool of potential appointees to top government positions. Key government officials tend to move into their government offices from positions in industry, finance, law, and universities. They are linked with an international elite that helps shape the world economy. According to the power elite model, Congress ultimately has minimal power. The elected representatives accede to the power elite. Elite theorists believe that government seldom regulates business. Instead, business co-opts politicians to support its interests by providing the financial support needed to run political election campaigns (Domhoff 2014).

Pluralists, however, believe that a powerful government serves as a balance to the enormous power of the corporate world. Big business and big government are safety checks against tyranny—and each is convinced that the other is too big. Table 13.1 shows the key differences between the pluralist and elite perspectives of power.

THINKING SOCIOLOGICALLY

Do you think your national society is controlled by pluralist interest groups or a power elite? Can an individual outside of a power elite help to influence policies in your nation? If so, how? If not, why not?

▼ TABLE 13.1

Pluralist and Power Elite Perspectives of Power

Perspective of Power	Power Distribution	Characteristics
Pluralist	• Power is distributed among various groups.	• People influence decision-making processes through interest groups (e.g., unions, environmental organizations, AARP, Tea Party, Indivisible). • Interest groups and big business act as checks on one another.
Power Elite	• Power is controlled by a small group of people.	• Robert Michels's *iron law of oligarchy*: elite rule is inevitable. • Vilfredo Pareto's *circulation of elites*: those who overthrow corrupt leaders become corrupt, themselves, once in power (and the cycle continues). • C. Wright Mills's *power elite*: an interconnected group of leaders in military, business, and political spheres control the government from behind the scenes. • G. William Domhoff's *"Who Rules America?" power elite model*: a small group of families go to the same schools, socialize together, and become interconnected leaders of large corporations, financial institutions, and top universities. They hold top government positions and control elected officials.

Individuals, Power, and Participation: Micro-Level Analysis

Whether you have health insurance or are subject to a military draft depends, in part, on the political and economic decisions made by the government in power. Political systems influence our personal lives in myriad ways, some of which are readily apparent: health and safety regulations, taxation, a military draft, and regulations on the food and drugs we buy. In this section, we explore the impact individuals have on the government and the variables that influence participation in political and economic policymaking processes. At the micro level, individuals decide to vote or otherwise participate in the political system. This private decision is, in turn, affected by where those individuals fall in the stratification system of society, not just by personal choices.

Participation in Democratic Processes

Citizens in democratic countries have the right to free and fair elections. Many social scientists, including sociologists, have tried to understand what influences citizens' decisions on whether and how to vote. Political sociologists want to know how participation affects (and is affected by) an individual's perception of his or her power in relationship to the state. They look at how such trends as growth in Hispanic and Asian groups, shifts of the population to different regions of the country and from rural to urban areas, changing family structures and shifting women's roles, the aging of Baby Boomers, and increasing resentment of the political status quo by many less educated citizens influence the electorate and elections (Teixeira and Halpin 2012). These factors combine with ideology and attitudes about government to influence participation in elections.

▲ Two women in Afghanistan cast their ballots during the 2014 presidential elections. In many parts of the world, voting is not just a treasured privilege, it is an act of courage.

Ideology and Attitudes About Politics and Economics. What kind of government do you think is best? If you believe that individuals are not naturally social people and, instead, are motivated only by selfish considerations and desire for power, you may feel as the 17th-century English philosopher Thomas Hobbes did—that order must be imposed by an all-powerful sovereign. In that scenario, individuals do not have rights, and rulers of states may control them in any way necessary. Control over people is more important than individual freedom and liberty because people cannot exist without the state.

On the other hand, you may believe, as did John Locke, another 17th-century political philosopher, that humans are naturally social and free and that governments have a right to exist only if they preserve that freedom. Humans, Locke argued, should have their needs and interests met by the state, and among these needs are liberty, ability to sustain life, and ownership of property. Unlike Hobbes, Locke believed that governments must have the consent of the people.

What kind of economic system do you favor? Do you believe in equal distribution of resources—wealth, property, and income—or do you think that those who are most able or have inherited high status should receive more of the wealth? Some social scientists, politicians, and voters think that individuals have different abilities and work ethics and are therefore entitled to different rewards. Some people are successful, and some are not. (Recall the structural-functional theory discussion in Chapter 7 on stratification about the inevitability of inequality.) Others think government should facilitate a more equal distribution of resources, so that all have similar life chances. Conflict theorists tend to support this view.

THINKING SOCIOLOGICALLY

How might your decision about how to vote (a micro-level decision) be affected by your ideology and attitudes about politics and economics? How might those decisions on how to vote make a difference in how state or provincial, national, or global systems work?

Levels of Participation in Politics. As mentioned in previous chapters, wealthier people are more likely to vote for various reasons. For example, they tend to

• have been socialized to believe they can make an impact on the political process,

- benefit from an educational background that allows them to understand the issues at hand and how their own self-interests are at stake,

- have and take the time to follow the news and political issues, and

- experience a more flexible schedule that allows them the time to vote.

Those with little money, on the other hand, tend to feel that politics has little relevance for them (apathy) or that they cannot affect the process and are disaffected by the scandals or corruption in politics (alienation from a system that does not value them). Participation in elections in the United States is the second lowest of the Global North democracies, as indicated in Figure 13.2. Note, however, that among *registered* voters, U.S. participation is among the highest. This highlights how policies that influence the ease of the registration process can influence voter turnout.

Structural factors also influence voting. The debates over voter registration in the United States are a case

▲ Citizens vote in an election in Manaus, Brazil, where voting is compulsory.

in point, with some states combing their voter lists for ineligible voters or making registration and voting difficult for some citizens, usually the elderly, minorities, and people in poverty who may have problems obtaining acceptable ID. By contrast, in 24 countries, including top-ranked Belgium, voting is compulsory, a

▼ FIGURE 13.2

International Voter Turnout

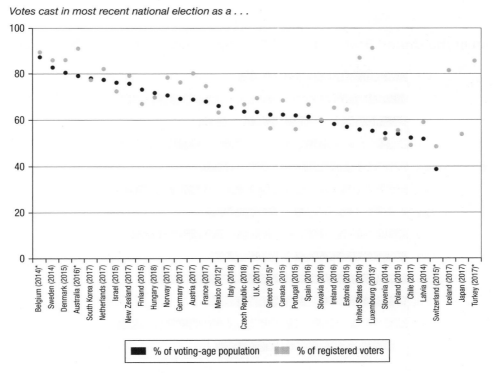

Source: Desilver 2017.

*National law makes voting compulsory.

Note: Current voting-age population estimates for Iceland, Japan, and Turkey are unavailable.

legal obligation of citizenship, and voter turnout tends to be close to 90% (Desilver 2017; Frankal 2011). Fines, community service, and even jail time are penalties for not voting. Elections are held over many days to ensure that people can get to the polls. Even inmates are expected to vote in some countries (Inter-Parliamentary Union 2016; McCrummen 2008; Paxton and Hughes 2007).

A higher percentage than normal of eligible U.S. voters turned out in the 2012 and 2016 presidential elections: 58.7% and 59.7%, respectively, but that means more people abstained from voting than voted for either of the top two candidates (41.6% not voting in 2016) (Ingraham 2016; U.S. Elections Project 2016). Figure 13.3 shows the trend in voting in presidential elections over the past 50 years. There is also considerable range in voter participation by state, with a high of 74.2% Minnesotans voting to a low in the mid 40% range in Hawaii and Utah (U.S. Election Project 2016).

In off-year elections—when many senators, congressional representatives, and state governors are elected—the turnout hovers in the low 40s or even below. If 40% of the eligible population votes and it is a very close election, only slightly more than 20% of the citizenry may have elected the new office holder. So voter turnout is an

▼ FIGURE 13.3

Turnout in U.S. Presidential Elections

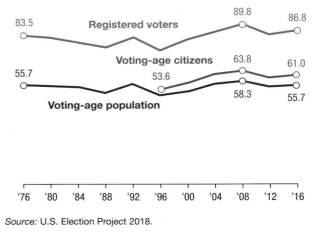

Votes cast as a share of . . .

Source: U.S. Election Project 2018.

important issue for a society that purports to be a democracy. In 2014, a nonpresidential election year, the overall national turnout was only 33.9%, and Indiana had the lowest turnout at 28.7% (Alter 2014; U.S. Elections Project 2016). Figure 13.4 indicates U.S. voter turnout since 1990.

▼ FIGURE 13.4

Voter Turnout in the United States: 1990–2014 (by Percentage of Eligible Voters)

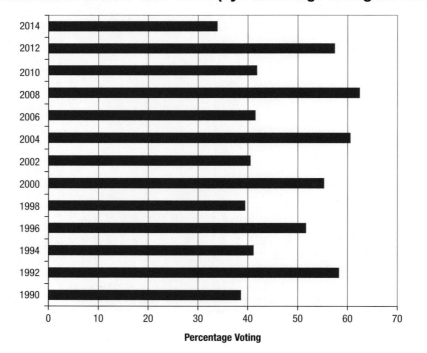

Source: U.S. Election Project 2016.

Power and Resource Distribution: Meso-Level Analysis

In southern Africa, Bantu tribal groups provide for heirs to take on leadership when a leader dies. When there is no male heir to the position, a female from the same lineage is appointed. This woman must assume the legal and social roles of a male husband, father, and chief by acting as a male and taking a "wife." The wife is assigned male sexual partners, who become the biological fathers of her children. This provides heirs for the lineage, but the female chief is their social father because she has socially become a male. This pattern has been common practice in many southern Bantu societies and among many other populations in four separate geographic areas of Africa. Anthropologists interpret this as a means of maintaining public positions of dominance and power in the hands of males in a family and community (D. O'Brien 1977). Ruling groups in society—in this case, a meso-level tribal society under the jurisdiction of a nation-state—have mechanisms for ensuring a smooth transition of power to keep the controlling structure functioning.

Meso-level political institutions include state or provincial governments, national political parties, and large formal organizations within the nation. Those political institutions also influence and are influenced by other meso-level institutions: family, education, religion, health care, and economics.

What Purposes Do Political and Economic Institutions Serve?

We have learned in earlier chapters that each institution has purposes or functions in society. Just as family, education, health care, and religion meet certain societal needs, so do the political and economic institutions. The following six activities are typical societal purposes (functions) of meso-level political and economic institutions. They set the stage for power and privilege carried out at the macro level in national and international arenas.

1. *To maintain social control.* We expect to live in safety, to live according to certain "rules," to be employed in meaningful work, and to participate in other activities prescribed or protected by law. Ideally, governments help clarify expectations and customs and implement laws that express societal values.

2. *To serve as an arbiter in disputes.* When disputes arise over property or the actions of another individual or group, a judicial branch of government can intervene. In some systems, such as the tribal

▲ One function of governments is to provide protection from external threats—the role of the military establishment. These soldiers are in training for that role.

groups mentioned earlier, a council of elders or powerful individuals performs judicial functions. In other cases, elected or appointed judges have the right to hear disputes, make judgments, and carry out punishment for infractions.

3. *To protect citizens.* Governments are responsible for protecting citizens from takeover by external powers or disruption from internal sources.

4. *To represent the group in relations with other groups or societies.* Individuals cannot negotiate agreements with foreign neighbors. Official representatives deal with other officials to negotiate arms and trade agreements, establish and maintain a nation's airways, determine fishing rights, and establish military bases in foreign lands, among other agreements.

The four functions listed thus far are clearly political in nature; the two that follow are areas of contention between political and economic realms.

5. *To make plans for the future of the group.* As individuals, we have little direct impact on the direction our society takes, but the official governmental body— be it elected, appointed, or imposed through force—shares responsibility with economic institutions for planning in the society. In some (but not all) socialist societies, this planning determines how many engineers, teachers, or nurses are needed. The appropriate number of people are then trained according to these projections. In other societies, power is much less direct. In capitalist systems, for instance, supply and demand are assumed to regulate the economic system, and

there is less governmental planning in economic matters than in socialist societies. The question of who does the planning is often a source of stress between the political and economic institutions: Are the planners elected politicians and public servants or private entrepreneurs?

6. *To provide for the needs of their citizens.* Governments differ greatly in the degree to which they attempt to meet the material needs of citizens. Some provide for most of the health and welfare needs of citizens, defined as *positive human rights*—to life, health, education, a healthy environment, and survival of one's culture (Frezzo 2015). Other governments tend to leave these largely to individuals, families, local community agencies, and other institutions, such as faith communities. Not everyone agrees that providing for needs is an inherent responsibility of the state. Some people believe that the economy will produce jobs, goods, and services for the population if the government gets out of the way and lets individuals make decisions based on their self-interests. Those who take this position define human rights in "negative" terms—that is, what governments can*not* do to people: abuse, humiliation, exploitation, exclusion, and interference with individual freedom (Frezzo 2015). The debates over health care and welfare systems in the United States point to conflicts over who should be responsible: the state or private individuals. Should such services be coordinated by the government or left to the "invisible hand" of market forces?

Clearly the role of political legislators is complex. Not only are they supposed to protect the self-interests of their constituents—those who elected them—but they are to make decisions about governmental policies that are in the best interest of the society as a whole. *Policy* (a course of action adopted and pursued by a government, ruler, or political party) is complex precisely because there are always unanticipated consequences, sometimes shocking to the advocates of that policy. One role of public sociologists—such as Lindsay Owens, described in the next Sociologists in Action feature—is to advise legislators.

The ways in which governments and economic institutions carry out the six functions of government are largely determined by society's dominant philosophies of power and political structures. Political and economic institutions, like family and religious institutions, come in many forms. These variations in political institutions reflect variations in human ideas of power.

Meso- and Macro-Level Systems of Power and Resource Distribution

Whereas *politics* refers to the social institution that determines and exercises power relations in society, *economics* is the social institution that deals with the production and distribution of goods and services. Both politics and economics focus on questions related directly to the concept of power and power relationships among and between individuals, organizations, nation-states, and societies. Economic and political systems overlap in part because those who have power also have access to resources. How goods are distributed to the members of society—a major function of economics—is often determined by who has political power.

Successful political campaigns, except at the most local level, require significant financial resources, so attaining political positions involves cultivating relationships with leaders in the economic system. Thus, there is a reciprocal relationship between economics and politics. In many countries, the government is the largest employer, purchaser of goods, controller of exports and imports, and regulator of industry and interest rates. In the United States, many government regulatory agencies, such as the Food and Drug Administration, Department of Agriculture, Consumer Financial Protection Bureau, and Justice Department, attempt to watch over the economic sector to protect consumers.

Government officials have a vested interest in the well-being of the economy, for should the economy fail, the state would be likely to fail as well. Recessions, depressions, and high rates of inflation put severe strains on governments that need stable economies to run properly. When problems occur, government officials are inclined to increase their roles in the economic sector. Witness the measures, such as bailouts of financially unstable banks and corporations, taken by governments to stabilize their economies when they are in jeopardy.

On September 29, 2008, the Dow Jones Industrial Average dropped an unprecedented 777 points and fell another 782 points a week later. President Bush and Congress immediately began to look for "stimulus packages" to keep the economy from going into a deep

USING SOCIOLOGICAL TRAINING IN GOVERNMENT POLICY WORK

I work as a policy advisor for a senator in the United States Congress. Certain aspects of my job appear, at first, to be wildly incompatible with my sociological training. For one, I am tasked with being an expert on hundreds of topics—from how payroll taxes are allocated between the two Social Security trust funds, to whether a big parent company has legal obligations to the employees in one of its franchises, to how securities regulation differs for fixed and variable annuities. In academia, I would not be considered an expert on any of these topics. I have not written a peer-reviewed article on them, given a colloquium talk on them, or covered them in a course lecture.

Senate offices, however, particularly the offices of relatively new members, are small. As a result, each policy expert covers an enormous range of topics. When an issue in one of the areas I am responsible for bubbles to the surface—because there is legislation on the floor, a committee hearing, or a constituent matter back in our home state—I have to get up to speed immediately. I do not have 3 months to dive into the academic literature. Instead, I rely on my sociological training to find information fast. I have to figure out quickly where I can get trustworthy information. I talk to experts—sometimes academics, sometimes Senate committee staff, and sometimes the Congressional Research Service—and then I read as much as I can as rapidly as I can and recommend a course of action. Although this was initially nerve-racking, I now find the intellectual challenge stimulating and rewarding.

The legislative process, by design, is slow and incremental, and the details of a legislative proposal—how much it costs, how it will be implemented, and how it interacts with current laws—can quickly overshadow larger policy aims. I find that my ability, as a sociologist, to step back and look at the big picture can be critically important.

My sociological training also leads me to ask certain key questions: What are the potential unintended consequences of this policy? Will the intended effect of the policy be stymied by firmly entrenched structural constraints? Will the effects of this policy differ for men or women, for people of color, or for people at different income levels? Sociologists bring a unique perspective to policymaking—a perspective that complements the extraordinary political and legal expertise of my colleagues.

I am not sure how long I will stay on the Hill, but I know that this experience will make me a more insightful scholar and teacher, and I know that my sociological training has made me a more effective policymaker. Above all, it is humbling and gratifying to be able to help a member of the U.S. Senate make a tangible difference in the lives of Americans.

★ ★ ★ ★ ★ ★

Lindsay Owens is an economic policy adviser for Senator Elizabeth Warren (D-Mass). Owens received her PhD from Stanford in 2014.

---

recession. When Barack Obama became president in 2009, turning the economy around became one of the key challenges of his presidency.

A dramatic drop in financial markets indicates a loss of the population's confidence in the economy and a mass reluctance to invest in it. Lending institutions cannot loan money easily, business stagnates, unemployment rates skyrocket, and the entire government may be held responsible for a lack of economic vitality. When a country goes into a recession, the party in power is often held responsible and will not likely be reelected if the recovery takes too long. Economic recessions can destroy the careers of politicians but can also create such dissatisfaction that the entire government may be at risk

of a citizen uprising, such as seen in Venezuela. Recession in one country also influences other countries around the world because of trade, international markets, and economic refugees seeking employment in other nations. For example, as Venezuela faces economic collapse, approximately 600,000 to 800,000 Venezuelans have entered neighboring Colombia in search of work and food (Wyss 2018).

Types of Governments. The major systems of government in the world range from fascist totalitarianism to democracy. However, each culture puts its own imprint on the system it uses, making for tremendous variation in actual practice.

▲ A stable economic system is essential to political stability, and extreme fluctuations in the economy threaten those in power. Indeed, market fluctuations in one country can influence financial stability in other countries because of global trade and international markets. This man is analyzing the stock market at a brokerage house in Hangzhou City, China.

▲ People gather to protest gun violence and call for sensible gun laws at a March for Our Lives rally in March 2018. Protests are one way citizens try to keep a government accountable and influence policy.

Authoritarian Governments. In **authoritarian governments**, *power is concentrated in the hands of an absolute monarch, dictator, or small group not accountable to the people.* They often have the backing of the military to keep them in power. Authoritarian regimes are common forms of government. Some are helpful to citizens—benevolent dictators—but almost all exert tremendous power and discourage dissent. The Castro brothers—Fidel, who died in 2016, and more recently Raúl—have maintained effective political control of Cuba since 1959. Although they are despised by many Cuban immigrants in the United States, they are admired by many Cubans (especially older Cubans) as ruling in the best interests of the people, even if autocratically (Clement 2015). For example, the literacy rate in Cuba has gone from 17% when the Castros took power to 99.8% in 2017, and many older people have accepted some loss of individual freedoms in exchange for universal education and health care (Dillinger 2017).

Totalitarian Governments. A **totalitarian government** is *any form of government that almost totally controls people's lives.* It differs from authoritarian governments in that the political leaders also control the social and economic institutions. Totalitarian states are often based on a specific political ideology and run by a single ruling group or party, referred to as an *oligarchy.* Russia under Joseph Stalin, Germany under Adolf Hitler, Libya under Muammar Gaddafi, and North Korea under Kim Jong-un are examples. The state typically controls the workplace, education, the media, and other aspects of life. All actions revolve around state-established objectives. Dissent and opposition are discouraged or forcefully

eliminated, with violent crackdowns on demonstrators. Interrogation by secret police, imprisonment, and torture are used to quiet dissenters. Terror is used as a tactic to deal with both internal and external dissent, but when it is used by the state to control the citizenry or to terrorize those of another nation, it is called *state terrorism.*

Throughout history, most people have lived under authoritarian or totalitarian systems. Under certain conditions, totalitarian regimes can turn into democratic ones, and of course, democratically elected leaders can change or ignore laws to retain their positions of power, as was the case for a number of elected leaders who changed the constitutions to allow for them to run again (Venezuela, Zimbabwe, Rwanda, and Russia are examples). The next Sociology Around the World provides an example of one totalitarian regime.

Democratic Systems of Government. In contrast to totalitarian regimes, **democratic governments** are *characterized by accountability of the government to citizens and a large degree of control by individuals over their own lives.* Democracies always have at least two political parties that compete in elections for power and that generally accept the outcome of elections. Mechanisms for the smooth transfer of power are laid out in a constitution or other legal document. Ideal-type democracies share the following characteristics, although few democracies fit this description exactly:

1. *Citizens participate in selecting the government.* There are free elections with anonymous ballots cast, widespread suffrage (voting rights), and competition between members of different parties running

THE KHMER ROUGE REVOLUTION: A TOTALITARIAN REGIME

▲ These skulls are the remains of people massacred by the Khmer Rouge in the Killing Fields of Cambodia.

When the Khmer Rouge faction took over the government of Cambodia in 1975, it abolished private property; relocated urban dwellers to rural areas; classified some people as peasants, workers, or soldiers—and killed the rest. The group's most impressive feat was the total evacuation of the capital city, Phnom Penh. It ordered the evacuation to remove urban civilization and isolate Cambodia from other economic and political influences, such as free markets and democracy, which the Khmer Rouge opposed.

This complete social and economic revolution under the leadership of Pol Pot was planned in Paris by a small group of intellectual revolutionaries. They believed that it would allow Kampuchea, their former name for the country, to rebuild from scratch, eliminating all capitalism, private property, and Western influence.

After urban dwellers were resettled in rural camps, the totalitarian regime tried to break down the family system by prohibiting contact between members, including sexual relations between husbands and wives. Approximately 1.7 million people (21% of the population), including defeated soldiers, bureaucrats, royalty, businesspeople, intellectuals with opposing views, Muslims, and Buddhist monks, were slaughtered for minor offenses. Hence, the term *killing fields* is used to describe the execution sites (Cambodian Genocide Program 2015).

Famine followed the killings, causing many Cambodians to flee their land, traveling by night and hiding by day to reach refugee camps across the border in Thailand. Pol Pot was finally overthrown in 1979, when Vietnam defeated Cambodia militarily and established a new government with Khmer Rouge defectors. Today, with increased global demand for manufacturing, the economy in Cambodia is growing, especially in the areas of garment work and tourism.

Violence still exists in Cambodia, however. Human Rights Watch reports chaos, corruption, poverty, and a reign of terror, with attacks on opposition leaders and social justice advocates. Killings, violence, and intimidation continue to surround elections (Human Rights Watch 2017).

for offices. Those who govern do so by the consent of the majority, but political minorities have rights, representation, and responsibilities.

2. *Civil liberties are guaranteed.* These usually include freedom of association, freedom of the press, freedom of speech, and freedom of religion. Such individual rights ensure dissent, and dissent creates more ideas about how to solve problems. These freedoms are therefore essential for a democracy to thrive.

3. *Government powers are limited by a constitution.* The government can intrude only into certain areas of individuals' lives. Criminal procedures and police power are clearly defined, thus prohibiting harassment or terrorism by police. The judicial system helps maintain a balance of power.

4. *Governmental structure and process are spelled out.* Generally, some officials are elected whereas others are appointed, but all are accountable to citizens. Representatives are given authority to pass laws, approve budgets, and hold the executive officer accountable for activities. The two main forms of democratic constitutional government are the parliamentary and presidential systems. In typical parliamentary governments, the head of government is a prime minister, chancellor, or premier, and there is also a president or monarch, with less power. Countries with this model include Belgium, Canada, Denmark, the United Kingdom, Japan, Sweden, Ireland, India, Israel, Pakistan, and Turkey. In presidential systems, the head of government is a president. Examples of presidential governments include France, Italy, the United States, Germany, Argentina, Brazil, Kenya, and the Philippines.

Proportional representation means that each party is given a number of seats corresponding to the percentage of votes it received in the election. In "winner-takes-all" systems, the individual with more than 50% of the votes gets the seat.

In the United States, each state votes indirectly through members of the Electoral College. The Electoral College consists of 538 electors; 270 are required to win the presidency. Each state has as many electors as they have representatives and senators (and the District of Columbia has 3 electors).

The electoral system has come under attack because the winner of the nationwide presidential popular vote can lose the election. This happened in five presidential elections in the United States: 1824, 1876, 1888, 2000, and 2016. In the most recent two instances, Al Gore and Hillary Clinton, respectively, received the most votes for president. Due to the system for electing the Electoral College, however, George W. Bush and Donald Trump gained the majority of Electoral College votes and won the presidency. In 2016, Hillary Clinton won the total popular vote with 2.8 million more votes, 48% compared to 45.9% for Donald Trump ("Presidential Election" 2018; U.S. Elections Project 2016). Defenders of this system of choosing the president argue that this protects the voice of each state, even if each individual voice is not given the same weight.

Constitutional governments may include representatives from two to a dozen or more parties (as has been the case in Switzerland). Most countries have four or five viable parties. In European countries, typical parties include Social Democrats, Christian Democrats, Communists, Liberals, Labour, and other parties tied to specific local or state issues, such as Green parties.

Modern electronic technology also has a complex relationship with democracy, enhancing it in some ways and undermining it in others. The next Sociology in Our Social World examines some of the impacts of electronic media on democracy.

THINKING SOCIOLOGICALLY

How can technology be problematic for representative democracy? How can it be beneficial? What are some ways technology has impacted elections in your country?

Types of Economic Systems. As societies become industrialized, one of two basic economic systems evolves: a planned system or a market system. Planned or centralized systems involve state-based planning and control of property, whereas market systems stress individual planning and private ownership of property, with much less governmental coordination or oversight. These basic types vary, depending on the peculiarities of the country and its economy. For instance, China has a highly centralized planned economy with government control, yet some private property and incentive plans exist, and these are expanding. The United States is a market system, yet the government puts many limitations on business enterprises and regulates the flow and value of money. Distinctions between the two major types rest on the degree of centralized planning and the ownership of property. In each type of system, decisions must be made concerning which goods to produce (and in what quantity), what to do in the event of shortages or surpluses, and how to distribute goods. Who has the power to make these decisions helps determine the type of system.

Market or Capitalist Economic Systems. **Market or capitalist economic systems** are *driven by the balance of supply and demand, allowing free competition to reward the efficient and the innovators with profits. They stress individual planning and private ownership of property.* As noted earlier, the goal of capitalism is profit, made through free competition for the available markets. Proponents of pure capitalism assume that the laws of supply and demand will allow some to profit, while others fail. Needed goods will be made, and the best product for the price will win out over the others. No planning by an oversight group is necessary, because the invisible

TECHNOLOGY AND DEMOCRACY

In the modern world, new challenges and issues face democracies. Electronic technology—the Internet and other telecommunications technologies—can be a boon to democracy, an opportunity for people around the world to gain information necessary to be an informed electorate, or it can be a burden that hinders thoughtful debate and civic engagement in ideas, these being essential ingredients of a functioning democracy (Barber 2006). For example, recent elections for U.S. president have permitted unlimited political contributions to political action committees (PACs) that fund negative campaign ads. These ads are often deceptive and require strong analytical skills to avoid being manipulated by them.

Cell phones and other telecommunications devices have been important tools for indigenous people, linking them to the outside world and combating oppressive governments. On the other hand, television news shows and online news and opinion sites are often known more for sound bites and polemical attacks on opponents than for reasoned debates in which opposing sides express views in search of a better solution than either side originally had. Technology can be used by elected officials and those running for elected positions in myriad ways. In representative democracies, such as the United States, one key contribution these technologies bring is speed—helping citizens stay in touch with their elected representatives. This allows them to follow and try to influence policymaking as it unfolds.

However, speed is not always good for democracy. Legislation requires the ability to debate and compromise, but digital media has the tendency to reduce political discourse to simplistic sound bites of opposites, as though only two choices are possible.

Technology can also invade citizens' privacy, even in democracies. For example, the leaking of classified information in 2013 revealed that the U.S. government keeps track of its citizens' communications by having direct access to the servers of Google, Apple, Facebook, and other Internet companies (Greenwald and MacAskill 2013). These intrusions are done in the name of protecting the public from terrorists, but some Americans believe that they violate their right to privacy.

Technology can also make electoral systems vulnerable to cyberattacks from other nations. In the 2016 election, for example, Russia infiltrated voter databases and software systems in 39 states in the United States. There is no evidence that the Russians tampered with actual votes in the election, but the episode highlighted the vulnerabilities of the U.S. electoral system in an era of cyberwarfare (Riley and Robertson 2017).

hand of the market will ensure sufficient quality control, production, and distribution of goods. This system also rewards innovative entrepreneurs who take risks and solve problems in new ways, resulting in potential growth and prosperity.

Capitalist manufacturers try to bring in more money than they pay out to produce goods and services. As Karl Marx described, because workers are a production cost, getting the maximum labor output for the smallest wage benefits capitalists (Marx [1844] 1963). Therefore, multinational corporations look throughout the world for the cheapest sources of labor with the fewest restrictions on employment and operations. The potential for (and practice of) labor exploitation leads most governments to exercise some control over manufacturing and the market, although the degree of control varies widely.

Capitalism was closest to its pure form during the Industrial Revolution, when some entrepreneurs gained control of large amounts of capital and resources, and legislation to control owners and protect workers did not yet exist. Using available labor and mechanical innovations, these entrepreneurs built industries and, soon, monopolies (exclusive control over supplying certain goods). Craftspeople, such as cobblers, could not compete with the efficiency of the new machine-run shops, and many were forced to become laborers in new industries to survive.

As noted in earlier chapters, Marx predicted that capitalism would cause citizens to split into two main classes: the *bourgeoisie*, capitalists who own the means of production (the "haves"), and the *proletariat*, those who sell their labor to capitalists (the "have-nots"). He argued that institutions such as education, politics, law, and religion work to preserve the privileges of the elite.

Religious ideology often stresses that workers should work hard and defer to authority. Furthermore, members of the economic and political elite usually encourage patriotism to distract the less privileged from their conflicts with the elite. According to Marx, the elite want the masses to draw the line between "us" and "them" based on national loyalty, not based on lines of economic self-interests (Gellner and Breuilly 2009). So, in Marxist thought, even patriotism is a tool of the elite to control the workers. However, Marx believed that ultimately the workers would realize their plight, develop a class consciousness, and rebel against their conditions. They would overthrow the "haves" and bring about a new and more egalitarian society.

The revolutions that Marx predicted have not occurred in most countries. Labor unions have protected workers from the severe exploitation that Marx witnessed in the early stages of industrialization in England, and capitalist governments have created and expanded a wide array of measures to protect workers, including antimonopoly legislation, social security systems, unemployment compensation, disability programs, welfare systems, and health care systems. Therefore, most workers have not been discontent to the point of trying to overthrow their governments. Marx's vision of a small group of owners controlling the economy has been borne out, however. For example, today, among the 100 wealthiest countries and corporations in the world, 69 are corporations and just 31 are countries (Global Justice Now 2016). Among individuals, just eight men own as much as the poorer *half* of the world's population (3.6 billion people) (Oxfam 2017).

One of the major criticisms of pure capitalism is that profit is the only value that drives the system. Human dignity and well-being, environmental protection, rights of ethnic groups, and other social issues are important only as they affect profits. This leaves some people deeply dissatisfied with capitalism.

Planned Economic Systems. In **planned (or centralized) economic systems**, *the government or another centralized group oversees production and distribution.* They deemphasize private control of property and economic autonomy and have the government do economic planning. Decisions concerning production and labor are, in theory, made with the "communal" good in mind. There is deep suspicion of the exploitation that can occur when individuals all pursue their own self-interests. Those who hold this philosophy believe that the market system also results in oligarchy—a system run by the financial elite in the pursuit of their own self-interests. Therefore, they believe the state needs to oversee the total economy. Cuba and North Korea have two of the few planned economic systems now in existence.

In reality, however, no system is totally planned, with the complete elimination of private property or differences in privilege. China, based on a planned, government-controlled system, made rapid progress in tackling hunger, illiteracy, drug addiction, and other problems by using its strong central government to establish 5-year economic development plans. Today, however, charges of corruption among those who control state-run companies and a desire for increased economic growth have led it to experiment with new economic plans, including limited private entrepreneurship, more imported goods, and trade and development agreements with other countries. China is now the largest trading nation and has surpassed the United States, in some measures, as the world's largest economy (Willige 2016).

One key criticism of planned systems is that placing both economic and political power in the hands of the same people can lead to control by a few leaders, resulting in tyranny. Marx believed that the worst form of government was *state capitalism*—a system in which the state controls the economy. His early writings, in particular, put much more emphasis on decentralization and even a withering away of the government (Marx [1844] 1963). So, it is ironic that the states perceived as communist today (China and Cuba) have such governments in authoritarian forms. They are far from what Marx would advocate. Multiple power centers in government, the business world, and the military can balance each other and help protect against dictatorships and tyranny (Heilbroner and Milberg 2007).

Mixed Economies. Some systems are mixed economies, sometimes called democratic socialism, because they try to balance societal needs and individual freedoms. **Democratic socialism** refers to *collective or group planning of the development of the society, but within a democratic political system.* Private profit is less important than in capitalism, and the good of the whole is paramount. Planning may include goals of protecting the environment, wealth redistribution through progressive taxation, universal health care, or supporting families through government-subsidized health care and family leave legislation, but individuals' rights to pursue their own self-interests are also allowed within certain parameters. Mixed economies seek checks and balances so that both political and economic decision makers are accountable to the public.

Several countries, including Sweden, the United Kingdom, Norway, Austria, Canada, France, and Australia, have incorporated some democratic socialist ideas into their governmental policies, especially in public services. Many Western European democracies redistribute income through progressive tax plans that tax according to people's ability to pay. The government uses these revenues to nationalize education, health plans and

▲ Hikers enjoy Grand Canyon National Park, one of 59 national parks and hundreds of national monuments publicly accessible because they are controlled by the federal government. This is one form of socialism that is very popular in the United States.

medical care, pensions, maternity leaves, and sometimes housing for its citizens (Heberlein 2016). Although much of the industry is privately run, the government regulates business and assesses high taxes to pay for government programs. Typically, public service industries such as transportation, communications, and power companies are government controlled.

Some programs and policies in the United States that follow the structure of democratic socialism include Social Security, Medicaid, Medicare, farm subsidies, federal unemployment insurance, the national parks system, public schools, environmental policies, and thousands of other programs that support and protect U.S. citizens. So, any government program that bails out the economy (such as rescuing a failing bank) or that protects consumers is part of a mixed economy that includes some socialist policies. Note that both Republican and Democratic administrations have supported such policies, and the policies have usually been popular. The popularity of Bernie Sanders—an ardent supporter of democratic socialism—in the 2016 U.S. presidential primaries is also an indication of the appeal of this approach with some Americans.

Just two and a half centuries ago, it was widely believed, perhaps rightly at that time, that democracy could not work. The notion of self-governance by the citizenry was discredited as a pipe dream. Yet this experiment in self-governance is continuing, despite some flaws and problems. In a speech to the British House of Commons in 1947, then prime minister Winston Churchill said that "democracy is the worst form of government, except for all those other forms that have been tried" (Churchill 2009). Some economists and social

philosophers have argued that if the people can plan for self-governance, they certainly should be able to plan for economic development in a way that does not put economic power solely in the hands of a political elite.

The institutions of politics and economics cannot be separated. In the 21st century, new political and economic relationships will emerge as each institution influences the other. Both institutions ultimately have close connections to power and privilege.

National and Global Systems: Macro-Level Analysis

Each nation-state develops its own systems of power and privilege in unique ways, depending on its history, leaders, needs, and relations with other nations. A macro-level analysis of national and global systems of governance and power includes individual nation-states, international organizations, multinational corporations, and terrorist groups that cross borders.

Power and the Nation-State

A *nation-state* is a political, geographical, and cultural unit with recognizable boundaries and a system of government. These boundaries change as disputes over territory are resolved by force or negotiation. For example, the boundaries of Israel have changed multiple times since the establishment of the nation in 1948.

There are officially 195 nation-states in the world today that are recognized by each other's governments in the United Nations, and 6 more with partial recognition, making 201 nation-states. The Vatican, Taiwan, Palestine, and Kosovo do not have UN representation, but the Vatican and Palestine now have UN *observer status* (Political Geography Now 2017). The number of nations increases as new independent nation-states continue to develop in Europe, Asia, and Africa. Kosovo and South Sudan are two of the newest nations. Kosovo declared its independence from Serbia in 2008, and South Sudan broke away from Sudan in 2011.

Within each nation-state, systems of power govern people through leaders, laws, courts, the tax structure, the military, and the economic system. Different forms of power dominate at different times in history and in different geographical settings.

The notions of the nation-state and of nationalism are so accepted that we rarely stop to think of them as social constructions of reality, created by people to meet group needs. In historical terms, though, nationalism is a rather recent or modern concept, emerging only after the

▲ The Avenue of the Nations in Geneva, Switzerland, displays all the flags of the member states of the United Nations.

creation of the nation-state (Gellner 1983, 1993; Gellner and Breuilly 2009). Medieval Europe, for example, knew no nation-states. One scholar writes that

> throughout the Middle Ages, the mass of inhabitants living in what is now known as France or England did not think of themselves as "French" or "English." They had little conception of a territorial nation (a "country") to which they owed an allegiance stronger than life itself (Billig 1995:21).

Their lives revolved around their local villages, and local feudal lords held the most power.

Some argue that nation-states have "no precedent in history" prior to the 16th century. Nation-states did not become widely acknowledged until they formed throughout Europe in the 19th century (Giddens 1986:166). This raises an interesting question: Why did nation-states emerge in Europe and then spread throughout the rest of the world? The answer to this puzzle of modern history has to do with the change to rational organizational structures (Billig 1995).

The nation is largely an imagined reality, something that exists because we choose to believe that it exists, but it can exert tremendous influence over us (B. Anderson 2006; McCrone 1998). For some people, belonging to the nation has become a substitute for religious faith or belonging to local ethnic groups (Theroux 2012). When nations face threat, populations tend to unify and rise to defend them—even at the cost of their own lives, if necessary.

Revolutions and Rebellions

From the 1980s to the present, significant social and political changes have taken place throughout the

▲ Revolutions can involve a violent attack on governments or nonviolent events such as this protest march by Burmese monks whom the government in Myanmar (Burma) brutally suppressed.

world. For example, the Berlin Wall was dismantled, leading to the reunification of East and West Germany. The government of South Africa that supported apartheid fell. The Baltic states of Estonia, Latvia, and Lithuania became independent. In Eastern Europe, political and social orders established since World War II underwent radical change. When the Soviet Union and Yugoslavia broke apart, national boundaries were redrawn. Internal strife resulted from ethnic divisions formerly kept under check by the strong centralized governments in these areas. The Arab Spring of 2011–2012 led to a number of dictators in the Middle East falling from power, and we are still seeing repercussions from those power changes.

Were these power changes around the world revolutions? **Revolution** refers to *social and political transformations of a nation that result when states fail to fulfill their expected responsibilities* (Skocpol 1979). Revolutions can be violent and generally result in altered distributions of power. Revolutions typically occur when the government does not respond to citizens' needs and when leadership emerges to challenge the existing regime. News reports from around the world frequently announce that nation-states have been challenged by opposition groups attempting to overthrow the regimes. This is the case in Syria and some other Middle Eastern nations today.

Meso-Macro Political Connection

State or provincial governments and national political parties are both meso-level organizations that operate beyond the local community but with less widespread influence than national or federal governments or global systems. Still, decisions at the state or provincial government level can have a major impact on political processes at the national level. Here we look at recent controversies about how to nominate and elect a president within the United States. Although the focus is on the U.S. political system, this discussion should be seen as illustrative of the tensions and peculiarities of the meso-macro link in any complex political system.

Some U.S. states have closed primaries, with only members of the respective political parties (e.g., Democrat and Republican) allowed to vote in their election of candidates for office. In other states, registered

Independents can vote in either primary election and help select either party's candidate in a primary election; these are called semiclosed primaries. Other states have open primaries, with Democrats and Republicans able to cross over and vote in the primary for the other party (Kamarck 2016; Real Clear Politics 2016).

In some U.S. states, each political party runs its own caucuses (face-to-face meetings of voters in homes, schools, and other buildings) to discuss policy and to carry out public votes. Each political party funds the process and sets the rules. In contrast, other states have primary elections, usually run by the state government. (See Table 13.2 for caucus and primary states.) However, even states that use a primary are not all the same. In most states, delegates to the convention are selected based on the proportion of the vote won by a candidate in that state. If a candidate wins 42% of the vote, she or he wins approximately 40% of the delegates. However, in 16 states on the Republican side, the delegate selection process is a winner-takes-all system. In such elections, if one candidate wins by a mere hundred votes, she or he wins all the delegates for that state. This is true even if the winner of that primary only captures 35% of the vote. In short, there is no uniformity. In addition, one state, New Hampshire, has in its state laws a mandate to the secretary of state that

▼ TABLE 13.2

Meso-Level Presidential Nomination Variations in the United States

Open Allow citizens to cross over to vote in the other party's primary	Semiclosed Allow Independents to vote in a party's primary	Closed Only party members may vote	States With Caucuses Rather Than Primaries Controlled by the political parties
AL AR GA IL IN MI MO MS MT SC TN TX VA VT WI	NH	AZ CT DE FL LA MD NM NY OR PA	Open: MN Closed: CO KS ME NV WY
Open in the Democratic but closed in the Republican processes: ND*	Semiclosed in Democratic but closed in Republican: CA OK SD UT**	Closed Democratic primary; closed Republican caucus: KY	Semiclosed in Democratic; closed in Republican: AK HI IA * * * * *
Open in Republican but semiclosed in Democratic: MA NC OH RI WV		Closed Republican caucus; closed Democratic caucus: ID NE	Caucus for Republican but not Democratic: ND KY UT
Open in Republican but closed in Democratic: NJ		Closed Republican primary; open Democratic caucus: WA	Caucus for Democratic but not Republican: ID NE WA

Sources: Kamarck 2016; Real Clear Politics 2016.

*North Dakota has an open primary for Democrats and a closed caucus for Republicans.

**Utah has a semiclosed primary for Democrats and a closed caucus for Republicans.

the state *must* have the first presidential primary, and this means the state has more influence on winnowing down the presidential candidates than other states (Kamarck 2016). (To see the processes for various states—whether winner-takes-all or proportional—go to www.realclear politics.com/epolls/2016/president/republican_delegate_count.html.)

THINKING SOCIOLOGICALLY

Some states never get any say in the nomination of candidates because the results are decided before they vote. New Hampshire, on the other hand, has written into its legal code a requirement directing the state's secretary of state that it must have the first primary election. Should these decisions be made at the state or the national level? Who has the authority to tell a state it cannot put into its constitution a regulation that it must have the first presidential primary?

Some state governments decide when primaries will be held, whereas elsewhere the political parties control the process of selecting nominees. Can a political party—a meso-level political entity—tell a state—another meso-level political entity—when to have its primary elections? On the other hand, can a state legislature tell a major national political party how to run its nomination process? The answers to these questions are not clear and have sometimes resulted in conflict, yet they can have profound effects on who becomes the president of the most powerful nation on earth.

In several states, the Republican primary is a "beauty contest" with no binding outcome. The results are purely advisory, and the delegates from that state are free to ignore the outcome of the election. The delegates are selected by party leaders in that state, not by the voters. The Democratic Party has no nonbinding elections, and all states distribute delegates based on the proportion of the vote won in that state (Kamarck 2016). So, both parties allow delegates not representing any constituency to help choose the presidential nominee. What are the implications for a democracy when there are such irregularities?

Even selection of the Electoral College, which truly decides who will be president after the general election, is not uniform in policy across the states. Two states—Nebraska and Maine—have proportional distribution of electors, and all the others have winner-takes-all. Should there be consistency among the states in the way the Electoral College is selected? Should state elections all be proportional or winner-takes-all? Should the president and vice president be elected by popular vote rather than the Electoral College? These are important issues for how a democracy operates.

Because the Constitution grants considerable autonomy to states to make these decisions, how does the nation ever get consistency? At the state (meso) level, legislatures are very protective of their right to make their own decisions. Yet governance of the nation and the nation's relationships with the global community may be at stake. As you can see, meso-level political power can shape power at the macro level, which then influences policies relevant to individual lives. The three levels are intimately linked. The next Engaging Sociology raises questions about where authority for decisions resides at each level in the social system.

Global Interdependencies: Cooperation and Conflicts

The most affluent countries in the Global North are democracies, but a democratic system of government may not be functional in poor countries with different cultural values and systems (Etounga-Manguelle 2000). Despite the movement toward political liberalization, democracy, and market-oriented reforms in countries such as Chile, Mexico, Nigeria, Poland, Senegal, Thailand, and Turkey, not all these societies are ready, willing, or able to adopt democratic forms of governance (L. Diamond 1992, 2008).

Foreign powers can do little to alter the social structure and cultural traditions of other societies, and as indicated, these structures are key to the successful development of democracy. If one tries to impose a system that is incompatible with the society's level of development and other institutional structures, authoritarian dictatorship rather than democracy may emerge as the traditional authority structure breaks down. We can see signs of this in Afghanistan and Iraq, two nations in which the United States tried to establish democratic forms of government. Certain preconditions tend to be necessary for the successful emergence of democracy:

- High levels of economic well-being
- The absence of extreme inequalities in wealth and income
- Social pluralism, including a particularly strong and autonomous middle class
- A market-oriented economy
- Influence in the world system of democratic states

POLITICAL DECISIONS: SOCIAL PROCESSES AT THE MICRO, MESO, AND MACRO LEVELS

Imagine that your state legislature is considering a change in the presidential election process. Your state representatives in the Electoral College would be selected according to the percentage of the popular vote in your state going to each candidate (Republican, Democratic, Libertarian, and Green Party). (*Note*: Currently, most—but not all—states distribute their electors on a winner-takes-all basis.)

1. Identify two possible micro-level consequences of this policy change. For example, how might it affect an individual's decision to vote?

2. Identify three consequences at the macro level. For example, how might the change affect how

presidential candidates spend their resources and time? How might Congress respond to such an initiative?

3. How does this illustrate the influence of meso-level organizations on micro and macro levels of the social system? For example, is it a problem for a *national* democracy when the delegate selection system is so variable at the meso level, or does this make elections even more democratic because states can make their own autonomous decisions? Explain your answer.

4. Which system—winner-takes-all or percentage of the popular vote—would produce the fairest outcome? Why?

- A culture relatively tolerant of diversity and that can accommodate compromise

- A functioning and impartial media that will hold the government accountable

- A literate population (80% or more) informed about issues

- A written constitution with guarantees of free speech and freedom of assembly (Bottomore 1979; Inglehart 1997)

THINKING SOCIOLOGICALLY

Why might some analysts believe that Iraq or Afghanistan—where the United States has attempted to set up democracies—may not be ready for a successful democratic government? Can you describe societies with which you are familiar that are—or are not—ready for democratic government? Why it is important for you, as a citizen of your own society, to be knowledgeable about other nations (and what will you do to become better informed)?

An outside power like the United States can help establish the structures necessary to support democracy but can seldom successfully impose those structures. If countries in the Global North want more democracies around the world, a more successful strategy would focus on supporting economic development in less

affluent countries. Again, politics and economics are intertwined.

Some Global South countries see discussions of democracy as a ploy—a cover-up used by dominant affluent nations for advancing their wealth. For example, some Global North nations have combined to form a coalition of nations calling itself the Group of Seven (or the G7—the United States, Japan, Germany, Canada, France, Great Britain, and Italy). Russia was in what was called the G8 but was asked to leave because of political disputes over the country of Ukraine. The G7 uses its collective power to regulate global economic policies to ensure stability (and thereby ensure that its members' interests are secure). The G7 has the power to control world markets through the World Trade Organization, the World Bank, and the International Monetary Fund (Brecher, Costello, and Smith 2012; Council on Foreign Relations 2016). Global South nations have responded to the G7 with an organization of poor countries that they call the G77 to create collective unity and gain enough power to determine their own destinies (Brecher et al. 2012; Eitzen and Zinn 2012; Hearn 2012). Figure 13.5 shows the location of G7 and G77 nations.

Political systems can face threats from internal sources such as disaffected citizens, the military, and interest groups vying for power, or they can be challenged by external sources such as other nations wanting land or resources or by coalitions of nations demanding change. This is the situation for North Korea and Iran, where

Countries of the G7 and of the G77

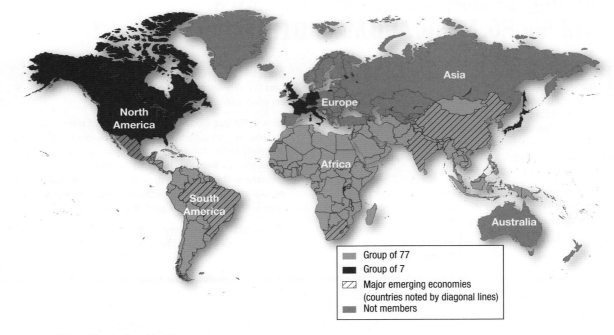

Source: www.g77.org. Map by Anna Versluis.

coalitions of nations have demanded that they drop their nuclear enrichment programs. Sometimes these power struggles erupt into violence. The following section discusses how war, terrorism, and rebellion challenge existing systems.

Violence on the Global Level. Although wars have always been brutal (Genghis Khan's ruthless campaigns are one example), since the invention of modern weaponry and chemical and nuclear weapons, no one has been safe from death and destruction in war. Weapons can destroy whole civilizations. A malfunctioning computer, a miscalculation, a deranged person, a misunderstanding between hostile factions, or a terrorist attack could kill millions of people.

War is *armed conflict occurring within, between, or among societies or groups*. It is sometimes called *organized mass violence* (Jacob and Danielsson 2016; Nolan 2002). War is a frequent but not inevitable condition of human existence. Many countries are now engaged in wars detrimental to their economies and morale. Some of these wars (between India and Pakistan, between the Palestinian Territories and Israel, and between rival factions in the Congo) have lasted many years. Others have been short and decisive, such as Operation Desert Storm, the war against Iraq under the first president Bush. Table 13.3 lists ongoing world conflicts as of 2015.

Why Do Nations Go to War? Leaders use moral, religious, or political ideology to legitimize war, although the cause may be conflicts over economic resources or ethnic tensions. Wars have been waged to support religions through crusades and jihads; to liberate a country from domination by a foreign power; to protect borders, resources, and cultural customs; and to capture resources, including slaves, land, and oil. War can also distract citizens from other problems in their country and may therefore be used by politicians intent on staying in power. The United States has been involved in numerous wars spanning from the colonial wars (1620–1774) to the war on terrorism (2001–present). The United States has been at war 193 out of the 243 years since the colonies declared independence. Indeed, during the entire 20th century, there were only 6 years when the United States was not engaged in some sort of military action around the world (Brandon 2005; Noguera and Cohen 2006). On the other hand, in some cultures, war is virtually unknown. These groups, often isolated, live in peace and cooperation, with little competition for land and resources. War is not inevitable but a product of societies and their leaders, created by and learned in societies.

▼ TABLE 13.3

Significant Ongoing Armed Conflicts, 2015

Main Warring Parties	Year Conflict Began
Middle East	
Syria vs. Free Syrian Army and other militants	2011
Iraq vs. Islamic State of Iraq and Syria (ISIS)	2003
Israel vs. Palestine	1948
Yemen: government forces vs. the rebel group Shabab al-Moumineen and other militants	2004
Turkey: government forces vs. the Kurdistan Workers' Party (PKK) and Kurdistan Freedom Falcons (TAK)	2003
Libya: fighting between militia groups	2012
Asia	
Afghanistan: U.S., UK, and coalition forces vs. al-Qaeda and Taliban	1978
Burma (Myanmar) vs. Kachin Independence Army (Kachin and Rakhine states)	1988
India vs. Kashmir Harkat-ul-Ansar, Northeast United People's Democratic Front, Maoist insurgents (and other splinter groups)	1947
Philippines vs. the Mindanaoan separatists (MILF/ASG), the Bransamoro Islamic Freedom Fighters (BIFF), the National Democratic Front (NDF), and New People's Army (NPA)	1969
Thailand vs. antigovernment insurgents	2004
Africa	
Algeria vs. al-Qaeda in the Islamic Maghreb	1992
Chad vs. Chadian Popular Front for Recovery (FPR)	1965
Democratic Republic of Congo vs. March 23 Movement (M23)	1990
Central African Republic vs. Christian vigilantes and ex-Séléka (rebel) soldiers	2014
Ethiopia vs. Ogaden National Liberation Front (ONLF)	2007
Kenya vs. Somali Islamists	1991
Nigeria vs. Boko Haram	1990
South Sudan vs. Sudan People's Liberation Army (SPLA) and Darfur	1983
Europe	
Russia vs. Chechen separatists in Chechnya	1999
Russian-backed separatists vs. Ukraine	2014

Note: Where multiple parties and long-standing but sporadic conflict are concerned, date of first combat deaths is given.

Source: Project Ploughshares 2016.

Note, however, that many businesses profit from war because their manufacturing power is put to full use. In fact, more money is spent on war than on prevention of disease, illiteracy, and hunger. Since 9/11, U.S. spending on war has reached $5.6 trillion, and the average American taxpayer has spent $23,386 on war since 2001 (Watson Institute International and Public Affairs 2017).

A concern of conflict theorists is that those with power have the most control over decisions to go to war, but citizens from the lower classes and racial minorities join the military, fight, and die in disproportionate numbers. Those with less privilege are more likely to join the military as an avenue to employment and job training. They join as enlistees who serve on the front lines and are more at risk.

All sociological theorists agree that war is not a natural or biological necessity but a social construction (Stoessinger 1993). Likewise, societies create ways to resolve and avoid war.

How Might Nations Avoid War? What can nations do to avoid war? Powerful nations have employed two primary methods: deterrence and negotiation. *Deterrence* is a theory of conflict management and a strategy aimed at preventing undesirable behavior by another group or country. Any parties contemplating action against others are deterred because the costs to them, should they strike, exceed any possible gains (Lebow 1981). This rational cost-benefit calculus is similar to rational choice theory, with which you are familiar. This approach was paramount during the Cold War between the United States and the Soviet Union, and many argue it worked because no nuclear war ensued. Today those who advocate building defense capability as a deterrent against nuclear attacks or war align themselves with this theory.

Many, however, argue that deterrence will not work against the growing threat of terrorists, because some terrorists are irrational, difficult to locate, and willing to incur loss of lives to achieve goals (Kroenig and Pavel 2012; U.S. Department of Defense 2012; van Ginkel 2015). Moreover, continual buildup of weapons increases mistrust and raises the potential for misunderstandings, mistakes, and disaster.

The world spent $1.686 trillion on military expenditures in 2016. The United States accounted for more than one third of world military spending, with $611 billion. China was second, with a budget of $215 billion. Russia was third, spending $69.2 billion. Saudi Arabia was fourth, spending $63.7 billion on its military, and India was fifth, with $55.9 billion in military expenditures (Stockholm International Peace Research Institute 2017). As mentioned, military spending usually comes at the expense of social programs such as education and health care, simply because there is not usually enough money to fund all these programs when the military consumes so much (Hinton 2010). Still, many people feel that protection of the citizenry is the government's most essential responsibility and deterrence is the way to achieve security.

Negotiation is the second approach to avoiding war and involves resolving conflicts by discussions to reach agreement. Diplomacy and treaties have set limits on nuclear weapons and their use. For example, President Obama negotiated a treaty with Russia in 2010 that led to a reduction in deployed, long-range nuclear warheads by 30% (Sheridan and Branigin 2010; Zeleny 2009). President Trump, on the other hand, has proposed to increase and expand the nuclear arsenal of the United States (Sonne 2018).

Some citizens, not satisfied to leave peacekeeping efforts to their government leaders, form and participate in nongovernmental peace organizations. These peace groups carry out efforts to prevent war, including protest marches, educational programs, and museum displays. The horrors depicted in the Hiroshima Peace Memorial Museum in Japan; the Killing Fields Museum in Cambodia; the Holocaust Memorial Museum in Washington, DC; the Anne Frank Museum in Amsterdam, Netherlands; the Kigali Genocide Memorial in Rwanda; and the Korean War and Vietnam Veterans Memorials in Washington, DC, all help sensitize the public and politicians to the effects of war. Interestingly, most war memorials in the United States glorify the wars and lionize the heroes who fought in them. In Europe, many memorials stress the pathos and agony of war. The Vietnam Veterans Memorial in Washington, DC, also sends a message about the sorrows of war. Peace advocates and veterans of the war have stood and wept together in front of that memorial.

Scholars draw several conclusions from studies of war in the past century: (a) No nation that began a major war in the 20th century emerged a clear winner; (b) in the nuclear age, war between nuclear powers could be suicidal; and (c) a victor's peace plan seldom lasts (e.g., the harsh peace settlement of World War I helped lead to World War II). Peace settlements based on equality tend to be much more permanent and durable. Economic issues, such as an inequitable distribution of resources, can incite a war. Therefore, a lasting peace requires attention to at least semi-equitable distribution of resources.

As long as conflict over resources, discrimination, hunger, and poverty exist, the roots of violence are present. The world is a complex interdependent system. When the linkages between peoples are based on ideologies that stress us-versus-them polarities and power differentials that alienate people, then war, terrorism, and violence will not disappear from the globe.

▲ The Vietnam Veterans Memorial in Washington, DC—like many European war memorials do—expresses and elicits a sense of the anguish and suffering of war. This man mourns the loss of a close friend and comrade.

Terrorism. "Got Him: Vengeance at Last! US Nails the Bastard" was the *New York Post*'s headline (Ortutay and Zongker 2011). For the 10 years following September 11, 2001, the search had been on. That was when three commercial airplanes became the missiles of terrorists, two crashing into the Twin Towers of the World Trade Center in New York City and one into the Pentagon in Washington, DC. Another crashed into the fields of Pennsylvania after the passengers heroically attacked the terrorists piloting the plane. Altogether more than 3,025 people from 68 nations died, and countless others were injured. This was an act of terrorism. Why did bin Laden and his followers do it? More recent events make us ask, why would a terrorist blow up children attending a concert or tourists on vacation? Most importantly, how can we prevent more such horrible acts?

Terrorism refers to the planned use of random, unlawful (or illegal) violence or threat of violence against civilians to create (or raise) fear and intimidate citizens to advance the terrorist group's political or ideological goals (U.S. Department of Defense 2012). Terrorism usually refers to acts of violence by private nonstate groups to advance revolutionary political goals, but state terrorism—government use of terror to control people—also proliferates. Terrorists are found at all points on the political continuum: anarchists, nationalists, religious fundamentalists, and members of ethnic advocacy groups. Worldwide, terrorist deaths decreased by 22% from 2014 through 2016. However, about two out of three nations experienced a terrorist attack in 2016 (Institute for Economics & Peace 2017).

What makes terrorism effective? Terrorists strike randomly and change tactics so that governments have no clear or effective way of dealing with them. This unpredictability causes public confidence in the ability of government to protect citizens to waver. Private terrorist groups tend to be most successful when attacking democratic governments. They seldom attack targets in oligarchic or dictatorial societies because these countries can ignore their demands despite the risk to innocent civilians and hostages' lives without fearing they will be voted out of office (Frey 2004).

Why Do Terrorists Commit Hostile Acts? In our anger against terrorists, we sometimes fail to look at why they commit these atrocities. Who are the terrorists, and what have they to gain? Without understanding the underlying causes of terrorism, we can do little to prevent it.

Few terrorists act alone. They tend to be members of or connected in some way (even if only through the Internet) to groups highly committed to an ideology or

▲ A protester addresses the "Bring Back Our Girls" protest group as they march to the presidential villa to deliver a protest letter to Nigeria's president Goodluck Jonathan in Abuja. The letter calls for the release of the Nigerian schoolgirls kidnapped by the Islamist militant group Boko Haram on May 22, 2014.

cause—religious, political, or both. Class, ethnic, racial, or religious alienation often lies at the roots of terrorism. The ideology of terrorist groups stresses us-versus-them perceptions of the world, viewing "them" as evil. Those committing terrorist acts often feel victimized by more powerful forces, and they sometimes see their lives as the only weapon they have to fight back. Many believe they have nothing to lose by committing terrorist acts, even suicidal terrorist acts. One person's terrorist may be someone else's freedom fighter—it is in *the eye of the beholder*.

Ahmad is a 20-year-old terrorist. All of his life, his family has been on the move, forced to work for others for barely a living wage and controlled by rules made up by other people—ones he feels are hostile to his group. When he was very young, his family's home was taken away, and the residents of his town scattered to other locations. He began to resent those whom he thought had dislocated his family, put neighbors in jail, and separated him from friends and relatives. Ahmad sees little future for himself or his people and little hope for education or a career of his choosing. He feels he has nothing to lose by joining a resistance organization to fight for what he sees as justice. Its members keep their identities secret. They are not powerful enough to mount an army to fight, so they rely on terrorist tactics against those they see as oppressors.

Ahmad puts the "greater good" of his religious and political beliefs and his group above his individual well-being. When he agrees to commit a terrorist act, he truly believes it is right and is the only way he can retaliate and bring attention to the suffering of his people. If killed, he knows he will be praised and become a martyr within his group. His family may even receive compensation for his death.

Political and religious beliefs are usually at the root of what leads terrorists to commit violent acts. Timothy McVeigh and Terry Nichols, convicted of bombing the Alfred P. Murrah Federal Building in Oklahoma City, Oklahoma, in 1995, had connections to paramilitary, antigovernment militia groups, many of which opposed government intervention in the private lives of U.S. residents. These groups are White supremacist and antigovernment (despite their fanatic pro-Americanism). Most such paramilitary groups consider themselves to be devoutly Christian, and they believe that their religion and "good intentions" justify their acts. Figure 8.9, "Active Hate Groups in 2017," on page 230 shows how such groups are scattered throughout the United States.

Structural explanations help predict when conditions are ripe for terrorism. Again, terrorism and war tend to be sparked by conflict and strife within and between societal systems. Ahmad learned his attitudes, hatreds, and stereotypes from his family, his friends, charismatic leaders, and media such as the Internet. These beliefs were reinforced by his religious beliefs, schools, and political leaders. However, their origin was anger and economic despair.

Conflict theory explanations of terrorism lie in the unequal distribution of world resources and the oppression of minority groups. Countries such as Germany, China, and the United States and multinational corporations control immense resources and capital and have considerable economic and cultural influence and power over peripheral nations. This inequity results in feelings of alienation and hostility—and sometimes terrorism.

Within nations, desperate fights for power among different ethnic and racial groups can lead some people to use terrorism as a weapon.

Sometimes, however, there is no clear, rational reason for terrorism. For example, Dylann Roof, a troubled high school dropout, drug user, and White supremacist, committed mass murder because he wanted to start a race war. James Hodgkinson, who shot at and gravely wounded Republican members of Congress and other members of the Republican baseball team during an early morning baseball practice in 2017, had a history of erratic, violent, and unstable behavior. From his Facebook posts and comments from his family, it seems that Hodgkinson wanted to "stop" Trump and other Republicans. Both he and Roof seemed to be energized by social media sources that promoted their anti-Republican or racist thoughts. Neither Hodgkinson nor Roof, however, seemed to have a coherent plan that connected their individual acts of terrorism to a larger political movement (Madhani 2017; Sanchez and Payne 2016). Importantly, neither had any problem getting his hands on a gun. Gun laws or lack thereof, a societal issue, can make terrorist acts harder or easier to commit, depending on the laws of a nation.

Terrorism, then, is a means by which even those with relatively little power can gain attention to their cause and (perhaps) some power in the global system, even if it involves hijackings, bombings, suicides, kidnappings, and political assassinations. Terrorists feel they are justified in their actions. The victims of these acts are understandably outraged.

Democracy comes in many forms and structures. If you want to live in a society where you have a voice, get involved in the political system and stay well informed about the policies your government is considering or has recently enacted. Political systems need diverse voices and critics—regardless of what party is currently in power—to create vibrant societies that represent the citizens. They also need healthy citizens. The next chapter focuses on the institution of health care and explores its interaction with other institutions—such as the economy and the political system.

WHAT HAVE WE LEARNED?

Political and economic systems are both sources of power and highly interlinked. Those who have high status in one institution tend to also have high status in the other. Political and economic institutions differ across societies. These differences influence levels of inequality across each society and the life chances of individuals within them.

- Power involves the ability to realize one's will, despite resistance.

- Power and economics impact our intimate (micro-level) lives, our (meso-level) organizations and institutions, and our (macro-level) national and global structures and policies.

- Leadership facilitates getting things done in any social group. It can be accomplished through raw power (coercion) or through authority (granted by the populace). Different types of leadership invest authority in the person, the position, or both.

- Various theories illuminate different aspects of political power and view U.S. policymaking processes very differently—as dominated by the power elite or as distributed among various groups so that no one group has complete power (pluralism).

- At the micro level of a political institution, individuals decide whether to vote or participate in politics. These decisions are not just individual choices but are shaped by the culture and structures of society.

- At the meso level, the political institution (when it functions well) works to resolve conflicts and to address social needs within the political system. This may be done with authoritarian or democratic structures. Within nations, meso-level policies can also have major implications for national power distribution.

- The economic system ensures production and distribution of goods in society, and the type of economy in a society determines who has the power to map the future and who has access to resources.

- At the macro level, nation-states have emerged only in the past few centuries as part of modernity.

- At the global level, issues of power, access to resources, alienation, and ideology shape economic policies, war, terrorism, and the prospects for lives of peace and prosperity for citizens around the planet.

DISCUSSION QUESTIONS

1. As you were growing up, did your parents encourage you to try to influence your local community or society? Why or why not? Was their perspective on power more like the pluralist or elite theoretical perspective? Explain. How have their views about power influenced your own?

2. Is your family of origin part of the *power elite*? What makes you think so? Are you a member of the power elite? Why or why not? If you are not, what do you think your chances are of becoming a member of the power elite? Why?

3. Do you think that large corporations have undue influence over the U.S. government? Why or why not?

4. If you had the choice, would you rather live in a society with a planned or centralized economic system or market or capitalist economic system? Why?

5. How do conflict theorists explain terrorism? Do you agree? Why or why not? How would you suggest the U.S. government try to stem terrorism? What theoretical perspective do you think is most helpful in terms of understanding and dealing with terrorism? Why?

KEY TERMS

authoritarian governments   402

authority   391

democratic governments   402

democratic socialism   406

market or capitalist economic system   404

planned (or centralized) economic systems   406

power   389

revolution   408

totalitarian government   402

war   412

CONTRIBUTING TO OUR SOCIAL WORLD: WHAT CAN WE DO?

At the Local (Micro) Level

- Consider getting involved in the *student government* on your campus. Most students do not know the power they have on their own campus. Organized students can have a major

impact. If you would like to see something changed on your campus, establish relationships with key administrators and organize other students. Consider running for a leadership position in a student club or the student government association. Doing so will help you learn how to gain and use power and to better understand the basic principles of the democratic process.

- *Model Legislature or Model UN programs* are found on most campuses and are usually administered through the department of political science. Consider joining yours and gain valuable knowledge and skills in debating and governing.

- *Arrange a campus visit by a local political candidate or office holder.* If this can be done through a sociology club, it would be especially appropriate to have the visitor discuss the political system as a social institution.

At the Organizational or Institutional (Meso) Level

- *Government internships.* Consider doing an internship in your *state or provincial legislature* (www.ncsl.org/legislative-staff .aspx?tabs=856,33,816) or in Congress (www.senate.gov/ reference/Index/Employment.htm and www.house.gov/ content/educate/internships.php) with a state or provincial legislator, the governor's office (Google "governor's office," "internship," and the name of your state), or with a court judge (Google "court judge," with the name of your district, and "internship").

- *Special interest parties.* Become involved in a special interest political group such as the Green Party (www.gp.org), the Libertarian Party (www.lp.org), the Socialist Party (http://

socialistparty-usa.net), the Tea Party (www.teaparty.org), Bread for the World (www.bread.org), People for the Ethical Treatment of Animals (www.peta.org), or any number of others.

- The Council on Foreign Relations' Internship Program offers outstanding volunteer opportunities for college students and graduate students focusing on international relations and pursuing a career in foreign policy or a related field. Learn more about this program at https://www.cfr.org/ career-opportunities/volunteer-internships.

At the National or Global (Macro) Level

- *Internships at the White House or one of the executive offices, such as the Departments of State, Agriculture, or Commerce,* can be a great learning experience. You can learn about the White House Internship Program and how to apply for one at www.whitehouse.gov/get-involved/internships. Google the name of a cabinet office to obtain contact information for the other executive offices.

- Explore *She Should Run* (www.sheshouldrun.org), an organization that aims to have 250,000 women running for office in 2030. The organization supports candidates and their campaigns.

- *Several agencies of the United Nations* hire interns. The general contact for relevant information is careers.un.org/lbw/home .aspx?viewtype=ip.

$SAGE edge™

Get the tools you need to sharpen your study skills. SAGE edge offers a robust online environment featuring an impressive array of free tools and resources.

Access practice quizzes, eFlashcards, video, and multimedia at **edge.sagepub.com/ballantine7e**

© iStockphoto.com/laflor

HEALTH CARE

An Anatomy of Health and Illness

▲ Health and illness are social matters, influenced by social interactions, affected by complex organizations intended to provide health care, and shaped by social policies at national and global levels. Sociological analyses look deeply into these processes.

MICRO

○ ME (AND MY MEDICAL PROVIDERS)

○ LOCAL ORGANIZATIONS AND COMMUNITY
Local community health clinics and hospitals are the local franchises of the health care institution.

MESO

○ NATIONAL ORGANIZATIONS, INSTITUTIONS, AND ETHNIC SUBCULTURES
State governments regulate health care and deal with public health issues.

MACRO

○ SOCIETY
National governments regulate drug companies for safety standards and fund research.

○ GLOBAL COMMUNITY
International organizations establish health programs and control pandemics.

WHAT WILL YOU LEARN IN THIS CHAPTER?

This chapter will help you to do the following:

14.1 Provide examples of health at the societal level; illustrate how health issues impact us at the micro, meso, and macro levels

14.2 Use the symbolic interaction perspective to show that illness is a social construction

14.3 Describe the role of the sick person

14.4 Explain modern hospitals as complex organizations with bureaucratic features

14.5 Describe how globalization influences health care issues at micro, meso, and macro levels

Micro: Small groups and local community	What does it mean for you to be sick or healthy? Why is being sick a social status and not just an individual concern? How does the health or illness of family and community members affect your functioning and that of your local community?
Meso: National institutions, complex organizations, and ethnic groups	What type of health care system keeps people healthiest? Why?
Macro: National and global systems	What are the costs to a nation of having a national health care system, and what are the costs of not having one? How do health care systems vary around the world?

Two tragic cases—each involving brain-dead, pregnant women on life support—show that health care is not just an individual matter. It can necessitate decisions by family, medical practitioners, and even politicians. In the case of brain-dead Marlise Munoz from Texas, her husband and family wanted her taken off life support, for she had expressed to them that she would never want to be kept alive that way. The hospital where she was admitted refused to do so, however, because Texas state law prohibited taking life support away from a pregnant woman, even though Munoz was only 14 weeks pregnant and the fetus was not viable. After nearly 2 months, Munoz's husband sued the hospital and she was taken off life support by order of the district court in Tarrant County, Texas (CBS News 2014). In the case of brain-dead Robyn Benson from

Victoria, British Columbia (Canada), 22 weeks pregnant, her family and doctors decided to keep her alive with feeding tubes and ventilators. The baby was successfully delivered by C-section 16 days later (Payne 2014). Who has the right to decide what to do in situations like this, when a patient cannot communicate?

Another end-of-life situation involved Debbie, a 20-year-old woman in Portland, Oregon, lying in pain and dying from ovarian cancer. She had not eaten or slept for 2 days and was struggling for air. She said to the young medical resident (doctor, in training) on duty, "Let's get this over with." The resident then gave her an injection of morphine, causing her to die 4 minutes later (Standler 2012). These cases and others like them raise great controversy in medical, legal, and religious communities. End-of-life legislation that determines if patients have the legal right to decide when to die is the topic of intense debate and varies across the United States and among nations throughout the world.

Today, anyone in the United States can sign a living will or right-to-die or do-not-resuscitate form, requesting that no extraordinary efforts be made to help keep the person alive when death would naturally occur (passive euthanasia). However, just six U.S. states (California, Colorado, Montana, Vermont, Oregon, and Washington) and the District of Columbia give competent, terminally ill adults the legal right to commit medically assisted suicide. In Montana, the state supreme court ruled in 2009 that the state's Rights of the Terminally Ill Act includes the right to assisted suicide. Montana has yet, however, to pass legislation on assisted suicide that establishes rules on how it must be carried out (Death with Dignity 2017; FindLaw 2015).

Since Brittany Maynard's widely publicized (including a *People* magazine cover) medically assisted suicide in 2014, calls for legalization have increased throughout the United States. Similar legislation has been proposed,

▲ Debbie Ziegler holds up a photograph of her daughter, Brittany Maynard, who suffered from terminal brain cancer before deciding to end her own life in 2014. Since then, Brittany's mother has advocated for the widespread legalization of assisted suicide.

and is now being debated, in more than half the states in the nation (Monir 2015). Belgium, the Netherlands, and Switzerland have permitted physician-assisted suicide since 1942, even for nonterminal patients ("Assisted Suicide" 2012).

Under Death with Dignity laws in the United States, patients themselves, not doctors, administer the drugs. Patients and doctors who carry out this law must go through many steps to ensure that patients making this decision are terminally ill and sure that they want to end their lives. They must

- prove residency in a state with a Death with Dignity law;

- be at least 18 years old;

- be able to make and communicate health care decisions for themselves;

- be diagnosed with a terminal illness, expected to lead to death within the next 6 months;

- have two physicians determine they have met the criteria above; and

- make two written requests for the prescription from the physician, witnessed by two people who are not family members or primary caregivers.

The physician filling out the prescription must share with the patient all other possible options (e.g., hospice and pain management) and attest that the patient is mentally competent (Death with Dignity 2018). A scenario like the one with Debbie and the medical resident would be considered illegal under the Death with Dignity laws.

Those who favor euthanasia argue that (a) physicians should be able to create comfortable environments for death to occur, (b) terminally ill individuals have a right—without interference by the state—to determine how they die and to make the decision to die, (c) legal safeguards are available to prevent abuse of physician-assisted suicide, (d) high rates of self-induced suicide already exist among terminally ill patients, (e) a majority of the public favors legalization of physician-assisted suicide, and (f) extending life with no hope of recovery is costly to families as well as to the medical care system.

Those opposed to euthanasia argue that (a) physicians are obligated to sustain life; (b) medical measures are available to relieve pain, so few have to suffer; (c) religious beliefs affirm the sanctity of life, which means supporting life at every turn; (d) terminally ill individuals who request to die often act out of depression, or they

may feel pressured to accept a facilitated death to save the family's resources; and (e) the legalization of euthanasia for the terminally ill may lead more depressed, disabled, and elderly people to commit suicide, reasoning that, if euthanasia at the end of life is acceptable, so is suicide for those suffering at other stages of life (G. Weiss and Lonnquist 2015).

Relatively few people have chosen to use the Death with Dignity laws to arrange their own deaths. For example, in Oregon in 2016, 204 people received lethal prescriptions and 133 people died by taking lethal prescriptions (9 used prescriptions from previous years). Similarly low numbers of assisted suicide deaths occur in the European nations that allow them ("Assisted Suicide" 2012; Monir 2015; Oregon Health Authority 2017).

The cost of dying differs tremendously, from nothing in many poor Global South countries with no health care for the dying, to many thousands of dollars per person in the United States. **Medicare** is *a government-run health insurance system for those 65 and older in the United States.* As the population ages, governments face great pressure to cover expenses. More than 1 out of every 4 Medicare dollars goes to medical bills incurred during the last year of patients' lives ($34,529 per person) (Cubanski and Neuman 2016). With projected increases in the percentage of elderly in the population, the Medicare system will deplete its funds by 2028 (The Boards of Trustees, Federal Hospital Insurance and Federal Supplementary Medical Insurance Trust Funds 2016).

Policy analysts point out that costs for elder care could be reduced and quality of care improved by providing more in-home services to allow people to die at home or in a hospice setting, rather than in an intensive care unit of a hospital. Efforts to encourage this have yielded some positive results. The percentage of people dying at home or in hospice increased, respectively, from 23% to 27% and from 21.6% to 42.2% from 2000 to 2009. Today, about half of all older Americans spend some time in hospice before they die (Jaslow 2013; Whoriskey and Keating 2015).

How we die, where we die, who is with us when we die, and whether we have a choice about when to die are decisions bound in cultural values, beliefs, and laws. Death and its various issues are but one aspect of the interrelationship between our physical condition and our social system. In this chapter, we consider why health is a social issue and examine theoretical perspectives on health and illness, the status and roles of sick people, modern health care systems, and health care policy issues at the national and global levels.

Why Is Health a Social Issue?

What role should social institutions play in our individual and group health issues? As you read the following examples, keep this question in mind and think about how government policies on health care and safety issues can impact the well-being of citizens and the productivity of a nation.

From 2000 to 2010, 15- to 19-year-olds in the United States were 82 times more likely to die from gun homicide than 15- to 19-year-olds in other OECD nations. Why? People in the United States make up just 4.4% of the world's population but own 42% of the world's guns. Federal gun laws and many state laws allow almost anyone to own a gun (aside from convicted felons, domestic abusers, and those committed to a mental institution or legally declared a mental defective). In almost every state (except Hawaii and Illinois), 18-year-olds may buy an AR-15, the semiautomatic rifle legally purchased and used in the 2018 shooting at Stoneman Douglas High School in Parkland, Florida. Only 23 states have minimum age requirements for owning a rifle (Fisher and Keller 2017; Giffords Law Center 2017; Thakrar, Forrest, Maltenfort, and Forrest, 2017). In a fiery speech, senior Emma Gonzalez demanded national lawmakers do something to prevent mass school shootings. Speaking at a rally a few days after the shooting, she declared

If all our government and president can do is send thoughts and prayers, then it's time for victims to be the change that we need to see. . . . We certainly do not understand why it should be harder to make plans with friends on weekends than it is to buy an automatic or semiautomatic weapon.

Gonzalez and other students called for government leaders to take actions to protect them and called for a ban on guns like the AR-15 (Almasy and Chavez 2018).

Government leaders can also impact driving fatality rates. In 1990, the United States had one of the lowest driving fatality rates among OECD nations. Today, it has one of the highest. Why? Other OECD nations have implemented stricter seat belt, speed, and alcohol policies and ramped up enforcement of them (International Transport Forum 2016; Leonhardt 2017).

The federal government in the United States has, however, set up several organizations, such as the Occupational Safety and Health Administration (OSHA), the Food and Drug Administration (FDA), and the Environmental Protection Agency (EPA), to protect citizens from threats to their health. For example,

OSHA requires factory owners to provide protective ear coverings for workers. The powers of these agencies are limited, however, and adequate funding for enforcement is always an issue.

Other examples of how government policies and the adequacy of their enforcement can impact the safety of citizens are easy to find. Consider the food industry: Food poisoning incidents in 2017 included the nationwide E. coli outbreak that led to the recall of I.M. Healthy brand nut butter and other products. The Dixie Dew factory in Kentucky that produced the contaminated soy paste for I.M. Healthy products had food safety violations recorded for at least the preceding 15 years (Beach 2017). In 2015, Blue Bell Creameries issued a recall of all its products due to a listeria contamination that led to at least three deaths. Documents released by the FDA shortly after the recall indicate that the company had been aware of the listeria problem since 2013 (Abrams 2015). The point is that an important role of governments is to protect people's health, whether through creating and enforcing gun laws and speed limits, inspecting food and workplaces, or other means.

We now turn to some of the other social forces related to health, illness, and death in the world. **Health** is *a state of physical, mental, and social well-being or the absence of disease.* **Illness**, or *lack of health*, affects the way we perform our individual responsibilities in the social world. Like any social institution, *health care*—our efforts to foster health and treat illness—affects how individuals and groups carry out their lives at the micro, meso, and macro levels.

Health at the Micro Level

Sociologists examine how our state of health affects our ability to carry out social responsibilities. Our everyday lives are shaped by our own state of health or illness and those of our loved ones and close associates. If a roommate, significant other, or child is ill, it affects our lives in a number of ways. It alters our schedules, costs us time and (usually) money, and causes us to worry. If a parent injures her back or a child has leukemia, the family's lives are influenced in profound and disruptive ways.

Health at the Meso Level

The health of individual citizens can impact how a society functions. One sick child can lead to a serious outbreak of influenza in the public schools, a meso-level institution. This could cause repercussions in workplaces throughout the community as parents struggle to deal with child care issues and visits to the doctor.

No doubt, if the outbreak spread dramatically, citizens would demand that their government act to address it. Thus, health status affects other institutions in the society, such as the government, family, educational system, and workplace.

To illustrate how health care connects to the major social institutions in society, consider the following examples:

- *Economy.* Economically successful nations have more money to devote to health care.

- *Education.* Well-educated citizens are more likely to develop health-enhancing lifestyles.

- *Family.* Families often have responsibility to care for the sick.

- *Political systems.* Governments often determine standards for health care and regulate medical drugs.

- *Religion.* Religious organizations establish support systems and health services, provide solace in times of illness and death, and sometimes offer faith-healing alternatives to supplement the established medical system.

These examples help reveal the interconnections between health and other institutions at the meso level.

Health at the Macro Level

Each society has a vested interest in the health of its citizenry because the general state of health affects the quality of life of the people and the state of the economy. Imagine a society in which citizens had "permission" to be sick frequently. How would that society continue to function? Cultural beliefs about illness and how to treat the sick vary by society.

Consider the case of the former Soviet Union. After the Soviet victory over Czarist Russia in 1917, the new revolutionary government was faced with an under-developed nation that still produced its food with human-powered plows and simple hoes. The task of leading the country out of the 16th century and into the 20th was formidable. It called for a total effort from the nation's workforce. The new government determined that absenteeism at work, regardless of cause, had to be kept very low. Accordingly, the government instituted rules that required workers who were ill to obtain a certificate allowing them to be absent from work because of illness (G. Weiss and Lonnquist 2015). To make sure only the

▲ Pharmaceutical chief Martin Shkreli bought out the company that invented Daraprim, a drug used to treat malaria. He then promptly raised the price about 5,000%, from $13.50 to $750 per pill. The public was outraged, and he was called to testify to Congress. One role of governments is to protect the public's health.

very sick could miss work, these certificates could be obtained only from government clinics, and each clinic could issue only a limited number of permits. In some cases, the government encouraged physicians to compete with one another to see how few certificates they could issue. Thus, absences due to minor illness were limited, and the human resources needed for rebuilding the nation were augmented. The macro-level needs were met at the expense of individuals.

Global health focuses on several issues, including possible pandemics of highly contagious diseases, which have become worldwide threats as global travel increases. A *pandemic* is a disease prevalent throughout an entire country that may infect a continent or reach around the world. Major efforts by international organizations and Global North countries contained the Ebola outbreak in West Africa beginning in March 2014, and efforts are underway to control the Zika virus that is fast spreading in countries around the world. Figure 14.1 illustrates the global nature of the HIV/AIDS pandemic. As of 2017, 36.9 million people around the world were living with HIV; only 21.7 million were receiving treatment. In 2017 alone, 940,000 people died of AIDS-related illness (Kaiser Family Foundation 2018b).

Controlling such diseases requires cooperation across national boundaries by organizations such as the United Nations. Smallpox, for example, remained a serious global threat from the Middle Ages until the World Health Organization of the United Nations eliminated the disease in the 1960s. Likewise, river blindness once afflicted thousands of West Africans but has been

▼ FIGURE 14.1

Adult HIV Prevalence Rate, 2017

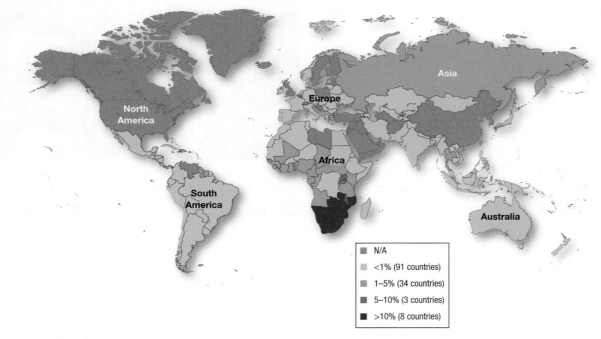

- N/A
- <1% (91 countries)
- 1–5% (34 countries)
- 5–10% (3 countries)
- >10% (8 countries)

Source: Kaiser Family Foundation 2018a.

Notes: Data are estimates. Prevalence rates include adults aged 15 to 49.

▲ A Guatemalan child infected with HIV marches outside the site of an AIDS conference in Guatemala City. Hundreds of people from different countries marched to bring attention to the lack of government aid and medical assistance for those infected with the virus that causes AIDS.

When you are sick, illness may seem like an individual problem, but as shown in the previous examples, it is far more than that. It is also a local, national, and global issue. This chapter examines health care at each level of analysis, from individual behaviors and decisions, to religious, political, and economic aspects, to the effects of stratification and ethnic status on the quality of health care one receives. Keep the social world model in mind as you read about health, illness, and health care.

THINKING SOCIOLOGICALLY

Why might diseases that affect a local community require international attention and solutions? What is a recent example?

eradicated due to international cooperation. Funding from organizations such as the Bill and Melinda Gates Foundation supports research, treatment, and eradication of killer diseases such as malaria, AIDS, and tuberculosis.

Theoretical Perspectives on Health and Illness

In the analysis of institutions, each major paradigm or perspective in sociology offers a lens for understanding different aspects of the institution. Let us consider how the major theoretical perspectives help us understand health and illness.

Micro-Level Theoretical Perspectives

Whereas once unruly schoolchildren faced punishments for being "bad," many now receive medications. New understandings of medical disorders have led to the diagnosis of millions of children with medical labels such as attention-deficit, autism spectrum, bipolar, and other disorders. Advances in medical science have also led to diagnosis and treatment of learning disabilities such as dyslexia, a disorder that makes it harder for children to achieve academic success. The changes in the labeling of such conditions result in decreased social stigma and different policies to deal with disorders.

Symbolic Interaction Perspective and Labeling Theory.

Symbolic interactionists point out that definitions of illness vary over time and from society to society. In recent years, the definition of illness in many Global North societies has expanded to encompass substance abuse and some forms of deviant behavior, giving physicians more power and authority over broad areas of social life. As noted, many behaviors once seen as criminal or "bad" are now viewed as symptoms of medical disorders.

Medicalization and Labeling. Medicalization refers to *handling some forms of deviance as well as some normal human functions (such as pregnancy and childbirth) in the health care system rather than the family, legal, or religious arenas.* In some cases, the shift is away from individual self-control and toward medical diagnosis and treatment.

Consider addictive behaviors such as alcoholism and drug abuse. Excessive alcohol use resulted in 88,000 deaths in the United States each year from 2006 to 2010 and was responsible for 1 in 10 deaths for adults ages 20 to 64 years (Centers for Disease Control and Prevention 2018). How we define alcoholism influences our understanding of the problem, whether we hold the patient to blame, and the course of treatment we pursue (Cockerham 2015). If we see alcoholism as a personal failing, we view the alcoholic as a moral degenerate who needs to start abiding by the norms of society. On the other hand, if we define alcoholism as a disease, we see the alcoholic as a sick person in need of help. The next Sociology in Our Social World explores social policy toward alcoholism.

As societal norms change, so do perceptions of behavior once considered a sign of mental or physical disorders. For example, until 1986, homosexuality appeared in the American Psychiatric Association's (APA) *Diagnostic and Statistical Manual of Mental Disorders.* Since that time, it has lost the label of mental disorder. The increasing acceptance of gay people in the United States has led, in this case, to demedicalization. We turn now to how forces at the meso and macro levels in our social world shape the experience of illness or health at the micro level.

Meso- and Macro-Level Theoretical Perspectives

Different cultures have different perspectives on illness. Consider the conflicting ideas of illness between the Hmong culture in the United States, made up of immigrants from regions of Laos, Thailand, Vietnam, and China, and the U.S. medical community. In *The Spirit Catches You and You Fall Down,* Anne Fadiman describes the contrasts between how an immigrant Hmong family views an epileptic child and how the hospital in the family's U.S. community sees the situation (Fadiman 1998). The Hmong family attributes the seizures to spirits, but the medical staff treats the epileptic seizures with Western medical methods that use drugs, surgery, and other science-based techniques.

Some Hispanic cultures practice a unique, ancient, and complex system of healing known as *curanderismo.* The origins can be found in traditional herbal medicine, precolonial religious belief systems, witchcraft, and Spanish Catholicism. Members of these subcultures view good health and a strong body as God's blessing for the faithful. Illness comes either when one has sinned or as a message from God to help the person learn to be good. The relationship between the *curandero,* or healer, and the patient is close, relying on psychological and spiritual as well as physical treatments. Many Hispanics combine Western medicine and curanderismo. For "non-Hispanic illnesses," the physician is the healer of choice. However, for culture-specific conditions such as *susto*

ALCOHOLISM, MEDICALIZATION, AND POLICY

▲ The label *alcoholic* has a number of implications, including the fact that the stigma associated with the term may prevent some people from seeking help. Many alcohol treatment centers have recast alcoholism as a disease, hoping that the redefinition would remove stigma.

Perhaps you know someone who struggles with an alcohol problem. The American Medical Association (AMA) officially designated alcoholism as an illness in 1956 (Jellinek 1960). *Alcoholism* is a dependency on alcohol (alcohol addiction), a chronic disease that includes strong craving, continued use of alcohol despite physical and social problems, and inability to limit drinking (CDC 2013c). The disease is often progressive and can be fatal.

Some health care professionals, however, argue that the disease concept is the wrong approach—that what is really at stake is "heavy drinking" as a way of life. Rather than treating a "disease," they feel that professionals should be concerned with approaches that will change the way in which individuals organize their behaviors. These researchers and practitioners argue that heavy drinkers can become nondrinkers or moderate drinkers who can control their drinking.

Some sociological theorists see medicalization as one more form of social control by the government and medical establishment. By labeling alcoholism as a disease, the medical profession gains more power and influence as an agent of social control (Conrad 2007). Whereas the Alcoholics Anonymous approach to alcoholism treatment involves laypeople in groups, helping each other stay away from alcohol in a spiritually oriented manner, the "medicalization of alcoholism" calls for treatment by professionals— psychiatrists, psychologists, hospitals, and clinics. Some people see these approaches as complementary, but others think they are incompatible (Conrad 2007; Roisen 2012).

A third possibility exists—that there is truth in both models based on individual differences. Treatment programs can be found based on both models, and the debate about the best approach continues. Recent approaches to alcoholism often combine medical and social-behavioral treatments, some of which have been illustrated on the TV show *Interventions* (A&E 2012; Roisen 2012). All approaches concur on the need to help alcoholics recognize that they require help.

▲ Doi Lan, a Lisu shaman in Thailand, gives an infant a liquid as part of a healing ceremony. Others wait for their turn to receive the healing powers of the respected shaman.

(characterized by extreme fright), the curandero may be consulted because many believe that such conditions are impervious to even the highest technology of the scientific physician (G. Weiss and Lonnquist 2015). The role of the curandero combines elements of a psychologist and healer.

Definitions of mental illness and treatment of the mentally ill can also vary greatly across societies. Consider the case of Manuel, a schizophrenic who "goes crazy" when the moon is full (from which the concept of lunacy derives) and is put in a Nicaraguan mental hospital during that time. Otherwise, he lives a relatively normal life with his parents. In another culture, he might be put in long-term hospital care or given drugs to control the condition (Fernando 2002).

All types of behavior (and their interpretation) vary from culture to culture, including reactions to pain (Galanti 2008). Many factors affect these reactions, from gender to age, education, socioeconomic status, power of the participant, and language being used to communicate. Cultural factors influence the nature, intensity, and duration of pain. As more advanced pain medications became available, attitudes have changed (Sussex 2016). For example, Asian patients rarely ask for pain medication, but patients from Mediterranean cultures readily ask for help to relieve the slightest pain. In a classic U.S. hospital-based study of reactions to pain, researchers observed that patients' responses fell into two main categories: stoic and emotive. Patients with Jewish and Italian cultural backgrounds tended to respond to pain emotionally, whereas patients of English background were usually stoic and tried to bravely endure pain. Those of Irish descent often denied pain altogether. Although the Jewish American and Italian American patients exhibited similar reactions to pain, their reasons for these reactions were different. The Jewish American patients took a long-term view toward pain. They were concerned about its meaning for their future, and their reactions did not subside when pain-relieving drugs were administered. The Italian American patients, on the other hand, were mainly concerned with the pain itself, and drugs relieved both the pain and their complaints (Lasch 2002; Thomas and Rose 1991; Zborowski 1952).

Other studies of culturally learned differences have linked expressive, emotive responses to Hispanic, Middle Eastern, and Mediterranean patients, whereas stoic patients were more often from northern European and Asian backgrounds (D'Arcy 2009; Galanti 2008). Even young children show cultural differences in reacting to pain (Azize et al. 2013). Sociological theories and cross-cultural knowledge help us to understand these and other cultural differences in approaches to health care.

Functionalist Perspective. Functional theorists focus primarily on the macro level of the health care system. Studies of suicide carried out by French sociologist Émile Durkheim (discussed in Chapter 5) illustrate that social conditions and events in the larger society and people's group affiliations affect inclinations to commit suicide. Other studies have linked illnesses such as heart disease, kidney failure, stroke, mental illness, and infant mortality to macro-level processes and trends in societies. For example, economic recessions cause social stress and disruption in lifestyles, which, in turn, can result in health problems.

According to functionalists, the purpose of the health care system in society is to maintain the social structure and a harmonious balance between individuals and institutions in society. Illness is potentially disruptive to the balanced social world because it "robs" the society of normal role functioning. As we saw in the Soviet example, if too many people claim the sick role at the same time, the tasks necessary to maintain the society cannot be performed. The primary task, or function, of the medical profession is to control illness and ensure that individuals can perform their social roles.

Functionalists like Talcott Parsons see positive value in the hierarchical structure of the medical profession and in the power of the physician over the patient (Parsons 1971). Parsons believed that having "experts" in charge led to better care for patients. That view, however, is not shared by all, as we will see shortly. We now turn to conflict theory for a different perspective on the health care system.

Conflict Perspective. Poverty, unemployment, low wages, malnutrition, and a host of other economic conditions affect people's access to and ability to receive health care and medicine in many countries. Differential access is a key theme in conflict theorists' approach to health issues. Consider the case of Nkosi, a 4-year-old boy in a rural Ghanaian village. He came down with an infection due to polluted water, causing diarrhea and vomiting. Nkosi was already weakened by malnutrition and parasites, and by the time his family got medical help, he was so dehydrated that he died. Why was health care for this easily treatable condition not available in time?

Nkosi had less access to medical treatment, immunizations, antibiotics, vitamins, and a balanced diet than children in Global North countries or even in urban areas of the Global South. Many children in poor countries around the world suffer from malnutrition and chronic disease before succumbing to pneumonia or other infections, diseases for which treatment is normally available.

Emerging infectious diseases such as AIDS, Brazilian purpuric fever, new strains of Ebola, and various insect- and bird-transported diseases such as Zika, bird flu, and swine flu (H1N1) add to the problems faced by health care workers in the Global South. Efforts by medical activists such as Dr. Paul Farmer, a U.S. infectious disease specialist and anthropologist, help poor countries. He set up an organization, Partners in Health, with the goal of conquering diseases among the world's poor (D. Alexander 2015; Kidder 2004). With life expectancy (average length of life) as low as 46 years in some drought-ridden and war-torn countries, the challenge is formidable.

Conflict theorists point out that individuals suffer different illnesses depending on the level of development of their society and their positions in it. As mentioned in Chapter 7, many low-income residents in Global North nations live in *food deserts*, areas that lack grocery stores and other means of access to affordable, healthy food. Residents in these food deserts tend to consume highly processed foods full of artificially cheap, corn-based ingredients; sugar-laden soft drinks; and other addictive foods that spark cravings for more such food. The 2004 movie *Supersize Me* illustrates this well. In 2013, the U.S. Congress began funding a program that increases the value of Supplemental Nutrition Assistance Programs (SNAP—once known as food stamps) benefits when people use them to buy vegetables and fruits. A 2017 survey of SNAP users at seven farmers markets revealed that 74% to 94% of users had bought or consumed more fruits and vegetables since the program started (Consumer Reports 2017).

Smoking in the United States has also become a health problem affecting a disproportionate number of poor and less educated people. Just 15% of adults in the United States still smoke, but more than 40% of those with just a high school education are addicted to cigarettes. Rural places in the southern United States have higher rates of smokers than urban areas. They also have fewer smoking cessation programs and provide less access to health care. Aware of that fact, and threatened by the overall decline in U.S. smokers, tobacco companies have aimed their efforts to curb taxes on cigarettes and other antismoking legislation in predominantly southern and rural states. In response, the Centers for Disease Control and Prevention started a national ad campaign targeted toward low-income U.S. residents (including the mentally ill, racial and ethnic minorities, and rural populations) (Wan 2017). Smoking cessation advocates also push for higher taxes on cigarettes, a strategy that has been proven to reduce smoking rates, especially among youth and low-income populations (Furman 2016).

Meanwhile, poor people in Global South countries die from ailments that are curable in rich countries. In Eswatini (formerly Swaziland), in sub-Saharan Africa, many people die of treatable diseases; however, the dominant killer is AIDS. No other nation has a higher percentage of its population infected by HIV/AIDS. Almost 1 in 3 adults have HIV (Médecins Sans Frontières, 2018). Due to high levels of rape and a strongly patriarchal society, young women are 3 times more likely to be infected with HIV than young men in Swaziland (Cowie 2015). Thanks in large part to PEPFAR (the U.S. President's Emergency Plan for AIDS Relief, instituted by George W. Bush), the number of treated adults has now surpassed the number of new infections, but great efforts must still be made to provide health care and preventative treatment for those with HIV/AIDS in this economically struggling nation (PEPFAR 2013).

At the global level, many multinational companies that build factories in the poor Global South provide examples of the profit motive's influence on health conditions. Businesses seeking large profit margins and cost-cutting opportunities may move operations to countries with lower health and safety standards than those in the Global North, which has more stringent health regulations. For example, many factories in Bangladesh spew untreated waste into the atmosphere without regard to the health of their workers or those living in the area. These textile and garment factories, through making clothes for companies such as Walmart, J.C. Penney, and H&M in the cheapest way possible, have helped create a pollution crisis. The pollution from their factories damages or destroys the food, water, and air sources people rely on to eat, drink, and breathe.

The 2013 collapse of factory buildings in Bangladesh, killing hundreds of workers, also illustrates a problem in Global South countries. Pressures from buyers in Global North multinational companies for manufacturers to produce cheap goods and corrupt government officials who fail to enforce regulations designed to provide safe buildings and control the treatment and dispersal of factory waste result in unsafe practices (Kashyap 2017).

▲ Abdur Rahman holds a family photo of his wife Cahyna Akhter, a garment worker who died when the Rana Plaza building collapsed, killing more than 1,000 people in 2013. Bangladeshi factory workers face risks from both unsafe working conditions and pollution created by the factories. Conflict theorists argue that self-interest of the affluent to increase profits results in unsafe conditions.

Conflict theorists also point out that most physicians work in affluent, urban areas and go into specialties that pay more than primary (general, family care) doctors receive. The most lucrative positions with the most prestige are generally located in major global urban areas and at well-known clinics, where people can pay for private care. As a result, a severe shortage of primary care doctors exists in rural areas of the world, including the rural United States (Snyderman and Sottile 2013). Conflict theorists emphasize that poverty and inequality—whether in the Global North or Global South—have major impacts on quality of life and health care. The next Engaging Sociology illustrates the impact a lack of health care can have on individuals in the United States.

Feminist Theory. Feminist theorists examine the impact of gender on health, illness, and health care, among other topics. They argue that the patriarchal control of women carries over to health care systems and reinforces the dependence and submission of women.

To regain control of women's health, some feminists have formed health organizations concerned with reproductive health. Such organizations may provide midwifery and natural childbirth services and help women deal with issues related to menopause. With increasing numbers of women physicians, attitudes toward women's health and communication practices between women and physicians have also started to change. Thanks to these changes, more doctors recognize the importance of listening to and working *with* patients on their health issues.

Some of the procedures practiced on women are unnecessary, according to feminists in medical professions. For example, many doctors recommend that women deliver their babies via cesarean section surgery rather than vaginally. In the United States, the percentage of cesarean births has risen dramatically from 5% in 1970 to 32% today. Some of them are necessary, but others may be for convenience or to avoid lawsuits (Lake 2012; Martin et al. 2017; R. Weiss 2010). According to feminist theorists, controlling women's reproductive health and defining women's normal biological experiences as medical problems reflect and support a patriarchal (male-dominated) society.

Gender also plays a role in doctors' specialty positions. Women now account for almost half of all those in medical school but, more than men, tend to opt for medical specialty areas with less prestige and less money but with more family-friendly emphases and hours. Women, for example, comprise 34% of all physicians in the United States but make up 62% of all pediatricians (Association of American Medical Colleges 2017).

Feminist theorists also point out that the social status of girls and women can be detrimental to their health. We have already noted the greater risk of sexually transmitted diseases for young women, due to widespread sexual violence against women. Also, many girls in Global South countries face pressure to marry at a young age, which can lead to major health problems. The risk of dying during childbirth increases the lower the age of the mother, yet 7.3 million girls under 18 in the Global South give birth each year, 2 million of them 14 and under (Vinograd 2013).

As you can see, each theory illuminates different issues in health, illness, and health care at the meso and macro levels. We now examine health and illness at a micro level. In doing so, we focus on the status and roles of the sick person.

Status and Roles of the Sick Person: Micro-Level Analysis

How do you know if you are sick? How you answer this question depends on your culture, as well as your physical symptoms (G. Weiss and Lonnquist 2015). A poor Central American woman illustrated this point. When asked if she was sick, she replied that she wished she knew what it meant to be sick. Sometimes she felt so bad she thought she could curl up and die, but she kept going because the kids needed her, and she lacked money to spend on a doctor. She did not have time to be sick. She asks, "How does one know when someone is sick?" Some of us can go to bed almost any time with any illness, but many of the world's people cannot be sick, not even when they need to be (Koos 1954).

To this woman, being sick was not just a physical condition or how she felt or any physical symptoms she displayed. From a cultural perspective, she had responsibilities that could not be ignored, little access to health care, and no money to buy medicine or care. So, who defines this poor woman as sick? She herself? Her friends and family? Her employer? A health care professional? The answer is ambiguous. Illness, then, is in part socially constructed. Health care providers, schools, and workplaces acknowledge illness only if certain society-defined conditions are present. Both individual (micro) and structural (meso or macro) factors influence health care decisions and treatment. The political and economic environment, access to medical services, and the predisposition by an individual to seek medical care all enter into health care decisions.

ENGAGING SOCIOLOGY

HEALTH CARE DURING A FINANCIAL CRISIS

Consider the following list of basic needs. Most of us provide these for our families through our jobs. Now imagine that you and your family are faced with a major financial crisis and you simply cannot meet all your needs:

- Health care and health insurance
- A car or other reliable transportation
- Food for the family
- Clothing—appropriate for the weather and your occupation
- Housing in a safe neighborhood
- Access to good schools for your children
- Other essentials

1. Which of these items would you give up? If that was still not sufficient to make ends meet, what decisions would you make to balance the budget?

2. Many people choose to postpone or sacrifice health insurance or doctors' visits. Describe how poor health care might affect your income *and* at least three of the items in the previous list.

3. Now consider items you chose to eliminate in Question 1. How might those decisions have a long-term impact on other aspects of your quality of life—*including* the health of family members?

THINKING SOCIOLOGICALLY

How do you determine whether you are sick? How do your obligations influence your perceptions of your health? Was it easier for you to be sick as a child than it is now? Why, or why not?

The Sick Role

Think of all the social relationships, engagements, and responsibilities affected when you are sick. You miss class and work and have to avoid your friends so that you do not infect them with your germs. Most people are sympathetic for a few days, but then they expect you to get back to your usual routines and responsibilities. Unless those around you perceive you as *very* ill, you probably cannot play the *sick role* for a long time without facing negative sanctions.

Ill people occupy a special status in society that requires them to perform a certain role. The **sick role** is *a special position in society in which one is temporarily relieved of responsibilities and accepts a position of dependence.* This role allows one to deviate from usual role expectations, and other people must pick up those responsibilities. Unlike other acts of deviance, however, the sick role is not punished—as long as the sick individual cooperates and acts to overcome illness, returning as soon as possible to fulfill his or her usual social

roles (Varul 2010). That can be difficult for people facing chronic illness, as seen in the following model.

In an early contribution to the sociology of health, Parsons (1951a) presented a functional theoretical model of the sick role, outlining four interrelated behavioral expectations—two rights and two obligations.

Right 1. The sick person has the right to be excused from normal social responsibility as needed to be restored to normal functioning in the society. For example, sick students expect to receive permission to miss class or to make up a missed exam.

Right 2. The sickness is not the individual's fault. The sick person did not mean to deviate from normal social expectations and cannot become well by self-decision or by willing it so.

Obligation 1. The sick person should define being sick as undesirable. To avoid the accusation of laziness or malingering, the sick person must not prolong illness unnecessarily to avoid social obligations.

Obligation 2. Those in the sick status should seek technically competent help and cooperate in getting well. In Western countries, the help most often comes from a medical doctor.

Parsons describes the physician's role as complementing the "sick role"—to restore routine behavior and "orderliness" in patients. The model presented by Parsons clearly relates to functionalist thought. Functionalists focus on integrating all aspects of medical care into a working social system (Parsons 1951a).

Some individuals, however, might like being excused from tasks and allowed to deviate from social responsibility (such as taking tests or doing an arduous task). Certainly, being sick requires a less demanding lifestyle than going to work or school or taking care of a family. The sick role can also legitimize failure by providing a ready excuse for poor performance at some task. People who believe they are permanently unable to fulfill their normal social roles may be motivated to define themselves as sick. Yet an excess of sick people could be disruptive to the social fabric, so it is necessary to develop means to control who enters the sick status and to guard against misuse of illness as an excuse for avoiding social responsibility. In most societies today, possible negative sanctions, ranging from colleagues' raised eyebrows to being fired, discourage many people from pretending to be sick to get out of work.

THINKING SOCIOLOGICALLY

Are you able to be sick? Why, or why not?

Individuals can also earn negative sanctions for engaging in unhealthy behavior. For example, if you smoke, there is a good chance that someone has chastised you for doing so. Your decisions about what you eat and drink, your use of alcohol and other drugs, and your sexual behavior affect your health. Any of these taken to extremes can result in illness.

When people become very sick many people do not know how they should treat them. Have you ever wondered what to say (or not to say) to someone diagnosed with a life-threatening disease? Coauthor Keith Roberts shared some advice in the following Sociology in Our Social World.

Attitudes toward illness and death vary from society to society. In countries with high infant mortality rates and low life expectancy, illness and death are all too familiar. As we describe in more detail in Chapter 15, many people in Global South nations have many children because they expect some to die before reaching adulthood.

Social Factors and Attitudes Toward Health, Illness, and Death. An American Peace Corps volunteer in a South American village could not understand the passive attitude of the mother, Mónica, as she held her dying baby. He offered to help Mónica get the baby to the clinic 15 miles away, but she seemed resigned to its death. The expectations that shaped Mónica's behavior were learned in her cultural setting. Three of her seven children had died already. In this rural Global South setting, as many as half of the babies born will die in infancy because of poor sanitation, lack of clean water, and lack of health care and medicine, often from curable illnesses. People come to accept infant deaths, often easily preventable, as part of life. Many parents do not even name their children until they have displayed indications of good health for several weeks after birth.

Social Predictors in Individual Health and Illness. Individual micro-level variables such as age,

▲ These two women are of similar age, both in their 30s. Health facilities make an enormous difference in one's life chances, one's health, and how one ages. The woman on the left lives in North America; the woman on the right raises a family in Senegal, West Africa.

SOCIOLOGY IN OUR SOCIAL WORLD

AWKWARD! WHAT TO SAY (OR NOT SAY) TO A FRIEND WITH A LIFE-THREATENING DISEASE

A person with a life-threatening disease experiences distancing and isolation, as if she or he is no longer fully part of the community. The person is treated as though he or she already has a foot in the casket or urn, and this diminishes the ill person. Because of this distancing, sociological studies have demonstrated that many ill people try to hide their illness, or at least the severity of it. That is a strain—one more added to the ambiguity and perhaps fear or confusion at the plethora of decisions to be made. So how do we engage with such people in a way that is not strained or stressful?

The most important thing is *no platitudes or shibboleths* such as these:

"Everything happens for a reason." Awkward! What? This can communicate that she or he somehow deserved this.

"God never gives you more than you can handle." Again, this can come across as mean-spirited.

"You are going to be okay. I just know it." Of course, you do *not* know it, and the person hearing it knows it is a vacuous platitude.

"What's your prognosis?" We are not immortal; no one knows what will happen around the bend, and if the prognosis is bad, he or she may not want to focus on it.

"Oh, my mom had it twice, and she beat it." It is not supportive when one makes it sound like a walk in the park that anyone should be able to conquer.

Silence or avoidance. Some people never mention the illness; it is the elephant in the room, and pretending it is not there can make some people feel invisible. However, the biggest mistake people can make is to become so afraid of misspeaking that one simply withdraws.

Genuineness, honesty, and support are always at the core of constructive interactions. Here are a few examples:

Let the person know he or she is in your thoughts, heart, and prayers. This is simple but *supportive*.

Ask if there are tangible ways you can be supportive—providing meals, raking leaves, clearing snow.

Express appreciation for what the person has meant to you, not in a morbid way but with empathy for the person's struggles.

If appropriate, some of the most eloquent statements of support are hugs (and few words).

Perhaps saying something like "I can't possibly fully enter into or understand what you are going through, but I would be most willing to listen if you want to talk about the experience or just need to vent. I do not want you to go through this alone." This can be followed up with a phone call and offer to meet for coffee. Your own thoughts are not what the person needs as much as your *presence*.

Excerpts taken from Keith A. Roberts, 2018, *Meaning Making with Malignancy: A Theologically Trained Sociologist Reflects on Living Meaningfully with Cancer*. Ch. 10. Covenant Books.

---

gender, ethnicity, income, social status, and urban or rural residence help determine patterns of health and illness. For example, *age* affects health in several ways. Those 65 years or older tend to have more health issues than younger people. Three out of four U.S. residents 65 or over have at least one chronic illness (Centers for Disease Control and Prevention 2016b), and, as noted earlier, one quarter of Medicare spending is for services in the last year of life.

Gender patterns are clear, too: In Global North cultures, women are more inclined to go to the doctor than are men, and they receive more preventive and reproductive care. In contrast, men tend to go to the doctor less and receive less preventative care. As a result, they tend to use emergency services more than women (G. Weiss and Lonnquist 2015).

Ethnic groups socialize individuals into lifestyles that help or harm their health. Ethnicity also influences people's perceptions of health, the medical interventions they seek, and their response to medical treatment. Recall the cases of Hispanic curanderismo and the different experiences of pain discussed earlier. Socialization into possible health care options ranges from modern medical practitioners to alternative medical practitioners (from traditional folk healers to modern chiropractors), nonmedical professions (e.g., social workers and clergy), lay advisers, and self-care (Pescosolido 1992). In the United States, African Americans, Hispanics, and Native Americans are less likely to have regular health care providers and more likely to use hospital emergency rooms and health clinics than White Americans. Life expectancy varies dramatically in areas across the country, with lower life expectancy in poor, rural areas (Dwyer-Lindgren et al. 2017).

On average, women of color receive less prenatal care than White women, and the infant mortality gap (i.e., the number of live-born infants who die in their first year per 1,000 births) reflects this disparity, as shown in Table 14.1. Although the infant mortality rate has declined in the United States over the past decade, it is still high compared with rates in other affluent countries. This stems largely from the lack of adequate health care available to Blacks and American Indians/Alaska Natives (Chen, Oster, and Williams 2013; Mathews and Driscoll 2017).

Wealthier individuals tend to seek professional help earlier for physical or psychological distress because they can better afford the cost and time for such treatment. Despite this fact, people in the lowest income group have more contact with physicians (7.6 doctor visits per year compared with an average of 6 for the entire population) (G. Weiss and Lonnquist 2015). This is one powerful indicator that lower-income people are less healthy.

Lower-income citizens in many states still do not have access to medical insurance, despite the existence of **Medicaid**, *the government-run insurance plan for low-income families.* More than 4 million "working poor" citizens who do not receive health insurance through their employers make too much to qualify for Medicaid (because they live in a state that refused to expand Medicaid under the Affordable Care Act [ACA]) but do not make enough money to qualify for subsidized health care under the ACA (Garfield et al. 2015). The percentage of uninsured people aged 19 to 64 in the United States dropped from 20.3% in 2013, when the ACA was implemented, to 12.7% in 2016, but as Figure 14.2 indicates, these gains have begun to reverse since the election of President Trump, rising to 15.5% in 2018 (Collins, Gunja, Doty, and Bhupal 2018). Differences in access to health care also relate to meso and macro levels of the social system, as discussed in the next sections.

Modern Health Care Systems: Meso-Level Analysis

At one time, health care was largely an issue addressed in homes by families. Today, in wealthy countries, health care has become institutionalized. Much of the treatment of diseases depends on research funded by governments or foundations, and bureaucratized corporations deliver care. This section explores the institution

▼ TABLE 14.1

Infant Deaths per 1,000 Live Births by Race and Ethnicity of Mother (in the United States)

Race or Ethnic Origin	Number per 1,000
All racial/ethnic groups	5.8
Black	10.9
American Indian/Alaska Native	7.6
Hispanic	5.0
White	4.9
Asian American	3.7

Source: Mathews and Driscoll 2017.

▼ FIGURE 14.2

Percentage of Uninsured U.S. Adults Ages 19 to 64

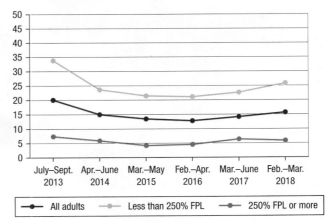

Source: Graph: The uninsured rate among working-age adults increased to 15.5 percent. From "First Look at Health Insurance in 2018 Finds ACA Gains Beginning to Reverse," Sara R. Collins et al., *To The Point,* The Commonwealth Fund, May 1, 2018.

Note: FPL refers to the federal poverty level; 250% FPL is about $31,150 for an individual and $61,500 for a family of four.

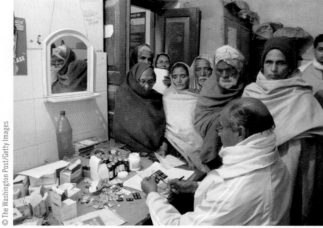

▲ Availability of health resources is an important structural factor in health. This primary health care center in rural India does not have a pharmacist. A filing clerk fills prescriptions.

of medicine: the organization of health care systems, hospitals as complex organizations, and changes of professional status for physicians.

Organization of Health Care Systems

Citizens' access to health care depends on the government's role in providing health care—whether health care is a right for all citizens or a privilege for those who can pay for it—and the type of health care available. Societies around the world struggle with issues of cost, quality and access to care, and medical technology. In the Global North, these struggles result from aging populations with more health needs. Nations in the Global South struggle with problems that result in high death rates from curable diseases and epidemics. Nations develop health care philosophies and systems based on population needs and their ability to address them.

Types of National Health Care Systems. The two most common national models for providing health care—socialized medicine and decentralized national health care programs—are based on the philosophy of health care as a human right. The United States had begun to move closer to the health-care-for-all philosophy with the passage of the Affordable Care Act, or Obamacare, signed into law in 2010. Figure 14.3 shows the countries of the world that have universal health care as of 2015.

Socialized medicine *provides a government-supported consumer service that assures equal access to health care for all citizens of a country* (Cockerham 2015). The political system controls the organization and financing

▼ FIGURE 14.3
Countries With Universal Health Care

■ Offers Universal Health Care ■ Does Not Offer Universal Health Care

Source: Wikimedia Commons 2018.

of health services and owns most facilities, pays providers directly, and allows private care for an extra fee. Global North countries that have different forms of socialized medicine systems include Canada, Great Britain, Israel, Norway, Sweden, and several other European countries.

Countries with decentralized national health programs have many of the same characteristics, but the government's role is different. The government has less direct control over health care and acts to regulate the system but not operate it (Cockerham 2015). Countries with decentralized systems include France, Germany, Japan, and the Netherlands.

A 2017 report that compared health care in 11 Global North nations revealed that the Netherlands, Australia, and the United Kingdom ranked highest and the United States lowest. All but the United States have universal health care. As you can see in Figure 14.4, the United States spends the most on health care but achieves the least results in access, administrative efficiency, equity, and health care outcomes.

The United States, unique among Global North countries, has a mix of socialized (Medicaid for poor and Medicare for elderly) and private health care programs (for which some qualified people may receive a government subsidy under the Affordable Care Act). Both types of programs tend to rely on *fee-for-service health care* in which doctors and hospitals are paid for each service they perform and decide the prices charged for every service. They typically can order as many tests as they feel necessary and decide the price for each. The fee-for-service aspect has led to doctors and hospitals charging enormous (and varying) fees for every conceivable thing used (e.g., ibuprofen and sponges) and exceedingly high health care costs (Brill 2015; Rosenthal 2017).

The Netherlands, which has a private health care system similar to the health care exchanges created under the Affordable Care Act, manages costs by providing every person with the same basic coverage with the same copayments. This cuts down on billing expenses that the United States incurs through insurance claims and the complicated and costly billing process just described. It also allows patients to know exactly what their medical costs will be, upfront (Schneider et al. 2017).

THINKING SOCIOLOGICALLY

What kind of access do you have to health care? Are you able to see a physician without worrying about the cost?

Why, or why not?

Most governments in Europe decided to support health care as a human right for all citizens and put their universal health care systems into place beginning in the late 1800s (in Germany) through the mid-1900s. Their motivations were to develop healthier populations, strengthen their military forces and economic systems, and reduce the possibility of revolution. The next Sociology Around the World describes the philosophy of the health care system in Canada, developed right after World War II.

THINKING SOCIOLOGICALLY

Would you rather live in a society with a higher tax rate and universal health care or one with a lower tax rate without universal coverage? How does your social class and level of health influence your decision? Which choice would be best for you? Which would be best for the overall society? Why?

▼ FIGURE 14.4

Health Care System Performance Compared to Spending

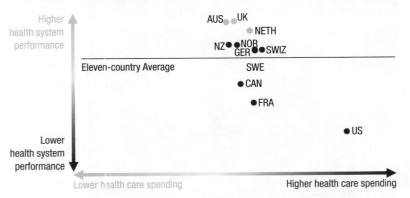

Source: Exhibit 5: Health Care System Performance Compared to Spending. From "Mirror, Mirror 2017: International Comparison Reflects Flaws and Opportunities for Better U.S. Health Care," by Schneider, Sarnak, Squires, Shah, and Doty. The Commonwealth Fund, 2017.

Note: Health care spending as a percent of GDP. Performance indicators include access, administrative efficiency, equity, and health care outcomes.

THE CANADIAN MODEL

Two principles underlie Canada's health care system: All Canadians should have the right to health care, and financial barriers to care should be eliminated. After World War II, the Canadian government established a group of health insurance plans (*socialized insurance*) that provided universal health insurance to improve the health of all Canadians. Most of the costs are shared by federal and provincial governments, with 70% paid by public funds and 30% by copayments, insurance, and other funding. The government, in consultation with medical professionals, sets prices for services (Canadian Health Care 2010).

Infant mortality and life expectancy rates, two key measures of a country's health status, reveal that Canada has lower infant mortality than the United States (4.5 deaths per 1,000 live births in Canada vs. 5.8 in the United States) (World Factbook 2017c). Canada also has higher life expectancy—81.9 years (21st in the world)—compared with 80 years (43rd in the world) in the United States (World Factbook 2017d). Taxes in Canada are 10% to 15% higher than those in the United States, but total cost per capita (per person) is 33% less for health care. In other words, the overall cost to consumers means somewhat higher taxes but lower health costs overall.

No system, including the Canadian one, is perfect. For example, in Canada, waiting periods for nonessential procedures are longer than those in the United States, and there are shortages of health care providers in some areas. As in the United States, if they have the funds, individual Canadians can sometimes pay for private, more rapid treatment. This fact indicates that even the Canadian universal health care system can treat patients differently depending on their resources.

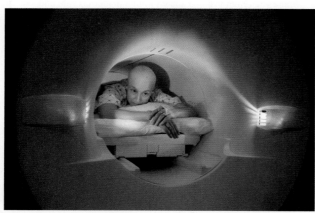

© REUTERS/Jim Bourg
© REUTERS/Jayanta Dey

▲ High-tech medical equipment (top) is expensive, but in places such as Ethiopia (bottom), hospitals have few resources, and physicians must use whatever limited technology is available.

Global health organizations serve many poor countries, primarily with immunizations and humanitarian aid during wars or epidemics. The Red Cross, Doctors without Borders, and other international aid organizations work to address the emergency needs of dislocated populations and those in war-torn nations. The World Health Organization, among other international organizations, helps provide immunizations and treatment for epidemics but does not provide services for ongoing health needs.

Hospitals as Complex Organizations. *Hospitals* are organizations that provide care and treatment for the sick and injured, providing centralized medical knowledge and technology for treatment of illnesses and accidents. Rational, systematic approaches to health care replaced individual folk remedies in the late colonial period in North America. The first colonial hospital opened in 1752, and the first medical school began accepting students in 1765. The focus of these early hospitals was on segregating the sick and destitute, who had nowhere else to go and might be contagious, from other members of society. At this time, most hospitals were small, but improvements in medical knowledge and competency began to change both these institutions and the entire medical profession. In the late 1800s, the number of hospitals, many of which were sponsored by religious organizations, grew rapidly.

The status of the hospital shifted dramatically in the early 1900s, due to advances in medical science. Trained staff, sterile conditions, and more advanced techniques and technology changed hospitals from being the last resort of the urban poor and the dying to places of healing for all classes. Small community hospitals became an essential element of town life.

The post–World War II period produced huge growth both in health care facilities and in the number of employees in the U.S. health care system. Medicines and vaccines controlled many infectious diseases that had formerly killed or disabled individuals. This period also saw the growth of medical schools and large medical facilities that provided not only patient care but also education and research. Thus began the dominance of the hospital in providing medical care. Today, many hospitals are centers of medical knowledge and technology, housing not only patients and surgical units but also laboratories and diagnostic centers, specialty clinics, and rehabilitation centers (Pescosolido et al. 2011).

Although medical health systems differ across societies, hospitals generally exhibit many characteristics similar to other large, bureaucratic organizations: hierarchical structures, rules and regulations, statuses based on competency and training (e.g., doctors and nurses), hiring and promotion based on merit, and contracts for work performed. Primary care physicians and other gatekeepers control client access to hospitals. Historically, U.S. hospitals were designed for the convenience of physicians. However, today two rather independent bureaucracies function within modern large-scale hospital organizations. Physicians dominate the medical operations, whereas lay administrators control other areas of the hospital (e.g., finance, human resources, and support services).

Health care systems act as major employers in most affluent nations. In the United States, for instance, hospitals directly employ 5.6 million people and support a total of 16 million jobs (American Hospital Association 2015). People in hospitals hold such jobs as nurses, hospital administrators, pharmacists, physical therapists, physician's assistants, nurse practitioners, imaging specialists (those who work with X-rays, MRIs, and the like), and aides and custodial staff; the number of employees continues to grow. Nurses—licensed registered nurses (3,316,111) and licensed practical nurses (832,619)—comprise the largest group of health care workers, with a total of six nurses per physician in the United States (Kaiser Family Foundation 2017). In a hospital, the nurse manages the patient care team under the authority of the physician, who is the prime decision-maker. Under the nurse's authority in this

hierarchical structure come increasing numbers of ancillary personnel.

As more for-profit corporations own and operate hospitals and other medical facilities in the United States, the power of the professional or medical line is giving way to corporate management—the lay or administrative line. Physicians have become the customers of the hospital, buying space and time to carry out their functions. Sometimes, the cost-saving goals of administrators and medical decisions of physicians come into conflict.

THINKING SOCIOLOGICALLY

Who controls the medical facilities in your community? What structure do the facilities have, and what roles predominate? Do you see evidence of a conflict between the cost-saving goals of administrators and medical decisions of physicians? How are the hospitals in your community regarded by the community? Why?

Changing Professional Status of Employees in the Health Care System

Some of you may be planning careers in the health care system. If you are taking the MCAT exams for medical school, you will find questions on social sciences, including sociology. These questions focus on understanding social structures (including the health care system); demographic characteristics and processes (such as migration, fertility, and mortality); social stratification (e.g., differences in health care depending on one's status in society); and social inequality (e.g., inequality in access to health care) (Kain 2012; Olsen 2016). This section covers these topics, some of which you have already reviewed, but now in the health care context.

Special features distinguish the hospital from other large-scale organizations or bureaucracies. The division of labor in the hospital is extensive and more highly specialized than in other formal organizations. The hospital has a hierarchical structure based on prestige and power, and hospitals depend on the cooperation of highly skilled people who must coordinate their work. Hospital employees rigidly follow patterns of authority and wear clothing and symbols indicating their positions in the hospital hierarchy. At the top of the stratification ladder, physicians exercise the most power and receive the highest financial and prestige rewards. Signs of their superior status include wearing long white coats or not wearing special uniforms at all.

Physicians rank among the most respected professionals in most societies. The widespread acceptance of physician authority is relatively recent, however. The status of physicians began to climb after medical discoveries in the 1800s led to greater success rates in treatment and more specialized training for physicians (Pescosolido and Boyer 2010). The transformation of physicians to a position of professional recognition gained great traction in the United States when some 250 physicians meeting in Philadelphia in May 1847 established the American Medical Association (AMA). This umbrella organization became the means for gaining legitimacy and power over health care practice (Cockerham 2015). The powerful new AMA delegitimized predominantly female health care areas such as midwifery and other holistic approaches such as osteopathy, chiropractic medicine, and homeopathy. Only one approach was granted credibility: *allopathy*, medical treatment supported by the American Medical Association and most Western medical organizations, involving remedies based on directly countering a patient's symptoms with drugs or surgery.

Included in the professionalization of doctors was the relationship with patients. Parsons presented a model of the doctor role that had rights and obligations, just as patients had. Among the expectations were that doctors would have a high degree of skill and knowledge, act for the patient and community welfare, be objective and emotionally detached, and be professional. These expectations are still valid in today's changing system (Parson 1951a).

Deprofessionalization is *the process though which a professional occupation loses autonomy, respect, and service orientation because the professionals come to be controlled by* nonprofessionals and outside forces such as financial concerns, government regulation, technological changes, and administrators or management. Although their position as physicians entails a high status in society, physicians have lost some control over health care to insurance companies and hospital administrators. Many physicians now work for managed care systems, by whose established guidelines for medical care they must abide, reducing their autonomy (Pescosolido and Boyer 2010).

We have explored issues of health care at the micro level (the role of sick people) and at the meso level (organization of health care and hospitals as complex organizations). We now move on to macro-level policy issues at the national and global level.

Health Care Issues at the National and Global Level: Macro-Level Analysis

Health Care System in the United States

The United States has the best health care system among Global North countries in terms of quality medical care, trained practitioners, facilities, and advanced medical technology. People from around the world seek training and care in the United States. It is also the worst system, with the highest cost per capita in the world, unequal access, inefficiencies, and competing interests. The Affordable Care Act (Obamacare) was designed to address some of these issues, but it is unclear how or if the health care system under the Trump administration will do so.

People like Eloise have suffered from some of the weaknesses of the U.S. health care system. She knew something was seriously wrong when she lost her appetite, vomited when she ate more than a few bites, and did not have her usual abundant energy. Without health insurance and fearing she would lose her job if she missed work to see a doctor, she tried home remedies and hoped the symptoms would go away. When she finally did go to the hospital, she was in serious condition. Eloise spent a

▲ The clothing worn by health care workers is significant. It communicates status, authority, and rights to certain prerogatives within the hospital or clinic. What sort of attire do nurses, technicians, and aides wear in your local hospital?

few days in intensive care and is now on a treatment plan, but without income from her job, she cannot pay the bills for herself and her child.

Because of cases like Eloise's, some critics claim that the U.S. health care system is, itself, a social problem. It developed without specific direction and responded to demands piecemeal, allowing practitioners, medical facilities, and insurance and drug companies to establish themselves and then protect their self-interests, sometimes at the expense of patients.

Health Care Advances. Medical research into gene therapy and new drug and technological therapies make biomedical research one of the most rapidly advancing medical fields. New therapies will help people live longer, more comfortable and productive lives—*if* they can afford and have access to the care. As science moves rapidly, ethical questions about the use of fetal tissue in experiments and treatments, cloning, prolonging life, and other issues challenge ethicists and lawmakers.

In addition to advances in medical science, there have been other positive steps taken to increase the health of the population. In the growing field of public health, professionals fight disease, promote health, and work to raise life expectancy rates. Recent public health accomplishments include improved motor vehicle safety, safer workplaces, control of more infectious diseases, greater access to family planning and prenatal care, and education of citizens about the dangers of tobacco and other unhealthy substances.

Problems in the U.S. Health Care System. Although the United States is the country of choice for many types of surgeries and the health care is exceptional for those with plenty of money, overall life expectancy rates in the country are alarming, as Figure 14.5 indicates. The bar in the middle, labeled OECD, is the average for all countries in the Organisation for Economic Co-operation and Development, all of which are Global North countries. The United States is below the average. It loses 3 times as many years of life to infectious diseases and 2 times as many to metabolic diseases as the average OECD nation (Kliff 2014). Much of this is because health care is so unevenly distributed in the United States.

Maldistribution of Health Care. In addition to a lack of doctors in rural and poor areas, inequality in U.S. health care also relates to the unequal distribution of doctors by state. Some states have higher ratios of physicians per residents than other states. Massachusetts has the

▼ FIGURE 14.5

Life Expectancy at Birth

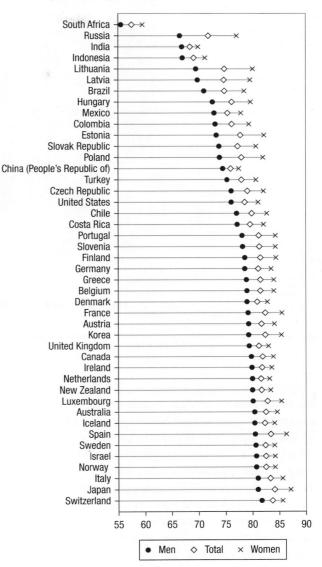

Source: OECD 2017a. Life Expectancy at Birth. https://data.oecd.org/healthstat/life-expectancy-at-birth.htm.

most "active patient care doctors" per 100,000 residents with 314; Mississippi has the fewest with 159. Figure 14.6 shows the variation.

THINKING SOCIOLOGICALLY

Given the previous discussion, how might where you live affect your access to health care and overall health?

Active Patient Care Physicians per 100,000 Population by State, 2014

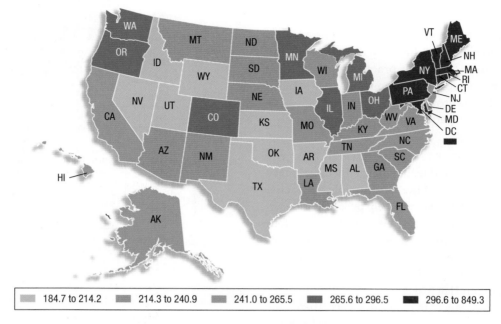

184.7 to 214.2	214.3 to 240.9	241.0 to 265.5	265.6 to 296.5	296.6 to 849.3

Source: Copyright © 2015 Association of American Medical Colleges. Reprinted with permission.

Health Care Cost and Funding. One of the most serious problems for health care systems and consumers in the United States is the cost of health care. Now at 18% of the gross domestic product, health care spending in the United States surpasses that of all other Global North countries, as Figure 14.7 reveals (Centers for Medicare and Medicaid Services 2017). Doctors, hospitals, and insurance companies use complicated codes to identify medical procedures and the cost for each one. Doctors and hospitals try to use the most expensive codes, whereas insurance companies that pay these bills try to deny high-cost claims. On average, hospitals charge the uninsured, with neither private nor government-sponsored (Medicare and Medicaid) insurance, 2.5 times the rate they charge the insured and 3 times the amount allowed by Medicare (Rosenthal 2017).

The cost of drugs in the United States is also higher than in most other countries. To find affordable medicine, some U.S. citizens are mail-ordering drugs from foreign pharmacies, a practice that critics say lacks quality controls and could be dangerous (Rosenthal 2013).

Out-of-pocket expenses (the costs of insurance plus deductibles) have doubled over the past 10 years and are now almost 10% of the median income in the United States (Schoen, Radley, and Collins 2015). The

Affordable Care Act offers some hope. For example, it encourages health providers to move away from the fee-for-service model.

Jimmy Kimmel's monologue that described his newborn's lifesaving surgery to address a heart defect brought the repercussions of lack of health care coverage home to millions of Americans. Arguing in favor of saving Obamacare (which President Trump vowed to repeal), Kimmel noted that "before 2014 [when Obamacare became law], if you were born with congenital heart disease like my son was, there was a good chance you would never be able to get health insurance because you had a preexisting condition. And if your parents didn't have medical insurance, you might not live long enough to even get denied because of a preexisting condition" (Russonello 2017).

Although, as we write these words in 2018, President Trump has not been able to totally dismantle the ACA, he has chipped away at it by taking such steps as cutting funding for advertising, reducing days people can enroll, eliminating the mandate for people to buy insurance, and cutting subsidies for health insurance companies that participate in the ACA (Luhby 2018). Moreover, although the Supreme Court upheld most of the Affordable Care Act, it also ruled that states cannot be

Health Spending by OECD Nations

India
Indonesia
China (People's Republic of)
Colombia
Mexico
South Africa
Turkey
Costa Rica
Russia
Brazil
Latvia
Chile
Poland
Lithuania
Hungary
Estonia
Slovak Republic
Greece
Czech Republic
Israel
Slovenia
Portugal
Korea
Spain
Italy
New Zealand
Finland
United Kingdom
Australia
Iceland
Japan
Belgium
Canada
France
Denmark
Netherlands
Austria
Ireland
Sweden
Germany
Norway
Luxembourg
Switzerland
United States

0k   2k   4k   6k   8k   10k   12k

| × Voluntary | ◇ Government/compulsory | • Total |

Source: OECD 2017b. Health Spending. https://data.oecd.org/healthres/health-spending.htm.

forced to expand Medicaid programs (government insurance for low-income residents primarily funded by the federal and state governments). Initially almost half of the states refused to do so, even though the federal government will pay for almost all the extended coverage. The expansion of Medicaid was a key part of the law, and the Supreme Court ruling (and the decision of some states) means that many poor citizens will remain without health insurance and that access to health care will become even more disparate among states. As seen in Figure 14.8,

34 states and the District of Columbia have adopted the Medicaid expansion, and 16 states have not.

Provisions of the Affordable Care Act declared constitutional by the Supreme Court include the following (National Conference of State Legislatures 2011):

- Requiring employers to provide health coverage for their workers, or pay penalties, with exceptions for employers with less than 50 employees

- Requiring individuals to have insurance (with some exceptions and with tax credits to help lower-income people pay for it)

- Requiring insurance companies to cover young adults until age 26 on parents' health insurance plan

- Prohibiting lifetime caps and limiting the use of annual caps on insurance coverage

- Prohibiting the exclusion of people with preexisting conditions from private (as well as public) insurance plans (individual health insurance plans—bought by individuals, not through an employer—were previously grandfathered and could refuse to cover someone because of a preexisting condition)

- Establishing a limit on the percentage of insurance payments used for nonmedical payments (e.g., salaries and other administrative costs)

Health Care Around the Globe

During a yearlong sabbatical in England, the Ballantine family signed up with a local surgeon, as the British call family physicians. Their sore throats, upset tummies, and

▼ FIGURE 14.8

Medicaid Expansion by State

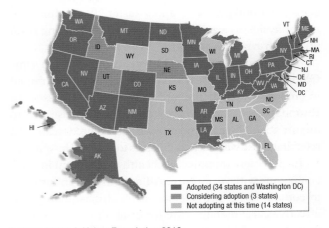

■ Adopted (34 states and Washington DC)
■ Considering adoption (3 states)
■ Not adopting at this time (14 states)

Source: Henry J. Kaiser Foundation 2018.

▲ Supporters (left) and opponents (right) of the Affordable Care Act rally on the sidewalk at the Supreme Court in Washington, DC, illustrating the controversy over national health care policy.

bruised feet were taken to the doctor at no direct cost. The school referred their daughter to the hospital eye clinic for glasses at no cost. Their son was diagnosed and treated for "glandular fever" (mononucleosis), again at no cost. In Great Britain, all citizens have access to treatment by family physicians and dentists, to the dispensing of prescribed drugs, to eye care, and to community nursing and health visitor services. Taxes fund universal health care coverage at an expense much less than that of the U.S. cost for health care, and the administrative costs are low.

The World Health Organization recommends at least 1 physician for every 600 citizens, but many nations do not reach this minimum. The maldistribution of physicians is a global, as well as a U.S., issue. As illustrated in Figure 14.9 in the next Engaging Sociology, the countries with the most doctors—the highest number of physicians per 1,000 people—are Greece (6.2), Belarus (5.2), Austria (4.9), Georgia (4.8), Norway (4.2), and Switzerland (4.1). The United States has 2.4 doctors per 1,000 people, and Canada has 2.0. The lowest numbers are found in Global South countries such as Colombia, Ghana, and Mauritania with 0.1 physicians per 1,000 people, and Afghanistan and Cambodia with 0.2 physicians per 1,000 people (NationMaster 2014). Moreover, most physicians are found in urban areas, leaving rural areas with even fewer doctors.

To help compensate for the paucity of doctors in some Global South countries, local rural residents are trained in emergency medicine and to recognize illnesses. In Rwanda, Africa, health care workers make house calls to inquire about diseases and provide the required treatment, referring those with serious illnesses to regional hospitals.

Each society organizes its health care system in ways congruous with its culture. All nations search for ways to contain costs; provide accessible, high-quality, and effective care; manage care for disabilities and chronic illnesses; and find treatments for infectious diseases

(Pescosolido and Boyer 2010). Western scientific medicine has spread throughout the world, but some of the ideas from other parts of the world now influence Western approaches to health and illness, as the following example from China illustrates.

The People's Republic of China: Medicine in a Communist State. Little was known outside China about China's health care system until the 1970s, when visitors, including health observers, were welcomed by the once-reclusive government. When the "bamboo curtain" that isolated China was raised in 1971, the outside world learned that, despite a background of poverty, the government had established an effective network of health services.

Several years ago, Jeanne, one of the coauthors of this text, met Xi (pronounced "She") on a train in China. He was returning to his village after completing a medical training course that covered first aid treatment, immunizations, and recognition of serious symptoms. He was one of more than a million "barefoot" doctors or *countryside doctors*—paramedics trained in basic medicine to provide health care for rural residents in China's villages. The program, begun in 1951, was very successful in curbing infectious diseases. In fact, the program has provided a model for reaching out into the countryside for several Global South countries, including Kenya and Rwanda.

Barefoot doctors were generally local peasants selected by fellow members of their agricultural communes. Many continued to work on the farm but, after some training, took responsibility for preventive medicine and some aspects of primary care in the local neighborhood. If they passed an exam they could become a village doctor, licensed to carry out additional medical procedures. They were paid the same as other agricultural workers. The barefoot doctor was generally the only medical practitioner that many of the 800 million people living in rural China ever saw. From a sociological perspective, a positive feature of these practitioners was their within-culture socialization. Given the homogeneity of peasant neighborhoods, the barefoot doctor had little difficulty understanding the local culture and its resistance to certain procedures.

Today, this program that provided a model for poor countries has all but collapsed in China—beginning in the late 1970s with the privatization of agriculture, private enterprises, and rapid growth. There were no longer collective farms with groups of people to finance the barefoot doctors. The government was also unwilling to train more of them. This left many villages with no primary care or immunization programs. Diseases that many thought had been eradicated began to resurface. Because most of the doctors in China live and work in

ACCESS TO HEALTH CARE FOR RICH AND POOR

▼ FIGURE 14.9

Number of Physicians per 1,000 People

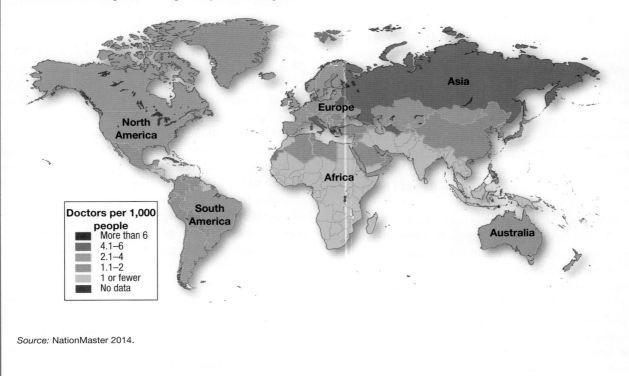

Source: NationMaster 2014.

Study the map in Figure 14.9. Then answer the following questions:

1. How do you think the scarcity of physicians in the Global South and rural areas in some affluent countries affects the health care of individuals and the functioning of communities and society?

2. How might a surplus of physicians influence health care?

3. How could a nation increase the number of qualified medical workers and people's access to health care?

4. How might health care differ depending on where one lives in the United States?

urban areas, many people in rural areas had to depend on home remedies (Casella 2009; Hou and Ke 2015). A remaining element of the rural medicine program is the Lifeline Express train in Xinjiang Province; it travels the countryside providing cataract eye surgery for residents across China. Today, the remaining village clinics provide basic services to poor and elderly, though they are poorly funded; doctors and health care workers often support themselves with money from medical drugs they sell (Babiarz, Yi, & Luo 2013; Hays 2011).

Recently, the central government allocated funds to increase basic coverage and improve hospitals in regional areas. The overall doctor-to-patient ratio is now 1.5 doctors per 1,000 people, but few physicians work in rural areas. Further, many of those trained as physicians in China choose to practice in African nations where the wages and social standing are higher (Hays 2011; World Factbook 2014).

Once introduced, Western-style medicine expanded rapidly in China, and Chinese practices expanded in Global North countries. After China opened itself up to the rest of the world in the 1970s, the number of medical personnel with training in Western medicine increased significantly. Many health care workers now blend Western medicine practices with traditional Chinese approaches. Increasingly, doctors are trained in both. The opening up of China also led to the spread of traditional Chinese medical practices to the West. Consider the example of acupuncture, an ancient Chinese method for treating certain physical problems and relieving pain.

One result of the spread of medical ideas around the world is the complementary and alternative medicines (CAM) movement in the United States and other Global North countries. CAM includes health care systems, practices, and products used to complement or replace conventional medicine. CAM therapies include acupuncture and chiropractic, natural products, special diets, and megavitamin therapy, and nearly 40% of U.S. citizens use one or more of these approaches (GoodTherapy.org 2012; NCCAM 2013).

Although acupuncture has been practiced for more than 5,000 years in China, only in the 1970s, when relations with China improved, did this treatment become known and practiced in the West. Many doctors in the Global North reject the practice as unscientific and ineffective, and some regulating agencies have put limits on its practice. However, many patients seek out those who can practice it. Some insurance companies cover the costs of acupuncture, and the World Health Organization recognizes more than 40 conditions that acupuncture can treat effectively (Weiss and Lonnquist 2015).

▲ Acupuncture is based on the idea that the body has 700 points that ease and control pain and stimulate body functions. This Asian-originated process of inserting fine sharp needles into selected points related to affected organs in the body is essentially painless, and doctors have even done operations without chemical anesthesia using acupuncture to block pain.

The Chinese health care system faces a variety of problems. In urban areas, air pollution and other environmental issues cause increasing numbers of health problems. In rural areas, many people practice only traditional folk medicine, and diseases, poor sanitation, and high smoking rates result in lowered life expectancy (Watts 2012).

China produces and consumes more tobacco than any other nation. Close to half (44%) of the world's cigarettes are consumed in China, harming smokers and all those around them exposed to secondhand smoke (World Health Organization 2017). Smoking is a primarily male activity in China, with 45% of men but just 2.1% of women smoking daily (Hunt 2015). Smoking-related illnesses result in 1 million deaths yearly in China (World Health Organization 2017).

Under enormous pressure, due to the increasingly toxic, highly polluted air, the Chinese government enacted strong new antismoking legislation for the capital of Beijing in 2015 and increased, slightly, the tax on cigarettes (World Health Organization 2017). Government efforts to control smoking have been uneven, however, for it has an economic stake in the success of tobacco sales. The China National Tobacco Corporation, a state-run monopoly, produces one out of every three cigarettes in the world. It makes much money for the government and employs millions of people (Hunt 2015).

Health care systems around the world illustrate the impact of national and global political and economic factors on the health care available to citizens. The political and economic systems of countries and the health of their economies influence their philosophies toward health care and the money each country puts into it. International events, such as wars and the spread of refugees, influence availability of health care within countries. International organizations, such as the World Health Organization, play a key role in addressing epidemics and pandemics throughout the world.

THINKING SOCIOLOGICALLY

What can countries learn by studying other health care systems? Give examples.

Globalization of Medical Problems. The international sale of body parts reveals how health care relates to social stratification and crosses national borders. In some countries, people at the bottom of the stratification system are so desperately poor that they sell parts of their body to help their families survive. For example, some mothers and fathers in poor slums of Mumbai and other cities in India and Pakistan sell one of their kidneys to those who plan to resell them to patients (primarily in Global North nations) in need of a new kidney and with the money to buy one. The individuals who sell their body parts tend to do so for money to pay for housing, food, education for their children, and dowries for their daughters to marry. In the process, their health can suffer due to complications during or after the surgery to remove their organ, and when the money is gone, life is even more difficult. Although laws passed in India in 1994 ban the sale of human organs, few violators face capture and punishment ("Body Parts for Sale" 2008; Scheper-Hughes 2014). At last report, the only nation where the sale of body organs was legal was Iran, which permits the sale of blood, breast milk, hair, eggs, sperm, and even the womb ("Body Parts for Sale" 2008; Kasperkevic 2014).

Three crimes are common in the organ trade: deceiving victims into giving up an organ, not paying an agreed price for removal of an organ, and treating persons for an ailment that may or may not exist and taking organs in the process. The most commonly trafficked are kidneys, the liver, and any other organ that can be removed (UN.GIFT 2014). Recently, sales of skin, bones, tissue, and dental implants from fresh corpses have grown, with a center of such activity in the Ukraine. The United States is the biggest market, with 2 million such products bought each year. These body parts allow those willing and wealthy enough to buy them to see with cornea transplants, walk with recycled tendons, and replace a dying kidney with a healthy one (Wilson, et al. 2012).

The global stratification of health care can also be seen in the different causes of death in affluent Global North versus poor Global South countries for the 55 million people who die worldwide every year (World Health Organization 2014c). Relatively few people in the Global North die of infectious diseases. Yet infectious diseases still cause most deaths in the Global South, reducing life expectancy in some poor countries to 50 years or less. Figures 14.10 and 14.11 show the leading causes of death in low- and high-income countries.

THINKING SOCIOLOGICALLY

What are some factors that account for the differences in causes of death between high- and low-income countries? What might be done to tackle these disparities?

▲ An unemployed man, Dwi Waryono, holds a placard advertising his kidney for sale in Jakarta. The placard reads "I was a blood donor. I will donate my kidney to pay for the cost of my children's schooling." For people in severe poverty, selling a body organ is a way to care for one's family, for it can raise several thousand dollars.

Globalization and the Mobility of Disease. Traveling humans throughout history have provided passage to pathogens on their bodies and in their luggage—great plagues, smallpox, syphilis, and others. Today, Ebola, SARS, polio, and other diseases thought to be under control many years ago are resurfacing (Ostroff 2013). Because far more people travel around the globe today than in the past, diseases can spread more widely and quickly.

Consider measles in the United States, which has reemerged in several areas. Measles, a vaccine-preventable disease, has ranged in number from 37 U.S. cases in 2004 to 220 in 2011, 187 in 2013, and over 600 cases in 2014 (it dropped to 70 in 2016). Why? One source of the disease is travelers returning from trips to foreign countries where the disease is still common. For example, one U.S. resident who visited the Philippines in 2014 brought back the disease and infected others (CDC 2015a, 2015d; Iannelli 2014). Also, measles can spread if it reaches a community where many people are not vaccinated (such as parts of California where the movement to "opt out" of vaccinations has gained traction). In 2014, there were 338 cases among the unvaccinated Amish in Ohio. This is one reason why California passed a law in 2015 making it mandatory for all public- and private-school children to be vaccinated against measles and other diseases (unless they cannot for medical reasons) (Centers for Disease Control 2017d; Perkins 2015). As seen in the next Sociologists in Action, some sociologists, like Richard Carpiano, are at the forefront of efforts to educate the public about

Top 10 Causes of Death in Low-Income Countries, 2016

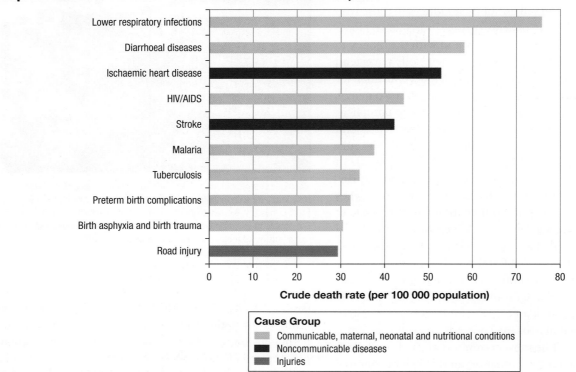

Source: World Health Organization 2018.

Top 10 Causes of Death in High-Income Countries, 2016

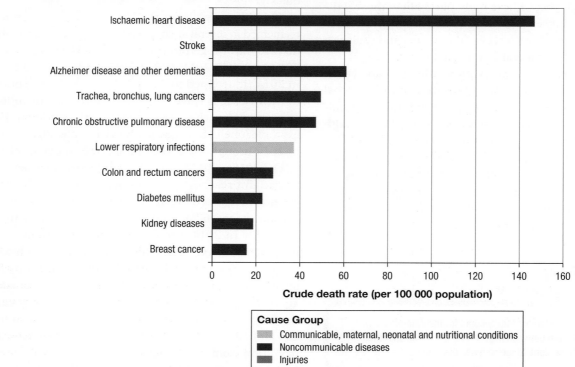

Source: World Health Organization 2018.

SOCIOLOGISTS IN ACTION
Richard M. Carpiano

CONNECTING PERSONAL HEALTH TO COMMUNITY LIFE

How might the communities we belong to affect our health? As a medical sociologist, I have been fascinated by this question. Our ability to experience a healthy life is a function of many factors. Yet most people—including those in the media—often only consider factors specific to our individual selves and bodies, such as our personal choices, behaviors, and genetics. Less often considered are our social environments. My research aims to better understand how our personal health behaviors, risks, and outcomes are influenced by community life—our social ties to family, friends, and others, as well as the neighborhoods, towns, and other place-based communities in which we live.

Throughout my career, I have had the opportunity to collaborate with researchers, clinicians, and social service and public health organizations in evaluating how community social conditions may contribute to a range of public health problems. My community-centered research took on a new focus, however, after reading news reports in 2015 about a measles outbreak that started in Disneyland. This troubling news sparked my concern over low child vaccination rates due, in large part, to increases in vaccine hesitancy: when parents refuse or delay some or all of the doctor-recommended vaccinations that could prevent their children and others in their communities from acquiring and spreading many infectious diseases. A major factor fueling this hesitancy is misinformation about vaccines often found online and circulated via parents' networks and antivaccine activist groups. Thus, these public health problems of child vaccination coverage and vaccine-preventable disease outbreaks are driven in large part by sociological factors.

Motivated by my concern about these vaccination issues and my prior research on community and health, I have become involved in multiple projects with researchers and public health agencies to better understand and ultimately address vaccine hesitancy and coverage. Some examples of these ongoing projects include

- investigating how and why child vaccination rates, knowledge, and attitudes vary across geographic areas and socioeconomic groups;

- assisting the Public Health Agency of Canada in designing questions to assess parents' vaccination knowledge, attitudes, and beliefs for inclusion in their childhood National Immunization Coverage Survey, which will collect information from several thousand parents throughout Canada; and

- studying how people in the United States and Canada react to vaccine-hesitant parents and which types of policies and laws they might support to ensure adequate vaccination coverage in their communities.

Some of these project findings have received significant news coverage. We were excited to speak with journalists because we feel a responsibility to communicate our findings to the public, so that people may be better informed about how these issues affect their families and communities.

Vaccinations are one example of the many health issues I have studied throughout my career. Regardless of the health issue of focus, I am grateful for any opportunity to use my skills as a sociologist to help shape policies that will allow people to enjoy healthier lives and communities.

★ ★ ★ ★ ★ ★

Richard M. Carpiano is Professor of Public Policy and Sociology at the University of California, Riverside.

how communities impact the health of individuals and to shape policies accordingly—including those around vaccinations.

The density and urbanization of the world's population (discussed in Chapter 15) also affects human health. For example, use of land and space influences the number of rodents and insects, the quality of water supplies, and the direct contact people have with one another. Currently, about half of the world's people live in urban areas, many in slums surrounding major cities. Problems such as open sewers, inadequate sanitation, lack of electricity, and polluted water pervade these slums. Overcrowding, combined with these problems, causes infectious diseases to spread more rapidly. Growing numbers of locations with shared circulated air (airplanes, domed stadiums, and air-conditioned office buildings

▲ A health care worker, wearing a protective suit, feeds an Ebola-infected child at a medical facility in Kailahun, Sierra Leone, the epicenter of the world's Ebola outbreak in 2014.

and hotels) also spread disease. Even climate change and antimicrobial resistance affect the spread of diseases (WHO 2013a).

The growing threat of pandemics is one cause for global concern, but the global disparity in the handling of treatable diseases remains an even more pressing issue. The uneven distribution of health care, doctors, and medicines around the world and resistance of some religious groups to inoculating their children has led to many preventable and curable diseases going untreated. Despite increasingly sophisticated medical technology, as long as there is inequality in countries of our social world, adequate health care will not reach all people and all countries equally.

THINKING SOCIOLOGICALLY

We live in a global world, yet our most immediate experiences are local. How might you and your family benefit if international agencies resolve health problems in Africa, Asia, and South America?

Our social institutions—from family, education, and religion to politics, economics, and health—maintain stability in societies. However, the world in which we live is a dynamic one. In the final two chapters, we turn to an examination of how change occurs. First, we examine two forces that have changed exponentially in the past two centuries—population patterns and urbanization. We close with an examination of the many manifestations of social change.

WHAT HAVE WE LEARNED?

Sickness and the role of sick people are social constructions that vary across societies. Although health is a private, personal concern, it is also a public concern, delivered through organizations dispensing health care and government practices determining access and funding of health care. Distant from your daily life but important to your well-being are the global health organizations that concern themselves with global epidemics. In addition, whether you can afford or have access to medical care depends in part on the economic conditions in your society and the marketplace of health care delivery.

KEY POINTS

• Sociology examines the social implications of health and illness—from the micro level of individuals coping with illness to the meso level of institutional interactions and complex organizations that manage health and illness to the global issues of controlling the spread of diseases around the world.

- Whether looking at the medicalization of social problems through labeling or examining functions and socioeconomic conflicts regarding health care in society, various social theories offer alternative lenses through which to view health care systems.

- At the micro level, we can look at issues such as the sick role; how social and cultural factors affect our responses to pain and ill health; and how our age, gender, and other personal aspects of identity relate to our responses to health and illness.

- Hospitals and other elements of organizational complexity; professionalism and deprofessionalization of medical personnel; and the linkages between institutions such as the economy, politics, education, and family are all aspects of health care at the meso level.

- Health care is a national issue that relates to the nation's resources, security of its citizens, and types of health care delivery.

- Globally, diseases spread around the planet much faster in our age of rapid travel and migrations. Different forms of health care have also spread throughout the world and influence the approaches we each choose in our own local communities.

- The disparity in health care within and among nations remains the most pressing health care issue facing societies today.

DISCUSSION QUESTIONS

1. Imagine that your state has a law on the ballot that would legalize assisted suicide, following the model of Oregon's law. Would you vote for or against the ballot question? Why? Would the conditions necessary for the legality of assisted suicide described in Oregon's law influence your vote? Why or why not? Why do you think most of those who participated in the Death with Dignity program in Oregon were Whites with college degrees?

2. Think of the last time you or someone close to you was seriously ill. What were the repercussions of the illness on the micro level? How did these repercussions relate to health care issues on the meso and macro levels?

3. What are three ways social class impacts health? Describe how social class has impacted your health and the health of your family members.

4. Do you think health care is a human right? Why or why not? How can equality or inequality in health care impact a society?

5. If you were a policymaker, how might you try to curb binge drinking or smoking among college students?

6. Do you think vaccinations should be mandatory for schoolchildren? Why or why not?

KEY TERMS

deprofessionalization   440
health   424
illness   424

Medicaid   435
Medicare   423
medicalization   427

sick role   432
socialized medicine   436

CONTRIBUTING TO OUR SOCIAL WORLD: WHAT CAN WE DO?

At the Local (Micro) Level

- The *Endocrine Society* (endocrinefacts.org/health-conditions/obesity) provides information on a wide range of resources related to studies on eating behavior, many of which are directly applicable to problems faced by students. Plan a support group for those facing weight issues.

- Can you find *healthy food on campus*? If your school does not offer enough healthy options, start a petition and present it to your campus administrators asking them to address this issue. Articles that describe some schools' attempts to go healthy can be found at www.bonappetit.com/gallery/7-healthiest-college-dining-halls and greatist.com/health/healthiest-colleges.

At the Organizational or Institutional (Meso) Level

- *Free or low-cost clinics.* Most communities provide health screening and other services to uninsured individuals and families. The U.S. Department of Health and Human Services has a locator website at findahealthcenter.hrsa.gov/Search_HCC.aspx that searches for free clinics by state and city. Most have volunteer and internship opportunities that afford interesting and valuable experiences, especially if you are considering a career in a health care field.

At the National or Global (Macro) Level

- *UNAIDS* works throughout the world to fight the pandemic. If you are interested in learning more about and possibly raising funds for this effort, go to www.unaids.org/en.

- *Doctors Without Borders/Médecins Sans Frontières (MSF)* "helps people worldwide where the need is greatest, delivering emergency medical aid to people affected by conflict, epidemics, disasters, or exclusion from health care." You can learn how to volunteer or gain a paid internship with them at www.doctorswithoutborders.org/work-office.

- *World Vision* (www.worldvision.org) helps children, their families, and their communities to combat malnutrition, AIDS, and other health- and poverty-related problems across the world. The organization's Hope Child program lists several suggestions for getting involved, including sponsorship of a child. *AVERT*, an international AIDS charity, provides material to educate yourself and your classmates about AIDS on the organization's website at www.avert.org/world aid.htm.

$SAGE edge™

Get the tools you need to sharpen your study skills. SAGE edge offers a robust online environment featuring an impressive array of free tools and resources.

Access practice quizzes, eFlashcards, video, and multimedia at **edge.sagepub.com/ballantine7e**

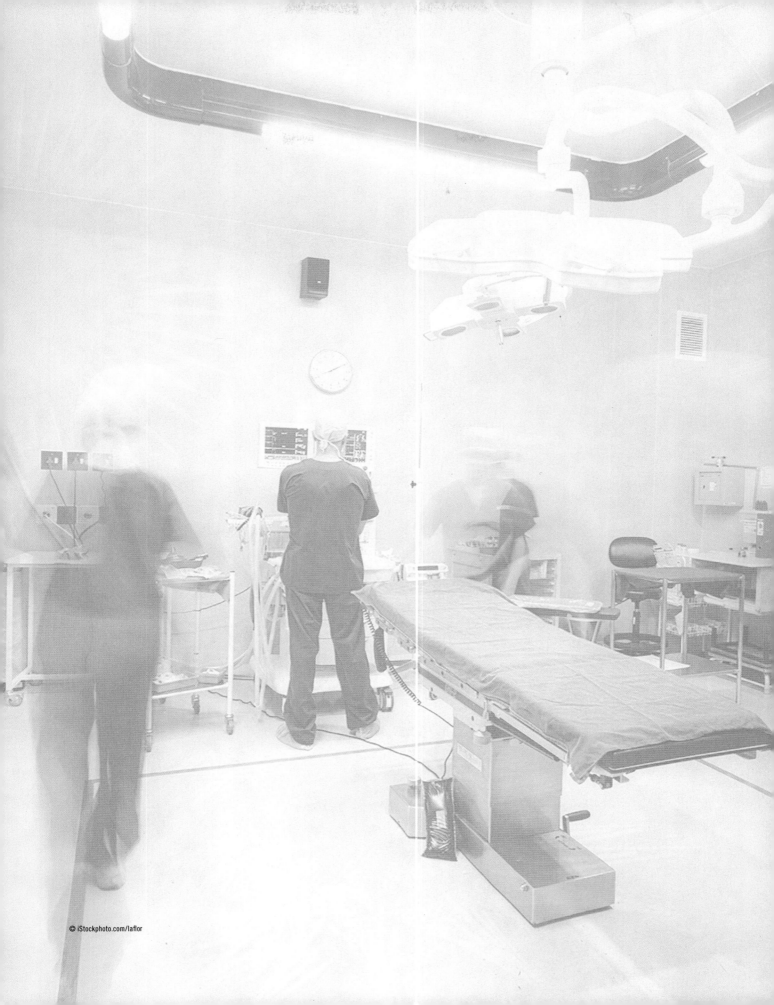

PART V

SOCIAL DYNAMICS

Social structures such as institutions tend to resist change. Nonetheless, this entire book demonstrates that societies are dynamic and changing. Globalization, a major theme in this book, is a process bringing transformation to our social world, as shown by the very different world inhabited by our grandparents. The macro- and meso-level dimensions of society have become increasingly powerful, which is exactly why we need a sociological imagination to understand how the events in our own micro worlds are influenced by the larger society.

This section looks at some of those dynamic, fluid, and vibrant processes: population changes, urbanization, climate change, expansion of technology, social movements, and more. In periods of rapid change, understanding how and why that change occurs can help us to influence the direction those changes take in our society. From rising global temperatures to terrorism and from robot-run factories to immigrants in our communities, we need to understand causes and consequences to respond constructively. To do so, we must grasp the micro-, meso-, and macro-level dimensions of change in our lives and the linkages between parts of our social world. We turn first to environmental sociology and look at population dynamics, urbanization, and climate change.

CHAPTER 15

© Dirk Meister/Moment/Getty Images

ENVIRONMENTAL SOCIOLOGY

Population, Urbanization, and Climate Change

▲ Humans are confined to this one moderate-sized planet on which we depend for survival. The challenges of controlling population size, migration patterns, the spread of disease, and climate change add to the need for global cooperation.

ME (AND MY NEIGHBORS)

LOCAL ORGANIZATIONS AND COMMUNITY

Local schools and community organizations serve the local population.

NATIONAL ORGANIZATIONS, INSTITUTIONS, AND ETHNIC SUBCULTURES

Population trends influence institutions such as politics, economics, and education.

SOCIETY

National governments set policies that influence birth incentives, birth control, and immigration.

GLOBAL COMMUNITY

Cross-national migration patterns can spread epidemics or meet pressing needs for labor.

WHAT WILL YOU LEARN IN THIS CHAPTER?

This chapter will help you to do the following:

15.1 Define environmental sociology

15.2 Illustrate the pattern of the world's population growth over time

15.3 Give examples of institutional influences on fertility, mortality, and migration

15.4 Describe individual decisions that affect population patterns

15.5 Discuss national and global urbanization trends

15.6 Explain why moving from rural to urban settings can lead to anomie

15.7 Explain three major environmental problems facing urban areas in the Global South

15.8 Describe how climate change is a social issue

THINK ABOUT IT

Micro: Small groups and local community	What is the population profile of your hometown (e.g., economic status of residents, ethnic and racial composition, and recent immigrant groups)? Where do you fit into that population profile?
Meso: National institutions, complex organizations, and ethnic groups	Why do people move from rural areas to urban areas? What problems might this pattern of movement create?
Macro: National and global systems	How do global issues relating to demographic changes, urbanization, and the environment affect your family and local community?

When Sally Ride, the first U.S. woman in space, looked down at Earth, she, like other astronauts who have the opportunity to see the planet from far above, experienced the *overview effect*. This occurs when Earth is viewed from a new angle, from the perspective of space. Ride described the impact it had on her.

> *Mountain ranges, volcanoes, and river deltas appeared in salt-and-flour relief, all leading me to assume the role of a novice geologist. In such moments, it was easy to imagine the dynamic upheavals that created jutting mountain ranges and the internal wrenching that created rifts and seas. I also became an instant believer in plate tectonics; India really is crashing into Asia, and Saudi Arabia and Egypt really are pulling apart, making the Red Sea wider. Even though their respective motion is really no more than mere inches a year, the view from overhead makes theory come alive.* (Quoted in Beaver 2012)

Ride's perspective changed, and, thus, her ability to recognize and understand the world also changed. Ride saw and noticed things she had not seen or noticed before because of this new view of the world. In this chapter, you will look at the environment from a sociological perspective and, in the process, see and notice patterns you may not have paid attention to before.

Environmental sociologists look at both natural communities (ecology) and human communities and how they interact with one another (Bell and Ashwood 2016). In doing so, they examine population growth, movements in population, and the impact humans have on the environment. Today, as the human population quickly increases, there are record numbers of displaced people moving across the world, and climate change threatens the very future of the human population.

We look first at population growth and then at urbanization and the impacts of climate change. The

previous chapters have moved from micro- to macro-level analysis. In this chapter, however, because of the nature of the material and the need to explain certain issues before the micro issues make sense, we discuss macro-level patterns in world population growth first. We then describe meso-level institutional influences and micro-level factors affecting population patterns. We close by looking at how climate change impacts all levels of society.

Macro-Level Patterns in World Population Growth

Table 15.1 illustrates the current state of the human population. As you can see, there are now more than 7.5 billion people on Earth, and the number is increasing rapidly.

The world's human population grew sporadically over the millennia, but the explosion of human beings on the planet in the past 2.5 centuries is stunning. If we collapsed all human history into one 24-hour day, the period since 1750 would consume 1 minute. Yet 25% of all humans have lived during this 1-minute period. In the 200 years from 1750 to 1950, the world's population mushroomed from 800 million to 2.5 billion. On October 12, 1999, the global population reached

▼ TABLE 15.1

Demographics of the World, 2017

	World
Population	7,576,951,385
Births per year	148,779,660
Deaths per year	58,619,319
Natural annual increase	90,160,341

Source: Countrymeters 2018.

▲ The overcrowding in some cities means that governments have a difficult time providing the infrastructure and services needed for the growing urban population. Rio de Janeiro, Brazil, is one example.

6 billion. It has now expanded to over 7.5 billion with almost all the latest growth in the Global South (Countrymeters 2018).

As societies develop, birthrates tend to go down. For example, typical European young people often wait until their late 20s or even 30s to start a family, postponing children until their education is complete and a job is in hand. They have access to effective birth control options, widely used throughout their societies. Unlike many children in the Global South, where birthrates are higher, most children born in the Global North will survive to old age with access to health care and good nutrition. Parents in the Global North do not feel as though they must have many children in order to see some grow to maturity. **Life expectancy**, the *number of years a person in a society can expect to live*, ranges widely across the world. It is 50.6 years in Chad, the nation with the lowest level, and 89.4 in Monaco, the country with the highest level of life expectancy (World Factbook 2017d).

Although some countries have birthrates below population replacement levels, the world's population continues to grow because of the skyrocketing growth rate in other countries and because of *population momentum* caused by the large number of individuals of childbearing age having children. After a baby boom, even though birthrates per couple may drop, the number of women of childbearing age becomes very high, resulting in continued growth in population size. Population growth is particularly an issue in many Global South nations in Africa, where climate change–induced desertification and surging populations have led to fierce competition for less and less fertile land and water resources (Gettleman 2017).

THINKING SOCIOLOGICALLY

Do you have a choice in how many children you will have? (Or, if you have children already, did you have a choice in how many you had?) Explain. What might influence (or what did influence) your decision to have a certain number of children? How might your decision differ if you lived in a different country? Should global patterns—which include food shortages and climate change—be a consideration in the size of your family and your neighbors' families? Why or why not?

We know this population information thanks to research gained through **demography**, *the study of human populations*. When demographers speak of **populations**, they mean *all permanent societies, states, communities, adherents of a common religious faith, racial or ethnic groups, kinship or clan groups, professions, and other identifiable categories of people*. Demographers examine various aspects of a population, including the size, location, movement, concentration in certain geographical areas, and changing characteristics. For example, the next Engaging Sociology asks you to imagine that the entire world population is only 100 people and look at how it would be composed given the current world distribution of certain characteristics.

Why did the world's population grow so slowly and then, recently, so rapidly? Sociologists look for patterns in population growth over time to answer these demographic questions.

IF THE WORLD WERE 100 PEOPLE

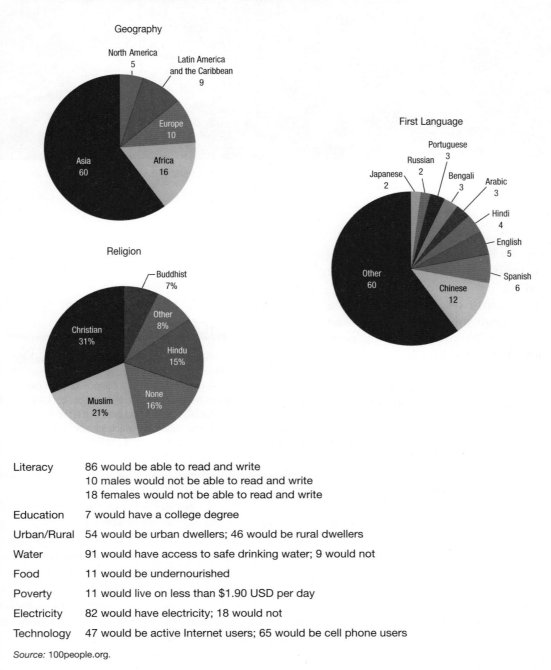

Geography

North America 5
Latin America and the Caribbean 9
Europe 10
Africa 16
Asia 60

First Language

Japanese 2
Russian 2
Portuguese 3
Bengali 3
Arabic 3
Hindi 4
English 5
Spanish 6
Chinese 12
Other 60

Religion

Buddhist 7%
Other 8%
Christian 31%
Hindu 15%
None 16%
Muslim 21%

Literacy	86 would be able to read and write
	10 males would not be able to read and write
	18 females would not be able to read and write
Education	7 would have a college degree
Urban/Rural	54 would be urban dwellers; 46 would be rural dwellers
Water	91 would have access to safe drinking water; 9 would not
Food	11 would be undernourished
Poverty	11 would live on less than $1.90 USD per day
Electricity	82 would have electricity; 18 would not
Technology	47 would be active Internet users; 65 would be cell phone users

Source: 100people.org.

Engaging Sociology

1. Did any of these facts surprise you? If so, which ones? Why? If not, where did you learn these facts?

2. In which ways are you highly privileged compared to most others in the world?

3. Which of the factors in this list cause the most suffering?

4. If you were a public sociologist and wanted to address two of these factors that affect world populations, which ones would you focus on? Why?

Patterns of Population Growth

Members of the small band of early *Homo sapiens* who inhabited the Olduvai Gorge moved gradually, haltingly, from this habitat into what are now other parts of Africa, Asia, and Europe. The process took thousands of years. At times, births outnumbered deaths and populations grew, but at other times, plagues, famines, droughts, and wars decimated populations. The large population we see today resulted from three phases of population evolution.

1. Humans, because of their thinking ability, competed satisfactorily in the animal kingdom to obtain the necessities for survival of the species.

2. With the agricultural revolution that occurred about 10,000 years ago and the resulting food surplus, mortality rates declined, and the population grew as more infants survived and people lived longer.

3. The biggest increase in population came with the Industrial Revolution, beginning about 300 years ago. Improved medical knowledge and sanitation helped bring the death rate down.

Industrialization not only brought about the social and economic changes in societies discussed in Chapter 3 (e.g., machines replacing human labor and mass production using resources in new ways), but it also led to the rapid growth of populations. The population explosion began with industrialization in Europe and spread to widely scattered areas of the globe. Figures 15.1 and 15.2 show population growth throughout history. The worldwide *rate* of population growth reached its peak in the 1960s (Countrymeters 2018). We now take a closer look at factors that impact population growth.

Predictors of Population Growth

Think for a moment about the impact that your age and sex have on your position in society and your activities. Are you of childbearing age? Do you depend on others for most of your needs, or do you support others? Your status is largely due to your age and sex and what they mean in your society. These demographic variables greatly influence your behavior and the behavior of others like you, and collectively they shape the population patterns of an entire society. In analyzing the impact of age and sex on human behavior, three concepts can be useful: youth and age dependency ratios, sex ratios, and age-sex population pyramids.

The *youth dependency ratio* is the number of children under age 15 divided by the number from 15 to 64. The

▼ FIGURE 15.1

Exponential World Population Growth From About 8000 BCE to 21st Century

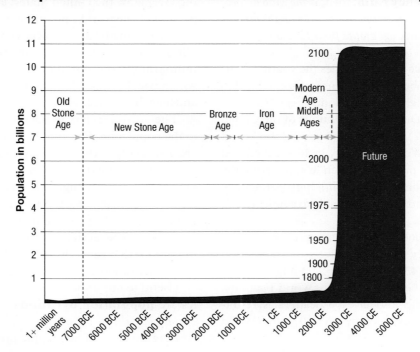

Source: Abu-Lughod 2001:50. Adapted from Fig. 2.12 in Abu-Lughod, Janet L. 1991. *Changing Cities: Urban Sociology.* New York: HarperCollins.

World Population Growth Rate, 1950–2050

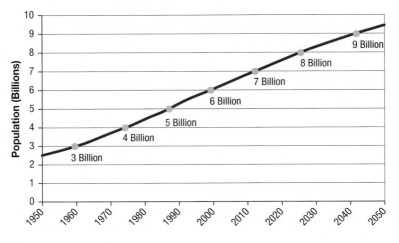

Source: U.S. Census Bureau 2015b.

age dependency ratio refers to the number of those older than 64 divided by those age 15 to 64. Although many of the world's young people under 15 help support themselves and their families, and many over 64 are likewise economically independent, these figures have been taken as the general ages when individuals are not contributing to the labor force. They represent the economic burden (especially in wealthy countries) of people in the population who must be supported by the working-age population. The **dependency ratio**, then, is *the ratio of those in both the young and aged groups compared with the number of people in the productive age groups from 15 to 64 years old* (Sengupta 2014).

In several resource-poor countries the youth dependency ratio (the number of dependent youth as related to working adults) is high. These include Niger (107.5%), Uganda (97.3), the Democratic Republic of the Congo (90.1), Zambia (89.7), and Afghanistan (82.3) (World Factbook 2017e). Working adults in less-developed countries have a tremendous burden in supporting the dependent population, especially if a high percentage of the population is urban and not able to support itself through farming.

Similarly, most Global North countries have relatively high age dependency ratios. The five with the highest age ratios are Japan (43.3%), Italy (35.1), Finland (32.4), Greece (32.2), and Germany (32.2) (World Factbook 2017e). These countries also have low death rates, resulting in an average life expectancy over 80 years (World Factbook 2017f).

Consider the case of Japan, which faces the problem of its "graying" or aging population. In 2016, 27.3%

of its population was 65 or older, and, as noted, the average life expectancy had reached 85 years (Index Mundi 2017). The death rate is higher than the birthrate, and the population is shrinking in size. Only 13% of the population is under 15 years old. With a declining population and almost no influx of immigrants, there are not enough replacement workers to support the aging population. Japan may provide a glimpse into the future for other rapidly aging societies, including Germany, the United States, and China. Thirteen percent of the world's population is age 60 and over, a rate increasing by 3% per year (United Nations 2017). These societies, however, vary in their approach to immigration and population control policies, which will impact both the demographic challenges they face and how they handle them.

The *sex ratio* refers to the ratio of males to females in the population. For instance, the more females there are, especially in their fertile years, the more potential there is for population growth. The sex ratio also determines the supply of eligible spouses. Other factors that influence marriage patterns include economic cycles, wars in which the proportion of males to females may decrease, sex-selective abortions favoring males, and migrations that generally take males from one area and add them to another.

Useful to our understanding of population dynamics are **population pyramids**, *pyramid-shaped diagrams that illustrate sex ratios and dependency ratios* (see Figure 15.3). The graphic presentation of the age and sex distribution of a population tells us a great deal about that population. The structures are called

Population Pyramids in Global North (Germany) and Global South (Uganda) Countries in 2018

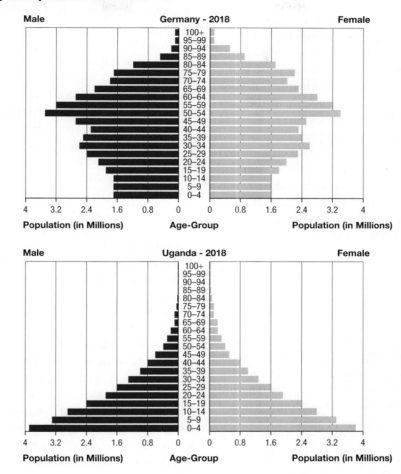

Source: Population Pyramid.net 2018a, 2018b.

pyramids because that is the shape they took until several decades ago. By looking up and down the pyramid, we can see the proportion of population at each age level. Looking to the right and left of the centerline tells us the balance of males to females at each age. The bottom line shows us the total population at each age.

The first pyramid shows the population of Germany with low birthrates and death rates. This is typical of Global North countries. The second pyramid—Uganda—is typical of Global South countries and illustrates populations with high birthrates and large dependent youth populations. As these images show, the world population has been getting both younger (the Global South) *and* older (the Global North), resulting in large numbers of people dependent on the working-age population, from 15 to 65 years of age. As Global South nations have more and more children,

they create more potential parents in later years, adding *momentum* to the world's population growth. Fewer deaths of infants and children, due to immunizations and disease control, result in lower mortality rates, younger populations, and higher potential numbers of births in the future.

THINKING SOCIOLOGICALLY

Consider your own country's population pyramid. You can find it at www.populationpyramid.net/world/2017. What can you tell about your country's age and sex ratios and level of development by studying the population pyramid? How might societies differ if they have a young versus an old population?

Population Patterns: Theoretical Explanations

The earliest historical writings reveal that interest in population size is nothing new. Scriptures written many centuries ago, such as the Quran and the Bible, encourage population growth to increase the ranks of the faithful. Of course, population expansion made sense at the time these holy tracts were written, when populations grew slowly. Government leaders throughout the ages have adopted various philosophies about the best size of populations. Ancient Greek philosopher Plato argued that the ideal city-state should have 5,040 citizens and that measures should be taken to increase or decrease the population to bring it in line with this figure (Plato [350 BCE] 1960). However, the first significant scholarly analysis that addressed global population issues came from Thomas Malthus (1766–1834), an English clergyman and social philosopher.

Malthus's Theory of Population. In his "Essay on the Principle of Population," Malthus argued that humans are driven to reproduce and will multiply excessively without checks imposed to slow population growth (Malthus [1798] 1926). He noted that an unchecked population increases geometrically: 2 parents could have 4 children, 16 grandchildren, 64 great-grandchildren, and so forth—just with a continuous average family size of 4 children. Meanwhile, the means of subsistence (food) increases at best only arithmetically or lineally (5, 10, 15, 20, 25). Therefore, population growth must be controlled. Malthus described two types of checks that control population growth: (1) positive checks that lead to higher death rates (e.g., wars, disease, epidemics, and food shortages leading to famine) and (2) preventative checks that result in lower birthrates (e.g., delaying marriage and practicing abstinence). Hoping to avoid the positive checks, Malthus advocated for implementing the preventative checks. He did not approve of contraception, viewing it as immoral.

Contemporary neo-Malthusians, like Paul and Anne Ehrlich, favor contraception rather than simple reliance on the moral restraint that Malthus proposed. They also add to the formula of "too many people and too little food" the additional problem of a "dying planet" caused by environmental damage. They argue that "the human predicament is driven by overpopulation, overconsumption of natural resources and the use of environmentally damaging technologies and socio-economic-political arrangements to service Homo Sapiens' aggregate consumption." Successfully addressing these threats and avoiding the "collapse" of global society will require dramatic cultural and political shifts across the world (Ehrlich and Ehrlich 1990, 2013:1).

Looking at the world today, we see examples of the "positive" population checks described by Malthus. War decimated the populations of several countries during the world wars and has taken its toll on other countries in Central and Eastern Europe, Africa, and the Middle East since then. Waterborne diseases, such as cholera and typhus, strike after floods, and the floods themselves are often caused by large populations clearing and using almost all the trees in their environment for fuel and building materials. Every year, famines strike parts of Africa and cause immense suffering. For example, in 2016, 50,000 children faced starvation due to famine in Somalia (World Famine Timeline 2016).

Disease has also taken a toll on the world's population. In some villages in sub-Saharan and East African countries, AIDS has wiped out large percentages of the population, and many children must fend for themselves. Orphaned children take care of their younger siblings. PEPFAR (President's Emergency Plan for AIDS Relief), begun under President George W. Bush and continued under President Barack Obama, distributes generic forms of antiviral drugs to those with AIDS and has helped bring the death toll down. Without this relief effort, the loss of life would be even more staggering in this region of the world. In his first budget proposal, President Trump sought to reduce funding for PEPFAR by 17%, but Congress passed and he signed a budget in 2018 that kept funding for PEPFAR at the same level as the previous year (Aizenman 2017; KFF 2018).

Although Malthus's work raised many issues still discussed today, his pessimistic vision of the future has not come to pass. He overemphasized *environmental determinism*, the idea that we can do little about the environment because it controls our lives. Malthus and neo-Malthusians were not able to anticipate the advances in agriculture that have increased the food supply tremendously. Nor did they foresee the importance of vaccines in controlling diseases. However, they have raised important issues that have helped government leaders in many parts of the world to plan for and take steps to control population growth.

THINKING SOCIOLOGICALLY

What are contemporary examples of what Malthus described as positive checks on population growth—war, disease, famine? Are family planning and contraception (a) suitable and (b) sufficient means to solve the problem of global overpopulation by humans? Can you think of other alternatives?

Demographic Transition: Explaining Population Growth and Expansion. Why should a change in the economic structure such as industrialization and movement from rural agricultural areas to cities have an impact on population size? The **demographic transition theory**, which *links trends in birthrates and death rates with patterns of economic and technological development*, offers one explanation. In 1929, geographer Warren Thompson first came up with this theory and included four stages. The fifth stage was added this century (Morgan 2011).

Stage 1. Populations have *high birthrates and death rates that tend to balance each other* over time. Births may outpace deaths until some disaster diminishes the increase. This has been the pattern for most of human history.

Stage 2. Populations still have high birthrates, but death rates decline (i.e., more people live longer) because of improvements in health care and sanitation, the establishment of public health programs, disease control and immunizations, and food availability and distribution. This imbalance between the continuing high number of births and the declining number of deaths means that the *population growth rate is very high*.

Stage 3. *Populations begin to level off* due to access to contraception, wage increases, urbanization, increases in education levels and the status of women, and other changes. Most industrial societies are in this stage.

Stage 4. *Birthrates and death rates are both low.* Birthrates in some Global North countries drop below replacement level, resulting in declining population. Death rates remain fairly constant and low, though lifestyle diseases caused by smoking, obesity, and lack of exercise may increase death rates in some areas.

Stage 5. This stage, which has not yet come into full existence, is emerging in some Global North societies. As death rates remain stable and birthrates decline, the total population will begin to decrease for the first time. Some Global North nations, like Japan and Germany, are in the beginning of Stage 5.

These stages are illustrated in Figure 15.4.

Demographic transition theory helps explain the developmental stages and population trends in countries around the world, but it does not consider some important factors that affect the size of populations.

1. People's age at marriage determines how many childbearing years they have. Late marriage means fewer years until menopause.

2. Contraceptive availability determines whether families can control their number of children.

3. A country's resources and land may determine how much population it can support.

▼ FIGURE 15.4

Stages of Demographic Transition

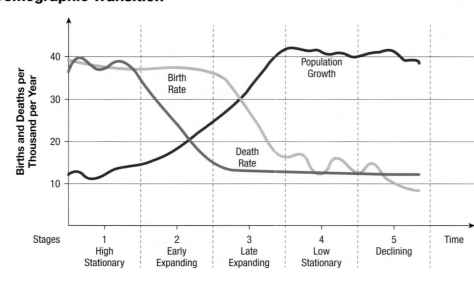

Source: SlideShare 2014.

4. The economic structure, religious beliefs, and political philosophies of a country affect attitudes toward birth control and family size.

5. Economic expansion rates influence a country's need for labor and its ability to create jobs.

The *wealth flow theory* suggests that two possible strategies operate in couples' personal decisions about family size. When wealth flows from children to parents—that is, when children are assets working on the family farm or laboring—parents have larger families. When wealth flows from parents to children—that is, when parents must support the children—families tend to have fewer children (Caldwell 1982). In the United States, middle-income, married couples who had a baby in 2015 could expect to spend $284,570 on that one offspring before the child turns 18. Note that this does *not* include college expenses (Lino 2017).

Elements of both the demographic transition and wealth flow theories describe why families in poor nations tend to have more children than those in wealthier nations. Consider the following:

1. Many poor societies are agricultural societies where more children equal more people to work the farm.

2. Poor societies have higher rates of child mortality, leading parents to have more children because they know some are likely to die at a young age.

3. Girls in poor societies tend to leave school early (if they attend at all) and to marry at a young age, leading to early and more childbearing.

4. Artificial contraception tends to be less available in poor nations.

With these facts in mind, those who study world poverty advocate for "a quality education for every child," improved health care, and access to contraceptives in poor nations (Sachs 2011, 2015, 2016).

Conflict Theorists' Explanations of Population Growth. Karl Marx did not agree with Malthus's idea that high fertility rates and population growth that outstrips food and resources produce poverty (Marx [1844] 2009). He believed that social and structural factors built into the economic system—inequitable distribution and control of resources—cause poverty. Capitalist structures lead to wealth for the owners and

▲ Overpopulation presents a challenge to food and water resources, and large populations damage the environment and provide little ecological recovery time. This photo shows the smog from fires, factories, and automobiles—called *brown haze*—that routinely hovers over Cape Town, South Africa, in the morning.

create overpopulation and poverty for workers. Workers are expendable, kept in competition for low wages, used when needed, and let go when unprofitable to capitalists. Marx's writing partner, Friedrich Engels, asserted that population growth in socialist societies could be controlled by the central government, as was done by the Chinese government when it imposed a one-child-per family policy in 1979 (Marx and Engels ([1881] 1975). (The policy in China has undergone several revisions since that time.)

Conflict theorists also point out the impact that capitalism has on the health of people living in poor areas, as exemplified by the dumping of toxic waste from industries into predominantly poor areas with high percentages of people of color. **Environmental racism**, *when environmental pollution disproportionately affects racial and ethnic minorities*, relates directly to the social status differences of groups in society. For example, in Dickson, Tennessee, a well where the African American Holt-Orsted family got their drinking water was being polluted with toxic chemicals that leaked from a nearby landfill. They continued to use this well, unaware of any problems, for 9 years. Although some of the neighbors—those who were White—were notified within 48 hours after local waste treatment agencies learned of the danger (in 1993), the Holt-Orsted family was not informed and in fact was told by county officials that things were fine (Holt 2007; Huang 2011). By the time that Sheila Holt-Orsted was finally informed (in 2002) that the water the family had been using for showering, cooking, and drinking was contaminated with cancer-causing agents, Sheila had breast cancer and her father had terminal prostate cancer. Four additional Holt-Orsted family members suffered from various other illnesses believed to be caused by the spills into the water supply. The family finally won their court case in 2011, but by then several family members had died from cancer (Holt 2007; Huang 2011).

The cost-saving measures that led to lead and other toxic chemicals leaching into the water supply in predominantly poor and racial minority Flint, Michigan, provides a more recent—and widespread—example. Over half of the Flint population is African American, and almost half of Flint residents live below the poverty line. The citizens of Flint's complaints about their discolored, foul-smelling, rash-inducing, lead-poisoning-causing water were ignored for over a year before the crisis was acknowledged (CNN 2017). As a report by the Michigan Civil Rights Commission (2017:4) notes, "the Flint water crisis is an example of environmental injustice" that would not have occurred in a more prosperous and Whiter city in Michigan.

In the United States, people of color are 2 to 3 times more likely than Whites to live in communities with hazardous waste problems and are exposed to 38% more toxins that cause cancer than are Whites (M. Bell 2012; Clark, Millet, and Marshall 2014; Mohai and Saha 2015). The Environmental Protection Agency now has an interactive environmental map that shows where U.S. low-income minority communities face the most environmental pollution (see www.epa.gov/ejscreen). Activists and researchers involved in the *environmental justice movement* work to address such problems.

One classic study in Chicago focused on the impact of efforts to make Chicago a more eco-friendly or "green" city by encouraging more recycling. However, there were substantial problems of pollution, disease risk, and other costs to the low-income, minority neighborhoods where the recycling plants were located (Pellow 2002). Today, if you send your old computer to a recycling center, it may end up on another continent—to be taken apart and burned by someone without gloves, a mask, or any other type of protection. To save money, many electronic recycling centers in Global North nations illegally hand off what they take in to people in developing nations like China, Pakistan, and Mexico, where governments are unable or unwilling to stop the unsafe disposal of e-waste. It is sobering to realize that environmentally friendly policies (recycling or donating—rather than throwing away—electronic devices) aimed at prolonging the health of Earth and the human population have often been implemented in ways that hurt those who have the fewest resources (Griner 2017; Hugo 2010; J. Korgen and Gallagher 2013).

▲ In a digital dump, a teenage boy can be seen burning electronic devices so that the metal components can be sold to local businesses. Note that he has no protective gear to wear when handling the materials.

Meso-Level Institutional Influences on Population Change

Meso-level analysis focuses on institutions and ethnic subcultures within a country. In this section, we examine how institutions influence birthrates and other population patterns. Populations change in three main ways: (1) *size* (overall number of people), (2) *composition* (the makeup of the population, including sex ratio, age distribution, and religious or ethnic representation in the population), and (3) *distribution* (density or concentration in various portions of the land).

The key *demographic processes* that cause population changes are **fertility** (*the birthrate*), **mortality** (*the death rate*), and **migration** (*movement of people from one place to another*). Populations change when births and deaths are not evenly balanced or when significant numbers of people move from one area to another. Migration does not change the size or composition of the world but can affect size or makeup in a micro- (family), meso- (institution or ethnic subculture), or macro-level (national) population. Fertility is the most easily controllable factor impacting population change.

Institutions and Population Patterns

Jeanne, one of the coauthors of this book, was riding in the back of a "mammy wagon," an open-sided truck that is a common means of transport in West Africa. Crowded in with the chickens and pigs and people, she did not expect the conversation that ensued. The man in his late 20s asked if she was married and for how long. Jeanne responded, "Yes, for 3 years." The man continued, "How many children do you have?" Jeanne answered,

▲ In an urban area in Cambodia (Kampuchea), residents crowd onto this truck, a common form of transportation. With a high fertility rate and migration from rural to urban areas, crowded transportation is common.

"None." The man commented, "Oh, I'm sorry!" Jeanne replied, "No, don't be sorry. We planned it that way!" This man had been married for 10 years to a woman 3 years younger than him and had eight children. The ninth was on the way. In answer to his pointed questions, Jeanne explained that she was not being cruel to her husband and that birth control was what prevented children, and no, it did not make sex less enjoyable. He expressed surprise that limiting the number of children was possible and rather liked the idea. He jumped at the suggestion that he visit the family planning clinic in the city. With his meager income, he and his wife were finding it hard to feed all their children. This story helps to illustrate the fact that knowledge of and access to family planning options are not uniformly available. Institutions affect access to those services.

Demographers consider micro-, meso-, and macro-level factors in attempting to understand fertility rates around the world. In the United States, almost half of all pregnancies are unplanned (Fine and Zolner 2016). Lack of access to contraception and laws affecting individual fertility decisions contribute to unexpected pregnancies in the United States and elsewhere (Tavernise 2015). As the use of effective, long-term contraceptives, particularly intrauterine devices, has gone up in the United States, the rate of unintended pregnancies has declined (Fine and Zolner 2016). Couples' decisions to use or not use contraception, their ideas about the acceptability of abortion, and whether they want to have children (and how many) can also have an impact on national and global rates of population change. So choices at the micro level make a difference at the macro level. Consider the following meso-level institutional factors affecting the size of the population.

Economic Factors and Population Patterns. Fertility fluctuates with actions in meso-level institutions such as the economy and the government. During economic depressions, for example, the rate of fertility tends to drop due to lack of family resources. Also, government policies to encourage or discourage births and access to health care influence decisions within families about fertility. For example, in the state of Colorado, the rate of teenagers giving birth dropped 40% and the abortion rate among teenagers fell 42% after Colorado (through a private grant) provided free intrauterine devices and implants to poor women and teenagers (Tavernise 2015).

The economic prosperity of nations also influences population growth. Figure 15.5 compares population trends in affluent Global North regions of the world—like Europe and North America—with the less affluent Global South regions—like Africa, Latin America, and Oceania, where poverty is widespread (Roser 2016).

THINKING SOCIOLOGICALLY

What does Figure 15.5 tell you about the lives of individuals in these different regions of the world?

Political Systems and Population Patterns. Some governments provide incentives to parents to have more children through *pronatalist policies* (those that encourage fertility), whereas others discourage high fertility with *antinatalist policies* (those that discourage fertility). Thus, meso-level social policies established by the political system can shape decisions of families at the micro level. Government policies can take several forms: (a) manipulating contraceptive availability; (b) promoting change in factors that affect fertility such as the status of women, education, availability of abortion, and degree of economic development; (c) using propaganda for or against having children; (d) creating incentives (parental leaves, benefits such as medical care and housing, and tax breaks) or penalties (such as fines) for having children; and (e) passing laws governing age of marriage, size of family, contraception, and abortion.

Antinatalist policies arise out of concern over available resources and differences in birthrates among population subgroups (particularly among those deemed inferior by the people in power). Throughout the 20th century in the

Population Growth by World Regions: 1950 to 2050

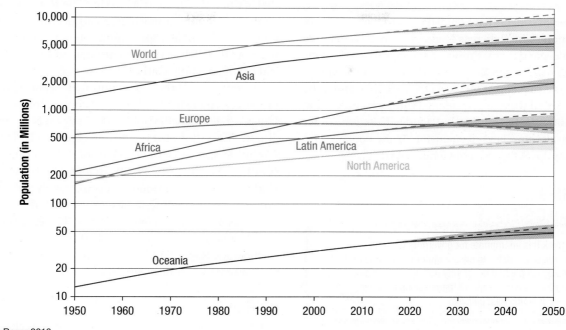

Source: Roser 2016.

Note: Based on United Nations population projections. Nearly all population growth will be in the Global South, though in Asia and Latin America it is leveling off. The dotted lines and shaded areas indicate speculation for trends that could vary depending on possible changes in key variables.

United States, federally financed sterilization programs operated in 60% of states and in Puerto Rico. Women from minority groups—including immigrant, American Indian, Hispanic, and Black women—and poor, disabled, imprisoned, or mentally ill women were targeted. Forced sterilizations are no longer legal but are still not unheard of in the United States. From 2006 to 2010, at least 148 women in California prisons underwent forced sterilization (Ko 2016; Krase 2014; Walden 2013).

As noted earlier, China instituted its antinatalist policy, which included the "one child" rule, in 1979. The government has discouraged traditional preferences for early marriage, large families, and many sons by using fines, group pressure, privileges for small families, and easy availability of birth control and abortion. The government has reduced the fertility rate to 1.55 children per family (World Factbook 2015).

Some of the results of the Chinese antinatalist policies were unanticipated, however. For a variety of reasons (including a lack of government support for the elderly), male babies tend to be preferred more than female babies. Faced with a limit of one child, many people decided to abort girls. Because of the policy, China now faces a rapidly aging population in which many

men will have difficulty finding a woman to marry. In 2014, the government began to allow parents to have a second child, if the mother or father was an only child (McKenzie 2015).

Examples of pronatalist government policies can be seen in Eastern Europe where governments are worried about the drop in birthrates. There are fewer young people to pay taxes and to do jobs needed in the society. Pronatalist policies established to raise birthrates include giving workers a day off to "have sex," free summer camps for young couples (without condoms), cars and monetary gifts for new parents, and additional benefits for parents and their children. Abortions and even birth control have been restricted in some Eastern European countries to curb dropping population numbers (Stracansky 2013). In the nation of Georgia, whose population fell from over 5 million in 1989 to 3.7 million in 2014, a nonprofit organization has set up a national online dating website. Singapore has put a limit on the number of small, one-bedroom apartments to force more people to live together (and procreate). South Korea, meanwhile, is expanding its government-supported child care programs as part of its efforts to grow its declining population.

In the United States, it is sometimes hard to pin a simple label of antinatalist or pronatalist on the administration in power. Over the past couple of decades, however, Republican presidents have tended to restrict birth control and abortion rights, whereas Democratic presidents have moved to expand them. President Obama enacted a contraception mandate in 2012 that declared contraception part of basic preventive medical coverage that should be available for all women. President Trump rescinded that mandate after he took office, but a judge halted the order while considering a lawsuit against it. As the book went to press in late 2018, the order remained halted.

THINKING SOCIOLOGICALLY

Do you think it is appropriate for governments to use enticements or penalties to encourage or discourage fertility decisions by couples? Why, or why not? Identify several possible positive and negative repercussions of either pronatalist or antinatalist policies.

Religion and Population Patterns. Religion is a primary shaper of norms and values in most societies, including those related to fertility. In some societies, children born out of wedlock are accepted into the mother's family. In other societies, a woman can be stoned to death for having a child or even sex out of wedlock.

Some religious groups oppose any intervention, such as birth control or abortion, in the natural processes of

© CHAIDEER MAHYUDDIN/AFP/Getty Images

▲ Nur Azizah binti Hanafiah, 22, receives a punishment of caning for having premarital sex with her boyfriend. Her community in the Aceh region of Indonesia follows a form of Islamic sharia law. In some societies, she would have been stoned to death for having premarital sex.

conception and birth. Roman Catholicism, for example, teaches that large families are a blessing from God and that artificial birth control is a sin. The Roman Catholic Church officially advocates natural family planning (NFP) to regulate conception, a less reliable method than "artificial" birth control, using medication, or physical barriers. Many Catholics, however, do use artificial birth control, and the recent outbreak of the Zika virus presents a challenge to the ban on contraceptives. In the United States, only 2% of Catholics rely on NFP whereas almost 70% rely on the birth control pill, an IUD (intrauterine device), or sterilization to control their family size (Guttmacher Institute 2013). In a poll by Unavision of Catholics on five continents, approximately 90% in four out of the five continents disagreed with the Catholic Church's teaching on contraceptives. The exception was Africa where, among those polled in Uganda and the Democratic Republic of Congo, only 44% disagreed with the Church's teaching on birth control (Unavision 2014).

Education and Population. If a country wants to control population growth, providing better access to schools and raising the education level of women is a key to success. The higher women's status in society—as measured by education level and job opportunities—the lower their fertility rate (Population Reference Bureau 2013b; Pradhan 2015; Testa 2014). Figure 15.6 shows the relationship between education and family size in five Global South countries (Population Reference Bureau 2016). Note that the higher the education level, the lower the fertility rate and population growth.

Lower population growth means less pressure on governments to provide emergency services, such as food and water rations, for booming populations, and more attention to services such as schools, health care, and jobs. Most population experts encourage governments and other meso-level institutions in fast-growing countries to act aggressively to control population size. Consequences of population fluctuations affect affluent parts of the world as well as poor parts. The impact of the baby boom in the United States illustrates this, as discussed in the next Sociology in Our Social World.

THINKING SOCIOLOGICALLY

Discuss what impact the baby boom and boomer echo have had on your opportunities for education and a career. How will retirements among Baby Boomers affect your opportunities?

THE SIGNIFICANCE OF THE BABY BOOM

At the end of World War II, the birthrate shot up temporarily in most countries involved in the war, as many young people who had been forced to delay marriage made up for lost time. The postwar economy was growing, people were employed in relatively well-paying positions, and the norms supported large families. In the United States, this baby boom lasted for 17 years, from 1946 to 1963.

The baby boom phenomenon has had many impacts. During the late 1960s, school boards and contractors were busy building schools to educate the growing number of children. By the 1980s, student numbers declined, and towns were consolidating schools and closing buildings. When the Baby Boomers entered the job market starting in the mid-1960s, there were great numbers of applicants for jobs, and employers could pay less. The supply was so great they were assured that someone would take the job.

Two decades later, it was much easier for young people to find jobs because there were fewer of them in that age range looking for entry-level positions. However, in some fields, Boomers in high-level positions have put off retirement, thus preventing younger workers from

taking their positions and earning higher incomes. In addition, trends in marketing and advertising have, for years, been dictated by the Baby Boomer generation because they are such a large segment of the consumer public.

By the 1960s, people's views of the ideal family size and the proper age for marriage changed. Zero-population-growth movements and environmental concerns slowed the rate of growth. The period from the late 1960s to early 1970s has been referred to as a "baby bust" or the "birth dearth." This fluctuation resulted in a population structure that did not look very much like a pyramid, as shown in Figure 15.8 on page 475.

In the mid-1970s and into the 1980s, when the baby boom generation started having babies, there was another baby boom—or a "boomer echo"—but it was much smaller because the Baby Boomers had smaller families. Currently, growth in the overall size of the U.S. population is due largely to immigration. White non-Hispanic deaths now outpace White non-Hispanic births. If not for immigration, the population in the United States might have actually begun to decline.

▼ FIGURE 15.6

Women's Education and Family Size—Selected Countries

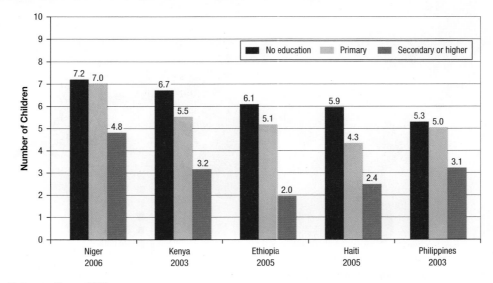

Source: Population Reference Bureau 2016.

Factors Affecting Mortality Rates

Recall that life expectancy refers to the average number of years a person in a society can expect to live. It indicates the overall health conditions in a country. Imagine living in Chad, Africa, where the life expectancy at birth is 57.5 years. In this low-income, largely agricultural society, families tend to have many children (5.9, on average). Of every 1,000 babies born alive, 71.7 will die within the first year. Most men and women live in rural areas, where most are subsistence farmers, working small plots that may not provide enough food to keep their families from starving (The World Factbook 2017a). When one plot is overfarmed and the soil depleted so that plants will no longer grow, the family moves to another and clears the land, depleting more arable land and cutting down trees that results in erosion of rich soil. This scenario repeats itself, leading to little arable land, food shortages, malnutrition, and a population susceptible to illnesses and disease. The limited medical care that exists is mostly available in urban areas.

Some other African countries face similar situations, with life expectancy in South Africa at 63.8, Zimbabwe at 60.4, and Somalia at 52.8. Average life expectancy for sub-Saharan Africa as a whole is about 59 years (The World Factbook 2017f).

▲ A sick and displaced Chadian woman watches as her malnourished infant sleeps at a health clinic run by Doctors without Borders. This mother knows that life expectancy for her child is less than 50 years and that many children die in infancy.

Why are these societies so dramatically different from Global North countries, many of which have average life expectancies into the 80s? The low life expectancy stems from lack of medical care, epidemics such as Ebola and AIDS, wars and civil strife, corrupt governments, droughts and famine, malnutrition, resulting susceptibility to diseases, and high infant mortality. Figure 15.7 shows the number of children who die before the age of 1 (per 1,000 live births) for various regions of

▼ FIGURE 15.7

Infant Mortality Rates Around the World (per 1,000 Live Births), 2018

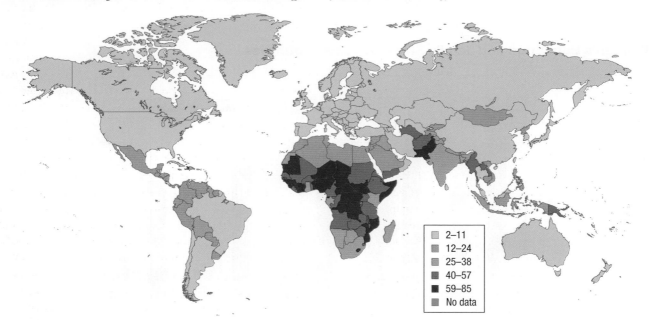

Legend:
- 2–11
- 12–24
- 25–38
- 40–57
- 59–85
- No data

Source: Population Reference Bureau (PRB), "Infant Mortality Rate Per 1,000 Live Births, 2018" (Washington, DC: PRB, 2018). All rights reserved. Reproduced by permission.

the world. This is another key indicator of a country's overall well-being.

Even within Global North nations, mortality rates can vary according to social class, geography, and social policies. In the United States, the life expectancy of the richest continues to rise—and pull away from that of the poor. The gap in life expectancy between the top 1% and bottom 1% in income in the United States has increased since 2001 (when it was 2.3% for men and 2.9% for women) to the current 14.6 years for men and 10.1 years for women. The good news is that new studies show that social policies can influence life expectancy for poor people. Those who live in areas with higher government expenditures and more positive health behaviors (such as lower smoking rates) have much higher life expectancy rates than those who live in other areas of the nation (Chetty et al. 2016).

Migration and Mobility: Where People Move and Why

Most of us have moved one or more times in our lives, a process called migration. Perhaps we have moved to a larger house down the block, maybe to another area for a job opportunity or school, or even to another country altogether. Over the history of the human race, people have migrated to the far reaches of the globe. Because of adaptability to climatic and geographic barriers, humans have dispersed to more areas of the world than any other species. Even inhospitable locations such as the Arctic North and the South Pole have human settlements.

As noted in previous chapters, the *push-pull* model points out that some people are pushed from their original locations by wars, plagues, famine, political or religious conflicts, economic crises, or other factors and pulled to new locations by economic opportunities or political and religious tolerance. Most people do not leave a location unless they have been forced out or have a viable alternative in the new location. They weigh the benefits of moving versus the costs.

Migration is often initiated at the micro level: A lucrative job offer in another location requires a move, the family dwelling becomes too small, a relative needs help, or a family member's health requires a different climate. However, if the risks are high, if the information about migration is scarce, or if the move involves negative factors such as leaving family, individuals may decide to stay put. Rational choice theorists focus on how individuals' assessment of costs and benefits impacts migration patterns.

Although the decision to move is often a micro-level personal or family one, the macro-level sociocultural

© Getty/Hoberman Collection/Contributor

▲ Humans are able to live in and have dispersed to some very inhospitable places, like Antarctica, where there is no sunshine at all for five to six months of the year, and temperatures have dropped as low as −135.8 degrees Fahrenheit. Antarctic communities are mostly research stations.

environment also influences it. Examples of large groups of people leaving an area because of aspirations to improve their life chances; hopes of retaining a way of life; or expulsion by political, economic, or religious forces have existed throughout history. Chinese railroad workers came to the United States for economic reasons. Amish and Mennonite settlers from Europe sought religious freedom and preservation of their way of life. The Amish, a group originating in Germany, left Germany en masse to find religious freedom, and members of this group now live entirely in North America. Italian immigration to the United States took place in a collective manner. When a family left Italy, they would usually move to a U.S. city where a relative, friend, or acquaintance lived. Thus, residents of entire apartment buildings in the North End of Boston were from the same extended family, and entire city blocks of people came from the same town or region of southern Italy (Gans 1962). Many European countries are multicultural environments today because of immigrants from former colonies.

Those living at the receiving end have not always been welcoming and in fact have often tried to isolate the newcomers in ghettos, preventing them from moving into other neighborhoods. Especially in difficult economic times, when competition for jobs is greatest, newcomers may find few employment opportunities (Foner 2005). Immigration laws in the United States reflect the nation's attitudes toward immigrants at different periods. The United States tended to welcome immigrants during boom economic times and tried to repel them during recessions and depressions. Exclusionary acts include the Chinese Exclusion Act of 1882, which ended Chinese immigration; the Gentlemen's Agreement of 1907, which halted Japanese immigration; and the National Origins Act of 1924, which heavily restricted immigration from Southern and Eastern Europe and excluded non-Whites.

The Immigration and Nationality Act of 1965 abolished the policies that excluded Asians, Africans, and Latin Americans and based immigration policy on family relationships and skills. Current debates in the U.S. Congress over immigration reform, however, reveal the persistent contentious nature of policies related to immigration, including undocumented migration from Latin America.

Social scientists study the impact of immigration, pointing out that immigration tends to yield significant economic gains for receiving countries, particularly employers (while native workers can face tighter job markets and lower pay because of greater competition for jobs) (Borjas 2016). Scholars who study migration—especially long-distance migration that involves crossing into another society—point out that migrants are usually hardworking, ambitious, optimistic, and healthy, for it takes considerable courage, motivation, and wherewithal to undertake a migration to a new land.

A recent study of immigrants to the United States shows people born elsewhere who later acquire U.S. citizenship are more likely than their native-born neighbors to marry, less likely to divorce, and more likely to avoid poverty. In the 10 poorest U.S. states, native-born citizens earn just $0.84 to every $1 earned by naturalized citizens. In the richest states, the ratio is $0.97 to $1. One reason for this difference in earnings comes from the fact that foreign-born naturalized citizens tend to bring with them the tools and attitudes they need to be successful.

▲ After crossing the Aegean Sea from Turkey on an inflatable boat in 2015, Syrian refugees arrive on the Greek island of Lesbos. Despite horrible weather and rough seas, migrants and refugees are risking their lives—and those of their children—in search of a better life within the European Union.

They had to have the wherewithal to leave their home country, find sponsors in the United States, navigate visa and green card requirements, and fulfill the requirements for U.S. citizenship. Those who can do all that tend to be self-reliant and willing to take risks, and have an entrepreneurial spirit (Bureau of Labor Statistics 2017b; Giridharadas 2014).

International Migration. Today, 244 million people, or 3.3% of the world's population, are migrants, people living in an area of the world different from the place of their birth. Half are women. These migrants change the size and characteristics of populations around the world, expanding some and emptying out others (Connor 2016).

International migration is especially common where political turmoil, wars, famines, or natural disasters ravage a country. More than 50 million migrants are *refugees*, those who flee in search of safety in times of war, political oppression, natural disaster, or religious persecution. Today, there are more refugees in the world than at any time since World War II.

The ongoing crisis in Syria has added significantly to the number of refugees. By July 2017, almost 5.5 million Syrians had registered as refugees with the United Nations (UNHCR 2017b). The tiny nations of Jordan and Lebanon have taken in well over 660,000 and 1 million refugees, respectively. Ten percent of the Jordanian population now consists of refugees, and that number increases daily (UNHCR 2015, 2017c).

THINKING SOCIOLOGICALLY

Think about your grandparents or great-grandparents. How long have your ancestors occupied the same house or lived in the same community? Do they go back more than one generation on the same property? If they have been mobile, what factors were critical in their decision to move? How has their mobility or stability influenced your family's experiences? How were they received in their new home?

Micro-Level Population Patterns

Understanding demography can be extremely important for comprehending social processes in your everyday life. Although most Global North countries do not have massive famines or population explosions, population fluctuations influence them in many ways. Consider the life choices you will make regarding education, employment, and retirement.

The wife of Keith, one of the coauthors of this book, once taught in a suburban school system at a time when the fertility rate was falling. The elementary school where she taught had four first-grade classrooms, with 28 children per room—112 first graders in the school. By the next year, the school felt the decline in the fertility rate 6 years earlier, and the number of first graders declined. Within 4 years, there were only 40 first graders in her school, with two classrooms and only 20 students per class. Some school systems lost half of their student population in a few years. One year, first-grade teachers were losing their jobs or having to move to another grade, and the next year, it was second-grade teachers who were scrambling. The third year, third-grade teachers were in oversupply, and so forth. With low demand, these were not times for college students to be pursuing teaching careers. A personal decision was being influenced by population trends—and this pattern continues.

We have already mentioned the impact of the baby boom (the high fertility rates from 1946 to about 1963) and the following baby bust (the drop in fertility for more than a decade following the baby boom). The population pyramid of the United States reveals the impact on the population (see Figures 15.8 and 15.9). As we can see, the U.S. population no longer looks anything like a pyramid. From these figures, we can tell a great deal about job prospects, retirement security, career decisions, and other outcomes of demographic changes. As that bulge for the Baby Boomer group moves into the senior citizens' category, society will have new challenges.

Retirement is another topic for which population patterns are critical. When Social Security was established in the United States in the 1930s, life expectancy from birth was 58 for men and 62 for women. The number of people in the age-dependent categories of under 15 and over 65 was low. For each person who received Social Security in 1945, 42 workers paid Social Security taxes. Forty people, each paying $255 a year, could easily support a retired person, receiving $10,000 per year. However, the average life expectancy has shifted, and the age-dependent population has increased (Social Security Administration 2013). In 2016, for every beneficiary of Social Security, just 2.3 workers paid Social Security taxes (Peter J. Petersen Foundation 2016). When commentators and politicians say Social Security is in trouble, they refer to problems created by changes in the composition of the U.S. population.

In the 1980s, the U.S. administration and Congress saw the problem coming and for the first time began to save funds in a Social Security account for the Baby Boomers. They also passed laws requiring Baby Boomers to work longer before they qualify for Social Security. The fact that there are so many Baby Boomers—and that an extremely high percentage of citizens over the age of 65 vote—makes

▼ FIGURE 15.8

United States, 2018

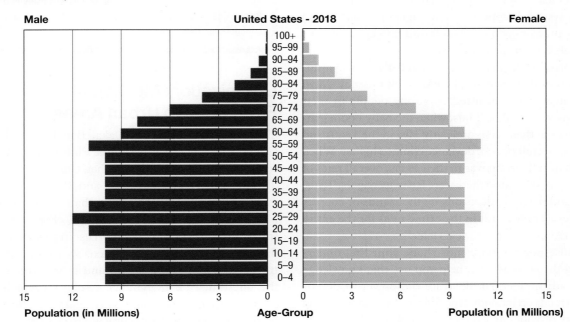

Source: Index Mundi 2015; PopulationPyramid.net 2018a.

United States, 2050

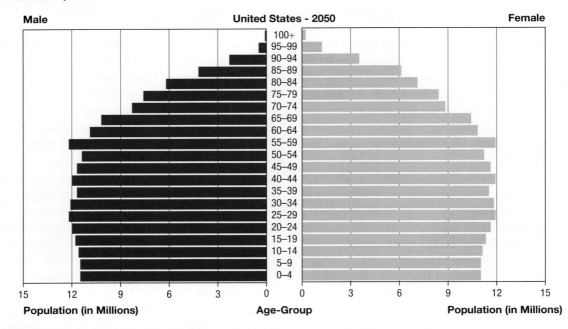

Source: Nationmaster 2011, "United States Population Pyramids"; PopulationPyramid.net 2018b.

it unlikely that the government will cut back on benefits to this group. Still, members of the younger generation may not receive as much Social Security income as do current retirees. Meanwhile, Medicare, the insurance program for retired adults, has less money on hand than does the Social Security system. It appears that the aging population and need for funds may have a profound influence on your own family budget and retirement.

As noted in Chapter 6, population patterns also influence rates of deviance and juvenile delinquency. Most deviant acts are committed by young people in their mid-teens to early 20s. Thus, when the baby boom generation was in their teens and early 20s, in the 1960s and 1970s, the overall rates of deviance climbed higher. When the birth dearth group was in their teens, overall rates of crime dropped because there were fewer teenagers. Thus, private and personal decisions by thousands of couples (micro level) may result in the crime rates for the entire country rising or falling 15 years later.

Because population trends shape your life, understanding those trends can help you use that knowledge to your advantage. To illustrate the power of demographic trends on individual decisions, the next Engaging Sociology provides an exercise in problem-solving using information from population pyramids of U.S. cities.

THINKING SOCIOLOGICALLY

Why do population experts predict the population pyramid will look like Figure 15.9 by 2050? What factors in society might lead to this? What kinds of problems do you think this sort of configuration might cause?

Urbanization: Movement From Rural to Urban Areas

Tokyo-Yokohama, Japan; Daka, Bangladesh; Tianjin, China; Moscow, Russia; Manila, Philippines; Mumbai, India; Karachi, Pakistan; Shanghai, China; and Istanbul, Turkey are *megacities* (cities and their surrounding metropolitan areas with more than 10 million people) (CityMayors 2018). They are characterized by traffic congestion and people rushing to their destinations. Carts, bicycles, and taxis weave in and out of traffic jams. The local spices and other aromas scent the air. Sidewalk merchants display vegetables and fruits unique to the country. Beggars and the homeless, often migrants from rural areas, dot the sidewalks, and merchants sell colorful wares. Cities provide a

POPULATION PYRAMIDS AND PREDICTING COMMUNITY NEEDS AND SERVICES

Study these three population pyramids. Based on what you see, answer the following questions:

1. Which community would likely have the lowest crime rate? Explain.

2. Which community would likely have the most cultural amenities (theaters, art galleries, concert halls, and so forth)? Explain.

3. Imagine you were an entrepreneur planning on starting a business in one of these communities.

   a. Name three businesses that you think would succeed in each community. Explain.

   b. Name one business that you think would not succeed in each community. Explain.

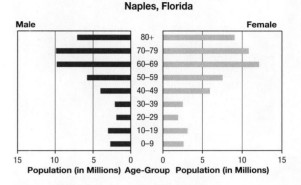

(Hint: Naples is a major retirement community.)

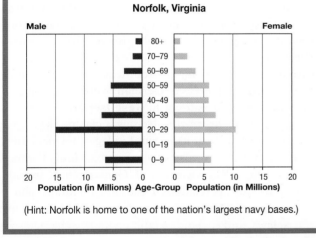

(Hint: Norfolk is home to one of the nation's largest navy bases.)

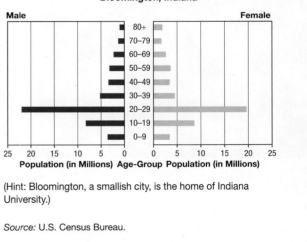

(Hint: Bloomington, a smallish city, is the home of Indiana University.)

Source: U.S. Census Bureau.

kaleidoscope of humanity as more of the world's population becomes urban.

With few jobs to support populations in rural areas (areas outside of cities and their surrounding suburbs), many people move to cities in hopes of finding employment. This *pattern of movement from rural areas to cities* is called **urbanization**. Today, more than half of all people in the world live in urban areas, and projections indicate that 7 out of 10 people will do so by 2050 (WHO 2013b).

The U.S. Census breaks down the geographic regions of the nation into urbanized areas (50,000 or more),

urban clusters (2,500–50,000), and rural areas (all nonurban areas). In 1900, 60.4% of Americans lived in nonurban, or rural, areas, whereas in 1960, 36% did so (U.S. Census Bureau 1995). By 2015, just 18.4% of the population lived in rural parts of the country, whereas 81.6% resided in urban areas (The World Factbook 2017g). The move from rural to urban areas has always stemmed from the increased opportunities for employment and investment that come with living around more people. Globalization has made this more important than ever, as markets and job opportunities have become transnational.

© SAJAD HUSSAIN/AFP/Getty Images

▲ In Mumbai many children have no choice but to sleep on the streets each night.

Population growth often spurs job growth. For example, in the United States, all but one of the 10 urban areas with the most population growth from 2000 to 2010 also increased its number of jobs. The exception was Atlanta, which had a slight decline (Kotkin 2013; Kotkin and Cox 2011). In many parts of the Global South, however, the rural poor who come to cities to find opportunities often just find disappointment and squalor. Many find themselves living without running water and electricity. Some do not even have access to a toilet.

Megacities around the world are part of urbanization, a global trend that has gained momentum over several centuries. The next Engaging Sociology feature invites you to explore some consequences of major urbanization trends in the world (Brunn et al. 2011).

Urbanization accompanies *modernization*, transformation from traditional, mostly agrarian societies to contemporary bureaucratized states, and *industrialization*, transformation from an agricultural base and handmade goods to manufacturing industries. We explore urbanization in this section as a demographic trend that has major social implications for how people live and interact.

Most people live their lives in *communities*: locations that provide dwellings, a sense of identity and belonging, neighbors and friends, social involvements, and access to necessities. Our most intimate microlevel interactions take place in these communities. Yet our communities also connect us to larger meso- and macro-level social structures, such as political and religious organizations, world health organizations, and international relief agencies (e.g., UNICEF). In this section, we consider the development of communities—from rural areas and small towns to urban areas such as megacities.

Cities as Micro-Level Living Environments

In the 17th and 18th centuries, when Europe was undergoing dramatic changes, small villages contrasted sharply with the rapidly growing urban centers. Ferdinand Tönnies (1855–1936) described these two extreme types of living environments on a continuum from **Gemeinschaft**, a German word indicating *a small traditional community*, to **Gesellschaft**, meaning *a large, impersonal urban area*. He saw social life as an evolution from family units to rural villages, towns, cities, nations, and finally cosmopolitan urban life (Tönnies [1887] 1963). Key elements of Gemeinschaft include family, friendship, relations to the land, common values, and traditions. On the other hand, formal relations, contracts, laws, and economies built on money characterize Gesellschaft. People in urban areas do not necessarily know one another or share common values. They tend to be employees of bureaucratic organizations and act as individuals rather than members of a collectivity.

A number of other theorists living in the Europe of the 19th century suggested similar contrasts between rural and urban life. Émile Durkheim (1858–1917) described the social bonds that held society together and the changes that arose from industrialization and urbanization. As discussed in Chapter 3, *mechanical solidarity* was Durkheim's term for the glue that holds a society together through shared beliefs, values, and traditions typical of rural areas and simple societies. In mechanical solidarity, social bonds were formed by homogeneity of thought.

ENGAGING SOCIOLOGY

WORLD URBANIZATION TRENDS

World Urbanization Prospects are reports published by the United Nations Population Division. They provide valuable data on past, present, and future urbanization trends in regions and subregions of the world. They also provide data on individual cities and urban areas. Consider the impact of major migration trends on the environment, friends and relatives left behind, dual-worker families, maintaining one's culture, new cultural ideas spreading, and more. The major findings of the most recent World Urbanization Prospects follow in Figures 15.10 and 15.11.

Engaging Sociology, Figure 15.10

- What do you learn from these graphs about world urbanization trends? Which continents seem to be urbanizing most rapidly?

- How might these trends affect people moving to urban areas?

- What might be some effects on global climate change, the possibility of globally transmitted diseases, political stability or instability, or the global economy?

- How might the global trend toward urbanization affect your own life?

Engaging Sociology, Figure 15.11

- When the size of the rural population declines, how might it affect the culture of a nation?

- Identify two positive and two negative consequences of this urbanization trend for a nation.

▼ FIGURE 15.10

Percentage of Population Residing in Urban Areas

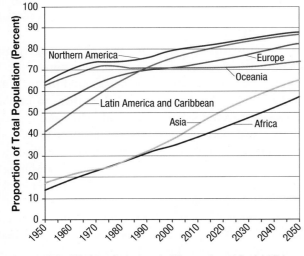

Source: United Nations, Department of Economic and Social Affairs, Population Division (2014). *World Urbanization Prospects: The 2014 Revision, Highlights.* Reprinted with the permission of the United Nations.

▼ FIGURE 15.11

Urban and Rural Population of the World, 1950–2050

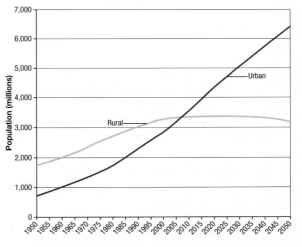

Source: United Nations, Department of Economic and Social Affairs, Population Division (2014). *World Urbanization Prospects: The 2014 Revision, Highlights.* Reprinted with the permission of the United Nations.

The social glue that holds modern industrial and postindustrial societies and people together is *organic solidarity*, the social coherence (glue) based on a division of labor with each member playing a highly specialized role in the society and each person depending on others due to interrelated, interdependent tasks. This interdependence of specialized tasks is the key to unity in more complex societies.

▲ This scene in Central Park, New York City, is possible because urban planners of the 19th century had the foresight to include several sizeable parks in the plans for the city.

THINKING SOCIOLOGICALLY

Consider a small town and a large city with which you are familiar. Do they seem to have unity and coherence based on organic or mechanical solidarity? Do the notions of Gemeinschaft and Gesellschaft seem to apply to them?

Life in the City

How does urban life affect people's thoughts and behavior? Sociologist Georg Simmel argued that two factors—the intensity and stimulation of city life and the economic effects on urban relations—cause people to have different attitudes, beliefs, and values from those in rural areas (Simmel [1902–1917] 1950). He thought that city dwellers have no choice but to be somewhat insensitive, to avoid intense relationships, and to keep most social relationships superficial to protect their privacy. However, he did not feel this was necessarily negative. Cities free people from the social constraints of close relationships in small towns. To visitors or strangers to city life, these behaviors seem callous and cold. However, they offer anonymity and freedom in a crowded environment (Goffman [1959] 2001).

Because urban residents live in heterogeneous, high-density areas, they seem to develop coping mechanisms for dealing with the people around them (Wirth 1964). They become removed from others to insulate themselves from too many personal claims and expectations. The depersonalization that results from lower commitment to a common community "goal" also leads to a higher tolerance for nonconformity in cities, resulting in more individual freedom and, as a result, a higher level of deviance (Wirth 1964).

Tolerance for nonconformity also promotes diverse subcultures. The larger numbers of people in cities make it possible for individuals with similar interests—from ethnic subcultures to LGBTQIA communities to artist groups—to draw together as clubs, organizations, or neighborhoods. These little social worlds "touch but do not interpenetrate" according to Claude Fischer (1984:37). If there are enough members of a group, each can maintain its own identity. So rather than creating isolated individuals who interact defensively with others, urban life may create choices about lifestyle and enhance a different kind of community base, intensifying the interactions.

As noted, for most of human history, humans lived in rural areas. *Rural sociology* considers patterns and behaviors among people at a distance from population centers. Over the past 3 centuries, and increasing rapidly over the past few decades, a rural exodus has been under way, with movement from rural to urban areas with more economic opportunities and better health care and education. Major population shifts from rural to urban areas came with industrialization in Europe and North America, followed by the same process in other areas of the world.

The early interpretations of urbanization, especially by European sociologists, were made through a rather pessimistic lens. The trend was seen largely as a decline of civil society. However, there are pluses as well as minuses in quality of life as people inhabit more densely populated areas. We consume less energy if we live in densely populated areas because there are fewer people using individual transportation (cars) to get to destinations because shared public transit is more possible. Many city planners have worked to make cities more habitable and "green," to encourage more people to live closer together in cities.

What do you see as the most important ways urban living impacts individuals or groups?

How Did Cities Evolve? Meso-Level Organizational Structures

Human settlements have gone through massive transitions over the past 100,000 years, from small agricultural settlements to bustling crowded metropolises with millions of people. The first step toward the development of urban life came when those living nomadic lives became more settled. Archaeological evidence indicates that the earliest settlements were in the Middle East and North Africa, about 125,000 years ago, when human nomads followed rivers into Arabia (Global Arab Network 2010). Other early settlements have been excavated in Ethiopia, Morocco, United Arab Emirates, South Africa, Pakistan, and Israel.

Starting about 10,000 years ago, with the advent of agriculture, domestication of animals, and the shift from food gathering to food production, small groups established permanent settlements. The settlements we recognize as cities today began to develop. *Cities* are large permanent settlements with nonagricultural specialists, a literate elite, and surplus food to support the social classes not involved in food production. In addition to having larger populations than the surrounding areas, they also perform functions (e.g., administrative, commercial, and cultural) for the larger geographic area.

Types of Cities

Organizational structures of cities have changed and evolved over time; in the following sections we focus on industrial and postindustrial cities.

Industrial Cities. The onset of industrialization in 17th- and 18th-century Europe started the trend toward urbanized nations, countries in which more than half of the population lives in urban areas. Rural peasants migrated to the cities in search of opportunities and to escape the tedium and poverty of agricultural existence and shortage of available farmland. A rapid influx of migrants often resulted in an unplanned urbanization process. Crowded conditions, poor sanitation, polluted water supplies, and poor working conditions all contributed to the misery of poor urban residents and to their short life expectancy compared with those living in the countryside.

Industrial cities became primarily commercial centers motivated by competition, a characteristic that differentiated them from preindustrial cities. The advent of power-driven machinery and the new capitalist factory system transformed and replaced the former craft and cottage industries and guild structures (Abu-Lughod 1991). Roads, waterways, and railroads made travel and communication between towns and cities easier and faster.

Around 1870, Great Britain became the first truly urban nation with more than 50% of the population living in urban areas. Economically changing conditions in the British Isles were conducive to urbanization and industrialization. Parliament had passed "enclosure acts" that enclosed common land people used for growing crops, so that they were clearly owned by just one person or family. Those who used to use those lands (but did not own them) to farm or pasture animals could no longer make a living and were pushed from the countryside to seek employment in cities. In addition, raw materials from colonies; new technology for manufacturing; and financing for industry were all falling into place (Benevolo 1995; Mumford 1961).

In the late 19th century in the United States, an increase in agricultural productivity aided urban growth. Fewer farms began to produce much more food than ever before, and the development of roads, trains, and other efficient means of transportation allowed farmers to move their produce to a growing urban population more easily.

Suburbs also began to develop during this period. With the advent of public transportation in the late 1800s and early 1900s, some city dwellers began to move to the outskirts of cities and beyond, to escape crowded city conditions. Private automobiles and telephones aided movement to the suburbs. Road systems were developed to accommodate the growing numbers of autos, and more businesses and services relocated to suburban areas.

Postindustrial Cities. Postindustrial cities have a high percentage of employees in the service sector—business headquarters, government and intergovernmental organizations, research and development, tourism, finance and banking, health, education, and telecommunications (Bell [1976] 1999). They are primarily found in the most technologically advanced, wealthy nations. Boston, Massachusetts, and Washington, DC, are examples of U.S. cities that fit most of these characteristics, as does La

Défense, an urban center on the outskirts of Paris, built as a commercial, service, and information exchange center to serve France.

In the transformation from industrial to postindustrial economies, from manufacturing to service economies, some people and some cities get left behind. Major economic restructuring has changed the fate of cities around the world, for better and for worse. Some cities have become international centers of finance, whereas others have become hollowed-out shells after losing their manufacturing base. For example, Detroit, once a booming industrial city, had to declare bankruptcy and now has miles of abandoned commercial buildings and housing within its city limits. Rust belt cities that have lost their industrial base, and therefore their tax base, struggle to reinvent themselves for the postindustrial economy. Some succeed; others fail (*The Economist* 2015; "Rustbelt Britain" 2013).

Cities such as Bengaluru (Bangalore), India, illustrate how some cities can contain both new high-tech industries that provide white-collar work and a large population of poor and uneducated people. These high-tech centers attract business from around the world. For example, with the competitive publication market, the publishers of this book have found it economically prudent to save on costs by outsourcing their production to India.

As many cities became overcrowded, people moved to the suburbs. Manufacturing firms, services, commerce, and retail trade followed, taking jobs and tax revenue with them (Clapson 2003; Gans 1982). Also, as populations spread out from cities, farmland and open lands disappeared; energy and water demands increased; and sprawl led to vast, crowded freeway systems.

As the world becomes more congested and cities continue to attract residents, cities start to merge or become continuous urban areas without rural areas between them. Those who have driven from Boston to Washington, DC—an area sometimes called BosWash—know the meaning of *megalopolis*, a spatial merging of two or more cities along major transportation corridors (Brunn et al. 2011).

Some urban areas are carefully planned. *New towns*, cities built in previously undeveloped areas as economically self-sufficient entities, provide all the needed urban amenities. Urban planners believe that these cities can relieve the congestion of urban areas, provide new economic bases and residences near jobs, and solve many problems faced by older cities. Some new towns, such as Columbia, Maryland; Brasília, Brazil (the relatively new capital); and Canberra, Australia, have been success stories.

In some urban areas, soaring real estate prices reflect new directions away from either suburbanization or deterioration of inner-city neighborhoods. The process of **gentrification** refers to *members of the middle and upper classes, mostly young White professionals, buying and renovating rundown properties in central-city locations and displacing poor residents.* In recent years, these neighborhoods, often adjacent to the central business districts, have become fashionable residential areas. For example, many neighborhoods in Washington, DC, and Brooklyn, New York, have become gentrified—some to the point that relatively few people can now afford to live in certain neighborhoods (like Capitol Hill in Washington, DC, and Williamsburg in Brooklyn). Walkability—the ability to walk to most "hot spots" in the city and dispense with owning a car—has become a primary standard for many young urbanites. This gentrification brings consumers and a tax base to the city.

For those low-income people who move because of rising costs, many are pushed into less attractive parts of town with fewer services and recreational areas, and often pay higher rents for less adequate housing. Some are rendered homeless. Others are pushed to the suburbs. From 2000 to 2015, poverty in suburban areas increased at a 50% higher rate than in city and rural areas in the United States (Kneebone 2017). Conflict theorists view gentrification and other urban developments that favor the wealthy and displace or exclude the poor as exploitation by real estate capitalists. In contrast, others argue that wealthy residents who choose the lifestyle of the city over suburbia help support viable, livable cities, bringing in an additional tax base.

THINKING SOCIOLOGICALLY

What are some positive and negative aspects of gentrification for individuals and cities? Explain.

The Urban Environment and Social Policy: Macro-Level Perspectives

In Cairo, Egypt, a huge sprawling graveyard full of large mausoleums, called the City of the Dead, has become home to thousands of families transplanted from rural areas. Cities in India such as Chennai (the former colonial name was Madras), Mumbai (Bombay), and Kolkata (Calcutta) have thousands of homeless migrants living on the sidewalks, on highway medians, and in river channels that flood during the rainy season. The laundry list of urban problems facing many city governments can seem overwhelming. They must cope with overcrowding; shortages of services, education, and health care; slums and squatters; traffic congestion; unemployment; and effects of global restructuring, including loss of agricultural land, environmental degradation, and influxes of immigrants and refugees. This section considers several of the many problems mentioned earlier in the chapter and now facing urban areas such as Cairo, Chennai, Mumbai, and Kolkata.

Rural Migrants and Overcrowding

Overcrowding exists in cities throughout the world but causes special problems in the Global South. As Figure 15.12 illustrates, from 1950 to 2014, the percentage of the world's population that is urban rather than rural tripled. Poor migrants set up shacks of any material available—tin, cardboard, leaves, mud, and sticks—in settlements known as *barriadas* in Spanish-speaking countries, favelas in Portuguese-speaking Brazil, and *bustees* in India. Most newcomers to cities are young. They are pulled to the city by hopes of finding jobs and often have been pushed from rural areas because of limited land on which to farm and too many mouths to feed.

Most Global South countries have little time or money to prepare infrastructure and provide services for the rapidly increasing numbers of urban residents. Technological development, job opportunities, and basic services have not kept up with the large migrations of would-be laborers. Lack of basic services has become a major problem, resulting in contagious diseases, like Ebola, that can cause deadly epidemics due to poor sanitary conditions. For fear of a worldwide pandemic, Global North countries contributed medical aid, doctors, and research funds to help curb the epidemics.

Lack of adequate housing is a worldwide problem as well. High birthrates in resource-poor countries exacerbate the challenges resulting from population increases greater than the rate of economic growth or the capacity of society to absorb. Lack of adequate planning and social policies have failed poor migrants in rapidly growing slums of many world cities.

Crime and Delinquency in the City

In many cities across the globe, crime is a serious issue, particularly among those experiencing large influxes of rural residents and immigrants. When people are transient, when they move frequently, they tend to experience

▲ With few places to live, rural migrants to Egypt's largest city, Cairo, find shelter in the large ancient mausoleums in the burial grounds of the City of the Dead.

anomie. They have less commitment to community norms and the well-being of the local community. Add to that the desperate situation of the very poor, and you have a recipe for crime.

In rural communities and tribal cultures, strict norms govern behavior, but in urban areas, cohesiveness of families and ties with tribal groups are lessened. Thus, crime is more likely to occur in this ambiguous social setting with fewer social ties that foster conformity to norms. When education, economic security, and social services increase, conformity again becomes a norm for these newcomers, replacing the sense of anomie experienced during the transition. Policy solutions, then, need to provide access to schools and jobs for new city dwellers and ways to build community and connectedness to neighbors.

Urban Planning for Structures That Meet Human Needs

Ideal city planning is quite a task. City planners must meet citizens' needs for housing, sanitation, education, food distribution, jobs, family life, and recreation. The problem is that most urban planners do not have the luxury of starting from scratch. They must work with decaying areas, being cognizant of meaningful landmarks and treasured sites. Planners may also have to undo mistaken or inadequate planning by previous administrations.

Leaders in some U.S. cities and states have begun to take more active roles on issues related to demographic and economic changes. For example, New York City has invested in diversifying the city's economy by recruiting a top-level university (Cornell) to develop a new high-tech graduate school. It is also creating an applied science district that will bring in new companies, new jobs, and

▼ FIGURE 15.12

Change in Urban and Rural Population as Proportion of Total Population, by Continent, 1950–2050

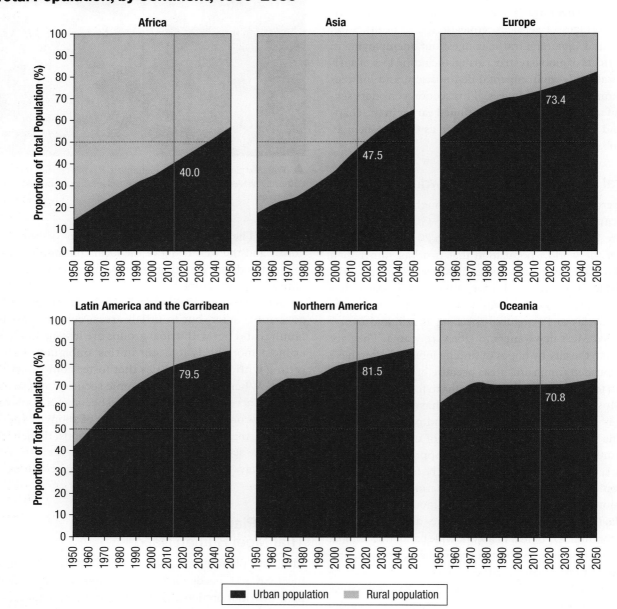

Source: United Nations, Department of Economic and Social Affairs, Population Division (2014). *World Urbanization Prospects: The 2014 Revision, Highlights.* Reprinted with the permission of the United Nations.

Note: Urban percentage at blue line is for 2014.

tax revenues for the city. Building on its expertise in high tech and sustainability, Portland, Oregon, has created a "We Build Green Cities" marketing campaign to promote its clean tech companies and created partnerships in other nations to expand the market for these companies. California has passed legislation to increase funding for low-income housing and make it easier for builders to create more housing as it confronts a lack of affordable housing in its cities and suburbs (Dillon 2017; Katz and Bradley 2013; Lieber 2015).

A number of global trends affect urban planning today.

1. The process of urbanization—people migrating to cities—will continue, exacerbating the already difficult situation of providing services for people in the world's crowded urban areas.

2. Information and transportation technologies allow people in any part of the globe to be in contact. However, this may also reduce the feelings of belonging to a specific place, thus reducing commitment to work on city problems.

3. International boundaries diminish in importance as the flow of information, goods, services, labor, and capital increasingly ignores national boundaries. For example, migration of Asians to cities around the world will continue and will have an impact on these cities.

4. Economies will increasingly rely on brain work, including invention of new technologies and high-tech manufacturing. Thus, the gap between the haves and have-nots is likely to continue.

5. Conflicts between cultural and political groups, including religious and political extremists (as described in previous chapters), will impact urban life.

6. Global climate change will impact cities, both directly (requiring adaptation or even evacuation) and indirectly (possible influxes of climate refugees).

7. *McDonaldization*—the creation of a consumer world dominated by American food, music, fashion, and entertainment—will continue, even as we see an increasing diversity of people within the United States (Ritzer 2018).

Awareness of these trends can help urban planners in their efforts to design cities to meet the needs of the future.

This basic population pattern—urbanization—has consequences at the most global levels and at the most micro levels of human life. Our social world model—which looks at the connections of micro, meso, and macro levels of the social system—makes us cognizant of the consequences of decisions made by millions of individuals and families. It also makes us mindful of the consequences of global trends and forces for individuals and for cities.

THINKING SOCIOLOGICALLY

Try planning an ideal city. First, list everything you need to consider, such as how big the city should be. Now think of organization: Who will handle what? Keep in mind services, maintenance, financing, and leadership.

Intersection of Demographics, Climate Change, and Environmental Policy

Traffic congestion and pollution are chronic problems, so intense in some cities that the slow movement of people and goods reduces productivity, jobs, health, and vital services. Increasing automobile use and the industrialization of the Global South adds to the pollution of our environment and intensifies climate change.

In regions of China, parents confine their children to their homes to keep them from breathing the outside air. In the spring of 2017, a combination of dust storms and pollution raised the AQI (air quality index) in Beijing so much it was beyond the measurable index. The most harmful pollution particles measured 684 micrograms per cubic meter, whereas the World Health Organization's recommended cap for such particles is 2.5 micrograms per cubic meter (Cummins and Wang 2017). A recent study indicates that one third of all deaths in China are related to air pollution. Parents of students at the International School in Beijing demanded that the school build an enclosed playground under a dome with filtered air, so their children will not have to breathe the polluted outside air while they play (Berlinger et al. 2017; Doane 2013).

In Global North countries, concern for these problems has brought some action and relief, but in impoverished countries where survival issues are pressing, environmental contamination is a low priority. Thus, the worst air pollution is now found in major cities in the Global South, such as Mexico City, São Paulo, and several Chinese cities, including Beijing. The overall impact, however, of air pollution—both past and present—affects the whole world. Human ways of living have impacted the world's climate—changing our weather and the very landscape of the Earth in the process.

© Getty/Kevin Frayer/Stringer

▲ A Chinese woman wears a mask and filter as she walks to work during heavy pollution in Beijing, China.

Climate Change

Climate change is happening now, and the only question that remains is *how severe* its repercussions will be (Greshko 2017). The overwhelming scientific consensus is that humans have contributed to the warming of our atmosphere and must take immediate steps to halt it or we will face more and more catastrophic environmental disasters. As Figure 15.13 reveals, atmospheric temperatures have increased markedly over the past century.

As temperatures increase, seawater expands, warming waters cause heavier rains, and ice over land melts. The results are rising seas levels and more precipitation. When Hurricane Harvey dropped 50 inches of rain causing death and destruction in and around Houston, Texas, the water in the Gulf of Mexico had reached record-breaking temperatures (Lowry 2017). Harvey was the third "500 year" flood to batter Houston within 3 years. As Ed Emmett, the chief executive of the county that includes Houston, put it, "Three 500-year floods in three years means either we're free and clear for the next 1,500 years . . . or something has seriously changed" (Kimmelman and Haner 2017).

Emmett continued, "The hard truth, scientists say, is that climate change will increasingly require moving—not just rebuilding—entire neighborhoods, reshaping cities, even abandoning coastlines" (Kimmelman and Haner 2017). The U.S. Geological Survey predicts that up to two thirds of the beaches in California will no longer exist by 2100 (USGS 2017). In fact, research by the real estate company Zillow shows that predicted rises in sea level by 2100 will lead to 300 U.S. cities losing at least half of their homes and the complete loss of 36 U.S. *cities* (Rao 2017). The World Atlas notes that climate change threatens the future of at least 52 *nations* (with 62 million people) and declares that 10 nations, including Bangladesh, are at great risk of disappearing completely due to rising water (World Atlas 2017). In other areas, rising temperatures and *lack* of rain have led to catastrophic droughts. Even nations with resources can become crippled due to global climate change. In recent years, residents in areas of Brazil and South Africa have faced water rationing and the threat of no water—at all—coming from their taps (Onishi and Sengupta 2018). Moreover, the economic and social costs from climate change increase every year. In the United States alone, the economic costs of air-pollution-related illnesses and extreme weather events will come to at least $360 billion *every year* within the next decade (Universal Ecological Fund 2017).

The Greenhouse Effect. The Earth's atmosphere has become warmer largely due to a human-created increase in the greenhouse effect. As Figure 15.14 illustrates, the greenhouse effect occurs when the Earth's atmosphere traps heat that radiates out from the Earth. Gases in the Earth's atmosphere like carbon dioxide, methane, and nitrous oxide prevent the heat from escaping.

Carbon dioxide (CO_2) is the most prevalent greenhouse gas. Released in huge quantities through the burning of fossil fuels (e.g., coal and oil) and deforestation, it has increased in the atmosphere by more than one third since the start of the Industrial Revolution. Its increase mirrors the increase in atmospheric temperature. Methane (CH_4), derived from sources such as the decomposition of waste in landfills and animal manure from farm-raised animals, is the most powerful greenhouse gas. Nitrous oxide (N_2O), created through industrial farming practices and the burning of fossil fuels, is another powerful greenhouse gas. Chlorofluorocarbons (CFCs), gases formed through various industrial practices, are also potent greenhouse gases but have been largely controlled though successful international agreements to protect the ozone layer in the atmosphere, which CFCs threatened (NASA 2017b).

Macro, Meso, and Micro Repercussions and Solutions. Repercussions of the current climate changes will be felt at the macro, meso, and micro levels of society. Nations will disappear and governments will

▼ FIGURE 15.13

Global Land-Ocean Temperature Index

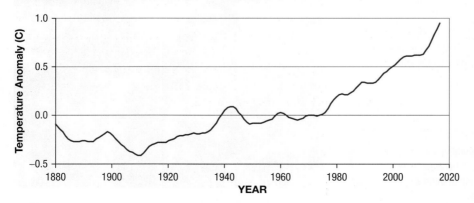

Source: NASA/GISS 2017.

▼ FIGURE 15.14

The Greenhouse Effect

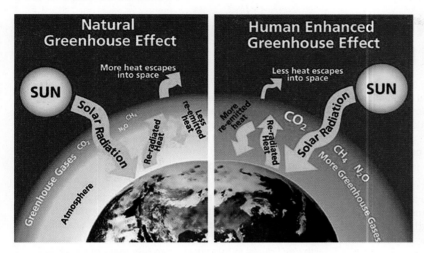

Source: Will Elder National Parks Service; Conservation in a Changing Climate 2015.

fall as millions of displaced people swarm over borders seeking livable land and safety. People will not be able to count on their governments to protect them from rising seas, desertification, rising temperatures, and extreme weather. Insurance companies will fold, as they find themselves unable to cover the costs of climate change. Individuals will seek safety in a world that seems unrecognizable to us now.

The good news is that humans have begun to take steps to recognize, prepare for, and mitigate the effects of climate change. A Pew survey across 38 nations reveals that climate change (along with ISIS) is the leading national security risk noted by most respondents (Poushter and Manevich 2017). Many global corporations have turned away from fossil fuels and begun to use more "green" energy. For example, Walmart plans to derive half of its power from green sources by 2025 and already has 350 stores that receive their energy from green sources on site (e.g., solar panels) (Renewable Energy World 2017).

Governments (with the Netherlands in the lead) have begun to prepare their shorelines for rising seas. Every nation on the planet signed the Paris Climate Change Agreement in 2016, agreeing to curb emissions. Even though President Trump declared in June 2017 that the

United States would withdraw from the agreement, most (56%) U.S. residents believe climate change is a national threat, and 160 U.S. mayors agreed to abide by the agreement (Poushter and Manevich 2017). In addition, 17 states have laws in place that require them to curb emissions contributing to climate change (Halper 2017). Moreover, 12 states follow the regulatory lead of California, which gained the right to maintain its own air pollution rules when the EPA was founded in 1970. It is committed to much stricter restrictions on carbon emissions than the Trump administration's (Tabuchi 2017). Finally, it has become a part of daily life among many individuals to recycle, moderate use of heat and air conditioning, use public transportation, and carry out other energy-reducing habits.

Directions for Policymakers

To improve the Earth's ecosystem, we must stabilize population growth in the Global South, develop plans for urban growth, and reduce human consumption and pollution. We must find a way to create **sustainable societies** *that can meet our current needs without harming future generations.* You can find sociologists at the forefront of efforts to confront environmental issues. In the next Sociologists in Action, Michael Haedicke describes how he helps policymakers address climate change in Louisiana. As he describes it, climate change is a grand issue that we must all tackle together.

Well over a decade after Hurricane Katrina, the city of New Orleans still struggles to prevent flooding when heavy rains fall—even without a hurricane (Gabour 2017). With a changing climate bringing more and more rain to the area, this fact does not bode well for the city or its residents. As Haedicke points out, individuals, cities, states, nations, and the global society must learn to work together to mitigate and adjust to climate change. If we do not learn how to mitigate these environmental challenges, our very survival is at risk.

ADDRESSING THE GRAND CHALLENGE OF CLIMATE CHANGE IN LOUISIANA

A changing climate, a growing global population, and widening social inequality all impact natural ecosystems and human welfare. It's no wonder that sustainability has been described as a "grand challenge" facing societies today. But how can sociology help societies meet this challenge?

One way to answer this question is to look closely at what the term *grand challenge* means. The answer might seem obvious: Grand challenges are big, important, and tough to solve. But there's more. Grand challenges are complicated because they require diverse groups of people, with different ideas and experiences, to work together. Sociology provides tools to understand social and cultural differences, which help to build these working relationships. It also highlights the ways in which different groups of people are connected and reveals common ground for negotiation and cooperation. Sustainability is a grand challenge, which means that no one group of people knows how to achieve it.

My research looks at one important place where people are trying to work out new approaches to sustainability: coastal Louisiana. Louisiana has been ground zero for recent environmental disasters, from Hurricane Katrina in 2005, which disproportionately harmed poor residents of color in New Orleans, to the BP oil spill in 2010, which devastated local ecosystems and businesses. As the state still works to recover from those disasters, coastal Louisiana must deal with the impact of rising sea levels associated with climate change.

Development along the Louisiana coastline has contributed to subsidence, meaning that the land is sinking even as the water is rising. Over the course of the 20th century, at least 1,880 square miles of land vanished into the Gulf of Mexico. Today, the state loses an average land size equal to a football field *every hour*.

To meet the environmental challenges facing their state, Louisiana's scientists, environmental activists, and political leaders are trying to figure out how to move Louisiana in the direction of environmental sustainability. My research looks at this process through interviews with key figures in this effort, from members of the U.S. Congress to local community organizers.

My interviews help to reveal the many issues that must be addressed if sustainability is to be achieved—from Louisiana's economic dependence on the oil industry that has made environmental protection difficult, to its history of racial inequality that has created various environmental justice issues. By bringing these different voices together through my sociological research, I am helping researchers, public officials, and the general public to understand the state's environmental challenges through the prisms of diverse groups. This sociological perspective reveals that we must work together to meet the grand challenge of sustainability.

★ ★ ★ ★ ★ ★ ★

Michael Haedicke is an environmental sociologist at Drake University who specializes in the study of food systems, environmental movements, and climate adaptation.

Many factors, including population dynamics, urbanization, and global warming, create change in a society. Some factors contributing to social dynamics push for innovation and change; other factors can retard change. The next chapter examines the larger picture of social transformation and change in our complex and multileveled social world.

WHAT HAVE WE LEARNED?

Population trends, including migration resulting in urbanization, provide a dynamic force for change in societies. Whether one is interested in understanding social problems, social policy, or factors that may affect one's own career, it is helpful to understand demographic processes. We ignore them at our peril—as individuals and as a society. If we overlook demographic patterns, family businesses can be destroyed, retirement plans obliterated, and the health of our communities sabotaged. Awareness of such patterns can enhance planning that leads to prosperity and enjoyment of our communities. Likewise, if we do not work to mitigate and prepare for the impact of climate change, individuals will suffer, nations will collapse, and the survival of the world will be at risk.

- Environmental sociologists look at both natural communities (ecology) and human communities and how they interact with one another.

- Population analysis (called demography) considers the composition, distribution, and size of a population and how variables of fertility, mortality, and migration impact society.

- The population of the world has increased dramatically since industrialization. Its implications for society can be viewed in population pyramids.

- Various theories explain the causes and repercussions of rapid population growth.

- Many institutions affect and are affected by fertility and mortality rates at the meso level—government, religion, the economy, education, and health care.

- Migration is also an important issue for society—whether the migration is international or internal—for it can change the size, distribution, and composition of a nation's citizenry.

- Population patterns can also affect individual decisions at the micro level, from career choices to business decisions to retirement plans.

- A major element of population migration has been urbanization. As populations become more densely concentrated, this creates a series of opportunities and problems for meeting human needs.

- At the macro level, urban environments must be understood as ecosystems that have dense poverty and homelessness, major pollution issues, and higher crime rates but also the potential to reduce environmentally harmful energy use.

- Climate change affects all levels of society—and must be addressed at all levels, including the international community, individual nations, corporations, states, cities, and individuals.

DISCUSSION QUESTIONS

1. Why is it important for policymakers, including urban planners, to understand demographic trends in their communities and nation? Why should *you* be interested in such knowledge? How might it impact your understanding of and positions on issues related to (a) immigration, (b) education, (c) health care, and (d) Social Security legislation?

2. How many children (if any) do you think you would ideally like to have? Why? What might make this ideal number change?

3. What are some examples of (a) pronatalist and (b) antinatalist policies? Do you approve of such policies? Why or why not? How might your perspective differ depending on the demographics of your nation?

4. How is the social status of girls and women related to a society's ability to control population growth? If you were a leader in the government of an overcrowded nation, why and how might you use this information to promote gender equality in your country? How might your ideas be perceived differently, depending on your sex?

5. What are some of the major reasons people leave their country of origin and move to another? Have you ever done so? Why? If not, under what circumstances would you be willing to leave the country in which you were born and move to another?

6. How do your attitudes toward those around you and your behavior differ in rural, suburban, and urban settings? Why?

7. What might be the repercussions of climate change on your life? On your children's lives? What can *you* do to help address climate change?

KEY TERMS

demographic transition theory 465

demography 459

dependency ratio 462

environmental racism 466

fertility 467

Gemeinschaft 478

gentrification 482

Gesellschaft 478

life expectancy 459

migration 467

mortality 467

population pyramids 462

populations 459

sustainable societies 487

urbanization 477

At the Local (Micro) Level

- The *U.S. Census Bureau* is always at work collecting, analyzing, and disseminating demographic information. It is a great source of data, ranging from information on your block to the whole nation. Invite a representative to your campus to discuss the bureau's activities. You can check internship and job opportunities with the Census Bureau at www.census.gov/about/census-careers/opportunities/programs/student.html.

- Check out your *local department of urban planning, urban and regional development, or community development* by Googling those terms and the name of your town, county, or province. Invite a representative to your campus or visit the department's offices. Discuss how population information is used in planning and service delivery contexts. Consider an internship with one of the organizations you find in your area.

- *Start a group to combat climate change.* The climate change organization 350.org has material on its website to help people interested in forming a local 350.org group.

At the Organizational or Institutional (Meso) Level

- *The Population Association of America (PAA)* "is a non-profit, scientific, professional organization that promotes research on population issues," according to its website. At www.populationassociation.org, you can find information on demographic issues and ways to get involved in efforts to address them.

At the National or Global (Macro) Level

- The *Population Reference Bureau* (www.prb.org/About.aspx) "informs people around the world about population, health, and the environment, and empowers them to use that information to advance the well-being of current and future generations." The organization offers fellowships for recent college graduates with a BA or BS.

- *Planned Parenthood* (www.plannedparenthood.org) promotes family planning education and outreach programs throughout the United States. The International Planned Parenthood Federation (www.ippf.org) works in 171 nations. The organizations use volunteers and interns, as well as provide long-term employment opportunities.

- *World Vision* (www.worldvision.org) is "a Christian humanitarian organization, dedicated to working with children, families, and their communities worldwide to reach their full potential by tackling the causes of injustice and poverty." The organization provides many ways you can get involved in efforts to alleviate poverty and promote justice around the world.

- *The Population Council* (www.popcouncil.org) promotes family planning to reduce poverty, create healthier populations and communities, empower women, and improve lives across the globe. You can find fact sheets and other information at their website. You can also look for possible job and internship opportunities at www.popcouncil.org/employment/index.asp.

$SAGE edge™

Get the tools you need to sharpen your study skills. SAGE edge offers a robust online environment featuring an impressive array of free tools and resources.

Access practice quizzes, eFlashcards, video, and multimedia at **edge.sagepub.com/ballantine7e**

CHAPTER 16

© REUTERS/Jonathan Ernst

PROCESS OF CHANGE

We Can Make a Difference!

▲ Individuals are profoundly influenced by changes in the meso and macro structures around them, but people are also capable of creating change, especially if they band together with others and approach change in an organized way.

MICRO

ME (AND MY FAMILY)

LOCAL ORGANIZATIONS
AND COMMUNITY
**Individuals and local groups
can work together to organize
and mobilize others and create
social change.**

MESO

NATIONAL ORGANIZATIONS,
INSTITUTIONS, AND ETHNIC
SUBCULTURES
**The environmental movement has put
pressure on governments to address global
climate change.**

MACRO

SOCIETY
**National government policies
about trade, war, or immigration
may cause change in families,
the economy, or international
relationships.**

GLOBAL COMMUNITY
**World Bank loans or United
Nations poverty programs may
result in change for poor nations
and stimulate international trade.**

WHAT WILL YOU LEARN IN THIS CHAPTER?

This chapter will help you to do the following:

16.1 Describe how the development of
technology brings about change in
societies and their environments

16.2 Give examples of how change takes
place at each level of analysis

16.3 Explain how stresses and strains can
lead to organizational change

16.4 Explain the six factors necessary for
collective behavior to occur

16.5 Provide examples of the difference
between planned and unplanned
change

16.6 Illustrate the stages of social
movements

THINK ABOUT IT

Micro: Small groups and local communities	What do you think needs to change in your community?
Meso: National institutions, complex organizations, and ethnic groups	How can complex organizations or social movements create, hamper, or shape change?
Macro: National and global systems	How can national governments affect the process of change in your country and in the world through training and support of technological innovation?

During the summer of 2017, a radio host in New York City interviewed 19 Bronx high school students enrolled in a journalism class at the Summer Arts Institute at Lehman College. Student after student mentioned how little they knew about how their community worked before they took the class at Lehman. As one student pointed out, "At first when I got in the class I didn't even know what the city council was." Another student said, "People don't know how to empower themselves . . . so they don't think anything is getting done." Now these students were reading the *New York Times* every day and reporting on New York City Council members and candidates for the council. These students emphasized how the knowledge they gained in the course made them feel that they could make a real difference in their community—and help change it for the better (Brian Lehrer Show 2017).

Does this sound familiar to you? By this point in the semester, you know that if you want to work effectively to change society, you need to know how society works. Once you have gained such information, you can take the next step and work to improve society. In this chapter we focus on how society changes and how you might influence it.

Social change refers to *variations or alterations over time in the structure, culture (including norms and values), and behavior patterns in a society.* Change can be rapid, caused by some disruption to the existing system, or be gradual and evolutionary. Often, change at one level in the social world occurs because of change at another level. Micro, meso, and macro levels of society often interconnect in the change process but are sometimes out of sync. In this chapter, we consider the complexity of change in our social world, explanations and theories of social change, the role of collective behavior in bringing about change, planned change in organizations, macro-level social movements, and technology and environmental actions as they affect and are affected by change.

Our social world model assumes that change, whether evolutionary or revolutionary, is inevitable and ever present in the social world. The impetus for change may begin at the micro, meso, or macro level of analysis. Studies of the change process are not complete, however, until the level under study is understood in relation to other levels in the model, for each level affects the others in multiple ways.

THINKING SOCIOLOGICALLY

> Why do you think so many students do not know how their community works? What should our education system do to address this issue? What should you do?

Complexity of Change in Our Social World

The Yir Yoront, a group of Australian aborigines, long believed that if their own ancestors did not do something, then they must not do it. It would be wrong and might cause evil to befall the group (Sharp 1990). However, contact with European cultures and missionaries brought new tools such as the steel ax, changing the role of men whose job it was to make stone axes. Gradually other European ways were introduced, changing the culture dramatically so that old ways were obsolete. The group's original culture disintegrated as it adopted others' ways, but a major contributor was the introduction of new technological ideas, especially the steel ax. In the 1940s, missionaries gave steel axes to the Yir Yoront women, and the hunting and gathering economy changed due to changing roles of women and men. Men, who used to control the stone axes, lost their high status in the community when they had to borrow axes and other tools from women, and thus the power structure of the community changed (BushTV 2010; Hotchkiss 2014).

Obviously, the Yir Yoront are not a people who favored change or innovation. In contrast, *progress* is a positive word in much of Australia and many other countries where change is seen as normal, even desirable. Technology, as well as traditions, cultural beliefs, and internal and external pressures, affects the degree and rate of change in society (B. Berman 2011).

Technology and Science

Technology refers to the practical application of tools, skills, and knowledge to meet human needs and extend human abilities. Throughout human history, there have been major transition periods when changes in the material culture brought about revolutions in human social structures and cultures (Toffler and Toffler 1980). For example, the agricultural revolution, which resulted from the use of the plow to till the soil, established new social arrangements and created food surpluses that allowed cities to flourish. With the Industrial Revolution came machines powered by steam and gasoline, resulting in mass production, population increases, urbanization, the division of labor in manufacturing, new forms of social stratification, and the socialist and capitalist political-economic systems. Today, postindustrial technology, based on the microchip, fuels the spread of information, communication, and transportation on a global level—even exploration of outer space. It also allows us to store and retrieve masses of information in seconds.

Sociologist William Ogburn (1886–1959) argued that change is brought about through three processes: discovery, invention, and diffusion. *Discovery* is a new way of seeing reality. The material objects or ideas have been present, but they are seen in a new light when the need arises or conditions are conducive to the discovery. It is usually accomplished by an individual or a small group, a micro-level activity (Ogburn [1922] 1938, 1961, 1964).

Invention refers to combining existing parts, materials, or ideas to form new ones. There was no light bulb or combustion engine lying in the forest waiting to be discovered. Human ingenuity was required to put together something that had not previously existed. Technological innovations often result from research and the expansion of science, increasingly generated in meso-level institutions and organizations in society.

Diffusion is the spread of an invention or discovery from one place to another. The spread of ideas such as capitalism, democracy, and religious beliefs has brought about changes in human relationships around the world.

▲ Technological innovation is now providing us with electricity through wind farms. The one depicted here is the first complete high-sea wind farm on the North Sea coast of Germany.

Likewise, the spread of various types of music, film technology, telephone systems, and computer hardware and software across the globe has had important ramifications for global interconnectedness. Diffusion often involves expansion of ideas across the globe (macro level), but it also requires individuals to adopt ideas at the micro level.

Science is *the systematic process of producing human knowledge; it uses empirical research methods to discover facts and test theories.* The question "How do we know what we know?" is often answered: "It's science." Whether social, biological, or physical, science provides a systematic way to approach the world and its mysteries. It uses empirical research methods to discover facts and test theories. Today, technology applies scientific knowledge to solve problems. Early human technology was largely the result of trial and error, not based on scientific knowledge or principles. Since the Industrial Revolution, many inventors and capitalists have seen science and technology as routes to human betterment and happiness. Science has become a major social institution in industrial and postindustrial societies, providing the bases of information and knowledge for sophisticated technology.

Indeed, one of the major transformations in modern society is the result of science becoming an institution. Prior to the 18th century, science was an avocation. People like Benjamin Franklin experimented in their homes or backyards, using whatever spare cash they had for materials, to satisfy their own curiosity. Science in the contemporary world is both a structure and social process. *Institutionalization* means creation of the organized, patterned, and enduring sets of social structures that provide guidelines for behavior and help the society meet its needs. Within these structures, actions are taken—the processes within the structure—that accomplish a goal such as conducting research. Innovation resulting in

▲ Thomas Edison had more than 1,000 patented inventions, including the light bulb, recorded sound, and movies, but perhaps his most influential invention was the research lab—where people are paid to invent and to conduct research. This was the seminal step in the institutionalization of science.

▲ In 2015 Arizona governor Doug Ducey opened the door for the first driverless taxis on public roads. This automated vehicle is taking a test-drive in Pittsburgh. As a society, we have little idea how such technological innovations may stimulate change to the larger society and our social structure.

change will be slow until a society has institutionalized science—providing extensive training and paying some people simply to do research. Modern science involves mobilizing financial resources and employing the most highly trained people (which, in turn, requires the development of educational institutions).

Specialization in science speeds up the rates of discovery. A researcher focuses on one area and gets much more in-depth understanding. Also, effective methods of communication across the globe mean that we do not need to wait several years for a research manuscript to cross the ocean and to be translated into another language. Competition in science (now global) means that

researchers move quickly on their findings. The first to create new drugs, devices, or other inventions tends to reap the most recognition and compensation.

We would not have automobiles, planes, missiles, space stations, computers, the Internet, and many of our modern conveniences without the institutionalization of science and without scientific application (technology). Science is big business, funded by industry and government. Most university researchers and some government-funded science institutes engage in *basic research* designed to discover new knowledge. Industry and some governmental agencies such as the military and the Department of Agriculture employ scientists to do *applied research* and discover practical uses for existing knowledge.

Scientific knowledge is usually cumulative, with each study adding to the existing body of research. However, radical new ideas can result in scientific revolutions (Kuhn 1970). Galileo's finding that the Earth revolves around the sun and Darwin's theory of evolution are two examples of radical new ideas that changed history. More recently, cumulative scientific knowledge has resulted in energy-efficient engines that power cars and computer technology that has revolutionized communication.

THINKING SOCIOLOGICALLY

Imagine what your life would have been like before home computers, e-mail, and the Internet. What would be different? (Note that you are imagining the world as it was only 30 years ago.) Ask your parents or grandparents what this recent past was like.

Technology and Change

A nation's research and development (R&D) is an important measure of investment in the future. For many years the biggest investors have been the United States and the European Union. They accounted for, respectively, 25.5% and 20.8% of global R&D spending in 2017. The levels for both the United States and the EU have been declining in recent years, however, while China has increased its investments in R&D. For the first time ever, China's share of the world's investment in R&D reached parity with the European Union (20.8%) in 2017 (The Industrial Research Institute 2017).

The decline in U.S. investment in research is especially troubling, given what we know about the relationship between economic growth and R&D (Battelle 2013). For example, the technological revolution in communications would not have come about without research and development. R&D has resulted in fiber-optic cable, wireless microwave cell phones, and satellite technologies that make it easier to communicate with people around the world.

Changes in technology do not, however, always have a positive effect on less affluent countries or areas within nations. Consider, for example, that changes in technology and the economy have forced many individuals to leave their native villages in search of paid labor positions in urban factories and the tourism industry, disrupting family lives. Meanwhile, U.S. rural populations continue to fall as jobs that pay well now exist primarily in technologically advanced regions of the nation (Thiede, Greiman, Weiler, Beda, and Conroy 2017).

These national and regional impacts, in turn, affect the lives of individuals. Technological advances help move some people up the social class ladder and others down it. With these changes brought about by technology also come changes in the nonmaterial culture—values, political ideologies, and human relationships. Many of these came out clearly in the 2016 presidential election when people in many economically hard-hit rural areas voted for a Republican presidential candidate for the first time in years. Clearly, technology can have a variety of social impacts—both positive and negative.

Change at the Individual Level: Micro-Level Analysis

One of the top U.S. entrepreneurs, Microsoft's founder Bill Gates, has used technological prowess and other skills to move up—way up—the economic ladder. Gates now has the power to influence the lives of millions of people. Although now retired from Microsoft, he is able to bring about change in organizations with his work through the Gates Foundation and his personal ability to motivate people and set wheels in motion.

Some people have persuasive power to influence decision-making, based on expertise, wealth, privileged position, access to information, or the ability to use coercive force. Any of us, if we feel strongly about an issue, can rally others and bring about change in society. Each individual in society has the potential to be a change agent.

Individuals are active agents, and they can either stimulate or resist change. Sometimes they prod organizations to change, insisting on more family-supportive policies (like an onsite day care center), better safety precautions for employees, or more environmentally friendly buildings and programs. For example, at the urging of students and others, colleges may develop more recycling

▲ Angelina Jolie (top) has used her fame as an Academy Award–winning actress to bring attention to problems of refugees, serving as a special envoy and goodwill ambassador for the United Nations High Commissioner for Refugees. Bill Gates (bottom) holds a child who is receiving a trial malaria vaccine at a medical research center in Mozambique. Gates announced a grant of $168 million to fight malaria, a disease that kills more than 1 million people a year, 90% of them children. Sometimes, social change occurs because of individual initiatives.

programs, more energy-efficient buildings or transportation systems, and more degree programs that involve study of the environment.

Sometimes individuals are not eager to change. They must be enticed or manipulated into change by organizations. When resistance does occur, most organizations—schools, businesses, and volunteer associations—use one or more of the following strategies to persuade individuals to accept change. They appeal to individuals' values, use persuasion by presenting hard data and logic, convince individuals that the benefits of change outweigh the costs, remove uncooperative individuals from the organization ("addition by subtraction"), provide rewards or sanctions for acceptance of change to alter the cost-benefit ratio, or compel individuals to change by an order from authority figures. In any case, individuals are critically important parts of social change.

Change at the Organizational or Institutional Level: Meso-Level Analysis

Global climate change, an issue connected to pollution and use of Earth's natural resources, affects people at all levels in the social system. As mentioned in Chapter 15, many meso-level organizations have developed policies and practices to reduce emission of pollutants and change the way they use resources. For example, many religious denominations have developed programs to be more "green" or "Earth-friendly." The United Church of Christ is one such group, passing a resolution in July 2009 encouraging local churches to become "Earthwise congregations." Mayflower United Church of Christ in Minneapolis was one of the first to seek the designation.

▲ A part of its "Earthwise" mission to protect the environment, this church in Minneapolis installed 240 solar panels in a commitment to be carbon neutral by 2030.

▲ People at the local level often try to influence policies at the meso level. At this farmer's market in Minneapolis, people lobby their neighbors and seek signatures for a petition about state legislation that would be welcoming to immigrants and protect refugees in the state.

The church has an action team that works on ways to help members have more energy-efficient homes, but it also brought a resolution to the congregation that by 2030, the church would be entirely carbon neutral. The resolution was approved, and fund-raising began to change the heating system to solar energy. The roof of the church is now covered with 240 solar panels. Within 18 months, the church reported a reduction of carbon emissions of almost 50% (Mayflower Church 2016; R. Riley 2014). Members of the congregation have also begun lobbying the state legislature for more public transit and especially more transportation that runs on electricity rather than oil-based fuels. Other United Church of Christ congregations are also taking actions, as are other communities of faith—inspired by denominational resolutions at the meso level.

Another example of meso-level change takes place at universities. Under pressure from college students, many have changed their policies about production of clothing with campus logos. Multinational corporations like Gap and Nike, seeking higher profits, fostered the growth of sweatshops in the Global South. Many professors, students, and concerned citizens in the United States and other Global North nations began to insist that these companies establish acceptable labor and human rights conditions in their factories in the Global South. Their efforts gradually grew into an anti-sweatshop movement with strong labor and religious support and tens of thousands of active participants. College students on hundreds of campuses in the United States have taken up the anti-sweatshop cause, holding sit-ins on many campuses to force their college bookstores to ban the use of college logos on products not produced under acceptable labor conditions. Many have also advocated for a $15 minimum wage—including for student workers on campuses (Brecher, Costello, and Smith 2012; USAS 2017; Wang and Currier 2015). In doing so, they have helped shape the conditions for workers everywhere.

Change at the National or Global Level: Macro-Level Analysis

Change also may begin at the national level in response to some concern, or it may be stimulated by a global organization (like the United Nations or the World Bank) or by a global issue, like climate change. In this section, we discuss national and then global forces that can bring about change.

Societal-Level Change. Look at the impact of national policies and trends on the global environment and the constant change we bring to our planet. To illustrate the increasingly complex and biologically interdependent social world, consider that pollution of the environment by any one country now threatens other countries. Carcinogens, acid rain, and other airborne chemicals carry across national boundaries (Zhang et al. 2017). As discussed in Chapter 15, global climate change, though the product of some nations more than others, affects the entire planet. As Figure 16.1 indicates, the United States and China are responsible for most carbon dioxide emissions.

According to scientists, Earth's surface has warmed by 1.5 degrees in the past century. That does not sound like much until one considers that during the last ice age, Earth's surface was only 7 degrees cooler than it is today. Small variations can make a huge difference, and those consequences are likely to be dire if the Earth's surface temperature increases by another 2 or 3 degrees. Currently, massive blocks of sea ice are melting each year at a rate that equals the size of Maryland and Delaware combined, and oceans are rising at a rate faster than at any time in the past 28 centuries (Gillis 2016b).

Global climate change will also lead to less drinkable water. In a warmer world, there is less snowfall, resulting in smaller mountain icecaps and, thus, a smaller spring runoff of crucial fresh water. Desertification of land also increases with rising temperatures. Less water leads to more competition (possibly violent) over what land still exists (Lem 2016).

THINKING SOCIOLOGICALLY

What do you think happens when people do not have enough water to survive? What happens when they try to move into someone else's territory to gain access to needed resources such as land and water? What might (a) the global society, (b) your national government, and (c) you do to reduce the likelihood of climate change–induced conflicts over land and water?

This global issue requires nations to work together for change, yet some nations resist change because they feel climate control efforts will impede economic progress.

▼ FIGURE 16.1

Share of Global Carbon Dioxide Emissions From Fuel Combustion, 2015

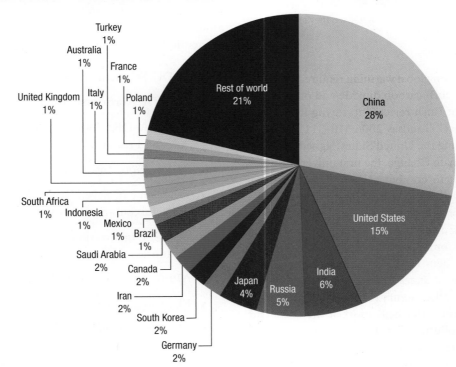

Source: Data from the International Energy Agency. Reprinted with permission from the Union of Concerned Scientists. https://www.ucsusa.org/global-warming/science-and-impacts/science/each-countrys-share-of-co2.html#.W1sVxtJKjlV.

Petermann Glacier, 5 August 2009

© Wikimedia

3xEiffel

Petermann Glacier 24 July 2011

© Wikimedia

▲ These before and after shots of the Petermann Glacier in Greenland show a massive loss of glacier in just one calving (breaking off of chunks of ice at the edge of a glacier). For many parts of the world, glaciers are a major source of fresh water, but they are melting because of global climate change.

affluent nations will also face increasing pressure from immigration (legal or not).

Yet fixing the environmental issues will be expensive for nations and may add to economic woes by temporarily hindering economic growth. Because slow-growth economies and recessions can lead to an unhappy public and political unrest, making changes to address climate change is not easy. However, such action is crucial because nations are still the most powerful units for allocating resources and setting policy.

Global Systems and Change. As the world becomes more interconnected and interdependent, impetus for change increasingly comes from global organizations, international and transnational government agencies, and multinational corporations. As discussed in other chapters, nongovernmental organizations (NGOs) work on such efforts as eradicating polio or controlling AIDS, Ebola, and malaria. Some promote human rights, and others support local social movements for clean water, environmental protection, and access to health. One NGO, Sociologists Without Borders, works transnationally to develop globally inclusive sociology curricula, advance human rights, and support the needs of vulnerable groups.

New and shifting alliances among international organizations and countries link together nations, form international liaisons, and create changing economic and political systems. The following international alliances among countries, for example, are based primarily on economic ties:

- SADC: Southern African Development Community

- NAFTA: North American Free Trade Agreement

- CAFTA-DR: Dominican Republic–Central America Free Trade Agreement

- WIPO: World Intellectual Property Organization

- G7: Group of Seven—the most affluent and most powerful countries in the world

- OPEC: Organization of the Petroleum Exporting Countries

- APEC: Asia-Pacific Economic Cooperation

- EU: European Union

- AU: African Union

The Kyoto Protocol on global warming required commitment by nations to curb carbon dioxide and other emissions, but President Bush rejected it, saying it did "not make economic sense" (Lindsay 2006:310–311). In 2015, 195 nations, including the United States, signed the Paris Agreement on Climate Change, the first universal legally binding agreement to combat global climate change. All governments pledged to reduce their emissions, and Global North nations promised to provide aid to Global South nations facing disproportionate threats from climate change (European Commission 2016). However, as noted in Chapter 15, President Trump announced his intention to withdraw the United States from the agreement, saying it was a "bad deal" for the country (Shear 2017).

Impoverished countries bear most of the costs and consequences of pollution. It is becoming increasingly clear, though, that rich nations will also pay a price. Not only will they have to face pollution, increasingly severe weather with intense storms, and rising waters, but if Global South countries cannot support their populations,

Consider NAFTA, which as of this writing was approaching its 25th anniversary. It was initiated in 1993 to establish free trade among Canada, the United States, and Mexico.

Promoters, including many global corporations, promised that the agreement would create thousands of new high-wage jobs, raise living standards in each of the countries, improve environmental conditions, and transform Mexico from a poor developing country into a booming new market. Opponents (including labor unions, environmental organizations, consumer groups, and religious communities) argued the opposite—that NAFTA would reduce wages; destroy jobs, especially in the United States; undermine democratic policymaking in North America by giving corporations a free rein; and threaten health, the environment, and food safety (U.S. Trade Representative 2012).

Analyses of NAFTA show mixed results. It has helped boost intraregional trade among Canada, Mexico, and the United States, but it has fallen short of generating the jobs and deeper regional economic integration its advocates promised decades ago (Council on Foreign Relations 2014). Trade has increased significantly, from $290 billion in 1993 to more than $1.1 trillion in 2016. There is some indication that tariffs are down and U.S. exports have increased (McBride and Sergie 2017). NAFTA has been more effective in increasing trade in agricultural commodities than nonagricultural products. Some analysts argue that NAFTA has improved environmental protections and labor rights, but many others argue the opposite (Zahniser, Angadjivand, and Hertz 2015). The truth is hard to determine, but there are probably both gains and losses. As talks at the macro level continue among the United States, Canada, and Mexico, NAFTA's future is in question, as are the effects possible changes could have at the micro level for businesses and farmers (Swanson 2018).

In the previous discussion of changes at different levels of analysis, one principle carries through all: Change at one level leads to change in other levels, as it has done in the global cases of climate change and NAFTA. Changes at the macro level affect individuals, just as changes at the micro level have repercussions at the meso and macro levels. Most of the gains have been to the Global North and most losses to poorer regions of the world (Witness for Peace 2016).

Social Change: Process and Theories

Process of Change

Something always triggers a social change. The impetus may come from within an organization or a society, a source of change known as *strain*. Sometimes it comes from outside an organization, what sociologists call *stress*. Let us first consider two examples of strain: (1) conflicting goals and (2) contrasting belief systems within an organization.

Conflicting goals are seen in the case of the platinum mining industry and its union workers. In the Lonmin South African platinum mines (providing materials for catalytic converters and jewelry), 44 workers died and 78 were injured in August 2012, and 2 more died in May 2014 during strikes against the company. In a report on the deaths at the mine, police, company managers, and union officers were blamed for letting the strike escalate to violent confrontation (St. Claire and Smith, 2015). Two feuding unions both demanded pay hikes, and in an ugly confrontation, police opened fire on an unruly crowd. Individual miners work in difficult, dangerous conditions to try to meet their basic needs for food and shelter for their families. Sometimes they must live at the mines away from their families for many months, but when jobs are scarce, one does what one must. Company goals focus on the bottom line: being profitable in a competitive environment. The company argues that it cannot afford to raise wages and still be competitive, yet its profit margin has dropped because of the strikes (Herskovitz 2012; "Lonmin Profit Plunges" 2014). This conflict and others like it demonstrate how the needs of the workers can be at odds with those of the company, creating *internal strain*.

Contrasting belief systems (political, religious, economic, and social) within a society can also have a major effect on the type and rate of change. For example, some religious groups oppose stem cell research, which often uses the cells of fetuses created in test tubes. Yet other members of those same religious groups may believe this research will alleviate the suffering of loved ones and save lives. Although both sides in the organization believe they are pro-life, the conflicts can be disruptive and cause internal strain (Religious Tolerance 2018).

Stresses, those pressures for change that come from the organization's external environment, can be traced to several sources: the natural environment and natural disasters, population dynamics, actions of leaders, new technologies, changes in other institutions, and major historical events. For example, the natural environment can bring about either slow or dramatic change in a society as seen in the effects of droughts in many parts of the world. In southern Spain, in the city of Murcia, dying orange and lemon trees littered the landscape in the summer of 2016. If the Earth's temperature rises 2 degrees Celsius, as expected, the entire region could become a desert (Vidal 2017).

Natural disasters such as floods, hurricanes, tsunamis, heavy snows, earthquakes, volcanic eruptions, mudslides, tornadoes, and other sudden events are not planned occurrences, but they can have dramatic consequences. Disease epidemics are often unpredictable, such as the 2010–2013 cholera epidemic in Haiti, the Ebola epidemic in several

▲ Natural disasters—floods, droughts, hurricanes, tornadoes, earthquakes, and volcanic eruptions—can be the cause of major social changes in a community. California and places like this—Lake Mead National Recreation Area in Nevada—can find the entire economy turned on its head by a severe drought.

▲ Syrian refugees wait on the Syrian side of the border to cross into Turkey. Immigration to avoid persecution and war can stimulate massive change for people and for countries.

African countries, and the Zika outbreak in Brazil and other nations (including parts of the United States) in 2016 (Chan 2017; UNICEF 2014). Natural disasters and diseases are important as dramatic change agents, and the sociology of disasters has become a specialty field within the discipline. The next Sociology in Our Social World describes one of the classic sociological studies of disaster.

THINKING SOCIOLOGICALLY

Think of a recent natural disaster with which you are familiar. If you oversaw the disaster relief effort, how might the findings from the Buffalo Creek study (discussed in the next Sociology in Our Social World feature) help you determine what steps you would take to help the community or communities impacted by the disaster?

As noted in Chapter 15, *population dynamics*—birthrates and death rates, size of populations, age distribution, and migration patterns—can be important contributors to external stress on organizations. Where populations are growing at extremely rapid rates, government systems may be unable to meet the basic needs of the people. Immigration due to political upheavals or motivated by anticipated economic opportunities can also create stress on the societies that receive the newcomers as they attempt to meet the immigrants' needs. For example, many refugees from the conflict in Syria fled to camps in the nearby countries of Turkey and Jordan and are now making their way to European countries to start new lives. Figure 16.2 shows the number of refugees in major host countries in 2015–2016.

Leaders influence change through their policy decisions or the social movements they help generate. India's

SOCIOLOGY IN OUR SOCIAL WORLD

DISASTERS AND THEIR AFTERMATH

Picture a series of small villages in mining country along Buffalo Creek, a mountain creek in West Virginia. At the top of the creek, a coal company has poured more than 1 million tons of wastewater and coal waste (shale, clay, slag, and low-quality coal) into a basin, creating a reservoir.

One late-winter morning, February 26, 1972, following days of heavy rains, the retaining wall broke, causing a massive flood of wastewater to cascade down the valley toward the homes of 5,000 residents. The first village hit disappeared entirely. Villages farther down the creek bed were crushed by filthy water and remains of homes, churches, stores, vehicles, and bodies. By the time the water subsided, the flood had taken with it almost everything in its path.

Sociologists were interested in the human cost to the survivors of this disaster—to their sense of self, their mental and emotional well-being, and their family and friendship ties. Before the flood, these communities had close-knit social networks, crime was virtually nonexistent, divorces were extraordinary, chemical abuse and mental problems were far below national norms, and neighborhoods were like extended families. Yet this close community was ripped apart in minutes. Even 3 years after the flood, time had not healed the social and emotional wounds: Among the survivors, few marriages remained intact, problems of deviance and delinquency were rife, and more than 90% of the people interviewed needed psychological counseling.

The federal government provided mobile homes and emergency food, but people were housed without considering existing ties with family members and neighbors. People found themselves surrounded by strangers, when they had few interpersonal resources to forge new relationships.

Mental health symptoms included psychic numbness (feeling mentally blank and emotionally limp), constant anxiety about death, guilt at having survived when so many had not, guilt for not saving people, loss of symbols of one's life—family heirlooms, photographs of loved ones, and other artifacts, and loss of trust in the order of the universe or a loving God.

The "collective trauma" was even more important to understand than the individual trauma; it included five dimensions:

1. *Disorientation.* Many experienced social displacement, difficulty orienting themselves in time and space up to 3 years after the flood.
2. *Loss of morale and morality.* People were more likely to commit deviant acts and feel that neighbors were immoral people.
3. *Loss of connection.* Marriages disintegrated, and people lost their sense of connection to others.
4. *Illness and identity.* Many felt that both the land and their bodies were polluted. Some were afraid of finding a body part if they farmed.
5. *Loss of a sense of safety.* People slept in their clothes and boots, and whenever it rained, they continually checked on the water levels.

This disaster at Buffalo Creek indicates how much of our personal mental health rests in the health of the larger community. Anomie (normlessness) can create anxiety and disorientation. It helps us understand that natural disasters and human catastrophes—the September 11 terrorist attacks, devastating storms such as Hurricane Katrina, and daily gang violence in El Salvador and Honduras—have pervasive effects on individuals and communities.

Work on collective trauma makes us aware of our dependency on the larger community to regain our footing after a disaster. Changes that disrupt our social ties can have severe and wide-ranging consequences.

Source: Kai Erikson 1976.

Mohandas (Mahatma) K. Gandhi taught the modern world nonviolent methods of bringing about change in political systems. The policies of Charles Taylor, former military dictator of Liberia, created long-term war that resulted in thousands of deaths. President Robert Mugabe of Zimbabwe locked his country in a downward spiral of economic turmoil and disease, killing thousands. These leaders' actions created internal strains in their own countries and external stressors resulting in discussions and sometimes change in the international community.

Technology also influences societal change. William F. Ogburn compiled a list of 150 social changes in the United States that resulted from the invention of the radio, such as instant access to information (Ogburn 1933). Other lists could be compiled for cell phones,

Number of Refugees by Major Host Countries, 2015–2016

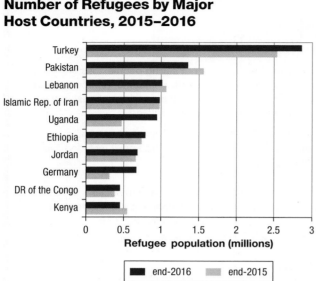

Refugee population (millions)

legend: ■ end-2016   ▨ end-2015

Source: UNHCR 2017d. Reprinted with permission from the United Nations High Commission for Refugees.

automobiles, television, computers, and newer technologies such as smartphones. Some of these changes give rise to secondary changes. For example, automobile use led to paved highways, complex systems of traffic patterns and rules, and the development of suburbs. The next Sociology in Our Social World explores several issues involving the automobile and change.

THINKING SOCIOLOGICALLY

What might be some long-term social consequences for our individual lives and societies of the widespread use of smartphones, smart speakers, and cars that can navigate themselves and warn us of hazards around us?

The diffusion or spread of technology throughout the world is likely to be uneven, especially in the early stages of the new technology. For example, computer technology has advanced rapidly, but those advances began in corporate boardrooms, military bases, and university laboratories. Policies of governing bodies—such as funding for school computers—determine the rate of public access. Thus, only gradually are computers reaching the world's citizenry through schools, libraries, and eventually private homes. Clearly, internal strains and external stressors give impetus to the processes of change. The question is how do these processes take place?

Theories of Social Change

Social scientists seek to explain the causes and consequences of social change, sometimes in the hope that change can be controlled or guided. Theories of change often reflect the events and belief systems of historical time periods. For example, conflict theory developed during periods of change in Europe. It gained adherents in the United States during the 1960s, when intense conflict over issues of race and ethnic relations, the morality of the Vietnam War, and changes in social values peaked. Theories such as structural functionalism that focused on social harmony were of little help.

The major social change theories can be categorized as micro level (symbolic interaction and rational choice theories) or meso and macro level (evolutionary, functional, conflict, and world systems theories). As we review these theories, many of them will be familiar to you from previous chapters. Here, we relate them to the process of change.

Micro-Level Theories of Change

Symbolic Interaction. According to symbolic interaction theory, human beings are always trying to make sense of the things they experience, figure out what an event or interaction means, and determine what action is required of them. Humans construct meanings that agree with or diverge from what others around them think. This capacity to define one's situation, such as concluding that one is oppressed, even though others have accepted the circumstances as normal, can be a powerful impetus to change. It can be the starting point of social movements, cultural changes, and revolutions.

Some sociologists believe that individuals are always at the core of social trends or movements, even if those movements are national or global (Blumer 1986; Giddens 1986; Simmel [1902–1917] 1950). After all, it is individuals who make decisions and act. Neither corporations nor bureaucracies nor nations make decisions—people do. Individuals who can convince others to follow them can make changes that impact whole societies. For example, there are leaders who have changed the world—for better (Mahatma Gandhi) or worse (Adolf Hitler). Even their followers, however, played roles in the changes led by these leaders. Their individual decisions to follow these leaders influenced the lives of many other people—and the course of history.

Social institutions and structures are always subject to maverick individuals "thinking outside the box" and changing how others see things. Individual actions can stimulate riots, social movements, planned change in

TECHNOLOGY AND CHANGE: THE AUTOMOBILE

Only a century ago, a newfangled novelty was spreading quickly from urban areas to the countryside: the automobile. At the turn of the 20th century, this strange horseless carriage was often referred to in rural areas as the "devil wagon." The introduction of this self-propelled vehicle was controversial; in the 1890s and early 1900s, some cities and counties had rules forbidding motorized vehicles. In Vermont, a walking escort had to precede the car by an eighth of a mile with a red warning flag, and in Iowa, motorists were required to telephone ahead to a town they planned to drive through to warn the community lest their horses be alarmed (M. Berger 1979; Clymer 1953; Glasscock 1937; L. Morris 1949). In most rural areas, motorists were expected to pull their cars to a stop or even to shut down the motor when a horse-drawn buggy came near. "Pig and chicken legal clauses" meant the automobile driver was liable for any injury, even if the injury was due to the animal running away (Scott-Montagu 1904).

Automobiles were restricted to cities for nearly a decade after their invention because roads were inadequate outside of the urban areas and vehicles often slid off muddy roads into ditches. Paving of roads became a necessity for automobile travel and, of course, made automobile travel much faster and more common. The expansion was stunning. Roughly 85,000 motored vehicles were in use in the United States in 1911. By 1930, the number was nearly 10 million, and in 2015 the number was close to 264 million (Berger 1979; Bureau of Transportation Statistics 2017; Statistica 2014).

Forms of entertainment began to change when people gained mobility. The Model T made cars affordable, so families no longer had only each other for socializing,

and entertainment became available virtually any night of the week (Berger 1979; McKelvie 1926). Thus, dependence on family was lessened, possibly weakening familial bonds and oversight (Berger 1979). Even courting was substantially changed, because individuals could go farther afield to find a possible life partner, couples could go more places on dates, and more privacy was available.

Transportation that made traversing distances easier changed how people related to a number of other institutions, as well. Motorized buses made transportation to schools possible, and attendance rates of rural children increased substantially (U.S. Department of Interior Office of Education 1930). Because people could drive farther to churches, they often chose to go to city churches, where the preachers were more skilled public speakers and the music was of higher quality (Berger 1979). Many country churches consolidated or closed (Wilson 1924). The automobile was also a boon to the mental health of isolated farm women, allowing them to visit with neighbors (Berger 1979; McNall and McNall 1983).

As people could live in less congested areas but still get to work in a reasonable amount of time via automobile, suburbs began to develop around cities. No longer did people locate homes close to shopping, schools, and places of worship. Still, a dispersed population needs to use more gasoline, thereby creating pollution. As the wealthy moved to expensive suburbs and paid higher taxes to support outstanding schools, socioeconomic and ethnic stratification between communities increased. These are some of the *unintended consequences* of the spread of the automobile. It sometimes takes decades before we can identify the consequences of technologies we adopt.

---

organizations, and a host of other outcomes that have the potential to transform society. If change feels threatening to some members who have a vested interest in the current arrangements, those individuals who advocate change may face resistance. Consider the recent U.S. debate on health care. Individuals who gained insurance under the Affordable Health Care Act (Obamacare) fought hard against those who wanted to repeal it.

Rational Choice. To rational choice theorists, behaviors are largely driven by individuals seeking rewards and reduced costs. They maintain that most individuals

engage in those activities that bring positive rewards and try to avoid actions that can have negative outcomes. A group seeking change can attempt to set up a situation in which the desired behavior is rewarded. The typology presented in Figure 16.3 shows the relationship between behaviors and sanctions.

Bringing about change may not, however, require a change in costs or rewards. It may be enough simply to change people's perception of the advantages and disadvantages of certain actions. Sometimes, people are not aware of all the rewards, or they have failed to accurately assess the costs of an action. For example, few citizens in

Relationship Between Behaviors and Sanctions

		Sanction	
		Formal	Informal
Behavior	Positive	Bonuses, advances, fringe benefits, recognition	Praise, smile, pat on the back
	Negative	Demotion, loss of salary	Ridicule, exclusion, talk behind back

the United States realize all the financial, health, and legal benefits of marriage. To change the marriage rates, we may not need more benefits to encourage marriage. We may do just as well to change the population's appraisal of the benefits already available.

Meso- and Macro-Level Theories of Change

Social Evolutionary Theories. Social evolutionary theories at the macro level assume that societies change slowly from simple to more complex forms. Early unilinear theories maintained that all societies moved through the same steps and that advancement or progress was desirable and would lead to a better society. These theories came to prominence during the Industrial Revolution, when European social scientists sought to interpret the differences between their own societies and the "primitive societies" of other continents. Europe was being stimulated by travel, exposure to new cultures, and a spawning of new philosophies, a period called the Enlightenment. Europeans witnessed the development of mines, railroads, ships, weaponry, cities, educational systems, and industries, which they defined as "progress" or "civilization." World travelers reported that other peoples

▲ The modes of transportation for goods and people vary around the world, often reflecting the level of development of the region or country. Sometimes, technological progress has high costs, including pollution.

and societies did not seem to have these developments. These reports provided the empirical evidence that early sociologist Auguste Comte used in proposing his theory of unilinear development from simple to complex societies. Unilinear theories came to legitimate colonial expansion and exploitation of other people and lands seen as less developed and "inferior."

In a more recent version of evolutionary theory, Patrick Nolan and Gerhard Lenski discuss five stages through which most societies progress: hunter-gatherer, horticultural, agrarian, industrial, and postindustrial (P. Nolan and Lenski 2014; see also Chapter 3). This does not mean that some stages are "better" than others. It simply means that this is the typical pattern of change to greater social complexity resulting from new technologies and more efficient harnessing of energy.

Contemporary evolutionary theories acknowledge that change takes place in multiple ways and not just in a straight line. The rapid spread of ideas and technologies means that societies today may move quickly from simple to complex, creating modern states. They skip steps or are selective about what aspects of technology they wish to adopt. For example, countries such as India and China are largely agricultural but are importing and developing the latest technology that allows them to skip over developmental steps. As noted in Chapter 7, many countries will not see landlines for phones but instead will have cell phones even in the more remote areas.

Some scholars disapprove of the term *developing countries* because it might imply that all societies are moving toward the type of social system characterized by the affluent or "developed" societies. As we have noted in earlier chapters, many now use the term *Global South* because poor countries are disproportionately located south of the 20th parallel north, whereas affluent nations are typically situated north of that latitude. Note that the term is a metaphor for all poor countries, meant to avoid an assumption of inevitable evolution toward Western cultures.

Functionalist Theories. Functional theorists assume that societies are basically stable systems held together by the shared norms and values of their members. The interdependent parts work together to make the society function smoothly. A change in one part of the society affects all the other parts, each changing in turn until the system resumes a state of equilibrium. Change can come from external or internal sources, from stresses in contacts with other societies or from strains within.

© Keith Roberts

Slow, nondisruptive change occurs as societies become more complex, and this may be a functional adaptation. Functional theorists, however, often see rapid change as dysfunctional or disruptive to stability. Because functionalists often view major change with suspicion, many sociologists have turned to conflict theories to help explain change, especially rapid or violent change.

Conflict Theories. Conflict theorists assume that societies are dynamic and that change and conflict are inevitable. According to Karl Marx, socioeconomic class conflict is the major source of tension leading to change in any society. Marx and Friedrich Engels predicted that the antagonistic relationship they saw developing between the workers (proletariat) and the owners of the production systems (bourgeoisie) in 19th-century England would lead to social revolution. From this, they believed a new world order would emerge in which the workers themselves would own the means of production. Thus, conflict between the owners and the workers would be the central factor driving social change (Marx and Engels [1848] 1969).

Other conflict theorists study variables such as gender, religion, politics, and ethnic or interest group problems in their analyses, believing that these factors can also be the grounds for oppression and us-versus-them differences (Dahrendorf 1959). Some see conflict as useful for society because it forces societies to adapt to new conditions and leads to healthy change (Coser 1956). Conflicts over slavery and gender inequality are examples of problems that cause stresses and strains, often resulting in an improved society.

World Systems Theory of Global Change. World systems theorists are conflict theorists who focus on how world history has influenced the status of individual countries today. Capitalist economies first appeared about 1500. Since then, except for a few isolated tribal groupings, almost all societies have been at least indirectly influenced by dominant capitalist world economic and political systems (Wallerstein 1974).

This theory divides the world system into three main parts: the core, semiperipheral, and peripheral areas (see Figure 16.4). *Core countries* include most Western European states, Australia and New Zealand, Japan, Canada, the United States, and a few others (Wallerstein 1974). Historically, they have controlled global decision-making; received the largest share of profits from the world economic system; and dominated the peripheral areas politically, economically, and culturally by controlling the flow of technology and capital into and out of those countries. *Peripheral countries*, most of which are

▼ FIGURE 16.4

World Systems Theory

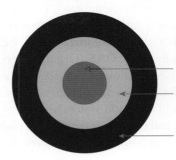

Core countries (wealthy countries of Europe, Japan, United States, Canada)

Semiperipheral countries (e.g., India, Mexico, China, Brazil)

Peripheral countries (many poor African, Asian, and Latin American nations)

in Africa, Asia, and South America, provide cheap labor and raw materials for the core countries' needs.

The *semiperipheral countries* hold an intermediate position, trading with both the core and peripheral countries. Brazil, Argentina, South Africa, India, the Philippines, Iran, Mexico, and the Baltic region of Eastern Europe are among the semiperipheral areas. Because most semiperipheral countries are industrializing, they serve as areas to which core-country businesses and multinational corporations can move for continued growth, often in partnerships, because semiperipheral states aspire to join the core countries. The core and semiperipheral countries process raw materials, often taken from peripheral countries for little in return, and may sell the final products back to the peripheral countries. The semiperipheral countries and the peripheral countries need the trade and the resources of the core countries, but they are also at a severe disadvantage in competition and are exploited by those at the core, resulting in an uneasy relationship.

Core countries have been a major force in the development of global institutions, such as the International Monetary Fund (IMF), that facilitate and attempt to control international capital flow. By creating the frameworks for debt restructuring for peripheral countries and some semiperipheral countries, the IMF attempts to restore sustainability and growth to countries that default on their loans. At least 95 countries have restructured their debt under IMF guidelines since the 1950s. A recent example is Greece, which has struggled to keep its economy from defaulting on its loan payments (Bergthaler et al. 2015; Das, Papaioannou, and Trebesch 2012). However, the IMF leaves countries little economic autonomy. The restructuring plans control what countries do even within their own national boundaries, creating debt dependencies on core countries that most poorer countries can never overcome. This often leads people in semiperipheral nations to resent the IMF and the core nations that control it (Dollars and Sense Collective 2012; Lienau 2016; Rothkopf 2012; Stiglitz 2012).

World systems theorists note that some groups of non-core countries have increased their collective power by forming alliances such as OPEC (Organization of the Petroleum Exporting Countries), OAS (Organization of African States), and SEATO (Southeast Asia Treaty Organization). These alliances present challenges to the historically core countries of the world system because of their combined economic and political power. For example, the price we pay at the gas pump reflects, in part, the power of OPEC to set prices.

When we understand international treaties and alliances as part of larger issues of conflict over resources and economic self-interests, the animosity of noncore countries toward core countries such as the United States begins to make sense. Likewise, the threat felt by the United States from countries that seem to be getting jobs once found in the United States is not entirely unfounded. The problem is an extraordinarily complex system that tends to leave the most vulnerable more at risk and the wealthiest even richer (Gibler 2012; McBride 2015; Oxfam 2017; Stiglitz 2012).

The climate crisis illustrates the world systems theory and rift between rich and poor nations. For example, tiny Pacific islands such as Nauru soon will be underwater due to global warming and water rising. Human activity, mostly from development in Global North countries, is causing what some groups of countries call *climate injustice*, and Global South nations harmed by climate change now demand compensation for damages. This world system outlook assumes that developed Global North countries are most to blame for climate change problems and therefore should be held accountable. However, nations like India and China, amid phenomenal economic growth, are now major contributors to increasing global carbon emissions. The causes of climate change are complex and not due solely to the actions of Global North countries (Myers and Kulish 2013; WorldAtlas 2017).

We have discussed examples of planned change, but sometimes behavior that results in change is unplanned, even spontaneous, as described in the following section.

THINKING SOCIOLOGICALLY

Where is your clothing made? Did a multinational corporation have it assembled in the Global South? What steps can you take to ensure that the workers who made your clothes receive tolerable working conditions and a fair wage?

Collective Behavior: Micro- to Meso-Level Change

On February 18, 2018, 3 days after a former classmate massacred 17 people at his school with an AR-15, high school junior Cameron Casky declared that students can no longer count on adults to protect them from gun violence. "We are losing our lives while the adults are playing around. . . . On March 24th you are going to see students in every major city marching. . . . We have our lives on the line here, and at the end of the day that is going to be what brings us to victory" (McLaughlin and Chavez 2018).

Individuals, like Cameron Casky and his classmates, often come together over some issue that irritates or even enrages them, and these gatherings can evolve into planned protests or mobs, riots, panics, or other forms of collective reaction to events. It is often at the micro or local level that change movements get started. These can evolve into large statewide, national, or even global movements with implications for the larger society, but because they begin with individuals in local communities deciding to take some sort of common action, we discuss them as micro- to meso-level events. Political demonstrations and stock market sell-offs are all forms of collective behavior that can stimulate change. In this section, we introduce a form of change that typically has uncertain outcomes.

Collective behavior is *spontaneous, unstructured, and disorganized actions that may violate norms; this behavior arises when people are trying to cope with stressful situations under unclear or uncertain conditions* (E. Goode 1992; Smelser 1963, 1988). Collective behavior falls into two main types: crowd behavior and mass behavior. It often starts as a response to an event or a stimulus. It could begin with a shooting or beating, a speech, a sports event, or a rumor. The key is that as individuals try to make sense of the situations they are in and respond based on their perceptions, collective social actions emerge.

Crowd behaviors—mobs, panics, riots, and demonstrations—are forms of collective behavior in which a crowd acts, at least temporarily, as a unified group (LeBon [1895] 1960). Crowds are often made up of individuals who see themselves as supporting a just cause. Because the protesters are anonymous in such a large group, they may not feel bound by normal social controls—either internal (normal moral standards) or external (fear of police sanctions).

Mass behavior occurs when individual people communicate or respond in a similar manner to ambiguous or uncertain situations, often based on common information from word-of-mouth rumors, websites, social networking, and television. Examples include fashions and fads, such as the mannequin challenge, hatch animals, and the *Hamilton* craze. Unlike social movements, these forms of collective behavior generally lack a hierarchy of authority and clear leadership, a division of labor, and a sense of group action.

Collective Behavior: Middle-Range Theories

Several explanations of individual involvement dominate the collective behavior literature. These are middle-range theories that seek to explain specific social behaviors or patterns. Social scientists studying group and crowd dynamics find that most members of crowds are respectable, law-abiding citizens, but faced with specific situations, they act out (Berk 1974; R. Turner and Killian 1993).

Based on principles of rational choice theory, the *minimax strategy* suggests that individuals try to minimize their losses or costs and maximize their benefits (Berk 1974). People are more likely to engage in crowd behavior if they feel the rewards outweigh the costs. Individuals may become involved in a riot if they feel the outcome—drawing attention to their plight, the possibility of improving conditions, solidarity with neighbors and friends, or looting goods—will be more rewarding than the status quo or possible negative sanctions.

Emergent norm theory points out that individuals have different emotions and attitudes guiding their behaviors in crowds than when they act alone (R. Turner and Killian 1993). The theory addresses the unusual situations, involving the breakdown of norms, in which most collective behavior takes place. Unusual situations may call for the development of new norms and even new definitions of acceptable behavior. The implication of this theory is that in ambiguous situations, people look to others for clues about what is happening or what is acceptable, and norms emerge in ambiguous contexts that may be considered inappropriate in other contexts. This is the most widely used approach to understanding collective behavior (R. Turner and Killian 1993).

Imagine you are at an athletic event. Someone in the crowd with a very loud voice begins to taunt a player from the visiting team. Initially some people around you laugh, but as the initiator begins to chant an insult, your friends and others around you begin to join in. Chances are good that in the camaraderie of the moment, you follow suit and start chanting the insult, too—even if it is disrespectful. Normally, you would not make such an insulting remark to someone's face, but in this situation where you are

▲ Crowds can stimulate change in a society, but they can also become unruly and unpredictable, so governments spend a good deal of money and time equipping and training officers to control crowds.

anonymous, the pattern of behavior emerged and you feel compelled to follow the crowd. This is an example of an emergent norm affecting an entire crowd.

Value-added theory (sometimes called structural-strain theory) describes the conditions for crowd behavior and social movements. Key elements are necessary for collective behavior, with each new variable adding to the total situation until conditions are sufficient for individuals to begin to act in common. At this point, collective behavior emerges (Smelser 1963). Six factors can result in collective behavior.

1. *Structural conduciveness*. Existing problems create a climate ripe for change. Consider the example of the independent country of Ukraine, caught between Russia and Western Europe. The (now-deposed) president of Ukraine stated that he planned to align Ukraine with the West, but, under pressure and promises from Russia, he changed his mind. This change angered many Ukrainians.

2. *Structural strain*. The social structure is not meeting the needs and expectations of the citizens, which creates widespread dissatisfaction with the status quo—the current arrangements. Ukrainians who felt the country would fare better if aligned with Western Europe demonstrated in the capital of Kiev.

3. *Spread of a generalized belief*. Common beliefs about the cause, effect, and solution of the problem evolve, develop, and spread. Charges spread that the pro-Russian president was corrupt, lived opulently, and had stolen money belonging to the Ukrainian people to support his lifestyle.

4. *Precipitating factor*. A dramatic event or incident occurs to incite people to action. The Ukrainian

president left the capital Kiev in fear after the guards defending him left their posts. President Putin of Russia amassed Russian troops on the Ukrainian border, charging that the president of Ukraine had been rightfully elected and that Crimea (then a section of Ukraine) should be part of Russia. Russian troops then entered Crimea, and Russia officially annexed it (declared it part of Russia).

5. *Mobilization for action*. Leaders emerge and set out a path of action, or an emergent norm develops that stimulates common action. Ukrainian leaders emerged to defend Ukraine against what they saw as Russian aggression. A newly elected Ukrainian president sent troops to eastern Ukraine to defend it against Russians living there who want to align it with Russia.

6. *Social controls are weak*. If the police, the military, or political or religious leaders are unable to counter the mobilization, a social movement or other crowd behavior may form. Ukraine's new president, parliament, and army resisted the efforts of the pro-Russian groups (assisted by Russian troops) in eastern Ukraine to establish a separate (pro-Russian) state, but Ukrainian forces and resources are much less than Russia's. As we write these words, the outcome remains unclear (and Russia still occupies Crimea).

When all six of these factors are present, some sort of collective behavior will emerge. Those interested in controlling volatile crowds must intervene and take control when one or more of these conditions exists (Flynn 2014; Smelser 1963).

THINKING SOCIOLOGICALLY

Think of an example of a crowd behavior or social movement. Which of the previous theories best explains it, and why?

▲ All six social factors that contribute to collective behavior were present in 2014 in Kiev, Ukraine, and the results were riots in the streets, the overthrow of the Ukrainian president, and the annexation of Crimea by Russia.

© AP Photo/Sergei Grits

Types of Collective Behavior

Collective behavior ranges from spontaneous violent mobs to temporary fads and fashions. Figure 16.5 shows the range of actions.

Mobs are emotional crowds that engage in violence against a specific target. Examples include lynchings, killings, and hate crimes. Near the end of the U.S. Civil War, self-appointed vigilante groups roamed the countryside in the South looking for Confederate army deserters, torturing and killing both those who harbored deserters and the deserters themselves. There were no courts and no laws, just "justice" in the eyes of the vigilantes. The members of these groups constituted mobs. The film *Cold Mountain* depicts these scenes vividly. Unless deterred, mobs often damage or destroy their target.

Riots—an outbreak of illegal violence against random or shifting targets committed by crowds expressing frustration or anger against people, property, or groups in power—begin when certain conditions occur. Often, a sense of frustration or deprivation sets the stage for a riot—hunger, poverty, poor housing, lack of jobs, discrimination, poor education, or an unresponsive or unfair judicial system. If the conditions for collective behavior are present, many types of incidents can be the

▼ FIGURE 16.5

Types of Collective Behavior

Spontaneous and often violent					Less spontaneous and seldom violent
	Crowd behavior			Mass behavior	
Mob	Riot	Panic	Rumor	Fad	Fashion

precipitating factor setting off a riot. For example, in the spring of 2015, residents of Baltimore, Maryland, became outraged when Freddie Gray died while in police custody. While some residents protested peacefully, others looted and burned down stores. The difference between riots and mobs is illustrated in Figure 16.6.

Panic occurs when many people become fearful or try to flee threatening situations beyond their control, sometimes putting their lives in danger. Panic can occur in a crowd situation, such as a restaurant or theater in which someone yells "Fire!" Or it can occur following rumors or information spread by the media. Panic started by rumors set off the run on the stock market in October 1929. A large number of actions by individuals caused the stock market crash in the United States, with repercussions around the world. In 2008, the collapse of the global investment banking and securities trader Bear, Stearns & Co. resulted in turmoil in the financial markets. Only radical intervention by the federal government abated the immediate panic. Panics can result in the collapse of an organization, destruction of communities, or death of innocent people.

Rumors are forms of mass behavior in which unsupported or unproven reports about a problem, issue, or concern circulate widely throughout the public. Rumors may spread only in a local area, but online rumors can spread more widely and rapidly. Without authoritative information, ambiguous situations can produce faulty information on which decisions are made and actions are based. *Urban legends*, one example of widely spread

▲ Jimmy Fallon challenges actress Lindsay Lohan to the Ice Bucket Challenge fad—a fund-raiser for combatting Lou Gehrig's disease, a neurodegenerative ailment that often results in death within 5 years. The money raised went to support medical research for this illness.

but unverified messages, are unsubstantiated stories that sound plausible and become widely circulated. The people telling these stories usually believe them (Mikkelson and Mikkelson 2012). The next Sociology in Our Social World provides an example. (Go to www.snopes.com/college/college.asp for some additional entertaining urban legends about professors, exam scams, embarrassments, and other college pranks.)

Fads are temporary behaviors, activities, or material objects that spread rapidly and are copied enthusiastically by large numbers of people. Body modification, especially tattooing, appeals mostly to young people of all social classes. Tattoo artists emblazon IDs, secret society and organization emblems, fraternity symbols, and decorations on all parts of customers' bodies. Body modification has taken place for centuries, but it goes through fads (University of Pennsylvania 2010). Sometimes, fads become institutionalized—that is, they gain a permanent place in the culture. Other fads die out, replaced by the next hot item. In 2015, one fund-raising fad, the "Ice Bucket Challenge," a gimmick to support research on ALS (also known as Lou Gehrig's disease), raised $115 million in just 6 weeks (Kristof 2015).

Fashions refer to a style of appearance and behavior temporarily favored by many people. Examples include clothing styles, music genres, color schemes in home decor, types of automobiles, and architectural designs. Fashions typically last longer than fads but sometimes survive less than a season, as can be seen in the clothing industry. (Following fashions can be fun but can also lead to waste and overconsumption that damages the environment and our bank accounts.)

▼ FIGURE 16.6
Difference Between Riots and Mobs

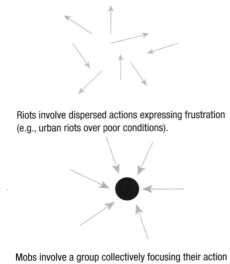

Riots involve dispersed actions expressing frustration (e.g., urban riots over poor conditions).

Mobs involve a group collectively focusing their action on a single individual or location (e.g., a lynch mob).

EXAM STORIES: TESTING THE TRUTH

College exams are quickly approaching, so it is a good time to look at the latest chapter in the tome of teacher-student legend and rumors.

One example was reported from Calgary, Alberta, by a civil engineering student at the University of Manitoba. This tale says a professor announced an open-book final examination in which the students could "use anything they are able to carry into the exam room." One innovative undergraduate, it is reported, carried in a graduate student who wrote his exam for him.

Another legend came from North Carolina. Supposedly, on the day before the final exam, the professor left his office unattended, with the door open and the examinations sitting on his desk. A student who came by to ask a question found the room empty and quickly left with one of the exams. However, the professor had printed the exact number of exams that he needed, and the next morning, he counted them again before going to the classroom. Discovering that he was one short, he suspected that it had been stolen, so he trimmed a half inch from the bottom of the remaining exams. When the exam papers were turned in, the student whose paper was longer than the others' received a failing grade.

Finally, two guys were taking introductory chemistry, and they had done so well on all the quizzes that by the last week of class they each had a solid A. These friends were so confident going into the final that on the weekend before the exam they partied. However, with hangovers on Monday, they overslept and missed the exam. They found the professor and told him they missed the final because they had been away, had had a flat tire on the way back to campus, and were without a spare. The professor thought this over and agreed that they could make up the final. The two studied intensely that night and went in the next day for the exam. The professor placed them in separate rooms and handed each of them a test booklet and told them to begin. The first problem was simple and was worth 5 points. They were both relieved. They did the first problem and then turned the page. The next question was "Which tire? (95 points)."

Campus legends such as these help reduce the strain of college life and spread the reputations of legendary professors. Furthermore, they keep alive hopes of someday outfoxing the professors—or the students, depending on which side you are on.

Source: www.snopes.com.

Each of these forms of collective behavior involves micro-level individual actions that cumulatively become collective responses to certain circumstances. Insofar as these various types of collective activity upset the standard routines of society and the accepted norms, they can unsettle the entire social system and cause lasting change (for good or bad). When we move to meso- and macro-level analyses, the established structures and processes of society become increasingly important. Much of the change at these levels is planned change.

Planned Change in Organizations: Meso-Level Change

The board of trustees of a small liberal arts college has witnessed recent drops in student enrollment that could cause the college to go out of business, but the college has a long tradition of fine education and devoted alumni. How does the college continue to serve future students and current alumni? The challenge is to plan change to keep the college solvent.

A company manufactures silicon chips for computers. Recently, the market has been flooded with inexpensive chips, primarily from Asia, where they are made more cheaply than this North American firm can possibly make them. Does the company succumb to the competition, figure out ways to meet it, or diversify its products? What steps should be taken to facilitate the change? Many companies in Silicon Valley, California, have faced exactly this challenge.

A Native American nation within the United States faces unemployment among its people due largely to discrimination by Anglos in the local community. Should the elders focus their energies and resources on electing sympathetic politicians, boycotting racist businesses, filing lawsuits, becoming entrepreneurs as a nation so they can hire their own people, or starting a local radio station so they will have a communication network for a social movement? What is the best strategy to help this proud nation recover from centuries of disadvantage?

All of these are real problems faced by real organizations. Anywhere we turn, organizations face questions involving change, questions that arise because of internal strains and external stresses. How organizational leaders deal with change will determine the survival and well-being of the organizations.

How Organizations Plan for Change

In a 2018 indictment related to Russian interference in the 2016 presidential election, United States government "officials detailed how the Russians repeatedly turned to Facebook and Instagram, often using stolen identities to pose as Americans, to sow discord among the electorate by creating Facebook groups, distributing divisive ads and posting inflammatory messages" (Frenkel and Benner 2018). After first trying to dismiss concerns raised shortly after the election, Facebook changed course as evidence mounted, admitting that 150 million people in the United States had seen the Russian propaganda on Facebook or Instagram (which is owned by Facebook). The company had not planned for this type of event, and it is now scrambling to simultaneously recover from this bad publicity, make its platforms safer, and keep increasing its users.

All organizations must change. Sometimes, as in the case for Facebook, change is forced on the organization. Such change can result from *stresses* from society (e.g., Russians trying to influence U.S. elections or competition from other organizations) or *strains* from individuals and groups within organizations pushing for new ideas. Often, a problem solved in one area can create unanticipated problems someplace else.

Organizational leaders must be prepared to guide their organization through planned and unplanned changes. Planned change involves strategic planning: deliberate, structured attempts, guided by stated goals, to alter the status quo of the social unit (Bennis, Benne, and Chin 1985; Ferhansyed 2008). The relationship between leaders and recipients of change is key to successful change, and employee commitment to change is necessary for that success (Hughes 2015; van der Voet 2015).

Several important questions should be considered before undertaking planned change: How can we identify what needs to be changed? How can we plan or manage the change process successfully? What kind of systems adapt well to change? Here, we outline three of the many approaches to planned change. Keep in mind the levels of analysis as you read about change models.

Models for Planning Organizational Change. Change models fall into two main categories: (1) closed-system models, which deal with the internal dynamics of the organization, and (2) open-system models (such as our social world model), which consider the organization and its environment. *Closed-system models*, often called classical or mechanistic models, focus on the internal dynamics of the organization. The goal of change using closed models is to move the organization closer to the ideal of bureaucratic efficiency and effectiveness. For example, time and motion studies analyze how much time it takes a worker to do a certain task and how it can be accomplished more efficiently. Each step in McDonald's process of getting a hamburger to the customer has been planned and timed for the greatest efficiency (Ritzer 2018).

In some closed-system models, top executives legislate change, and it filters down to the workers. Other organizations follow a closed-system change model with an organizational development approach. They involve participants in the organization in decision-making leading to change. The leadership is more democratic and supportive of workers, and the atmosphere is transparent—open, honest, and accountable to workers and investors. This model emphasizes that change comes about through adjusting workers' values, beliefs, and attitudes regarding new demands on the organization. Many variations on this theme have evolved, with current efforts including team building and change of the organizational culture to improve worker morale.

Open-system models combine both internal processes and the external environment. The latter provides the organization with inputs (workers and raw materials) and feedback (acceptability of the product or result). In turn, the organization has outputs (products) that affect the larger society. There are three implications of this model: (1) Change is an ever-present and ongoing process, (2) all parts of the organization and its immediate environment are linked, and (3) change in one part influences the other parts. Change can be initiated from within or from outside the organization. The model in Figure 16.7 illustrates the open system.

▼ FIGURE 16.7

Open System Model

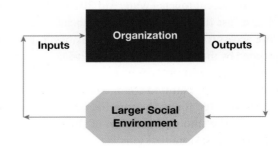

Process of Planned Change. A huge issue in the Global South is the availability of clean drinking water. For example, in parts of Africa, women must spend as much as 6 hours a day carrying water to their homes. Because older daughters care for the younger siblings while the mother is away, many girls cannot attend school. Sometimes the water found is not clean, leading to water-related diseases and more lost school days. Moreover, one in three schools has no clean water or toilets, causing many menstruating girls to stay away when on their periods. This, in turn, has implications for the continuation of poverty (WaterAid 2017). Scientists and public policy NGOs work to plan changes and address such problems. Consider the following example.

With global climate change, the glaciers on top of mountains such as Mount Kenya are melting. Although that mountain peak has been snow-covered for more than 10,000 years, the glaciers are expected to be completely gone in approximately 30 years. When the snow on the mountaintop disappears, the water supply for hundreds of thousands of people and animals will disappear (Cousteau 2008; Mangat 2017). One British NGO bringing about change in this area is WaterAid, launched in 1981. It has grown to become an international NGO that focuses entirely on water and sanitation issues, including hygiene. WaterAid now assists communities throughout the world to develop the most appropriate technologies for clean water, given the geographical features and changes in resources in their areas. This is an issue that requires careful planning and strategic use of resources if change is to be effective and have positive outcomes.

Using planned change, since 1981 WaterAid has reached 26.8 million people with safe water and 27 million people with decent toilets (WaterAid 2016, 2018). Some sociologists use their understanding of social processes to improve access to safe water and water management. This is illustrated by the work of Ruth Meinzen-Dick, described in the next Sociologists in Action.

The process of planned change is like a puzzle with pieces that differ for each organization but must fit together for the smooth operation of the organization. The goal of most organizations is to continually fulfill their respective missions and to avoid threats or conflict. They tend to prefer to change in a slow, carefully planned way because unplanned change can be disruptive to the system. We turn next to an exploration of change at the macro level.

Social Movements: Macro-Level Change

If you are making more than the minimum wage, you may owe The Fight for $15 movement a thank you. The Fight for $15 began in 2012 with 200 fast-food workers in New York City who had the courage to collectively walk away from their jobs and demand a raise and union rights. Today, it is a global movement of low-wage workers (including fast-food employees, childcare teachers, home health aides, and adjunct professors) that has raised wages for millions. In this section, we define social movements and look at how they form and affect the larger society.

What Is a Social Movement?

Social movements are *consciously organized attempts outside of established institutions to enhance or resist change through group action.* Movements focus on a common interest of members, such as abortion policy. They have an organization, defined leadership, and one or more goals that aim to correct some perceived wrongs existing in their nation or even around the globe. Social movements are most often found in industrial or postindustrial societies although they can occur anywhere groups of people have a concern or frustration.

Social movements entail large groups of people who hold little power individually but do have power as united

▲ Homecare workers take part in a National Day of Action Fight for $15 protest at the Massachusetts State House in Boston in November 2016.

SOCIOLOGISTS IN ACTION
Ruth Meinzen-Dick

NATURAL RESOURCE MANAGEMENT IN DEVELOPING COUNTRIES

What does a sociologist have to say about natural resource management? This is a question Ruth Meinzen-Dick has often been asked during her career. For 24 years, she has studied how farmers organize and relate to government and other organizations through her work at the International Food Policy Research Institute (IFPRI), part of a larger network of international agricultural research organizations.

Meinzen-Dick's interest in water management came from growing up in a dry part of India, where water was critical. After earning a doctorate in sociology, she returned to India to study how small-scale irrigation systems were operated and found that farmers' organizations played an important role, even though the systems were formally under government management. Other students and faculty from different fields at Cornell University were finding similar patterns of farmer-managed irrigation systems in other parts of the world, so Meinzen-Dick was able to be part of a larger effort to understand the human side of water management. This was not just an academic exercise. Even while still in graduate school, Meinzen-Dick had a consultancy with the World Bank to review the extent of farmer participation in their irrigation programs.

During her work at IFPRI, Meinzen-Dick has been able to continue studying what brings people together to manage water systems in developing countries and to compare this with the factors that encourage collective action for managing forests, rangelands, and other natural resources. This has involved field research in countries such as India, Pakistan, Zimbabwe, Kenya, and Uganda. She brought all this research together by coordinating the international network Collective Action and Property Rights (CAPRi). This network helps people working on different aspects of agricultural research and natural resource management in developing countries to understand that the social institutions of property rights and collective action play a major role in shaping how people use and share resources. The CAPRi program provides training in quantitative and qualitative research methods to researchers and practitioners interested in collective action, property rights, and research strategies.

Much of Meinzen-Dick's professional life has involved working across disciplines. It has been especially important for her to communicate the findings of sociological research clearly to nonsociologists. Institutional economics and a strong background in quantitative analysis have been especially helpful for her in communicating with her colleagues—mostly economists. She says, "It is exhilarating when the research team achieves changes in government policies or development programs such as allowing farmers to have more voice in water management."

★ ★ ★ ★ ★ ★

Ruth Meinzen-Dick received her master's and PhD degrees in development sociology at Cornell University, with minors in agricultural economics and international agriculture. She is a senior research fellow at the International Food Policy Research Institute (IFPRI), with research in water resource management.

---

groups that promote or resist social change. The concerns leading to social movements often result from the way resources—human rights, jobs, income, housing, money for education and health care, and power—are distributed. In turn, *countermovements*—social movements against the goals of the original movement—may develop, representing other opinions (J. McCarthy and Zald 1977).

Many individuals join social movements to change the world or their part of the world and affect the direction of history. In fact, some social movements have been successful in doing just that. Consider the movements around the world that have protected lands, forests, rivers, and oceans, seeking environmental protection for the people whose survival depends on these natural resources. For example, the Chipko movement (meaning "embrace") fought the logging of forests by commercial industries in a number of areas in India. Villagers, mostly women, successfully used Gandhi-style nonviolent methods to oppose the deforestation. Their tactics have been used by environmental activists in many parts of the world who wish to save our ecosystem (Petruzzello 2017).

Stages of Social Movements

Why do people become involved in social movements such as PETA (People for the Ethical Treatment of

Animals), pro-choice or pro-life movements, or school safety or pro-gun rights movements? Social movements begin because of cultural conflicts in society and because people who want to create—or resist—social change come together. Movements take the time and energy of individual volunteers, and these human resources must be focused as the movement evolves.

The *first stage* of a social movement involves setting the purpose of the movement. Long-standing problems or recent events may create dissatisfaction and discontent in the general public or a part of the public. This discontent can galvanize people to take collective action.

Sociologists have identified four conditions that give rise to the *preliminary stage* of a social movement.

1. The individuals involved *share some basic values and ideals*. They often occupy similar social statuses or positions and share concerns.

2. Social movements need to have a *preexisting communication network* that allows alienated or dissatisfied people to share their discontent (Farley 2011). The civil rights movement used churches and colleges. Today, many social movements use social media to communicate.

3. A *strain and a precipitating event* galvanize people around the issue. Effective leadership emerges—leaders who can mobilize people, organize the movement, and garner resources to fund the movement.

4. The people in the movement develop a *sense of efficacy*, a sense of confidence that they can be successful and change the system. Sometimes, as in the case of the civil rights movement, a sense of efficacy comes from a religious conviction that God will not let the movement fail (Farley 2011).

The *second stage* in the development of a movement is popularization, in which individuals coalesce their efforts, define their goals and strategies, develop recruitment tactics, and identify leaders. The social movement enters the public arena. The leaders present the social problems and solutions as seen by the members of the social movement. Now the social movement enters the *third stage*, becoming institutionalized and a formal organization. This organized effort generates the resources and members for the social change efforts.

In some movements, the final *fourth stage* is fragmentation and demise. The group may have achieved its goals and decided to disband. Or the organization may reach its demise for other reasons, including a lack of resources, loss of leadership, or co-optation by powerful mainline organizations. In the latter case, radical renewal movements may arise among those still strongly committed to the original cause (Mauss 1975).

Social movements sometimes focus on regional or even organizational modification, but typically, their focus is on national or global issues. For example, Amnesty International's primary interest is in challenging countries with human rights violations. It publishes information on violations around the world and encourages supporters to advocate for those who face government persecution. One way to classify social movements is by their purpose or goals, as seen in the following section.

Types of Social Movements

Stonewall is a gay, lesbian, and bisexual rights movement that began when patrons of the Stonewall gay bar fought back against a police raid in New York in 1969. After that incident, the concern about gay rights erupted from a small number of activists into a widespread movement for rights and acceptance. Stonewall now has gone global, with chapters in many countries and across continents.

Proactive social movements such as Stonewall advocate moving forward with a new initiative—proposing something that did not exist before. Another example is the effort by the Nonhuman Rights Project to give mammals such as chimpanzees legal rights of personhood. The Supreme Court ruled in the *Citizens United* case that corporations can be considered "persons." Now the Nonhuman Rights Project and Harvard professor Steven Wise argue that dogs, cats, elephants, and other animals should be protected with rights of persons (such as the right to bodily integrity) because they are aware, thinking, feeling, compassionate, communicating beings (Nonhuman Rights Project 2016). Regardless of whether you think this is an idea whose time has come or a harebrained notion, it would clearly change many aspects of society and move us in an entirely new direction.

Reactive social movements resist change, reacting against something that exists or against new trends or social policies. The alt-right provides an example of a current reactive social movement. It is composed of various organizations and individuals who find unity in the belief that White identity—and civilization, itself—is under attack from those advocating for acceptance of diversity and multiculturalism; they are reacting to changes in society by resisting change (Southern Poverty Law Center 2017a).

Note that both liberals and conservatives can be involved in a reactive movement. When businesses want to build a corporation or plant in an area that will wipe out a native forest or destroy a historic area, liberals can be at the forefront of fighting "progress." The designation *proactive* or *reactive* only tells us whether a group supports or resists a change. There are other aspects of social movements and other ways of thinking about movements, as expressed in the five main types of social movements: expressive, social reform, revolutionary, resistance or regressive, and globalized.

Expressive movements take place in groups, but they *focus on changing individuals and saving people from lifestyles the movement considers corrupt.* Many expressive movements are religious, such as the born-again Christian movements, Zen Buddhism, Scientology, and the Christian Science Church. Expressive movements also include secular psychotherapy movements and self-help or self-actualization groups.

Social reform movements *seek to change some specific dimension of society, usually involving legislative policy modification or appeals to the courts.* They are typically proactive. Movement members generally support the society as a whole but think things could be better if attention were given to issues such as environmental protection, women's rights, same-sex marriage, "just and fair" globalization, reducing the national debt, or abortion policy.

The Special Olympics International provides an example of a social reform movement. Begun by Eunice Kennedy Shriver in 1968, it gives those with intellectual or physical disabilities an opportunity to excel in sports. Over 3 million athletes from 150 countries now participate in these games (see www.specialolympics.org).

The 2017 Special Olympic World Winter Games were held in Austria, featuring athletes with physical, mental, and sensorial disabilities. These events bring attention to the movement and issues faced by those with disabilities. Of particular interest were the advances the movement has helped to stimulate in physical adaptations for amputees, such as ice hockey using two sticks.

Revolutionary movements *attempt to transform society to bring about total change in society by overthrowing existing power structures and replacing them with new ones; these movements often resort to violent means to achieve goals.* These movements are always proactive. When we read in the paper that there has been a coup, we are learning about the ousting of an existing government such as when, in 2017, the president of Venezuela, Nicolas Maduro, dissolved the National Assembly and the Supreme Court (which he controlled) and took control of legislative powers.

Resistance or regressive movements *try to protect an existing system, protect part of that system, or return to what a system had been by overthrowing current laws and practices. They see societal change as a threat to values or practices and wish to maintain the status quo or return to a former status by reversing the change process* (Eitzen and Zinn 2012; Inglehart and Baker 2001). Thus, they are always reactive. ISIS, or ISIL as it is sometimes called, is a regressive movement against modernization, especially against the Western pattern of giving freedom and autonomy to women. Recently, the movement controlled parts of Syria and Iraq for several years, imposing a harsh brand of Islamic law in the areas under its control. ISIS, like the Taliban in Afghanistan, insists that its version of Islam is pure in that it follows a literal understanding of the Muslim holy book. Members of the movement maintain that someone who commits adultery should be stoned to death; the hands or arms of thieves should be amputated; and women who deviate from the Taliban interpretation of Muslim law should be mutilated, publicly beaten, and sometimes executed (G. Wood 2015).

Global transnational movements are *mobilized groups that take place across societies as international organizations.* Such groups focus on issues that affect the global community, such as the status of women, child labor, the rights of indigenous peoples, environmental degradation, global climate change, and disease pandemics. Free the Slaves, an antislavery movement started by sociologist Kevin Bales, provides one example of a global transnational movement. Members of this movement have researched and written about the plight of the 40 million slaves in the world, "forced to work without pay, under threat of violence and unable to walk away" (Free the Slaves 2018; International Labour Organization 2017).

Often these transnational movements are proactive—but not always. The movement by some environmental groups to halt the use of genetically modified organisms (GMOs) in food production provides an example of a reactive transnational social movement. Members of this movement argue (among other things) that GMOs can create new allergens, bugs resistant to insecticide, and unknown health risks for those who eat genetically modified food (Diaz and Fridovich-Keil 2016).

Figure 16.8 summarizes the types of movements and the focus of each, from the micro to the macro level.

Globalization and Social Movements

Social movements provide compelling evidence that humans make choices and are capable of countering macro- and meso-level forces. As Stanley Eitzen and Maxine Baca Zinn put it, "Powerful social structures constrain what we do, but they can never control (us) entirely. Human beings are not passive actors. . . . Individuals

▼ FIGURE 16.8

Types of Movements

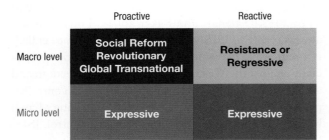

	Proactive	Reactive
Macro level	Social Reform Revolutionary Global Transnational	Resistance or Regressive
Micro level	Expressive	Expressive

▲ A statue of Nelson Mandela, who voted for the first time in South Africa in 1994. He had been a political prisoner for 26 years before becoming president of South Africa and winning the Nobel Peace Prize. Mandela provides a model for those committed to nonviolent revolutionary change.

acting alone, or with others, can shape, resist, challenge, and sometimes change the social structures that impinge on them. These actions constitute *human agency*" (Eitzen and Zinn 2012:269).

Globalization from below refers to the efforts by common people in small groups and protest movements to fight back against global economic forces that have primarily benefited the wealthy few at the expense of the masses (Della Porta et al. 2006; Eitzen and Zinn 2012). These countermovements seek to protect workers, defend the environment, and combat the bone-crunching poverty that plagues so much of the Global South and many of the poor and working classes in the Global North. The argument goes like this:

It is the activity of people—going to work, paying taxes, buying products, obeying government officials, staying off private property—that continually re-creates the power of the powerful. . . . [The system, for all its power and resources, depends on common people to do the basic jobs that keep the

society running.] This dependency gives people a potential power over the society—but one that can be realized only if they are prepared to reverse their acquiescence. . . . Social movements can be understood as the collective withdrawal of consent to established institutions. (Brecher et al. 2012:279)

The movement against corporate-dominated globalization can be understood as individuals and countries withdrawing consent for globalization dominated by global corporations (Brecher et al. 2012). There are thousands of small resistance actions against what are sometimes perceived to be the oppressive policies of transnational corporations (Hearn 2012). They involve micro-level actions to bring change at the macro level. Consider the following example.

Under heavy pressure from the World Bank, the Bolivian government sold off the public water system of its third-largest city, Cochabamba, to a subsidiary of the San Francisco–based Bechtel Corporation, which promptly doubled the price of water for people's homes. Early in 2000, the people of Cochabamba rebelled, shutting down the city with general strikes and blockades. The government declared a state of siege, and a young protester was shot and killed. Word spread all over the world from the remote Bolivian highlands via the Internet. Hundreds of e-mail messages poured into Bechtel from all over the world, demanding that it leave Cochabamba. Amid local and global protests, the Bolivian government, which had said that Bechtel must not leave, suddenly reversed itself and signed an accord accepting every demand of the protesters (Brecher et al. 2012:284; Wearewater 2017).

Many concerned citizens in the Global North now buy fair trade–certified goods such as coffee, cocoa, and fruits. This is an effort by individuals to support *globalization from below*—a different model of how to change the world. Activists believe that actions by individuals and small groups—globalization from below—can have a real impact on global problems. Consider how effective you think the actions taken by individuals and local groups can be by thinking about the issues in the next Engaging Sociology.

In summary, some social change is planned by organizations (planned change), some is initiated by groups outside the organizational structure (social movements), and some is unplanned and spontaneous (collective behavior). The most important point, however, is that actions taken by individuals affect the larger social world, sometimes even having global ramifications. Likewise, national and international changes and social movements influence the lives of individuals.

The following Sociologists in Action describes how a graduate student and his friends figured out how to help others bring about social change.

MICRO TO MACRO: CHANGE FROM THE BOTTOM UP

The idea of globalization "from the bottom up" suggests that the actions of a lot of people at the micro or local level can have a significant impact on how things develop at the macro level. Think about that process and what forces can enhance or retard that kind of change.

1. Are you familiar with cases in which "globalization from below" has made a difference in local, national, or international events? If so, what are those? If not, do a Google search of the Zapatistas of Mexico or of their leader, Subcomandante Marcos. What are the pros and cons of this movement? Do you think the Zapatistas have any chance of bringing change to the poor, disfranchised people of southern Mexico? Why or why not?

2. Identify three structural challenges that might make it hard for people at the micro level to change the national and global forces that interfere with the quality of their lives.

3. Identify three reasons to be optimistic about why change from the bottom up can be successful.

SOCIOLOGISTS IN ACTION
Ellis Jones

EMPOWERING EVERYDAY PEOPLE: DEMOCRATIZING ACCESS TO SOCIAL CHANGE

On April 22, 1990, something changed for me. It was a Sunday. I was a student at the University of Southern California, and a friend invited me to walk down to a fair that was going on nearby. I did not have any plans, so I decided to join him. Apparently, it was something called Earth Day. There were tables and booths everywhere, and people were excitedly milling about from one to the next. Every booth I visited offered me a different way to make a positive environmental impact: recycling, composting, conserving water, reusing old clothes, and the list went on and on.

At the end of that day, I felt absolutely inspired to make the world a better place. In my mind, the environmental movement had experienced a stroke of true genius. They were not asking people to join groups, attend meetings, or organize rallies. Instead, they had opened up a completely new realm of action for people—their own everyday lives. By engaging people in micro-activism rather than asking them to commit to the much more intensive work undertaken by full-time activists, they were essentially democratizing access to social change. It was a way to expand the environmental movement to almost anyone despite their limits of time, money, skills, or circumstances.

The more I thought about this potential, the more I became convinced that what people really needed was a book—a single resource—that would contain as many actions on environmental protection, human rights, social justice, animal rights, feminism, and LGBTQIA issues as possible. I was absolutely sure that someone would write it and that I, in turn, would be first in line to buy it. Ten years later, I was a sociology graduate student at the University of Colorado, Boulder. I had waited, patiently, for the imaginary author of this hypothetical book to appear, and he or she had yet to step forward.

I decided right then that I had waited long enough. So I roped in two of my closest friends (also fellow

(Continued)

sociology grad students), and we spent the next year writing a book that collected all of the actions we could find, from every source we could get our hands on, and distilled the results into a single book. We added a section summarizing the latest data on some of the most significant social and environmental problems we seemed to be facing at the beginning of the 21st century, and the result was *The Better World Handbook: Small Changes That Make a Big Difference*. It has since sold 25,000 copies, been added to more than 300 college and university libraries worldwide, and been adopted in sociology classrooms across the country. In a very practical sense, sociology provided the three of us with the tools we needed to uncover, understand, and translate our world's social and environmental problems into a form that allows each of us to personally contribute to their resolution.

★ ★ ★ ★ ★ ★

Ellis Jones received his doctorate from the University of Colorado at Boulder and is now an assistant professor of sociology at College of the Holy Cross in Worcester, Massachusetts.

In the opening to this book, we asked whether you as an individual can make a difference. You now know the answer is a resounding "Yes!" This final Engaging Sociology provides a plan you can follow to make a difference.

ENGAGING SOCIOLOGY

MAKING A DIFFERENCE

Because bringing about change requires cooperation, working in a group context is often essential. Flexibility, openness to new ideas, and willingness to entertain alternative suggestions are also key factors in successful change-making. The following steps provide a useful strategy for planning change.

1. *Identify the issue.* Be specific and focus on what is to be changed. Without clear focus, your target for change can get muddied or lost in the attempt.

2. *Research the issue and use those findings.* Learn as much as you can about the situation or problem to be changed. Use informants, interviews, written materials, observation, existing data (such as U.S. Census Bureau statistics), or anything that helps you understand the issues. That will enable you to find the information you need to thoroughly understand the issue you wish to address.

3. *Find out what has already been done and by whom.* Other individuals or groups may be working on the same issue. Be sure you know what findings and intervention have already taken place. This can also

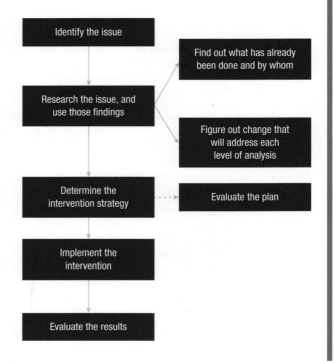

help determine whether attempts at change have been tried, what has been successful, and whether further change is needed.

4. *Change must consider each level of analysis.* When planning a strategy, you may focus on one level of analysis, but be sure to consider what interventions are needed at other levels to make the change effective or to anticipate the effects of change on other levels.

5. *Determine the intervention strategy.* Map out the intervention and the steps to carry it out. Identify resources needed and plan each step in detail.

6. *Evaluate the plan.* Get feedback on the plan from those involved in the issue and from unbiased colleagues. If possible, involve those who will be affected by the intervention in the planning and evaluation of the change. When feasible, test the intervention plan before implementing it.

7. *Implement the intervention.* Put the plan into effect, watching for any unintended consequences. Ask for regular feedback from those affected by the change.

8. *Evaluate the results.* Assess what is working, what is not, and how the constituents that experience the change are reacting. Sociological knowledge and skills should help guide this process.

Engaging Sociology

1. Use the steps to plan how you might bring about a change that would make a difference at your college, in your community, in your country, or in the world.

2. Go to Contributing to Our Social World: What Can We Do? at the end of this and other chapters to find ways in which you can be actively involved in bettering society.

WHAT HAVE WE LEARNED?

Sociology teaches us that the choices we make facilitate change at each level in our social world. It also helps us to learn how to work with groups to make a difference.

As you face individual challenges to bring about change in your social world, keep in mind this message: Change at one level affects all other levels. Sociology as a discipline is focused on gathering accurate information about the society in which we live. Sociologists often use their knowledge to advocate for changes that they think will make a better society. We hope that through this book and your course you have gained important sociological insights that will help you contribute to the dialogue about how to make our social world a better, more humane place.

KEY POINTS

- Science and technology can stimulate change. Science has its greatest impact for change when it is institutionalized and becomes a part of the society.

- Social change—variation or alteration over time in behavior patterns, culture, or structure in a society—typically involves change at one level of the social system that ripples through the other levels: micro, meso, and macro.

- *Strains* within an organization or group can induce change, as can *stresses* imposed from the outside environment.

- Sociological theories—whether micro or macro—offer explanations for the causes of change.

- At the micro level, change is often initiated through collective behavior, which can take several forms: crowds, mobs, riots, rumors, fads, and fashions.

- At the meso level, change in organizations is often managed through a planned process.

- Social movements often provide impetus for change at the macro level. Social changes can be induced at the micro level, but they can have impacts even at the global level.

- Social structures constrain what we do, but individuals, especially when acting in concert with others, can challenge, resist, and change the social systems that constrain them. We can change our society through *human agency*.

DISCUSSION QUESTIONS

1. What is the latest technological device you or your family has acquired? How has it changed your life? What are the (a) intended and (b) unintended consequences of your having it?

2. Describe a time when you participated in a form of collective behavior (crowds, mobs, riots, rumors, fads, and fashions). How does the information in this chapter help you to better understand your participation?

3. Every organization must adapt to change. Describe how an organization to which you belong coped with change. Was the adaptation successful? Why or why not? What was your role? Did you feel as though you had some influence over the adaptation strategy? Why or why not?

4. What type of social movement helped bring about the dramatic increase in support for same-sex marriage over the past decade? Why? How do the results of this movement indicate the power of social movements to influence society at the micro, meso, and macro levels?

5. If you were to join a social movement today, which would you join? Why? What would you hope to achieve?

KEY TERMS

collective behavior   508

expressive movements   517

global transnational movements   517

resistance or regressive movements   517

revolutionary movements   517

science   495

social change   494

social movements   514

social reform movements   517

CONTRIBUTING TO OUR SOCIAL WORLD: WHAT CAN WE DO?

At the Local (Micro) Level

- *Campus-wide movements.* A wide range of social issues, including international peace, environmental issues, human rights, and specific student concerns such as campus safety and the rising cost of higher education may have movements represented on your campus. Consider participating in such activities. If you feel strongly about an issue for which no movement exists, consider organizing one with a few like-minded students. You can find tools to create a campus movement at www.campusactivism.org/index .php or www.campusactivism.org/displayresource-471.htm.

- Students can sponsor a TEDx event on campus around a special issue or theme or organize an event with broader appeal. This creates an opportunity for students to take leadership in designing, promoting, and organizing this event. See directions at the TED site: https://www.ted.com/participate/organize-a-local-tedx-event/community-resources/event-type-resources/university-event-resources.

- Students can develop pop-up marketplaces for local social enterprises and other vendors. See the example of the Social Change Marketplace at Bryant University: www .socialchangemarketplace.com.

- Many *community movements* bring about change at the local level, sometimes with national and even international effects. Check with your professors, service learning and campus activities offices, and chambers of commerce to find community movements in your area.

At the Organizational or Institutional (Meso) Level

- *Invite a movement leader to campus.* Consider inviting movement leaders to your campus for a lecture or organize a conference that features several experts in a field. The environment, civil rights, and modern slavery are topics that have wide appeal. Professors who teach classes that cover these issues may be able to help you find a good speaker. Work with your sociology club or student government to provide funding for the speaker.

- *Volunteer Match* seeks to connect individuals with movements of interest to them. Its website (www.volunteermatch.org) has suggestions for getting involved in your local area.

At the National or Global (Macro) Level

- *The Malala Fund* works to secure free education for every girl in the world. Begun by Malala Yousafzai, the young Pakistani education activist who survived an attempted assassination by the Taliban, the fund advocates for girls in various ways in which you can participate, if you would like to do so. You can learn more about it by going to the Malala Fund website at www.malala.org.

⑨SAGE edge™

Get the tools you need to sharpen your study skills. SAGE edge offers a robust online environment featuring an impressive array of free tools and resources.

Access practice quizzes, eFlashcards, video, and multimedia at **edge.sagepub.com/ballantine7e**

GLOSSARY

Ability grouping. Places students into different-level groups within classes, 338

Absolute poverty. Not having resources to meet basic needs, 209

Achieved status. Social status that is chosen or earned by decisions one makes, the interest or effort one puts into an activity, and sometimes by personal ability, 127

Achieved stratification systems. Societal systems that allow individuals to earn positions through their ability, efforts, and choices, 205

Agents of socialization. The transmitters of culture—the people, organizations, and institutions that help us define our identity and teach us how to thrive in our social world, 105

Agricultural societies. Societies that rely primarily on raising crops for food but make use of technological advances such as the plow, irrigation, animals, and fertilization to continuously cultivate the same land, 63

Anomie. The state of normlessness that occurs when rules for behavior in society break down under extreme stress from rapid social change or conflict, 130

Arranged marriages. A pattern of mate selection in which someone other than the couple—elder males, parents, or a matchmaker—selects the marital partners, 303

Ascribed status. Social status that is often assigned at birth and that does not change during an individual's lifetime; age cohort, sex, and ethnicity are examples, 127

Ascribed stratification systems. Societal systems in which characteristics beyond the control of the individual—such as family background, age, sex, and race—determine one's position in society, 205

Assimilation. The structural and cultural merging of minority and dominant groups, 237

Authoritarian governments. Governments in which power is concentrated in the hands of an absolute monarch, dictator, or small group not accountable to the people, 402

Authority. Power that is considered legitimate and rightful by those subject to it, 391

Beliefs. Ideas we hold about life, about the way society works, and about where we fit into the world, 76

Bureaucracies. Specific types of large formal organizations that have the purpose of maximizing efficiency. They are characterized by formal relations among participants, clearly laid-out procedures and rules, and the pursuit of shared goals, 133

Caste systems. The most rigid ascribed stratification systems. Individuals are born into a status, which they retain throughout life. That status is deeply embedded in religious, political, and economic norms and institutions, 205

Cause-and-effect-relationships. Relationships in which one variable stimulates a change in another, 42

Civil religion. The set of beliefs, rites, and symbols that sacralize the values of the society and place the nation in the context of transcendent meaning, often giving it divine significance, 365

Collective behavior. Actions that are spontaneous, unstructured, and disorganized and that may violate norms; this behavior arises when people are trying to cope with stressful situations and under unclear or uncertain conditions, 508

Conflict theory. Theory that contends that conflict is inevitable in any group or society, 35

Consensus crimes. Crimes that members of society generally agree are serious, 147

Content analysis. Analysis that entails the systematic categorizing and recording of information from written or recorded sources—printed materials, videos, radio broadcasts, or artworks, 44

Control group. A group in which the subjects are not exposed to the variable the researcher wants to test, 44

Controls. Steps used by researchers to eliminate all variables except those related to the hypothesis—especially those variables that might be spurious, 42

Correlation. A relationship between variables with change in one variable associated with change in another, 42

Counterculture. A group with expectations and values that contrast sharply with the dominant values of a particular society, 81

Crime. Deviant actions for which there are formal penalties imposed by the government, such as fines, jail, or prison sentences, 144

Cultural capital. The knowledge, skills, language mastery, style of dress, and values that provide a person with access to a particular status in society, 187

Cultural relativism. Requires setting aside cultural and personal beliefs and prejudices to understand another group or society through the eyes of its members and using its own community standards, 72

Culture. The way of life shared by a group of people—the knowledge, beliefs, values, rules or laws, language, customs, symbols, and material products (such as food, houses, and transportation) within a society that help meet human needs, 58

Democratic governments. Governments characterized by accountability to citizens and a large degree of control by individuals over their own lives, 402

Democratic socialism. Collective or group planning of the development of society, but within a democratic political system, 406

Demographic transition theory. Links trends in birthrates and death rates with patterns of economic and technological development, 465

Demography. The study of human populations, 459

Denominations. Centralized coordinating bodies or associations that link local congregations with a similar history and theology, 360

Dependency ratio. The ratio of those in both the young and aged groups compared with the number of people in the productive age group from age 15 through age 64, 462

Dependent variable. The variable in a cause-and-effect relationship that is affected by and comes after the independent variable in time sequence, 42

Deprofessionalization. The process through which a professional occupation loses autonomy, respect, and service orientation because the professionals come to be controlled by nonprofessionals and outside forces such as financial concerns, government regulations, technological changes, and administrators or management, 440

Deviance. The violation of social norms, 144

Differential association theory. Theory that focuses on the learning of deviant behavior from those with whom we interact (e.g., family, peers, fellow employees), 148

Discrimination. Differential treatment and harmful actions against minorities, 227

Dysfunctions. Actions that undermine the stability or equilibrium of society, 34

Elective affinity. The pattern of people belonging to religious groups that espouse values and characteristics compatible with their social status and self-interests, 371

Empirical knowledge. Knowledge founded on information gained from evidence (facts), rather than intuition, 40

Endogamy. Norms that require individuals to marry inside certain human boundaries based on whatever the societal members see as protecting the homogeneity of the group, 302

Environment. The setting in which the social unit works, including everything that influences the social unit, such as its physical and organizational surroundings and technological innovations, 16

Environmental racism. When environmental pollution disproportionately affects racial and ethnic minorities, 466

Equal educational opportunity. A system in which children are provided with equal facilities, financing, and access to school programs, 340

Estate systems. Characterized by the concentration of economic and political power in the hands of a small minority of political-military elite, with the peasantry tied to the land, 206

Ethnic group. A group within the human species that is based on cultural factors: language, religion, dress, foods, customs, beliefs, values, norms, a shared group identity or feeling, and sometimes loyalty to a homeland, monarch, or religious leader, 225

Ethnocentrism. The tendency to view one's own group and its cultural expectations as right, proper, and superior to others, 70

Evidence. Facts and observations that can be objectively observed and carefully measured using the five senses (sometimes enhanced by scientific instruments), 40

Exogamy. Norms governing the choice of a mate that require individuals to marry outside of their own immediate group, 302

Experimental groups. Groups in which subjects are exposed to the variable being studied; this process is to test the effects of that variable on human behavior, 44

Experiments. Procedures in which all variables except the one being studied are controlled so researchers can study the effects on the variable under study, 44

Expressive movements. Focus on changing individuals and saving people from lifestyles the social movement considers corrupt, 517

Extended family. Two or more adult generations that share tasks and living quarters. This may include brothers, sisters, aunts, uncles, cousins, and grandparents, 308

Family of orientation. The family into which we are born or adopted, 295

Family of procreation. The family we create ourselves, 296

Feminist theory. Theory that critiques the hierarchical power structures that disadvantage women and other minorities, 38

Fertility. The birthrate, 467

Formal agents of socialization. Official or legal agents (e.g., families, schools, teachers, and religious organizations) whose purpose it is to socialize the individual into the values, beliefs, and behaviors of the culture, 107

Formal education. Schooling that takes place in a prescribed setting with the goal of teaching a set curriculum, 322

Formal organizations. Modern rational organizations composed of complex secondary groups deliberately formed to pursue and achieve certain goals, 133

Formal sanctions. Rewards or punishments conferred by recognized officials, 77

Free-choice marriage. A pattern of mate selection in which the partners select each other based primarily on romance and love, 303

Functional theory. See *structural-functional theory*, 34

Functions. Consequences of an action or behavior, 34

Game stage. Stage in the process of developing a social self when a child develops the ability to take the role of multiple others concurrently and to conform to societal expectations, 102

Gemeinschaft. German term meaning "small traditional community," 478

Gender. A society's notions of masculinity and femininity—socially constructed meanings associated with being male or female—and how individuals construct their identity in terms of gender within these constraints, 257

Gender roles. Those commonly assigned tasks or expected behaviors linked to an individual's sex-determined statuses, 257

Generalized other. A composite of societal expectations that a child learns from family, peers, and other organizations, 102

Genocide. The systematic effort of one group, usually the dominant group, to destroy a minority group by killing them, 236

Gentrification. Refers to members of the middle and upper class, mostly young White professionals, buying and renovating rundown properties in central-city locations and displacing poor residents, 482

Gesellschaft. German term meaning "large, impersonal urban area," 478

Glass ceiling. Processes that limit the progress of women and others, 267

Global culture. Behavioral standards, symbols, values, and material objects that have become common across the globe, 84

Global transnational movements. Mobilized groups that take place across societies as international organizations, 517

Globalization. The process by which the entire world is becoming a single interdependent sociocultural entity, more uniform, more integrated, and more interdependent, 6

Groups. Units involving two or more people who interact with each other because of shared interests, goals, experiences, and needs, 129

Hate crimes. Criminal offenses committed against a person, property, or group that are motivated by the offender's bias against a religious, ethnic, or racial group; national origin; gender; or sexual orientation, 161

Health. A state of physical, mental, and social well-being or the absence of disease, 424

Herding societies. Societies in which the food-producing strategy is based on the domestication of animals, whose care is the central focus of their activities, 62

Heterosexism. An assumption that every person is heterosexual, legitimizing heterosexuality as the only normal lifestyle and marginalizing persons who do not identify as heterosexual, 277

Hidden curriculum. The implicit messages learned in school through the other three *R*s of school: rules, routines, and regulations, 328

Homophobia. Intense fear and hatred of homosexuality and homosexuals, whether male or female, 277

Horticultural societies. Societies in which the food-producing strategy is based on the domestication of plants, using digging sticks and wooden hoes to cultivate small gardens, 62

Hunter-gatherer societies. Societies in which people rely on the vegetation and animals occurring naturally in their habitat to sustain life, 61

Hypothesis. An educated guess or prediction, 40

I. The spontaneous, unpredictable, impulsive, and largely unorganized aspect of the self, 101

Ideal culture. Consists of practices, beliefs, and values that are regarded as most desirable in society and are consciously taught to children, 76

Illness. Lack of health, 424

Imitation stage. A period when children under 3 years old are preparing for role-taking by observing others and imitating their behaviors, sounds, and gestures, 101

Income. Money received from work or investments, 192

Independent variable. The variable in a cause-and-effect relationship that comes first in a time sequence and causes a change in another variable, 42

Industrial societies. Societies that rely primarily on mechanized production, resulting in greater division of labor based on expertise, 63

Inequality. A social condition in which privileges, opportunities, and substantial rewards are given to people in some positions in society but denied to others, 183

Informal agents of socialization. Unofficial influential agents that shape values, beliefs, and behaviors in which socialization is not the express purpose, 107

Informal sanctions. Unofficial rewards or punishments such as smiles, frowns, gossip, or ignoring someone, 77

In-group. A group to which an individual feels a sense of loyalty and belonging; it also may serve as a reference group, 132

Institutional racial discrimination. Any meso-level institutional arrangement that favors one racial group over another; this favoritism may result in intentional or unintentional consequences for minority groups, 232

Institutions. Organized, patterned, and enduring sets of social structures that provide guidelines for behavior and help each society meet its basic survival needs. Although institutions operate mostly at the meso level, they also act to integrate micro and macro levels of society, 288

Interaction. The exchange of verbal and nonverbal messages, 93

Interviews. Research conducted by talking directly with people and asking questions in person or by telephone, 43

Labeling theory. Theory that explains how people can be labeled deviant after committing a deviant act, which can then lead them to carry out further acts that reflect that label, 149

Language. The foundation of every culture. It conveys verbal, written, and nonverbal messages among members of society, 77

Latent functions. Unplanned or unintended consequences of actions or of social structures, 34

Laws. Norms formally encoded by those holding political power in society, 77

Levels of analysis. Social groups from the smallest to the largest, 12

Life expectancy. The number of years a person in a particular society can expect to live, 459

Lifestyle. Includes attitudes, values, beliefs, behavior patterns, and other aspects of one's place in the world, shaped by socialization, 195

Looking-glass self. A reflective process that develops our self based on our interpretations and internalization of the reactions of others to us, 99

Macro-level analysis. Analysis of the largest social units in the social world, including entire nations, global forces (such as international organizations), and international social trends, 18

Manifest functions. The planned outcomes of interactions, social organizations, or institutions, 34

Market or capitalist economic systems. Economic systems driven by the balance of supply and demand, allowing free competition to reward the efficient and the innovative with profits. They stress individual planning and private ownership of property, 404

Master status. An individual's social status that becomes most important and takes precedence over other statuses, 128

Material culture. Includes all the objects we can see or touch—all the artifacts of a group of people, 73

Me. The part of the self that has learned the rules of society through interaction and role taking; it controls the *I* and its desires, 101

Means of production. Property, machinery, and other means of creating saleable goods or services, 34

Mechanical solidarity. Social cohesion and integration based on the similarity of individuals in the group, including shared beliefs, values, and emotional ties between members of the group, 61

Medicaid. The government-run health insurance plan for low-income families in the United States, 435

Medicalization. Handling of some forms of deviance as well as some normal human functions (such as pregnancy and childbirth) in the health care system rather than the family, legal, or religious arenas, 427

Medicare. A government-run health insurance system for those 65 and older in the United States, 423

Meritocracy. A social group or organization in which people are allocated to positions according to their abilities and credentials, as in level of education attained, 201

Meso-level analysis. Analysis of intermediate-size social units, smaller than the nation but large enough to encompass more than the local community or region, 17

Microculture. A culture that develops at the micro level in groups or organizations and affects only a segment of one's life or influences a limited period of one's life, 79

Micro-level analysis. Analysis with a focus on individual or small-group interaction in specific situations, 17

Migration. Movement of people from one place to another, 467

Minority groups. Groups of people with distinct physical or cultural characteristics who are singled out from others in their society for differential and unequal treatment, 218

Monogamy. Marriage of two individuals, 307

Mortality. The death rate, 467

Myths. Stories that transmit values and embody ideas about life and the world, 358

National culture. Common values and beliefs that tie citizens of a nation together, 83

National society. A population of people, usually living within a specified geographic area, who are connected by common ideas, cooperate for the attainment of common goals, and are subject to a particular political authority, 15

New religious movements (NRMs). The beginning phase of an entirely new religion, 362

Nonmaterial culture. The thoughts, language, feelings, beliefs, values, and attitudes that make up much of our culture, 74

Nonverbal communication. Interactions without words using facial expressions, the head, eye contact, body posture, gestures, touch, walk, status symbols, and personal space, 123

Norms. Rules of behavior shared by members of a society and rooted in the value system, 76

Nuclear family. Consists of two parents and their children—or any two of the three, 308

Objectivity. The quality of taking steps to ensure that one's personal opinions or values do not bias or contaminate data collection and analysis, 40

Observational studies. Studies that involve systematic, planned observation and recording of interactions and other human behavior in natural settings (where the activity normally takes place, rather than in a laboratory), 44

Organic solidarity. Refers to social cohesion (glue) based on division of labor, with each member playing a highly specialized role in the society and each person depending on others due to interdependent, interrelated tasks, 61

Organized crime. Ongoing criminal enterprises run by an organized group whose ultimate purpose is economic gain through illegitimate means, 162

Out-group. A group to which an individual does not belong and competes with or acts in opposition to an in-group, 132

Past-in-present discrimination. Practices from the past that may no longer be allowed but that continue to affect people today, 234

Peer groups. People who are roughly equal in some status within the society, such as the same age or occupation, 106

Planned (or centralized) economic systems. Economic systems in which the government or another centralized group oversees production and distribution, 406

Play stage. Involves a child, usually ages 3 to 5, having the ability to see things (role-take) from the perspective of one person at a time; simple role-taking or play-acting, 101

Pluralism. Occurs when each ethnic or racial group in a country maintains its own culture and separate set of institutions but has recognized equality in the society, 237

Pluralist power theorists. Theorists who argue that power is not held exclusively by an elite group but is shared among many power centers, each of which has its own self-interests to protect, 207

Polygamy. Marriage of one person to more than one partner at the same time, 307

Population pyramids. Pyramid-shaped diagrams that illustrate sex ratios and dependency ratios, 462

Population transfer. The removal, often forced, of a minority group from a region or country, 237

Populations. All permanent societies, states, communities, adherents of a common religious faith, racial or ethnic groups, kinship or clan groups, professions, and other identifiable categories of people, 459

Postindustrial societies. Societies that have moved from human labor and manufacturing to automated production and service jobs, largely processing information, 64

Power. Ability of a person or group to realize its own will in groups, even against the resistance of others who disagree, 389

Power elite. Top leaders in corporations, politics, and the military, 207

Prejudice. Preconceived attitudes about a group, usually negative and not based on facts, 227

Primary deviance. A violation of a norm that may be an isolated act or an initial act of rule breaking, 149

Primary groups. Groups characterized by cooperation among close, intimate, long-term relationships, 131

Public order crimes. See *victimless crimes*, 159

Public sociologists. Sociologists who strive to better understand how society operates and to make practical use of their sociological findings, 47

Questionnaires. A set of questions and other types of items designed to solicit information appropriate to analysis of research questions, 43

Race. A socially created concept that identifies a group as "different," usually based on ancestry or certain physical characteristics, 219

Rational choice (exchange) theory. Theory that focuses on humans as fundamentally concerned with self-interests, making rational decisions based on weighing costs and rewards of the projected outcome, 32

Rationality. The attempt to reach maximum efficiency with rules that are rationally designed to accomplish goals, 38

Rationalization. The attempt to maximize efficiency by creating rules and procedures focused solely on accomplishing goals, 133

Real culture. The way things in society are actually done, 76

Recidivism rates. The likelihood that someone who is arrested, convicted, and imprisoned will later be a repeat offender, 174

Reference groups. Groups composed of members who act as role models and establish standards against which members evaluate their conduct, 132

Relative poverty. Occurs when one's income falls below the poverty line, resulting in an inadequate standard of living relative to others in the individual's country, 209

Reproduction of class. The socioeconomic positions of one generation passing on to the next, 339

Resistance or regressive movements. Movements that try to protect an existing system, protect part of that system, or return to what a system had been by overthrowing current laws and practices. They see societal change as a threat to values or practices and wish to maintain the status quo or return to a former status by reversing the change process, 517

Resocialization. The process of shedding one or more positions and taking on others, which involves learning new norms, behaviors, and values suitable to the newly acquired status, 104

Revolution. Social and political transformations of a nation that result when states fail to fulfill their expected responsibilities, 408

Revolutionary movements. Movements that attempt to transform society to bring about a total change in society by overthrowing existing power structures and replacing them with new ones; these movements often resort to violent means to achieve goals, 517

Rituals. Ceremonies or repetitive practices, often used to invoke a sense of awe of the sacred and to make certain ideas sacred, 358

Role conflict. Conflict between the roles of two or more social statuses, 129

Role strain. Tension among roles within a social status, 129

Roles. The expected behaviors, rights, obligations, responsibilities, and privileges assigned to a social status, 128

Role-taking. The process by which individuals take others into account by imagining themselves in the position of that other, 99

Sample. A group of systematically chosen people who represent a much larger group to study, 41

Sanctions. Rewards and penalties that reinforce norms, 77

School climate. A general social environment that characterizes aspects of a school's social climate, 329

Science. The systematic process of producing human knowledge; it uses empirical research methods to discover facts and test theories, 495

Secondary analysis. Analysis that uses existing data, information that has already been collected in other studies—including data banks, such as the national census, 44

Secondary deviance. Occurs when an individual continues to violate a norm and begins to take on a deviant identity as a result of being labeled as deviant, 149

Secondary groups. Groups characterized by formal, impersonal, and businesslike relationships; often temporary and based on a specific limited purpose or goal, 131

Secularization. The diminishing influence and role of religion in everyday life, 377

Self. The perceptions we have of who we are, 98

Self-fulfilling prophecy. Occurs when a belief or a prediction becomes a reality, in part because of the prediction, 150

Sex. A biological term referring to genetic, anatomical, and hormonal differences between males and females, 255

Sexuality. Culturally shaped meanings both of sexual acts and of how we experience our own bodies—especially in relation to the bodies of others, 256

Shadow education. Learning opportunities outside of school, such as tutoring, test prep, and summer programs, 341

Sick role. A special position in society in which one is temporarily relieved of responsibilities and accepts a position of dependence, 432

Side-effect discrimination. Practices in one institutional area that have a negative impact because they are linked to practices in another institutional area. Because institutions are interdependent, discrimination in one results in unintentional discrimination in others, 232

Significant others. Parents, guardians, relatives, siblings, or important individuals whose primary and sustained interactions with the individual are especially influential for the individual, 101

Slavery. When an individual or a family is bound in servitude as the property of a person or household, bought and sold, and forced to work, 183

Social capital. Connections or networks with people who have influence, 187

Social change. Variations or alterations over time in the behavior patterns, culture (including norms and values), and behavior patterns in a society, 494

Social class. The wealth, power, and prestige rankings that individuals hold in society, 108

Social construction of reality. The process by which individuals and groups shape their reality through social interaction, 85

Social control theory. Theory that examines the processes a society or group uses to ensure conformity to its norms and expectations, 152

Social institutions. Organized, patterned, and enduring sets of social structures that provide guidelines for behavior and help each society meet its basic survival needs, 14

Social interaction. Two or more individuals purposefully relating to each other, 122

Social mobility. The extent of individual movement up or down in the class system, changing one's social position in society—especially relative to one's parents, 198

Social movements. Consciously organized attempts outside of established institutional mechanisms to enhance or resist change through group action, 514

Social networks. Individuals linked together by one or more social relationships, connecting them to the larger society, 121

Social processes. Processes that take place through actions of people in institutions and other social units or structures, 16

Social reform movements. Movements that seek to change some specific dimension of society, usually involving legislative policy modification or appeals to the courts, 517

Social stratification. How individuals and groups are layered or ranked in society according to their access to and possession of valued resources, 186

Social structure. The stable patterns of interactions, statuses (positions), roles (responsibilities), and organizations that provide stability for the society and bring order to individuals' lives, 14

Social units. Interconnected parts of the social world ranging from small groups to societies, 14

Social world model. A framework that helps us view the levels of analysis in our social surroundings as an interconnected series of small groups, organizations, institutions, and societies, 14

Socialization. The lifelong process of learning to become a member of the social world, beginning at birth and continuing until death, 92

Socialized medicine. Provides a government-supported consumer service that ensures equal access to health care for all citizens of a country, 436

Society. An organized and interdependent group of individuals who live together in a specific geographical area and who interact more with each other than they do with outsiders; they cooperate for the attainment of common goals and share a common culture over time, 58

Sociological imagination. The recognition of the complex and interactive relationship between micro-level individual experiences and macro-level public issues, 8

Sociology. The scientific study of social life, social change, and the social causes and consequences of human behavior, 5

Spurious relationships. Relationships in which the variables are not casually related but are seen to be, often because of another unseen variable, 42

Status. A social position in society, 127

Stigmatize. Branding a person in a way that discredits that person's claim to a "normal" identity, 150

Strain theory. Theory that contends that the opportunity or limitations embedded in the structures of society may contradict and undermine the goals and aspirations society encourages for its members, creating strains that lead to deviance, 154

Stratification. See *social stratification*, 186

Structural-functional theory. Theory that assumes that all parts of the social structure (groups, organizations, and institutions), the culture (values and beliefs), and social processes (e.g., legislators working to create a law, an instructor teaching a child, or laws passed to bring about positive social change) work together to make the whole society run smoothly and harmoniously, 34

Subculture. The culture of a meso-level subcommunity that distinguishes itself from the dominant culture of the larger society. It is smaller than the nation but, unlike a microculture, is large enough to support people throughout the life span, 80

Subjugation. The subordination of one group to another that holds power and authority, 236

Sustainable societies. Societies that meet our current needs without harming future generations, 487

Symbol. An object or an action that represents something else and therefore has meaning beyond its own existence (e.g., flags and wedding rings), 31

Symbolic interaction theory (also called social constructionism or interpretative theory). Theory that sees humans as active agents who create shared meanings of symbols and events and then interact on the basis of those meanings, 31

Technology. The practical application of tools, skills, and knowledge to meet human needs and extend human abilities, 65

Terrorism. The calculated use of unlawful violence to inculcate fear; intended to coerce or to intimidate governments or societies in the pursuit of goals that are generally political, religious, or ideological, 166

Theocracy. Government in which religious leaders rule society in accordance with God's presumed wishes, 365

Theoretical perspective. A basic view of society that guides sociologists' research and analysis. Theoretical perspectives are the broadest theories in sociology, providing overall approaches to understanding the social world and social problems, 30

Theories. Statements or explanations regarding how and why two or more facts are related to each other and the connections between these facts, 30

Totalitarian government. Any form of government that almost totally controls people's lives, 402

Transgender. Describes someone who is challenging, questioning, or changing gender from that assigned at birth to a chosen gender—male to female, female to male, transitioning between genders, or genderqueer (challenging gender norms), 256

Triangulation. The use of two or more methods of data collection to enhance the amount and type of data for analysis and the accuracy of the findings, 45

Urbanization. The pattern of movement from rural areas to cities, 477

Values. Shared judgments about what is desirable or undesirable, right or wrong, and good or bad. They express the basic ideals of any group of people, 74

Variables. Concepts (ideas) that can vary in frequency of occurrence from one time, place, or person to another, 40

Victimless crimes (also called public order crimes). Acts committed by or between individual consenting adults, 159

War. Armed conflict occurring within, between, or among societies or groups, 412

Wealth. The worth of a person based on his or her financial holdings (stocks, bank accounts, and investment income) and property (homes, cars) minus debt, 192

White-collar (or occupational) crime. The violation of law committed by an individual or group in the course of a legitimate, respected occupation or financial activity, 164

REFERENCES

AAANativeArts. 2011. "Facts About Alaskan Natives." Retrieved April 19, 2011 (www.aaanativearts.com/alaskan-natives/index .html).

AAUW. 2017. "Three-Fourths of Schools Report Zero Incidents of Sexual Harassment in Grades 7-12." October 24. Retrieved February 7, 2018 (www.aauw.org/article/schools-report-zero-incidents-of-sexual-harassment/).

Abadi, Ponta. 2013. "Kids' Toys: More Gendered Than Ever." *Ms. Magazine*, June 5. Retrieved January 16, 2014 (http://mismagazine.com/blog/2013/06/05/kids-toys-more-gendered-than-ever).

ABC News/Washington Post Poll. 2011. "One in Four U.S. Women Reports Workplace Harassment." November 16. Retrieved October 23, 2017 (http://www.langerresearch.com/wp-content/uploads/1192a1SexualHarassment.pdf).

Abrams, Rachel. 2015. "Blue Bell Knew About Listeria Issues, F.D.A. Says." *New York Times*, May 7. Retrieved June 30, 2015 (www.nytimes.com/2015/05/08/business/blue-bell-knew-about-listeria-issues-fda-says.html?ref=topics).

Abu-Lughod, Janet L. 1991. *Changing Cities: Urban Sociology*. New York: HarperCollins.

Abu-Lughod, Janet L. 2001. *New York, Chicago, Los Angeles: America's Global Cities*. Minneapolis: University of Minnesota Press.

ACT. 2016. "The AACT Profile Report: National Graduating Class 2016." Retrieved September 8, 2018 (https://www.ACT.org/content/dam/act/unsecured/documents/P_99_999999_N_S_N00_ACT-GCPR_National.pdf).

ACT. 2017. "The ACT Profile Report: National Graduating Class 2017." Retrieved November 16, 2017 (http://www.ACT.org/content/dam/act/unsecured/documents/cccr2017/P_99_999999_N_S_N00_ACT-GCPR_National.pdf).

Adelstein, Jake. 2015. "The Yakuza: Inside Japan's Murky Underworld." *CNN*, December 16. Retrieved February 17, 2018 (https://www.cnn.com/2015/09/15/asia/yakuza-yamaguchi gumi-explainer/index.html).

Adler, Patricia A. and Peter Adler. 1991. *Backboards and Blackboards: College Athletes and Role Engulfment*. New York: Columbia University Press.

Adler, Patricia A. and Peter Adler. 2004. "The Gloried Self." Pp. 117–26 in *Inside Social Life*, 4th ed., edited by Spencer E. Cahill. Los Angeles: Roxbury.

A&E. 2012. "Intervention." Retrieved July 16, 2012 (www.aetv .com).

AFL-CIO. 2016. "Executive Paywatch: CEO Pay and Corporate Income Tax Avoidance." Retrieved May 5, 2017 (http://archives .aflcio.org/Corporate-Watch/Paywatch-2016).

Agius, Silvan. 2013. "Third Gender: A Step Toward Ending Intersex Discrimination." Retrieved January 16, 2014 (Spiegel.de/international/Europe/third-gender-option-in-germany-a-small-step-for-intersex-recognition-a-917650.html).

Aizenman, Nurith. 2017. "Trump's Proposed Budget Would Cut $2.2 Billion from Global Health Spending." *NPR*, May 25.

Retrieved July 20, 2017 (http://www.npr.org/sections/goatsandsoda/2017/05/25/529873431/trumps-proposed-budget-would-cut-2-2-billion-from-global-health-spending).

Alagha, Joseph. 2017. "Ibn Khaldun: A Sociology of History." *International Sociology* 32(2):180–88.

Alarcon, Arthur L. and Paula M. Mitchell. 2011. "Executing the Will of the Voters? A Roadmap to Mend or End the California Legislature's Multi-Billion Dollar Death Penalty Debacle." *Loyola of Los Angeles Law Review* 44(June):S41.

Alatas, Syed Farid. 2006. "Ibn Khaldun and Contemporary Sociology." *International Sociology* 21(6):782–95.

Alexander, Dan. 2015. "Bill Clinton Honors Paul Farmer, the Doctor Out to Save the World." *Forbes*, January 4. Retrieved July 1, 2015 (www.forbes.com/sites/randalllane/2013/10/03/this-guy-may-have-solved-the-healthcare-model-for-1-billion-people/).

Alliance for Excellent Education. 2018. "The High Cost of High School Dropouts: The Economic Case for Reducing the High School Dropout Rate." Retrieved June 10, 2018 (http://all4ed.org/take-action/action-academy/the-economic-case-for-reducing-the-high-school-dropout-rate/).

Almasy, Steve and Nicole Chavez. 2018. "Student Who Survived School Shooting to Lawmakers: 'Shame on You.'" *CNN*, February 17. Retrieved February 17, 2018 (https://www.cnn .com/2018/02/17/us/florida-school-shooting/index.html).

Alper, Becka A. 2015. "Millennials Are Less Religious than Older Americans, but Just as Spiritual." *Pew Research Center*, November 23. Retrieved December 16, 2015 (www .pewresearch.org/fact-tank/2015/11/23/millennials-are-less religious-than-older-americans-but-just-as-spiritual/).

Alter, Charlotte. 2014. "Voter Turnout in Midterm Elections Hits 72 Year Low." *Time*, November 10. Retrieved January 27, 2016 (http://timer.com/3576090/midterm-elections-turnout-world-war-two/).

Altheide, David, Patricia A. Adler, Peter Adler, and Duane Altheide. 1978. "The Social Meanings of Employee Theft." P. 90 in *Crime at the Top*, edited by John M. Johnson and Jack D. Douglas. Philadelphia: Lippincott.

Alvarez, Lizette. 2013. "Girl's Suicide Points to Rise in Apps Used by Cyberbullies." *New York Times*, September 13. Retrieved January 16, 2014 (www.nytimes.com/2013/09/14/us/suicide-of-girl-after-bullying-raises-worries-on-websites .html?ref=cyberbullying&_r=0).

Amato, Paul R. 2000. "The Consequences of Divorce for Adults and Children." *Journal of Marriage and the Family* 62(November):1269–87.

American Academy of Pediatrics. 2016. "Poverty and Child Health in the United States." March 7. Retrieved May 19, 2018 (http://pediatrics.aappublications.org/content/pediatrics/early/2016/03/07/peds.2016-0339.full.pdf).

American Anthropological Association. [May 19, 1998] 2016. "AAA Statement on Race." Retrieved May 22, 2017 (http://www.americananthro.org/ConnectWithAAA/Content.aspx? ItemNumber=2583).

American Hospital Association. 2015. "Economic Contribution Often Overlooked." January 21. Retrieved July 2, 2015 (file:///C:/Users/Kathleen/Downloads/econcontribution.pdf).

American Library Association. 2016. "Top Ten Most Frequently Challenged Books of 2015." Retrieved August 17, 2016 (http://www.ala.org/bbooks/frequentlychallengedbooks/top10).

American Medical Association. 2012. *Physician Characteristics and Distribution in the U.S.*, 2012 ed. Washington, DC: Author.

American Sociological Association. 2009. *21st Century Careers with an Undergraduate Degree in Sociology.* Washington, DC: Author.

America's Promise Alliance. 2018. "Building a Grad Nation: Progress and Challenge in Raising High School Graduation Rates." Retrieved August 27, 2018 (gradnation .americaspromise.org/2018-building-grad-nation-report).

Ammerman, Nancy. 1990. *Baptist Battles: Social Change and Religious Conflict in the Southern Baptist Convention.* New Brunswick, NJ: Rutgers University Press.

Ammerman, Nancy. 2006. "Denominationalism/Congregationalism." Pp. 353–72 in *Handbook of Religion and Social Institutions*, edited by Helen Rose Ebaugh. New York: Springer.

Ammerman, Nancy. 2009. "Congregations: Local, Social, and Religious." Pp. 562–80 in *Oxford Handbook of the Sociology of Religion*, edited by Peter Clarke. New York, Oxford: Oxford University Press.

Ammerman, Nancy. 2013. *Sacred Stories, Spiritual Tribes: Finding Religion in Everyday Life.* New York: Oxford University Press.

Amnesty International. 2012. "Death Penalty 2011: Alarming Levels of Executions in the Few Countries that Kill." March 27. Retrieved April 16, 2012 (www.amnesty.org/en/news/death-penalty-2011-alarming-level-executions-few-countries-kill-2012-03-27).

Amnesty International. 2016. "Private Prisons." Retrieved September 19, 2016 (www.aclu.org/issues/mass-incarceration/privatization-criminal-justice/private-prisons).

ANAD. 2015. "Eating Disorders Statistics." Retrieved September 6, 2015 (www.anad.org/get-information/about-eating-disorders/eating-disorders-statistics/).

Anderson, Benedict. 2006. *Imagined Communities: Reflections on the Origin and Spread of Nationalism*, rev. ed. London: Verso.

Anderson, David A. and Mykol Hamilton. 2005. "Gender Role Stereotyping of Parents in Children's Picture Books: The Invisible Father." *Sex Roles: A Journal of Research* 52(3/4):145.

Anderson, Elijah. 2000. *Code of the Street: Decency, Violence, and the Moral Life of the Inner City.* New York: Norton.

Anderson, Kurt. 2017. "How America Lost its Mind." *The Atlantic*, September. Retrieved March 28, 2018 (www.theatlantic.com/magazine/archive/2017/09/how-america-lost-its-mind/534231/).

Anderson, Margaret and Patricia Hill Collins. 2016. *Race, Class, and Gender: An Anthology*, 4th ed. Belmont, CA: Wadsworth.

Anderson, Monica. 2015. "A Rising Share of the U.S. Black Population Is Foreign Born." *Pew Research Center*, April 9. Retrieved June 18, 2015 (www.pewsocialtrends.org/2015/04/09/a-rising-share-of-the-u-s-black-population-is-foreign-born/).

Anderson, Monica and Jingjing Jiang. 2018. "Teens, Social Media & Technology." *Pew Research Center*, May 31. Retrieved August 30, 2018 (http://www.pewinternet.org/2018/05/31/teens-social-media-technology-2018/).

Andolfatto, David. 2017. "Why Do Unemployment Rates Vary by Race and Ethnicity?" *Federal Reserve Bank of St. Louis*, February 6. Retrieved May 10, 2017 (https://www.stlouisfed.org/on-the-economy/2017/february/why-unemployment-rates-vary-races-ethnicity).

Anglican Church in North America. 2013. "About." Retrieved July 13, 2013 (http://anglicanchurch.net/?/main/page/about-acna).

Antoun, Richard T. 2008. *Understanding Fundamentalism: Christian, Islamic, and Jewish Movements*, 2nd ed. Walnut Creek, CA: AltaMira.

Anxiety and Depression Association of America. 2016. "Facts and Statistics." August. Retrieved May 24, 2017 (https://www.adaa.org/about-adaa/press-room/facts-statistics).

Anyon, Jean. 1980. "Social Class and the Hidden Curriculum of Work." *Journal of Education* 162(1):67–92.

Arrighi, Barbara A. 2000. *Understanding Inequality: The Intersection of Race, Ethnicity, Class, and Gender.* Lanham, MD: Rowman & Littlefield.

ASA (American Sociological Association). 2017. *The Sociology Major in the Changing Landscape of Higher Education: Curriculum, Careers, and Online Learning.* Washington, DC: Author.

Aseltine, Robert H., Jr. 1995. "A Reconsideration of Parental and Peer Influences on Adolescent Deviance." *Journal of Health and Social Behavior* 36(2):103–21.

Aslan, Reza. 2011. *No God but God: The Origins, Evolution, and Future of Islam*, updated ed. New York: Random House.

"Assisted Suicide: Over My Dead Body." 2012. *The Economist*, October 20. Retrieved March 13, 2017 (http://www.economist.com/news/international/21564830-helping-terminally-ill-die-once-taboo-gaining-acceptance).

Associated Press. 2015. "Pope Francis Indicates Little Concern Over Condom Use in Fight Against Aids." *The Guardian*, November 30. Retrieved June 6, 2017 (https://www.theguardian.com/world/2015/nov/30/pope-francis-condoms-aids-hiv-africa).

Association of American Colleges and Universities and Hart Research Associates. 2013. "It Takes More than a Major: Employer Priorities for College Learning and Student Success." *Washington, DC*. Retrieved May 22, 2013 (www.aacu.org/leap/documents/2013_EmployerSurvey.pdf).

Association of American Medical Colleges. 2017. "Active Physicians by Sex and Specialty, 2015." Retrieved June 22, 2017 (https://www.aamc.org/data/workforce/reports/458712/1-3-chart.html).

Audette, Nicole. 2014. "Congo: Rape as a Weapon of War and Wealth." *Christian Science Monitor*. Retrieved May 11, 2014 (www.csmonitor.com/World/Africa/Africa-Monitor/2014/0321/Congo-Rape-as-a-weapon-of-war-and wealth).

Aulette, Judy Root. 2010. *Changing American Families.* Boston: Allyn & Bacon.

Autor, David, David Dorn, and Gordon Hanson. 2017. "When Work Disappears: Decline and the Falling Marriage-Market Value of Men." *NBER Working Paper No. 23173*, February. Retrieved September 25, 2017 (http://www.ddorn.net/papers/Autor-Dorn-Hanson-MarriageMarket.pdf).

Avery, Beth and Phil Hernandez. 2017. "Ban the Box: U.S. Cities, Counties, and States Adopt Fair Hiring Policies." *National Employment Law Project*, August 1. Retrieved August 6, 2017 (http://www.nelp.org/publication/ban-the-box-fair-chance-hiring-state-and-local-guide/).

Azize, Pary M., Ruth Endacott, Allegra Cattani, and Ann Humphreys. 2013. "Cultural Responses to Pain in UK Children of Primary School Age: A Mixed-Methods Study." *Nursing & Health Sciences*, August 29. Retrieved March 4, 2014 (http://onlinelibrary.wiley.com/doi/10.1111/nhs.12084/abstract).

Babbie, Earl. 2014. *The Basics of Social Research*, 6th ed. Belmont, CA: Thomsen/Wadsworth.

Babiarz, Kimberly Singer, Hongmei Yi, and Renfu Luo. 2013. "Meeting the Health-Care Needs of the Rural Elderly: The

Unique Role of Village Doctors." *China & World Economy* 21(3):44–60.

Bagby, Ihsan. 2003. "Imams and Mosque Organization in the United States: A Study of Mosque Leadership and Organizational Structure in American Mosques." Pp. 113–34 in *Muslims in the United States*, edited by Philippa Strum and Danielle Tarantolo. Washington, DC: Woodrow Wilson International Center for Scholars.

Bainbridge, William S. and Rodney Stark. 1981. "Suicide, Homicide, and Religion: Durkheim Reassessed." *Annual Review of the Social Sciences of Religion* 5:33–56.

Bales, Kevin. 1999. *Disposable People: New Slavery in the Global Economy*. Berkeley: University of California Press.

Bales, Kevin. 2004. *Disposable People: New Slavery in the Global Economy*, 2nd ed. Berkeley: University of California Press.

Bales, Kevin. 2012. *Disposable People: New Slavery in the Global Economy*, 3rd ed. Berkeley: University of California Press.

Ballantine, Jeanne H. and Floyd M. Hammack. 2012. *The Sociology of Education: A Systematic Analysis*, 7th ed. Upper Saddle River, NJ: Prentice Hall.

Ballantine, Jeanne H., Floyd M. Hammack, and Jenny Stuber. 2017. *The Sociology of Education: A Systematic Analysis*, 8th ed. New York: Routledge/Taylor & Francis.

Barash, David. 2002. "Evolution, Males, and Violence." *Chronicle Review*, May 24:B7.

Barber, Benjamin R. 2006. "The Uncertainty of Digital Politics: Democracy's Relationship with Information Technology." Pp. 61–69 in *Globalization: The Transformation of Social Worlds*, edited by D. Stanley Eitzen and Maxine Baca Zinn. Belmont, CA: Wadsworth.

Barlow, Philip L. and Terry L. Givens, eds. 2015. *The Oxford Handbook to Mormonism*. New York: Oxford University Press.

Barrett, David, George Kurian, and Todd Johnson, eds. 2001. *World Christian Encyclopedia*, Vol. 2. New York: Oxford University Press.

Barron, James. 2017. "In an Era of Fake News, Teaching Students to Parse Facts from Fiction." *New York Times*, March 20. Retrieved May 20, 2018 (www.nytimes.com/2017/03/20/nyregion/fake-news-brooklyn-middle-school.html?smprod=nytcore-ipad&smid=nytcore-ipad-share).

Barry, Ellen and Mansi Choksi. 2013. "Gang Rape in India, Routine and Invisible." *New York Times*, October 26. Retrieved January 17, 2014 (www.nytimes.com/2013/10/27/world/asia/gang-rape-in-india-routine-and-invisible.html?_r=0).

Basso, Keith H. 1996. *Wisdom Sits in Places: Landscape and Language Among the Western Apache*. Albuquerque: University of New Mexico Press.

Battelle. 2013. "2014 Global R&D Funding Forecast." December. Retrieved February 24, 2014 (www.battelle.org/docs/tpp/2014_global_rd_funding_forecast.pdf).

Beach, Coral. 2017. "FDA Shuts Down Soy Nut Butter Maker Linked to E. Coli Outbreak." *Food Safety News*, March 31. Retrieved June 17, 2017 (http://www.foodsafetynews.com/2017/03/fda-shuts-down-soy-nut-butter-maker-linked-to-e-coli-outbreak/#.WUUxgpDyvIU).

Beaton, Caroline. 2017. "Top Employers Say Millenials Need These 4 Skills in 2017." *Forbes*, January 6. Retrieved April 30, 2018 (www.forbes.com/sites/carolinebeaton/2017/01/06/top-employers-say-millenials-need-these-4-skills-in-2017/#71c9a8897fe4).

Beaver, David. 2012. "Sally Ride: Beauty of the Earth Is Only Half of It." *The Overview Institute*. Retrieved June 29, 2013 (www.overviewinstitute.org/featured-articles/45-sally-ride-beauty-of-the-earth-is-only-half-of-it).

Beckwith, Carol. 1993. *Nomads of Niger*. New York: Harry N. Abrams.

Beeman, Angie. 2015. "Walk the Walk but Don't Talk the Talk: The Strategic Use of Color-Blind Ideology in an Interracial Social Movement Organization." *Sociological Forum* 30(1):127–47.

Behm-Morawitz, Elizabeth, Jennifer Lewallen, and Brandon Miller. 2016. "Real Mean Girls? Reality Television Viewing, Social Aggression, and Gender-Related Beliefs Among Female Emerging Adults." *Psychology of Popular Media Culture* 5(4):340–55.

Belding, Theodore C. 2004. "Nobility and Stupidity: Modeling the Evolution of Class Endogamy." Retrieved August 7, 2008 (http://arxiv.org/abs/nlin.AO/0405048).

Bell, Daniel. 1973. *The Coming of Post-Industrial Society: A Venture in Social Forecasting*. New York: Basic Books.

Bell, Daniel. [1976] 1999. *The Coming of Post-Industrial Society: A Venture in Social Forecasting*, Special anniversary edition. New York: Basic Books.

Bell, Michael Mayerfeld. 2012. *An Invitation to Environmental Sociology*, 4th ed. Thousand Oaks, CA: Sage/Pine Forge.

Bell, Michael Mayerfeld and Loka L. Ashwood. 2016. *An Invitation to Environmental Sociology*, 5th ed. Thousand Oaks, CA: Sage.

Bellah, Robert N. 1970. "Civil Religion in America." Pp. 168–215 in *Beyond Belief: Essays on Religion in a Post-Traditionalist World*. New York: Harper & Row.

Bellah, Robert N. 1992. *The Broken Covenant: American Civil Religion in Time of Trial*. Chicago: University of Chicago Press.

Bellis, Rich. 2016. "Here's Everywhere in America You Can Still Get Fired for Being Gay or Trans." *Fast Company*, March 3. Retrieved May 24, 2017 (https://www.fastcompany.com/3057357/heres-everywhere-in-america-you-can-still-get-fired-for-being-lgbt).

Benevolo, Leonardo. 1995. *The European City*. Cambridge, MA: Blackwell.

Bennis, Warren G., Kenneth D. Benne, and Robert Chin. 1985. *The Planning of Change*, 4th ed. New York: Holt, Rinehart and Winston.

Benokraitis, Nijole V. 2015. *Marriages and Families: Changes, Choices, and Constraints—2010 Census Update*, 8th ed. Englewood Cliffs, NJ: Prentice Hall.

Beran, Tanya. 2012. "Bullying: What Are the Differences Between Boys and Girls?" Education.*com*, January 24. Retrieved January 17, 2014 (www.education.com/reference/article/Ref_Bullying_Differences).

Berger, Helen. 1999. *A Community of Witches: Contemporary Neo-Paganism and Witchcraft in the United States*. Columbia: University of South Carolina Press.

Berger, Michael L. 1979. *The Devil Wagon in God's Country: The Automobile and Social Change in Rural America, 1893–1929*. Hamden, CT: Archon.

Berger, Peter L. and Thomas Luckmann. 1966. *The Social Construction of Reality*. Garden City, NY: Doubleday.

Bergthaler, Wolfgang, Kenneth Kang, Yan Liu, and Dermot Monaghan. 2015. "Tackling Small and Medium Sized Enterprise Problem Loans in Europe." *International Monetary Fund*, March. Retrieved September 11, 2015 (www.imf.org/external/pubs/ft/sdn/2015/sdn1504.pdf).

Berk, Richard A. 1974. *Collective Behavior*. Dubuque, IA: Brown.

Berlinger, Josh, Steve George, and Serenitie Wang. 2017. "Beijing's Smog: A Tale of Two Cities." *CNN*, January 16. Retrieved July

25, 2017 (http://www.cnn.com/2017/01/15/health/china-beijing-smog-tale-of-two-cities/index.html).

Berman, Bruce J. 2011. "Of Magic, Invisible Hands and Elfs: How not to Study Ethnicity in Africa." Paper presented at the ECAS4, Uppsala, Sweden, June 14–18.

Bernard, Tara Siegel, Tiffany Hsu, Nicole Perlroth, and Ron Lieber. 2017. "Equifax Says CyberAttack May Have Affected 143 Million in the U.S." *New York Times*, September 7. Retrieved September 9, 2017 (https://www.nytimes.com/2017/09/07/business/equifax-cyberattack.html).

Bernardo, Richie. 2018. "2018's Most & Least Educated States in America." *Wallethub*. Retrieved September 8, 2018 (https://wallethub.com/edu/most-educated-states/31075/).

Bettie, Julie. 2003. *Women Without Class: Girls, Race, and Identity*. Berkeley: University of California Press.

Bhagat, Srnriti, Moira Burke, Carlos Diuk, Ismail Onur Filiz, and Sergey Edunov. 2016. "Three and a Half Degrees of Separation." February 4. Retrieved March 18, 2018 (http://research.fb.com/three-and-a-half-degrees-of-separation/).

Bhuiyan, Johana. 2017. "Uber Has Published Its Much Sought After Diversity Numbers for the First Time." *Recode*. March 28. Retrieved September 3, 2018 (https://www.recode.net/2017/3/28/15087184/uber-diversity-numbers-first-three-million).

Bialik, Kristen and Jens Manuel Krogstad. 2017. "115th Congress Sets New High for Racial, Ethnic Diversity." *Pew Research Center*, January 24. Retrieved May 11, 2017 (http://www.pewresearch.org/fact-tank/2017/01/24/115th-congress-sets-new-high-for-racial-ethnic-diversity/).

Bian, Lin, Sarah-Jane Leslie, and Andrei Cimpian. 2017. "Gender Stereotypes About Intellectual Ability Emerge Early and Influence Children's Interests." *Science* 355(6323): 389–91.

Bianco, Marcie. 2017. "Feminist Activism in the 21st Century Begins with a 'Post.'" *Gender News*, February 13. The Clayman Institute for Gender Research, Stanford University. Retrieved May 23, 2017 (http://gender.stanford.edu/news/2017/feminist-activism-21st-century-begins-post).

Billig, Michael. 1995. *Banal Nationalism*. Thousand Oaks, CA: Sage.

Bjorklund-Young, Alanna. 2016. "Family Income and the College Completion Gap." *Johns Hopkins Institute for Education Policy*, March. Retrieved November 9, 2017 (http://edpolicy.education.jhu.edu/wp-content/uploads/2016/03/FamilyincomeandcollegegapmastheadFINAL.pdf).

Black's Law Dictionary. 2015. "What Is Dowry." Retrieved January 7, 2016 (http://thelawdictionary.org/dowry/).

Blau, Peter M. 1956. *Bureaucracy in Modern Society*. New York: Random House.

Blau, Peter M. 1964. *Exchange and Power in Social Life*. New York: John Wiley.

Blau, Peter and Otis Dudley Duncan. 1967. *The American Occupational Structure*. New York: John Wiley.

Blee, Kathleen M. 2008. "White Supremacy as Extreme Deviance." Pp. 108–17 in *Extreme Deviance*, edited by Erich Goode and D. Angus Vail. Thousand Oaks, CA: Pine Forge.

Bloom, Linda. 2017. "Breaking the Silence to Build Support." *United Methodist News*, March 9. Retrieved June 8, 2017 (http://www.umc.org/news-and-media/breaking-the-silence-to-build-support).

Blumer, Herbert. 1986. *Symbolic Interactionism: Perspective and Method*. Berkeley: University of California Press.

The Boards of Trustees, Federal Hospital Insurance and Federal Supplementary Medical Insurance Trust Funds. 2016. "2016 Annual Report of the Boards of Trustees of the Federal Hospital Insurance and Federal Supplementary Medical Insurance Trust Funds." June 22. Retrieved June 22, 2017 (https://www.cms.gov/Research-Statistics-Data-and-Systems/Statistics-Trends-and-Reports/ReportsTrustFunds/Downloads/TR2016.pdf).

"Body Parts for Sale." 2008. Science and Society. *ABC News*, May 6. Retrieved January 11, 2010 (blogs.abcnews.com/scienceandsociety/2008/05/body-parts-for.html).

Boger, John Charles and Gary Orfield. 2009. *School Resegregation: Must the South Turn Back?* Chapel Hill: University of North Carolina Press.

Boli, John. 2002. "Globalization." Pp. 307–13 in *Education and Sociology: An Encyclopedia*, edited by David L. Levinson, Peter W. Cookson, Jr., and Alan R. Sadovnik. New York: RoutledgeFalmer.

Bonacich, Edna. 1972. "A Theory of Ethnic Antagonism: The Split Labor Market." *American Sociological Review* 37(October):547–59.

Bonacich, Edna. 1976. "Advanced Capitalism and Black/White Relations in the United States: A Split Labor Market Interpretation." *American Sociological Review* 41:34–51.

Bond, Jeff. 2010. "The Anthropology of Garbage." *Columns*, March. Retrieved August 15, 2013 (www.washington.edu/alumni/columns/march10/garbage.html).

Bonilla-Silva, Eduardo. 2003. *Racism Without Racists: Color-Blind Racism and the Persistence of Racial Inequality in the United States*. Berkeley: University of California Press.

Bonilla-Silva, Eduardo. 2009. *Racism Without Racists: Color-Blind Racism and the Persistence of Racial Inequality in America*, 3rd ed. Lanham, MD: Rowman & Littlefield.

Bonilla-Silva, Eduardo. 2017. "What We Were, What We Are, and What We Should Be: The Racial Problem of American Sociology." *Social Problems* 64(2):179–87.

Bonilla-Silva, Eduardo and David G. Embrick. 2005. "Black, Honorary White, White: The Future of Race in the United States?" In *Negotiating the Color Line: Doing Race in the Color-Blind Era and Implications for Racial Justice*, edited by David Brunsma and Lynne Rienner. Boulder, CO: Lynne Rienner.

Borg, Marcus. 2001. *Reading the Bible Again for the First Time*. New York: HarperCollins.

Borjas, Carlos. 2016. "Yes, Immigration Hurts American Workers." *Politico*, September/October. Retrieved July 24, 2017 (http://www.politico.com/magazine/story/2016/09/trump-clinton-immigration-economy-unemployment-jobs-214216).

Bottomore, Tom. 1979. *Political Sociology*. New York: Harper & Row.

Bourdieu, P. and J. C. Passeron. 1977. *Reproduction in Education, Society and Culture*. London: Sage.

Bower, Bruce. 2016. "Year in Review: How Humans Populated the Globe." *Science News*, December 14. 190(13):25. Retrieved May 10, 2017 (https://www.sciencenews.org/article/ancient-human-migration-top-science-stories-2016).

Bowles, Samuel and Herbert Gintis. 1976. *Schooling in Capitalist America*. New York: Basic Books.

Bowles, Samuel and Herbert Gintis. 2002. "Schooling in Capitalist America Revisited." *Sociology of Education* 75(1):1–18.

Boy, Angie and Andrzej Kulczycki. 2008. "What We Know About Intimate Partner Violence in the Middle East and North Africa." *Violence Against Women* 14(1):53–70.

Bozelko, Chandra. 2017. "Give Working Prisoners Dignity: and Decent Wages." *National Review*, January 11. Retrieved August 3, 2017 (http://www.nationalreview.com/article/443747/prison-labor-laws-wages).

Brandon, Mark E. 2005. "War and American Constitutional Order." In *The Constitution in Wartime: Beyond Alarmism and Complacency*, edited by Mark Tushner. Durham, NC: Duke University Press.

Brasher, Brenda E. 2004. *Give Me that On-Line Religion*. New Brunswick, NJ: Rutgers University Press.

Brecher, Jeremy, Tim Costello, and Brendan Smith. 2012. "Globalization and Social Movements." Pp. 272–90 in *Globalization: The Transformation of Social Worlds*, 3rd ed., edited by D. Stanley Eitzen and Maxine Baca Zinn. Belmont, CA: Wadsworth.

Brettell, Caroline B. and Carolyn F. Sargent. 2012. *Gender in Cross-Cultural Perspective*, 6th ed. Englewood Cliffs, NJ: Pearson.

Brewer, Graham. 2017. "As Native Americans Face Job Discrimination: A Tribe Works to Employ Its Own." *NPR*, November 18. Retrieved November 19, 2017 (https://www.npr.org/2017/11/18/564807229/as-native-americans-face-job-discrimination-a-tribe-works-to-employ-its-own?sc=17&f=1001&utm_source=iosnewsapp&utm_medium=Email&utm_campaign=app).

Brian Lehrer Show. 2017. "The World According to the Journalists of Tomorrow." July 25. Retrieved July 25, 2017 (http://www.wnyc.org/story/journalists-tomorrow).

Brill, Steven. 2015. *America's Bitter Pill: Money, Politics, Backroom Deals, and the Fight to Fix Our Broken Healthcare System*. New York: Random House.

Briner, Raphaël. 2015. "The New 2015 Top 500 NGOs Is Out." *Global Journal*, February 14. Retrieved January 25, 2016 (www.theglobaljournal.net/article/view/1171/).

Brinkerhoff, David B., Lynn K. White, Suzanne T. Ortega, and Rose Weitz. 2014. *Essentials of Sociology*, 9th ed. New York: Cengage Learning.

Brint, Steven, Mary F. Contreras, and Michael T. Matthews. 2001. "Socialization Messages in Primary Schools: An Organizational Analysis." *Sociology of Education* 74(July):157–80.

Bromley, David G. and Anson D. Shupe, Jr. 1981. *Strange Gods: The Great American Cult Scare*. Boston: Beacon.

Brookings. 2017. "The 'Word Gap' and 1 City's Plan to Close It." Retrieved January 31, 2018 (www.brookings.edu/blog/brown-center-chalkboard-2017/07/10/the-word-gap-and-one-citys-plan-to-close-it/).

Brookover, Wilbur B. and Edsel L. Erickson. 1975. *Sociology of Education*. Homewood, IL: Dorsey.

Brookover, Wilbur B., Edsel L. Erickson, and Alan McEvoy. 1996. *Creating Effective Schools: An In-Service Program*. Holmes Beach, FL: Learning Publications.

Brooks, David. 2018. "Good Leaders Make Good Schools." *New York Times*, March 12. Retrieved March 14, 2018 (https://www.nytimes.com/2018/03/12/opinion/good-leaders-schools.html).

Broom, Leonard and Philip Selznick. 1963. *Sociology: A Text with Adapted Readings*, 3rd ed. New York: Harper & Row.

Brown, Anna. 2017. "5 Key Findings About LGBT Americans." *Pew Research Center*, June 13. Retrieved May 29, 2018 (http://www.pewresearch.org/fact-tank/2017/06/13/5-key-findings-about-lgbt-americans/).

Bruner, Jerome. 1996. *The Culture of Education*. Cambridge, MA: Harvard University Press.

Brunn, Stanley D., Maureen Hays-Mitchell, and Donald J. Zeigler. 2011. *Cities of the World: World Regional Urban Development*, 4th ed. Lanham, MD: Rowman and Littlefield.

Brunsma, David. 2006. *Mixed Messages: Doing Race in the Color-Blind Era*. Boulder, CO: Lynne Rienner.

Brym, Robert J. and John Lie. 2007. *Sociology: Your Compass for a New World*, 3rd ed. Belmont, CA: Wadsworth.

Bump, Philip. 2016. "Radical Islam Accounts for Few Recent Mass Shootings: But Also Some of the Deadliest." June 12. Retrieved June 10, 2018 (www.washingtonpost.com/news/the-fix/wp/2016.06/12/islamic-terrorism-accounts-for-few-recent-mass-shootings-but-also-some-of-the-deadliest/?noredirect=on&utm_term=.b294ddc8dfa9).

Bureau of Justice Statistics. 2016. "Criminal Victimization." October. Retrieved May 24, 2017 (https://www.bjs.gov/content/pub/pdf/cv15_sum.pdf).

Bureau of Justice Statistics. 2017. "Sexual Victimization in Prisons and Jails Reported by Inmates, 2011-12-Update." July 24. Retrieved May 10, 2018 (https://www.bjs.gov/index.cfm?iid=4654&ty=pbdetail).

Bureau of Labor Statistics. 2016. "Women More Likely than Men to have Earned a Bachelor's Degree by Age 29." *TED: The Economics Daily*, April 16. Retrieved May 8, 2017 (https://www.bls.gov/opub/ted/2016/women-more-likely-than-men-to-have-earned-a-bachelors-degree-by-age-29.htm).

Bureau of Labor Statistics. 2017a. "Unemployment Rates and Earnings by Educational Attainment, 2016." April 20. Retrieved May 8, 2017 (https://www.bls.gov/emp/ep_chart_001.htm).

Bureau of Labor Statistics. 2017b. "Foreign-Born Workers Made 83.1 Percent of the Earnings of Their Native-Born Counterparts in 2016." May 24. Retrieved March 26, 2018 (https://www.bls.gov/opub/ted/2017/foreign-born-workers-made-83-point-1-percent-of-the-earnings-of-their-native-born-counterparts-in-2016.htm).

Bureau of Labor Statistics. 2017c. "Unemployment Rate 2.5 Percent for College Grads, 7.7 Percent for High School Dropouts, January 2017." February 7. Retrieved June 10, 2018 (www.bls.gov/opub/ted/2017/unemployment-rate-2-point-5-percent-for-college-grads-7-point-7-percent-for-high-school-dropouts-january-2017.htm).

Bureau of Labor Statistics. 2017d. "Economics News Release: Persons with a Disability—Labor Force Characteristics Summary." June 21. Retrieved November 20, 2017 (https://www.bls.gov/news.release/disabl.nr0.htm).

Bureau of Labor Statistics. 2017e. "Household Data Annual Averages 37. Median Weekly Earnings of Full-Time Wage and Salary Workers by Selected Characteristics." February 8. Retrieved May 24, 2017 (https://www.bls.gov/cps/tables.htm#weekearn).

Bureau of Labor Statistics. 2018a. *Occupational Outlook Handbook: Sociology*. Washington, DC: Bureau of Labor Statistics, Department of Labor.

Bureau of Labor Statistics. 2018b. "Household Data Annual Averages 37. Median Weekly Earnings of Full-Time Wage and Salary Workers by Selected Characteristics." January 19. Retrieved February 5, 2018 (https://www.bls.gov/cps/cpsaat37.pdf).

Bureau of Transportation Statistics. 2017. "Table 1-11: Number of U.S. Aircraft, Vehicles, Vessels, and Other Conveyances." July. Retrieved July 26, 2017 (https://www.rita.dot.gov/bts/sites/rita.dot.gov.bts/files/publications/national_transportation_statistics/html/table_01_11.html).

Burn, Shawn Meghan. 2011. *Women Across Cultures: A Global Perspective*, 3rd ed. New York: McGraw-Hill.

Burnett, John. 2017. "Will the Private Prison Business See a Trump Bump?" *NPR*, January 4. Retrieved August 3, 2017 (http://www.npr.org/2017/01/04/508048666/will-the-private-prison-business-see-a-trump-bump).

BushTV. 2010. "Kowanyama Keeping Culture Alive." Retrieved September 12, 2014 (http://www.youtube.com/watch?v=QCcBaVEUFlo).

Byanyima, Winnie. 2015. "Richest 1% Will Own More than All the Rest by 2016." Oxfam International, January 19. Retrieved January 29, 2015 (www.oxfam.org/en/pressroom/pressreleases/2015-01-19/richest-1-will-own-more-all-rest-2016).

Cahalan, Margaret, Laura Perna, Mika Yamashita, Roman Ruiz, and Khadish Franklin. 2016. *Indicators of Higher Education Equity in the United States: 2016 Historical Trend Report.* Washington, DC: Pell Institute for the Study of Opportunity in Higher Education, Council for Opportunity in Education and Alliance for Higher Education and Democracy of the University of Pennsylvania. Retrieved November 17, 2015 (www.pellinstitute.org/downloads/publications-Indicators_of_Higher_Education_Equity_in_the_US_45_Year_Trend_Report.pdf).

Cahill, Spencer E., Kent Sandstrom, and Carissa Froyum. 2013. *Inside Social Life,* 7th ed. New York: Oxford University Press.

Caldwell, John C. 1982. *Theory of Fertility Decline.* New York: Academic Press.

Calhoun, Craig, ed. 2007. *Sociology in America: A History.* Chicago: University of Chicago Press.

Cambodian Genocide Program. 2015. "The CGP, 1994–2015." Yale University. Retrieved January 28, 2016 (www.yale.edu/cgp/).

Campbell, Colin. 2017. "Which Games Are Women and Girls Playing?" *Polygon,* January 20. Retrieved February 3, 2018 (www.polygon.com/2017/1/20/14337282/games-for-women-and-girls).

Campbell, Ernest Q. and Thomas F. Pettigrew. 1959. *Christians in Racial Crisis.* Washington, DC: Public Affairs Press.

Canadian Health Care. 2010. "Introduction." Retrieved May 14, 2011 (www.canadian-healthcare.org/).

Cancian, Francesca M. 1992. "Feminist Science: Methodologies That Challenge Inequality." *Gender and Society* 6(4):623–42.

Carbone, June and Naomi Cahn. 2014. *Marriage Markets: How Inequality Is Remaking the American Family.* Oxford: Oxford University Press.

Carlson, Allan C. and Paul T. Mero. 2005. *The Natural Family: A Manifesto.* The Howard Center for Family, Religion and Society and the Sutherland Institute. Retrieved July 11, 2013 (http://familymanifesto.net/fmDocs/FamilyManifesto.pdf).

Caron, Christina. 2017. "Californians Will Soon Have Nonbinary as a Gender Option on Birth Certificates." *New York Times,* October 19. Retrieved October 19, 2017 (https://www.nytimes.com/2017/10/19/us/birth-certificate-nonbinary-gender-california.html?_r=0).

Carrothers, Robert M. and Denzel E. Benson. 2003. "Symbolic Interactionism in Introductory Textbooks: Coverage and Pedagogical Implications." *Teaching Sociology* 31(2):162–81.

Carson, E. Ann. 2018. "Prisoners in 2016." Bureau of Justice Statistics, January. Retrieved February 5, 2018 (https://www.bjs.gov/content/pub/pdf/p16.pdf).

Carter, Michael J. and Celene Fuller. 2015. Sociopedia.*isa.* Retrieved May 2, 2018 (www.sagepub.net/isa/resources/pdf/symbolic%20interactionism.pdf).

Carver-Thomas, Desiree and Linda Darling-Hammond. 2017. "Teacher Turnover: Why It Matters and What We Can Do About It." *Learning Policy Institute.* Retrieved September 7, 2018 (https://learningpolicyinstitute.org/product/teacher-turnover-report).

Casasanto, Daniel. 2008. "Who's Afraid of the Big Bad Whorf? Crosslinguistic Differences in Temporal Language and Thought." *Language Learning* 58(1):63–79.

Casella, Alexander. 2009. "Rural China Misses 'Barefoot Doctors.'" *Asia Times,* January 16. Retrieved January 10, 2010 (www.atimes.com/atimes/China/KA16Ad04.html).

Cashman, Geer Fay. 2017. "Women and Jihad: The Motivation of Female Suicide Bombers." *Jerusalem Post,* February 6. Retrieved January 27, 2018 (www.jpost.com/Arab-Israeli-Conflict/Women-and-Jihad-The-motivation-of female-suicide-bombers-480666).

Cashmore, Ellis and Barry Troyna. 1990. *Introduction to Race Relations.* London: Routledge.

Castiello, Umberto, Cristina Becchio, Stefania Zoia, Cristian Nelini, Luisa Sartori, Laura Blason, Giuseppina D'Ottavio, Maria Bulgheroni, and Vittorio Gallese. 2010. "Wired to Be Social: The Ontogeny of Human Interaction." *PLoS One* 5(10). Retrieved October 19, 2010 (www.plosone.org/article/info%3Adoi%2F10.1371%2Fjournal.pone.0013199).

Catalyst. 2017. "Women CEOs of the Fortune 500." April 25. Retrieved May 23, 2017 (http://www.catalyst.org/knowledge/women-ceos-sp-500).

CBS News. 2014. "Experts Weigh in on Texas Law Keeping Brain-Dead Pregnant Woman Alive." *CBS News,* January 3. Retrieved March 3, 2014 (www.cbsnews.com/news/experts-weight-in-on-texas-law-keeping-brain-dead-woman-alive/).

CBS News. 2017. "White Supremacist Activity on the Rise on College Campuses Since Election." *CBS News,* May 3. Retrieved July 31, 2017 (http://www.cbsnews.com/news/white-supremacist-activity-on-the-rise-on-college-campuses-since-election/).

Center for American Women and Politics. 2017. "Women in the U.S. Congress 2017." Retrieved May 22, 2017 (http://www.cawp.rutgers.edu/women-us-congress-2017).

Center for Constitutional Rights. 2017. "CCR News: Remembering 9/11." September 11. Retrieved January 28, 2018 (http://ccrjustice.org/home/blog/2017/09/11/ccr-news-remembering-911).

Center for Responsive Politics. 2017. "Election Overview." April 19. Retrieved May 7, 2017 (https://www.opensecrets.org/overview/index.php?cycle=2016&display=T&type=A).

Centers for Disease Control and Prevention. 2009. "Overweight and Obesity." July 27–29. Retrieved November 4, 2009 (www.cdc.gov/obesity/index.html).

Centers for Disease Control and Prevention. 2013c. "NCHS Data Brief; Trends in Inpatient Hospital Deaths: National Hospital Discharge Survey, 2000–2010." Retrieved July 16, 2013 (www.cdc.gov/nchs/data/databriefs/db118.htm).

Centers for Disease Control and Prevention. 2015a. *Epidemiology and Prevention of Vaccine-Preventable Diseases,* 13th ed., April. Retrieved March 14, 2017 (https://www.cdc.gov/vaccines/pubs/pinkbook/downloads/appendices/e/reported-cases.html).

Centers for Disease Control and Prevention. 2015b. "Measles Cases and Outbreaks, January 1 to August 29, 2014." Retrieval September 7, 2014 (www.cdc.gov/measles/cases-outbreaks.html).

Centers for Disease Control and Prevention. 2015c. "Births: Method of Delivery." January 22. Retrieved July 1, 2015 (www.cdc.gov/nchs/fastats/delivery.htm).

Centers for Disease Control and Prevention. 2015d. "Health Expenditures." April 29. Retrieved July 2, 2015 (www.cdc.gov/nchs/fastats/health-expenditures.htm).

Centers for Disease Control and Prevention. 2015e. "Measles Cases in the U.S." June 30. Retrieved July 2, 2015 (www.cdc.gov/measles/cases-outbreaks.html).

Centers for Disease Control and Prevention. 2016a. "HIV/AIDS: Basic Statistics." Retrieved April 11, 2016 (www.cdc.gov/hiv/basic/statistics.html).

Centers for Disease Control and Prevention. 2016b. "Chronic Disease Prevention and Health Promotion: Multiple Chronic Conditions." Retrieved June 21, 2017 (https://www.cdc.gov/chronicdisease/about/multiple-chronic.htm).

Centers for Disease Control and Prevention. 2016c. "Adult Obesity Facts." September 1. Retrieved July 29, 2017 (https://www.cdc.gov/obesity/data/adult.html).

Centers for Disease Control and Prevention. 2017a. "Provisional Number of Marriages and Marriage Rate: United States, 2000–2016." Retrieved September 7, 2018 (https://www.cdc.gov/nchs/data/dvs/national_marriage_divorce_rates_00-16.pdf).

Centers for Disease Control and Prevention. 2017b. "Divorce Rates by State: 1990, 1995, and 1999–2016." January 13. Retrieved September 7, 2018 (https://www.cdc.gov/nchs/data/dvs/state_divorce_rates_90_95_99-16.pdf).

Centers for Disease Control and Prevention. 2017c. "National Vital Statistics Reports." January 5(66):1.

Centers for Disease Control and Prevention. 2017d. "Measles Cases and Outbreaks." Retrieved June 22, 2017 (https://www.cdc.gov/measles/cases-outbreaks.html).

Centers for Disease Control and Prevention. 2018a. "Fact Sheet: Alcohol Use and Your Health." January 3. Retrieved February 10, 2018 (www.cdc.gov/alcohol/fact-sheets/alcohol-use.htm).

Centers for Disease Control and Prevention. 2018b. "Fewer U.S. High School Students Having Sex, Using Drugs." Retrieved September 7, 2018 (https://www.cdc.gov/media/releases/2018/p0614-yrbs.html).

Centers for Disease Control and Prevention/National Center for Health Statistics. 2015. "National Vital Statistics System: National Marriage and Divorce Rate Trends—Provisional Number of Divorces and Annulments and Rate: United States, 2000–2014." Retrieved August 2016 (www.cdc.gov/nchs/nvss/marriage_divorce_tables.htm).

Centers for Medicare & Medicaid Services. 2017. "2016-2025 Projections of National Health Expenditures Data Released." Retrieved June 21, 2017 (https://www.cms.gov/Newsroom/MediaReleaseDatabase/Press-releases/2017-Press-releases-items/2017-02-15-2.html).

The Century Foundation. 2016. "The Benefits of Socioeconomically and Racially Integrated Schools and Classrooms." February 10. Retrieved May 16, 2017 (https://tcf.org/content/facts/the-benefits-of-socioeconomically-and-racially-integrated-schools-and-classrooms/).

Chalfant, Morgan. 2017. "Trump Signs Cybercrime Bill." *The Hill*, November 2. Retrieved February 17, 2018 (http://thehill.com/policy/cybersecurity/358511-trump-signs-cyber-crime-bill).

Chalfant, Paul H. and Charles W. Peck. 1983. "Religious Affiliation, Religiosity, and Racial Prejudice: A New Look at Old Relationships." *Review of Religious Research* 25(December):155–61.

Chamberlain, Houston Stewart. [1899] 1911. *The Foundations of the Nineteenth Century*, translated by John Lees. London, New York: John Lane.

Chambliss, William J. 1973. "The Saints and the Roughnecks." *Society* 11(December):24–31.

Chan, Margaret. 2017. "'Zika' We Must Be Ready for the Long Haul." *World Health Organization*, February 1. Retrieved July 26, 2017 (http://www.who.int/mediacentre/commentaries/2017/zika-long-haul/en/).

Chappell, Bill. 2017. "Census Finds a More Diverse America as Whites Lag Growth." *NPR*, June 22. Retrieved March 15, 2018 (www.npr.org/sections/thetwo-way/2017/06/22/533926978/census-finds-a-more-diverse-america-as-whites-lag-growth).

Charities Aid Foundation. 2012. "World Giving Index 2012." December. Retrieved June 15, 2013 (www.cafonline.org/PDF/WorldGivingIndex2012WEB.pdf).

Charles, Camille Z., Vincent J. Roscigno, and Kimberly C. Torres. 2007. "Racial Inequality and College Attendance: The Mediating Role of Parental Investments." *Social Science Research* 36(1):329–52.

Charon, Joel. 2010. *Symbolic Interactionism: An Introduction, an Interpretation, an Integration*, 10th ed. Englewood Cliffs, NJ: Prentice Hall.

Chase, Cheryl. 2000. "Genital Surgery on Children Below the Age of Consent: Intersex Genital Mutilation." In *Psychological Perspectives on Human Sexuality*, edited by L. Szuchman and F. Muscarella. New York: Wiley.

Chase-Dunn, Christopher and E. N. Anderson. 2006. *The Historical Evolution of World-Systems*. New York: Palgrave Macmillan.

Chaves, Mark. 2004. *Congregations in America*. Cambridge, MA: Harvard University Press.

Chaves, Mark and Philip S. Gorski. 2001. "Religious Pluralism and Religious Participation." *Annual Review of Sociology* 27:261–81.

Chen, Alice, Emily Oster, and Heidi Williams. 2016. "Why Is Infant Mortality Higher in the United States Than in Europe?" *American Economic Journal. Economic Policy* 8(2):89–124 (http://doi.org/10.1257/pol.20140224).

Cheng, Siwei and Yu Xie. 2013. "Structural Effect of Size on Interracial Friendship." *Proceedings of the National Academy of Sciences*, April 15.

Cherlin, Andrew. 1978. "Remarriage as an Incomplete Institution." *American Journal of Sociology* 84(3):634–50.

Cherry, Kendra. 2012. "Understanding Body Language." About.*com Psychology*. Retrieved September 25, 2012 (http://psychology.about.com/od/nonverbalcommunication/ss/understanding-body-language.htm).

Chetty, Raj and Nathaniel Hendren. 2015. "Executive Summary, April 2015. The Impacts of Neighborhoods on Intergenerational Mobility Childhood Exposure Effects and County-Level Estimates." *Harvard University*, April. Retrieved June 25, 2015 (www.equality-of-opportunity.org/images/nbhds_exec_summary.pdf).

Chetty, Raj, Nathaniel Hendren, Maggie R. Jones and Sonya R. Porter. 2018. "Race and Economic Opportunity in the United States: An Intergenerational Perspective." *The Equality of Opportunity Project*, March. Retrieved March 19, 2018 (http://www.equality-of-opportunity.org/assets/documents/race_paper.pdf).

Chetty, Raj, Nathaniel Hendren, Patrick Kline, and Emmanuel Saez. 2014. "Where Is the Land of Opportunity? The Geography of Intergenerational Mobility in the United States." *The Equality of Opportunity Project*, June. Retrieved June 11, 2015 (www.equality-of-opportunity.org/images/mobility_geo.pdf).

Chetty, Raj, Michael Stepner, Sarah Abraham, Shelby Lin, Benjamin Scuderi, Nicholas Turner, Augustin Bergeron, and David Cutler. 2016. "The Association Between Income and Life Expectancy in the United States, 2001–2014." *Journal of the American Medical Association*. Retrieved April 11, 2016 (http://jama.jamanetwork.com/article.aspx? articleid=2513561).

Cheung, Cecilia Sin-Sze and Eva M. Pomerantz. 2012. "Why Does Parents' Involvement Enhance Children's Achievement? The Role of Parent-Oriented Motivation." *Journal of Educational Psychology* 14(3):820–32.

ChildStats.gov. 2013. "America's Children: Key National Indicators of Well-Being, 2013." Retrieved February 25, 2014 (www.childstats.gov/americaschildren/famsoc2.asp).

ChildStats.gov. 2017. "America's Children in Brief: Key National Indicators of Well-Being, 2016." Retrieved June 2, 2017 (https://www.childstats.gov/americaschildren/index.asp).

Child Trends. 2013a. "Child Support Receipt." Retrieved February 19, 2014 (www.childtrends.org/wp-content/uploads/212/07/84_Child_Support_Receipt.pdf).

Child Trends. 2013b. "High School Dropout Rates." Retrieved April 3, 2014 (www.childtrends.org/?indicators=high-school-dropout-rates).

Child Trends. 2018. "2018 High School Drop Out Rates." Retrieved September 7, 2018 (https://www.childtrends.org/indicators/high-school-dropout-rates).

Christiano, Kevin J., William H. Swatos, Jr., and Peter Kivisto. 2008. *Sociology of Religion: Contemporary Developments*, Rev. ed. Walnut Creek, CA: AltaMira.

Churches, Kimberly. 2017. "Of Course Sexual Harassment Is Rampant. It Starts in Our Schools." October 26. Retrieved February 7, 2018 (fortune.com/2017/10/26/sexual-harassment-assault-mark-halperin-george-hw-bush/).

Churchill, Winston. 2009. *Churchill by Himself: The Definitive Collection of Quotations*, edited by Richard Langworth. Jackson, TN: Public Affairs.

CityMayors 2018. "Largest Cities in the World." Retrieved September 17, 2018 (http://www.citymayors.com/statistics/largest-cities-population-125.html).

Clapson, Mark. 2003. *Suburban Century: Social Change and Urban Growth in England and the USA*. Oxford and New York: Berg.

Clark, Lara, Dylan B. Millet, and Julian D. Marshall. 2014. "National Patterns in Environmental Injustice and Inequality: Outdoor NO_2 Air Pollution in the United States." *PLOS One* 9(4). Retrieved July 6, 2015 (www.plosone.org/article/fetchObject.action?uri=info:doi/10.1371/journal.pone.0094431&representation=PDF).

Clarke, Ronald R., ed. 1997. *Situational Crime Prevention: Successful Case Studies*, 2nd ed. New York: Harrow and Heston.

Clausen, John A. 1986. *The Life Course: A Sociological Perspective*. Englewood Cliffs, NJ: Prentice Hall.

Clement, Scott. 2015. "Do Cubans Like the Castros?" *Washington Post*, April 9. Retrieved January 28, 2016 (www.washingtonpost.com/news/worldviews/wp/2015/04/09/do-cubans-like-the-castros/).

Clymer, Floyd. 1953. *Those Wonderful Old Automobiles*. New York: Bonanza.

CNN. 2017. "Flint Water Crisis Fast Facts." June 14. Retrieved July 20, 2017 (http://www.cnn.com/2016/03/04/us/flint-water-crisis-fast-facts/index.html).

CNN Freedom Project. 2017. "The Cost of a Slave Today." Retrieved May 15, 2018 (https://www.cnn.com/videos/world/2017/01/05/freedom-project-slave-cost.cnn/video/playlists/slavery-in-numbers/).

CNNMoney. 2017. "Education vs. Prison Costs." Retrieved November 16, 2017 (http://money.cnn.com/infographic/economy/education-vs-prison-costs/).

CNN Wire. 2017. "Harvard Fight Could Redirect 40 Years of Affirmative Action." August 6. Retrieved May 8, 2018 (wgntv.com/2017/08/06/Harvard-fight-could-redirect-40-years-of affirmative-action/).

Coates, Jennifer. 2013. *Women, Men, and Language*. New York: Routledge.

Cockerham, William C. 2015. *Medical Sociology*, 12th ed. Englewood Cliffs, NJ: Prentice Hall.

Cohn, D'Vera. 2015. "How Many Same-Sex Married Couples in the U.S.? Maybe 170,000." *Pew Research Center*, June 24. Retrieved September 9, 2015 (www.pewresearch.org/fact-tank/2015/06/24/how-many-same-sex-married-couples-in-the-u-s-maybe-170000/).

Cohn, D'Vera, Paul Taylor, Mark Hugo Lopez, Catherine A. Gallagher, Kim Parker, and Kevin T. Maass. 2013. "Gun Homicide Rate Down 49% Since 1993 Peak; Public Unaware." *Pew Research Social & Demographic Trends*, May 7. Retrieved June 1, 2013 (www.pewsocialtrends.org/2013/05/07/gun-homicide-rate-down-49-since-1993-peak-public-unaware/).

Coleman, James S. 1968. "The Concept of Equality of Educational Opportunity." *Harvard Education Review* 38(Winter):7–22.

Coleman, James S. 1975. "What Is Meant by 'An Equal Educational Opportunity'?" *Oxford Review of Education* 1(1):27–29.

Coleman, James. 1990. *Equality and Achievement in Education*. Boulder, CO: Westview.

Coleman, James William. 2006. *The Criminal Elite: Understanding White Collar Crime*, 6th ed. New York: Worth.

Coleman-Jensen, Alisha, Matthew P. Rabbitt, Christian A. Gregory, and Anita Singh. 2016. "Household Food Security in the United States in 2015." *ERR-215, U.S. Department of Agriculture, Economic Research Service*, September 2016. Retrieved May 9, 2017 (https://www.ers.usda.gov/webdocs/publications/79761/err-215.pdf?v=42636).

College Board. 2015. "Total Group Profile Report." Retrieved February 17, 2016 (http://secure-media.collegeboard.org/digitalServices/pdf/sat/total-group-2015.pdf).

College Board. 2016. "Total Group Profile Report." Retrieved November 1, 2017 (https://secure-media.collegeboard.org/digitalServices/pdf/sat/total-group-2016.pdf).

Collins, Chuck and Josh Hoxie. 2015. "Billionaire Bonanza: The Forbes 400 and the Rest of US." *Institute for Policy Studies*, December 1. Retrieved May 7, 2017 (https://www.ips-dc.org/billionaire-bonanza/).

Collins, Patricia Hill. 2008. *Black Feminist Thought: Knowledge, Consciousness, and the Politics of Empowerment*. New York: Routledge.

Collins, Patricia Hill and Sirma Bilge. 2016. *Intersectionality*. Malden, MA: Polity Press.

Collins, Peter A., Robert C. Boruchowitz, Matthew J. Hickman, and Mark A. Larrañaga. 2016. "An Analysis of the Economic Costs of Seeking the Death Penalty in Washington State." *Seattle Journal for Social Justice* 4(3):727–79.

Collins, Randall. 1971. "A Conflict Theory of Sexual Stratification." *Social Problems* 19(Summer):2–21.

Collins, Randall. 2014. "Conflict Theory of Educational Stratification." *American Sociological Review* 38:47–54.

Collins, Sara R., Munira Z. Gunja, Michelle M. Doty, and Herman K. Bhupal. 2018. "First Look at Health Insurance Coverage in 2018 Finds ACA Gains Beginning to Reverse." *The Commonwealth Fund*. Retrieved September 17, 2018 (https://www.commonwealthfund.org/blog/2018/first-look-health-insurance-coverage-2018-finds-aca-gains-beginning-reverse?redirect_source=/publications/blog/2018/apr/health-coverage-erosion).

Colorado Department of Public Health & Environment. 2016. "Survey: Parents Biggest Influence on Youth Health Behaviors." June 20. Retrieved July 31, 2017 (https://www.colorado.gov/pacific/cdphe/news/HKCS2015).

Common Core Standards Initiative. 2017. "Standards in Your State." Retrieved November 22, 2017 (http://www.corestandards.org/standards-in-your-state/).

Comte, Auguste. [1855] 2003. *The Positive Philosophy of Auguste Comte, freely translated and condensed by Harriet Martineau.* Whitefish, MO: Kessinger.

Conley, Dalto. 2014. "Recognizing When Kids Benefit from Their Parents' Divorce." *The Atlantic*, April 16. Retrieved January 15, 2016 (www.theatlantic.com/health/archive/2014/04/recognizing-when-kids-benefit-from-their-parents-divorce/284589/).

Connor, Phillip. 2016. "International Migration: Key Findings from the U.S., Europe and the World." *Pew Research Center*, December 15. Retrieved July 24, 2017 (http://www.pewresearch.org/fact-tank/2016/12/15/international-migration-key-findings-from-the-u-s-europe-and-the-world/).

Conrad, Peter. 2007. *The Medicalization of Society: On the Transformation of Human Conditions into Treatable Disorders.* Baltimore: Johns Hopkins University Press.

Consumer Reports. 2017. "The New War on Obesity." Pp. 48–53, October.

Conyers, Addrain and Thomas C. Calhoun. 2015. "Labeling Theory." Pp. 263–64 in *The Handbook of Deviance*, edited by Erich Goode. Malden, MA: Wiley.

Cook, Karen S., Jodi O'Brien, and Peter Kollock. 1990. "Exchange Theory: A Blueprint for Structure and Process." Pp. 158–81 in *Frontiers of Social Theory: The New Syntheses*, edited by George Ritzer. New York: Columbia University Press.

Cooley, Charles Horton. 1902. *Human Nature and the Social Order.* New York: Scribner.

Cooley, Charles Horton. [1909] 1983. *Social Organization: A Study of the Larger Mind.* New York: Schocken Books.

Coontz, Stephanie. 2016. *The Way We Never Were: American Families and the Nostalgia Trap*, Rev. ed. New York: Basic Books.

Cooper, David and Teresa Kroeger. 2017. "Employers Steal Billions from Worker's Paychecks Each Year." *Economic Policy Institute*, May 10. Retrieved August 1, 2017 (http://www.epi.org/publication/employers-steal-billions-from-workers-paychecks-each-year-survey-data-show-millions-of-workers-are-paid-less-than-the-minimum-wage-at-significant-cost-to-taxpayers-and-state-economies/).

Copp, Jennifer E., Peggy C. Giordano, Monica A. Longmore, and Wendy D. Manning. 2013. "Stay/Leave Decision-Making in Non-violent and Violent Dating Relationships." *2013 Working Paper Series.* Center for Family and Demographic Research. Retrieved January 17, 2014 (www.bgsu.edu/organizations.cfdr).

Corak, Miles. 2016. "The Poverty and Inequality Report." *Pathways.* Retrieved September 18, 2017 (https://inequality.stanford.edu/sites/default/files/Pathways-SOTU-2016-Economic-Mobility-3.pdf).

Coser, Lewis A. 1956. *The Functions of Social Conflict.* New York: Free Press.

Coser, Lewis A. 1964. *The Functions of Social Conflict.* New York: Free Press.

Council on Foreign Relations. 2014. "NAFTA's Economic Impact." Retrieved February 23, 2014 (www.cfr.org/trade/naftas-economic-impact/p15790).

Council on Foreign Relations. 2016. "The Group of Seven (G7)." Retrieved January 29, 2016 (www.cfr.org/international-organizations-and-alliances/group-seven-g7/p32957).

Council of State Governments. 2016. "State Affirmative Action Bans on College Campuses." March 15. Retrieved May 17, 2017 (http://knowledgecenter.csg.org/kc/content/state-affirmative-action-bans-college-campuses).

Council of State Governments Justice Center. 2015. "Three Core Elements of Programs that Reduce Recidivism: Who, What, and How Well." July 7. Retrieved August 3, 2017 (https://csgjusticecenter.org/jr/posts/three-core-elements-of-programs-that-reduce-recidivism-who-what-and-how-well/).

Countrymeters. 2018. "World Population." Retrieved March 22, 2018 (http://countrymeters.info/en/World#population_2017).

Cousteau, Jacques-Yves. 2008. "The Great Ocean Adventure." *Lecture at Hanover College*, January 15.

Cowie, Sam. 2015. "Rape and HIV a Common Reality for Young Swazi Women." *Al Jazeera*, April 7. Retrieved July 1, 2015 (www.aljazeera.com/indepth/features/2015/03/rape-hiv-common-reality-young-swazi-women-150331055924861.html).

Cramer & Associates. 2016. "Giving USA 2016." Retrieved June 7, 2017 (http://www.beneschlaw.com/files/uploads/Documents/GivingUSA-2016_Findings_Final.pdf).

Crary, David and Denise Lavoie. 2013. "As Boston Buries Its Dead, More Evidence Gathered." *AP*, April 23. Retrieved August 23, 2014 (http://bigstory.ap.org/article/more-details-sought-mute-boston-bomb-suspect).

CRDC. 2017. "CRDC Data Set for School Year 2017–18: Response to First Round Public Comment." Retrieved February 7, 2018 (edweek.org/edweek/campaign-k-12/July%202017_Response_to_60_Day_Public_Comment_FINAL%20%281%29.pdf).

Croft, Jay and Tristan Smith. 2017. "Dylann Roof Pleads Guilty to State Charges in Church Massacre." *CNN*, April 10. Retrieved May 11, 2017 (http://www.cnn.com/2017/04/10/us/dylann-roof-guilty-plea-state-trial/).

Croft, Michelle and Grover J. "Russ" Whitehurst. 2010. "The Harlem Children's Zone Revisited." *The Brookings Institute*, July 28. Retrieved January 10, 2014 (www.brookings.edu/blogs/up-front/posts/2010/07/28-hcz-whitehurst).

Crosby, Faye J. 2004. *Affirmative Action Is Dead; Long Live Affirmative Action.* New Haven, CT: Yale University Press.

Cubanski, Juliette and Tricia Neuman. 2016. "Medicare Spending at the End of Life: A Snapshot of Beneficiaries Who Died in 2014 and the Cost of Their Care." The Henry J. Kaiser Foundation, July 14. Retrieved June 22, 2017 (http://www.kff.org/report-section/medicare-spending-at-the-end-of-life-findings/).

Cultural Survival. 2010. "Wodaabe." Retrieved July 7, 2013 (www.culturalsurvival.org/publications/cultural-survival-quarterly/cameroon/wodaabe).

Cummins, Anna and Serenitie Wang. 2017. "Sandstorm Pushes Beijing Smog Off Pollution Charts." *CNN*, May 4. Retrieved July 25, 2017 (http://www.cnn.com/2017/05/04/asia/beijing-sand-storm-pollution-beyond-index/index.html).

Curtiss, S. 1977. *Genie: A Psycholinguistic Study of a Modern-Day "Wild Child."* New York: Academic Press.

Cuzzort, R. P. and Edith W. King. 2002. *Social Thought into the Twenty-First Century*, 6th ed. Belmont, CA: Wadsworth.

DaCosta, Kimberly McClain. 2007. *Making Multiracials: State, Family, and Market in the Redrawing of the Color Line.* Stanford, CA: Stanford University Press.

Dahl, Robert A. 1961. *Who Governs?* New Haven, CT: Yale University Press.

Dahrendorf, Ralf. 1959. *Class and Class Conflict in Industrial Societies.* Palo Alto, CA: Stanford University Press.

Dalton, Harlon. 2012. "Failing to See." Pp. 15–18 in *White Privilege*, edited by Paula S. Rothenberg. New York: Worth.

Danilova, Maria. 2017. "Does Free Mean Better for Students Choosing SAT Prep Courses?" *U.S. News*, May 8. Retrieved November 21, 2017 (https://www.usnews.com/news/business/articles/2017-05-08/ap-ahead-in-test-prep-industry-more-options-available).

Danwatch. 2016. "Bitter Coffee." Retrieved May 3, 2017 (https://www.danwatch.dk/en/undersogelse/bitter-coffee-2/).

D'Arcy, Yvonne. 2009. "The Effect of Culture on Pain." *Nursing Made Incredibly Easy!* 7(3):5–7.

Darwin, Charles. [1859] 1909. *On the Origin of Species.* New York: P. F. Collier.

Das, Udaibir S., Michael G. Papaioannou, and Christoph Trebesch. 2012. "Sovereign Debt Restructurings 1950–2010: Literature Survey, Data, and Stylized Facts." International Monetary Fund, August. Retrieved September 8, 2014 (www.un.org/esa/ffd/ecosoc/debt/2013/IMF_wp12_203.pdf).

Davenport, Coral and Marjorie Connelly. 2015. "Most Americans Support Government Action on Climate Change, Poll Finds." *Environmental Economics*, January 30. Retrieved September 13, 2015 (www.env-econ.net/2015/01/most-americans-support-government-action-on-climate-change-poll-finds.html).

Davis, Kingsley. 1940. "Extreme Social Isolation of a Child." *American Journal of Sociology* 45:554–65.

Davis, Kingsley. 1947. "A Final Note on a Case of Extreme Isolation." *American Journal of Sociology* 52:432–37.

Davis, Kingsley and Wilbert Moore. 1945. "Some Principles of Stratification." *American Sociological Review* 10(April):242–45.

Davis, Lois M., Robert Bozick, Jennifer Steele, Jessica Saunders, and Jeremy N. V. Miles. 2013. "Evaluating the Effectiveness of Correctional Education." *The Rand Corporation.* Retrieved March 22, 2018 (https://www.rand.org/pubs/research_reports/RR266.html).

Death Penalty Information Center. 2018. "Facts About the Death Penalty." August 14. Retrieved September 1, 2018 (https://deathpenaltyinfo.org/documents/FactSheet.pdf).

Death with Dignity. 2017. "Death with Dignity Laws." Retrieved March 13, 2017 (https://www.deathwithdignity.org/learn/access/).

Death with Dignity. 2018. "Frequently Asked Questions." Retrieved September 17, 2018 (https://www.deathwithdignity.org/faqs/#safeguards).

Debenham, Lucy. 2014. "Communication: What Percent Is Body Language?" August 18. Retrieved August 29, 2014 (www.bodylanguageexpert.co.uk/communication-what-percent-age-body-language.html).

Debenham, Lucy. 2018. "Communication: What Percentage is Body Language?" April 30. Retrieved May 8, 2018 (www.bodylanguageexpert.co.uk/communication-what-percentage-body-language.html).

Deerwester, Karen. 2013. "Boy Toys or Girl Toys: Children Are What They Play." *Examiner*, November 8. Retrieved January 16, 2014 (www.examiner.com/article/boy-toys-or-girl-toys-children-are-what-they-play).

Delehanty, John. 2015. "Prophets of Resistance: Social Justice Activists Contesting Comfortable Church Culture." *Sociology of Religion* 54(Winter):1–22.

Della Porta, Donatella, Massimillano Andretta, Lorenzo Mosca, and Herbert Reiter. 2006. *Globalization From Below: Transnational Activists and Protest Networks.* Minneapolis: University of Minnesota Press.

De los Santos, Isaiah. 2017. "Do the Blazers Get Penalized More for Wearing Black Uniforms?" Retrieved March 28, 2018 (www.blazersedge.com/2017/12/18/16786364/trail-blazers-nike-icon-jerseys-fouls-home-record).

Deming, David J. 2015. "The Growing Importance of Social Skills in the Labor Market." *NBER Working Paper No. 21473.* The National Bureau of Economic Research, August. Retrieved October 19, 2015 (www.nber.org/papers/w21473).

DeMitchell, Todd A. and John J. Carney. 2005. "Harry Potter and the Public School Library." *Phi Delta Kappan* (October):159–65.

Denali Commission. 2011. "Denali Commission Performance and Accountability Report, Agency Financial Report Fiscal Year 2011." Anchorage, AK: Author.

Dennis, Alex. 2017. "The Strange Survival and Apparent Resurgence of Sociobiology." *History of the Human Sciences* 31(1):19–35.

DeParle, Jason and Sabrina Tavernise. 2012. "For Women Under 30, Most Births Occur Outside Marriage." *New York Times*, February 17. Retrieved June 5, 2012 (www.nytimes.com/2012/02/18/us/for-women-under-30-most-births-occur-outside-marriage.html?pagewanted=all).

DePaulo, Bella. 2017. "What Is the Divorce Rate, Really?" *Psychology Today*, February 2. Retrieved June 10, 2018 (www.psychologytoday.com/us/blog/living-single/201702/what-is-the-divorce-rate-really).

Desilver, Drew. 2017. "U.S. Trails Most Developed Countries in Voter Turnout." *Pew Research Center*, May 15. Retrieved June 20, 2017 (http://www.pewresearch.org/fact-tank/2017/05/15/u-s-voter-turnout-trails-most-developed-countries/).

Desmond, Matthew. 2017. "How Home Ownership Became the Engine of American Inequality." *New York Times Magazine*, May 9. Retrieved May 11, 2017 (https://www.nytimes.com/2017/05/09/magazine/how-homeownership-became-the-engine-of-american-inequality.html?smprod=nytcore-ipad&smid=nytcore-ipad-share).

Deutsch, Albert. 1944. The First U.S. Census of the Insane (1840) and Its Use as Pro-Slavery Propaganda. *Bulletin of the History of Medicine* 15:472.

De Waal, Frans. 2016. *Are We Smart Enough to Know How Smart Animals Are?* New York: W. W. Norton.

Diamond, Jared M. 1999. *Guns, Germs, and Steel: The Fates of Human Societies.* New York: Norton.

Diamond, Jared M. 2005. *Collapse: How Societies Choose to Fail or Succeed.* New York: Viking.

Diamond, Jared M. 2012. *The World Until Yesterday.* New York: Penguin Books.

Diamond, Larry. 1992. "Introduction: Civil Society and the Struggle for Democracy." Pp. 1–28 in *The Democratic Revolution: Struggles for Freedom and Pluralism in the Developing World*, edited by Larry Diamond. New York: Freedom House.

Diamond, Larry. 2008. *The Spirit of Democracy: The Struggle to Build Free Societies Throughout the World.* New York: Henry Holt.

Diana, Mario and Doug McAdam, eds. 2003. *Social Movements and Networks: Relational Approaches to Collective Action.* Oxford, England: Oxford University Press.

Diaz, Julia M. and Judith L. Fridovich-Keil. 2016. "Genetically Modified Organisms." *Encyclopedia Britannica*, November. Retrieved July 28, 2017 (https://www.britannica.com/science/genetically-modified-organism).

Dickerson, Caitlin. 2017. "Trump Plan Would Curtail Protections for Detained Immigrants." *New York Times*, April 13. Retrieved August 3, 2017 (https://www.nytimes.com/2017/04/13/us/

detained-immigrants-may-face-harsher-conditions-under-trump.html?_r=0).

Diekman, Amanda B. and Sarah K. Murmen. 2004. "Learning to Be Little Women and Little Men: The Inequitable Gender Equality of Nonsexist Children's Literature." *Sex Roles: A Journal of Research* 50(5/6):373.

Diggs, Nancy Brown. 2011. *Hidden in the Heartland*. East Lansing: Michigan State University Press.

Diggs, Nancy Brown. 2014. *Breaking the Cycle: How Schools Can Overcome Urban Challenges*. New York: Rowman and Littlefield.

Dillinger, Jennifer. 2017. "25 Countries with the Highest Literacy Rates." *World Atlas*, March 21. Retrieved June 14, 2017 (http://www.worldatlas.com/articles/the-highest-literacy-rates-in-the-world.html).

Dillon, Liam. 2017. "California Senate Passes Package of Bills Aiming to Address Housing Crisis." *Los Angeles Times*, June 1. Retrieved July 24, 2017 (http://www.latimes.com/politics/essential/la-pol-ca-essential-politics-updates-california-senate-passes-package-of-1496339298-htmlstory.html).

Dilon, Michele. 2009. *Introduction to Sociological Theory: Theorists, Concepts, and Their Applicability to the Twenty-First Century*. Malden, MA: Wiley-Blackwell.

Doane, Beth. 2013. "Beijing Pollution Forces Children to Play Under Dome." *CBS News*, July 17. Retrieved July 9, 2015 (www.cbsnews.com/news/beijing-pollution-forces-students-to-play-under-dome/).

Dobbelaere, Karel. 1981. *Secularization: A Multidimensional Concept*. Beverly Hills, CA: Sage.

Dobbelaere, Karel. 2000. "Toward an Integrated Perspective of the Processes Related to the Descriptive Concept of Secularization." Pp. 21–39 in *The Secularization Debate*, edited by William H. Swatos Jr. and Daniel V. A. Olson. Lanham, MD: Rowman & Littlefield.

Dobbin, Frank and Alexandra Kalev. 2016. "Why Diversity Programs Fail." *Harvard Business Review*, July/August. Retrieved May 14, 2018 (https://hbr.org/2016/07/why-diversity-programs-fail).

Dobbin, Frank and Alexander Kalev. 2017. "Training Programs and Reporting Systems Won't End Sexual Harassment: More Women Will." *Harvard Business Review*, November 15. Retrieved December 18, 2017 (https://hbr.org/2017/11/training-programs-and-reporting-systems-wont-end-sexual-harassment-promoting-more-women-will).

Dobbs, David. 2013. "The Social Life of Genes." *Pacific Standard*, September 3. Retrieved December 17, 2013 (www.psmag.com/health/the-social-life-of-genes-64616/).

Dockterman, Eliana. 2014. "Chore Wars: How the Division of Domestic Duties Really Affects a Couple's Sex Life." *Time*, February 18. Retrieved February 28, 2014 (http://healthland.time.com/2014/02/18/chore-wars-how-the-division-of-domestic-duties-really-affects-a-couples-sex-life/#ixzz2udTcoUJ0).

Dollars and Sense Collective. 2012. Pp. 81–91 in *Globalization: The Transformation of Social Worlds*, 3rd ed., edited by D. Stanley Eitzen and Maxine Baca Zinn. Belmont, CA: Wadsworth.

Domhoff, William G. 2008. "Who Rules America: Power, Politics, and Social Change." Retrieved March 24, 2008 (http://sociology.ucsc.edu/whoruleesamerica).

Domhoff, William G. 2014. *Who Rules America? The Triumph of the Corporate Rich*, 7th ed. New York: McGraw-Hill.

Domhoff, William G. 2018. "Who Rules America: Power, Politics, and Social Change." Retrieved March 17, 2018 (www2.ucsc.edu/whorulesamerica?).

Donovan, Josephine. 2012. *Feminist Theory*, 4th ed. New York: Bloomsbury.

Dorell, Oren. 2017. "Alleged Russian Political Meddling Documents in 27 Countries Since 2004." USA Today, September 7. Retrieved February 5, 2018 (https://www.usatoday.com/story/news/world/2017/09/07/alleged-russian-political-meddling-documented-27-countries-since-2004/619056001/).

Dowd, James. 2017. "The Center Holds: From Subcultures to Social Worlds." November 26. Retrieved March 30, 2018 (www.researchgate.net/publication/271690925_The_Center_Holds_From_Subcultures_to_Social_Worlds).

Downey, Douglas B. and Shana Pribesh. 2004. "When Race Matters: Teachers' Evaluations of Students' Classroom Behavior." *Sociology of Education* 77(4):267–82.

Drafke, Michael. 2008. *The Human Side of Organizations*. Englewood Cliffs, NJ: Prentice Hall.

Drori, Gili S. 2006. *Global E-Litism: Digital Technology, Social Inequality, and Transnationality*. New York: Worth.

Drug Policy Alliance. 2017. "New FBI Report Shows Drug Arrests Increased in 2016, as Drug War Rages On." September 25. Retrieved September 1, 2018 (http://www.drugpolicy.org/press-release/2017/09/new-fbi-report-shows-drug-arrests-increased-2016-drug-war-rages).

Drury, Flora. 2015. "The Wodaabe Wife-Stealing Festival." *Daily Mail*, July 7. Retrieved March 15, 2018 (www.dailymail.co.uk/news/article-3149684/The-Wodaabe-wife-stealing-festival).

Du Bois, W. E. B. [1899] 1967. *The Philadelphia Negro: A Social Study*. New York: Schocken.

Dufur, Mikaela J. and Seth L. Feinberg. 2007. "Artificially Restricted Labor Markets and Worker Dignity in Professional Football." *Journal of Contemporary Ethnography* 36(5):505–36.

Duhigg, Charles and David Kocieniewski. 2013. "How Apple Sidesteps Billions in Taxes." *New York Times*, April 28. Retrieved May 31, 2013 (www.nytimes.com/2012/04/29/business/apples-tax-strategy-aims-at-low-tax-states-and-nations.html?pagewanted=all&_r=0).

Duncan, Greg J. and Richard J. Murnane. 2011. "Introduction: The American Dream, Then and Now." Pp. 3–26 in *Whither Opportunity? Rising Inequality, Schools, and Children's Life Chances*, edited by Greg J. Duncan and Richard J. Murnane. New York: Russell Sage Foundation and Spencer Foundation.

Dunn, James, ed. 2015. *Fundamentalisms: Threats and Ideologies in the Modern World*. London: I. B. Tauris.

Dunn, Jeff. 2017. "TV Is Still Media's Biggest Platform: But the Internet Is Quickly Gaining Ground." *Business Insider*, June 9. Retrieved May 8, 2018 (www.businessinsider.com/tv-vs-internet-media-consumption-average-chart-2017-6).

Durkheim, Émile. [1893] 1947. *The Division of Labor in Society*, translated by George Simpson. New York: Free Press.

Durkheim, Émile. [1912] 1947. *Elementary Forms of Religious Life*. Glencoe, IL: Free Press.

Durkheim, Émile. [1922] 1956. *Education and Society*, translated by Sherwood D. Fox. Glencoe, IL: Free Press.

Durkheim, Émile. [1895] 1982. *The Rules of the Sociological Method*, edited by Steven Lukes and translated by W. D. Halls. New York: Free Press.

Durkheim, Émile. [1897] 1964. *Suicide*. Glencoe, IL: Free Press.

Durkheim, Émile. [1915] 2002. *Classical Sociological Theory*, edited by Craig Calhoun. Malden, MA: Blackwell.

Durward, Rosemary and Lee Marsden, eds. 2009. *Religion, Conflict and Military Intervention*. London: Ashgate.

Dusenbery, Maya and Jaeah Lee. 2012. "Charts: The State of Women's Athletics, 40 Years After Title IX." *Mother Jones*, June 22. Retrieved May 2, 2013 (www.motherjones.com/politics/2012/06/charts-womens-athletics-title-nine-ncaa).

Dworkin, Anthony Gary and Pamela F. Tobe. 2012. "Teacher Burnout in Light of School Safety, Student Misbehavior, and Changing Accountability Standards." Pp. 199–211 in *Schools and Society: A Sociological Approach to Education*, edited by Jeanne H. Ballantine and Joan Z. Spade. Thousand Oaks, CA: Sage Pine Forge.

Dworkin, Anthony Gary and Rosalind J. Dworkin. 1999. *The Minority Report: An Introduction to Racial, Ethnic, and Gender Relations*, 3rd ed. Fort Worth, TX: Harcourt Brace.

Dwyer-Lindgren Laura, Amelia Bertozzi-Villa, Rebecca W. Stubbs, Chloe Morozoff, Johan P. Mackenbach, Frank J. van Lenthe, Ali H. Mokdad, and Christopher J. L. Murray. 2017. "Inequalities in Life Expectancy Among US Counties, 1980 to 2014 Temporal Trends and Key Drivers." *JAMA Internal Medicine* (Published online May 08, 2017; 10.1001/jamainternmed.2017.0918).

Dye, Thomas R. 2002. *Who's Running America? The Bush Restoration*, 7th ed. Upper Saddle River, NJ: Prentice Hall.

Dye, Thomas R. 2014. *Who's Running America? The Obama Reign*, 8th ed. Upper Saddle River, NJ: Prentice Hall.

Dye, Thomas and Harmon Zeigler. 1983. *The Irony of Democracy*. North Scituate, MA: Duxbury Press.

Dyer, Richard. 2012. "The Matter of Whiteness." Pp. 9–14 in *White Privilege*, edited by Paula S. Rothenberg. New York: Worth.

Dynarski, Susan M. 2015a. "Helping the Poor in Education: The Power of a Simple Nudge." *New York Times*, January 17. Retrieved June 23, 2015 (http://www.nytimes.com/2015/01/18/upshot/helping-the-poor-in-higher-education-the-power-of-a-simple-nudge.html?emc=eta1&abt=0002&abg=1).

Dynarski, Susan M. 2015b. "For the Poor, the Graduation Gap Is Even Wider than the Enrollment Gap." *New York Times*, June 2. Retrieved October 20, 2016 (www.nytimes.com/2015/06/02/upshot/for-the-poor-the-graduation-gap-is-even-wider-than-the-enrollment-gap.html).

Earls, Felton M. and Albert J. Reiss. 1994. *Breaking the Cycle: Predicting and Preventing Crime*. Washington, DC: National Institute of Justice.

Ebaugh, Helen Rose Fuchs. 2005. *Handbook of Religion and Social Institutions*. New York: Springer.

The Economist. 2015. "American Manufacturing: The Two Worlds of Deindustrialization." March 4. Retrieved July 24, 2017 (https://www.economist.com/blogs/freeexchange/2015/03/american-manufacturing).

The Economist. 2016. "Re-Educating Rita." *Special Report: Artificial Intelligence and Education*, June 25. Retrieved May 9, 2017 (http://www.economist.com/news/special-report/21700760-artificial-intelligence-will-have-implications-policymakers-education-welfare-and).

The Economist. 2017a. "Wasting Indian Minds: India Has Made Primary Education Universal, But Not Good." June 7. Retrieved November 9, 2017 (https://www.economist.com/news/leaders/21723105-worlds-biggest-school-system-also-one-worst-india-has-made-primary-education).

The Economist. 2017b. "The Glass Ceiling Index." March 8. Retrieved May 23, 2017 (http://www.economist.com/blogs/graphicdetail/2017/03/daily-chart-0).

The Economist. 2017c. "Prison Labour Is a Billion-Dollar Industry, with Uncertain Returns for Inmates." March 16. Retrieved

August 3, 2017 (https://www.economist.com/news/united-states/21718897-idaho-prisoners-roast-potatoes-kentucky-they-sell-cattle-prison-labour).

The Economist. 2018. "The Glass-Ceiling Index." February 15. Retrieved September 6, 2018 (https://www.economist.com/graphic-detail/2018/02/15/the-glass-ceiling-index).

Edwards, Harry. 2000. "Crisis of the Black Athlete on the Eve of the 21st Century." *Society* 37(3):9–13.

Egalite, Anna J. Spring. 2016. "How Family Background Influences Student Achievement." *EducationNext* 16(2). Retrieved November 2, 2017 (http://educationnext.org/how-family-background-influences-student-achievement/).

eHarmony. 2017. "Who We Are." Retrieved June 2, 2017 (http://www.eharmony.com/about/eharmony/).

Ehrlich, Paul and Anne Ehrlich. 1990. *The Population Explosion*. New York: Simon and Schuster.

Ehrlich, Paul and Anne Ehrlich. 2013. "Can a Collapse of Global Civilization Be Avoided?" *Proceedings of the Royal Society B* 280(1754). http://dx.doi.org/10.1098/rspb.2012.2845

Eitzen, D. Stanley and Maxine Baca Zinn. 2012. "Changing Global Structures: Resistance and Social Movements." Pp. 269–71 in *Globalization: The Transformation of Social Worlds*, 3rd ed., edited by D. Stanley Eitzen and Maxine Baca Zinn. Belmont, CA: Wadsworth.

Elkins, Kathleen. 2018. "The Royal Wedding Costs an Estimated $42.8 Million—And 94% of It Is for Security." May 19. Retrieved July 12, 2018 (https://www.cnbc.com/2018/05/18/the-royal-wedding-may-cost-43-million-and-94-percent-of-that-is-for-security.html).

Ellison, Christopher G. and Daniel A. Powers. 1994. "The Contact Hypothesis and Racial Attitudes Among Black Americans." *Social Science Quarterly* 75(2):385–400.

Ellison, Christopher G., J. A. Burr, and P. L. McCall. 1997. "Religious Homogeneity and Metropolitan Suicide Rates." *Social Forces* 76(1):273–99.

Emerson, Ralph Waldo. 1904. "Astraea." *The Complete Works*, Vol. IX. Poems (no publisher listed); Emerson, 1904. *Poems*. Boston: Houghton Mifflin & Co.

Emery, Robert E. 2013. *Cultural Sociology of Divorce: An Encyclopedia*. Thousand Oaks, CA: Sage.

Engels, Friedrich. [1884] 1942. *The Origin of the Family, Private Property, and the State*. New York: International.

Erickson, Fritz and John A. Vonk. 2012. "100 People: A World Portrait." Retrieved January 4, 2014 (www.100people.org/statistics_100stats.php).

Erikson, Kai T. 1976. *Everything in Its Path: Destruction of Community in the Buffalo Creek Flood*. New York: Simon & Schuster.

Eshleman, J. Ross and Richard A. Bulcroft. 2010. *The Family*, 12th ed. Boston: Allyn & Bacon.

Espelage, Dorothy L., Jun Sung Hong, Sarah Rinehart, and Namrata Doshi. 2016. "Understanding Types, Locations, & Perpetrators of Peer-to-Peer Sexual Harassment in U.S. Middle Schools: A Focus on Sex, Racial, and Grade Differences." *Children and Youth Services Review* 71:174–84.

Esperitu, Yen Le. 1992. *Asian American Panethnicity: Bridging Institutions and Identities*. Philadelphia: Temple University Press.

Estrellado, Alicia F. and Jennifer (M. I.) Loh. 2013. "Factors Associated with Battered Filipino Women's Decision to Stay in or Leave an Abusive Relationship." *Journal of Interpersonal Violence*, November 7. Retrieved January 17, 2014 (http://jiv.sagepub.com/content/early/2013/11/07/08862605 13505709.abstract).

Etounga-Manguelle, Daniel. 2000. "Does Africa Need a Cultural Adjustment Program?" Pp. 65–77 in *Culture Matters: How Values Shape Human Progress*, edited by Lawrence E. Harrison and Samuel P. Huntington. New York: Basic Books.

European Commission. 2016. "Climate Action." Retrieved August 12, 2016 (http://ec.europa.eu/clima/policies/international/ negotiations/paris/index_en.htm).

European Commission. 2017. "Attitudes Towards the Impact of Digitisation and Automation on Daily Life." May 10. Retrieved December 29, 2017 (https://ec.europa.eu/digital-single-market/ en/news/attitudes-towards-impact-digitisation-and-automation-daily-life).

Eurostat. 2018. "Mortality and Life Expectancy Statistics." Retrieved August 30, 2018 (ec.europa.eu/eurostat/statistics-explained/index.php/Mortality_and_life_expectancy_statistics).

Fadiman, Anne. (1998). *The Spirit Catches You and You Fall Down: A Hmong Child, Her American Doctors, and the Collision of Two Cultures*. New York: Farrar, Straus and Giroux.

Fallon, Kathleen M., Liam Swiss, and Jocelyn Viterna. 2012. "Resolving the Democracy Paradox: Democratization and Women's Legislative Representation in Developing Nations, 1975 to 2009." *American Sociological Review* 77(3):380–408.

Family Research Council. 2014. "Marriage and Family." Retrieved September 16, 2014 (http://www.frc.org/Marriage-and-Family).

FAO (Food and Agriculture Organization) of the United Nations. 2016. *State of the World's Forests: Forests and Agriculture: Land-Use Challenges and Opportunities*. Rome: Author.

Farley, John E. 2011. *Majority-Minority Relations, Census Update*. New York: Pearson

Farrer, Claire R. 2011. *Thunder Rides a Black Horse: Mescalero Apaches and the Mythic Present*, 3rd ed. Long Grove, IL: Waveland.

Fathi, David C. 2009. "Prison Nation." *Human Rights Watch*, April 9. Retrieved April 15, 2009 (www.hrw.org/en/news/2009/04/09/ prison-nation).

Fausto-Sterling, Anne. 1992. *Myths of Gender: Biological Theories About Women and Men*, 2nd ed. New York: Basic Books.

Fausto-Sterling, Anne. 2000. "The Five Sexes, Revisited." *Sciences* 40(July/August):118.

Feagin, Joe R. 2012. *The White Frame: Centuries of Racial Framing and Counter-Framing*, 2nd ed. New York: Routledge.

Feagin, Joe R. and Clairece Booher Feagin. 1986. *Discrimination American Style: Institutional Racism and Sexism*. Malabar, FL: Krieger.

Feagin, Joe R. and Clairece Booher Feagin. 2012. *Racial and Ethnic Relations*, 9th ed. Englewood Cliffs, NJ: Prentice Hall.

Federal Bureau of Investigation. 2017. "UCR." Retrieved May 10, 2018 (https://ucr.fbi.gov/hate-crime/2016/topic-pages/ incidentsandoffenses).

Federal Communications Commission. 2016. "2016 Broadband Progress Report." January 29. Retrieved May 11, 2017 (https:// www.fcc.gov/reports-research/reports/broadband-progress-reports/2016-broadband-progress-report).

Federal Register. 2018. "Annual Update of the HHS Poverty Guidelines." January 8. Retrieved March 27, 2018 (https://www .federalregister.gov/documents/2018/01/18/2018-00814/annual-update-of-the-hhs-poverty-guidelines).

Feeding America. 2017. "What Is Food Insecurity?" Retrieved May 8, 2017 (http://www.feedingamerica.org/hunger-in-america/ what-is-hunger-and-food-insecurity.html).

Felbab, Brown. 2017. "The Hellish Road to Good Intentions: How to Break Political-Criminal Alliances in Contexts of Transition." *United Nations University Centre for Policy Research Crime-Conflict Nexus Series: No 7*, April. Retrieved August 1, 2017 (https://www.brookings.edu/wp-content/uploads/2017/05/the-hellish-road-to-good-intentions-how-to-break-political-criminal-alliances-in-contexts-of-transition.pdf).

Fensterwald, John. 2015. "Half of New Teachers Quit Profession in 5 Years? Not True, New Study Says." *Edsource*, July 16. Retrieved October 25, 2017 (https://edsource.org/2015/half-of-new-teachers-quit-profession-in-5-years-not-true-new-study-says/83054).

Ferhansyed. 2008. "Fundamental Terminology of Planned Change." Retrieved December 21, 2009 (http://organization development .wordpress.com/2008/08/10/fundamental-terminology-of-organization-development).

Fernandez, Eleazar S. 2011. Burning Center, Porous Borders: The Church in a Globalized World. Eugene, OR: Wipf and Stock.

Fernando, Suman. 2002. *Mental Health, Race and Culture*, 2nd ed. New York: Palgrave.

Fields, Julian. 2015. "Speaking Without Words: Body Language and Non-Verbal Cues in Communication." *Lifesize*, June 23. Retrieved August 29, 2015 (www.lifesize.com/video-conferencing-blog/speaking-without-words/).

FindLaw. 2015. "Death with Dignity." *Laws by State*. Retrieved June 30, 2015 (http://healthcare.findlaw.com/patient-rights/death-with-dignity-laws-by-state.html).

Fine, Lawrence B. and Mia R. Zolner. 2016. "Declines in Unintended Pregnancy in the United States, 2008–2011." *New England Journal of Medicine* 374:843–52. Retrieved July 20, 2017 (http://www.nejm.org/doi/full/10.1056/ NEJMsa1506575#t=article).

"Finery for Infants." 1893, July 23. *New York Times*, p. 11. Retrieved September 6, 2018 (https://timesmachine.nytimes.com/ timesmachine/1893/07/23/109265111.pdf).

Finke, Roger and Christopher P. Scheitle. 2013. "Sources of Religious Pluralism: Revisiting the Relationship Between Pluralism and Participation." Pp. 170–90 in *Religions as Brands: New Perspectives on the Marketization of Religion and Spirituality*, edited by Jean-Claude Usunier and Jörg Stolz. Surrey, England: Ashgate.

Finke, Roger and Rodney Stark. 1992. *The Churching of America: Winners and Losers in the Religious Economy*. New Brunswick, NJ: Rutgers University Press.

Fischer, Claude S. 1984. *The Urban Experience*, 2nd ed. San Diego, CA: Harcourt Brace Jovanovich.

Fish, Virginia Kemp. 1986. "The Hull House Circle: Women's Friendships and Achievements." Pp. 185–227 in *Gender, Ideology, and Action: Historical Perspectives on Women's Public Lives*, edited by Janet Sharistanian. Westport, CT: Greenwood.

Fisher, Max and Josh Keller. 2017. "What Explains U.S. Mass Shootings? International Comparisons Suggest an Answer." *New York Times*, November 7. Retrieved February 17, 2018 (https:// www.nytimes.com/2017/11/07/world/americas/mass-shootings-us-international.html).

"Flag-Burning Amendment Fails by a Vote." 2006. CNN.com, June 28. Retrieved August 16, 2008 (http://www.cnn.com/2006/ POLITICS/06/27/flag.burning/).

Flood, Rebecca. 2017. "Judge Grants Person the Right to Be Genderless in Landmark Ruling." *Independent*, March 26. Retrieved May 23, 2017 (http://www.independent.co.uk/ news/world/americas/judge-gender-genderless-legal-patch-us-landmark-ruling-a7651036.html).

Florida, Richard. 2004. *Cities and the Creative Class*. New York: Routledge.

Florida, Richard. 2017. "Creativity Is the Basis of the Future." March 20. Retrieved March 28, 2018 (www.geopolitika.hu/en/2017/03/20/richard-florida-creativity-is-the-basis-of-the-future/).

Florio, Jenna. 2018. "2018 Games Clouded by Investigation of Corruption." *International and Comparative Law Review* 25(1).

Flynn, Simone I. 2014. "Social Movement Theory: Value-Added Theory." *Research Starters*. Retrieved February 24, 2014 (http://connection.ebscohost.com/c/essays/36268048/social-movement-theory-value-added-theory).

Foley, Emily and Lacey Harris. 2014. "Case Studies on Isolated Children: Anna and Isabelle." October 9. Retrieved May 7, 2018 (http://prezi.com/12b_qdyv6ype/case-studies-on-isolated-children-anna-and-isabelle/).

Foner, Nancy. 2005. *In a New Land: A Comparative View of Immigration*. New York: New York University Press.

Food and Agriculture Organization, International Fund for Agricultural Development, World Food Program. 2015. *The State of Food Insecurity in the World 2015. Strengthening the Enabling Environment for Food Security and Nutrition*. Retrieved May 8, 2017 (http://www.fao.org/3/a4ef2d16-70a7-460a-a9ac-2a65a533269a/i4646e.pdf).

Food Empowerment Project. 2015. "Child Labor and Slavery in the Chocolate Industry." Retrieved July 19, 2015 (www.foodispower.org/slavery-chocolate/).

Foster, Brooke Lea. 2015. "What Is It Like to Be Poor at an Ivy League school?" *Boston Globe*, April 9. Retrieved June 11, 2015 (www.bostonglobe.com/magazine/2015/04/09/what-like-poor-ivy-league-school/xPtql5uzDb6r9AUFER8R0O/story.html).

Frank, Mark G. and Thomas Gilovich. 1988. "The Dark Side of Self- and Social Perception: Black Uniforms and Aggression in Professional Sports." *Journal of Personality and Social Psychology* 54(1):74–85.

Frankal, Elliot. 2011. "Compulsory Voting Around the World." *The Guardian*, October 4. Retrieved May 21, 2014 (guardian.co.uk/politics.guardian.co.uk).

Frater, Jamie. 2012. "10 Things You Probably Don't Know About the Amish." *Listverse*, October 29. Retrieved December 15, 2015 (https://listverse.com/2012/10/29/10-things-you-probably-dont-know-about-the-amish/).

Frederick, David A., Gaganjyot Sandhu, Patrick J. Morse, and Viren Swami. 2016. "Correlates of Appearance and Weight Satisfaction in a U.S. National Sample: Personality, Attachment Style, Television Viewing, Self-Esteem, and Life Satisfaction." *Body Image* 17(June):191–203.

Free the Children. 2015. "Our Story: A Connection a World Away." Retrieved November 25, 2015 (www.freethechildren.com/).

Free the Slaves. 2018. "About Slavery." Retrieved May 3, 2017 (http://www.freetheslaves.net/about-slavery/slavery-today/).

Freilich, Joshua D. and Graeme R. Newman. 2017. "Situational Crime Prevention." *Oxford Research Encyclopedia of Criminology*. Retrieved July 29, 2017 (http://criminology.oxfordre.com/view/10.1093/acrefore/9780190264079.001.0001/acrefore-9780190264079-e-3).

Frenkel, Sheera and Katie Benner. 2018. "To Stir Discord in 2016, Russians Turned Most Often to Facebook." *New York Times*, February 17. Retrieved February 19, 2018 (https://www.nytimes.com/2018/02/17/technology/indictment-russian-tech-facebook.html).

Frey, Bruno S. 2004. *Dealing with Terrorism: Stick or Carrot?* Cheltenham, UK: Edward Elgar.

Frey, Carl Benedikt and Michael Osborne. 2013. "The Future of Employment." *Oxford Martin Programme on Technology and Employment*. Retrieved December 29, 2017 (https://www.oxfordmartin.ox.ac.uk/downloads/academic/future-of-employment.pdf).

Frezzo, Mark. 2015. *The Sociology of Human Rights*. Malden, MA: Polity Press.

Furman, Jason. 2016. "Six Lessons from the U.S. Experience with Tobacco Taxes." *World Bank Conference: Winning the Tax Wars: Global Solutions for Developing Countries*, May 24. Retrieved June 22, 2017 (https://obamawhitehouse.archives.gov/sites/default/files/page/files/20160524_cea_tobacco_tax_speech.pdf).

Gabour, Jim. 2017. "New Orleans Under Water: 12 Years After Katrina, Officials Can't Get It Right." August 15. *The Guardian*. Retrieved September 17, 2018 (https://www.theguardian.com/us-news/2017/aug/15/new-orleans-flooding-rain-water-louisiana).

Gaines, Cork. 2017. "Number of Minority NFL Head Coaches." *Business Insider*, January 13, 2017 (http://www.businessinsider.com/nfl-head-coaches-race-2017-1).

Galanti, Geri-Ann. 2008. *Caring for Patients from Different Cultures*, 4th ed. Philadelphia: University Pennsylvania Press.

Galeotti, Mark. 2017. "Crimintern: How the Kremlin Uses Russia's Criminal Networks in Europe." *European Council on Foreign Relations*, April 18. Retrieved August 1, 2017 (http://www.ecfr.eu/publications/summary/crimintern_how_the_kremlin_uses_russias_criminal_networks_in_europe).

Gallagher, Charles. 2004. "Transforming Racial Identity Through Affirmative Action." Pp. 153–70 in *Race and Ethnicity: Across Time, Space and Discipline*, edited by Rodney D. Coates. Leiden, Holland: Brill.

Gallup. 2015a. "Gay and Lesbian Rights." Retrieved September 6, 2016 (www.gallup.com/poll/1651/gay-lesbian-rights.aspx).

Gallup. 2015b. "Religion." Retrieved December 16, 2015 (www.gallup.com/poll/1690/religion.aspx).

Gallup. 2016. "Five Key Findings on Religion in the US." December 23. Retrieved June 8, 2017 (http://www.gallup.com/poll/200186/five-key-findings-religion.aspx?g_source=How+Important+Is+Religion+in+Your+Life&g_medium=search&g_campaign=tiles).

Gallup. 2017. "In US, Belief in Creationist View of Humans at New Low." May 22. Retrieved June 8, 2017 (http://www.gallup.com/poll/210956/belief-creationist-view-humans-new-low.aspx?g_source=creationism&g_medium=search&g_campaign=tiles).

Gans, Herbert J. 1962. *The Urban Villagers: Group and Class in the Life of Italian-Americans*. New York: Free Press.

Gans, Herbert J. 1971. "The Uses of Poverty: The Poor Pay All." *Social Policy* 2(2):20–24.

Gans, Herbert. 1982. *The Levittowners: Ways of Life and Politics in a New Suburban Community*. New York: Columbia University Press.

Gans, Herbert J. 1994. "Positive Functions of the Undeserving Poor: Uses of the Underclass in America." *Politics and Society* 22(3):269–83.

Gans, Herbert J. 1995. *The War Against the Poor*. New York: Basic Books.

Gans, Herbert J. 2007. "No, Poverty Has Not Disappeared." In *Sociological Footprints*, edited by Leonard Cargan and Jeanne Ballantine. Belmont, CA: Wadsworth.

Gardner, Howard. 1987. "The Theory of Multiple Intelligences." *Annual Dyslexia* 37:19–35.

Gardner, Howard. 1999. *Intelligence Reframed: Multiple Intelligences for the 21st Century*. New York: Basic Books.

Gardom, James. 2011. "The End of Secularisation." *Cambridge GodThink*, March 30. Retrieved July 12, 2013 (http://godthink .org.uk/2011/03/30/the-end-of-secularisation/).

Garfield, Rachel, Anthony Damico, Jessica Stephens, and Saman Rouhani. 2015. "The Coverage Gap: Uninsured Poor Adults in States that Do Not Expand Medicaid—An Update." *Kaiser Family Foundation*. Retrieved June 27, 2015 (http://kff.org/ health-reform/issue-brief/the-coverage-gap-uninsured-poor-adults-in-states-that-do-not-expand-medicaid-an-update/).

Gatto, John Taylow. 2003. *The Prussian Connection*. New York: The Odysseus Group.

Gaudiano, Nicole. 2018. "New Year of the Woman? Over 100 Female Candidates Set to Win Seats in Congress, Make History." *USA Today*, November 7. Retrieved November 14, 2018 (www .usatoday.com/story/news/politics/elections/2018/11/06/women-candidates-midterms/1845639002/).

Geiger, Abigail. 2016. "Sharing Chores a Key to Good Marriage, Say Majority of Married Adults." *Pew Research Center*. Retrieved June 2, 2017 (http://www.pewresearch.org/fact-tank/2016/11/30/ sharing-chores-a-key-to-good-marriage-say-majority-of-married-adults/).

Geiger, Abigail. 2017. "U.S. Private Prison Population Has Declined in Recent Years." *Pew Research Center*, April 11. Retrieved August 3, 2017 (http://www.pewresearch.org/fact-tank/2017/04/11/u-s-private-prison-population-has-declined-in-recent-years/).

Gellner, Ernest. 1983. *Culture, Identity, and Politics*. Cambridge, UK: Cambridge University Press.

Gellner, Ernest. 1993. "Nationalism." Pp. 409–11 in *Blackwell Dictionary of Twentieth Century Thought*, edited by William Outhwaite and Tom Bottomore. Oxford, UK: Basil Blackwell.

Gellner, Ernest and John Breuilly. 2009. *Nations and Nationalism*, 2nd ed. Ithaca, NY: Cornell University Press.

Gender Equity Resource Center. 2013. "Definition of Terms: Heterosexism." Retrieved February 10, 2014 (http://geneq .berkeley.edu/lgbt_resources_definiton_of_terms#hetero sexism).

Gettleman, Jeffrey. 2017. "Vanishing Land Fuels 'Looming Crisis' Across Africa." *New York Times*, July 29. Retrieved July 29, 2017 (https://www.nytimes.com/2017/07/29/world/africa/africa-climate-change-kenya-land-disputes.html?smprod=nytcore-ipad&smid=nytcore-ipad-share&_r=0).

Gibler, John. 2012. "Mexico's Ghost Towns." Pp. 68–72 in *Globalization: The Transformation of Social Worlds*, 3rd ed., edited by D. Stanley Eitzen and Maxine Baca Zinn. Belmont, CA: Wadsworth.

Gidda, Mirren. 2017. "Private Prison Company Geo Group Gave Generously to Trump and Now Has Lucrative Contract." *Newsweek*, May 11. Retrieved August 3, 2017 (http://www .newsweek.com/geo-group-private-prisons-immigration-detention-trump-596505).

Giddens, Anthony. 1986. *The Constitution of Society*. Berkeley: University of California Press.

Giffords Law Center. 2017. "Minimum Age to Purchase and Possess." Retrieved February 17, 2018 (http://lawcenter .giffords.org/gun-laws/policy-areas/who-can-have-a-gun/ minimum-age/).

Gilbert, Dennis. 2011. *The American Class Structure in an Age of Growing Inequality*, 8th ed. Thousand Oaks, CA: Sage.

Gilleard, Chris and Paul Higgs. 2015. "Connecting Life Span Development with the Sociology of Life Course: A New Direction." *Sociology*, May 12.

Retrieved August 31, 2015 (soc.sagepub.com/content/ early/2015/05/12/0038038515577906,full).

Gillis, Justin. 2016. "Seas Are Rising at Fastest Rate in Last 28 Centuries." *New York Times*. Retrieved February 27, 2016 (www.nytimes.com/2016/02/23/science/sea-level-rise-global-warming-climate-change.html?smid=nytcore-ipad-share&smprod=nytcore-ipad).

Giridharadas, Anand. 2014. "The Immigrant Advantage." *New York Times*, May 25. *Sunday Review*, pp. 1, 5.

Giuletti, Corradio, Mirco Tonin, and Michael Vlassopoulos. 2017. "Racial Discrimination in Local Public Services: A Field Experiment in the US." *Journal of the European Economic Association* (https://doi.org/10.1093/jeea/jvx045).

Givens, David B. 2012. "Nonverbal Communication." *Center for Nonverbal Studies*. Retrieved September 25, 2012 (http://center-for-nonverba-studies.org/nvcom.htm).

Glasberg, Davita Silfen and Deric Shannon. 2011. *Political Sociology: Oppression, Resistance, and the State*. Thousand Oaks, CA: Sage.

GLAAD. 2018. *Accelerating Acceptance 2018*. Retrieved January 30, 2018 (http://www.glaad.org/files/aa/Accelerating%20 Acceptance%202018.pdf).

Glasscock, C. B. 1937. *The Gasoline Age: The Story of the Men Who Made It*. Indianapolis, IN: Bobbs-Merrill.

Global Arab Network. 2010. "British Archaeologist: 125,000 Years Ago First Human Settlement Began in Oman." April 9. Retrieved July 30, 2012 (www.english.globalarabnetwork. com/201004095443/Cu5000-years-ago-first-human-settlement-began-in-oman.html).

Global Hunger Index. 2018. "2017 Global Hunger Index." Retrieved September 3, 2018 (http://ghi.ifpri.org/).

Global Journal. 2013. "Top 100 NGOs." Retrieved June 28, 2013 (http://theglobaljournal.net/top100NGOs/).

Global Justice Now. 2016. "The Case for a UN Treaty on Transnational Corporations and Human Rights." *Controlling Corporations*. Retrieved June 14, 2017 (http://www.globaljustice .org.uk/sites/default/files/files/resources/controlling_corporations_ briefing.pdf).

Global Partnership for Education. 2017. "Out of School Children." Retrieved November 7, 2017 (http://www.globalpartnership.org/ focus-areas/out-of-school-children).

Global Security. 2009. "Guantanamo Bay Detainees." Retrieved April 14, 2012 (www.globalsecurity.org/military/facility/ guantanamo-bay_detainees.htm).

Global Sports Development. 2013. "Steroid Use Among High School Athletes: Research Articles." November 12. Retrieved January 17, 2014 (http://globalsportsdevelopment.org/steroid-use-among-high-school-athletes/).

"Global Warming and Climate Change." 2013. *New York Times*, January 8. Retrieved February 5, 2013 (http://topics.nytimes .com/top/news/science/topics/globalwarming/index.html).

Globe Women. 2013. "WEXPO: Women's Online Marketplace." Retrieved January 23, 2013 (http://www.wexpo.biz/).

Goffman, Erving. 1961. *Asylums: Essays on the Social Situation of Mental Patients and Other Inmates*. New York: Anchor.

Goffman, Erving. 1967. *Interaction Ritual*. New York: Anchor.

Goffman, Erving. [1959] 2001. *Presentation of Self in Everyday Life*. New York: Penguin.

Gonzalez-Perez, Margaret. 2011. "The False Islamization of Female Suicide Bombers." *Gender Issues* 28(1/2):50–65.

Goode, Erich. 1992. *Collective Behavior*. New York: Harcourt Brace Jovanovich.

Goode, William J. 1970. *World Revolution and Family Patterns*. New York: Free Press.

Goodman, Marc D. and Susan W. Brenner. 2002. "The Emerging Consensus on Criminal Conduct in Cyberspace." *International Journal of Law and Information Technology* 10(2):139–223.

Goodstein, Laurie. 2016. "Jimmy Carter, Seeing Resurgence of Racism, Plans Baptist Conference for Unity." *New York Times*, May 23. Retrieved September 5, 2016 (http://www.nytimes.com/2016/05/24/us/jimmy-carter-racism-baptist-conference-unity-donald-trump.html).

GoodTherapy.org. 2012. "Complementary and Alternative Medicine (CAM)." Retrieved August 3, 2012 (www.goodtherapy.org/complementary-alternative-medicine.html).

Gordon, Milton. 1970. "The Subsociety and the Subculture." Pp. 150–63 in *The Sociology of Subcultures*, edited by David O. Arnold. Berkeley, CA: Gendessary.

Gore, Al. 2012. "Global Warming Is Real." *EarthSky*, April 30. Retrieved September 7, 2012 (http://earthsky.org/human-world/al-gore-at-hampshire-college-global-warming-is-real).

Gorski, Phillip S. 2000. "Historicizing the Secularization Debate: Church, State, and Society in Late Medieval and Early Modern Europe, ca 1300 to 1700." *Social Forces* (February):138–67.

Gorski, Philip and Ates Altinordu. 2008. "After Secularization." *Annual Review of Sociology* 34:55–85.

Gottfredson, Michael R. and Travis Hirschi. 1990. *A General Theory of Crime*. Palo Alto, CA: Stanford University Press.

Gould, Stephen J. 1997. *The Mismeasure of Man*. New York: Norton.

Gouldner, Alvin W. 1960. "The Norm of Reciprocity: A Preliminary Statement." *American Sociological Review* 25(2):161–78.

Governing. 2017. "State Marijuana Laws in 2017 Map." Retrieved July 31, 2017 (http://www.governing.com/gov-data/state-marijuana-laws-map-medical-recreational.html).

Gowen, Annie. 2018. "An 8-Year-Old Girl's Gang Rape and Murder Trigger New Outrage Over India's Rape Culture." *Washington Post*, April 19. Retrieved April 30, 2018 (www.washingtonpost.com/world/asia_pacific/an-8-year-old-girls-gang-rape-and-murder-trigger-new-outrage-over-indias-rape-culture/2018/04/18/15b66724-4254-11e8-b2d).

Gracey, Harry L. 1967. "Learning the Student Role: Kindergarten as Academic Boot Camp." Pp. 215–26 in *Readings in Introductory Sociology*, 3rd ed., edited by Dennis Wrong and Harry L. Gracey. New York: Macmillan.

Grall, Timothy. 2016. "Custodial Mothers and Fathers and Their Child Support: 2013. Current Population Reports." U.S. Census Bureau, January. Retrieved June 2, 2017 (https://www.census.gov/content/dam/Census/library/publications/2016/demo/P60-255.pdf).

Gramlich, John. 2018a. "5 Facts About Crime in the U.S." *Pew Research Center*, January 30. Retrieved February 5, 2018 (http://www.pewresearch.org/fact-tank/2018/01/30/5-facts-about-crime-in-the-u-s//).

Gramlich, John. 2018b. "America's Incarceration Rate Is at a Two-Decade Low." *Pew Research Center*, May 2. Retrieved September 1, 2018 (http://www.pewresearch.org/fact-tank/2018/05/02/americas-incarceration-rate-is-at-a-two-decade-low/).

Grandpa Junior. 2006. "If You Were Born Before 1945." Retrieved July 20, 2006 (www.grandpajunior.com/1945.shtml).

Granovetter, Mark. 2007. "Introduction for the French Reader." *Sociologica* 1(Suppl.):1–10.

Gratton, Lynda. 2012. "The Globalisation of Work: and People." *BBC News*, September 6. Retrieved June 11, 2015 (www.bbc.com/news/business-19476254).

Greeley, Andrew M. 1972. *The Denominational Society*. Glenview, IL: Scott, Foresman.

Green, Erica L. 2018. "Senate Leaders Reconsider Pell Grants for Prisoners." *New York Times*, February 15. Retrieved March 22, 2018 (https://www.nytimes.com/2018/02/15/us/politics/pell-grants-prisoners.html).

Greenemeier, Larry. 2017. "When Hatred Goes Viral: Inside Social Media's Efforts to Combat Terrorism." *Scientific American*, June 5. Retrieved June 9, 2017 (https://www.scientificamerican.com/article/when-hatred-goes-viral-inside-social-medias-efforts-to-combat-terrorism/).

Greenspan, Sam. 2018. "11 State Laws about Marrying Your Cousins, from Strictest to Loosest." February 24. Retrieved March 28, 2018 (11points.com/11-state-laws-marrying-cousins-strictest-loosest/).

Greenwald, Glenn and Ewen MacAskill. 2013. "NSA Prism Program Taps in to User Data of Apple, Google and Others." *The Guardian*, June 6. Retrieved June 30, 2013 (www.guardian.co.uk/world/2013/jun/06/us-tech-giants-nsa-data).

Greshko, Michael. 2017. "Climate Change Now Impacting U.S., Report Warns." *National Geographic*, August 8. Retrieved August 17, 2017 (http://news.nationalgeographic.com/2017/08/climate-change-government-draft-review-usa-environment-spd/).

Grille, Robin. 2005. *Parenting for a Peaceful World*. Richmond, VA: Children's Project.

Griner, Allison. 2017. "Looks Are Deceiving in Chinese Town that Was US E-Waste Dumping Site." *Reveal*, January 6. Retrieved July 17, 2017 (https://www.revealnews.org/article/looks-are-deceiving-in-chinese-town-that-was-us-e-waste-dumping-site/).

Grossman, Cathy Lynn. 2012. "Number of U.S. Mosques Up 74% Since 2000." *USA Today*, February 29. Retrieved June 7, 2012 (www.usatoday.com/news/religion/story/2012-02-29/islamic-worship-growth-us/53298792/1).

The Guardian. 2016. "Nestlé Admits Slave Labour Risk on Brazil Coffee Plantations." March 2. Retrieved May 3, 2017 (https://www.theguardian.com/global-development/2016/mar/02/nestle-admits-slave-labour-risk-on-brazil-coffee-plantations).

The Guardian. 2018. "Boko Haram Returns More Than 100 School Girls Kidnapped Last Month." March 21. Retrieved May 7, 2018 (www.theguardian.com/world/2018/mar/21/boko-haram-returns-some-of-the-girls-it-kidnapped-last-month).

Gunaratna, Rohan. 2018. "Global Threat Forecast." *Journal of the International Centre for Political Violence and Terrorism Research* 10(1):1–64.

Gunnarsdottir, Hrafnhildur, Ylva Bjereld, Gunnel Hensing, Max Petzold, and Lene Povlsen. 2015. "Associations Between Parents' Subjective Time Pressure and Mental Health Problems Among Children in the Nordic Countries: A Population Based Study." *BMC Public Health* 15:353. Retrieved May 23, 2017 (https://www.ncbi.nlm.nih.gov/pmc/articles/PMC4397869/).

Guttmacher Institute. 2013. "Contraceptive Use in the United States." August. Retrieved March 17, 2014 (www.guttmacher.org/pubs/fb_contr_use.html).

Hackett, Conrad and David McClendon. 2017. "Christians Remain World's Largest Religious Group, but They Are Declining in Europe." *Pew Research Center*, April 5. Retrieved June 6, 2017 (http://www.pewresearch.org/fact-tank/2017/04/05/christians-remain-worlds-largest-religious-group-but-they-are-declining-in-europe/).

Hagan, Frank E. 2016. *Introduction to Criminology*, 9th ed. Thousand Oaks, CA: Sage.

Hagan, John and Wenona Rymond-Richmond. 2009. *Darfur and the Crime of Genocide*. Cambridge, UK: Cambridge University Press.

"Haiti." 2015. *The Economist*, July 12. Retrieved July 20, 2015 (http://country.eiu.com/haiti).

Hales, Craig M., Margaret D. Carroll, Cheryl D. Fryar, and Cynthia L. Ogden. 2017. "Prevalence of Obesity Among Adults and Youth: United States, 2015–2016." NCHS Data Brief, No. 288. Hyattsville, MD: National Center for Health Statistics. Retrieved September 1, 2018 (https://www.cdc.gov/nchs/data/databriefs/db288.pdf).

Hall, Edward T. 1981. *The Silent Language*. New York: Anchor Books.

Hall, Edward T. 1983. *The Dance of Life*. Garden City, NY: Anchor Books/Doubleday.

Hall, Edward T. and Mildred Reed Hall. 1992. *An Anthropology of Everyday Life*. New York: Doubleday.

Hall, Richard H. 2002. *Organizations: Structures, Processes, and Outcomes*, 7th ed. Englewood Cliffs, NJ: Prentice Hall.

Halper, Evan. 2017. "A California-Led Alliance of Cities and States Vows to Keep the Paris Climate Accord Intact." *Los Angeles Times*, June 2. Retrieved July 19, 2017 (http://www.latimes.com/politics/la-na-pol-paris-states-20170602-story.html).

Hamilton, Lombard. 2014. "Ancestry: Who Do You Think You Are?" *Stat Chat From the Demographics Research Group at UVA*. Retrieved September 5, 2014 (http://statchatva.org/2014/03/13/ancestry-who-do-you-think-you-are/).

Hammersley, Martyn and Glenn Turner. 1980. "Conformist Pupils." In *Pupil Strategies: Explorations in the Sociology of the School*, edited by Peter Woods. London: Croom Helm.

Handel, Gerald, Spencer Cahill, and Frederick Elkin. 2007. *Children and Society: The Sociology of Children and Childhood Socialization*. New York: Oxford University Press.

Handwerk, Brian. 2004. "Female Suicide Bombers: Dying to Kill." *National Geographic*, December 13. Retrieved July 5, 2008 (http://news.nationalgeographic.com/news/2004/12/1213_041213_tv_suicide_bombers.html).

Haner, Josh, Edward Wong, Derek Watkins, and Jeremy White. 2016. "Living in China's Expanding Deserts." *New York Times*, October 24. Retrieved May 2, 2017 (https://www.nytimes.com/interactive/2016/10/24/world/asia/living-in-chinas-expanding-deserts.html?emc=eta1&_r=0).

Hansen, Randall and Katharine Hansen. 2003. "What Do Employers Really Want? Top Skills and Values Employers Seek From Job-Seekers." *Quintessential Careers*. Retrieved June 23, 2008 (www.quintcareers.com/job_skills_values.html).

Harikrishnan, Charmy. 2017. "Indian Youth Is a Strange Mix of Conservative and Liberal Attitudes: Survey." *Economic Times*, April 23. Retrieved May 25, 2017 (http://economictimes.indiatimes.com/news/politics-and-nation/indian-youth-is-a-strange-mix-of-conservative-and-liberal-attitudes/articleshow/58319013.cms).

Harris, Judith Rich. 2009. *The Nurture Assumption: Why Children Turn Out the Way They Do*, Rev. and updated edition. New York: Free Press.

Harris, Marvin. 1989. *Cows, Pigs, War, and Witches: The Riddles of Culture*. New York: Random House.

Harrison, Matthew S. 2010. "Colorism: The Often Un-discussed '-ism' in America's Workforce." *The Jury Expert*, January. Retrieved June 19, 2015 (www.thejuryexpert.com/wp-content/uploads/HarrisonTJEJan2010.pdf).

Harrison, Matthew S. and Keisha M. Thomas. 2009. "The Hidden Prejudice in Selection: A Research Investigation on Skin Color Bias." *Journal of Applied Social Psychology* 39(1):134–68.

Hart, Betty and Todd R. Risley. 2003. "The Early Catastrophe: The 30 Million Word Gap by Age 3." *American Educator* 27(1):4–9.

Hattery, Angela and Earl Smith. 2012. *African American Families Today: Myths and Realities*. Lanham, MD: Rowman and Littlefield.

Hays, Jeffrey. 2011. "China's Barefoot Doctors: What Happened?" *CR Studies*, August 5. Retrieved August 2, 2012 (www.wengewang.org/read.php?tid=30852).

Hearn, Kelly. 2012. "Big Oil Wreaks Havoc in the Amazon, but Communities Are Fighting Back." Pp. 313–16 in *Globalization: The Transformation of Social Worlds*, 3rd ed., edited by D. Stanley Eitzen and Maxine Baca Zinn. Belmont, CA: Wadsworth.

Heberlein, Tom. 2016. "Low Taxes? We Get Just What We Pay for." *The Cap Times*. Retrieved April 18, 2016 (http://host.madison.com/ct/opinion/column/tom-heberlein-low-taxes-we-get-just-what-we-pay/article_edafbda2-b379-5afc-8836-a482b4312b42.html).

Heilbroner, Robert L. and William Milberg. 2007. *The Making of Economic Society*, 12th ed. Englewood Cliffs, NJ: Prentice Hall.

Hendry, Joy. 1987. *Becoming Japanese: The World of the Preschool Child*. Honolulu: University of Hawaii Press.

Henley, Jon. 2008. "Did a Pair of Twins Really Get Married by Mistake?" *The Guardian*, January 15. Retrieved August 29, 2015 (www.theguardian.com/lifeandstyle/2008/jan/15/familyandrelationships.jonhenley).

Henry J. Kaiser Foundation. 2018. September 11. "Status of State Action on the Medicaid Expansion Decision." Retrieved September 17, 2018 (https://www.kff.org/health-reform/state-indicator/state-activity-around-expanding-medicaid-under-the-affordable-care-act/?currentTimeframe=0&sortModel=%7B%22colId%22:%22Location%22,%22sort%22:%22asc%22%7D).

Hensley, Christopher, M. Koscheski, and Richard Tewksbury. 2005. "Examining the Characteristics of Male Sexual Assault Targets in a Southern Maximum-Security Prison." *Journal of Interpersonal Violence* 20(6):667–79.

Hepworth, Kimberly. 2010. "Eating Disorders Today: Not Just a Girl Thing." *Journal of Christian Nursing*, July/September. Retrieved January 17, 2014 (http://nursing.ceconnection.com/nu/public/modules/2224).

Herman, Jody L., Andrew R. Flores, Taylor N. T. Brown, Bianca D. M. Wilson, and Kerith J. Conron. 2017. "Age of Individuals Who Identify as Transgender in the United States." *The Williams Institute, UCLA School of Law*. Retrieved May 23, 2017 (http://williamsinstitute.law.ucla.edu/wp-content/uploads/TransAgeReport.pdf).

Herskovitz, Jon. 2012. "Militant South African Union Tells Lonmin to Pay Up." *Reuters*, September 7. Retrieved September 8, 2012 (www.reuters.com/article/2012/09/07/us-safrica-mines-idUSBRE8860U820120907).

Hewitt, John P. and David Shulman. 2011. *Self and Society: A Symbolic Interactionist Approach to Social Psychology*, 11th ed. Englewood Cliffs, NJ: Prentice Hall.

HG.org Legal Resources. 2014. "Covenant Marriage Laws in the U.S." Retrieved February 19, 2014 (www.hg.org/divorce-law-covenant-marriage.html).

"High School Dropouts Cost $1.8 Billion Every Year." 2013. *New York Post*, February 25. Retrieved July 18, 2015 (http://nypost.com/2013/02/25/high-school-dropouts-const-1-8-billion-every-year/).

Hinckley, Story. 2018. "California Keeps Girls in School By Providing Feminine Products." *Christian Science Monitor*,

January 19. Retrieved March 12, 2018 (https://www.csmonitor.com/EqualEd/2018/0119/California-keeps-girls-in-school-by-providing-feminine-products).

Hinton, Christopher. 2010. "Global Military Spending to Outpace GDP Growth in 2010." Market Watch, June 18. Retrieved May 10, 2011 (www.marketwatch.com/story/worlds-militaries-see-another-budget-busting-year-2010-06-18).

Hirschi, Travis. [1969] 2002. *Causes of Delinquency*. Berkeley: University of California Press.

Hochschild, Arlie. 1989. *The Second Shift: Working Parents and the Revolution at Home*. New York: Viking.

Hochschild, Arlie Russell. 2016. *Strangers in Their Own Land*. New York: The New Press.

Hochschild, J., V. Weaver, and T. Burch. 2012. *Creating a New Racial Order: How Immigration, Multiracialism, Genomics, and the Young Can Remake Race in America*. Princeton NJ: Princeton University Press.

Hollander, Sophia. 2014. "Canada to Resign From Harlem Children's Zone." *Wall Street Journal*, February 10. Retrieved June 23, 2015 (http://www.wsj.com/articles/SB1000142405270230410450457937468357919231).

Holt, Sheila. 2007. *Talk of the Nation*. National Public Radio Interview by Cheryl Covley, March 26.

Homans, George C. 1974. *Social Behavior: Its Elementary Forms*. New York: Harcourt, Brace Jovanovich.

Hoover, Amanda. 2017. "Forced to Work? 60,000 Undocumented Immigrants May Sue Detention Center." *Christian Science Monitor*, March 1. Retrieved August 3, 2017 (https://www.csmonitor.com/USA/Justice/2017/0301/Forced-to-work-60-000-undocumented-immigrants-may-sue-detention-center).

Horwitz, Sari. 2017. "How Jeff Sessions Wants to Bring Back the War on Drugs." *Washington Post*, April 8. Retrieved August 2, 2017 (https://www.washingtonpost.com/world/national-security/how-jeff-sessions-wants-to-bring-back-the-war-on-drugs/2017/04/08/414ce6be-132b-11e7-ada0-1489b735b3a3_story.html?utm_term=.cc7860e59d9f).

Hostetler, John A. 1993. *Amish Society*, 4th ed. Baltimore: Johns Hopkins University Press.

Hotchkiss, Gord. 2014. "The Unintended Consequences of Technology." *Media Post*, November 6. Retrieved September 10, 2015 (www.mediapost.com/publications/article/237717/the-unintended-consequences-of-technology.html).

Hou, Jianlin and Yang Ke. 2015. Addressing the Shortage of Health Professionals in Rural China: Issues and Progress—Comment on "Have Health Human Resources Become More Equal Between Rural and Urban Areas After the New Reform?" *International Journal of Health Policy and Management* 4(5): 327–28 (http://doi.org/10.15171/ijhpm.2015.57).

Houlis, Anna Marie. 2011. "Gender Stereotypes in Picture Books Are Blamed for Affecting Children." June 13. Retrieved May 23, 2012 (http://annamariehoulis.wordpress.com/2011/06/13/gender-stereotypes-in-picture-books-are-blamed-for-affecting-children/).

"How Finnish Schools Shine." 2012. *The Guardian*, May 21. Retrieved July 8, 2013 (www.guardian.co.uk/teacher-network/teacher-blog/2012/apr/09/finish-school-system).

Howard, Adam. 2007. *Learning Privilege: Lessons of Power and Identity in Affluent Schooling*. New York: Taylor & Francis.

Howard, Jacqueline. 2017. "Kids Under 9 Spend More than 2 Hours a Day on Screens, Report Shows." *CNN*, October 19. Retrieved May 8, 2018 (www.cnn.com/2017/10/19/health/children-smartphone-tablet-use-report/index.html).

Huang, Al. 2011. "'Poster Child' for Environmental Racism Finds Justice in Dickson, TN." *NRDC Switchboard*, December 8. Retrieved March 14, 2014 (http://archive.is/AsHA).

Huddy, Leonie and Stanley Feldman. 2006. "Worlds Apart: Blacks and Whites React to Hurricane Katrina." *Du Bois Review* 3(1):97–113. Retrieved July 7, 2011 (http://journals.cambridge.org/action/displayAbstract?fromPage=online&aid=462978).

Hudson, Heather E. 2011. "Digital Diversity: Broadband and Indigenous Populations in Alaska." *Journal of Information Policy* 1:378–93. Retrieved September 25, 2012 (jip.vmhost.psu.edu/ojs/index.php/jip/article/download/42/37).

Huggler, Justin and Roland Oliphant. 2017. "Russia Is Targeting French, Dutch and German Elections with Fake News, EU Task Force Warns." *The Telegraph*, January 24. Retrieved February 5, 2018 (http://www.telegraph.co.uk/news/2017/01/24/russia-targetting-european-elections-fake-news-eu-task-force/).

Hughes, Mark. 2015. "Leading Changes: Why Transformation Explanations Fail." *Leadership*, February 9. Retrieved September 10, 2015 (http://lea.sagepub.com/content/early/2015/02/09/1742715015571393.abstract).

Hugo, Peter. 2010. "A Global Graveyard for Dead Computers in Ghana." *New York Times Magazine*. Retrieved July 10, 2013 (www.cnn.com/2011/10/17/opinion/sachs-global-population).

Human Planet. 2012. "Wodaabe Flirtation Festival." Retrieved January 16, 2014 (http://dsc.discovery.com/tv-shows/human-planet/videos/wodaabe-flirtation-festival.htm).

Human Rights First. 2015. "Guantanamo by the Numbers." *Fact Sheet*, January 15. Retrieved January 27, 2015 (www.humanrightsfirst.org/sites/default/files/gtmo-by-the-numbers.pdf).

Human Rights Watch. 2016a. "Iraq: Women Suffer under ISIS." Retrieved August 19, 2016 (https://www.hrw.org/news/2016/04/05/iraq-women-suffer-under-isis).

Human Rights Watch. 2016b. "Every 25 Second: The Human Toll of Criminalizing Drug Use in the United States." October 12. Retrieved July 31, 2017 (https://www.hrw.org/report/2016/10/12/every-25-seconds/human-toll-criminalizing-drug-use-united-states).

Human Rights Watch. 2017. "Cambodia: Events of 2016." *World Report 2017*. Retrieved June 14, 2017 (https://www.hrw.org/world-report/2017/country-chapters/cambodia).

Hunt, Katie. 2015. "Beijing Rolls Out China's Toughest Smoking Ban . . . but Will It Work?" *CNN*, June 1. Retrieved July 2, 2015 (www.cnn.com/2015/06/01/asia/china-beijing-smoking-crackdown/).

Hunter College Women's Studies Collective. 2005. *Women's Realities, Women's Choices: An Introduction to Women's Studies*, 3rd ed. New York: Oxford University Press.

Hurst, Charles E. 2006. *Social Inequality: Forms, Causes and Consequences*, 6th ed. Boston: Allyn & Bacon.

Iannaccone, Laurence R. 2010. "The Economics of Religion: Invest Now, Repent Later?" *Faith and Economics* 55(Spring):1–10.

Iannelli, Vincent. 2014. "Measles Outbreaks 2014." Retrieved March 10, 2014 (http://pediatrics.about.com/od/measles-outbreaks.htm).

Ibrahim, Murtala. 2013. "The Rise and Proliferation of New Religious Movements (NRMs) in Nigeria." *International Journal of Humanities and Social Science* 3:15(August):181–90.

Ice. 2015. "'Ice': An Exhibition at the Anchorage Museum." Paper presented at the Collaboration with Inuit Elders, Anchorage, Alaska.

Illing, Sean. 2018. "Technology Isn't Just Changing Society: It's Changing What It Means to Be Human." February

23. Retrieved March 30, 2018 (www.vox.com/technology/2018/2/23/16992816/facebook-twitter-artificial-intelligence-crispr).

IMDb. 2017. "'Gay' Feature Films Released 2016-01-01 to 2016-12-31." Retrieved May 24, 2017 (http://www.imdb.com/search/title?at=0&keywords=gay&sort=alpha&title_type=feature&year=2016,2016).

Index Mundi. 2017. "Japan Demographics Profile 2017." July 9. Retrieved July 20, 2017 (http://www.indexmundi.com/japan/demographics_profile.html).

Indian Health Service. 2016. "Disparities." March. Retrieved September 5, 2016 (https://www.ihs.gov/newsroom/factsheets/disparities/).

Industrial Research Institute. 2017. "2017 R&D Trends Forecast: Results from the Industrial Research Institute's Annual Survey." Research Technology Management. *January–February18–25*. Retrieved July 28, 2017 (http://www.tandfonline.com/doi/full/10.1080/08956308.2017.1255049?scroll=top&needAccess=true).

Ingersoll, Richard M. and Gregory J. Collins. 2017. "The Status of Teaching as a Profession." Pp. 199–212 in *Schools and Society: A Sociological Approach to Education*, 6th ed., edited by Jeanne H. Ballantine, Joan Z. Spade, and Jenny M. Stuber. Los Angeles: Sage.

Inglehart, Ronald. 1997. *Modernization and Postmodernization: Cultural, Economic, and Political Change in 43 Societies*. Princeton, NJ: Princeton University Press.

Inglehart, Ronald and Wayne E. Baker. 2001. "Modernization's Challenge to Traditional Values: Who's Afraid of Ronald McDonald?" *The Futurist* 35(2):16–22.

Ingraham, Christopher. 2016. "Now We Know What Happens to Teens When You Make Pot Legal." *Washington Post*, June 21. Retrieved July 31, 2017 (https://www.washingtonpost.com/news/wonk/wp/2016/06/21/colorado-survey-shows-what-marijuana-legalization-will-do-to-your-kids/?utm_term=.ba46dfc524a6).

In Sickness and in Wealth: Health in America. 2008. *Unnatural Causes*, July 3. Retrieved May 13, 2014 (www.youtube.com/watch?v=w98GSXBEyQw).

Institute for Economics & Peace. 2017. "Global Terrorism Index 2015." Retrieved April 3, 2015 (http://economicsandpeace.org/wp-content/uploads/2015/11/Global-Terrorism-Index-2015.pdf).

International Beliefs and Values Institute. 2012. "Mission." Staunton, VA: Mary Baldwin College. Retrieved March 23, 2012 (www.ibavi.org).

International Institute for Democracy and Electoral Assistance. 2016. "Voter Turnout: Most Recent Parliamentary Elections." Retrieved April 18, 2016 (www.idea.int/vt/field.cfm?field=221).

International Lesbian, Gay, Bisexual, Trans and Intersex Association. 2017. "Maps—Sexual Orientation Laws." Retrieved September 6, 2018 (https://ilga.org/maps-sexual-orientation-laws).

International Labour Organisation. 2017a. "Cambodia." Retrieved January 18, 2014 (www.ilo.org/asia/countries/cambodia/lang—en/index.htm).

International Labour Organization. 2017b. "Forced Labour, Modern Slavery and Human Trafficking." Retrieved May 3, 2017 (http://www.ilo.org/global/topics/forced-labour/lang--en/index.htm).

International Transport Forum. 2016. "Road Safety Annual Report 2016." July 15 (http://dx.doi.org/10.1787/irtad-2016-en).

Inter-Parliamentary Union. 2016. "Women in National Parliaments." Retrieved March 3, 2016 (www.ipu.org/wmn-e/classif.htm).

Inter-Parliamentary Union. 2018a. "Women in National Parliaments: World Average." January 1. Retrieved March 26, 2018 (http://archive.ipu.org/wmn-e/world.htm).

Inter-Parliamentary Union. 2018b. "Women in National Parliaments: World Classification." January 1. Retrieved March 26, 2018 (http://archive.ipu.org/wmn-e/classif.htm).

Interuniversity Consortium for Political and Social Research. 2011. "Voting Behavior: The 2008 Election." Retrieved May 16, 2012 (http://www.icpsr.umich.edu/icpsrweb/SETUPS 2008/voting.jsp).

Ireland, Corydon. 2016. "The Costs of Inequality: Education's the One Key that Rules Them All." *Harvard Gazette*, February 15. Retrieved May 8, 2017 (http://news.harvard.edu/gazette/story/2016/02/the-costs-of-inequality-educations-the-one-key-that-rules-them-all/).

Irvine, Leslie. 2004. *If You Tame Me: Understanding Our Connection with Animals*. Philadelphia: Temple University Press.

Irwin, John. 1985. *The Jail: Managing the Underclass in American Society*. Berkeley: University of California Press.

Irwin, John and Barbara Owen. 2007. *The Warehouse Prison: Disposal of the New Dangerous Class*. New York: Oxford University Press.

Irwin, Neil. 2015. "Why American Workers without Much Education Are Being Hammered." April 21. Retrieved February 4, 2016 (www.nytimes.com/2015/04/22/upshot/why-workers-without-much-education-are-being-hammered.html?ref=topics).

Jackson, Philip W. 1968. *Life in Classrooms*. New York: Holt, Rinehart & Winston.

Jacob, Frank and Sarah Danielsson, eds. 2017. *War and Geography: The Spatiality of Organized Mass Violence*. Paderborn, Germany: Schoeningh Ferdinand GMBH.

Jaeger, Mads Meier. 2011. "Does Cultural Capital Really Affect Academic Achievement? New Evidence From Combined Sibling and Panel Data." *Sociology of Education* 84(October):281–98.

James, Deanna. 2013. "The Psychology of Eating Disorders." *PsychCentral*, August 8. Retrieved January 18, 2014 (http://psychcentral.com/blog/archives/2013/08/08/the-psychology-of-eating-disorders/).

James, William. [1890] 1934. *The Principles of Psychology*. Mineola, NY: Dover.

Jan, Tracy. 2017. "With NAFTA in Trump's Crosshairs, Mexico's Border Factories Brace for the Unknown." *Washington Post*, February 21. Retrieved May 24, 2017 (https://www.washingtonpost.com/business/economy/with-nafta-in-trumps-crosshairs-mexicos-border-factories-brace-for-the-unknown/2017/02/21/f91a3960-ee49-11e6-b4ff-ac2cf509efe5_story.html?utm_term=.7bc75e57acfd).

The Japan Times. 2016. "Still a Struggle for Working Women." *Editorial*, April 8. Retrieved May 7, 2017 (http://www.japantimes.co.jp/opinion/2016/04/08/editorials/still-a-struggle-for-working-women/#.WQ9EJojyvIU).

Jaschik, Scott. 2013. "Prestige vs. Major." *Inside Higher Education*, December 10. Retrieved January 4, 2014 (www.insidehighered.com/news/2013/12/10/study-examines-impact-major-vs-impact-college-prestige-womens-earnings).

Jaschik, Scott. 2016a. "ACT Scores Drop as More Take Test." *Inside Higher Education*, August 24. Retrieved November 16, 2017 (https://www.insidehighered.com/news/2016/08/24/average-act-scores-drop-more-people-take-test).

Jaschik, Scott. 2016b. "SAT Scores Drop." *Inside Higher Education*, September 3. Retrieved April 11, 2016 (www.insidehighered.com/news/2015/09/03/sat-scores-drop-and-racial-gap-remains-large).

Jaschik, Scott. 2016c. "ACT Scores Are Flat." *Inside Higher Education*, August 26. Retrieved April 11, 2016 (www .insidehighered.com/news/2015/08/26/act-scores-year-flat-and-racial-gaps-persist).

Jaslow, Ryan. 2013. "End of Life Care for Elderly Often Too Aggressive, Study Says." *CBS News*, February 6. Retrieved July 16, 2013 (www.cbsnews.com/8301-204_162-57567998/end-of-life-care-for-elderly-often-too-aggressive-study-says/).

Jelen, Ted, ed. 2002. *Sacred Markets, Sacred Canopies: Essays on Religious Markets and Religious Pluralism*. New York: Rowman & Littlefield.

Jellinek, E. M. 1960. *The Disease Concept of Alcoholism*. New Haven, CT: Hillhouse.

Jewish Outreach Institute. 2015. "What Are the Different Denominations of Judaism?" Retrieved December 15, 2015 (www.joi.org/qa/denom.shtml).

Jewkes, Rachel, Robert Morrell, Jeff Hearn, Emma Lundqvist, David Blackbeard, Graham Lindegger, Michael Quayle, Yandisa Sikweyiya, and Lucas Gottzén. 2015. "Hegemonic Masculinity: Combining Theory and Practice in Gender Interventions." *Culture, Health & Sexuality* 17(Suppl. 2):96–111. Retrieved May 24, 2017 https://www.ncbi.nlm.nih.gov/pmc/articles/PMC4706037/).

Jiroute, Jamie J. and Nora S. Newcombe. 2015. "Building Blocks for Developing Spatial Skills: Evidence From a Large, Representative U.S. Sample." *Psychological Science* 26(3):302–10.

Johnson, Carolyn Y. 2012. "Scientists Begin to Unravel the Long-Lasting Biological Effects of Early-Life Adversity, Social Isolation." *Boston Globe*, September 21. Retrieved August 30, 2015 (www.boston.com/news/science/2012/09/21/scientists-begin-unravel-the-long-lasting-biological-effects-early-life-adversity-social-isolation/j28yh2lHWj3P8vYY1CpGPO/story/html).

Johnson, Richard. 2017. "College Football's Lack of Black Head Coaches Is the Result of a Flawed Pipeline." *SB Nation*. Retrieved January 31, 2018 (www.sbnation.com/college-football/2017/8/9/15959410/black-coaches-rooney-rule-assistants-quarterbacks).

Johnson, Robert. 2002. *Hard Time: Understanding and Reforming the Prison*. Belmont, CA: Wadsworth/Thompson Learning.

Jordan, Winthrop D. 2012. *White Over Black: American Attitudes Toward the Negro 1550–1812*, 2nd ed. (Published for the Omohundro Institute of Early American History). Chapel Hill: University of North Carolina.

Jordon, Miriam. 2014. "Georgia Town Is Case Study in Immigration Debate." *Wall Street Journal*, December 30. Retrieved November 8, 2017 (https://www.wsj.com/articles/in-immigration-debate-business-can-trump-politics-1419971756).

Jourdan, Adam. 2013. "Divided Church of England Renews Pledge to Ordain Women Bishops." *Reuters*, July 8. Retrieved July 12, 2013 (http://uk.reuters.com/article/2013/07/08/uk-britain-church-women-idUKBRE9670SC20130708).

Kahn, Samantha. 2018. "Sexual Violence on Campus: What Numbers Can and Can't Tell Us." *National Center for Health Research*. Retrieved September 6, 2018 (http://www.center4research.org/sexual-violence-campus-numbers-can-cant-tell-us/).

Kain, Edward L. 2012. "Changes in the MCAT Have Implications for Sociology Department Planning." *ASA Footnotes* 40(9). Retrieved May 31, 2016 (www.asanet.org/footnotes/dec12/mcat_1212.html).

Kaiser Family Foundation. 2015. "Infant Mortality Rate (Deaths Per 1,000 Live Births)." Retrieved April 21, 2016 (http://kff.org/other/state-indicator/infant-death-rate/).

Kaiser Family Foundation. 2017. "Total Number of Professionally Active Nurses." April. Retrieved June 22, 2017 (http://www.kff.org/other/state-indicator/total-registered-nurses/?currentTimeframe=0&sortModel=%7B%22colId%22:%22Location%22,%22sort%22:%22asc%22%7D).

Kaiser Family Foundation. 2018a. "Figure 1, Adult HIV Prevalence 2017." Retrieved September 17, 2018 (https://www.kff.org/global-health-policy/fact-sheet/the-global-hivaids-epidemic/).

Kaiser Family Foundation. 2018b. "The Global HIV/AIDS Epidemic." July 25. Retrieved July 26, 2018 (https://www.kff.org/global-health-policy/fact-sheet/the-global-hivaids-epidemic/).

Kamarck, Elaine C. 2016. *Primary Politics*, 2nd ed. Washington, DC: Brookings Institution.

Kamarck, Kristy, N. 2016. "Women in Combat: Issues for Congress." *Congressional Research Service*, December 13. Retrieved May 18, 2017 (https://fas.org/sgp/crs/natsec/R42075.pdf).

Kamenetz, Anya. 2018. "Let's Stop Talking About The '30 Million Word Gap.'" June 1. NPR. Retrieved September 3, 2018 (https://www.npr.org/sections/ed/2018/06/01/615188051/lets-stop-talking-about-the-30-million-word-gap).

Kanter, Rosabeth Moss. 1977. *Men and Women of the Corporation*. New York: Basic Books.

Kanter, Rosabeth Moss. 2005. *Commitment and Community*. Cambridge, MA: Harvard University Press.

Kaplan, Howard B. and Robert J. Johnson. 1991. "Negative Social Sanctions and Juvenile Delinquency: Effects of Labeling in a Model of Deviant Behavior." *Social Science Quarterly* 72(1):117.

Kashyap, Aruna. 2017. "'Soon There Won't Be Much to Hide' Transparency in the Apparel Industry." Retrieved September 17, 2018 (https://www.hrw.org/world-report/2018/essay/transparency-in-apparel-industry).

Kasperkevic, Jana. 2014. "How Much Can You Get for Selling Your Body (Parts)?" *The Guardian*. Retrieved May 27, 2014 (www.theguardian.com/money/us-money-blog/2014/jan/31/flu-government-sell-egg-sperm-body).

Katz, Jackson. 2006. *The Macho Paradox: Why Some Men Hurt Women and How All Men Can Help*. Naperville, IL: Sourcebooks.

Katz, Jackson. 2016. Man Enough? *Donald Trump, Hillary Clinton, and the Politics of Presidential Masculinity*. Northhampton, MA: Interlink Books

Katz, Jonathan and Jennifer Bradley. 2013. *The Metropolitan Revolution*. Washington, DC: The Brookings Institution.

Kean, Sam. 2007. "What's in a Name?" *New York Times*, October 28. Retrieved May 21, 2012 (www.nytimes.com/2007/10/28/magazine/28wwln-idealab-t.html).

Kearney, Melissa S., Brad Hershbein, and Elisa Jacome. 2015. "Profiles of Change: Employment, Earnings and Occupations from 1990–2013." The Hamilton Project. Retrieved February 4, 2016 (www.hamiltonproject.org/assets/legacy/files/downloads_and_links/Employment_Earnings_Occupations_Changes_1990-2013_FINAL_1.pdf).

Kemp, Simon. 2018. "Digital in 2018: World's Internet Users Pass the 4 Billion Mark." *We Are Social: Global Digital*, January 30. Retrieved May 8, 2018 (https://wearesocial.com/blog/2018/01/global-digital-report-2018).

Kennedy, Sheela and Stephen Ruggles. 2014. "Breaking Up Is Hard to Count: The Rise of Divorce in the United States, 1980–2010." *Demography* 51(2):587–98.

Kerbo, Harold R. 2008. *Social Stratification and Inequality*, 7th ed. Boston: McGraw-Hill.

KFF (Henry J. Kaiser Family Foundation). 2018. "Congress Releases FY18 Omnibus." March 22. Retrieved March 26, 2018 (https://www.kff.org/news-summary/congress-releases-fy18-omnibus/).

Khanna, Nikki. 2016. "The Connections Among Racial Identity, Social Class, and Public Policy." *In Race Policy and Multiracial Americans*, edited by Kathleen Odell Korgen. Chicago and Bristol England: Policy Press

Khazaleh, Lorenz. 2009. "Internet Fatwas Cautiously Support Divorce Among Women." *CULCOM*, October 29. Retrieved January 4, 2010 (www.culcom.uio.no/english/news/2009/bogstad.html).

Kheel, Rebecca. 2017. "Trump Officials Signal Intent to Begin Refilling Guantanamo." *The Hill*, July 8. Retrieved August 2, 2017 (http://thehill.com/policy/defense/341051-trump-officials-signal-intent-to-begin-refilling-guantanamo).

Kidder, Tracy. 2004. *Mountains Beyond Mountains*. New York: Random House.

Kids Count. 2017. "Children in Single-Parent Families by Race." Retrieved June 2, 2017 (http://datacenter.kidscount.org/data/tables/107-children-in-single-parent-families-by#detailed/1/any/false/573,869,36,868,867/10,11,9,12,1,185,13/432,431).

Kielburger, Craig. 2009. *Free the Children*. Toronto: Me to We Books.

Kihal-Talantkite, Wahida, Denis Zmirou-Navier, Cindy Padilla, and Séverine Deguen. 2017. "Systematic Literature Review of Reproductive Outcome Associated with Residential Proximity to Polluted Sites." *International Journal of Health Geographics* 16:20 (https://doi.org/10.1186/s12942-017-0091-y).

Kilbourne, Jean. 1999. *Deadly Persuasion*. New York: Free Press.

Kimmel, Michael S. and Michael A. Messner. 2013. *Men's Lives*, 8th ed. Boston: Allyn & Bacon.

Kimmelman, Michael and Josh Haner. 2017. "Lessons from Hurricane Harvey: Houston's Struggle Is America's Tale." *New York Times*, November 11. Retrieved November 11, 2017 (https://www.nytimes.com/interactive/2017/11/11/climate/houston-flooding-climate.html).

Kindlon, Dan and Michael Thompson. 2000. *Raising Cain: Protecting the Emotional Life of Boys*. New York: Ballantine Books.

King, Neil, Jr. 2012. "Vote Data Show Changing Nation." *Wall Street Journal*, November 8. Retrieved June 7, 2013 (http://online.wsj.com/article/SB10001424127887324073504578105360833569352.html#project%3DEXITPOLLS2012%26articleTabs%3Darticle).

Kinsey Institute for Research in Sex, Gender, and Reproduction. 2012. Retrieved May 20, 2012 (www.kinseyinstitute.org).

Kitano, Harry H., Pauline Aqbayani, and Diane de Anda. 2005. *Race Relations*, 6th ed. Englewood Cliffs, NJ: Prentice Hall.

Klein, Joanna. 2018. "They Hunt. They Gather. They're Very Good at Talking About Smells." *New York Times*, January 19. Retrieved May 20, 2018 (www.nytimes.com/2018/01/19/science/smells-descriptions-hunter-gatherers.html?smprod-nytcore-ipad&smid-nytcore-ipad-share).

Kleinman, Johathan. 2014. "Top 10 Energy Efficiency Predictions for 2015." Clearesult, December 9. Retrieved August 28, 2015 (www.clearesult.com/insights/top-10-energy-efficient-predictions-2015).

Kliff, Sarah. 2014. "Think America Has the World's Best Health Care System? You Won't After Seeing This Chart." *Washington Post*, January 7. Retrieved March 12, 2014 (www.washingtonpost.com/blogs/wonkblog/wp/2014/01/07/think-america-has-the-worlds-best-health-care-system-you-wont-after-seeing-this-chart/).

Kneebone, Elizabeth. 2017. "Testimony: The Changing Geography of U.S Poverty." *The Brookings Institute*, February 15. Retrieved July 24, 2017 (https://www.brookings.edu/testimonies/the-changing-geography-of-us-poverty/).

Ko, Lisa. 2016. "Unwanted Sterilization and Eugenics Programs in the United States." *PBS*, January 29. Retrieved July 21, 2017 (http://www.pbs.org/independentlens/blog/unwanted-sterilization-and-eugenics-programs-in-the-united-states/).

Kochhar, Rakesh and Richard Fry. 2014. "Wealth Inequality Has Widened Along Racial, Ethnic Lines Since End of Great Recession." *Pew Research Center*, December 12. Retrieved June 15, 2015 (www.pewresearch.org/fact-tank/2014/12/12/racial-wealth-gaps-great-recession).

Kodish, Bruce I. 2003. "What We Do with Language: What It Does with Us." *ETC: A Review of General Semantics* 60:383–95.

Kohn, Melvin. 1989. *Class and Conformity: A Study of Values*, 2nd ed. Chicago: University of Chicago Press.

Kolata, Gina. 2016. "Why Do Obese Patients Get Worse Care? Many Doctors Don't See Past the Fat." *New York Times*, September 25. Retrieved July 29, 2017 (https://www.nytimes.com/2016/09/26/health/obese-patients-health-care.html).

Koos, Earl. 1954. *The Health of Regionville*. New York: Columbia University Press.

Korgen, Jeffry and Charles Gallagher. 2013. *The True Cost of Low Prices*. New York: Orbis Books.

Korgen, Kathleen, ed. 2016. *Race Policy and Multiracial Americans*. Bristol, UK: Policy Press.

Korgen, Kathleen Odell and David Brunsma. 2012. "Avoiding Race or Following the Racial Scripts? Obama and Race in the Recessionary Part of the Colorblind Era." In *Obama and the Biracial Factor: The Battle for a New American Majority*, edited by Andrew Jolivette. Bristol, UK: Policy Press.

Korgen, Kathleen Odell, Jonathan M. White, and Shelley K. White. 2013. *Sociologists in Action: Sociology, Social Change, and Social Justice*, 2nd ed. Thousand Oaks, CA: Sage.

Korte, Charles and Stanley Milgram. 1970. "Acquaintance Networks Between Racial Groups." *Journal of Personality and Social Psychology* 15:101–8.

Koschate-Reis, Miriam. 2009. "The Social Psychology of Embarrassment." Research Project at the School of Psychology, University of St. Andrews. Retrieved March 31, 2012 (http://sites.google.com/site/embarrassmentproject/home).

Kotkin, Joel. 2013. "America's Fastest—and Slowest—Growing Cities." *Forbes*, March 18. Retrieved July 1, 2013 (www.forbes.com/sites/joelkotkin/2013/03/18/americas-fastest-and-slowest-growing-cities/).

Kotkin, Joel and Wendell Cox. 2011. "Cities and the Census." *City Journal*, April 6. Retrieved July 1, 2013 (www.city-journal.org/2011/eon0406jkwc.html).

Kottak, Conrad Phillip. 2014. *Anthropology: Appreciating Human Diversity*, 16th ed. New York: McGraw-Hill

Kozol, Jonathan. 2006. *The Shame of the Nation: The Restoration of Apartheid Schooling in America*. New York: Crown.

Kozol, Jonathan. 2012. *Fire in the Ashes: Twenty-Five Years Among the Poorest Children in America*. New York: Random House Crown.

Kramer, Laura and Ann Beutel. 2014. *The Sociology of Gender: A Brief Introduction*, 4th ed. New York: Oxford University Press.

Krase, Kathryn. 2014. "History of Forced Sterilization and Current U.S. Abuses." *Our Bodies Ourselves*, October 1. Retrieved July 21, 2017 (http://www.ourbodiesourselves.org/health-info/forced-sterilization/).

Kristof, Nicholas. 2015. "Payday for Ice Bucket Challenge's Mocked Slacktivists." *New York Times*, September 2. Retrieved February 11, 2016 (www.nytimes.com/2015/09/03/opinion/nicholas-kristof-payday-for-ice-bucket-challenges-mocked-slacktivists.html?_r=0).

Kristof, Nicholas and Sheryl WuDunn. 2009. *Half the Sky: Turning Oppression into Opportunity for Women Worldwide*. New York: Alfred A. Knopf.

Kroenig, Matthew and Barry Pavel. 2012. "How to Deter Terrorism." *Washington Quarterly* 35(2):21–36.

Krueger, Megan. 2015. "Kids Books that Defy Gender Stereotypes." *MetroParent*, January 11. Retrieved September 2, 2015 (www.metroparent.com/daily/parenting/parenting-issues-tips/kids-books-defy-gender-stereotypes/).

Krupnik, Igor, Claudio Aporta, Shari Gearheard, Gita J. Laidler, and Lene Kielsen Holm. 2010. *SIKU: Knowing our Ice—Documenting Inuit Sea Ice Knowledge and Use*. New York: Springer.

Kruse, Adam J. 2016. "Cultural Bias in Testing: A Review of Literature and Implications for Music Education." *National Association for Music Education* 35(1):23–31.

Kübler-Ross, Elizabeth. 1997. *Death, the Final Stage of Growth*, Rev. ed. New York: Scribner.

Kuhn, Manford. 1964. "Major Trends in Symbolic Interaction Theory in the Past Twenty-Five Years." *Sociological Quarterly* 5:61–84.

Kuhn, Thomas. 1970. *The Structure of Scientific Revolutions*, 2nd ed. Chicago: University of Chicago Press.

Kundnani, Arun. 2012. "Radicalisation: The Journey of a Concept." *Race and Class* 54(December):3–25.

LaFraniere, Sharon and Andrew W. Lehren. 2015. "The Disproportionate Risks of Driving while Black." *New York Times*, October 24. Retrieved December 8, 2015 (www.nytimes.com/2015/10/25/us/racial-disparity-traffic-stops-driving-black.html?smid=nytcore-ipad-share&smprod=nytcore-ipad).

Lahaie, Curtis. 2016. "New GLSEN National School Climate Survey." *GLSEN*, December 14. Retrieved November 1, 2017 (https://www.glsen.org/article/LGBTQIA-secondary-students-still-face-hostility-school-considerable-improvements-show-progress).

Lake, Nell. 2012. "Labor, Interrupted." *Harvard Magazine*, November–December. Retrieved July 15, 2013 (http://harvardmagazine.com/2012/11/labor-interrupted).

Lake, Robert. 1990. "An Indian Father's Plea." *Teacher Magazine* 2(September):48–53.

Lambert, Yves. 2000. "Religion in Modernity as a New Axial Age: Secularization or New Religious Forms?" Pp. 95–125 in *The Secularization Debate*, edited by William H. Swatos, Jr., and Daniel V. A. Olson. Lanham, MD: Rowman & Littlefield.

Langlois, Christine. 2015. "The Accidental Activists: Craig and Marc Kielburger." *Canadian Living*. Retrieved November 25, 2015 (www.canadianliving.com/life/community/the_accidental_activists_craig_and_marc_kielburger.php).

Langton, Lynn, Michael Planty, and Nathan Sandholtz. 2013. "Hate Crime Victimization, 2003–2011." Bureau of Justice Statistics, March 21. Retrieved June 1, 2013 (www.bjs.gov/index.cfm?ty=pbdetail&iid=4614).

Lareau, Annette. 2003. *Unequal Childhoods: Class, Race, and Family Life*. Berkeley: University of California Press.

Larsen, Jensine. 2013. "The Day Women of the Congo Seized Control of the Internet." *Huffington Post*, March 5. Retrieved May 3, 2013 (www.huffingtonpost.com/news/congo-rape-weapon-of-war).

Lasch, Kathryn E. 2002. "Culture and Pain." Pain: Clinical Updates, December. *International Association for the Study of Pain* X(5):1–9.

Lashbrook, Jeffrey. 2009. "Social Class Differences in Family Life." P. 224 in *Our Social World*, 2nd ed., edited by Jeanne H. Ballantine and Keith A. Roberts. Thousand Oaks, CA: Sage.

Lauzen, Martha M. 2017. "The Celluloid Ceiling: Behind-the-Scenes Employment of Women on the Top 100, 250, and 500 Films of 2016." Retrieved May 23, 2017 (http://womenintvfilm.sdsu.edu/wp-content/uploads/2017/01/2016_Celluloid_Ceiling_Report.pdf).

Lavy, Victor and Edith Sand. 2015. "On the Origins of Gender Human Capital Gaps: Short and Long Term Consequences of Teachers' Stereotypical Biases." *National Bureau of Economic Research Working Paper No. 20909*, January 15. Retrieved September 3, 2015 (www.nber.org/papers/w20909).

Lawrence, Alison. 2009. "Cutting Correction Costs: Earned Time Policies for State Prisoners." *National Conference of State Legislatures*. Retrieved June 2, 2013 (www.ncsl.org/documents/cj/earned_time_report.pdf).

Lazare, Aaron. 2004. *On Apology*. New York: Oxford University Press.

Lazaridis, Gabriella. 2011. *Security, Insecurity and Migration in Europe*. Farnham, UK: Ashgate.

LeBon, Gustave. [1895] 1960. *The Crowd: A Study of the Popular Mind*. New York: Viking.

Lebow, R. N. 1981. *Between Peace and War: The Nature of International Crisis*. Baltimore: Johns Hopkins University Press.

Lechner, Frank J. and John Boli. 2012. *World Culture: Origins and Consequences*, 4th ed. Malden, MA: Blackwell.

Lee, Jennifer and Frank D. Bean. 2004. "America's Changing Color Lines: Immigration, Race/Ethnicity, and Multiracial Identification." *Annual Review of Sociology* 30(August):222–42.

Lee, Jennifer and Frank D. Bean. 2007. "Reinventing the Color Line: Immigration and America's New Racial/Ethnic Divide." *Social Forces* 86(2):561–86.

Lee, Richard B. 1984. *The Dobe !Kung*. New York: Holt, Rinehart & Winston.

Lehman, Edward C., Jr. 1985. *Women Clergy: Breaking Through Gender Barriers*. New Brunswick, NJ: Transaction.

Lem, Pola. 2016. "Could a Lack of Water Cause Wars?" *Scientific American*, May 4. Retrieved July 25, 2017 (https://www.scientificamerican.com/article/could-a-lack-of-water-cause-wars/).

Lemert, Edwin M. 1951. *Social Pathology*. New York: McGraw-Hill.

Lemert, Edwin M. 1972. *Human Deviance, Social Problems, and Social Control*. New York: Prentice Hall.

Lenhart, Amanda. 2015. "Teens, Technology and Friendships." *Pew Research Center*, August 6. Retrieved September 3, 2015 (http://www.pewinternet.org/2015/08/06/teens-technology-and-friendships/).

Lenski, Gerhard E. 1966. *Human Societies*. New York: McGraw-Hill.

Leon, Kim. 2009. "Covenant Marriage: What Is It and Does It Work?" Retrieved June 6, 2012 (http://missourifamilies.org/features/divorcearticles/divorcefeature23.htm).

Leonhardt, David. 2015. "Middle-Class Black Families, in Low-Income Neighborhoods." *New York Times*, June 24. Retrieved June 25, 2015 (www.nytimes.com/2015/06/25/upshot/middle-class-black-families-in-low-income-neighborhoods.html?abt=0002&abg=1).

Leonhardt, David. 2017. "America Is Now an Outlier on Driving Deaths." *New York Times*, November 19. Retrieved February 17, 2018 (https://www.nytimes.com/2017/11/19/opinion/america-is-now-an-outlier-on-driving-deaths.html).

Leslie, Gerald R. and Sheila K. Korman. 1989. *The Family in Social Context*, 7th ed. New York: Oxford University Press.

Levinson, Stephen C. 2000. "Yeli Dnye and the Theory of Basic Color Terms." *Journal of Linguistic Anthropology* 1:3–55.

Lewis, Oscar. 1961. *The Children of Sánchez: Autobiography of a Mexican Family*. New York: Random House.

Li, Shanshan Li, Meir J. Stampfer, David R. Williams, and Tyler J. VanderWeele. 2016. "Association of Religious Service Attendance with Mortality Among Women." *JAMA Internal Medicine* 176(6):777–85. Retrieved June 6, 2017 (http://jamanetwork.com/journals/jamainternalmedicine/fullarticle/2521827).

Lieber, Jessica. 2015. "Introducing the Bridge, the Innovation Hub of New York City's $2 Billion Tech Campus." *FastCompany*. Retrieved July 8, 2015 (www.fastcoexist.com/3047388/introducing-the-bridge-the-innovation-hub-of-new-york-citys-2-billion-tech-campus).

Lienau, Odette. 2016. "The Challenge of Legitimacy in Sovereign Debt Restructuring." *Harvard International Law Journal* 57(1):151–214.

Lincoln, Erik and Laurence Mamiya. 1990. *The Black Church in the African American Experience*. Durham, NC: Duke University Press.

Lindow, Megan. 2009. "South Africa's Rape Crisis: 1 in 4 Men Say They've Done It." *Time/World*, June 20. Retrieved February 27, 2012 (www.time.com/time/world/article/0,8599,190 6000,00.html).

Lindsay, James M. 2006. "Global Warming Heats Up." Pp. 307–13 in *Globalization: The Transformation of Social Worlds*, edited by D. Stanley Eitzen and Maxine Baca Zinn. Belmont, CA: Wadsworth.

Lindsey, Linda L. 2015. *Gender Roles: A Sociological Perspective*, 6th ed. Englewood Cliffs, NJ: Prentice Hall.

Lino, Mark. 2017. "The Cost of Raising a Child." *USDA*, January 13. Retrieved July 20, 2017 (https://www.usda.gov/media/blog/2017/01/13/cost-raising-child).

Linton, Ralph. 1937. *The Study of Man*. New York: D. Appleton-Century.

Lipka, Michael. 2017a. "Muslims and Islam: Key Findings in the U.S. and Around the World." *Pew Research Center*, February 27. Retrieved May 11, 2017 (http://www.pewresearch.org/fact-tank/2017/02/27/muslims-and-islam-key-findings-in-the-u-s-and-around-the-world/).

Lipka, Michael. 2017b. "A Closer Look at Catholic America." September 14. Retrieved June 8, 2017 (http://www.pewresearch.org/fact-tank/2015/09/14/a-closer-look-at-catholic-america/).

Lips, Hilary M. 2013. *Sex and Gender: An Introduction*, 6th ed. Boston: McGraw-Hill.

Liptak, Adam. 2008. "U.S. Prison Population Dwarfs that of Other Nations." April 23. *New York Times*. Retrieved April 15, 2012 (www.nytimes.com/2008/04/23/world/americas/23iht-23prisons.12253738.html).

Liptak, Adam. 2013. "Justices Step Up Scrutiny of Race in College Entry." *New York Times*, June 24. Retrieved June 25, 2013 (www.nytimes.com/2013/06/25/us/affirmative-action-decision.html?pagewanted=1&_r=0&hp).

Liptak, Adam. 2015. "Supreme Court Ruling Makes Same-Sex Marriage a Right Nationwide." *New York Times*, June 26. Retrieved October 23, 2015 (www.nytimes.com/2015/06/27/us/supreme-court-same-sex-marriage.html?_r-0).

Liptak, Adam. 2016. "Supreme Court Upholds Affirmative Action Program at University of Texas." *New York Times*, June 23. Retrieved July 20, 2016 (www.nytimes.com/2016/06/24/us/politics/supreme-court-affirmative-action-university-of-texas.html).

The Local. 2017. "French Firms Told They Can Ban Staff from Wearing Muslim Headscarves at Work." March 14. Retrieved May 24, 2017 (https://www.thelocal.fr/20170314/french-firms-told-they-can-ban-the-muslim-headscarf-at-work).

Lofgren, Orvar. 1999. *On Holiday: A History of Vacationing*. Berkeley: University of California Press.

Lofgren, Orvar. 2010. "The Global Beach." Pp. 37–55 in *Tourists and Tourism*, 2nd ed., edited by Sharon Bohn Gmelch. Long Grove, IL: Waveland Press.

Londoño, Ernesto. 2017. "President Bachelet of Chile Is the Last Woman Standing in the American." *New York Times*, July 24. Retrieved July 24, 2017 (https://www.nytimes.com/2017/07/24/world/americas/michelle-bachelet-president-of-chile.html?smprod=nytcore-ipad&smid=nytcore-ipad-share).

"Lonmin Profit Plunges on South Africa Platinum Strike." 2014. BBC News, May 12. Retrieved September 7, 2014 (www.bbc.com/news/business-27369966).

López, Gustavo and Jynnah Radford. 2017. "Statistical Portrait of the Foreign-Born Population in the United States." *Pew Research Center*, May 3. Retrieved May 10, 2017 (http://www.pewhispanic.org/2017/05/03/statistical-portrait-of-the-foreign-born-population-in-the-united-states-2015/).

Lorber, Judith. 2009. *Gender Inequality: Feminist Theories and Politics*. New York: Oxford University Press.

Lorber, Judith and Lisa Jean Moore. 2011. *Gendered Bodies: Feminist Perspectives*, 2nd ed. New York: Oxford University Press.

Lorillard, Didi. 2011. "What's Going on with the Venerable State of Marriage?" *GoLocal Lifestyle*. Retrieved June 4, 2012 (www.golocalprov.com/lifestyle/modern-manners-etiquette-sharing-household-chores/).

Lotfi, Yaser, Ali Ayar, and Simin Shams. 2012. "The Relation Between Religious Practice and Committing Suicide: Common and Suicidal People in Darehshahr, Iran." *Procedia: Social and Behavioral Sciences* July 16–18(50):1051–60.

Loveless, Tom. 2009. "Tracking and Detracking: High Achievers in Massachusetts Middle Schools." Thomas B. *Fordham Institute*. Retrieved April 17, 2010 (http://edexcellence.net/.../news_tracking-and-detracking-high-achievers-in-massachusetts-middle-schools).

Loveless, Tom. 2013. "The Resurgence of Ability Grouping and Persistence of Tracking." *Brookings Institution*, March 18. Retrieved June 23, 2015 (www.brookings.edu/research/reports/2013/03/18-tracking-ability-grouping-loveless).

Lowry, Michael R. 2017. "2017 Continues to Be the Warmest on Record for the Gulf of Mexico. Surely Not a Good Sign Going into Severe Season." February 28. Retrieved August 29, 2017 (https://twitter.com/MichaelRLowry/status/836614194401267712).

Lucas, Jeffrey W. 2003. "Status Processes and the Institutionalization of Women as Leaders." *American Sociological Review* 68(3):464–80.

Luhby, Tami. 2018. "8 Ways Trump Hurt Obamacare in His First Year. *CNN Money*, January 20. Retrieved June 6, 2018 (http://money.cnn.com/2018/01/20/news/economy/obamacare-trump-year-one/index.html).

Luhman, Reid and Stuart Gilman. 1980. *Race and Ethnic Relations: The Social and Political Experience of Minority Groups*. Belmont, CA: Wadsworth.

Lutz, Ashley. 2012. "These 6 Corporations Control 90% of the Media in America." *Business Insider*, June 14. Retrieved June 30, 2016 (www.businessinsider.com/these-6-corporations-control-90-of-the-media-in-america-2012-6).

Lynch, Robert. 2015. "The Economic and Fiscal Consequences of Improving U.S. Educational Outcomes." *The Washington*

Center for Equitable Growth. Retrieved June 23, 2015 (http://equitablegrowth.org/research/achievement-gap/).

Lyttelton, Oliver. 2017. "The 50 Best Crime Movies of the 21st Century So Far." *The Playlist*. Retrieved January 28, 2018 (http://theplaylist.net/the-50-best-crime-movies-of-the-21st-century-so-far-20170627/).

Machalek, Richard and Michael W. Martin. 2010. "Evolution, Biology, and Society: A Conversation for the 21st Century Classroom." *Teaching Sociology* 38(1):35–45.

Machiavelli, Niccolò. [1532] 2010. *The Prince*. Hollywood, FL: Simon & Brown.

MacLeod, Jay. 2008. *Ain't No Makin' It: Aspirations and Attainment in a Low-Income Neighborhood*, 3rd ed. Boulder, CO: Westview.

MacMillan, Thomas. 2018. "The Classic Study that Showed the World Is Smaller than You Think." *The Cut*, March 14. Retrieved March 17, 2018 (www.thecut.com/2018/03/the-history-of-the-six-degrees-of-separation-study.html).

Madhani, Aamer. 2017. "James Hodgkinson's Neighbors Recall Strange Behavior, Simmering Anger." *USA Today*, June 15. Retrieved June 15, 2017 (https://www.usatoday.com/story/news/nation/2017/06/15/james-hodgkinson-neighbors-recall-strange-behavior-simmering-anger/102877828/).

"The Madoff Case: A Timeline." 2009. *Wall Street Journal*, March 12. Retrieved November 5, 2009 (http://online.wsj.com/article/SB112966954231272304.html?mod=googlenews.wsj).

Maglaty, Jeanne. 2011. "When Did Girls Start Wearing Pink?" Retrieved May 9, 2013 (www.smithsonianmag.com/arts-culture/When-Did-Girls-Start-Wearing-Pink.html).

Mahendru, Ritu. 2017. "The Women in Afghanistan's Moral Prisons." *The Diplomat*, March 8. Retrieved July 31, 2017 (http://thediplomat.com/2017/03/the-women-in-afghanistans-moral-prisons/).

Makhmalbaf, Mohsen, producer. 2003. *Kandahar: The Sun Behind the Moon* (Film).

Malala Fund. 2017. "About the Malala Fund." Retrieved May 22, 2017 (https://www.malala.org/about).

"Male Dominance Causes Rape." 2008. *Journal of Feminist Insight*, December 8. Retrieved April 8, 2011 (http://journaloffeministinsight.blogspot.com/2008/12/male-dominance-causes-rape.html).

Malthus, Thomas R. [1798] 1926. *First Essay on Population 1798*. London: Macmillan.

Manevich, Dorothy and Hanyu Chwe. 2017. "Globally, More People See U.S. Power and Influence as a Major Threat." *Pew Research Center*, August 1. Retrieved May 4, 2018 (www.pewresearch.org/fact-tank/2017/08/01/u-s-power-and-influence-increasingly-seen-as-threat-in-other-countries/).

Mangat, Rupi. 2017. "The Vanishing Glaciers of Mount Kenya." *The East African*, January 14. Retrieved July 27, 2017 (http://www.theeastafrican.co.ke/magazine/The-vanishing—glaciers-of-Mount-Kenya—/434746-3516298-12ef2p/index.html).

Mann, Charles C. 2005. *1491: New Revelations of the Americas Before Columbus*. New York: Alfred A. Knopf.

Maquila Solidarity Network. 2017. "Support Grows for Cambodian Garment Workers After Violent Government Crackdown." January 17. Retrieved January 18, 2014 (http://en.maquilasolidarity.org/).

Marcotte, Amanda. 2015. "Teen Girls Love Video Games, but They're Really Quiet About It." *Slate*, August 18. Retrieved September 3, 2015 (www.slate.com/blogs/xx_factor/2015/08/18/teen_girls_play_video_games_but_they_minimize_their_contact_with_other_players.html).

Marger, Martin N. 2012. *Race and Ethnic Relations: American and Global Perspectives*, 9th ed. Belmont, CA: Wadsworth.

Marjoribanks, Tim and Karen Farquharson. 2011. "Sports, Race and Racism." In *Sport and Society in the Global Age*, Pp. 43–47. New York: Palgrave Macmillan.

Markoff, John and Somini Sengupta. 2011. "Separating You and Me? 4.74 Degrees." *New York Times*, November 21. Retrieved September 25, 2012 (www.nytimes.com/2011/11/22/technolgoy/between-you-and-me-4-74-degrees.html).

Marques, Luana, Margarita Alegria, Anne E. Becker, Chih-nan Chen, Angela Fang, Anne Chosak, and Juliana Belo Diniz. 2011. "Comparative Prevalence, Correlates of Impairment, and Service Utilization for Eating Disorders Across U.S. Ethnic Groups: Implications for Reducing Ethnic Disparities in Health Care Access for Eating Disorders." *International Journal of Eating Disorders* 44(5):412–20. Retrieved July 29, 2017 (https://www.ncbi.nlm.nih.gov/pmc/articles/PMC3011052/).

Martell, Luke. 2016. *The Sociology of Globalization*. Cambridge, UK: Polity Books.

Martin, Jenny Beth and Mark Meckler. 2012. *Tea Party Patriots: The Second American Revolution*. New York: Henry Holt.

Martin, Joyce A., Brady E. Hamilton, Michelle J. K. Osterman, Anne K. Driscoll, and T. J. Mathews. 2017. Births: Final Data for 2015. *National Vital Statistics Report*, January 5. 66(1). Retrieved June 22, 2017 (https://www.cdc.gov/nchs/data/nvsr66/nvsr66_01.pdf).

Martineau, Harriet. [1837] 1962. *Society in America*. Garden City, NY: Doubleday.

Martineau, Harriet. 1838. *How to Observe Manners and Morals*. London: Charles Knight & Co.

Martinez, Martha A. 2008. "Split Labor Market." Pp. 1275–77 in *Encyclopedia of Race, Ethnicity, and Society*, edited by Richard T. Schaefer. Thousand Oaks, CA: Sage.

Marty, Martin E. and R. Scott Appleby, eds. 1991. *Fundamentalism Observed*. Chicago: University of Chicago Press.

Marty, Martin E. and Scott Appleby, eds. 2004. *Accounting for Fundamentalism: The Dynamic Character of Movements*. Chicago: Chicago University Press.

Marx, Karl. [1844] 1963. "Contribution to the Critique of Hegel's Philosophy of Right." Pp. 43–59 in *Karl Marx: Early Writings*, translated and edited by T. B. Bottomore. New York: McGraw-Hill.

Marx, Karl. [1844] 1964. *The Economic and Philosophical Manuscripts of 1844*. New York: International.

Marx, Karl and Friedrich Engels. [1848] 1969. *The Communist Manifesto*. Baltimore: Penguin.

Marx, Karl and Friedrich Engels. 1955. *Selected Work in Two Volumes*. Moscow: Foreign Language.

Mascaro, Jennifer S., Kelly E. Rentscher, Patrick D. Hackett, Matthias R. Mehl, and James K. Rilling. 2017. *Behavioral Neuroscience* 131(3):262–73.

Masci, David. 2016. "How Income Varies among U.S. Religious Groups." October 11. Pew Research Center. Retrieved September 19, 2018 (http://www.pewresearch.org/fact-tank/2016/10/11/how-income-varies-among-u-s-religious-groups/).

Mashal, Mujib. 2017. "Their Identities Denied, Afghan Women Ask 'Where Is My Name?'" *New York Times*, July 30. Retrieved July 31, 2017 (https://www.nytimes.com/2017/07/30/world/asia/afghanistan-womens-rights-whereismyname.html?_r=0).

Mathews, T. J. and Anne K. Driscoll. 2017. "Trends in Infant Mortality in the United States, 2005–2014." *NCHS Data Brief No. 279*. Centers for Disease Control, March. Retrieved June 21, 2017 (https://www.cdc.gov/nchs/data/databriefs/db279.pdf).

Matthew, Dayna and Richard Reeves. 2017. "Trump Won White Voters, but Serious Inequities Remain for Black Americans." January 13. Retrieved September 1, 2018 (https://www.brookings.edu/blog/social-mobility-memos/2017/01/13/trump-won-white-voters-but-serious-inequities-remain-for-black-americans/).

Matthews, Chris. 2014. "Fortune 5: The Biggest Organized Crime Groups in the World." *Fortune*, September 14. Retrieved June 7, 2015.

Mauss, Armand. 1975. *Social Problems as Social Movements.* Philadelphia: Lippincott.

Mayeda, David. 2013. "Preventing Violence Against Women and Girls." *Sociology in Focus*, April 3. Retrieved July 18, 2015 (www.sociologyinfocus.com/2013/04/03/preventing-violence-against-women-girls-steubenville-sport/).

Mayflower Church. 2016. "Social Justice: Earthwise Congregation." Retrieved February 10, 2016 (www.mayflowermpls.org/social-justice/earthwise).

McAdam, Doug. 1999. Political Process and the Development of Black Insurgency, 1930–1970, 2nd ed. Chicago: University of Chicago Press.

McBride, James. 2015. "Prospects for the Global Economy in 2016." Council on Foreign Relations, December 23. Retrieved February 11, 2016 (www.cfr.org/global/prospects-global-economy-2016/p37400).

McBride, James and Mohammed Alie Sergie. 2017. "NAFTA's Economic Impact." *Council on Foreign Relations*, January 24. Retrieved July 26, 2017 (https://www.cfr.org/backgrounder/naftas-economic-impact).

McBride, Maureen. 2015. "What Works to Reduce Prejudice and Discrimination? A Review of the Evidence." *Scottish Government*, October 14. Retrieved May 17, 2017 (http://www.gov.scot/Publications/2015/10/2156/4).

McCabe, Janice, Emily Fairchild, Liz Grauerholz, Bernice A. Pescosolido, and Daniel Tope. 2011. "Gender in Twentieth-Century Children's Books: Patterns of Disparity in Titles and Central Characters." *Gender and Society* 25(2):197–226.

McCarthy, John D. and Mayer N. Zald. 1977. "Resource Mobilization and Social Movements: A Partial Theory." *American Journal of Sociology* 82(6):1212–41.

McCarthy, Justin. 2017. "Record-High Support for Legalizing Marijuana Use in U.S." *Gallup*, October 25. Retrieved October 25, 2017 (http://news.gallup.com/poll/221018/record-high-support-legalizing-marijuana.aspx).

McCoy, Terrence. 2014. "India's Gang Rapes: And the Failure to Stop Them." *Washington Post*, May 30. Retrieved May 28, 2015 (www.washingtonpost.com/news/morning-mix/wp/2014/05/30/indias-culture-of-gang-rape-and-the-failure-to-stop-it/).

McCrone, David. 1998. *The Sociology of Nationalism.* London: Routledge.

McCrummen, Stephanie. 2008. "Women Run the Show in a Recovering Rwanda." *Washington Post*, October 27. Retrieved May 6, 2011 (www.washingtonpost.com/wp-dyn/content/article/2008/10/26/AR2008102602197.html).

McEvoy, Alan W. and Jeff B. Brookings. 2008. *If She Is Raped: A Guidebook for the Men in Her Life*, 4th ed., abridged. Tampa, FL: Teal Ribbon Books.

McFarland, Daniel A., James Moody, David Diehl, Jeffrey A. Smith, and Reuben J. Thomas. 2014. "Network Ecology and Adolescent Social Structure." November 5. *American Sociological Review* 79(6):1088–121.

McFarland, Joel, Patrick Stark, and Jiashan Cui. 2018. "Trends in High School Dropout and Completion Rates in the U.S.: 2014." *National Center for Educational Statistics, Department of Education*, February 2018.

McGuire, Meredith. 2002. *Religion: The Social Context*, 5th ed. Belmont, CA: Wadsworth.

McGuire, Meredith B. 2008. *Lived Religion: Faith and Practice in Everyday Life*. New York: Oxford University Press.

McIntosh, Peggy. 2002. "White Privilege: Unpacking the Invisible Knapsack." Pp. 97–101 in *White Privilege: Essential Readings on the Other Side of Racism*, edited by Paula S. Rothenberg. New York: Worth.

McKelvie, Samuel R. 1926. "What the Movies Meant to the Farmer." *Annals of the American Academy of Political and Social Science* 128(November):131.

McKenzie, David. 2015. "For China, Three Decades of One-Child Policy Proves Hard to Undo." *CNN*, March 30. Retrieved July 6, 2015 (www.cnn.com/2015/03/30/asia/china-one-child-policy-undo/).

McKie, Linda and Samantha Callan. 2012. *Understanding Families: A Global Introduction.* Thousand Oaks, CA: Sage.

McKinsey & Company. 2018. "Women in the Workplace 2017." Retrieved July 16, 2018 (https://womenintheworkplace.com).

McLaughlin, Eliott C. and Nicole Chavez. 2018. "Parkland Students Say, 'We Are Going to Be the Last Mass Shooting.'" *CNN*, February 18. Retrieved February 19, 2018 (https://www.cnn.com/2018/02/18/us/florida-school-shooting-updates/index.html).

McNall, Scott G. and Sally Allen McNall. 1983. *Plains Families: Exploring Sociology Through Social History.* New York: St. Martin's Press.

McPhail, Deborah, Brenda Beagan, and Gwen E. Chapman. 2012. "'I Don't Want to Be Sexist but . . .' Denying and Re-inscribing Gender Through Food." *Food, Culture & Society* 15(3):473–89.

Mead, Frank, Samuel Hill, and Craig Atwood, eds. 2005. *Handbook of Denominations in the United States*, 12th ed. Nashville, TN: Abingdon Press.

Mead, George Herbert. [1934] 1962. *Mind, Self, and Society.* Chicago: University of Chicago Press.

"Mean Girls Cliques." 2014. (www.youtube.com/watch?v=RRtoekw7m80).

Mears, Bill. 2014. "Michigan's Ban on Affirmative Action Upheld by Supreme Court." *CNN Justice*, April 23. Retrieved May 11, 2014 (www.cnn.com/2014/04/22/justice/scotus-michigan-affirmative-action/).

Médecins Sans Frontières. 2018. "Eswatini (formerly Swaziland)." Retrieved September 17, 2018 (https://www.msf.org/eswatini).

Mehan, Hugh. 1992. "Understanding Inequality in Schools: The Contribution of Interpretive Studies." *Sociology of Education* 65(1):1–20.

Mehrabian, Albert. 1971. *Silent Messages: Implicit Communication of Emotions and Attitudes.* Belmont, CA: Wadsworth.

Mehsud, Saud. 2012. "Pakistani Girl Shot by Taliban Defied Threats for Years." *Reuters*, October 10. Retrieved October 11, 2012 (www.reuters.com/article/2012/10/10/us-pakistan-girl-family-idUSBRE8990T720121010).

Meier, Robert F. 2017. "Sociological Perspectives on Criminal Behavior." In *The Cambridge Handbook of Sociology*. Cambridge, UK: Cambridge University Press.

Meixell, Brady and Ross Eisenbrey. 2014. "An Epidemic of Wage Theft Is Costing Workers Hundreds of Millions of Dollars a Year." *Economic Policy Institute*, September 11. Retrieved June 7, 2015 (www.epi.org/publication/epidemic-wage-theft-costing-workers-hundreds/).

Melton, Gordon J. and Martin Blaumann, eds. 2010. *Religions of the World*, 2nd ed. Santa Barbara, CA: Greenwood.

Melton, Gordon J., James Bevereley, Constance Jones, and Pamela S. Nadell. 2009. *Melton's Encyclopedia of American Religions*, 8th ed. Detroit, MI: Gale/Cengage.

Meltzer, Bernard. 1978. "Mead's Social Psychology." Pp. 15–27 in *Symbolic Interactionism: A Reader in Social Psychology*, 3rd ed., edited by J. Manis and B. Meltzer. Boston: Allyn & Bacon.

Meltzer, Bernard N., John W. Petras, and Larry T. Reynolds. 1975. *Symbolic Interactionism: Genesis, Varieties and Criticism*. London: Routledge & Kegan Paul.

Merriam-Webster. 2014. "Black." Retrieved April 9, 2014 (www.merriam-webster.com/dictionary/black).

Merton, Robert K. 1938. "Social Structure and Anomie." *American Sociological Review* 3(October):672–82.

Merton, Robert K. 1948. "The Self Fulfilling Prophecy." *The Antioch Review* 8(2):193–210.

Merton, Robert K. 1968. *Social Theory and Social Structure*, 2nd ed. New York: Free Press.

Merton, Robert K. [1942] 1973. *The Sociology of Science: Theoretical and Empirical Investigations*. Chicago: University of Chicago Press.

Messerschmidt, James W., Patricia Yancey Martin, Michael A. Messner, and Raewyn Connell. 2018. *Gender Reckonings: New Social Theory and Research*. New York: New York University Press.

Michels, Robert. [1911] 1967. *Political Parties*. New York: Free Press.

Michigan Civil Rights Commission. 2017. "The Flint Water Crisis: Systemic Racism Through the Lens of Flint." February 17. Retrieved July 20, 2017 (https://www.michigan.gov/documents/mdcr/VFlintCrisisRep-F-Edited3-13-17_554317_7.pdf).

Mikkelson, Barbara and David P. Mikkelson. 2012. "Urban Legends." Retrieved January 1, 2012 (www.snopes.com/college/college.asp).

Milgram, Stanley. 1967. "The Small World Problem." *Psychology Today* 1:61–67.

Miller, Claire Cain. 2015a. "How Mark Zuckerberg's Example Helps Fight Stigma of Family Leave." *New York Times*, December 2. Retrieved January 14, 2016 (http://nyti.ms/1IoLBXz).

Miller, Claire Cain. 2015b. "More than Their Mothers, Young Women Plan Career Pauses." *New York Times*, July 22. Retrieved September 14, 2015 (http://nyti.ms/1JxIeIa).

Miller, Claire Cain. 2015c. "Why What You Learned at Preschool Is Crucial at Work." *New York Times*, October 16. Retrieved August 29, 2016 (www.nytimes.com/2015/10/18/upshot/how-the-modern-workplace-has-become-more-like-preschool.html?_r=0).

Miller, Claire Cain. 2018. "Salaried or Hourly? The Gaps in Family-Friendly Policies Begin to Close." *New York Times*, January 24. Retrieved January 24, 2018 (https://www.nytimes.com/2018/01/24/upshot/parental-leave-company-policy-salaried-hourly-gap.html?hp&action=click&pgtype=Homepage&clickSource=story-heading&module=second-column-region&region=top-news&WT.nav=top-news).

Miller, Claire Cain and Liz Alderman. 2014. "Why U.S. Women Are Leaving Jobs Behind." *New York Times*, December 12. Retrieved September 14, 2015 (http;//nyti.ms/1zJZTL6).

Miller, Michael. 2015. "How a Curmudgeonly Old Reporter Exposed the FIFA Scandal That Toppled Sepp Blatter." *Washington Post*, June 3. Retrieved June 3, 2015 (www.washingtonpost.com/news/morning-mix/wp/2015/06/03/how-a-curmudgeonly-old-reporter-exposed-the-fifa-scandal-that-toppled-sepp-blatter/).

Mills, Theodore M. 1984. *The Sociology of Small Groups*, 2nd ed. Englewood Cliffs, NJ: Prentice Hall.

Mills, Wright C. 1956. *The Power Elite*. New York: Oxford University Press.

Mills, Wright C. 1959. *The Sociological Imagination*. New York: Oxford University Press.

Mindful Relations. 2015. "Mindful Parenting: Beware of the 'Boy Code.'" Retrieved September 2, 2015 (www.mindfulrelations.org/mindful-parenting-beware-of-boy-code/).

Minor, Dylan, Nicola Persico, and Deborah M. Weiss. 2017. *SSRN*, May 4. Retrieved August 7, 2017 (https://ssrn.com/abstract=2851951).

"Mobility, Measured." 2014. *The Economist*, February 1. Retrieved August 24, 2016 (http://www.economist.com/news/united-states/21595437-america-no-less-socially-mobile-it-was-generation-ago-mobility-measured).

Mohai, Paul and Robin Saha. 2015. "Which Came First, People or Pollution? Assessing the Disparate Siting and Post-Siting Demographic Change Hypotheses of Environmental Injustice." *Environmental Research Letters*, November 18. Retrieved July 20, 2017 (doi:10.1088/1748-9326/10/11/115008; https://phys.org/news/2016-01-minority-low-income-neighborhoods-hazardous-sites.html#jCp).

Monahan, Susanne C., William A. Mirola, and Michael O. Emerson. 2016. *Sociology of Religion: A Reader*, 2nd ed. New York: Routledge.

Mondal, Puja. 2015. "Major Changes that Occurred in the Family Patterns After Industrialization." Retrieved September 8, 2015 (www.yourarticlelibrary.com/sociology/kinship-and-family/major-changes-that-occurred-in-the-family-patterns-after-industrialization/31300/).

Monir, Malak. 2015. "Half the States Look at Right-to-Die Legislation." *USA Today*, April 16. Retrieved June 30, 2015 (www.usatoday.com/story/news/politics/2015/04/15/death-with-dignity-laws-25-states/25735597/).

Monroe, Burt L., Christopher Boylan, and Ryan McMahon. 2017. "NFL Draft Profiles Are Full of Racial Stereotypes. And that Matters for When Quarterbacks Get Drafted." Monkey Cage. *Washington Post*, April 27, 2017 (https://www.washingtonpost.com/news/monkey-cage/wp/2017/04/27/nfl-draft-profiles-are-full-of-racial-stereotypes-and-that-matters-for-when-quarterbacks-get-drafted/?utm_term=.5d051e33c9a8).

Morey, Peter and Amina Yaqin. 2011. *Framing Muslims: Stereotyping and Representation After 9/11*. Cambridge, MA: Harvard University Press.

Morgan, Edward. 2011. "Looking at the New Demography." *New Geography*, December 27. Retrieved July 26, 2017 (http://www.newgeography.com/content/002591-looking-new-demography).

Morris, Aldon D. 2015. *The Scholar Denied: W.E.B. Du Bois and the Birth of Modern Sociology*. Oakland: University of California Press.

Morris, Edward W. 2005. "From 'Middle Class' to 'Trailer Trash': Teachers' Perceptions of White Students in a Predominately Minority School." *Sociology of Education* 78(2):99–121.

Morris, Joan M. and Michael D. Grimes. 1997. *Caught in the Middle: Contradictions in the Lives of Sociologists from Working Class Backgrounds*. Westport, CT: Praeger.

Morris, Lloyd R. 1949. *Not So Long Ago*. New York: Random House.

Mou, Yi and Wei Peng. 2009. "Gender and Racial Stereotypes in Popular Video Games." *IGI Global OnDemand*.

Moynihan, Mary M., Victoria L. Banyard, Alison C. Cares, Sharyn J. Potter, Linda M. Williams, and Jane G. Stapleton. 2015.

"Encouraging Responses in Sexual and Relationship Violence Prevention: What Program Effects Remain 1 Year Later?" *Journal of Interpersonal Violence* 30(1):110–32.

Mumford, Lewis. 1961. *The City in History: Its Origins, Transformations, and Prospects*. New York: Harcourt, Brace, & World.

Munchener Ruckversicherungs-Gesellschaft, NatCatService. 2018. "Loss Events Worldwide 2017: Geographic Overview." Retrieved August 27, 2018 (www.munichre.com/site/corporate/get/params_E976667823_Dattachment/1627370/MunichRe-NatCat-2017-World-Map.pdf).

Murphy, Caryle. 2015. "Interfaith Marriage Is Common in U.S., Particularly Among the Recently Wed." *Pew Research Center*, June 2. Retrieved January 12, 2016 (www.pewresearch.org/fact-tank/2015/06/02/interfaith-marriage/).

Murphy, Heather. 2017. "What Experts Know About Rape." *New York Times*, October 30. Retrieved March 20, 2018 (www.nytimes.com/2017/10/30/healthy/men-rape-sexual-assault.html).

Musu-Gillette, Lauren and Stephen Cornman. 2016. "Financing Education: National, State, and Local Funding and Spending for Public Schools in 2013." *NCES Blog*, January 25. Retrieved November 22, 2017 (https://nces.ed.gov/blogs/nces/post/financing-education-national-state-and-local-funding-and-spending-for-public-schools-in-2013).

Mydans, Seth. 2002. "In Pakistan, Rape Victims Are the 'Criminals.'" *New York Times*, May 17, p. A3.

Myers, Steven Lee and Nicholas Kulish. 2013. "Growing Clamor About Inequities of Climate Crisis." *New York Times*, November 16. Retrieved February 24, 2014 (www.nytimes.com/2013/11/17/world/growing-clamor-about-inequities-of-climate-crisis.html?_r=0).

Myrdal, Gunnar. 1964. *An American Dilemma*. New York: McGraw-Hill.

Nadeau, Barbie Latza. 2017. "Heads Roll at the Vatican over Missionary Condom Scandal." *The Daily Beast*, January 25. Retrieved June 6, 2017 (http://www.thedailybeast.com/heads-roll-at-the-vatican-over-missionary-condom-scandal).

Nagel, Joane. 1994. "Constructing Ethnicity: Creating and Recreating Ethnic Identity and Culture." *Social Problems* 41(1):152–76.

Nall, Jeff. 2012. "Combating Slavery in Coffee and Chocolate Production." *Toward Freedom*, January 5. Retrieved May 1, 2012 (http://www.towardfreedom.com/labor/2673-combat ing-slavery-in-coffee-and-chocolate-production).

NASA. 2017. "Global Climate Change: A Blanket Around the Earth." July 14. Retrieved July 18, 2017 (https://climate.nasa.gov/causes/).

National Alliance to End Homelessness. 2017. "Snapshot of Homelessness." Retrieved May 5, 2017 (http://www.endhomelessness.org/pages/snapshot_of_homelessness).

National Center for Complementary and Alternative Medicine. 2013. "Complementary, Alternative or Integrative Health: What's in a Name?" *National Institutes of Health*, May. Retrieved March 10, 2014 (http://nccam.nih.gov/health/whatiscam).

National Center for Education Statistics. 2015a. "Postsecondary Attainment: Differences by Socioeconomic Status." *Institute of Educational Sciences*, May. Retrieved November 17, 2015 (http://nces.ed.gov/programs/coe/indicator_tva.asp).

National Center for Education Statistics. 2015b. "School Composition and the Black-White Achievement Gap." Retrieved May 22, 2017 (https://nces.ed.gov/nationsreportcard/subject/studies/pdf/school_composition_and_the_bw_achievement_gap_2015.pdf).

National Center for Education Statistics. 2017a. "Dropout Rates." Retrieved June 10, 2018 (https://nces.ed.gov/fastfacts/display.asp?id=16).

National Center for Education Statistics. 2017b. "Fast Facts: Students with Disabilities, Inclusion of." Retrieved November 20, 2017 (https://nces.ed.gov/fastfacts/display.asp?id=59).

National Center for Education Statistics. 2017c. "Private School Enrollment." Retrieved November 9, 2017 (https://nces.ed.gov/programs/coe/indicator_cgc.asp).

National Center for Education Statistics. 2017d. "The Condition of Education 2017." Retrieved November 16, 2017 (https://nces.ed.gov/programs/coe/pdf/coe_coi.pdf).

National Conference of State Legislatures. 2011. "The Affordable Care Act: A Brief Summary." Retrieved July 13, 2013 (www.ncsl.org/portals/1/documents/health/hraca.pdf).

National Consumers League. 2013. "Parents: Take Control Over Your Child's Viewing, Surfing, and Texting Habits." Retrieved December 6, 2013 (www.ncinet.org/technology/149-parental-controls/537-parental-controls).

National Dropout Prevention Center/Network. 2015. "Mission." Retrieved August 29, 2016 (http://dropoutprevention.org/who-we-are/our-mission/).

National Geographic. 2017. "Toxic Waste." Retrieved August 1, 2017 (http://www.nationalgeographic.com/environment/global-warming/toxic-waste/).

National Institute of Drug Abuse. 2016. "Sex and Gender Differences in Drug Abuse." September. Retrieved May 24, 2017 (https://www.drugabuse.gov/publications/research-reports/substance-use-in-women/sex-gender-differences-in-substance-use).

National Institutes of Health. 2012. "Stem Cell Information: Stem Cell Basics." February 13. Retrieved March 7, 2012 (http://stemcells.nih.gov/info/basics/basics4.asp).

National Partnership for Women and Families. 2015. "An Unlevel Playing Field: America's Gender-Based Wage Gap, Binds of Discrimination, and a Path Forward." April. Retrieved September 5, 2015 (www.nationalpartnership.org/research-library/workplace-fairness/fair-pay/an-unevel-playing-field-americas-gender-based-wage-gap-binds-if discrimination-and-a-path-forward.pdf).

National School Boards Association. 2017. "Addressing Teacher Turnover in High-Poverty, High-Minority Urban Schools." Retrieved February 5, 2018 (www.nsba.org/newsroom/addressing-teacher-turnover-high-poverty-high-minority-urban-schools).

NationMaster. 2014. "Physicians per 1,000 People." Retrieved September 15, 2014 (http://www.nationmaster.com/country-info/stats/Health/Physicians/Per-1%2C000-people).

NationMaster. 2017. "Crime: Japan and United States Compared." Retrieved September 19, 2018 (http://www.nationmaster.com/country-info/compare/Japan/United-States/Crime).

Nation of Islam. N.d. "What the Muslims Want." Retrieved May 16, 2017 (https://www.noi.org/muslim-program/).

NCES. 2015. "Undergraduate Enrollment." *The Condition of Education*, May. Retrieved February 5, 2016 (nces.ed.gov/programs/coe/indicator_cha.asp).

Neuhauser, Alan. 2018. "Trump Had Ties to Russian Mob Figures: Testimony." *U.S. News*, January 18. Retrieved February 17, 2018 (https://www.usnews.com/news/national-news/articles/2018-01-18/trump-had-ties-to-russian-mob-figures-fusion-gps-founder-testifies).

Neuman, Michelle J. 2005. "Global Early Care and Education: Challenges, Responses, and Lessons." *Phi Delta Kappan* (November):188–92.

Newman, David M. 2017. *Exploring the Architecture of Everyday Life: Brief Edition.* Thousand Oaks, CA: Sage.

Newman, Lily Hay. 2017. "The Biggest Cybersecurity Disasters of 2017 so Far." *Wired*, July 1. Retrieved August 2, 2017 (https://www.wired.com/story/2017-biggest-hacks-so-far/).

Newman, Matthew L., Carla J. Groom, Lori D. Handelman, and James W. Pennebaker. 2008. "Gender Differences in Language Use: An Analysis of 14,000 Text Samples." *Discourse Process* 45:211–36.

Newport, Frank. 2012a. "Nearly One in Five Americans Would Not Vote for a Mormon Presidential Candidate." *Gallup*, June 21. Retrieved September 24, 2012 (www.gallup.com/video/155270/Nearly-One-Five-Americans-Not-Vote-Mormon-Candidate.aspx).

Newport, Frank. 2012b. "The Highly Religious Choose Romney, the Less Religious, Obama." *Gallup*. Retrieved September 24, 2012 (www.gallup.com/video/154112/Highly-Religious-Choose-Romney-Less-Religious-Obama.aspx).

Newport, Frank. 2012c. "In U.S., 46% Hold Creationist View of Human Origins." *Gallup*, June 1. Retrieved September 24, 2012 (www.gallup.com/poll/155003/Hold-Creationist-View-Human-Origins.aspx).

Newport, Frank. 2012d. "Hispanic Catholics Pro-Obama; Non-Hispanic Catholics Pro Romney." *Gallup*, May 1. Retrieved September 24, 2012 (www.gallup.com/poll/154424/Hispanic-Catholics-Pro-Obama-Non-Hispanic-Catholics-Pro Romney.aspx).

Newport, Frank. 2012e. "More than Nine in Ten Americans Continue to Believe in God." *Gallup*. Retrieved September 26, 2012 (www.gallup.com/poll/147887/americans-continue-believe-god.aspx).

Newport, Frank. 2015. "Fewer Americans Identify as Middle Class. *Gallup*, April 28. Retrieved May 8, 2017 (http://www.gallup.com/poll/182918/fewer-americans-identify-middle-class-recent-years.aspx).

NG Advisor. 2017. "NGO Advisor Announces the Top 500 NGOs WORLD 2017." January 9. Retrieved June 13, 2017 (https://www.ngoadvisor.net/2017-edition-top-500-ngos-rankings/).

Nielsen. 2014. "The Total Audience Report." Retrieved September 14, 2015 (ir.nielsen.com/files/doc_presentations/2015/total-audience-report-q4-2014.pdf).

Nielsen. 2016. "The Total Audience Report: Q1 2016." Retrieved May 23, 2017 (http://www.nielsen.com/us/en/insights/reports/2016/the-total-audience-report-q1-2016.html).

Nixon, Ron. 2012. "New Rules for School Meals Aim at Reducing Obesity." *New York Times*, January 25. Retrieved February 7, 2015 (www.nytimes.com/2012/01/26/us/politics/new-school-lunch-rules-aimed-at-reducing-obesity.html?_r=0).

Nock, Steven L. Laura Ann Sanchez, and James D. Wright. 2008. *Covenant Marriage: The Movement to Reclaim Tradition in America.* New Brunswick, NJ: Rutgers University Press.

Noel, Donald. 1968. "A Theory of the Origin of Ethnic Stratification." *Social Problems* 16(Fall):157–72.

Noguera, Pedro A. 2011. "A Broader and Bolder Approach Uses Education to Break Cycle of Poverty." *Phi Delta Kappan* 93(3):9–14.

Noguera, Pedro and Robby Cohen. 2006. "Patriotism and Accountability: The Role of Educators in the War on Terrorism." *Phi Delta Kappan* 87(8):573–78.

Nolan, Cathal J. 2002. "Terrorism." Pp. 1648–49 and "War" in *The Greenwood Encyclopedia of International Relations*. London: Greenwood.

Nolan, Patrick and Gerhard Lenski. 2014. *Human Societies: An Introduction to Macrosociology*, 12th ed. New York: Oxford University Press.

Nolan, Patrick D., Jennifer Triplett, and Shannon McDonough. 2010. "Sociology's Suicide: A Forensic Autopsy." *The American Sociologist* 41:292–305.

Nonhuman Rights Project. 2016. "About Us." Retrieved February 12, 2016 (www.nonhumanrightsproject.org/about-us-2/).

Norton, M. and D. Ariely. 2011. "Building a Better America: One Wealth Quintile at a Time." *Perspectives in Psychological Science* 6(1):9–12.

NPR. 2014. "Black Preschoolers Far More Likely to Be Suspended." Retrieved November 2, 2017 (http://www.npr.org/sections/codeswitch/2014/03/21/292456211/black-preschoolers-far-more-likely-to-be-suspended).

NPR. 2016. "Why America's Schools Have a Money Problem." Retrieved September 8, 2016 (https://www.npr.org/2016/04/18/474256366/why-americas-schools-have-a-money-problem).

Nunn, Lisa. 2014. *Defining Student Success: The Role of School and Culture.* New Brunswick, NJ: Rutgers University Press.

Oakes, Jeannie, Amy Stuart Wells, Makeba Jones, and Amanda Datnow. 1997. "Detracking: The Social Construction of Ability, Cultural Politics, and Resistance to Reform." *Teacher's College Record* 98(3):482–510.

O'Brien, Denise. 1977. "Female Husbands in Southern Bantu Societies." In *Sexual Stratification: A Cross-Cultural View*, edited by Alice Schlegel. New York: Columbia University Press.

O'Brien, Jody. 2011. *The Production of Reality*, 5th ed. Thousand Oaks, CA: Sage.

O'Brien, Sara Ashley. 2017. "Uber Has More Work to Do Winning Over Drivers." *CNN*. December 18. Retrieved September 3, 2018 (https://money.cnn.com/2017/12/18/technology/uber-drivers-180-days-of-change/index.html).

O'Connel, Sanjida. 1993. "Meet My Two Husbands." *Guardian*, March 4, Sec. 2, p. 12.

O'Connor, Liz, Gus Lubin, and Dina Spector. 2013. "The Largest Ancestry Groups in the United States." *Business Insider*, August 13. Retrieved September 5, 2014 (www.business insider.com/largest-ethnic-groups-in-america-2013-8).

O'Shea, Chiade. 2005. "The Rape Victim Who Fought Back." *BBCNews*, March 8. Retrieved September 1, 2018 (http://news.bbc.co.uk/2/hi/south_asia/4330335.stm).

OECD. 2015. "OECD PISA 2015." Retrieved October 23, 2017 (http://www.oecd.org/pisa/).

OECD. 2016a. "OECD. CO2.2: Child Poverty." August 25. Retrieved May 9, 2017 (http://www.oecd.org/els/soc/CO_2_2_Child_Poverty.pdf).

OECD. 2016b. "SF3.1: Marriage and Divorce Rates." August 25. Retrieved June 2, 2017 (https://www.oecd.org/els/family/SF_3_1_Marriage_and_divorce_rates.pdf).

OECD. 2017a. "Health Spending (Indicator)." June 21, 2017 (doi:10.1787/8643de7e-en).

OECD. 2017b. "Life Expectancy at Birth (Indicator)." June 22, 2017 (doi:10.1787/27e0fc9d-en).

Ofcom. 2017. "Children and Parents: Media Use and Attitudes Report." Retrieved May 8, 2018 (www.ofcom.org.uk/_data/assets/pdf_file/0020/108182/children-parents-media-use-attitudes-2017.pdf).

Ogburn, William F. 1933. *Recent Social Trends*. New York: McGraw-Hill.

Ogburn, William F. [1922] 1938. *Social Change, with Respect to Culture and Original Nature.* New York: Viking.

Ogburn, William F. 1961. "The Hypothesis of Cultural Lag." Pp. 1270–73 in *Theories of Society: Foundations of Modern Sociological Theory*, Vol. 2, edited by Talcott Parsons, Edward Shils, Kaspar D. Naegele, and Jesse R. Pitts. New York: Free Press.

Ogburn, William F. 1964. In *On Culture and Social Change: Selected Papers*, edited by Otis Dudley Duncan. Chicago: University of Chicago Press.

O'Hara, Mary Emily. 2016. "Nation's First Known Intersex Birth Certificate Issued in NYC." *NBC News*, December 29. Retrieved May 18, 2017 (http://www.nbcnews.com/feature/nbc-out/nation-s-first-known-intersex-birth-certificate-issued-nyc-n701186).

O'Keefe, Brian. 2016. "Bitter Sweets." *Fortune*, March 1. Retrieved May 3, 2017 (http://fortune.com/big-chocolate-child-labor/).

Olsen, Lauren D. 2016. "It's on the MCAT for a Reason: Premedical Students and the Perceived Utility of Sociology." *Teaching Sociology* 44(2):72–83.

Olson, Roger E., Craig D. Atwood, Frank S. Mead, and Samuel S. Hill. 2018. *Handbook of Denominations in the United States*, 14th ed. Nashville, TN: Abingdon Press

Onishi, Norimitsu and Somini Sengupta. 2018. "Dangerously Low on Water, Cape Town Now Faces 'Day Zero.'" *New York Times*. Retrieved February 1, 2018 (https://www.nytimes.com/2018/01/30/world/africa/cape-town-day-zero.html?smprod=nytcore-ipad&smid=nytcore-ipad-share).

Oregon Health Authority. 2017. "Oregon Death with Dignity Act: Data Summary 2016." February 10. Retrieved June 22, 2017 (http://www.oregon.gov/oha/PH/PROVIDERPARTNERRESOURCES/EVALUATIONRESEARCH/DEATHWITHDIGNITYACT/Documents/year19.pdf).

Organisation for Economic Co-operation and Development (OECD). 2015. *The ABCs of Gender Equity in Education: Aptitude, Behavior, Confidence.* PISA, OECD Publishing.

Organisation for Economic Co-operation and Development (OECD). 2017. "PF2.1: Key Characteristics of Parental Leave Systems." Retrieved September 6, 2018 (https://www.oecd.org/els/soc/PF2_1_Parental_leave_systems.pdf).

Ortutay, Barbara and Brett Zongker. 2011. "Newspapers See Big Demand from Bin Laden News." *Seattle Times*, May 3. Retrieved August 8, 2016 (www.seattletimes.com/business/newspapers-see-big-demand-from-bin-laden-news/).

Ostroff, Stephen M. 2013. "Perspectives: The Role of the Traveler in Translocation of Disease." In *Travelers' Health*. Retrieved March 10, 2014 (www.cdc.gov/travel/yellow book/2014/chapter-1-introduction/perspective-the-role-of-the-traveler-in-translocation-of-disease).

Oswalt, Angela. 2018. "Early Childhood Emotional and Social Development: Identity and Self-Esteem." *Gulf Bend Center.* Retrieved May 8, 2018 (www.gulfbend.org/poc/view_doc.php?type=doc&id=12766&cn=462).

Oxfam. 2017a. "An Economy for the 99%." January. Retrieved May 9, 2017 (https://www.oxfam.org/sites/www.oxfam.org/files/file_attachments/bp-economy-for-99-percent-160117-en.pdf).

Oxfam. 2017b. "Just 8 Men Own Same Wealth as Half the World." January 16. Retrieved June 14, 2017 (https://www.oxfam.org/en/pressroom/pressreleases/2017-01-16/just-8-men-own-same-wealth-half-world).

Oyez. 2015. *Davis v. Monroe County Board of Education.* Chicago-Kent College of Law. Retrieved June 22, 2015 (www.oyez.org/cases/1990-1999/1998/1998_97_843).

Papalia, Diane and Gabriela Martorell. 2015. *Experience Human Development*, 13th ed. New York: McGraw-Hill.

Papalia, Diane E., Gabriela Martorell, and Ruth Duskin Feldman. 2014. *A Child's World: Infancy Through Adolescence*, 13th ed. Dubuque, IA: McGraw-Hill Education.

Pareto, Vilfredo. [1911] 1955. "Mathematical Economics." In *Encyclopedie des Sciences Mathematique.* New York: Macmillan.

Park, Haeyoun and Iaryna Mykhyalyshyn. 2016. "L.G.B.T. People Are More Likely to Be Targets of Hate Crimes than Any Other Minority Group." *New York Times*, June 16. Retrieved July 31, 2017 (https://www.nytimes.com/interactive/2016/06/16/us/hate-crimes-against-lgbt.html).

Parker, Kim and Renee Stepler. 2017. "As U.S. Marriage Rate Hovers at 50%, Education Gap in Marital Status Widens." *Pew Research Center*, September 14. Retrieved June 10, 2018 (www.pewresearch.org/fact-tank/2017/09/14/as-u-s-marriage-rate-hovers-at-50-education-gap-in-marital-status-widens/).

Parker, Laura. 2017. "A Gamer Channel's Mission: Send the Trolls Packing." *New York Times*, July 19. Retrieved September 6, 2018 (https://www.nytimes.com/2017/07/19/technology/personaltech/a-gamer-channels-mission-send-the-trolls-packing.html).

Parker-Pope, Tara. 2013. "Are Doctors Nicer to Thinner Patients?" *New York Times*, April 29. Retrieved October 29, 2013 (http://well.blogs.nytimes.com/2013/04/29/overweight-patients-face-bias/).

Parloff, Roger. 2015. "Big Business Asks Supreme Court to Save Affirmative Action." December 9. Retrieved May 8, 2018 (fortune.com/2015/12/09/supreme-court-affirmative-action/).

Parsons, Talcott. 1951a. *The Social System.* New York: Free Press.

Parsons, Talcott. 1951b. *Toward a General Theory of Action.* New York: Harper & Row.

Parsons, Talcott. 1971. *The System of Modern Societies.* Englewood Cliffs, NJ: Prentice-Hall.

Parsons, Talcott and Robert F. Bales. 1953. *Family, Socialization, and Interaction Process.* Glencoe, IL: Free Press.

Patel, Jugal K., Troy Griggs, and Claire Cane Miller. 2017. "We Asked 615 Men How They Conduct Themselves at Work." *New York Times*, December 28. Retrieved December 28, 2017 (https://www.nytimes.com/interactive/2017/12/28/upshot/sexual-harassment-survey-600-men.html?hp&action=click&pgtype=Homepage&clickSource=story-heading&module=photo-spot-region&region=top-news&WT.nav=top-news).

Patnaik, Ankita. 2015. "'Daddy's Home!' Increasing Men's Use of Paternity Leave." *Council on Contemporary Families*, April 2. Retrieved June 2, 2017 (https://contemporaryfamilies.org/ccf-briefing-report-daddys-home/).

Patten, Eileen and Gretchen Livingston. 2016. "Why Is the Teen Birth Rate Falling?" *Pew Research Center.* Retrieved November 8, 2017 (http://www.pewresearch.org/fact-tank/2016/04/29/why-is-the-teen-birth-rate-falling/).

Paxton, Pamela and Melanie M. Hughes. 2007. *Women, Politics, and Power: A Global Perspective.* Thousand Oaks, CA: Pine Forge Press.

Paxton, Pamela and Tess Pearce. 2009. "How Does Social Class Affect Socialization Within the Family?" *Exploring Social Science Research*, April 24. Retrieved March 1, 2011 (http://ibssblog.wordpress.com/2009/04/24/how-dues-social-class-affect-socialisation-within-the-family/).

Payne, Ed. 2014. "Doctors Keep Brain-Dead Pregnant Woman on Life Support Until Baby's Birth." *CNN*, February 4. Retrieved February 3, 2014 (www.cnn.com/2014/02/04/world/americas/canada-brain-dead-woman/).

Pazzanese, Christina. 2013. "Understanding India's Rape Crisis." Retrieved January 17, 2013 (http://news.harvard.edu/gazette/story/2013/09/udnerstanding-indias-rape-crisis/).

Pearson. 2018. "Study Finds Mobile Technology Gets Parents Reading to Young Children and Improves Home Literacy Environment." April 17. Retrieved May 7, 2018 (www.pearson.com/corporate/news/media/news-announcements/2018/04/study-finds-mobile-technology-gets-parents-reading-to-young-chil.html).

Pearson, Michael and Joe Sutton. 2015. "Black Football Players at Missouri: We'll Sit Out Until System President Resigns." *CNN*, November 9. Retrieved December 8, 2015 (www.cnn.com/2015/11/08/us/missouri-football-players-protest/).

Peek, Lori. 2011. *Behind the Backlash: Muslim Americans After 9/11*. Philadelphia: Temple University Press.

Pellow, David Naguib. 2002. Garbage Wars: The Struggle for Environmental Justice in Chicago. Cambridge, MA: MIT Press.

PEPFAR. 2013. "Secretary of State John Kerry Marks Tenth Anniversary of PEPFAR." Retrieved July 15, 2013 (www.pepfar.gov/press/releases/2013/210773.htm).

Perez, Marvin G. 2013. "Coffee Consumption Increases in U.S., Association Survey Shows." *Bloomberg News*, March 22. Retrieved February 14, 2014 (www.bloomberg.com/news/2013-03-22/coffee-consumption-increases-in-u-s-association-survey-shows.html).

Perkins, Lucy. 2015. "California Governor Signs School Vaccination Law." *NPR*, June 30. Retrieved July 2, 2015 (www.npr.org/sections/thetwo-way/2015/06/30/418908804/california-governor-signs-school-vaccination-law).

Perrin, Andrew and Jingjing Jiang. 2018. "About a Quarter of U.S. Adults Say They Are 'Almost Constantly' Online." *Pew Research Center*, March 14. Retrieved May 8, 2018 (www.pewresearch.org/fact-tank/2018/03/14/about-a-quarter-of-americans-report-going-online-almost-constantly/).

Persell, Caroline Hodges. 2005. "Race, Education, and Inequality." Pp. 286–324 in *Blackwell Companion to Social Inequalities*, edited by M. Romero and E. Margolis. Oxford, UK: Blackwell.

Persell, Caroline Hodges and Peter W. Cookson, Jr. 1985. "Chartering and Bartering: Elite Education and Social Reproduction." *Social Problems* 33(2):114–29.

Pescosolido, Bernice A. 1992. "Beyond Rational Choice: The Social Dynamics of How People Seek Help." *American Journal of Sociology* 97(4):1113.

Pescosolido, Bernice A. and Carol A. Boyer. 2010. "The American Health Care System: Beginning the 21st Century with High Risk, Major Challenges, and Great Opportunities." Pp. 391–411 in *The New Blackwell Companion to Medical Sociology*, edited by William C. Cockerham. Malden, MA: Wiley-Blackwell.

Pescosolido, Bernice A., Jack K. Martin, Jane D. McLeod, and Anne Rogers, eds. 2011. *The Sociology of Health, Illness, and Healing: Blueprint for the 21st Century*. New York: Springer.

Peter J. Peterson Foundation. 2016. "Worker-to-Beneficiary Ratio in the Social Security Program." June 30. Retrieved July 24, 2017 (http://www.pgpf.org/chart-archive/0004_worker-benefit-ratio).

Petropoulos, Aggelos and Richard Engel. 2017. "A Panama Tower Carries Trump's Name and Ties to Organized Crime." *NBC News*, November 17. Retrieved February 17, 2018 (https://www.nbcnews.com/news/investigations/panama-tower-carries-trump-s-name-ties-organized-crime-n821706?cid=eml_nbn_20171117).

Petruzzello, Melissa. 2017. "Chipko Movement." *Encyclopedia Britannica*. Retrieved July 27, 2017 (https://www.britannica.com/topic/Chipko-movement).

Pettigrew, Thomas F., Linda R. Tropp, Ulrich Wagner, and Oliver Christ. 2011. "Recent Advances in Intergroup Contact Theory." *International Journal of Intercultural Relations* 35(May):271–80.

Pew Charitable Trusts. 2012. "Pursuing the American Dream: Economic Mobility Across Generations." Retrieved June 7, 2013 (www.pewstates.org/uploadedFiles/PCS_Assets/2012/Pursuing_American_Dream.pdf).

Pew Forum on Religion and Public Life. 2012a. "'Nones' on the Rise: One-in-Five Adults Have No Religious Affiliation." Retrieved October 10, 2012 (www.pewforum.org/uploadedFiles/Topics/Religious_Affiliation/Unaffiliated/NonesOnTheRise-full.pdf October 9).

Pew Forum on Religion and Public Life. 2012b. "U.S. Religious Landscape Survey." September 18. Retrieved September 18, 2012 (http://religions.pewforum.org/reports).

Pew Forum on Religion and Public Life. 2016. "Religious Landscape Study." Retrieved August 25, 2016 (www.pewforum.org/religious-landscape-study).

Pew Research Center. 2013. "Canada's Changing Religious Landscape." June 27. Retrieved June 8, 2017 (http://www.pewforum.org/2013/06/27/canadas-changing-religious-landscape/).

Pew Research Center. 2015a. "Changing Attitudes on Gay Marriage." July 29. Retrieved September 6, 2015 (www.pewforum.org/2015/07/29/graphics-slideshow-changing-attitudes-on-gay-marriage/).

Pew Research Center. 2015b. "Recently Wed Americans More Likely to Marry Outside the Faith." June 2. Retrieved January 12, 2016 (www.pewresearch.org/fact-tank/2015/06/02/interfaith-marriage/).

Pew Research Center. 2015c. "Teens, Social Media & Technology Overview 2015." April 8. Retrieved September 3, 2015 (www.pewinternet.org/2015/04/09/teens-social-media-technology-2015/pi_2015-04-09_teensandtech_16/).

Pew Research Center. 2015d. "Parenting in America." December 17. Retrieved June 2, 2017 (http://www.pewsocialtrends.org/2015/12/17/1-the-american-family-today/).

Pew Research Center. 2015e. "U.S. Catholics Open to Non-Traditional Families: 45% of Americans are Catholic or Connected to Catholicism." September 2. Retrieved June 7, 2017 (http://www.pewforum.org/2015/09/02/u-s-catholics-open-to-non-traditional-families/).

Pew Research Center. 2015f. "America's Changing Religious Landscape: Christians Decline Sharply as Share of Population; Unaffiliated and Other Faiths Continue to Grow." May 12. Retrieved June 26, 2015 (www.pewforum.org/files/2015/05/RLS-05-08-full-report.pdf).

Pew Research Center. 2015g. "Multiracial in America: Proud, Diverse and Growing in Numbers." June. Retrieved May 10, 2017 (http://www.pewsocialtrends.org/2015/06/11/multiracial-in-america/#the-size-of-the-multiracial-population).

Pew Research Center. 2015h. "The Future of World Religions: Population Growth Projections, 2010–2050." April 2. Retrieved June 26, 2015 (www.pewforum.org/2015/04/02/religious-projections-2010-2050/).

Pew Research Center. 2015i. "The American Middle Class Is Losing Ground." December 9. Retrieved September 4, 2018 (http://www.pewsocialtrends.org/2015/12/09/the-american-middle-class-is-losing-ground/).

Pew Research Center. 2015j. "For Children, Growing Diversity in Family Living Arrangements." December 14. Retrieved

September 7, 2018 (http://www.pewsocialtrends.org/2015/12/17/parenting-in-america/st_2015-12-17_parenting-11/).

Pew Research Center. 2016a. "Social Networking Fact Sheet." Retrieved April 12, 2016 (http://www.pewinternet.org/fact-sheets/social-networking-fact-sheet/).

Pew Research Center. 2016b. "Changing Attitudes on Gay Marriage." May 12. Retrieved June 8, 2017 (http://www.pewforum.org/2016/05/12/changing-attitudes-on-gay-marriage/).

Pew Research Center. 2016c. "Education Distribution by Religious Group." *Religion and Public Life.* Retrieved April 1, 2016 (www.pewforum.org/religious-landscape-study/educational-distribution/).

Pew Research Center. 2016d. "Income Distribution by Religious Group." *Religion and Public Life.* Retrieved April 1, 2016 (www.pewforum.org/religious-landscape-study/income-distribution/).

Pew Research Center. 2016e. "Views About Anti-Americanism Among U.S. Muslims Have Grown More Partisan." February 2. Retrieved July 14, 2018 (http://www.pewforum.org/2016/02/03/republicans-prefer-blunt-talk-about-islamic-extremism-democrats-favor-caution/pf_2016-02-02_views-islam-politics-05/).

Pew Research Center. 2016f. "Explore Religious Groups in the U.S. by Tradition, Family and Denomination." *Religious Landscape Study.* Retrieved April 25, 2016 (www.pewforum.org/religious-landscape-study/).

Pew Research Center. 2016g. "Religious Landscape Study: Gender Composition." *Religious Landscape Study.* Retrieved August 15, 2016 (www.pewforum.org/religious-landscape-study/gender-composition).

Pew Research Center. 2017a. "The Changing Global Religious Landscape." April 5. Retrieved June 8, 2017 (http://www.pewforum.org/2017/04/05/the-changing-global-religious-landscape/).

Pew Research Center. 2017b. "More Worry than Optimism About Potential Developments in Automation." October 3. Retrieved December 29, 2017 (http://www.pewinternet.org/2017/10/04/automation-in-everyday-life/pi_2017-10-04_automation_0-01/).

Pew Research Center. 2018a. "Social Media Use By Education." Retrieved August 30, 2018 (http://www.pewinternet.org/chart/social-media-use-by-education/).

Pew Research Center. 2018b. "Social Media Use by Income." Retrieved August 30, 2018 (http://www.pewinternet.org/chart/social-media-use-by-income/).

Pew Research Center. 2018c. "Social Media Use by Gender." Retrieved August 30, 2018 (http://www.pewinternet.org/chart/social-media-use-by-gender/).

Pew Research Center. 2018d. "Support for Same-Sex Marriage Grows, Even Among Groups That Had Been Skeptical." Retrieved September 6, 2018 (http://www.people-press.org/2017/06/26/support-for-same-sex-marriage-grows-even-among-groups-that-had-been-skeptical/).

Pew Research Center Religious Landscape Study. 2018. "Religious Composition of Adults with Some College Education." Retrieved September 19, 2018 (http://www.pewforum.org/religious-landscape-study/educational-distribution/some-college/).

Phillips, Richard. 2013. "Animal Communication." Lecture at Tuesdays with a Liberal Arts Scholar. *University of Minnesota,* May 6.

Phillips, Tom. 2015. "China Ends One-Child Policy After 35 Years." *The Guardian,* October 29. Retrieved January 4, 2015 (www.theguardian.com/world/2015/oct/29/china-abandons-one-child-policy).

Phys.Org. 2009. "Humans Spread Out of Africa Later." Retrieved October 9, 2012 (http://phys.org/news171286860.html).

Piaget, Jean. 1989. *The Child's Conception of the World.* Savage, MD: Littlefield, Adams Quality Paperbacks.

Pickard, Ruth and Daryl Poole. 2007. "The Study of Society and the Practice of Sociology." Previously unpublished essay.

Pinker, Steven. 2002. The Blank Slate: The Modern Denial of Human Nature. New York: Viking.

Plato. [ca. 350 BCE] 1960. *The Laws.* New York: Dutton.

Police Accountability Task Force. 2016. "Recommendations for Reform: Restoring Trust Between the Chicago Police and the Communities They Serve." April. Retrieved May 10, 2017 (https://chicagopatf.org/wp-content/uploads/2016/04/PATF_Final_Report_Executive_Summary_4_13_16-1.pdf).

Political Geography Now. 2015. "How Many Countries Are There in the World in 2015?" September 12. Retrieved January 28, 2016 (www.polgeonow.com/2011/04/how-many-countries-are-there-in-world.html).

Political Geography Now. 2017. "How Many Countries Are There in the World in 2017?" June 14. Retrieved June 14, 2017 (http://www.polgeonow.com/2011/04/how-many-countries-are-there-in-world.html).

Pollack, William. 1999. *Real Boys: Rescuing Our Sons from the Myths of Boyhood.* New York: Owl Books.

PopulationPyramid.net. 2018a. "United States of America 2018." Retrieved March 26, 2018 (https://www.populationpyramid.net/united-states-of-america/2017/).

PopulationPyramid.net. 2018b. "United States of America 2015." Retrieved March 26, 2018 (http://www.populationpyramid.net/united-states-of-america/2050/).

Population Reference Bureau. 2012. "World Population Data Sheet." Retrieved August 25, 2012 (www.prb.org/pdf12/2012-population-data-sheet_eng.pdf).

Population Reference Bureau. 2013a. "Rate of Natural Increase." Retrieved March 17, 2014 (www.prb.org/DataFinder/Topic/Rankings.aspx?ind=16).

Population Reference Bureau. 2013b. "Total Fertility Rate, 2012." Retrieved February 7, 2013 (http://www.prb.org/DataFinder/Topic/Rankings.aspx?ind=17).

Population Reference Bureau. 2016. "Women's Education and Family Size in Selected Countries, 2000's" in *Human Population: Women.* Retrieved March 18, 2017 (www.prb.org/Publications/Lesson-Plans/HumanPopulation/Women.aspx).

Population Reference Bureau. 2017. "Infant Mortality Rate." Retrieved July 26, 2018 (https://www.prb.org/international/indicator/infant-mortality/snapshot).

Potok, Mark. 2013a. "DOJ Study: More Than 250,000 Hate Crimes a Year, Most Unreported." *Southern Poverty Law Center,* March 26. Retrieved June 1, 2013 (www.splcenter.org/blog/2013/03/26/doj-study-more-than-250000-hate-crimes-a-year-a-third-never-reported/).

Potok, Mark. 2013b. "Editorial: Boston and Beyond." *Intelligence Report* 150. Retrieved June 17, 2013 (www.splcenter.org/get-informed/intelligence-report/browse-all-issues/2013/summer/boston-and-beyond).

Potok, Mark. 2015. "The Year in Hate and Extremism." *Intelligence Report* 149. Retrieved July 20, 2016 (www.splcenter.org/fighting-hate/intelligence-report/2013/editorial-boston-and-beyond).

Potter, Sharyn J. and Mary M. Moynihan. 2011. "Bringing in the Bystander In-Person Prevention Program to a U.S. Military

Installation: Results From a Pilot Study." *Military Medicine* 176(8):870–75.

Poushter, Jacob. 2014. "What's Morally Acceptable? It Depends on Where in the World You Live." *Pew Research Center*, April 15. Retrieved August 29, 2015 (www.pewresearch.org/fact-tank/2014/04/15/whats-morally-acceptable-it-depends-on-where-in-the-world-you-live/).

Poushter, Jacob and Dorothy Manevich. 2017. "Globally, People Point to ISIS and Climate Change as Lading Security Threats." *Pew Research Center*. Retrieved August 2, 2017 (http://www.pewglobal.org/2017/08/01/globally-people-point-to-isis-and-climate-change-as-leading-security-threats/).

"The Power of High Expectations: Closing the Gap in Your Classroom." 2011. Retrieved June 22, 2015 (http://teachingasleadership.org/sites/default/files/Related-Readings/DCA_Ch2_2011.pdf).

Pradhan, Elina. 2015. "The Relationship Between Women's Education and Fertility." *The World Economic Forum*. Retrieved April 3, 2016 (www.weforum.org/agenda/2015/11/the-relationship-between-womens-education-and-fertility/).

Prasad, Leena and Vikram Srivastava. 2016. "Dowry Deaths: India's Shame." CounterCurrents.org, July 6. Retrieved February 5, 2018 (https://countercurrents.org/2016/07/06/dowry-deaths-indias-shame/).

"Presidential Election Results: Donald J. Trump Wins." 2017. *New York Times*, August 9. Retrieved September 14, 2018 (https://www.nytimes.com/elections/results/president).

Preston, David L. 1988. The Social Organization of Zen Practice: Constructing Transcultural Reality. Cambridge, UK: Cambridge University Press.

"Prison Labour Is a Billion-Dollar Industry, with Uncertain Returns for Inmates." 2017. *The Economist*, March 16. Retrieved August 3, 2017 (https://www.economist.com/news/united-states/21718897-idaho-prisoners-roast-potatoes-kentucky-they-sell-cattle-prison-labour).

Prison Policy Initiative. 2015. "Correctional Education and the School-to-Prison Pipeline." Retrieved February 4, 2016 (www.prisonpolicy.org/research/education/).

"Pro Football Is Still America's Favorite Sport." 2016. January 26. Harris Poll. (http://www.theharrispoll.com/sports/Americas_Fav_Sport_2016.html).

Project Ploughshares. 2016. "Armed Conflict Report: 2016." Retrieved September 14, 2018 (http://ploughshares.ca/wp-content/uploads/2016/10/PloughsharesAnnualReportReport2016.pdf).

Proudman, Charlotte Rachael. 2012. "Sex and Sharia: Muslim Women Punished for Failed Marriages." *The Independent*, April 2. Retrieved May 24, 2012 (http://blogs.independent.co.uk/2012/04/02/sex-and-sharia-muslim-women-punished-for-failed-marriages/).

Putt, Gina. 2014. "Life Events and the Life Cycle: Crises of Adulthood." *Decoded Science*, March 3. Retrieved August 31, 2015 (www.decodedscience.com/life-events-life-cycle-crises-adulthood/43230).

Pyle, Ralph E. 2006. "Trends in Religious Stratification: Have Religious Group Socioeconomic Distinctions Declined in Recent Decades?" *Sociology of Religion* 67(Spring):61–79.

Quinney, Richard. 2002. Critique of Legal Order: Crime Control in Capitalist Society. New Brunswick, NJ: Transaction.

Quora. 2016. "Is It Legal for Someone to Marry His Sister?" February 29. Retrieved March 28, 2018 (www.quora.com/Is-it-legal-for-someone-to-marry-his-sister).

Rabuy, Bernadette and Daniel Kopf. 2015. "Prisons of Poverty: Uncovering the Pre-incarceration Rates of the Imprisoned." *Prison Policy Initiative*, July 9. Retrieved February 5, 2018 (https://www.prisonpolicy.org/reports/income.html).

Radcliffe-Brown, A. R. 1935. "On the Concept of Functional in Social Science." *American Anthropologist* 37(3):394–402.

Radelet, Michael L. and Traci L. Lacock. 2009. "Do Executions Lower Homicide Rates? The Views of Leading Criminologists." *Journal of Criminal Laws and Criminology* 99(2).

Raina, Shruti. 2012. "Gender Bias in Education." *International Journal of Research Pedagogy and Technology in Education* 1(2):37–45. Retrieved July 10, 2013 (http://ijems.net/issue02Dec.IJEMSp05.pdf).

Rankin, Bruce H. and Işik A. Aytaç. 2006. "Gender Inequality in Schooling: The Case of Turkey." *Sociology of Education* 79(1):25–43.

Rao, Krishna. 2017. "Climate Change and Housing: Will a Rising Tide Sink All Homes?" *Zillow*, June 2. Retrieved July 18, 2017 (https://www.zillow.com/research/climate-change-underwater-homes-12890/).

Rappoport, Leon. 2003. *How We Eat: Appetite, Culture and the Psychology of Food.* Toronto, Ontario, Canada: ECW Press.

Real Clear Politics. 2016. "Republican Delegate Count" and "Democratic Delegate Count." Retrieved March 18, 2016 (www.realclearpolitics.com/elections/2016/).

Reardon, Sean F., Lindsay Fox, and Joseph Townsend. 2015. "Neighborhood Income Composition by Household Race and Income, 1990–2009." *Annals of the American Academy of Political and Social Science* 660(1):78–97.

Refugees Deeply. 2018. "The Top Refugee Issues to Watch in 2018." Retrieved April 16, 2018 (www.newsdeeply.com/refugees/articles/2018-01-12/the-top-refugee-issues-to-monitor-in-2018).

Reilly, Mollie. 2016. "Same-Sex Couples Can Now Adopt Children in All 50 States." *Huffington Post*, March 31. Retrieved August 3, 2016 (http://www.huffingtonpost.com/entry/mississippi-same-sex-adoption_us_56fdb1a3e4b083f5c607567).

Reiman, Jeffrey and Paul Leighton. 2017. *The Rich Get Richer and the Poor Get Prison*, 11th ed. London: Routledge.

Religious Tolerance. 2015. "The Status of Women, Currently and Throughout History." Retrieved November 30, 2012 (http://www.religioustolerance.org/women.htm).

Religious Tolerance. 2018. "Stem Cell Research: All Viewpoints." Retrieved March 4, 2014 (http://www.religioustolerance.org/res_stem.htm).

Religious Worlds. 2007. "New Religious Movements." Retrieved August 14, 2008 (www.religiousworlds.com/newreligions.html).

Renewable Energy World. 2017. "Walmart Secures 40 MWh of Energy Storage for Southern California Stores." *Renewable Energy World*, April 17. Retrieved July 19, 2017 (http://www.renewableenergyworld.com/articles/2017/04/walmart-secures-40-mwh-of-energy-storage-for-southern-california-stores.html).

Residents of Hull House. [ca. 1895] 1970. *Hull House Maps and Papers*. New York: Arno.

Reuters. 2017. "Pentagon: Military to Accept Transgender Recruits in 2018." December 30. Retrieved May 8, 2018 (https://nypost.com/2017/12/30/pentagon-military-to-accept-transgender-recruits-in-2018/).

Reuters. 2018. "Homeland Security Unveils New Cyber Security Strategy Amid Threats." *New York Times*, May 15. Retrieved May 21, 2018 (https://www.nytimes.com/reuters/2018/05/15/business/15reuters-usa-cyber.html).

Rhoades, Kimberley A. 2008. "Children's Responses to Interparental Conflict: A Meta-Analysis of Their Associations with Child Adjustment." *Child Development* 79(6):1942–56.

Rice, William. 2013. "Types of Terrorism." *Prezi*, March 8. Retrieved May 13, 2014 (http://prezi.com/zyhuxjslaame/copy-of-types-of-terrorism/).

Rich, Motoko. 2014. "New Federal Guidelines Aim to Rid Schools of Racial Inequality." *New York Times*, October 1. Retrieved June 23, 2015 (www.nytimes.com/2014/10/02/education/new-federal-guidelines-aim-to-rid-schools-of-racial-inequality.html?emc=eta1).

"Richest People in the World: Forbes' Top 20 Billionaires of 2018." 2018. CBS News. Retrieved September 3, 2018 (https://www.cbsnews.com/pictures/richest-people-in-world-forbes/11/).

Riley, Michael, Ben Elgin, Dune Lawrence, and Carol Matlack. 2014. "Missed Alarms and 40 Million Stolen Credit Card Numbers: How Target Blew It." *Bloomberg Business Week*, March 13. Retrieved June 8, 2015 (www.businessweek.com/articles/2014-03-13/target-missed-alarms-in-epic-hack-of-credit-card-data).

Riley, Michael and Jordon Robertson. 2017. "Russian Cyber Hacks on U.S. Electoral System Far Wider than Previously Known." *Bloomberg*, June 13. Retrieved August 2, 2017 (https://www.bloomberg.com/news/articles/2017-06-13/russian-breach-of-39-states-threatens-future-u-s-elections).

Riley, Robin. 2014. "Journey of Hope: The Mayflower Carbon Neutral Story." Retrieved February 16, 2015 (www.youtube.com/watch?v=_Qx1UGTEWMA&list=UUfUaer6k7cf-z6RV2JjAUOA).

Riordan, Cornelius. 2004. *Equality and Achievement: An Introduction to the Sociology of Education.* Upper Saddle River, NJ: Prentice Hall.

Risman, Barbara J. and Pallavi Banerjee. 2013. "Talking About Race: Tween-agers in a Post-Civil Rights Era." *Sociological Forum* 28(2):213–35.

Ritzer, George. 2011. *Globalization: The Essentials.* Malden, MA: Wiley.

Ritzer, George. 2013. *Introduction to Sociology.* Thousand Oaks, CA: Sage.

Ritzer, George. 2015. *The McDonalization of Society*, 8th ed. Thousand Oaks, CA: Sage.

Ritzer, George. 2018. *The McDonaldization of Society*, 9th ed. Thousand Oaks, CA: Sage.

Ritzer, George and Douglas J. Goodman. 2004. *Sociological Theory*, 6th ed. New York: McGraw-Hill.

Ritzer, George and Paul Dean. 2014. *Globalization: A Basic Text.* New York: Wiley.

Roberts, Christine. 2012. "Most 10 Year-Olds Have Been on a Diet." *Daily News.* Retrieved January 17, 2014 (www.nydailynews.com/news/national/diets-obsess-tweens-study-article-1.1106653).

Roberts, Keith A. 2018. *Meaning Making with Malignancy.* Murrells Inlet, SC: Covenant Books.

Roberts, Keith A. and David Yamane. 2016. *Religion in Sociological Perspective*, 6th ed. Thousand Oaks, CA: Sage/Pine Forge Press.

Roberts, Keith A. and Karen A. Donahue. 2000. "Professing Professionalism: Bureaucratization and Deprofessionalization in the Academy." *Sociological Focus* 33(4):365–83.

Roberts, Yvonne. 2018. "If Adolescence Now Lasts Until 24, What Does that Mean for the Rest of Us?" January 21. Retrieved May 7, 2018 (www.theguardian.com/society/2018/jan/21/adulthood-extended-adolescence-when-will-we-grow-uo).

Robles, Frances, Jason Horowitz, and Shaila Dewan. 2015. "Dylann Roof, Suspect in Charleston Shooting, Flew the Flags of White Power." *New York Times*, June 18. Retrieved June 19, 2015 (www.nytimes.com/2015/06/19/us/on-facebook-dylann-roof-charleston-suspect-wears-symbols-of-white-supremacy.html).

Robson, David. 2013. "There Really Are 50 Eskimo Words for 'Snow.'" *Washington Post*, January 14. Retrieved October 1, 2015 (www.washingtonpost.com/national/health-science/there-really-are-50-eskimo-words-for-snow/2013/01/14/e0e3f4e0-59a0-11e2-beee-6e38f5215402_story.html).

Rockquemore, Kerry Ann and David Brunsma. 2008. *Beyond Black: Biracial Identity in America*, 2nd ed. Lanham, MD: Lexington Books.

Rodrigue, Edward and Richard V. Reeves. 2015. "Social Mobility Memos: Five Bleak Facts on Black Opportunity." January 15. Retrieved May 8, 2017 (https://www.brookings.edu/blog/social-mobility-memos/2015/01/15/five-bleak-facts-on-black-opportunity/).

Roethlisberger, Fritz J. and William J. Dickson. 1939. *Management and the Worker.* Cambridge, MA: Harvard University Press.

Roisen, Ron. 2012. "Mrs. Marty Mann and the Early Medicalization of Alcoholism." *The Atlantic*, February 22. Retrieved July 16, 2012 (www.theatlantic.com/health/archive/2012/02/mrs-marty-mann-and-the-early-medicalization-of-alcoholism/252286/).

Roof, Wade Clark. 1999. *Spiritual Marketplace: Baby Boomers and the Remaking of American Religion.* Princeton, NJ: Princeton University Press.

Rosenbaum, James E. 1999. "If Tracking Is Bad, Is Detracking Better? A Study of a Detracked High School." *American Schools* (Winter):24–47.

Rosenbaum, Janet. 2018. "Educational and Criminal Justice Outcomes 12 Years After School Suspension." *Youth and Society*, January 17. Retrieved March 14, 2018 (https://doi.org/10.1177/0044118X17752208).

Rosenberg, Tina. 2017. "In Kenya, Phones Replace Bank Tellers." *New York Times*, May 9. Retrieved May 9, 2017 (https://www.nytimes.com/2017/05/09/opinion/in-kenya-phones-replace-bank-tellers.html?smprod=nytcore-ipad&smid=nytcore-ipad-share).

Rosenqvist, Erik. 2017. "Two Functions of Peer Influence on Upper-Secondary Education Application Behavior." *Sociology of Education* 91(1):72–89.

Rosenthal, Elisabeth. 2013. "As Drug Costs Rise, Bending the Law Is One Remedy." *New York Times*, October 22. Retrieved March 12, 2014 (http://nyti.ms/17HuF6G).

Rosenthal, Elisabeth. 2017. "Those Indecipherable Medical Bills? They Are One Reason Health Care Costs So Much." *New York Times*, March 29. Retrieved June 21, 2017 (https://www.nytimes.com/2017/03/29/magazine/those-indecipherable-medical-bills-theyre-one-reason-health-care-costs-so-much.html?smprod=nytcore-ipad&smid=nytcore-ipad-share&_r=0).

Roser, Max. 2016. "Future World Population Growth." *Our World in Data.* Retrieved April 24, 2016 (http://ourworldindata.org/future-world-population-growth/).

Rossi, Alice S. 1984. "Gender and Parenthood." *American Sociological Review* 49(February):1–19.

Rothenberg, Paula S. 2014. *Race, Class, and Gender in the United States: An Integrated Study*, 9th ed. New York: Worth.

Rothenberg, Paula S. 2015. *White Privilege: Essential Readings on the Other Side of Racism*, 5th ed. New York: Worth.

Rothkopf, David. 2012. "Two Septembers." Pp. 100–103 in *Globalization: The Transformation of Social Worlds*, 3rd ed., edited by D. Stanley Eitzen and Maxine Baca Zinn. Belmont, CA: Wadsworth.

Rothman, Robert A. 2005. *Inequality and Stratification: Race, Class, and Gender*, 5th ed. Englewood Cliffs, NJ: Prentice Hall.

Rumbaut, Ruben G. and Alejandro Portes. 2001. *Ethnicities: Children of Immigrants in America*. Los Angeles: University of California Press.

Rumberger, Russell W. 2011. *Dropping Out: Why Students Drop Out of High School and What Can Be Done About It*. Cambridge, MA: Harvard University Press.

Russonello, Giovanni. 2017. "Jimmy Kimmel's Emotional Monologue: His New Son's Heart Condition." *New York Times*, May 2. Retrieved June 17, 2017 (https://www.nytimes.com/2017/05/02/arts/television/jimmy-kimmel-baby-son-wife.html).

"Rustbelt Britain: The Urban Ghosts." 2013. *The Economist*, October 12. Retrieved March 17, 2014 (www.economist.com/news/britain/21587799-these-days-worst-urban-decay-found-not-big-cities-small-ones-urban-ghosts).

Rydgren, Jens. 2004. "Mechanisms of Exclusion: Ethnic Discrimination in the Swedish Labour Market." *Journal of Ethnic and Migration Studies* 30(4):687–716.

Sachs, Jeffrey D. 2011. "With 7 Billion on Earth, a Huge Task Before Us." Retrieved July 10, 2013 (www.cnn.com/2011/10/17/opinion/sachs-global-population).

Sachs, Jeffrey D. 2015. "Financing Education for All." *Project Syndicate*. Retrieved July 6, 2015 (www.project-syndicate.org/commentary/financing-education-poor-children-by-jeffrey-d-sachs-2015-03).

Sachs, Jeffrey D. 2016. "Financing Health and Education for All." *Project Syndicate*, May 31. Retrieved July 20, 2017 (https://www.project-syndicate.org/commentary/financing-universal-health-education-by-jeffrey-d-sachs-2016-05#comments).

Sadker, Myra and David Sadker. 2005. *Teachers, Schools, and Society*, 7th ed. Boston: McGraw-Hill.

Sahadi, Jeanne. 2016. "Dads Get More of a (Paid) Break at Work." *CNNMoney*, June 17. Retrieved June 2, 2017 (https://contemporaryfamilies.org/ccf-briefing-report-daddys-home/).

Saharan Vibe. 2007. "Wodaabe Beauty Ceremony." February 19. Retrieved November 6, 2009 (saharanvibe.blogspot.com/2007/02/wodaabe-beauty-ceremony.html).

Salchegger, Silvia. 2016. "Selective School Systems and Academic Self-Concept: How Explicit and Implicit School-Level Tracking Relate to the Big-Fish-Little-Pond Effect Across Cultures." *Journal of Educational Psychology* 108(3):405–23.

Salzman, Michael B. 2008. "Globalization, Religious Fundamentalism and the Need for Meaning." *International Journal of Intercultural Relations* 32(July):318–27.

Sampath, G. 2016. "Why Children Drop Out from Primary School." *The Hindu*, December 11. Retrieved November 9, 2017 (http://www.thehindu.com/news/national/Why-children-drop-out-from-primary-school/article16792949.ece).

Sample, Ian. 2015. "Hope Raised for New Genetic Therapy to Prevent Inherited Diseases." *The Guardian*, April 23. Retrieved November 22, 2015 (www.theguardian.com/science/2015/apr/23/hopes-raised-for-new-genetic-therapy-to-prevent-inherited-diseases).

Sanchez, Ray and Ed Payne. 2016. "Charleston Church Shooting: Who Is Dylan Roof?" *CNN*, December 16. Retrieved September 14, 2018 (https://www.cnn.com/2015/06/19/us/charleston-church-shooting-suspect/index.html).

Sanday, Peggy and Ruth Gallagher Goodenough, eds. 1990. *Beyond the Second Sex*. Philadelphia: University of Pennsylvania Press.

Sandberg, Sheryl. 2013. *Lean In: Women, Work, and the Will to Lead*. New York: Alfred A. Knopf.

Sandberg, Sheryl and Adam Grant. 2015. "Speaking While Female." *New York Times*, January 12. Retrieved September 1, 2015 (http://nyti.ms/1A7Xwyw).

Sanger, David E. 2018. "Trump's National Security Chief Calls Russian Interference 'Incontrovertible.'" *New York Times*. Retrieved February 17, 2018 (https://www.nytimes.com/2018/02/17/world/europe/russia-meddling-mcmaster.html).

Sapir, Edward. 1929. "The Status of Linguistics as a Science." *Language* 5:207–14.

Sapir, Edward. 1949. In *Selected Writings of Edward Sapir in Language, Culture, and Personality*, edited by David G. Mandelbaum. Berkeley: University of California Press.

Sapiro, Virginia. 2003. *Women in American Society: An Introduction to Women's Studies*, 5th ed. Mountain View, CA: Mayfield.

Sapolsky, Robert. 2014. "The Trouble with Testosterone." In *The Kaleidoscope of Gender*, 4th ed., edited by Joan Z. Spade and Catherine G. Valentine. Thousand Oaks, CA: Sage.

Sargeant, Kimon Howland. 2000. *Seeker Churches: Promoting Traditional Religion in a Nontraditional Way*. New Brunswick, NJ: Rutgers University Press.

Savage, Charlie. 2017. "Justice Dept. to Take on Affirmative Action in College Admissions." *New York Times*, August 1. Retrieved February 18, 2018 (https://www.nytimes.com/2017/08/01/us/politics/trump-affirmative-action-universities.html).

Sawicki, John. 2016. "Why Terrorists Use Female and Child Suicide Bombers." *July*–August. Retrieved July 28, 2017 (https://www.chausa.org/publications/health-progress/article/july-august-2016/why-terrorists-use-female-and-child-suicide-bombers).

Schaefer, Richard T. 2012. *Racial and Ethnic Groups*, 13th ed. Upper Saddle River, NJ: Prentice Hall.

Schaefer, Richard T. and Jenifer Kunz. 2007. *Racial and Ethnic Groups*. Upper Saddle River, NJ: Pearson/Prentice Hall.

Scheiber, Noam. 2015. "Rising Economic Insecurity Tied to Decades-Long Trend in Employment Practices." *New York Times*, July 12. Retrieved July 13, 2015 (www.nytimes.com/2015/07/13/business/rising-economic-insecurity-tied-to-decades-long-trend-in-employment-practices.html).

Scheiber, Noam and Patricia Cohen. 2015. "For the Wealthiest, a Private Tax System that Saves Them Billions." *New York Times*, December 29. Retrieved April 18, 2016 (www.nytimes.com/2015/12/30/business/economy/for-the-wealthiest-private-tax-system-saves-them-billions.html?emc=eta1).

Scheper-Hughes, Nancy. 2014. "Human Traffic: Exposing the Brutal Organ Trade." *New Internationalist*, May. Retrieved July 2, 2015 (http://newint.org/features/2014/05/01/organ-trafficking-keynote/).

Scherrer, Christoph and Anil Shah. 2017. "The Return of Commercial Prison Labor." *MROnline*, April 18. Retrieved August 3, 2017 (https://mronline.org/2017/04/18/the-return-of-commercial-prison-labor/).

Schmalleger, Frank. 2006. *Criminology Today: An Integrative Introduction*, 4th ed. Upper Saddle River, NJ: Prentice Hall.

Schmalleger, Frank. 2012. *Criminology Today: An Integrative Introduction*, 6th ed. Upper Saddle River, NJ: Prentice Hall.

Schneider, Eric C., Dana O. Sarnak, David Squires, Arnav Shah, and Michelle M. Doty. 2017. "Mirror, Mirror 2017: International Comparison Reflects Flaws and Opportunities for Better U.S. Health Care." July. Retrieved August 7, 2017 (http://www.commonwealthfund.org/interactives/2017/july/mirror-mirror/).

Schoen, Cathy, David Radley, and Sara R. Collins. 2015. "State Trends in the Cost of Employer Health Insurance Coverage,

2003–2013." *The Commonwealth Fund*, January. Retrieved July 2, 2015 (https://timedotcom.files.wordpress.com/2015/01/1798_schoen_state_trends_2003_2013.pdf?la=en).

Schoepflin, Todd. 2011. "Doing Gender." *Creative Sociology*, August 10. Retrieved May 25, 2012 (http://creativesociology.blogspot.com/2011/08/doing-gender.html).

Schwartz, Hunter. 2015. "There Are 390,000 Gay Marriages in the U.S. The Supreme Court Could Quickly Make It Half a Million." *Washington Post*, April 28. Retrieved September 9, 2015 (www.washingtonpost.com/news/the-fix/wp/2015/04/28/heres-how-many-gay-marriages-the-supreme-court-could-make-way-for/).

Schwartz, Nelson D. 2013. "Where Factory Apprenticeship Is Latest Model from Germany." *New York Times*, November 30. Retrieved May 13, 2014 (www.nytimes.com/2013/12/01/business/where-factory-apprenticeship-is-latest-model-from-germany.html?_r=0).

Science Focus. 2016. "Future Technology: 22 Ideas About to Change Our World." December 2. Retrieved March 28, 2018 (www.sciencefocus.com/feature/future/future-technology-22-ideas-about-to-change-our-world).

Scobie, Omid. 2016. "Prince Harry Defends Girlfriend Meghan Markle Against 'Racist and Sexist' Trolls: What He Said." *US Magazine*, November 8. Retrieved February 18, 2018 (https://www.usmagazine.com/celebrity-news/news/prince-harry-defends-girlfriend-against-racist-sexist-trolls-w449086/).

Scott-Montagu, John. 1904. "Automobile Legislation: A Criticism and Review." *North American Review* 179(573):168–77.

Semega, Jessica L., Kayla R. Fontenot, and Melissa A. Kollar. 2017. "Income and Poverty in the United States: 2016 Current Population Reports." United States Census Bureau, September. Retrieved September 18, 2017 (https://www.census.gov/content/dam/Census/library/publications/2017/demo/P60-259.pdf).

Sengupta, Somini. 2014. "U.N. Report Says Progress for Women Is Unequal." *New York Times*, February 12. Retrieved February 20, 2014 (www.nytimes.com/2014/02/13/world/un-report-says-progress-for-women-is-unequal.html?_r=0).

Sentencing Project. 2018. "Trends in U.S. Corrections." Retrieved September 1, 2018 (https://sentencingproject.org/wp-content/uploads/2016/01/Trends-in-US-Corrections.pdf).

Sernau, Scott. 2010. *Social Inequality in a Global Age*. Thousand Oaks, CA: Sage/Pine Forge Press.

Šeta, Đermana. 2016. "Forgotten Women: The Impact of Islamophobia on Muslim Women." *European Network Against Racism*. Retrieved May 24, 2017 (http://enar-eu.org/IMG/pdf/20095_forgottenwomenpublication_v5_1_.pdf).

Shackle, Samira. 2012. "Mukhtar Mai: The Gang Rape Victim Who Defied Her Attackers." *New Statesman*, October 19. Retrieved April 24, 2014 (www.newstatesman.com/world-affairs/2012/10/mukhtar-mai-gang-rape-victim-who-defided-her-attackers).

Sharkey, Patrick. 2017. "Community and the Crime Decline: The Causal Effects of Local Nonprofits on Violent Crime." *American Sociological Review* 82(6):1214–40.

Sharp, Henry S. 1991. "Memory, Meaning, and Imaginary Time: The Construction of Knowledge in White and Chipewayan Cultures." *Ethnohistory* 38(2):149–73.

Sharp, Lauriston. 1990. "Steel Axes for Stone-Age Australians." Pp. 410–24 in *Conformity and Conflict*, 7th ed., edited by James P. Spradley and David W. McCurdy. Glenview, IL: Scott Foresman.

Shaw, Clifford R. and Henry D. McKay. 1929. *Delinquency Areas*. Chicago: University of Chicago Press.

Shaw, Susan M. and Janet Lee. 2005. *Women's Voices, Feminist Visions: Classic and Contemporary Readings*, 3rd ed. Boston: McGraw-Hill.

Shear, Michael D. 2017. "Trump Will Withdraw U.S. from Climate Agreement." *New York Times*, June 1. Retrieved July 25, 2017 (https://www.nytimes.com/2017/06/01/climate/trump-paris-climate-agreement.html).

Sheridan, Mary Beth and William Branigin. 2010. "Senate Ratifies New U.S.-Russia Nuclear Weapons Treaty." *Washington Post*, December 22. Retrieved June 28, 2013 (www.washingtonpost.com/wp-dyn/content/article/2010/12/21/AR2010122104371.html?sid=ST2010122205900).

Sherif, Muzafer and Carolyn Sherif. 1953. *Groups in Harmony and Tension*. New York: Harper & Row.

Sherkat, Darren E. and Christopher G. Ellison. 1999. "Recent Developments and Current Controversies in the Sociology of Religion." *Annual Review of Sociology* 25:363–94.

Siegel, Larry J. 2011. *Criminology: Theories, Patterns, and Typologies*, 11th ed. Belmont, CA: Thomson/Wadsworth.

Siegel, Larry and Clemens Bartollas. 2016. *Corrections Today*. Boston: Cengage.

Simmel, Georg. 1904. "The Sociology of Conflict." *American Journal of Sociology* 4(January):490–525. Retrieved October 4, 2015 (www.jstor.org/stable/2762175?seq=1#page_scan_tab_contents).

Simmel, Georg. [1902–1917] 1950. *The Sociology of Georg Simmel*, translated by Kurt Wolff. Glencoe, IL: Free Press.

Simmel, Georg. [1922] 1955. *Conflict and the Web of Group Affiliations*, translated and edited by Kurt Wolff. Glencoe, IL: Free Press.

Sinclair Broadcast Group. 2018. "Mosques Experiencing Growth in U.S." WJLA.*com*, May 29. Retrieved May 29, 2018 (http://wjla.com/news/nation-world/mosques-experiencing-growth-in-us).

Singer, Max. 2018. *Militant Islam's War against the West*. Ramat Gan, Israel: BESA.

Sizer, Theodore R. 1984. *Horace's Compromise: The Dilemma of the American High School*. Boston: Houghton Mifflin.

Skocpol, Theda. 1979. *States and Social Revolutions: A Comparative Analysis of France, Russia, and China*. Cambridge, UK: Cambridge University Press.

Skocpol, Theda and Vanessa Williamson. 2012. *The Tea Party and the Remaking of Republican Conservatism*. New York: Oxford University Press.

Slaughter, Anne-Marie. 2015. *Unfinished Business: Women Men Work Family*. London: Oneworld.

SlideShare. 2014. "Population Pyramids 2014." Retrieved September 16, 2014 (http://www.slideshare.net/sbsgeog/population-pyramids-2014).

Smelser, Neil J. 1963. *Theory of Collective Behavior*. New York: Free Press.

Smelser, Neil J. 1988. "Social Structure." Pp. 103–29 in *Handbook of Sociology*, edited by Neil J. Smelser. Newbury Park, CA: Sage.

Smelser, Neil J. 1992. "The Rational Choice Perspective: A Theoretical Assessment." *Rationality and Society* 4: 381–410.

Smith, Aaron and Monica Anderson. 2016. "5 Facts About Online Dating." *Pew Research Center*, February 29. Retrieved September 7, 2015 (www.pewresearch.org/fact-tank/2015/04/20/5-facts-about-online-dating/).

Smith, Aaron and Monica Anderson. 2018. "Social Media Use in 2018." Pew Research Center, March 1. Retrieved May 8, 2018 (www.pewinternet.org/2018/03/01/social-media-use-in-2018/).

Smith, Amelia. 2015. "Polio-Related Murders Kill More than the Disease Itself." *Newsweek*, November 28. Retrieved June 30, 2015 (http://europe.newsweek.com/polio-related-murders-kill-more-disease-itself-287880).

Smith, Christian and Robert Faris. 2005. "Socioeconomic Inequality in the American Religious System: An Update and Assessment." *Journal for the Scientific Study of Religion* 44(1):95–104.

Smith, Gregory A. 2017a. "A Growing Share of Americans Say It's Not Necessary to Believe in God to Be Moral." *Pew Research Center*, October 16. Retrieved March 30, 2018 (www.pewresearch.org/fact-tank/2017/10/16/a-growing-share-of-americans-say-its-not-necessary-to-believe-in-god-to-be-moral/).

Smith, Gregory A. 2017b. "Views of Transgender Issues Divide Along Religious Lines." *Pew Research Center*, November 27. Retrieved May 29, 2018 (http://www.pewresearch.org/fact-tank/2017/11/27/views-of-transgender-issues-divide-along-religious-lines/).

Smith, Gregory A. and David Masci. 2018. "7 Facts About American Catholics." *Pew Research Center*, September 4. Retrieved September 13, 2018 (http://www.pewresearch.org/fact-tank/2018/09/04/7-facts-about-american-catholics/).

Smith, Mark K. 2008. "Howard Gardner and Multiple Intelligences." *The Encyclopedia of Informal Education*. Retrieved April 17, 2011 (http://www.infed.org/thinkers/gardner.htm).

Smith, Nick. 2014. *Justice Through Apologies: Remorse, Reform, and Punishment*. Cambridge, England: Cambridge University Press.

Smith, Sharon J., Jieru Chen, Kathleen C. Basile, Leah K. Gilbert, Melissa T. Merrick, Nimesh Patel, Margie Walling, and Anurag Jain. 2017. The National Intimate Partner and Sexual Violence Survey (NISVS): 2010-2012 State Report. April. Atlanta, GA: National Center for Injury Prevention and Control, Centers for Disease Control and Prevention.

Snow, David A. and L. Anderson. 1993. *Down on Their Luck: A Study of Homeless Street People*. Berkeley: University of California Press.

Snyder, Denson R. 1971. *The Hidden Curriculum*. New York: Alfred A. Knopf.

Snyderman, Nancy and Chiara Sottile. 2013. "'It's Getting a Lot Harder to Do This': Doctor Shortage Strains Practices." *NBC News*, May 25. Retrieved July 15, 2013 (http://dailynightly.nbcnews.com/_news/2013/05/25/18042694-it-is-getting-a-lot-harder-to-do-this-doctor-shortage-strains-practices?lite).

Soble, Johathan. 2015. "To Rescue Economy, Japan Turns to Supermom." *New York Times*, January 1. Retrieved September 14, 2015 (http://nyti.ms/1zDywPg).

Social Security Administration. 2013. "Social Security Basic Facts." Retrieved July 1, 2013 (www.ssa.gov/pressoffice/basicfact.htm).

Sommer, Eric. 2014. "How Five American Companies Control What You Think." *RT Question More*, May 14. Retrieved January 25, 2016 (www.rt.com/op-edge/158920-us-ukraine-media-control/).

Sommerville, John C. 2002. "Stark's Age of Faith Argument and the Secularization of Things: A Commentary." *Review of Religious Research* (Fall):361–72.

Sonne, Paul. 2018. "Pentagon Unveils New Nuclear Weapons Strategy, Ending Obama-Era Push to Reduce U.S. Arsenal." *Washington Post*, February 2. Retrieved February 11, 2018 (https://www.washingtonpost.com/world/national-security/pentagon-unveils-new-nuclear-weapons-strategy-ending-obama-era-push-to-reduce-us-arsenal/2018/02/02/fd72ad34-0839-11e8-ae28-e370b74ea9a7_story.html).

Sons of Union Veterans of the Civil War. 2010. "The United States' Flag Code." Retrieved December 12, 2011 (http://suvcw.org/flag.htm).

Southern Poverty Law Center. 2017a. "Alternative Right." Retrieved July 27, 2017 (https://www.splcenter.org/fighting-hate/extremist-files/ideology/alternative-right).

Southern Poverty Law Center. 2017b. "Hate Groups Increase for Second Consecutive Year as Trump Electrifies Radical Right." February 15. Retrieved May 11, 2017 (https://www.splcenter.org/news/2017/02/15/hate-groups-increase-second-consecutive-year-trump-electrifies-radical-right).

Southern Poverty Law Center. 2017c. "Nation of Islam." Retrieved February 2, 2018 (www.splcenter.org/fighting-hate/extremist-files/group/nation-islam).

Southern Poverty Law Center. 2018. "Hate Map 2017." Retrieved March 22, 2018 (https://www.splcenter.org/hate-map).

Spade, Joan Z. 2004. "Gender in Education in the United States." Pp. 287–95 in *Schools and Society: A Sociological Approach to Education*, 2nd ed., edited by Jeanne H. Ballantine and Joan Z. Spade. Belmont, CA: Wadsworth.

Spencer, Kyle. 2016. "As Other Districts Grapple with Segregation, This One Makes Integration Work." *New York Times*, December 12. Retrieved May 22, 2017 (https://www.nytimes.com/2016/12/12/nyregion/as-other-districts-grapple-with-segregation-this-one-makes-integration-work.html).

Sprey, Jetse. 1969. The Family as a System in Conflict." *Journal of Marriage and Family* 31(4):699–706.

Standler, Ronald B. 2012. "Annotated Legal Cases on Physician-Assisted Suicide in the USA." *Carbon Mitigation Initiative*, July 12. Retrieved July 16, 2013 (cmi.princeton.edu/).

Stanton, Glenn. 2018. "What Is the Actual Divorce Rate?" *Focus on the Family*. Retrieved March 15, 2018 (www.focusonthefamily.com/about/focus-findings/marriage/what-is-actual-divorce-rate).

Staples, Brent. 2001. "Black Men and Public Space." Pp. 244–46 in *The Production of Reality*, edited by Jodi O'Brien and Peter Kollock. Thousand Oaks, CA: Pine Forge Press.

Stark, Rodney. 2000. "Secularization, R.P.I." Pp. 41–66 in *The Secularization Debate*, edited by William H. Swatos Jr. and Daniel V. A. Olson. Lanham, MD: Rowman & Littlefield.

Stark, Rodney and Roger Finke. 2000. *Acts of Faith: Explaining the Human Side of Religion*. Berkeley: University of California Press.

Startz, Dick. 2017. "What Should We Pay Teachers?" *Brookings*. Retrieved September 9, 2018 (https://www.brookings.edu/blog/brown-center-chalkboard/2017/09/20/what-should-we-pay-teachers/).

State of Alaska. 2006. "Workplace Alaska: How to Apply." Retrieved July 5, 2006 (http://notes3.state.ak.us/WA/MainEntry.nsf/WebData/HTMLHow+to+Apply/?open).

Statista. 2014. "Number of Vehicles Registered in the United States from 1990 to 2011." Retrieved February 23, 2014 (www.statista.com/statistics/183505/number-of-vehicles-in-the-united-stastes-since-1990/).

Statista. 2016a. "Number of Monthly Active Facebook Users Worldwide as of 4th Quarter 2016." Retrieved February 26, 2017 (http: www.statista.com/statistics/264810/number-of-monthly-active-facebook-users-worldwide/).

Statista. 2016b. "Reported Violent Crime Rate in the United States from 1990 to 2014." Retrieved April 5, 2016 (www.statista.com/statistics/191219/reported-violent-crime-rate-in-the-usa-since-1990/).

Statista. 2017a. "Average Life Expectancy in North America for Those Born in 2017, by Gender and Region (in Years)."

Retrieved May 7, 2018 (www.statista.com/statistics/274513/life-expectancy-in-north-america?).

Statista. 2017b. "Number of People Who Conducted Volunteer Work Within the Last 12 Months in the United States from Spring 2008 to Spring 2017 (in Millions)." Retrieved May 8, 2018 (wwwstatista.com/statistics/227432/number-of-volunteer-workers-usa/).

Statista. 2018a. "Most Popular Social Networks Worldwide as of April 2018, Ranked by Number of Active Users (in Millions)." Retrieved May 8, 2018 (www.statista.com/statistics/272014/global-social-networks-ranked-by-number-of-users/).

Statista. 2018b. "Social Media: Statistics and Facts." Retrieved May 7, 2018 (www.statista.com/topics/1164/social-networks/).

Statista. 2018c. "Number of Smartphone Users Worldwide from 2014 to 2020 (in Billions)." Retrieved May 7, 2018 (https://www.statista.com/statistics/330695/number-of-smartphone-users-worldwide/).

St. Claire, Pat and Karen Smith. 2015. "South African Mine Massacre: Report Says Many Share in the Blame." *CNN*, June 25. Retrieved September 11, 2015 (www.cnn.com/2015/06/25/africa/south-africa-mine-massacre-report/).

Steele, Tracey L. 2005. *Sex, Self, and Society: The Social Context of Sexuality*. Belmont, CA: Thomson Wadsworth.

Stephen, Eric M., Jennifer Rose, Lindsay Kenney, Francine Rosselli-Navarra, and Ruth S. Weissman. 2014. "Adolescent Risk Factors for Purging in Young Women: Findings From the National Longitudinal Study of Adolescent Health." *Journal of Eating Disorders* 2(1). Retrieved January 16, 2014 (www.jeatdisord.com/).

Stern, Jessica. 2003. Terror in the Name of God: Why Religious Militants Kill. New York: HarperCollins.

Stetka, Bret. 2017. "Extended Adolescence: When 25 is the New 18." *Scientific American*, September 19. Retrieved May 7, 2018 (www.scientificamerican.com/article/extended-adolescence-when-25-is-the-new-181/).

Stewart, Susan D. 2007. *Brave New Stepfamilies: Diverse Paths Toward Stepfamily Living*. Thousand Oaks, CA: Sage.

Stiglitz, Joseph E. 2012. "A Real Cure for the Global Economic Crackup." Pp. 104–9 in *Globalization: The Transformation of Social Worlds*, 3rd ed., edited by D. Stanley Eitzen and Maxine Baca Zinn. Belmont, CA: Wadsworth.

Stockholm International Peace Research Institute. 2017. "World Military Spending: Increases in the USA and Europe, Decreases in Oil-Exporting Countries." April 24. Retrieved June 15, 2017 (https://www.sipri.org/media/press-release/2017/world-military-spending-increases-usa-and-europe).

Stoessinger, John. 1993. *Why Nations Go to War*. New York: St. Martin's Press.

Stracansky, Pavol. 2013. "Curbs on Abortion Spread Across East Europe." *Inter Press Service*, July 12. Retrieved March 17, 2014 (www.ipsnews/net/2013/07/curbs-on-abortion-spread-across-east-europe/).

Straus, Murray A. 2017. *Physical Violence in American Families: Risk Factors and Adaptations to Violence in 8,145 Families*. New York: Routledge.

Straus, Murray A., Richard J. Gelles, and Suzanne K. Steinmetz. 2006. *Behind Closed Doors: Violence in the American Family*. New Brunswick, NJ: Transaction.

Strauss, Valerie. 2011. "ACT Scores Show Problems with College Readiness." *Washington Post*, August 17. Retrieved July 8, 2013 (www.washingtonpost.com/blogs/answer-sheet/post/2011-act-scores-show-problems-with-college-read iness/2011/08/16/gIQABKu4JJ_blog.html).

Strauss, Valerie. 2017. "Arizona's Ban on Mexican American Studies was Racist, U.S. Court Rules." *Washington Post*, August 23. Retrieved November 2, 2017 (https://www.washingtonpost.com/news/answer-sheet/wp/2017/08/23/arizonas-ban-on-mexican-american-studies-was-racist-u-s-court-rules/?utm_term=.4a9d1f2b62cf).

Stryker, Sheldon. 1980. *Symbolic Interactionism: A Social Structural Version*. Menlo Park, CA: Benjamin Cummings.

Stryker, Sheldon. 2000. "Identity Competition: Key to Differential Social Involvement." Pp. 21–40 in *Identity, Self, and Social Movements*, edited by Sheldon Styker, Timothy Owens, and Robert White. Minneapolis: University of Minnesota Press.

Sullivan, Brian. 2013. "HUD Repots Continued Decline in U.S. Homelessness Since 2010." HUD.gov, November 21. Retrieved February 17, 2014 (http://portal.hud.gov/hudportal/HUD?src=/press/press_releases_media_advisories/2013/HUDNo.13-173).

Suri, Tavneet and William Jack. 2017. "The Long-Term Effects of Access to Mobile Money in Kenya." *IPA*. Retrieved May 9, 2017 (http://www.poverty-action.org/study/long-term-effects-access-mobile-money-kenya).

Sussex, Roland. 2016. "How Different Cultures Experience and Talk about Pain." January 1. Retrieved February 10, 2018 (https://bodyinmind.org/cultures-pain/).

Sutherland, Anne. 1986. *Gypsies: The Hidden Americans*. Prospect Heights, IL: Waveland.

Sutherland, Anne. 2001. "Complexities of U.S. Law and Gypsy Identity." Pp. 231–42 in *Gypsy Law: Romani Legal Traditions and Culture*, edited by Walter O. Weyrauch. Berkeley: University of California Press.

Sutherland, Edwin H., Donald R. Cressey, and David Luckenbil. 1992. *Criminology*. Dix Hills, NY: General Hall.

Sutton, Joe. 2013. "Maryland Governor Signs Death Penalty Repeal." *CNN*, May 2. Retrieved June 2, 2013 (www.cnn.com/2013/05/02/us/maryland-death-penalty).

Svrluga, Susan. 2015. "U. Missouri President, Chancellor Resign Over Handling of Racial Incidents." *Washington Post*, November 9. Retrieved December 8, 2015 (www.washingtonpost.com/news/grade-point/wp/2015/11/09/missouris-student-government-calls-for-university-presidents-removal/).

Swan, Rita. 2017. "Religious Attitudes on Corporal Punishment." CHILD. *Inc*. Retrieved June 7, 2017 (http://childrenshealthcare.org/?page_id=146).

Swank, Eric, Breanne Fahs, and David M. Frost. 2013. "Region, Social Identities and Disclosure Practices as Predictors of Heterosexist Discrimination Against Sexual Minorities in the United States." *Sociological Inquiry* 83(2):238–58.

Swanson, Ana. 2018 "Signs of Progress in Nafta Talks but Countries Remain Deeply Divided." January 29. Retrieved February 18, 2018 (www.nytimes.com/2018/01/29/us/politics/nafta-talks-conclude-in-montreal-with-signs-of-progress-and-rish.html).

Sway, Marlene. 1988. *Familiar Strangers: Gypsy Life in America*. Urbana: University of Illinois Press.

Tabuchi, Hiroko. 2017. "U.S. Climate Change Policy Made in California." *New York Times*, September 27. Retrieved September 27, 2017 (https://www.nytimes.com/2017/09/27/climate/california-climate-change.html?hp&action=click&pgtype=Homepage&clickSource=story-heading&module=first-column-region&region=top-news&WT.nav=top-news).

Tamney, Joseph B. 1992. *The Resilience of Christianity in the Modern World*. Albany: State University of New York Press.

Tanner, Lindsey. 2014. "AMA Officially Designates Cheerleading a Sport." *USA Today*, June 10. Retrieved September 4, 2015 (www.usatoday.com/story/news/nation/2014/06/10/ama-cheerleading-sport/10272941/).

Taseer, Shehrbano. 2011. "True Survivor." *The Daily Beast*, May 1. Retrieved April 12, 2012 (www.thedailybeast.com/newsweek/2011/05/01/true-survivor.html).

Tavernise, Sabrina. 2015. "Colorado's Effort Against Teenage Pregnancies Is a Startling Success." *New York Times*, July 5. Retrieved July 6, 2015 (www.nytimes.com/2015/07/06/science/colorados-push-against-teenage-pregnancies-is-a-startling-success.html).

Tavernise, Sabrina. 2016. "Disparity in Life Spans of the Rich and the Poor Is Growing." *New York Times*, February 12. Retrieved February 15, 2016 (www.nytimes.com/2016/02/13/health/disparity-in-life-spans-of-the-rich-and-the-poor-is-growing.html?smid=nytcore-ipad-share&smprod=nytcore-ipad).

Tea Party. 2016. "About Us." Retrieved January 25, 2016 (www.teaparty.org/about-us/).

Teixeira, Ruy and John Halpin. 2012. "The Obama Coalition in the 2012 Election and Beyond." Center for American Progress, December. Retrieved November 19, 2013 (www.americanprogress.org/wp-content/uploads/2012/12/ObamaCoalition-5.pdf).

Terra Networks. 2013. "Kony 2012 Viral Campaign Sheds Light on Ugandan Violence." Retrieved March 30, 2012 (http://en.terra.com/latin-in-america/news/kony_2012_viral_campaign_sheds_light_on_ugandan_violence/hof18171/ECID=US_ENGLISH_terrausa_SEMSearch_Kony).

Testa, Maria Rita. 2014. "On the Positive Correlation Between Education and Fertility Intentions in Europe: Individual- and Country-Level Evidence." *Advances in Life Course Research* 21(September):28–42.

Thakrar, Ashish P., Alexandra D. Forrest, Mitchell G. Maltenfort, and Christopher B. Forrest. 2018. "Child Mortality in the US and 19 OECD Comparator Nations: A 50-Year Time-Trend Analysis." *Health Affairs* 37(1) (https://doi.org/10.1377/hlthaff.2017.0767).

Thiede, Brian, Lillie Greiman, Stephan Weiler, Steven C. Beda, and Tessa Conroy. 2017. "Six Charts That Illustrate the Divide Between Rural and Urban America." *The Conversation*, March 16. Retrieved September 18, 2018 (http://theconversation.com/six-charts-that-illustrate-the-divide-between-rural-and-urban-america-72934).

Theroux, David J. 2012. "Secular Theocracy: The Foundations and Folly of Modern Tyranny." *The Independent Institute*, January 11. Retrieved July 13, 2012 (www.independent.org/newsroom/article.asp?id=3206).

Thomas, V. J. and F. D. Rose. 1991. "Ethnic Differences in the Experience of Pain." *Social Science and Medicine* 32(9):1063–66.

Thomason, Andy. 2017. "What You Need to Know About Race-Conscious Admissions in 2017." *Chronicle of Higher Education*, August 2. Retrieved May 8, 2018 (www.chronicle.com/article/What-You-Need-to-Know-About/240820).

Thompson, A. C. 2009. "Katrina's Hidden Race War." *The Nation*, January 5. Retrieved July 7, 2011 (www.thenation.com/article/katrinas-hidden-race-war).

Thomson, Helen. 2015. "Study of Holocaust Survivors Finds Trauma Passed on to Children's Genes." *The Guardian*, August 21. Retrieved November 16, 2015 (www.theguardian.com/science/2015/aug/21/study-of-holocaust-survivors-finds-trauma-passed-on-to-childrens-genes?CMP=share_btn_fb).

Thorne, Barrie. 1993. *Gender Play: Girls and Boys in School*. New Brunswick, NJ: Rutgers University Press.

Timsit, Annabelle. 2017. "Things Could Get Very Ugly Following Europe's Refugee Crisis." *The Atlantic*, October 27. Retrieved March 28, 2018 (www.theatlantic.com/international/archive/2017/10/qa-sasha-polakow-suransky-immigantion-europe/543537/).

Tipton, Steven M. 1990. "The Social Organization of Zen Practice: Constructing Transcultural Reality." *American Journal of Sociology* 96(2):488–90.

Title IX. 2015. "Athletics Under Title IX." Retrieved September 4, 2015 (www.titleix.info/10-key-areas-of-title-ix/athletics.aspx).

Toffler, Alvin and Heidi Toffler. 1980. *The Third Wave*. New York: Morrow.

Tolbert, Pamela S. and Richard H. Hall. 2008. *Organizations: Structures, Processes, and Outcomes*, 10th ed. Upper Saddle River, NJ: Prentice Hall.

Tönnies, Ferdinand. [1887] 1963. *Community and Society*. New York: Harper & Row.

"Top 100 Boy's Names for 2018." 2018a. Mom 365. Retrieved September 5, 2018 (https://www.mom365.com/baby-names/top-boy-names).

"Top 100 Girl's Names for 2018." 2018b. Mom 365. Retrieved September 5, 2018 (https://www.mom365.com/baby-names/top-girl-names).

Torok, Robyn. 2015. "ISIS and the Institution of Online Terrorist Recruitment." *Middle East Institute*, January 29. Retrieved November 19, 2015 (www.mei.edu/content/map/isis-and-institution-online-terrorist-recruitment).

Transparency International. 2017a. "Corruption Perceptions Index." Retrieved February 10, 2018 (www.transparency.org/research/cpi/overview).

Transparency International. 2017b. "Corruption in the USA: The Difference a Year Makes." December 12. Retrieved February 5, 2018 (https://www.transparency.org/news/feature/corruption_in_the_usa_the_difference_a_year_makes).

Transparency International. 2018. "Corruption Perceptions Index 2017." February 21. Retrieved March 22, 2018 (https://www.transparency.org/news/feature/corruption_perceptions_index_2017#research).

Traub, Amy, Laura Sullivan, Tatjana Meschede, and Tom Shapiro. 2017. "The Asset Value of Whiteness." *Demos and IASP*, February 13. Retrieved May 10, 2017 (http://www.demos.org/sites/default/files/publications/Asset%20Value%20of%20Whiteness_0.pdf).

Trust in Education. 2013. "Life as an Afghan Woman." Retrieved September 6, 2018 (http://www.trustineducation.org/resources/life-as-an-afghan-woman/).

Tull, Matthew. 2012. "The Consequences of Male Gender Role Stress." Retrieved February 6, 2014 (http://ptsd.about.com/od/relatedconditions/a/MaleGenderRoleStres.htm).

Turner, Bryan S. 1991a. "Politics and Culture in Islamic Globalism." Pp. 161–81 in *Religion and Global Order*, edited by Roland Robertson and William R. Garrett. New York: Paragon.

Turner, Bryan S. 1991b. *Religion and Social Theory*. London: Sage.

Turner, Jonathan H. 2003. *The Structure of Sociological Theory*, 7th ed. Belmont, CA: Wadsworth.

Turner, Kathleen. 2015. "Femme Fatale: The Rise of Female Suicide Bombers." *War on the Rocks*, December 14. Retrieved January 27, 2018 (https://warontherocks.com/2015/12/femme-fatale-the-rise-of-female-suicide-bombers/).

Turner, Ralph H. and Lewis M. Killian. 1993. "The Field of Collective Behavior." Pp. 5–20 in *Collective Behavior and Social Movements*, edited by Russell L. Curtis, Jr. and Benigno E. Aguirre. Boston: Allyn & Bacon.

UN Department of Economic and Social Affairs. 2014. "World Urbanization Prospects: 2014 Revision." Retrieved April 24, 2016 (http://esa.un.org/unpd/wup/Publications/Files/WUP2014-Highlights.pdf).

UN News Center. 2010. "Senior UN Official Cites Evidence of Growing Support for Abolishing Death Penalty." February 24. Retrieved March 8, 2011 (www.un.org/apps/news/story.asp?NewsID=33877&Cr=death+penalty&Cr1=).

UN Women. 2016. "Facts and Figures: Ending Violence Against Women." February. Retrieved May 25, 2017 (http://www.unwomen.org/en/what-we-do/ending-violence-against-women/facts-and-figures#notes).

UN Women. 2017. "Facts and Figures: Ending Violence Against Women." August. Retrieved March 20, 2018 (www.unwomen.org/en/what-we-do/ending-violence-against-women/facts-and-figures).

UN Women. 2018. "Six Activists Who Are Using Social Media For Change Offline." June 29. Retrieved September 6, 2018 (http://www.unwomen.org/en/news/stories/2018/6/compilation-social-media-day).

Unavision. 2014. "Voice of the People." Retrieved July 24, 2017 (http://univision.data4.mx/resultados_catolicos/eng/ENG_catholic-survey.pdf).

UNESCO. 2015. "Education 2030: Incheon Declaration and Framework for Action for the Implementation of Sustainable Development Goal 4." Retrieved October 19, 2017 (http://unesdoc.unesco.org/images/0024/002456/245656E.pdf).

UNESCO. 2016. "Policy Paper 27/Fact Sheet 37: Leaving No One Behind: How Far on the Way to Universal Primary and Secondary Education?" Retrieved September 9, 2018 (http://uis.unesco.org/sites/default/files/documents/fs37-leaving-no-one-behind-how-far-on-the-way-to-universal-primary-and-secondary-education-2016-en.pdf).

UNESCO. 2017a. "Learning to Live Together: Trans-nationalism." Retrieved April 16, 2018 (www.unesco.org/new/en/social-and-human-sciences/themes/international-migration/glossary/trans-nationalism/).

UNESCO. 2017b. "International Literacy Day 2017." January 9. Retrieved October 19, 2017 (http://uis.unesco.org/en/news/international-literacy-day-2017).

UNESCO Institute for Statistics. 2017. "Youth Literacy Rate, Population 15–24 Years." Retrieved September 9, 2018 (http://uis.unesco.org/en/news/international-literacy-day-2017).

UN.GIFT. 2014. "Trafficking for Organ Trade." *Global Initiative to Fight Human Trafficking*. Retrieved March 10, 2014 (www.ungift.org/knowledgehub/en/about/trafficking-for-organ-trade.html).

UNHCR. 2015. "Syria Regional Refuge Response." Retrieved July 8, 2015 (http://data.unhcr.org/syrianrefugees/regional.php).

UNHCR. 2017a. "Global Trends: Forced Displacement in 2016." Retrieved July 27, 2018 (http://www.unhcr.org/globaltrends2016/).

UNHCR. 2017b. "Figures at a Glance." Retrieved July 24, 2017 (http://www.unhcr.org/en-us/figures-at-a-glance.html).

UNHCR. 2017c. "Syria Emergency." Retrieved July 24, 2017 (http://www.unhcr.org/en-us/syria-emergency.html).

UNHCR 2017d. "Major Refugee-Hosting Countries." Retrieved September 18, 2018 (http://www.unhcr.org/globaltrends2016/).

UNICEF. 2014. "Update on Haiti's Children." Retrieved February 23, 2014 (www.unicefusa.org/work/emergencies/Haiti/?gclid=CJ6zxOK847wCFdE-Mgodt1IANg).

UNICEF. 2015. "Education Is Vital to Meeting All Millennium Development Goals." February. Retrieved June 23, 2015 (http://data.unicef.org/education/overview#sthash.MYUmyFbM.dpuf).

Union of Concerned Scientists. 2017. "Each Country's Share of CO2 Emissions." November 20. Retrieved September 18, 2018 (https://www.ucsusa.org/global-warming/science-and-impacts/science/each-countrys-share-of-co2.html#.W6EqJuhKjIU).

United National Environmental Programme. 2017. "Towards a Pollution Free Planet." Retrieved August 2, 2017 (http://wedocs.unep.org/bitstream/handle/20.500.11822/21213/Towards_a_pollution_free_planet_advance%20version.pdf?sequence=2&isAllowed=y).

United Nations. 2017. "World Population Prospects: The 2017 Revision." Ageing. Retrieved February 12, 2018 (www.un.org/en/sections/issues-depth/ageing/).

United Nations Human Rights Office of Commissioner. 2017. "Committee on the Rights of the Child." Retrieved June 12, 2017 (http://www.ohchr.org/EN/HRBodies/CRC/Pages/CRCIndex.aspx).

United Nations Population Fund. 2014. "Big Gains Made on Women's Health, but Access Still Unequal." Retrieved February 20, 2014 (info@populationandsustainability.org).

United Nations Population Fund. 2017. "Gender-Biased Selection." Retrieved May 18, 2017 (http://www.unfpa.org/gender-biased-sex-selection).

United States Government Accountability Office. 2018. "K-12 EDUCATION Discipline Disparities for Black Students, Boys, and Students with Disabilities." March. Retrieved May 29, 2018 (https://www.gao.gov/assets/700/690828.pdf).

Universal Ecological Fund. 2017. "The Economic Case for Climate Action in the United States." September. Retrieved September 27, 2017 (https://feu-us.org/case-for-climate-action-us2/).

University of Michigan Documents Center. 2003. "Documents in the News—1997/2003: Affirmative Action in College Admissions." Retrieved April 17, 2010 (www.lib.umich.edu/files/libraries/govdocs/pdf/affirm/pdf).

University of Pennsylvania. 2010. "Body Modification." Retrieved November 18, 2010 (penn.museum/sites/body_modification/bodmodpierce.shtml).

UNODC. 2018. "UNODC Launches Handbook on Children Recruited and Exploited by Terrorist Groups." January 26. Retrieved May 7, 2018 (www.unodc.org/unodc/en/frontpage/2018/January/unodc-launches-handbook-on-children-recruited-and-exploited-by-terrorist-groups.html).

U.S. Bureau of Labor Statistics. 2018. "Table 1. Time Spent in Primary Activities and Percent of Civilian Population Engaging in Each Activity, Averages per Day by Sex, 2017 Annual Averages." June 28. Retrieved July 24, 2018 (https://www.bls.gov/news.release/atus.t01.htm).

U.S. Census Bureau. 1995. "Table 1. Urban and Rural Population: 1900 to 1990." Retrieved July 24, 2017 (https://www.census.gov/population/censusdata/urpop0090.txt).

U.S. Census Bureau. 2015a. "Subject Definitions." August 25. Retrieved May 24, 2017 (https://www.census.gov/programs-surveys/cps/technical-documentation/subject-definitions.html#family).

U.S. Census Bureau. 2015b. "How the Census Bureau Measures Poverty." Retrieved November 17, 2015 (www.census.gov/hhes/www/poverty/about/overview/measure.html).

U.S. Census Bureau. 2016a. "Detailed Years of School Completed by People 25 Years and Over by Sex, Age Groups, Race and Hispanic Origin: 2015." Retrieved March 30, 2016 (www.census.gov/hhes/socdemo/education/data/cps/2015/tables.html).

U.S. Census Bureau. 2016b. "Table P-28. Educational Attainment—Workers 18 Years Old and Over by Mean Earnings, Age and Sex." Retrieved May 23, 2017 (https://www.census.gov/data/tables/time-series/demo/income-poverty/historical-income-people.html).

U.S. Census Bureau. 2017a. "Marriage and Divorce." November 16. Retrieved March 15, 2018 (www.census.gov/topics/families/marriage&divorce.html).

U.S. Census Bureau. 2017b. "U.S. and World Population Clock." May 25. Retrieved May 25, 2017 (https://www.census.gov/popclock/).

U.S. Census Bureau. 2017c. "Current Population Survey Tables PINC-03. Educational Attainment-People 25 Years Old and Over, by Total Money Earnings, Work Experience, Age, Race, Hispanic Origin, and Sex." Retrieved July 13, 2018 (https://www.census.gov/data/tables/time-series/demo/income-poverty/cps-pinc/pinc-03.html).

U.S. Census Bureau. 2017d. "Figure CH-1 Living Arrangements of Children: 1960 to Present." November 15. Retrieved March 27, 2018 (https://www.census.gov/content/dam/Census/library/visualizations/time-series/demo/families-and-households/ch-1.pdf).

U.S. Census Bureau. 2017e. "Table H-5. Race and Hispanic Origin of Householder—Households by Median and Mean Income: 1967 to 2016." Retrieved July, 13 2017 (www.census.gov/data/tables/time-series/demo/income-poverty/historical-income-households.html).

U.S. Census Bureau. 2017f. "Figure 11.3: Percent of Population 25 Years and Older, and 25 to 29 Years Old, with Bachelors Degree or Higher by Sex: 1947–2016." Retrieved September 9, 2018 (https://www.census.gov/library/visualizations/time-series/demo/cps-historical-time-series.html).

U.S. Census Bureau. 2018. "Preliminary Estimate of Weighted Average Poverty Thresholds for 2017." Retrieved September 3, 2018 (https://www.census.gov/data/tables/time-series/demo/income-poverty/historical-poverty-thresholds.html).

U.S. Debt Clock. 2016. "U.S. National Debt Clock." Retrieved January 25, 2016 (www.usdebtclock.org/).

U.S. Department of Defense. 2012. "Department of Defense Antiterrorism Program Memo: Instruction No. 2000.12." March 1. Retrieved July 28, 2012 (www.dtic.mil/whs/directives/corres/pdf/200012p.pdf).

U.S. Department of Defense. 2014. "U.S. Department of Defense (DoD) Definition of Terrorism." April 4. Retrieved January 28, 2018 (www.secbrief.org/2014/04/definition-of-terroris/).

U.S. Department of Education. 2015. "US High School Graduate Rate Hits New Record High." Retrieved April 11, 2016 (www.ed.gov/news/press-releases/us-high-school-graduation-rate-hits-new-record-high-0).

U.S. Department of Education for Civil Rights. 2012. "Title VI Enforcement Highlights." Retrieved July 8, 2013 (www2.ed.gov/documents/press-releases/title-vi-enforcement.pdf).

U.S. Department of Health and Human Services. 2015. "2015 Poverty Guidelines." September 3. Retrieved September 8, 2015 (aspe.hhs.gov/woa5-poverty-guidelines).

U.S. Department of Housing and Urban Development. 2016. "The 2016 Annual Homeless Assessment Report (AHAR) to Congress." November. Retrieved May 9, 2017 (https://www.hudexchange.info/resources/documents/2016-AHAR-Part-1.pdf).

U.S. Department of Interior Office of Education. 1930. *Availability of Public School Education in Rural Communities* (Bulletin No. 34, edited by Walter H. Gaummitz). Washington, DC: Government Printing Office.

U.S. Department of Justice. 2017. "Prison Rape Elimination Act of 2003 PREA Data Collection Activities, 2017." June. Retrieved August 3, 2017 (https://www.bjs.gov/content/pub/pdf/pdca17.pdf).

U.S. Department of Labor. 2013. "Employee Rights and Responsibilities Under the Family and Medical Leave Act." Retrieved February 19, 2014 (www.dol.gov/whd/regs/compliance/posters/fmlean.pdf).

U.S. Department of State. 2015. "South Africa 2015 Crime and Safety Report." Retrieved May 28, 2015 (www.osac.gov/pages/ContentReportDetails.aspx?cid=17042).

U.S. Department of State. 2017. "Trafficking in Persons Report." June. Retrieved July 30, 2017 (https://www.state.gov/documents/organization/271339.pdf).

U.S. Elections Project. 2016. "Turnout 1980–2012." Retrieved January 27, 2016 (http://elections.gmu.edu/voter_turnout.htm).

U.S. Equal Employment Opportunity Commission. 2016. "Select Task Force on the Study of Harassment in the Workplace." June. Retrieved October 23, 2017 (https://www.eeoc.gov/eeoc/task_force/harassment/upload/report.pdf).

U.S. Flag Code. 2008. "U.S. Flag Code (4 US Code 1)." Retrieved August 28, 2008 (http://suvcw.org/flag.htm).

U.S. Geological Survey. 2017. "Disappearing Beaches: Modeling Shoreline Change in Southern California." March 17. Retrieved August 17, 2017 (https://www.usgs.gov/news/disappearing-beaches-modeling-shoreline-change-southern-california).

U.S. Government Accountability Office. 2015. "Financial Audit: Bureau of the Fiscal Service's Fiscal Years 2015 and 2014 Schedules of Federal Debt." November 13. Retrieved January 25, 2016 (www.gao.gov/products/GAO-16-160).

U.S. Trade Representative. 2012. "Joint Stats from 2012 NAFTA Commission Meeting." Retrieved September 8, 2012 (www.ustr.gov/).

USAS. 2017. "Student Worker Organizing." Retrieved July 25, 2017 (http://usas.org/student-workers-need-15/).

Uzoma, Kay. 2015. "How Much TV Does the Average Child Watch Each Day?" *Livestrong*, May 25. Retrieved September 14, 2015 (www.livestrong.com/article/222032-how-much-tv-does-the-average-child-watch-each-day/).

Van der Voet, Joris. 2015. "Change Leadership and Public Sector Organizational Change." *The American Review of Public Administration*, March 22. Retrieved September 10, 2015 (http://arp.sagepub.com/content/early/2015/03/18/0275074015574769.abstract).

Van Ginkel, Bibi. 2015. "The (In-)Effectiveness of 'Deterrence' as an Instrument." *Clingendael Netherlands Institute of International Relations*, March 30. Retrieved June 15, 2017 (https://www.clingendael.nl/publication/effectiveness-deterrence-instrument-against-jihadist-terrorist-threats).

Vance, J. D. 2016. *Hillbilly Elegy.* New York: HarperCollins.

Varul, Matthias Zick. 2010. "Talcott Parsons, the Sick Role and Chronic Illness." *Body Society* 16(2):72–94.

Veblen, Thorstein. 1902. *The Theory of the Leisure Class: An Economic Study of Institutions.* New York: Macmillan.

Verbeek, Stjin and Rinus Penninx. 2009. "Employment Equity Policies in Work Organisations." Pp. 69–94 in *Equal Opportunity and Ethnic Inequality in European Labour Markets: Discrimination, Gender, and Policies of Diversity,* edited by Karen Kraal, Judith

Roosblad, and John Wrench. Amsterdam: University of Amsterdam Press.

Victor, Barbara. 2003. *Army of Roses: Inside the World of Palestinian Women Suicide Bombers*. Emmaus, PA: Rodale Books.

Victor, Daniel. 2017. "Hackers Threaten 'Game of Thrones' as HBO Confirms Cyberattack." *New York Times*, July 31. Retrieved August 2, 2017 (https://www.nytimes.com/2017/07/31/business/media/hbo-hack-game-of-thrones.html).

Vidal, John. 2017. "From Heatwaves to Hurricanes, Floods to Famine: Seven Climate Change Hotspots." *The Guardian*, June 23. Retrieved July 26, 2017 (https://www.theguardian.com/environment/2017/jun/23/from-heatwaves-to-hurricanes-floods-to-famine-seven-climate-change-hotspots).

Vijayakumar, Gowri. 2012. "Girls and Education: A Global Approach." May 20. Retrieved January 28, 2013 (www.socwomen.org/web/images/stories/resources/fact_sheets/fact_2_2012-girlseducation.pdf).

Vinograd, Cassandra. 2013. "Teen Pregnancy: 7.3 Million Teenage Births in Developing World, UN Says." Retrieved March 12, 2014 (www.huffingtonpost.com/2013/10/30/teen-pregnancy-developing-world_n_4176898.html).

Wade, Lisa. 2012. "The New Elite: Attributing Privilege and Class vs. Merit." *Sociological Images: Inspiring Sociological Imaginations Everywhere*, June 21. Retrieved September 14, 2012 (http://thesocietypages.org/socimages/2012/06/21/the-new-elite-attributing-privilege-to-class-vs-merit/).

Walden, Rachel. 2013. "CIR Prison Investigation Opens Another Chapter on Sterilization of Women in U.S." *Our Bodies Ourselves*, July 10. Retrieved July 21, 2017 (http://www.ourbodiesourselves.org/2013/07/cir-prison-investigation-opens-another-chapter-on-sterilization-of-women-in-u-s/).

Walk Free Foundation. 2018. "The Global Slavery Index 2018." Retrieved September 3, 2018 (https://www.globalslaveryindex.org/2018/findings/highlights/).

Wall Street Journal. 2016. "Why It's Hard to Shatter Japan's Glass Ceiling." May 16. Retrieved May 24, 2017 (http://www.wsj.com/video/why-its-hard-to-shatter-japans-glass-ceiling/2D85643F-3C76-4211-BEE5-CF88D183C36C.html).

The Wallace Foundation. 2013. "The School Principal as Leader: Guiding Schools to Better Teaching and Learning." January. Retrieved March 14, 2018 (http://www.wallacefoundation.org/knowledge-center/Documents/The-School-Principal-as-Leader-Guiding-Schools-to-Better-Teaching-and-Learning-2nd-Ed.pdf).

Wallenstein, Peter. 2002. *Tell the Court I Love My Wife: Race, Marriage, and Law: An American History*. New York: Macmillan.

Wallerstein, Immanuel. 1974. *The Modern World System*. New York: Academic Press.

Walters, Glenn D. 2015. "The Decision to Commit Crime: Rational or Nonrational?" *Criminology, Criminal Justice Law, and Society* 16(3):1–18.

Walters, Joanna. 2015. "Tablets and Smartphones May Affect Social and Emotional Development, Scientists Speculate." *The Guardian*, February 2. Retrieved August 30, 2015 (www.theguardian.com/technology/2015/feb/01/toddler-brains-research-smartphones-damage-social-development).

Wan, William. 2017. "America's New Tobacco Crisis: The Rich Stopped Smoking, The Poor Didn't." *Washington Post*, June 13. Retrieved June 22, 2017 (https://www.washingtonpost.com/national/americas-new-tobacco-crisis-the-rich-stopped-smoking-the-poor-didnt/2017/06/13/a63b42ba-4c8c-11e7-9669-250d0b15f83b_story.html?utm_term=.0dbd6f5e0ad4).

Wang, Julia and Morgan Currier. 2015. "Students Force 16 Universities to End Sweatshop Contracts." *Popular Resistance*, February 3. Retrieved February 10, 2016 (www.popularresistance.org/students-force-16-universities-to-end-sweatshop-contracts/).

War Child. 2014. "Child Soldier: Some Words Don't Belong Together." Retrieved August 21, 2014 (www.warchild.org.uk/issues/child-soldiers?gclid=CJ_78cL7bYCFSdgMgod11wAmQ).

Ward, Martha, and Monica Edelstein. 2016. *A World Full of Women*, 6th ed. London: Routledge: Taylor & Francis Group.

Warner, R. Stephen. 1993. "Work in Progress Toward a New Paradigm for the Sociological Study of Religion in the United States." *American Journal of Sociology* 98(5):1044–1093.

WaterAid. 2013. "Precipitation for Education." Retrieved February 10, 2013 (www.wateraid.org/other/Print.asp).

WaterAid. 2016. "Facts and Statistics." Retrieved February 19, 2018 (https://www.wateraid.org/us/facts-and-statistics).

WaterAid. 2017. "As Children Around the World Go Back to School, One in Three Have No Clean Water or Toilets." September 4. Retrieved February 18, 2018 (www.wateraid.org/us/media/as-children-around-the-world-go-back-to-school-one-in-three-have-no-clean-water-or-toilets).

WaterAid. 2018. "Why WaterAid." Retrieved June 7, 2018 (https://www.wateraid.org/us/why-wateraid).

Waters, Tony. 2012. *Schooling, Childhood, and Bureaucracy: Bureaucratizing the Child*. Basingstoke, UK: Palgrave Macmillan.

Watson Institute International & Public Affairs. 2017. "Costs of War." Retrieved February 10, 2018 (Watson.brown.edu/costofwar/;http://news.brown.edu/articles/2017/11/costssummary).

Watts, Jonathan. 2012. "Air Pollution Could Become China's Biggest Health Threat, Expert Warns." *The Guardian*, March 16. Retrieved August 2, 2012 (www.guardian.co.uk/environment/2012/mar/16/air-pollution-biggest-threat-china).

Way, Niobe. 2011. *Deep Secrets: Boys' Friendships and the Crisis of Connection*. Cambridge, MA: Harvard University Press.

Wearewater. 2017. "Resilient Bolivia, an Example to Overcome the Water Crisis." March 10. Retrieved February 18, 2018 (www.wearewater.org/en/resilient-bolivia-an-example-to-overcome-the-water-crisis_280381).

Weaver, Janelle. 2010. "Social Life Starts in the Womb." *Science*, October 12. Retrieved October 19, 2010 (http://news.sciencemag.org/sciencenow/2010/10/scienceshot-social-life-starts-in.html?rss=1&utm_source=twitterfeed&utm_medium=twitter).

Weaver, Mary Anne. 2015. "Her Majesty's Jihadist." *New York Times Magazine*, April 14. Retrieved November 19, 2015 (www.nytimes.com/2015/04/19/magazine/her-majestys-jihadist.html?_r=0).

Weber, Max. 1946. *From Max Weber: Essays in Sociology*, translated and edited by Hans H. Gerth and C. Wright Mills. New York: Oxford University Press.

Weber, Max. 1947. *The Theory of Social and Economic Organization*, translated and edited by A. M. Henderson and Talcott Parsons. New York: Oxford University Press.

Weber, Max. [1904–1905] 1958. *The Protestant Ethic and the Spirit of Capitalism*, translated by Talcott Parsons. New York: Scribner.

Weinberg, George. 1972. *Society and the Healthy Homosexual*. New York: St. Martin's Press.

Weiss, Gregory L. and Lynne E. Lonnquist. 2015. *The Sociology of Health, Healing, and Illness*, 7th ed. Englewood Cliffs, NJ: Prentice Hall.

Weiss, Robin Elise. 2010. "Pregnancy and Childbirth." Retrieved January 9, 2010 (pregnancy.about.com/od/cesareansections/ss/cesarian.htm).

Weissmann, Jordan. 2014. "Americans Have No Idea How Bad Inequality Really Is." *Slate*, September 26. Retrieved April 8, 2016 (www.slate.com/articles/business/moneybox/2014/09/americans_have_no_idea_how_bad_inequality_is_new_harvard_business_school.html).

Wells, Amy Stuart and Jeannie Oakes. 1996. "Potential Pitfalls of Systemic Reform: Early Lessons from Research on Detracking." *Sociology of Education* 69(Extra Issue):135–43.

Wells, Cheryl. 2008. "Suns, Moons, Clocks, and Bells: Native Americans and Time." USC History Seminar, December, SOS 250, Department of History, University of Wyoming.

Wendling, Elodie, Timothy B. Kellison, and Michael Sagas. 2018. "A Conceptual Examination of College Athletes' Role Conflict Through the Lens of Conservation of Resources Theory." *Quest* 70(1):28–47.

Wessinger, Catherine. 2000. *How the Millennium Comes Violently: From Jonestown to Heaven's Gate*. New York: Seven Bridges.

West, Candace and Don H. Zimmerman. 1987. "Doing Gender." *Gender and Society* 1(2):125–51.

Whitham, Monica M. 2017. "Paying it Forward and Getting It Back: The Benefits of Shared Social Identity in Generalized Exchange." *Sociological Perspectives* 61(1):81–98.

Whorf, Benjamin Lee. 1956. *Language, Thought, and Reality*. New York: John Wiley.

Whoriskey, Peter and Dan Keating. 2015. "The Business of Hospice." *Washington Post*, December 26. Retrieved June 30, 2015 (www.washingtonpost.com/business/economy/2014/12/26/a7d90438-692f-11e4-b053-65cea7903f2e_story.html).

Whyte, William H. 1956. *The Organization Man*. New York: Simon and Schuster.

Wike, Richard, Bruce Stokes, and Jacob Poushter. 2015. "America's Global Image." *Pew Research Center*, June 23. Retrieved August 29, 2015 (www.pewglobal.org/2015/06/23/1-americas-global-image/).

Wikipedia. 2018. "Cousin Marriage Law in the United States by State." Retrieved August 29, 2018 (https://en.wikipedia.org/wiki/Cousin_marriage_law_in_the_United_States_by_state).

Wilcox, Bradford W. and Wendy Wang. 2017. "The Marriage Divide." *American Enterprise Institute*, September 25. Retrieved September 25, 2017 (http://www.aei.org/wp-content/uploads/2017/09/The-Marriage-Divide.pdf).

Williams, Brian K., Stacey C. Sawyer, and Carl M. Wahlstrom. 2017. *Marriages, Families, and Intimate Relationships*, 3rd ed. Boston: Allyn & Bacon.

Williams, Christine L. 2013. "The Glass Escalator, Revisited: Gender Inequality in Neoliberal Times." *Gender and Society* 27(5):609–29.

William, Julius Wilson. 1996. *When Work Disappears: The World of the New Urban Poor*. New York: Knopf.

Williams, Pete. 2017. "Supreme Court Rejects Gavin Grimm's Transgender Bathroom Rights Case." *New York Times*, March 6. Retrieved May 17, 2017 (http://www.nbcnews.com/news/us-news/u-s-supreme-court-rejects-transgender-rights-case-n729556).

Williams, Robin Murphy, Jr. 1970. *American Society: A Sociological Interpretation*, 3rd ed. New York: Alfred Knopf.

Williams, Timothy. 2018. "Inside a Private Prison: Blood, Suicide, and Poorly Paid Guards." *New York Times*, April 3. Retrieved April 4, 2018 (https://www.nytimes.com/2018/04/03/us/mississippi-private-prison-abuse.html).

Willige, Andrea. 2016. "The World's Top Economy: The US vs China in Five Charts." *World Economic Forum*, December 5. Retrieved June 14, 2017 (https://www.weforum.org/agenda/2016/12/the-world-s-top-economy-the-us-vs-china-in-five-charts/).

Willis, Paul. 1979. *Learning to Labor: How Working Class Kids Get Working Class Jobs*. Aldershot, Hampshire, England: Saxon House.

Wilson, Edward O. 1978. "What Is Sociobiology?" Pp. 1–12 in *Sociobiology and Human Nature: An Interdisciplinary Critique and Defense*, edited by Michael S. Gregory, Anita Silvers, and Diane Sutch. San Francisco: Jossey-Bass.

Wilson, Edward O. 1980. *Sociobiology*. Cambridge, MA: Belknap.

Wilson, Edward O. 2000. *Sociobiology: The New Synthesis*, Twenty-fifth anniversary ed. Cambridge, MA: Harvard University Press.

Wilson, Edward O. 2012. *The Social Conquest of Earth*. New York: Liveright.

Wilson, Kate, Vlad Lavrov, Martina Keller, Thomas Jajer, and Gerard Ryle. 2012. "Skin, Bones and Tissue for Sale: How the Dead Are Being Used for Grisly Trade in Human Body Parts." *Daily Mail*, July 17. Retrieved August 2, 2012 (www.dailymail.co.uk/news/article-2175006/Skin-bones-tissue-sale-How-dead-used-grisly-trade-human-body-parts.html).

Wilson, Megan. 2012. "Big Business Sides with Obama on Affirmative Action Case Before High Court." *The Hill*, October 28. Retrieved May 31, 2013 (http://thehill.com/homenews/administration/264329-big-business-sides-with-obama-on-affirmative-action-case-before-supreme-court).

Wilson, Reid. 2015. "In Major Cities, Murder Rates Drop Precipitously." *Washington Post*, January 2. Retrieved June 7, 2015 (www.washingtonpost.com/blogs/govbeat/wp/2015/01/02/in-major-cities-murder-rates-drop-precipitously/).

Wilson, Warren H. 1924. "What the Automobile Has Done to and for the Country Church." *Annals of the American Academy of Political and Social Science* 116(November):85–6.

Winders, Bill. 2004. "Changing Racial Inequality: The Rise and Fall of Systems of Racial Inequality in the U.S." Paper presented at the Annual Meeting of the American Sociological Association, San Francisco.

Winslow, Robert W. and Sheldon X. Zhang. 2008. *Criminology: A Global Perspective*. Upper Saddle River, NJ: Pearson Prentice Hall.

Wirth, Louis. 1964. "Urbanism as a Way of Life." *American Journal of Sociology* 44(1):1–24.

Witherell, Sharon. 2016. "Open Doors 2016 Executive Summary." Retrieved May 7, 2017 (https://www.iie.org/Why-IIE/Announcements/2016-11-14-Open-Doors-Executive-Summary).

Witness for Peace. 2016. "Free Trade Agreements." Retrieved February 10, 2016 (www.witnessforpeace.org/section.php?id=99).

Wolff, K., and J. Holmes. 2011. "Linguistic Relativity." *Wiley Interdisciplinary Reviews: Cognitive Science* 2(3):253–65.

Wong, Alia. 2015. "Where Girls Are Missing Out on High-School Sports." *The Atlantic*, June 26. Retrieved September 4, 2015 (www.theatlantic.com/education/archive/2015/06/girls-high-school-sports-inequality/396782/).

Wood, Graeme. 2015. "What ISIS Really Wants." *The Atlantic*, March. Retrieved September 13, 2015 (www.theatlantic.com/magazine/archive/2015/03/what-isis-really-wants/384980/).

Wood, Julia. 2008. *Gendered Lives: Communication, Gender, and Culture*, 8th ed. Belmont, CA: Wadsworth.

Wood, Julia T. and Nina M. Reich. 2006. "Gendered Communication Styles." Pp. 177–86 in *Intercultural Communication*, 11th ed., edited by Larry A. Samovar, Richard E. Porter, and Edwin R. McDaniel. Belmont, CA: Wadsworth.

Woodward, J. R. 2004. "Professional Football Scouts: An Investigation of Racial Stacking." *Sociology of Sport Journal* 21(4):356–75.

World Atlas. 2017. "10 Countries that Could Disappear with Global Warming." Retrieved July 18, 2017 (http://www.worldatlas.com/articles/10-countries-that-could-disappear-with-global-warming.html).

World Bank. 2016. "Individuals Using the Internet, Users (% of Population)." Retrieved August 30, 2018 (https://data.worldbank.org/indicator/IT.NET.USER.ZS?view=map).

World Bank. 2017a. "Population Density (People per sq. km of Land Area)." Retrieved July 20, 2017 (http://data.worldbank.org/indicator/EN.POP.DNST).

World Bank. 2017b. "Educating Girls, Ending Child Marriage." August 24. Retrieved November 16, 2017 (http://www.worldbank.org/en/news/immersive-story/2017/08/22/educating-girls-ending-child-marriage).

World Bank. 2018a. "Intentional Homicides (per 100,000 People)." Retrieved September 1, 2018 (http://data.worldbank.org/indicator/VC.IHR.PSRC.P5?view=map).

World Bank. 2018b. "GNI, Atlas Method (Current US$)." Retrieved September 3, 2018 (https://data.worldbank.org/indicator/NY.GNP.PCAP.PP.CD?view=map).

World Christian Database. 2015. "World Religion at Your Fingertips." Retrieved December 14, 2015 (www.worldchristiandatabase.org/wcd/).

World Economic Forum. 2015. "The Global Information Technology Report 2015." Retrieved June 11, 2015 (http://reports.weforum.org/global-information-technology-report-2015/report-highlights/#keyfindings).

World Economic Forum. 2017. "The Global Gender Gap Report 2017." Retrieved September 6, 2018 (http://www3.weforum.org/docs/WEF_GGGR_2017.pdf).

World Factbook. 2014. "China." Retrieved September 15, 2014 (https://www.cia.gov/library/publications/the-worldfactbook/geos/ch.html).

World Factbook. 2015. "China: People and Society." Retrieved July 6, 2015 (www.cia.gov/library/publications/resources/the-world-factbook/geos/sn.html).

World Factbook. 2017a. "Africa: Chad." Retrieved July 24, 2017 (https://www.cia.gov/library/publications/the-world-factbook/geos/cd.html).

World Factbook. 2017b. "Country Comparison: GDP per Capita." Retrieved February 18, 2018 (https://www.cia.gov/library/publications/the-world-factbook/rankorder/2004rank.html).

World Factbook. 2017c. "Country Comparison: Infant Mortality Rate." Retrieved February 18, 2018 (https://www.cia.gov/library/publications/the-world-factbook/rankorder/2091rank.html).

World Factbook. 2017d. "Country Comparison: Life Expectancy at Birth." Retrieved February 18, 2018 (https://www.cia.gov/library/publications/the-world-factbook/rankorder/2102rank.html).

World Factbook. 2017e. "Field Listing: Dependency Ratios." Retrieved July 20, 2017 (https://www.cia.gov/library/publications/resources/the-world-factbook/fields/2261.html).

World Factbook. 2017f. "Field Listing: Life Expectancy at Birth." Retrieved July 20, 2017 (https://www.cia.gov/library/publications/resources/the-world-factbook/fields/2102.html#138).

World Factbook. 2017g. "Urbanization." Retrieved July 24, 2017 (https://www.cia.gov/library/publications/resources/the-world-factbook/fields/2212.html#228).

World Famine Timeline. 2016. "Famine." Retrieved April 4, 2016 (www.mapreport.com/subtopics/d/0.html#2013).

World Health Organization. 2011. "The Top 10 Causes of Death." Retrieved August 29, 2012 (www.who.int/mediacentre/factsheets/fs310/en/index.html).

World Health Organization. 2013a. "Antimicrobial Resistance." *Fact Sheet 194*, May. Retrieved March 10, 2014 (www.who.int/mediacentre/factsheets/fs194/en/).

World Health Organization. 2013b. "Urban Population Growth." Retrieved July 1, 2013 (www.forbes.com/sites/joelkotkin/2013/03/18/americas-fastest-and-slowest-growing-cities/).

World Health Organization. 2014. "The Top 10 Causes of Death." Retrieved May 28, 2014 (www.who.int/mediacentre/factsheets/fs310/en/index1.html).

World Health Organization. 2017. *The Bill China Cannot Afford: Health, Economic and Social Costs of China's Tobacco Epidemic.* Manila, Philippines: World Health Organization Regional Office for the Western Pacific. Retrieved June 22, 2017 (http://www.wpro.who.int/china/publications/2017_china_tobacco_control_report_en.pdf?ua=1).

World Health Organization. 2018. "The Top Ten Causes of Death." May 24. Retrieved June 6, 2018 (http://www.who.int/news-room/fact-sheets/detail/the-top-10-causes-of-death).

World of Children. 2012. "Craig Kielburger: The Power of Youth." October 18. Retrieved March 30, 2018 (https://worldofchildren.org/craig-kielburger-the-power-of-youth).

WorldWideLearn. 2007. "Guide to College Majors in Sociology." Retrieved June 23, 2008 (www.worldwidelearn.com/online-education-guide/social-science/sociology-major.htm).

Wyss, Jim. 2018. "How Many Venezuelans Have Crossed the Border? Colombia Is Counting." *Miami Herald*, April 6. Retrieved May 31, 2018 (http://www.miamiherald.com/news/nation-world/world/americas/colombia/article208083819.html).

Yablonski, Lewis. 1959. "The Gang as a Near-Group." *Social Problems* 7(Fall):108–17.

Yamamoto, Yoko. 2015. "Gender and Social Class Differences in Japanese Mothers' Beliefs About Children's Education and Socialization." *Gender and Education* 28(1):72–88.

Yamane, David. 1997. "Secularization on Trial: In Defense of a Neosecularization Paradigm." *Journal for the Scientific Study of Religion* 36(1):109–22.

Yamane, David. 2007. "Civil Religion." Pp. 506–507 in *The Blackwell Encyclopedia of Sociology*, Vol. II, edited by George Ritzer. Oxford: Blackwell.

Yeginsu, Ceylan. 2017. "Slavery Ensares Thousands in U.K. Here's One Girl's Story." *New York Times*, November 18. Retrieved November 19, 2017 (https://www.nytimes.com/2017/11/18/world/europe/uk-modern-slavery.html?smprod=nytcore-ipad&smid=nytcore-ipad-share&_r=0).

Yehuda, Rachel, Nikolaos P. Daskalakis, Linda M. Bierer, Heather N. Bader, Torsten Klengel, Holsboer Florian, and Elisabeth B. Binder. 2015. "Holocaust Exposure Induced Intergenerational Effects on FKBP5 Methylation." *Biological Psychiatry*, August 6. Retrieved November 16, 2015 (www.biologicalpsychiatryjournal.com/article/S0006-3223(15)00652-6/abstract).

Yinger, Milton J. 1960. "Contraculture and Subculture." *American Sociological Review* 25(October):625–35.

Yoon, Mi Yung. 2011a. "More Women in the Tanzanian Legislature: Do Numbers Matter?" *Journal of Contemporary African Studies* 29(January):83–98.

Yoon, Mi Yung. 2011b. "Factors Hindering 'Larger' Representation of Women in Parliament: The Case of Seychelles." *Commonwealth and Comparative Politics* 49(February):98–114.

Yu, Tianyi, Gregory S. Pettit, Jennifer E. Lansford, Kenneth A. Dodge, and John E. Bates. 2010. "The Interactive Effects of Marital Conflict and Divorce on Parent–Adult Children's Relationships." *Journal of Marriage and Family* 72(2): 282–92.

Yukich, Grace. 2013. *One Family Under God: Immigration Politics and Progressive Religion in America*. New York: Oxford University Press.

Zahniser, Steven, Sahar Angadjivand, and Thomas Hertz. 2015. "NAFTA at 20: With Regional Trade Liberalization Complete, Focus Shifts to Other Methods of Deepening Economic Integration." U.S. *Department of Agriculture*, April 6. Retrieved February 10, 2016 (www.ers.usda.gov/amber-waves/2015-april/nafta-at-20-with-regional-trade-liberalization-complete,-focus-shifts-to-other-methods-of-deepening-economic-integration.aspx).

Zaidi, Tariq. 2017. "In Pictures: The Men Competing for Love in the Deserts of Chad." February 27. Retrieved March 15, 2018 (www.bbc.com/news/world-africa-39070587).

Zaimov, Stoyan. 2013. "African Anglicans Say Gay Bishops Affirmation Shatters Hopes of Reconciliation." *The Christian World*, January 10. Retrieved July 12, 2013 (www.christianpost .com/news/african-anglicans-say-gay-bishops-affirmation-shatters-hopes-of-reconciliation-88038/).

Zajda, Joseph, ed. 2015. *Globalisation, Ideology and Politics of Education Reform*. Heidelberg, Switzerland: Springer.

Zapotosky, Matt, and Chico Harlan. 2016. "Justice Department Says It Will End Use of Private Prisons." *Washington Post*, August 18. Retrieved September 19, 2016 (www.washingtonpost.com/news/post-nation/wp/2016/08/18/justice-department-says-it-will-end-use-of-private-prisons/?utm_term=.b3a308b2daa7).

Zborowski, Mark. 1952. "Cultural Components in Response to Pain." *Journal of Social Issues* 8(4):16–30.

Zdan, Rick. 2017. "Pluralism." In *The Cambridge Handbook of Sociology*, edited by Kathleen Odell Korgen. Cambridge, England: Cambridge University Press.

Zeleny, Jeff. 2009. "Obama Vows, 'We Will Rebuild' and 'Recover.'" *New York Times*, February 25. Retrieved February 25, 2009 (www.nytimes.com/2009/02/25/us/politics/25 obama.html?scp=1&sq=obama%20vows%20we%20will%20 rebuild&st=cse).

Zhang, Qiang, Xujia Jiang, Dan Tong, Steven J. Davis, Hongyan Zhao, Guannan Geng, Tong Feng, Bo Zheng, Zifeng Lu, David G. Streets, Ruijing Ni, Michael Brauer, Aaron van Donkelaar, Randall V. Martin, Hong Huo, Zhu Liu, Da Pan, Haidong Kan, Yingying Yan, Jintai Lin, Kebin He, and Dabo Guan. 2017. "Transboundary Health Impacts of Transported Global Air Pollution and International Trade." *Nature* 543:705–9.

Zimbardo, Philip C. 2004. "Power Turns Good Soldiers into 'Bad Apples.'" *Boston Globe*, May 9. Retrieved July 5, 2008 (www.boston.com/news/globe/editorial_opinion/oped/artic les/2004/05/09/power_turns_good_soldiers_into_bad_apples).

Zimbardo, Philip C., Craig Haney, Curtis Banks, and David Jaffe. 1973. "The Mind Is a Formidable Jailer: A Pirandellian Prison." *New York Times*, April 8:38–60.

INDEX

Binge drinking, 9 (photo)
Binge eating, 151
bin Laden, Osama, 415
Biosocial theories, 94
Bird flu, 429
Birthrates, 316
    among teens, 335, 335 (figure)
    decline in, 459
    in demographic transition, 465
    See also Fertility
Births, to married and unmarried women,
        309 (table)
Bisexual, 256
Black (color), racism and negative images of,
        79, 79 (photo)
Black Lives Matter, 229, 231, 240, 250
Black men
    economic inequality experienced by, 225
    in public sphere, 100
Black Panther (film), 265 (photo)
Blacks
    collective Black, 227
    defining who is black, 222
    immigrants as part of Black population in U.S., 227 (figure)
    pulled over for driving while Black, 224, 225 (photo)
    social mobility and, 225
    See also Whites
Blame the victims of poverty, 310
Body images, gender expectations and, 280
Body language, of women, 270 (photo)
Body parts, global trade in, 446–447
Body time, 73
Boeing, 173
Boko Haram, 84, 96, 345, 415
Bolivia, public water system and, 518
Bonilla-Silva, Eduardo, 226
Books, banned, 334, 334 (table)
"Boomer echo," 471
Borders, war and protection of, 412
Border wall, Mexican-U.S., 244 (photo)
Boston Marathon bombing, 5, 5 (photo), 111, 161
Boston (Massachusetts), as postindustrial city, 481, 482
BosWash, 482
Botswana Bushmen, 62 (photo)
Bourgeoisie, 35–36, 192, 405
Boy code, 261, 262
Boys
    educational attainment of, 328
    gender socialization of, 261, 262
    steroid use, 264
Boys and Girls Clubs, 177
BRAC, 394
Brahman, 206
Brazil
    favela in, 28, 28 (photo), 33, 36, 39
Brazil, voting in, 397 (photo)
Bread for the World, 394, 418
Breastfeeding babies at work, 268–269
Bribery, 167
Bride burnings, 277
"Bring Back Our Girls" protest (Nigeria), 415 (photo)
Brown haze, 466 (photo)

Buddhism/Buddhists
    branches of, 361
    future trends in population of, 377
    number of (global), 356 (figure)
Buddhist monks, 65 (photo), 354 (photo)
Buffalo Creek disaster, 503
Buffett, Warren, 209
Bureaucracies, 133–138, 133 (figure)
    characteristics of, 135–136
    defined, 133–134
    issues in, 136–138
    religious, 355
    school, 332–333
Bureau of Justice Statistics, 158
Bush, George W., 400, 404, 464, 500
Businesses, profiting from war, 413
Bustees, 483
Bystander sexual harassment training, 269

CAFTA-DR (Dominican Republic-Central America
        Free Trade Agreement), 500
Cairo (Egypt), homeless migrants in City of the Dead,
        482, 483 (photo)
Calhoun, John, 221
Calling (religious), 367
Calvinist Puritan movement, 361
Cambodia
    crowded transportation in, 468 (photo)
    Khmer Rouge, 403
Canada
    Canadian health care model, 438
    decline in religious influence in, 374
    demographic changes and religious landscape in, 377
    men taking parental leave in, 311
    as national society, 83
Canada, Geoffrey, 344
Cape Town (South Africa), brown haze over, 466 (photo)
Capitalism, 35–36, 404–406
    deviance and, 155
    Protestant ethic and, 367–368
    state, 406
Capitalists, 192
Capital punishment, 173–174
CARE International, 116, 214
Carpiano, Richard, 447, 449
Carter, Jimmy, 231
Cartwright, Edmund, 64 (figure)
Casky, Cameron, 508
Caste systems, 205–206
Castro brothers (Fidel and Raul), 402
Catholic Relief Services, 384
Caucuses, 409
Causality, 41, 42
Causation, 40
Cause-and-effect relationships, 42
Celestial burial master, 105 (photo)
Cell phones, 67, 109, 112, 120
    smartphones, 120, 212, 263
Census questionnaires, 43 (photo)
Central Park (New York City), 480 (photo)
Cesarean section surgery, rise in rate of, 430
Chad, life expectancy in, 472

Kenneavy, Kristin, 50
Kenya
    impact of smartphones in, 212
    schoolgirls in, 340 (photo)
Khaldun, Ibn, 29
Khan Academy, 341
Khmer Rouge, 403
Kidneys, sale of, 447, 447 (photo)
Kielburger, Craig, 92
Kielburger, Marc, 92
Kielburger, Theresa, 92
Kigali Genocide Memorial, 414
"Killer apps," 69
Killing fields (Cambodia), 403
Killing Fields Museum, 414
Kim Jong-un, 402
Kimmel, Jimmy, 442
Kindergarten, 329
King, Martin Luther, Jr., 146, 240, 366
Kirk, David, 114–115
Kiva, 141, 214
Koch, Charles, 209
Koch, David, 209
Kony, Joseph, 96
Korean War Memorial, 414
Kosher food preparation rules, 356, 359
Kosovo, 407
Kshatriyas, 206
Ku Klux Klan, 229
!Kung people, 61–62
Kyoto Protocol, 500

Labeling theory, 149–150
    on health and illness, 427
Labor unions, 406
Lake Mead National Recreation Area, 502 (photo)
Lan, Doi, 428 (photo)
Lancaster, Bill, 163
Land-ocean temperature index, 486 (figure)
Language
    in college classroom, 32
    defined, 77
    as foundation of culture, 77–78
    gender and use of, 258
    nonverbal, 74 (photo), 78, 123–124
    role-taking and, 101
    social stratification and, 189
    spoken, 78
    symbolic interaction theory and, 31
    world's most spoken, 78 (figure)
    written, 78
Language barriers, for parents of schoolchildren, 333
Laos, digital divide and, 212 (photo)
La Raza Unida, 240
Lareau, Annette, 310
Latent functions, 34
    of education, 337, 337 (table)
Latin America, changes in urban and rural population as proportion
        of total population, 484 (figure)
Latinos, 222
    See also Hispanics
Laughter, Albert, 358 (photo)

Laws
    defined, 77
    to improve group relations, 244
    interracial marriage, 147
    no-fault divorce, 314
    same-sex marriage, 147
    on sexual orientation, 278 (figure)
    Sharia, 267, 470
    U.S. immigration, 473–474
Leaders
    gaining legitimate power, 391–393
    influence on social change, 502–503
    in planned change in organizations, 513
Leadership Conference on Civil and Human Rights, 250
Leadership development in schools, gender inequality in, 265–267
Leadership roles, 388
Learned helplessness, 149
Lee, Ann, 393
Left wing terrorist groups, 166 (table)
Legitimacy of power, 390–394
Lenski, Gerhard, 193, 506
Lesbian clergy, 381
Levels of analysis, 12, 16–19
    education and, 17 (table)
    macro-level analysis, 18–19
    meso-level analysis, 17–18
    micro-level analysis, 17
    social world model and, 43 (figure)
Levin, Jack, 162, 163
LGBTQIA people, 277–279
LGBTQIA students
    climate for, 326
    LGBTQIA-friendly student organizations, 326 (photo)
Libertarian Party, 418
Life chances
    of Black men, 225
    individual, 194–195
Life expectancy
    at birth, 441 (figure)
    in Chad, 472
    defined, 459
    individual life chances and, 194–195
    rise in, 103–104
    in selected poor and rich countries, 196 (table)
Lifeline Express train (China), 445
Lifestyles, 195–197
    defined, 195
Linguistic relativity theory, 78
LinkedIn, 110 (figure), 122
Linnaeus, 221
Literacy, 322
    global literacy rates, 322, 323 (figure)
Living will, 422
Local schools, 323–331
    individuals within, 324–325
    local community influences on, 334–335
Locke, John, 396
Lohan, Lindsay, 511 (photo)
Long childhood, 94–95
Looking-glass self, 98–101, 99 (figure)
    obesity and, 151
    race and, 221

Multiracial populations, 226–227
  percentage of multiracial U.S. adults, 228 (figure)
Mumbai, homeless in, 478 (photo)
Munoz, Marlise, 422
Murder rate, 168, 169 (figure)
Murdock, George, 306–307
Muslim Americans, hate crimes against, 161, 228
Muslims
  anti-Muslim sentiment following 9/11, 371
  arranged marriage and, 303
  face covering by women, 255 (photo)
  growth in number of, 377
  number of (global), 356 (figure)
  prayer ritual, 352
  suspicions of for maintaining international networks of
      faithful, 366
  wearing of hijab, 275, 345 (photo), 357
  See also Islam
Myanmar (Burma), protest march in, 408 (photo)
Myrdal, Gunnar, 74
Myths, 358–359
  defined, 358

NAFTA (North American Free Trade Agreement),
    500–501
Names for children, gender socialization and, 261
Nassar, Larry, 269
National Association for the Advancement of Colored People
    (NAACP), 36, 141, 240
National Basketball Association (NBA), 133
National Computer Forensics Institute, 168
National crime, 166–169
National Crime Victimization Survey (NCVS), 158
National culture, 83
National Day of Action Fight for $15 protest, 514 (photo)
National family issues, 312–315
National Football League (NFL)
  NFL players kneeling during national anthem, 240, 367
  racial stereotypes in, 232, 233
National health care issues, 440–450
National health care systems, 436–438
Nationalism, 407–408
  religion and, 379
Nationalist terror groups, 166 (table)
National level, social change at, 498–501
National-level influences on schools, 335–336
National networks, 138–139
National Organization for Women (NOW), 284
National organizations/institutions, 5–6
National Origins Act of 1924, 474
National parliaments, nations with highest percentage of women in,
    259, 260 (table)
National Rifle Association (NRA), 394
National society, defined, 15
Nation of Islam, 361
Nation-state, 6
  exercise of power and, 389, 407–408
Native Alaskan language, 78–79
Native Americans
  concepts of time and, 72–73
  discrimination faced by, 224–225, 224 (figure)
  endogamy among, 302

forced assimilation in boarding schools, 237
  social mobility and, 225
Natural disasters
  loss events worldwide, 18, 18 (figure)
  social change and, 501–502
  See also individual events
Natural family planning (NFP), 470
Natural resource management in Global South, 515
Natural sciences, 9
Nature *vs.* nurture, 93–94
Nauru, 508
Navajo medicine man, 358 (photo)
Nazi Germany, religious opposition to, 365
Negative sanctions, 107
Negotiation, to avoid war, 414
Neo-Nazi hate groups, 229
Neo-Pagans, 364
Nepalese family, 296 (photo)
Netflix, 311
Netherlands, health care in, 437
Netsilik Inuits
  myth, 358
  religious beliefs of, 352
Networking via Facebook, 123
New American Schools, 346
Newcomen, Thomas, 64 (figure)
NEW Leadership National Network at the Center for American
    Women and Politics, 284
New Orleans, effect of Hurricane Katrina on, 487, 488
New religious movements (NRMs), 355, 362–363
New towns, 482
Nichols, Terry, 416
Nielsen, Kirstjen, 167
Nigeria
  ancestor worship in, 352
  "Bring Back Our Girls" protest, 415 (photo)
  schoolgirl kidnapping in, 96, 415
Nike, 12, 498
No-fault divorce, 314, 315–316
Nolan, Patrick, 506
Nonconformity, cities and tolerance for, 480
Nongovernmental organizations (NGOs), 64, 394, 500
Nongovernmental peace organizations, 414
Nonhuman Rights Project, 516
Nonmaterial culture, 74–79
Nonverbal communication, 74 (photo)
  culture and, 123–124
  defined, 123
Nonverbal language, 78
Nonviolent resistance, 240
Norms
  bureaucracy and, 136
  defined, 76
  definition of family and, 295
  governing choice of marriage partners, 301–303
  guiding behavior, 123
  religion and legitimization of, 369
  school, 328
  violations of, 77 (table)
North America, changes in urban and rural population as
    proportion of total population, 484 (figure)
Northern Ireland, religious conflict in, 366

defined as deviant, 146
in education system, 325–328
individual, 194–197
institutions, organizations and individual, 133 (figure)
master, 128
role and, 128–129
of sick person, 431–435
types of status relationships, 127 (figure)
Status assignment, family and, 298
Status inconsistency, 197, 207
Status set, 127, 129 (figure)
STEM, gender gap in, 265
Stem cell research, religious group opposition to, 501
Stephenson, George, 65 (figure)
Stereotypes
about Black men, 100
gender, 260
of Roma people, 245
Steroid use, boys and media message about, 264
Stickball, 186 (photo)
Stigmas, 39
Stigmatize, labels that, 150
Stigmatizing fatness, 151
Stoneman Douglas High School shooting, 5, 424, 508
Stonewall, 516
Strain
rise of social movements and, 516
social change and, 501, 506, 513
Strain theory, 154, 154 (figure)
coping strategies in schools and, 331
on occupational crime, 164–165
Stratification systems, 205–207
Streaming, 341, 343
"Street people," 149
Street protests, 153 (photo)
Stress, social change and, 501, 513
Stress-coping strategies, role conflict and, 129
Strict affirmative action, 245–246
Structural conduciveness, collective behavior and, 509
Structural-functional theories of deviance
anomie, 153–154
social control theory, 152–153
strain theory, 154
Structural-functional theory, 34–35, 39 (figure)
critique of, 35
on dominant-minority group relations, 241
on family, 297–299
on gender stratification, 273–274
on justice system, 169
at meso and macro levels, 86
on power and privilege, 390
on social change, 504
on socialization, 97
on social stratification, 190–191
Structural strain, collective behavior and, 509
Structural-strain theory, 509
Structural system, religion as, 353, 354–355
Students
cultural and social capital and first-generation, 204
labeling of, 322
social stratification and college prep, 189
stratification and tracking, 341–342

types of interactions with reciprocal status holders, 128, 128 (figure)
See also Education
Subcultures, 80–82
social class and, 108
terrorist groups and, 84
Subjugation, 236–237, 236 (figure)
defined, 236
Subramaniam, Mangala, 282
Sub-Saharan Africa
Christianity in, 377
HIV/AIDS in, 430
lack of gender equity in education in, 345
life expectancy in, 472
poverty in, 183
Suburbs, 481, 482, 505
Success, cultural ideas of, 330–331
Sudras, 206
Suicide, 429
Durkheim on, 130–131, 152, 369, 429
medically-assisted, 422–423
Suicide bombers, 130 (photo), 131, 144
Suicide (Durkheim), 130
Sunni Islam, 219, 361
Supersize Me (film), 430
Survivalist groups, 82
Survival needs, institutions and meeting, 288
Survival of the fittest, 221
Sustainable societies, 487
Susto, 427–428
Sweatshops, 281
anti-sweatshop cause, 498
Swine flu, 429
Symbolic interaction theory, 31–32, 39 (figure)
analysis of social construction of race, 221–222
on classrooms, 324
critique of, 31–32
differential association theory, 148–149
on family, 296–297
on gender stratification, 272
on health and illness, 427
labeling theory, 149–150
looking-glass self and, 99
as micro level, 84–85
on power and privilege, 390–391
on religion, 357
on social change, 504–505
on social interaction, 125–126
on social stratification, 188–189
Symbolism of flag, 392
Symbols
defined, 31
indicating marriage, 299 (photo)
religious, 357
ritual, 358–359
role-taking and, 101
social interaction and, 125
Syrian refugees, 58, 316 (photo), 474, 474 (photo), 502 (photo)
Systema Naturae (Linnaeus), 221

Taboos, 76–77
incest, 76–77, 77 (table), 302
Taliban, 84, 255, 259, 517

effect on populations, 464
  reasons for engaging in, 412–413
  religion and, 353, 379–380
  significant ongoing armed conflicts, 413 (table)
Ward, Lester, 47
War refugees, socialization of, 111
Waryono, Dwi, 447 (photo)
Washington, DC, as postindustrial city, 481, 482
Washington, George, 238
WaterAid, 514
Water management, in Global South, 515
Watson, Emma, 254
Way of life, 58
Wealth
  access to health care and, 435
  defined, 192
  race and differences in, 223, 224 (figure)
  unequal distribution of, 191–192
Wealth flow theory, 466
Wealth inequality, 182 (photo), 192
  in United States, 211 (figure)
Weber, Max, 30, 38
  on elective affinity, 371
  on ideal-type bureaucracies, 135
  on legitimate and illegitimate power, 391
  on power, 389
  on Protestant ethic and capitalism, 367–368
  on rationalization of social life, 133
  on social class ranking, 207
  on social stratification, 192
  on status inconsistency, 197
  Verstehen, 300
WE Charity, 116
Weinstein, Harvey, 269
Welfare, 211
WE organization, 214
Western Electric plant study, 136
Western-style medicine, in China, 445–446
WhatsApp, 110 (figure), 122
White-collar crime, 164–166
White-collar middle class, 207
White (color), racism and positive images of, 79, 79 (photo)
Whites
  concept of time, 72–73
  high school dropout rate and, 11
  honorary, 226–227
  invisible privileges of, 230
  in three-tiered racial hierarchy, 226
White supremacist groups
  increase in, 161–162
  terrorism and, 416
Whitney, Eli, 64 (figure)
Who Rules America? (Domhoff), 395, 395 (table)
Wicca, 363, 364
Williams, Betty, 207
Williams, Roger, 374
Wind farms, 495 (photo)
Wind-Wolf (Native American child), 231–232
WIPO (World Intellectual Property Organization), 500
"Wisdom literature," 266
Wise, Steven, 516
Witchcraft, 363, 364

Wodaabe people
  gender characteristics among, 7
  gender norms of, 254–255, 255 (photo)
Women
  body language of, 270 (photo)
  family size and education of, 470, 471 (figure)
  feminization of higher education and, 326
  feminization of poverty, 209–210
  health and social status of, 430
  as migrants, 474
  percentage of men's earnings, 276 (table)
  rape and, 276
  spirituality gap, 373 (figure)
  stress and gender role expectations, 280
  violence against, 275 (*see also* Domestic violence; Intimate partner violence (IPV))
Women of color, discrimination against, 276
Women's Marches, 274–275
Wonder Woman (film), 264, 265 (photo)
Word gap, 200–201
Work
  breastfeeding babies at, 268–269
  gendered organizations, 267–269
Work environment, institutionalized gender discrimination and, 270
Workers, 192
Workers' centers, 141
Workfare, 211
Working class, 207
Working-class parenting, 310
Working-class parents
  as agents of socialization, 108–109
  interactions with schools, 333
Working-class schools, stress on order and discipline in, 329
Work-life conflicts, 307
Workplace, sexual harassment in the, 269
World Bank, 33, 64, 248, 518
World Christian Encyclopedia, 361
World Court, 64, 84
World Education (organization), 116
World Health Organization (WHO), 64, 248
  on acupuncture, 446
  air pollution cap, 485
  elimination of smallpox and, 425
  function of, 438
  physician-patient ratio recommendations, 444
World of Warcraft, 263
World population growth
  explosive population growth of, 458–459, 461 (figure), 462 (figure)
  institutional influences on population change, 467–474
  macro-level patterns in, 458–467
  micro-level population patterns in, 474–476
  patterns of, 461, 461 (figure), 462 (figure)
  predictors of, 461–463
  theoretical explanations for population patterns, 464–467
  women's education and family size, 471 (figure)
  by world regions, 469 (figure)
  See also Urbanization
World systems theory, 168–169
  of global change, 507–508, 507 (figure)
World Trade Organization (WTO), 14, 33, 248
World Urbanization Prospects, 479

ABOUT THE AUTHORS

 **Jeanne H. Ballantine** is University Professor of Sociology Emerita at Wright State University, a state university of about 17,000 students in Ohio. She has also taught at several 4-year colleges, including an "alternative" college and a traditionally Black college, and at international programs in universities abroad. She has been teaching introductory sociology for more than 35 years with a mission to introduce the uninitiated to the field, to help students see the usefulness and value in sociology, and to present a global approach. She has been active in the teaching movement, shaping curriculum, writing and presenting research on teaching, and offering workshops and consulting in regional, national, and international forums. She is a Fulbright Senior Scholar and serves as a Departmental Resources Group consultant and evaluator.

Jeanne has written several textbooks, all with the goal of reaching the student audience. As the original director of the Center for Teaching and Learning at Wright State University, she scoured the literature on student learning and served as a mentor to teachers in a wide variety of disciplines. Local, regional, and national organizations have honored her for her teaching and for her contributions to helping others become effective teachers. In 1986, the American Sociological Association's Section on Undergraduate Education (now called the Section on Teaching and Learning in Sociology) recognized her with the Hans O. Mauksch Award for Distinguished Contributions to Teaching of Sociology. In 2004, she was honored by the American Sociological Association with its Distinguished Contributions to Teaching Award. In 2010, the North Central Sociological Association awarded her the J. Milton Yinger Award for Distinguished Career in Sociology.

 **Keith A. Roberts** was Emeritus Professor of Sociology at Hanover College, a private liberal arts college of about 1,100 students in Indiana. He taught introductory sociology for 35 years with a passion for active learning strategies and a focus on "deep learning" by students that transformed the way they see the world. Prior to teaching at Hanover, he taught at a 2-year regional campus of a large university.

He was active in the teaching movement, writing on teaching and serving as a consultant to sociology departments across the country in his capacity as a member of the American Sociological Association Departmental Resources Group. He wrote a very popular textbook on the sociology of religion, coauthored a book on writing in the undergraduate curriculum, published and led many workshops on the Scholarship of Teaching and Learning, and for 22 years ran an annual workshop for high school sociology teachers. He chaired the Selection Committee for the SAGE Innovations and Professional Development Awards. He was honored for his teaching and teaching-related work at local, state, regional, and national levels. The American Sociological Association's Section on Teaching and Learning awarded him the Hans O. Mauksch Award for Distinguished Contributions to Teaching of Sociology in 2000. He was honored with the American Sociological Association's Distinguished Contributions to Teaching Award in 2010. In 2012, the North Central Sociological Association awarded Keith the J. Milton Yinger Award for Distinguished Career in Sociology.

Kathleen Odell Korgen is Professor of Sociology at William Paterson University, a comprehensive university in Wayne, New Jersey. In addition to her research on racial identity and race relations, she has written extensively in support of the public sociology movement and active learning. Kathleen enjoys teaching her students that sociology is a remarkably useful discipline and highlights how "Sociologists in Action" make a positive impact on society. Her published works on race relations and racial identity include *Race Policy and Multiracial Americans* (2016), *Multiracial Identity and Social Class* (2010), *Crossing the Racial Divide: Close Friendships between* *Black and White Americans* (2002), and *From Black to Biracial: Transforming Racial Identity among Americans* (1998, 1999). Her works on public sociology and active learning include *The Engaged Sociologist: Connecting the Classroom to the Community* (with Jonathan White, 2007, 2009, 2011, 2014) and *Sociologists in Action: Sociology, Social Change, and Social Justice* (2011, 2014), *Sociologist in Action: Inequalities* (with Jonathan White and Shelley White, 2015), *Sociology in Action* (with Maxine Atkinson, 2018), and *Social Problems in Action* (with Mary Nell Trautner and Maxine Atkinson, forthcoming). Kathleen is also the editor of *The Cambridge Handbook of Sociology* (2017).

Kathleen works as a consultant for other sociology departments as a member of the American Sociological Association Departmental Resources Group and received William Paterson University's awards for Excellence in Scholarship/Creative Expression and for Excellence in Teaching.